My Life

Bill Clinton

My Life

RANDOM HOUSE LARGE PRINT

Grateful acknowledgment is made to the following for permission
to reprint previously published material:
Harcourt, Inc.: Excerpt from **The People, Yes** by Carl Sandburg.
Copyright © 1936 by Harcourt Brace & Company.
Copyright renewed 1964 by Carl Sandburg.
Reprinted by permission of Harcourt, Inc.
Random House Inc.: Excerpt from **On The Pulse Of Morning** by
Maya Angelou. Copyright © 1993 by Maya Angelou.
Reprinted by permission of Random House, Inc.
The Washington Post: Excerpt from "Opinion Roundup GOP
Distorts History" by Edwin Yoder. Originally from **The Atlanta
Journal and Constitution** (March 9, 1994). Copyright © 1994
by The Washington Post Writers Group. Reprinted by permission
of The Washington Post.

**The Library of Congress has established
a Cataloging-in-Publication record for this title.**

0-375-43519-0

www.randomlargeprint.com

FIRST LARGE PRINT EDITION

10 9 8 7 6 5 4 3 2 1

This Large Print edition published in accord with
the standards of the N.A.V.H.

To my mother, who gave me a love of life

To Hillary, who gave me a life of love

To Chelsea, who gave joy and meaning to it all

And to the memory of my grandfather,
who taught me to look up to people others looked
down on, because we're not so different after all

My Life

PROLOGUE

When I was a young man just out of law school and eager to get on with my life, on a whim I briefly put aside my reading preference for fiction and history and bought one of those how-to books: **How to Get Control of Your Time and Your Life,** by Alan Lakein. The book's main point was the necessity of listing short-, medium-, and long-term life goals, then categorizing them in order of their importance, with the A group being the most important, the B group next, and the C the last, then listing under each goal specific activities designed to achieve them. I still have that paperback book, now almost thirty years old. And I'm sure I have that old list somewhere buried in my papers, though I can't find it. However, I do remember the A list. I wanted to be a good man, have a good marriage and children, have good friends, make a successful political life, and write a great book.

Whether I'm a good man is, of course, for God to judge. I know that I am not as good as my strongest supporters believe or as I hope to become, nor as bad as my harshest critics assert. I have been graced beyond measure by my family life with Hillary and Chelsea. Like all families' lives, ours is not perfect, but it has been wonderful. Its flaws, as all the world knows, are mostly mine, and its continuing promise is grounded in their love. No person I know ever had more or better friends. Indeed, a strong case can be made that I rose to the presidency on the shoulders of my personal friends, the now legendary FOBs.

My life in politics was a joy. I loved campaigns and I loved governing. I always tried to keep things moving in the right direction, to give more people a chance to live their dreams, to lift people's spirits, and to bring them together. That's the way I kept score.

As for the great book, who knows? It sure is a good story.

ONE

Early on the morning of August 19, 1946, I was born under a clear sky after a violent summer storm to a widowed mother in the Julia Chester Hospital in Hope, a town of about six thousand in southwest Arkansas, thirty-three miles east of the Texas border at Texarkana. My mother named me William Jefferson Blythe III after my father, William Jefferson Blythe Jr., one of nine children of a poor farmer in Sherman, Texas, who died when my father was seventeen. According to his sisters, my father always tried to take care of them, and he grew up to be a handsome, hardworking, fun-loving man. He met my mother at Tri-State Hospital in Shreveport, Louisiana, in 1943, when she was training to be a nurse. Many times when I was growing up, I asked Mother to tell me the story of their meeting, courting, and marriage. He brought a date with some kind of medical emergency into the ward where she was working, and they talked and flirted while the other woman was being treated. On his way out of the hospital, he touched the finger on which she was wearing her boyfriend's ring and asked her if she was married. She stammered "no"—she was single. The next day he sent the other woman flowers and her heart sank. Then he called Mother for a date, explaining that he always sent flowers when he ended a relationship.

Two months later, they were married and he was off to war. He served in a motor pool in the invasion of Italy, repairing jeeps and tanks. After the war, he returned to Hope for Mother and they moved to Chicago, where he got back his old job as a salesman for the Manbee Equipment Company. They bought a little house in the suburb of Forest Park but couldn't move in for a couple of months, and since Mother was pregnant with me, they decided she should go home to Hope until they could get into the new house. On May 17, 1946, after moving their furniture into their new home, my father was driving from Chicago to Hope to fetch his wife. Late at night on Highway 60 outside of Sikeston, Missouri, he lost control of his car, a 1942 Buick, when the right front tire blew out on a wet road. He was thrown clear of the car but landed in, or crawled into, a drainage ditch dug to reclaim swampland. The ditch held three feet of water. When he was found, after a two-hour search, his hand was grasping a branch above the waterline. He had tried but failed to pull himself out. He drowned, only twenty-eight years old, married two years and eight months, only seven months of which he had spent with Mother.

That brief sketch is about all I ever really knew about my father. All my life I have been hungry to fill in the blanks, clinging eagerly to every photo or story or scrap of paper that would tell me more of the man who gave me life.

When I was about twelve, sitting on my uncle Buddy's porch in Hope, a man walked up the steps, looked at me, and said, "You're Bill Blythe's son. You look just like him." I beamed for days.

In 1974, I was running for Congress. It was my first race and the local paper did a feature story on my mother. She was at her regular coffee shop early in the morning discussing the article with a lawyer friend when one of the breakfast regulars she knew only casually came up to her and said, "I was there, I was the first one at the wreck that night." He then told Mother what he had seen, including the fact that my father had retained enough consciousness or survival instinct to try to claw himself up and out of the water before he died. Mother thanked him, went out to her car and cried, then dried her tears and went to work.

In 1993, on Father's Day, my first as President, the **Washington Post** ran a long investigative story on my father, which was followed over the next two months by other investigative pieces by the Associated Press and many smaller papers. The stories confirmed the things my mother and I knew. They also turned up a lot we didn't know, including the fact that my father had probably been married three times before he met Mother, and apparently had at least two more children.

My father's other son was identified as Leon Ritzenthaler, a retired owner of a janitorial service, from northern California. In the article, he said he had written me during the '92 campaign but had received no reply. I don't remember hearing about his letter, and considering all the other bullets we were dodging then, it's possible that my staff kept it from me. Or maybe the letter was just misplaced in the mountains of mail we were receiving. Anyway, when I read about Leon, I got in touch with him and later met him and his wife, Judy, during one of my stops in northern California. We had a happy visit and since then we've corresponded in holiday seasons. He and I look alike, his birth certificate says his father was mine, and I wish I'd known about him a long time ago.

Somewhere around this time, I also received information confirming news stories about a daughter, Sharon Pettijohn, born Sharon Lee Blythe in Kansas City in 1941, to a woman my father later divorced. She sent copies of her birth certificate, her parents' marriage license, a photo of my father, and a letter to her mother from my father asking about "our baby" to Betsey Wright, my former chief of staff in the governor's office. I'm sorry to say that, for whatever reason, I've never met her.

This news breaking in 1993 came as a shock to Mother, who by then had been battling cancer for some time, but she took it all in stride. She said young people did a lot of things during the Depression and the war that people in another time might disapprove of. What mattered was that my father was the love of her life and she had no doubt of his love for her. Whatever the facts, that's all she needed to know as her own life moved toward its end. As for me, I wasn't quite sure what to make of it all, but given the life I've led, I could hardly be surprised that my father was more complicated than the idealized pictures I had lived with for nearly half a century.

In 1994, as we headed for the celebration of the fiftieth anniversary of D-day, several newspapers published a story on my father's war record, with a snapshot of him in uniform. Shortly afterward, I received a letter from Umberto Baron of Netcong, New Jersey, recounting his own experiences during the war and after. He said that he was a young boy in Italy when the Americans arrived, and that he loved to go to their camp, where one soldier in particular befriended him, giving him candy and showing him how engines worked and how to repair them. He knew him only as Bill. After the war, Baron came to the United States, and, inspired by what he had learned from the soldier who called him "Little GI Joe," he opened his own garage and started a family. He told me he had lived the American dream, with a thriving business and three children. He said he owed so much of his success in life to that young soldier, but hadn't had the opportunity to say good-bye then, and had often wondered what had happened to him. Then, he said, "On Memorial Day of this year, I was thumbing through a copy of the New York **Daily News** with my morning coffee when suddenly I felt as if I was struck by lightning. There in the lower left-hand corner of the paper was a photo of Bill. I felt chills to learn that Bill was none other than the father of the President of the United States."

In 1996, the children of one of my father's sisters came for the first time to our annual family Christmas party at the White House and brought me a gift: the condolence letter my aunt had received from her congressman, the great Sam Rayburn, after my father died. It's just a short form letter and appears to have been signed with the autopen of the day, but I hugged that letter with all the glee of a six-year-old boy getting his first train set from Santa Claus. I hung it in my private office on the second floor of the White House, and looked at it every night.

Shortly after I left the White House, I was boarding the USAir shuttle in Washington for New York when an airline employee stopped me to say that his stepfather had just told him he had served in the war with my father and had liked him very much. I asked for the old vet's phone number and address, and the man said he didn't have it but would get it to me. I'm still waiting, hoping there will be one more human connection to my father.

At the end of my presidency, I picked a few special places to say goodbye and thanks to the American people. One of them was Chicago, where Hillary was born; where I all but clinched the Democratic nomination on St. Patrick's Day 1992; where many of my most ardent supporters live and many of my most important domestic initiatives in crime, welfare, and education were proved effective; and, of course, where my parents went to live after the war. I used to joke with Hillary that if my father hadn't lost his life on that rainy Missouri highway, I would have grown up a few miles from her and we probably never would have met. My last event was in the Palmer House Hotel, scene of the only photo I have of my parents together, taken just before Mother came back to Hope in 1946. After the speech and the good-byes, I went into a small room where I met a woman, Mary Etta Rees, and her two daughters. She told me she had grown up and gone to high school with my mother, then had gone north to Indiana to work in a war industry, married, stayed, and raised her children. Then she gave me another precious gift: the letter my twenty-three-year-old mother had written on her birthday to her friend, three weeks after my father's death, more than fifty-four years earlier. It was vintage Mother. In her beautiful hand, she wrote of her heartbreak and her determination to carry on: "It seemed almost unbelievable at the time but you see I am six months pregnant and the thought of our baby keeps me going and really gives me the whole world before me."

My mother left me the wedding ring she gave my father, a few moving stories, and the sure knowledge that she was loving me for him too.

My father left me with the feeling that I had to live for two people, and that if I did it well enough, somehow I could make up for the life he should have had. And his memory infused me, at a younger age than most, with a sense of my own mortality. The knowledge that I, too, could die young drove me both to try to drain the most out of every moment of life and to get on with the next big challenge. Even when I wasn't sure where I was going, I was always in a hurry.

TWO

I was born on my grandfather's birthday, a couple of weeks early, weighing in at a respectable six pounds eight ounces, on a twenty-one-inch frame. Mother and I came home to her parents' house on Hervey Street in Hope, where I would spend the next four years. That old house seemed massive and mysterious to me then and still holds deep memories today. The people of Hope raised the funds to restore it and fill it with old pictures, memorabilia, and period furniture. They call it the Clinton Birthplace. It certainly is the place I associate with awakening to life—to the smells of country food; to buttermilk churns, ice-cream makers, washboards, and clotheslines; to my "Dick and Jane" readers, my first toys, including a simple length of chain I prized above them all; to strange voices talking over our "party line" telephone; to my first friends, and the work my grandparents did.

After a year or so, my mother decided she needed to go back to New Orleans to Charity Hospital, where she had done part of her nursing training, to learn to be a nurse anesthetist. In the old days, doctors had administered their own anesthetics, so there was a demand for this relatively new work, which would bring more prestige to her and more money for us. But it must have been hard on her, leaving me. On the other hand, New Orleans was an amazing place after the war, full of young people, Dixieland music, and over-the-top haunts like the Club My-

Oh-My, where men in drag danced and sang as lovely ladies. I guess it wasn't a bad place for a beautiful young widow to move beyond her loss.

I got to visit Mother twice when my grandmother took me on the train to New Orleans. I was only three, but I remember two things clearly. First, we stayed just across Canal Street from the French Quarter in the Jung Hotel, on one of the higher floors. It was the first building more than two stories high I had ever been in, in the first real city I had ever seen. I can remember the awe I felt looking out over all the city lights at night. I don't recall what Mother and I did in New Orleans, but I'll never forget what happened one of the times I got on the train to leave. As we pulled away from the station, Mother knelt by the side of the railroad tracks and cried as she waved good-bye. I can see her there still, crying on her knees, as if it were yesterday.

For more than fifty years, from that first trip, New Orleans has always had a special fascination for me. I love its music, food, people, and spirit. When I was fifteen, my family took a vacation to New Orleans and the Gulf Coast, and I got to hear Al Hirt, the great trumpeter, in his own club. At first they wouldn't let me in because I was underage. As Mother and I were about to walk away, the doorman told us that Hirt was sitting in his car reading just around the corner, and that only he could let me in. I found him—in his Bentley no less—tapped on the window, and made my case. He got out, took Mother and me into the club, and put us at a table near the front. He and his group played a great set—it was my first live jazz experience. Al Hirt died while I was President. I wrote his wife and told her the story, expressing my gratitude for a big man's long-ago kindness to a boy.

When I was in high school, I played the tenor saxophone solo on a piece about New Orleans called **Crescent
City Suite.** I always thought I did a better job on it
because I played it with memories of my first sight of the
city. When I was twenty-one, I won a Rhodes scholarship
in New Orleans. I think I did well in the interview in part
because I felt at home there. When I was a young law professor, Hillary and I had a couple of great trips to New
Orleans for conventions, staying at a quaint little hotel in
the French Quarter, the Cornstalk. When I was governor
of Arkansas, we played in the Sugar Bowl there, losing to
Alabama in one of the legendary Bear Bryant's last great
victories. At least he was born and grew up in Arkansas!
When I ran for President, the people of New Orleans
twice gave me overwhelming victory margins, assuring
Louisiana's electoral votes for our side.

Now I have seen most of the world's great cities, but
New Orleans will always be special—for coffee and
beignets at the Morning Call on the Mississippi; for the
music of Aaron and Charmaine Neville, the old guys at
Preservation Hall, and the memory of Al Hirt; for jogging
through the French Quarter in the early morning; for
amazing meals at a host of terrific restaurants with John
Breaux, Sheriff Harry Lee, and my other pals; and most of
all, for those first memories of my mother. They are the
magnets that keep pulling me down the Mississippi to
New Orleans.

While Mother was in New Orleans, I was in the care of
my grandparents. They were incredibly conscientious
about me. They loved me very much; sadly, much better
than they were able to love each other or, in my grandmother's case, to love my mother. Of course, I was bliss-

fully unaware of all this at the time. I just knew that I was loved. Later, when I became interested in children growing up in hard circumstances and learned something of child development from Hillary's work at the Yale Child Study Center, I came to realize how fortunate I had been. For all their own demons, my grandparents and my mother always made me feel I was the most important person in the world to them. Most children will make it if they have just one person who makes them feel that way. I had three.

My grandmother, Edith Grisham Cassidy, stood just over five feet tall and weighed about 180 pounds. Mammaw was bright, intense, and aggressive, and had obviously been pretty once. She had a great laugh, but she also was full of anger and disappointment and obsessions she only dimly understood. She took it all out in raging tirades against my grandfather and my mother, both before and after I was born, though I was shielded from most of them. She had been a good student and ambitious, so after high school she took a correspondence course in nursing from the Chicago School of Nursing. By the time I was a toddler she was a private-duty nurse for a man not far from our house on Hervey Street. I can still remember running down the sidewalk to meet her when she came home from work.

Mammaw's main goals for me were that I would eat a lot, learn a lot, and always be neat and clean. We ate in the kitchen at a table next to the window. My high chair faced the window, and Mammaw tacked playing cards up on the wooden window frame at mealtimes so that I could learn to count. She also stuffed me at every meal, because conventional wisdom at the time was that a fat baby was a healthy one, as long as he bathed every day. At least once a day, she read to me from "Dick and Jane" books until I could read them myself, and from **World Book Encyclopedia** volumes, which in those days were sold door-to-door by salesmen and were often the only books besides the Bible in working people's houses. These early instructions probably explain why I now read a lot, love card games, battle my weight, and never forget to wash my hands and brush my teeth.

I adored my grandfather, the first male influence in my life, and felt pride that I was born on his birthday. James Eldridge Cassidy was a slight man, about five eight, but in those years still strong and handsome. I always thought he resembled the actor Randolph Scott.

When my grandparents moved from Bodcaw, which had a population of about a hundred, to the metropolis Hope, Papaw worked for an icehouse delivering ice on a horse-drawn wagon. In those days, refrigerators really were iceboxes, cooled by chunks of ice whose size varied according to the size of the appliance. Though he weighed about 150 pounds, my grandfather carried ice blocks that weighed up to a hundred pounds or more, using a pair of hooks to slide them onto his back, which was protected by a large leather flap.

My grandfather was an incredibly kind and generous man. During the Depression, when nobody had any money, he would invite boys to ride the ice truck with him just to get them off the street. They earned twenty-five cents a day. In 1976, when I was in Hope running for attorney general, I had a talk with one of those boys, Judge John Wilson. He grew up to be a distinguished, successful lawyer, but he still had vivid memories of those days. He told me that at the end of one day, when my grandfather gave him his quarter, he asked if he could have two dimes and a nickel so that he could feel he had more money. He got them and walked home, jingling the change in his pockets. But he jingled too hard, and one of the dimes fell out. He looked for that dime for hours to no avail. Forty years later, he told me he still never walked by that stretch of sidewalk without trying to spot that dime.

It's hard to convey to young people today the impact the Depression had on my parents' and grandparents' generation, but I grew up feeling it. One of the most memorable stories of my childhood was my mother's tale of a Depression Good Friday when my grandfather came home from work and broke down and cried as he told her he just couldn't afford the dollar or so it would cost to buy her a new Easter dress. She never forgot it, and every year of my childhood I had a new Easter outfit whether I wanted it or not. I remember one Easter in the 1950s, when I was fat and self-conscious. I went to church in a light-colored short-sleeved shirt, white linen pants, pink and black Hush Puppies, and a matching pink suede belt. It hurt, but my mother had been faithful to her father's Easter ritual.

When I was living with him, my grandfather had two jobs that I really loved: he ran a little grocery store, and he supplemented his income by working as a night watchman at a sawmill. I loved spending the night with Papaw at the sawmill. We would take a paper bag with sandwiches for supper, and I would sleep in the backseat of the car. And on clear starlit nights, I would climb in the sawdust piles, taking in the magical smells of fresh-cut timber and sawdust. My grandfather loved working there, too. It got him out of the house and reminded him of the mill work he'd done as a young man around the time of my mother's birth. Except for the time Papaw closed the car door on my fingers in the dark, those nights were perfect adventures.

The grocery store was a different sort of adventure. First, there was a huge jar of Jackson's cookies on the counter, which I raided with gusto. Second, grown-ups I didn't know came in to buy groceries, for the first time exposing me to adults who weren't relatives. Third, a lot of my grandfather's customers were black. Though the South was completely segregated back then, some level of racial interaction was inevitable in small towns, just as it had always been in the rural South. However, it was rare to find an uneducated rural southerner without a racist bone in his body. That's exactly what my grandfather was. I could see that black people looked different, but because he treated them like he did everybody else, asking after their children and about their work, I thought they were just like me. Occasionally, black kids would come into the store and we would play. It took me years to learn about segregation and prejudice and the meaning of poverty, years to learn that most white people weren't like my grandfather and grandmother, whose views on race were among the few things she had in common with her husband. In fact, Mother told me one of the worst whippings she ever got was when, at age three or four, she called a black woman "Nigger." To put it mildly, Mammaw's whipping her was an unusual reaction for a poor southern white woman in the 1920s.

My mother once told me that after Papaw died, she found some of his old account books from the grocery store with lots of unpaid bills from his customers, most of them black. She recalled that he had told her that good people who were doing the best they could deserved to be able to feed their families, and no matter how strapped he was, he never denied them groceries on credit. Maybe that's why I've always believed in food stamps.

After I became President, I got another firsthand account of my grandfather's store. In 1997, an African-American woman, Ernestine Campbell, did an interview for her hometown paper in Toledo, Ohio, about her grandfather buying groceries from Papaw "on account" and bringing her with him to the store. She said that she remembered playing with me, and that I was "the only white boy in that neighborhood who played with black kids." Thanks to my grandfather, I didn't know I was the only white kid who did that.

Besides my grandfather's store, my neighborhood provided my only other contact with people outside my family. I experienced a lot in those narrow confines. I saw a house burn down across the street and learned I was not the only person bad things happened to. I made friends with a boy who collected strange creatures, and once he invited me over to see his snake. He said it was in the closet. Then he opened the closet door, shoved me into the darkness, slammed the door shut, and told me I was in the dark alone with the snake. I wasn't, thank goodness, but I was sure scared to death. I learned that what seems funny to the strong can be cruel and humiliating to the weak.

Our house was just a block away from a railroad underpass, which then was made of rough tar-coated timbers. I liked to climb on the timbers, listen to the trains rattle overhead, and wonder where they were going and whether I would ever go there.

And I used to play in the backyard with a boy whose yard adjoined mine. He lived with two beautiful sisters in a bigger, nicer house than ours. We used to sit on the grass for hours, throwing his knife in the ground and learning to make it stick. His name was Vince Foster. He was kind to me and never lorded it over me the way so many older boys did with younger ones. He grew up to be a tall, handsome, wise, good man. He became a great lawyer, a strong supporter early in my career, and Hillary's best friend at the Rose Law Firm. Our families socialized in Little Rock, mostly at his house, where his wife, Lisa, taught Chelsea to swim. He came to the White House with us, and was a voice of calm and reason in those crazy early months.

There was one other person outside the family who influenced me in my early childhood. Odessa was a black woman who came to our house to clean, cook, and watch me when my grandparents were at work. She had big buck teeth, which made her smile only brighter and more beautiful to me. I kept up with her for years after I left Hope. In 1966, a friend and I went out to see Odessa after visiting my father's and grandfather's graves. Most of the black people in Hope lived near the cemetery, across the road from where my grandfather's store had been. I remember our visiting on her porch for a good long while. When the time came to go, we got in my car and drove away on dirt streets. The only unpaved streets I saw in Hope, or later in Hot Springs when I moved there, were in black neighborhoods, full of people who worked hard, many of them raising kids like me, and who paid taxes. Odessa deserved better.

The other large figures in my childhood were relatives: my maternal great-grandparents, my great-aunt Otie and great-uncle Carl Russell, and most of all, my great-uncle Oren—known as Buddy, and one of the lights of my life—and his wife, Aunt Ollie.

My Grisham great-grandparents lived out in the country in a little wooden house built up off the ground. Because Arkansas gets more tornadoes than almost any other place in the United States, most people who lived in virtual stick houses like theirs dug a hole in the ground for a storm cellar. Theirs was out in the front yard, and had a little bed and a small table with a coal-oil lantern on it. I still remember peering into that little space and hearing my great-grandfather say, "Yes, sometimes snakes go down there too, but they won't bite you if the lantern's lit." I never found out whether that was true or not. My only other memory of my great-grandfather is that he came to visit me in the hospital when I broke my leg at age five. He held my hand and we posed for a picture. He's in a simple black jacket and a white shirt buttoned all the way up, looking old as the hills, straight out of **American Gothic.**

My grandmother's sister Opal—we called her Otie— was a fine-looking woman with the great Grisham family laugh, whose quiet husband, Carl, was the first person I knew who grew watermelons. The river-enriched, sandy soil around Hope is ideal for them, and the size of Hope's melons became the trademark of the town in the early fifties when the community sent the largest melon ever grown up to that time, just under two hundred pounds, to President Truman. The better-tasting melons, however, weigh sixty pounds or less. Those are the ones I saw my great-uncle Carl grow, pouring water from a washtub into the soil around the melons and watching the stalks suck it up like a vacuum cleaner. When I became President, Uncle Carl's cousin Carter Russell still had a watermelon stand in Hope where you could get good red or the sweeter yellow melons.

Hillary says the first time she ever saw me, I was in the Yale Law School lounge bragging to skeptical fellow students about the size of Hope watermelons. When I was President, my old friends from Hope put on a watermelon feed on the South Lawn of the White House, and I got to tell my watermelon stories to a new generation of young people who pretended to be interested in a subject I began to learn about so long ago from Aunt Otie and Uncle Carl.

My grandmother's brother Uncle Buddy and his wife, Ollie, were the primary members of my extended family. Buddy and Ollie had four children, three of whom were gone from Hope by the time I came along. Dwayne was an executive with a shoe manufacturer in New Hampshire. Conrad and Falba were living in Dallas, though they both came back to Hope often and live there today. Myra, the youngest, was a rodeo queen. She could ride like a pro, and she later ran off with a cowboy, had two boys, divorced, and moved home, where she ran the local housing authority. Myra and Falba are great women who laugh through their tears and never quit on family and friends. I'm glad they are still part of my life. I spent a lot of time at Buddy and Ollie's house, not just in my first six years in Hope, but for forty more years until Ollie died and Buddy sold the house and moved in with Falba.

Social life in my extended family, like that of most people of modest means who grew up in the country, revolved around meals, conversation, and storytelling. They couldn't afford vacations, rarely if ever went to the movies, and didn't have television until the mid- to late 1950s. They went out a few times a year—to the county fair, the watermelon festival, the occasional square dance or gospel singing. The men hunted and fished and raised vegetables and watermelon on small plots out in the country that they'd kept when they moved to town to work.

Though they never had extra money, they never felt

poor as long as they had a neat house, clean clothes, and enough food to feed anyone who came in the front door. They worked to live, not the other way around.

My favorite childhood meals were at Buddy and Ollie's, eating around a big table in their small kitchen. A typical weekend lunch, which we called dinner (the evening meal was supper), included ham or a roast, corn bread, spinach or collard greens, mashed potatoes, sweet potatoes, peas, green beans or lima beans, fruit pie, and endless quantities of iced tea we drank in large goblet-like glasses. I felt more grown up drinking out of those big glasses. On special days we had homemade ice cream to go with the pie. When I was there early enough, I got to help prepare the meal, shelling the beans or turning the crank on the ice-cream maker. Before, during, and after dinner there was constant talk: town gossip, family goings-on, and stories, lots of them. All my kinfolks could tell a story, making simple events, encounters, and mishaps involving ordinary people come alive with drama and laughter.

Buddy was the best storyteller. Like both of his sisters, he was very bright. I often wondered what he and they would have made of their lives if they had been born into my generation or my daughter's. But there were lots of people like them back then. The guy pumping your gas might have had an IQ as high as the guy taking your tonsils out. There are still people like the Grishams in America, many of them new immigrants, which is why I tried as President to open the doors of college to all comers.

Though he had a very limited education, Buddy had a fine mind and a Ph.D. in human nature, born of a lifetime of keen observation and dealing with his own demons and those of his family. Early in his marriage he had a drinking problem. One day he came home and told his wife he knew his drinking was hurting her and their family and he was never going to drink again. And he never did, for more than fifty years.

Well into his eighties, Buddy could tell amazing stories highlighting the personalities of dogs he'd had five or six decades earlier. He remembered their names, their looks, their peculiar habits, how he came by them, the precise way they retrieved shot birds. Lots of people would come by his house and sit on the porch for a visit. After they left he'd have a story about them or their kids—sometimes funny, sometimes sad, usually sympathetic, always understanding.

I learned a lot from the stories my uncle, aunts, and grandparents told me: that no one is perfect but most people are good; that people can't be judged only by their worst or weakest moments; that harsh judgments can make hypocrites of us all; that a lot of life is just showing up and hanging on; that laughter is often the best, and sometimes the only, response to pain. Perhaps most important, I learned that everyone has a story—of dreams and nightmares, hope and heartache, love and loss, courage and fear, sacrifice and selfishness. All my life I've been interested in other people's stories. I've wanted to know them, understand them, feel them. When I grew up and got into politics, I always felt the main point of my work was to give people a chance to have better stories.

Uncle Buddy's story was good until the end. He got lung cancer in 1974, had a lung removed, and still lived to be ninety-one. He counseled me in my political career, and if I'd followed his advice and repealed an unpopular car-tag increase, I probably wouldn't have lost my first gubernatorial reelection campaign in 1980. He lived to see me elected President and got a big kick out of it. After

Ollie died, he kept active by going down to his daughter Falba's donut shop and regaling a whole new generation of kids with his stories and witty observations on the human condition. He never lost his sense of humor. He was still driving at eighty-seven, when he took two lady friends, aged ninety-one and ninety-three, for drives separately once a week. When he told me about his "dates," I asked, "So you like these older women now?" He snickered and said, "Yeah, I do. Seems like they're a little more settled."

In all our years together, I saw my uncle cry only once. Ollie developed Alzheimer's and had to be moved to a nursing home. For several weeks afterward, she knew who she was for a few minutes a day. During those lucid intervals, she would call Buddy and say, "Oren, how could you leave me in this place after fifty-six years of marriage? Come get me right now." He would dutifully drive over to see her, but by the time he got there, she would be lost again in the mists of the disease and didn't know him.

It was during this period that I stopped by to see him late one afternoon, our last visit at the old house. I was hoping to cheer him up. Instead, he made me laugh with bawdy jokes and droll comments on current events. When darkness fell, I told him I had to go back home to Little Rock. He followed me to the door, and as I was about to walk out, he grabbed my arm. I turned and saw tears in his eyes for the first and only time in almost fifty years of love and friendship. I said, "This is really hard, isn't it?" I'll never forget his reply. He smiled and said, "Yeah, it is, but I signed on for the whole load, and most of it was pretty good." My uncle Buddy taught me that everyone has a story. He told his in that one sentence.

THREE

After the year in New Orleans, Mother came home to Hope eager to put her anesthesia training into practice, elated at being reunited with me, and back to her old fun-loving self. She had dated several men in New Orleans and had a fine time, according to her memoir, **Leading with My Heart,** which I'm sure would have been a bestseller if she had lived to promote it.

However, before, during, and after her sojourn in New Orleans, Mother was dating one man more than anyone else, the owner of the local Buick dealership, Roger Clinton. She was a beautiful, high-spirited widow. He was a handsome, hell-raising, twice-divorced man from Hot Springs, Arkansas' "Sin City," which for several years had been home to the largest illegal gambling operation in the United States. Roger's brother Raymond owned the Buick dealership in Hot Springs, and Roger, the baby and "bad boy" of a family of five, had come to Hope to take advantage of the war activity around the Southwestern Proving Ground and perhaps to get out of his brother's shadow.

Roger loved to drink and party with his two best buddies from Hot Springs, Van Hampton Lyell, who owned the Coca-Cola bottling plant across the street from Clinton Buick, and Gabe Crawford, who owned several drugstores in Hot Springs and one in Hope, later built Hot Springs' first shopping center, and was then married to Roger's gorgeous niece, Virginia, a woman I've always loved, who was the very first Miss Hot Springs. Their idea of a good time was to gamble, get drunk, and do crazy, reckless things in cars or airplanes or on motorcycles. It's a wonder they didn't all die young.

Mother liked Roger because he was fun, paid attention to me, and was generous. He paid for her to come home to see me several times when she was in New Orleans, and he probably paid for the train trips Mammaw and I took to see Mother.

Papaw liked Roger because he was nice both to me and to him. For a while after my grandfather quit the icehouse because of severe bronchial problems, he ran a liquor store. Near the end of the war, Hempstead County, of which Hope is the county seat, voted to go "dry." That's when my grandfather opened his grocery store. I later learned that Papaw sold liquor under the counter to the doctors, lawyers, and other respectable people who didn't want to drive the thirty-three miles to the nearest legal liquor store in Texarkana, and that Roger was his supplier.

Mammaw really disliked Roger because she thought he was not the kind of man her daughter and grandson should be tied to. She had a dark side her husband and daughter lacked, but it enabled her to see the darkness in others that they missed. She thought Roger Clinton was nothing but trouble. She was right about the trouble part, but not the "nothing but." There was more to him than that, which makes his story even sadder.

As for me, all I knew was that he was good to me and had a big brown and black German shepherd, Susie, that he brought to play with me. Susie was a big part of my childhood, and started my lifelong love affair with dogs.

Mother and Roger got married in Hot Springs, in June 1950, shortly after her twenty-seventh birthday. Only

Gabe and Virginia Crawford were there. Then Mother and I left her parents' home and moved with my new step-father, whom I soon began to call Daddy, into a little white wooden house on the south end of town at 321 Thirteenth Street at the corner of Walker Street. Not long afterward, I started calling myself Billy Clinton.

My new world was exciting to me. Next door were Ned and Alice Williams. Mr. Ned was a retired railroad worker who built a workshop behind his house filled with a large sophisticated model electric-train setup. Back then every little kid wanted a Lionel train set. Daddy got me one and we used to play with it together, but nothing could compare to Mr. Ned's large intricate tracks and beautiful fast trains. I spent hours there. It was like having my own Disneyland next door.

My neighborhood was a class-A advertisement for the post–World War II baby boom. There were lots of young couples with kids. Across the street lived the most special child of all, Mitzi Polk, daughter of Minor and Margaret Polk. Mitzi had a loud roaring laugh. She would swing so high on her swing set the poles of the frame would come up out of the ground, as she bellowed at the top of her lungs, "Billy sucks a bottle! Billy sucks a bottle!" She drove me nuts. After all, I was getting to be a big boy and I did no such thing.

I later learned that Mitzi was developmentally disabled. The term wouldn't have meant anything to me then, but when I pushed to expand opportunities for the disabled as governor and President, I thought often of Mitzi Polk.

A lot happened to me while I lived on Thirteenth Street. I started school at Miss Marie Purkins' School for Little Folks kindergarten, which I loved until I broke my leg one day jumping rope. And it wasn't even a moving rope. The rope in the playground was tied at one end to a tree and at the other end to a swing set. The kids would line up on one side and take turns running and jumping over it. All the other kids cleared the rope.

One of them was Mack McLarty, son of the local Ford dealer, later governor of Boys State, all-star quarterback, state legislator, successful businessman, and then my first White House chief of staff. Mack always cleared every hurdle. Luckily for me, he always waited for me to catch up.

Me, I didn't clear the rope. I was a little chunky anyway, and slow, so slow that I was once the only kid at an Easter egg hunt who didn't get a single egg, not because I couldn't find them but because I couldn't get to them fast enough. On the day I tried to jump rope I was wearing cowboy boots to school. Like a fool, I didn't take the boots off to jump. My heel caught on the rope, I turned, fell, and heard my leg snap. I lay in agony on the ground for several minutes while Daddy raced over from the Buick place to get me.

I had broken my leg above the knee, and because I was growing so fast, the doctor was reluctant to put me in a cast up to my hip. Instead, he made a hole through my ankle, pushed a stainless steel bar through it, attached it to a stainless steel horseshoe, and hung my leg up in the air over my hospital bed. I lay like that for two months, flat on my back, feeling both foolish and pleased to be out of school and receiving so many visitors. I took a long time getting over that leg break. After I got out of the hospital, my folks bought me a bicycle, but I never lost my fear of riding without the training wheels. As a result, I never stopped feeling that I was clumsy and without a normal sense of balance until, at the age of twenty-two, I finally started riding a bike at Oxford. Even then I fell a few times, but I thought of it as building my pain threshold.

I was grateful to Daddy for coming to rescue me when I broke my leg. He also came home from work a time or two to try to talk Mother out of spanking me when I did something wrong. At the beginning of their marriage he really tried to be there for me. I remember once he even took me on the train to St. Louis to see the Cardinals, then our nearest major league baseball team. We stayed overnight and came home the next day. I loved it. Sadly, it was the only trip the two of us ever took together. Like the only time we ever went fishing together. The only time we ever went out into the woods to cut our own Christmas tree together. The only time our whole family took an out-of-state vacation together. There were so many things that meant a lot to me but were never to occur again. Roger Clinton really loved me and he loved Mother, but he couldn't ever quite break free of the shadows of self-doubt, the phony security of binge drinking and adolescent partying, and the isolation from and verbal abuse of Mother that kept him from becoming the man he might have been.

One night his drunken self-destructiveness came to a head in a fight with my mother I can't ever forget. Mother wanted us to go to the hospital to see my great-grandmother, who didn't have long to live. Daddy said she couldn't go. They were screaming at each other in their bedroom in the back of the house. For some reason, I walked out into the hall to the doorway of the bedroom. Just as I did, Daddy pulled a gun from behind his back and fired in Mother's direction. The bullet went into the wall between where she and I were standing. I was stunned and so scared. I had never heard a shot fired before, much less seen one. Mother grabbed me and ran across the street to the neighbors. The police were called. I can still see them leading Daddy away in handcuffs to jail, where he spent the night.

I'm sure Daddy didn't mean to hurt her and he would have died if the bullet had accidentally hit either of us. But something more poisonous than alcohol drove him to that level of debasement. It would be a long time before I could understand such forces in others or in myself. When Daddy got out of jail he had sobered up in more ways than one and was so ashamed that nothing bad happened for some time.

I had one more year of life and schooling in Hope. I went to first grade at Brookwood School; my teacher was Miss Mary Wilson. Although she had only one arm, she didn't believe in sparing the rod, or, in her case, the paddle, into which she had bored holes to cut down on the wind resistance. On more than one occasion I was the recipient of her concern.

In addition to my neighbors and Mack McLarty, I became friends with some other kids who stayed with me for a lifetime. One of them, Joe Purvis, had a childhood that made mine look idyllic. He grew up to be a fine lawyer, and when I was elected attorney general, I hired Joe on my staff. When Arkansas had an important case before the U.S. Supreme Court, I went, but I let Joe make the argument. Justice Byron "Whizzer" White sent me a note from the bench saying that Joe had done a good job. Later, Joe became the first chairman of my Birthplace Foundation.

Besides my friends and family, my life on Thirteenth Street was marked by my discovery of the movies. In 1951 and 1952, I could go for a dime: a nickel to get in, a nickel for a Coke. I went every couple of weeks or so. Back then, you got a feature film, a cartoon, a serial, and a newsreel. The Korean War was on, so I learned about that. Flash Gordon and Rocket Man were the big serial heroes. For cartoons, I preferred **Bugs Bunny, Casper the Friendly Ghost,** and **Baby Huey,** with whom I probably identified. I saw a lot of movies, and especially liked the westerns. My favorite was **High Noon**—I probably saw it half a dozen times during its run in Hope, and have seen it more than a dozen times since. It's still my favorite movie, because it's not your typical macho western. I loved the movie because from start to finish Gary Cooper is scared to death but does the right thing anyway.

When I was elected President, I told an interviewer that my favorite movie was **High Noon.** At the time, Fred Zinnemann, its director, was nearly ninety, living in London. I got a great letter from him with a copy of his annotated script and an autographed picture of himself with Cooper and Grace Kelly in street clothes on the **High Noon** set in 1951. Over the long years since I first saw **High Noon,** when I faced my own showdowns, I often thought of the look in Gary Cooper's eyes as he stares into the face of almost certain defeat, and how he keeps walking through his fears toward his duty. It works pretty well in real life too.

FOUR

In the summer after my first-grade year, Daddy decided he wanted to go home to Hot Springs. He sold the Buick dealership and moved us to a four hundred–acre farm out on Wildcat Road a few miles west of the city. It had cattle, sheep, and goats. What it didn't have was an indoor toilet. So for the year or so we lived out there, on the hottest summer days and the coldest winter nights, we had to go outside to the wooden outhouse to relieve ourselves. It was an interesting experience, especially when the nonpoisonous king snake that hung around our yard was peering up through the hole at me when I had to go. Later, when I got into politics, being able to say I had lived on a farm with an outhouse made a great story, almost as good as being born in a log cabin.

I liked living on the farm, feeding the animals, and moving among them, until one fateful Sunday. Daddy had several members of his family out to lunch, including his brother Raymond and his children. I took one of Raymond's daughters, Karla, out into the field where the sheep were grazing. I knew there was one mean ram we had to avoid, but we decided to tempt fate, a big mistake. When we were about a hundred yards away from the fence, the ram saw us and started to charge. We started running for the fence. Karla was bigger and faster and made it. I stumbled over a big rock. When I fell I could see I wasn't going to make the fence before the ram got to me, so I retreated to a small tree a few feet away in the hope I could keep away from him by running around the tree until help came. Another big mistake. Soon he caught me and knocked my legs out from under me. Before I could get up he butted me in the head. Then I was stunned and hurt and couldn't get up. So he backed up, got a good head start, and rammed me again as hard as he could. He did the same thing over and over and over again, alternating his targets between my head and my gut. Soon I was pouring blood and hurting like the devil. After what seemed an eternity my uncle showed up, picked up a big rock, and threw it hard, hitting the ram square between the eyes. The ram just shook his head and walked off, apparently unfazed. I recovered, left with only a scar on my forehead, which gradually grew into my scalp. And I learned that I could take a hard hit, a lesson that I would relearn a couple more times in my childhood and later in life.

A few months after we moved to the farm, both my folks were going to town to work. Daddy gave up on being a farmer and took a job as a parts manager for Uncle Raymond's Buick dealership, while Mother found more anesthesia work in Hot Springs than she could handle. One day, on the way to work, she picked up a woman who was walking to town. After they got acquainted, Mother asked her if she knew anyone who would come to the house and look after me while she and Daddy were at work. In one of the great moments of good luck in my life, she suggested herself. Her name was Cora Walters; she was a grandmother with every good quality of an old-fashioned countrywoman. She was wise, kind, upright, conscientious, and deeply Christian. She became a member of our family for eleven years. All her family were good people, and after she left us, her daughter Maye Hightower came to work for Mother and stayed thirty more years until Mother died. In another age, Cora Walters would have made a fine minister. She made me a better person by her example, and certainly wasn't responsible for any of my sins, then or later. She was a tough old gal, too. One day she helped me kill a huge rat that was hanging around our house. Actually, I found it and she killed it while I cheered.

When we moved out to the country, Mother was concerned about my going to a small rural school, so she enrolled me in St. John's Catholic School downtown, where I attended second and third grade. Both years my teacher was Sister Mary Amata McGee, a fine and caring teacher but no pushover. I often got straight As on my six-week report card and a C in citizenship, which was a euphemism for good behavior in class. I loved to read and compete in spelling contests, but I talked too much. It was a constant problem in grade school, and as my critics and many of my friends would say, it's one I never quite got over. I also got in trouble once for excusing myself to go to the bathroom and staying away too long during the daily rosary. I was fascinated by the Catholic Church, its rituals and the devotion of the nuns, but getting on my knees on the seat of my desk and leaning on the back with the rosary beads was often too much for a rambunctious boy whose only church experience before then had been in the Sunday school and the summer vacation Bible school of the First Baptist Church in Hope.

After a year or so on the farm, Daddy decided to move into Hot Springs. He rented a big house from Uncle Raymond at 1011 Park Avenue, in the east end of town. He led Mother to believe he'd made a good deal for it and had bought the house with his income and hers, but even with their two incomes, and with housing costs a considerably smaller part of the average family's expenses than now, I can't see how we could have afforded it. The house was up on a hill; it had two stories, five bedrooms, and a fascinating little ballroom upstairs with a bar on which stood a big rotating cage with two huge dice in it. Apparently the first owner had been in the gambling business. I spent many happy hours in that room, having parties or just playing with my friends.

The exterior of the house was white with green trim, with sloping roofs over the front entrance and the two sides. The front yard was terraced on three levels with a sidewalk down the middle and a rock wall between the middle and ground levels. The side yards were small, but large enough for Mother to indulge her favorite outdoor hobby, gardening. She especially loved to grow roses and did so in all her homes until she died. Mother tanned easily and deeply, and she got most of her tan while digging dirt around her flowers in a tank top and shorts. The back had a gravel driveway with a four-car garage, a nice lawn with a swing set, and, on both sides of the driveway, sloping lawns that went down to the street, Circle Drive.

We lived in that house from the time I was seven or eight until I was fifteen. It was fascinating to me. The grounds were full of shrubs, bushes, flowers, long hedges laced with honeysuckle, and lots of trees, including a fig, a pear, two crab apples, and a huge old oak in the front.

I helped Daddy take care of the grounds. It was one thing we did do together, though as I got older, I did more and more of it myself. The house was near a wooded area, so I was always running across spiders, tarantulas, centipedes, scorpions, wasps, hornets, bees, and snakes, along with more benign creatures like squirrels, chipmunks, blue jays, robins, and woodpeckers. Once, when I was mowing the lawn, I looked down to see a rattlesnake sliding along with the lawn mower, apparently captivated by the vibrations. I didn't like the vibes, so I ran like crazy and escaped unscathed.

Another time I wasn't so lucky. Daddy had put up a huge three-story birdhouse for martins, which nest in groups, at the bottom of the back driveway. One day I was mowing grass down there and discovered it had become a nesting place not for martins but for bumblebees. They swarmed me, flying all over my body, my arms, my face. Amazingly, not one of them stung me. I ran off to catch my breath and consider my options. Mistakenly, I assumed they had decided I meant them no harm, so after a few minutes I went back to my mowing. I hadn't gone ten yards before they swarmed me again, this time stinging me all over my body. One got caught between my belly and my belt, stinging me over and over, something bumblebees can do that honeybees can't. I was delirious and had to be rushed to the doctor, but recovered soon enough with another valuable lesson: tribes of bumblebees give intruders one fair warning but not two. More than thirty-five years later, Kate Ross, the five-year-old daughter of my friends Michael Ross and Markie Post, sent me a letter that said simply: "Bees can sting you. Watch out." I knew just what she meant.

My move to Hot Springs gave my life many new experiences: a new, much larger and more sophisticated city; a new neighborhood; a new school, new friends, and my introduction to music; my first serious religious experience in a new church; and, of course, a new extended family in the Clinton clan.

The hot sulfur springs, for which the city is named, bubble up from below ground in a narrow gap in the Ouachita Mountains a little more than fifty miles west and slightly south of Little Rock. The first European to see them was Hernando de Soto, who came through the valley in 1541, saw the Indians bathing in the steaming springs, and, legend has it, thought he had discovered the fountain of youth.

In 1832, President Andrew Jackson signed a bill to protect four sections of land around Hot Springs as a federal reservation, the first such bill Congress ever enacted, well before the National Park Service was established or Yellowstone became our first national park. Soon more hotels sprung up to house visitors. By the 1880s, Central Avenue, the main street, snaking a mile and a half or so through the gap in the mountains where the springs were, was sprouting beautiful bathhouses as more than 100,000 people a year were taking baths for everything from rheumatism to paralysis to malaria to venereal disease to general relaxation. In the first quarter of the twentieth century, the grandest bathhouses were built, more than a million baths a year were taken, and the spa city became known around the world. After its status was changed from federal reservation to national park, Hot Springs became the only city in America that was actually in one of our national parks.

The city's attraction was amplified by grand hotels, an opera house, and, beginning in the mid-nineteenth century, gambling. By the 1880s, there were several open gambling houses, and Hot Springs was on its way to being both an attractive spa and a notorious town. For decades before and during World War II, it was run by a boss worthy of any big city, Mayor Leo McLaughlin. He ran the gambling with the help of a mobster who moved down from New York, Owen Vincent "Owney" Madden.

After the war, a GI ticket of reformers headed by Sid McMath broke McLaughlin's power in a move that, soon after, made the thirty-five-year-old McMath the nation's youngest governor. Notwithstanding the GI reformers, however, gambling continued to operate, with payoffs to state and local politicians and law-enforcement officials, well into the 1960s. Owney Madden lived in Hot Springs as a "respectable" citizen for the rest of his life. Mother once put him to sleep for surgery. She came home afterward and laughingly told me that looking at his X-ray was like visiting a planetarium: the twelve bullets still in his body reminded her of shooting stars.

Ironically, because it was illegal, the Mafia never took over gambling in Hot Springs; instead, we had our own local bosses. Sometimes the competing interests fought, but in my time, the violence was always controlled. For example, the garages of two houses were bombed, but at a time when no one was home.

For the last three decades of the nineteenth century and the first five of the twentieth, gambling drew an amazing array of characters to town: outlaws, mobsters, military heroes, actors, and a host of baseball greats. The legendary pool shark Minnesota Fats came often. In 1977, as attorney general, I shot pool with him for a charity in Hot Springs. He killed me in the game but made up for it by regaling me with stories of long-ago visits, when he played the horses by day, then ate and gambled up and down Central Avenue all night, adding to his pocketbook and his famous waistline.

Hot Springs drew politicians too. William Jennings Bryan came several times. So did Teddy Roosevelt in

1910, Herbert Hoover in 1927, and Franklin and Eleanor Roosevelt for the state's centennial in 1936. Huey Long had a second honeymoon with his wife there. JFK and Lyndon Johnson visited before they were Presidents. So did Harry Truman, the only one who gambled—at least the only one who didn't hide it.

The gambling and hot-water attractions of Hot Springs were enhanced by large brightly lit auction houses, which alternated with gambling spots and restaurants on Central Avenue on the other side of the street from the bathhouses; by Oaklawn racetrack, which offered fine Thoroughbred racing for thirty days a year in the spring, the only legal gambling in the city; by slot machines in many of the restaurants, some of which even kids were allowed to play if they were sitting on their parents' laps; and by three lakes near the city, the most important of which was Lake Hamilton, where many of the city's grandees, including Uncle Raymond, had large houses. Thousands of people flocked to the lake's motels for summer vacation. There was also an alligator farm in which the largest resident was eighteen feet long; an ostrich farm, whose residents sometimes paraded down Central Avenue; Keller Breland's IQZoo, full of animals and featuring the alleged skeleton of a mermaid; and a notorious whorehouse run by Maxine Harris (later Maxine Temple Jones), a real character who openly deposited her payoffs in the local authorities' bank accounts and who in 1983 wrote an interesting book about her life: **"Call Me Madam": The Life and Times of a Hot Springs Madam.** When I was ten or eleven, on a couple of occasions my friends and I entertained ourselves for hours by calling Maxine's place over and over, tying up her phone and blocking calls from real customers. It infuriated her and she cursed us out with salty and creative language we'd never before heard from a woman, or a man, for that matter. It was hilarious. I think she thought it was funny, too, at least for the first fifteen minutes or so.

For Arkansas, a state composed mostly of white Southern Baptists and blacks, Hot Springs was amazingly diverse, especially for a town of only 35,000. There was a good-sized black population and a hotel, the Knights of the Pythias, for black visitors. There were two Catholic churches and two synagogues. The Jewish residents owned some of the best stores and ran the auction houses. The best toy store in town was Ricky's, named by the Silvermans after their son, who was in the band with me. Lauray's, the jewelry store where I bought little things for Mother, was owned by Marty and Laura Fleishner. And there was the B'nai B'rith's Leo N. Levi Hospital, which used the hot springs to treat arthritis. I also met my first Arab-Americans in Hot Springs, the Zorubs and the Hassins. When David Zorub's parents were killed in Lebanon, he was adopted by his uncle. He came to this country at nine unable to speak any English and eventually became valedictorian of his class and governor of Boys State. Now he is a neurosurgeon in Pennsylvania. Guido Hassin and his sisters were the children of the World War II romance of a Syrian-American and an Italian woman; they were my neighbors during high school. I also had a Japanese-American friend, Albert Hahm, and a Czech classmate, René Duchac, whose émigré parents owned a restaurant, The Little Bohemia. There was a large Greek community, which included a Greek Orthodox church and Angelo's, a restaurant just around the corner from Clinton Buick. It was a great old-fashioned place, with its long soda fountain–like bar and tables covered with red-and-white checked tablecloths. The house specialty was a three-way: chili, beans, and spaghetti.

My best Greek friends by far were the Leopoulos family. George ran a little café on Bridge Street between Central Avenue and Broadway, which we claimed was the shortest street in America, stretching all of a third of a block. George's wife, Evelyn, was a tiny woman who believed in reincarnation, collected antiques, and loved Liberace, who thrilled her by coming to her house for dinner once while he was performing in Hot Springs. The younger Leopoulos son, Paul David, became my best friend in fourth grade and has been like my brother ever since.

When we were boys, I loved to go with him to his dad's café, especially when the carnival was in town, because all the carnies ate there. Once they gave us free tickets to all the rides. We used every one of them, making David happy and me dizzy and sick to my stomach. After that I stuck to bumper cars and Ferris wheels. We've shared a lifetime of ups and downs, and enough laughs for three lifetimes.

That I had friends and acquaintances from such a diverse group of people when I was young may seem normal today, but in 1950s Arkansas, it could have happened only in Hot Springs. Even so, most of my friends and I led pretty normal lives, apart from the occasional calls to Maxine's bordello and the temptation to cut classes during racing season, which I never did, but which proved irresistible to some of my classmates in high school.

From fourth through sixth grades, most of my life ran up and down Park Avenue. Our neighborhood was interesting. There was a row of beautiful houses east of ours all the way to the woods and another row behind our house on

Circle Drive. David Leopoulos lived a couple of blocks away. My closest friends among the near neighbors were the Crane family. They lived in a big old mysterious-looking wooden house just across from my back drive. Edie Crane's Aunt Dan took the Crane kids, and often me, everywhere—to the movies, to Snow Springs Park to swim in a pool fed by very cold springwater, and to Whittington Park to play miniature golf. Rose, the oldest kid, was my age. Larry, the middle child, was a couple of years younger. We always had a great relationship except once, when I used a new word on him. We were playing with Rose in my backyard when I told him his epidermis was showing. That made him mad. Then I told him the epidermises of his mother and father were showing too. That did it. He went home, got a knife, came back, and threw it at me. Even though he missed, I've been leery of big words ever since. Mary Dan, the youngest, asked me to wait for her to grow up so that we could get married.

Across the street from the front of our house was a collection of modest businesses. There was a small garage made of tin sheeting. David and I used to hide behind the oak tree and throw acorns against the tin to rattle the guys who worked there. Sometimes we would also try to hit the hubcaps of passing cars and, when we succeeded, it made a loud pinging noise. One day one of our targets stopped suddenly, got out of the car, saw us hiding behind a bush, and rushed up the driveway after us. After that, I didn't lob so many acorns at cars. But it was great fun.

Next to the garage was a brick block that contained a grocery, a Laundromat, and Stubby's, a small family-run barbeque restaurant, where I often enjoyed a meal alone, just sitting at the front table by the window, wondering about the lives of the people in the passing cars. I got my first job at thirteen in that grocery store. The owner, Dick Sanders, was already about seventy, and, like many people his age back then, he thought it was a bad thing to be left-handed, so he decided to change me, a deeply left-handed person. One day he had me stacking mayonnaise right-handed, big jars of Hellmann's mayonnaise, which cost eighty-nine cents. I misstacked one and it fell to the floor, leaving a mess of broken glass and mayo. First I cleaned it up. Then Dick told me he'd have to dock my pay for the lost jar. I was making a dollar an hour. I got up my courage and said, "Look, Dick, you can have a good left-handed grocery boy for a dollar an hour, but you can't have a clumsy right-handed one for free." To my surprise, he laughed and agreed. He even let me start my first business, a used–comic-book stand in front of the store. I had carefully saved two trunkloads of comic books. They were in very good condition and sold well. At the time I was proud of myself, though I know now that if I'd saved them, they'd be valuable collectors' items today.

Next to our house going west, toward town, was the Perry Plaza Motel. I liked the Perrys and their daughter Tavia, who was a year or two older than I. One day I was visiting her just after she'd gotten a new BB gun. I must have been nine or ten. She threw a belt on the floor and said if I stepped over it she'd shoot me. Of course, I did. And she shot me. It was a leg hit so it could have been worse, and I resolved to become a better judge of when someone's bluffing.

I remember something else about the Perrys' motel. It was yellow-brick—two stories high and one room wide, stretching from Park Avenue to Circle Drive. Sometimes people would rent rooms there, and at other motels and rooming houses around town, for weeks or even months at a time. Once a middle-aged man did that with the backmost room on the second floor. One day the police came and took him away. He had been performing abortions there. Until then, I don't think I knew what an abortion was.

Farther down Park Avenue was a little barbershop, where Mr. Brizendine cut my hair. About a quarter mile past the barbershop, Park Avenue runs into Ramble Street, which then led south up a hill to my new school, Ramble Elementary. In fourth grade I started band. The grade school band was composed of students from all the city's elementary schools. The director, George Gray, had a great, encouraging way with little kids as we squawked away. I played clarinet for a year or so, then switched to tenor saxophone because the band needed one, a change I would never regret. My most vivid memory of fifth grade is a class discussion about memory in which one of my classmates, Tommy O'Neal, told our teacher, Mrs. Caristianos, he thought he could remember when he was born. I didn't know whether he had a vivid imagination or a loose screw, but I liked him and had finally met someone with an even better memory than mine.

I adored my sixth-grade teacher, Kathleen Schaer. Like a lot of teachers of her generation, she never married and devoted her life to children. She lived into her late eighties with her cousin, who made the same choices. As gentle and kind as she was, Miss Schaer believed in tough love. The day before we had our little grade school graduation ceremony, she held me after class. She told me I should be graduating first in my class, tied with Donna Standiford. Instead, because my citizenship grades were so low—we might have been calling it "deportment" by then—I had been dropped to a tie for third. Miss Schaer said, "Billy, when you grow up you're either going to be governor or get in a lot of trouble.

It all depends on whether you learn when to talk and when to keep quiet." Turns out she was right on both counts.

When I was at Ramble, my interest in reading grew and I discovered the Garland County Public Library, which was downtown, near the courthouse and not far from Clinton Buick Company. I would go there for hours, browsing among the books and reading lots of them. I was most fascinated by books about Native Americans and read children's biographies of Geronimo, the great Apache; Crazy Horse, the Lakota Sioux who killed Custer and routed his troops at Little Bighorn; Chief Joseph of the Nez Percé, who made peace with his powerful statement, "From where the sun now stands, I will fight no more forever"; and the great Seminole chief Osceola, who developed a written alphabet for his people. I never lost my interest in Native Americans or my feeling that they had been terribly mistreated.

My last stop on Park Avenue was my first real church, Park Place Baptist Church. Though Mother and Daddy didn't go except on Easter and sometimes at Christmas, Mother encouraged me to go, and I did, just about every Sunday. I loved getting dressed up and walking down there. From the time I was about eleven until I graduated from high school, my teacher was A. B. "Sonny" Jeffries. His son Bert was in my class and we became close friends. Every Sunday for years, we went to Sunday school and church together, always sitting in the back, often in our own world. In 1955, I had absorbed enough of my church's teachings to know that I was a sinner and to want Jesus to save me. So I came down the aisle at the end of Sunday service, professed my faith in Christ, and asked to be baptized. The Reverend Fitzgerald came to the house to talk to Mother and me. Baptists require an informed profession of faith for baptism; they want people to know what they are doing, as opposed to the Methodists' infant-sprinkling ritual that took Hillary and her brothers out of hell's way.

Bert Jeffries and I were baptized together, along with several other people on a Sunday night. The baptismal pool was just above the choir loft. When the curtains were opened, the congregation could see the pastor standing in a white robe, dunking the saved. Just ahead of Bert and me in the line was a woman who was visibly afraid of the water. She trembled down the steps into the pool. When the preacher held her nose and dunked her, she went completely rigid. Her right leg jerked straight up in the air and came to rest on the narrow strip of glass that protected the choir loft from splashes. Her heel stuck. She couldn't get it off, so when the preacher tried to lift her up, he couldn't budge her. Since he was looking at her submerged head, he didn't see what had happened, so he just kept jerking on her. Finally he looked around, figured it out, and took the poor woman's leg down before she drowned. Bert and I were in stitches. I couldn't help thinking that if Jesus had this much of a sense of humor, being a Christian wasn't going to be so tough.

Besides my new friends, neighborhood, school, and church, Hot Springs brought me a new extended family in the Clintons. My step-grandparents were Al and Eula Mae Cornwell Clinton. Poppy Al, as we all called him, came from Dardanelle, in Yell County, a beautiful wooded place seventy miles west of Little Rock up the Arkansas River. He met and married his wife there after her family migrated from Mississippi in the 1890s. We called my new grandmother Mama Clinton. She was one of a huge

Cornwell family that spread out all over Arkansas. Together with the Clintons and my mother's relatives, they gave me kinfolk in fifteen of Arkansas' seventy-five counties, an enormous asset when I started my political career in a time when personal contacts counted more than credentials or positions on the issues.

Poppy Al was a small man, shorter and slighter than Papaw, with a kind, sweet spirit. The first time I met him we were still living in Hope and he dropped by our house to see his son and his new family. He wasn't alone. At the time, he was still working as a parole officer for the state and he was taking one of the prisoners, who must have been out on furlough, back to the penitentiary. When he got out of the car to visit, the man was handcuffed to him. It was a hilarious sight, because the inmate was huge; he must have been twice Poppy Al's size. But Poppy Al spoke to him gently and respectfully and the man seemed to respond in kind. All I know is that Poppy Al got his man safely back on time.

Poppy Al and Mama Clinton lived in a small old house up on top of a hill. He kept a garden out back, of which he was very proud. He lived to be eighty-four, and when he was over eighty, that garden produced a tomato that weighed two and a half pounds. I had to use both hands to hold it.

Mama Clinton ruled the house. She was good to me, but she knew how to manipulate the men in her life. She always treated Daddy like the baby of the family who could do no wrong, which is probably one reason he never grew up. She liked Mother, who was better than most of the other family members at listening to her hypochondriacal tales of woe and at giving sensible, sympathetic advice. She lived to be ninety-three.

Poppy Al and Mama Clinton produced five children, one girl and four boys. The girl, Aunt Ilaree, was the second-oldest child. Her daughter Virginia, whose nickname was Sister, was then married to Gabe Crawford and was a good friend of Mother's. The older she got, the more of an idiosyncratic character Ilaree became. One day Mother was visiting her and Ilaree complained she was having trouble walking. She lifted up her skirt, revealing a huge growth on the inside of her leg. Not long afterward, when she met Hillary for the first time, she picked up her skirt again and showed her the tumor. It was a good beginning. Ilaree was the first of the Clintons to really like Hillary. Mother finally convinced her to have the tumor removed, and she took the first flight of her life to the Mayo Clinic. By the time they cut the tumor off it weighed nine pounds, but miraculously it had not spread cancer cells to the rest of her leg. I was told the clinic kept that amazing tumor for some time for study. When jaunty old Ilaree got home, it was clear she had been more afraid of her first flight than of the tumor or the surgery.

The oldest son was Robert. He and his wife, Evelyn, were quiet people who lived in Texas and who seemed sensibly happy to take Hot Springs and the rest of the Clintons in small doses.

The second son, Uncle Roy, had a feed store. His wife, Janet, and Mother were the two strongest personalities outside the blood family, and became great friends. In the early fifties Roy ran for the legislature and won. On election day, I handed out cards for him in my neighborhood, as close to the polling station as the law would allow. It was my first political experience. Uncle Roy served only one term. He was very well liked but didn't run for reelection, I think because Janet hated politics. Roy and Janet played dominoes with my folks almost every week for years, alternating between our home and theirs.

Raymond, the fourth child, was the only Clinton with any money or consistent involvement in politics. He had been part of the GI reform effort after World War II, although he wasn't in the service himself. Raymond Jr., "Corky," was the only one who was younger than I. He was also brighter. He literally became a rocket scientist, with a distinguished career at NASA.

Mother always had an ambiguous relationship with Raymond, because he liked to run everything and because, with Daddy's drinking, we often needed his help more that she wanted it. When we first moved to Hot Springs, we even went to Uncle Raymond's church, First Presbyterian, though Mother was at least a nominal Baptist. The pastor back then, the Reverend Overholser, was a remarkable man who produced two equally remarkable daughters: Nan Keohane, who became president of Wellesley, Hillary's alma mater, and then the first woman president of Duke University; and Geneva Overholser, who was editor of the **Des Moines Register** and endorsed me when I ran for President, and who later became the ombudsman for the **Washington Post,** where she aired the legitimate complaints of the general public but not the President.

Notwithstanding Mother's reservations, I liked Raymond. I was impressed with his strength, his influence in town, and his genuine interest in his kids, and in me. His egocentric foibles didn't bother me much, though we were as different as daylight and dark. In 1968, when I was giving pro–civil rights talks to civic clubs in Hot Springs, Raymond was supporting George Wallace for President. But in 1974, when I launched an apparently impossible campaign for Congress, Raymond and Gabe Crawford co-signed a $10,000 note to get me started. It was all the money in the world to me then. When his wife of more than forty-five years died, Raymond got reacquainted with a widow he had dated in high school and they married, bringing happiness to his last years. For some reason I can't even remember now, Raymond got mad at me late in his life. Before we could reconcile he got Alzheimer's. I went to visit him twice, once in St. Joseph's Hospital and once in a nursing home. The first time I told him I loved him, was sorry for whatever had come between us, and would always be grateful for all he'd done for me. He might have known who I was for a minute or two; I can't be sure. The second time, I know he didn't know me, but I wanted to see him once more anyway. He died at eighty-four, like my aunt Ollie, well after his mind had gone.

Raymond and his family lived in a big house on Lake Hamilton, where we used to go for picnics and rides in his big wooden Chris-Craft boat. We celebrated every Fourth of July there with lots of fireworks. After his death, Raymond's kids decided with sadness that they had to sell the old house. Luckily my library and foundation needed a retreat, so we bought the place and are renovating it for that purpose, and Raymond's kids and grandkids can still use it. He's smiling down on me now.

Not long after we moved to Park Avenue, in 1955 I think, my mother's parents moved to Hot Springs to a little apartment in an old house on our street, a mile or so toward town from our place. The move was motivated primarily by health concerns. Papaw's bronchiectasis continued to advance and Mammaw had had a stroke. Papaw got a job at a liquor store, which I think Daddy owned a part of, just across from Mr. Brizendine's barbershop. He

had a lot of free time, since even in Hot Springs most people were too conventional to frequent liquor stores in
broad daylight, so I often visited him there. He played a
lot of solitaire and taught me how. I still play three different kinds, often when I'm thinking through a problem
and need an outlet for nervous energy.

Mammaw's stroke was a major one, and in the aftermath she was racked by hysterical screaming. Unforgiv-
ably, to calm her down, her doctor prescribed morphine,
lots of it. It was when she got hooked that Mother
brought her and Papaw to Hot Springs. Her behavior
became even more irrational, and in desperation Mother
reluctantly committed her to the state's mental hospital,
about thirty miles away. I don't think there were any drug-
treatment facilities back then.

Of course I didn't know anything about her problem at
the time; I just knew she was sick. Then Mother drove me
over to the state hospital to see her. It was awful. It was
bedlam. We went into a big open room cooled by electric
fans encased in huge metal mesh to keep the patients from
putting their hands into them. Dazed-looking people
dressed in loose cotton dresses or pajamas walked around
aimlessly, muttering to themselves or shouting into space.
Still, Mammaw seemed normal and glad to see us, and we
had a good talk. After a few months, she had settled down
enough to come home, and she was never again on morphine. Her problem gave me my first exposure to the kind
of mental-health system that served most of America back
then. When he became governor, Orval Faubus modern-
ized our state hospital and put a lot more money into it.
Despite the damage he did in other areas, I was always
grateful to him for that.

FIVE

I n 1956, I finally got a brother, and our family finally
got a television set. My brother, Roger Cassidy Clinton, was born on July 25, his father's birthday. I was so
happy. Mother and Daddy had been trying to have a baby
for some time (a couple of years earlier she'd had a miscar-
riage). I think she, and probably he too, thought it might
save their marriage. Daddy's response was not auspicious.
I was with Mammaw and Papaw when Mother delivered
by caesarean section. Daddy picked me up and took me to
see her, then brought me home and left. He had been
drinking for the last few months, and instead of making
him happy and responsible, the birth of his only son
prompted him to run back to the bottle.

Along with the excitement of a new baby in the house
was the thrill of the new TV. There were lots of shows and
entertainers for kids: cartoons, **Captain Kangaroo** and
Howdy Doody, with Buffalo Bob Smith, whom I especially liked. And there was baseball: Mickey Mantle and
the Yankees, Stan Musial and the Cardinals, and my all-
time favorite, Willie Mays and the old New York Giants.

But strange as it was for a kid of ten years old, what
really dominated my TV viewing that summer were the
Republican and Democratic conventions. I sat on the
floor right in front of the TV and watched them both,
transfixed. It sounds crazy, but I felt right at home in the
world of politics and politicians. I liked President Eisen-

hower and enjoyed seeing him renominated, but we were Democrats, so I really got into their convention. Governor Frank Clement of Tennessee gave a rousing keynote address. There was an exciting contest for the vice-presidential nomination between young Senator John F. Kennedy and the eventual victor, Senator Estes Kefauver, who served Tennessee in the Senate with Al Gore's father. When Adlai Stevenson, the nominee in 1952, accepted his party's call to run again, he said he had prayed "this cup would pass from me." I admired Stevenson's intelligence and eloquence, but even then I couldn't understand why anyone wouldn't want the chance to be President. Now I think what he didn't want was to lead another losing effort. I do understand that. I've lost a couple of elections myself, though I never fought a battle I didn't first convince myself I could win.

I didn't spend all my time watching TV. I still saw all the movies I could. Hot Springs had two old-fashioned movie houses, the Paramount and the Malco, with big stages on which touring western stars appeared on the weekends. I saw Lash LaRue, all decked out in cowboy black, do his tricks with a bullwhip, and Gail Davis, who played Annie Oakley on TV, give a shooting exhibition.

Elvis Presley began to make movies in the late fifties. I loved Elvis. I could sing all his songs, as well as the Jordanaires' backgrounds. I admired him for doing his military service and was fascinated when he married his beautiful young wife, Priscilla. Unlike most parents, who thought his gyrations obscene, Mother loved Elvis, too, maybe even more than I did. We watched his legendary performance on **The Ed Sullivan Show** together, and laughed when the cameras cut off his lower body movements to protect us from the indecency. Beyond his music, I identified with his small-town southern roots. And I thought he had a good heart. Steve Clark, a friend of mine who served as attorney general when I was governor, once took his little sister, who was dying of cancer, to see Elvis perform in Memphis. When Elvis heard about the little girl, he put her and her brother in the front row, and after the concert he brought her up onstage and talked to her for a good while. I never forgot that.

Elvis's first movie, **Love Me Tender,** was my favorite and remains so, though I also liked **Loving You, Jailhouse Rock, King Creole,** and **Blue Hawaii.** After that, his movies got more saccharine and predictable. The interesting thing about **Love Me Tender,** a post–Civil War western, is that Elvis, already a national sex symbol, got the girl, Debra Paget, but only because she thought his older brother, whom she really loved, had been killed in the war. At the end of the film, Elvis gets shot and dies, leaving his brother with his wife.

I never quite escaped Elvis. In the '92 campaign, some members of my staff nicknamed me Elvis. A few years later, when I appointed Kim Wardlaw of Los Angeles to a federal judgeship, she was thoughtful enough to send me a scarf Elvis had worn and signed for her at one of his concerts in the early seventies, when she was nineteen. I still have it in my music room. And I confess: I still love Elvis.

My favorite movies during this time were the biblical epics: **The Robe, Demetrius and the Gladiators, Samson and Delilah, Ben-Hur,** and especially **The Ten Commandments,** the first movie I recall paying more than a dime to see. I saw **The Ten Commandments** when Mother and Daddy were on a brief trip to Las Vegas. I took a sack lunch and sat through the whole thing twice for the price of one ticket. Years later, when I welcomed

Charlton Heston to the White House as a Kennedy Center honoree, he was president of the National Rifle Association and a virulent critic of my legislative efforts to keep guns away from criminals and children. I joked to him and the audience that I liked him better as Moses than in his present role. To his credit, he took it in good humor.

In 1957, my grandfather's lungs finally gave out. He died in the relatively new Ouachita Hospital, where Mother worked. He was only fifty-six years old. Too much of his life had been occupied with economic woes, health problems, and marital strife, yet he always found things to enjoy in the face of his adversity. And he loved Mother and me more than life. His love, and the things he taught me, mostly by example, including appreciation for the gifts of daily life and the problems of other people, made me better than I could have been without him.

Nineteen fifty-seven was also the year of the Little Rock Central High crisis. In September, nine black kids, supported by Daisy Bates, the editor of the **Arkansas State Press,** Little Rock's black newspaper, integrated Little Rock Central High School. Governor Faubus, eager to break Arkansas' tradition of governors serving only two terms, abandoned his family's progressive tradition (his father had voted for Eugene Debs, the perpetual Socialist candidate for President) and called out the National Guard to prevent the integration. Then President Dwight Eisenhower federalized the troops to protect the students, and they went to school through angry mobs shouting racist epithets. Most of my friends were either against integration or apparently unconcerned. I didn't say too much about it, probably because my family was not especially political, but I hated what Faubus did. Though

Faubus had inflicted lasting damage to the state's image, he had assured himself not only a third two-year term but another three terms beyond that. Later he tried comebacks against Dale Bumpers, David Pryor, and me, but the state had moved beyond reaction by then.

The Little Rock Nine became a symbol of courage in the quest for equality. In 1987, on the thirtieth anniversary of the crisis, as governor I invited the Little Rock Nine back. I held a reception for them at the Governor's Mansion and took them to the room where Governor Faubus had orchestrated the campaign to keep them out of school. In 1997, we had a big ceremony on the lawn of Central High for the fortieth anniversary. After the program, Governor Mike Huckabee and I held open the doors of Central High as the nine walked through. Elizabeth Eckford, who at fifteen was deeply seared emotionally by vicious harassment as she walked alone through an angry mob, was reconciled with Hazel Massery, one of the girls who had taunted her forty years earlier. In 2000, at a ceremony on the South Lawn of the White House, I presented the Little Rock Nine with the Congressional Gold Medal, an honor initiated by Senator Dale Bumpers. In that late summer of 1957, the nine helped to set all of us, white and black alike, free from the dark shackles of segregation and discrimination. In so doing, they did more for me than I could ever do for them. But I hope that what I did do for them, and for civil rights, in the years afterward honored the lessons I learned more than fifty years ago in my grandfather's store.

In the summer of 1957 and again after Christmas that year, I took my first trips out of Arkansas since going to New Orleans to see Mother. Both times I got on a Trailways bus bound for Dallas to visit Aunt Otie. It was a luxurious bus for the time, with an attendant who served little sandwiches. I ate a lot of them.

Dallas was the third real city I had been in. I visited Little Rock on a fifth-grade field trip to the state Capitol, the highlight of which was a visit to the governor's office with the chance to sit in the absent governor's chair. It made such an impression on me that years later I often took pictures with children sitting in my chair both in the governor's office and in the Oval Office.

The trips to Dallas were remarkable to me for three reasons, beyond the great Mexican food, the zoo, and the most beautiful miniature golf course I'd ever seen. First, I got to meet some of my father's relatives. His younger brother, Glenn Blythe, was the constable of Irving, a suburb of Dallas. He was a big, handsome man, and being with him made me feel connected to my father. Sadly, he also died too young, at forty-eight, of a stroke. My father's niece, Ann Grigsby, had been a friend of Mother's since she married my father. On those trips she became a lifetime friend, telling me stories about my father and about what Mother was like as a young bride. Ann remains my closest link to my Blythe family heritage.

Second, on New Year's Day 1958, I went to the Cotton Bowl, my first college football game. Rice, led by quarterback King Hill, played Navy, whose great running back Joe Bellino won the Heisman Trophy two years later. I sat in the end zone but felt as if I were on a throne, as Navy won 20–7.

Third, just after Christmas I went to the movies by myself on an afternoon when Otie had to work. I think **The Bridge on the River Kwai** was showing. I loved the movie, but I didn't like the fact that I had to buy an adult ticket even though I wasn't yet twelve. I was so big for my age, the ticket seller didn't believe me. It was the first time in my life someone refused to take my word. This hurt, but I learned an important difference between big impersonal cities and small towns, and I began my long preparation for life in Washington, where no one takes your word for anything.

I started the 1958–59 school year at the junior high school. It was right across the street from Ouachita Hospital and adjacent to Hot Springs High School. Both school buildings were dark red brick. The high school was four stories high, with a great old auditorium and classic lines befitting its 1917 vintage. The junior high was smaller and more pedestrian but still represented an important new phase of my life. The biggest thing that happened to me that year, however, had nothing to do with school. One of the Sunday-school teachers offered to take a few of the boys in our church to Little Rock to hear Billy Graham preach in his crusade in War Memorial Stadium, where the Razorbacks played. Racial tensions were still high in 1958. Little Rock's schools were closed in a last-gasp effort to stop integration, its kids dispersed to schools in nearby towns. Segregationists from the White Citizens Council and other quarters suggested that, given the tense atmosphere, it would be better if the Reverend Graham restricted admission to the crusade to whites only. He replied that Jesus loved all sinners, that everyone needed a chance to hear the word, and therefore that he would cancel the crusade rather than preach to a segregated audience. Back then, Billy Graham was the living embodiment of Southern Baptist authority, the largest religious figure in the South, perhaps in the nation. I wanted to hear him

preach even more after he took the stand he did. The segregationists backed down, and the Reverend Graham
delivered a powerful message in his trademark twenty
minutes. When he gave the invitation for people to come
down onto the football field to become Christians or to
rededicate their lives to Christ, hundreds of blacks and
whites came down the stadium aisles together, stood
together, and prayed together. It was a powerful counter-
point to the racist politics sweeping across the South. I
loved Billy Graham for doing that. For months after that I
regularly sent part of my small allowance to support his
ministry.

Thirty years later, Billy came back to Little Rock for
another crusade in War Memorial Stadium. As governor, I
was honored to sit on the stage with him one night and
even more to go with him and my friend Mike Coulson to
visit my pastor and Billy's old friend W. O. Vaught, who
was dying of cancer. It was amazing to listen to these two
men of God discussing death, their fears, and their faith.
When Billy got up to leave, he held Dr. Vaught's hand in
his and said, "W.O., it won't be long now for both of us.
I'll see you soon, just outside the Eastern Gate," the
entrance to the Holy City.

When I became President, Billy and Ruth Graham visited Hillary and me in the White House residence. Billy
prayed with me in the Oval Office, and wrote inspiring
letters of instruction and encouragement in my times of
trial. In all his dealings with me, just as in that crucial crusade in 1958, Billy Graham lived his faith.

Junior high school brought a whole new set of experiences
and challenges, as I began to learn more about my mind,
my body, my spirit, and my little world. I liked most of

what I learned about myself but not all of it. And some of what came into my head and life scared the living hell out of me, including anger at Daddy, the first stirrings of sexual feelings toward girls, and doubts about my religious convictions, which I think developed because I couldn't understand why a God whose existence I couldn't prove would create a world in which so many bad things happened.

My interest in music grew. I was now going to junior high band practices every day, looking forward to marching at football game halftimes and in the Christmas parade, to the concerts, and to the regional and state band festivals, at which judges graded the bands as well as solo and ensemble performances. I won a fair number of medals in junior high, and when I didn't do so well, it was invariably because I tried to perform a piece that was too difficult for me. I still have some of the judges' rating sheets on my early solos, pointing out my poor control in the lower register, bad phrasing, and puffy cheeks. The ratings got better when I grew older, but I never quite cured the puffy cheeks. My favorite solo in this period was an arrangement of **Rhapsody in Blue,** which I loved to try to play and once performed for guests at the old Majestic Hotel. I was nervous as could be, but determined to make a good impression in my new white coat, with red plaid bow tie and cummerbund.

My junior high band directors encouraged me to improve and I decided to try. Arkansas had a number of summer band camps back then on university campuses and I wanted to go to one of them. I decided to attend the camp at the main University of Arkansas campus in Fayetteville because it had a lot of good teachers and I wanted to spend a couple of weeks on the campus where I assumed I'd go to college one day. I went there every summer for seven years, until the summer after high school graduation. It proved to be one of the most important experiences in my growing up. First, I played and played. And I got better. Some days I would play for twelve hours until my lips were so sore I could hardly move them. I also listened to and learned from older, better musicians.

Band camp also proved an ideal place for me to develop political and leadership skills. The whole time I was growing up, it was the only place being a "band boy" instead of a football player wasn't a political liability. It was also the only place being a band boy wasn't a disadvantage in the adolescent quest for pretty girls. We all had a grand time, from the minute we got up for breakfast at a university dining hall until we went to bed in one of the dorms, all the while feeling very important.

I also loved the campus. The university is the oldest land-grant college west of the Mississippi. As a high school junior I wrote a paper on it and as governor I supported an appropriation to restore Old Main, the oldest building on campus. Built in 1871, it is a unique reminder of the Civil War, marked by two towers, with the northern one higher than its southern counterpart.

The band also brought me my best friend in junior high, Joe Newman. He was a drummer, and a good one. His mother, Rae, was a teacher in our school, and she and her husband, Dub, always made me feel welcome in their big white wood-frame house on Ouachita Avenue, near where Uncle Roy and Aunt Janet lived. Joe was smart, skeptical, moody, funny, and loyal. I liked to play games or just talk with him. I still do—we've stayed close over the years.

My main academic interest in junior high was math. I was lucky enough to be among the first group in our town to take algebra in the eighth, not the ninth, grade, which meant I'd have a chance to take geometry, algebra II, trigonometry, and calculus by the time I finished high school. I loved math because it was problem-solving, which always got my juices flowing. Although I never took a math class in college, I always thought I was good at it until I had to give up helping Chelsea with her homework when she was in ninth grade. Another illusion bites the dust.

Mary Matassarin taught me algebra and geometry. Her sister, Verna Dokey, taught history, and Verna's husband, Vernon, a retired coach, taught eighth-grade science. I liked them all, but even though I was not particularly good at science, it was one of Mr. Dokey's lessons that stayed with me. Though his wife and her sister were attractive women, Vernon Dokey, to put it charitably, was not a handsome man. He was burly, a bit heavy around the waist, wore thick glasses, and smoked cheap cigars in a cigar holder with a small mouthpiece, which gave his face a peculiar pinched look when he sucked on it. He generally affected a brusque manner, but he had a great smile, a good sense of humor, and a keen understanding of human nature. One day he looked out at us and said, "Kids, years from now you may not remember anything you learned about science in this class, so I'm going to teach you something about human nature you should remember. Every morning when I wake up, I go into my bathroom, splash water on my face, shave, wipe the shaving cream off, then look in the mirror and say, 'Vernon, you're beautiful.' You remember that, kids. Everybody wants to feel like they're beautiful." And I have remembered, for more than forty years. It's helped me understand things I would have missed if Ver-

non Dokey hadn't told me he was beautiful, and I hadn't
come to see that, in fact, he was.

I needed all the help I could get in understanding people
in junior high school. It was there that I had to face the
fact that I was not destined to be liked by everyone, usually for reasons I couldn't figure out. Once when I was
walking to school and was about a block away, an older
student, one of the town "hoods," who was standing in
the gap between two buildings smoking a cigarette,
flicked the burning weed at me, hitting the bridge of my
nose and nearly burning my eye. I never did figure out
why he did it, but after all, I was a fat band boy who didn't
wear cool jeans (Levi's, preferably with the stitching on
the back pockets removed).

Around that same time, I got into an argument about
something or other with Clifton Bryant, a boy who was a
year or so older, but smaller than I was. One day my
friends and I decided to walk home from school, about
three miles. Clifton lived in the same end of town, and he
followed us home, taunting me and hitting me on the
back and shoulders over and over. We walked like that all
the way up Central Avenue to the fountain and the right
turn to Park Avenue. For more than a mile I tried to
ignore him. Finally I couldn't take it anymore. I turned,
took a big swing, and hit him. It was a good blow, but by
the time it landed he had already turned to run away, so it
caught him only in the back. As I said, I was slow. When
Clifton ran away home, I yelled at him to come back and
fight like a man. He kept on going. By the time I got
home, I had calmed down and the "atta boys" I got from
my buddies had worn off. I was afraid I might have hurt
him, so I made Mother call his house to make sure he was

okay. We never had any trouble after that. I had learned I could defend myself, but I hadn't enjoyed hurting him and I was a little disturbed by my anger, the currents of which would prove deeper and stronger in the years ahead. I now know that my anger on that day was a normal and healthy response to the way I'd been treated. But because of the way Daddy behaved when he was angry and drunk, I associated anger with being out of control and I was determined not to lose control. Doing so could unleash the deeper, constant anger I kept locked away because I didn't know where it came from.

Even when I was mad I had sense enough not to take on every challenge. Twice in those years, I took a pass, or, if you're inclined to be critical, a dive. Once I went swimming with the Crane kids in the Caddo River, west of Hot Springs, near a little town called Caddo Gap. One of the local country boys came up to the riverbank near where I was swimming and shouted some insult at me. So I mouthed off back at him. Then he picked up a rock and threw it at me. He was twenty yards or so away, but he hit me right in the head, near the temple, and drew blood. I wanted to get out and fight, but I could see he was bigger, stronger, and tougher than I, so I swam away. Given my experiences with the ram, Tavia Perry's BB gun, and similar mistakes I still had ahead of me, I guess I did the right thing.

The second time I took a pass in junior high I know I did the right thing. On Friday nights there was always a dance in the gym of the local YMCA. I loved rock-and-roll music and dancing and went frequently, starting in eighth or ninth grade, even though I was fat, uncool, and hardly popular with the girls. Besides, I still wore the wrong jeans.

One night at the Y, I strolled into the poolroom next to the gym, where the Coke machine was, to get something to drink. Some older high school boys were shooting pool or standing around watching. One of them was Henry Hill, whose family owned the old bowling alley downtown, the Lucky Strike Lanes. Henry started in on me about my jeans, which, that night, were especially raunchy. They were carpenter's jeans, with a right side loop to hang a hammer in. I was insecure enough without Henry grinding on me, so I sassed him back. He slugged me in the jaw as hard as he could. Now, I was big for my age, about five nine, 185 pounds. But Henry Hill was six foot six with an enormous reach. No way was I going to hit back. Besides, to my amazement, it didn't hurt too badly. So I just stood my ground and stared at him. I think Henry was surprised I didn't go down or run off, because he laughed, slapped me on the back, and said I was okay. We were always friendly after that. I had learned again that I could take a hit and that there's more than one way to stand against aggression.

By the time I started ninth grade, in September 1960, the presidential campaign was in full swing. My homeroom and English teacher, Ruth Atkins, was also from Hope and, like me, a stomp-down Democrat. She had us read and discuss Dickens's **Great Expectations,** but left lots of time for political debate. Hot Springs had more Republicans than most of the rest of Arkansas back then, but their roots were far less conservative than the current crop. Some of the older families had been there since the Civil War and became Republicans because they were against secession and slavery. Some families had Republican roots in Teddy Roosevelt's progressivism. Others supported Eisenhower's moderate conservatism.

The Arkansas Democrats were an even more diverse group. Those in the Civil War tradition were Democrats because their forebears had supported secession and slavery. A larger group swelled the ranks of the party in the Depression, when so many unemployed workers and poor farmers saw FDR as a savior and later loved our neighbor from Missouri, Harry Truman. A smaller group were immigrant Democrats, mostly from Europe. Most blacks were Democrats because of Roosevelt, and Truman's stand for civil rights, and their sense that Kennedy would be more aggressive than Nixon on the issue. A small group of whites felt that way too. I was one of them.

In Miss Atkins's class most of the kids were for Nixon. I remember David Leopoulos defending him on the grounds that he had far more experience than Kennedy, especially in foreign affairs, and that his civil rights record was pretty good, which was true. I didn't really have anything against Nixon at this point. I didn't know then about his Red-baiting campaigns for the House and Senate in California against Jerry Voorhis and Helen Gahagan Douglas, respectively. I liked the way he stood up to Nikita Khrushchev. In 1956, I had admired both Eisenhower and Stevenson, but by 1960, I was a partisan. I had been for LBJ in the primaries because of his Senate leadership, especially in passing a civil rights bill in 1957, and his poor southern roots. I also liked Hubert Humphrey, because he was the most passionate advocate for civil rights, and Kennedy, because of his youth, strength, and commitment to getting the country moving again. With Kennedy the nominee, I made the best case I could to my classmates.

I badly wanted him to win, especially after he called Coretta King to express his concern when her husband was jailed, and after he spoke to the Southern Baptists in Houston, defending his faith and the right of Catholic Americans to run for President. Most of my classmates, and their parents, disagreed. I was getting used to it. A few months earlier, I had lost the student council president's race to Mike Thomas, a good guy, who would be one of four classmates to be killed in Vietnam. Nixon carried our county, but Kennedy squeaked by in Arkansas with 50.2 percent of the vote, despite the best efforts of Protestant fundamentalists to convince Baptist Democrats that he would be taking orders from the pope.

Of course, the fact that he was a Catholic was one of the reasons I wanted Kennedy to be President. From my own experiences at St. John's School and my encounters with the nuns who worked with Mother at St. Joseph's Hospital, I liked and admired Catholics—their values, devotion, and social conscience. I was also proud that the only Arkansan ever to run for national office, Senator Joe T. Robinson, was the running mate of the first Catholic candidate for President, Governor Al Smith of New York, in 1928. Like Kennedy, Smith carried Arkansas, thanks to Robinson.

Given my affinity for Catholics, it's ironic that, besides music, my major extracurricular interest from ninth grade on was the Order of DeMolay, a boys' organization sponsored by the Masons. I always thought the Masons and DeMolays were anti-Catholic, though I didn't understand why. DeMolay was, after all, a pre-Reformation martyr who died a believer at the hands of the Spanish Inquisition. It was not until I was doing research for this book that I learned that the Catholic Church had condemned Masons going back to the early eighteenth century as a dangerous authority-threatening institution, while the

Masons don't ban people of any faith and, in fact, have had a few Catholic members.

The purpose of DeMolay was to foster personal and civic virtues and friendship among its members. I enjoyed the camaraderie, memorizing all the parts of the rituals, moving up the offices to be master counselor of my local chapter, and going to the state conventions, with their vigorous politics and parties with the Rainbow Girls, DeMolay's sister organization. I learned more about politics by participating in the state DeMolay election, though I never ran myself. The cleverest man I supported for state master counselor was Bill Ebbert of Jonesboro. Ebbert would have made a great mayor or congressional committee chairman in the old days when seniority ruled. He was funny, smart, tough, and as good at deal making as LBJ. Once he was barreling down an Arkansas highway at ninety-five miles per hour when a state police car, with siren screaming, gave chase. Ebbert had a shortwave radio, so he called the police to report a serious car wreck three miles behind. The police car got the message and quickly changed direction, leaving the speeding Ebbert home free. I wonder if the policeman ever figured it out.

Even though I enjoyed DeMolay, I didn't buy the idea that its secret rituals were a big deal that somehow made our lives more important. After I graduated out of DeMolay, I didn't follow a long line of distinguished Americans going back to George Washington, Benjamin Franklin, and Paul Revere into Masonry, probably because in my twenties I was in an anti-joining phase, and I didn't like what I mistakenly thought was Masonry's latent anti-Catholicism, or the segregation of blacks and whites into different branches (though when I was exposed to black Prince Hall Masonic conventions as governor, the members seemed to be having more fun on their own than the Masons I had known).

Besides, I didn't need to be in a secret fraternity to have secrets. I had real secrets of my own, rooted in Daddy's alcoholism and abuse. They got worse when I was fourteen and in the ninth grade and my brother was only four. One night Daddy closed the door to his bedroom, started screaming at Mother, then began to hit her. Little Roger was scared, just as I had been nine years earlier on the night of the gunshot. Finally, I couldn't bear the thought of Mother being hurt and Roger being frightened anymore. I grabbed a golf club out of my bag and threw open their door. Mother was on the floor and Daddy was standing over her, beating on her. I told him to stop and said that if he didn't I was going to beat the hell out of him with the golf club. He just caved, sitting down in a chair next to the bed and hanging his head. It made me sick. In her book, Mother says she called the police and had Daddy taken to jail for the night. I don't remember that, but I do know we didn't have any more trouble for a good while. I suppose I was proud of myself for standing up for Mother, but afterward I was sad about it, too. I just couldn't accept the fact that a basically good person would try to make his own pain go away by hurting someone else. I wish I'd had someone to talk with about all this, but I didn't, so I had to figure it out for myself.

I came to accept the secrets of our house as a normal part of my life. I never talked to anyone about them—not a friend, a neighbor, a teacher, a pastor. Many years later when I ran for President, several of my friends told reporters they never knew. Of course, as with most secrets, some people did know. Daddy couldn't be on good behavior with everyone but us, though he tried. Whoever else knew—family members, Mother's close friends, a couple of policemen—didn't mention it to me, so I thought I had a real secret and kept quiet about it. Our family policy was "don't ask, don't tell."

The only other secret I had in grade school and junior high was sending part of my allowance to Billy Graham after his Little Rock crusade. I never told my parents or friends about that, either. Once when I was on my way to the mailbox near our driveway off Circle Drive with my money for Billy, I saw Daddy working in the backyard. To avoid being seen, I went out the front down to Park Avenue, turned right, and cut back through the driveway of the Perry Plaza Motel next door. Our house was on a hill. Perry Plaza was on flat land below. When I got about halfway through the drive, Daddy looked down and saw me anyway with the letter in my hand. I proceeded to the mailbox, put the letter in, and came home. He must have wondered what I was doing, but he didn't ask. He never did. I guess he had enough secrets of his own to carry.

The question of secrets is one I've thought about a lot over the years. We all have them and I think we're entitled to them. They make our lives more interesting, and when we decide to share them, our relationships become more meaningful. The place where secrets are kept can also provide a haven, a retreat from the rest of the world, where one's identity can be shaped and reaffirmed, where being alone can bring security and peace. Still, secrets can be an awful burden to bear, especially if some sense of shame is attached to them, even if the source of the shame is not the secret holder. Or the allure of our secrets can be too strong, strong enough to make us feel we can't live without them, that we wouldn't even be who we are without them.

Of course, I didn't begin to understand all this back when I became a secret-keeper. I didn't even give it much thought then. I have a good memory of so much of my childhood, but I don't trust my memory to tell me exactly what I knew about all this and when I knew it. I know only that it became a struggle for me to find the right balance between secrets of internal richness and those of hidden fears and shame, and that I was always reluctant to discuss with anyone the most difficult parts of my personal life, including a major spiritual crisis I had at the age of thirteen, when my faith was too weak to sustain a certain belief in God in the face of what I was witnessing and going through. I now know this struggle is at least partly the result of growing up in an alcoholic home and the mechanisms I developed to cope with it. It took me a long time just to figure that out. It was even harder to learn which secrets to keep, which to let go of, which to avoid in the first place. I am still not sure I understand that completely. It looks as if it's going to be a lifetime project.

SIX

I don't know how Mother handled it all as well as she did. Every morning, no matter what had happened the night before, she got up and put her game face on. And what a face it was. From the time she came back home from New Orleans, when I could get up early enough I loved sitting on the floor of the bathroom and watching her put makeup on that beautiful face.

It took quite a while, partly because she had no eyebrows. She often joked that she wished she had big bushy ones that needed plucking, like those of Akim Tamiroff, a famous character actor of that time. Instead, she drew her eyebrows on with a cosmetic pencil. Then she put on her makeup and her lipstick, usually a bright red shade that matched her nail polish.

Until I was eleven or twelve, she had long dark wavy hair. It was really thick and beautiful, and I liked watching her brush it until it was just so. I'll never forget the day she came home from the beauty shop with short hair, all her beautiful waves gone. It was not long after my first dog, Susie, had to be put to sleep at age nine, and it hurt almost as badly. Mother said short hair was more in style and more appropriate for a woman in her mid-thirties. I didn't buy it, and I never stopped missing her long hair, though I did like it when, a few months later, she stopped dyeing the gray streak that had run through the middle of her hair since she was in her twenties.

By the time she finished her makeup, Mother had already run through a cigarette or two and a couple of cups of coffee. Then after Mrs. Walters got there, she'd head off to work, sometimes dropping me at school when our starting times were close enough. When I got home from school, I'd keep busy playing with my friends or with Roger. I loved having a little brother, and all my pals liked having him around, until he got big enough to prefer his own friends.

Mother usually got home by four or five, except when the racetrack was open. She loved those races. Though she rarely bet more than two dollars across the board, she took it seriously, studying the racing form and the tout sheets, listening to the jockeys, trainers, and owners she got to know, debating her options with her racetrack friends. She made some of the best friends of her life there: Louise Crain and her husband, Joe, a policeman who later became chief and who used to drive Daddy around in his patrol car when he was drunk until his anger died down; Dixie Seba and her husband, Mike, a trainer; and Marge Mitchell, a nurse who staffed the clinic at the track for people who had health problems while there and who, along with Dixie Seba, and later Nancy Crawford, Gabe's second wife, probably came as close as anyone ever did to being Mother's real confidante. Marge and Mother called each other "Sister."

Shortly after I came home from law school I had the chance to repay Marge for all she'd done for Mother and for me. When she was dismissed from her job at our local community mental-health center, she decided to challenge the decision and asked me to represent her at the hearing, where even my inexperienced questioning made it obvious that the termination was based on nothing but a personal conflict with her supervisor. I tore the case against her to shreds, and when we won I was thrilled. She deserved to get her job back.

Before I got Mother into politics, most of her friends were involved in her work—doctors, nurses, hospital personnel. She had a lot of them. She never met a stranger, worked hard to put her patients at ease before surgery, and genuinely enjoyed the company of her co-workers. Of course, not everybody liked her. She could be abrasive with people she thought were trying to push her around or take advantage of their positions to treat others unfairly. Unlike me, she actually enjoyed making some of these people mad. I tended to make enemies effortlessly, just by being me, or, after I got into politics, because of the positions I took and the changes I tried to make. When Mother really didn't like people, she worked hard to get them foaming at the mouth. Later in her career, it cost her, after she had fought for years to avoid going to work for an MD anesthesiologist and had some problems with a couple of her operations. But most people did like her, because she liked them, treated them with respect, and obviously loved life.

I never knew how she kept her energy and spirit, always filling her days with work and fun, always being there for my brother, Roger, and me, never missing our school events, finding time for our friends, too, and keeping all her troubles to herself.

I loved going to the hospital to visit her, meeting the nurses and doctors, watching them care for people. I got to watch an actual operation once, when I was in junior high, but all I remember about it is that there was a lot of cutting and a lot of blood and I didn't get sick. I was fascinated by the work surgeons do and thought I might like to do it myself one day.

Mother took a lot of interest in her patients, whether they could pay or not. In the days before Medicare and Medicaid there were a lot who couldn't. I remember one poor, proud man coming to our door one day to settle his account. He was a fruit picker who paid Mother with six bushels of fresh peaches. We ate those peaches for a long time—on cereal, in pies, in homemade ice cream. It made me wish more of her patients were cash poor!

I think Mother found enormous relief from the strains of her marriage in her work and friends, and at the races. There must have been many days when she was crying inside, maybe even in physical pain, but most people didn't have a clue. The example she set stood me in good stead when I became President. She almost never discussed her troubles with me. I think she figured I knew about all I needed to know, was smart enough to figure out the rest, and deserved as normal a childhood as possible under the circumstances.

When I was fifteen, events overtook the silent strategy. Daddy started drinking and behaving violently again, so Mother took Roger and me away. We had done it once before, a couple of years earlier, when we moved for a few weeks into the Cleveland Manor Apartments on the south end of Central Avenue, almost to the racetrack. This time, in April 1962, we stayed about three weeks at a motel while Mother searched for a house. We looked at several houses together, all much smaller than the one we lived in, some still out of her price range. Finally, she settled on a three-bedroom, two-bath house on Scully Street, a one-block-long street in south Hot Springs about a half mile west of Central Avenue. It was one of the new, all-electric Gold Medallion houses with central heat and air—we had window-unit air conditioners back on Park Avenue—and

I think it cost $30,000. The house had a nice living room and dining room just left of the front entrance. Behind it was a large den that connected to the dining area and kitchen, with a laundry room off it just behind the garage. Beyond the den was a good-sized porch we later glassed in and outfitted with a pool table. Two of the bedrooms were to the right of the hall, to the left was a large bathroom, and, behind it, a bedroom with a separate bathroom with a shower. Mother gave me the big bedroom with the shower, I think because she wanted the big bathroom with its larger makeup area and mirror. She took the next biggest bedroom in the back, and Roger got the small one.

Though I loved our house on Park Avenue, the yard I worked hard to keep up, my neighbors and friends and familiar haunts, I was glad to be in a normal house and to feel safe, maybe more for Mother and Roger than for me. By then, even though I knew nothing of child psychology, I had begun to worry that Daddy's drinking and abusive behavior would scar Roger even more than it would scar me, because he'd lived with it all his life and because Roger Clinton was his natural father. Knowing my father was someone else, someone I thought of as strong, trustworthy, and reliable, gave me more emotional security and the space necessary to see what was happening with some detachment, even sympathy. I never stopped loving Roger Clinton, never stopped pulling for him to change, never stopped enjoying being with him when he was sober and engaged. I was afraid even then that little Roger would come to hate his father. And he did, at a terrible cost to himself.

As I relate these events from long ago, I see how easy it is to fall into the trap Shakespeare's Marc Antony spoke of in his eulogy for Julius Caesar: allowing the evil that men do to live after them, while the good is interred with their bones. Like most alcoholics and drug addicts I've known, Roger Clinton was fundamentally a good person. He loved Mother and me and little Roger. He had helped Mother to see me when she was finishing school in New Orleans. He was generous to family and friends. He was smart and funny. But he had that combustible mix of fears, insecurities, and psychological vulnerabilities that destroys the promise of so many addicts' lives. And as far as I know, he never sought help from those who knew how to give it.

The really disturbing thing about living with an alcoholic is that it isn't always bad. Weeks, sometimes even whole months, would pass while we'd enjoy being a family, blessed with the quiet joys of an ordinary life. I'm grateful that I haven't forgotten all those times, and when I do, I've still got a few postcards and letters Daddy sent to me and some I sent to him to remind me.

Some of the bad times tend to be forgotten, too. When I recently reread my deposition in Mother's divorce filings, I saw that in it I recounted an incident three years earlier when I called her attorney to get the police to take Daddy away after a violent episode. I also said he'd threatened to beat me the last time I stopped him from hitting her, which was laughable, because by that time I was bigger and stronger than he was sober, much less drunk. I'd forgotten both instances, perhaps out of the denial experts say families of alcoholics engage in when they continue to live with them. For whatever reason, those particular memories remained blocked after forty years.

Five days after we left, on April 14, 1962, Mother filed for divorce. Divorce can happen quickly in Arkansas, and she certainly had grounds. But it wasn't over. Daddy was desperate to get her, and us, back. He fell apart, lost a lot of weight, parked for hours near our house, even slept on our concrete front porch a couple of times. One day he asked me to take a ride with him. We drove up behind our old house on Circle Drive. He stopped at the bottom of our back driveway. He was a wreck. He hadn't shaved in three or four days, though I don't think he'd been drinking. He told me he couldn't live without us, that he had nothing else to live for. He cried. He begged me to talk to Mother and ask her to take him back. He said he would straighten up and never hit her or scream at her again. When he said it, he really believed it, but I didn't. He never understood, or accepted, the cause of his problem. He never acknowledged that he was powerless in the face of liquor and that he couldn't quit all by himself.

Meanwhile, his entreaties were beginning to get to Mother. I think she was feeling a little uncertain about her ability to take care of us financially—she didn't make really good money until Medicaid and Medicare were enacted a couple of years later. Even more important was her old-school view that divorce, especially with kids in the house, was a bad thing, which it often is if there's no real abuse. I think she also felt that their problems must be partly her fault. And she probably did trigger his insecurities; after all, she was a good-looking, interesting woman who liked men and worked with a lot of attractive ones who were more successful than her husband. As far as I know, she never carried on with any of them, though I couldn't blame her if she had, and when she and Daddy were apart, she did see a dark-haired handsome man who gave me some golf clubs I still have.

After we had been on Scully Street just a few months and the divorce had been finalized, Mother told Roger and me that we needed to have a family meeting to discuss Daddy. She said he wanted to come back, to move into our new house, and she thought it would be different this time, and then she asked what we thought. I don't remember what Roger said—he was only five and probably confused. I told her that I was against it, because I didn't think he could change, but that I would support whatever decision she made. She said that we needed a man in the house and that she would always feel guilty if she didn't give him another chance. So she did; they remarried, which, given the way Daddy's life played out, was good for him, but not so good for Roger or for her. I don't know what effect it had on me, except that later, when he got ill, I was very glad to be able to share his last months.

Although I didn't agree with Mother's decision, I understood her feelings. Shortly before she took Daddy back, I went down to the courthouse and had my name changed legally from Blythe to Clinton, the name I had been using for years. I'm still not sure exactly why I did it, but I know I really thought I should, partly because Roger was about to start school and I didn't want the differences in our lineage ever to be an issue for him, partly because I just wanted the same name as the rest of my family. Maybe I even wanted to do something nice for Daddy, though I was glad Mother had divorced him. I didn't tell her in advance, but she had to give her permission. When she got a call from the courthouse, she said okay, though she probably thought I had slipped a gear. It wouldn't be the last time in my life that my decisions and my timing were open to question.

The deterioration of my parents' marriage, the divorce and reconciliation, took up a lot of my emotional energy at the end of junior high and through my sophomore year in the old high school just up the hill.

Just as Mother threw herself into work, I threw myself into high school, and into my new neighborhood on Scully Street. It was a block full of mostly newer, modest houses. Just across the street was a completely empty square block, all that was left of the Wheatley farm, which had covered a much larger area not long before. Every year Mr. Wheatley planted the whole block with peonies. They brightened the spring and drew people from miles around, who waited patiently for him to cut them and give them away.

We lived in the second house on the street. The first house, on the corner of Scully and Wheatley, belonged to the Reverend Walter Yeldell, his wife, Kay, and their kids, Carolyn, Lynda, and Walter. Walter was pastor of Second Baptist Church and later president of the Arkansas Baptist Convention. He and Kay were wonderful to us from the first day. I don't know how Brother Yeldell, as we called him, who died in 1987, would have fared in the harshly judgmental environment of the Southern Baptist Convention of the nineties, when wrong-thinking "liberals" were purged from the seminaries and the church hardened its positions rightward on every social issue but race (it apologized for the sins of the past). Brother Yeldell was a big, broad man who weighed well over 250 pounds. Beneath a shy demeanor, he had a terrific sense of humor and a great laugh. So did his wife. They didn't have a pompous bone between them. He led people to Christ through instruction and example, not condemnation and ridicule. He wouldn't have been a favorite of some of the recent Baptist overlords or today's conservative talk-show hosts, but I sure liked talking to him.

Carolyn, the oldest Yeldell child, was my age. She loved music, had a wonderful voice, and was an accomplished pianist. We spent countless hours around her piano singing. She also accompanied my saxophone solos from time to time, probably not the first time an accompanist was better than the soloist. Carolyn soon became one of my closest friends and a part of our regular gang, along with David Leopoulos, Joe Newman, and Ronnie Cecil. We went to movies and school events together, and spent lots of time playing cards and games or just goofing off, usually at our house. In 1963, when I went to American Legion Boys Nation and took the now famous photo with President Kennedy, Carolyn was elected to Girls Nation, the only time that ever happened to hometown neighbors. Carolyn went to the University of Indiana and studied voice. She wanted to be an opera singer but didn't want the lifestyle. Instead she married Jerry Staley, a fine photographer, had three kids, and became a leader in the field of adult literacy. When I became governor I put her in charge of our adult literacy program, and she and her family lived in a great old house about three blocks from the Governor's Mansion, where I often visited for parties, games, or singing the way we did in the old days. When I became President, Carolyn and her family moved to the Washington area, where she went to work for, and later led, the National Institute for Literacy. She stayed on for a while after I left the White House, then followed her father into the ministry. The Staleys are still a good part of my life. It all started on Scully Street.

The house on the other side of us belonged to Jim and Edith Clark, who had no kids of their own but treated me like theirs. Among our other neighbors were the Frasers, an older couple who always supported me when I got into politics. But their greatest gift to me came by accident. Over the holidays in 1974, after I lost a heartbreaking race for Congress and was still feeling pretty low, I saw the Frasers' little granddaughter, who must have been five or six. She had a severe medical condition that made her bones weak and was in a body cast up to her chest that also splayed her legs outward to take the pressure off her spine. It was very awkward for her to navigate with her crutches, but she was a tough little girl with that total lack of self-consciousness that secure young children have. When I saw her I asked if she knew who I was. She said, "Sure, you're still Bill Clinton." I needed to be reminded of that just then.

The Hassins, the Syrian-Italian family I mentioned earlier, were packed, all six of them, in a tiny little house at the end of the street. They must have spent all their money on food. Every Christmas and on several other occasions during the year they fed the whole block huge Italian meals. I can still hear Mama Gina saying, "A-Beel, a-Beel, you gotta eat some more."

And then there were Jon and Toni Karber, who were both book readers and the most intellectual people I knew, and their son Mike, who was in my class. And Charley Housley—a man's man who knew about hunting, fishing, and fixing things, the things that matter to small boys—who took Roger under his wing. Though our new house and yard were smaller than our old one, and the immediate surroundings less beautiful, I came to love my new home and neighborhood. It was a good place for me to live out my high school years.

SEVEN

Ⓗigh school was a great ride. I liked the school-work, my friends, the band, DeMolay, and my other activities, but it bothered me that Hot Springs' schools still weren't integrated. The black kids still went to Langston High School, which claimed as its most famous alumnus the legendary Washington Red-skins back Bobby Mitchell. I followed the civil rights movement on the evening news and in our daily paper, the **Sentinel-Record,** along with Cold War events like the Bay of Pigs and the U-2 incident with Francis Gary Pow-ers. I can still see Castro riding into Havana at the head of his ragtag but victorious army. But as with most kids, pol-itics took a backseat to daily life. And apart from Daddy's occasional relapses, I liked my life a lot.

It was in high school that I really fell in love with music. Classical, jazz, and band music joined rock and roll, swing, and gospel as my idea of pure joy. For some reason I didn't get into country and western until I was in my twenties, when Hank Williams and Patsy Cline reached down to me from heaven.

In addition to the marching and concert bands, I joined our dance band, the Stardusters. I spent a year dueling for first chair on tenor sax with Larry McDougal, who looked as if he should have played backup for Buddy Holly, the rocker who died tragically in a bad-weather plane crash in 1959 along with two other big stars, the Big

Bopper and seventeen-year-old Richie Valens. When I was President I gave a speech to college students in Mason City, Iowa, near where Holly and his pals had played their last gig. Afterward I drove to the site, the Surf Ballroom, in neighboring Clear Lake, Iowa. It's still standing and ought to be turned into a shrine for those of us who grew up on those guys.

Anyway, McDougal looked and played as if he belonged with them. He had a ducktail hairdo, crew cut on top, long hair greased back on the sides. When he stood for a solo, he gyrated and played with a blaring tone, more like hard-core rock and roll than jazz or swing. I wasn't as good as he was in 1961, but I was determined to get better. That year we entered a competition with other jazz bands in Camden in south Arkansas. I had a small solo on a slow, pretty piece. At the end of the performance, to my astonishment, I won the prize for "best sweet soloist." By the next year, I had improved enough to be first chair in the All-State Band, a position I won again as a senior, when Joe Newman won on drums.

In my last two years I played in a jazz trio, the 3 Kings, with Randy Goodrum, a pianist a year younger and light-years better than I was or ever could be. Our first drummer was Mike Hardgraves. Mike was raised by a single mom, who often had me and a couple of Mike's other friends over for card games. In my senior year Joe Newman became our drummer. We made a little money playing for dances, and we performed at school events, including the annual Band Variety Show. Our signature piece was the theme from **El Cid.** I still have a tape of it, and it holds up pretty well after all these years, except for a squeak I made in my closing riff. I always had problems with the lower notes.

My band director, Virgil Spurlin, was a tall, heavyset man with dark wavy hair and a gentle, winning demeanor. He was a pretty good band director and a world-class human being. Mr. Spurlin also organized the State Band Festival, which was held over several days every year in Hot Springs. He had to schedule all the band performances and hundreds of solo and ensemble presentations in classrooms in the junior and senior high school buildings. He scheduled the days, times, and venues for all the events on large poster boards every year. Those of us who were willing stayed after school and worked nights for several days to help him get the job done. It was the first large organizational effort in which I was ever involved, and I learned a lot that I put to good use later on.

At the state festivals, I won several medals for solos and ensembles, and a couple for student conducting, of which I was especially proud. I loved to read the scores and try to get the band to play pieces exactly as I thought they should sound. In my second term as President, Leonard Slatkin, conductor of the Washington National Symphony, asked me if I would direct the orchestra in Sousa's "Stars and Stripes Forever" at the Kennedy Center. He told me all I had to do was wave the baton more or less in time and the musicians would do the rest. He even offered to bring me a baton and show me how to hold it. When I told him that I'd be delighted to do it but that I wanted him to send me the score of the march so I could review it, he almost dropped the phone. But he brought the score and the baton. When I stood before the orchestra I was nervous, but we got into it, and away we went. I hope Mr. Sousa would have been pleased.

My only other artistic endeavor in high school was the junior class play, **Arsenic and Old Lace,** a hilarious farce about two old maids who poison people and stash them in the house they share with their unsuspecting nephew. I got the role of the nephew, which Cary Grant played in the movie. My girlfriend was played by a tall, attractive girl, Cindy Arnold. The play was a big success, largely because of two developments that weren't part of the script. In one scene, I was supposed to lift up a window seat, find one of my aunts' victims, and feign horror. I practiced hard and had it down. But on play night, when I opened the seat, my friend Ronnie Cecil was crammed into it, looked up at me, and said, "Good evening," in his best vampire voice. I lost it. Luckily, so did everyone else. Something even funnier happened offstage. When I kissed Cindy during our only love scene, her boyfriend— a senior football player named Allen Broyles, who was sitting in the front row—let out a loud comic groan that brought the house down. I still enjoyed the kiss.

My high school offered calculus and trigonometry, chemistry and physics, Spanish, French, and four years of Latin, a range of courses many smaller schools in Arkansas lacked. We were blessed with a lot of smart, effective teachers and a remarkable school leader, Johnnie Mae Mackey, a tall, imposing woman with thick black hair and a ready smile or a stern scowl as the occasion demanded. Johnnie Mae ran a tight ship and still managed to be the spark plug of our school spirit, which was a job in itself, because we had the losingest football team in Arkansas, back when football was a religion, with every coach expected to be Knute Rockne. Every student from back then can still remember Johnnie Mae closing our pep rallies leading the Trojan yell, fist in the air, dignity discarded, voice roaring, "Hullabloo, Ke-neck, Ke-neck,

Hullabloo, Ke-neck, Ke-neck, Wo-Hee, Wo-Hi, We win or die! Ching Chang, Chow Chow! Bing Bang, Bow Wow! Trojans! Trojans! Fight, Fight, Fight!" Fortunately, it was just a cheer. With a 6–29–1 record in my three years, if the yell had been accurate, our mortality rate would have been serious.

I took four years of Latin from Mrs. Elizabeth Buck, a delightful, sophisticated woman from Philadelphia who had us memorize lots of lines from Caesar's **Gallic Wars.** After the Russians beat us into space with **Sputnik,** President Eisenhower and then President Kennedy decided Americans needed to know more about science and math, so I took all the courses I could. I was not very good in Dick Duncan's chemistry class, but did better in biology, though I remember only one remarkable class, in which the teacher, Nathan McCauley, told us we die sooner than we should because our bodies' capacity to turn food into energy and process the waste wears out. In 2002, a major medical study concluded that older people could increase their life span dramatically by sharply decreasing food intake. Coach McCauley knew that forty years ago. Now that I am one of those older people, I am trying to take his advice.

My world history teacher, Paul Root, was a short, stocky man from rural Arkansas who combined a fine mind with a homespun manner and an offbeat, wicked sense of humor. When I became governor, he left his teaching position at Ouachita University to work for me. One day in 1987, I came upon Paul in the state Capitol talking to three state legislators. They were discussing Gary Hart's recent downfall after the story broke about Donna Rice and the **Monkey Business.** The legislators were all giving Gary hell in their most sanctimonious voices. Paul, a devout Baptist, director of his church choir, and certified straight arrow, listened patiently while the legislators droned on. When they stopped for breath, he deadpanned, "You're absolutely right. What he did was awful. But you know what else? It's amazing what being short, fat, and ugly has done for my moral character." The legislators shut up, and Paul walked off with me. I love that guy.

I enjoyed all my English courses. John Wilson made Shakespeare's **Julius Caesar** come alive to Arkansas fifteen-year-olds by having us put the meaning of the play in ordinary words and asking us repeatedly whether Shakespeare's view of human nature and behavior seemed right to us. Mr. Wilson thought old Will had it about right: life is comedy and tragedy.

In junior English honors class, we had to write an auto-biographical essay. Mine was full of self-doubt I didn't understand and hadn't admitted to myself before. Here are some excerpts:

> I am a person motivated and influenced by so many diverse forces I sometimes question the sanity of my existence. I am a living paradox—deeply religious, yet not as convinced of my exact beliefs as I ought to be; wanting responsibility yet shirking it; loving the truth but often times giving way to falsity. . . . I detest selfishness, but see it in the mirror every day. . . . I view those, some of whom are very dear to me, who have never learned how to live. I desire and struggle to be different from them, but often am almost an exact likeness. . . . What a boring little word—I! I, me, my, mine . . . the only things that enable worthwhile uses of these words are the universal good qualities which we are not too often able

to place with them—faith, trust, love, responsibility, regret, knowledge. But the acronyms to these symbols of what enable life to be worth the trouble cannot be escaped. I, in my attempts to be honest, will not be the hypocrite I hate, and will own up to their ominous presence in this boy, endeavoring in such earnest to be a man. . . .

My teacher, Lonnie Warneke, gave me a grade of 100, saying the paper was a beautiful and honest attempt to go "way down inside" to fulfill the classic demand to "know thyself." I was gratified but still unsure of what to make of what I'd found. I didn't do bad things; I didn't drink, smoke, or go beyond petting with girls, though I kissed a fair number. Most of the time I was happy, but I could never be sure I was as good as I wanted to be.

Miss Warneke took our small class on a field trip to Newton County, my first trip into the heart of the Ozarks in north Arkansas, our Appalachia. Back then it was a place of breathtaking beauty, hardscrabble poverty, and rough, all-consuming politics. The county had about six thousand people spread over more than a couple of hundred square miles in hills and hollows. Jasper, the county seat, had a little more than three hundred people, a WPA-built courthouse, two cafés, a general store, and one tiny movie theater, where our class went one night to watch an old Audie Murphy western. When I got into politics I came to know every township in Newton County, but I fell in love with it at sixteen, as we navigated the mountain roads, learning about the history, geology, flora, and fauna of the Ozarks. One day we visited the cabin of a mountain man who had a collection of rifles and pistols dating back to the Civil War, then explored a cave the Confederates had used for munitions storage. The guns still fired, and remnants of the arsenal were still in the cave, visible manifestation of how real a century-old conflict was in places where time passed slowly, grudges died hard, and handed-down memories hung on and on. In the mid-seventies, when I was attorney general, I was invited to give the commencement address at Jasper High School. I urged the students to keep going in the face of adversity, citing Abraham Lincoln and all the hardships and setbacks he'd overcome. Afterward, the leading Democrats took me out into a bright starlit Ozark night and said, "Bill, that was a fine speech. You can give it down in Little Rock anytime. But don't you ever come up here and brag on that Republican President again. If he'd been that good, we wouldn't have had the Civil War!" I didn't know what to say.

In Ruth Sweeney's senior English class, we read **Macbeth** and were encouraged to memorize and recite portions of it. I made it through a hundred lines or so, including the famous soliloquy that begins, "Tomorrow, and tomorrow, and tomorrow creeps in this petty pace from day to day, to the last syllable of recorded time" and ends, "Life's but a walking shadow, a poor player that struts and frets his hour upon the stage and then is heard no more. It is a tale told by an idiot, full of sound and fury, signifying nothing." Almost thirty years later, when I was governor, I happened to visit a class in Vilonia, Arkansas, on a day the students were studying **Macbeth,** and I recited the lines for them, the words still full of power for me, a dreadful message I was always determined would not be the measure of my life.

The summer after my junior year, I attended the annual weeklong American Legion Boys State program at Camp

Robinson, an old army camp with enough primitive wooden barracks to house a thousand sixteen-year-old boys. We were organized by cities and counties, divided equally into two political parties, and introduced as candidates and voters to local, county, and state politics. We also developed platforms and voted on issues. We heard addresses from important figures, from the governor on down, and got to spend one day at the state Capitol, during which the Boys State governor, the other elected officials and their "staffs," and the legislators actually got to occupy the state offices and legislative chambers.

At the end of the week, both parties nominated two candidates for the Boys Nation program, to be held toward the end of July at the University of Maryland in College Park, near the nation's capital. An election was held, and the top two vote-getters got to go as Arkansas' senators. I was one of them.

I went to Camp Robinson wanting to run for Boys Nation senator. Though the most prestigious post was governor, I had no interest in it then, or in the real job itself, for years thereafter. I thought Washington was where the action was on civil rights, poverty, education, and foreign policy. Besides, I couldn't have won the governor's election anyway, since it was, in the Arkansas vernacular, "saucered and blowed"—over before it started. My longtime friend from Hope, Mack McLarty, had it in the bag. As his school's student-council president, a star quarterback, and a straight-A student, he had begun lining up support all across the state several weeks earlier. Our party nominated Larry Taunton, a radio announcer with a wonderful silken voice full of sincerity and confidence, but McLarty had the votes and won going away. We were all sure he would be the first person our age to be elected governor, an impression reinforced four years later when he was elected student body president at the University of Arkansas, and again just a year after that when, at twenty-two, he became the youngest member of the state legislature. Not long after that, Mack, who was in the Ford business with his father, devised a then-novel leasing scheme for Ford trucks, which eventually made him and Ford Motor Company a fortune. He gave up politics for a business career that led him to the presidency of Arkansas-Louisiana Gas Company, our largest natural gas utility. But he stayed active in politics, lending leadership and fund-raising skills to many Arkansas Democrats, especially David Pryor and me. He stayed with me all the way to the White House, first as chief of staff, then as special envoy to the Americas. Now he is Henry Kissinger's partner in a consulting business and owns, among other things, twelve car dealerships in São Paulo, Brazil.

Though he lost the governor's race, Larry Taunton got a big consolation prize: as the only boy besides McLarty with 100 percent name recognition, he was a lock cinch for one of the two Boys Nation slots; he had only to file. But there was a problem. Larry was one of two "stars" in his hometown delegation. The other was Bill Rainer, a bright, handsome multi-sport athlete. They had come to Boys State agreeing that Taunton would run for governor, Rainer for Boys Nation. Now, though both were free to run for Boys Nation, there was no way two boys from the same town were going to be elected. Besides, they were both in my party and I had been campaigning hard for a week. A letter I wrote to Mother at the time recounts that I had already won elections for tax collector, party secretary, and municipal judge, and that I was running for county judge, an important position in real Arkansas politics.

At the last minute, not long before the party met to hear our campaign speeches, Taunton filed. Bill Rainer was so stunned he could hardly get through his speech. I still have a copy of my own speech, which is unremarkable, except for a reference to the Little Rock Central High turmoil: "We have grown up in a state ridden with the shame of a crisis it did not ask for." I did not approve of what Faubus had done, and I wanted people from other states to think better of Arkansas. When the votes were counted, Larry Taunton finished first by a good margin. I was second with a pretty good cushion. Rainer finished well back. I had come to really like Bill, and I never forgot the dignity with which he bore his loss.

In 1992, when Bill was living in Connecticut, he contacted my campaign and offered to help. Our friendship, forged in the pain of youthful disappointment, enjoyed a happy renewal.

Larry Taunton and I defeated our opponents from the other party after another day of campaigning and I arrived in College Park on July 19, 1963, and eager to meet the other delegates, vote on important issues, hear from cabinet members and other government officials, and visit the White House, where we hoped to see the President.

The week passed quickly, the days packed with events and legislative sessions. I remember being particularly impressed by Secretary of Labor Willard Wirtz and completely caught up in our debates over civil rights. Many of the boys were Republicans and supporters of Barry Goldwater, who they hoped would defeat President Kennedy in 1964, but there were enough progressives on civil rights, including four of us from the South, for our legislative proposals to carry the day.

Because of my friendship with Bill Rainer and my more

liberal views on civil rights, I had a tense relationship with Larry Taunton the whole week of Boys Nation. I'm glad that, after I became President, I got to meet the grown-up Larry Taunton and his children. He seemed to be a good man who'd built a good life.

On Monday, July 22, we visited the Capitol, took pictures on the steps, and met our state's senators. Larry and I had lunch with J. William Fulbright, chairman of the Foreign Relations Committee, and John McClellan, chairman of the Appropriations Committee. The seniority system was alive and well, and no state had more power from it than Arkansas. In addition, all four of our congressmen held important positions: Wilbur Mills was chairman of the Ways and Means Committee; Oren Harris, chairman of the Commerce Committee; "Took" Gathings, ranking member of the Agriculture Committee; and Jim Trimble, who had been in Congress "only" since 1945, a member of the powerful Rules Committee, which controls the flow of legislation to the House floor. Little did I know that within three years I would be working for Fulbright on the Foreign Relations Committee staff. A few days after the lunch, Mother got a letter from Senator Fulbright saying that he had enjoyed our lunch and that she must be proud of me. I still have that letter, my first encounter with good staff work.

On Wednesday, July 24, we went to the White House to meet the President in the Rose Garden. President Kennedy walked out of the Oval Office into the bright sunshine and made some brief remarks, complimenting our work, especially our support for civil rights, and giving us higher marks than the governors, who had not been so forward-leaning in their annual summer meeting. After accepting a Boys Nation T-shirt, Kennedy walked down the steps and began shaking hands. I was in the front, and being bigger and a bigger supporter of the President's than most of the others, I made sure I'd get to shake his hand even if he shook only two or three. It was an amazing moment for me, meeting the President whom I had supported in my ninth-grade class debates, and about whom I felt even more strongly after his two and a half years in office. A friend took a photo for me, and later we found film footage of the handshake in the Kennedy Library.

Much has been made of that brief encounter and its impact on my life. My mother said she knew when I came home that I was determined to go into politics, and after I became the Democratic nominee in 1992, the film was widely pointed to as the beginning of my presidential aspirations. I'm not sure about that. I have a copy of the speech I gave to the American Legion in Hot Springs after I came home, and in it I didn't make too much of the handshake. I thought at the time I wanted to become a senator, but deep down I probably felt as Abraham Lincoln did when he wrote as a young man, "I will study and get ready, and perhaps my chance will come."

I had some success in high school politics, getting elected president of the junior class, and I wanted to run for president of the student council, but the accrediting group that oversaw our high school decided that Hot Springs students were not allowed to be involved in too many activities and ordered restrictions. Under the new rules, since I was the band major, I was ineligible to run for student council or class president. So was Phil Jamison, the captain of the football team and the odds-on favorite to win.

Not running for high school student-council president didn't hurt me or Phil Jamison too much. Phil went on to the Naval Academy, and after his naval career he did important work in the Pentagon on arms control issues. When I was President, he was involved in all our important work with Russia, and our friendship gave me a close account of our efforts from an operational level, which I would not have received had I not known him.

In one of the dumber political moves of my life, I allowed my name to be put up for senior class secretary by a friend who was angry about the new activity restrictions. My next-door neighbor Carolyn Yeldell defeated me handily, as she should have. It was a foolish, selfish thing for me to do, and proof positive of one of my rules of politics: Never run for an office you don't really want and don't have a good reason to hold.

Notwithstanding the setbacks, sometime in my sixteenth year I decided I wanted to be in public life as an elected official. I loved music and thought I could be very good, but I knew I would never be John Coltrane or Stan Getz. I was interested in medicine and thought I could be a fine doctor, but I knew I would never be Michael DeBakey. But I knew I could be great in public service. I was fascinated by people, politics, and policy, and I thought I could make it without family wealth, or connections, or establishment southern positions on race and other issues. Of course it was improbable, but isn't that what America is all about?

EIGHT

One other memorable event happened to me in the summer of 1963. On August 28, nine days after I turned seventeen, I sat alone in a big white reclining chair in our den and watched the greatest speech of my lifetime, as Martin Luther King Jr. stood in front of the Lincoln Memorial and spoke of his dream for America. In rhythmic cadences reminiscent of old Negro spirituals, his voice at once booming and shaking, he told a vast throng before him, and millions like me transfixed before television sets, of his dream that "one day on the red hills of Georgia, the sons of former slaves and the sons of former slave owners will be able to sit down together at the table of brotherhood," and that "my four little children will one day live in a nation where they will not be judged by the color of their skin but by the content of their character."

It is difficult to convey more than forty years later the emotion and hope with which King's speech filled me; or what it meant to a nation with no Civil Rights Act, no Voting Rights Act, no open housing law, no Thurgood Marshall on the Supreme Court; or what it meant in the American South, where schools were still mostly segregated, the poll tax was used to keep blacks from voting or to round them up to vote as a bloc for the status quo crowd, and the word "nigger" was still used openly by people who knew better.

I started crying during the speech and wept for a good while after Dr. King finished. He had said everything I believed, far better than I ever could. More than anything I ever experienced, except perhaps the power of my grandfather's example, that speech steeled my determination to do whatever I could for the rest of my life to make Martin Luther King Jr.'s dream come true.

A couple of weeks later, I started my senior year in high school, still on a high from Boys Nation, and determined to enjoy my last shot at childhood.

The most challenging course I took in high school was calculus. There were seven of us in the class; it had never been offered before. I recall two events with clarity. One day the teacher, Mr. Coe, handed back an exam on which I had all the right answers but a grade reflecting that I'd missed one. When I asked about it, Mr. Coe said I hadn't worked the problem properly and therefore must have gotten the correct answer by accident, so he couldn't give me credit for it; in the textbook, the problem required several more steps than I had used. Our class had one true genius, Jim McDougal (no, not the Whitewater one), who asked if he could see my paper. He then told Mr. Coe he should give me credit because my solution was as valid as the one in the textbook, indeed better, because it was shorter. He then volunteered to demonstrate the validity of his opinion. Mr. Coe was just as much in awe of Jim's brain as the rest of us, so he told him to go ahead. Jim then proceeded to fill two full blackboards with symbolic mathematical formulas analyzing the problem and demonstrating how I had improved on the textbook solution. You could have fooled me. I had always liked solving puzzles, still do, but I was just clawing my way through a maze. I didn't have a clue about what Jim was saying, and

I'm not sure Mr. Coe did either, but at the end of his bravura performance I got my grade changed. That incident taught me two things: that in problem-solving, sometimes good instincts can overcome intellectual inadequacy; and that I had no business pursuing advanced mathematics any further.

Our class met at fourth period, just after lunch. On November 22, Mr. Coe was called out of class to the office. When he returned, he was white as a sheet and could hardly speak. He told us President Kennedy had been shot and probably killed in Dallas. I was devastated. Just four months before, I had seen him in the Rose Garden, so full of life and strength. So much of what he did and said—the inaugural address; the Alliance for Progress in Latin America; the cool handling of the Cuban Missile Crisis; the Peace Corps; the stunning line from the "Ich bin ein Berliner" speech: "Freedom has many difficulties, and democracy is not perfect, but we have never had to put a wall up to keep our people in"—all these embodied my hopes for my country and my belief in politics.

After class, all the students in the annex where our class met walked back to the main building. We were all so sad, all of us but one. I overheard an attractive girl who was in the band with me say that maybe it was a good thing for the country that he was gone. I knew her family was more conservative than I was, but I was stunned and very angry that someone I considered a friend would say such a thing. It was my first exposure, beyond raw racism, to the kind of hatred I would see a lot of in my political career, and that was forged into a powerful political movement in the last quarter of the twentieth century. I am thankful that my friend outgrew it. When I was campaigning in Las Vegas in 1992, she came to one of my events. She had become a social worker and a Democrat. I treasured our reunion and the chance it gave me to heal an old wound.

After I watched President Kennedy's funeral and was reassured by Lyndon Johnson's sober assumption of the presidency with the moving words "All that I have I would have given gladly not to be standing here today," I slowly returned to normal life. The rest of senior year passed quickly with DeMolay and band activities, including a senior band trip to Pensacola, Florida, and another trip to All-State Band; and lots of good times with my friends, including lunches at the Club Café, with the best Dutch apple pie I've ever had, movies, dances at the Y, ice cream at Cook's Dairy, and barbeque at McClard's, a seventy-five-year-old family place with arguably the best barbeque and unquestionably the best barbeque beans in the whole country.

For several months that year, I dated Susan Smithers, a girl from Benton, Arkansas, thirty miles east of Hot Springs on the highway to Little Rock. Often on Sundays, I would go to Benton to church and lunch with her family. At the end of the meal Susan's mother, Mary, would put a pile of peach or apple fried pies on the table, and her father, Reese, and I would eat them until I practically had to be carried away. One Sunday after lunch, Susan and I went for a drive to Bauxite, a town near Benton named for the ore used to make aluminum, which was dug out of open pit mines there. When we got to town we decided to drive out to see the mines, going off the road onto what I thought was hard clay soil, right up to the edge of a huge open pit. After walking around the site, we got back in the car to go home, and our mood took a sharp downward turn. My car's wheels had sunk deep into the soft, wet ground. The wheels turned over and over, but we didn't move an inch. I found some old boards, dug down behind the wheels, and put them in the space for traction. Still no luck. After two hours, I had burned all the tread off the tires, it was getting dark, and we were still stuck. Finally I gave up, walked to town, asked for help, and called Susan's parents. Eventually help came and we were towed out of the huge ruts, my tires as smooth as a baby's behind. It was way past dark when I got Susan home. I think her folks believed our story, but her dad sneaked a look at my tires just to be sure. In that more innocent time, I was mortified.

As my senior year drew to a close, I became increasingly anxious about college. For some reason, I never even considered applying to any Ivy League school. I knew just where I wanted to go, and I applied only there: the Georgetown University School of Foreign Service. I didn't want to go into the foreign service and I had never even seen the Georgetown campus when I was at Boys Nation, but I wanted to go back to Washington; Georgetown had the best academic reputation in the city; the intellectual rigor of the Jesuits was legendary and fascinating to me; and I felt that I needed to know all I could about international affairs, and that somehow I would absorb all I could learn about domestic issues just by being in Washington in the mid-sixties. I thought I would get in, because I was fourth in my class of 327, my College Board scores were pretty good, and Georgetown tried to have at least one student from every state (an early affirmative action program!). Still, I was worried.

I had decided that if I got turned down at Georgetown, I'd go to the University of Arkansas, which had an open admissions policy for Arkansas high school graduates, and where the smart money said aspiring politicians should go anyway. In the second week of April, my acceptance notice from Georgetown arrived. I was happy, but by then I'd begun to question the wisdom of going. I didn't get a scholarship and it was so expensive: $1,200 for tuition and $700 for room and fees, plus books, food, and other expenses. Although we were a comfortable middle-class family by Arkansas standards, I was worried that my folks couldn't afford it. And I was worried about being so far away and leaving Mother and Roger alone with Daddy, though age was slowing him down. My guidance counselor, Edith Irons, was adamant that I should go, that it was an investment in my future that my parents should make. Mother and Daddy agreed. Also, Mother was convinced that once I got there and proved myself I'd get some financial help. So I decided to give it a shot.

I graduated from high school on the evening of May 29, 1964, in a ceremony at Rix Field, where we played our football games. As fourth-ranked student, I got to give the benediction. Subsequent court decisions on religion in public schools, had they been law then, might have taken us prayer leaders off the program. I agree that tax money should not be used to advance purely religious causes, but I was honored to get in the last word at the end of my high school years.

My benediction reflected my deep religious convictions as well as a little politics as I prayed that God would "leave within us the youthful idealism and moralism which have made our people strong. Sicken us at the sight of apathy, ignorance, and rejection so that our generation will remove complacency, poverty, and prejudice from the hearts of free men. . . . Make us care so that we will never know the misery and muddle of life without purpose, and so that when we die, others will still have the opportunity to live in a free land."

I know that some nonreligious people may find all this offensive or naïve but I'm glad I was so idealistic back then, and I still believe every word I prayed.

After graduation, I went with Mauria Jackson to our senior party at the old Belvedere Club, not far from our Park Avenue house. Since Mauria and I were both unattached at the time and had been in grade school together at St. John's, it seemed like a good idea, and it was.

The next morning, I headed into my last summer as a boy. It was a typical, good, hot Arkansas summer, and it passed quickly, with a sixth and final trip to the university band camp, and a return to Boys State as a counselor. That summer I helped Daddy for a couple of weeks with the annual inventory at Clinton Buick, something I had done a few times before. It's hard to remember today, when records are computerized and parts can be ordered from efficient distribution centers, that in those days we kept parts in stock for cars more than ten years old, and counted them all by hand every year. The small parts were in little cubbyholes in very tall shelves set close together, making the back of the parts department very dark, in stark contrast to the bright showroom in front, which was only large enough to accommodate one of the new Buicks.

The work was tedious, but I liked doing it, mostly because it was the only thing I did with Daddy. I also enjoyed being at the Buick place, visiting with Uncle Raymond, with the salesmen on the car lot full of new and used cars, and with the mechanics in the back. There were three men back there I especially liked. Two were black. Early Arnold looked like Ray Charles and had one of the greatest laughs I ever heard. He was always wonderful to me. James White was more laid-back. He had to be: he was trying to raise eight kids on what Uncle Raymond was paying him and what his wife, Earlene, earned by working at our house for Mother after Mrs. Walters left. I lapped up James's armchair philosophy. Once, when I remarked on how quickly my high school years had flown by, he said, "Yeah, time's goin' by so fast, I can't hardly keep up with my age." Then I thought it was a joke. Now it's not so funny.

The white guy, Ed Foshee, was a genius with cars and later opened his own shop. When I went away to school, we sold him the Henry J I drove, one of six badly burned cars Daddy had repaired at the Buick dealership in Hope. I hated to part with that car, leaking hydraulic brakes and all, and I'd give anything to get it back now. It gave my friends and me a lot of good times, and one not-so-good one. One night, I was driving out of Hot Springs on Highway 7 on slick pavement, just behind a black car. As we were passing Jessie Howe's Drive-In, the car in front stopped dead in its tracks, apparently to see what was showing on the big screen. One of its brake lights was out, and I didn't see it stop until it was too late. The combination of inattention, slow reflexes, and iffy brakes plowed me right into the back of the black car, driving my jaw into the steering wheel, which promptly broke in half. Luckily, no one was seriously hurt, and I had insurance to cover the other car's damage. The guys at Clinton Buick fixed the Henry J as good as new, and I was grateful that the steering wheel had broken instead of my jaw. It didn't hurt any worse than when Henry Hill had slugged me a few years earlier, and not nearly as badly as when the ram had almost butted me to death. By then I was more philosophical about such things, with an attitude rather like the wise man who said, "It does a dog good to have a few fleas now and then. It keeps him from worrying so much about being a dog."

NINE

The summer ended too quickly, as all childhood summers do, and on September 12 Mother and I flew to Washington, where we would spend a week sightseeing before I started freshman orientation. I didn't know exactly what I was getting into, but I was full of anticipation.

The trip was harder on Mother than on me. We were always close, and I knew that when she looked at me, she often saw both me and my father. She had to be worried about how she was going to raise little Roger and deal with big Roger without me to help out on both fronts. And we were going to miss each other. We were enough alike and enough different that we enjoyed being together. My friends loved her, too, and she loved having them at our house. That would still happen, but usually only when I was home at Christmas or in the summer.

I couldn't have known then as I know now how much she worried about me. Recently, I came across a letter she wrote in December 1963 as part of my successful application for the Elks Leadership Award, which was given to one or two high school seniors each year in towns with Elks Clubs. She wrote that her letter "relieves in a small way a guilt complex I have about Bill. Anesthesia is my profession and it has always taken time that I felt rightfully belonged to him. And, because of this, the credit for what he is and what he has done with his life actually belongs to him. Thus, when I look at him I see a 'self-made' man." Was she ever wrong about that! It was she who taught me to get up every day and keep going; to look for the best in people even when they saw the worst in me; to be grateful for every day and greet it with a smile; to believe I could do or be anything I put my mind to if I were willing to make the requisite effort; to believe that, in the end, love and kindness would prevail over cruelty and selfishness. Mother was not conventionally religious then, though she grew to be as she aged. She saw so many people die that she had a hard time believing in life after death. But if God is love, she was a godly woman. How I wish I'd told her more often that I was the furthest thing in the world from a self-made man.

Despite all the apprehension about the big changes in our lives, Mother and I were both giddy with excitement by the time we got to Georgetown. Just a couple of blocks away from the main campus was the so-called East Campus, which included the School of Foreign Service and other schools that had women and were religiously and racially more diverse. The college was founded in 1789, George Washington's first year as President, by Archbishop John Carroll. A statue of him anchors the grand circle at the entrance to the main campus. In 1815, President James Madison signed a bill granting Georgetown a charter to confer degrees. Although our university has from the beginning been open to people of all faiths, and one of the greatest Georgetown presidents, Father Patrick Healy, was from 1874 to 1882 the first African-American president of a predominantly white university, the Yard was all male, almost all Catholic, and all white. The School of Foreign Service was founded in 1919 by Father Edmund A. Walsh, a staunch anti-Communist, and when

I got there the faculty was still full of professors who had fled from or suffered from Communist regimes in Europe and China and who were sympathetic to any anti-Communist activity by the U.S. government, including in Vietnam.

The politics weren't all that was conservative at the Foreign Service School. So was the curriculum, the rigor of which reflected the Jesuit educational philosophy, the **Ratio Studiorum,** developed in the late sixteenth century. For the first two years, six courses a semester were required, totaling eighteen or nineteen hours of class time, and there were no electives until the second semester of the junior year. Then there was the dress code. In my freshman year, men were still required to wear dress shirt, jacket, and tie to class. Synthetic-fabric "drip-dry" shirts were available, but they felt awful, so I went to Georgetown determined to fit the five-dollar-a-week dry-cleaning bill for five shirts into my twenty-five-dollar-a-week allowance for food and other expenses. And there were the dorm rules: "Freshmen are required to be in their rooms and studying weeknights, and must have their lights out by midnight. On Friday and Saturday evenings, freshmen must return to their rooms for the night by 12:30 a.m. . . . Absolutely no guests of the opposite sex, alcoholic beverages, pets, or firearms are allowed in University dormitories." I know things have changed a bit since then, but when Hillary and I took Chelsea to Stanford in 1997, it was still somewhat unsettling to see the young women and men living in the same dorm. Apparently the NRA hasn't yet succeeded in lifting the firearms restriction.

One of the first people I met when Mother and I went through the front gate was the priest in charge of freshman orientation, Father Dinneen, who greeted me by saying Georgetown couldn't figure out why a Southern Baptist with no foreign language except Latin would want to go to the Foreign Service School. His tone indicated that they also couldn't quite figure out why they had let me in. I just laughed and said maybe we'd figure it out together in a year or two. I could tell Mother was concerned, so after Father Dinneen went on to other students, I told her that in a little while they'd all know why. I suspect I was bluffing, but it sounded good.

After the preliminaries, we went off to find my dorm room and meet my roommate. Loyola Hall is at the corner of 35th and N streets just behind the Walsh Building, which houses the Foreign Service School and is connected to it. I was assigned Room 225, which was right over the front entrance on 35th and overlooked the house and beautiful garden of Rhode Island's distinguished senator Claiborne Pell, who was still in the Senate when I became President. He and his wife, Nuala, became friends of Hillary's and mine, and thirty years after staring at the exterior of their grand old house, I finally saw the inside of it.

When Mother and I got to the door of my dorm room, I was taken aback. The 1964 presidential campaign was in full swing, and there, plastered on my door, was a Goldwater sticker. I thought I'd left them all behind in Arkansas! It belonged to my roommate, Tom Campbell, an Irish Catholic from Huntington, Long Island. He came from a staunch conservative Republican family, and had been a football player at Xavier Jesuit High School in New York City. His father was a lawyer who won a local judgeship running on the Conservative Party line. Tom was probably more surprised than I was by his assigned roommate. I was the first Southern Baptist from Arkansas he'd ever met, and to make matters worse, I was a hard-core Democrat for LBJ.

Mother wasn't about to let a little thing like politics stand in the way of good living arrangements. She started talking to Tom as if she'd known him forever, just as she always did with everyone, and before long she won him over. I liked him too and figured we could make a go of it. And we have, through four years of living together at Georgetown and almost forty years of friendship.

Soon enough, Mother left me with a cheerful, stiff-upper-lip parting, and I began to explore my immediate surroundings, beginning with my dorm floor. I heard music coming from down the hall—"Tara's Theme" from **Gone with the Wind**—and followed it, expecting to find another southerner, if not another Democrat. When I came to the room where the music was playing, I found instead a character who defied categories, Tommy Caplan. He was sitting in a rocking chair, the only one on our floor. I learned that he was an only child from Baltimore, that his father was in the jewelry business, and that he had known President Kennedy. He spoke with an unusual clipped accent that sounded aristocratic to me, told me he wanted to be a writer, and regaled me with Kennedy tales. Though I knew I liked him, I couldn't have known then that I had just met another person who would prove to be one of the best friends I'd ever have. In the next four years Tommy would introduce me to Baltimore; to his home on Maryland's Eastern Shore; to the Episcopal church and its liturgy; in New York to the Pierre Hotel and its great Indian curry, to the Carlyle Hotel and my first experience with expensive room service, and to the "21" Club, where several of us celebrated his twenty-first birthday; and to Massachusetts and Cape Cod, where I nearly drowned after failing to hold on to a barnacle-covered rock in an effort that shredded my hands, arms, chest, and legs. Trying desperately to get back to shore, I was saved by a fortuitous long, narrow sandbar and a helping hand from Tommy's old school friend, Fife Symington, later Republican governor of Arizona. (If he could have foreseen the future, he might have had second thoughts!) In return, I introduced Tommy to Arkansas, southern folkways, and grassroots politics. I think I made a good trade.

Over the next several days, I met other students and started classes. I also figured out how to live on twenty-five dollars a week. Five dollars came off the top for the required five dress shirts, and I decided to eat on a dollar a day Monday through Friday, and allocate another dollar to weekend meals, so that I'd have fourteen dollars left to go out on Saturday night. In 1964, I could actually take a date to dinner for fourteen dollars, sometimes a movie too, though I had to let the girl order first to make sure our combined order plus a tip didn't go over my budget. Back then there were a lot of good restaurants in Georgetown where fourteen dollars would go that far. Besides, in the first few months I didn't have a date every Saturday, so I was often a little ahead on my budget.

It wasn't too hard to get by on a dollar a day the rest of the time—I always felt I had plenty of money, even enough to cover the extra cost of a school dance or some other special event. At Wisemiller's Deli, just across Thirty-sixth Street from the Walsh Building, where most of my classes were, I got coffee and two donuts for twenty cents every morning, the first time in my life I ever drank coffee, a habit I still try to lick now and then, with limited success. At lunch, I splurged to thirty cents. Half of it bought a Hostess fried pie, apple or cherry; the other half went for a sixteen-ounce Royal Crown Cola. I loved those RCs and was really sad when they quit producing them. Dinner was more expensive, fifty cents. I usually ate at the Hoya Carry Out, a couple of blocks from our dorm, which despite its name had a counter where you could enjoy your meal. Eating there was half the fun. For fifteen cents, I got another big soft drink, and for thirty-five cents, a great tuna fish sandwich on rye, so big you could barely get your mouth around it. For eighty-five cents you could get a roast beef sandwich just as big. Once in a while, when I hadn't blown the whole fourteen dollars the previous Saturday night, I would get one of those.

But the real attractions of the Hoya Carry Out were the proprietors, Don and Rose. Don was a husky character with a tattoo on one of his bulging biceps, back when tattoos were a rarity rather than a common sight on the bodies of rock stars, athletes, and hip young people. Rose had a big beehive hairdo, a nice face, and a great figure, which she showed off to good effect in tight sweaters, tighter pants, and spiked heels. She was a big draw for boys with small budgets and large imaginations, and Don's good-natured but vigilant presence guaranteed that all we did was eat. When Rose was at work, we ate slowly enough to ensure good digestion.

In my first two years, I rarely ventured beyond the confines of the university and its immediate surroundings, a small area bordered by M Street and the Potomac River to the south, Q Street to the north, Wisconsin Avenue to the east, and the university to the west. My favorite haunts in Georgetown were the Tombs, a beer hall in a cellar below the 1789 Restaurant, where most of the students went for beer and burgers; Billy Martin's restaurant, with good food and atmosphere within my budget; and the Cellar

Door, just down the hill from my dorm on M Street. It had great live music. I heard Glenn Yarborough, a popular sixties folksinger; the great jazz organist Jimmy Smith; and a now forgotten group called the Mugwumps, who broke up shortly after I came to Georgetown. Two of the men formed a new, more famous band, the Lovin' Spoonful, and the lead singer, Cass Elliot, became Mama Cass of the Mamas and the Papas. Sometimes the Cellar Door opened on Sunday afternoon, when you could nurse a Coke and listen to the Mugwumps for hours for just a dollar.

Though occasionally I felt cooped up in Georgetown, most days I was happy as a clam, absorbed in my classes and friends. However, I was also grateful for my few trips out of the cocoon. Several weeks into my first semester, I went to the Lisner Auditorium to hear Judy Collins sing. I can still see her, standing alone on the stage with her long blond hair, floor-length cotton dress, and guitar. From that day on, I was a huge Judy Collins fan. In December 1978, Hillary and I were on a brief vacation to London after the first time I was elected governor. One day as we window-shopped down King's Road in Chelsea, the loudspeaker of a store blared out Judy's version of Joni Mitchell's "Chelsea Morning." We agreed on the spot that if we ever had a daughter we'd call her Chelsea.

Though I didn't leave the Georgetown environs often, I did manage two trips to New York my first semester. I went home with Tom Campbell to Long Island for Thanksgiving. LBJ had won the election by then, and I enjoyed arguing politics with Tom's father. I goaded him one night by asking if the nice neighborhood they lived in had been organized under a "protective" covenant, under which homeowners committed not to sell to members of proscribed groups, usually blacks. They were common until the Supreme Court ruled them unconstitutional. Mr. Campbell said yes, the area they lived in had been established under a covenant, but it ran not against blacks but Jews. I lived in a southern town with two synagogues and a fair number of anti-Semites who referred to Jews as "Christ killers," but I was surprised to find anti-Semitism alive and well in New York. I guess I should have been reassured to know the South didn't have a corner on racism or anti-Semitism, but I wasn't.

A few weeks before the Thanksgiving trip, I got my first bite at the Big Apple when I traveled to New York City with the Georgetown band, pretty much a ragtag outfit. We practiced only once or twice a week, but we were good enough to be invited to play a concert at a small Catholic school, St. Joseph's College for Women in Brooklyn. The concert went fine, and at the mixer afterward I met a student who invited me to walk her home and have a Coke with her and her mother. It was my first foray into one of the endless apartment buildings that house the vast majority of New Yorkers, poor to rich. There was no elevator, so we had to walk up several flights to reach her place. It seemed so small to me then, accustomed as I was to Arkansas' one-story houses with yards, even for people of modest means. All I remember about the encounter is that the girl and her mother seemed incredibly nice, and I was amazed that you could develop such outgoing personalities living in such confined spaces.

After I said good night, I was on my own in the big city. I hailed a cab and asked to go to Times Square. I had never seen so many bright neon lights. The place was loud, fast, and throbbing with life, some of it on the seamy side. I saw my first streetwalker, hitting on a hapless archetype: a pathetic-looking guy wearing a dark suit, crew cut, and thick black horn-rimmed glasses and carrying a briefcase. He was both tempted and terrified. Terror won out. He walked on; she smiled, shrugged, and went back to work. I checked out the theaters and storefronts, and one bright sign caught my eye—Tad's Steaks—advertising big steaks for $1.59.

It seemed too good to pass up, so I went in, got my steak, and found a table. Sitting near me were an angry boy and his heartbroken mother. He was giving her a verbal beating with the words, "It's cheap, Mama. It's cheap." She kept saying the salesman had told her it was nice. Over the next few minutes I pieced the story together. She had saved up enough money to buy her son a record player that he wanted badly. The problem was that it was a standard high-fidelity system, called "hi-fi," but he wanted one of the new stereo systems that had much better sound, and apparently more status among fashion-conscious kids. With all her scrimping, his mother couldn't afford it. Instead of being grateful, the kid was screaming at her in public, "Everything we have is cheap! I wanted a nice one!" It made me sick. I wanted to slug him, to scream back at him that he was lucky to have a mother who loved him so much, who put food on his plate and clothes on his back with what was almost certainly a deadly dull job that paid too little. I got up and walked out in disgust, without finishing my bargain steak. That incident had a big impact on me, I guess because of what my own mother had done and endured. It made me more sensitive to the daily struggles of women and men who do things we want someone else to do but don't want to pay much for. It made me hate ingratitude more and resolve to be more grateful myself. And it made me even more determined to enjoy life's lucky breaks without taking them too seriously, knowing that one turn of fate's screw could put me back to square one or worse.

Not long after I got back from New York, I left the band to concentrate on my studies and student government. I won the election for freshman class president in one of my better campaigns, waged to an electorate dominated by Irish and Italian Catholics from the East. I don't remember how I decided to go for it, but I had a lot of help and it was exciting. There were really no issues and not much patronage, so the race boiled down to grassroots politics and one speech. One of my campaign workers wrote me a note showing the depth of our canvassing: "Bill: problems in New Men's; Hanover picking up lots of votes. There are possibilities on 3rd (Pallen's) floor Loyola—down at the end towards the pay phone. Thanks to Dick Hayes. See you tomorrow. Sleep well Gentlemen. King." King was John King, a five-foot-five dynamo who became the coxswain of the Georgetown crew team and study partner of our classmate Luci Johnson, the President's daughter, who once invited him to dinner at the White House, earning our admiration and envy.

On the Tuesday before the election, the class gathered to hear our campaign speeches. I was nominated by Bob Billingsley, a gregarious New Yorker whose Uncle Sherman had owned the Stork Club and who told me great stories of all the stars who had come there from the twenties on. Bob said I had a record of leadership and was "a person who will get things done, and done well." Then came my turn. I raised no issue and promised only to serve "in whatever capacity is needed at any time," whether I won or lost, and to give the election "a spirit which will make our class a little bit stronger and a little bit prouder when the race is over." It was a modest effort, as it should have been; as the saying goes, I had much to be modest about.

The stronger of my two opponents tried to inject some gravity into an inherently weightless moment when he told us he was running because he didn't want our class to fall "into the bottomless abyss of perdition." I didn't know much about that—it sounded like a place you'd go for collaborating with Communists. This bottomless remark was over the top, and was my first big break. We worked like crazy and I was elected. After the votes were counted, my friends collected a lot of nickels, dimes, and quarters so that I could call home on the nearest pay phone and tell my family I had won. It was a happy conversation. I could tell there was no trouble on the other end of the line, and Mother could tell I was getting over my homesickness.

Though I enjoyed student government, the trips to New York, and just being in the Georgetown area, my classes were the main event of my freshman year. For the first time I had to work to learn. I had one big advantage: all six of my courses were taught by interesting, able people. We all had to study a foreign language. I chose German because I was interested in the country and impressed by the clarity and precision of the language. Dr. von Ihering, the German professor, was a kindly man who had hidden from the Nazis in the loft of a farmhouse after they began burning books, including the children's books he wrote. Arthur Cozzens, the geography professor, had a white goatee and a quaint professional manner. I was bored in his class until he told us that, geologically, Arkansas was one of the most interesting places on earth, because of its diamond, quartz crystal, bauxite, and other mineral deposits and formations.

I took logic from Otto Hentz, a Jesuit who had not yet been ordained as a priest. He was bright, energetic, and concerned about the students. One day he asked me if I'd like to have a hamburger with him for dinner. I was flattered and agreed, and we drove up Wisconsin Avenue to a Howard Johnson's. After a little small talk, Otto turned serious. He asked me if I had ever considered becoming a Jesuit. I laughed and replied, "Don't I have to become a Catholic first?" When I told him I was a Baptist and said, only half in jest, that I didn't think I could keep the vow of celibacy even if I were Catholic, he shook his head and said, "I can't believe it. I've read your papers and exams. You write like a Catholic. You think like a Catholic." I used to tell this story to Catholic groups on the campaign trail in Arkansas, assuring them I was the closest thing they could get to a Catholic governor.

Another Jesuit professor, Joseph Sebes, was one of the most remarkable men I've ever known. Lean and stoop-shouldered, he was a gifted linguist whose primary interest was Asia. He had been working in China when the Communists prevailed, and spent some time in captivity, much of it in a small hole in the ground. The abuse damaged his stomach, cost him a kidney, and kept him in poor health for much of the rest of his life. He taught a course called Comparative Cultures. It should have been entitled Religions of the World: we studied Judaism, Islam, Buddhism, Shintoism, Confucianism, Taoism, Hinduism, Jainism, Zoroastrianism, and other faiths. I loved Sebes and learned a lot from him about how people the world over defined God, truth, and the good life. Knowing how many of the students came from foreign countries, he offered everyone the chance to take the final exam orally—in nine languages. In the second semester I got an

A, one of only four that were given, and one of my proudest academic achievements.

My other two teachers were real characters. Robert Irving taught English to freshmen who were unprepared for his rapid-fire, acid commentary on the propensity of freshmen to be verbose and imprecise. He wrote withering comments in the margins of essays, calling one of his students "a capricious little bilge pump," responding to another's expression of chagrin with "turned into a cabbage, did you?" My papers received more pedestrian rebukes: in the margins or at the end, Dr. Irving wrote "awk" for awkward, "ugh," "rather dull, pathetic." On one paper I saved, he finally wrote "clever and thoughtful," only to follow it by asking me to "next time be a sport" and write my essay on "better paper"! One day Dr. Irving read aloud an essay one of his former students had written on Marvell to illustrate the importance of using language with care. The student noted that Marvell loved his wife even after she died, then added the unfortunate sentence, "Of course physical love, for the most part, ends after death." Irving roared, "For the most part! For the most part! I suppose to some people, there's nothing better on a warm day than a nice cold corpse!" That was a little rich for a bunch of eighteen-year-old Catholic school kids and one Southern Baptist. Wherever he is today, I dread the thought of Dr. Irving reading this book, and can only imagine the scorching comments he's scribbling in the margins.

The most legendary class at Georgetown was Professor Carroll Quigley's Development of Civilizations, a requirement for all freshmen, with more than two hundred people in each class. Though difficult, the class was wildly popular because of Quigley's intellect, opinions, and antics. The antics included his discourse on the reality of paranormal phenomena, including his claim to have seen a table rise off the floor and a woman take flight at a séance, and his lecture condemning Plato's elevation of absolute rationality over observed experience, which he delivered every year at the end of the course. He always closed the lecture by ripping apart a paperback copy of Plato's **Republic,** then throwing it across the room, shouting, "Plato is a fascist!"

The exams were filled with mind-bending questions like "Write a brief but well-organized history of the Balkan Peninsula from the start of the Würm Glacier to the time of Homer" and "What is the relationship between the process of cosmic evolution and the dimension of abstraction?"

Two of Quigley's insights had a particularly lasting impact. First, he said that societies have to develop organized instruments to achieve their military, political, economic, social, religious, and intellectual objectives. The problem, according to Quigley, is that all instruments eventually become "institutionalized"—that is, vested interests more committed to preserving their own prerogatives than to meeting the needs for which they were created. Once this happens, change can come only through reform or circumvention of the institutions. If these fail, reaction and decline set in.

His second lasting insight concerned the key to the greatness of Western civilization, and its continuing capacity for reform and renewal. He said our civilization's success is rooted in unique religious and philosophical convictions: that man is basically good; that there is truth, but no finite mortal has it; that we can get closer to the truth only by working together; and that through faith and good works, we can have a better life in this world and a reward in the next. According to Quigley, these ideas gave our civilization its optimistic, pragmatic character and an unwavering belief in the possibility of positive change. He summed up our ideology with the term "future preference," the belief that "the future can be better than the past, and each individual has a personal, moral obligation to make it so." From the 1992 campaign through my two terms in office, I quoted Professor Quigley's line often, hoping it would spur my fellow Americans, and me, to practice what he preached.

By the end of my first year, I had been dating my first long-term girlfriend for a few months. Denise Hyland was a tall, freckle-faced Irish girl with kind, beautiful eyes and an infectious smile. She was from Upper Montclair, New Jersey, the second of six children of a doctor who was studying to be a priest before he met her mother. Denise and I broke up at the end of our junior year, but our friendship has endured.

I was glad to be going home, where at least I'd have old friends and my beloved hot summer. I had a job waiting for me at Camp Yorktown Bay, a Navy League camp for poor kids mostly from Texas and Arkansas, on Lake Ouachita, the largest of Hot Springs' three lakes and one of the cleanest in America. You could see the bottom clearly at a depth of more than thirty feet. The man-made lake was in the Ouachita National Forest, so development around it, with the attendant pollution runoff, was limited.

For several weeks, I got up early every morning and drove out to the camp, twenty miles or so away, where I supervised swimming, basketball, and other camp activities. A lot of the kids needed a week away from their lives.

One came from a family of six kids and a single mother and didn't have a penny to his name when he arrived. His mother was moving and he didn't know where he'd be living when he got back. I talked with one boy who tried unsuccessfully to swim and was in bad shape when he was pulled out of the lake. He said it was nothing: in his short life, he'd already swallowed his tongue, been poisoned, survived a bad car wreck, and lost his father three months earlier.

The summer passed quickly, full of good times with my friends and interesting letters from Denise, who was in France. There was one last terrible incident with Daddy. One day he came home early from work, drunk and mad. I was over at the Yeldells', but luckily, Roger was home. Daddy went after Mother with a pair of scissors and pushed her into the laundry room off the kitchen. Roger ran out the front door and over to the Yeldells' screaming, "Bubba, help! Daddy's killing Dado!" (When Roger was a baby he could say "Daddy" before he could say "Mother," so he created the term "Dado" for her, and he used it for a long time afterward.) I ran back to the house, pulled Daddy off Mother, and grabbed the scissors from him. I took Mother and Roger to the living room, then went back and reamed Daddy out. When I looked into his eyes I saw more fear than rage. Not long before, he had been diagnosed with cancer of the mouth and throat. The doctors recommended radical, and disfiguring, surgery, but he refused, so they treated him as best they could. This incident took place early in the two-year period leading to his death, and I think it was his shame at the way he'd lived and his fear of dying that drove him to what would be his last bad outburst. After that, he still drank, but he became more withdrawn and passive.

This incident had a particularly devastating effect on my brother. Almost forty years later, he told me how humiliated he'd felt running for assistance, how helpless he felt that he couldn't stop his father, how irrevocable his hatred was after that. I realized then how foolish I'd been, in the immediate aftermath of the episode, to revert to our family policy of just pretending nothing had happened and going back to "normal." Instead, I should have told Roger that I was very proud of him; that it was his alertness, love, and courage that had saved Mother; that what he did was harder than what I had done; that he needed to let go of his hatred, because his father was sick, and hating his father would only spread the sickness to him. Oh, I often wrote to Roger and called him a lot when I was away; I encouraged him in his studies and activities and told him I loved him. But I missed the deep scarring and the trouble it would inevitably bring. It took Roger a long time and a lot of self-inflicted wounds to finally get to the source of the hurt in his heart.

Though I still had some concerns about Mother's and Roger's safety, I believed Daddy when he promised he was through with violence, and besides, he was losing the capacity to generate it, so I was ready when the time came to go back to Georgetown for my second year. In June, I had been awarded a $500 scholarship, and the requirement to wear tie and shirt to class had been scrapped, so I was looking forward to a more affluent existence on my twenty-five dollars a week. I also had been reelected president of my class, this time with a real program concentrating on campus issues, including nondenominational religious services and a community-service initiative we took over from the outgoing senior class: GUCAP, the Georgetown University Community Action Program, which sent student volunteers into poor neighborhoods to help kids with their studies. We also tutored adults working for high school diplomas through an extension program, and did whatever else we could to help families struggling to get by. I went a few times, although not as often as I should have. Along with what I knew from growing up in Arkansas, I saw enough of inner-city Washington to convince me that volunteer charity alone would never be enough to overcome the grinding combination of poverty, discrimination, and lack of opportunity that held so many of my fellow citizens back. It made my support for President Johnson's civil rights, voting rights, and anti-poverty initiatives even stronger.

My second year, like the first, was primarily focused on class work, really for the last time. From then on, through my final two years at Georgetown, the stay in Oxford, and law school, my formal studies increasingly fought a losing battle with politics, personal experiences, and private explorations.

For now, there was more than enough to hold my attention in the classroom, starting with second-year German, Mary Bond's absorbing course on major British writers, and Ulrich Allers's History of Political Thought. Allers was a gruff German who noted these few words on a paper I wrote on the ancient Athenian legal system: "Plodding but very decent." At the time, I felt damned with faint praise. After I had been President a few years, I would have killed to be called that.

I made a C in Joe White's microeconomics class first semester. Professor White also taught macroeconomics second semester, and I got an A in that class. I suppose both grades were harbingers, since as President I did a good job with the nation's economy and a poor job with my personal economic situation, at least until I left the White House.

I studied European history with Luis Aguilar, a Cuban expatriate who had been a leader of the democratic opposition to Batista before he was overthrown by Castro. Once, Aguilar asked me what I intended to do with my life. I told him that I wanted to go home and get into politics but that I was becoming interested in a lot of other things too. He replied wistfully, "Choosing a career is like choosing a wife from ten girlfriends. Even if you pick the most beautiful, the most intelligent, the kindest woman, there is still the pain of losing the other nine." Though he loved teaching and was good at it, I had the feeling that for Professor Aguilar, Cuba was those other nine women rolled into one.

My most memorable class sophomore year was Professor Walter Giles's U.S. Constitution and Government, a course he taught largely through Supreme Court cases. Giles was a redheaded, crew-cut confirmed bachelor whose life was filled by his students, his love for the Constitution and social justice, and his passion for the Washington Redskins, win or lose. He invited students to his house for dinners, and a lucky few even got to go with him to see the Redskins play. Giles was a liberal Democrat from Oklahoma, not common then and rare enough today to place him under the protection of the Endangered Species Act.

I think he took an interest in me partly because I was from a state that bordered his own, though he liked to kid me about it. By the time I got to his class I had embraced my lifelong affinity for sleep deprivation and had developed the sometimes embarrassing habit of falling asleep for five or ten minutes in class, after which I'd be fine. I sat in the front row of Giles's big lecture class, a perfect foil for his biting wit. One day as I was napping, he noted loudly that a certain Supreme Court ruling was so crystal clear anyone could understand it, "unless, of course, you're from some hick town in Arkansas." I awoke with a start to peals of laughter from my classmates and never fell asleep on him again.

TEN

After my sophomore year I went home without a
job but with a clear idea of what I wanted to do. It
was the end of an era in Arkansas—after six terms,
Orval Faubus wasn't running for reelection as governor.
Finally our state would have a chance to move beyond the
scars of Little Rock and the stains of cronyism that also
tainted his later years. I wanted to work in the governor's
race, both to learn about politics and to do what little I
could to put Arkansas on a more progressive course.

The pent-up ambitions from the Faubus years propelled several candidates into the race, seven Democrats
and one very big Republican, Winthrop Rockefeller, the
fifth of the six children of John D. Rockefeller Jr., who left
his father's empire to oversee the charitable efforts of the
Rockefeller Foundation; left his father's conservative, anti-
labor politics under the influence of his more liberal wife,
Abby, and the great Canadian liberal politician Mackenzie
King; and, finally, left his father's conservative religious
views to found the interdenominational Riverside Church
in New York City with Harry Emerson Fosdick.

Winthrop had seemed destined to be the black sheep of
the family. He was expelled from Yale and went to work in
the Texas oil fields. After distinguished service in World
War II, he married a New York socialite and reacquired his
reputation as a hard-partying dilettante. In 1953, he moved
to Arkansas, partly because he had a wartime buddy from

there who interested him in the possibilities of setting up a ranching operation, and partly because the state had a thirty-day divorce law and he was eager to end his brief first marriage. Rockefeller was a huge man, about six feet four, weighing about 250 pounds. He really took to Arkansas, where everybody called him Win, not a bad name for a politician. He always wore cowboy boots and a white Stetson hat, which became his trademark. He bought a huge chunk of Petit Jean Mountain, about fifty miles west of Little Rock, became a successful breeder of Santa Gertrudis cattle, and married his second wife, Jeannette.

As he settled into his adopted state, Rockefeller worked hard to shed the playboy image that had dogged him in New York. He built up the small Arkansas Republican Party and worked to bring industry to our poor state. Governor Faubus appointed him chairman of the Arkansas Industrial Development Commission, and he brought in a lot of new jobs. In 1964, impatient with Arkansas' backward image, he challenged Faubus for governor. Everybody appreciated what he had done, but Faubus had an organization in every county; most people, especially in rural Arkansas, still supported his segregationist position over Rockefeller's pro–civil rights stance; and Arkansas was still a Democratic state.

Also, the painfully shy Rockefeller was a poor speaker, a problem aggravated by his legendary drinking habits, which also made him so late so often that he made me look punctual. Once, he arrived inebriated and more than an hour late to address the chamber of commerce banquet in Wynne, county seat of Cross County, in eastern Arkansas. When he got up to speak, he said, "I'm glad to be here in—" When he realized he didn't know where he was, he whispered to the master of ceremonies, "Where am I?" The man whispered back, "Wynne." He asked again and got the same answer. Then he boomed out, "Damn it, I know my name! Where am I?" That story crossed the state like wildfire, but was usually told good-naturedly, because everybody knew Rockefeller was an Arkansan by choice and had the state's best interests at heart. In 1966, Rockefeller was running again, but even with Faubus gone, I didn't think he could make it.

Besides, I wanted to back a progressive Democrat. My sentimental favorite was Brooks Hays, who had lost his seat in Congress in 1958 for supporting the integration of Little Rock Central High. He was defeated by a segregationist optometrist, Dr. Dale Alford, in a write-in campaign, which succeeded partly because of the use of stickers with his name on them that could be plastered on ballots by voters who couldn't write but were "smart" enough to know that blacks and whites shouldn't go to school together. Hays was a devout Christian who had served as president of the Southern Baptist Convention before the majority of my fellow Baptists decided that only conservatives could lead them, or the country. He was a marvelous man, bright, humble, funny as all get-out, and kind to a fault, even to his opponent's young campaign workers.

Ironically, Dr. Alford was in the race for govenor, too, and he couldn't win either, because the racists had a far more fervent champion in Justice Jim Johnson, who had risen from humble roots in Crossett, in southeast Arkansas, to the state supreme court on rhetoric that won the endorsement of the Ku Klux Klan in the governor's race. He thought Faubus was too soft on civil rights; after all, he had appointed a few blacks to state boards and commissions. With Faubus, who had genuine populist impulses, racism was a political imperative. He preferred improving schools and nursing homes, building roads, and reforming the state mental hospital to race-baiting. It was just the price of staying in office. With Johnson, racism was theology. He thrived on hate. He had sharp features and bright, wild eyes, giving him a "lean and hungry" look that would have made Shakespeare's Cassius green with envy. And he was a savvy politician who knew where his voters were. Instead of going to the endless campaign rallies where the other candidates spoke, he traveled all over the state on his own, with a country-and-western band, which he used to pull in a crowd. Then he would whip them into a frenzy with tirades against blacks and their traitorous white sympathizers.

I didn't see it at the time, but he was building strength among people the other candidates couldn't reach: people upset with federal activism in civil rights, scared by the Watts riots and other racial disturbances, convinced the War on Poverty was socialist welfare for blacks, and frustrated with their own economic conditions. Psychologically, we're all a complex mixture of hopes and fears. Each day we wake up with the scales tipping a bit one way or the other. If they go too far toward hopefulness, we can become naïve and unrealistic. If the scales tilt too far the other way, we can get consumed by paranoia and hatred. In the South, the dark side of the scales has always been the bigger problem. In 1966, Jim Johnson was just the man to tip them in that direction.

The best candidate with a good shot at winning was another supreme court justice and a former attorney general, Frank Holt. He had the support of most of the courthouse crowd and the big financial interests, but he was more progressive on race than Faubus, and completely honest and decent. Frank Holt was admired by just about everybody who knew him (except those who thought he was too easygoing to make any real change), had wanted to be governor all his life, and also wanted to redeem his family's legacy: his brother, Jack, who was more of an old-fashioned southern populist, had lost a hot Senate race to our conservative senior senator, John McClellan, a few years before.

My uncle Raymond Clinton was a big supporter of Holt's and told me he thought he could get me on the campaign. Holt already had secured the support of a number of student leaders from Arkansas colleges, who called themselves the "Holt Generation." Before long I got hired at fifty dollars a week. I think Uncle Raymond paid my way. Since I had been living on twenty-five dollars a week at Georgetown, I felt rich.

The other students were a little older and a lot better connected than I was. Mac Glover had been president of the University of Arkansas student body; Dick King was president of the student body at Arkansas State Teachers College; Paul Fray was president of the Young Democrats at Ouachita Baptist; Bill Allen was a former Arkansas Boys State governor and student leader at Memphis State, just across the Mississippi River from Arkansas; Leslie Smith was a beautiful, smart girl from a powerful political family who had been Arkansas Junior Miss.

At the start of the campaign, I was definitely a second stringer in the Holt Generation. My assignments included nailing "Holt for Governor" signs on trees, trying to get people to put his bumper stickers on their cars; and handing out his brochures at rallies around the state. One of the most important rallies, then and later when I became a candidate, was the Mount Nebo Chicken Fry. Mount

Nebo is a beautiful spot overlooking the Arkansas River in Yell County, in western Arkansas, where the Clintons originally settled. People would show up for the food, the music, and a long stream of speeches by candidates, beginning with those running for local office and ending with those running for governor.

Not long after I got there and began working the crowd, our opponents started to arrive. Judge Holt was running late. When his opponents began speaking, he still wasn't there. I was getting worried. This was not an event to miss. I went to a pay phone and somehow tracked him down, which was a lot harder before cell phones. He said that he just couldn't get there before the speeches were over, and that I should speak for him. I was surprised and asked if he was sure. He said I knew what he stood for and I should just tell the people that. When I told the event organizers Judge Holt couldn't make it and asked if I could speak in his place, I was scared to death; it was much worse than speaking for myself. After I finished, the people gave me a polite reception. I don't remember what I said, but it must have been okay, because after that, along with my sign and bumper-sticker duties, I was asked to stand in for Judge Holt at a few smaller rallies he couldn't attend. There were so many, no candidate could make them all. Arkansas has seventy-five counties, and several counties held more than one rally.

After a few weeks, the campaign decided that the judge's wife, Mary, and his daughters, Lyda and Melissa, should go on the road to cover places he couldn't. Mary Holt was a tall, intelligent, independent woman who owned a fashionable dress shop in Little Rock; Lyda was a student at Mary Baldwin College in Staunton, Virginia, where Woodrow Wilson was born; Melissa was in high school.

They were all attractive and articulate, and they all adored Judge Holt and were really committed to the campaign. All they needed was a driver. Somehow I was chosen.

We crisscrossed the state. We were gone a week at a time, coming back to Little Rock to wash our clothes and recharge for another lap. It was great fun. I really got to know the state and learned a lot from hours of conversation with Mary and her daughters. One night we went to Hope for a rally on the courthouse steps. Because my grandmother was in the crowd, Mary graciously invited me to speak to the hometown folks, though Lyda was supposed to do it. I think they both knew I wanted the chance to show that I'd grown up. The crowd gave me a good listen and I even got a nice write-up in the local paper, the **Hope Star,** which tickled Daddy because when he had the Buick dealership in Hope, the editor disliked him so much he got an ugly mongrel dog, named him Roger, and frequently let the dog loose near the Buick place so that he could go down the street after him shouting, "Come here, Roger! Here, Roger!"

That night I took Lyda to see the house where I had spent my first four years and the wooden railroad overpass where I'd played. The next day we went out to the cemetery to visit the graves of Mary Holt's family, and I showed them my father's and grandfather's graves.

I treasure the memories of those road trips. I was used to being bossed around by women, so we got along well, and I think I was useful to them. I changed flat tires, helped a family get out of a burning house, and got eaten alive by mosquitoes so big you could feel them puncture your skin. We passed the hours of driving by talking about politics, people, and books. And I think we got some votes.

Not long before the Hope rally, the campaign decided

to put on a fifteen-minute TV program featuring the students who were working for Judge Holt; they thought it would position him as the candidate of Arkansas' future. Several of us spoke for a couple of minutes about why we were supporting him. I don't know if it did any good, but I enjoyed my first TV appearance, though I didn't get to watch it. I had to speak at yet another rally in Alread, a remote community in Van Buren County, in the mountains of north-central Arkansas. The candidates who made it way up there usually got the votes, and I was beginning to realize that we needed all we could get.

As the hot summer weeks passed, I saw more and more evidence that the Old South hadn't given up the ghost, and the New South wasn't yet powerful enough to chase it away. Most of our schools were still segregated, and resistance remained strong. One county courthouse in the Mississippi Delta still had "white" and "colored" designations on the doors of the public restrooms. When I asked one elderly black lady in another town to vote for Judge Holt, she said she couldn't because she hadn't paid her poll tax. I told her that Congress had eliminated the poll tax two years earlier and all she had to do was register. I don't know if she did.

Still, there were signs of a new day. While campaigning in Arkadelphia, thirty-five miles south of Hot Springs, I met the leading candidate for the south Arkansas congressional seat, a young man named David Pryor. He was clearly a progressive who thought if he could just meet enough people he could persuade most of them to vote for him. He did it in 1966, did it again in the governor's race in 1974, and again in the Senate race in 1978. By the time he retired, much to my dismay, from the Senate in 1996, David Pryor was the most popular politician in Arkansas, with a fine progressive legacy. Everybody thought of him as their friend, including me.

The kind of retail politics Pryor mastered was important in a rural state like Arkansas, where more than half the people lived in towns with fewer than five thousand people, and tens of thousands just lived "out in the country." We were still in the days before television ads, especially negative ones, assumed the large role in elections they have now. Candidates mostly bought television time to look into the camera and talk to voters. They also were expected to visit the courthouses and main businesses in every county seat, go into the kitchen of every café, and campaign in sale barns, where livestock are auctioned. The county fairs and pie suppers were fertile territory. And, of course, every weekly newspaper and radio station expected a visit and an ad or two. That's how I learned politics. I think it works better than TV air wars. You could talk, but you had to listen, too. You had to answer voters' tough questions face-to-face. Of course, you could still be demonized, but at least your adversaries had to work harder to do it. And when you took a shot at your opponent, you had to take it, not hide behind some bogus committee that expected to make a killing from your time in office if its attacks destroyed the other candidate.

Though the campaigns were more personal, they were far from just personality contests. When there were big issues at stake, they had to be addressed. And if a strong tide of public opinion was rolling in, and you couldn't go with the flow in good conscience, you had to be tough, disciplined, and quick to avoid being washed away.

In 1966, Jim Johnson—or "Justice Jim," as he liked to be called—was riding the tide and making big, ugly waves. He attacked Frank Holt as a "pleasant vegetable," and implied that Rockefeller had had homosexual relations with black men, a laughable charge considering his earlier well-earned reputation as a ladies' man. Justice Jim's message was simply the latest version of an old southern song sung to white voters in times of economic and social uncertainty: You're good, decent, God-fearing people; "they're" threatening your way of life; you don't have to change, it's all their fault; elect me and I'll stand up for you just as you are and kick the hell out of them. The perennial political divide, Us versus Them. It was mean, ugly, and ultimately self-defeating for the people who bought it, but as we still see, when people feel discontented and insecure it often works. Because Johnson was so extreme in his rhetoric, and largely invisible on the traditional campaign trail, most political observers thought it wouldn't work this time. As election day neared, Frank Holt refused to answer his attacks, or the attacks from other candidates, who assumed he was way ahead and also began to hit him for being the "old-guard machine" candidate. We didn't have many polls back then and most people didn't put much stock in the few that floated around.

Holt's strategy sounded good to the idealistic young people around him, like me. He simply replied to all charges with a statement that he was completely independent, that he wouldn't respond to unsubstantiated attacks or attack his opponents in return, and that he wanted to win on his own merits "or not at all." I finally learned that phrases like "or not at all" are often used by candidates who forget that politics is a contact sport. The strategy can work when the public mood is secure and hopeful and when the candidate has a platform of serious, specific policy proposals, but in the summer of 1966 the mood was mixed at best, and the Holt platform was too general to inspire much intense feeling. Besides, those who most wanted a candidate who simply embodied opposition to segregation could vote for Brooks Hays.

Despite the attacks on him, most people thought Frank Holt would lead the ticket, but without a majority, and then would win the runoff two weeks later. On July 26, the people spoke, more than 420,000 of them. The results surprised the pundits. Johnson led with 25 percent of the vote, Holt was second with 23 percent, Hays was third with 15 percent, Alford got 13 percent, and the other three split the rest.

We were shocked but not without hope. Judge Holt and Brooks Hays had gotten slightly more votes between them than the segregationist combo of Johnson and Alford. Also, in one of the more interesting legislative races, a long-serving old-guard House member, Paul Van Dalsem, was defeated by a young, progressive, Yale-educated lawyer, Herb Rule. A couple of years earlier Van Dalsem had infuriated supporters of the rising women's movement by saying women should be kept at home, "barefoot and pregnant." That got Herb, later Hillary's partner at the Rose Law Firm, an army of female volunteers, who dubbed themselves "Barefoot Women for Rule."

The outcome of the runoff election was very much up in the air, because runoffs are about voter turnout, about which candidate will do a better job of getting his own voters back to the polls, and a better job of persuading those who voted for candidates who were eliminated or people who didn't vote the first time to support him. Judge Holt tried hard to make the runoff a choice between the Old South and the New South. Johnson didn't exactly undermine that framing of the race when he went on TV to tell the voters that he stood "with Daniel in the lion's den" and "with John the Baptist in Herod's court" in opposing godless integration. I think somewhere in that talk Justice Jim even got on Paul Revere's horse.

Though the Holt strategy was smart and Johnson was willing to fight it out as Old versus New, there were two problems with Holt's approach. First, the Old South voters were highly motivated to vote and they were sure Johnson was their champion, while the New South voters weren't so sure about Holt. His refusal to really take the gloves off until late in the race reinforced their doubts and reduced their incentive to vote. Second, an undetermined number of Rockefeller supporters wanted to vote for Johnson because they thought he'd be easier than Holt for their man to beat, and anyone, Republican or Democrat, could vote in the Democratic runoff as long as he or she hadn't voted in the Republican primary. Only 19,646 people had done that, since Rockefeller was unopposed. On runoff election day, only 5,000 fewer people voted than in the first primary. Each candidate got twice as many votes as the first time, and Johnson won by 15,000 votes, 52 to 48 percent.

I was sick about the outcome. I had come to care deeply about Judge Holt and his family, to believe he would have been a better governor than he was a candidate, and to dislike what Justice Jim stood for even more. The only bright spot was Rockefeller, who actually had a chance to win. He was a better organized candidate the second time around. He spent money as if it was going out of style, even buying hundreds of bicycles for poor black kids. In the fall he won with 54.5 percent of the vote. I was very proud of my state. I had gone back to Georgetown by then and didn't watch the campaign unfold firsthand, but a lot of people commented that Johnson seemed less animated in the general election. Perhaps it was because his financial support was limited, but there was also a rumor that he might have gotten some "encouragement" from Rockefeller to cool it. I have no idea if that was true or not.

Except for a brief interregnum in the Carter years, when I was President Carter's point man in Arkansas, and when he wanted a federal appointment for his son, Jim Johnson remained way out there on the right, where he grew more and more hostile toward me. In the 1980s, like so many southern conservatives he became a Republican. He ran again for the supreme court and lost. After that, he made his mischief in the background. When I ran for President, he planted ingenious stories, directly and indirectly, with anyone gullible enough to believe them, and got some surprising takers among the so-called eastern liberal media he loved to revile, especially for Whitewater tales. He's a canny old rascal. He must have had a great time conning them, and if the Republicans in Washington had succeeded in running me out of town, he'd have had a good claim to the last laugh.

After the campaign I got to wind down by taking my first trip to the West Coast. A regular customer of Uncle Raymond's wanted a new Buick he didn't have in stock. Uncle Raymond found one at a dealership in Los Angeles, where it was being used as a "demonstrator," a car prospective customers could test-drive to see how they liked it. Dealers often swapped these cars or sold them to one another at a discount. My uncle asked me to fly out to L.A. and drive the car back, along with Pat Brady, whose mother was his secretary, and who had been in my high school class and the band. If we both went, we could drive straight through. We were eager to go, and back then student fares were so cheap Raymond could fly us out for nearly nothing and still make a profit on the car.

We flew into LAX, got the car, and headed home, but not in a straight line. Instead, we took a minor detour to Las Vegas, a place we thought we'd never have another chance to see. I still remember driving across the flat desert at night with the windows down, feeling the warm, dry air and seeing the bright lights of Vegas beckoning in the distance.

Las Vegas was different then. There were no big theme hotels like the Paris or the Venetian, just the Strip, with its gambling and entertainment. Pat and I didn't have much money, but we wanted to play the slot machines, so we picked a place, got a roll of nickels each, and went to work. Within fifteen minutes I had hit one jackpot and Pat had pulled two. This did not go unnoticed by the regular hostages to the one-armed bandits. They were convinced we were good luck, so every time we left a machine without hitting, people rushed to it, jostling for the right to pull up the jackpot we had left waiting for them. We couldn't understand it. We were convinced that we'd completely used up years of luck in those few minutes, and we didn't want to squander it. We got back on the road with most of our winnings still bulging in our pockets. I don't think anyone carries that many nickels anymore.

After we turned the car in to Uncle Raymond, who didn't seem to mind the side trip, I had to get ready to go back to Georgetown. At the end of the campaign, I had spoken to Jack Holt about my interest in going to work for Senator Fulbright, but I didn't know if anything would come of it. I had written Fulbright for a job the previous spring and had received a letter back saying there were no vacancies but they'd keep my letter on file. I doubted things had changed, but a few days after getting back to Hot Springs, I got a call early in the morning from Lee Williams, Fulbright's administrative assistant. Lee said Jack Holt had recommended me and there was a job opening as an assistant clerk on the Foreign Relations Committee. He said, "You can have a part-time job for $3,500 or a full-time job for $5,000." Even though I was sleepy, I couldn't miss that one. I said, "How about two part-time jobs?" He laughed and said I was just the kind of person he was looking for and I should report for work Monday morning. I was so excited I could have popped. The Foreign Relations Committee under Fulbright had become the center of national debate over foreign policy, especially the escalating war in Vietnam. Now I would witness the drama unfold firsthand, albeit as a flunky. And I would be able to pay for college without any help from Mother and Daddy, taking the financial burden off them and the guilt burden off me. I had worried about how in the world they could afford Daddy's medical treatments on top of the costs of Georgetown. Though I never told anyone at the time, I was afraid I'd have to leave George-town and come home, where college was so much less expensive. Now, out of the blue, I had the chance to stay on at Georgetown and work for the Foreign Relations Committee. I owe so much of the rest of my life to Jack Holt for recommending me for that job, and to Lee Williams for giving it to me.

ELEVEN

A couple of days after Lee Williams called I was packed and ready to drive back to Washington in a gift. Since my new job required me to get to Capitol Hill every day, Mother and Daddy gave me their "old car," a three-year-old white convertible Buick LeSabre with a white and red leather interior. Daddy got a new car every three years or so and turned the old one in to be sold on the used-car lot. This time I replaced the used-car lot and I was ecstatic. It was a beautiful car. Though it got only seven or eight miles to the gallon, gas was cheap, dropping under thirty cents per gallon when there was a "gas war" on.

On my first Monday back in Washington, as instructed, I presented myself in Senator Fulbright's office, the first office on the left in what was then called the New Senate Office Building, now the Dirksen Building. Like the Old Senate Office Building across the street, it is a grand marble edifice, but much brighter. I had a good talk with Lee, then was taken upstairs to the fourth floor, where the Foreign Relations Committee had its offices and hearing room. The committee also had a much grander space in the Capitol building, where the chief of staff, Carl Marcy, and a few of the senior staff worked. There was also a beautiful conference room where the committee could meet privately.

When I arrived at the committee office, I met Buddy

Kendrick, the documents clerk, who would be my supervisor, fellow storyteller, and provider of homespun advice over the next two years; Buddy's full-time assistant, Bertie Bowman, a kind, bighearted African-American who moonlighted as a cabdriver and also drove Senator Fulbright on occasion; and my two student counterparts, Phil Dozier from Arkansas and Charlie Parks, a law student from Anniston, Alabama.

I was told I would be taking memos and other materials back and forth between the Capitol and Senator Fulbright's office, including confidential material for which I would have to receive proper government clearance. Beyond that, I would do whatever was required, from reading newspapers and clipping important articles for the staff and interested senators to answering requests for speeches and other materials, to adding names to the committee's mailing list. Keep in mind that this was before computers and e-mail, even before modern copying machines, though while I was there we did graduate from copies made on carbon paper while typing or writing to rudimentary "Xerox" copies. Most of the newspaper articles I clipped were never copied; they were simply put into a big folder every day with a routing sheet that had the names of the committee staff from the chairman on down. Each person would receive and review them, check off his or her name on the sheet, and pass them along. The main mailing lists were kept in the basement. Each name and address was typed onto a small metal plate, then the plates were stored in alphabetical order in file cabinets. When we sent a mailing out, the plates were put into a machine that inked them and stamped the imprints on envelopes as they passed through.

I enjoyed going to the basement to type new names and

addresses on plates and put them in file drawers. Since I was always exhausted, I often took a nap down there, sometimes just leaning against the file cabinets. And I really loved reading the newspapers and clipping articles for the staff to read. For nearly two years, every day, I read the **New York Times,** the **Washington Post,** the now defunct **Washington Star,** the **Wall Street Journal,** the **Baltimore Sun,** and the **St. Louis Post-Dispatch,** the last because it was thought the committee should see at least one good "heartland" newspaper. When McGeorge Bundy was President Kennedy's national security advisor, he remarked that any citizen who read six good newspapers a day would know as much as he did. I don't know about that, but after I did what he recommended for sixteen months, I did know enough to survive my Rhodes scholarship interview. And if Trivial Pursuit had been around back then, I might have been national champion.

We also handled requests for documents. The committee produced a lot of them: reports on foreign trips, expert testimony in hearings, and full hearing transcripts. The deeper we got into Vietnam, the more Senator Fulbright and his allies tried to use the hearing process to educate Americans about the complexities of life and politics in North and South Vietnam, the rest of Southeast Asia, and China.

The document room was our regular workplace. In the first year I worked my half day in the afternoon from one to five. Because the committee hearings and other business often ran beyond that, I often stayed after five o'clock and never begrudged it. I liked the people I worked with, and I liked what Senator Fulbright was doing with the committee.

It was easy to fit the job into my daily schedule, partly because in junior year only five courses were required instead of six, partly because some classes started as early as 7 a.m. Three of my requirements—U.S. History and Diplomacy, Modern Foreign Governments, and Theory and Practice of Communism—complemented my new work. Scheduling was also easier because I didn't run again for president of the class.

Every day, I looked forward to the end of classes and the drive to Capitol Hill. It was easier to find parking then. And it was a fascinating time to be there. The vast majority that had carried Lyndon Johnson to his landslide victory in 1964 was beginning to unravel. In a few months the Democrats would see their majorities in the House and Senate diminish in the 1966 midterm elections, as the country moved to the right in reaction to riots, social unrest, and the rise of inflation, and President Johnson escalated both domestic spending and our involvement in Vietnam. He claimed our country could afford both "guns and butter," but the people were beginning to doubt it. In his first two and a half years as President, Johnson had enjoyed the most stunning legislative successes since FDR: the Civil Rights Act of 1964, the Voting Rights Act of 1965, sweeping anti-poverty legislation, and Medicare and Medicaid, which at last guaranteed medical care for the poor and elderly.

Now, more and more, the attention of the President, the Congress, and the country was turning to Vietnam. As the death toll mounted with no victory in sight, rising opposition to the war took many forms, from protests on campuses to sermons from pulpits, from arguments in coffee shops to speeches on the floor of Congress. When I went to work for the Foreign Relations Committee, I didn't know enough about Vietnam to have a strong opinion, but I was so supportive of President Johnson that I gave him the benefit of the doubt. Still, it was clear that events were conspiring to undermine the magic moment of progress ushered in by his landslide election.

The country was dividing over more than Vietnam. The Watts riots in Los Angeles in 1965 and the rise of militant black activists pushed their sympathizers to the left and their opponents to the right. The Voting Rights Act, of which LBJ was particularly and justifiably proud, had a similar effect, especially as it began to be enforced. Johnson was an uncommonly shrewd politician. He said when he signed the voting rights legislation that he had just killed the Democratic Party in the South for a generation. In fact, the so-called Solid South of the Democrats had been far from solid for a long time. The conservative Democrats had been falling away since 1948, when they recoiled at Hubert Humphrey's barn-burning civil rights speech at the Democratic convention and Strom Thurmond bolted the party to run for President as a Dixiecrat. In 1960, Johnson helped Kennedy hold enough southern states to win, but Kennedy's commitment to enforcing court-ordered integration of southern public schools and universities drove more conservative whites into the Republican fold. In 1964, while losing in a landslide, Goldwater carried five southern states.

However, in 1966 a lot of the white segregationists were still southern Democrats, people like Orval Faubus and Jim Johnson and Governor George Wallace of Alabama. And the Senate was full of them, grand characters like Richard Russell of Georgia and John Stennis of Mississippi and some others who had no grandeur at all, just power. But President Johnson was right about the impact of the Voting Rights Act and the other civil rights efforts. By 1968, Richard Nixon and George Wallace, running for President as an independent, would both out-poll Humphrey in the South, and since then, the only Democrats to win the White House were two southerners, Jimmy Carter and I. We won enough southern states to get in, with huge black support and a few more white voters than a non-southerner could have gotten. The Reagan years solidified the hold of the Republican Party on white conservative southerners, and the Republicans made them feel welcome.

President Reagan even went so far as to make a campaign speech defending states' rights and, by implication, resistance to federal meddling in civil rights, in Philadelphia, Mississippi, where civil rights workers Andrew Goodman, Michael Schwerner, and James Chaney, two whites and one black, were martyred to the cause in 1964. I always liked President Reagan personally and wished he hadn't done that. In the 2002 midterm elections, even with Colin Powell, Condi Rice, and other minorities holding prominent positions in the Bush administration, Republicans were still winning elections on race, with white backlashes in Georgia and South Carolina over Democratic governors removing the Confederate flag from the Georgia State flag and from the South Carolina Capitol building. Just two years earlier, George W. Bush had campaigned at the notoriously right-wing Bob Jones University in South Carolina, where he declined to take a stand on the flag issue, saying it was a matter for the state to decide. When a Texas school insisted on hoisting the Confederate flag every morning, Governor Bush said it was not a state but a local issue. And they called me slick! President Johnson foresaw all this in 1965, but he did the right thing anyway, and I'm grateful he did.

In the summer of 1966, and even more after the elections that fall, all the foreign and domestic conflicts were apparent in the deliberations of the U.S. Senate. When I went to work there, the Senate was full of big personalities and high drama. I tried to absorb it all. The president pro tempore, Carl Hayden of Arizona, had been in Congress since his state entered the Union in 1912 and in the Senate for forty years. He was bald, gaunt, almost skeletal. Senator Fulbright's brilliant speechwriter Seth Tillman once cracked that Carl Hayden was "the only ninety-year-old man in the world who looks twice his age." The Senate majority leader, Mike Mansfield of Montana, had enlisted to fight in World War I at fifteen, then had become a college professor with a specialty in Asian affairs. He held the post of majority leader for sixteen years, until 1977, when President Carter appointed him ambassador to Japan. Mansfield was a fitness fanatic who walked five miles a day well into his nineties. He was also a genuine liberal and, behind his taciturn façade, something of a wit. He had been born in 1903, two years before Senator Fulbright, and lived to be ninety-eight. Shortly after I became President, Mansfield had lunch with Fulbright. When he asked Fulbright his age and Fulbright said he was eighty-seven, Mansfield replied, "Oh, to be eighty-seven again."

The Republican leader, Everett Dirksen of Illinois, had been essential to passing some of the President's legislation, providing enough liberal Republican votes to overcome the opposition of segregationist southern Democrats. Dirksen had an amazing face, with a large mouth and lots of wrinkles, and an even more amazing voice. Deep and full, it boomed out one pithy phrase after another. Once he hit Democratic spending habits with this ditty: "A billion here, a billion there, pretty soon you're talking about real money." When Dirksen talked it was like hearing the voice of God or a pompous snake-oil salesman, depending on your perspective.

The Senate looked a lot different then from how it looks today. In January 1967, after the Democrats had lost four seats in the midterm elections, they still had a margin of sixty-four to thirty-six—a far more lopsided group than what we usually find today. But the differences then were deep, too, and the lines were not only drawn on party affiliation. A few things have not changed: Robert Byrd of West Virginia still serves in the Senate. In 1966, he was already the authoritative voice on the rules and history of the body.

Eight states of the Old South still had two Democratic senators each, down from ten before the 1966 elections, but most of them were conservative segregationists. Today, only Arkansas, Florida, and Louisiana are represented by two Democrats. Oklahoma had two Democrats, California two Republicans. Today it's the reverse. In the inter-mountain West, now solidly Republican, Utah, Idaho, and Wyoming each had one progressive Democratic senator. Indiana, a conservative state, had two liberal Democratic senators, one of whom, Birch Bayh, is the father of current Senator Evan Bayh, a gifted leader who might be President someday, but who's not as liberal as his dad was. Minnesota was represented by the brilliant but diffident intellectual Gene McCarthy and future vice president Walter Mondale, who succeeded Hubert Humphrey when he became President Johnson's vice president. Johnson picked Humphrey over Connecticut senator Tom Dodd, one of the chief prosecutors of Nazis at the Nuremberg War Crimes Tribunal. Dodd's son, Chris, now represents Connecticut in the Senate. Al Gore's father was in his last term and was a hero to young southerners like me because he and his Tennessee colleague, Estes Kefauver, were the only two southern senators who refused to sign the so-called Southern Manifesto in 1956, which called for resistance to court-ordered school integration. The fiery populist Ralph Yarborough represented Texas, though the rightward future of the state was emerging with the election in 1961 of a Republican senator, John Tower, and a young Republican congressman from Houston, George Herbert Walker Bush. One of the most interesting senators was Oregon's Wayne Morse, who started out as a Republican, then became an independent, and was by 1966 a Democrat. Morse, who was long-winded but smart and tough, and Democrat Ernest Gruening of Alaska were the only two senators to oppose the Tonkin Gulf resolution in 1964, which LBJ claimed gave him authority to wage the war in Vietnam. The only woman in the Senate was a Republican who smoked a pipe, Margaret Chase Smith of Maine. By 2004, there were fourteen women senators, nine Democrats and five Republicans. Back then there were also a number of influential liberal Republicans, alas, a virtually extinct group today, including Edward Brooke of Massachusetts, the Senate's only African-American; Mark Hatfield of Oregon; Jacob Javits of New York; and George Aiken of Vermont, a crusty old New Englander who thought our Vietnam policy was nuts and tersely suggested we should simply "declare victory and get out."

By far the most famous first-term senator was Robert Kennedy of New York, who joined his brother Ted in 1965, after defeating Senator Kenneth Keating for the seat Hillary now holds. Bobby Kennedy was fascinating.

He radiated raw energy. He's the only man I ever saw who could walk stoop-shouldered, with his head down, and still look like a coiled spring about to release into the air. He wasn't a great speaker by conventional standards, but he spoke with such intensity and passion it could be mesmerizing. And if he didn't get everyone's attention with his name, countenance, and speech, he had Brumus, a large, shaggy Newfoundland, the biggest dog I ever saw. Brumus often came to work with Senator Kennedy. When Bobby walked from his office in the New Senate Building to the Capitol to vote, Brumus would walk by his side, bounding up the Capitol steps to the revolving door on the rotunda level, then sitting patiently outside until his master returned for the walk back. Anyone who could command the respect of that dog had mine too.

John McClellan, Arkansas' senior senator, was not merely an ardent conservative. He was also tough as nails, vindictive when crossed, a prodigious worker, and adept at obtaining power and using it, whether to bring federal money home to Arkansas or to pursue people he saw as evildoers. McClellan led a life of ambition and anguish, the difficulties of which bred in him an iron will and deep resentments. The son of a lawyer and farmer, at age seventeen he became the youngest person ever to practice law in Arkansas, when he passed an oral examination with honors after reading law books he had checked out of the traveling library of the Cumberland Law School. After he served in World War I, he returned home to find that his wife had become involved with another man and he divorced her, a rare occurrence in Arkansas that long ago. His second wife died of spinal meningitis in 1935, when he was in the House of Representatives. Two years later, he married his third wife, Norma, who was with him for forty years until he died. But his sorrows were far from over. Between 1943 and 1958 he lost all three of his sons: the first to spinal meningitis, the next in a car accident, the last in a small-plane crash.

McClellan lived an eventful but difficult life, the sorrows of which he drowned in enough whiskey to float the Capitol down the Potomac River. After a few years, he decided drunkenness was inconsistent with both his values and his self-image and he gave up liquor completely, sealing the only crack in his armor with his iron will.

By the time I got to Washington, he was chairman of the powerful Appropriations Committee, a position he used to get our state a great deal of money for things like the Arkansas River Navigation System. He served another twelve years, a total of six terms, dying in 1977 after announcing he would not seek a seventh. When I worked on the Hill, McClellan seemed a remote, almost forbidding figure, which is how he wanted to be perceived by most people. After I became attorney general in 1977, I spent quite a bit of time with him. I was touched by his kindness and his interest in my career, and wished he had been able to show the side of him I saw to more people and to reflect it more in his public work.

Fulbright was as different from McClellan as daylight from dark. His childhood had been more carefree and secure, his education more extensive, his mind less dogmatic. He was born in 1905 in Fayetteville, a beautiful Ozark Mountain town in north Arkansas where the University of Arkansas is located. His mother, Roberta, was the outspoken progressive editor of the local paper, the **Northwest Arkansas Times.** Fulbright went to the hometown university, where he was a star student and quarterback of the Arkansas Razorbacks. When he was twenty, he went to Oxford on a Rhodes scholarship. When he returned two years later, he was a committed internationalist. After law school and a brief stint in Washington as a government lawyer, he came home to teach at the university with his wife, Betty, a delightful, elegant woman who turned out to be a better retail politician than he was and who kept his morose side in check through more than fifty years of marriage, until she died in 1985. I'll never forget one night in 1967 or '68. I was walking alone in Georgetown when I saw Senator and Mrs. Fulbright leaving one of the fashionable homes after a dinner party. When they reached the street, apparently with no one around to see, he took her in his arms and danced a few steps. Standing in the shadows, I saw what a light she was in his life. At thirty-four, Fulbright was named president of the University of Arkansas, the youngest president of a major university in America. He and Betty seemed headed for a long and happy life in the idyllic Ozarks. But after a couple of years, his apparently effortless rise to prominence was abruptly interrupted when the new governor, Homer Adkins, fired him because of his mother's sharply critical editorials.

In 1942, with nothing better to do, Fulbright filed for the open congressional seat in northwest Arkansas. He won, and in his only term in the House of Representatives, he sponsored the Fulbright Resolution, which presaged the United Nations in its call for American participation in an international organization to preserve peace after the end of World War II. In 1944, Fulbright ran for the U.S. Senate and for a chance to get even. His main opponent was his nemesis, Governor Adkins. Adkins had a flair for making enemies, a hazardous trait in politics. Besides getting Fulbright fired, he had made the mistake of opposing John McClellan just two years earlier, going so far as to have the tax returns of McClellan's major supporters audited. As I said, McClellan never forgot or forgave a slight. He worked hard to help Fulbright defeat Adkins, and Fulbright did it. They both got even.

Despite the thirty years they served together in the Senate, Fulbright and McClellan were never particularly close. Neither was prone to personal relationships with other politicians. They did work together to advance Arkansas' economic interests, and voted with the southern bloc against civil rights; beyond that, they didn't have much in common.

McClellan was a pro-military, anti-Communist conservative who wanted to spend tax dollars only on defense, public works, and law enforcement. He was bright but not subtle. He saw things as black or white. He spoke in blunt terms, and if he ever had any doubts about anything, he never revealed them for fear of looking weak. He thought politics was about money and power.

Fulbright was more liberal than McClellan. He was a good Democrat who liked and supported President Johnson until they fell out over the Dominican Republic and Vietnam. He favored progressive taxation, social programs to reduce poverty and inequality, federal aid to education, and more generous American contributions to international institutions charged with alleviating poverty in poor countries. In 1946, he sponsored legislation creating the Fulbright program for international education exchange, which has funded the education of hundreds of thousands of Fulbright scholars from the United States and sixty other countries. He thought politics was about the power of ideas.

On civil rights, Fulbright never spent much time defending his voting record on the merits. He simply said he had to vote with the majority of his constituents on issues like civil rights, areas about which they knew as much as he did, which is just a euphemistic way of saying he didn't want to get beat. He signed the Southern Manifesto after he watered it down a little, and didn't vote for a civil rights bill until 1970, during the Nixon administration, when he also took a leading role in defeating President Nixon's anti–civil rights nominee to the Supreme Court, G. Harrold Carswell.

Despite his civil rights stance, Fulbright was far from gutless. He hated sanctimonious demagogues parading as patriots. When Senator Joe McCarthy of Wisconsin was terrorizing innocent people with his blanket accusations of Communist ties, he intimidated most politicians into silence, even those who loathed him. Fulbright cast the only vote in the Senate against giving McCarthy's special investigative subcommittee more money. He also co-sponsored the resolution censuring McCarthy, which the Senate finally passed after Joseph Welch exposed him to the whole country for the fraud he was. McCarthy came along too soon—he would have been right at home in the crowd that took over the Congress in 1995. But back in the early fifties, a period so vulnerable to anti-Communist hysteria, McCarthy was the nine hundred–pound gorilla. Fulbright took him on before his other colleagues would.

Fulbright didn't shy away from controversy in foreign affairs, either, an area in which, unlike civil rights, he knew more than his constituents did or could know. He decided just to do what he thought was right and hope he could sell it to the voters. He favored multilateral cooperation over unilateral action; dialogue with, not isolation from, the Soviet Union and Warsaw Pact nations; more generous foreign assistance and fewer military interventions; and the winning of converts to American values and interests by the force of our example and ideas, not the force of arms.

Another reason I liked Fulbright was that he was interested in things besides politics. He thought the purpose of politics was to enable people to develop all their faculties and enjoy their fleeting lives. The idea that power was an end in itself, rather than a means to provide the security and opportunity necessary for the pursuit of happiness, seemed to him stupid and self-defeating. Fulbright liked to spend time with his family and friends, took a couple of vacations a year to rest and recharge his batteries, and read widely. He liked to go duck hunting, and he loved golf, shooting his age when he was seventy-eight. He was an engaging conversationalist with an unusual, elegant accent. When he was relaxed, he was eloquent and persuasive. When he got impatient or angry, he exaggerated his speech patterns in a tone of voice that made him seem arrogant and dismissive.

Fulbright had supported the Tonkin Gulf resolution in August 1964, giving President Johnson the authority to respond to apparent attacks on American vessels there, but by the summer of 1966, he had decided our policy in Vietnam was misguided, doomed to fail, and part of a larger pattern of errors that, if not changed, would bring disastrous consequences for America and the world. In 1966, he published his views on Vietnam and his general critique of American foreign policy in his most famous book, **The Arrogance of Power.** A few months after I joined the committee staff, he autographed a copy for me.

Fulbright's essential argument was that great nations

get into trouble and can go into long-term decline when they are "arrogant" in the use of their power, trying to do things they shouldn't do in places they shouldn't be. He was suspicious of any foreign policy rooted in missionary zeal, which he felt would cause us to drift into commitments "which though generous and benevolent in content, are so far reaching as to exceed even America's great capacities." He also thought that when we brought our power to bear in the service of an abstract concept, like anti-communism, without understanding local history, culture, and politics, we could do more harm than good. That's what happened with our unilateral intervention in the Dominican Republic's civil war in 1965, where, out of fear that leftist President Juan Bosch would install a Cuban-style Communist government, the United States supported those who had been allied with General Rafael Trujillo's repressive, reactionary, often murderous thirty-year military dictatorship, which ended with Trujillo's assassination in 1961.

Fulbright thought we were making the same mistake in Vietnam, on a much larger scale. The Johnson administration and its allies saw the Vietcong as instruments of Chinese expansionism in Southeast Asia, which had to be stopped before all the Asian "dominoes" fell to communism. That led the United States to support the anti-Communist, but hardly democratic, South Vietnamese government. As South Vietnam proved unable to defeat the Vietcong alone, our support was expanded to include military advisors, and finally to a massive military presence to defend what Fulbright saw as "a weak, dictatorial government which does not command the loyalty of the South Vietnamese people." Fulbright thought Ho Chi Minh, who had been an admirer of Franklin Roosevelt for his opposition to colonialism, was primarily interested in making Vietnam independent of all foreign powers. He believed that Ho, far from being a Chinese puppet, shared the historic Vietnamese antipathy for, and suspicion of, its larger neighbor to the north. Therefore, he did not believe we had a national interest sufficient to justify the giving and taking of so many lives. Still, he did not favor unilateral withdrawal. Instead, he supported an attempt to "neutralize" Southeast Asia, with American withdrawal conditioned on agreement by all parties to self-determination for South Vietnam and a referendum on reunification with North Vietnam. Unfortunately, by 1968, when peace talks opened in Paris, such a rational resolution was no longer possible.

As nearly as I could tell, everyone who worked on the committee staff felt the way Fulbright did about Vietnam. They also felt, increasingly, that the political and military leaders of the Johnson administration consistently overstated the progress of our military efforts. And they set out systematically to make the case for a change in policy to the administration, the Congress, and the country. As I write this, it seems reasonable and straightforward. But Fulbright, his committee colleagues, and the staff were in fact walking a high political tightrope across dangerous rocks. War hawks in both parties accused the committee, and Fulbright in particular, of giving "aid and comfort" to our enemies, dividing our country, and weakening our will to fight on to victory. Still, Fulbright persevered. Though he endured harsh criticism, the hearings helped to galvanize anti-war sentiment, especially among young people, more and more of whom were participating in anti-war rallies and "teach-ins."

In the time I was there, the committee held hearings on

such subjects as attitudes of Americans toward foreign policy, China-U.S. relations, possible conflicts between U.S. domestic goals and foreign policy, the impact of the dispute between China and the Soviet Union on the Vietnam conflict, and the psychological aspects of international relations. Distinguished critics of our policy appeared, people like Harrison Salisbury of the **New York Times**; George Kennan, former ambassador to the USSR and author of the idea of "containment" of the Soviet Union; Edwin Reischauer, former ambassador to Japan; distinguished historian Henry Steele Commager; retired General James Gavin; and professor Crane Brinton, an expert on revolutionary movements. Of course, the administration sent up its witnesses, too. One of the most effective was Undersecretary of State Nick Katzenbach, who had a leg up with me at least, because of his civil rights work in President Kennedy's Justice Department. Fulbright also met privately with Secretary of State Dean Rusk, usually for early-morning coffee in Fulbright's office.

I found the dynamics between Rusk and Fulbright fascinating. Fulbright himself had been on Kennedy's short list for secretary of state. Most people thought he was eliminated because of his anti–civil rights record, especially his signing of the Southern Manifesto. Rusk was also a southerner, from Georgia, but he was sympathetic to civil rights and had not faced the political pressure Fulbright had, since he was not in Congress but a member of the foreign policy establishment. Rusk saw the Vietnam conflict in simple, stark terms: It was the battleground of freedom and communism in Asia. If we lost Vietnam, communism would sweep through Southeast Asia with devastating consequences.

I always thought the dramatically different ways Fulbright and Rusk viewed Vietnam were due in part to the very different times when they were young Rhodes scholars in England. When Fulbright went to Oxford in 1925, the Treaty of Versailles ending World War I was being implemented. It imposed harsh financial and political burdens on Germany, and redrew the map of Europe and the Middle East after the collapse of the Austro-Hungarian and Ottoman empires. The humiliation of Germany by the victorious European powers, and the postwar isolationism and protectionism of the United States, reflected in the Senate's rejection of the League of Nations and the passage of the Smoot-Hawley Tariff Act, led to an ultra-nationalist backlash in Germany, the rise of Hitler, and then World War II. Fulbright was loath to make that mistake again. He rarely saw conflicts in black and white, tried to avoid demonizing adversaries, and always looked for negotiated solutions first, preferably in a multilateral context.

By contrast, Rusk was at Oxford in the early thirties, when the Nazis came to power. Later, he followed the hopeless attempts of Prime Minister Neville Chamberlain of Great Britain to negotiate with Hitler, an approach given one of history's most stinging rebukes: appeasement. Rusk equated Communist totalitarianism with Nazi totalitarianism, and despised it as much. The movement of the Soviet Union to control and communize Central and Eastern Europe after World War II convinced him communism was a disease that infected nations with a hostility to personal freedom and an unquenchable aggressiveness. And he was determined not to be an appeaser. Thus, he and Fulbright came to Vietnam from different sides of an unbridgeable intellectual and emotional divide, formed decades before Vietnam appeared on America's radar screen.

The psychological divide was reinforced on the pro-war side by the natural tendency in wartime to demonize one's adversary and by the determination Johnson, Rusk, and others had not to "lose" Vietnam, thus doing lasting damage to America's prestige, and to their own. I saw the same compulsion at work in peacetime when I was President, in my ideological battles with the Republican Congress and their allies. When there is no understanding, respect, or trust, any compromise, much less an admission of error, is seen as weakness and disloyalty, a sure recipe for defeat.

To the Vietnam hawks of the late sixties, Fulbright was the poster boy of gullible naïveté. Naïveté is a problem all well-meaning people have to guard against. But hardheadedness has its own perils. In politics, when you find yourself in a hole, the first rule is to quit digging; if you're blind to the possibility of error or determined not to admit it, you just look for a bigger shovel. The more difficulties we had in Vietnam, the more protests mounted at home, the more troops we sent in. We topped out at more than 540,000 in 1969, before reality finally forced us to change course.

I watched all this unfold with amazement and fascination. I read everything I could, including the material stamped "confidential" and "secret" that I had to deliver from time to time, which showed clearly that our country was being misled about our progress, or lack of it, in the war. And I saw the body count mount, one at a time. Every day Fulbright got a list of the boys from Arkansas who had been killed in Vietnam. I got in the habit of dropping by his office to check the list, and one day I saw the name of my friend and classmate Tommy Young. Just a few days before he was to return home, his jeep ran over a mine. I was so sad. Tommy Young was a big, smart, ungainly, sensitive guy who I thought would grow up to have a good life. Seeing his name on the list, along with others I was sure had more to give and get in life, triggered the first pangs of guilt I felt about being a student and only touching the deaths in Vietnam from a distance. I briefly flirted with the idea of dropping out of school and enlisting in the military—after all, I was a democrat in philosophy as well as party; I didn't feel entitled to escape even a war I had come to oppose. I talked to Lee Williams about it. He said that I'd be crazy to quit school, that I should keep doing my part to end the war, that I wouldn't prove anything by being one more soldier, perhaps one more casualty. Rationally, I could understand that and I went on about my business, but I never felt quite right about it. After all, I was the child of a World War II veteran. I respected the military, even if I thought many of those in charge were clueless, with more guts than brains. So began my personal bout with guilt, one that was fought by many thousands of us who loved our country but hated the war.

Those long-distant days are not easy to re-create for those who didn't live through them. For those who did, little needs to be said. The war took its toll at home, too, even on its most self-confident opponents. Fulbright liked and admired President Johnson. He enjoyed being part of a team he thought was moving America forward, even on civil rights, where he couldn't help. He always wore his game face to work, but he hated being a reviled, isolated outsider. Once, coming to work early in the morning, I saw him walking alone down the corridor toward his office, lost in sadness and frustration, actually bumping into the wall a time or two as he trudged to his damnable duty.

Although the Foreign Relations Committee had to concern itself with other things, Vietnam overshadowed everything else for the committee members and for me. In my first two years at Georgetown, I saved virtually all my class notes, papers, and exams. From my third year, about all I have are two not at all impressive Money and Banking papers. In the second semester I even withdrew from the only course I ever dropped at Georgetown, Theory and Practice of Communism. I had a good reason, though it had nothing to do with Vietnam.

In the spring of 1967, Daddy's cancer had returned, and he went to the Duke Medical Center in Durham, North Carolina, for several weeks of treatment. Every weekend I would drive the 266 miles from Georgetown to see him, leaving Friday afternoon, returning late Sunday night. I couldn't do it and make the communism course, so I bagged it. It was one of the most exhausting but important times of my young life. I would get into Durham late Friday night, then go get Daddy and spend Saturday with him. We'd spend Sunday morning and early afternoon together, then I'd head back to school and work.

On Easter Sunday, March 26, 1967, we went to church in the Duke Chapel, a grand Gothic church. Daddy had never been much of a churchgoer, but he really seemed to enjoy this service. Maybe he found some peace in the message that Jesus had died for his sins, too. Maybe he finally believed it when we sang the words to that wonderful old hymn "Sing with All the Sons of Glory": "Sing with all the sons of glory, sing the resurrection song! Death and sorrow, Earth's dark story, to the former days belong. All around the clouds are breaking, soon the storms of time shall cease; In God's likeness man, awaking, knows the everlasting peace." After church, we drove over to Chapel Hill, home of the University of North Carolina. The place was in full bloom, awash in the dogwoods and redbuds. Most southern springtimes are beautiful; this one was spectacular and remains my most vivid Easter memory.

On those weekends, Daddy talked to me in a way he never had before. Mostly it was small talk, about my life and his, Mother and Roger, family and friends. Some of it was deeper, as he reflected on the life he knew he would be leaving soon enough. But even with the small stuff, he spoke with an openness, a depth, a lack of defensiveness I'd never heard before. On those long, languid weekends, we came to terms with each other, and he accepted the fact that I loved and forgave him. If he could only have faced life with the same courage and sense of honor with which he faced death, he would have been quite a guy.

TWELVE

A long toward the end of my junior year, it was election time again. I had decided a year or so earlier that I would run for president of the student council. Though I had been away from campus a lot, I'd kept up with my friends and activities, and given my earlier successes, I thought I could win. But I was more out of touch than I knew. My opponent, Terry Modglin, was vice president of our class. He had been preparing for the race all year, lining up support and devising a strategy. I presented a specific but conventional platform. Modglin tapped into the growing sense of discontent on college campuses across America, and the specific opposition many students were expressing to the rigidity of Georgetown's academic requirements and campus rules. He called his campaign the "Modg Rebellion," a takeoff on "The Dodge Rebellion," the slogan of the automobile company. He and his supporters portrayed themselves in white hats fighting against the Jesuit administration and me. Because of my good relations with the school administrators, my job and car, my orthodox campaign, and my glad-handing manner, I became the establishment candidate. I worked hard, and so did my friends, but I could tell we were in trouble from the intensity of Modglin and his workers. For example, our signs were disappearing at an alarming rate. In retaliation, one night close to the election, some of my guys tore down Modglin's signs, put them in the back of a car, then drove off and dumped them. They would be caught and reprimanded.

That sealed it. Modglin beat the hell out of me, 717–570. He deserved to win. He had outthought, outorganized, and outworked me. He also wanted it more. Looking back, I see I probably shouldn't have run in the first place. I disagreed with the majority of my classmates about the need for relaxing the required curriculum; I liked it the way it was. I had lost the singular focus on campus life that had provided the energy for my victories in the earlier races for class president. And my daily absence from campus made it easier to portray me as an establishment backslapper gliding his way through the turmoil of the time. I got over the loss soon enough and by the end of the year was looking forward to staying in Washington for the summer, working for the committee and taking some courses. I couldn't know that the summer of '67 was the calm before the storm, for me and for America.

Things slow down in the summer in Washington, and the Congress is usually in recess all of August. It's a good time to be there if you're young, interested in politics, and don't mind the heat. Kit Ashby and another of my classmates, Jim Moore, had rented an old house at 4513 Potomac Avenue, just off MacArthur Boulevard, a mile or so behind the Georgetown campus. They invited me to live with them and to stay on for senior year, when we would be joined by Tom Campbell and Tommy Caplan. The house overlooked the Potomac River. It had five bedrooms, a small living room, and a decent kitchen. It also had two decks off the second-floor bedrooms, where we could catch some sun in the daytime and, on occasion, sleep at night in the soft summer air. The house had belonged to a man who wrote the national plumbing code back in the early 1950s. There was still a set of those fascinating volumes on the living-room bookshelves, incongruously kept upright by a bookend of Beethoven at his piano. It was the only interesting artifact in the whole house. My roommates bequeathed it to me, and I still have it.

Kit Ashby was a doctor's son from Dallas. When I worked for Senator Fulbright, he worked for Senator Henry "Scoop" Jackson of Washington State, who, like LBJ, was a domestic liberal and a Vietnam hawk. Kit shared his views and we had a lot of good arguments. Jim Moore was an army brat who had grown up all over. He was a serious historian and genuine intellectual whose views on Vietnam fell somewhere between Kit's and mine. In that summer and the senior year that followed, I formed a lasting friendship with both of them. After Georgetown, Kit went into the Marine Corps, then became an international banker. When I was President, I appointed him ambassador to Uruguay. Jim Moore followed his father into the army, then had a very successful career managing state pension investments. When a lot of states got in trouble with them in the 1980s, I got some good free advice from him on what we should do in Arkansas.

We all had a great time that summer. On June 24, I went to Constitution Hall to hear Ray Charles sing. My date was Carlene Jann, a striking girl I had met at one of the numerous mixers the area girls' schools held for Georgetown boys. She was nearly as tall as I was and had long blond hair. We sat near the back of the balcony and were among the tiny minority of white people there. I had loved Ray Charles since I heard his great line from

"What'd I Say": "Tell your mama, tell your pa, I'm gonna send you back to Arkansas." By the end of the concert Ray had the audience dancing in the aisles. When I got back to Potomac Avenue that night, I was so excited I couldn't sleep. At 5 a.m., I gave up and went for a three-mile run. I carried the ticket stub from that concert in my wallet for a decade.

Constitution Hall had come a long way since the 1930s, when the Daughters of the American Revolution had denied the great Marian Anderson permission to sing there because she was black. But a lot of younger blacks had moved way beyond wanting access to concert halls. Rising discontent over poverty, continuing discrimination, violence against civil rights activists, and the disproportionate number of blacks fighting and dying in Vietnam had sparked a new militancy, especially in America's cities, where Martin Luther King Jr. was competing for the hearts and minds of black America against the much more militant idea of "Black Power."

In the mid-sixties, race riots of varying size and intensity swept through non-southern ghettos. Before 1964, Malcolm X, the Black Muslim leader, had rejected integration in favor of black-only efforts to fight poverty and other urban problems, and predicted "more racial violence than white Americans have ever experienced."

In the summer of 1967, while I was enjoying Washington, there were serious riots in Newark and Detroit. By the end of the summer there had been more than 160 riots in American cities. President Johnson appointed a National Advisory Commission on Civil Disorders, chaired by Otto Kerner, the governor of Illinois, which found that the riots were the result of police racism and brutality, and the absence of economic and educational opportunities for blacks. Its ominous conclusion was summed up in a sentence that became famous: "Our nation is moving toward two societies, one black, one white—separate and unequal."

Washington was still fairly quiet in that troubled summer, but we got a small taste of the Black Power movement when, every night for several weeks, black activists took over Dupont Circle, not far from the White House, at the intersection of Connecticut and Massachusetts avenues. A friend of mine got to know a few of them and took me down one night to hear what they had to say. They were cocky, angry, and sometimes incoherent, but they weren't stupid, and though I disagreed with their solutions, the problems at the root of their grievances were real.

Increasingly, the lines between the militancy of the civil rights movement and that of the anti-war movement were beginning to blur. Though the anti-war movement began as a protest of middle-class and affluent white college students and their older supporters among intellectuals, artists, and religious leaders, many of its early leaders also had been involved in the civil rights movement. By the spring of 1966, the anti-war movement had outgrown its organizers, with large demonstrations and rallies all across America, fueled in part by popular reaction to the Fulbright hearings. In the spring of 1967, 300,000 people demonstrated against the war in New York City's Central Park.

My first exposure to serious anti-war activists came that summer when the liberal National Student Association (NSA) held its convention at the University of Maryland campus, where I had attended Boys Nation just four years earlier. The NSA was less radical than the Students for a Democratic Society (SDS) but firmly anti-war. Its credibility had been damaged the previous spring when it was revealed that for years the organization had been taking money from the CIA to finance its international operations. Despite this, it still commanded the support of a lot of students all over America.

One night I went out to College Park to the convention to see what was going on. I ran into Bruce Lindsey, from Little Rock, whom I had met in the 1966 governor's campaign when he was working for Brooks Hays. He had come to the meeting with Southwestern's NSA delegate, Debbie Sale, also an Arkansan. Bruce became my close friend, advisor, and confidant as governor and President— the kind of friend every person needs and no President can do without. Later, Debbie helped me get a foothold in New York. But at the NSA convention in 1967, we were just three conventional-looking and conventional-acting young Arkansans who were against the war and looking for company.

The NSA was full of people like me, who were uncomfortable with the more militant SDS but still wanted to be counted in the ranks of those working to end the war. The most notable speech of the convention was given by Allard Lowenstein, who urged the students to form a national organization to defeat President Johnson in 1968. Most people at the time thought it was a fool's errand, but things were changing quickly enough to make Al Lowenstein a prophet. Within three months, the antiwar movement would produce 100,000 protesters at the Lincoln Memorial. Three hundred of them turned in their draft cards, which were presented to the Justice Department by two older anti-warriors, William Sloane Coffin, the chaplain of Yale University, and Dr. Benjamin Spock, the famous baby doctor.

Interestingly, the NSA also had a history of opposing strict totalitarianism, so there were representatives of the Baltic "captive nations" there, too. I had a conversation with the woman representing Latvia. She was a few years older than I, and I had the feeling that going to these kinds of meetings was her career. She spoke with conviction about her belief that one day Soviet Communism would fail and Latvia would again be free. At the time I thought she was three bricks shy of a full load. Instead, she turned out to be as prophetic as Al Lowenstein.

Besides my work for the committee and my occasional excursions, I took three courses in summer school—in philosophy, ethics, and U.S. Diplomacy in the Far East. For the first time I read Kant and Kierkegaard, Hegel and Nietzsche. In the ethics class I took good notes, and one day in August another student, who was smart as a whip but seldom attended class, asked me if I'd take a few hours and go over my notes with him before the final exam. On August 19, my twenty-first birthday, I spent about four hours doing that, and the guy got a B on the test. Twenty-five years later, when I became President, my old study partner Turki al-Faisal, son of the late Saudi king, was head of Saudi Arabia's intelligence service, a position he held for twenty-four years. I doubt his philosophy grade had much to do with his success in life, but we enjoyed joking about it.

The professor for U.S. Diplomacy, Jules Davids, was a distinguished academic who later helped Averell Harriman write his memoirs. My paper was on Congress and the Southeast Asia resolution. The resolution, more commonly known as the Tonkin Gulf resolution, was passed on August 7, 1964, at the request of President Johnson, after two U.S. destroyers, the USS **Maddox** and the USS **C. Turner Joy,** allegedly were attacked by North Vietnamese vessels on August 2 and 4, 1964, and the United States retaliated with attacks on North Vietnamese naval bases and an oil storage depot. It authorized the President to "take all necessary measures to repel any armed attack against the forces of the United States and to prevent further aggression," and "to take all necessary steps, including the use of armed force," to assist any nation covered by the SEATO Treaty "in defense of its freedom."

The main point of my paper was that, except for Senator Wayne Morse, no one had seriously examined or even questioned the constitutionality, or even the wisdom, of the resolution. The country and the Congress were hopping mad and wanted to show we wouldn't be pushed around or run out of Southeast Asia. Dr. Davids liked my paper and said it was worthy of publication. I wasn't so sure; there were too many unanswered questions. Beyond the constitutional ones, some distinguished journalists had questioned whether the attacks had even occurred, and at the time I finished the paper, Fulbright was asking the Pentagon for more information on the incidents. The committee's review of Tonkin Gulf ran into 1968, and the investigations seemed to confirm that at least on the second date, August 4, the U.S. destroyers were not fired upon. Seldom in history has a non-event led to such huge consequences.

Within a few months, those consequences would come crashing down on Lyndon Johnson. The swift and nearly unanimous passage of the Tonkin Gulf resolution became a painful example of the old proverb that life's greatest curse is the answered prayer.

THIRTEEN

M y senior year was a strange combination of interesting college life and cataclysmic personal and political events. As I look back on it, it seems weird that anyone could be absorbed in so many big and little things at the same time, but people inevitably search for the pleasures and deal with the pain of normal life under difficult, even bizarre circumstances.

I took two particularly interesting courses, an international law seminar and a European history colloquium. Dr. William O'Brien taught the international law course, and he permitted me to do a paper on the subject of selective conscientious objection to the draft, examining other nations' conscription systems as well as America's, and exploring the legal and philosophical roots of the conscientious-objection allowances. I argued that conscientious objection should not be confined to those with a religious opposition to all wars, because the exception was grounded not in theological doctrine but in personal moral opposition to military service. Therefore, though judging individual cases would be difficult, the government should allow selective conscientious objection if its assertion was determined to be genuine. The end of the draft in the 1970s made the point moot.

The European history colloquium was essentially a survey of European intellectual history. The professor was Hisham Sharabi, a brilliant, erudite Lebanese who was passionately committed to the Palestinian cause. There were, as I recall, fourteen students in a course that ran fourteen weeks each semester and met for two hours once a week. We read all the books, but each week a student would lead off the discussion with a ten-minute presentation about the book of the week. You could do what you wanted with the ten minutes—summarize the book, talk about its central idea, or discuss an aspect of particular interest—but you had to do it in these ten minutes. Sharabi believed that if you couldn't, you didn't understand the book, and he strictly enforced the limit. He did make one exception, for a philosophy major, the first person I ever heard use the word "ontological"—for all I knew, it was a medical specialty. He ran on well past the ten-minute limit, and when he finally ran out of gas, Sharabi stared at him with his big, expressive eyes and said, "If I had a gun, I would shoot you." Ouch. I made my presentation on Joseph Schumpeter's **Capitalism, Socialism, and Democracy.** I'm not sure how good it was, but I used simple words and, believe it or not, finished in just over nine minutes.

I spent much of the fall of 1967 preparing for November's Conference on the Atlantic Community (CONTAC). As chairman of CONTAC's nine seminars, my job was to place the delegates, assign paper topics, and recruit experts for a total of eighty-one sessions. Georgetown brought students from Europe, Canada, and the United States together in a series of seminars and lectures to examine issues facing the community. I had participated in the conference two years earlier, where the most impressive student I met was a West Point cadet from Arkansas who was first in his class and a Rhodes scholar, Wes Clark. Our relations with some European countries were strained by European opposition to the Vietnam War, but the importance of NATO to European security in the Cold War made a serious rupture out of the question. The conference was a great success, thanks largely to the quality of the students.

Later in the fall, Daddy had gotten sick again. The cancer had spread, and it was clear that further treatment wouldn't help. He was in the hospital for a while, but he wanted to come home to die. He told Mother he didn't want me to miss too much school, so they didn't call me right away. One day he said, "It's time." Mother sent for me and I flew home. I knew it was coming, and I just hoped he would still know me when I got there, so that I could tell him I loved him.

By the time I arrived, Daddy had gone to bed for good, getting up only to go to the bathroom, and then only with help. He had lost a lot of weight and was weak. Every time he tried to get up, his knees buckled repeatedly; he was like a puppet whose strings were being pulled by jerking hands. He seemed to like it when Roger and I helped him. I guess taking him back and forth to the toilet was the last thing I ever did for him. He took it all in good humor, laughing and saying, wasn't it a hell of a mess and wasn't it good that it would be over soon. When he became so weak and unstrung he couldn't walk even with help, he had to give up the bathroom and use a bedpan, which he hated doing in front of the nurses—friends of Mother's who had come to help.

Though he was fast losing control of his body, his mind and voice were clear for about three days after I got home, and we had some good talks. He said we would be all right when he was gone and he was sure I would win a Rhodes scholarship when the interviews came in about a month.

After a week, he was seldom more than half conscious, though he had surges of mental activity almost to the end. Twice he woke to tell Mother and me he was still there. Twice when he should have been too far gone or too drugged to think or speak (the cancer was way down in his chest cavity now, and there was no point in letting him suffer on aspirin, which is all he would take until then), he amazed us all by asking me if I was sure I could take all this time away from school, and if not, it wasn't really necessary for me to stay, since there wasn't much left to happen and we had had our last good talks. When he couldn't speak at all anymore, he would still wake and focus on someone and make sounds so that we could understand simple things like when he wanted to be turned over in the bed. I could only wonder at what else was passing through his mind.

After his final attempt to communicate, he lasted one and a half horrible days. It was awful, hearing the hard, sharp thrusts of his breathing and seeing his body bloat into disfigurement that did not look like anything I'd ever seen. Somewhere near the end, Mother came in and saw him, burst into tears, and told him she loved him. After all he had put her through, I hoped she meant it, more for her sake than for his.

Daddy's last days brought a classic country deathwatch into our house. Family and friends streamed in and out to offer their sympathy. Most of them brought food so we wouldn't have to cook, and so we could feed the other visitors. Since I hardly slept, and ate with everyone who came by, I gained ten pounds in the two weeks I was home. But it was comforting to have all that food and all those friends when there was nothing to do but wait for death to make its final claim.

It was raining on the day of the funeral. Often when I was a boy, Daddy would stare out the window into a storm and say, "Don't bury me in the rain." It was one of those old sayings without which you can't make conversation in the South, and I never paid all that much attention when he said it. Somehow, though, it registered with me that it was important to him, that he had some deep dread about being put to rest in the rain. Now that was going to happen, after all he had done through his long illness to deserve better.

We worried about the rain on the drive to the chapel and all through the funeral, as the preacher droned on, saying nice things about him that weren't true, that he would have scorned and laughed at had he heard them. Unlike me, Daddy never thought much of funerals in general and would not have liked his own very much, except for the hymns, which he had picked. When the funeral was over, we almost ran outside to see if it was still raining. It was, and on the slow drive to the cemetery we couldn't grieve for worrying about the weather.

Then, as we turned off the street into the narrow way of the cemetery, inching toward the freshly dug grave, Roger was the first to notice that the rain had stopped, and he almost shouted to us. We were unbelievably, irrationally overjoyed and relieved. But we kept the story to ourselves, allowing ourselves only small, knowing smiles, like the one we had seen so often on Daddy's face since he had come to terms with himself. On his last long journey to the end that awaits us all, he found a forgiving God. He was not buried in the rain.

A month after the funeral, I came home again for the Rhodes scholarship interview—I'd been interested since high school. Every year thirty-two American Rhodes scholars are chosen for two years of study at Oxford, paid for by the trust established in 1903 by Cecil Rhodes's will. Rhodes, who made a fortune in South Africa's diamond mines, provided for scholarships for young men from all the present and former British colonies who had demonstrated outstanding intellectual, athletic, and leadership qualities. He wanted to send people to Oxford who were interested and accomplished in more than academics, because he thought they would be more likely to "esteem the performance of public duties" over purely private pursuits. Over the years, selection committees had come to discount a lack of athletic prowess if a candidate had excelled in some other nonacademic field. In a few more years, the trust would be amended to allow women to compete. A student could apply in either the state where he lived or the one where he went to college. Every December, each state nominated two candidates, who then went to one of eight regional competitions in which scholars were chosen for the coming academic year. The selection process required the candidate to provide between five and eight letters of recommendation, write an essay on why he wanted to go to Oxford, and submit to interviews at the state and regional levels by panels composed of former Rhodes scholars, with a chairman who wasn't one. I asked Father Sebes, Dr. Giles, Dr. Davids, and my sophomore English professor, Mary Bond, to write letters, along with Dr. Bennett and Frank Holt from back home, and Seth Tillman, Senator Fulbright's speechwriter, who taught at the Johns Hopkins School of Advanced International Studies and had become a friend and mentor to me. At Lee Williams's suggestion, I also asked Senator Fulbright. I hadn't wanted to bother the senator because of his preoccupation with and deepening gloom over the war, but Lee said he wanted to do it, and he gave me a generous letter.

The Rhodes committee asked the recommenders to note my weaknesses along with my strengths. The Georgetown people said, charitably, that I wasn't much of an athlete. Seth said that, while I was highly qualified for the scholarship, "he is not particularly competent in the routine work which he does for the Committee; this work is below his intellectual capacity and he often seems to have other things on his mind." That was news to me; I thought I was doing a good job at the committee, but as he said, I had other things on my mind. Maybe that's why I had a hard time concentrating on my essay. Finally, I gave up trying to write it at home and checked in to a hotel on Capitol Hill about a block from the New Senate Office Building, to have complete quiet. It was harder than I thought it would be to explain my short life and why it made sense for them to send me to Oxford.

I began by saying that I had come to Washington "to prepare for the life of a practicing politician"; I asked the committee to send me to Oxford "to study in depth those subjects which I have only begun to investigate," in the hope that I could "mold an intellect that can stand the pressures of political life." I thought at the time that the essay was a pretty good effort. Now it seems a bit strained and overdone, as if I were trying to find the kind of voice in which a cultivated Rhodes scholar should speak. Maybe it was just the earnestness of youth and living in a time when so many things were overdone.

Applying in Arkansas was a big advantage. Because of the size of our state and its college population, there were fewer competitors; I probably wouldn't have made it to the regional level if I'd been from New York, California, or some other big state, competing against students from Ivy League schools that had well-honed systems to recruit and train their best students for the Rhodes competition. Of the thirty-two scholars elected in 1968, Yale and Harvard produced six each, Dartmouth three, Princeton and the Naval Academy two. The winners are more spread out today, as they should be in a country with hundreds of fine undergraduate schools, but the elite schools and the service academies still do very well.

The Arkansas committee was run by Bill Nash, a tall, spare man who was an active Mason and senior partner of the Rose Law Firm in Little Rock, the oldest west of the Mississippi, with its roots dating back to 1820. Mr. Nash was an old-fashioned, high-minded man who walked several miles to work every day, rain or shine. The committee included another Rose Law Firm partner, Gaston Williamson, who also served as the Arkansas member of the regional committee. Gaston was big, burly, and brilliant, with a deep, strong voice and a commanding manner. He had opposed what Faubus did at Central High and had done what he could to beat back the forces of reaction. He was extremely helpful to and supportive of me during the whole selection process and a source of wise advice later, when I became attorney general and governor. After Hillary went to work at Rose in 1977, he befriended and counseled her too. Gaston adored Hillary. He supported me politically and liked me well enough, but I think he always thought I wasn't quite good enough for her.

I got through the Arkansas interviews and was off to New Orleans for the finals. We stayed in the French Quarter at the Royal Orleans Hotel, where the interviews were held for the finalists from Arkansas, Oklahoma, Texas, Louisiana, Mississippi, and Alabama. The only preparation I did the night before was to reread my essay, read **Time, Newsweek,** and **U.S. News & World Report** cover to cover, and get a good night's sleep. I knew there would be unexpected questions and I wanted to be sharp. And I didn't want my emotions to get the better of me. New Orleans brought memories of previous trips: when I was a little boy watching Mother kneel by the railroad tracks and cry as Mammaw and I pulled away in the train; when we visited New Orleans and the Mississippi Gulf Coast on the only out-of-state vacation our whole family took together. And I couldn't get Daddy and his confident deathbed prediction that I would win out of my mind. I wanted to do it for him, too.

The chairman of the committee was Dean McGee of Oklahoma, head of the Kerr-McGee Oil Company and a powerful figure in Oklahoma business and political life. The member who impressed me most was Barney Monaghan, the chairman of Vulcan, a steel company in Birmingham, Alabama. He looked more like a college professor than a southern businessman, impeccably dressed in a three-piece suit.

The hardest question I got was about trade. I was asked whether I was for free trade, protectionism, or something in between. When I said I was pro–free trade, especially for advanced economies, my questioner shot back, "Then how do you justify Senator Fulbright's efforts to protect Arkansas chickens?" It was a good trick question, designed to make me feel I had to choose, on the spur of the moment, between being inconsistent on trade or disloyal to Fulbright. I confessed I didn't know anything about the chicken issue, but I didn't have to agree with the senator on everything to be proud to work for him. Gaston Williamson broke in and bailed me out, explaining that the issue wasn't as simple as the question implied; in fact, Fulbright had been trying to open foreign markets to our chickens. It had never occurred to me that I could blow the interview because I didn't know enough about chickens. It never happened again. When I was governor and President, people were amazed at how much I knew about how chickens are raised, processed, and marketed at home and abroad.

At the end of all twelve interviews, and a little time for deliberation, we were brought back into a reception room. The committee had selected one guy from New Orleans, two from Mississippi, and me. After we talked briefly to the press, I called Mother, who had been waiting anxiously by the phone, and asked her how she thought I'd look in English tweeds. Lord, I was happy—happy for Mother after all she'd lived through to get me to that day, happy that Daddy's last prediction came true, happy for the honor and the promise of the next two years. For a while the world just stopped. There was no Vietnam, no racial turmoil, no trouble at home, no anxieties about myself or my future. I had a few more hours in New Orleans, and I enjoyed the city they call "the Big Easy" like a native son.

When I got home, after a visit to Daddy's grave, we plunged into the holiday season. There was a nice write-up in the paper, even a laudatory editorial. I spoke to a local civic club, spent good time with my friends, and enjoyed a raft of congratulatory letters and phone calls. Christmas was nice but bittersweet; for the first time since my brother was born, there were only three of us.

After I returned to Georgetown there was one more piece of sad news. On January 17, my grandmother died.

A few years earlier, after she had had a second stroke, she asked to go home to Hope to live in the nursing home downtown in what was the old Julia Chester Hospital. She requested and got the same room Mother was in when I was born. Her death, like Daddy's, must have set loose contradictory feelings in Mother. Mammaw had been hard on her. Perhaps because she was jealous that Papaw loved his only child so much, too often she made her daughter the target of her outbursts of rage. Her tantrums lessened after Papaw died, when she was hired as a nurse to a nice lady who took her on trips to Wisconsin and Arizona and fed some of her hunger to go beyond the circumstances of her confined, predictable life. And she had been wonderful to me in my first four years, when she taught me to read and count, clean my plate, and wash my hands. After we moved to Hot Springs, whenever I made straight A's in school she sent me five dollars. When I turned twenty-one, she still wanted to know if "her baby had his handkerchief." I wish she could have understood herself better and cared for herself and her family more. But she did love me, and she did her best to get me off to a good start in life.

I thought I had made a pretty good start, but nothing could have prepared me for what was about to happen. Nineteen sixty-eight was one of the most tumultuous and heartbreaking years in American history. Lyndon Johnson started the year expecting to hold his course in Vietnam, continue his Great Society assault on unemployment, poverty, and hunger, and pursue reelection. But his country was moving away from him. Though I was sympathetic to the zeitgeist, I didn't embrace the lifestyle or the radical rhetoric. My hair was short, I didn't even drink, and some of the music was too loud and harsh for my taste. I didn't hate LBJ; I just wanted to end the war, and I was afraid the culture clashes would undermine, not advance, the cause. In reaction to the youth protests and "countercultural" lifestyles, Republicans and many working-class Democrats moved to the right, flocking to hear conservatives like the resurgent Richard Nixon and the new governor of California, Ronald Reagan, a former FDR Democrat.

The Democrats were moving away from Johnson, too. On the right, Governor George Wallace announced that he would run for President as an independent. On the left, young activists like Allard Lowenstein were urging anti-war Democrats to challenge President Johnson in the Democratic primaries. Their first choice was Senator Robert Kennedy, who had been pressing for a negotiated settlement in Vietnam. He declined, fearing that if he ran, given his well-known dislike of the President, he would appear to be pursuing a vendetta rather than a principled crusade. Senator George McGovern of South Dakota, who was up for reelection in his conservative state, also declined. Senator Gene McCarthy of Minnesota did not. As the party's heir apparent to Adlai Stevenson's legacy of intellectual liberalism, McCarthy could be maddening, even disingenuous, in his efforts to appear almost saintly in his lack of ambition. But he had the guts to take on Johnson, and as the year dawned, he was the only horse the anti-warriors had to ride. In January, he announced that he would run in the first primary contest in New Hampshire.

In February, two events in Vietnam further hardened opposition to the war. The first was the impromptu execution of a person suspected of being a Vietcong by the chief of the South Vietnamese National Police, General Loan.

Loan shot the man in the head in broad daylight on the street in Saigon. The killing was captured on film by the great photographer Eddie Adams, whose picture caused more Americans to question whether our allies were any better than our enemies, who were also undeniably ruthless.

The second, and far more significant, event was the Tet offensive, so named because it took place during the Vietnamese holiday of Tet, which marked their new year. North Vietnamese and Vietcong forces launched a series of coordinated attacks on American positions all over South Vietnam, including strongholds like Saigon, where even the American embassy was under fire. The attacks were rebuffed and the North Vietnamese and Vietcong sustained heavy casualties, leading President Johnson and our military leaders to claim victory, but in fact, Tet was a huge psychological and political defeat for America, because Americans saw with their own eyes, in our first "television war," that our forces were vulnerable even in places they controlled. More and more Americans began to question whether we could win a war the South Vietnamese couldn't win for themselves, and whether it was worth sending even more soldiers into Vietnam when the answer to the first question seemed to be no.

On the home front, the Senate majority leader, Mike Mansfield, called for a bombing halt. President Johnson's secretary of defense, Robert McNamara, and his close advisor Clark Clifford, along with former secretary of state Dean Acheson, told the President it was time to "review" his policy of continuing escalation to achieve a military victory. Dean Rusk continued to support the policy, and the military had asked for 200,000 more troops to pursue it. Racial incidents, some of them violent, continued across the country. Richard Nixon and George Wallace formally declared their candidacies for President. In New Hampshire, McCarthy's campaign was gathering steam, with hundreds of anti-war students pouring into the state to knock on doors for him. Those who didn't want to cut their hair and shave worked in the back room of his campaign headquarters stuffing envelopes. Meanwhile, Bobby Kennedy continued to fret about whether he should get in the race too.

On March 12, McCarthy got 42 percent of the vote in New Hampshire to 49 percent for LBJ. Though Johnson was a write-in candidate who never came to New Hampshire to campaign, it was a big psychological victory for McCarthy and the anti-war movement. Four days later, Kennedy entered the race, announcing in the same Senate caucus room where his brother John had begun his campaign in 1960. He sought to defuse charges that he was driven by ruthless personal ambition by saying that McCarthy's campaign had already exposed the deep divisions within the Democratic Party, and he wanted to give the country a new direction. Of course, now he had a new "ruthlessness" problem: he was raining on McCarthy's parade, after McCarthy had challenged the President when Kennedy wouldn't.

I saw all this unfold from a peculiar perspective. My housemate Tommy Caplan was working in Kennedy's office, so I knew what was going on there. And I had begun dating a classmate who was volunteering at McCarthy's national headquarters in Washington. Ann Markusen was a brilliant economics student, captain of the Georgetown women's sailing team, a passionate anti-war liberal, and a Minnesota native. She admired McCarthy and, like many young people who worked for him, hated Kennedy for trying to take the nomination away from him. We had some ferocious arguments, because I was glad Kennedy was in. I had watched him perform as attorney general and senator and thought he cared more about domestic issues than McCarthy, and I was convinced he would be a much more effective President. McCarthy was a fascinating man, tall, gray-haired, and handsome, an Irish Catholic intellectual with a fine mind and a biting wit. But I had watched him on the Foreign Relations Committee, and he was too detached for my taste. Until he entered the New Hampshire primary, he seemed curiously passive about what was going on, content to vote the right way and say the right things.

By contrast, just before Bobby Kennedy announced for President, he was working hard to pass a resolution sponsored by Fulbright to give the Senate a say before LBJ could put 200,000 more troops in Vietnam. He had also been to Appalachia to expose the depth of rural poverty in America, and had made an amazing trip to South Africa, where he challenged young people to fight apartheid. McCarthy, though I liked him, gave me the impression he'd rather be home reading St. Thomas Aquinas than going into a tar-paper shack to see how poor people lived or flying halfway around the world to speak against racism. Every time I tried to make these arguments to Ann, she gave me hell, saying if Bobby Kennedy had been more principled and less political he would have done what McCarthy did. The underlying message, of course, was that I also was too political. I was really crazy about her then and hated to be on her bad side, but I wanted to win and I wanted to elect a good man who would also be a good President.

My interest grew more personal on March 20, four days after Kennedy announced for President, when President

Johnson ended all draft deferments for graduate students, except for those in medical school, putting my future at Oxford in doubt. Johnson's decision triggered another shot of Vietnam guilt: like Johnson, I didn't believe graduate students should have draft deferments, but I didn't believe in our Vietnam policy either.

On Sunday night, March 31, President Johnson was scheduled to address the nation about Vietnam. There was speculation about whether he would escalate the war or cool it a little in the hope of starting negotiations, but nobody really saw what was coming. I was driving on Massachusetts Avenue, listening to the speech on my car radio. After speaking for some time, Johnson said he had decided to sharply restrict the bombing of North Vietnam, in the hope of finding a resolution to the conflict. Then, as I was passing by the Cosmos Club, just northwest of Dupont Circle, the President dropped his own bombshell: "With American sons in the fields far away, and our world's hopes for peace in the balance every day, I do not believe I should devote another hour or another day of my time to any personal partisan causes. . . . Accordingly, I shall not seek, and I will not accept, the nomination of my party for another term as your President." I pulled over to the curb in disbelief, feeling sad for Johnson, who had done so much for America at home, but happy for my country and for the prospect of a new beginning.

The feeling didn't last long. Four days later, on the night of April 4, Martin Luther King Jr. was killed on the balcony outside his room at the Lorraine Motel in Memphis, where he had gone to support striking sanitation workers. In the last couple of years of his life, he had broadened his civil rights agenda to include an assault on urban poverty and outspoken opposition to the war. It was politically necessary to fend off the challenge to his leadership from younger, more militant blacks, but it was clear to all of us who watched him that Dr. King meant it when he said he could not advance civil rights for blacks without also opposing poverty and the war in Vietnam.

The night before he was killed, Dr. King gave an eerily prophetic sermon to a packed house at Mason Temple Church. In an obvious reference to the many threats on his life, he said, "Like anybody I would like to live a long life. Longevity has its place. But I'm not concerned about that now. I just want to do God's will. And He's allowed me to go up to the mountain. And I've looked over, and I've seen the promised land. I may not get there with you, but I want you to know tonight that we as a people will get to the promised land. So I'm happy tonight. I'm not worried about anything. I'm not fearing any man. Mine eyes have seen the glory of the coming of the Lord!" The next evening, at 6 p.m., he was shot dead by James Earl Ray, a chronically disaffected, convicted armed robber who had escaped from prison about a year earlier.

Martin Luther King Jr.'s death shook the nation as no other event had since President Kennedy's assassination. Campaigning in Indiana that night, Robert Kennedy tried to calm the fears of America with perhaps the greatest speech of his life. He asked blacks not to be filled with hatred of whites and reminded them that his brother, too, had been killed by a white man. He quoted the great lines of Aeschylus about pain bringing wisdom, against our will, "through the awful grace of God." He told the crowd before him and the country listening to him that we would get through this time because the vast majority of blacks and whites "want to live together, want to improve the quality of our life, and want justice for all human beings who abide in our land." He ended with these words: "Let us dedicate ourselves to what the Greeks wrote so many years ago: to tame the savageness of man and make gentle the life of this world. Let us dedicate ourselves to that, and say a prayer for our country and for our people."

Dr. King's death provoked more than prayer; some feared, and others hoped, it marked the death of nonviolence, too. Stokely Carmichael said that white America had declared war on black America and there was "no alternative to retribution." Rioting broke out in New York, Boston, Chicago, Detroit, Memphis, and more than one hundred other cities and towns. More than forty people were killed and hundreds were injured. The violence was especially bad in Washington, predominantly directed against black businesses all along Fourteenth and H streets. President Johnson called out the National Guard to restore order, but the atmosphere remained tense.

Georgetown was at a safe distance from the violence, but we had a taste of it when a few hundred National Guardsmen camped out in McDonough Gym, where our basketball team played its games. Many black families were burned out of their homes and took refuge in local churches. I signed up with the Red Cross to help deliver food, blankets, and other supplies to them. My 1963 white Buick convertible, with Arkansas plates and the Red Cross logo plastered on the doors, cut a strange figure in the mostly empty streets, which were marked by still-smoking buildings and storefronts with broken glass from looting. I made the drive once at night, then again on Sunday morning, when I took Carolyn Yeldell, who had flown in for the weekend, with me. In the daylight it felt safe, so we got out and walked around a little, looking at the riot's wreckage. It was the only time I've ever felt insecure in a black neighborhood. And I thought, not for the first or last time, that it was sad and ironic that the primary victims of black rage were blacks themselves.

Dr. King's death left a void in a nation desperately in need of his allegiance to nonviolence and his belief in the promise of America, and now in danger of losing both. Congress responded by passing President Johnson's bill to ban racial discrimination in the sale or rental of housing. Robert Kennedy tried to fill the void, too. He won the Indiana primary on May 7, preaching racial reconciliation while appealing to more conservative voters by talking tough on crime and the need to move people from welfare to work. Some liberals attacked his "law and order" message, but it was politically necessary. And he believed in it, just as he believed in ending all draft deferments.

In Indiana, Bobby Kennedy became the first New Democrat, before Jimmy Carter, before the Democratic Leadership Council, which I helped to start in 1985, and before my campaign in 1992. He believed in civil rights for all and special privileges for none, in giving poor people a hand up rather than a handout: work was better than welfare. He understood in a visceral way that progressive politics requires the advocacy of both new policies and fundamental values, both far-reaching change and social stability. If he had become President, America's journey through the rest of the twentieth century would have been very different.

On May 10, peace talks between the United States and North Vietnam began in Paris, bringing hope to Americans who were eager for the war to end, and relief to Vice President Hubert Humphrey, who had entered the race in late April and who needed some change in our fortunes to have any chance to win the nomination or the election. Meanwhile, social turmoil continued unabated. Columbia University in New York was shut down by protesters for the rest of the academic year. Two Catholic priests, brothers Daniel and Philip Berrigan, were arrested for stealing and burning draft records. And in Washington, barely a month after the riots, civil rights activists went on with Martin Luther King Jr.'s plans for a Poor People's Campaign, setting up a tent encampment on the Mall, called Resurrection City, to highlight the problems of poverty. It rained like crazy, turning the Mall to mud and making living conditions miserable. One day in June, Ann Markusen and I went down to see it and show support. Boards had been laid down between the tents so that you could walk without sinking into the mud, but after a couple of hours of wandering around and talking to people, we were covered in it anyway. It was a good metaphor for the confusion of the time.

May ended with the race for the Democratic nomination in doubt. Humphrey began gaining delegates from party regulars in states without primary elections, and McCarthy defeated Kennedy in the Oregon primary. Kennedy's hopes for the nomination were riding on the California primary on June 4. My last week in college was spent in high anticipation of the outcome, four days before our graduation.

On Tuesday night, Robert Kennedy won California, thanks to a big showing among minority voters in Los Angeles County. Tommy Caplan and I were thrilled. We stayed up until Kennedy gave his victory speech, then went to bed; it was nearly three in the morning in Washington.

A few hours later I was awakened by Tommy, who was shaking me and shouting, "Bobby's been shot! Bobby's been shot!" A few minutes after we had turned off the television and gone to bed, Senator Kennedy was walking through the kitchen at the Ambassador Hotel when a young Arab, Sirhan Sirhan, who was angry at Kennedy because of his support for Israel, rained a hail of bullets down on him and those surrounding him. Five others were wounded; they all recovered. Bobby Kennedy was operated on for a severe wound to the head. He died a day later, only forty-two, on June 6, Mother's forty-fifth birthday, two months and two days after Martin Luther King Jr. was killed.

On June 8, Caplan went to New York for the funeral at St. Patrick's Cathedral. Senator Kennedy's admirers, both the famous and the anonymous, had streamed past his casket all day and all night before the service. President Johnson, Vice President Humphrey, and Senator McCarthy were there. So was Senator Fulbright. Ted Kennedy gave a magnificent eulogy for his brother, closing with words of power and grace I will never forget: "My brother need not be idealized, or enlarged in death beyond what he was in life. He should be remembered simply as a good and decent man, who saw wrong and tried to right it, saw suffering and tried to heal it, saw war and tried to stop it. Those of us who loved him, and who take him to his rest today, pray that what he was to us and what he wished for others will someday come to pass for all the world."

That is what I wanted, too, but it seemed further away than ever. We went through those last few college days in a numb fog. Tommy took the funeral train from New York to Washington, barely making it back for graduation. All the other graduation events had been canceled, but the commencement ceremony itself was set to go on as planned. Even that didn't work out, providing the first levity in days. Just as the commencement speaker, home-town mayor Walter Washington, got up to speak, a tremendous storm cloud came out. He spoke for about thirty seconds, congratulating us, wishing us well, and saying that if we didn't get inside right then, we'd all drown. Then the rain came and we hightailed it. Our class was ready to vote for Mayor Washington for President. That night, Tommy Caplan's parents took Tommy, Mother, Roger, me, and a few others out to dinner at an Italian restaurant. Tommy carried the conversation, at one point saying that understanding some subject or other required a "mature intellect." My eleven-year-old brother looked up and said, "Tom, am I a mature intellect?" It was good to end a roller-coaster day and a heartbreaking ten weeks with a laugh.

After a few days to pack up and say last good-byes, I drove back to Arkansas with my roommate Jim Moore to work on Senator Fulbright's reelection campaign. He seemed vulnerable on two counts: first, his outspoken opposition to the Vietnam War in a conservative, pro-military state already upset with all the upheaval in America; and sec-ond, his refusal to adapt to the demands of modern congressional politics, which required senators and con-gressmen to come home on most weekends to see their constituents. Fulbright had gone to Congress in the 1940s, when expectations were very different. Back then members of Congress were expected to come home dur-ing vacations and the long summer recess, to answer their mail and phone calls, and to see their constituents when they came to Washington. On the weekends when Congress was in session, they were free to stay in town, relax, and reflect, like most other working Americans. When they did go back home on long breaks, they were expected to keep office hours in the home office and to take a few trips out to the heartland to see the folks. Intensive interaction with voters was reserved for campaigns.

By the late sixties, the availability of easy air travel and extensive local news coverage were rapidly changing the rules for survival. More and more, senators and congressmen were coming home on most weekends, traveling to more places when they got there, and making pronouncements for the local media whenever they could.

Fulbright's campaign encountered no little resistance from people who disagreed with him on the war or thought he was out of touch, or both. He thought the idea of flying home every weekend was nuts and once said to me, in reference to his colleagues who did it, "When do they ever get time to read and think?" Sadly, the pressures on members of Congress to travel constantly have grown only more intense. The rising costs of television, radio, and other advertising and the insatiable appetite for news coverage put many senators and congressmen on a plane every weekend and often out many weeknights for fundraisers in the Washington area. When I was President, I often remarked to Hillary and my staff that I thought one reason congressional debate had grown so harshly negative was that too many members of Congress were in a constant state of exhaustion.

In the summer of '68, exhaustion wasn't Fulbright's problem, though he was weary from fighting over Vietnam. What he needed was not rest, but a way to reconnect with voters who felt alienated from him. Luckily, he was blessed with weak opponents. His main adversary in the primary was none other than Justice Jim Johnson, who was back to his old routine, traveling to county seats with a country band, bashing Fulbright as soft on communism. Johnson's wife, Virginia, was attempting to emulate George Wallace's wife, Lurleen, who had succeeded her husband as governor. The Republican Senate candidate was an unknown small-business man from east Arkansas, Charles Bernard, who said Fulbright was too liberal for our state.

Lee Williams had come down to run the campaign, with a lot of help from the young but seasoned politician who ran Senator Fulbright's Little Rock office, Jim McDougal (the Whitewater one), an old-fashioned populist who told great stories in colorful language and worked his heart out for Fulbright, whom he revered.

Jim and Lee decided to reintroduce the senator to Arkansas as "just plain Bill," a down-to-earth Arkansan in a red-checked sport shirt. All the campaign's printed materials and most of the TV ads showed him that way, though I don't think he liked it, and on most campaign days he still wore a suit. To hammer the down-home image into reality, the senator decided to make a grass-roots campaign trip to small towns around the state, accompanied only by a driver and a black notebook filled with the names of his past supporters that had been compiled by Parker Westbrook, a staffer who seemed to know everyone in Arkansas who had the slightest interest in politics. Since Senator Fulbright campaigned only every six years, we just hoped all the folks listed in Parker's black notebook were still alive and kicking.

Lee Williams gave me the chance to drive the senator for a few days on a trip to southwest Arkansas, and I jumped at it. I was fascinated by Fulbright, grateful for the letter he had written for me to the Rhodes Scholarship Committee, and eager to learn more about what small-town Arkansans were thinking. They were a long way from urban violence and anti-war demonstrations, but a lot of them had kids in Vietnam.

One day Fulbright was being followed by a national television crew as we pulled in to a small town, parked, and went into a feed store where farmers bought grain for their animals. With cameras rolling, Fulbright shook hands with an old character in overalls and asked him for his vote. The man said he couldn't give it because Fulbright wouldn't stand up to the "Commies" and he'd let them "take over our country." Fulbright sat down on a pile of feed bags stacked on the floor and struck up a conversation. He told the man he'd stand up to the Communists at home if he could find them. "Well, they're all over," the man replied. Then Fulbright commented, "Really? Have you seen any around here? I've been looking all over and I haven't seen the first one." It was funny to watch Fulbright do his thing. The guy thought they were having a serious conversation. I'm sure the TV audience got a kick out of it, but what I saw bothered me. The wall had gone up in that man's eyes. It didn't matter that he couldn't find a Commie to save his soul. He had turned Fulbright off, and no amount of talking could bring the wall in his mind down again. I just hoped there were enough other voters in that town and the hundreds like it who were still reachable.

Notwithstanding the feed-store incident, Fulbright was convinced that small-town voters were mostly wise, practical, and fair-minded. He thought they had more time to reflect on things and were not all that easy for his right-wing critics to stampede. After a couple of days of visiting places where all the white voters seemed to be for George Wallace, I wasn't so sure. Then we came to Center Point, and one of the more memorable encounters of my life in politics. Center Point was a little place of fewer than two hundred people. The black notebook said the man to see was Bo Reece, a longtime supporter who lived in the best house in town. In the days before television ads, there was a Bo Reece in most little Arkansas towns. A couple of weeks before the election, people would ask, "Who's Bo for?" His choice would be made known and would get about two-thirds of the vote, sometimes more.

When we pulled up in front of the house, Bo was sitting on his porch. He shook hands with Fulbright and me, said he'd been expecting him, and invited us in for a visit. It was an old-fashioned house with a fireplace and comfortable chairs. As soon as we were settled, Reece said, "Senator, this country's got lots of troubles. A lot of things aren't right." Fulbright agreed, but he didn't know where Bo Reece was going, and neither did I—maybe straight to Wallace. Then Bo told a story I'll remember as long as I live: "The other day I was talking to a planter friend of mine who grows cotton in east Arkansas. He has a bunch of sharecroppers working for him. [Sharecroppers were farmhands, usually black, who were literally paid with a small share of the crops. They often lived in run-down shacks on the farm and were invariably poor.] So I asked him, 'How are your sharecroppers doing?' And he said, 'Well, if we have a bad year, they break even.' Then he laughed and said, 'And if we have a good year, they break even.'" Then Bo said, "Senator, that ain't right and you know it. That's why we've got so much poverty and other troubles in this country, and if you get another term you've got to do something about it. The blacks deserve a better deal." After all the racist talk we'd been hearing, Fulbright nearly fell out of his chair. He assured Bo he'd try to do something about it when he was reelected, and Bo pledged to stick with him.

When we got back in the car, Fulbright said, "See, I told you, there's a lot of wisdom in these small towns. Bo sits on that porch and thinks things through." Bo Reece had a big impact on Fulbright. A few weeks later at a campaign rally in El Dorado, a south Arkansas oil town that was a hotbed of racism and pro-Wallace sentiment, Fulbright was asked what was the biggest problem facing America. Without hesitation he said, "Poverty." I was proud of him and grateful to Bo Reece.

When we were driving from town to town on those hot country roads, I would try to get Fulbright to talk. The conversations left me with great memories but sharply curtailed my career as his driver. One day we got into it over the Warren Court. I strongly favored most of its decisions, especially in civil rights. Fulbright disagreed. He said, "There is going to be a terrible backlash against this Supreme Court. You can't change society too much through the courts. Most of it has to come through the political system. Even if it takes longer, it's more likely to stick." I still think America came out way ahead under the Warren Court, but there's no doubt we've had a powerful reaction to it for more than thirty years now.

Four or five days into our trip, I started up one of those political discussions with Fulbright as we were driving out of yet another small town to our next stop. After about five minutes Fulbright asked me where I was going. When I told him, he said, "Then you better turn around. You're headed in exactly the opposite direction." As I sheepishly made the U-turn, he said, "You're going to give Rhodes scholars a bad name. You're acting like a damned egghead who doesn't know which way to drive."

I was embarrassed, of course, as I turned around and got the senator back on schedule. And I knew my days as a driver were over. But what the heck, I was just shy of my twenty-second birthday and had just had a few days of experiences and conversations that would last a lifetime. What Fulbright needed was a driver who could get him to the next place on time, and I was happy to go back to headquarters work, to the rallies and picnics and the long dinners listening to Lee Williams, Jim McDougal, and the other old hands tell Arkansas political stories.

Not long before the primary, Tom Campbell came for a visit on his way to Texas for his Marine Corps officer training. Jim Johnson was having one of his courthouse-steps, country-band rallies that night in Batesville, about an hour and a half north of Little Rock, so I decided to show Tom a side of Arkansas he'd only heard about before. Johnson was in good form. After warming up the crowd, he held up a shoe and shouted, "You see this shoe? It was made in Communist Romania [he pronounced it "Rooo-main-yuh"]! Bill Fulbright voted to let these Communist shoes come into America and take jobs away from good Arkansas people working in our shoe factories." We had a lot of those folks back then and Johnson promised them and all the rest of us that when he got to the Senate there would be no more Commie shoes invading America. I had no idea whether we in fact were importing shoes from Romania, whether Fulbright had voted for a failed attempt to open our border to them, or whether Johnson made the whole thing up, but it made a good tale. After the speech Johnson stood on the steps and shook hands with the crowd. I patiently waited my turn. When he shook my hand, I told him he made me ashamed to be from Arkansas. I think my earnestness amused him. He just smiled, invited me to write him about my feelings, and moved on to the next handshake.

On July 30, Fulbright defeated Jim Johnson and two lesser-known candidates. Justice Jim's wife, Virginia, barely made it into the gubernatorial runoff, beating a young reformer named Ted Boswell by 409 votes out of more than 400,000 votes cast, despite the best efforts of the Fulbright folks to help him in the closing days of the campaign and in the six days following, when everybody was hustling to keep from getting counted out or to get some extra votes in the unreported precincts. Mrs. Johnson lost the runoff by 63 to 37 percent to Marion Crank, a state legislator from Foreman in southwest Arkansas, who had the courthouse crowd and the Faubus machine behind him. Arkansas had finally had enough of the Johnsons. We were not yet in the New South of the seventies, but we did have sense enough not to go backward.

In August, as I was winding down my involvement in the Fulbright campaign and getting ready to go to Oxford, I spent several summer nights at the home of Mother's friends Bill and Marge Mitchell on Lake Hamilton, where I was always welcome. That summer I met some interesting people at Marge and Bill's. Like Mother, they loved the races and over the years got to know a lot of the horse people, including two brothers from Illinois, W. Hal and "Donkey" Bishop, who owned and trained horses. W. Hal Bishop was more successful, but Donkey was one of the most memorable characters I've ever met. He was a frequent visitor in Marge and Bill's home. One

night we were out at the lake talking about my generation's experiences with drugs and women, and Donkey
mentioned that he used to drink a lot and had been married ten times. I was amazed. "Don't look at me like that,"
he said. "When I was your age, it wasn't like it is now. If
you wanted to have sex, it wasn't even enough to say you
loved 'em. You had to marry 'em!" I laughed and asked if
he remembered all their names. "All but two," he replied.
His shortest marriage? "One night. I woke up in a motel
with a horrible hangover and a strange woman. I said,
'Who in the hell are you?' She said, 'I'm your wife, you
SOB!' I got up, put my pants on, and got out of there." In
the 1950s, Donkey met a woman who was different from
all the rest. He told her the whole truth about his life and
said if she'd marry him, he would never drink or carouse
again. She took the unbelievable chance, and he kept his
word for twenty-five years, until he died.

Marge Mitchell also introduced me to two young people who had just started teaching in Hot Springs, Danny
Thomason and Jan Biggers. Danny came from Hampton,
seat of Arkansas' smallest county, and he had a world of
good country stories to prove it. When I was governor, we
sang tenor side by side in the Immanuel Baptist Church
choir every Sunday. His brother and sister-in-law, Harry
and Linda, became two of Hillary's and my closest friends
and played a big role in the '92 presidential campaign and
our White House years.

Jan Biggers was a tall, pretty, talkative girl from Tucker-
man, in northeast Arkansas. I liked her, but she had segregationist views from her upbringing, which I deplored.
When I left for Oxford, I gave her a cardboard box full of
paperback books on civil rights and urged her to read
them. A few months later, she ran off with another

teacher, John Paschal, the president of the local NAACP. They wound up in New Hampshire, where he became a builder, she kept teaching, and they had three children. When I ran for President, I was happily surprised to find that Jan was the Democratic chair in one of New Hampshire's ten counties.

Though I was preparing to go to Oxford, August was one of 1968's craziest months, and it was hard to look ahead. It began with the Republican convention in Miami Beach, where New York governor Nelson Rockefeller's bid to defeat a resurgent Richard Nixon showed just how weak the moderate wing of the party had become, and where Governor Ronald Reagan of California first emerged as a potential President with his appeal to "true" conservatives. Nixon won on the first ballot, with 692 votes to 277 for Rockefeller and 182 for Reagan. Nixon's message was simple: he was for law and order at home, and peace with honor in Vietnam. Though the real political turmoil lay ahead when the Democrats met in Chicago, the Republicans had their share of turbulence, aggravated by Nixon's vice-presidential choice, Governor Spiro Agnew of Maryland, whose only national notoriety had come from his hard-line stance against civil disobedience. Baseball Hall of Famer Jackie Robinson, the first black to play in the major leagues, resigned his post as an aide to Rockefeller because he could not back a Republican ticket he saw as "racist." Martin Luther King Jr.'s successor, the Reverend Ralph Abernathy, moved the Poor People's Campaign from Washington to Miami Beach in hopes of influencing the Republican convention in a progressive way. They were disappointed by the platform, the floor speeches, and Nixon's appeals to the ultra-conservatives. After the

Agnew nomination was announced, what had been a peaceful gathering against poverty turned into a riot. The National Guard was called out, and the by now pre-dictable scenario unfolded: tear gas, beating, looting, fires. When it was over, three black men had been killed, a three-day curfew was imposed, and 250 people were arrested and later released to quiet charges of police bru-tality. But all the trouble only strengthened the law-and-order hand Nixon was playing to the so-called silent majority of Americans, who were appalled by what they saw as the breakdown of the fabric of American life.

The Miami strife was just a warm-up for what the Democrats faced when they met in Chicago later that month. At the beginning of the month, Al Lowenstein and others were still looking for an alternative to Humphrey. McCarthy was still hanging in there, with no real prospect of winning. On August 10, Senator George McGovern announced his own candidacy, clearly hoping to get the support of those who had been for Robert Kennedy. Meanwhile, Chicago was filling up with young people opposed to the war. A small number intended to make real trouble; the rest were there to stage various forms of peaceful protest, including the Yippies, who planned a "countercultural" "Festival of Life" with most of the celebrants high on marijuana, and the National Mobi-lization Committee, which had a more conventional protest in mind. But Mayor Richard Daley wasn't taking any chances: he put the entire police force on alert, asked the governor to send in the National Guard, and prepared for the worst.

On August 22, the convention claimed its first victim, a seventeen-year-old Native American shot by police who claimed he fired on them first near Lincoln Park, where the people gathered every day. Two days later, a thousand demonstrators refused to vacate the park at night as ordered. Hundreds of police waded into the crowd with nightsticks, as their targets threw rocks, shouted curses, or ran. It was all on television.

That was how I experienced Chicago. It was surreal. I had gone to Shreveport, Louisiana, with Jeff Dwire, the man my mother was involved with and was soon to marry. He was an unusual man: a World War II veteran of the Pacific theater who had permanently injured his abdominal muscles when he parachuted out of his damaged plane and landed on a coral reef; an accomplished carpenter; a slick Louisiana charmer; and the owner of the beauty salon where Mother got her hair done (he had worked his way through college as a hairdresser). He had also been a football player, a judo instructor, a home builder, a seller of oil-well equipment, and a securities salesman. He was married but separated from his wife, and he had three daughters. He had also served nine months in prison in 1962 for stock fraud. In 1956, he had raised $24,000 for a company that was going to make movies about colorful Oklahoma characters, including the gangster Pretty Boy Floyd. The U.S. attorney concluded the company spent the money as soon as it came in and never had any intention to make the movies. Jeff claimed he left the operation as soon as he knew it was a scam, but it was too late. I respected him for telling me about all this soon after we met. Whatever had really happened, Mother was serious about him and wanted us to spend some time together, so I agreed to go to Louisiana with him for a few days while he pursued his involvement with a pre-fab housing company. Shreveport was a conservative city in northwest Louisiana, not far from the Arkansas border, with an ultra–right wing newspaper that gave me a hard spin every morning on what I had seen on television the night before. The circumstances were bizarre, but I sat glued to the TV for hours, taking time out to go to a few places and eat with Jeff. I felt so isolated. I didn't identify with the kids raising hell or with Chicago's mayor and his rough tactics, or with the people who were supporting him, which included most of the folks I had grown up among. And I was heartsick that my party and its progressive causes were disintegrating before my eyes.

Any hope that the convention might produce a unified party was dashed by President Johnson. In his first statement since his brother's funeral, Senator Edward Kennedy called for a unilateral bombing halt and a mutual withdrawal of U.S. and North Vietnamese forces from South Vietnam. His proposal was the basis of a compromise platform plank agreed to by the Humphrey, Kennedy, and McCarthy leaders. When General Creighton Abrams, the U.S. commander in Vietnam, told LBJ a bombing halt would endanger America's troops, the President demanded Humphrey abandon the Vietnam compromise plank in the platform, and Humphrey gave in. Later, in his autobiography, Humphrey said, "I should have stood my ground. . . . I should not have yielded." But he did, and the dam broke.

The convention opened on August 26. The keynoter was Senator Dan Inouye of Hawaii, a brave Japanese-American veteran of World War II, to whom I awarded the Congressional Medal of Honor in 2000, a belated recognition of the heroism that had cost him an arm, and very nearly his life, while his own people were being herded into detention camps back home. Inouye expressed sympathy for the protesters and their goals, but urged them not to abandon peaceful means. He spoke against "violence and anarchy," but also condemned apathy and prejudice "hiding behind the reach of law and order," a clear slap at Nixon and perhaps at the Chicago police tactics too. Inouye struck a good balance, but things were too far out of kilter to be righted by the power of his words.

More than Vietnam divided the convention. Some of the southern delegations were still resisting the party rule that the delegate-selection process be open to blacks. The credentials committee, including Arkansas congressman David Pryor, voted to accept the Mississippi challenge delegation led by civil rights activist Aaron Henry. The other southern delegations were seated, except for Georgia's, which was split, with half the seats given to a challenge slate headed by young state representative Julian Bond, now chairman of the NAACP; and Alabama's, which had sixteen of its delegates disqualified because they wouldn't pledge to support the party's nominee, presumably because Alabama's Governor Wallace was running as an independent.

Despite these disputes, the main point of contention was the war. McCarthy seemed miserable, back to his old diffident self, resigned to defeat, detached from the kids who were getting harassed or beaten every night in Lincoln Park or Grant Park when they refused to leave. In a last-minute effort to find a candidate most Democrats thought was electable and acceptable, people from Al Lowenstein to Mayor Daley sounded out Ted Kennedy. When he gave a firm no, Humphrey's nomination was secure. So was the Vietnam plank Johnson wanted. About 60 percent of the delegates voted for it.

The night the convention was to name its nominee, fif-

teen thousand people gathered in Grant Park to demonstrate against the war and Mayor Daley's tough tactics.
After one of them started to lower the American flag, the
police stormed into the crowd, beating and arresting people. When the demonstrators marched toward the Hilton,
the police teargassed them and beat them again on Michigan Avenue. All the action was beamed into the convention hall by television. Both sides were inflamed.
McCarthy finally addressed his supporters in Grant Park,
telling them he would not abandon them and would not
endorse Humphrey or Nixon. Senator Abe Ribicoff of
Connecticut, in nominating McGovern, condemned the
"Gestapo tactics in the streets of Chicago." Daley leapt to
his feet and, with the TV cameras on him, hurled an angry
epithet at Ribicoff. When the speeches were over, the balloting began. Humphrey won handily, with the vote completed at about midnight. His choice for vice president,
Senator Edmund Muskie of Maine, breezed through
shortly afterward. Meanwhile, the protests continued outside the convention hall, led by Tom Hayden and black
comedian Dick Gregory. The only uplifting thing to happen inside the hall, besides Inouye's keynote, was the final-
day film tribute to Robert Kennedy, which brought the
delegates to a frenzy of emotion. Wisely, President Johnson had ordered that it not be shown until after
Humphrey was nominated.

In a final indignity, after the convention, the police
stormed into the Hilton to beat and arrest McCarthy volunteers who were having a farewell party. They claimed
the young people, while drowning their sorrows, had
thrown objects down on them from the McCarthy staff's
fifteenth-floor room. The next day, Humphrey stood
foursquare behind Daley's handling of the "planned and

premeditated" violence and denied that the mayor had done anything wrong.

The Democrats limped out of Chicago divided and discouraged, the latest casualties in a culture war that went beyond differences over Vietnam. It would reshape and realign American politics for the rest of the century and beyond, and frustrate most efforts to focus the electorate on the issues that most affect their lives and livelihoods, as opposed to their psyches. The kids and their supporters saw the mayor and the cops as authoritarian, ignorant, violent bigots. The mayor and his largely blue-collar ethnic police force saw the kids as foul-mouthed, immoral, unpatriotic, soft, upper-class kids who were too spoiled to respect authority, too selfish to appreciate what it takes to hold a society together, too cowardly to serve in Vietnam.

As I watched all this in my little hotel room in Shreveport, I understood how both sides felt. I was against the war and the police brutality, but growing up in Arkansas had given me an appreciation for the struggles of ordinary people who do their duty every day, and a deep skepticism about self-righteous sanctimony on the right or the left. The fleeting fanaticism of the left had not yet played itself out, but it had already unleashed a radical reaction on the right, one that would prove more durable, more well financed, more institutionalized, more resourceful, more addicted to power, and far more skilled at getting and keeping it.

Much of my public life was spent trying to bridge the cultural and psychological divide that had widened into a chasm in Chicago. I won a lot of elections and I think I did a lot of good, but the more I tried to bring people together, the madder it made the fanatics on the right. Unlike the kids in Chicago, they didn't want America to come back together. They had an enemy, and they meant to keep it.

FOURTEEN

I spent September getting ready for Oxford, saying good-bye to friends, and watching the presidential campaign unfold. I was eligible for the draft so I checked in with the local board chairman, Bill Armstrong, about when I could expect to be called. Though graduate deferments had been abolished the previous spring, students were allowed to finish the term they were in. Oxford had three eight-week terms a year, divided by two five-week vacation periods. I was told that I wouldn't be in the October call, and that I might get to stay beyond one term, depending on how many people my local draft board had to supply. I wanted to go to Oxford badly, even if I got to stay only a couple of months. The Rhodes Trust would allow people to do their military service and come to Oxford afterward, but since I had decided to be in the draft, with no end in sight in Vietnam, it didn't seem prudent to think about afterward.

On the political front, though I thought we were deader than a doornail coming out of Chicago, and Humphrey was sticking with LBJ's Vietnam policy, I still wanted him to win. Civil rights alone was enough reason. Race still divided the South, and increasingly, with the spread of court-ordered busing of children out of their local schools to achieve racial balance across school districts, the rest of the country was dividing as well. Ironically, Wallace's candidacy gave Humphrey a chance, since most of his voters were law-and-order segregationists who would have voted for Nixon in a two-man race.

The country's cultural clashes continued to erupt. Anti-war demonstrators went after Humphrey more than Nixon or Wallace. The vice president was also bedeviled by continuing criticism of Mayor Daley's police tactics during the convention. While a Gallup poll said 56 percent of Americans approved of the police conduct toward the demonstrators, most of them were not in the Democratic base, especially in a three-way race including Wallace. As if all this were not enough, the established order was further upset by two sets of protesters at the Miss America Pageant in Atlantic City. A black group protested the absence of black contestants. A women's liberation group protested the pageant itself as degrading to women. For good measure, some of them burned their bras, proof positive to many old-fashioned Americans that something had gone terribly wrong.

In the presidential campaign, Nixon appeared to be coasting to victory, attacking Humphrey as weak and ineffectual and saying as little as possible about what he would do as President, except to pander to segregationists (and court Wallace voters) by promising to reverse the policy of withholding federal funds from school districts that refused to comply with federal court orders to integrate their schools. Nixon's running mate, Spiro Agnew, was the campaign's attack dog, aided by his speechwriter Pat Buchanan. His harshness and verbal gaffes were becoming legendary. Humphrey suffered loud demonstrators everywhere he went. By the end of the month, Nixon was holding steady at 43 percent in the polls, while Humphrey had dropped twelve points to 28 percent, just seven points ahead of Wallace at 21 percent. On the last day of September, in desperation, Humphrey publicly broke with President Johnson on Vietnam, saying that he would stop the bombing of North Vietnam as "an acceptable risk for peace." Finally, he had become his own man, but there were only five weeks to go.

By the time Humphrey made his "free at last" speech, I was in New York getting ready to set sail for Oxford. Denise Hyland and I had a terrific lunch with Willie Morris, then the young editor of **Harper's Magazine.** In my senior year at Georgetown, I had read his wonderful memoir, **North Toward Home,** and had become a lifetime fan. After I won the Rhodes, I wrote Willie, asking if I could come to see him when I was in New York. In the spring he received me in his office on Park Avenue. I enjoyed the visit so much I asked to see him again before I left, and for some reason, maybe southern manners, he made the time.

On October 4, Denise went with me to Pier 86 on the Hudson River, where I would board the SS **United States** for England. I knew where the huge ocean liner was headed, but I had no idea where I was going.

The **United States** was then the fastest liner on the seas, but the trip still took nearly a week. It was a long-standing tradition for the Rhodes group to sail together so that they could get acquainted. The ship's leisurely pace and group dining did give us time to get to know one another (after the obligatory period of "sniffing each other out" like a pack of wary, well-bred hunting dogs), to meet some other passengers, and to decompress a little out of the hothouse American political environment. Most of us were so earnest we almost felt guilty about enjoying the trip; we were surprised to meet people who were far less obsessed with Vietnam and domestic politics than we were.

The most unusual encounter I had was with Bobby Baker, the notorious political protégé of Lyndon Johnson's who had been secretary of the Senate when the President was Senate majority leader. A year earlier, Baker had been convicted of tax evasion and various other federal offenses, but was still free while his case was on appeal. Baker seemed carefree, consumed with politics, and interested in spending time with the Rhodes scholars. The feeling wasn't generally reciprocated. Some of our group didn't know who he was; most of the rest saw him as the embodiment of the political establishment's corrupt cronyism. I didn't approve of what he apparently had done, but was fascinated by his stories and insights, which he was eager to share. It took only a question or two to get him started.

With the exception of Bobby Baker and his entourage, I mostly hung around with the other Rhodes scholars and the other young people on board. I especially liked Martha Saxton, a brilliant, lovely, aspiring writer. She was spending most of her time with another Rhodes scholar, but eventually I got my chance, and after our romance was over, we became lifelong friends. Recently, she gave me a copy of her latest book, **Being Good: Women's Moral Values in Early America.**

One day a man invited a few of us to his suite for cocktails. I had never had a drink before and had never wanted one. I hated what liquor had done to Roger Clinton and was afraid that it might have the same effect on me. But I decided the time had come to overcome my lifelong fear. When our host asked me what I wanted, I said Scotch and soda, a drink I had made for others when I worked as a bartender for a couple of private parties in Georgetown. I had no idea what it would taste like, and when I tried it I didn't like it very much. The next day I tried a bourbon and water, which I liked a little better. After I got to Oxford, I drank mostly beer, wine, and sherry, and when I came home, I enjoyed gin and tonic and beer in the summertime. A few times in my twenties and early thirties I had too much to drink. After I met Hillary we enjoyed champagne on special occasions, but fortunately, liquor never did much for me. Also, in the late seventies I developed an allergy to all alcoholic drinks except vodka. On balance, I'm glad I broke free of my fear of tasting liquor on the ship, and I'm relieved I never had a craving for it. I've had enough problems without that one.

By far the best part of the voyage was just what it was supposed to be: being with the other Rhodes scholars. I tried to spend some time with all of them, listening to their stories and learning from them. Many had far more impressive academic records than I did, and a few had been active in anti-war politics, on campuses or in the McCarthy and Kennedy campaigns. Several of those I liked most became lifetime friends, and an amazing number played an important part in my presidency: Tom Williamson, a black Harvard football player, who served as counsel to the Labor Department in my first term; Rick Stearns, a Stanford graduate, who got me into the national McGovern campaign and whom I appointed a federal judge in Boston; Strobe Talbott, editor of the **Yale Daily News,** who became my special advisor on Russia and deputy secretary of state after a distinguished career at **Time** magazine; Doug Eakeley, later my law school housemate, whom I appointed chair of the Legal Services Corporation; Alan Bersin, another Harvard football player from Brooklyn, whom I appointed U.S. attorney in San Diego, where he's now superintendent of schools; Willie Fletcher from Seattle, Washington, whom I appointed to the Ninth Circuit Court of Appeals; and Bob Reich, the already famous spark plug of our group, who served as secretary of labor in my first term. Dennis Blair, a Naval Academy grad, was an admiral in the Pentagon when I became President and later commander of our forces in the Pacific, but he got there without any help from me.

Over the next two years, we would all experience Oxford in different ways, but we shared in the uncertainties and anxieties of the times at home, loving Oxford, yet wondering what the devil we were doing there. Most of us threw ourselves into our new lives more than into our tutorials or lectures. Our conversations, personal reading, and trips seemed more important, especially to those of us who thought we were on borrowed time. After two years, a smaller percentage of the Americans would actually receive degrees than in any previous class of Rhodes scholars. In our own way, filled with youthful angst, we probably learned more at Oxford about ourselves, and about things that would matter for a lifetime, than most of our predecessors had.

After five days and a brief stop in Le Havre, we finally arrived at Southampton, where we caught our first glimpse of Oxford in the person of Sir Edgar "Bill" Williams, the warden of Rhodes House. He was waiting for us on the dock in a bowler hat, raincoat, and umbrella, looking more like an English dandy than like the man who, during World War II, had served as chief of intelligence to Field Marshal Montgomery.

Bill Williams herded us onto a bus for the ride to Oxford. It was dark and rainy so we didn't see much. When we got to Oxford, it was about 11 p.m. and the whole town was shut down tight as a drum, except for a little lighted truck selling hot dogs, bad coffee, and junk food on High Street, just outside University College, where I had been assigned. The bus let us off and we walked through the door into the main quadrangle, built in the seventeenth century, where we were met by Douglas Millin, the head porter, who controlled access to the college. Millin was a crusty old codger who took the college job after he retired from the navy. He was very smart, a fact he took pains to hide behind torrents of good-natured verbal abuse. He especially liked to work the Americans over. The first words I heard from him were directed at Bob Reich, who is less than five feet tall. He said he'd been told he was getting four Yanks, but they'd sent him only three and a half. He never stopped making fun of us, but behind it he was a wise man and a shrewd judge of people.

I spent a lot of time over the next two years talking to Douglas. In between the "bloody hells" and various other English epithets, he taught me how the college really worked, told me stories of the main professors and staff, and discussed current affairs, including the differences between Vietnam and World War II. Over the next twenty-five years, whenever I got back to England, I dropped in to see Douglas for a reality check. At the end of 1978, after I had been elected governor of Arkansas the first time, I took Hillary to England for a much-needed vacation. When we got to Oxford, I was feeling pretty proud of myself as we walked through the front door of the college. Then I saw Douglas. He didn't miss a beat. "Clinton," he said, "I hear you've just been elected king of some place with three men and a dog." I loved Douglas Millin.

My rooms were in the back of the college, behind the

library, in Helen's Court, a quaint little space named after the wife of a previous master of the college. Two buildings faced each other across a small walled-in space. The older building on the left had two doors to two sets of student rooms on the ground floor and the second floor. I was assigned to the rooms on the left side of the second floor at the far entrance. I had a small bedroom and a small study that were really just one big room. The toilet was on the first floor, which often made for a cold walk down the stairs. The shower was on my floor. Sometimes it had warm water. The modern building on the right was for graduate students, who had two-story flats. In October 2001, I helped Chelsea unpack her things in the flat with a bedroom directly opposite the rooms I had occupied thirty-three years earlier. It was one of those priceless moments when the sunshine takes away all life's shadows.

I woke up on my first morning in Oxford to encounter one of the curiosities of Oxford life, my "scout" Archie, who took care of the rooms in Helen's Court. I was used to making my own bed and looking after myself, but gradually I gave in to letting Archie do the job he had been doing for almost fifty years by the time he got stuck with me. He was a quiet, kind man for whom I and the other boys developed real affection and respect. At Christmas and on other special occasions, the students were expected to give their scout a modest gift, and modest was all most of us could afford on the annual Rhodes stipend of $1,700. Archie let it be known that what he really wanted was a few bottles of Guinness stout, a dark Irish beer. I gave him a lot of it in my year in Helen's Court and occasionally shared a sip with him. Archie really loved that stuff, and thanks to him, I actually developed a taste for it too.

University life is organized around its twenty-nine colleges, then still divided by gender; there were far fewer women's colleges. The University's main role in students' lives is to provide lectures, which students may or may not attend, and to administer exams, which are given at the end of the entire course of study. Whether you get a degree and how distinguished it is depends entirely on your performance during examination week. Meanwhile, the primary means of covering the material is the weekly tutorial, which normally requires you to produce a short essay on the subject to be discussed. Each college has its own chapel, dining hall, and library. Most have remarkable architectural features; some have stunning gardens, even parks and lakes, or touch on the River Cherwell, which borders the old city on the east. Just below Oxford, the Cherwell runs into the Isis, part of the Thames, the massive river that shapes so much of London.

I spent most of the first two weeks walking around Oxford, an ancient and beautiful city. I explored its rivers, parks, tree-lined paths, churches, the covered market, and, of course, the colleges.

Though my college didn't have large grounds, and its oldest buildings date only to the seventeenth century, it suited me fine. In the fourteenth century, the fellows of the college forged documents to show that it was Oxford's oldest, with roots in the ninth-century rule of Alfred the Great. Indisputably, Univ, as everyone calls it, is one of the three oldest colleges, founded along with Merton and Balliol in the thirteenth century. In 1292, the governing statutes contained a set of strict rules, including a ban on singing ballads and speaking English. On a few rowdy nights, I almost wished my contemporaries were still confined to whispering in Latin.

University's most famous student, Percy Bysshe Shelley, enrolled in 1810 as a chemistry student. He lasted about a year, expelled not because he had used his knowledge to set up a small still in his room to make liquor, but because of his paper "The Necessity of Atheism." By 1894, Univ had reclaimed Shelley, in the form of a beautiful marble statue of the dead poet, who drowned off the coast of Italy in his late twenties. Visitors to the college who never read his poetry can tell, just by gazing on his graceful death pose, why he had such a hold on the young people of his time. In the twentieth century, Univ's undergraduates and fellows included three famous writers: Stephen Spender, C. S. Lewis, and V. S. Naipaul; the great physicist Stephen Hawking; two British prime ministers, Clement Attlee and Harold Wilson; Australian prime minister Bob Hawke, who still owns the college speed record in beer drinking; the actor Michael York; and the man who killed Rasputin, Prince Felix Yusupov.

While beginning to learn about Oxford and England, I was also trying to follow election developments from afar and was eagerly awaiting the absentee ballot with which I would cast my first vote for President. Although urban violence and student demonstrations continued, Humphrey was doing better. After his semi–declaration of independence from LBJ on Vietnam, he drew fewer protests and more support from young people. McCarthy finally endorsed him, in a typically halfhearted way, adding that he would not be a candidate for reelection to the Senate in 1970 or for President in 1972. Meanwhile, Wallace committed a crippling error by naming former air force chief of staff Curtis LeMay as his vice-presidential partner. LeMay, who had urged President Kennedy to bomb Cuba during the missile crisis five years earlier, made his debut as a candidate by saying nuclear bombs were "just another weapon in the arsenal" and that "there are many times when it would be most efficient to use them." LeMay's remarks put Wallace on the defensive and he never recovered.

Meanwhile, Nixon kept at the strategy with which he was coasting to victory, refusing repeated invitations to debate Humphrey; he was bothered only by the universal unfavorable comparison of Spiro Agnew to Humphrey's running mate, Senator Muskie, and by the fear that Johnson would achieve an "October surprise" breakthrough in the Paris peace talks with a bombing halt. We now know that the Nixon campaign was being fed inside information about the talks by Henry Kissinger, who, as a consultant to Averell Harriman, was involved enough with the Paris talks to know what was going on. We also know that Nixon's campaign manager, John Mitchell, lobbied South Vietnam's president, Thieu, through Nixon's friend Anna Chennault, not to give in to LBJ's pressure to join the peace talks along with the government's South Vietnamese opposition, the National Liberation Front. Johnson knew about the Nixon team's efforts because of Justice Department–approved wiretaps on Anna Chennault and the South Vietnamese ambassador to Washington. Finally, on the last day of October, President Johnson announced a full bombing halt, Hanoi's agreement to South Vietnam's participation in the talks, and U.S. approval of a role for the National Liberation Front.

November opened with high hopes for Humphrey and his supporters. He was moving up fast in the polls and clearly thought the peace initiative would put him over the top. On November 2, the Saturday before the election, President Thieu announced that he wouldn't go to

Paris because the NLF was included. He said that would force him into a coalition government with the Communists, and he would deal only with North Vietnam. The Nixon camp was quick to imply that LBJ had jumped the gun on his peace initiative, acting to help Humphrey without having all his diplomatic ducks in a row.

Johnson was furious, and gave Humphrey the information on Anna Chennault's efforts to sabotage the initiative on Nixon's behalf. There was no longer a need to keep it from the public to avoid undermining President Thieu, but amazingly, Humphrey refused to use it. Because the polls showed him in a virtual dead heat with Nixon, he thought he might win without it, and apparently he was afraid of a possible backlash because the facts didn't prove that Nixon himself knew what others, including John Mitchell, were doing on his behalf. Still, the implication was strong that Nixon had engaged in activity that was virtually treasonous. Johnson was furious at Humphrey. I belicve LBJ would have leaked the bombshell if he had been running, and that if the roles had been reversed, Nixon would have used it in a heartbeat.

Humphrey paid for his scruples, or his squeamishness. He lost the election by 500,000 votes, 43.4 percent to 42.7 percent to 13.5 percent for Wallace. Nixon won 301 electoral votes, 31 over a majority, with close victories in Illinois and Ohio. Nixon got away with the Kissinger-Mitchell-Chennault gambit, but as Jules Witcover speculates in his book on 1968, **The Year the Dream Died,** it may have been a more costly escape than it appeared. Its success may have contributed to the Nixon crowd's belief that they could get away with anything, including all the shenanigans that surfaced in Watergate.

On November 1, I began to keep a diary in one of two

leather-bound volumes Denise Hyland had given me when I left the United States. When Archie woke me with the good news about the bombing halt, I wrote: "I wish I could have seen Senator Fulbright today—one more instance of vindication for his tireless and tenacious battle." The next day I speculated that a cease-fire might lead to a troop reduction and my not being drafted, or at least "allow many of my friends already in the service to escape Vietnam. And maybe some now in those jungles can be saved from early death." Little did I know that half our deaths were still to come. I closed my first two installments by "extolling the same virtue: hope, the fiber of my being, which stays with me even on nights like tonight when I have lost all power of analysis and articulation." Yes, I was young and melodramatic, but I already believed in what I was to term "a place called Hope" in my 1992 Democratic convention speech. It's kept me going through a lifetime.

On November 3, I forgot about the election for a while during a lunch with George Cawkwell, the dean of graduates at Univ. He was a big, imposing man who still looked every inch the rugby star he once had been, as a Rhodes scholar from New Zealand. At our first meeting, Professor Cawkwell had really dressed me down about my decision to change my course of studies. Soon after I arrived in Oxford, I had transferred out of the undergraduate program in politics, philosophy, and economics, called PPE, and into the B.Litt. in politics, which required a fifty thousand–word dissertation. I had covered virtually all the first year's work in PPE at Georgetown, and because of the draft, I didn't expect to have a second year at Oxford. Cawkwell thought I'd made a terrible mistake in passing up the weekly tutorials, in which essays are read, criticized, and defended. Largely because of Cawkwell's argument, I switched courses again, to the B.Phil. in politics, which does include tutorials, essays, exams, and a shorter thesis.

Election day, November 5, was also Guy Fawkes Day in England, the observance of his attempt to burn down Parliament in 1605. My diary says: "Everyone in England celebrates the occasion; some because Fawkes failed, some because he tried." That night we Americans had an election-watch party at Rhodes House. The largely pro-Humphrey crowd was cheering him on. We went to bed not knowing what happened, but we did know that Fulbright had won handily, a relief, since he had prevailed in the primary over Jim Johnson and two little-known contenders with only 52 percent of the vote. A great cheer went up at Rhodes House when his victory was announced.

On November 6, we learned that Nixon had won and that, as I wrote, "Uncle Raymond and his cronies carried Arkansas for Wallace, our first deviation from the national (Democratic) ticket since achieving statehood in 1836. . . . I must send my ten dollars to Uncle Raymond, for I bet him last November that Arkansas, the most 'liberal' of the Southern states, would never go for Wallace, which just goes to show how wrong these pseudo-intellectuals can be!" ("Pseudo-intellectual" was a favorite Wallace epithet for anyone with a college degree who disagreed with him.) I noted that, unlike the South Vietnamese government, I was terribly disappointed that "after all that has occurred, after Humphrey's remarkable recovery, it has come to the end I sensed last January: Nixon in the White House."

Adding insult to injury, my absentee ballot never

arrived and I missed my first chance to vote for President. The county clerk had mailed it by surface mail, not airmail. It was cheaper but it took three weeks, arriving long after the election.

The next day, I got back to my life. I called Mother, who had by then decided to marry Jeff Dwire and was so blissfully happy she made me feel good, too. And I mailed that ten-dollar check to Uncle Raymond, suggesting that the United States establish a national George Wallace Day, similar to Guy Fawkes Day. Everyone could celebrate: some because he ran for President, the rest of us because he ran so poorly.

The rest of the month was a blizzard of activity that pushed politics and Vietnam to the back of my brain for a while. One Friday, Rick Stearns and I hitchhiked and rode buses to Wales and back, while Rick read Dylan Thomas poems to me. It was the first time I had heard "Do Not Go Gentle into That Good Night." I loved it, and love it still when brave souls "rage against the dying of the light."

I also took several trips with Tom Williamson. Once we decided to do a role reversal on the bad stereotypes of subservient blacks and racist southern overlords. When the nice English driver stopped to pick us up, Tom said, "Boy, get in the backseat." "Yes suh," I replied. The English driver thought we were nuts.

Two weeks after the election I scored my first touchdown, called a "try," for Univ's rugby team. It was a big thing for a former band boy. Though I never really understood its subtleties, I liked rugby. I was bigger than most English boys and could normally make an acceptable contribution by running to the ball and getting in the opposition's way, or pushing hard in the second row of the "scrum," a strange formation in which the two sides push against each other for control of the ball, which is placed on the ground between them. Once, we went to Cambridge for a match. Though Cambridge is more serene than Oxford, which is larger and more industrialized, the opposing team played hard and rough. I got a blow on the head and probably sustained a minor concussion. When I told the coach I was dizzy, he reminded me that there were no substitutes and our side would be one man short if I came out: "Just get back on the field and get in someone's way." We lost anyway, but I was glad I hadn't quit the field. As long as you don't quit, you've always got a chance.

In late November, I wrote my first essay for my tutor, Dr. Zbigniew Pelczynski, a Polish émigré, on the role of terror in Soviet totalitarianism ("a sterile knife cutting into the collective body, removing hard growths of diversity and independence"), attended my first tutorial, and went to my first academic seminar. Apart from those meager efforts, I spent the rest of the month sort of wandering around. I went twice to Stratford-upon-Avon, Shakespeare's home, to see plays of his; to London twice, to see Ann Markusen's former Georgetown housemates Dru Bachman and Ellen McPeake, who were living and working there; to Birmingham to play basketball badly; and to Derby to speak to high school students and answer their questions about America on the fifth anniversary of President Kennedy's death.

As December began, I made plans for my surprise homecoming for Mother's wedding, filled with foreboding about my future and hers. A lot of Mother's friends were dead set against her marrying Jeff Dwire, because he had been to prison and because they thought he was still untrustworthy. To make things worse, he hadn't been able to finalize his divorce from his long-estranged wife.

Meanwhile, the uncertainty of my own life was reinforced when my friend Frank Aller, a Rhodes scholar at Queen's College, just across High Street from Univ, received his draft notice from his hometown selective-service board in Spokane, Washington. He told me he was going home to prepare his parents and girlfriend for his decision to refuse induction and to stay in England indefinitely to avoid going to jail. Frank was a China scholar who understood Vietnam well, and thought our policy was both wrong and immoral. He was also a good middle-class boy who loved his country. He was miserable on the horns of his dilemma. Strobe Talbott, who lived just down the street in Magdalen College, and I tried to console and support him. Frank was a good-hearted man who knew we were as opposed to the war as he was, and he tried to console us in return. He was particularly forceful with me, telling me that, unlike him, I had the desire and ability to make a difference in politics and it would be wrong to throw my opportunities away by resisting the draft. His generosity only made me feel more guilty, as the angst-ridden pages of my diary show. He was cutting me more slack than I could allow myself.

On December 19, I landed in a huge snowfall in Minneapolis for a reunion with Ann Markusen. She was home from her Ph.D. studies at Michigan State and as uncertain about her future, and ours, as I was. I loved her, but I was too uncertain of myself at that point in my life to make a commitment to anyone else.

On December 23, I flew home. The surprise came off. Mother cried and cried. She, Jeff, and Roger all seemed happy about the coming marriage, so happy that they didn't give me too much grief about my newly long hair. Christmas was merry in spite of last-ditch efforts by two of Mother's friends to get me to try to talk her out of marrying Jeff. I took four yellow roses to Daddy's grave and prayed that his family would support Mother and Roger in their new endeavor. I liked Jeff Dwire. He was smart, hardworking, good with Roger, and clearly in love with Mother. I was for the marriage, noting that "if all the skeptical well-wishers and the really pernicious ill-wishers are right about Jeff and Mother, their union can hardly prove more of a failure than did its predecessors—his too," and for a while, I forgot all the tumult of 1968, the year that broke open the nation and shattered the Democratic Party; the year that conservative populism replaced progressive populism as the dominant political force in our nation; the year that law and order and strength became the province of Republicans, and Democrats became associated with chaos, weakness, and out-of-touch, self-indulgent elites; the year that led to Nixon, then Reagan, then Gingrich, then George W. Bush. The middle-class backlash would shape and distort American politics for the rest of the century. The new conservatism would be shaken by Watergate, but not destroyed. Its public support would be weakened, as right-wing ideologues promoted economic inequality, environmental destruction, and social divisions, but not destroyed. When threatened by its own excesses, the conservative movement would promise to be "kinder and gentler" or more "compassionate," all the while ripping the hide off Democrats for alleged weakness of values, character, and will. And it would be enough to provoke the painfully predictable, almost Pavlovian reaction among enough white middle-class voters to carry the day. Of course it was more complicated than that. Sometimes conservatives' criticisms of the Democrats had validity, and there were always moderate Republicans and conservatives of good-will who worked with Democrats to make some positive changes.

Nevertheless, the deeply embedded nightmares of 1968 formed the arena in which I and all other progressive politicians had to struggle over our entire careers. Perhaps if Martin Luther King Jr. and Robert Kennedy had lived, things would have been different. Perhaps if Humphrey had used the information about Nixon's interference with the Paris peace talks, things would have been different. Perhaps not. Regardless, those of us who believed that the good in the 1960s outweighed the bad would fight on, still fired by the heroes and dreams of our youth.

FIFTEEN

ew Year's morning 1969—I opened the year on a happy note. Frank Holt had just been reelected to the supreme court, only two years after his defeat in the governor's race. I drove to Little Rock, to the judge's swearing-in ceremony. Predictably, he had urged us not to spend New Year's Day on this modest ritual, but more than fifty of us diehards showed up anyway. My diary says: "I told him I wasn't about to pull out just because he was winning!" Ironically, as a "new" justice, he was assigned to the old offices of Justice Jim Johnson.

On January 2, Joe Newman and I drove Mother home to Hope to tell what remained of her family that she was going to marry Jeff the next day. When we got home, Joe and I took the "The Roger Clintons" sign off the mailbox. With his sharp sense of irony, Joe laughed and said, "It's kinda sad that it comes off so easily." Despite the harbingers of doom, I thought the marriage would work. As I wrote in my diary, "If Jeff is nothing more than a con man, as some still insist, then color me conned."

The next night, the ceremony was short and simple. Our friend Reverend John Miles led them through their vows. Roger lit the candles. I was best man. There was a party afterward at which Carolyn Yeldell and I played and sang for the wedding guests. Some preachers would have refused church sanction to the wedding because Jeff was divorced, and so recently. Not John Miles. He was a pugnacious, tough, liberal Methodist who believed Jesus was sent by his Father God to give us all second chances.

On January 4, thanks to my friend Sharon Evans, who knew Governor Rockefeller, I was invited to lunch with the governor at his ranch on Petit Jean Mountain. I found Rockefeller friendly and articulate. We discussed Oxford and his son Winthrop Paul's desire to go there. The governor wanted me to keep in touch with Win Paul, who had spent a lot of his childhood in Europe, when he began his studies at Pembroke College in the fall.

After lunch, I had a good talk with Win Paul, after which we headed southwest for a rendezvous with Tom Campbell, who had driven to Arkansas from Mississippi, where he was in marine flight training. The three of us drove to the Governor's Mansion, which Win Paul had invited us to see. We were all impressed, and I left thinking I had just seen an important piece of Arkansas history, not the place that in a decade would become my home for twelve years.

On January 11, I flew back to England on the same plane with Tom Williamson, who was educating me about being black in America, and Frank Aller, who recounted his difficult holiday, in which his conservative father made getting a haircut, but not reporting for the draft, a precondition of Christmas at home. When I got back to Univ, I found in my stack of mail a remarkable letter from my old friend and baptismal partner, Marine Private Bert Jeffries. I recorded some excerpts of his stunning, sad message:

> . . . Bill, I've already seen many things and been through a lot no man of a right mind would want to see or go through. Over here, they play for keeps. And it's either win or lose. It's not a pretty sight to

see a buddy you live with and become so close to, to have him die beside you and you know it was for no good reason. And you realize how easily it could have been you.

I work for a Lieutenant Colonel. I am his bodyguard. . . . On the 21st of November we came to a place called Winchester. Our helicopter let us off and the Colonel, myself, and two other men started looking over the area . . . there were two NVAs [North Vietnamese Army soldiers] in a bunker, they opened up on us. . . . The Colonel got hit and the two others were hit. Bill, that day I prayed. Fortunately I got the two of them before they got me. I killed my first man that day. And Bill, it's an awful feeling, to know you took another man's life. It's a sickening feeling. And then you realize how it could have been you just as easily.

The next day, January 13, I went to London for my draft exam. The doctor declared me, according to my fanciful diary notes, "one of the healthiest specimens in the western world, suitable for display at medical schools, exhibitions, zoos, carnivals, and base training camps." On the fifteenth I saw Edward Albee's **A Delicate Balance,** which was "my second surrealistic experience in as many days." Albee's characters forced the audience "to wonder if some day near the end they won't wake up and find themselves hollow and afraid." I was already wondering that.

President Nixon was inaugurated on January 20. His speech was an attempt at reconciliation, but it "left me pretty cold, the preaching of good old middle-class religion and virtues. They will supposedly solve our problems with the Asians, who do not come from the Judeo-

Christian tradition; the Communists, who do not even believe in God; the blacks, who have been shafted so often by God-fearing white men that there is hardly any common ground left between them; and the kids, who have heard those same song-and-dance sermons sung false so many times they may prefer dope to the audacious self-delusion of their elders." Ironically, I believed in Christianity and middle-class virtues, too; they just didn't lead me to the same place. I thought living out our true religious and political principles would require us to reach deeper and go further than Mr. Nixon was prepared to go.

I decided to get back into my own life in England for whatever time I had left. I went to my first Oxford Union debate—Resolved: that man created God in his own image, "a potentially fertile subject poorly ploughed." I went north to Manchester, and marveled at the beauty of the English countryside "quilted by those ancient rock walls without mortar or mud or cement." There was a seminar on "Pluralism as a Concept of Democratic Theory," which I found boring, just another attempt "to explain in more complex (therefore, more meaningful, of course) terms what is going on before our own eyes. . . . It is only so much dog-dripping to me because I am at root not intellectual, not conceptual about the actual, just damn well not smart enough, I reckon, to run in this fast crowd."

On January 27, the actual reared its ugly head again, as a few of us threw a party for Frank Aller on the day he officially became a draft resister, "walking along the only open road." Despite the vodka, the toasts, the attempts at humor, the party was a bust. Even Bob Reich, easily the wittiest of us, couldn't make it work. We simply could not lift the burden from Frank's shoulders "on this, the day when he put his money where his mouth was." The next day Strobe Talbott, whose draft status was already 1-Y because of an old football injury, became really unsuited for military service when his eyeglasses met up with John Isaacson's squash racket on the Univ court. The doctor spent two hours pulling glass out of his cornea. He recovered and went on to spend the next thirty-five years seeing things most of us miss.

For a long time, February has been a hard month for me, dominated by fighting the blues and waiting for spring to come. My first February in Oxford was a real zinger. I fought it by reading, something I did a lot of at Oxford, with no particular pattern except what my studies dictated. I read hundreds of books. That month I read John Steinbeck's **The Moon Is Down,** partly because he had just died and I wanted to remember him with something I hadn't read before. I reread Willie Morris's **North Toward Home,** because it helped me to understand my roots and my "better self." I read Eldridge Cleaver's **Soul on Ice** and pondered the meaning of soul. "Soul is a word I use often enough to be Black, but of course, and I occasionally think unfortunately, I am not. . . . The soul: I know what it is—it's where I feel things; it's what moves me; it's what makes me a man, and when I put it out of commission, I know soon enough I will die if I do not retrieve it." I was afraid then that I was losing it.

My struggles with the draft rekindled my long-standing doubts about whether I was, or could become, a really good person. Apparently, a lot of people who grow up in difficult circumstances subconsciously blame themselves and feel unworthy of a better fate. I think this problem arises from leading parallel lives, an external life that takes its natural course and an internal life where the secrets are hidden. When I was a child, my outside life was filled with friends and fun, learning and doing. My internal life was full of uncertainty, anger, and a dread of ever-looming violence. No one can live parallel lives with complete success; the two have to intersect. At Georgetown, as the threat of Daddy's violence dissipated, then disappeared, I had been more able to live one coherent life. Now the draft dilemma brought back my internal life with a vengeance. Beneath my new and exciting external life, the old demons of self-doubt and impending destruction reared their ugly heads again.

I would continue to struggle to merge the parallel lives, to live with my mind, body, and spirit in the same place. In the meantime, I have tried to make my external life as good as possible, and to survive the dangers and relieve the pain of my internal life. This probably explains my profound admiration for the personal courage of soldiers and others who put their lives at risk for honorable causes, and my visceral hatred of violence and abuse of power; my passion for public service and my deep sympathy for the problems of other people; the solace I have found in human companionship and the difficulty I've had in letting anyone into the deepest recesses of my internal life. It was dark down there.

I had been down on myself before, but never like this, for this long. As I said, I first became self-aware enough to know that those feelings rumbled around beneath my sunny disposition and optimistic outlook when I was a junior in high school, more than five years before I went to Oxford. It was when I wrote an autobiographical essay for Ms. Warneke's honors English class and talked about the "disgust" that "storms my brain."

The storms were really raging in February 1969, and I tried to put them out by reading, traveling, and spending lots of time with interesting people. I would meet many of them at 9 Bolton Gardens in London, a spacious apartment that became my home away from Oxford on many weekends. Its full-time occupant was David Edwards, who had shown up at Helen's Court one night with Dru Bachman, Ann Markusen's Georgetown housemate, dressed in a zoot suit, a long coat with a lot of buttons and pockets, and flared pants. Before then, I'd seen zoot suits only in old movies. David's place in Bolton Gardens became an open house for a loose collection of young Americans, Britons, and others floating in and out of London. There were plenty of meals and parties, usually funded disproportionately by David, who had more money than the rest of us and was generous to a fault.

I also spent a lot of time alone at Oxford. I enjoyed the solitude of reading and was especially moved by a passage in Carl Sandburg's **The People, Yes**:

> Tell him to be alone often and get at himself
> and above all tell himself no lies about himself.
>
> . . .
>
> Tell him solitude is creative if he is strong
> and the final decisions are made in silent rooms.
>
> . . .
>
> He will be lonely enough
> to have time for the work
> he knows as his own.

Sandburg made me think something good could come of my wondering and worrying. I had always spent a lot of time alone, being an only child until I was ten, with both parents working. When I got into national politics, one of the more amusing myths propagated by people who didn't know me was that I hate to be by myself, probably because I relish the company of others, from huge crowds to small dinners and card games with friends. As President, I worked hard to schedule my time so that I'd have a couple of hours a day alone to think, reflect, plan, or do nothing. Often I slept less just to get the alone time. At Oxford, I was alone a lot, and I used the time to do the sorting out Sandburg said a good life requires.

In March, with spring coming, my spirits lifted along with the weather. During our five-week vacation break, I took my first trip to the Continent, taking a train to Dover to see the white cliffs, then going by ferry to Belgium, where I took a train to Cologne, Germany. At 9:30 p.m., I stepped out of the station into the shadow of the magnificent medieval cathedral just up the hill, and understood why Allied pilots in World War II risked their lives to avoid destroying it by flying too low in their efforts to bomb the nearby rail bridge over the Rhine River. I felt close to God in that cathedral, as I have every time I've returned to it. The next morning I met up with Rick Stearns, Ann Markusen, and my German friend Rudy Lowe, whom I'd met in 1967 at CONTAC in Washington, D.C., to tour Bavaria. In Bamberg, Rudy's thousand-year-old hometown, he took me to see the East German border nearby, where there was an East German soldier standing guard in a high outpost behind barbed wire on the edge of the Bavarian Forest.

While I was traveling, President Eisenhower died, "one of the final fragments that remained of the American Dream." So did my relationship with Ann Markusen, a casualty of the times and my incapacity for commitment.

It would be a long time before we reestablished our friendship.

Back in Oxford, George Kennan came to speak. Kennan had grave reservations about our Vietnam policy, and my friends and I were eager to hear him. Unfortunately, he stayed away from foreign policy, and instead launched into a diatribe against student demonstrators and the whole anti-war "counterculture." After some of my cohorts, especially Tom Williamson, debated him for a while, the show was over. Our consensus reaction was neatly summed up in a droll comment by Alan Bersin: "The book was better than the movie."

A couple of days later, I had an amazing dinner and argument with Rick Stearns, probably the most politically mature and savvy of our group. My diary notes that Rick "tore into my opposition to the draft," saying that the end of it would ensure that the poor would bear an even larger burden of military service. Instead, "Stearns wants national service, with alternate means of fulfillment to the military, but with inducements of shorter service time and higher salaries to keep the military force to acceptable levels. He believes everyone, not just the poor, should give community service." Thus was planted a seed that more than twenty years later, in my first presidential campaign, would blossom into my proposal for a national community service program for young people.

In the spring of 1969, the only national service was military, and its dimensions were measured by the callous term "body count." By mid-April, the count included my boyhood friend Bert Jeffries. In the agony of the aftermath, his wife gave birth a month prematurely to their child, who, like me, would grow up with received memories of a father. When Bert died, he was serving in the marines with two of his closest friends from Hot Springs, Ira Stone and Duke Watts. His family got to select one person to bring his body home, a choice of some consequence since, under military regulations, that person didn't have to go back. They chose Ira, who had already been wounded three times, in part because Duke, who had had his own narrow escapes from death, had only a month left on his tour. I cried for my friend, and wondered again whether my decision to go to Oxford was not motivated more by the desire to go on living than by opposition to the war. I noted in my diary that "the privilege of living in suspension . . . is impossible to justify, but, perhaps unfortunately, only very hard to live with."

Back home, the war protests continued unabated. In 1969, 448 universities had strikes or were forced to close. On April 22, I was surprised to read in **The Guardian** that Ed Whitfield from Little Rock had led an armed group of blacks to occupy a building on the campuses of Cornell University in Ithaca, New York. Just the summer before, Ed had been criticized by young militant blacks in Little Rock when we worked together to help Fulbright get reelected.

A week later, on April 30, the war finally came directly home to me, with a strange twist that was a metaphor for those bizarre times. I received my draft notice: I was ordered to report for duty on April 21. It's clear the notice had been mailed on April 1, but like my absentee ballot a few months earlier, it had been sent by surface mail. I called home to make sure the draft board knew I hadn't been a draft resister for nine days and asked what I should do. They told me the surface mailing was their mistake, and besides, under the rules, I got to finish the term I was in, so I was instructed to come home for induction when I finished.

I decided to make the most of what seemed certain to be the end of my Oxford stay, savoring every moment of the long English spring days. I went to the little village of Stoke Poges to see the beautiful churchyard where Thomas Gray is buried and read his "Elegy Written in a Country Churchyard," then to London to a concert and a visit to Highgate Cemetery, where Karl Marx is buried beneath a large bust that is a powerful likeness of him. I spent as much time as I could with the other Rhodes scholars, especially Strobe Talbott and Rick Stearns, from whom I was still learning. Over breakfast at George's, an old-fashioned café on the second floor of Oxford's covered market, Paul Parish and I discussed his application for conscientious-objector status, which I supported with a letter to his draft board.

In late May, along with Paul Parish and his lady friend, Sara Maitland, a witty, wonderful Scottish woman who later became a fine writer, I went to the Royal Albert Hall in London to hear the great gospel singer Mahalia Jackson. She was magnificent, with her booming voice and powerful, innocent faith. At the end of the concert, her young audience crowded around the stage, cheering and begging for an encore. They still hungered to believe in something larger than themselves. So did I.

On the twenty-eighth, I gave a farewell party at Univ for my friends: fellows from the college I'd played rugby and shared meals with; Douglas and the other porters; my scout, Archie; the Warden and Mrs. Williams; George Cawkwell; and an assortment of American, Indian, Caribbean, and South African students I'd gotten to know. I just wanted to thank them for being a big part of my year.

My friends gave me a number of going-away gifts: a walking stick, an English wool hat, and a paperback copy of Flaubert's **Madame Bovary,** which I still have.

I spent the first part of June seeing Paris. I didn't want to go home without having done so. I took a room in the Latin Quarter, finished reading George Orwell's **Down and Out in Paris and London,** and saw all the sights, including the amazing small memorial to the Holocaust just behind Notre Dame. It's easy to miss, but worth the effort. You walk downstairs at the end of the island into a small space, turn around, and find yourself peering into a gas chamber.

My guide and companion on the trip was Alice Chamberlin, whom I had met through mutual friends in London. We walked through the Tuileries, stopping at the ponds to watch the children and their sailboats; ate interesting and cheap Vietnamese, Algerian, Ethiopian, and West Indian food; scaled Montmartre; and visited the church called Sacré Coeur—where in reverence and humor I lit a candle for my friend Dr. Victor Bennett, who had died a few days before and who, for all his genius, was irrationally anti-Catholic. I was trying to cover all his bases. It was the least I could do after all he'd done for Mother, Daddy, and me.

By the time I got back to Oxford, it was light almost around the clock. In the wee hours of one morning, my English friends took me to the rooftop of one of Univ's buildings to watch the sun rise over the beautiful Oxford skyline. We were so pumped up we broke into the Univ kitchen, pinched some bread, sausages, tomatoes, and cheese, went back to my room for breakfast.

On June 24, I went to say good-bye to Bill Williams. He wished me well and said he expected me to become a "disgustingly enthusiastic, pompous old alumnus." That night I had my last Oxford meal at a pub with Tom Williamson and his friends. On the twenty-fifth, I said good-bye to Oxford—permanently, I believed. I went to London to meet Frank, Mary, and Lyda Holt. After we attended a night session of Parliament, and Judge and Mrs. Holt went home, I took Lyda to meet some friends for my last dinner in England, grabbed a couple of hours' sleep at David Edwards's place, then got up early and headed for the airport with six friends who came along to see me off. We didn't know when, if ever, we'd see each other again. I hugged them and ran for the plane.

SIXTEEN

I arrived in New York at 9:45 p.m., nine hours late, thanks to delays on both ends. By the time I got to Manhattan, it was after midnight, so I decided to stay up all night to catch an early-morning flight. I woke up Martha Saxton, and we sat and talked for two hours on the front steps of her place on the Upper West Side, then went to an all-night diner, where I got my first good hamburger in months, talked to two cabdrivers, read E. H. Carr's **What Is History?,** and thought about the extraordinary year I'd lived through and what lay ahead. And I stared at my nicest going-away gift: two little memory cards with French sayings entitled "L'Amitié" and "Sympathie." They had been given to me by Anik Alexis, a beautiful black Caribbean woman who was living in Paris and going out with Tom Williamson. Nikki had saved those cards for eight years, since she was a schoolgirl. I treasured them because they reflected the gifts I had tried to give, share, and draw out of others. I framed them and have put them up in every place I've lived for the past thirty-five years.

I left the diner with less than twenty dollars to get home to Arkansas, yet I wrote in the last page of my diary that I felt like "a wealthy man indeed, full of good fortune, and friends, and hope and convictions a bit more specific and well thought out than the ones with which I started this book last November." In that crazy time, my mood went up and down like an elevator. For good or ill, Denise Hyland had sent me a second diary in the spring to chronicle whatever happened next.

When I got home at the end of June, I had about a month before reporting for induction, during which I was free to make other military arrangements. There were no available spots in the National Guard or reserves. I looked into the air force, but learned I couldn't become a jet pilot because I didn't have fusion vision. I had a weak left eye, which had often tilted outward when I was very young. It had largely corrected itself, but my vision still didn't come to a single point, and apparently the consequences in flight could be severe. I also took a physical for a naval officer program but failed it, too, this time because of poor hearing, a problem I hadn't noticed and wouldn't until a decade later when I entered politics and often couldn't hear or understand people talking to me in crowds. The best option left seemed to be enrolling in law school and joining the Army Reserve Officers' Training Corps at the University of Arkansas.

On July 17, I went to Fayetteville and in two hours was accepted by both. The officer in charge of the program, Colonel Eugene Holmes, told me he was taking me because I would be of greater service to the country as an officer than as a draftee. His second in command, Lieutenant Colonel Clint Jones, seemed more conservative and skeptical of me, but we had a pleasant talk about his daughter, whom I had known and liked in Washington. Joining ROTC meant that I would go on active duty after law school. Apparently, they couldn't formally enroll me until the next summer, because I had to go to summer camp before I could enter ROTC classes, but signing a letter of intent was enough for the draft board to waive my induction date and give me a 1-D Reservist classification. I had mixed feelings. I knew I had a chance to avoid Vietnam, "but somebody will be getting on that bus in ten days and it may be that I should be getting on it too."

But ten days later I was not on the bus. Instead, I was in my car driving to Texas for a reunion with my Georgetown roommates who were already in the military, Tom Campbell, Jim Moore, and Kit Ashby. On the way there and back, I was alert to things that would reorient me to America. Houston and Dallas were crowded with large new apartment complexes, sprawling in no apparent pattern. I imagined that they were the wave of the future and I wasn't sure I wanted to go there. I read some cultural significance into the bumper stickers and personalized license plates I saw. My favorite bumper sticker said "Don't Blame Jesus If You Go to Hell." By far the best license tag was, unbelievably, attached to a hearse: "Pop Box." Apparently readers were supposed to fear hell but laugh at death.

I wasn't at the laughing stage yet, but I had always been aware of, and not all that uncomfortable with, my own mortality. Probably because my father had died before I was born, I started thinking about death at an early age. I've always been fascinated by cemeteries and enjoy spending time in them. On the way home from Texas I stopped in Hope to see Buddy and Ollie and visit the graves of my father and grandparents. As I picked the weeds from around their tombstones, I was struck again by how few years they'd had on earth: twenty-eight for my father, fifty-eight for Papaw, sixty-six for Mammaw (and back in Hot Springs, fifty-seven for my stepfather). I knew I might not have a long life and I wanted to make the most of it. My attitude toward death was captured by the punch line in an old joke about Sister Jones, the most devout woman in her church. One Sunday her normally boring minister preached the sermon of his life. At the end he shouted, "I want everyone who wants to go to heaven to stand up." The congregation leapt to their feet, everyone except Sister Jones. Her pastor was crestfallen. He said, "Sister Jones, don't you want to go to heaven when you die?" The good lady jumped right up and said, "Oh yes, preacher. I'm sorry. I thought you were trying to get up a load to go right now!"

The next six weeks in Hot Springs were more interesting than I could have imagined. I worked one week helping a sixty-seven-year-old man put up one of Jeff's pre-fab houses in the small settlement of Story, west of Hot Springs. The old guy worked me into the ground every day and shared a lot of his homespun wisdom and country skepticism with me. Just a month before, **Apollo 11** astronauts Buzz Aldrin and Neil Armstrong had left their colleague, Michael Collins, aboard spaceship **Columbia** and walked on the moon, beating by five months President Kennedy's goal of putting a man on the moon before the decade was out. The old carpenter asked me if I really believed it had happened. I said sure, I saw it on television. He disagreed; he said that he didn't believe it for a minute, that "them television fellers" could make things look real that weren't. Back then, I thought he was a crank. During my eight years in Washington, I saw some things on TV that made me wonder if he wasn't ahead of his time.

I spent most evenings and a lot of days with Betsey Reader, who had been a year ahead of me in school and was working in Hot Springs. She was a wonderful antidote to my unrelenting anxieties: wise, wistful, and kind. We were asked to go to the YMCA to be a semi-adult presence at some events for high schoolers and we sort of adopted three of them. Jeff Rosensweig, the son of my pediatrician, who was very knowledgeable about politics; Jan Dierks, a quiet, intelligent girl who was interested in civil rights; and Glenn Mahone, a hip, articulate black guy, who had a large Afro and liked to wear African dashikis, long, colorful shirts worn outside the pants. We went everywhere together and had a grand time.

Hot Springs had a couple of racial incidents that summer, and tensions were high. Glenn and I thought we could relieve them by forming an interracial rock band and hosting a free dance in the Kmart parking lot. He would sing and I'd play my sax. On the appointed night a big crowd showed up. We played up on a flatbed truck, and they danced and mingled on the pavement. Everything went well for about an hour. Then a handsome young black man asked a pretty blond girl to dance. They were good together—too good. It was too much for some of the rednecks to bear. A fight broke out, then another, and another. Before we knew it we had a full-fledged brawl on our hands and police cars in the parking lot. So ended my first initiative in racial reconciliation.

One day Mack McLarty, who had been elected to the legislature just out of college, came to Hot Springs for a Ford dealers' convention. He was already married and settled into serious business and politics. I wanted to see him and decided to play a little joke on him in front of his highly conventional colleagues. I made arrangements to meet him on the plaza outside our convention center. He didn't know I'd grown long hair and a beard. That was bad enough, but I took three people with me: two English girls who had stopped in Hot Springs on a cross-country bus trip and looked the way you look after two or three days on a bus; and Glenn Mahone with his Afro and dashiki. We looked like refugees from the Woodstock festival. When Mack walked out onto the plaza with two of his friends, we must have caused him heartburn. But he never broke a sweat; he just greeted me and introduced us around. Underneath his starched shirt and short hair were a heart and a brain that sympathized with the peace and civil rights movements. He's stuck with me through thick and thin for a lifetime, but I never put him to a sterner test.

As the summer wore on, I felt worse and worse about my decision to join the ROTC and go to Arkansas Law School. I had a hard time sleeping, and spent most nights in the den in the white reclining chair in which I'd watched Martin Luther King Jr.'s "I have a dream" speech six years earlier. I'd read until I could nod off for a few hours. Because I had joined the ROTC late, I couldn't go to the required summer camp until the following summer, so Colonel Holmes agreed to let me go back to Oxford for a second year, which meant that I wouldn't begin my post–law school military service for four years rather than three. I was still disturbed by my decision.

A conversation with Reverend John Miles's brother made me more uncertain. Warren Miles quit school at eighteen to join the marines and go to Korea, where he was wounded in action. He came home and went to Hendrix College, where he won a Rhodes scholarship. He encouraged me to bag the safety of my present course, join the marines, and go to Vietnam, where at least I'd really learn something. He dismissed my opposition to the war out of hand, saying there was not a thing I could do about the fact of the war, and as long as it was there, decent people ought to go, experience, learn, remember. It was a hell of an argument. But I already remembered. I remembered what I'd learned working on the Foreign Relations Committee, including the classified evidence that the American people were being misled about the war. And I remembered Bert Jeffries's letter telling me to stay away. I was really torn. As the son of a World War II veteran, and as someone who grew up on John Wayne movies, I had always admired people who served in the military. Now I searched my heart, trying to determine whether my aversion to going was rooted in conviction or cowardice. Given the way it played out, I'm not sure I ever answered the question for myself.

Near the end of September, while working my way back to Oxford, I flew to Martha's Vineyard for a reunion of anti-war activists who had worked for Gene McCarthy. Of course, I hadn't done so. Rick Stearns invited me, I think because he knew I wanted to come and they wanted another southerner. The only other one there was Taylor Branch, a recent graduate of the University of North Carolina, who had just been in Georgia registering blacks to vote. Taylor went on to a distinguished career in journalism, helped John Dean of Watergate fame and basketball great Bill Russell write their autobiographies, then wrote his magnificent Pulitzer Prize–winning book, **Parting the Waters,** the first volume of a planned trilogy on Martin Luther King Jr. and the civil rights movement. Taylor and I formed a friendship that would lead us into the Texas McGovern campaign together in 1972, and then, in 1993, into an almost monthly oral history of my presidency, without which many of my memories of those years would be lost.

Besides Rick and Taylor, there were four other men at the reunion whom I kept up with over the years: Sam Brown, one of the most prominent leaders of the student anti-war movement, later got involved in Colorado politics and, when I was President, served the United States with the Organization for Security and Cooperation in Europe; David Mixner, who had begun organizing fellow migrant workers at fourteen, visited me several times in England and later moved to California, where he became active in the struggle against AIDS and for gay rights, and supported me in 1992; Mike Driver became one of my most cherished friends over the next thirty years; and Eli Segal, whom I met in the McGovern campaign, became chief of staff of the Clinton-Gore campaign.

All of us who gathered that weekend have since led lives we couldn't have imagined as autumn dawned in 1969. We just wanted to help stop the war. The group was planning the next large protest, known as the Vietnam Moratorium, and I made what little contribution I could to their deliberations. But mostly I was thinking about the draft, and feeling more and more uncomfortable with the way I'd handled it. Just before I left Arkansas for Martha's Vineyard, I wrote a letter to Bill Armstrong, chairman of my local draft board, telling him I didn't really want to do the ROTC program and asking him to withdraw my 1-D deferment and put me back in the draft. Strobe Talbott came to Arkansas to visit and we discussed whether I should mail it. I didn't.

The day I flew out, our local paper carried the front-page news that Army Lieutenant Mike Thomas, who had defeated me for student council president in junior high school, had been killed in Vietnam. Mike's unit came under attack and took cover. He died when he went back into the line of fire to rescue one of his men who was trapped in their vehicle; a mortar shell killed them both. After his death, the army gave him a Silver Star, a Bronze Star, and a Purple Heart. Now almost 39,000 Americans had perished in Vietnam, with 19,000 casualties still to come.

On September 25 and 26, I wrote in my diary: "Reading **The Unfinished Odyssey of Robert Kennedy** [by David Halberstam], I was reminded again that I don't believe in deferments. . . . I cannot do this ROTC." Sometime in the next few days, I called Jeff Dwire, told him I wanted to be put back in the draft, and asked him to tell Bill Armstrong. On October 30, the draft board reclassified me 1-A. On October 1, President Nixon had ordered a change in Selective Service System policy to allow graduate students to finish the entire school year they were in, not just the term, so I wouldn't be called until July. I don't remember, and my diary doesn't indicate, whether I asked Jeff to talk to the local board before or after I learned that graduate deferments had been extended to a full academic year. I do remember feeling relieved both that I'd get to spend some more time at Oxford and that the draft situation was resolved: I was reconciled to the fact that I'd probably be called up at the end of the Oxford year.

I also asked Jeff to talk to Colonel Holmes. I still felt an obligation to him: he had helped keep me from induction on July 28. Even though I was now 1-A again, if he held me to my commitment to the ROTC program beginning with next summer's camp, I thought I would have to do it. Jeff indicated that the colonel accepted my decision, but thought I was making a mistake.

On December 1, pursuant to a bill signed by President Nixon five days earlier, the United States instituted a draft lottery, with a drawing in which all the days of the year were pulled out of a bowl. The order in which your birth-day came up determined the order in which you could be drafted. August 19 came up 311. Even with the high lottery number, for months afterward, I thought I had a fair chance of being drafted. On March 21, 1970, I got a letter from Lee Williams saying that he had talked to Colonel Lefty Hawkins, the head of the Arkansas Selective Service System, who told him we would all be called.

When I got the high draft number, I called Jeff again and asked him to tell Colonel Holmes that I hadn't gone back into the draft knowing this would happen and that I understood that he could still call me on the ROTC obligation. Then, on December 3, I sat down and wrote Colonel Holmes. I thanked him for protecting me from the draft the previous summer, told him how much I admired him, and said I doubted that he would have admired me had he known more about my political beliefs and activities: "At least you might have thought me more fit for the draft than for ROTC." I described my work for the Foreign Relations Committee, "a time when not many people had more information about Vietnam at hand than I did." I told him that, after I left Arkansas the previous summer, I did some work for the Vietnam Moratorium in Washington and in England. I also told him I had studied the draft at Georgetown, and had concluded it was justified only when, as in World War II, the nation and our way of life were at stake. I expressed sympathy with conscientious objectors and draft resisters. I told him Frank Aller, whom I identified only as my roommate, was "one of the bravest, best men I know. His country needs men like him more than they know. That he is considered a criminal is an obscenity." Then I admitted I had considered being a resister myself, and accepted the draft "in spite of my beliefs for one reason: to maintain my political viability within the system." I also admitted that I had asked to be accepted in the ROTC program because it was the only way I could "possibly, but not positively, avoid both Vietnam and resistance." I confessed to the colonel that "after I signed the ROTC letter of intent I began to wonder whether the compromise I had made with myself was not more objectionable than the draft would have been, because I had no interest in the ROTC program in itself and all I seemed to have done was to protect myself from physical harm . . . after we had made our agreement and you had sent my 1-D deferment to my draft board, the anguish and loss of self-regard and self-confidence really set in." Then I told the colonel that I had written a letter to the draft board on September 12 asking to be put back into the draft but never mailed it. I didn't mention that I had asked Jeff Dwire to get me reclassified 1-A and that the local draft board had done so at the October meeting, because I knew Jeff had already told the colonel that. I said that I hoped that "my telling this one story will help you to understand more clearly how so many fine people have come to find themselves still loving their country but loathing the military, to which you and other good men have devoted years, lifetimes, of the best service you could give." It was how I felt at the time, as a young man deeply troubled and conflicted about the war. In any case, I still considered myself bound to the ROTC commitment if Colonel Holmes called me on it. Because he didn't reply to my letter, I didn't know for several months what he would do.

In March 1970, at about the same time I heard from Lee Williams that he expected all the lottery numbers to be called, I received two tapes made by my family while David Edwards was visiting them in Hot Springs. The first tape contains a lot of good-natured bantering around our pool table, ending with Roger playing the saxophone for me while our German shepherd, King, howled. The second tape has personal messages from Mother and Jeff. Mother told me how much she loved me and urged me to get more rest. Jeff gave me an update on family matters, then spoke these words:

> I took the liberty of calling the Colonel a few days ago and visiting with him a little. He wishes you well and hopes you'll find time to drop by and say hello to him on your return. I would not be concerned at all regarding the ROTC program as far as he is concerned, because he apparently understands more about the general overall situation of our young people than people would give him credit for.

So by the second week of March 1970, I knew I was free of the ROTC obligation, but not the draft.

As it turned out, Lee Williams was wrong. The deescalation of the war reduced the need for new troops to the point that my number was never called. I always felt bad about escaping the risks that had taken the lives of so many of my generation whose claim to a future was as legitimate as mine. Over the years—as governor, when I was in charge of the Arkansas National Guard, and especially after I became President—the more I saw of America's military, the more I wished I'd been a part of it when I was young, though I never changed my feelings about Vietnam.

If I hadn't gone to Georgetown and worked on the Foreign Relations Committee, I might have made different decisions about military service. During the Vietnam era, 16 million men avoided military service through legal means; 8.7 million enlisted; 2.2 million were drafted; only 209,000 were alleged to have dodged the draft or resisted, of whom 8,750 were convicted.

Those of us who could have gone to Vietnam but didn't were nevertheless marked by it, especially if we had friends who were killed there. I was always interested to see how others who took a pass and later got into public life dealt with military issues and political dissent. Some of them turned out to be superhawks and hyperpatriots, claiming that personal considerations justified their failure to serve while still condemning those who opposed a war they themselves had avoided. By 2002, Vietnam apparently had receded so far into the shadows of the American psyche that in Georgia, Republican congressman Saxby Chambliss, who had a Vietnam-era deferment, was able to defeat Senator Max Cleland, who lost three limbs in Vietnam, by questioning his patriotism and commitment to America's security.

In stark contrast to the activities of the nonserving superhawks, America's efforts to reconcile and normalize relations with Vietnam were led by distinguished Vietnam veterans in Congress, like Chuck Robb, John McCain, John Kerry, Bob Kerrey, Chuck Hagel, and Pete Peterson, men who had more than paid their dues and had nothing to hide or prove.

When I returned to Oxford in early October for my surprise second year, the circumstances of my life were almost as complicated as they had been in Arkansas. I didn't have a place to stay, because until the end of summer I hadn't thought I was coming back, and we got guaranteed rooms in college only the first year. I lived with Rick Stearns for a couple of weeks, during which we worked on and participated in our own Vietnam Moratorium observance at the U.S. embassy in London on October 15, in support of the main event back in the United States. I also helped to organize a teach-in at the London School of Economics.

Eventually, I found a home for the rest of my stay at Oxford with Strobe Talbott and Frank Aller, at 46 Leckford Road. Someone else who had been slated to live with them left, and they needed me to share the rent. We paid about thirty-six pounds a month—$86.40 at the exchange rate of $2.40 a pound. The place was pretty rundown but more than adequate for us. On the first floor there was a small sitting room and a bedroom for me, along with a kitchen and a bathroom, which was the first thing you saw when you entered the house. The bathroom door had a glass window covered with a portrait of a woman in pre-Raphaelite style on a thin sheet that made it look like stained glass from a distance. It was the most elegant part of the house. Strobe's and Frank's bedrooms and workspaces were on the second and third floors. We had a small, scraggly walled-in yard in the back.

Unlike me, Strobe and Frank were doing serious work. Frank was writing a thesis on the epic Long March in the Chinese civil war. He had been to Switzerland to see Edgar Snow, whose famous book **Red Star Over China** chronicles his unique experiences with Mao and his revolutionaries in Yenan. Snow had given Frank some of his unpublished notes to use, and it was clear that he was going to produce a scholarly work of real significance.

Strobe was working on an even bigger project, Nikita Khrushchev's memoirs. Khrushchev was known in the United States for his confrontations with Kennedy and

Nixon, but as Cold War Soviets went, he was a reformer and a fascinating character. He had built the beautiful Moscow subway system and denounced Stalin's murderous excesses. After more orthodox conservative forces removed him from power and installed Brezhnev and Kosygin, Khrushchev secretly recorded his memoirs on tape, and arranged, I think through friends in the KGB, to get them to Jerry Schecter, then **Time** magazine's bureau chief in Moscow. Strobe was fluent in Russian and had worked for **Time** in Moscow the previous summer. He flew to Copenhagen to meet Schecter and get the tapes. When he got back to Oxford, he began the laborious process of typing Khrushchev's words out in Russian, then translating and editing them.

On many mornings, I would make breakfast for Frank and Strobe as they began their work. I was a pretty fair short-order cook. I'd take them the products of "Mother Clinton's Country Kitchen" and check on their work. I was especially fascinated to hear Strobe recount Khrushchev's tales of Kremlin intrigue. Strobe's seminal book, **Khrushchev Remembers,** made a major contribution in the West to the understanding of the inner workings and tensions of the Soviet Union, and raised the hope that someday internal reform might bring more freedom and openness.

On November 15, the second, larger Moratorium service was held, with more than five hundred people marching around Grosvenor Square in front of the U.S. Embassy. We were joined by Father Richard McSorley, a Jesuit on the Georgetown faculty who had long been active in the peace movement. As a chaplain in World War II, McSorley survived the Bataan death march, and he later became close to Robert Kennedy and his family.

After the demonstration, we had a prayer service at St. Mark's Church near the embassy. Father McSorley recited the peace prayer of St. Francis of Assisi, and Rick Stearns read John Donne's famous lines that end "Never send to know for whom the bell tolls; it tolls for thee."

After Thanksgiving, Tom Williamson and I flew to Dublin to meet Hillary Hart and Martha Saxton, whom I had been seeing on and off for several months. More than thirty years later, Martha reminded me that on that trip I said she was too sad for me. Actually, back then, as anguished as I was about Vietnam, I was too sad for her, or anyone else. But even sad, I loved Ireland, and felt at home there. I hated to leave after just a weekend.

By Saturday, December 6, three days after I wrote the letter to Colonel Holmes, I was in London at David Edwards's flat for a big event, the Arkansas-Texas football game. Both teams were undefeated. Texas was ranked first and Arkansas second in the national polls. They were playing for the national championship in the last regular-season game of the one hundredth year of college football. I rented a shortwave radio, which wasn't too expensive but required a fifty-pound deposit, a lot of money for me. David whipped up a big pot of good chili. We had a few friends over who thought we had lost our minds as we whooped and hollered through a football game so exciting it was billed as the Game of the Century. For a few hours, we were innocent again, totally caught up in the contest.

The game and its cultural and political contexts have been beautifully chronicled by Terry Frei in his book **Horns, Hogs, and Nixon Coming.** Frei subtitled his book **Texas v. Arkansas in Dixie's Last Stand,** because it was the last major sporting event involving two all-white teams.

A few days earlier, the White House had announced that President Nixon, a fanatic football fan, would attend the game and present the national championship trophy to the winner. Nine members of Congress would accompany him, including his Vietnam nemesis Senator Fulbright, who had played for the Razorbacks more than forty years earlier, and a young Texas congressman, George H. W. Bush. Also slated to come were White House aides Henry Kissinger and H. R. Haldeman, and Ron Ziegler, the press secretary.

Arkansas kicked off to Texas, forced a fumble on the first possession, and scored less than a minute and a half into the game. At halftime, with Arkansas still leading 7–0, President Nixon was interviewed. He said, "I expect to see both teams score in the second half. The question is whether Texas's superior manpower, and I mean probably a stronger bench, may win in the last quarter. That's the way I see it." On the first play of the fourth quarter, with Arkansas leading 14–0, the Texas quarterback, James Street, made an amazing forty-two-yard touchdown run on a busted play. Texas went for the two-point conversion, got it, and was behind only 14–8. On the next possession, Arkansas immediately took the ball down to the Texas seven. With the best field-goal kicker in the country, Arkansas could have kicked a field goal, making the score 17–8 and requiring Texas to score twice to win. But a pass play was called. The pass fell a little bit short and was intercepted. With just under five minutes left, Texas had a fourth down and three yards to go on its own forty-three-yard line. The quarterback completed a miraculous pass to a well-defended receiver at the Arkansas thirteen-yard line. Two plays later, Texas scored and took the lead, 15–14. On its last drive,

Arkansas moved the ball down the field on short passes, mostly to its talented tailback, Bill Burnett, who was having a good day running the ball and who would soon become Colonel Eugene Holmes's son-in-law. After a thrilling game, Texas intercepted an Arkansas pass, ran the last minute and twenty-two seconds off the clock, and won 15–14.

It had been a magnificent game. Even several of the Texas players said neither team should have lost. The only really bad taste in my mouth came from President Nixon's prediction at halftime that Texas might well win the game in the fourth quarter. For years afterward, I think I held that against him almost as much as Watergate.

The fact that David Edwards and I went to the trouble of renting a shortwave radio to listen to a football game won't surprise anyone who grew up in America's sports-mad culture. Supporting the Razorback football team was central to the idea of being an Arkansan. Before our family got a television, I listened to all the games on my radio. In high school, I carried equipment for the Razorback band just to get into the games. At Georgetown, I watched all the Razorback games that were televised. When I moved back home, as a law professor, attorney general, and governor, I got to virtually every home game. When Eddie Sutton became the basketball coach and his wife, Patsy, took an active role in my 1980 campaign, I also began going to all the basketball games I could. When Coach Nolan Richardson's Arkansas team won the NCAA Championship over Duke in 1994, I was in the arena.

Of all the great football games I ever watched, only the Game of the Century had any impact on my political career. Though the anti-war demonstrators weren't

shown on national television, they were there. One of
them was perched up in a tree on the hill overlooking the
stadium. The next day, his picture was in many of the
daily and weekly papers in Arkansas. Five years later, in
1974, shortly before my first congressional election, my
opponent's campaign workers called newspapers all over
the congressional district asking if they had kept a copy of
"that picture of Bill Clinton up in the tree demonstrating
against Nixon at the Arkansas-Texas game." The rumor
spread like wildfire and cost me a lot of votes. In 1978,
when I ran for governor the first time, a state trooper in
south Arkansas swore to several people that he was the
very one who pulled me out of the tree that day. In 1979,
my first year as governor, and ten years after the Game,
when I was answering questions at a high school assembly
in Berryville, about an hour's drive east of Fayetteville, a
student asked me whether I had really been in the tree.
When I asked who had heard the rumor, half the students
and three-quarters of the teachers raised their hands. In
1983, fourteen years after the Game, I went to Tonti-
town, a small community north of Fayetteville, to crown
the queen of the annual Grape Festival. After I did, the
sixteen-year-old girl looked at me and said, "Did you
really get up in that tree without any clothes on and
demonstrate against President Nixon and the war?"
When I said no, she replied, "Oh, shoot. That's one reason I've always been for you!" Even though I had even
lost my clothes as the story ripened, the worm seemed to
be turning on it. Alas, not long afterward, Fayetteville's
irreverently liberal weekly paper, **The Grapevine,** finally
put the loony old tale to rest with a story on the real pro-
tester, including the picture of him in the tree. The
author of the article also said that when Governor Clin-

ton was young, he was far too "preppy" to do anything as adventurous as that.

That long-ago football game was a chance for me to enjoy a sport I loved, and to feel closer to home. I had just started reading Thomas Wolfe's **You Can't Go Home Again** and was afraid it might turn out that way for me. And I was about to go farther away from home than I had ever been, in more ways than one.

At the end of the first week of December, during our long winter break, I began a forty-day trip that would take me from Amsterdam through the Scandinavian countries to Russia, then back to Oxford through Prague and Munich. It was, and remains, the longest trip of my life.

I went to Amsterdam with my artist friend Aimée Gautier. The streets were covered with Christmas lights and lined with charming shops. The famous red-light district featured perfectly legal prostitutes sitting on display in their windows. Aimée jokingly asked if I wanted to go into one of the places, but I declined.

We toured the main churches, saw the Van Goghs at the Municipal Museum and the Vermeers and Rembrandts at the Rijksmuseum. At closing time, we were asked to leave the wonderful old place. I went to the cloakroom to pick up our coats. There was only one other person left in line to pick up his. When he turned around, I found myself facing Rudolf Nureyev. We exchanged a few words and he asked me if I wanted to go get a cup of tea. I knew Aimée would love it, but just outside the front door, a handsome, frowning young man was anxiously pacing, obviously waiting for Nureyev, so I took a pass. Years later, when I was governor, I found myself in the same hotel with Nureyev in Taipei, Taiwan. We finally got our cup of tea late one night after we had fulfilled our respective obligations. Obviously he didn't recall our first meeting.

In Amsterdam, I said good-bye to Aimée, who was going home, and left on the train to Copenhagen, Oslo, and Stockholm. At the border between Norway and Sweden, I was almost put out in the middle of nowhere.

At a tiny railroad station, the guards searched the luggage of all the young people, looking for drugs. In my bag they found a lot of Contac pills, which I was taking to a friend in Moscow. Contac was relatively new and for some reason wasn't yet on the Swedish government's list of approved drugs. I tried to explain that the pills were just for colds, widely available in American drugstores and without any addictive qualities. The guard confiscated the Contac pills, but at least I wasn't thrown out into the snowy desolation for drug trafficking, where I might have become an interesting piece of ice sculpture, perfectly preserved until the spring thaw.

After a couple of days in Stockholm, I took an overnight ferry to Helsinki. Late in the night, as I was sitting by myself at a table in the dining area reading a book and drinking coffee, a fight broke out at the bar. Two very drunk men were fighting over the only girl there. Both men were too inebriated to defend themselves but managed to land blows on each other. Before long they were both gushing blood. One of them was a member of the crew, with two or three of his mates just standing there watching. Finally I couldn't stand it anymore. I got up and walked over to stop the fight before they did themselves serious damage. When I got about ten feet from them, one of the other crewmen blocked my way and said, "You can't stop the fight. If you try, they'll both turn on you.

And we'll help them." When I asked why, he just smiled and replied, "We're Finns." I shrugged, turned away, picked up my book, and went to bed, having absorbed another lesson about different cultures. I bet neither one of them got the girl.

I checked into a small hotel and began touring the city with Georgetown classmate Richard Shullaw, whose father was deputy chief of mission in the American embassy there.

On Christmas Day, the first I'd ever spent away from home, I walked out onto Helsinki Bay. The ice was thick, and there was enough snow on it to give some traction. Amid all the natural beauty I saw a small wooden house a few yards from the shore, and a small round hole in the ice a few yards out. The house was a sauna, and soon a man came out in a skimpy swimsuit. He marched straight out onto the ice and lowered himself into the hole and its frigid water. After a couple of minutes, he got out, went back into the sauna, and repeated the ritual. I thought he was crazier than the two guys in the bar. In time I came to enjoy the hot steam of the sauna, but despite my growing love for Finland during several trips since, I could never get into the ice water.

On New Year's Eve, I boarded the train to Moscow with an interim stop in Leningrad's Finland Station. It was the same route Lenin had taken in 1917 when he returned to Russia to take over the revolution. It was on my mind because I had read Edmund Wilson's marvelous book **To the Finland Station.** When we came to the Russian border, another isolated outpost, I met my first real live Communist, a pudgy, cherubic-looking guard. When he eyed my bags suspiciously, I expected him to check for drugs. Instead, he asked in his heavily accented

English, "Dirty books? Dirty books? Got any dirty books?" I laughed and opened my book bag, pouring out Penguin paperback novels by Tolstoy, Dostoevsky, and Turgenev. He was so disappointed. I guess he longed for contraband that would enliven those long, lonely nights on the frigid frontier.

The Soviet train was filled with spacious compartments. Each car had a giant samovar full of hot tea that was served along with black bread by an elderly woman. I shared my berth with an interesting man who had been the coach of the Estonian boxing team in the 1936 Olympics, three years before the Soviet Union absorbed the Baltic states. We both spoke enough German to communicate a little. He was a lively fellow who told me with absolute confidence that one day Estonia would be free again. In 2002, when I traveled to Tallinn, Estonia's beautiful old capital, I told this story to the audience I addressed. My friend, former president Lennart Meri, was at the speech and did some quick research for me. The man's name was Peter Matsov. He died in 1980. I think often of him and our New Year's Eve train ride. I wish he had lived another decade to see his dream come true.

It was nearly midnight and the dawn of a new decade when we pulled into Leningrad. I got out and walked for a few minutes, but all I saw were policemen dragging inebriated celebrants off the streets in a driving snowstorm. It would be nearly thirty years before I got to see the splendor of the city. By then the Communists were gone and its original name, St. Petersburg, had been restored.

On New Year's morning 1970, I began an amazing five days. I had prepared for the trip to Moscow by getting a guidebook and a good street map in English since I couldn't read the Russian Cyrillic script.

I checked into the National Hotel, just off Red Square. It had a huge high-ceiling lobby, comfortable rooms, and a nice restaurant and bar.

The only person I knew in Moscow was Nikki Alexis, who had given me the two friendship cards I loved when I went home from Oxford the previous summer. She was an amazing woman, born in Martinique in the West Indies, living in Paris because her father was a diplomat there. Nikki was studying at Lumumba University, named after the Congolese leader who was murdered in 1961, apparently with the complicity of the U.S. Central Intelligence Agency. Most of the students were poor people from poor countries. The Soviets obviously hoped that by educating them they'd be making converts when they went home.

One night I took a bus out to Lumumba University to have dinner with Nikki and some of her friends. One of them was a Haitian woman named Helene whose husband was studying in Paris. They had a daughter who was living with him. They had no money to travel and hadn't seen each other in almost two years. When I left Russia a few days later, Helene gave me one of those trademark Russian fur hats. It wasn't expensive but she had no money. I asked her if she was sure she wanted me to have it. She replied, "Yes. You were kind to me and you made me have hope." In 1994, when, as President, I made the decision to remove Haiti's military dictator, General Raoul Cedras, and return the democratically elected President Jean-Bertrand Aristide, I thought of that good woman for the first time in years, and wondered if she ever went back to Haiti.

Around midnight, I rode the bus to my hotel. There was only one other person on it. His name was Oleg Rakito and he spoke better English than I did. He asked me

lots of questions and told me he worked for the government, virtually admitting he was assigned to keep an eye
on me. He said he'd like to continue our conversation at
breakfast the next morning. As we ate cold bacon and eggs
he told me he read **Time** and **Newsweek** every week and
loved the British pop star Tom Jones, whose songs he got
on bootlegged tapes. If Oleg was pumping me for information because I had had a security clearance when I
worked for Senator Fulbright, he came up dry. But I
learned some things from him about the thirst of a young
person behind the Iron Curtain for real information about
the outside world. That stayed with me all the way to the
White House.

Oleg wasn't the only friendly Russian I encountered.
President Nixon's policy of détente was having noticeable
results. A few months earlier, Russian television had
shown the Americans walking on the moon. People were
still excited about it and seemed to be fascinated by all
things American. They envied our freedom and assumed
we were all rich. I guess, compared with most of them, we
were. Whenever I took the subway, people would come up
to me and say proudly, "I speak English! Welcome to
Moscow." One night I shared dinner with a few hotel
guests, a local cabdriver, and his sister. The girl had a bit
too much to drink and decided she wanted to stay with
me. Her brother had to drag her out of the hotel into the
snow and shove her into his cab. I never knew whether he
was afraid being with me would guarantee her a grilling by
the KGB, or he just thought I was unworthy of his sister.

My most interesting Moscow adventure began with a
chance encounter in the hotel elevator. When I got in,
there were four other men in the car. One of them was
wearing a Virginia Lions Club pin. He obviously thought

I was a foreigner, with my long hair and beard, rawhide boots, and British navy pea jacket. He drawled, "Where you from?" When I smiled and said, "Arkansas," he replied, "Shoot, I thought you were from Denmark or someplace like that!" The man's name was Charlie Daniels. He was from Norton, Virginia, hometown of Francis Gary Powers, the U-2 pilot who had been shot down and captured in Russia in 1960. He was accompanied by Carl McAfee, a lawyer from Norton who had helped to arrange Powers's release, and a chicken farmer from Washington State, Henry Fors, whose son had been shot down in Vietnam. They had come all the way to Moscow to see if the North Vietnamese stationed there would tell the farmer whether his son was dead or alive. The fourth man was from Paris and, like the men from Virginia, a member of the Lions Club. He had joined them because the North Vietnamese spoke French. They all just came to Moscow without any assurances that the Russians would permit them to talk with the Vietnamese or that, if they did, any information would be forthcoming. None of them spoke Russian. They asked if I knew anyone who could help them. My old friend Nikki Alexis was studying English, French, and Russian at Patrice Lumumba University. I introduced her to them and they spent a couple of days together making the rounds, checking in with the American embassy, asking the Russians to help, finally seeing the North Vietnamese, who apparently were impressed that Mr. Fors and his friends would make such an effort to learn the fate of his son and several others who were missing in action. They said they would check into it and get back to them. A few weeks later, Henry Fors learned that his son had been killed when his plane was shot down. At least he had some peace of mind. I thought of Henry Fors when I worked to resolve POW/MIA cases as President and to help the Vietnamese find out what had happened to more than 300,000 of their people still unaccounted for.

On January 6, Nikki and her Haitian friend Helene put me on the train to Prague, one of the most beautiful old cities in Europe, still reeling from the Soviet repression of Alexander Dubček's Prague Spring reform movement in August 1968. I had been invited to stay with the parents of Jan Kopold, who played basketball with me at Oxford. The Kopolds were nice people whose personal history was closely entwined with that of modern Czechoslovakia. Mrs. Kopold's father had been editor in chief of the Communist newspaper **Rude Pravo,** died fighting the Nazis in World War II, and had a bridge in Prague named for him. Both Mr. and Mrs. Kopold were academics and had been big supporters of Dubček. Mrs. Kopold's mother also lived with them. She took me around town during the day when the Kopolds were working. They lived in a nice apartment in a modern high-rise with a beautiful view of the city. I stayed in Jan's room and was so excited I woke up three or four times a night just to stare at the skyline.

The Kopolds, like all the Czechs I met, held on to the belief that their chance at freedom would come again. They deserved it as much as anyone on earth. They were intelligent, proud, and determined. The young Czechs I met were especially pro-American. They supported our government in Vietnam because we were for freedom and the Soviets weren't. Mr. Kopold once said to me, "Even the Russians cannot defy forever the laws of historical development." Sure enough, they couldn't. In twenty years, Václav Havel's peaceful "Velvet Revolution" would reclaim the promise of Prague Spring.

Ten months after I left the Kopolds to go back to Oxford, I received the following notice from them, written on simple white paper with black borders: "With immense pain we want to inform his friends that on July 29 in the University Hospital in Smyrna, Turkey, died at the young age of 23 Jan Kopold. . . . For a long time it was his great desire to visit what remains of the Hellenic culture. It was not far from Troy that he fell from a height and succumbed from the injuries he sustained." I really liked Jan, with his ready smile and good mind. When I knew him, he was tortured by the conflict between his love of Czechoslovakia and his love of freedom. I wish he had lived to enjoy both.

After six days in Prague, I stopped in Munich to celebrate Faschingsfest with Rudy Lowe, then returned to England with renewed faith in America and democracy. For all its faults, I had discovered that my country was still a beacon of light to people chafing under communism. Ironically, when I ran for President in 1992, the Republicans tried to use the trip against me, claiming that I had consorted with Communists in Moscow.

With a new term, I got back into my tutorials in politics, including studies on the relevance of scientific theories to strategic planning; the problem of making a conscript army into a patriotic one, from Napoleon to Vietnam; and the problems China and Russia posed for U.S. policy. I read Herman Kahn on the probabilities of nuclear war, different destruction levels, and post-attack behavior. It was Strangelove-like and unconvincing. I noted in my diary that "what happens after the fireworks begin may not pursue the set course of any scientific systems and analysts' models."

While I was enduring another sunless English winter, letters and cards from home streamed in. My friends were getting jobs, getting married, getting on with their lives. Their normalcy looked pretty good after all the anguish I'd felt over Vietnam.

March and the coming of spring brightened things up a bit. I read Hemingway, tended to tutorials, and talked to my friends, including a fascinating new one. Mandy Merck had come to Oxford from Reed College in Oregon. She was hyperkinetic and highly intelligent, the only American woman I met at Oxford who was more than a match for her British counterparts in fast, free-flowing conversation. She was also the first openly lesbian woman I'd known. March was a big month for my awareness of homosexuality. Paul Parish came out to me, too, and was mortally afraid of being branded a social pariah. He suffered for a long time. Now he's in San Francisco, and, in his own words, "safe and legal." Mandy Merck stayed in England and became a journalist and gay-rights advocate. Back then, her brilliant banter brightened my spring.

Rick Stearns threw me for a loop one night when he told me I was unsuited for politics. He said Huey Long and I both had great southern political styles, but Long was a political genius who understood how to get and use power. He said my gifts were more literary, that I should be a writer because I wrote better than I spoke, and besides, I wasn't tough enough for politics. A lot of people have thought that over the years. Rick was close to right, though. I never loved power for power's sake, but whenever I got hit by my opponents, I usually mustered enough toughness to survive. Besides, I didn't think I could do anything else as well.

In early 1970, having received Jeff Dwire's tape

recounting his conversation with Colonel Holmes and the high lottery number, I knew I was out of ROTC and wouldn't be drafted at least until late in the year. If I wasn't called, I was torn between coming back to Oxford for a third year, which the Rhodes scholarship would cover, or going to Yale Law School, if I was accepted.

I loved Oxford, maybe too much. I was afraid if I came back for a third year, I might drift into a comfortable but aimless academic life that would disappoint me in the end. Given my feelings about the war, I wasn't at all sure I'd ever make it in politics, but I was inclined to go back home to America and give it a chance.

In April, during the break between second and third terms, I took one last trip—to Spain, with Rick Stearns. I had been reading up on Spain and was totally mesmerized by it, thanks to André Malraux's **Man's Hope,** George Orwell's **Homage to Catalonia,** and Hugh Thomas's masterly **The Spanish Civil War.** Malraux explored the dilemma war presents to intellectuals, many of whom were drawn to the fight against Franco. He said the intellectual wants to make distinctions, to know precisely what he is fighting for and how he must fight, an attitude that is by definition anti-Manichean, but every warrior is by definition a Manichean. To kill and stay alive he must see things starkly as black and white, evil and good. I recognized the same thing in politics years later when the Far Right took over the Republican Party and the Congress. Politics to them was simply war by other means. They needed an enemy and I was the demon on the other side of the Manichean divide.

I never got over the romantic pull of Spain, the raw pulse of the land, the expansive, rugged spirit of the people, the haunting memories of the lost civil war, the Prado, the beauty of the Alhambra. When I was President, Hillary and I became friends with King Juan Carlos and Queen Sofia. (On my last trip to Spain, President Juan Carlos had remembered my telling him of my nostalgia about Granada and took Hillary and me back there. After thirty years I walked through the Alhambra again, in a Spain now democratic and free of Francoism, thanks in no small part to him.)

At the end of April when I got back to Oxford, Mother called to tell me that David Leopoulos's mother, Evelyn, had been murdered, stabbed four times in the heart in her antique store. The crime was never solved. I was reading Thomas Hobbes's **Leviathan** at the time and I remember thinking he might be right that life is "poor, nasty, brutish and short." David came to see me a few weeks later on his way back to army duty in Italy, and I tried to lift his spirits. His loss finally provoked me to finish a short story on Daddy's last year and a half and his death. It got pretty good reviews from my friends, provoking me to write in my diary, "Perhaps I can write instead of be a doorman when my political career is in shambles." I had fantasized from time to time about being a doorman at New York's Plaza Hotel, at the south end of Central Park. Plaza doormen had nice uniforms and met interesting people from all over the world. I imagined garnering large tips from guests who thought that, despite my strange southern accent, I made good conversation.

In late May, I was accepted at Yale and decided to go. I finished up my tutorials on the concept of opposition, the British prime minister, and political theory, preferring Locke to Hobbes. On June 5, I gave one last speech to an American military high school graduation. I sat on a stage with generals and colonels, and in my speech told why I loved America, respected the military, and opposed the Vietnam War. The kids liked it, and I think the officers respected the way I said it.

On June 26, I took the plane to New York, after emotional good-byes, especially with Frank Aller, Paul Parish, and David Edwards, this time for real. Just like that, it was over, two of the most extraordinary years of my life. They began on the eve of Richard Nixon's election and ended as the Beatles announced they were breaking up and released their last movie to loving, mourning fans. I had traveled a lot and loved it. I had also ventured into the far reaches of my mind and heart, struggling with my draft situation, my ambivalence about my ambition, and my inability to have anything other than brief relationships with women. I had no degree, but I had learned a lot. My "long and winding road" was leading me home, and I hoped that, as the Beatles sang in "Hey Jude," I could at least "take a sad song and make it better."

SEVENTEEN

In July, I went to work in Washington for Project Purse-strings, a citizens' lobby for the McGovern-Hatfield amendment, which called for a cutoff of funding for the Vietnam War by the end of 1971. We had no chance to pass it, but the campaign to do so provided a vehicle to mobilize and highlight growing bipartisan opposition to the war.

I got a room for the summer at the home of Dick and Helen Dudman, who lived in a great old two-story house with a big front porch in northwest Washington. Dick was a distinguished journalist. He and Helen both opposed the war and supported the young people who were trying to stop it. They were wonderful to me. One morning they invited me down to breakfast on the front porch with their friend and neighbor Senator Gene McCarthy. He was serving his last year in the Senate, having announced back in 1968 that he wouldn't run again. That morning he was in an open, expansive mood, offering a precise analysis of current events and expressing some nostalgia at leaving the Senate. I liked McCarthy more than I expected to, especially after he loaned me a pair of shoes to wear to the black-tie Women's Press Dinner, which I think the Dudmans got me invited to. President Nixon came and shook a lot of hands, though not mine. I was seated at a table with Clark Clifford, who had come to Washington from Missouri with President Truman and had served as a close advisor and then as defense secretary to President Johnson in his last year in office. On Vietnam, Clifford noted dryly, "It's really one of the most awful places in the world to be involved." The dinner was a heady experience for me, especially since I kept my feet on the ground in Gene McCarthy's shoes.

Shortly after I started at Pursestrings, I took a long weekend off and drove to Springfield, Massachusetts, for the wedding of my Georgetown roommate Marine Lieutenant Kit Ashby.

On the way back to Washington, I stopped in Cape Cod to visit Tommy Caplan and Jim Moore, who had also been at Kit's wedding. At night, we went to see Carolyn Yeldell, who was singing on the Cape with a group of young entertainers for the summer. We had a great time, but I stayed too long. When I got back on the road, I was dead tired. Before I even made it out of Massachusetts on the interstate highway, a car pulled out of a rest stop right in front of me. The driver didn't see me, and I didn't see him until it was too late. I swerved to miss him, but I hit the left rear of his car hard. The man and woman in the other car seemed to be dazed but unhurt. I wasn't hurt either, but the little Volkswagen bug Jeff Dwire had given me to drive for the summer was badly mangled. When the police came, I had a big problem. I had misplaced my driver's license on the move home from England and couldn't prove I was a valid driver. There were no computerized records of such things back then, so I couldn't be validated until the morning. The officer said he'd have to put me in jail. By the time we got there it was about 5 a.m. They stripped me of my belongings and took my belt so that I couldn't strangle myself, gave me a cup of coffee, and put me in a cell with a hard metal bed, a blanket, a smelly stopped-up toilet, and a light that stayed on. After a couple of hours of semi-sleep, I called Tommy Caplan for help. He and Jim Moore went to court with me and posted my bond. The judge was friendly but reprimanded me about not having my license. It worked: after my night in jail, I was never without my license again.

Two weeks after my trip to Massachusetts, I was back in New England to spend a week in Connecticut working for Joe Duffey in the Democratic primary election for the U.S. Senate. Duffey was running as the peace candidate, aided primarily by the people who had made a good showing for Gene McCarthy two years earlier. The incumbent senator, Democrat Tom Dodd, was a longtime fixture in Connecticut politics. He had prosecuted Nazis at the Nuremberg War Crimes Tribunal and had a good progressive record, but he had two problems. First, he had been censured by the Senate for the personal use of funds that had been raised for him in his official capacity. Second, he had supported President Johnson on Vietnam, and Democratic primary voters were much more likely to be anti-war. Dodd was hurt and angered by the Senate censure and not ready to give up his seat without a fight. Rather than face a hostile electorate in the Democratic primary, he filed as an Independent to run in the November general election. Joe Duffey was an ethics professor at Hartford Seminary Foundation and president of the liberal Americans for Democratic Action. Though he was a coal miner's son from West Virginia, his strongest supporters were prosperous, well-educated, anti-war liberals who lived in the suburbs, and young people drawn to his record on civil rights and peace. His campaign co-chairman was Paul Newman, who worked hard in the campaign. His finance committee included the photographer Margaret Bourke-White, artist Alexander Calder,

New Yorker cartoonist Dana Fradon, and an extraordinary array of writers and historians, including Francine du Plessix Gray, John Hersey, Arthur Miller, Vance Packard, William Shirer, William Styron, Barbara Tuchman, and Thornton Wilder. Their names looked pretty impressive on the campaign stationery, but they weren't likely to impress many voters among blue-collar ethnics.

Between July 29 and August 5, I was asked to organize two towns in the Fifth Congressional District, Bethel and Trumbull. Both were full of old white wooden houses with big front porches and long histories that were chronicled in the local registers. In Bethel, we put in phones the first day and organized a telephone canvass, to be followed by personal deliveries of literature to all the undecided voters. The office was kept open long hours by dedicated volunteers, and I was pretty sure Duffey would get his maximum possible vote there. Trumbull didn't have a fully operational headquarters; the volunteers were phoning some voters and seeing others. I urged them to keep an office open from 10 a.m. to 7 p.m., Monday through Saturday, and to follow the Bethel canvassing procedure, which would guarantee two contacts with all persuadable voters. I also reviewed the operations in two other towns that were less well organized and urged the state headquarters to at least make sure they had complete voter lists and the capacity to do the phone canvass.

I liked the work and met a lot of people who would be important in my life, including John Podesta, who served superbly in the White House as staff secretary, deputy chief of staff, and chief of staff, and Susan Thomases, who, when I was in New York, let me sleep on the couch in the Park Avenue apartment where she still lives, and who became one of Hillary's and my closest friends and advisors.

When Joe Duffey won the primary, I was asked to coordinate the Third Congressional District for the general election. The biggest city in the district was New Haven, where I'd be going to law school, and the district included Milford, where I would be living. Doing the job meant that I'd miss a lot of classes until the election was over in early November, but I thought I could make it with borrowed notes and hard study at the end of term.

I loved New Haven with its cauldron of old-fashioned ethnic politics and student activists. East Haven, next door, was overwhelmingly Italian, while nearby Orange was mostly Irish. The towns farther away from New Haven tended to be wealthier, with the ethnic lines more blurred. The two towns at the eastern end of the district, Guilford and Madison, were especially old and beautiful. I spent a lot of time driving to the other towns in the district, making sure our people had a good campaign plan in place, and the support and materials they needed from the central headquarters. Since my Volkswagen had been ruined in the wreck in Massachusetts, I was driving a rust-colored Opel station wagon, which was better suited to delivering campaign materials anyway. I put a lot of miles on that old station wagon.

When my campaign work permitted, I attended classes in constitutional law, contracts, procedure, and torts. The most interesting class by far was Constitutional Law, taught by Robert Bork, who was later put on the Court of Appeals for the District of Columbia, and in 1987 was nominated for the Supreme Court by President Reagan. Bork was extremely conservative in his legal philosophy, aggressive in pushing his point of view, but fair to students who disagreed. In my one memorable exchange with him, I pointed out that his argument on the question at issue was circular. He replied, "Of course it is. All the best arguments are."

After the primary election, I did my best to bring the supporters of the other candidates into the Duffey campaign, but it was tough. I'd go into the heavily ethnic blue-collar areas and make my best pitch, but I could tell I was hitting a lot of stone walls. Too many white ethnic Democrats thought Joe Duffey, whom Vice President Agnew had called a "Marxist revisionist," was too radical, too identified with dope-smoking anti-war hippies. Many of the ethnic Democrats were turning against the war, too, but they still didn't feel comfortable in the company of those who had been against it before they were. The campaign to win them over was complicated by the fact that Senator Dodd was running as an Independent, so the disgruntled Democrats had someplace else to go. Joe Duffey ran a fine campaign, pouring his heart and mind into it and inspiring young people all across the country, but he was defeated by the Republican candidate, Congressman Lowell Weicker, a maverick who later left the Republican Party and served as governor of Connecticut as an Independent. Weicker got just under 42 percent of the vote, enough to beat Duffey handily. Duffey got less than 34 percent, with Senator Dodd garnering almost 25 percent. We got killed in ethnic towns like East Haven and West Haven.

I don't know if Duffey would have won if Dodd hadn't run, but I was sure the Democratic Party was headed for minority status unless we could get back the kind of folks who voted for Dodd. After the election I talked about it for hours with Anne Wexler, who had done a superb job as campaign manager. She was a great politician and related well to all kinds of people, but in 1970 most voters weren't buying the message or the messengers. Anne became a great friend and advisor to me over the years. After she and Joe Duffey got married, I stayed in touch with them. When I was in the White House, I appointed him to run the United States Information Agency, which oversaw the Voice of America, where he took America's message to a world more receptive to him than the Connecticut electorate had been in 1970. I thought of it as Joe's last campaign, and he won it.

The brightest spot in November 1970 was the election of a young Democratic governor, Dale Bumpers, in Arkansas. He handily defeated former governor Faubus in the primary and won the general election over Governor Rockefeller in a landslide. Bumpers was an ex-marine and a great trial lawyer. He was funny as all get-out and could talk an owl out of a tree. And he was a genuine progressive who had led his small hometown of Charleston, in conservative western Arkansas, to peacefully integrate its schools, in stark contrast to the turmoil in Little Rock. Two years later he was reelected by a large margin, and two years after that he became one of our U.S. senators. Bumpers proved that the power of leadership to lift and unite people in a common cause could overcome the South's old politics of division. That's what I wanted to do. I didn't mind backing candidates who were almost certain to lose when we were fighting for civil rights or against the war. But sooner or later, you have to win if you want to change things. I went to Yale Law School to learn more about policy. And in case my political aspirations didn't work out, I wanted a profession from which I could never be forced to retire.

After the election, I settled into law school life, cramming for exams, getting to know some of the other students, and enjoying my house and my three housemates. Doug

Eakeley, my fellow Rhodes scholar at Univ, found a great old house on Long Island Sound in Milford. It had four bedrooms, a good-sized kitchen, and a large screened-in porch that opened right onto the beach. The beach was perfect for cookouts, and when the tide was out, we had enough room for touch-football games. The only drawback to the place was that it was a summer house, with no insulation against the whipping winter winds. But we were young and got used to it. I still vividly remember spending one cold winter day after the election sitting on the porch with a blanket wrapped around me reading William Faulkner's **The Sound and the Fury.**

My other housemates at 889 East Broadway were Don Pogue and Bill Coleman. Don was more left wing than the rest of us, but he looked more blue collar. He was built like a concrete block and was strong as an ox. He drove a motorcycle to law school, where he engaged all comers in endless political debate. Luckily for us, he was also a good cook and was usually on good behavior, thanks to his equally intense but more nuanced English girlfriend, Susan Bucknell. Bill was one of the growing number of black students at Yale. His father was a liberal Republican lawyer—they still existed back then—who had clerked for Justice Felix Frankfurter on the Supreme Court and had served as secretary of transportation under President Ford. On the surface, Bill was the most laid-back of our group.

Besides my roommates, I knew only a few other students when I got back to Yale after the Duffey campaign, including my Boys Nation friend from Louisiana Fred Kammer, and Bob Reich. Because he was the secretary of our Rhodes class, Bob kept up with everyone and was a continuing source of information and humorous misinformation on what our old crowd was up to.

Bob was living in a house near campus with three other students, one of whom, Nancy Bekavac, became a special friend of mine. She was a passionate liberal whose anti-war convictions had been confirmed the previous summer when she worked in Vietnam as a journalist. She wrote beautiful poems, powerful letters, and great class notes, which she let me use when I showed up for class two months late.

Through Bill Coleman, I got to meet a number of the black students. I was interested in how they came to Yale, and what they planned to do with what, back then, was still an unusual opportunity for African-Americans. Besides Bill, I became friends with Eric Clay from Detroit, whom I later appointed to the U.S. court of appeals; Nancy Gist, a Wellesley classmate of Hillary's who served in the Justice Department when I was President; Lila Coleburn, who gave up law to become a psychotherapist; Rufus Cormier, a big, quiet man who'd starred at guard on the Southern Methodist University football team; and Lani Guinier, whom I tried to appoint assistant attorney general for civil rights, a sad story the details of which I'll relate later. Supreme Court Justice Clarence Thomas was a classmate too, but I never got to know him.

Near the end of the term, we heard that Frank Aller had decided to return to America. He moved back to the Boston area and went home to Spokane to face the draft music. He was arrested, arraigned, then released pending trial. Frank had decided that whatever impact he'd had by resisting had been achieved, and he didn't want to spend the rest of his life out of America, looking forward to a cold, bitter middle age in some Canadian or British university, forever defined by Vietnam. One night in December, Bob Reich said it seemed foolish for Frank to risk jail when there was so much he could do out of the country. My diary notes my reply: "A man is more than the sum of all the things he can do." Frank's decision was about who he was, not what he could do. I thought it was the right one. Not long after he got back, Frank had a psychiatric exam in which the doctor found him depressed and unfit for military service. He took his draft physical and, like Strobe, was declared 1-Y, draftable only in a national emergency.

On Christmas Day, I was back home in Hot Springs, a long way from Helsinki Bay, where I'd walked on the ice the previous Christmas. Instead, I walked the grounds of my old elementary school, counted my blessings, and marked the changes in my life. Several of my close friends were getting married. I wished them well and wondered whether I would ever do so.

I was thinking a lot about the past and my roots. On New Year's Day, I finished C. Vann Woodward's **The Burden of Southern History,** in which he noted southerners' "peculiar historical consciousness," what Eudora Welty called "the sense of place." Arkansas was my place. Unlike Thomas Wolfe, whose cascading prose I so admired, I knew I could go home again. Indeed, I had to. But first, I had to finish law school.

I got to spend my second term at Yale as a proper law student with the heaviest class load of my stay there. My Business Law professor was John Baker, Yale Law's first black faculty member. He was very good to me, gave me some research work to supplement my meager income, and invited me to his house for dinner. John and his wife had gone to Fisk University, a black school in Nashville,

Tennessee, in the early sixties, when the civil rights movement was in full flower. He told me fascinating stories about the fear they lived with and the joy he and his classmates found in the work of the movement.

I took Constitutional Law with Charles Reich, who was as liberal as Bob Bork was conservative, and the author of one of the seminal "countercultural" books about the 1960s, **The Greening of America.** My Criminal Law professor, Steve Duke, was a witty, acerbic man and a fine teacher with whom I later did a seminar on white-collar crime. I really enjoyed Political and Civil Rights, taught by Tom Emerson, a dapper little man who had been in FDR's administration and whose textbook we used. I also took Professor William Leon McBride's National Law and Philosophy, did some legal services work, and got a part-time job. For a few months, I drove to Hartford four times a week to help Dick Suisman, a Democratic businessman I'd met in the Duffey campaign, with his work on the city council. Dick knew I needed the work, and I think I was some help to him.

In late February, I flew to California for a few days to be with Frank Aller, Strobe Talbott, and Strobe's girlfriend, Brooke Shearer. We met in Los Angeles at the home of Brooke's extraordinarily welcoming and generous parents, Marva and Lloyd Shearer, who, for many years, wrote America's most widely read celebrity gossip column, Walter Scott's Personality Parade. Then in March I went up to Boston, where Frank was living and looking for work as a journalist, to see him and Strobe again. We walked in the woods behind Frank's house and along the New Hampshire coast nearby. Frank seemed glad to be home, but still sad. Even though he had escaped the draft and prison, he seemed caught in the throes of a depression, like that which Turgenev said "only the very young know and which has no apparent reason." I thought he'd get over it.

The spring lifted my spirits as it always did. The political news was a mixed bag. The Supreme Court unanimously upheld busing to achieve racial balance. The Chinese accepted an American invitation to reciprocate the visit of the American Ping-Pong team to China by sending their team to the United States. And the war protests continued. Senator McGovern came to New Haven on May 16, plainly with the intention of running for President in 1972. I liked him and thought he had a chance to win, because of his heroic record as a bomber pilot in World War II, his leadership of the Food for Peace program in the Kennedy administration, and the new rules for delegate selection for the next Democratic convention. McGovern was heading a commission to write them, for the purpose of ensuring a more diverse convention in terms of age, race, and gender. The new rules, plus the weight of anti-war liberals in the primaries, virtually assured that the old political bosses would have less influence and the party activists more in the 1972 nominating process. Rick Stearns had been working for the commission, and I was sure he'd be tough and smart enough to devise a system favorable to McGovern.

While law school and politics were going well, my personal life was a mess. I had broken up with a young woman who went home to marry her old boyfriend, then had a painful parting with a law student I liked very much but couldn't commit to. I was just about reconciled to being alone and was determined not to get involved with anyone for a while. Then one day, when I was sitting at the back of Professor Emerson's class in Political and Civil Rights, I spotted a woman I hadn't seen before. Apparently she attended even less frequently than I did. She had thick dark blond hair and wore eyeglasses and no makeup, but she conveyed a sense of strength and self-possession I had rarely seen in anyone, man or woman. After class I followed her out, intending to introduce myself. When I got a couple of feet from her, I reached out my hand to touch her shoulder, then immediately pulled it back. It was almost a physical reaction. Somehow I knew that this wasn't another tap on the shoulder, that I might be starting something I couldn't stop.

I saw the girl several times around school over the next few days, but didn't approach her. Then one night I was standing at one end of the long, narrow Yale Law Library talking to another student, Jeff Gleckel, about joining the **Yale Law Journal.** Jeff urged me to do it, saying it would assure me a good clerkship with a federal judge or a job with one of the blue-chip law firms. He made a good case, but I just wasn't interested; I was going home to Arkansas, and in the meantime preferred politics to the law review. After a while I suddenly stopped paying attention to his earnest entreaty because I saw the girl again, standing at the other end of the room. For once, she was staring back at me. After a while she closed her book, walked the length of the library, looked me in the eye, and said, "If you're going to keep staring at me and I'm going to keep staring back, we ought to at least know each other's names. Mine's Hillary Rodham. What's yours?" Hillary, of course, remembers all this, but in slightly different words. I was impressed and so stunned I couldn't say anything for a few seconds. Finally I blurted my name out. We exchanged a few words, and she left. I don't know what poor Jeff Gleckel thought was going on, but he never talked to me about the law review again.

A couple of days later, I was coming down the steps to the ground floor of the law school when I saw Hillary again. She was wearing a bright flowered skirt that nearly touched the floor. I was determined to spend some time with her. She said she was going to register for next term's classes, so I said I'd go, too. We stood in line and talked. I thought I was doing pretty well until we got to the front of the line. The registrar looked up at me and said, "Bill, what are you doing back here? You registered this morning." I turned beet red, and Hillary laughed that big laugh of hers. My cover was blown, so I asked her to take a walk with me to the Yale Art Gallery to see the Mark Rothko exhibit. I was so eager and nervous that I forgot the university workforce was on strike and the museum was closed. Luckily, there was a guard on duty. I pleaded my case and offered to clean up the branches and other litter in the museum's garden if he'd let me in.

The guard took a look at us, figured it out, and let us in. We had the whole exhibit to ourselves. It was wonderful, and I've liked Rothko ever since. When we were done, we went out to the garden, and I picked up the sticks. I suppose I was being a scab for the first and only time in my life, but the union didn't have a picket line outside the museum and, besides, politics was the last thing on my mind. After I paid my cleaning-up dues, Hillary and I stayed in the garden for another hour or so. There was a large, beautiful Henry Moore sculpture of a seated woman. Hillary sat in the woman's lap, and I sat beside her talking. Before long, I leaned over and put my head on her shoulder. It was our first date.

We spent the next several days together, just hanging

around, talking about everything under the sun. The next weekend Hillary went up to Vermont on a long-planned visit to the man she had been dating. I was anxious about it. I didn't want to lose her. When she got home late Sunday night I called her. She was sick as a dog, so I brought her some chicken soup and orange juice. From then on we were inseparable. She spent a lot of time at our house on the beach and quickly won over Doug, Don, and Bill.

She didn't do so well with my mother when she came to visit a few weeks later, partly because she tried to cut her own hair just before Mother arrived. It was a minor fiasco; she looked more like a punk rocker than someone who had just walked out of Jeff Dwire's beauty salon. With no makeup, a work shirt and jeans, and bare feet coated with tar from walking on the beach at Milford, she might as well have been a space alien. The fact that I was obviously serious about her gave Mother heartburn. In her book, Mother called Hillary a "growth experience." It was a girl with "no makeup, Coke-bottle glasses, and brown hair with no apparent style" versus a woman with hot-pink lipstick, painted-on eyebrows, and a silver stripe in her hair. I got a kick out of watching them try to figure each other out. Over time they did, as Mother came to care less about Hillary's appearance and Hillary came to care more about it. Underneath their different styles, they were both smart, tough, resilient, passionate women. When they got together, I didn't stand a chance.

By mid-May, I wanted to be with Hillary all the time. As a result, I met several of her friends, including Susan Graber, a Wellesley classmate of hers whom I later appointed to a federal judgeship in Oregon; Carolyn Ellis, a bright, funny Lebanese woman from Mississippi who could "out-southern" me and is now chancellor of the

University of Mississippi; and Neil Steinman, the brightest man I met at Yale, who raised the first funds for me in Pennsylvania in 1992.

I learned about Hillary's childhood in Park Ridge, Illinois; her four years at Wellesley, where she switched her politics from Republican to Democrat because of civil rights and the war; her post-graduation trip to Alaska, where she slimed fish for a living; and her interest in legal services for poor people and in children's issues. I also heard about her famous commencement speech at Wellesley in which she articulated our generation's contradictory feelings of alienation from the political system and determination to make America better. The speech got a lot of national publicity and was her first brush with fame beyond the boundaries of her immediate environment. What I liked about her politics was that, like me, she was both idealistic and practical. She wanted to change things, and she knew that doing so required persistent effort. She was as tired as I was of our side getting beat and treating defeat as evidence of moral virtue and superiority. Hillary was a formidable presence in law school, a big fish in our small but highly competitive pond. I was more of a floating presence, drifting in and out.

A lot of the students we both knew talked about Hillary as if they were a little intimidated by her. Not me. I just wanted to be with her. But time was running out on us. Hillary had accepted a summer job at Treuhaft, Walker, and Burnstein, a law firm in Oakland, California, and I had been asked to take a job as coordinator of the southern states for Senator McGovern. Until I met Hillary, I was really looking forward to it. I was going to be based in Miami, and the job required traveling throughout the South putting state campaigns together. I knew I'd be good at it, and though I didn't think McGovern could do very well in the general election in the South, I believed he could win a fair number of convention delegates during the primary season. Regardless, I'd have the political experience of a lifetime. It was a rare opportunity for a twenty-five-year-old, one I got from a combination of my friendship with Rick Stearns, who had an important post in the campaign, and affirmative action: they had to have at least one southerner in a responsible position!

The problem was, I no longer wanted to do it. I knew if I went to Florida, Hillary and I might be lost to each other. Though I found the prospect of the campaign exciting, I feared, as I wrote in my diary, that it would simply be "a way of formalizing my aloneness," letting me deal with people in a good cause but at arm's length. With Hillary there was no arm's length. She was in my face from the start, and, before I knew it, in my heart.

I screwed up my courage and asked Hillary if I could spend the summer with her in California. She was incredulous at first, because she knew how much I loved politics and how deeply I felt about the war. I told her I'd have the rest of my life for my work and my ambition, but I loved her and wanted to see if it could work out for us. She took a deep breath and agreed to let me take her to California. We had been together only about a month.

We stopped briefly in Park Ridge to meet her family. Her mother, Dorothy, was a lovely, attractive woman, whom I got along with from the start, but I was as alien to Hillary's father as Hillary was to Mother. Hugh Rodham was a gruff, tough-talking Republican who, to say the least, was suspicious of me. But the more we talked, the more I liked him. I resolved to keep at it until he came around. Soon we drove on to Berkeley, California, near her job in Oakland, where she would be staying in a small house owned by her mother's half sister, Adeline. After a day or two I drove back across the country to Washington, to tell Rick Stearns and Gary Hart, Senator McGovern's campaign manager, that I couldn't go to Florida after all. Gary thought I had lost my mind to pass up such an opportunity. I suppose Rich did, too. To them, I suppose I did look like a fool, but your life is shaped by the opportunities you turn down as well as by those you seize.

I did feel bad about leaving the campaign, and I offered to go to Connecticut for a couple of weeks to set up an organization there. As soon as I had signed up people in every congressional district, I headed back to California, this time by the southern route so that I could stop at home.

I enjoyed the drive west, including a visit in the Grand Canyon. I got there in the late afternoon and crawled out on a rock jutting over the canyon's edge to watch the sun go down. It was amazing the way the rocks, compressed into distinct layers over millions of years, changed colors as the canyon darkened from the bottom up.

After I left the canyon, I had a blistering drive across Death Valley, America's hottest spot, then turned north to my summer with Hillary. When I walked into her house in Berkeley, she greeted me with a peach pie—my favorite—that she'd baked herself. It was good, and it didn't last long. During the day, when she was at work, I walked all over the city, read books in the parks and coffee shops, and explored San Francisco. At night we'd go to movies or local restaurants or just stay in and talk. On July 24, we drove down to Stanford to hear Joan Baez sing in the open amphitheater. So that all her fans could see her, she charged only $2.50 for admission, a striking contrast to the high ticket prices of today's big concerts. Baez sang her old hits and, for one of the first times in public, "The Night They Drove Old Dixie Down."

When the summer ended, Hillary and I were nowhere near finished with our conversation, so we decided to live together back in New Haven, a move that doubtless caused both our families concern. We found an apartment on the ground floor of an old house at 21 Edgewood Avenue, near the law school.

The front door of our apartment opened into a tiny living room, behind which was a smaller dining-room area and an even smaller bedroom. Behind the bedroom were an old kitchen and a bathroom so small the toilet seat sometimes scraped against the bathtub. The house was so old that the floors sank from the walls to the middle at an angle so pronounced I had to put little wooden blocks under the inside legs of our small dining table. But the price was right for penurious law students: seventy-five dollars a month. The nicest thing about the place was the fireplace in the living room. I still remember sitting in front of the fire on a cold winter day as Hillary and I read Vincent Cronin's biography of Napoleon together.

We were too happy and too poor to be anything but proud of our new home. We enjoyed having friends over for meals. Among our favorite guests were Rufus and Yvonne Cormier. They were both children of African-American ministers in Beaumont, Texas, who grew up in the same neighborhood and had gone together for years before they married. While Rufus studied law, Yvonne was getting her Ph.D. in biochemistry. Eventually she became a doctor and he became the first black partner of the big Houston law firm Baker and Botts. One night at dinner, Rufus, who was one of the best students in our class, was bemoaning the long hours he spent studying. "You know," he said in his slow drawl, "life is organized backwards. You spend the best years studying, then working. When you retire at sixty-five, you're too old to enjoy it. People should retire between the ages of twenty-one and thirty-five, then work like hell till they die." Of course, it didn't work out that way. We're all closing in on sixty-five and still at it.

I really got into my third semester of law school, with courses in Corporate Finance, Criminal Procedure, Taxation, Estates, and a seminar in Corporate Social Responsibility. The seminar was taught by Burke Marshall, a legendary figure for his work as assistant attorney general for civil rights under Robert Kennedy, and Jan Deutsch, reputed to be the only person, up to that time, to make the Honors grade in all his classes at Yale Law. Marshall was small and wiry, with bright dancing eyes. He barely spoke above a whisper, but there was steel in his voice, and in his spine. Deutsch had an unusual, clipped, stream-of-consciousness speaking style, which moved rapidly from one unfinished sentence to another. This was apparently the result of a severe head injury incurred when he was hit by a car and flew a long distance in the air before coming down hard on concrete. He was unconscious for several weeks and woke up with a metal plate in his head. But he was brilliant. I figured out his speaking style and was able to translate him to classmates who couldn't unpack his words. Jan Deutsch was also the only man I'd ever met who ate all of an apple, including the core. He said all the good minerals were there. He was smarter than I was, so I tried it. Once in a while I still do, with fond memories of Professor Deutsch.

Marvin Chirelstein taught me both Corporate Finance

and Taxation. I was lousy in Taxation. The tax code was riddled with too many artificial distinctions I couldn't care less
about; they seemed to me to provide more opportunities
for tax lawyers to reduce their clients' obligation to help pay
America's way than to advance worthy social goals. Once,
instead of paying attention to the class, I read Gabriel García Márquez's **One Hundred Years of Solitude**. At the end
of the hour, Professor Chirelstein asked me what was so
much more interesting than his lecture. I held up the book
and told him it was the greatest novel written in any language since William Faulkner died. I still think so.

I redeemed myself in Corporate Finance when I aced
the final exam. When Professor Chirelstein asked me how
I could be so good at Corporate Finance and so bad at
Taxation, I told him it was because corporate finance was
like politics: within a given set of rules, it was a constant
struggle for power, with all parties trying to avoid getting
shafted but eager to shaft.

In addition to my classwork I had two jobs. Even with
a scholarship and two different student loans, I needed the
money. I worked a few hours a week for Ben Moss, a local
lawyer, doing legal research and running errands. The
research got old after a while, but the errands were interesting. One day I had to deliver some papers to an address
in an inner-city high-rise. As I was climbing the stairs to
the third or fourth floor, I passed a man in the stairwell
with a glazed look in his eyes and a hypodermic needle
and syringe hanging from his arm. He had just shot himself full of heroin. I delivered the papers and got out of
there as quickly as I could.

My other job was less hazardous but more interesting.
I taught criminal law to undergraduates in a law-
enforcement program at the University of New Haven.

My position was funded under the Federal Law Enforcement Assistance program, which had just started under Nixon. The classes were designed to produce more professional law officers who could make arrests, searches, and seizures in a constitutional manner. I often had to prepare my lectures late in the evening before the day I delivered them. To stay awake, I did a lot of my work at the Elm Street Diner, about a block away from our house. It was open all night, had great coffee and fruit pie, and was full of characters from New Haven's night life. Tony, a Greek immigrant whose uncle owned the place, ran the diner at night. He gave me endless free refills of coffee as I toiled away.

The street outside the diner was the border dividing the territory of two groups of streetwalking prostitutes. From time to time the police took them away, but they were always quickly back at work. The streetwalkers often came into the diner to get coffee and warm up. When they found out I was in law school, several would plop down in my booth in search of free legal advice. I did my best, but none took the best advice: get another job. One night, a tall black transvestite sat down across from me and said his social club wanted to raffle off a television to make money; he wanted to know if the raffle would run afoul of the law against gambling. I later learned what he was really worried about was that the television was stolen. It had been "donated" to the club by a friend who ran a fencing operation, buying stolen goods and reselling them at a discount. Anyway, I told him that other groups held raffles all the time and it was highly unlikely that the club would be prosecuted. In return for my wise counsel, he gave me the only fee I ever received for legal advice in the Elm Street Diner, a raffle ticket. I didn't win the television, but I felt well paid just at having the ticket with the name of the social club on it in bold print: The Black Uniques.

On September 14, as Hillary and I were walking into the Blue Bell Café, someone came up to me and said it was urgent that I call Strobe Talbott. He and Brooke were visiting his parents in Cleveland. My stomach was in knots as I fed change into the pay phone outside the café. Brooke answered the phone and told me Frank Aller had killed himself. He had just been offered a job to work in the Saigon bureau of the **Los Angeles Times,** had accepted it, and had gone home to Spokane, apparently in good spirits, to get his clothes together and prepare for the move to Vietnam. I think he wanted to see and write about the war he opposed. Perhaps he wanted to put himself in harm's way to prove he wasn't a coward. Just when things were working out on the surface of his life, whatever was going on inside compelled him to end it.

His friends were stunned, but we probably shouldn't have been. Six weeks earlier, I had noted in my diary that Frank was really in the dumps again, having to that point failed to find a newspaper job in Vietnam or China. I said he had "fallen finally, physically and emotionally, to the strains, contractions, pains of the last few years, which he has endured, mostly alone." Frank's close, rational friends assumed that getting his external life back on track would calm his inner turmoil. But as I learned on that awful day, depression crowds out rationality with a vengeance. It's a disease that, when far advanced, is beyond the reasoned reach of spouses, children, lovers, and friends. I don't think I ever really understood it until I read my friend Bill Styron's brave account of his own battle with depression and suicidal thoughts, **Darkness Visible: A Memoir of Madness.** When Frank killed himself, I felt both grief and anger—at him for doing it, and at myself for not seeing it coming and pushing him to get professional help. I wish I had known then what I know now, though maybe it wouldn't have made any difference.

After Frank's death, I lost my usual optimism and my interest in courses, politics, and people. I don't know what I would have done without Hillary. When we first got together, she had a brief bout with self-doubt, but she was always so strong in public I don't think even her closest friends knew it. The fact that she opened herself to me only strengthened and validated my feelings for her. Now I needed her. And she came through, reminding me that what I was learning, doing, and thinking mattered.

In the spring term, I was bored in all my classes but Evidence, taught by Geoffrey Hazard. The rules for what is and isn't admissible in a fair trial and the process of making an honest and reasoned argument on the facts available were fascinating to me and left a lasting impression. I always tried to argue the evidence in politics as well as law.

Evidence counted a lot in my major law school activity that term, the annual Barristers Union trial competition. On March 28, Hillary and I competed in the semifinals, from which four students plus two alternates would be chosen to participate in a full-blown trial to be written by a third-year student. We did well and both made the cut.

For the next month we prepared for the Prize Trial, **State v. Porter.** Porter was a policeman accused of beating a long-haired kid to death. On April 29, Hillary and I prosecuted Mr. Porter, with help from our alternate, Bob Alsdorf. The defense lawyers were Mike Conway and Tony Rood, with Doug Eakeley as their alternate. The judge was former Supreme Court Justice Abe Fortas. He took his role seriously and played it to the hilt, issuing ruling after ruling on both sides and objections, all the while evaluating the four of us to decide who would win the prize. If my performance in the semifinals was the best public speaking of my law school career, my effort in the Prize Trial was the worst. I had an off day and didn't deserve to win. Hillary, on the other hand, was very good. So was Mike Conway, who gave an effective, emotional closing argument. Fortas gave Conway the prize. At the time I thought Hillary didn't get it in part because the dour-faced Fortas disapproved of her highly unprosecutorial outfit. She wore a blue suede jacket, bright—and I mean bright—orange suede flared pants, and a blue, orange, and white blouse. Hillary became a fine trial lawyer, but she never wore those orange pants to court again.

Apart from the Prize Trial, I poured my competitive instincts into the McGovern campaign. Early in the year, I cleaned out my bank account to open a headquarters near the campus. I had enough money, about $200, to pay a month's rent and put in a telephone. In three weeks, we had eight hundred volunteers and enough small contributions to reimburse me and keep the place open.

The volunteers were important for the coming primary campaign, which I assumed we'd have to wage against the Democratic organization and its powerful boss, Arthur Barbieri. Four years earlier, in 1968, the McCarthy forces had done well in the primary in New Haven, partly because the Democratic regulars had taken Vice President Humphrey's victory for granted. I had no illusions that Barbieri would make that mistake again, so I decided to try to persuade him to endorse McGovern. To say it was a long shot is a gross understatement. When I walked into his office and introduced myself, Barbieri was cordial but business-like. He sat back in his chair with his hands folded across his chest, displaying two huge diamond rings, one big circular one with lots of stones, the other with his initials, AB, completely filled with diamonds. He smiled and told me that 1972 would not be a replay of 1968, that he had already lined up his poll workers and a number of cars to take his people to the polls. He said he had dedicated $50,000 to the effort, a huge sum in those days for a town the size of New Haven. I replied that I didn't have much money, but I did have eight hundred volunteers who would knock on the doors of every house in his stronghold, telling all the Italian mothers that Arthur Barbieri wanted to keep sending their sons to fight and die in Vietnam. "You don't need that grief," I said. "Why do you care who wins the nomination? Endorse McGovern. He was a war hero in World War II. He can make peace and you can keep control of New Haven." Barbieri listened and replied, "You know, kid, you ain't so dumb. I'll think about it. Come back and see me in ten days." When I returned, Barbieri said, "I've been thinking about it. I think Senator McGovern is a good man and we need to get out of Vietnam. I'm going to tell my guys what we're going to do, and I want you to be there to make the pitch."

A few days later, I took Hillary with me to the extraordinary encounter with Barbieri's party leaders at a local Italian club, the Melebus, in the basement of an old building downtown. The décor was all red and black. It was very dark, very ethnic, very un-McGovern. When Barbieri told his guys that they were going to support McGovern so that no more boys from New Haven would die in Vietnam, there were groans and gasps. "Arthur, he's almost a Commie," one man blurted out. Another said, "Arthur, he sounds like a fag," referring to the senator's High Plains nasal twang. Barbieri never flinched. He introduced me, told them about my eight hundred volunteers, and let me give my pitch, which was heavy on McGovern's war record and work in the Kennedy administration. By the time the evening was over, they came around.

I was ecstatic. In the entire primary process, Arthur Barbieri and Matty Troy of Queens in New York City were the only old-line Democratic bosses to endorse McGovern. Not all our troops were pleased. After the endorsement was announced, I got an angry late-night call from two of our stalwarts in Trumbull with whom I'd worked in the Duffey campaign. They couldn't believe I'd sold out the spirit of the campaign with such a nefarious compromise. "I'm sorry," I shouted into the phone, "I thought our objective was to win," and I hung up. Barbieri proved to be loyal and effective. At the Democratic convention, Senator McGovern got five of our congressional district's six votes on the first ballot. In the November vote, New Haven was the only Connecticut city that went for him. Barbieri was as good as his word. When I became President, I tracked him down. He was in ill health and had long since retired from politics. I invited him to the White House, and we had a good visit in the Oval Office not long before he died. Barbieri was what James Carville calls a "sticker." In politics, there's nothing better.

Apparently my work in Connecticut redeemed me in the eyes of the McGovern campaign. I was asked to join the national staff and work the Democratic National Convention in Miami Beach, concentrating on the South Carolina and Arkansas delegations.

Meanwhile, Hillary had gone to Washington to work

for Marian Wright Edelman at the Washington Research Project, an advocacy group for children, which would soon be called the Children's Defense Fund. Her job was to investigate all-white southern academies that were established in response to court-ordered public school integration. In the North, white parents who didn't want their kids in inner-city schools could move to the suburbs. That wasn't an option in small southern towns—the suburbs were cow pastures and soybean fields. The problem was that the Nixon administration was not enforcing the law banning such schools from claiming tax-exempt status, a move that plainly encouraged southern whites to leave public schools.

I started my job for McGovern in Washington, first checking in with Lee Williams and my other friends on Senator Fulbright's staff, then going to see Congressman Wilbur Mills, the powerful chairman of the House Ways and Means Committee. Mills, who was a Washington legend for his detailed knowledge of the tax code and his skill in running his committee, had announced that he would be Arkansas' "favorite son" candidate at the Miami convention. Such candidacies were usually launched in the hope of preventing a state's delegation from voting for the front-runner, although back then a favorite son occasionally thought lightning might strike and he would at least wind up on the ticket as the vice-presidential nominee. In Mills's case, his candidacy served both purposes. The Arkansas Democrats thought McGovern, who was far ahead in the delegate count, was sure to be trounced at home in the general election, and Mills doubtless thought he would be a better President. Our meeting was cordial. I told Chairman Mills that I expected the delegates to be loyal to him but that I would be working them to get their support on important procedural votes and on a second ballot if Senator McGovern needed one.

After the Mills meeting I flew to Columbia, South Carolina, to meet as many of the convention delegates there as possible. Many were sympathetic to McGovern, and I thought they would help us on crucial votes, despite the fact that their credentials were subject to challenge on the grounds that the delegation did not have as much racial, gender, and age diversity as the new rules written by the McGovern Commission required.

Before Miami, I also went to the Arkansas Democratic Convention in Hot Springs to court my home-state delegates. I knew that Governor Bumpers, who would chair the delegation in Miami, thought McGovern would hurt the Democrats in Arkansas, but as in South Carolina, a lot of the delegates were anti-war and pro-McGovern. I left for Miami feeling pretty good about both the delegations I was working.

At the convention in mid-July, the major candidates had their headquarters in hotels around Miami and Miami Beach, but their operations were run out of trailers outside the Convention Center. The McGovern trailer was overseen by Gary Hart as national campaign manager, with Frank Mankiewicz as national political director and public spokesman, and my friend Rick Stearns as the director of research and caucus state operations. Rick knew more about the rules than anyone else. Those of us who were working the delegations were on the floor, following instructions from the trailer. The McGovern campaign had come a long way, thanks to an array of committed volunteers, Hart's leadership, Mankiewicz's handling of the press, and Stearns's strategizing. With their help, McGovern had outfought and outpolled politicians who were more established, more charismatic, or both: Hubert Humphrey; Ed Muskie; Mayor John Lindsay of New York, who had switched parties to run; Senator Henry Jackson of Washington State; and George Wallace, who was paralyzed by a would-be assassin's bullet during the campaign. Congresswoman Shirley Chisholm of New York also ran, becoming the first African-American to do so.

We thought McGovern had enough votes to win on the first ballot if he could weather the challenge to the California delegation. The new McGovern rules required each state with a primary election to apportion its delegates as closely as possible to the percentage of votes they got. However, California still had a winner-take-all system and was asserting its right to keep it because the state legislature hadn't changed its election law by convention time. Ironically, McGovern favored the California system over his own rules because he had won the primary with 44 percent of the votes but had all of the state's 271 delegates pledged to him. The anti-McGovern forces argued that McGovern was a hypocrite and that the convention should seat only 44 percent, or 120 delegates, for him, with the other 151 being pledged to the other candidates in proportion to their share of the California primary vote. The Credentials Committee of the convention was anti-McGovern and voted to uphold the California challenge, seating only 120 of his delegates, and putting his first-ballot victory in doubt.

The Credentials Committee's decisions could be overturned by a majority of the convention delegates. The McGovern forces wanted to do that with California. So did the South Carolina delegation, which was in danger of losing its votes because it had also been found in violation of the rules; only 25 percent of the delegation were women, rather than the required half. McGovern was nominally against the South Carolina position because of that underrepresentation.

What happened next was complicated and not worth going into detail about. Essentially, Rick Stearns decided that we should lose the South Carolina vote, bind our opponents to a procedural rule that benefited our challenge; then we would win the California vote. It worked. The South Carolina delegation was seated, and our opponents smelled victory. But by the time they realized they had been tricked, it was too late; we picked up all 271 delegates and clinched the nomination. The California challenge was probably the greatest example of political jujitsu at a party convention since primary elections became the dominant mode of selecting delegates. As I've said, Rick Stearns was a genius on the rules. I was elated. Now McGovern was virtually guaranteed a first-ballot victory, and the folks from South Carolina, whom I had come to like a lot, could stay.

Alas, it was all downhill from there. McGovern entered the convention well behind but still within striking distance of President Nixon in the opinion polls, and we expected to pick up five or six points during the week, thanks to several days of intense media coverage. Getting that kind of bounce, however, requires the kind of disciplined control of events our forces had demonstrated with the delegate challenges. For some reason, it evaporated after that. First, a gay-rights group staged a sit-in at McGovern's hotel and refused to budge until he met with them. When he did, the media and the Republicans portrayed it as a cave-in that made him look both weak and too liberal. Then, on Thursday afternoon, after he picked Senator Tom Eagleton of Missouri to be his running mate,

McGovern allowed other names to be put in nomination against him during the voting that night. Six more people got in the race, complete with nominating speeches, and a long roll-call vote. Though Eagleton's victory was a foregone conclusion, the other six got some votes. So did Roger Mudd of CBS News, the television character Archie Bunker, and Mao Tse-tung. It was a disaster. The useless exercise had taken all the prime-time television hours, when nearly eighteen million households were watching the convention. The intended media events—Senator Edward Kennedy's speech nominating McGovern and the nominee's own acceptance speech—were pushed back into the wee hours of the morning. Senator Kennedy was a champ and gave a rousing speech. McGovern's was good, too. He called on America to "come home . . . from deception in high places . . . from the waste of idle hands . . . from prejudice. . . . Come home to the affirmation that we have a dream . . . to the conviction that we can move our country forward . . . to the belief that we can seek a newer world." The problem was that McGovern began to talk at 2:48 a.m., or "prime time in Samoa," as the humorist Mark Shields quipped. He had lost 80 percent of his television audience.

As if that weren't enough, it soon became public that Eagleton had had treatment, including electric shock therapy, for depression. Unfortunately, back then there was still a great deal of ignorance about the nature and range of mental-health problems, as well as the fact that previous Presidents, including Lincoln and Wilson, had suffered from periodic depression. The idea that Senator Eagleton would be next in line to be President if McGovern were elected was unsettling to many people, even more so because Eagleton hadn't told McGovern about it.

If McGovern had known and picked him anyway, perhaps we could have made real progress in the public's understanding of mental health, but the way it came out raised questions not only about McGovern's judgment but also about his competence as well. Our vaunted campaign operation hadn't even vetted Eagleton's selection with Missouri's Democratic governor, Warren Hearnes, who knew about the mental-health issue.

Within a week after the Miami convention, we were in even worse shape than when the Democrats had exited Chicago four years earlier, looking both too liberal and too inept. After the Eagleton story came out, McGovern first said he stood by his running mate "1,000 percent." A few days later, under withering, unrelenting pressure from his own supporters, he dropped him. Then it took until the second week of August to get a replacement. Sargent Shriver, President Kennedy's brother-in-law, said yes after Ted Kennedy, Senator Abe Ribicoff of Connecticut, Governor Reubin Askew of Florida, Hubert Humphrey, and Senator Ed Muskie all declined to join the ticket. I was convinced that most Americans would vote for a peace candidate who was progressive but not too liberal, and before Miami I thought we could sell McGovern. Now we were back to square one. After the convention, I went to Washington to see Hillary, so exhausted I slept more than twenty-four hours straight.

A few days later, I packed up to go to Texas to help coordinate the general election campaign there. I knew it was going to be tough when I flew from Washington to Arkansas to pick up a car. I sat next to a young man from Jackson, Mississippi, who asked me what I was doing. When I told him, he almost shouted, "You're the only white person I've ever met for McGovern!" Later, when I was home watching John Dean testify about the misdeeds of the Nixon White House before Senator Sam Ervin's Watergate Committee, the phone rang. It was the young man whom I'd met on the airplane. He said, "I just called so you could say, 'I told you so.' " I never heard from him again, but I appreciated the call. It was amazing how far public opinion moved in just two years as Watergate unfolded.

In the summer of 1972, however, going to Texas was a fool's errand, although it was a fascinating one. Starting with John Kennedy in 1960, Democratic presidential campaigns often assigned out-of-staters to oversee important state campaigns on the theory that they could bring competing factions together and make sure all decisions put the candidate's interests, not parochial concerns, first. Whatever the theory, in practice, outsiders could inspire resentment on all sides, especially for a campaign as troubled as McGovern's, in an environment as fractured and contentious as Texas.

The campaign decided to send two of us to Texas, me and Taylor Branch, whom, as I've said, I'd first met on Martha's Vineyard in 1969. As an insurance policy, the campaign named a successful young Houston lawyer, Julius Glickman, to be the third member of our triumvirate. Since Taylor and I were both southerners and not averse to cooperating, I thought we might be able to make it work in Texas. We set up a headquarters on West Sixth Street in Austin, not far from the state Capitol, and shared an apartment on a hill just across the Colorado River. Taylor ran the headquarters operation and controlled the budget. We didn't have much money, so it was fortunate that he was tightfisted, and better than I was at saying no to people. I worked with the county organizations, and Julius lined up what support he could get from prominent Texans he knew, and we had a great staff of enthusiastic young people. Three of them became especially close friends of Hillary's and mine: Garry Mauro, who became Texas land commissioner and took a leading role in my presidential campaign; and Roy Spence and Judy Trabulsi, who founded an advertising agency that became the largest in America outside New York City. Garry, Roy, and Judy would support me and Hillary in all our campaigns.

The Texan who had by far the greatest impact on my career was Betsey Wright, a doctor's daughter from the small West Texas town of Alpine. She was just a couple years older than I was but much more experienced in grass-roots politics, having worked for the state Democratic Party and Common Cause. She was brilliant, intense, loyal, and conscientious almost to a fault. And she was the only person I had ever met who was more fascinated by and consumed with politics than I was. Unlike some of our more inexperienced colleagues, she knew we were getting the daylights beaten out of us, but she worked eighteen-hour days anyway. After I was defeated for governor in 1980, Hillary asked Betsey to come to Little Rock to help organize my files for a comeback. She did, and she stayed to run my successful campaign in 1982. Later, Betsey served as chief of staff in the governor's office. In 1992, she played a pivotal role in the presidential campaign, defending me and my record from the endless barrage of personal and political attacks with a skill and strength no one else could have mustered and maintained. Without Betsey Wright, I could not have become President.

After I had been in Texas a few weeks, Hillary joined me and the campaign, having been hired by Anne Wexler to do voter registration for the Democratic Party. She got on well with the rest of the staff, and brightened even my toughest days.

The Texas campaign got off to a rocky start, mostly because of the Eagleton disaster, but also because a lot of the local Democrats didn't want to be identified with McGovern. Senator Lloyd Bentsen, who had defeated the fiery liberal Senator Ralph Yarborough two years earlier, declined to be the campaign chairman. The gubernatorial nominee, Dolph Briscoe, a South Texas rancher who years later became a friend and supporter of mine, didn't even want to appear in public with our candidate. Former governor John Connally, who had been riding in the car with President Kennedy when he was killed nine years earlier and had been a close ally of President Johnson, was leading a group called Democrats for Nixon.

Still, Texas was too big to write off, and Humphrey had carried it four years earlier, though by only 38,000 votes. Finally, two elected state officials agreed to co-chair the campaign, Agriculture Commissioner John White and Land Commissioner Bob Armstrong. White, an old-fashioned Texas Democrat, knew we couldn't win but wanted the Democratic ticket to make the best showing possible in Texas. John later became chairman of the Democratic National Committee. Bob Armstrong was an ardent environmentalist who loved to play guitar and hang out with us at Scholtz's Beer Garden, the local bowling alley, or the Armadillo Music Hall, where he took Hillary and me to see Jerry Jeff Walker and Willie Nelson.

I thought things were looking up in late August when Senator McGovern and Sargent Shriver were slated to come to Texas to see President Johnson. Shriver was a likable man with a buoyant personality who brought energy and gravitas to the ticket. He had been a founder of the Legal Services Corporation, which provides legal assistance to the poor, President Kennedy's first director of the Peace Corps, and President Johnson's first director of the War on Poverty.

McGovern and Shriver's meeting with President Johnson went reasonably well but delivered few political benefits because Johnson insisted there be no press and because he already had issued a lukewarm endorsement of McGovern to a local newspaper a few days before they met. The main thing I got out of it was an autographed picture of the President, which he had signed when Taylor had gone out to the LBJ Ranch a few days before the meeting to finalize the arrangements. Probably because we were pro–civil rights southerners, Taylor and I liked Johnson more than most of our McGovern co-workers did.

After the meeting, McGovern went back to his hotel suite in Austin to meet with some of his main supporters and staff people. There were a lot of complaints about the disarray in the campaign. It certainly was disorganized. Taylor and I hadn't been there long enough to establish ourselves, much less a smooth organization, and our liberal base was dispirited after its candidate, Sissy Farenthold, lost a bruising primary battle for governor to Dolph Briscoe. For some reason, the highest-ranking state official who did support McGovern, Secretary of State Bob Bullock, wasn't even invited to meet him. McGovern wrote him an apology, but it was a telling oversight.

Not long after McGovern left Texas, the campaign decided we needed some adult supervision, so they sent down a crusty gray-haired Irishman from Sioux City, Iowa, Don O'Brien, who had been active in John

Kennedy's campaign and had served as the U.S. attorney under Robert Kennedy. I liked Don O'Brien a lot, but he was an old-fashioned chauvinist who got on the nerves of a lot of our independent young women. Still, we made it work, and I was relieved because now I could spend even more time on the road. Those were my best days in Texas.

I went north to Waco, where I met the liberal insurance magnate, and a future supporter of mine, Bernard Rapoport; east to Dallas, where I met Jess Hay, a moderate but loyal Democratic businessman who also stayed my friend and supporter, and a black state senator, Eddie Bernice Johnson, who became one of my strongest allies in Congress when I was elected President; then to Houston, where I met and fell in love with the godmother of Texas liberals, Billie Carr, a big, raucous woman who reminded me a little of Mother. Billie took me under her wing and never let me go until the day she died, even when I disappointed her by being less liberal than she was.

I had my first extensive contacts with Mexican-Americans, commonly called Chicanos back then, and came to love their spirit, culture, and food. In San Antonio, I discovered Mario's and Mi Tierra, where I once ate three meals in eighteen hours.

I worked South Texas with Franklin Garcia, a tough labor organizer with a tender heart, and his friend Pat Robards. One night Franklin and Pat drove Hillary and me over the Rio Grande to Matamoros, Mexico. They took us to a dive with a mariachi band, a halfhearted stripper, and a menu that featured **cabrito,** barbequed goat head. I was so exhausted I fell asleep while the stripper was dancing and the goat head was looking up at me.

One day when I was driving alone in rural South Texas, I stopped at a filling station for gas and struck up a conversation with the young Mexican-American who was filling my tank and asked him to vote for McGovern. "I can't," he said. When I asked why, he replied, "Because of Eagleton. He should not have abandoned him. A lot of people have troubles. You have to stick with your friends." I never forgot his wise advice. When I was President, Hispanic-Americans knew I had tried to be their friend, and they stuck with me.

In the last week of the campaign, though all was lost, I had two memorable experiences. Congressman Henry B. Gonzales hosted the Bexar County Democratic Dinner in San Antonio at the Menger Hotel near the Alamo, where more than two hundred Texans under Jim Bowie and Davy Crockett died fighting for Texas's independence from Mexico. More than sixty years later, Teddy Roosevelt had stayed at the Menger while he was training the Rough Riders for their epic battle on San Juan Hill in Cuba. The Menger serves fantastic mango ice cream, to which I became addicted. On election eve 1992, when we stopped in San Antonio, my staff bought four hundred dollars' worth of it, and everyone on the campaign plane ate it all night long.

The speaker at the dinner was the House majority leader, Hale Boggs of Louisiana. He made an impassioned speech for McGovern and the Democrats. The next morning I got him up early to catch a plane to Alaska, where he was scheduled to campaign with Congressman Nick Begich. The following day, on a swing through the snowcapped mountains, their plane crashed and was never found. I admired Hale Boggs and wished we'd overslept that day. He left a remarkable family behind. His wife, Lindy, a lovely woman and a first-rate politician herself, took his New Orleans House seat and was one of my strongest supporters in Louisiana. I appointed her U.S. ambassador to the Vatican.

The other notable event occurred during Sargent Shriver's last visit to Texas. We had a great rally in McAllen, deep in South Texas, and rushed back to the airport, almost on time, to fly to Texarkana, where Congressman Wright Patman had raised a crowd of several thousand people on State Line Boulevard, the border between Arkansas and Texas. For some reason, our plane didn't take off. After a few minutes, we learned that a pilot flying a single-engine plane had become disoriented in the foggy night sky above McAllen and was circling the airport, waiting to be talked down. In Spanish. First they had to find an instrument-rated pilot who could speak Spanish, then they had to calm the guy down and bring him in. As the drama unfolded, I was sitting across from Shriver, briefing him on the Texarkana stop. If we had any doubt how low the campaign's fortunes had sunk, this removed it. Shriver took it all in stride and asked the flight attendants to serve dinner. Soon there were two planes full of staff and a large press corps eating steak on the tarmac in McAllen. When we finally got to Texarkana, more than three hours late, the rally had disbanded, but about two hundred diehards, including Congressman Patman, came to the airport to greet Shriver. He jumped off the plane and shook hands with every one of them as if it were the first day of a close election.

McGovern lost Texas 67 to 33 percent, a slightly better showing than he made in Arkansas, where only 31 percent of the voters supported him. After the election, Taylor and I stayed around a few days to thank people and wrap things up. Then Hillary and I went back to Yale, after a brief vacation in Zihuatanejo on Mexico's Pacific Coast.

It's built up now, but then it was still a little Mexican hamlet with bumpy unpaved streets, open bars, and tropical birds in the trees.

We got through our finals in good shape, especially considering our long absence. I had to work hard to master the arcane rules of Admiralty Law, which I took only because I wanted to have a course taught by Charles Black, an eloquent, courtly Texan who was well liked and respected by the students and who was especially fond of Hillary. Much to my surprise, the jurisdiction of admiralty law extended to any waterway in the United States that had been navigable in its original condition. That included lakes built from damming once-navigable rivers around my hometown.

In the spring term of 1973, I took a full class load but was preoccupied with going home and with what was going to happen with Hillary. Both of us especially enjoyed staging that year's Barristers Union Prize Trial. We wrote a trial based on the characters in the movie **Casablanca.** Ingrid Bergman's husband was killed, and Humphrey Bogart was put on trial for it. Burke Marshall's friend and former colleague in the Justice Department, John Doar, came to New Haven with his young son to judge the trial. Hillary and I hosted him and were very impressed. It was easy to understand why he had been so effective in enforcing civil rights rulings in the South. He was quiet, direct, smart, and strong. He judged well, and Bogie was acquitted by the jury.

One day after my class in Corporate Tax, Professor Chirelstein asked me what I was going to do when I graduated. I told him I was going home to Arkansas and supposed I would just hang up a shingle on my own since I had no job offers. He said there was a sudden, unexpected vacancy on the faculty of the University of Arkansas Law School at Fayetteville. He suggested that I apply for the position and volunteered to recommend me. It had never occurred to me that I could or should get a teaching job, but I was intrigued by the idea. A few days later, in late March, I drove home for Easter break. When I got to Little Rock, I pulled off the highway, went to a pay phone, called the law school dean, Wylie Davis, introduced myself, told him what I'd heard about the vacancy, and said I'd like to apply. He said I was too young and inexperienced. I laughed and told him I'd been hearing that for years, but if he was hard up, I'd be good for him, because I'd work hard and teach any courses he wanted. Besides, I wouldn't have tenure, so he could fire me at any time. He chuckled and invited me to Fayetteville for an interview; I flew there in the first week of May. I had strong letters of recommendation from Professor Chirelstein, Burke Marshall, Steve Duke, John Baker, and Caroline Dinegar, chairman of the political science department at the University of New Haven, where I had taught Constitutional Law and Criminal Law to undergraduates. The interviews went well, and on May 12, I got a letter from Dean Davis offering me a position as an assistant professor at a salary of $14,706. Hillary was all for it, and ten days later I accepted.

It wasn't much money, but teaching would enable me to work off my National Defense Education loan rather than pay it off. My other law school loan was unique in that it required me and my classmates to pay our loans down with a small fixed percentage of our annual incomes until the aggregate debt of our class was retired. Obviously, those who made more paid more, but we all knew that when we borrowed the money. My experience with the Yale loan program was the stimulus for my desire to change the federal student-loan program when I became President, so that students would have the option of repaying their loans over a longer period of time as a fixed percentage of their income. That way, they would be less likely to drop out of school for fear of not being able to repay their loans, and less reluctant to take jobs with high social utility but low pay. When we gave students the option of income-contingent loans, a lot of them took it.

Though I hadn't been the most diligent student, I was pleased with my law school years. I had learned a lot from some brilliant and dedicated professors, and from my fellow students, more than twenty of whom I would later appoint to positions in the administration or the federal judiciary. I had come to a keener appreciation of the role the law plays in maintaining a sense of order and fairness in our society, and in providing a means to make social progress. Living in New Haven gave me a sense of the reality and ethnic diversity of urban America. And, of course, it was in New Haven that I met Hillary.

Thanks to the Duffey and McGovern campaigns, I had made some good friends who shared my passion for politics and learned more about the mechanics of electioneering. I had also learned again that winning elections as a progressive requires great care and discipline in crafting and presenting a message and a program that gives people the confidence to change course. Our society can absorb only so much change at a time, and when we move forward we must do it in a way that reaffirms our core convictions of opportunity and responsibility, work and family, strength and compassion—the values that have been the bedrock of America's success. Most people have their hands full raising their kids, doing their jobs, and paying the bills. They don't think about government policy as much as liberals do, nor are they as obsessed with power as the new right conservatives. They have a lot of common sense, and a desire to understand the larger forces shaping their lives, but can't be expected to abandon the values and social arrangements that at least enable them to survive and feel good about themselves. Since 1968, conservatives have been very good at convincing middle America that progressive candidates, ideas, and policies are alien to their values and threatening to their security. Joe Duffey was a coal miner's son who was morphed into a weak, ultra-liberal elitist. George McGovern was a genuine war hero, sent to the Senate by the conservatives of rural South Dakota, who was turned into a spineless, wild-eyed leftist who wouldn't stand up for America but would tax and spend it into oblivion. In both cases, the candidates and their campaigns made mistakes that reinforced the images their opponents were trying hard to create. I already knew enough about how difficult it was to push the rocks of civil rights, peace, and anti-poverty programs up the political hill to know we couldn't expect to win all the time, but I was determined to stop helping our opponents win without a fight. Later, both as governor and as President, I made some of the same mistakes all over again, but not as many as I would have had I not been given the chance to work for those two good men, Joe Duffey and George McGovern.

I was happy to be going home to the prospect of interesting work, but I still didn't know what to do about Hillary, or what was best for her. I had always believed she had as much (or more) potential to succeed in politics as I did, and I wanted her to have her chance. Back then, I wanted it for her more than she did, and I thought coming to Arkansas with me would end the prospect of a political career for her. I didn't want to do that, but I didn't want to give her up, either. Hillary had already decided against working for a big firm or clerking for a judge in favor of a position with Marian Edelman's Children's Defense Fund in its new office in Cambridge, Massachusetts, so we were going to be a long way away from each other.

That was all we knew when we finished law school and I took Hillary on her first overseas trip. I gave her a tour of London and Oxford, then we went west to Wales, then back into England to the Lake District, which I hadn't seen before. It's beautiful and romantic there in the late spring. One evening at sunset, on the shore of Lake Ennerdale, I asked Hillary to marry me. I couldn't believe I'd done it. Neither could she. She said she loved me but couldn't say yes. I couldn't blame her, but I didn't want to lose her. So I asked her to come home to Arkansas with me to see how she liked it. And to take the Arkansas bar exam, just in case.

EIGHTEEN

I n June, Hillary flew to Little Rock for a visit. I took her home the long way, to show her a part of the state I loved. We drove west up the Arkansas River for seventy miles to Russellville, then south down Highway 7 through the Ouachita Mountains and National Forest, stopping from time to time to look at the beautiful vistas. We spent a couple of days in Hot Springs with Mother, Jeff, and Roger, then went back to Little Rock for a prep course on the Arkansas Bar exam, which proved helpful enough that both of us passed.

After the bar, Hillary went back to Massachusetts to start her job with the Children's Defense Fund, and I went to Fayetteville to begin my new life as a law professor. I found the perfect place to live, a beautiful little house designed by the famous Arkansas architect Fay Jones, whose stunning Thorncrown Chapel in nearby Eureka Springs won international awards and accolades. The house was on more than eighty acres of land about eight miles east of Fayetteville, on Highway 16. The land's eastern border was the middle fork of the White River. A few dozen cattle grazed the pasture. The house, built in the mid-1950s, was essentially a one-room structure, long and thin, divided down the middle, with the bathroom dropped like a block in the center. Both the front and back walls were a series of sliding glass doors, which, along with skylights in the bedroom and bathroom, guaranteed lots of light. Running in front of the whole length of the living room was a screened-in porch, which jutted out from the house as the land sloped down to the road. The house proved to be a godsend of peace and quiet, especially after I started my first campaign. I loved to sit on the porch and near the fireplace, and to walk in the field by the river with the cattle.

The house did have a couple of drawbacks. Mice visited every night. When I realized I couldn't get rid of them and they kept to themselves in the kitchen, I started leaving them bread crumbs. The outdoors was full of spiders, ticks, and other menaces. They didn't bother me much, but when a brown recluse spider bit Hillary, her leg swelled up enormously and took a long time to go back down. And the place was impossible to secure. We had a rash of burglaries across northwest Arkansas that summer. The culprit was hitting lots of rural houses up and down High-way 16. One evening when I came home, it looked as if someone had been there, but nothing was missing. Perhaps I'd scared him off. On impulse, I sat down and wrote a letter to the burglar, in case he came back:

Dear Burglar:

Things in my house were so much the same, I could not tell whether or not you actually entered the house yesterday. If not, here is what you will find—a TV which cost $80 new one and a half years ago; a radio which cost $40 new three years ago; a tiny record player that cost $40 new three years ago; and a lot of keepsakes, little things, very few of which cost over $10. Almost all the clothes are over two or three years old. Hardly worth risking jail for.

William J. Clinton

I taped the letter to the fireplace. Unfortunately, the ploy didn't work. The next day when I was at work, the guy came back and took the TV, the radio, the record player, and one thing I purposely left off the list: a beautifully engraved German military sword from World War I. I was heartsick about losing it because Daddy had given it to me, and because, just a year earlier, the only other valuable thing I owned, the Selmer Mark VI tenor saxophone Mother and Daddy had given me in 1963, had been stolen out of my car in Washington. Eventually I replaced the sax with a 1935 Selmer "cigar cutter" model, but the sword proved irreplaceable.

I spent the last weeks of a very hot August preparing my classes and running around the university track in the hottest hours of the day, getting my weight down to 185 pounds for the first (and last) time since I was thirteen. In September, I began to teach my first classes: Antitrust, which I had studied at Yale and enjoyed very much, and Agency and Partnership, dealing with the nature of contractual relationships and the legal responsibilities that arise out of them. I had sixteen students in Antitrust and fifty-six in A and P. Antitrust law is rooted in the idea that the government should prevent the formation of monopolies as well as other noncompetitive practices in order to preserve a functioning, fair free-market economy. Since I knew that not all the students had a good grounding in economics, I tried hard to make the material clear and the principles understandable. Agency and Partnership, by contrast, seemed straightforward enough. I was afraid the students would get bored and also miss the importance and occasional difficulty of determining the exact nature of the relationships between parties in a common enterprise, so I tried to think of interesting and illuminating examples to keep the classroom discussion going. For example, the Watergate hearings and the White House response to the ongoing revelations had raised a lot of questions about the perpetrators of the break-in. Were they agents of the President, and if not, for whom and on whose authority were they acting? In all the classes I taught, I tried to get a lot of students involved in the discussions and to make myself easily available to them in my office and around the law school.

I enjoyed writing exams, which I hoped would be interesting, challenging, and fair. In the accounts I've read of my teaching years, my grading has been questioned, with the implication that I was too easy, either because I was too soft or too eager not to offend potential supporters when I ran for office. At Yale, the only grades were Honors, Pass, or Fail. It was usually pretty hard to get Honors and virtually impossible to fail. At many other law schools, especially those where the admissions standards were more lax, the grading tended to be tougher, with the expectation that 20 to 30 percent of a class should fail. I didn't agree with that. If a student got a bad grade, I always felt like a failure too, for not having engaged his or her interest or effort. Almost all the students were intellectually capable of learning enough to get a C. On the other hand, I thought a good grade should mean something. In my big classes, ranging from fifty to ninety students, I gave two or three A's and about the same number of D's. In one class of seventy-seven, I gave only one A, and only once did I flunk a student. Usually the students who were going to flunk would withdraw rather than risk an F. In two smaller classes, I gave more A's because the students worked harder, learned more, and deserved them.

Although the University of Arkansas law school's first

black students had entered twenty-five years earlier, it was
not until the early seventies that a substantial number of
them finally began to enter state law schools across the
South. Many were not well prepared, especially those
whose education had been confined to poor segregated
schools. About twenty black students took my courses
between 1973 and 1976, and I got to know the others.
Almost all of them were working very hard. They wanted
to succeed, and several of them lived under enormous
emotional pressure because they were afraid they couldn't
make it. Sometimes their fears were justified. I'll never forget reading one black student's exam paper with a mixture
of disbelief and anger. I knew he had studied like a demon
and understood the material, but his exam didn't show it.
The right answers were in there, but finding them required
digging through piles of misspelled words, bad grammar,
and poor sentence construction. An A's worth of knowledge was hidden in the bushes of an F presentation, flawed
by things he hadn't learned going all the way back to elementary school. I gave him a B−, corrected the grammar
and spelling, and decided to set up tutoring sessions to
help transform the black students' hard work and native
intelligence into better results. I think they helped, both
substantively and psychologically, though several of the
students continued to struggle with their writing skills and
with the emotional burden of having one foot through the
door of opportunity and the other held back by the heavy
weight of past segregation. When many of those students
went on to distinguished careers as lawyers and judges, the
clients they represented and the parties they judged probably had no idea how high a mountain they had had to
climb to reach the bar or the bench. When the Supreme
Court upheld the principle of affirmative action in 2003, I

thought of my black students, of how hard they worked and all they had to overcome. They gave me all the evidence I'd ever need to support the Court's ruling.

Besides my interaction with the students, the best thing about being a law professor was being part of a faculty filled with people I liked and admired. My best friends on the faculty were two people my age, Elizabeth Osenbaugh and Dick Atkinson. Elizabeth was a brilliant Iowa farm girl, a good Democrat, and a devoted teacher who became good friends with Hillary, too. Eventually, she went back to Iowa to work in the Attorney General's office. When I was elected President, I persuaded her to come to the Justice Department, but after a few years she again went back home, largely because she thought it would be better for her young daughter, Betsy. Sadly, Elizabeth died of cancer in 1998, and her daughter went to live with Elizabeth's brother. I have tried to keep in touch with Betsy over the years; her mother was one of the finest people I've ever known. Dick Atkinson was a friend from law school who had grown dissatisfied with private practice in Atlanta. I suggested he consider teaching and urged him to come to Fayetteville for an interview. He did, and was offered and accepted a position on our faculty. The students loved Dick, and he loved teaching. In 2003, he would become Dean of the Arkansas Law School. Our most famous and fascinating professor was Robert Leflar, the most eminent legal scholar our state ever produced, a recognized authority in torts, conflicts of law, and appellate judging. In 1973, he was already past the mandatory retirement age of seventy and was teaching a full load for a dollar a year. He had been on the faculty since he was twenty-six. For several years before I knew him, Bob had commuted weekly between Fayetteville and New York, where he taught a course in appellate judging to federal and state judges at New York University Law School, a course that more than half the Supreme Court justices had taken. He was never late for class in either place.

Bob Leflar was a small, wiry man with huge, piercing eyes, and he was still as strong as an ox. He couldn't have weighed more than 150 pounds, but while working in his yard he carried around big chunks of flagstone that I could hardly lift. After every Razorback football homecoming game, Bob and his wife, Helen, hosted a party in their home. Sometimes guests would play touch football in the front yard. I remember one game in particular, when Bob and I and another young lawyer played against two big young guys and a nine-year-old boy. The game was tied and we all agreed that whoever scored next would win. Our side had the ball. I asked Bob if he really wanted to win. He said, "I sure do." He was as competitive as Michael Jordan. So I told the third man on our team to center the ball, let the rusher come after me, and go block the tall man defending the backfield to the right. The nine-year-old was covering Bob, on the assumption that I'd throw the ball to the taller, younger man, or that if Bob got the ball the kid would be able to touch him. I told Bob to block the kid to the right too, then run hard left, and I'd throw the ball to him right before the rusher got to me. When the ball was snapped, Bob was so excited he knocked the boy to the ground and ran left. He was wide open when our teammate completed his blocking assignment. I lobbed the ball to Bob and he ran across the goal line, the happiest seventy-five-year-old man in America. Bob Leflar had a steel-trap mind, the heart of a lion, a tough will, and a childlike love of life. He was sort of a Democratic version of Strom Thurmond. If we had more like him, we'd win more often. When Bob died at ninety-three, I thought he was still too young to go.

Law school policies were set by the faculty at regular meetings. On occasion I thought they ran too long and got too mired in details best left to the dean and other administrators, but I learned a lot about academic governance and politics in them. Generally, I deferred to my colleagues when there was a consensus because I felt they knew more than I did and had a longer-term commitment to the academic life. I did urge the faculty to undertake more pro bono activities and to relax the "publish or perish" imperative for professors in favor of greater emphasis on classroom teaching and spending more out-of-class time with students.

My own pro bono work included handling minor legal problems for students and a young assistant professor; trying—unsuccessfully—to persuade more doctors in Springdale, just north of Fayetteville, to accept poor patients on Medicaid; preparing a brief for the U.S. Supreme Court in an antitrust case at the request of Attorney General Jim Guy Tucker; and, in my first appearance as a lawyer in court, filing a brief to defend my friend State Representative Steve Smith in an election-law dispute in Madison County.

Huntsville, the county seat and Orval Faubus's hometown, had a little more than a thousand people. The Democrats held all the courthouse offices, from the judge and sheriff on down, but there were a lot of Republicans in the hills and hollows of north Arkansas, most of them descendants of people who had opposed secession in 1861. The Republicans had made a good showing in 1972, aided by the Nixon landslide, and they felt that if they could get enough absentee ballots thrown out, they might reverse the results of the local elections.

The case was tried in the old Madison County courthouse before Judge Bill Enfield, a Democrat who later became a friend and supporter of mine. The Democrats were represented by two real characters: Bill Murphy, a Fayetteville lawyer whose great passions were the American Legion, which he served as Arkansas commander, and the Democratic Party; and a local lawyer, W. Q. Hall, known as "Q," a one-armed wit with a sense of humor as sharp as the hook affixed to his left arm. The people hauled in to testify about why they voted absentee offered a vivid picture of the fierce loyalties, rough politics, and economic pressures that shaped the lives of Arkansas hill people. One man had to defend voting absentee at the last minute, without having applied in advance, as the law required. He explained that he worked for the state Game and Fish Commission, and he went down to vote on the day before the election because he had just been ordered to take the state's only bear trap over slow mountain roads to Stone County on election day. His vote was allowed. Another man was called back from his job in Tulsa, Oklahoma, to testify. He admitted that he had lived in Tulsa for more than ten years but still voted by absentee ballot in Madison County in every election, though he was no longer a legal resident there. When the Republican lawyer pressed him on it, he said with great emotion that Madison County was his home; that he had gone to Tulsa only because he couldn't make a living in the hills; that he didn't know or care anything about politics there; and that in another ten years or so, as soon as he could retire, he was coming home. I can't remember whether his vote was counted, but his attachment to his roots left a lasting impression on me.

Steve Smith testified about his role in gathering absentee ballots from residents in his father's nursing home. The law seemed to allow people associated with nursing homes to help residents fill out their ballots, but required the ballots to be mailed by a family member or someone with specific written authorization to do so. Steve had picked up all the ballots and dropped them in the nearest mailbox. I presented the judge with what I thought was a very persuasive brief, arguing that it was nonsensical to say Steve couldn't mail them; no one had suggested that he had tampered with them, or that the residents didn't want him to mail them. For all we knew, not all the elderly residents even had family members who could perform the chore. Judge Enfield ruled against me and Steve, but upheld enough of the absentee votes for County Judge Charles Whorton, Sheriff Ralph Baker, and their crew to stay in office.

I had lost my part of the case but gained invaluable insight into the lives of Arkansas hill people. And I had made friends with some of the most effective politicians I would ever know. If a new person moved into Madison County, they would know within a week if he or she was a Democrat or a Republican. The Republicans had to come to the courthouse to register to vote. The county clerk went to the Democrats' homes to register them. Two weeks before each election they called all the Democrats, asking for their votes. They were called again on election morning. If they hadn't voted by late afternoon, someone went to their homes and took them to the polls. On the day of my first general election, in 1974, I called Charles Whorton to see how we were doing. He said heavy rain had washed a bridge out in a remote part of the county and some of our folks couldn't get to the polls, but they were working hard and thought we would win by about 500 votes. I carried Madison County by 501 votes.

A couple of months after I moved to Fayetteville, I felt completely at home there. I loved teaching, going to Razorbacks football games, driving around in the mountains, and living in a university community of people who cared about the things I did. I made friends with Carl Whillock, a university vice president who had short gray hair and a very reserved manner. I first met him at lunch at Wyatt's Cafeteria in the big shopping mall on a hill between Fayetteville and Springdale. Everyone at our table was criticizing President Nixon except Carl, who didn't say a word. I had no idea what he thought, so I asked him. I'll never forget his monotone reply: "I agree with Harry Truman. He said Richard Nixon is the kind of man who would take wooden nickels off a dead man's eyes." In the old days, wooden nickels were the round wood objects morticians put on the eyes of corpses to keep them closed during the embalming process. Carl Whillock was a book you couldn't judge by its cover. Beneath his buttoned-down appearance was a tough mind and a brave heart.

I especially liked two women professors whose husbands were in the state legislature. Ann Henry taught at the Business School; her husband, Morriss, was an ophthalmologist and our state senator. Ann and Morriss became special friends to Hillary and me, and when we married, they hosted our wedding reception at their home. Diane Kincaid was a professor in the political science department, then married to State Representative Hugh Kincaid. Diane was beautiful, brilliant, and politically savvy. When Hillary moved to Fayetteville, Diane and Hillary became more than friends; they were soul mates, finding in each other's company the kind of understanding, stimulation, support, and love that come along all too rarely in life.

Though Fayetteville, like all of northwest Arkansas, was growing fast, it still had a quaint little town square with an old post office in the middle, which was later converted into a restaurant and bar. Retail stores, offices, and banks lined the four sides of the square, and every Saturday morning it was filled with a farmers' market offering fresh produce. My cousin Roy Clinton ran the Campbell-Bell Department Store on the northwest corner of the square. I traded with him and learned a lot about my new hometown. The courthouse was just a block off the square. The local lawyers who practiced there and had offices nearby included an impressive collection of wily older lawyers and bright young ones, many of whom would soon become strong supporters.

The local political hangout was Billie Schneider's Steakhouse on Highway 71, north of town. Billie was a hard-boiled, gravel-voiced, tough-talking woman who'd seen it all but never lost her consuming, idealistic passion for politics. All the local politicos hung out at her place, including Don Tyson, the chicken magnate whose operation would become the largest agricultural company in the world, and Don's lawyer, Jim Blair, a six-foot-five-inch idiosyncratic genius who would become one of my closest friends. A few months after I moved to Fayetteville, Billie closed the steakhouse and opened a bar and disco in the basement of a hotel across the street from the courthouse. All the same folks hung out there, but she also developed a big following among university students, whom she mobilized to work for her candidates in elections. Billie was a big part of my life until the day we buried her.

I left my mountain lair for a few days over Thanksgiving to visit Hillary in Cambridge. She and I didn't resolve our situation, but she did agree to come visit me over the Christmas holidays. I loved her and wanted to be with her, but I understood her reservations. I was passionate and driven, and nothing in my background indicated I knew what a stable marriage was all about. She knew that being married to me would be a high-wire operation in more ways than one. Also, Arkansas must still have seemed an alien place for her to settle, though she no longer felt it was the other side of the moon. And as I've said, I wasn't sure it was right for her. I still thought she should have her own political career. At that point in my life I thought that work was more important than having a personal life. I had met many of the ablest people of my generation, and I thought she was head and shoulders above them all in political potential. She had a big brain, a good heart, better organizational skills than I did, and political skills that were nearly as good as mine; I'd just had more experience. I loved her enough both to want her and to want the best for her. It was a high-class dilemma.

When I got back to Arkansas, political talk had begun in earnest. Like Democrats everywhere, our people were stirred up by Senator Sam Ervin's Watergate hearings and the continuation of the war. It appeared that we would have a chance to make some gains in the midterm congressional elections, especially after the price of oil shot up and gasoline began to be rationed. However, the local Democrats did not believe the prospects of unseating our congressman, John Paul Hammerschmidt, were very good. Hammerschmidt had a very conservative voting record and was a strong defender of President Nixon. But he also had a friendly, low-key manner, came home and traveled his district on most weekends, and had a fabulous casework operation, helping little towns get water and sewer grants and securing government benefits for constituents, often from programs he had voted to slash back in Washington. Hammerschmidt was in the lumber business, had good support from the small-business people in the district, and took care of the large timber, poultry, and trucking interests, which made up a significant portion of the economy.

I talked to several people that fall about whether they would be interested in running, including Hugh and Diane Kincaid, Morriss and Ann Henry, Steve Smith, and state representative Rudy Moore, who was Clark Whillock's brother-in-law. Everyone thought the race needed to be made, but no one wanted to make it; it seemed too unwinnable. Also, it seemed that Governor Bumpers, who was immensely popular, was likely to challenge Senator Fulbright in the Democratic primary. Fulbright was from Fayetteville, and most of my friends, though they liked Bumpers, felt obligated to help the senator in what was sure to be an all-uphill battle.

As it became clear that no one in our area who could run a strong race was willing to do it, I began to think about running myself. It seemed absurd on the face of it. I had been home only six months after nine years away. I was just three months into my new job. I had no contacts in most of the district. On the other hand, Fayetteville, with its students and liberal Democrats, was not a bad place to start. Hot Springs, where I grew up, was the biggest town in the south end of the district. And Yell County, where the Clintons were from, was part of it, too. All told, I had relatives in five of the district's twenty-one counties. I was young, single, and willing to work all hours of the day and night. And even if I didn't win, if I made a good showing I didn't think it would hurt me in any future campaigns I might undertake. Of course, if I got waxed, my long-hoped-for political career could be over before it began.

I had a lot to think about when Hillary came to visit me shortly after Christmas. We were talking it over in my house one morning in early January when the phone rang. It was John Doar, with whom Hillary and I had spent some time the previous spring when he came to Yale to judge our **Casablanca** Prize Trial. He told me that he had just agreed to become the chief counsel for the House Judiciary Committee's inquiry into whether President Nixon should be impeached, and that Burke Marshall had recommended me to him. He wanted me to take a leave of absence from the law school, come to work, and help him recruit some other good young lawyers. I told him I was thinking about running for Congress, but I'd consider the offer and call him back the next day. I had to think fast, and as would so often happen in the years ahead, I turned to Hillary for judgment and advice. By the time I called John back, I had made up my mind. I thanked him for the offer but declined, saying that I had decided to make the long-shot race for Congress instead, because there were lots of gifted young lawyers who would give anything to work for him on the impeachment inquiry but no one else to take on the fight in Arkansas. I could tell John thought I was making a foolish mistake, and by every rational standard I was. But, as I've said before, a lot of your life is shaped by the opportunities you turn down as much as those you take up.

I suggested to John that he ought to sign up Hillary and

our Yale classmates Mike Conway and Rufus Cormier. He laughed and said Burke Marshall had recommended them too. Eventually they all went to work for John and did an outstanding job. Doar wound up with an extraordinary array of talented young people, proving that, as I had expected, he didn't need me to have a great staff.

A couple of days before Hillary had to go back to Cambridge, I took her to Huntsville, about twenty-five miles east of my house, to see former governor Faubus. If I was going to run for Congress, I'd have to pay a courtesy call on him sooner or later. Besides, much as I disapproved of what he'd done at Little Rock, he was bright and had a brain full of Arkansas political lore, which I wanted to pick. Faubus lived in a beautiful big Fay Jones house his supporters had built for him when, after twelve years, he left the governor's office with no money. He was then living with his second wife, Elizabeth, an attractive Massachusetts woman who still wore a 1960s beehive hairdo and who, before her marriage, had had a brief career as a political commentator in Little Rock. She was extremely conservative, and was in stark contrast in both looks and outlook to the governor's first wife, Alta, who was a good hill-country populist and the editor of the local paper, the **Madison County Record.**

Hillary and I were ushered into the Faubus home and seated at a big round table in an all-glass alcove looking out on the Ozarks and the town below. For the next four or five hours, I asked questions and Orval talked, delivering a fascinating account of Arkansas history and politics: what life was like during the Depression and World War II, why he was still defending what he had done in Little Rock, and how he thought President Nixon's problems might or might not affect the congressional race. I didn't say much; I would just ask a new question when Faubus finished answering the previous one. Hillary didn't say anything. Surprisingly, for more than four hours Elizabeth Faubus didn't either. She just kept us supplied with coffee and cookies.

Finally, when it was obvious the interview was winding down, Elizabeth Faubus stared hard at me and said, "This is all very well, Mr. Clinton, but how do you feel about the international conspiracy to overthrow the United States?" I stared right back and replied, "Why, I'm against it, Mrs. Faubus. Aren't you?" Not long afterward, the Faubuses moved to Houston, where Orval was distraught after Elizabeth was brutally murdered in their apartment. When I was inaugurated governor in 1979, I invited all the former governors to attend, including Faubus. It was a controversial move among my progressive supporters, who felt I'd given the old rascal new life. The way it played out proved them right, a classic example of the old adage that no good deed goes unpunished. Still, I'd do it all over again just to have the Red-menace exchange with Elizabeth Faubus.

After Hillary left, I went to see Dean Davis, told him I wanted to run for Congress, and promised to keep up with all my class work and to make time for the students. I was assigned to teach Criminal Procedure and Admiralty in the spring term and had already done quite a bit of the preparation work. To my surprise, Wylie gave me his blessing, probably because it was too late to get anyone else to teach the courses.

Arkansas' Third District comprised twenty-one counties in the northwest quadrant of the state and was one of America's most rural congressional districts. It included the big counties of Washington and Benton in the extreme north-west; seven northern counties in the Ozarks; eight counties in the Arkansas River valley below; and four in the Oua-chita Mountains in the southwest. Thanks to Wal-Mart, Tyson Foods and other poultry companies, and trucking companies like J. B. Hunt, Willis Shaw, and Harvey Jones, the towns in Benton and Washington counties were grow-ing more prosperous, and more Republican. Eventually, the growth of evangelical Christian churches and the influx of retirees from the Midwest combined with the success of the big companies to make northwest Arkansas the most Republican and most conservative part of the state, with the exception of Fayetteville, where the university kept things in closer balance.

In 1974, Fort Smith, on the Oklahoma border, was both the district's biggest city, with a population of 72,286, and its most conservative. In the 1960s, the city fathers had turned down urban-renewal funds, which they believed were the first step to socialism, and when Water-gate figure John Mitchell was indicted a few years later, his lawyers said Fort Smith was one of only three places in America where he could get a fair trial. What he would have gotten there was a hero's welcome. East of Fort Smith down the Arkansas River, and in the mountains to the north, the counties tended to be populist, socially conser-vative, and pretty evenly divided between Republicans and Democrats.

The mountain counties, especially Madison, Newton, and Searcy, were still fairly isolated. A few new people moved in, but many families had been on the same land for more than a hundred years. They spoke in a unique way, using vivid expressions I had never heard before. My favorite was a description of someone you really don't like:

"I wouldn't piss in his ear if his brain was on fire." The rural counties in the southern part of the district tended to be more Democratic but still conservative, and the largest county, Garland, with Hot Springs as the county seat, usually voted Republican in presidential elections and had a lot of new Republican retirees from up north. The congressman was very popular there.

There were very few blacks, most of them concentrated in Fort Smith; Hot Springs, the district's second-largest city; and in the river valley towns of Russellville and Dardanelle in the southeast part of the district. Organized labor had a fairly strong presence in Fayetteville, Fort Smith, and Hot Springs, but not much elsewhere. Because of bad mountain roads and the predominance of old cars and pickups, the district had the highest gasoline usage per registered vehicle of any in the United States, a factor of no small importance given the rising price and shortage of gas. It also had the highest percentage of disabled veterans of any congressional district. Congressman Hammerschmidt was a World War II veteran who courted veterans heavily. In the previous election, the social and fiscal conservative forces had overwhelmed the hard-core Democrats and economic populists, as Nixon defeated McGovern 74 to 26 percent. Hammerschmidt got 77 percent. No wonder no one else wanted to make the race.

A few days after Hillary left, Carl Whillock took me on my first campaign trip, a swing across the district's northern counties. We stopped first in Carroll County. In Berryville, a town of about 1,300, I visited the store of Si Bigham, a prominent local Democrat, who had his four-year-old grandson with him. More than twenty years later, that little boy, Kris Engskov, would become my personal aide in the White House. I also met the local Methodist minister, Vic Nixon, and his wife, Freddie. They were liberal Democrats who opposed the Vietnam War, and they agreed to support me. They wound up doing far more. Freddie became my county coordinator, charmed the socks off the leaders in all the rural voting precincts, and later worked for me in the governor's office, where she never stopped trying to convince me that the death penalty was wrong. When Hillary and I got married, Vic performed the ceremony.

We drove on east to Boone County and then drove to Mountain Home, county seat of the district's northeasternmost county, Baxter. Carl wanted me to meet Hugh Hackler, a businessman who told us right off the bat that he was committed to another candidate in the primary. Still, we started talking. When he found out I was from Hot Springs, he told me Gabe Crawford was a good friend of his. When I replied that Gabe had been Daddy's best friend, Hugh got out of his commitment to the other guy and supported me. I also met Vada Sheid, who owned a furniture store and was the county treasurer. She noticed a loose button on my shirt and sewed it on while we visited. She became a supporter that day, too. She never sewed another button for me, but after I became governor and she went to the state Senate, her votes often bailed me out in other ways.

After we left Mountain Home, we drove south to Searcy County. We stopped in St. Joe, which had about 150 people, to see the county Democratic chairman, Will Goggins. Will was over eighty, but still sharp as a tack, physically strong, and passionate about his politics. When he said he'd be for me, I knew it meant a lot of votes, as you'll see. In the county seat of Marshall, I met George Daniel, who ran the local hardware store. George's younger brother, James, was a student at the law school who gave me one of my first thousand-dollar contributions; his older brother, Charles, was the county's doctor. I got a lot of laughs out of George's homespun humor and learned one searing lesson. A Vietnam veteran who'd been away from the county for several years came into his store one day and bought a pistol. He said he wanted to do some target practice. A day later he killed six people. It turned out he had just walked away from Fort Roots, the federal mental-health facility for veterans in North Little Rock, where he'd been for several years, apparently because of trauma from his war experiences. It took George Daniel a long time to get over that. And it was the best argument I ever encountered for the kind of background checks on gun buyers required by the Brady bill, which I finally signed into law in 1993, after nineteen more years of avoidable killings by known felons, stalkers, and people with mental disorders.

When Carl and I got back to Fayetteville, I was higher than a kite. I had always liked one-on-one "retail" politics when I was working for other candidates. Now I really loved going into the little towns, or stopping at country stores, cafés, and filling stations along the road. I was never very good at asking for money, but I liked going into people's homes and businesses and asking for their votes. Besides, you could never tell when you would meet a colorful character, hear an interesting story, learn something worth knowing, or make a new friend.

That first day on the campaign trail would be followed by scores of others just like it. I would set out in the morning from Fayetteville, work as many towns and counties as I could until late at night, then head back home if I had to teach the next day or, if I didn't, stay with a hospitable

Democrat so that I could go on to the next county in the morning.

The next Sunday I went back east to finish up the mountain counties. I almost didn't make it. I had forgotten to fill the tank of my 1970 American Motors Gremlin before the weekend. Because of the gasoline shortage, federal law required filling stations to be closed on Sunday. But I had to get back to the hills. In desperation, I called the president of our local natural-gas company, Charles Scharlau, and asked him if he would let me have a tank of gas from the pump in his equipment yard. He told me to go on down there and he'd take care of it. To my astonishment he showed up and filled my gas tank himself. Charles Scharlau single-handedly kept my fledgling campaign going.

First I drove to Alpena to see the county Democratic chairman, Bo Forney, whom I had missed on my first stop there. I found his little house with no trouble. There was a pickup truck with a gun rack in the front yard, standard equipment for mountain men. Bo met me at the front door in jeans and a white T-shirt over his ample girth. He was watching TV and didn't say much as I made my pitch for his support. When I finished, he said that Hammerschmidt needed beating, and that although he would win his hometown of Harrison by a large margin, he thought we could do some good in the rural part of Boone County. Then he gave me the names of some people to see, told me I'd get more votes if I got a haircut, said he'd support me, and went back to his television. I wasn't sure what to make of Bo until I took a closer look at his pickup on my way back to the car. It had a bumper sticker that said "Don't Blame Me. I Voted for McGovern." Later, when I asked Bo about the bumper sticker, he said he didn't care what the critics said about McGovern, the Democrats were for the common people and the Republicans weren't, and that's all there was to it. When I was President and Bo was in ill health, our mutual friend and fellow yellow-dog Democrat Levi Phillips brought him to spend the night with us in the White House. Bo had a good time, but refused to sleep in the Lincoln Bedroom. He couldn't forgive him for the Republican Party's excesses during the Reconstruction Era after the Civil War, or for its devotion to the wealthy and powerful throughout the twentieth century. Now that Bo and Mr. Lincoln are both in heaven, I like to think they've gotten together and resolved their differences.

After Alpena, I went to Flippin, a town of about a thousand in Marion County, which had more miles of unpaved roads than any other in our state. I went to see two young men I wanted to run my campaign there, Jim "Red" Milligan and Kearney Carlton. They put me between them in Red's pickup and took off down one of those dirt roads to Everton, a tiny place in the most remote part of the county, to see Leon Swofford, who owned the only store and whose support was worth a couple of hundred votes. About ten miles out of town, Red stopped the truck in the middle of nowhere. We were engulfed in dust. He took out a pack of Red Man chewing tobacco, put a wad in his mouth, then handed it to Kearney, who followed suit. Then Kearney handed it to me and said, "We want to see what you're made of. If you're man enough to chew this tobacco, we'll be for you. If you're not, we'll kick you out and let you walk back to town." I thought about it and said, "Open the damn door." They glared at me for about five seconds, then roared with laughter and took off down the road to Swofford's store. We got the votes there, and a lot more over the years. If they had measured me by my taste for Red Man, I might still be wandering the back roads of Marion County.

A few weeks later, I'd be tested like that again. I was in Clarksville in the Arkansas River valley with my twenty-two-year-old county leader, Ron Taylor, who was from a prominent political family and politically wise well beyond his years. He took me out to the county fair to see the county sheriff, whose support Ron said we had to have to carry the county. We found him at the rodeo grounds, holding the reins of a horse. The rodeo was about to begin with a parade of horses marching around the arena. The sheriff handed me the reins and told me to join the parade and I'd be introduced to the crowd. He promised that the horse was well behaved. I was wearing a dark suit and tie and wing-tipped shoes. I hadn't been on a horse since I was five, and then only to pose for a picture in a cowboy outfit. I had turned down the chewing tobacco, but I took the reins and mounted the horse. After a lifetime of watching cowboy movies, I thought, how hard could it be? When the opening ceremony started, I rode out into the arena just as if I knew what I was doing. About a quarter of the way around the arena, right after I'd been introduced, the horse stopped and reared up on its hind legs. Miraculously, I didn't fall off. The crowd clapped. I think they believed I'd done it on purpose. The sheriff knew better, but he supported me anyway.

I finished my round of the Ozarks in Newton County, one of the most beautiful places in America, home of the Buffalo River, which recently had been named the first river protected by Congress under the Wild and Scenic Rivers Act. I stopped first in Pruitt, a small settlement on the Buffalo, to see Hilary Jones. Though he lived in a modest home, he was a road builder and might have been the wealthiest man in the county. His family's Democratic heritage went all the way back to the Civil War and before, and he had the genealogical books to prove it. He was deeply rooted in his land along the river. His family had lost a lot of it in the Depression, and when he came home from World War II he worked for years to put it all back together again. The Buffalo's designation as a protected river was his worst nightmare. Most landowners along the river were given life tenancies; they couldn't sell the land to anyone but the government in their lifetimes, and when they died only the government could buy it. Because Hilary's homestead was on the main highway, the government was going to take it by eminent domain in the near future and make it part of the headquarters operation. He and his wife, Margaret, had eight children. They wanted the kids to have their land. There was an old cemetery on it where people born in the 1700s were buried. Whenever anyone died destitute and alone in the county, Hilary paid for the burial in his cemetery. I supported protecting the river, but I thought the government should have let the old homesteaders keep their land under a scenic easement, which would have precluded any development or environmental degradation but allowed families to pass the land on from generation to generation. When I became President, my experience with the folks on the Buffalo gave me a better understanding than most Democrats of the resentments a lot of western ranchers had when environmental considerations clashed with what they saw as their prerogatives.

Hilary Jones finally lost his fight with the government. It took a lot out of him, but it never killed his passion for politics; he moved into a new house and carried on. He spent a memorable night with Hillary and me in the White House. He almost cried when Hillary took him into the map room to show him the war map FDR was using when he died in Warm Springs, Georgia, in 1945. He worshipped FDR. Unlike Bo Forney, he spent the night in the Lincoln Bedroom. When he visited us in the White House, I kidded him about sleeping in Lincoln's bed, which Bo Forney had turned down. Hilary said at least he had "slept on the side of the bed that was under Andrew Jackson's picture."

From the day I met him until the day I flew home from the White House to speak at his funeral, Hilary Jones was my man in Newton County. He embodied the wild, beautiful spirit of a special place I had loved since I first saw it at sixteen.

The county seat, Jasper, was a town of fewer than four hundred people. There were two cafés, one frequented by Republicans, the other by Democrats. The man I wanted to see, Walter Brasel, lived beneath the Democratic café, which his wife ran. I got there on a Sunday morning and he was still in bed. As I sat in the little living room, he got up and began to put his pants on with the door from the living room to the bedroom open. He wasn't fully awake, slipped, and was rotund enough to literally roll over a couple of times until he was ten or fifteen feet out into the living room. I wanted his support, so I couldn't laugh. But he did. He said he'd once been young, thin, and fast, the starting guard on the Coal Hill High School basketball team, which he had led to the state championship over Little Rock Central High in the 1930s; he'd gained all his weight in the years when he was the county bootlegger, and never lost it. After a while, he said he'd be for me, maybe just so he could go back to bed.

Next, I drove out into the country to see Bill Fowler, who had a farm in Boxley. Bill had served as the Arkansas representative in the Agricultural Soil and Conservation Service in the Johnson administration. As we stood on a hillside with a spectacular view of the mountains, he said he would support me, but he didn't think Hammerschmidt would "have enough of Nixon's crap on him to stink by election day." He then offered this assessment of the President: "I hate to say this about a Republican, but Nixon could have been a wonderful President. He's brilliant and he's got a sackful of guts. But he's just sorry, and he can't help it." I thought about what he said all the way back to Fayetteville.

During the early weeks of the campaign, besides the retail politics I tried to work through the mechanics. As I've mentioned, Uncle Raymond and Gabe Crawford co-signed a note for $10,000 to get me started, and I began to raise money, at first mostly in the Fayetteville area, then across the district and eventually throughout the state. Several of my friends from Georgetown, Oxford, and Yale and the McGovern and Duffey campaigns sent small checks. My largest contributor was my friend Anne Bartley, Governor Winthrop Rockefeller's stepdaughter, who later ran the Arkansas office in Washington, D.C., when I was governor. Eventually thousands of people gave, often one-, five-, or ten-dollar bills as we passed the bucket at rallies.

On February 25, I formally announced my candidacy with my family and a few friends at the Avanelle Motel, where Mother went for coffee most mornings before work.

Uncle Raymond gave me a little house in a good location for the Hot Springs headquarters. Mother, my Park Avenue neighbor Rose Crane, and Bobby Hargraves, a young lawyer whose sister I had worked with in Washington, set up a first-class operation. Rose later moved to Little Rock and joined my administration when I became governor, but Mother kept building the organization and put it to work in future campaigns. The main headquarters was in Fayetteville, where my banker friend George Shelton agreed to be campaign chairman and F. H. Martin, a young lawyer I played basketball with, signed on as treasurer. I rented an old house on College Avenue, which was kept open mostly by college students, and often on weekends by my cousin Roy's fifteen-year-old daughter, Marie Clinton, alone. We painted big CLINTON FOR CONGRESS signs and put them on both sides of the house. They're still there, having been painted over many times as new enterprises moved in. Today there's one word over the old signs: TATTOO. Eventually, my childhood friend Patty Howe opened a headquarters in Fort Smith, and others cropped up around the district as we got closer to the election.

By the time I went to Little Rock to file on March 22, I had three opponents: State Senator Gene Rainwater, a crew-cut conservative Democrat from Greenwood, just south of Fort Smith; David Stewart, a handsome young lawyer from Danville in Yell County; and Jim Scanlon, the tall, gregarious mayor of Greenland, a few miles south of Fayetteville. I was most worried about Stewart because he was attractive, articulate, and from the Clintons' home county, which I had hoped would go for me.

The first big political event of the campaign was on April 6: the River Valley Rally in Russellville, a college town in the east end of the district. It was an obligatory event, and all the candidates for federal, state, and local

office were there, including Senator Fulbright and Governor Bumpers. Senator Robert Byrd of West Virginia was
the featured speaker. He gave an old-time fire-and-
brimstone speech and entertained the crowd by playing
the fiddle. Then the candidates' speeches started, with the
congressional candidates scheduled to speak last. By the
time everyone else had taken three to five minutes, it was
past ten o'clock. I knew the crowd would be tired and
bored by the time we got up, but I took a gamble and
chose to speak last. I figured it was my only chance to
make an impression.

I had worked hard on the speech and had hammered it
down to two minutes. It was a passionate call for a
stronger Congress that would represent ordinary people
against the concentration of power in the Republican
administration and its allied economic interests. Though I
had written the speech out, I gave it from memory and
poured my heart into it. Somehow it struck a responsive
chord with the audience, who, though tired after a long
evening, found the energy to rise to their feet and cheer.
As the crowd walked out, my volunteers gave them copies
of the speech. I was off to a good start.

When the event was over, Governor Bumpers came up
to me. After complimenting me on the speech, he said he
knew I had worked for Senator Fulbright and thought he
shouldn't be trying to unseat him. Then he stunned me by
saying, "In twelve years or so, you may be facing the same
decision regarding running against me. If you think it's
the right thing to do, go on and run, and remember I told
you to do it." Dale Bumpers was one smart cookie. He
could have made a handsome living as a psychologist.

The next seven weeks were a blur of rallies, sale barns,
pie suppers, money-raising, and retail politics. I got a big

financial and organizational boost when the AFL-CIO, at its meeting in Hot Springs, endorsed me. The Arkansas Education Association also endorsed me because of my support for federal aid to education.

I spent a lot of time in the counties where I was less well known and that were less well organized than the Ozark Mountain counties: Benton County in the extreme northwest, the counties bordering both sides of the Arkansas River, and the southwest counties in the Ouachita Mountains. In Yell County my campaign was run by my cousin Mike Cornwell, the local funeral-home operator. Since he had buried all the kinfolk there, he knew everyone, and he had an upbeat personality that kept him going in the uphill battle against his neighbor in Danville, David Stewart. There were an amazing number of people who took active roles in the campaign: idealistic young professional and business people, gifted local labor leaders, county and city officials, and die-hard Democrats, from high school students to seniors in their seventies and eighties.

By primary election day, we had outorganized and outworked the opposition. I got 44 percent of the vote, with Senator Rainwater barely edging out David Stewart for a spot in the runoff, 26 to 25 percent. Mayor Scanlon, who had no money but waged a game fight, got the rest.

I thought we would win handily in the June 11 runoff unless there was a very small turnout, in which case anything could happen. I didn't want my supporters to take the vote lightly and was alarmed when Will Goggins, the Democratic chairman of Searcy County, announced that all the voting there would be done in the courthouse on the square in Marshall. There was no way people living out in the country would drive thirty or forty miles over winding roads to vote in just one race. When I called and tried to talk him into opening more polling places, Will laughed and said, "Now, Bill, calm down. If you can't beat Rainwater without a big turnout here, you don't have a chance against Hammerschmidt. I can't afford to open rural polling places when only two or three people will vote. We'll need that money in November. You'll get whatever votes we cast."

On June 11, I won 69 to 31 percent, carrying the small turnout in Searcy County 177 to 10. After the November election, when I called Will to thank him for all his help, he said he wanted to put my mind at rest about something: "I know you think I rigged that runoff vote for you, but I didn't. Actually, you won 177 to 9. I gave Rainwater another vote because I couldn't stand to see anyone not in double figures."

The primary campaign was exhilarating for me. I had thrown myself into one unfamiliar circumstance after another and learned an enormous amount about people—the impact of government on their lives, and how their views of politics are shaped by both their interests and their values. I had also kept up with my teaching schedule. It was hard, but I enjoyed it and believed I did it pretty well except for one inexcusable mistake. After I gave exams in the spring, I had to grade them while the campaign was in full swing. I took my Admiralty exams in the car with me, grading them as we rode or at night when the campaign work was over. Somehow in the travel, I lost five of them. I was mortified. I offered the students the option of retaking the exam or getting full credit without a specific grade. They all took the credit, but one of them was particularly upset about it, because she was a good student who probably would have made an A, and because she was a good Republican who had worked for Congressman

Hammerschmidt. I don't think she ever forgave me for losing the exam or for running against her old boss. I sure thought about it when, more than twenty years later, that former student, federal judge Susan Webber Wright, became the presiding judge in the Paula Jones case. Susan Webber Wright was plenty smart, and maybe I should have just given her an A. At any rate, for the general election, I took leave without pay from the law school.

During the summer I kept up the hectic pace, with breaks for my brother's high school graduation, my tenth high school reunion, and a trip to Washington to see Hillary and meet some of her co-workers on the impeachment inquiry staff. Hillary and all her colleagues were working themselves to a frazzle under John's stern demands to be thorough, fair, and absolutely closed-lipped. I was worried about how exhausted she was—she was thinner than I had ever seen her, so thin her lovely but large head seemed to be too big for her body.

Over the weekend I took her away for some rest and relaxation to the Outer Banks of North Carolina. We had a great time together and I was beginning to think Hillary might actually join me in Arkansas when the inquiry was finished. Earlier in the year on a trip to Fayetteville, she'd been invited by Dean Davis to interview for a position on the law faculty. She came back a few weeks later, impressed the committee, and was offered a job, so now she could both teach and practice law in Arkansas. The question was whether she would. At the moment I was more worried about how tired and skinny she was.

I went back home to the campaign and a far bigger health problem in my family. On July 4, I spoke at the Mount Nebo Chicken Fry for the first time since I represented Frank Holt there in 1966. Jeff, Mother, and Rose Crane drove up to hear me and help me work the crowd. I could tell Jeff wasn't feeling well and learned he hadn't been working much. He said it was too hard to stand all day. I suggested he come up to Fayetteville and spend a couple of weeks with me, where he could work the phones and give the headquarters some adult supervision. He took me up on the offer and seemed to enjoy it, but when I'd come home from the road at night, I could see he was ill. One night I was shocked to see him kneeling by the bed and stretched across it. He said he couldn't breathe lying down anymore and was trying to find a way to sleep. When he could no longer work a full day at headquarters, he went home. Mother told me his problem had to be a result of his diabetes or the medicine he had been taking for it for years. At the VA hospital in Little Rock, he was diagnosed with cardiomegaly, an enlargement and deterioration of the heart muscle. Apparently there was no cure for it. Jeff went home and tried to enjoy what was left of his life. A few days later when I was in Hot Springs campaigning, I met him briefly for coffee. He was on his way to the dog races in West Memphis, dapper as always, decked out in white shirt, pants, and shoes. It was the last time I ever saw him.

On August 8, President Nixon, his presidency doomed by the tapes he had kept of his conversations with aides, announced his intention of resigning the following day. I thought the President's decision was good for our country but bad for my campaign. Just a couple of days before the announcement, Congressman Hammerschmidt had defended Nixon and criticized the Watergate investigation in a front-page interview in the **Arkansas Gazette.** My campaign had been gaining momentum, but with the albatross of Nixon lifted from Hammerschmidt's shoulders, you could feel the air go out of it.

I got a second wind when Hillary called me a few days later to tell me she was coming to Arkansas. Her friend Sara Ehrman was driving her. Sara was more than twenty years older than Hillary and had seen in her the full promise of the new opportunities open to women. She thought Hillary was nuts to be coming to Arkansas after having done such good work and making so many friends in Washington, so she took her own good time getting Hillary to her destination, while trying to change her mind every few miles or so. When they finally got to Fayetteville it was Saturday night. I was at a rally in Bentonville, not far north, so they drove up to meet me. I tried to give a good speech, as much for Hillary and Sara as for the crowd. After I shook hands, we went back to Fayetteville and our future.

Two days later, Mother called to tell me Jeff had died in his sleep. He was only forty-eight years old. She was devastated, and so was Roger. Now she had lost three husbands and he had lost two fathers. I drove home and took care of the funeral arrangements. Jeff had wanted to be cremated, so we had to ship his body off to Texas because Arkansas didn't have a crematorium back then. When Jeff's ashes came back, in accordance with his instructions they were scattered over Lake Hamilton near his favorite fishing dock, while Mother and her friend Marge Mitchell watched.

I delivered the eulogy at his funeral. I tried to put into a few words the love he gave to Mother; the fathering guidance he gave to Roger; the friendship and wise counsel he gave to me; the kindness he showed to children and people down on their luck; the dignity with which he bore the pain of his past and his final illness. As Roger said so often in the days after he died, "He tried so hard." Whatever he was before he came into our lives, during his six short years with us he was a very good man. We all missed him for a long time.

Before Jeff got sick, I knew next to nothing about diabetes. It subsequently killed my 1974 campaign chairman, George Shelton. It afflicts two children of my friend and former chief of staff Erskine Bowles, as well as millions of other Americans, with a disproportionate impact on our minority population. When I became President, I learned that diabetes and its complications account for a staggering 25 percent of all Medicaid costs. That's a big reason why, as President, I supported stem cell research and a diabetes self-care program that the American Diabetes Association called the most important advance in diabetes care since the development of insulin. I did it for Erskine's kids, for George Shelton, and for Jeff, who would have wanted more than anything to spare others his pain and premature end.

A few days after the funeral, Mother urged me, in her "get up and go on" way, to resume campaigning. Politics stops for death, but not for very long. So I went back to work, though I made sure to call and see Mother more often, especially after Roger left for Hendrix College in Conway in the fall. He was so concerned about her, he almost didn't go. Mother and I finally talked him into it.

As September arrived, I was still behind in the polls 59 to 23 percent after eight months of backbreaking work. Then I got lucky. On September 8, five days before the state Democratic convention in Hot Springs, President Ford granted Richard Nixon an unconditional pardon for all crimes he "committed or may have committed" while

President. The country strongly disagreed. We were back in business.

At the state convention, all the attention was focused on my race. Governor Bumpers had defeated Senator Fulbright by a large margin in the primary, and there were no other serious contests on the ballot. I hated seeing Fulbright lose, but it was inevitable. The convention delegates were pumped up and we added fuel to the fire by packing the Hot Springs Convention Center with hometown friends and extra supporters from all over the district.

I gave a barn burner of a speech, articulating what I believed in a way that I hoped would unite the conservative and liberal populist elements in the district. I began by blasting President Ford's pardon of former President Nixon. One of my better lines was: "If President Ford wants to pardon anybody, he ought to pardon the administration's economic advisors."

Over the years, I changed my mind about the Nixon pardon. I came to see that the country needed to move on, and I believe President Ford did the right, though unpopular, thing, and I said so when we were together in 2000 to celebrate the two hundredth anniversary of the White House. But I haven't changed my mind about Republican economic policies. I still believe FDR was right when he said, "We have always known that heedless self-interest was bad morals. We now know that it is bad economics." That has even greater application today than it did in 1974.

We left Hot Springs on a roll. With seven weeks to go we had a chance, but a lot of work to do. Our headquarters operation was getting better and better. My best young volunteers were getting to be experienced pros.

They got some very good suggestions from the person the Democratic Party sent down to help us. His name was Jody Powell, and his boss, Governor Jimmy Carter of Georgia, had assumed a leading role in helping Democrats win in 1974. A couple of years later, when Jimmy Carter ran for President, a lot of us remembered and were grateful. When Hillary came down, she helped, too, as did her father and her younger brother, Tony, who put up signs all over north Arkansas and told the Republican retirees from the Midwest that the Rodhams were Midwest Republicans but that I was all right.

Several of my law students proved to be dependable drivers. When I needed them during my congressional campaign, there were a couple of airplanes I could borrow to fly around in. One of my pilots, sixty-seven-year-old Jay Smith, wore a patch over one eye and wasn't instrument-rated, but he had been flying in the Ozarks for forty years. Often when we hit bad weather, he swooped down below the clouds to follow a river valley through the mountains, all the while telling me stories or bragging on Senator Fulbright for knowing Vietnam was a mistake before anyone else did.

Steve Smith did a brilliant job of research on issues and Hammerschmidt's voting record. He came up with a series of ingenious pamphlets comparing my positions on issues to his votes on them, and we put out one a week for the last six weeks of the campaign. They got good coverage in the local papers, and Steve turned them into effective newspaper ads. For example, the Arkansas River valley from Clarksville to the Oklahoma border south of Fort Smith was full of coal miners who had worked for decades in the open pit mines that scarred the landscape until federal laws forced the land to be restored. Many of the miners had debilitating black-lung disease from all the years of breathing the coal dust and were entitled to benefits from the federal government. The congressman's casework operation helped them get the benefits, but when the Nixon administration wanted to cut back the program, he voted for the cutbacks. Folks in the river valley didn't know that until Steve Smith and I told them.

I also had a number of positive proposals, some of which I advocated for twenty years, including a fairer tax system, a national health-insurance program, public funding of presidential elections, a lean and more effective federal bureaucracy, more federal education funding and creation of a federal Department of Education (it was then still an office in the Department of Health, Education and Welfare), and incentives to promote energy conservation and solar power.

Thanks largely to financial support from the national labor unions, which my friend and regional AFL-CIO leader Dan Powell pushed hard for, we got enough money to do some television ads. Old Dan Powell was talking about me becoming President when I was still twenty-five points behind for Congress. All I did was stand in front of a camera and talk. It forced me to think in twenty-eight-second segments. After a while, I didn't need a stopwatch to tell me whether I was a second or two long or short. Production costs were low for the ads.

The TV ads may have been rudimentary, but our radio ads were great. One memorable ad, produced in Nashville, featured a country singer who sounded just like Arkansas-born Johnny Cash. It opened, "If you're tired of eating beans and greens and forgotten what pork and beefsteak means, there's a man you ought to be listening to." It went on to slam the Nixon administration for financing huge grain sales to the Soviet Union, which drove up the price of food and animal feed, hurting poultry and cattle operations. The song said, "It's time to push Earl Butz [Nixon's agriculture secretary] away from the trough." In between verses came this refrain: "Bill Clinton's ready, he's fed up too. He's a lot like me, he's a lot like you. Bill Clinton's gonna get things done, and we're gonna send him to Washington." I loved that spot. Don Tyson, whose costs of poultry production had soared with the grain sales and whose brother, Randal, was working hard for me, made sure I had enough money to run the song to death on rural radio.

As we moved closer to election day, the support got stronger and so did the opposition. I got the endorsement of the **Arkansas Gazette,** the state's largest newspaper, plus several papers in the district. I began to campaign hard in Fort Smith, where there was strong support from the black community, especially after I joined the local chapter of the NAACP. I found good support all over heavily Republican Benton County. Across the river from Fort Smith, four or five people practically worked themselves to death trying to turn Crawford County for me. I got a great reception in Scott County, south of Fort Smith, at the annual fox and wolf hunters' field trial. It was an all-night event out in the country, at which men who loved their dogs as much as their kids (and took just as good care of them) showed the dogs and then cut them loose to chase foxes and bay at the moon while the women kept mountains of food out on picnic tables all through the night. I was even getting some strong support from Harrison, the congressman's hometown, from a few brave souls who weren't afraid to take on the small-town establishment.

One of the most exciting rallies of the election occurred one fall afternoon on the White River, not far from the infamous Whitewater property I later invested in but never saw. The Democrats in the area were all stirred up because the Nixon Justice Department was trying to send the Democratic sheriff of Searcy County, Billy Joe Holder, to jail for income tax evasion. Under our 1876 constitution, the salaries of the state and local officials have to be approved by a vote of the people; they had last been raised in 1910. County officials made just $5,000 a year. The governor made only $10,000, but at least he had a mansion, and his transportation and food costs were covered. A lot of the local officials were forced to use their expense accounts, which as I recall were about $7,000 a year, just to live. The Justice Department wanted Sheriff Holder to go to jail for not paying income tax on his personal expenditures from the account. I believe the Holder case was the smallest income tax–evasion prosecution ever brought by the federal government, and the hill people were convinced it was politically motivated. If so, it backfired. After an hour and a half of deliberations, the jury returned a verdict of not guilty. It turned out they voted to acquit right away, then stayed in the jury room more than an hour longer just to make it look right. Billy Joe walked out of the courthouse and drove straight to our rally, where he was greeted like a hero home from war.

On the way back to Fayetteville, I stopped in Harrison, where the trial was held, to discuss it with Miss Ruth Wilson, a public accountant who did tax work for lots of hill people. I told Miss Ruth that I understood she had helped Holder's lawyer, my friend F. H. Martin, with the jury selection. She said she had. I asked her half jokingly if she had packed it with Democrats. I'll never forget her reply:

"No, Bill, I didn't. Actually, there were a fair number of Republicans on that jury. You know, those young men who came down from Washington to prosecute the sheriff were smart fellows, and they looked real good in their expensive suits. But they just didn't know our folks. It's the strangest thing. Nine of those twelve jurors had been audited by the Internal Revenue Service in the last two years." I was glad Ruth Wilson and her boys were on my side. After she worked over those Washington lawyers, the Justice Department began to ask prospective jurors in tax cases about their own experiences with the IRS.

With about two weeks to go, the congressman finally got his campaign in gear. He had seen a poll that said if he didn't, my momentum might carry me to a narrow victory. His people pulled out all the stops. His business friends and the Republicans went to work. Someone began calling all the papers asking for the nonexistent photo of me demonstrating against President Nixon at the 1969 Arkansas-Texas game, giving birth to the infamous "tree story" I mentioned earlier. In Hot Springs, the chamber of commerce had a big dinner to thank him for all he'd done. Several hundred people showed up, and it received extensive coverage in the local paper. Across the district, Republicans scared businesspeople by charging that I had so much support from unions, I would be a puppet for organized labor in Congress. In Fort Smith, six thousand postcards we sent to political supporters identified in our phone canvass were never delivered. Apparently my labor support didn't extend to the postal workers there. The cards were found a few days after the election in the trash outside the main post office. The state branch of the American Medical Association came out strongly for Hammerschmidt, hitting me for my efforts to get doctors in the Springdale area to treat poor people on Medicaid. Hammerschmidt even got federal revenue-sharing funds to pave the streets of Gilbert, a small town in Searcy County, a few days before the election. He carried it 38–34, but it was the only township in the county he won.

I got an inkling of just how effective his work had been the weekend before the election when I went to a closing rally at the Hot Springs Convention Center. We didn't have as many people there as had attended his dinner a few days before. Our people had worked their hearts out, but they were tired.

Still, on election day, I thought we might win. As we gathered in my headquarters to watch the returns, we were nervous but hopeful. We led in the vote count until nearly midnight, because the largest and most Republican county, Sebastian, reported late. I carried twelve of the fifteen counties with fewer than eight thousand total votes, including every voting box along the Buffalo River in Newton and Searcy counties. But I lost five of the six biggest counties, suffering narrow defeats of fewer than five hundred votes each in Garland County, where I grew up, and Washington County, where I lived, losing Crawford County by eleven hundred votes and getting killed in Benton and Sebastian counties, where my combined losses were twice the total margin of victory. We each won one county by about two to one. He won Sebastian County, the biggest, and I won Perry County, the smallest. It seems ironic now, when rural Americans vote overwhelmingly Republican in national elections, that I began my political career with a profoundly rural base, born of intense personal contact and responsiveness to both their resentments and their real problems. I was on their side, and they knew it. The final total vote was 89,324 to 83,030, about 52 to 48 percent.

The Democrats had a good night nationally, picking up forty-nine House seats and four seats in the Senate, but we just couldn't overcome Hammerschmidt's enormous popularity and his last-minute push. When the campaign began, his approval rating was 85 percent. I had whittled it down to 69 percent, while mine had gone from zero to 66 percent, very good but not good enough. Everybody said I made a good showing and had a bright future. That was nice to hear, but I'd wanted to win. I was proud of our campaign and I felt that somehow I had let the steam go out of it in the last few days, and in so doing let down all the people who worked so hard for me and the changes we wanted to make. Maybe if I'd had the money and the sense to run effective television ads on the congressman's voting record, it would have made a difference. Probably not. Nevertheless, in 1974, I saw firsthand, in thousands of encounters, that middle-class voters would support government activism to solve their problems, and those of the poor, but only if the effort was made with due care for their tax dollars, and if efforts to increase opportunity were coupled with an insistence on responsibility.

After I spent a few days traveling and calling around to thank people, I went into a funk. I spent most of the next six weeks at Hillary's house, a nice place near campus. Mostly I just lay on the floor, nursing my regrets and trying to figure out how I was going to pay off my campaign debt of over $40,000. My new salary of $16,450 was more than enough to live on and pay off my law school debts, but nowhere near enough to cover the debt from the campaign. Sometime in December, there was a big band dance at the university, which Hillary coaxed me into taking her to. After we danced a few hours, I began to feel better. Still, it would be a good while before I realized the congressman had done me a favor by beating me. If I had won and gone to Washington, I'm sure I never would have been elected President. And I would have missed the eighteen great Arkansas years that lay ahead.

NINETEEN

In January 1975, I went back to my teaching, the only full year I did it uninterrupted by politics. In the spring term, I taught Antitrust and held a seminar in White-Collar Crime; in summer school, Admiralty and Federal Jurisdiction; in the fall, White-Collar Crime again and Constitutional Law. In Constitutional Law, I spent two full weeks on **Roe** v. **Wade,** the Supreme Court decision that gave women a constitutional privacy right to an abortion in the first two trimesters of pregnancy, the approximate amount of time it takes a fetus to become "viable"—that is, able to live outside the mother's womb. After viability, the Court ruled, the state could protect a child's interest in being born against the mother's decision not to have it, unless her life or health would be threatened by continued pregnancy or childbirth. Some of my students who saw Constitutional Law as just another course in which they had to memorize the rule of law in each case couldn't understand why I spent so much time on **Roe.** It was easy to remember the three-trimester rule and the reasoning behind it.

I made them delve deeper, because I thought then, and still believe, that **Roe** v. **Wade** is the most difficult of all judicial decisions. Whatever they decided, the Court had to play God. Everyone knows life begins biologically at conception. No one knows when biology turns into humanity or, for the religious, when the soul enters the body. Most abortions that don't involve the life or health of the mother are chosen by scared young women and girls who don't know what else to do. Most people who are pro-choice understand that abortions terminate potential life and believe that they should be legal, safe, and rare and that we should support young mothers who decide to complete their pregnancies, as most of them do. Most ardent pro-lifers are all for prosecuting doctors but grow less certain when their argument that an abortion is a crime is carried to its logical conclusion: prosecuting the mother for murder. Even the fanatics who bomb abortion clinics don't target the women who keep them in business. Also, as we've learned first with Prohibition and later with our drug laws, which have more support than a total ban on abortion does, it's hard to apply the criminal law to acts that a substantial portion of the citizenry doesn't believe should be labeled crimes.

I thought then and still believe that the Court reached the right conclusion, though, as so often happens in American politics, its action sparked a powerful reaction, the growth of an active, effective national anti-abortion movement, which over time drastically reduced the practical availability of abortions in many places and drove large numbers of voters into the new right wing of the Republican Party. Regardless of what opinion polls show about voters' positions on abortion, our national ambivalence about it means that its impact on elections depends on which side feels more threatened. For most of the last thirty years, for example, during which a woman's right to choose has been secure, pro-choice voters have felt free to vote for or against candidates on other issues, while for anti-abortion voters, the other issues often didn't matter. Nineteen ninety-two was an exception. The highly publicized court of appeals decision in the **Webster** case, narrowing the right to choose, combined with the prospect of Supreme Court vacancies in the near future, threatened and galvanized the pro-choice voters, so I and other pro-choice candidates weren't hurt by our position that year. After I was elected, with the right to choose secure again, pro-choice suburbanites again felt free to vote for anti-abortion Republicans for other reasons, while pro-life Democrats and independents, who approved of my record on economic and other social issues, nevertheless often felt compelled to support pro-life candidates who were almost always conservative Republicans.

In 1975, I didn't know or care much about the politics of abortion. I was interested in the Supreme Court's herculean effort to reconcile conflicting convictions about law, morality, and life. In my opinion they did about the best they could do, lacking access to the mind of God. Whether my students agreed with me or not, I wanted them to think hard about it.

In the fall, I got a new teaching assignment: I was asked to come down to the university's Little Rock campus once a week to teach a night seminar in Law and Society to students who worked during the day in law enforcement. I was eager to do it and enjoyed my interaction with people who seemed genuinely interested in how their work in police departments and sheriffs' offices fit into the fabric of both the Constitution and citizens' daily lives.

Besides teaching, I kept my hand in politics and did some interesting legal work. I was appointed to head a state Democratic Party committee on affirmative action. It was designed to assure increased participation by women and minorities in party affairs without falling into the trap of the McGovern rules, which gave us delegates to the national convention who were representative of every demographic group but often hadn't ever really worked for the party and couldn't get any votes. The assignment gave me a chance to travel the state meeting Democrats, both black and white, who cared about the issue.

The other thing that kept me politically active was the necessity to pay off my campaign debt. I finally did it in much the way we financed the campaign, with lots of small-dollar events and with the help of some generous larger givers. I got my first $250 from Jack Yates, a fine lawyer in Ozark who, along with his partner, Lonnie Turner, had worked hard for me in the election. Jack gave me the check within two weeks after the election. At the time, I wasn't sure where my next dollar was coming from and I never forgot it. Sadly, a couple of months after he helped me, Jack Yates died of a heart attack. After the funeral, Lonnie Turner asked me if I would take over Jack's black-lung cases. The Nixon administration had promulgated new rules making it harder to get benefits and requiring the cases of people already receiving them to be reviewed. In many cases, the benefits were being revoked. I began to drive down to the Ozarks once or twice a week to review the files and interview the old miners, with the understanding that any pay I got would come from fees from the cases I won.

Lonnie knew I cared a lot about the issue and was familiar with how the program worked. It's true that when the black-lung program was first implemented the evaluations were too lax and some people did get benefits who didn't need them, but as so often happens with government programs, the attempt to correct the problem went too far in the other direction.

Even before I took over Jack Yates's cases, I had agreed

to try to help another man in his fight for black-lung benefits. Jack Burns Sr., from a small town south of Fort Smith, was the father of the administrator of Ouachita Hospital in Hot Springs, where Mother worked. He was about five feet four inches tall and couldn't have weighed much more than one hundred pounds. Jack was an old-fashioned man of quiet dignity, who was severely damaged by black lung. He was entitled to the benefits, and he and his wife badly needed them to help pay their bills. In the months we worked together, I came to respect both his patience and his determination. When we won his case, I was almost as happy as he was.

I think there were more than one hundred cases like Jack Burns's in the stack of files Lonnie Turner gave me. I enjoyed going down to Ozark from Fayetteville over the winding road known as the "Pig Trail" to work on them. The cases were heard first by an administrative law judge, Jerry Thomasson, who was a fair-minded Republican. They could then be appealed to the federal judge in Fort Smith, Paul X. Williams, who was a sympathetic Democrat. So was his longtime clerk, Elsijane Trimble Roy, who was a great help to me. I was elated when President Carter appointed her Arkansas' first female federal judge.

While I continued my teaching, politics, and law work, Hillary was settling into life in Fayetteville. I could tell she really liked being there, maybe even enough to stay. She taught Criminal Law and Trial Advocacy, and oversaw both the legal-aid clinic and the students who did work for prison inmates. Some of the crusty old lawyers and judges and a few of the students didn't know what to make of her at first, but eventually she won them over. Because there is a constitutional right to a lawyer in a criminal case, our judges assigned local lawyers to represent poor defendants, and since poor criminal defendants almost never paid, the bar wanted Hillary's clinic to handle their cases. In its first year, it served more than three hundred clients and became an established institution at the law school. In the process, Hillary earned the respect of our legal community, helped a lot of folks who needed it, and established the record that, a few years later, led President Carter to appoint her to the board of directors of the national Legal Services Corporation.

Jimmy Carter was our featured speaker on Law Day, near the end of the spring term. It was clear that he was running for President. Hillary and I spoke with him briefly, and he invited us to continue the conversation down in Little Rock, where he had another engagement. Our talk confirmed my sense that he had a good chance to be elected. After Watergate and all the country's economic problems, a successful southern governor who wasn't involved in Washington's politics and could appeal to people the Democrats had lost in 1968 and 1972 seemed like a breath of fresh air. Six months earlier, I had gone to Dale Bumpers and urged him to run, saying, "In 1976, someone like you is going to be elected. It might as well be you." He seemed interested but said it was out of the question; he had just been elected to the Senate, and Arkansas voters wouldn't support him if he immediately started running for President. He was probably right, but he would have been a terrific candidate and a very good President.

Besides our work and normal social life with friends, Hillary and I had a few adventures in and around Fayetteville. One night we drove south down Highway 71 to Alma to hear Dolly Parton sing. I was a big Dolly Parton fan, and she was, you might say, in particularly good form that night. But the most enduring impact of the evening was that it was my first exposure to the people who brought her to Alma, Tony and Susan Alamo. At the time, the Alamos sold fancy performance outfits in Nashville to many of the biggest country music stars. That's not all they did. Tony, who looked like Roy Orbison on speed, had been a promoter of rock-and-roll concerts back in California, when he met Susan, who had grown up near Alma but had moved out west and become a television evangelist. They teamed up, and he promoted her as he had his rock and rollers. Susan had white-blond hair and often wore floor-length white dresses to preach on TV. She was pretty good at it, and he was great at marketing her. They built a small empire, including a large farming operation manned by devoted young followers as transfixed by them as the young acolytes of the Reverend Sun Myung Moon were by their leader. When Susan got cancer, she wanted to come home to Arkansas. They bought a big house in Dyer, her hometown, opened the place in Alma, where Dolly Parton sang, as well as a smaller version of their Nashville country outfit store just across the road, and had a big truckload of food from their California farm delivered each week to feed them and their Arkansas contingent of young laborers. Susan got on TV at home, and enjoyed some success until she finally succumbed to her illness. When she died, Tony announced that God had told him he was going to raise her from the dead someday, and he put her body in a glass box in their home to await the blessed day. He tried to keep their empire going with the promise of Susan's return, but a promoter is lost without his product. Things went downhill. When I was governor, he got into a big fight with the government over taxes and staged a brief, nonviolent standoff of sorts around his house. A couple of years later, he got involved with a younger woman. Lo and behold, God spoke to him again and told him Susan wasn't coming back after all, so he took her out of the glass box and buried her.

In the summer, I taught both semesters of summer school to earn some extra money and had a good time hanging around Fayetteville with Hillary and our friends. One day, I drove her to the airport for a trip back east. As we were driving down California Drive, we passed a beautiful little jagged brick house set back on a rise with a stone wall bracing up the front yard. There was a FOR SALE sign in the yard. She remarked on how pretty the place was. After I dropped her off, I checked the house out. It was a one-story structure of about eleven hundred square feet, with a bedroom, a bathroom, a kitchen with breakfast room attached, a small dining room, and a gorgeous living room that had a beamed ceiling half again as high as the others in the house, a good-looking offset fireplace, and a big bay window. There was also a large screened-in porch that could double as a guest bedroom most of the year. The house had no air conditioning, but the big attic fan did a good job. The price was $20,500. I bought the house with a $3,000 down payment, big enough to get the monthly mortgage payments down to $174.

I moved what little furniture I had into my new house and bought enough other things so that the place wasn't totally bare. When Hillary came back from her trip, I said, "Remember that little house you liked so much? I bought it. You have to marry me now, because I can't live there alone." I took her to see the house. It still needed a lot of work, but my rash move did the trick. Although she had never even told me she was prepared to stay in Arkansas, she finally said yes.

On October 11, 1975, we were married in the big living room of the little house at 930 California Drive, which had been replastered under the watchful eye of Marynm Bassett, a fine decorator who knew our budget was limited. For example, she helped us pick out bright yellow wallpaper for the breakfast room, but we put it on ourselves, an experience that reaffirmed my limitations as a manual laborer. Hillary wore an old-fashioned Victorian lace dress that I loved, and the Reverend Vic Nixon married us in the presence of Hillary's parents and brothers, Mother, Roger (who served as best man), and a few close friends: Hillary's closest friend from Park Ridge, Betsy Johnson Ebeling, and her husband, Tom; her Wellesley classmate Johanna Branson; my young cousin Marie Clinton; my campaign treasurer, F. H. Martin, and his wife, Myrna; our best friends on the law faculty, Dick Atkinson and Elizabeth Osenbaugh; and my childhood friend and tireless campaign worker Patty Howe. Hugh Rodham never thought he'd be giving his midwestern Methodist daughter to a Southern Baptist in the Arkansas Ozarks, but he did it. By then I had been working on him and the rest of the Rodhams for four years. I hoped I had won them over. They certainly had captured me.

After the ceremony, a couple hundred of our friends gathered at Morriss and Ann Henry's house for a reception, and that evening we danced the night away at Billie Schneider's place in the Downtown Motor Inn. At about 4 a.m., after Hillary and I had gone to bed, I got a call from my younger brother-in-law, Tony, who was at the Washington County jail. While he was driving one of the guests home after the party, he was pulled over by a state trooper, not because he was speeding or weaving on the road, but because his tipsy rider was dangling her feet out of the car's back window. After he stopped Tony, the deputy could see he had been drinking, so he hauled him in. When I got down to the jail to bail him out, Tony was shivering. The jailer told me that our sheriff, Herb Marshall, a Republican whom I liked, kept the jail real cold at night to keep the drunks from throwing up. As we were leaving, Tony asked me if I would get another man released who was in town making a movie with Peter Fonda. I did. He was shaking worse than Tony, so badly that when he got in his car to drive away, he rammed right into Hillary's little yellow Fiat. Even though I bailed him out, the guy never paid me for the costs of the car repair. On the other hand, at least he didn't leave his dinner on the floor of the county jail. So ended my first night as a married man.

For the longest time I'd never thought I'd get married. Now that I was, it felt right, but I wasn't sure where it would lead us.

Probably more has been written or said about our marriage than about any other in America. I've always been amazed at the people who felt free to analyze, criticize, and pontificate about it. After being married for nearly thirty years and observing my friends' experiences with separations, reconciliations, and divorces, I've learned that marriage, with all its magic and misery, its contentments and disappointments, remains a mystery, not easy for those in it to understand and largely inaccessible to outsiders. On October 11, 1975, I didn't know any of that. All I knew then was that I loved Hillary, the life, work, and friends we now had in common, and the promise of what we could do together. I was proud of her, too, and thrilled to be in a relationship that might not ever be perfect, but would certainly never be boring.

After our sleepless wedding night, we went back to work. We were in the middle of a school term, and I had black-lung hearings to attend. Two months later, we finally had a honeymoon in Acapulco, an unusual one, with Hillary's whole family and the girlfriend of one of her brothers along. We all spent a week together in a beautiful penthouse suite, walking on the beach, enjoying the restaurants. I know it was different, but we had a great time. I adored Hillary's mother, Dorothy, and enjoyed spending time with her father and brothers, playing pinochle and swapping stories. Like me, they were storytellers, and all of them could spin a good yarn.

I read one book in Acapulco, Ernest Becker's **The Denial of Death**—heavy reading for a honeymoon, but I was only a year older than my father was when he died, and I had just taken a big step. It seemed like a good time to keep exploring the meaning of life.

According to Becker, as we grow up, at some point we become aware of death, then the fact that people we know and love die, then the fact that someday we, too, will die. Most of us do what we can to avoid it. Meanwhile, in ways we understand only dimly if at all, we embrace identities and the illusion of self-sufficiency. We pursue activities, both positive and negative, that we hope will lift us beyond the chains of ordinary existence and perhaps endure after we are gone. All this we do in a desperate push against the certainty that death is our ultimate destiny. Some of us seek power and wealth, others romantic love, sex, or some other indulgence. Some want to be great, others to do good and be good. Whether we succeed or fail, we are still going to die. The only solace, of course, is to believe that since we were created, there must be a Creator, one to whom we matter and will in some way return.

Where does Becker's analysis leave us? He concludes: "Who knows what form the forward momentum of life will take in the time ahead. . . . The most that any one of us can seem to do is to fashion something—an object or ourselves—and drop it into the confusion, make an offering of it, so to speak, to the life force." Ernest Becker died shortly before **The Denial of Death** was published, but he seemed to have met Immanuel Kant's test of life: "How to occupy properly that place in creation that is assigned to man, and how to learn from it what one must be in order to be a man." I've spent a lifetime trying to do that. Becker's book helped convince me it was an effort worth making.

In December, I had another political decision to make. Many of my supporters wanted me to run for Congress again. The debt was paid off, and they wanted a rematch. I thought Congressman Hammerschmidt would be harder to beat this time, even if Jimmy Carter won the party's nomination. More important, I had lost my desire to go to Washington; I wanted to stay in Arkansas. And I was getting more interested in state government, thanks in part to the opportunity Attorney General Jim Guy Tucker had given me to write a brief to the U.S. Supreme Court on behalf of our state in an antitrust case involving the setting of interest rates on credit cards. Jim Guy was running for Congress, for the seat vacated by the retirement of Wilbur Mills, so the attorney general's job would be open and it had a lot of appeal for me.

While I was mulling it over, my friend David Edwards,

who was working for Citibank, called and asked us to go to Haiti with him. He said he had enough frequent flier miles built up to pay for our tickets, and he wanted to give us the trip as a wedding present. Barely a week after we returned from Mexico, we were off again.

By late 1975, Papa Doc Duvalier had passed from the scene, succeeded by his son, a portly young man whom everybody called Baby Doc. We saw him one day when he drove across the big square from his official residence in Port-au-Prince to lay a wreath at the monument to Haitian independence, a statue of a powerful freed slave blowing on a conch. His security force, the infamous Tontons Macoutes, were everywhere, and intimidating with their sunglasses and machine guns.

The Duvaliers had managed to dominate, pillage, and mismanage Haiti until it was the poorest county in our hemisphere. Port-au-Prince was still beautiful in places but had the feel of faded glory. I remember especially the frayed carpeting and broken pews in the National Cathedral. Despite the politics and poverty, I found the Haitians fascinating. They seemed lively and intelligent, and they produced beautiful folk art and captivating music. I marveled at the way so many of them seemed not only to survive but to enjoy life.

I was particularly intrigued by the voodoo religion and culture to which I had had some limited exposure in New Orleans, and that existed alongside Catholicism in Haiti. The name of the traditional Haitian religion comes from the Fon language of Benin in West Africa, where voodoo originated. It means "God" or "spirit," without the connotations of black magic and witchcraft attached to it in so many movies. Voodoo's central ritual is a dance during which spirits possess believers. On the most interesting day of the trip, I got the chance to observe voodoo in practice. David's Citibank contact in Port-au-Prince offered to take him, Hillary, and me to a nearby village to meet an unusual voodoo priest. Max Beauvoir had spent fifteen years outside Haiti, studying at the Sorbonne in Paris and working in New York. He had a beautiful blond French wife and two bright young daughters. He had been a practicing chemical engineer until his voodoo-priest grandfather, on his deathbed, chose Max to succeed him. Max was a believer, and he did it, though it must have proved a challenge for his French wife and westernized kids.

We arrived in the late afternoon, an hour or so before the dance ceremony, which Max opened to paying tourists as a way of covering some of the costs of his operation. He explained that in voodoo, God is manifest to humans through spirits that represent forces of light and darkness, good and evil, which are more or less in balance. After Hillary, David, and I finished our brief course in voodoo theology, we were escorted back to an open area and seated with other guests who had come to witness the ceremony, in which spirits are called forth and enter into the bodies of dancing believers. After several minutes of rhythmic dancing to pounding drums, the spirits arrived, seizing a woman and a man. The man proceeded to rub a burning torch all over his body and walk on hot coals without being burned. The woman, in a frenzy, screamed repeatedly, then grabbed a live chicken and bit its head off. Then the spirits left and those who had been possessed fell to the ground.

A few years after I witnessed this extraordinary event, a Harvard University scientist named Wade Davis, in Haiti searching for an explanation for the phenomenon of zombies, or walking dead, also went to see Max Beauvoir. According to his book **The Serpent and the Rainbow,** with the help of Max and his daughter, Davis managed to unravel the mystery of zombies, those who apparently die and rise to life again. They are administered a dose of poison by secret societies as punishment for some offense. The poison, tetrodotoxin, is extracted from puffer fish. In proper doses, it can paralyze the body and reduce respiration to such low levels that even the attending doctor believes the person is dead. When the poison wears off, the person wakes up. Similar cases had been reported in Japan, where puffer fish is a delicacy if properly prepared, and deadly if not.

I describe my brief foray into the world of voodoo because I've always been fascinated by the way different cultures try to make sense of life, nature, and the virtually universal belief that there is a nonphysical spirit force at work in the world that existed before humanity and will be here when we all are long gone. Haitians' understanding of how God is manifest in our lives is very different from that of most Christians, Jews, or Muslims, but their documented experiences certainly prove the old adage that the Lord works in mysterious ways.

By the time we got back from Haiti, I had determined to run for attorney general. I took another leave from teaching at the law school and got to work. I had two opponents in the Democratic primary: George Jernigan, the secretary of state; and Clarence Cash, who was head of the consumer protection division in Jim Guy Tucker's office. Both were articulate and not much older than I. Jernigan seemed to be the more formidable of the two, with a lot of friends in Governor Pryor's organization, at several county courthouses, and among conservatives across the state. Strangely, no Republicans filed, making it the only time I ever ran without opposition in the general election.

I knew I'd have to run the campaign out of Little Rock. Besides being the capital city, it is in the center of the state and has both the biggest vote and the largest fund-raising potential. I set up headquarters in an old house a couple of blocks from the Capitol building. Wally DeRoeck, a young banker from Jonesboro, agreed to be my campaign chairman. Steve Smith, who had done such good work in the Congress race, signed on as campaign manager. The office was run by Linda McGee, who did a terrific job on a shoestring budget: We ran the whole campaign on less than $100,000. Somehow Linda kept the place open long hours, paid the bills, and managed the volunteers. I was offered a place to stay by Paul Berry, whom I had met and liked when he ran Senator McClellan's Arkansas office and who was then a vice president at Union Bank. Apart from everything else, he insisted on my sleeping in his apartment's only bed, even if I got in from the road at two or three in the morning. Night after night I'd drag in to find him asleep on the couch in the living room, with a light on in the kitchen, where he'd left out my favorite snack, peanut butter and carrots.

Longtime friends like Mack McLarty and Vince Foster helped me break into the Little Rock business and professional communities. I still had good support from labor leaders, though some of it fell off when I refused to sign a petition supporting labor's effort to repeal Arkansas' right-to-work law by putting the question on the November ballot. Right-to-work laws enable people to work in plants with unionized workforces without paying union dues. Back then, the law appealed to my libertarian side. I later learned that Senator McClellan was so impressed by my position that he asked Paul Berry to call his main supporters and tell them he was for me. A few years later, I changed my mind about right to work. It's wrong, I think, for someone to reap the superior salaries, health care, and retirement plans normally found in union plants without making a contribution to the union that secures those benefits.

My base in the Third District seemed secure. All the folks who had worked for me in 1974 were willing to go again. I got some extra help from Hillary's brothers, both of whom had moved to Fayetteville and enrolled at the university. They also added a lot of fun to our lives. One night, Hillary and I went over to their place for dinner and spent the whole evening listening to Hugh regale us with tales of his adventures in Colombia with the Peace Corps—stories that sounded as if they came straight out of **One Hundred Years of Solitude** but that he swore were all true. He also made us piña coladas that tasted like fruit juice but packed quite a punch. After two or three I was so sleepy that I went outside and climbed into the back of my Chevy El Camino pickup truck, which I had inherited from Jeff Dwire. The back was covered in Astro-turf, so I slept like a lamb. Hillary drove me home, and the next day I went back to work. I loved that old truck and drove it until it completely wore out.

Out in the state, I found strong support in and around Hope, where I was born, and in the five or six counties outside the Third District where I had relatives. I got off to a good start among blacks in central, south, and east Arkansas, thanks to former students who were practicing law in those areas. And I had support from Democratic activists who had cheered my race against Hammer-schmidt from the sidelines or been involved in the work of my affirmative action committee. Despite all that, there were still gaping holes in the organization. Most of the campaign was an attempt to fill them.

As I traveled the state, I had to contend with the rise of a new political force, the Moral Majority, founded by the Reverend Jerry Falwell, a conservative Baptist minister from Virginia who had won a large television following and was using it to build a national organization committed to Christian fundamentalism and right-wing politics. In any part of the state, I might find myself shaking hands with someone who would ask if I was a Christian. When I said yes, I would be asked if I was a born-again Christian. When I said yes, there would be several more questions, apparently supplied by Falwell's organization. Once when I was campaigning in Conway, about thirty miles east of Little Rock, I was in the county clerk's office, where absentee ballots are cast. One of the women who worked there started in on me with the questions. Apparently, I gave the wrong answer to one of them, and before I left the courthouse she had cost me four votes. I didn't know what to do. I wasn't about to answer a question about religion falsely, but I didn't want to keep losing votes. I called Senator Bumpers, a good liberal Methodist, for advice. "Oh, I get that all the time," he said. "But I never let them get past the first question. When they ask me if I'm a Christian, I say, 'I sure hope so, and I've always tried to be. But I really think that's a question only God can judge.' That usually shuts them up." After Bumpers finished, I laughed and told him now I knew why he was a senator and I was just a candidate for attorney general. And for the rest of the campaign, I used his answer.

The funniest thing that happened in the race occurred in Mississippi County, in far northeast Arkansas. The county had two cities, Blytheville and Osceola, and a host of towns dominated by planters who farmed huge plots of land. Typically, their farmworkers and the small merchants whose incomes they made possible voted for the planters' choice, normally the most conservative person running—in this case, Secretary of State Jernigan. The county also had a strong local organization, headed by the county judge, "Shug" Banks, who was also for Jernigan. It looked hopeless, but the county was too big to ignore, so I devoted one Saturday to working Blytheville and Osceola. I was by myself and, to put it mildly, it was a discouraging day. In both towns, though I found some support, thanks to my former law students, most people I met either were against me or didn't know who I was and didn't care to learn. Still, I shook every available hand, finishing in Osceola about eleven at night. I finally gave up when I realized I still had a three-hour drive back to Little Rock and didn't want to fall asleep at the wheel.

As I was driving south through a string of little settlements, I remembered that I hadn't eaten all day and was hungry. When I came to a place called Joiner, I saw a light on in a beer joint. In the hope that it also served food, I pulled over and went in. The only people there were the man at the bar and four guys playing dominoes. After ordering a hamburger, I went outside to call Hillary from the pay phone. When I walked back in, I decided to introduce myself to the domino players. The first three, like so many people I'd met that day, didn't know who I was and didn't care. The fourth man looked up and smiled. I'll never forget his first words: "Kid, we're going to kill you up here. You know that, don't you?" I replied that I'd gotten that impression after a day of campaigning, but I was sorry to hear it confirmed. "Well, we are," he continued.

"You're a long-haired hippie professor from the university. For all we know, you're a Communist. But I'll tell you something. Anybody who would campaign at a beer joint in Joiner at midnight on Saturday night deserves to carry one box. So you hide and watch. You'll win here. But it'll be the only damn place you win in this county."

The man's name was R. L. Cox, and he was as good as his word. On election night, I was crushed in the other voting precincts controlled by the big farmers, but I got 76 votes in Joiner and my two opponents got 49. It was the only place in Mississippi County I carried, except for two black precincts in Blytheville that were turned the weekend before the election by a black funeral-home operator, LaVester McDonald, and the local newspaper editor, Hank Haines.

Luckily, I did better almost everywhere else, winning more than 55 percent of the total vote and carrying sixty-nine of the seventy-five counties, thanks to a big vote in south Arkansas, where I had lots of relatives and good friends, and a whopping 74 percent in the Third Congressional District. All the people who had worked so hard for me in 1974 were finally rewarded with a victory.

The summer after the election was a happy time for Hillary and me. We spent the first two months just having fun in Fayetteville with our friends. Then, in mid-July, we took a trip to Europe, stopping in New York to attend one night of the Democratic convention, after which we flew to Paris to meet up with David Edwards, who was working there. After a couple of days, we set out for Spain. Just after we crossed the Pyrenees, I got a message asking me to call the Carter campaign. When I returned the call from the village of Castro Urdiales, I was asked to chair the campaign in Arkansas, and I accepted immediately. I strongly supported Jimmy Carter, and though I was scheduled to teach in the fall at Fayetteville, I knew I could do the job. Carter was immensely popular in Arkansas because of his progressive record, his farming experience, his genuine commitment to his Southern Baptist faith, and his personal contacts, which included four prominent Arkansans who had been in his class at the Naval Academy. The issue in Arkansas was not whether the state would vote for him but by how much. After all the lost elections, the prospect of winning two in one year was too tempting to pass up.

We finished our vacation in Spain with a stop in Guernica, the town memorialized in Picasso's remarkable painting of its bombing in the Spanish civil war. When we got there, a Basque festival was in progress. We liked the music and dancing but had a hard time with one of the native delicacies, cold fish in milk. We explored the nearby caves with their prehistoric drawings and spent a glorious day in the shadow of the snowcapped Pyrenees on a hot beach that had a little restaurant with good, inexpensive food and beer at a nickel a glass. At the border on the way back into France—by this time it was early August, the vacation month in Europe—cars were stretched out before us as far as we could see, testament to the good sense of Europeans that life is more than work. For me, that adage would get harder and harder to live by.

When we got back home, I went to Little Rock to set up a campaign operation with Craig Campbell, a former executive of the state Democratic Party, who worked for Stephens, Inc., in Little Rock, then the largest investment bank in America outside Wall Street. It was owned by Witt and Jack Stephens. Witt Stephens was a longtime power in state politics. Jack, who was ten years younger, had gone to the Naval Academy with Jimmy Carter. Craig was a big, good-looking, fun-loving guy who was deceptively sensitive in personal and political ways that made him very effective.

I traveled the state to make sure we had a functioning organization in every county. One Sunday night, I went to a little black church just outside Little Rock. The pastor was Cato Brooks. When we got there, the place was already rocking to the music of a great gospel choir. During the second or third song, the door flew open and a young woman who looked like Diana Ross, in black knee-high boots and a tight knit dress, strode down the aisle, waved to the choir, and sat down at the organ. I had never heard organ music like that before. It was so powerful I wouldn't have been surprised if the instrument had levitated and left the church under its own power. When Cato got up to preach, four or five of the men of the church gathered around him, sitting on folding chairs. He chanted and sang virtually his entire sermon in rhythmic cadences punctuated by the sound of the spoons that the men were beating on their knees. After the sermon, the Reverend Brooks introduced me to speak for Carter. I was fired up, but I was nowhere near as good as Cato. When I sat down, he told me the church would be for Carter and suggested I leave because they were going to be there for another hour or so. A few steps outside the church, a voice behind me said, "Hey, white boy, you want some help with your campaign?" It was the organist, Paula Cotton. She became one of our best volunteers. Cato Brooks moved to Chicago not long after the campaign. He was too good to keep down on the farm.

While I was working in Arkansas, Hillary joined the

Carter campaign, too, taking on a much tougher assignment. She became the field coordinator in Indiana, a state that traditionally votes Republican in presidential elections but that the Carter staff hoped his farm roots would give him a chance to win. She worked hard and had some interesting adventures, which she eagerly recounted to me in daily phone conversations and during my one trip to Indianapolis.

The fall campaign was a roller coaster. Carter came out of the convention in New York with a thirty-point lead over President Ford, but the country was more evenly divided than that. President Ford made an impressive effort to catch up, mostly by questioning whether a southern governor, whose main promise was to give us a government as honest as the American people, had the experience to be President. In the end, Carter defeated Ford by about 2 percent of the popular vote and by 297 electoral votes to 240. The election was too close for our side to prevail in Indiana, but we carried Arkansas with 65 percent, just two points less than President Carter's 67 percent margin in his native Georgia and seven points better than the next largest victory margin, in West Virginia.

After the campaign, Hillary and I settled back into our home for a few months as I completed my final teaching assignments, in Admiralty and Constitutional Law. In three years and three months I had taught eight courses in five semesters and a summer session, taught two courses to law-enforcement officers in Little Rock, run for office twice, and managed the Carter campaign. And I had loved every minute of it, regretting only the time it took me away from our life and friends in Fayetteville, and that little house at 930 California Drive that brought Hillary and me so much joy.

TWENTY

For the last couple of months of 1976, I commuted to Little Rock to prepare for my new job. Paul Berry got me some office space on the eighteenth floor of the Union Bank building, where he worked, so I could interview prospective staff members.

A lot of idealistic and able people applied for jobs. I persuaded Steve Smith to become my chief of staff, to make sure we came up with some good policy initiatives while handling the work that came in the door. There were only twenty lawyers on the staff. Some very good ones wanted to stay on with me. I hired some new lawyers, among them young women and black attorneys—enough to make our legal staff 25 percent female and 20 percent black, both numbers unheard of in those days.

Sometime in December, Hillary and I found a house at 5419 L Street in the Hillcrest section of Little Rock, a nice old neighborhood close to downtown. At 980 square feet, it was even smaller than our home in Fayetteville and cost a lot more, $34,000, but we could afford it, because in the previous election the voters had approved an increase in the salaries of state and local officials for the first time since 1910, raising the attorney general's salary to $26,500 a year. And Hillary found a good job at the Rose Law Firm, which was full of experienced, highly regarded lawyers and bright younger ones, including my friend Vince Foster and Webb Hubbell, a huge former football star for the Razorbacks who would become one of Hillary's and my closest friends. From then on, she earned much more than I did every year until the year I became President and she gave up her practice.

In addition to issuing opinions on questions of state law, the attorney general's office prosecuted and defended civil suits on behalf of the state; represented the state in criminal appeals to the state supreme court and in criminal cases in federal court; provided legal advice to state boards and commissions; and protected consumer interests through lawsuits, lobbying the legislature, and appearing in utility-rate cases before the state Public Service Commission (PSC). The workload was large, varied, and interesting.

The year got off to a fast start. The legislature went into session in early January and there was a PSC hearing on a request for a large rate increase for Arkansas Power and Light Company, based on the cost of AP&L's participation in a large nuclear power plant at Grand Gulf, Mississippi, that was being built by its parent company, Middle South Utilities (now Entergy). Since Middle South didn't serve customers directly, the costs of the Grand Gulf plant had to be allocated among its subsidiaries serving Arkansas, Louisiana, Mississippi, and the city of New Orleans. The Grand Gulf case would consume a lot of my time and attention over the next few years. I had two problems with it: first, because the parent company was building the plant, advance approval by our state PSC was not required, even though our ratepayers were required to pay for 35 percent of it; and second, I thought we could meet the increased demand for electricity much less expensively through energy conservation and more efficient use of existing plants.

In preparing for the hearing, Wally Nixon, a lawyer on my staff, came across the work of Amory Lovins, which demonstrated the enormous potential and economic benefits of energy conservation and solar power. I thought what he said made sense and I got in touch with him. At the time, the conventional wisdom among business and political leaders was that economic growth required constantly increasing electricity production. No matter how strong the evidence supporting it, conservation was viewed as a harebrained fantasy of fuzzy-headed intellectuals. Unfortunately, too many people still look at it that way.

For more than twenty years, as attorney general, governor, and President, I tried to push an alternative-energy policy, using the work of Amory Lovins and others to support my argument. Though I made some modest progress in all three jobs, the opposition remained fierce, especially after the conservatives took over Congress in 1995. Al Gore and I tried for years without success to get them to adopt a 25 percent tax credit for the production or purchase of clean energy and energy conservation technology, with mountains of evidence to support our position. The Republicans blocked it every time. I used to joke that one of the most significant achievements of my second term was that I had finally found a tax cut Newt Gingrich and Tom DeLay wouldn't support.

Working with the state legislature was fascinating, not only because the issues were interesting and unpredictable, but also because the House and Senate were full of colorful people, and because sooner or later half the state seemed to show up to lobby for or against some measure. One day early in the legislative session, I appeared at a committee hearing to speak against a measure. The room was packed with people representing interests who were for it, including Vince Foster. And Hillary. He had brought her along for the experience, not knowing I would be appearing for the other side. We just smiled at each other and did our jobs. Luckily, the Rose firm had gotten an opinion from the American Bar Association saying it could hire the wife of the attorney general and setting out the steps necessary to avoid conflicts of interest. Hillary followed them to the letter. After I became governor, and she was a full partner at the Rose firm, she gave up her portion of the annual profits made from state bond business, legal work the firm had been doing since the 1940s.

When I took office, there was a serious backlog of opinions and other work. We often worked until midnight to catch up, and in the process we developed a great rapport and had a terrific time. On Fridays, when the legislature wasn't in session, I allowed casual dress and encouraged everyone to go for a long lunch at a nearby haunt that had first-rate hamburgers, pinball machines, and a shuffleboard game. The old unpainted shack also had a big canoe on the roof and an ominous name, the Whitewater Tavern.

The growing strength of the Moral Majority and like-minded groups gave rise to some legislation that many moderate and progressive legislators didn't want to pass but didn't want to be on record as voting against. The obvious tactic was to get the attorney general to say the bill was unconstitutional. This was an example of another of Clinton's laws of politics: If someone can shift the heat from himself to you, he'll do it every time.

The funniest bills were offered by Representative Arlo Tyer of Pocahontas, in northeast Arkansas. Arlo was a

decent man who wanted to stay one step ahead of the
Moral Majority. He introduced a bill to make it illegal to
show X-rated movies anywhere in Arkansas, even to
adults. I was asked whether the bill was an unconstitutional restriction on the freedom of speech. I could just see
the headlines: "Attorney General Comes Out for Dirty
Movies!" I called Bob Dudley, a district judge from Arlo's
hometown, to find out why he'd introduced the bill. "Do
you have a lot of X-rated movies up there?" I asked. Dudley, who was a real wit, said, "No. We don't have any
movie theaters at all. He's just jealous of the rest of you
seeing all that stuff."

As soon as the movie bill died, Arlo came up with
another gem: a $1,500-a-year tax on every couple in
Arkansas who lived together without benefit of wedlock.
The headline alarm bell went off in my brain again: "Clinton Comes Out for Living in Sin!" I went to see Representative Tyer on this one. "Arlo," I asked, "how long do a
man and a woman have to cohabit to pay this tax? A year,
a month, a week? Or is a one-night stand enough?" "You
know, I hadn't thought about that," he replied. "And what
about enforcement?" I went on. "Are you and I going to
get baseball bats and knock down doors to see who's doing
what with whom?" Arlo shrugged and said, "I hadn't
thought about that either. Maybe I better pull that bill
down." I walked back to my office relieved to have dodged
another bullet. To my surprise, some of my staff seemed
disappointed. A couple of them had decided they wanted
the bill to pass and our office to enforce it. They had even
imagined their new uniforms: T-shirts emblazoned with
the acronym SNIF, for Sex No-no Investigation Force.

We had a tougher time when it came to gay rights. Two
years earlier, Attorney General Jim Guy Tucker had spear-

headed a new criminal code through the legislature. It simplified and clarified the definitions of more than one hundred years of complicated and overlapping crimes. It also eliminated so-called status offenses, which had been condemned by the Supreme Court. A crime requires committing a forbidden act, intentionally or recklessly; just being something society deems undesirable isn't enough. For example, being a drunk wasn't a crime. Neither was being a homosexual, though it had been before the new code was adopted.

Representative Bill Stancil took a lot of heat from the conservative pastors in his hometown of Fort Smith for his vote in favor of the revised criminal code. They said he had voted to legalize homosexuality. Stancil was a good man who had been one of Arkansas' best high school football coaches. He was a muscular, square-jawed, broken-nosed guy, and subtlety wasn't his strong point. He couldn't believe he had voted for homosexuality and was determined to rectify his error before the religious right could punish him for it, so he introduced a bill to make homosexual acts a crime. For good measure, he criminalized bestiality too, causing one of his wittier colleagues to remark that he obviously didn't have many farmers in his district. Stancil's bill described in excruciating detail every conceivable variation of both kinds of forbidden intercourse. A pervert could read it and escape the urge to buy pornographic material for a whole week.

There was no way to beat the bill on a direct vote. Moreover, the Supreme Court was a long way from its 2003 decision declaring that consensual homosexual relations are protected by the right to privacy, so getting an opinion from me saying the bill was unconstitutional wasn't an option. The only possible strategy was to delay the bill to death. In the House, three young liberals who were great allies of mine—Kent Rubens, Jody Mahoney, and Richard Mays—decided to offer an interesting amendment. Word got out that something was afoot, and I joined a packed gallery above the House chamber to watch the fireworks go off. One of the guys rose and praised Stancil's bill, saying it was about time someone stood up for morality in Arkansas. The only problem, he said, was that the bill was too weak, and he wanted to offer a "little amendment" to strengthen it. Then, with a straight face, he proposed the addition, making it a Class D felony for any member of the legislature to commit adultery in Little Rock while the legislature was in session.

The entire gallery was engulfed in peals of laughter. On the floor, however, the silence was deafening. For many legislators from small towns, coming to Little Rock for the session was the only fun they had—the equivalent of two months in Paris. They were not amused, and several of them told the three wise guys they'd never pass another bill unless the amendment was withdrawn. It was. The bill sailed through and was sent to the Senate.

We had a better chance to kill it there, because it was assigned to a committee chaired by Nick Wilson, a young senator from Pocahontas who was one of the brightest and most progressive members of the legislature. I thought he might be persuaded to keep the bill bottled up until the legislature adjourned.

On the last day of the session, the bill was still in Nick's committee and I was counting the hours until adjournment. I called him about it several times and hung around until I was almost an hour late in leaving for a speech in Hot Springs. When I could finally wait no longer, I called him one last time. He said they would adjourn in half an hour and the bill was dead, so I left. Fifteen minutes later, a powerful senator who favored the bill offered Nick Wilson a new building for the vocational technical school in his district if he'd let the bill go through. As Speaker Tip O'Neill used to say, all politics is local. Nick let the bill go, and it passed easily. I was sick. A few years later, the present congressman from Little Rock, Vic Snyder, tried to repeal the bill when he was in the state Senate. He failed too. As far as I know, the law was never enforced, but we had to wait for the 2003 Supreme Court decision to invalidate the law.

Another really interesting problem I faced as attorney general was literally a matter of life and death. One day I got a call from the Arkansas Children's Hospital. It had just recruited a gifted young surgeon who was being asked to operate on Siamese twins who were joined at the chest, using the same systems to breathe and pump blood. The systems couldn't support them both much longer, and without surgery to separate them, they both would die. The problem was that the surgery would certainly kill one of them. The hospital wanted an opinion saying that the doctor couldn't be prosecuted for manslaughter for killing the twin who wouldn't survive the surgery. Strictly speaking, I couldn't guarantee him that, because an attorney general's opinion protects the person receiving it from civil suits but not from criminal prosecution. Nevertheless, the opinion would be a powerful deterrent to an overzealous prosecutor. I gave him an official letter stating my opinion that the certain death of one of the twins to save the life of the other would not be a crime. The doctor performed the operation. One twin died. But the other one lived.

Most of the work we did was far more conventional

than the examples I've cited. For two years, we worked hard to issue truly well-written opinions, do a good job for the state agencies and with the criminal cases, improve the quality of nursing-home care, and hold down utility rates, including a vigorous effort to keep the cost of a pay-phone call down to a dime, when nearly every other state was raising it to twenty-five cents.

Apart from my work, I got around the state as much as I could to broaden my contacts and strengthen my organization for the next election. In January 1977, I gave my first speech as an elected official at a Rotary Club banquet in Pine Bluff, the largest city in southeast Arkansas. I had gotten 45 percent of the vote there in 1976, but I needed to do better in future races. The five hundred people at the dinner provided a good opportunity to improve. It was a long evening, with a lot of speeches and an interminable number of introductions. Often the people who run such events are afraid that everyone who isn't introduced will go home mad. If so, there weren't many unhappy people after that dinner. It was nearly 10 p.m. when my host got up to introduce me. He was more nervous than I was. The first words out of his mouth were "You know, we could stop here and have had a very nice evening." I know he meant to suggest the best was yet to come, but that's not how it came out. Thank goodness, the crowd laughed, and I got a good reception to my speech, mostly because it was short.

I also attended several events in the black community. One day I was invited by the Reverend Robert Jenkins to his inauguration as the new pastor of Morning Star Baptist Church. It was a little white wooden church in North Little Rock with enough pews to seat 150 people comfortably. On a very hot Sunday afternoon, there were about three hundred people there, including ministers and choirs from several other churches, and one other white person, our county judge, Roger Mears. Every choir sang and every preacher offered congratulations. When Robert got up to preach, the congregation had been there a good while. But he was young, handsome, a powerful speaker, and he held their attention. He began slowly, saying he wanted to be an accessible pastor but not a misunderstood one. "I want to say a special word to the ladies of the church," he said. "If you need a pastor, you can call on me anytime of the day or night. But if you need a man, call on the Lord. He'll get you one." Such candor would have been unthinkable in a mainline white church, but his crowd appreciated it. He got a loud chorus of amens.

As Robert got into his sermon, the temperature seemed to rise. All of a sudden an older lady sitting near me stood up, shaking and shouting, seized by the spirit of the Lord. A moment later a man got up in an even louder and more uncontrolled state. When he couldn't calm down, a couple of the churchmen escorted him to a little room in the back of the church that held the choir robes and closed the door. He continued to shout something unintelligible and bang against the walls. I turned around just in time to see him literally tear the door off its hinges, throw it down, and run out into the churchyard screaming. It reminded me of the scene at Max Beauvoir's in Haiti, except these people believed they had been moved by Jesus.

Not long afterward, I saw white Christians have similar experiences, when my finance officer in the attorney general's office, Dianne Evans, invited me to the annual summer camp meeting of the Pentecostals in Redfield, about thirty miles south of Little Rock. Dianne was the daughter of Pentecostal ministers, and like other devout women of her faith, she wore modest clothes and no makeup and didn't cut her hair, which she rolled up into a bun. Back then, the strict Pentecostals didn't go to movies or sporting events. Many wouldn't even listen to nonreligious music on the car radio. I was interested in their faith and practices, especially after I got to know Dianne, who was smart, extremely competent at her job, and had a good sense of humor. When I kidded her about all the things Pentecostals couldn't do, she said they had all their fun in church. I was soon to discover how right she was.

When I got to Redfield, I was introduced to the state leader of the Pentecostals, Reverend James Lumpkin, and other prominent ministers. Then we went out into the sanctuary, which held about three thousand people. I sat up on the stage with the preachers. After my introduction and other preliminaries, the service got going with music as powerful and rhythmic as anything I had heard in black churches. After a couple of hymns, a beautiful young woman got up from one of the pews, sat down at the organ, and began to sing a gospel song I had never heard before, "In the Presence of Jehovah." It was breathtaking. Before I knew it, I was so moved I was crying. The woman was Mickey Mangun, the daughter of Brother Lumpkin and wife of the Reverend Anthony Mangun, who, along with Mickey and his parents, pastored a large church in Alexandria, Louisiana. After a rousing sermon by the pastor, which included speaking "in tongues"—uttering whatever syllables the Holy Spirit brings out—the congregation was invited to come to the front and pray at a row of knee-high altars. Many came, raising their hands, praising God, and also speaking in tongues. It was a night I would never forget.

I made that camp meeting every summer but one

between 1977 and 1992, often taking friends with me. After a couple of years, when they learned I was in my church choir, I was invited to sing with a quartet of balding ministers known as the Bald Knobbers. I loved it and fit right in, except for the hair issue.

Every year I witnessed some amazing new manifestation of the Pentecostals' faith. One year the featured pastor was an uneducated man who told us God had given him the power to memorize the Bible. He quoted more than 230 verses in his sermon. I had my Bible with me and checked his memory. I stopped after the first twenty-eight verses; he never missed a word. Once I saw a severely handicapped young man who came every year answer the altar call in his automated wheelchair. He was near the back of the church, which sloped down to the front. He rolled his wheelchair on full speed and barreled down the aisle. When he got about ten feet from the altar, he slammed on the brakes, throwing himself out of the wheelchair into the air and landing perfectly on his knees just at the altar, where he proceeded to lean over and praise God just like everybody else.

Far more important than what I saw the Pentecostals do were the friendships I made among them. I liked and admired them because they lived their faith. They are strictly anti-abortion, but unlike some others, they will make sure that any unwanted baby, regardless of race or disability, has a loving home. They disagreed with me on abortion and gay rights, but they still followed Christ's admonition to love their neighbors. In 1980, when I was defeated for reelection as governor, one of the first calls I got was from one of the Bald Knobbers. He said three of the ministers wanted to come see me. They arrived at the Governor's Mansion, prayed with me, told me they loved me just as much now as they had when I was a winner, and left.

Besides being true to their faith, the Pentecostals I knew were good citizens. They thought it was a sin not to vote. Most of the preachers I knew liked politics and politicians, and they could be good practical politicians themselves. In the mid-eighties, all over America, fundamentalist churches were protesting state laws requiring that their child-care centers meet state standards and be licensed. It had become a very hot issue in some places, with at least one minister in a midwestern state choosing to go to jail rather than comply with the child-care standards. The issue had the potential to explode in Arkansas, where we had had some problems with a religious child-care center and where new state standards for child care were pending. I called in a couple of my Pentecostal pastor friends and asked what the real problem was. They replied that they had no problem meeting the state health and safety standards; their problem was in the demand that they get a state license and display it on the wall. They considered child care to be a critical part of their ministry, which they thought should be free from state interference under the First Amendment's guarantee of freedom of religion. I gave them a copy of the new state standards and asked them to read them and tell me what they thought. When they came back the next day, they said the standards were fair. I then proposed a compromise: religious child-care centers wouldn't have to be certified by the state if the churches agreed to remain in substantial compliance with them and to allow regular inspections. They took the deal, the crisis passed, the standards were implemented, and as far as I know, the church-run centers never had any problems.

One Easter in the eighties, Hillary and I took Chelsea to see the Easter Messiah service at the Manguns' church in Alexandria. The sound and light systems were first-rate, the scenery was realistic, including live animals, and all the performers were members of the church. Most of the songs were original and beautifully performed. When I was President and happened to be in Fort Polk, near Alexandria, at Eastertime, I went back to the Messiah service and talked the traveling press corps into coming with me, along with Louisiana's two black congressmen, Cleo Fields and Bill Jefferson. In the middle of the service, the lights went out. A woman began to sing a well-known hymn in a powerful deep voice. The reverend leaned over to Congressman Jefferson and asked, "Bill, you think this church member is white or black?" Bill said, "She's a sister. No doubt about it." After a couple of minutes, the lights came back up, revealing a small white woman in a long black dress with her hair piled up on her head. Jefferson just shook his head, but another black man sitting a couple of rows ahead of us couldn't contain himself. He blurted out, "My God, it's a white librarian!" By the end of the show, I saw several of my normally cynical press-corps people with tears in their eyes as the power of the music pierced the walls of their skepticism.

Mickey Mangun and another Pentecostal friend, Janice Sjostrand, sang at the dedicatory church service at my first inauguration and brought the house down. As he was leaving the church, Colin Powell, the chairman of the Joint Chiefs of Staff, leaned over to me and asked, "Where did you find white women who could sing like that? I didn't know there were any." I smiled and told him knowing people like them was one reason I got elected President.

During my second term, when the Republicans were trying to run me out of town and a lot of the pundits were saying I was dead meat, Anthony Mangun called me and asked if he and Mickey could come see me for twenty minutes. I said, "Twenty minutes? You're going to fly all the way up here for twenty minutes?" He replied, "You're busy. That's all it'll take." I told him to come on up. A few days later, Anthony and Mickey sat alone with me in the Oval Office. He said, "You did a bad thing but you're not a bad man. We raised our children together. I know your heart. Don't give up on yourself. And if you're going down, and the rats start to leave the sinking ship, call me. I rode up with you, and I want to go down with you." Then we prayed together and Mickey gave me a tape of a beautiful song she had written to shore me up. It was entitled "Redeemed." After twenty minutes, they got up and flew home.

Knowing the Pentecostals has enriched and changed my life. Whatever your religious views, or lack of them, seeing people live their faith in a spirit of love toward all people, not just their own, is beautiful to behold. If you ever get a chance to go to a Pentecostal service, don't miss it.

Toward the end of 1977, the political talk started again. Senator McClellan had announced his retirement after almost thirty-five years in the Senate, setting the stage for an epic battle to be his successor. Governor Pryor, who had come close to defeating McClellan six years earlier, was going to run. So were Jim Guy Tucker and the congressman from the Fourth District in south Arkansas, Ray Thornton, who had achieved prominence as a member of the House Judiciary Committee during the Nixon impeachment proceedings. He was also the nephew of Witt and Jack Stephens, so he had guaranteed financing for his campaign.

I had to decide whether to get into the Senate race too. A recent poll had me in second place, about ten points behind the governor and a little ahead of the two congressmen. I had been an elected official less than a year, but unlike the congressmen, I represented the entire state, was home all the time, and had the good fortune to have a job that, when well done, naturally engenders public approval. Not many people are against consumer protection, better care of the elderly, lower utility rates, and law and order.

But I decided to run for governor instead. I liked state government and wanted to stay home. Before I could get into the race, I had one last big case to handle as attorney general. I did it long distance. After Christmas, Hillary and I went to Florida to see Arkansas play Oklahoma in the Orange Bowl. Coach Lou Holtz, in his first year at Arkansas, had led the Razorbacks to a 10–1 season and a sixth-place national ranking; their only loss was at the hands of top-ranked Texas. Oklahoma was ranked second nationally, having also lost to Texas, but more narrowly.

No sooner had we arrived than a firestorm broke out in Arkansas involving the football team. Coach Holtz suspended three players from the team, which prevented them from playing in the bowl game, for their involvement in an incident in the players' dorm involving a young woman. They weren't just any three players. They were the starting tailback, who was the leading rusher in the Southwest Conference; the starting fullback; and the starting flanker, who had blinding speed and was a genuine pro prospect. The three of them accounted for most of the team's offense. Although no criminal charges were filed, Holtz said that he was suspending the players because they had violated the "do right" rule, and that he was coaching his charges to be good men as well as good football players.

The three players filed a lawsuit seeking reinstatement, claiming the suspension was arbitrary and may have been based on racial considerations, since the three players were black and the woman was white. They also lined up support on the team. Nine other players said they wouldn't play in the Orange Bowl either unless the three were reinstated.

My job was to defend Holtz's decision. After talking with Frank Broyles, who had become athletic director, I decided to stay in Florida, where I could consult closely with him and Holtz. I asked Ellen Brantley on my staff to handle things in the federal court in Little Rock. Ellen had gone to Wellesley with Hillary and was a brilliant attorney; I thought it wouldn't do any harm to have a woman arguing our side of the case. Meanwhile, the support for Holtz and playing the game began to build among the players.

For a few hectic days, I spent eight or more hours a day on the phone, talking to Ellen back in Little Rock and to Broyles and Holtz in Miami. The pressure and criticism were getting to Holtz, especially the charge that he was a racist. The only evidence against him was the fact that when he had coached at North Carolina State, he had endorsed ultra-conservative Senator Jesse Helms for reelection. After spending hours talking to Holtz, I could tell he wasn't a racist, nor was he political. Helms had been decent to him and he had returned the favor.

On December 30, three days before the game, the players dropped their suit and released their twelve allies from their commitment not to play. It still wasn't over. Holtz was so upset he told me that he was going to call Frank Broyles and resign. I immediately called Frank and told him not to answer the phone in his room that night no matter what. I was convinced Lou would wake up in the morning wanting to win the game.

For the next two days the team worked like crazy. They had been eighteen-point underdogs to start, and after the three stars were out, the game was taken off the odds chart. But the players whipped one another up into a frenzy.

On the night of January 2, Hillary and I sat in the Orange Bowl watching Oklahoma go through warm-ups. The day before, top-ranked Texas had lost to Notre Dame in the Cotton Bowl. All Oklahoma had to do was beat crippled Arkansas to win the national championship. Along with everybody else, they thought it was going to be a cakewalk.

Then the Razorbacks took the field. They trotted out in a straight line and slapped the goal post before they started their drills. Hillary watched them, grabbed my arm, and said, "Just look at them, Bill. They're going to win." With smothering defense and a record-setting 205 yards rushing from reserve back Roland Sales, the Razorbacks routed Oklahoma 31–6, perhaps the biggest and certainly the most unlikely victory in the storied history of Arkansas football. Lou Holtz is a high-strung, skinny little fellow who paced the sidelines in a way that reminded Hillary of Woody Allen. I was grateful that this bizarre episode gave me the chance to know him well. He's brilliant and gutsy, perhaps the best on-the-field coach in America. He's had other great seasons at Arkansas, Minnesota, Notre Dame, and South Carolina, but he'll never have another night quite like that one.

With the Orange Bowl case behind me, I went home to make my next move. After Senator McClellan publicly announced his retirement, I went to see him to thank him for his service and ask his advice. He strongly urged me to run for his seat; he didn't want David Pryor to win it and had no particular ties to Tucker and Thornton. He said that the worst I could do was lose, as he had done on his first try, and that if I lost, I was young and could try again, as he had. When I told him I was thinking of running for governor, he said that was a bad idea, that all you did in the governor's office was make people mad. In the Senate you could do big things for the state and the nation. The governor's office, he said, was a short trip to the political graveyard. Historically, McClellan's analysis was right. While Dale Bumpers had ridden the wave of New South prosperity and progressivism from the governor's office to the Senate, he was the exception to the rule. Times were tough in Pryor's tenure and he was facing a stiff challenge whether I ran or not. And it was hard to serve as governor longer than four years. Since Arkansas adopted a two-year term in 1876, only two governors, Jeff Davis before World War I and Orval Faubus, had served more than four years. And Faubus had to do wrong at Central High to hang on.

McClellan, at age eighty-two, was still sharp as a tack, and I respected his advice. I was also surprised by his encouragement. I was much more liberal than he was, but the same could be said for all his potential successors. For some reason, we got along, in part because I had been away at law school when Governor Pryor ran against him and therefore couldn't have helped Pryor, which I would have done had I been home. I also respected the serious

work McClellan had done to crack organized-crime networks. They were a threat to all Americans, regardless of
their political views or economic circumstances. Not long
after our meeting, Senator McClellan died before he
could finish his term.

Despite his advice and the assurances of support for the
Senate race that I'd received from around the state, I
decided to run for governor. I was excited by the prospect
of what I could accomplish, and I thought I could win.
Though my age, thirty-one, was more likely to be an issue
against me in a race for governor than one for the Senate,
because of the heavy management and decision-making
responsibilities, the competition wasn't as stiff as it was in
the Senate race.

Four other candidates ran in the Democratic primary:
Joe Woodward, a lawyer from Magnolia in south Arkansas
who had been active in Dale Bumpers's campaigns; Frank
Lady, a lawyer from northeast Arkansas, who was a conservative evangelical Christian, the favored candidate of
the Moral Majority voters, and the first, but not the last,
of my opponents to publicly criticize Hillary, explicitly for
practicing law and implicitly for retaining her maiden
name when we married; Randall Mathis, the articulate
county judge of Clark County, just south of Hot Springs;
and Monroe Schwarzlose, a genial old turkey farmer from
southeast Arkansas. Woodward promised to be the
strongest candidate. He was intelligent and articulate and
had contacts all over the state because of his work with
Bumpers. Still, I started with a big lead. All I had to do
was keep it. Because all the real interest was in the Senate
race, I just had to run hard, avoid mistakes, and go on
doing a good job as attorney general.

Despite its relative lack of drama, the campaign had its

interesting moments. The "tree story" surfaced again when a state policeman who was supporting Joe Woodward swore he had taken me out of that infamous tree back in 1969. In Dover, north of Russellville, I answered another challenge to my manhood by participating in a tug-of-war with a bunch of very large log haulers. I was the smallest man on either team and they put me in front. We pulled the rope back and forth across a hole full of water and mud. My side lost, and I wound up caked in mud, with my hands torn and bleeding from pulling the rope so hard. Fortunately, a friend who had urged me to compete gave me a new pair of khakis so that I could return to the campaign trail. In St. Paul, a town of about 150 near Huntsville, I was shaking hands with all the marchers in the Pioneer Day parade, but I chickened out when I saw a man walking right toward me with his pet on a leash. It was a full-grown bear. I don't know who was reassured by the leash, but I sure wasn't.

Believe it or not, tomatoes played a role in the 1978 campaign. Arkansas grows a lot of them in Bradley County, most of them picked by migrant laborers who travel from South Texas through Arkansas up the Mississippi River all the way to Michigan, following the warming weather and ripening crops. As attorney general, I had gone to Hermitage, in the southern part of the county, to a community meeting on the problems the small farmers were having in implementing new federal standards for their workers' housing. They simply couldn't afford it. I got them some help from the Carter administration so that they could build the required facilities and stay in business. The people were very grateful, and after I announced for governor they scheduled a Bill Clinton Appreciation Day, which included the high school band leading a parade down the main street. I was excited about it and glad a reporter from the **Arkansas Gazette** was driving down with me to cover the story. On the way, she asked me a lot of questions about the campaign and the issues. I said something that called into question my support for the death penalty, and that became the day's story. The whole town of Hermitage turned out, but the event, and the work that gave rise to it, remained a secret to the rest of the state. I complained about it for days until finally my staff decided the only way to shut me up was to make fun of me. They had T-shirts printed up with the words "You Should Have Seen the Crowd at Hermitage!" At least I got about all the votes down there and I learned to be more careful in dealing with reporters.

A few weeks later, I was back in Bradley County to work the tomato vote again at Warren's annual Pink Tomato Festival, and I entered the tomato-eating contest. Three of the seven or eight competitors were young men much bigger than I was. We each got a paper sack full of tomatoes, which had been carefully weighed. When the bell sounded, we ate as many as we could in the allotted time, which I think was five minutes, a long time for a crowd to watch grown men behave like pigs at the trough. Any part of the tomato that was not consumed had to be put back in the sack, so that the exact weight of tomatoes consumed could be determined. Like a fool, I tried to win. I always did. I finished third or fourth and felt pretty sick for a couple of days. It wasn't all for nothing, though; I got most of the votes in Warren, too. But I never entered the contest again.

The U.S. Congress had passed the equal-rights amendment to the Constitution and referred it to the states for ratification, but the requisite three-quarters of the state legislatures had not ratified it and never would. Even so, it was still a hot-button issue among Arkansas' social conservatives, for several reasons. Senator Kaneaster Hodges, whom David Pryor had appointed to finish Senator McClellan's term, had given an eloquent speech on the Senate floor in support of the ERA. Our friend Diane Kincaid had bested Phyllis Schlafly, the nation's leading opponent of the amendment, in a highly publicized debate before the Arkansas legislature. And Hillary and I were on record supporting it. The opponents of the ERA predicted an end to civilization as we knew it if the amendment passed: women in combat, unisex bathrooms, broken families where uppity women no longer were subject to their husbands.

Because of the ERA, I had a minor run-in with Frank Lady's supporters at a rally of about five hundred people in Jonesboro, in northeast Arkansas. I was giving my campaign speech outlining my proposals for education and economic development when an older woman in a Lady T-shirt started screaming at me, "Talk about the ERA! Talk about the ERA!" Finally I said, "Okay. I'll talk about it. I'm for it. You're against it. But it won't do as much harm as you think it will or as much good as those of us who support it wish it would. Now let's get back to schools and jobs." She wouldn't let it go. She screamed, "You're just promoting homosexuality!" I looked at her, smiled, and said, "Ma'am, in my short life in politics, I've been accused of everything under the sun. But you're the first person who ever accused me of promoting homosexuality." The crowd roared. Even some of the Lady supporters laughed. And then I got to finish my talk.

On primary election day, I got 60 percent of the vote and carried seventy-one of the seventy-five counties. The

vote in the Senate race was split almost evenly among
Pryor, Tucker, and Thornton. The governor got 34 percent, and Jim Guy Tucker got a few more votes than Ray
Thornton, so there would be a runoff. The conventional
wisdom was that Pryor was in trouble because, as an
incumbent governor, he should have polled well over 40
percent. Because I liked him and had enjoyed working
with him in state government, I urged him to seek advice
from my new pollster, Dick Morris, a young political consultant who had been active in New York City politics.
Morris was a brilliant, abrasive character, brimming with
ideas about politics and policy. He believed in aggressive,
creative campaigns, and was so cocksure about everything
that a lot of people, especially in a down-home place like
Arkansas, found him hard to take. But I was stimulated by
him. And he did me a lot of good, partly because I refused
to be put off by his manner and partly because I had good
instincts about when he was right and when he was wasn't.
One thing I really liked about him was that he would tell
me things I didn't want to hear.

In the fall campaign, my opponent was a cattleman and
the chairman of the state Republican Party, Lynn Lowe.
The race was uneventful except for the press conference
on the steps of the Capitol in which his campaign accused
me of being a draft dodger. I referred them to Colonel
Holmes. I won the election with 63 percent of the vote,
carrying sixty-nine of the seventy-five counties.

At thirty-two, I was the governor-elect of Arkansas,
with two months to assemble a staff, put together a legislative program, and wrap up my work as attorney general. I had really enjoyed the job, and thanks to the hard
work and dedication of a fine staff, we had accomplished a
lot. We cleaned out the backlog of requests for legal opin-

ions, issuing a record number of them; recovered more than $400,000 in consumer claims, more than in the previous five years of the division's existence combined; told the state boards that regulate professions that they could no longer ban price advertising by the professional groups they regulated, a common practice in those days all across America; pushed for better nursing-home care and an end to age discrimination against the elderly; intervened in more utility-rate hearings than the office had ever done before, saving the ratepayers millions of dollars; drafted and passed legislation to compensate victims of violent crime; and protected the privacy rights of citizens with regard to personal information held by state agencies. One other thing I accomplished was especially important to me. I convinced the required three-quarters of both legislative chambers to amend the state's voting rights law to restore the right to vote to convicted felons upon completion of their sentences. I argued that once the offender had paid in full, he should be restored to full citizenship. I did it for Jeff Dwire, a hardworking, tax-paying citizen, who never got a pardon and who died a thousand deaths every election day. Sadly, more than twenty-five years later the federal government and most states still haven't followed suit.

TWENTY-ONE

We started planning for my first term after the primary election in May and really got going after November, converting the headquarters into a transition office. Rudy Moore and Steve Smith, who had both served in the legislature, helped me as we prepared budgets, drafted bills to enact my policy priorities, analyzed the major management challenges, and began to hire a staff and cabinet.

In December, the Democratic Party held its midterm convention in Memphis. I was asked to travel across the Mississippi River to moderate a health-care panel featuring Joe Califano, President Carter's secretary of health, education, and welfare, and Senator Edward Kennedy, the Senate's chief advocate for universal health coverage. Califano was articulate in his defense of the President's more incremental approach to health-care reform, but Kennedy won the crowd with an emotional plea for ordinary Americans to have the same coverage that his wealth provided for his son, Teddy, when he got cancer. I enjoyed the experience and the national exposure, but was convinced that the convention only highlighted our intra-party differences, when it was supposed to unite and reinvigorate Democrats in nonpresidential election years. The midterm meetings were later abandoned.

Not long before Christmas, Hillary and I took a much-needed vacation to England. We spent Christmas Day with my friend from Oxford, Sara Maitland, and her husband, Donald Lee, an American who had become a priest in the Church of England. It was Donald's first Christmas church service. He had to be a little nervous, but he began the service with a surefire winner, a children's sermon. He sat down on the steps in front of a lovely nativity scene and asked all the children to come and sit with him. When they settled down, he said, "Children, this is a very special day." They nodded. "Do you know what day this is?" "Yes," they said. Donald beamed and asked, "What day is it?" In unison, they all shouted, "Monday!" I don't know how he carried on. Perhaps he was consoled by the fact that in his church, kids told the literal truth.

In a month, it was time to move into the Governor's Mansion and get ready for the inauguration. The mansion was a big colonial-style house of about ten thousand square feet in the beautiful old Quapaw Quarter of Little Rock, not far from the Capitol. The main house was flanked by two smaller ones, with the one on the left serving as a guest house and the one on the right providing a headquarters for the state troopers who watched the place and answered the phone twenty-four hours a day. The mansion had three large, handsome public rooms, a big kitchen, and a little breakfast room on the first floor; a spacious basement, which we converted into a rec room complete with pinball machine; and living quarters on the second floor. Despite its overall size, the mansion's living area occupied just five small rooms and two modest bathrooms. Still, it was such a step up from our little house on L Street that we didn't have enough furniture to fill the five rooms.

The hardest thing about the transition was getting used to the security. I had always prided myself on my self-sufficiency and prized my private time. I had been self-supporting since I was twenty, and over the years had gotten used to cleaning house, running errands, and cooking. When Hillary and I got together, we shared the household duties. Now other people cooked the meals, cleaned the house, and ran the errands. Since I was sixteen, I had enjoyed driving alone in my own car, listening to music and thinking. I couldn't do that anymore. I liked to jog every day, usually before or after work. Now, I was being followed by a trooper in an unmarked car. It really bothered me at first—it made me want to run up one-way streets the wrong way. In time I got used to it and came to appreciate the work the folks at the mansion and the troopers did; they gave me more time for the job. Because the troopers drove me, I got a lot of paperwork done in transit. Eventually we agreed that I'd drive myself to church on Sundays. It wasn't much of a concession, since my church and the Methodist church Hillary attended were both within a mile of the mansion, but I really looked forward to my Sunday freedom ride. One of the troopers ran with me when he was on duty, and I liked that a lot better than being followed. After I had been in office several years and there was clearly no imminent threat, I often ran alone in the mornings, but along a predictable downtown route with lots of people around. Frequently I ended those runs at the McDonald's or the local bakery, both about a half mile from the mansion, where I'd get a cup of water, then walk back home.

The troopers did have real security work to do on occasion. In my first term, an escapee from one of our mental institutions called the mansion and said he was going to kill me. Since he had decapitated his mother a few years earlier, they took it seriously. He was caught and returned to confinement, which might have been his subconscious desire when he called. One day, a massive man carrying a railroad spike walked into the governor's office and said he needed to meet with me all alone. He was not admitted. In 1982, when I was trying to regain the governor's office, a man called and said he'd had a message from God telling him my opponent was the instrument of the Lord and I was the instrument of the devil and he was going to do God's will and eliminate me. He turned out to be an escapee from a Tennessee mental institution. He had an odd-caliber revolver and went from gun store to gun store trying to buy ammunition for it, and because he couldn't produce any identification, he didn't succeed. Still, I had to wear an uncomfortable bulletproof jacket for several days near the end of the campaign. Once, when the front door was accidentally left unlocked, a deranged but harmless woman got halfway up the stairs to our living quarters before the troopers caught her as she was calling out to me. Another time, a small, wiry man in combat boots and shorts was apprehended trying to break down the front door. He was high on some kind of drug mixture that made him so strong it took two troopers bigger than I am to subdue him, and then only after he'd thrown one of them off and put his head through a window in the troopers' quarters. He was carried away in a straitjacket strapped to a stretcher. Later, when he sobered up, the man apologized to the troopers and thanked them for keeping him from doing anyone harm.

The troopers who served me became an issue in my first term as President when two of them who were disgruntled and had financial problems spread stories about me for a modest amount of money and fame and the hope of a bigger payoff. But most of those who served on the security detail were fine people who did their jobs well, and several of them became good friends. In January 1979, I wasn't sure I'd ever get used to twenty-four-hour security coverage, but I was so excited about my job I didn't have much time to think about it.

In addition to the traditional inaugural ball, we hosted a night of Arkansas entertainment called "Diamonds and Denim." All the performers were Arkansans, including the great soul singer Al Green, who later turned to gospel music and the ministry, and Randy Goodrum, the pianist in our high school trio, the 3 Kings. At thirty-one, he had already won a Grammy award for his songwriting. I joined him on sax for "Summertime," the first time we'd played together since 1964.

The inauguration was a big event. Hundreds of people from all over the state came, as did friends Hillary and I had made over the years, including my old roommate Tommy Caplan; Dave Matter, who managed my losing campaign at Georgetown; Betsey Wright; my pro–civil rights Boys Nation buddies from Louisiana, Fred Kammer and Alston Johnson; and three friends from Yale, Carolyn Ellis, Greg Craig, and Steve Cohen. Carolyn Yeldell Staley also came home from Indiana to sing.

I worked hard on my inaugural address. I wanted both to capture the historical moment and to tell my fellow Arkansans more about the values and ideals I was bringing to the governor's office. The night before, Steve Cohen had given me an idea I added to the speech when he'd said he was feeling two things he hadn't in a long time, "pride and hope." I said some things in that speech that I believe as strongly today as I did then, words that capture what I've tried to do in all my public work, including the presidency:

For as long as I can remember, I have believed passionately in the cause of equal opportunity, and I will do what I can to advance it.

For as long as I can remember, I have deplored the arbitrary and abusive exercise of power by those in authority, and I will do what I can to prevent it.

For as long as I can remember, I have rued the waste and lack of order and discipline that are too often in evidence in governmental affairs, and I will do what I can to diminish them.

For as long as I can remember, I have loved the land, air, and water of Arkansas, and I will do what I can to protect them.

For as long as I can remember, I have wished to ease the burdens of life for those who, through no fault of their own, are old or weak or needy, and I will try to help them.

For as long as I can remember, I have been saddened by the sight of so many of our independent, industrious people working too hard for too little because of inadequate economic opportunities, and I will do what I can to enhance them. . . .

The next day I went to work for what would prove to be two of the most exhilarating and exhausting, rewarding and frustrating years of my life. I was always in a hurry to get things done, and this time my reach often exceeded my grasp. I think a fair summary of my first gubernatorial term is that it was a policy success and a political disaster.

In the legislative session I had two major spending priorities, education and highways, and a host of other substantive reforms in health, energy, and economic development. In 1978, Arkansas ranked last among all states in per capita education spending. A study of our schools conducted by Dr. Kern Alexander, a nationally recognized expert in education policy from the University of Florida, concluded that our system was dismal: "From an educational standpoint, the average child in Arkansas would be much better off attending the public schools of almost any other state in the country." We had 369 school districts, many too small to offer needed courses in math and science. There were no state standards or evaluation systems. And teacher pay was pitifully low in most places.

The legislature passed almost all my education proposals, prodded by the Arkansas Education Association, which represented most of the teachers; the associations representing the administrators and school board members; and pro-education legislators, including Clarence Bell, the powerful chairman of the Senate Education Committee. They approved a 40 percent increase in funding over the next two years, including a $1,200 teacher pay raise in each year; a 67 percent increase for special education; increases for textbook costs, transportation, and other operations; and, for the first time, aid to school districts for programs for gifted and talented children and for transporting kindergarten students, a big step toward universal kindergarten.

The money was tied to efforts to raise standards and improve quality, something I always tried to do. We passed the first state programs mandating testing to measure pupil performance and indicate areas that needed improvement, a requirement that all teachers take the National Teacher Examination before they could be certified, and a bill prohibiting the firing of teachers for "arbitrary, capricious, or discriminatory" reasons. We also established the Arkansas Governor's School for gifted and talented students, which met for the first time at Hendrix College in the summer of 1980. Hillary and I spoke to the first class. It was one of my proudest achievements, and it's still going strong.

In two other areas I was less successful. The Alexander report recommended reducing the number of school districts to two hundred, which would have saved a lot of money on administrative costs. But I couldn't even pass a bill to create a commission to study it, because so many small towns believed that if they didn't have their own districts, "city folks" would close their schools and destroy their communities.

The other area in which I met resistance involved the formula by which school aid was distributed. Several school districts had filed a suit contending that our system was unfair, and that, when coupled with differences in local property-tax revenues, the inequalities in spending per child across the state were so great they were unconstitutional. The formula didn't take adequate account of differences in property values or student population shifts, and it gave more money per student to the very small districts, where the overhead costs per student were much higher. This system was hard to change, because giving more to some districts meant giving less to others. Both groups were well represented in the legislature, and when the losers saw the printouts showing what the changes would do to their districts, they fought hard to stop them. We adjusted the formula, but not by much. It would take a 1983 state supreme court decision invalidating the school formulas before we could really change things.

The highway program I proposed was designed to deal with the deterioration of our state highways, county roads, and city streets, and the need for new construction.

Arkansas hadn't had a good road program in more than a decade, and potholes and slow travel were costing people time and money. There was a lot of support for a road program, but there were big disagreements about how to fund it. I proposed a hefty tax package featuring large increases for heavy trucks, which did most of the damage, and substantial ones for cars. At the time, car tags, like truck licenses, were priced according to vehicle weight. I thought this was unfair, since the weight differences for cars, unlike trucks, were not significant in terms of road damage, and the heavier cars were older and usually belonged to people with lower incomes. Instead, I proposed to set fees for car tags based on the value of the car, with the owners of the most expensive new ones paying $50 and of the oldest, least valuable paying $20. Under my proposal, the owners of old, heavy cars would not have had to pay more.

Some of the seasoned legislators said we shouldn't raise the license fees at all, and instead should finance the road program with an increase in fuel taxes. Organized labor was against that because ordinary drivers would have to pay substantially more over the course of a year, though they wouldn't feel it since the tax would be buried in the price of fuel purchases. I agreed with labor on the merits, but a gas-tax increase would have been far less politically damaging than what I did.

None of the organized groups except the highway contractors supported my proposal. The trucking, poultry, and timber interests said they couldn't afford the increases on their big trucks, and they got them reduced. The new-car dealers said I wanted to charge their customers too much, and licensing based on value would be an administrative nightmare. I thought their arguments were partic-

ularly weak, but the legislature bought them. The highway lobby was represented in the Senate by Knox Nelson,
a wily legislator and road contractor himself, who wanted
the money but didn't really care how it was raised. In the
end, the legislature approved a large increase in revenue
from car tags but within the old weight structure, nearly
doubling the price for heavy cars from $19 to $36. I had a
decision to make. I could sign the bill into law and have a
good road program paid for in an unfair way, or veto it
and have no road program at all. I signed the bill. It was
the single dumbest mistake I ever made in politics until
1994, when I agreed to ask for a special prosecutor in the
Whitewater case when there was not a shred of evidence
to justify one.

In Arkansas, people's car license fees come due every
year on their birthdays, when they have to go to the revenue offices in their local counties to renew them. After the
increase went into effect on July 1, every single day, for a
whole year, a new group of people would come into their
revenue offices to find their birthday present from me: the
price of their car tags had doubled. Many of them were
country people who had driven more than twenty miles to
the county seat to buy their new tags. Often they had no
checkbooks and had brought only enough cash to pay the
previous cost of the tags, so they had to drive all the way
back home, get more cash out of the family stash, and
come back. When they got back and had to wait in line, as
they often did, the only thing they had to look at in the
spartan revenue offices was a picture of the governor smiling down on them.

In late 1978, when I was first elected governor, Hilary
Jones had made a prophetic comment to me. He said the
hill people had carried me through three elections, but I

would have to get my votes in the cities now. When I
asked him why, he replied that I was going to work on
schools and economic development, which the state
needed, but that anything I did to raise school standards
would threaten the rural schools; that I'd never be able to
get many new jobs into poor rural areas; and that the
recent U.S. Supreme Court ruling that government
employees who weren't in policy-making positions could
no longer be replaced for political reasons meant that I
couldn't even fire the current state employees in the rural
counties and bring our people in. "I'll still do all I can for
you," Hilary said, "but it'll never be like it was up here
again." As he was about so many things, Hilary was right
on target. Over the course of my winning campaigns for
governor, I got more and more support from Independent
and Republican voters in the cities and suburbs, but I
never recovered the depth of support I had enjoyed
among white rural voters in the Third District and much
of the rest of the state. Now, on top of all the things I
couldn't help, I had shot myself in the foot with the car-
tag increase, blowing five years of hard work among rural
Arkansans—and a lot of blue-collar city people, too—
with the stroke of a pen.

The pattern of good policy and bad politics wasn't confined to legislative matters. I organized the governor's
office without a chief of staff, giving different areas of
responsibility to Rudy Moore, Steve Smith, and John
Danner, a policy analyst from California whose wife,
Nancy Pietrafesa, was on old friend of Hillary's. Nancy
was working in the administration, too, on education.
President Kennedy had organized his White House in a
similar way, but his guys all had short hair, boring suits,
white shirts, and dark, narrow ties. Rudy, Steve, and John

all had beards and were less constrained in their dress code. My conservative critics in the legislature had a field day with them. Eventually, several inter-office conflicts broke out. I decided to make Rudy chief of staff, have Steve oversee a lot of the policy initiatives, and release John Danner and his wife, Nancy, from their responsibilities. With an inexcusable loss of nerve, I asked Rudy to tell them. He did it and they quit. Although I tried to talk to them about it later, our relationship never recovered. I doubt that they ever forgave me for not handling it myself, and I don't blame them. They were good people who worked hard and had good ideas; through inexperience, I had put them in an impossible situation. It was my mistake.

I also got into hot water for bringing in a lot of people from out of state to run the Department of Health, the Department of Human Services and its divisions of Social Services and Mental Health, the Department of Education, and the new Department of Energy. They were able and well intentioned, but they needed more contacts and experience dealing with their constituencies to make the big changes we were seeking.

These problems were aggravated by my own lack of experience and my youth. I looked even younger than my thirty-two years. When I became attorney general, George Fisher, the talented cartoonist for the **Arkansas Gazette,** drew me in a baby carriage. When I became governor he promoted me to a tricycle. It wasn't until I became President that he took me off the tricycle and put me in a pickup truck. And he was a supporter. It should have set off an alarm bell, but it didn't.

After a nationwide search, Dr. Robert Young, who had run a successful rural health clinic in West Virginia, was appointed director of the Department of Health. I wanted him to deal with the serious problems of health-care access and quality in Arkansas' rural areas. Dr. Young and Orson Berry, director of the Rural Health Office, came up with an innovative plan to establish clinics that required a doctor to be in attendance at least once every two weeks, with nurse practitioners and physician's assistants manning them full-time and providing the diagnostic services and treatment for which they were trained. Despite the insufficient number of doctors willing to practice in rural areas, studies showed that most patients preferred a nurse practitioner or physician's assistant because they spent more time with patients; and a nurse-midwife program in Mississippi County had cut the infant mortality rate there in half.

Arkansas doctors strongly opposed the plan. Dr. Jim Webber, representing the family physicians, said, "We don't believe a little bit of care is better than nothing." Notwithstanding the doctors' opposition, the Carter administration approved a grant funding our plan. We opened four rural clinics, started building three others, and expanded the Mississippi County Nurse Midwife Program with nurse practitioners. And the work we did won praise across the nation.

We tried to work with the physicians whenever we could. I supported appropriations to build an intensive-care nursery at the Arkansas Children's Hospital to care for extremely premature and other endangered newborns, and to establish a radiation-therapy institute at the University Medical Center to provide better treatment to cancer patients. I appointed Hillary to chair a Rural Health Advisory Committee, to recommend further improvements and help prioritize the large number of requests for help from rural communities. We worked harder to recruit doctors to rural areas, set up a loan fund to provide up to $150,000 of state money to any doctor who would set up a clinic in a town with six thousand or fewer people, and allowed family practitioners in small towns to apply for $6,000 a year in income supplements. The doctors strongly supported all these initiatives, which were especially remarkable because the economic downturn in 1980 forced severe cutbacks in the Department of Health's budget. Still, the doctors never forgave Dr. Young, or me, for not consulting them more and not going more slowly on the rural health clinics. By August 1980, the Arkansas Medical Society was asking for his resignation. When I left office in 1981, some of my initiatives were cut back, illustrating the point that you can have good policy without good politics, but you can't give people good government without both.

Energy was a huge issue because of OPEC's steep increases in the price of oil, which raised prices for everything else, too. In this area, we had good policy and better politics, though I still made some powerful enemies. I got the legislature to upgrade the Arkansas Energy Office to a cabinet-level department and attempted to build a broad coalition of ratepayers, utilities, businesses, and government to save ratepayers money; give utilities, businesses, and homeowners incentives to promote conservation; and help develop new sources of clean energy. I thought we could become more self-sufficient and a national leader in both conservation and alternative fuels. We passed legislation allowing tax deductions for energy conservation and renewable energy expenditures for residential, commercial, and industrial use, and exempted mixed fuels that were at least 10 percent alcohol from the state gas tax. We provided energy audits to industrial and commercial businesses and gave 50 percent matching grants to schools, hospitals, and other public institutions for the purchase and installation of energy conservation programs. The federal government provided funds for such initiatives, and we were the first state in the country to get them. When I took office, according to federal government statistics our energy conservation program was the worst in the country. After a year, we ranked ninth overall and third in industrial conservation.

Our efforts at utility regulation were mostly successful but much more controversial. I wanted the Energy Department to be able to intervene in the Public Service Commission's rate hearings and to be able to get information on, and inspect, nuclear power facilities. The legislature, prodded by its senior member, Max Howell, who was liberal on education and taxes but close to the utilities, watered down my first request and refused to fund the second. When I persuaded Arkansas Power and Light to offer interest-free conservation loans to its customers and charge the cost of making them to the ratepayers, everyone who understood the issue applauded, knowing it was a far cheaper way of increasing energy availability than building new power plants. Unfortunately, a number of legislators, who thought conservation amounted to subversion of the free-enterprise system, raised so much hell that AP&L felt compelled to shelve the program. The utility did continue to support our extensive efforts to weatherize the homes of low-income people, which made them cooler in the summer and warmer in the winter, and cut their utility bills considerably.

Alas, even our conservation efforts didn't escape controversy. An investigative reporter discovered that one of the projects we funded was a boondoggle. It was designed to train low-income people to chop wood and distribute it to other poor people to burn in their stoves. The Special Alternative Wood Energy Resources project had a descriptive acronym, SAWER, but a lousy record. It had spent $62,000 to train six woodchoppers and cut three cords of wood. I fired the director and got someone else who fixed the program, but it was the waste that stuck in the public's mind. To most Arkansans, $62,000 was a lot of money.

On the regulatory front, we were outgunned on two big issues. First, we did our best to stop what was called "pancaking" by utilities. If they asked for a 10 percent rate increase and got only 5 percent, they could collect the 10 percent while they appealed the decision in court. Meanwhile, they could file for another rate increase and do it all over again, thus pancaking unapproved rates on top of one another. Even if the utilities lost their appeals, which they usually did, the effect of the pancaking was to force ratepayers, including many poor people, to give them massive low-interest loans. It was wrong, but once again the utilities had more swat with the legislature than I did, killing the anti-pancaking bill in committee.

Second, I continued to fight with AP&L and its parent, Middle South Utilities, over the plan to make Arkansas ratepayers foot the bill for 35 percent of the Grand Gulf nuclear plants in Mississippi, while AP&L proposed to build six coal-fired plants in Arkansas, and demand for electricity in our state was declining so much that AP&L was planning to sell electricity from one of its existing plants to out-of-state users. Under the law, utilities were entitled to a profit, euphemistically called a "rate of return," on all their expenses. And under the Grand Gulf plan, Arkansas ratepayers would have to pay for more than a third of the construction costs, plus the rate of return, even if they never used any of the power. AP&L had no ownership in the plant; it belonged to an independent subsidiary with no ratepayers, and its construction and financing plan had to be approved only by the federal government, which subjected the project to far less than adequate scrutiny. When these facts were published in the **Arkansas Gazette** they caused a firestorm of protest. AP&L was urged to pull out of Grand Gulf by the chairman of the Public Service Commission. We organized a massive postcard campaign to the Federal Energy Regulatory Commission, urging it to reverse the Grand Gulf decision and give Arkansas relief. All to no avail.

The Grand Gulf arrangement was eventually upheld by the District of Columbia Court of Appeals, which had jurisdiction over cases involving federal regulatory agencies. The opinion was written by Judge Robert Bork, my old Constitutional Law professor. Just as he had been at Yale, he was all for states' rights when it came to restrictions on individual liberty. On the other hand, when big business was involved, he thought the federal government should have the final say and protect business from meddlesome state efforts to look out for ordinary citizens. In 1987, in testimony I researched and wrote myself for the Senate Judiciary Committee, Bork's decision in the Grand Gulf case was one of the grounds I cited for opposing his nomination to the U.S. Supreme Court.

I worked hard on an energy plan against stiff opposition, but I had made a powerful adversary in AP&L, which had offices in most counties. And I wasn't through making enemies. I was upset by what I thought were excessive clear-cutting practices by some of our timber companies and appointed Steve Smith to head a task force to look into it. Steve was still in his firebrand phase. He scared the timber folks and made them mad. All I wanted the clear-cutters to do was to reduce the size of their big cuts and leave adequate buffers along roads and streams to reduce soil erosion. My loudest critics claimed I wanted to put every log hauler and mill worker out of business. We got nowhere, and Steve got disgusted and went home to the hills not long afterward.

I even made some people mad in my economic development work. That's hard to do. I was determined to broaden the state's efforts beyond the traditional function of recruiting new industries, to include the expansion of existing industries and aid to small and minority businesses and farmers in marketing their products at home and abroad. We dramatically increased the activity of our state's European office in Brussels and I took the first Arkansas trade mission to the Far East—to Taiwan, Japan, and Hong Kong. We became the first state in America to have our own program for handling hazardous waste products approved by the federal government. We were also successful in the traditional work of recruiting new industries, with increased investments over previous years of 75 percent in 1979 and 64 percent in 1980. How could I make anybody mad with that record? Because I changed the name of the department, from the Arkansas Industrial Development Commission to the Department of Economic Development, to reflect its new, broader scope of activity. The AIDC, it turned out, was a sacred brand name to many influential businesspeople who had served on the commission and to local chamber of commerce directors all over the state who had worked with the agency. They were not satisfied by my appointment of Jim Dyke, a successful Little Rock businessman, to lead the new department. If I hadn't changed its name, I could have done all the same things without the adverse fallout. In 1979 and 1980, I seemed to have an affinity for adverse fallout.

I made a similar mistake in education. I appointed Dr. Don Roberts, superintendent of schools in Newport News, Virginia, to be director of education. Don had been an administrator in the Little Rock system a few years earlier, so he knew a lot of the players, and he had a friendly, low-key manner and got along well with most of them. He implemented the reforms I passed in the legislature, plus one of his own, a teacher-training program called PET, Program for Effective Teaching. The problem was that to get Don in, I had to ask for the resignation of the department's longtime director, Arch Ford. Arch was a fine gentleman who had devoted decades of dedicated service to Arkansas' schoolchildren. It was time for him to retire, though, and this time, I didn't make the mistake of letting someone else ask him to go. But I could have handled it better, giving him a big send-off and taking pains to make it look like his idea. I just blew it.

In the human services area, we got generally good reviews. We took the sales tax off prescription drugs, a measure especially helpful to seniors, and increased the homestead-property tax exemption for them by two-thirds. All told, more than twenty-five bills directly benefiting the elderly were passed, including tougher standards for nursing homes and an expansion of home health care.

Nineteen seventy-nine was the International Year of the Child. Hillary, who was serving as chair of the Arkansas Advocates for Children and Families, an organization she had helped to found, took the lead in pushing some meaningful changes, including passing a Uniform Child

Custody Act to eliminate custody problems for families moving in and out of our state; reducing the average daily population of our youth-service detention centers by 25 percent; developing better inpatient and community-based treatment for severely disturbed children; and placing 35 percent more children with special needs in adoptive homes.

Finally, I got involved in welfare reform for the first time. The Carter administration named Arkansas one of a handful of states to participate in a "workfare" experiment, in which able-bodied food-stamp recipients were required to register for work in order to keep getting the stamps. The experience sparked my abiding interest in moving toward a more empowering, work-oriented approach to helping poor people, one that I carried with me all the way to the White House and the signing of the Welfare Reform bill of 1996.

As 1980 dawned, I felt good about the governorship and my life. I had made some powerful interests angry, and gripes about the car tags were growing, but I had a long list of progressive legislative and administrative initiatives of which I was very proud.

In September, our friends Diane Kincaid and Jim Blair were married in Morriss and Ann Henry's backyard, where Hillary and I had had our wedding reception four years earlier. I performed the ceremony, as the Arkansas Constitution allows governors to do, and Hillary served as both bridesmaid and best man. The politically correct Blairs referred to her as "best person." I couldn't argue with that.

Besides being the best, Hillary was pregnant—very pregnant. We badly wanted to have a child and had been trying for some time without success. In the summer of 1979, we decided to make an appointment with a fertility expert in San Francisco as soon as we got back from a short vacation in Bermuda, but we had a wonderful time, so wonderful we never made it to San Francisco. Soon after we got home, Hillary found out she was pregnant. She kept working for several months, and we attended Lamaze classes in anticipation of my participating in a natural childbirth. I really enjoyed those classes and the time we spent with the other expectant parents, who were mostly middle-class working people just as excited as we were. A few weeks before her delivery date, Hillary was having a few problems. Her doctor told her she absolutely couldn't travel. We had complete confidence in him and understood that she had to observe his travel ban. Unfortunately, that meant she couldn't go with me to the annual Washington meeting of the National Governors Association, including dinner at the White House with President and Mrs. Carter. I went to the conference; took Carolyn Huber, who had left the Rose Law Firm to run the Governor's Mansion for us, to the White House dinner, called home every few hours, and returned as soon as I could on the night of February 27.

Fifteen minutes after I walked into the Governor's Mansion, Hillary's water broke, three weeks early. I was nervous as a cat, carrying around my list of Lamaze materials to take to Arkansas Baptist Hospital. The state troopers who worked at the mansion were nervous, too. I asked them to get the bag of ice cubes for Hillary to suck on while I gathered the other stuff. They did—a nine-pound bag, enough to last her through a week of labor. With the trunk loaded with Hillary's ice, the troopers got us to the hospital in no time. Soon after we arrived, we learned

Hillary would have to give birth by cesarean section because the baby was "in breech," upside down in the womb. I was told that hospital policy did not permit fathers in the delivery room when an operation was necessary. I pleaded with the hospital administrator to let me go in, saying that I had been to surgeries with Mother and that they could cut Hillary open from head to toe and I wouldn't get sick or faint, whereas Hillary was on edge, because she had never been a hospital patient in her entire life and she needed me there. They relented. At 11:24 p.m., I held Hillary's hand and looked over the screen blocking her view of the cutting and bleeding to see the doctor lift our baby out of her body. It was the happiest moment of my life, one my own father never knew.

Our little girl was a healthy six pounds, one and three quarters ounces, and she cried on cue. While Hillary was in the recovery room, I carried Chelsea out to Mother and anyone else who was available to see the world's most wonderful baby. I talked to her and sang to her. I never wanted that night to end. At last I was a father. Despite my love for politics and government and my growing ambitions, I knew then that being a father was the most important job I'd ever have. Thanks to Hillary and Chelsea, it also turned out to be the most rewarding.

When we got home from the hospital, Chelsea had a ready-made extended family in the Governor's Mansion staff, including Carolyn Huber and Eliza Ashley, who had cooked there forever. Liza thought I looked too young to be governor in part because I was thin; she said if I were "more stout" I'd look the part, and she was determined to make it happen. She's a great cook, and unfortunately she succeeded.

The Rose firm gave Hillary four months of parental

leave to get Chelsea off to a good start. Because I was the boss, I could control when I went to the office, so I arranged my work to be home a lot in those first few months. Hillary and I talked often about how fortunate we were to have had that critical time to bond with Chelsea. Hillary told me that most other advanced countries provided paid parental leave to all citizens, and we believed that other parents should have the same priceless opportunity we'd had. I thought about those first months with Chelsea in February 1993, when I signed my first bill into law as President, the Family and Medical Leave Act, which allows most American workers three months off when a baby is born or a family member is ill. By the time I left office, more than thirty-five million Americans had taken advantage of the law. People still come up to me, tell me their stories, and thank me for it.

After we got Chelsea settled in, I went back to work in a year that would be dominated by politics and disasters. Often the two were indistinguishable.

One of the things candidates don't discuss much and voters don't consider carefully in races for governor or President is crisis management. How will the Chief Executive handle natural or man-made disasters? I had more than my fair share in my first term as governor. The state was deluged in winter ice storms when I took office. I called out the National Guard to get generators to people without electricity, clear rural roads, and pull vehicles out of ditches. In the spring of 1979, we had a string of tornadoes, which required me to ask President Carter to officially declare Arkansas a disaster area, making us eligible for federal funds. We opened disaster-assistance centers to help people who'd lost their homes, businesses, and farm crops. We had to do it all over again when the spring of 1980 brought more tornadoes.

In the summer of 1980, we had a terrible heat wave that killed more than one hundred people and brought the worst drought in fifty years. Senior citizens were most at risk. We kept the senior centers open longer and provided state and federal money to buy electric fans, rent air conditioners, and help pay electric bills. We also got strong support from the Carter administration in the form of low-interest loans for poultry producers who'd lost millions of chickens, and farmers whose fields had burned up. The roads were collapsing under the heat, and we had a record number of fires, nearly eight hundred, forcing me to ban outdoor burning. Rural Arkansas was not in a positive frame of mind heading toward the November election.

Besides the natural disasters, we had some crises brought on by human accident or design. The damage they caused was more psychological than physical or financial, but it was profound. In the spring of 1979, the Ku Klux Klan and its national director, David Duke, decided to hold a meeting in Little Rock. I was determined to avoid the violence that had erupted between Klansmen and protesters recently during a similar rally in Decatur, Alabama. My public safety director, Tommy Robinson, studied the Decatur situation and put in place stringent security measures to avoid a repeat. We had a lot of state troopers and local police on the ground, with instructions to arrest people at the first sign of disorder. Eventually, six people were arrested, but no one was hurt, thanks largely to the deterrent effect of the large police presence. I felt good about how we handled the Klan situation, and it increased my confidence that we could deal properly with anything that might happen in the future. A year later, something much bigger came up.

In the spring of 1980, Fidel Castro deported 120,000 political prisoners and other "undesirables," many of them with criminal records or mental problems, to the United States. They sailed to Florida, seeking asylum and creating a massive problem for the Carter administration. I knew immediately that the White House might want to send some of the Cubans to Fort Chaffee, a large installation near Fort Smith, because it had been used as a relocation center in the mid-seventies for Vietnamese refugees. That relocation was largely successful, and many Vietnamese families were still living in western Arkansas and doing well.

When I discussed the issue with Gene Eidenberg, the White House official handling the Cuban issue for the President, I told him the Vietnamese effort had worked well in part because of preliminary screenings in the Philippines and Thailand to weed out those who shouldn't be admitted to the United States in the first place. I suggested he put an aircraft carrier or other large vessel off the coast of Florida and do the same kind of screening. I knew that most of the refugees weren't criminals or crazy, but they were being portrayed that way in the press, and the screening process would build public support for those who did come in. Gene said screening would be pointless because there was no place to send the rejects. "Sure there is," I said. "We still have a base at Guantánamo, don't we? And there must be a gate in the fence that divides it from Cuba. Take them to Guantánamo, open the door, and march them back into Cuba." Castro was making America look foolish and the President look powerless. Jimmy Carter already had his hands full with inflation and the

Iranian hostage crisis; he didn't need this. My proposal seemed to me to be a good way for the President to look strong, turn lemons into lemonade, and pave the way for public acceptance of the refugees who were allowed to stay. When the White House dismissed my suggestion out of hand, I should have known we were in for a long, rough ride.

On May 7, the White House notified me that Fort Chaffee would be used to resettle some of the Cubans. I urged the White House to take strong security precautions and made a statement to the press saying the Cubans were fleeing "a Communist dictatorship" and pledging to "do all I can to fulfill whatever responsibilities the President imposes upon Arkansans" to facilitate their resettlement. By May 20, there were nearly twenty thousand Cubans at Fort Chaffee. Almost as soon as they arrived, disturbances by young, restless Cubans, tired of being fenced in and uncertain about their future, became a staple of daily life inside the fort. As I have said, Fort Smith was a very conservative community, and most people were none too happy in the first place about the Cubans coming. When reports of the disturbances were publicized, people in Fort Smith and nearby towns became frightened and angry, especially those who lived in the little town of Barling, which borders the fort. As Sheriff Bill Cauthron, who was strong and sensible throughout the crisis, said in an interview: "To say that they [local residents] are scared is an understatement. They are arming themselves to the teeth, and that only makes the situation more volatile."

On Monday night, May 26, a couple hundred refugees charged the barricades and ran out of the fort through an unguarded gate. At dawn the next morning, primary election day, I called sixty-five National Guardsmen to Fort

Chaffee, flew to Fayetteville with Hillary to vote, then went to the fort, where I spent the day talking to people on the ground and at the White House. The commanding officer, Brigadier General James "Bulldog" Drummond, was an impressive man with a sterling combat record. When I complained that his troops had let the Cubans off base, he told me he couldn't stop them; he had been told by his immediate superior that a federal statute, the **posse comitatus** law, prohibits the military from exercising law-enforcement authority over civilians. Apparently, the army had concluded that the law covered the Cubans, though their legal status was uncertain. They weren't citizens or legal immigrants, but they weren't illegal aliens either. Since they had broken no law, Drummond was told he couldn't keep them at the fort against their will just because the local population detested and feared them. The general said his sole mission was to keep order on the base. I called the President, explained the situation, and demanded that someone be given authority to keep the Cubans on the base. I was afraid people in the area were going to start shooting them. There had been a run on handguns and rifles in every gun store within fifty miles of Chaffee.

The next day I again spoke to the President, who said that he was sending more troops and that they would maintain order and keep the Cubans inside the base. Gene Eidenberg told me that the Justice Department was sending the Pentagon a letter saying the military had the legal authority to do so. By the end of the day, I was able to relax a little and to ponder the primary election, in which my only opponent, the old turkey farmer Monroe Schwarzlose, got 31 percent of the vote, thirty times the vote he had received in the 1978 primary. The rural folks were sending me a message about the car tags. I hoped they had gotten it out of their system, but they hadn't.

On the night of June 1, all hell broke loose. One thousand Cubans ran out of the fort, right past federal troops, and onto Highway 22, where they began walking toward Barling. Once again, the troops didn't lift a finger to stop them. So I did. The only barrier between the Cubans and several hundred angry and armed Arkansans was composed of state troopers under the command of Captain Deloin Causey, a dedicated and coolheaded leader; the National Guardsmen; and Sheriff Bill Cauthron's deputies. I had given Causey and the National Guard strict instructions not to let the Cubans pass. I knew what would happen if they did: a bloodbath that would make the Little Rock Central High crisis look like a Sunday afternoon picnic. The Cubans kept coming at our people and began throwing rocks. Finally, Causey told the state police to fire shots over their heads. Only then did they turn around and go back to the fort. When the smoke cleared, sixty-two people had been injured, five of them from the shotgun blasts, and three of Fort Chaffee's buildings had been destroyed. But no one was killed or hurt too badly.

I flew up to Chaffee as soon as I could to meet with General Drummond. We had a real shouting match. I was outraged that his troops hadn't stopped the Cubans after the White House had assured me the Pentagon had received Justice Department approval to do so. The general didn't flinch. He told me he took his orders from a two-star general in San Antonio, Texas, and no matter what the White House had said to me, his orders hadn't changed. Drummond was a real straight shooter; he was obviously telling the truth. I called Gene Eidenberg, told him what Drummond had said, and demanded an explanation. Instead I got a lecture. Eidenberg said he'd been told I was overreacting and grandstanding after my disappointing primary showing. It was obvious that Gene, whom I considered a friend, didn't understand the situation, or me, as well as I had thought he did.

I was fit to be tied. I told him that since he obviously didn't have confidence in my judgment, he could make the next decision: "You can either come down here and fix this right now, tonight, or I'm going to shut the fort down. I'll put National Guardsmen at every entrance and no one will go in or out without my approval."

He was incredulous. "You can't do that," he said. "It's a federal facility."

"That may be," I shot back, "but it's on a state road and I control it. It's your decision."

Eidenberg flew to Fort Smith on an air force plane that night. I picked him up, and before we went to the fort I took him on a tour of Barling. It was well after midnight, but down every street we drove, at every house, armed residents were on alert, sitting on their lawns, on their porches, and, in one case, on the roof. I'll never forget one lady, who looked to be in her seventies, sitting stoically in her lawn chair with her shotgun across her lap. Eidenberg was shocked by what he saw. After we finished the tour he looked at me and said, "I had no idea."

After the tour, we met with General Drummond and other federal, state, and local officials for an hour or so. Then we talked to the horde of press people who had gathered. Eidenberg promised that the security problem would be fixed. Later that day, June 2, the White House said the Pentagon had received clear instructions to maintain order and keep the Cubans on the base. President

Carter also acknowledged that the people of Arkansas had suffered needless anxiety and promised that no more Cubans would be sent to Fort Chaffee.

Delays with the screening process seemed to be the root cause of the turmoil, and the people doing the screening made an effort to speed it up. When I went to visit the fort not long afterward, the situation was calmer and everyone seemed to be in a better frame of mind.

While things seemed to be settling down, I was still troubled by what had happened, or hadn't, between May 28, when Eidenberg told me the army had been ordered to keep the Cubans from leaving Chaffee, and June 1, when they let one thousand of them escape. Either the White House hadn't told me the truth, or the Justice Department was slow in getting its legal opinion to the Pentagon, or someone in the Pentagon had defied a lawful order of the Commander in Chief. If that's what happened, it amounted to a serious breach of the Constitution. I'm not sure the whole truth ever came out. As I learned when I got to Washington, after things go wrong, the willingness to take responsibility often vanishes.

In August, Hillary and I went to Denver for the summer meeting of the National Governors Association. All the talk was of presidential politics. President Carter seemed to have survived a vigorous challenge to his renomination from Senator Edward Kennedy, but Kennedy had not withdrawn. We had breakfast with the famous criminal lawyer Edward Bennett Williams, whom Hillary had known for years and who had wanted her to come to work for him after law school. Williams was strongly for Kennedy, and believed he'd have a better chance to defeat Ronald Reagan in the fall campaign because the President was bedeviled by a bad economy and the ten-month-long captivity of our hostages in Iran.

I disagreed with him on the politics and the merits. Carter had done a lot of good things as President, wasn't responsible for the OPEC price increases that had fueled the inflation, and had few good options for dealing with the hostage crisis. Besides, despite the problems with the Cubans, the Carter White House had been good to Arkansas, giving financial aid and support for our reform efforts in education, energy, health, and economic development. I had also been given remarkable access to the White House, for both business and pleasure. In the latter category, the best visit was when I took Mother to hear Willie Nelson sing on the South Lawn of the White House at a picnic the President hosted for NASCAR. After the event, Mother and I accompanied Nelson and the President's son Chip to the Hay-Adams Hotel, across Lafayette Square from the White House, where Willie sat at the piano and sang for us until two in the morning.

For all those reasons, I was feeling good about my relationship with the White House as the National Governors Association meeting began. The Democratic governors and their Republican counterparts held separate meetings. I had been elected vice chairman of the Democratic governors at the winter meeting, thanks to my nomination by Governor Jim Hunt of North Carolina, who would become one of my closest friends among the governors and an ally in the fight for education reform all the way through the White House years. Bob Strauss, the chairman of the Democratic National Committee, asked me to get the Democratic Governors Association to endorse President Carter over Senator Kennedy. After a quick canvass of the governors present, I told Strauss the vote would

My father, William
Jefferson Blythe, 1944

My father and my mother, Virginia
Cassidy Blythe, at the Palmer House Hotel,
Chicago,
1946

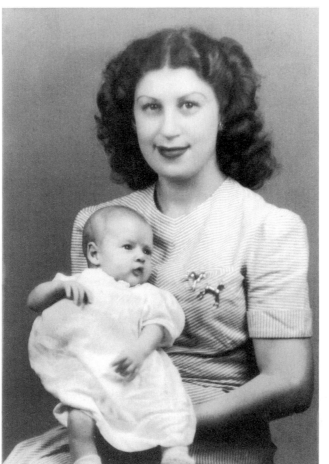

Mother and I

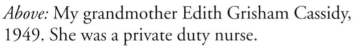

Here I am in 1949
Above, far left: at
my father's gravesi[de]
on the afternoon
Mother left for
nurse's training in
New Orleans;
above, center: in ou[r]
backyard; *above,*
right: posing for a
photo for Mother'[s]
Day

Above: My grandmother Edith Grisham Cassidy,
1949. She was a private duty nurse.

Below: My grandfather James Eldridge Cassidy
(right) in his grocery store in Hope, Arkansas, 1946

Miss Marie Purkins' School for Little Folks in Hope. I'm at the far left, with Vince Foster next to me and Mack McLarty in the back row.

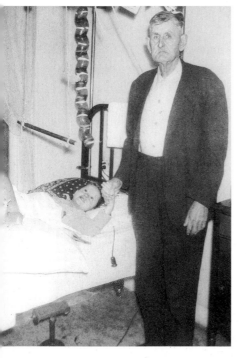

With my great-uncle Buddy Grisham, one of the lights of my life, during my first presidential campaign

My great-grandfather Lem Grisham came to visit me in the hospital when I broke my leg, March 1952.

Mother and Daddy, 1965

Daddy (my stepfather, Roger Clinton)

Below: My brother, Roger, and I with Cora Walters, the wonderful woman who took care of us

Below, right: From my high school yearbook: the Three Blind Mice, better known as the 3 Kings— Randy Goodrum on piano, Joe Newman on drums

Daddy and I at home in Hope 1951

I'm in the front, right behind the photographer, as President John F. Kennedy addresses the Boys Nation delegates in the Rose Garden on July 24, 1963.

David Leopoulos and I as emcees of the Hot Springs High School Band Variety Show, 1964

Mother, Roger, our dog Susie, and I in the snow at our Park Avenue house, 1961

At a picnic with friends, including Carolyn Yeldell, David Leopoulos, Ronnie Cecil, and Mary Jo Nelson

Frank Holt meeting and greeting in his shirtsleeves during his 1966 campaign for governor. (I'm in the light-colored suit.)

With my brother and my room-mates at our graduation from Georgetown, 1968: (from left) Kit Ashby, Tommy Caplan, Jim Moore, and Tom Campbell

Above: My Oxford roommates: Strobe Talbott (left) and Frank Aller. I'm in my bearded phase.

Right: I surprised Mother by flying home for her wedding to Jeff Dwire, January 3, 1969. Reverend John Miles officiated, and I was best man. Roger's in the front.

With my mentor J. William Fulbright and his administrative assistant, Lee Williams, September 1989. During my Georgetown years, I was assistant clerk on Fulbright's Foreign Relations Committee.

Hillary and I with our Yale Law School Barristers Union classmates

Above: Campaigning for George McGovern in San Antonio, Texas, 1972

Right: Teaching at the University of Arkansas Law School, Fayetteville

Right: With George Shelton, my campaign chairman, and F. H. Martin, treasurer. While they passed away before my presidency, their sons both served in my administration.

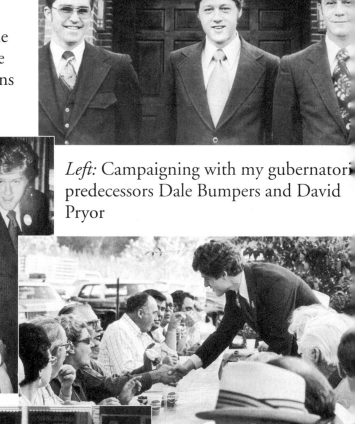

Left: Campaigning with my gubernatorial predecessors Dale Bumpers and David Pryor

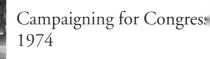

Campaigning for Congress 1974

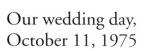

Our wedding day, October 11, 1975

Celebrating my thirty-second birthday during the campaign. Hillary is in dark glasses.

Addressing the Arkansas legislature after I was sworn in as governor, January 9, 1979

The youthful leaders of Arkansas, 1979: Secretary of State Paul Riviere, 31; State Senator Cliff Hoofman, 35; me, 32; State Auditor Jimmie Lou Fisher, 35; and Attorney General Steve Clark, 31

With Chelsea and Zeke

Hillary, Carolyn Huber, Emma Phillips, Chelsea, and Liza Ashley celebrate Liza's birthday in the Governor's Mansion in 1980.

Above: My announcement for governor in 1982. Hillary inscribe the picture "Chelsea's second birthday, Bill's second chance."

Left: With three of my strongest Arkansas supporters: Maurice Smit Jim Pledger, and Bill Clark, 1998

Below, left: Visiting Arkansas Delta Project leaders, with whom I worke to bring economic development to their region

Below: Parents and students at the Governor's Mansion for High School Honors Day, celebrating th valedictorians and salutorians of Arkansas high schools

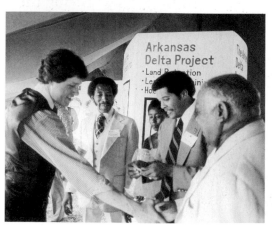

Above: At the Sanyo Electric plant in Japan
Left: My workday at the Tosco plant

Left to right:
Henry Oliver;
Gloria Cabe;
Carol Rasco

At the Grand Ole Opry, Nashville, during the governors' conference, 1984. I'm standing next to Minnie Pearl; Hillary is at the far left.

Left: Chelsea's first day of school. *Middle:* Betsey Wright and I surprise Hillary for her birthday, 1983. *Right:* Chelsea is enjoying the sight of me holding "Boa Derek" for Proclamation Day.

Dancing with Chelsea and with Hillary at the Governor's Inaugural Ball, January, 1991

With Dr. Billy Graham and my pastor, Dr. W. O. Vaught, fall 1989

With (clockwise, from left) Lottie Shackleford, Bobby Rush, Ernie Green, Carol Willis, Avis Lavelle, Bob Nash, and Rodney Slater at the National Democratic Convention, July 1992

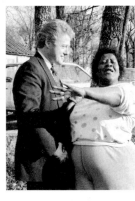

The 1992 campaign *Left:* Tipper Gore took this picture of the huge crowd in Keene, New Hampshire; *below, left:* in the "war room" James Carville and Paul Begala high five; *below:* campaigning in Stone Mountain, Georgia; *bottom:* Wall Street turns out for Hillary and me.

On the West Coast in 1992. *Top, left:* Cinco de Mayo; *top, right:* rally in Seattle; *right:* at a prayer meeting after the Los Angeles riots; *above:* greeting supporters in Los Angeles

Left: The Rodham family: (from left) Maria, Hugh, Dorothy, Hillary, and Tony. Hillary's father, Hugh, is seated.

The campaign team

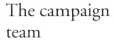

The bus tour

Hillary and I, Tipper and Al Gore, President Jimmy Carter, and (at left) Habitat for Humanity founder Millard Fuller celebrate Tipper's and my joint birthday.

President George H. W. Bush, Ross Perot, and I at the University of Richmond debate

The Arsenio Hall Show

My first day as President-elect. *Above, right:* with Mother; *below:* at Carolyn Yeldell Staley's house: (front row) Mother, Thea Leopoulos; (second row) Bob Aspell, me, Hillary, Glenda Cooper, Linda Leopoulos; (top row) Carolyn Staley, David Leopoulos, Mauria Aspell, Mary Jo Rodgers, Jim French, Tommy Caplan, Phil Jamison, Dick Kelley, Kit Ashby, Tom Campbell, Bob Dangremond, Patrick Campbell, Susan Jamison, Gail and Randy Goodrum, Thaddeus Leopoulos, Amy Ashby, Jim and Jane Moore, Tom and Jude Campbell, Will Staley

be twenty to four for Carter. We had a civilized debate, with Strauss speaking for the President and Governor Hugh Carey of New York arguing for Kennedy. After the 20–4 vote, Strauss and I spoke briefly to the press, touting the endorsement as a show of confidence in and political boost for President Carter at a time when he needed it.

About fifteen minutes later, I was told the White House was trying to reach me on the phone. Apparently the President wanted to thank me for helping line up the governors' support. Appearances can be deceiving. What the President wanted to tell me was that the weather was about to turn cold in Pennsylvania and Wisconsin, where the rest of the Cubans were being housed. Because those forts weren't insulated from the winter weather, he said it would be necessary to move the refugees. Then came the kicker. Now that the security problems were solved at Fort Chaffee, they would be moved there. I responded, "Mr. President, you promised that no more refugees would be sent to Arkansas. Send them to a fort in some warm place out west you're not going to win in November anyway." The President replied that he'd considered that but couldn't do it because it would cost $10 million to outfit a facility out west. I said, "Mr. President, your word to the people of Arkansas is worth $10 million." He disagreed, and we ended the conversation.

Now that I've been President, I have some idea of the pressures Jimmy Carter was under. He was dealing with both rampant inflation and a stagnant economy. The American hostages in Iran had been held by the Ayatollah Khomeini for almost a year. The Cubans weren't rioting anymore, so they were the least of his problems. Pennsylvania and Wisconsin had both voted for him in 1976, and they had more electoral votes than Arkansas, which he had won with almost two-thirds of the vote. I was still more than twenty points ahead of my opponent, Frank White, in the polls, so how could I be hurt?

At the time I saw it differently. I knew the President would be hurt badly by breaking his commitment to Arkansas. Whether or not the forts in Wisconsin and Pennsylvania had to be closed for weather or for political reasons, sending the remaining Cubans to the one place he had promised not to, in order to save $10 million, was nuts. I called Rudy Moore and my campaign chairman, Dick Herget, to see what they thought I should do. Dick said I should fly directly to Washington to see the President. If I couldn't change his mind, I should talk to the press outside the White House and withdraw my support for his reelection. But I couldn't do that, for two reasons. First, I didn't want to look like a modern version of Orval Faubus and other southern governors who resisted federal authority in the civil rights years. Second, I didn't want to do anything to help Ronald Reagan beat Carter. Reagan was running a great campaign, with a big head of steam, fueled by the hostages, the bad economy, and the intense support of right-wing groups outraged about everything from abortion to Carter's turning the Panama Canal over to Panama.

Gene Eidenberg asked me not to announce the relocation until he could come to Arkansas and put the best face on it. The story leaked anyway, and Gene's visit to Arkansas did little to help. He made a convincing case that there would be no further security problems, but he couldn't deny that the President was breaking a clear commitment to the state that had been more supportive of him than any other outside his native Georgia. I won a larger role in controlling the security arrangements and made some improvements, but I was still the President's man in Arkansas who had failed to hold him to his word.

I returned home from Denver to a very volatile political situation. My opponent in the general election, Frank White, was gaining ground. White was a big man with a booming voice and a bombastic style that belied his background as a graduate of the Naval Academy, savings-and-loan executive, and former director of the Arkansas Industrial Development Commission under Governor Pryor. He had strong support from all the interest groups I'd taken on, including utility, poultry, trucking, and timber companies, and the medical associations. He was a born-again Christian with the strong backing of the state chapter of the Moral Majority and other conservative activists. And he had the pulse of the country people and blue-collar workers upset about the car tags. He also had the advantage of a generally disgruntled mood, due to the economy and the drought. When the bad economy led state revenues to decline below projections, I was forced to lower state spending to balance the budget, including education cuts that reduced the second year's $1,200 pay raise for teachers to about $900. Many teachers didn't care about the state's budget problems; they had been promised $1,200 for two years and they wanted the second installment. When it didn't come, the intensity of their support for me faded considerably.

Back in April, Hillary and I had seen Frank White at an event and I told her that no matter what the polls said, he was starting with 45 percent of the vote. I had made that many people mad. After the announcement that all the refugees would be housed at Fort Chaffee, White had his mantra for the election: Cubans and Car Tags. That's all he talked about for the rest of the campaign. I campaigned hard in August but without much success. At factory gates, workers changing shifts said they wouldn't vote for me because I had made their economic woes worse and betrayed them by raising the car tags. Once while campaigning in Fort Smith, near the bridge to Oklahoma, when I asked a man for his support, he gave a more graphic version of the answer I'd heard hundreds of times: "You raised my car tags. I wouldn't vote for you if you were the only SOB on the ballot!" He was angry and red in the face. In exasperation, I pointed over the bridge to Oklahoma and said, "Look over there. If you lived in Oklahoma your car tags would be more than twice as expensive as they are now!" Suddenly all the red drained out of his face. He smiled, put his hand on my shoulder, and said, "See, kid, you just don't get it. That's one reason I live on this side of the border."

At the end of August, I went to the Democratic National Convention with the Arkansas delegation. Senator Kennedy was still in the race, though he was clearly going to lose. I had some good friends working for Kennedy who wanted me to encourage him to withdraw before the balloting and make a generous speech supporting Carter. I liked Kennedy and thought it was best for him to be gracious, so that he wouldn't be blamed if Carter lost. The blood between the two candidates was bad, but my friends thought I might be able to persuade him. I went to the senator's hotel suite and gave it my best shot. Kennedy ultimately did withdraw and endorse the President, though when they appeared on the platform together he didn't do a very good job of faking an enthusiasm he clearly didn't feel.

By convention time, I was the chairman of the Democratic Governors Association and was invited to give a five-minute address. National conventions are noisy and chaotic. The delegates normally listen only to the keynote address and the presidential and vice-presidential acceptance speeches. If you're not giving one of those three, your only chance of being heard over the constant din of floor talk is to be compelling and quick. I tried to explain the painful, profoundly different economic situation we were experiencing, and to argue that the Democratic Party had to change to meet the challenge. Ever since World War II, Democrats had taken America's prosperity for granted; their priorities were extending its benefits to more and more people and fighting for social justice. Now we had to deal with inflation and unemployment, big government deficits, and the loss of our competitive edge. Our failure to do so had driven more people to support Republicans or to join the growing cadre of alienated nonvoters. It was a good speech that took less than the allotted five minutes, but nobody paid much attention to it.

President Carter left the convention with all the problems he had when it started, and without the boost a genuinely enthusiastic, united party usually gives its nominee. I returned to Arkansas determined to try to salvage my own campaign. It kept getting worse.

On September 19, I was home in Hot Springs after a long day of politics when the commander of the Strategic Air Command called me to say that there had been an explosion in a Titan II missile silo near Damascus, Arkansas, about forty miles northwest of Little Rock. The story was unbelievable. An air force mechanic was repairing the missile when he dropped his three-pound wrench. It fell seventy feet to the bottom of the silo, bounced up, and punctured the tank full of rocket fuel. When the highly toxic fuel mixed with the air, it caused a fire, then a huge explosion that blew the 740-ton concrete top off the silo, killed the mechanic, and injured twenty other air force personnel who were near the opening. The explosion also destroyed the missile and catapulted its nuclear warhead into the cow pasture where the silo was located. I was assured that the warhead wouldn't detonate, that no radioactive material would be released, and that the military would remove it safely. At least my state wasn't going to be incinerated by Arkansas' latest brush with bad luck. I was beginning to feel snakebit, but tried to make the best of the situation. I instructed my new director of public safety, Sam Tatom, to work out an emergency evacuation plan with federal officials in case something went wrong with one of the seventeen remaining Titan II missiles.

After all the other things we'd been through, now Arkansas had the world's only cow pasture with its very own nuclear warhead. A few days after the incident, Vice President Mondale came to our state Democratic convention in Hot Springs. When I asked him to make sure the military cooperated with us on a new emergency plan for the missiles, he picked up the phone and called Harold Brown, the secretary of defense. His first words were "Damn it, Harold, I know I asked you to do something to get the Cuban problem off Arkansas' mind, but this is a little extreme." Contrary to his restrained public demeanor, Mondale had a great sense of humor. He knew we were both tanking, and he still made it funny.

The last few weeks of the campaign were dominated by a new phenomenon in Arkansas politics: completely negative television ads. There was a tough one on the car tags. But White's most effective campaign ad showed rioting Cubans, with a strong voice-over telling viewers that the governors of Pennsylvania and Wisconsin cared about their people and they got rid of the Cubans, but I cared more about Jimmy Carter than the people of Arkansas, "and now we've got them all." When Hillary and I first saw it, we thought it was so outrageous that no one would believe it. A poll taken right before the ad started running had shown that 60 percent of the people thought I'd done a good job at Fort Chaffee, while 3 percent thought I'd been too tough and 20 percent, the hard-core right, too weak. I could have satisfied them only by shooting every refugee that left the fort.

We were wrong about the ads. They were working. In Fort Smith, local officials, including Sheriff Bill Cauthron and Prosecuting Attorney Ron Fields, strongly defended me, saying I had done a good job and had taken risks to protect the people around the fort. As we all know now, a press conference will not counter the effect of a powerful negative ad. I was sinking in the quicksand of Cubans and car tags.

Several days before the election, Hillary called Dick Morris, whom I had replaced with Peter Hart because my people hated dealing with Dick's abrasive personality. She asked him to do a poll to see if there was anything we could do to pull it out. To his credit, Dick did the poll, and with characteristic bluntness said that I would probably lose. He made a couple of suggestions for ads, which we followed, but as he predicted, it was too little, too late.

On election day, November 4, Jimmy Carter and I got 48 percent of Arkansas' vote, down from his 65 percent in 1976 and my 63 percent in 1978. However, we lost in very different ways. The President carried fifty of the seventy-five counties, holding on to the Democratic strongholds where the Cuban issue cut into but didn't eliminate his margin of victory, and getting annihilated in the more conservative Republican areas in western Arkansas, where there was a high turnout, fueled by voters' anger over his broken pledge on the Cubans, and by Reagan's alliance with Christian fundamentalists and their opposition to abortion and the Panama Canal treaties. Arkansas still hadn't gone over to the Republicans. Carter's 48 percent was seven points better than his national percentage. If it hadn't been for the broken pledge, he would have carried the state.

By contrast, I carried only twenty-four counties, including those with heavy black populations and a few where there was more support for or less opposition to the highway program. I lost all eleven counties in Democratic northeast Arkansas, almost all the rural counties in the Third District, and several in south Arkansas. I had been killed by the car tags. The main effect of the Cuban ad was to take away voters who had been supporting me despite their reservations. Public approval of my performance on the Cuban issue kept my poll ratings higher than they would have been in the face of the car tags, the interest groups' opposition, and the dour economic situation. What happened to me in 1980 was strikingly similar to what happened to President George H. W. Bush in 1992. The Gulf War kept his poll numbers high, but underneath there was a lot of discontent. When people decided they weren't going to vote for him on the war issue, I moved ahead. Frank White used the Cuban ad to do the same thing to me.

In 1980, I ran better than President Carter in the Republican areas in western Arkansas, where there was more direct knowledge of how I had handled the Cuban situation. In Fort Smith and Sebastian County, I actually led the Democratic ticket, because of Fort Chaffee. Carter got 28 percent.

Senator Bumpers, who had practiced law there for more than twenty years but who had committed the unpardonable sin of voting to "give away" the Panama Canal, got 30 percent. I got 33 percent. That's how bad it was.

On election night I was in such bad shape I didn't think I could bear to face the press. Hillary went down to the headquarters, thanked the workers, and invited them to the Governor's Mansion the next day. After a fitful night's sleep, Hillary, Chelsea, and I met with a couple hundred of our die-hard supporters on the back lawn of the mansion. I gave them the best speech I could, thanking them for all they'd done, telling them to be proud of all we'd accomplished, and offering my cooperation to Frank White. It was a pretty upbeat talk considering the circumstances. Inside, I was full of self-pity and anger, mostly at myself. And I was filled with regret that I would no longer be able to do the work I loved so much. I expressed the regret but kept the whining and anger to myself.

At that moment, there didn't seem to be much future for me in politics. I was the first Arkansas governor in a quarter of a century denied a second two-year term, and probably the youngest ex-governor in American history. John McClellan's warning about the governor's office being a graveyard seemed prophetic. But since I had dug my own grave, the only sensible thing to do seemed to be to start climbing out.

On Thursday, Hillary and I found a new home. It was a pretty wooden house, built in 1911, on Midland Avenue in the Hillcrest area of Little Rock, not too far from where we'd lived before moving into the Governor's Mansion. I called Betsey Wright and asked her if she'd come help me get my files organized before I left office. To my joy, she agreed. She moved into the Governor's Mansion and worked every day with my friend State Representative Gloria Cabe, who had also been defeated for reelection after supporting all my programs.

My remaining two months in office were tough on my staff. They needed to find jobs. The usual route out of politics is through one of the big companies that do a lot of business with state government, but we had angered all of them. Rudy Moore did a good job trying to help everyone and make sure we cleared up all outstanding public business before we turned the office over to Frank White. He and my scheduler, Randy White, also reminded me, in my periods of self-absorption, that I needed to show more concern for my staff and their future welfare. Most of them had no savings to sustain a long job hunt. Several had young children. And many had worked only for the state, including a number of people who had been with me in the attorney general's office. Though I really liked the people who had worked for me and felt grateful to them, I'm afraid I didn't demonstrate that as clearly as I should have on many of the days after I lost.

Hillary was especially good to me in that awful period, balancing love and sympathy with an uncanny knack for keeping me focused on the present and the future. The fact that Chelsea didn't have a clue that anything bad had happened helped me realize that it was not the end of the world. I got great calls of encouragement from Ted Kennedy, who said I'd be back, and Walter Mondale, who showed extraordinary good humor in the face of his own disappointing defeat. I even went to the White House to say good-bye to President Carter and thank him for all the good things his administration had done to help Arkansans. I was still upset about his broken pledge and how it contributed to my defeat and led to his loss in

Arkansas, but I felt history would be kinder to him because of his energy and environmental policies, especially the establishment of the massive Arctic National Wildlife Refuge in Alaska, and his accomplishments in foreign policy—the Camp David agreement between Israel and Egypt, the Panama Canal treaties, and the elevation of the human rights issue.

Like the rest of the employees of the governor's office, I had to find a job, too. I got several interesting offers or inquiries from out of state. My friend John Y. Brown, governor of Kentucky, who had made a fortune with Kentucky Fried Chicken, asked if I'd be interested in applying for the presidency of the University of Louisville. In typical John Y. short-speak, he made the pitch: "Good school, nice house, great basketball team." California governor Jerry Brown told me his chief of staff, Gray Davis, himself a future governor, was leaving and asked me to replace him. He said that he couldn't believe I'd been thrown out over car tags, that California was a place full of people who had moved there from other states and I'd fit right in, and that he'd guarantee my ability to influence policy in areas I cared about. I was approached about taking over the World Wildlife Fund, a Washington-based conservation group, which did work I admired. Norman Lear, producer of some of the most successful television shows in history, including **All in the Family,** asked me to become head of the People for the American Way, a liberal group established to counter conservative assaults on First Amendment freedoms. And several people asked me to run for chairman of the Democratic National Committee against Charles Manatt, a successful Los Angeles lawyer with Iowa roots. The only job offer I got in Arkansas was from Wright, Lindsey & Jennings, a fine law firm, which asked me to become "of counsel" for $60,000 a year, almost twice what I'd made as governor.

I took a hard look at the Democratic committee job, because I loved politics and thought I understood what needed to be done. In the end, I decided it wasn't right for me. Besides, Chuck Manatt wanted it badly and probably already had the votes to win before I got interested. I discussed it with Mickey Kantor, a partner of Manatt's whom I had gotten to know when he served with Hillary on the board of the Legal Services Corporation. I liked Mickey a lot and trusted his judgment. He said if I wanted another chance at elected office, I shouldn't try for the party job. He also advised against becoming Jerry Brown's chief of staff. The other out-of-state jobs had some appeal to me, especially the one at the World Wildlife Fund, but I knew they didn't make sense. I wasn't ready to give up on Arkansas or myself, so I accepted the offer from Wright, Lindsey & Jennings.

Almost immediately after I lost, and for months afterward, I asked everybody I knew why they thought it had happened. Some of the answers, beyond Cubans, car tags, and making all the interest groups angry at the same time, surprised me. Jimmy "Red" Jones, whom I had appointed adjutant general of the Arkansas National Guard after he'd had a long career as state auditor, said I had alienated the voters with too many young beards and out-of-staters in important positions. He also thought Hillary's decision to keep her maiden name had hurt; it might be all right for a lawyer, but not for a first lady. Wally DeRoeck, who had been my chairman in 1976 and 1978, said I got so caught up in being governor that I stopped thinking about everything else. He told me that after I became governor, I never asked him about his children again. In harsher language, my friend George Daniel, who owned the hardware store in Marshall up in the hills, said the same thing: "Bill, the people thought you were an asshole!" Rudy Moore told me I had complained a lot about how much trouble I was in but never seemed to really focus on my political problems hard and long enough to figure out what to do about them. Mack McLarty, my oldest friend, who knew me like the back of his hand, said he thought I was preoccupied all year by the arrival of Chelsea. He said I had always been saddened by the fact that I never knew my own father, that I really wanted to focus on being Chelsea's father, except when something like the Cuban crisis tore me away, and that I just didn't have my heart in the campaign.

After I was out of office a few months, it became clear to me that all these explanations had some validity. By that time, more than a hundred people had come up to me and said they'd voted against me to send a message but wouldn't have done it if they'd known I was going to lose. I thought of so many things I could have done if I'd had my head on straight. And it was painfully clear that thousands of people thought I'd gotten too big for my britches, too obsessed with what I wanted to do and oblivious to what they wanted me to do. The protest vote was there, all right, but it didn't make the difference. The post-election polls showed that 12 percent of the voters said they'd supported me in 1978 but voted the other way in 1980 because of the car tags. Six percent of my former supporters said it was because of the Cubans. With all my other problems and mistakes, if I had been free of either of these two issues, I would have won. But if I hadn't been defeated, I probably never would have become President. It was a near-death experience, but an invaluable one, forcing me to be more sensitive to the political problems inherent in progressive politics: the system can absorb only so much change at once; no one can beat all the entrenched interests at the same time; and if people think you've stopped listening, you're sunk.

On my last day in the governor's office, after taking a picture of ten-month-old Chelsea sitting in my chair holding the telephone, I went up to the legislature to give my farewell address. I recounted the progress we'd made, thanked the legislators for their support, and pointed out that we still had America's second-lowest tax burden and that, sooner or later, we would have to find a politically acceptable way to broaden our revenue base to make the most of our potential. Then I walked out of the Capitol and into private life, a fish out of water.

TWENTY-TWO

Wright, Lindsey & Jennings was, by Arkansas standards, a large firm with a fine reputation and a varied practice. The support staff were able and friendly and went out of their way to help settle me in and make me feel at home. The firm also allowed me to bring my secretary, Barbara Kerns, who had been with me for four years by then and knew all my family, friends, and supporters. It even provided Betsey Wright office space so that she could keep working on my files and, as it turned out, plan the next campaign. I did some legal work and brought in a couple of modest clients, but I'm sure the lifeline the firm threw me didn't make it any money. All the firm really got out of it was my everlasting gratitude and some legal business defending me when I became President.

Though I missed being governor and the excitement of politics, I enjoyed the more normal pace of my life, coming home at a reasonable hour, being with Hillary as we watched Chelsea grow into her life, going out to dinner with friends, and getting to know our neighbors, especially the older couple who lived directly across the street, Sarge and Louise Lozano. They adored Chelsea and were always there to help out.

I resolved to stay away from public speaking for several months, with one exception. In February, I drove to Brinkley, about an hour east of Little Rock on the interstate, to speak at the Lions Club banquet. The area had voted for me in 1980, and my strongest supporters there all urged me to come. They said it would lift my spirits to be with folks who were still supporters, and it did. After the dinner, I went to a reception at the home of my county leaders, Don and Betty Fuller, where I was gratified and a little surprised to meet people who actually wanted me to be governor again. Back in Little Rock, most people were still trying to get on good terms with the new governor. One man whom I'd appointed to a position in state government and who wanted to stay on under Governor White actually crossed the street in downtown Little Rock one day when he saw me walking toward him. He was afraid to be seen shaking hands with me in broad daylight.

While I was grateful for the kindness of my friends in Brinkley, I didn't go out speaking again in Arkansas for several months. Frank White was beginning to make mistakes and lose some legislative battles, and I didn't want to get in his way. He kept his campaign pledge to pass bills changing the name of the Economic Development Department back to the Arkansas Industrial Development Commission and abolishing the Department of Energy. But when he tried to abolish the rural health clinics Hillary and I had established, large numbers of people who depended on them showed up to protest. His bill was defeated, and he had to be content with stopping the building of more clinics that would have served others who really needed them.

When the governor introduced a bill to roll back the car-tag increase, the director of the Highway Department, Henry Gray, the highway commissioners, and the road builders put up strong resistance. They were building and repairing roads and making money. A lot of legislators listened to them, because their constituents liked the roadwork even if they had resisted paying for it. In the end, White got a modest rollback in the fees, but most of the money stayed in the program.

The governor's biggest legislative problem arose, ironically, out of a bill he passed. The so-called creation science bill required that every Arkansas school that taught the theory of evolution had to spend an equal amount of time teaching a theory of creation consistent with the Bible: that humans did not evolve out of other species around one hundred thousand years ago, but instead were created by God as a separate species a few thousand years ago.

For much of the twentieth century, fundamentalists had opposed evolution as being inconsistent with a literal reading of the biblical account of human creation, and in the early 1900s, several states, including Arkansas, outlawed the teaching of evolution. Even after the Supreme Court struck down such bans, most science texts didn't discuss evolution until the 1960s. By the late sixties, a new generation of fundamentalists were at it again, this time arguing that there was scientific evidence to support the Bible's creation story, and evidence that cast doubt on the theory of evolution. Eventually, they came up with the idea of requiring that schools that taught evolution had to give comparable attention to "creation science."

Because of intense lobbying efforts by fundamentalist groups like FLAG (Family, Life, America under God) and the governor's support, Arkansas was the first state to legally embrace the creation science notion. The bill passed without much difficulty: we didn't have many scientists in the legislature, and many politicians were afraid to offend the conservative Christian groups, who were riding high after electing a President and a governor. After Governor White signed the bill, there was a storm of protest from educators who didn't want to be forced to teach religion as science, from religious leaders who wanted to preserve the constitutional separation of church and state, and from ordinary citizens who didn't want Arkansas to become the laughingstock of the nation.

Frank White became an object of ridicule for the opponents of the creation science law. George Fisher, the **Arkansas Gazette** cartoonist who drew me on a tricycle, began presenting the governor with a half-peeled banana in his hand, implying that he hadn't fully evolved and was perhaps the proverbial "missing link" between humans and chimpanzees. When he started feeling the heat, Governor White protested that he hadn't read the bill before he signed it, digging himself into a deeper hole. Eventually, the creation science bill was declared unconstitutional by Judge Bill Overton, who did a masterly job at the trial and wrote a clear, compelling opinion saying the bill required the teaching of religion, not science, and therefore breached the Constitution's wall between church and state. Attorney General Steve Clark declined to appeal the decision.

Frank White had problems that went beyond the legislative session. His worst move was sending prospective appointees for the Public Service Commission to be interviewed by the Arkansas Power and Light Company, which had been seeking substantial increases in utility rates for the last few years. When the story came out, the press pounded the governor over it. People's electric rates were going up far more steeply than the car tags had. Now they had a governor who wanted to give AP&L prior approval of the people who would decide whether or not the company got to raise its rates even higher.

Then there were the verbal gaffes. When the governor announced a trade mission to Taiwan and Japan, he told the press how glad he was to be going to the Middle East. The incident gave George Fisher the inspiration for one of his funniest cartoons: the governor and his party getting off an airplane in the middle of a desert, complete with palm trees, pyramids, robed Arabs, and a camel. With banana in hand, he looks around and says, "Splendid! Whistle us up a rickshaw!"

While all this was going on, I made a few political trips out of state. Before I lost, I had been invited by Governor John Evans to speak at the Idaho Jefferson-Jackson Day dinner. After I got beat he asked me to come on anyway.

I went to Des Moines, Iowa, for the first time, to speak to a Democratic Party workshop for state and local officials. My friend Sandy Berger asked me to come to Washington to have lunch with Pamela Harriman, wife of the famous Democratic statesman Averell Harriman, who had been FDR's envoy to Churchill and Stalin, governor of New York, and our negotiator at the Paris peace talks with North Vietnam. Harriman met Pamela during World War II when she was married to Churchill's son and living at 10 Downing Street. They married thirty years later, after his first wife died. Pamela was in her early sixties and still a beautiful woman. She wanted me to join the board of Democrats for the 80's, a new political action committee she had formed to raise money and promote ideas to help Democrats come back into power. After the lunch, I accompanied Pam to her first television interview. She was nervous and wanted my advice. I told her to relax and speak in the same conversational tone she'd used during our lunch. I joined her board and over the next few years spent a number of great evenings at the Harrimans' Georgetown house, with its political memorabilia and impressionist art treasures. When I became President, I named Pamela Harriman ambassador to France, where she had gone to live after World War II and the breakup of her first marriage. She was wildly popular and immensely effective with the French, and very happy there until she died, on the job, in 1997.

By the spring, the governor looked vulnerable in the next election and I began to think of a rematch. One day, I drove from Little Rock to Hot Springs to see Mother. About halfway there, I pulled into the parking lot of the gas station and store at Lonsdale. The man who owned it was active in local politics, and I wanted to see what he thought about my chances. He was friendly but noncommittal. As I walked back to my car, I ran into an elderly man in overalls. He said, "Aren't you Bill Clinton?" When I said I was and shook his hand, he couldn't wait to tell me he had voted against me. "I'm one of those who helped beat you. I cost you eleven votes—me, my wife, my two boys and their wives, and five of my friends. We just leveled you." I asked him why and got the predictable reply: "I had to. You raised my car tags." I pointed to a spot on the highway not far from where we were standing and said, "Remember that ice storm we had when I took office? That piece of road over there buckled and cars were stuck in the ditch. I had to get the National Guard to pull them out. There were pictures of it in all the papers. Those roads had to be fixed." He replied, "I don't care. I still didn't want to pay it." For some reason, after all he'd said, I blurted out, "Let me ask you something. If I ran for governor again, would you consider voting for me?" He smiled and said, "Sure I would. We're even now." I went right to the pay phone, called Hillary, told her the story, and said I thought we could win.

I spent most of the rest of 1981 traveling and calling around the state. The Democrats wanted to beat Frank White, and most of my old supporters said they'd be with me if I ran. Two men with a deep love for our state and a passion for politics took a particular interest in helping me. Maurice Smith owned a 12,000-acre farm and the bank in his little hometown of Birdeye. He was about sixty years old, short and thin, with a craggy face and a deep, gravelly voice he used sparingly but to great effect. Maurice was smart as a whip and good as gold. He had been active in Arkansas politics a long time—and was a genuine progressive Democrat, a virtue his whole family shared. He didn't have a racist or an elitist bone in his body, and he had supported both my highway program and my education program. He wanted me to run again, and he was prepared to take the lead role in raising the funds necessary to win and in getting support from well-respected people who hadn't been involved before. His biggest coup was George Kell, who had made the Hall of Fame playing baseball for the Detroit Tigers and was still the radio announcer for the Tiger games. Throughout his stellar baseball career, Kell had kept his home in Swifton, the small northeast Arkansas town where he grew up. He was a legend there and had lots of admirers all over the state. After we got acquainted, he agreed to serve as the campaign treasurer.

Maurice's support gave my campaign instant credibility, which was important because no Arkansas governor had ever been elected, defeated, and elected again, though others had tried. But he gave me much more. He became my friend, confidant, and advisor. I trusted him completely. He was somewhere between a second father and an older brother to me. For the rest of my time in Arkansas, he was involved in all my campaigns and the work of the governor's office. Because Maurice loved the give-and-take of politics, he was especially effective in pushing my programs in the legislature. He knew when to fight and when to deal. He kept me out of a lot of the trouble I'd had in the first term. By the time I became President, Maurice was in ill health. We spent one happy evening on the third floor of the White House reminiscing about our times together.

I never met a single person who didn't like and respect Maurice Smith. A few weeks before he died, Hillary was back in Arkansas and went to the hospital to see him. When she returned to the White House, she looked at me and said, "I just love that man." In the last week of his life, we talked twice on the telephone. He told me he didn't think he'd get out of the hospital this time and just wanted me to know "I'm proud of everything we did together and I love you." It was the only time he ever said that.

When Maurice died in late 1998, I went home to speak at his funeral, something I had to do too much of as President. On the way down to Arkansas, I thought of all he had done for me. He was finance chairman of all my campaigns, master of ceremonies at every inauguration, my chief of staff, a member of the university board of trustees, director of the Highway Department, chief lobbyist for legislation for the disabled—the favorite cause of his wife, Jane. But most of all, I thought of the day after I lost the 1980 election, when Hillary, Chelsea, and I were standing on the lawn of the Governor's Mansion. As I slumped under the weight of my defeat, a small man put his hand on my shoulder, looked me in the eye, and said in that wonderful raspy voice, "That's all right. We'll be back." I still miss Maurice Smith.

The other man in that category was L. W. "Bill" Clark, a man I barely knew before he sought me out in 1981 to discuss what I'd have to do to regain the governor's office. Bill was a strongly built man who loved a good political fight and had a keen understanding of human nature. He was from Fordyce in southeast Arkansas and owned a mill that shaped white oak lumber into staves for the casks that hold sherry and whiskey. He sold a lot of them in Spain. He also owned a couple of Burger King restaurants. One day in the early spring, he invited me to go to the races with him at Oaklawn Park in Hot Springs. I had been out of office only a couple of months, and Bill was surprised that so few people came up to our box to say hello. Instead of discouraging him, the cool treatment I got fired his competitive instincts. He decided he was going to get me back to the governor's office come hell or high water. I went to his Hot Springs lake house several times in 1981 to talk politics and meet friends he was trying to recruit to help us. At those small dinners and parties, I met several people who agreed to take leading roles in the campaign in south Arkansas. Some of them had never supported me before, but Bill Clark brought them over. I owe Bill Clark a lot for all he did for me over the next eleven years, to help me win elections and pass my legislative program. But mostly I owe him for believing in me at a time when I wasn't always able to believe in myself.

While I was out on the hustings, Betsey Wright was working hard to get the mechanics in place. In the last several months of 1981, she, Hillary, and I talked to Dick Morris about how to launch my campaign, flying to New York at Dick's suggestion to meet with Tony Schwartz, a famous expert in political media, who rarely left his Manhattan apartment. I found Schwartz and his ideas about how to influence both the thoughts and feelings of voters fascinating. It was clear that if I wanted to win in 1982, just two years after being thrown out of office, I had to walk a fine line with Arkansans. I couldn't tell the voters they'd made a mistake in defeating me. On the other hand, if I wore the hair shirt too much, I would have a hard time convincing voters to give me another chance to serve. It was a problem we all thought hard about, as Betsey and I labored over the lists and devised strategies for the primary and general elections.

Meanwhile, as 1981 drew to a close, I took two very different trips that prepared me for the battle ahead. At the invitation of Governor Bob Graham, I went to Florida to address the state Democratic convention, which met in the Miami area every two years in December. I gave an impassioned plea for the Democrats to fight back in the face of Republican attack ads. I said it was all well and good to let them strike the first blow, but if they hit us hard below the belt, we should "take a meat ax and cut their hands off." It was a bit melodramatic, but the right wing had taken over the Republican Party and changed the rules of political combat, while their hero, President Reagan, smiled and appeared to stay above it all. The Republicans thought they could win election wars indefinitely with their verbal assault weapons. Perhaps they could, but I for one was determined never to practice unilateral disarmament again.

The other trip I took was a pilgrimage with Hillary to the Holy Land, led by the pastor of Immanuel Baptist Church, W. O. Vaught. In 1980, at Hillary's urging, I had joined Immanuel and begun to sing in the choir. I hadn't been a regular churchgoer since I left home for George-town in 1964, and I'd stopped singing in the church choir a few years before then. Hillary knew that I missed going to church, and that I admired W. O. Vaught because he had forsaken the hellfire-and-brimstone preaching of his early ministry in favor of carefully teaching the Bible to his congregation. He believed that the Bible was the inerrant word of God but that few people understood its true meaning. He immersed himself in the study of the earliest available versions of the scriptures, and would give a series of sermons on one book of the Bible or an impor-tant scriptural subject before going on to something else. I looked forward to my Sundays in the choir loft of the church, looking at the back of Dr. Vaught's bald head and following along in my Bible, as he taught us through the Old and New Testaments.

Dr. Vaught had been going to the Holy Land since 1938, ten years before the state of Israel came into being. Hillary's parents came down from Park Ridge to stay with Chelsea so that we could join the group he led in Decem-ber 1981. We spent much of our time in Jerusalem, retrac-ing the steps Jesus walked and meeting local Christians. We saw the spot where Christians believe Jesus was cruci-fied and the small cave where Christ is believed to have been buried and from which He arose. We also went to the Western Wall, holy to Jews, and to the Muslim holy sites, the Al-Aqsa Mosque and the Dome of the Rock, the point from which Muslims believe Mohammed rose to heaven and his rendezvous with Allah. We went to the Church of the Holy Sepulcher; to the Sea of Galilee, where Jesus walked on water; to Jericho, possibly the world's oldest city; and to Masada, where a band of Jewish warriors, the Maccabees, withstood a long, furious

Roman assault until they were finally overcome and entered the pantheon of martyrs. Atop Masada, as we looked down on the valley below, Dr. Vaught reminded us that history's greatest armies, including those of Alexander the Great and Napoleon, had marched through it, and that the book of Revelation says that at the end of time, the valley will flow with blood.

That trip left a lasting mark on me. I returned home with a deeper appreciation of my own faith, a profound admiration for Israel, and for the first time, some understanding of Palestinian aspirations and grievances. It was the beginning of an obsession to see all the children of Abraham reconciled on the holy ground in which our three faiths came to life.

Not long after I got home, Mother got married to Dick Kelley, a food broker she had known for years and had been seeing for a while. She had been single for more than seven years, and I was happy for her. Dick was a big, attractive guy who loved the races as much as she did. He also loved to travel and did a lot of it. He would take Mother all over the world. Thanks to Dick, she went to Las Vegas often but also got to Africa before I did. The Reverend John Miles married them in a sweet ceremony at Marge and Bill Mitchell's place on Lake Hamilton, which ended with Roger singing Billy Joel's "Just the Way You Are." I would come to love Dick Kelley and grow ever more grateful for the happiness he brought Mother, and me. He would become one of my favorite golf companions. Well into his eighties, when he played his handicap and I played mine, he beat me more than half the time.

In January 1982, golf was the last thing on my mind; it

was time to start the campaign. Betsey had taken to Arkansas like a duck to water and had done a great job putting together an organization of my old supporters and new people who were disenchanted with Governor White. Our first big decision was how to begin. Dick Morris suggested that before I made a formal announcement I should go on television to acknowledge the mistakes that led to my defeat and ask for another chance. It was a risky idea, but the whole idea of running just two years after I had lost was risky. If I lost again, there would be no more comebacks, at least not for a long time.

We cut the ad in New York at Tony Schwartz's studio. I thought the only way it would work was if it contained both an honest acknowledgment of my past mistakes and the promise of the kind of positive leadership that had attracted popular support the first time I ran. The ad aired without prior notice on February 8. My face filled the screen as I told the voters that since my defeat I had traveled the state talking with thousands of Arkansans; that they had told me I'd done some good things but made big mistakes, including raising the car-tag fees; and that our roads needed the money but I was wrong to raise it in a way that hurt so many people. I then said that when I was growing up, "my daddy never had to whip me twice for the same thing"; that the state needed leadership in education and economic development, areas in which I had done a good job; and that if they'd give me another chance, I'd be a governor who had learned from defeat that "you can't lead without listening."

The ad generated a lot of conversation and seemed at least to have opened the minds of enough voters to give me a chance. On February 27, Chelsea's birthday, I made my official announcement. Hillary gave me a picture of the three of us at the event, with the inscription "Chelsea's second birthday, Bill's second chance."

I promised to focus on the three issues I thought were most important to the state's future: improving education, bringing in more jobs, and holding down utility rates. These were also the issues on which Governor White was most vulnerable. He had cut the car-tag fees $16 million, while his Public Service Commission had approved $227 million in rate increases for Arkansas Power and Light, hurting both consumers and businesses. The down economy had cost us a lot of jobs, and state revenue was too meager to allow anything to be done for education.

The message was well received, but the big news on that day was Hillary's declaration that she was taking my name. From now on, she would be known as Hillary Rodham Clinton. We had been discussing it for weeks. Hillary had been convinced to do it by the large number of our friends who said that, though the issue never showed up as a negative in our polls, it bothered a lot of people. Even Vernon Jordan had mentioned it to her when he came to Little Rock to visit us a few months earlier. Over the years Vernon had become a close friend of ours. He was one of the nation's foremost civil rights leaders, and he was a person on whom his friends could always rely. He was a southerner and older than we were by enough years to understand why the name issue mattered. Ironically, the only person outside our inner circle to mention it to me was a young progressive lawyer from Pine Bluff who was a big supporter of mine. He asked me if Hillary's keeping her maiden name bothered me. I told him that it didn't, and that I had never thought about it until someone brought it up. He stared at me in disbelief and said, "Come on, I know you. You're a real man. It's got to bother you!" I was amazed. It was neither the first nor the last time that something other people cared about didn't mean a thing to me.

I made it clear to Hillary that the decision was hers alone and that I didn't think the election would turn on her name. Not long after we started seeing each other, she had told me that keeping her maiden name was a decision she had made as a young girl, long before it became a symbol of women's equality. She was proud of her family heritage and wanted to hang on to it. Since I wanted to hang on to her, that was fine by me. Actually, it was one of the many things I liked about her.

In the end, Hillary decided, with her typical practicality, that keeping her maiden name wasn't worth offending the people who cared about it. When she told me, my only advice was to tell the public the truth about why she was doing it. My TV ad carried a genuine apology for real mistakes. This wasn't the same thing, and I thought we'd both look phony if we presented her new name as a change of heart. In her statement, she was very matter-of-fact about it, essentially telling the voters she'd done it for them.

We opened the primary campaign leading in the polls but facing formidable opposition. At the outset, the strongest candidate was Jim Guy Tucker, who had lost the Senate race four years earlier to David Pryor. Since then he had made a good deal of money in cable television. He appealed to the same progressive base I did, and the scars of his defeat had had two more years than mine to heal. I had a better organization in the rural counties than he did, but more rural voters were still mad at me. They had a third alternative in Joe Purcell, a decent, low-key man who had been attorney general and lieutenant governor and done a good job with both positions. Unlike Jim Guy and me, he had never made anybody mad. Joe had wanted to be governor for a long time, and though he was no longer in the best of health, he thought he could win by portraying himself as everybody's friend and less ambitious than his younger competitors. Two other candidates also filed: state senator Kim Hendren, a conservative from northwest Arkansas, and my old nemesis, Monroe Schwarzlose. Running for governor was keeping him alive.

My campaign would have collapsed in the first month if I hadn't learned the lessons of 1980 about the impact of negative television ads. Right off the bat, Jim Guy Tucker put up an ad criticizing me for commuting the sentences of first-degree murderers in my first term. He highlighted the case of a man who got out and killed a friend just a few weeks after his release. Since the voters hadn't been aware of that issue, my apology ad didn't immunize me from it, and I dropped behind Tucker in the polls.

The Board of Pardons and Paroles had recommended the commutations in question for two reasons. First, the board and the people running the prison system felt it would be much harder to maintain order and minimize violence if the "lifers" knew they could never get out no matter how well they behaved. Second, a lot of the older inmates had extensive health problems that cost the state a lot of money. If they were released, their health costs would be covered by the Medicaid program, which was funded mostly by the federal government.

The case featured in the ad was truly bizarre. The man whom I made eligible for parole was seventy-two years old and had served more than sixteen years for murder. In all that time, he had been a model prisoner with only one disciplinary mark against him. He was suffering from arteriosclerosis, and the prison doctors said he had about a year to live and probably would be completely incapacitated within six months, costing the prison budget a small fortune. He also had a sister in southeast Arkansas who was willing to take him in. About six weeks after he was paroled, he was drinking beer with a friend in the other man's pickup truck, with a gun rack in the back. They got into a fight and he grabbed the gun, shot the man dead, and took his Social Security check. Between the time of his arrest and his trial for that offense, the judge released the helpless-looking old man into his sister's custody. A few days after that, he got on the back of a motorcycle driven by a thirty-year-old man and rode north, all the way up to Pottsville, a little town near Russellville, where they tried to rob the local bank by driving the motorcycle right through the front door. The old boy was sick all right, but not in the way the prison doctors thought.

Not long afterward, I was in Pine Bluff in the county clerk's office. I shook hands with a woman who told me the man who'd been killed in his pickup was her uncle. She was kind enough to say, "I don't hold you responsible. There's no way in the wide world you could have known he'd do that." Most voters weren't as forgiving. I promised not to commute the sentences of any more first-degree murderers and said I'd require greater participation by victims in the decisions of the Board of Pardons and Paroles.

And I hit back at Tucker, following my own admonition to take the first hit, then counterpunch as hard as I could. With the help of David Watkins, a local advertising executive who was also from Hope, I ran an ad criticizing Jim Guy's voting record in Congress. It was poor because he had started running for the Senate not long after he began his term in the House of Representatives, so he wasn't there to vote much. One of the attendance ads featured two people sitting around a kitchen table, talking about how they wouldn't get paid if they showed up for work only half the time. We traded blows like that for the rest of the campaign. Meanwhile, Joe Purcell traveled around the state in a van, shaking hands and staying out of the TV-ad war.

Besides the air war, we waged a vigorous ground campaign. Betsey Wright ran it to perfection. She drove people hard, and lost her temper from time to time, but everybody knew she was brilliant, committed, and the hardest-working person in our campaign. We were so much on the same wavelength that she often knew what I was thinking, and vice versa, before we ever said a word. It saved a lot of time.

I started the campaign by traveling around the state with Hillary and Chelsea in a car driven by my friend and campaign chairman, Jimmy "Red" Jones, who had been state auditor for more than twenty years and who still had a good following among small-town leaders. Our strategy was to win Pulaski and the other big counties, carry the south Arkansas counties where I had a leg up, hold a large majority of the black vote, and turn the eleven counties in northeast Arkansas, which had all switched their support from me to Frank White in 1980. I went after those eleven counties with the same zeal I'd brought to winning the rural counties of the Third District in 1974. I made sure I campaigned in every little town in the region, often spending the night with new supporters. This strategy also got votes in the larger cities, where people were impressed when the pictures of me shaking hands in places candidates never visited appeared in their newspapers.

Betsey and I also signed up three young black leaders who proved invaluble. Rodney Slater left Attorney General Steve Clark's staff to help. Even back then, he was a powerful speaker, drawing on his deep knowledge of the scriptures to fashion powerful arguments for our cause. I had known Carol Willis when he was a student at the law school in Fayetteville. He was a great old-fashioned politician who knew all the players in the rural areas like the back of his hand. Bob Nash, who was working on economic development for the Rockefeller Foundation, helped on nights and weekends.

Rodney Slater, Carol Willis, and Bob Nash stayed with me for the next nineteen years. They worked for me the whole time I was governor. When I was President, Rodney served as federal highway administrator and secretary of transportation. Carol kept our fences mended with black America at the Democratic National Committee. Bob started as under secretary of agriculture, then came to the White House as director of personnel and appointments. I don't know what I would have done without them.

Perhaps the defining moment of the primary campaign came at a meeting of about eighty black leaders from the Delta who came to hear from Jim Guy Tucker and me so that they could decide which one of us to support. Tucker had already won the endorsement of the Arkansas Education Association by promising teachers a big pay raise without a tax increase. I had countered with the endorsement of several teachers and administrators who knew the state's bad economy wouldn't permit Tucker's promise to be kept and who remembered what I had done for education in my first term. I could still win with a split among educators, but not with a split among blacks in the Delta. I had to have nearly all of them.

The meeting was held in Jack Crumbly's barbeque place in Forrest City, about ninety miles east of Little

Rock. Jim Guy had come and gone by the time I got there, leaving a good impression. It was late and I was tired, but I made the best case I could, emphasizing the black appointments I'd made and my efforts to help long-ignored rural black communities get money for water and sewer systems.

After I finished, a young black lawyer from Lakeview, Jimmy Wilson, got up to speak. He was Tucker's main supporter in the Delta. Jimmy said I was a good man and had been a good governor, but that no Arkansas governor who had lost for reelection had ever been elected again. He said Frank White was terrible for blacks and had to be defeated. He reminded them that Jim Guy had a good civil rights record in Congress and had hired several young black people to work for him. He said Jim Guy would be as good for blacks as I would, and he could win. "I like Governor Clinton," he said, "but he's a loser. And we can't afford to lose." It was a persuasive argument, all the more so because he had the guts to do it with me sitting there. I could feel the crowd slipping away.

After a few seconds of silence, a man stood up in the back and said he'd like to be heard. John Lee Wilson was the mayor of Haynes, a small town of about 150 people. He was a heavy man of medium height, dressed in jeans and a white T-shirt, which bulged with the bulk of his huge arms, neck, and gut. I didn't know him very well and had no idea what he would say, but I'll never forget his words.

"Lawyer Wilson made a good speech," he began, "and he may be right. The governor may be a loser. All I know is, when Bill Clinton became governor, the crap was running open in the streets of my town, and my babies was sick because we didn't have no sewer system. Nobody paid any attention to us. When he left office, we had a sewer system and my babies wasn't sick anymore. He did that for a lot of us. Let me ask you something. If we don't stick with folks who stick with us, who will ever respect us again? He may be a loser, but if he loses, I'm going down with him. And so should you." As the old saying goes, it was all over but the shouting, one of those rare moments when one man's words actually changed minds, and hearts.

Unfortunately, John Lee Wilson died before I was elected President. Near the end of my second term, I made a nostalgic trip back to east Arkansas to speak at Earle High School. The school principal was Jack Crumbly, the host of that fateful meeting almost two decades earlier. In my remarks, I told the story of John Lee Wilson's speech for the first time in public. It was televised across east Arkansas. One person who watched it, sitting in her little house in Haynes, was John Lee Wilson's widow. She wrote me a very moving letter saying how proud John would have been to have the President praising him. Of course I praised him. If it hadn't been for John Lee, I might be writing wills and divorce settlements instead of this book.

As we got close to election day, my support went up and down among voters who couldn't decide whether to give me another chance. I was worried about it until I met a man in a café one afternoon in Newark, in northeast Arkansas. When I asked for his vote, he said, "I voted against you last time, but I'm going to vote for you this time." Although I knew the answer, I still asked him why he voted against me. "Because you raised my car tags." When I asked him why he was voting for me, he said, "Because you raised my car tags." I told him I needed every vote I could get, and I didn't want to make him mad, but it didn't make any sense for him to vote for me for the same reason he'd voted against me before. He smiled and said, "Oh, it makes all the sense in the world. You may be a lot of things, Bill, but you ain't dumb. You're the very least likely one to ever raise those car tags again, so I'm for you." I added his impeccable logic to my stump speech for the rest of the campaign.

On May 25, I won the primary election with 42 percent of the vote. Under the counterassault of my ads and the strength of our organization, Jim Guy Tucker fell to 23 percent. Joe Purcell had parlayed his issue- and controversy-free campaign into 29 percent of the vote and a spot in the runoff, two weeks away. It was a dangerous situation. Tucker and I had driven each other's negative ratings up with the attack ads, and Purcell appealed to the Democrats who hadn't gotten over the car-tag increase. There was a good chance he could win just by being the un-Clinton. I tried for ten days to smoke him out, but he was shrewd enough to stay in his van and shake a few hands. On the Thursday night before the election, I did a poll that said the race was dead even. That meant I'd probably lose, since the undecided vote usually broke against the incumbent, which I effectively was. I had just put up an ad highlighting our differences on whether the Public Service Commission, which sets electric rates, should be elected rather than appointed, a change I favored and Joe opposed. I hoped it would make a difference, but I wasn't sure.

The very next day, I was handed the election in the guise of a crippling body blow. Frank White badly wanted Purcell to win the runoff. The governor's negative ratings were even higher than mine, and I had the issues and an organized campaign on my side. By contrast,

White felt certain that Joe Purcell's poor health would become a decisive factor in the general election campaign, guaranteeing White a second term. On Friday night, when it was too late for me to counter on television, Frank White began running a TV ad attacking me for raising the car-tag fee and telling people not to forget it. He got the time to run it heavily all weekend by persuading his business supporters to pull their commercials so that he could put the attack ad up. I saw the ad and knew it would turn a close race. I couldn't get a response to it on television until Monday, and by then it would be too late. This was an unfair advantage that was later disallowed by a federal regulation requiring stations to place ads that respond to last-minute attacks over the weekend, but that was no help to me.

Betsey and I called David Watkins and asked him to open his studio so that I could cut a radio ad. We worked on the script and met David about an hour before midnight. By that time Betsey had lined up some young volunteers to drive the ad to radio stations all over the state in time for them to be run early Saturday morning. In my radio response, I asked people if they'd seen White's ad attacking me and asked them to think about why he was interfering with a Democratic primary. There was only one answer: he wanted to run against Joe Purcell, not me, because I would beat him and Joe couldn't. I knew most Democratic primary voters intensely opposed the governor and would hate the thought of being manipulated by him. David Watkins worked all night long making enough copies of our ad to saturate the state. The kids started driving them to the radio stations at about four in the morning, along with checks from the campaign to purchase a heavy buy. The radio spot was so effective that by Saturday night, White's own television ad was working for me. On Monday we put our response up on television too, but we had already won the battle by then. The next day, June 8, I won the runoff 54 to 46 percent. It was a near-run thing. I had won most of the big counties and those with a substantial number of black voters, but was still struggling in the rural Democratic counties where the car-tag issue wouldn't die. It would take another two years to repair the damage completely.

The fall campaign against Frank White was rough but fun. This time the economy was hurting him, not me, and he had a record I could run against. I hit him on his utility ties and lost jobs, and ran positive ads on my issues. He had a great attack ad featuring a man trying to scrape the spots off a leopard; it said that, just like a leopard, I couldn't change my spots. Dick Morris did a devastating ad taking White to task for letting utilities have big rate increases while cutting back from four to three the number of monthly prescriptions the elderly could get under Medicaid. The tagline was: "Frank White—Soft on utilities. Tough on the elderly." Our funniest radio ad came in response to a barrage of false charges. Our announcer asked if it wouldn't be nice to have a guard dog that would bark every time a politician said something that wasn't true. Then a dog barked, "Woof, woof!" The announcer repeated each charge, and the dog barked again just before he answered it. There were, as I recall, four "woof, woof's" in all. By the time it had run a few days, workers were good-naturedly barking "Woof, woof!" at me when I shook hands at plant gates during shift changes. White further solidified the black vote by saying blacks would vote for a duck if it ran as a Democrat. Shortly after that,

Bishop L. T. Walker of the Church of God in Christ told his people they had to get "Old Hoghead" out of office.

There comes a time in every campaign when you know in your bones whether you're going to win or lose. In 1982, it happened to me in Melbourne, the county seat of Izard County in north Arkansas. I had lost the county in 1980 over the car tags despite the fact that the local legislator, John Miller, had voted to raise them. John was one of the most senior members of the legislature and probably knew more about all aspects of state government than anyone else in Arkansas. He was working hard for me and arranged for me to tour the local McDonnell Douglas plant, which made component parts for airplanes.

Even though the workers belonged to the United Auto Workers union, I was nervous, because most of them had voted against me just two years before. I was met at the front door by Una Sitton, a good Democrat who worked in the front office. Una shook my hand and said, "Bill, I think you're going to enjoy this." When I opened the door to the plant, I was almost knocked over by the loud sound of Willie Nelson singing one of my favorite songs, Steve Goodman's "City of New Orleans." I walked in to the opening line of the chorus: "Good morning, America, how are you? Don't you know me, I'm your native son." The workers cheered. All of them but one were wearing my campaign buttons. I made my way down each aisle, shaking hands to the music and fighting back the tears. I knew the election was over. My people were bringing their native son home.

Near the end of almost all my campaigns, I turned up at the morning shift at the Campbell's Soup factory in Fayetteville, where the workers prepared turkeys and chickens for soups. At 5 a.m., it was the earliest shift change in Arkansas. In 1982, it was cold and rainy when I began shaking hands in the dark. One man joked that he had intended to vote for me, but was having second thoughts about voting for someone with no better sense than to campaign in the dark in a cold rain.

I learned a lot on those dark mornings. I'll never forget seeing one man drop his wife off. When the door to their pickup opened, there were three young children sitting between them. The man told me they had to get the kids up at a quarter to four every morning. After he took his wife to work, he dropped the kids off with a babysitter who took them to school, because he had to be at work by seven.

It's easy for a politician in this mass-media culture to reduce electioneering to fund-raisers, rallies, advertisements, and a debate or two. All that may be enough for the voters to make an intelligent decision, but the candidates miss out on a lot, including the struggles of people who have their hands full just getting through the day and doing the best they can for their kids. I had made up my mind that if those folks gave me another chance, I'd never forget them.

On November 2, they gave me that chance. I won 55 percent of the vote, carrying fifty-six of the seventy-five counties, losing eighteen counties in Republican western Arkansas and one in south Arkansas. Most of the white rural counties came back, though the margins in several were close. The margin wasn't close in the largest county, Pulaski. I swept the eleven counties in northeast Arkansas where we had worked especially hard. And the black vote was staggering.

One black leader I particularly liked, Emily Bowens, was mayor of the small community of Mitchellville in southeast Arkansas. I had helped her in my first term, and she repaid the debt in full: I won Mitchellville 196–8 in the primary runoff with Purcell. When I called her to thank her for getting me 96 percent of the vote, she apologized for the eight votes we lost. "Governor, I'll find those eight people and straighten them out by November," she promised. On November 2, I carried Mitchellville 256–0. Emily had turned the eight and registered fifty-two more.

After the election, I heard from people all over the country. Ted Kennedy and Walter Mondale called just as they had in 1980. And I received some wonderful letters. One came from an unlikely source: General James Drummond, who had commanded the troops during the Cuban crisis at Fort Chaffee two years earlier. He said he was glad I won, because "while it may have seemed that we marched to different drums at Fort Chaffee . . . I appreciated and admired your leadership, your principles, and your willingness to stand up and be counted for the people of Arkansas." I admired Drummond too, and his letter meant more to me than he could have known.

The Democrats did well all over the country and especially in the South, winning a majority of the thirty-six governorships, picking up seats in the House of Representatives, up for grabs largely because of America's troubled economy. Among the new governors were two old ones besides me: George Wallace of Alabama, who had apologized to black voters for his racist past from his wheelchair; and Michael Dukakis of Massachusetts, who, like me, had been defeated after his first term and had just defeated the man who beat him.

My supporters were ecstatic. After a long, history-making campaign, they had every right to their raucous celebration. By contrast, I was feeling strangely subdued. I was happy but didn't feel like gloating over my victory. I didn't blame Frank White for beating me last time or for wanting to be governor again. Losing had been my fault. What I mostly felt on election night, and for days afterward, was a deep, quiet gratitude that the people of the state I loved so much were willing to give me another chance. I was determined to vindicate their judgment.

TWENTY-THREE

On January 11, 1983, I took the oath of office for the second time, before the largest crowd ever to attend an inauguration in our state. The celebrants had brought me back from the political grave, and their support would keep me in the governor's office for ten more years, the longest period I ever stayed in one job.

The challenge I faced was to keep my promise to be more responsive to the people while maintaining my commitment to move our state forward. The task was complicated, and made more important, by the dismal state of the economy. The state's unemployment rate was 10.6 percent. In December, as governor-elect, I had gone to Trumann, in northeast Arkansas, to shake hands with six hundred workers at the Singer Plant, which had made wooden cabinets for sewing machines for decades, as they walked out of the plant for the last time. The plant closing, one of many we had endured over the last two years, dealt a body blow to the economy of Poinsett County and had a discouraging impact on the whole state. I can still see the look of despair on so many of the Singer workers' faces. They knew that they had worked hard, and that their livelihoods were being swept away by forces beyond their control.

Another consequence of the poor economy was a falloff in state revenues, leaving too little money for education and other essential services. It was clear to me that, if we were going to get out of this fix, I had to focus the state's attention, and mine, on education and employment. For the next decade, that's what I did. Even when my administration took important initiatives in health care, the environment, prison reform, and other areas, or in appointing more minorities and women to important positions, I tried never to let the spotlight stray too far from schools and jobs. They were the keys to opportunity and empowerment for our people, and to maintaining the political support I needed to keep pursuing positive changes. I had learned in my first term that if you give equal time to all the things you do, you run the risk of having everything become a blur in the public's mind, leaving no clear impression that anything important was being done. My longtime friend George Frazier from Hope once told an interviewer, "If he has a flaw, and we all do, I think Bill's flaw is that he sees so much that needs to be done." I never cured that flaw, and I kept trying to do a lot, but for the next decade I focused most of my energy, and my public statements, on schools and jobs.

Betsey Wright had done such a good job with the campaign that I was convinced she could manage the governor's office. In the beginning I also asked Maurice Smith to serve as executive secretary, to add some maturity to the mix and to ensure cordial relations with the senior legislators, lobbyists, and power brokers. I had a strong education team with Paul Root, my former world history teacher, and Don Ernst. My legal counsel, Sam Bratton, who had been with me in the attorney general's office, was also an expert in education law.

Carol Rasco became my aide for health and human services. Her qualifications were rooted in experience: Her older child, Hamp, was born with cerebral palsy. She fought for his educational and other rights, and in the process acquired a detailed knowledge of state and federal programs for the disabled.

I persuaded Dorothy Moore, from Arkansas City in deep southeast Arkansas, to greet people and answer phones in the reception area. Miss Dorothy was already in her seventies when she started, and she stayed until I left the governor's office. Finally, I got a new secretary. Barbara Kerns had had enough of politics and stayed behind at the Wright firm. In early 1983, I hired Lynda Dixon, who took care of me for a decade and continued to work in my Arkansas office when I became President.

My most notable appointment was Mahlon Martin as director of finance and administration, arguably the most important job in state government after the governorship. Before I appointed him, Mahlon was city manager of Little Rock, and a very good one. He was black, and an Arkansan through and through—he always wanted to take the first day of deer season off from work. In tough times, he could be creative in finding solutions to budget problems, but he was always fiscally responsible. In one of our two-year budget cycles in the 1980s, he had to cut spending six times to balance the books.

Shortly after I became President, Mahlon began a long, losing battle against cancer. In June 1995, I went back to Little Rock to dedicate the Mahlon Martin Apartments for low-income working people. Mahlon died two months after the dedication. I never worked with a more gifted public servant.

Betsey saw to it that my time was scheduled differently than it had been in my first term. I had been perceived as being inaccessible then, in part because I accepted so many daytime speaking engagements out in the state.

Now I spent more time in the office and more personal time with legislators when they were in session, including after-hours card games I really enjoyed. When I did attend out-of-town events, it was usually at the request of one of my supporters. Doing those events rewarded people who had helped me, reinforced their positions in their communities, and helped to keep our organization together.

No matter how far away the event was or how long it lasted, I always came home at night so that I could be there when Chelsea woke up. That way I could have breakfast with her and Hillary and, when Chelsea got old enough, take her to school. I did that every day until I started running for President. I also put a little desk in the governor's office where Chelsea could sit and read or draw. I loved it when we were both at our desks working away. If Hillary's law practice took her away at night or overnight, I tried to be at home. When Chelsea was in kindergarten, she and her classmates were asked what their parents did for a living. She reported that her mother was a lawyer and her father "talks on the telephone, drinks coffee, and makes 'peeches." At bedtime, Hillary, Chelsea, and I would say a little prayer or two by Chelsea's bed, then Hillary or I would read Chelsea a book. When I was so tired I fell asleep reading, as I often did, she would kiss me awake. I liked that so much I often pretended to be asleep when I wasn't.

A week into my new term, I gave my State of the State address to the legislators, recommending ways to deal with the severe budget crisis and asking them to do four things I thought would help the economy: expand the Arkansas Housing Development Agency's authority to issue revenue bonds to increase housing and create jobs; establish enterprise zones in high-unemployment areas in order to provide greater incentives to invest in them; give a jobs tax credit to employers who created new jobs; and create an Arkansas Science and Technology Authority, patterned in part on the Port Authority of New York and New Jersey, to develop the scientific and technological potential of the state. These measures, all of which were enacted into law, were forerunners of similar initiatives that passed when I became President in another time of economic trouble.

I argued hard for my utility reforms, including the popular election of Public Service Commission members, but I knew I couldn't pass most of them, because Arkansas Power and Light Company and the other utilities had so much influence in the legislature. Instead, I had to be content to appoint commissioners I thought would protect the people and the state's economy without bankrupting the utilities.

I proposed and passed some modest educational improvements, including a requirement that all districts offer kindergarten, and a law allowing students to take up to half their courses in a nearby school district if the home district didn't offer them. That was important because so many of the smaller districts didn't offer chemistry, physics, advanced math, or foreign languages. I also asked the legislature to raise cigarette, beer, and liquor taxes and to allocate more than half of our projected new revenues to the schools. That was all we could do, given our financial condition and the fact that we were awaiting a state supreme court decision on a case claiming that, because our school financing system was so unequal in its distribution of funds, it was unconstitutional. If the court ruled for the plaintiffs, as I hoped it would, I would have to call a special session of the legislature to deal with it. As it was, the legislature was required to meet only sixty days every two years. Though the legislators usually stayed a few days longer, something often came up after they had gone home that required me to call them back. The supreme court decision would do that. Such a session would be difficult, but it might give us the chance to do something really big for education, because the legislature, the public, and the press could focus on it in a way that was impossible in a regular session, when so many other things were going on.

In April, the National Commission on Excellence in Education, appointed by U.S. Secretary of Education Terrel Bell, issued a stunning report entitled **A Nation at Risk.** The report noted that on nineteen different international tests, American students were never first or second and were last seven times; 23 million American adults, 13 percent of all seventeen-year-olds, and up to 40 percent of minority students were functionally illiterate; high school students' average performance on standardized tests was lower than it had been twenty-six years earlier, when **Sputnik** was launched; scores on the principal college entrance exam, the Scholastic Aptitude Test, had been declining since 1962; one-quarter of all college math courses were remedial—that is, teaching what should have been learned in high school or earlier; business and military leaders reported having to spend increasing amounts of money on remedial education; and finally, these declines in education were occurring at a time when the demand for highly skilled workers was increasing sharply.

Just five years earlier, Dr. Kern Alexander had said children would be better off in the schools of almost any state other than Arkansas. If our whole nation was at risk, we had to be on life support. In 1983, 265 of our high schools offered no advanced biology, 217 no physics, 177 no foreign language, 164 no advanced math, 126 no chemistry. In the 1983 regular session, I asked the legislature to authorize a fifteen-member Education Standards Committee to make specific recommendations on new curriculum standards. I put together an able and fully representative committee and asked Hillary to chair it. She had done an excellent job chairing the Rural Health Committee and the board of the national Legal Services Corporation in my first term. She was very good at running committees, she cared about children, and by naming her I was sending a strong signal about how important education was to me. My reasoning was sound, but it was still a risky move, because every significant change we proposed was sure to rattle some interest group.

In May, the state supreme court declared our school financing system unconstitutional. We had to write a new aid formula, then fund it. There were only two alternatives: take money away from the wealthiest and smallest districts and give it to the poorest and fastest-growing ones, or raise enough new revenues so that we could equalize funding without hurting the presently overfunded districts. Since no district wanted its schools to lose money, the court decision gave us the best opportunity we'd ever have to raise taxes for education. Hillary's committee held hearings in every county in the state in July, getting recommendations from educators and the public. She gave me their report in September, and I announced that I would call the legislature into session on October 4 to deal with education.

On September 19, I delivered a televised address to explain what was in the education program, to advocate a one-cent increase in the sales tax and a hike in the severance tax on natural gas to pay for it, and to ask the people to endorse it. Despite the support we had built for the program, there was still a strong anti-tax feeling in the state, aggravated by the poor economy. In the previous election, one man in Nashville, Arkansas, asked me to do just one thing if I won: spend his tax dollars as if I lived like him, on $150 a week. Another man helping to build Little Rock's new Excelsior Hotel asked me to remember that while the state needed more taxes, he was in his last day on the job and didn't have another one waiting. I had to win those people to the cause.

In my speech, I argued that we couldn't create more jobs without improving education, citing examples from my own efforts to recruit high-technology companies. Then I said we couldn't make real advances as long as "we are last in spending per child, teacher salaries, and total state and local taxes per person." What we needed to do was to both raise the sales tax and approve standards recommended by Hillary's committee, "standards which, when implemented, will be among the nation's best."

The standards included required kindergarten; a maximum class size of twenty through third grade; counselors in all elementary schools; uniform testing of all students in third, sixth, and eighth grades, with mandatory retention of those who failed the eighth-grade test; a requirement that any school in which more than 15 percent of students failed to develop a plan to improve performance and, if its students didn't improve within two years, be subject to management changes; more math, science, and foreign language courses; a required high school curriculum of four years of English and three years of math, science, and history or social studies; more time on academic work during the school day and an increase in the school year from 175 to 180 days; special opportunities for gifted children; and a requirement that students stay in school until the age of sixteen. Until then, students could leave after the eighth grade, and a lot of them did. Our dropout rate was more than 30 percent.

The most controversial proposal I made was to require all teachers and administrators to take and pass the National Teacher Examination in 1984, "by the standards now applied to new college graduates who take the test." I recommended that teachers who failed be given free tuition to take regular courses and be able to take the test as many times as possible until 1987, when the school standards would be fully effective.

I also proposed improvements in vocational and higher education, and a tripling of the adult education program to help dropouts who wanted to get a high school diploma.

At the end of the speech, I asked the people to join Hillary and me in wearing blue ribbons to demonstrate support for the program and our conviction that Arkansas could be a "blue ribbon" state, in the front ranks of educational excellence. We ran television and radio ads asking for support, distributed thousands of postcards for people to send their legislators, and passed out tens of thousands of those blue ribbons. Many people wore them every day until the legislative session was over. The public was beginning to believe we could do something special.

It was an ambitious program: Only a handful of states then required as strong a core curriculum as the one I proposed. None required students to pass an eighth-grade test before going to high school. A few required them to pass tests in the eleventh or twelfth grade to get a diploma, but to me, that was like closing the barn door after the cow is out. I wanted the students to have time to catch up. No state required elementary school counselors, though more and more young children were coming to school from troubled homes with emotional problems that inhibited their learning. And no state allowed its education department to force management changes in nonperforming schools. Our proposals went well beyond those of the **Nation at Risk** report.

The biggest firestorm by far was generated by the teacher-testing program. The Arkansas Education Association (AEA) went ballistic, accusing me of degrading teachers and using them as scapegoats. For the first time in my life, I was charged with racism, on the assumption that a higher percentage of black teachers would fail the test. Cynics accused Hillary and me of grandstanding to increase our popularity among people who would otherwise oppose any tax increase. While it was true that the teacher test was a strong symbol of accountability to many people, the case for the test came out of the hearings the Standards Committee had held across the state. Many people complained about particular teachers who didn't know the subjects they were teaching or who lacked basic literacy skills. One woman handed me a note the teacher had sent home with her child. Of the twenty-two words in it, three were misspelled. I had no doubt that most teachers were able and dedicated, and I knew that most of those with problems had probably had inferior educations themselves; they would have the chance to improve their skills and take the test again. But if we were going to raise taxes to increase teacher pay, and if the standards were going to work for the kids, the teachers had to be able to teach them.

The legislature met for thirty-eight days to consider the fifty-two bills in my agenda and related items offered by the lawmakers themselves. Hillary made a brilliant presentation before the House and Senate, prompting Representative Lloyd George of Yell County to say, "It looks like we might have elected the wrong Clinton!" We had opposition from three quarters: the anti-tax crowd; rural school districts that feared they would be consolidated because they couldn't meet the standards; and the AEA, which threatened to defeat every legislator who voted for teacher testing.

We countered the argument that the test was degrading to teachers with a statement from several teachers at Little Rock Central High, widely recognized as the best in the state. They said they were glad to take the test, in order to reinforce public confidence. To beat back the argument that the test was racist, I persuaded a group of prominent black ministers to support my position. They argued that black children were most in need of good teachers, and those who failed the test would be given other chances to pass. I also got invaluable support from Dr. Lloyd Hackley, the African-American chancellor of the University of Arkansas at Pine Bluff, a predominantly black institution. Hackley had done an amazing job at UAPB and was a member of Hillary's Education Standards Committee. In 1980, when college graduates first had to take a test to be certified to teach, 42 percent of the UAPB students failed. By 1986, the pass rate had increased dramatically. Dr. Hackley's nursing graduates improved the most in the same period. He argued that black students had been held back more by low standards and low expectations than by discrimination. The results he got proved him right. He believed in his students and got a lot out of them. All our children need educators like him.

Near the end of the legislative session, it looked as if the

AEA might be able to beat the testing bill. I went back and forth to the Senate and House repeatedly to twist arms and make deals for votes. Finally, I had to threaten not to allow my own sales-tax bill to pass if the testing wasn't passed along with it.

It was a risky gambit: I could have lost both the tax and the testing law. Organized labor opposed the sales-tax raise, saying it was unfair to working families because I had failed to secure an income tax rebate as an offset for the sales tax on food. Labor's opposition brought some liberal votes to the anti-tax side, but they couldn't get a majority. There was a lot of support for the program from the outset, and by the time the tax vote came up, we had passed a new formula and the standards were approved. Without a sales-tax increase, many districts would lose state aid under the new formula, and most of them would have to enact large local property-tax increases to meet the standards. By the last day of the session, we had it all: the standards, the teacher-testing law, and an increase in the sales tax.

I was elated, and totally exhausted, as I piled into the car to drive sixty miles north to appear at the annual governor's night in Fairfield Bay, a retirement village full of middle-class folks who'd come to Arkansas from up north because it was warmer but still had four seasons and low taxes. Most of them, including the retired educators, supported the education program. One amateur carpenter made me a little red schoolhouse with a plaque on it commemorating my efforts.

As the smoke cleared from the session, Arkansas began to get a lot of positive national coverage for our education reforms, including praise from Secretary of Education Bell. However, the AEA didn't give up; it filed a lawsuit against the testing law. Peggy Nabors, the AEA president, and I had a heated debate on the **Phil Donahue Show,** one of several arguments we had in the national media. The company that owned the National Teacher Examination refused to let us use it for existing teachers, saying it was a good measure of whether someone should be allowed to teach in the first place but not of whether a teacher who couldn't pass it should be able to keep teaching. So we had to develop a whole new test. When the test was first given to teachers and administrators in 1984, 10 percent failed. About the same percentage failed in subsequent attempts. In the end, 1,215 teachers, about 3.5 percent of our total, had to leave the classroom because they couldn't pass the test. Another 1,600 lost their certification because they never took it. In the 1984 election, the AEA refused to endorse me and many of education's best friends in the legislature because of the testing law. Their efforts managed to defeat only one legislator, my old friend Senator Vada Sheid from Mountain Home, who had sewn a button on my shirt when I first met her in 1974. The teachers went door-to-door for her opponent, Steve Luelf, a Republican lawyer who had moved to Arkansas from California. They didn't talk about the teacher test. Unfortunately, neither did Vada. She made a mistake common to candidates who take a position supported by a disorganized majority but opposed by an organized and animated minority. The only way to survive the onslaught is to make the issue matter as much in the voting booth to those who agree with you as it does to those who disagree. Vada just wanted the whole thing to go away. I always felt bad about the price she paid for helping our children.

Over the next two years, teacher pay went up $4,400,

the fastest growth rate in the nation. Although we still ranked forty-sixth, we were finally above the national average in teacher pay as a percentage of state per capita income, and almost at the national average in per-pupil expenditures as a percentage of income. By 1987, the number of our school districts had dropped to 329, and 85 percent of the districts had increased their property-tax rates, which can be done only by a popular vote, to meet the standards.

Student test scores rose steadily across the board. In 1986, the Southern Regional Education Board gave a test to eleventh graders in five southern states. Arkansas was the only state to score above the national average. When the same group was tested five years earlier, in 1981, our students scored below the national average. We were on our way.

I continued to push for educational improvements for the rest of my time as governor, but the new standards, funding, and accountability measures laid the foundation for all the later progress. Eventually I reconciled with the AEA and its leaders, as we worked together year after year to improve our schools and our children's future. When I look back on my career in politics, the 1983 legislative session on education is one of the things I'm proudest of.

In the summer of 1983, the governors met in Portland, Maine. Hillary, Chelsea, and I had a great time, getting together with my old friend Bob Reich and his family, and going with the other governors to a cookout at Vice President Bush's house in the beautiful oceanside town of Kennebunkport. Three-year-old Chelsea marched up to the vice president and said she needed to go to the bathroom. He took her by the hand and led her there. Chelsea appreciated it, and Hillary and I were impressed by George Bush's kindness. It wouldn't be the last time.

Nevertheless, I was upset with the Reagan administration, and had come to Maine determined to do something about it. It had just dramatically tightened the eligibility rules for federal disability benefits. Just as with the black-lung program ten years earlier, there had been abuses of the disability program, but the Reagan cure was worse than the problem. The regulations were so strict they were ridiculous. In Arkansas, a truck driver with a ninth-grade education had lost his arm in an accident. He was denied disability benefits on the theory that he could get a desk job doing clerical work.

Several Democrats in the House, including Arkansas congressman Beryl Anthony, were trying to overturn the rules. Beryl asked me to get the governors to call for their reversal. The governors were interested in the issue, because a lot of our disabled constituents were being denied benefits, and because we were being held partly responsible. Although the program was funded by the federal government, it was administered by the states.

Since the matter wasn't on our agenda, I had to get the relevant committee to vote to overturn the rules by two-thirds, then get 75 percent of the governors present to support the committee action. It was important enough to the White House that the administration sent two assistant secretaries from the Department of Health and Human Services to work against my efforts. The Republican governors were in a bind. Most of them agreed that the rules needed to be changed and certainly didn't want to defend them in public, but they wanted to stick with their President. The Republican strategy was to kill our proposal in committee. My head count indicated we

would win in the committee by a single vote, but only if
all our votes showed up. One of those votes was Governor
George Wallace. Ever since he had been confined to a
wheelchair by a would-be assassin's bullet, it took him a
couple of hours every morning to get ready to face the
day. On this morning, George Wallace had to get up two
hours earlier than usual to go through his painful preparations. He came to the meeting and cast a loud "aye" vote
for our resolution, after telling the committee how many
Alabama working people, black and white, had been hurt
by the new disability rules. The resolution passed out of
the committee, and the National Governors Association
adopted it. Subsequently, Congress overturned the regulations, and a lot of deserving people got the help they
needed to survive. It might not have happened if George
Wallace hadn't returned to the populist roots of his youth
on an early Maine morning when he stood tall in his
wheelchair.

At the end of the year, our family accepted an invitation
from Phil and Linda Lader to attend their New Year's
weekend gathering in Hilton Head, South Carolina,
called Renaissance Weekend. The event was then only a
couple of years old. Fewer than one hundred families
gathered to spend three days talking about everything
under the sun, from politics and economics to religion
and our personal lives. The attendees were of different
ages, religions, races, and backgrounds, all bound together
by a simple preference for spending the weekend in serious talk and family fun rather than all-night parties and
football games. It was an extraordinary bonding experience. We revealed things about ourselves and learned
things about other people that would never have come out

under normal circumstances. And all three of us made a lot of new friends, many of whom helped in 1992 and served in my administration. We went to Renaissance Weekend virtually every year after that until the millennium weekend, 1999–2000, when the national celebration at the Lincoln Memorial required our presence in Washington. After I became President, the event had swelled to more than 1,500 people and had lost some of its earlier intimacy, but I still enjoyed going.

In early 1984, it was time to run for reelection again. Even though President Reagan was far more popular in Arkansas, and across the country, than he had been in 1980, I felt confident. The whole state was excited about implementing the school standards, and the economy was getting a little better. My main primary opponent was Lonnie Turner, the Ozark lawyer I'd worked with on black-lung cases back in 1975, after his partner, Jack Yates, died. Lonnie thought the school standards were going to close rural schools, and he was mad about it. It made me sad because of our long friendship and because I thought he should have known better. In May, I won the primary easily, and after a few years we made up.

In July, Colonel Tommy Goodwin, the director of the state police, asked to see me. I sat with Betsey Wright in stunned silence as he told me that my brother had been videotaped selling cocaine to an undercover state police officer, one who ironically had been hired in an expansion of state anti-drug efforts I had asked the legislature to fund. Tommy asked me what I wanted him to do. I asked him what the state police would normally do in a case like this. He said Roger wasn't a big-time dealer but a cocaine addict who was selling the stuff to support his habit. Typically, with someone like him, they'd set him up a few more times on videotape to make sure they had him dead to rights, then squeeze him with the threat of a long prison term to make him give up his supplier. I told Tommy to treat Roger's case just like any other. Then I asked Betsey to find Hillary. She was at a restaurant downtown. I went by to pick her up and told her what had happened.

For the next six miserable weeks, no one outside the state police knew, except Betsey, Hillary, and, I believe, my completely trustworthy press secretary, Joan Roberts. And me. Every time I saw or talked to Mother I was heartsick. Every time I looked in the mirror I was disgusted. I had been so caught up in my life and work that I'd missed all the signs. Shortly after Roger went to college in 1974, he formed a rock band that was good enough to make a living from playing clubs in Hot Springs and Little Rock. I went to hear him several times and thought that with Roger's distinctive voice and the band's musical ability, they had real promise. He clearly loved doing it, and though he went back to Hendrix College a couple of times, he would soon drop out again to return to the band. When he was working, he stayed up all night and slept late. During the racing season, he played the horses heavily. He also bet on football games. I never knew how much he won or lost, but I never asked. When our family gathered for holiday meals, he invariably came late, seemed on edge, and got up a time or two during dinner to make phone calls. The warning signs were all there. I was just too preoccupied to see them.

When Roger was finally arrested, it was big news in Arkansas. I made a brief statement to the press, saying that I loved my brother but expected the law to take its course, and asking for prayers and privacy for my family. Then I told my brother and Mother the truth about how long I'd known. Mother was in shock, and I'm not sure the reality registered on her. Roger was angry, though he got over it later when he came to terms with his addiction. We all went to counseling. I learned that Roger's cocaine habit, about four grams a day, was so bad it might have killed him if he hadn't had the constitution of an ox, and that his addiction was rooted, in part, in the scars of his childhood and perhaps a genetic predisposition to addiction he shared with his father.

From the time he was arrested until almost the date of his court appearance, Roger couldn't admit that he was an addict. Finally one day, as we were sitting at the breakfast table, I told him that if he wasn't an addict, I wanted him to go to jail for a very long time, because he had been selling poison to other people for money. Somehow, that got through to him. After he admitted his problem, he began the long road back.

The case had been taken over by the U.S. attorney, Asa Hutchinson. Roger gave up his supplier, an immigrant even younger than he was, who got cocaine from family or friends in his home country. Roger pleaded guilty to two federal offenses before Judge Oren Harris, who had been chairman of the Commerce Committee in the House of Representatives before going to the bench. Judge Harris was in his early eighties but still sharp and very wise. He sentenced Roger to three years on one charge and two years on the other, and suspended the three-year sentence because of his cooperation. Roger served fourteen months, most of it in a federal facility for nonviolent offenders, which was hard on him but probably saved his life.

Hillary and I were in court with Mother when he was sentenced. I was impressed by the way the whole thing was handled by Judge Harris, and by the U.S. attorney. Asa Hutchinson was professional, fair, and sensitive to the agony my family was experiencing. I wasn't at all surprised when later he was elected to Congress from the Third District.

In the summer, I led the Arkansas delegation to the Democratic convention in San Francisco to see Walter Mondale and Geraldine Ferraro nominated and to give a five-minute tribute to Harry Truman. We were in trouble to start with, and it was all over when Mondale said he would propose a hefty tax increase to reduce the budget deficit. It was a remarkable act of candor, but he might as well have proposed a federal car-tag fee. Still, the city put on a great convention. San Francisco had lots of pleasant small hotels within walking distance of the convention center, and well-organized traffic, so we avoided the crushing traffic jams that characterize many conventions. The Arkansas host, Dr. Richard Sanchez, was heavily invested in the efforts to treat and prevent the relatively new disease of AIDS, which was sweeping the city. I asked Richard about the problem and what could be done about it. That was my first real exposure to a battle that would claim a lot of my attention in the White House and afterward.

I had to leave San Francisco early to return to Arkansas to recruit a high-tech industry for our state. In the end it didn't pan out, but I couldn't have done any good staying in California anyway. We were headed for defeat. The economy was rebounding and the President told us it was "morning again in America," while his surrogates sneered at those of us on the other side as "San Francisco Democrats," a not-so-veiled allusion to our ties to the city's large gay population. Even Vice President Bush fell into the macho mode, saying he was going to "kick a little ass."

In the November election, Reagan defeated Mondale 59 to 41 percent. The President won 62 percent of the vote in Arkansas. I received 63 percent in my race against Woody Freeman, an appealing young businessman from Jonesboro.

After our family enjoyed Chelsea's fifth Christmas and our second Renaissance Weekend, it was time for a new legislative session, this one devoted to modernizing our economy.

Even though the overall economy was improving, unemployment was still high in states like Arkansas that were dependent on agriculture and traditional industries. Most of America's job growth of the eighties came in the high-technology and service sectors, and was concentrated in and around urban areas, primarily in states on or near the East and West coasts. The industrial and agricultural heartland was still in bad shape. The pattern was so pronounced that people began to refer to America as having a "bicoastal" economy.

It was obvious that in order to accelerate job and income growth, we had to restructure our economy. The development package I presented to the legislature had some financial components that were new to Arkansas but already in place in other states. I proposed to broaden the state's housing agency into a Development and Finance Authority that would be able to issue bonds to finance industrial, agricultural, and small-business projects. I recommended that the state's public pension funds set targets of investing at least 5 percent of their assets in Arkansas. We were a capital-poor state; we didn't need to export public funds when there were good investment options at home. I recommended allowing state-chartered banks to hold assets they foreclosed on for longer periods of time, primarily to avoid dumping farmland in an already depressed market, which would make it even harder for farmers to hold on. I also asked the legislature to allow state-chartered banks not only to lend money, but also to make modest equity investments in farms and businesses that couldn't borrow any more money, with the provision that the farmer or small-business person had a right to buy the bank out within three years. Other farm-state governors were especially interested in this bill, and one of them, Bill Janklow of South Dakota, passed a version of it through his legislature.

The economic proposals were innovative but too complex to be well understood or widely supported. However, after I made appearances at several committee hearings to answer questions and did a lot of one-on-one lobbying, the legislature passed them all.

More than a decade after the U.S. Supreme Court decision in **Roe** v. **Wade** authorized it, our legislature banned abortions performed in the third trimester of pregnancy. The bill was sponsored by Senator Lu Hardin of Russellville, a Christian whom I liked very much, and Senator Bill Henley, a Catholic who was Susan McDougal's brother. The bill passed easily, and I signed it into law. A decade later, when congressional Republicans were pushing a bill to ban so-called partial-birth abortions with no exemption for the health of the mother, I urged them instead to adopt a federal statute banning late-term abortions unless the life or health of the mother was at stake. Because several states still hadn't passed laws like the one I signed in 1985, the bill I proposed would have outlawed more abortions than the bill banning the partial-birth procedure, which normally is used to minimize damage to the mother's body. The GOP leadership turned me down.

Besides the economic package and the abortion bill, the legislature adopted my proposals to set up a fund to compensate victims of violent crime; strengthen our efforts to reduce and deal with child abuse; establish a fund to provide health care for indigents, mostly poor pregnant women, not covered by the federal Medicaid program; make Martin Luther King Jr.'s birthday a state holiday; and create a program to provide better training for school principals. I had become convinced that school performance depended more on the quality of a principal's leadership than on any other single factor. The years ahead only strengthened that conviction.

The only real fireworks in a session otherwise devoted to good government and harmless legislative sideshows came from the herculean effort of the AEA to repeal the teacher-testing law just weeks before the test was scheduled to be given for the first time. In a clever move, the teachers got Representative Ode Maddox to sponsor the repeal. Ode was a highly respected former superintendent in his little town of Oden. He was a good Democrat who kept a large old photograph of FDR up in the school auditorium into the 1980s. He was also a friend of mine. Despite the best efforts of my supporters, the repeal passed the House. I immediately put an ad on the radio telling the people what had happened and asking them to call the Senate in protest. The switchboard was flooded with calls and the bill was killed. Instead, the legislature passed a bill that I supported requiring all certified educators, not just those working in 1985, to take and pass the test by 1987 to keep their certification.

The AEA said teachers would boycott the test. The

week before it was given, 4,000 teachers demonstrated outside the Capitol and heard a representative of the National Education Association accuse me of "assassinating the dignity of the public schools and its children." A week later, more than 90 percent of our 27,600 teachers showed up for the test.

Before the legislature went home, we had one last bit of fireworks. The Highway Department had gone all over the state pushing a new road program, to be financed by an increase in gasoline and diesel taxes. The department sold it to the local business and farm leaders, and it passed rather handily, creating a problem for me. I liked the program and thought it would be good for the economy, but in the election I had pledged not to support a major tax increase. So I vetoed the bill and told its sponsors I wouldn't fight their efforts to override it. The override passed easily, the only time in twelve years one of my vetoes was overturned.

I also engaged in some national political activity in 1985. In February, I narrated the Democrats' response to President Reagan's State of the Union address. The State of the Union was a great forum for Reagan's speaking skills, and whoever gave our brief response had a hard time making any impression. Our party took a different tack that year, featuring the new ideas and economic achievements of several of our governors and mayors. I also got involved in the newly formed Democratic Leadership Council, a group dedicated to forging a winning message for the Democrats based on fiscal responsibility, creative new ideas on social policy, and a commitment to a strong national defense.

The summer governors' conference, held in Idaho, was marked by an unusual partisan fight over a fund-raising letter for the Republican governors signed by President Reagan. The letter took some hard shots at their Democratic colleagues for being too liberal with tax-and-spend policies, a violation of our unwritten commitment to keep the governors' meetings bipartisan. The Democrats were so angry we threatened to block the election of Republican governor Lamar Alexander of Tennessee to the chairmanship of the National Governors Association, normally a routine action since he was the vice chair and the chairmanship rotated by party every year. I liked Lamar and doubted he had his heart in the attack on his Democratic colleagues; after all, he, too, had raised taxes to fund higher school standards. I helped to broker a resolution to the conflict, in which the Republicans apologized for the letter and said they wouldn't do it again, and we voted for Lamar for chairman. I was elected vice chairman. We did a lot of good work in the governors' conferences in the seventies and eighties. In the 1990s, when the Republican governors gained the majority and got more in line with their national party, the old cooperative spirit diminished. That might have been good politics, but it impaired the search for good policy.

On our way to Idaho, Hillary, Chelsea, and I stopped for a few happy days in Montana, thanks largely to Governor Ted Schwinden. After we spent the night with him, Ted got us up at dawn to take a helicopter up the Missouri River and watch the wildlife waking up to the day. Then we took a four-wheel-drive vehicle equipped with rail connectors along the Burlington Northern rail line for a couple hundred miles, a trip that included a dramatic crossing of a three-hundred-foot-deep gorge. And we drove a rented car up the "highway to the sun," where we watched marmosets scramble around above the snow line, then spent a few days at Kootenai Lodge on Swan Lake. After all my travels, I still think western Montana is one of the most beautiful places I've ever seen.

The political trips I took were a minor diversion from my main mission after the legislature went home in 1985, and for the rest of the decade: building the Arkansas economy. I enjoyed the challenge, and I got pretty good at it. First, I had to stop bad things from happening. When International Paper announced plans to close a mill in Camden that had been operating since the 1920s, I flew to New York to see the company president, John Georges, and asked him what it would take to keep the mill open. He gave me a list of five or six things he wanted. I delivered on all but one, and he kept the plant open. When my friend Turner Whitson called to tell me the shoe plant in Clarksville was closing, I turned for help to Don Munro, who had managed to keep six shoe-making facilities open in Arkansas during the worst of the eighties recession. I offered him $1 million in assistance and he took over the plant. The workers found out about their jobs being saved at a meeting to help them file for unemployment and retraining benefits.

When the Sanyo company told me it was planning to close its television-assembly plant in Forrest City, Dave Harrington and I flew to Osaka, Japan, to see Satoshi Iue, the president of Sanyo, a vast company with more than 100,000 employees worldwide. I had become friends with Mr. Iue over the years. After I was defeated for governor in 1980, he sent me a beautiful piece of Japanese calligraphy that said "Though the river may force you to change course, hold fast to what you believe." I had it framed, and when I was reelected in 1982, it hung at the entrance to our bedroom so that I would see it every day. I told Mr. Iue that we couldn't handle the loss of Sanyo's jobs in eastern Arkansas, where the Delta counties all had unemployment rates higher than 10 percent. I asked him if he would keep the plant open if Wal-Mart would sell Sanyo's televisions. After he agreed, I flew back to Arkansas and asked Wal-Mart to help. In September 2003, Satoshi Iue came to Chappaqua for lunch. By then, Wal-Mart had bought more than twenty million of those television sets.

It wasn't all rescue missions. We also made some new things happen, financing new high-tech ventures, involving the universities in helping start new businesses, taking successful trade and investment missions to Europe and Asia, and supporting the expansion of successful plants like the ones run by the Daiwa Steel Tube Industries in Pine Bluff and the Dana Company in Jonesboro, which made transmissions with the help of skilled workers and amazing robots.

Our biggest coup was getting NUCOR Steel Company to come to northeast Arkansas. NUCOR was a highly profitable company that made steel by melting already-forged metal rather than creating it from scratch. NUCOR paid workers a modest weekly wage and a bonus based on profits—a bonus that usually accounted for more than half the workers' income. By 1992, the Arkansas NUCOR workers' average income was about $50,000. Moreover, NUCOR gave every employee an extra $1,500 a year for every child he or she had in college. One of its employees educated eleven children with the company's help. NUCOR had no corporate jet and operated with a tiny headquarters staff out of rented space in North Carolina. The founder, Ken Iverson, inspired great loyalty the old-fashioned way: he earned it. In the only year NUCOR's earnings were down in the 1980s, Iverson sent a letter to his employees apologizing for the cut in their pay, which was applied across the board because NUCOR had a strict no-layoff policy. The benefits and burdens were shared equally, except for the boss. Iverson said it wasn't the workers' fault that market conditions were poor, but he should have figured out a way to deal with them. He told his workers he was taking a 60-percent pay cut, three times theirs, a dramatic departure from the common practice for the last two decades of raising executive pay at a far greater rate than that of other employees, whether the company is doing well or not. Needless to say, no one at NUCOR wanted to quit.

When the Van Heusen shirt company announced it was closing its Brinkley plant, Farris and Marilyn Burroughs, who had been involved with the workers and community for years, decided to buy it and keep it open, but they needed more customers for their shirts. I asked David Glass, the president of Wal-Mart, if he would stock them. Again, Wal-Mart came to the rescue. Shortly afterward, I hosted a lunch for Wal-Mart executives and our economic development people to encourage the company to buy more products made in America and to advertise this practice as a way to increase sales. Wal-Mart's "Buy America" campaign was a great success and helped to reduce resentment against the giant discounter for putting small-town merchants out of business. Hillary loved the program and supported it strongly when she went on the Wal-Mart board a couple of years later. At its high-water mark, Wal-Mart's merchandise was about 55 percent American made, about 10 percent more than that of its nearest competitor. Unfortunately, after a few years Wal-Mart abandoned the policy in its marketing drive to be the lowest-cost retailer, but we made the most of it in Arkansas while it lasted.

The work I did in education and economic development convinced me that Arkansas, and America, had to make some big changes if we wanted to preserve our economic and political leadership in the global economy. We simply weren't well educated or productive enough. We had been losing ground in average incomes since 1973, and by the 1980s, four in ten workers were experiencing declining incomes. The situation was intolerable, and I was determined to do what I could to change it.

My efforts helped to broaden my political base, garnering support from Republicans and conservative independents who had never voted for me before. Even though Arkansas had been in the top ten states in new-job growth as a percentage of total employment in two of the last three years, I couldn't convert everybody. When the oil refinery in El Dorado was about to close, costing us more than three hundred good union jobs, I helped convince some businesspeople from Mississippi to buy and operate it. I knew how much it meant to those workers' families and to the local economy, and I looked forward to shaking hands at the plant gate at the next election. It was a home run, until I met a man who angrily said he wouldn't vote for me under any circumstances. When I responded, "Don't you know I saved your job?" he replied, "Yeah, I know you did, but you don't care a thing about me. You only did it so you'd have one more poor sucker to tax. That's why you want me to have a job, so you can tax me. I wouldn't vote for you for all the money in the world." You can't win 'em all.

In early 1986, I launched my campaign for reelection,

this one for a four-year term. In 1984, the voters had passed an amendment to change executive terms from two to four years for the first time since our Reconstruction Era Constitution was adopted in 1874. If I won, I would become the second-longest-serving Arkansas governor after Orval Faubus. He won his longevity because of Little Rock Central High. I wanted to win mine on schools and jobs.

Ironically, my main opponent in the primary was Faubus himself. He was still angry at me because, in my first term, I refused to have the state buy his beautiful Fay Jones house in Huntsville and put it into the state park system to be used as a retreat. I knew he was strapped for cash, but so was the state, and I couldn't justify the expense. Faubus was going to rail against the new education standards, saying they had brought consolidation and high taxes to rural areas, which hadn't gotten any of the new jobs I was always bragging about.

And once I got by Faubus, Frank White was waiting. He was trying to win the best two out of three. Between the two of them, I knew a lot of charges would fly. I felt confident that Betsey Wright, Dick Morris, David Watkins, and I could deal with whatever came up, but I was concerned about how Chelsea would react to people saying bad things about her father. She was six and had begun to watch the news and even to read the paper. Hillary and I tried to prepare her for what White and Faubus might say about me and how I would respond. Then, for several days, we would take turns playing one of the candidates. One day Hillary was Frank White, I was Faubus, and Chelsea was me. I accused her of ruining the small schools with misguided education ideas. She shot back, "Well, at least I didn't use the state police to spy on my political enemies the way you did!" Faubus had actually done that in the aftermath of the Central High crisis. Not bad for a six-year-old.

I won the primary with more than 60 percent of the vote, but Faubus pulled a third of it. Even at seventy-six, he still had some juice in rural areas. Frank White took up where Faubus left off. Although he had called teachers "greedy" when they pushed for higher pay during his tenure, he got the endorsement of the Arkansas Education Association in the Republican primary when he changed his position from support of the teacher test to opposition. Then he started in on Hillary and me.

White began by saying the new education standards were too burdensome and needed to be changed. I hit that one out of the park, saying if he were elected, he would "delay them to death." Then he went after Hillary, alleging she had a conflict of interest because the Rose firm was representing the state in its fight against the Grand Gulf nuclear plants. We had a good response to that charge, too. First, the Rose firm was working to save Arkansans money by lifting the burden of the Grand Gulf plants, while White, as a board member of one of the Middle South Utilities companies, had voted three times to go forward with construction of the plants. Second, the Public Service Commission hired the Rose firm because all the other big firms were representing utilities or other parties in the case. Both the legislature and the attorney general approved the hiring. Third, the money the state paid to the Rose firm was subtracted from the firm's income before Hillary's partnership profits were calculated, so she made no money from it. White seemed more interested in defending the utility's effort to soak Arkansas ratepayers than protecting them from a conflict of interest. I asked him if his attacks on Hillary meant he wanted to run for first lady instead of governor. Our campaign even made bumper stickers and buttons that said, "Frank for First Lady."

White's final charges did him in. He had been working for Stephens, Inc., then the largest bond house outside Wall Street. Jack Stephens had supported me when I first ran for governor, but then he drifted to the right, heading Democrats for Reagan in 1984, and by 1986 he had become a Republican. His older brother, Witt, was still a Democrat and supporting me, but Jack ran the bond house. And Frank White was his guy. For many years, Stephens had controlled the state's bond business. When I dramatically expanded the volume of bond issues, I insisted that we open all of them to competitive bidding by national firms, and that we let more Arkansas firms have the opportunity to sell the bonds. The Stephens firm still got its fair share, but it didn't control all the issues as it had in the past and would again if White won the election. One of the Arkansas firms that got some business was headed by Dan Lasater, who built a successful bond firm in Little Rock before he lost it all to a cocaine habit. Lasater had been a supporter of mine and a friend of my brother's, with whom he had partied hard when they were both chained to cocaine, as too many young people were in the 1980s.

When Betsey Wright and I were preparing for our television debate with White, we learned that he was going to challenge me to take a drug test with him. The ostensible reason was to set a good example, but I knew White was hoping I wouldn't do it. The blizzard of rumors spawned by Lasater's downfall included one that I had been part of Dan's party circle. It wasn't true. Betsey and I decided to take a drug test before the debate. When White hit me on television with his challenge, I smiled and said Betsey and I had already taken a test and he and his campaign manager, Darrell Glascock, should follow suit. Glascock had been subjected to his share of rumors too. Their clever trick had backfired.

White turned up the heat with the nastiest TV ad I'd ever seen. He showed Lasater's office, followed by a tray of cocaine, with an announcer saying I'd taken campaign contributions from a cocaine-using felon, then given him state bond business. The clear implication was that I'd given Lasater preferred treatment and at the least I had known about his cocaine habit when I did. I invited the **Arkansas Gazette** to review the records of the Development Finance Authority, and the paper ran a front-page story showing how many more bond houses had done business with the state since I'd taken over from Governor White. The number had gone from four to fifteen, and Stephens still had handled over $700 million of bond business, more than twice as much as any other Arkansas firm. I also hit back with a TV ad that began by asking people if they'd seen White's ad and actually showing a few seconds of it. Then my ad cut to a picture of Stephens, Inc., with the announcer saying White worked there and the reason he was attacking me was that neither Stephens nor anyone else controlled the state's business any longer, but they would if White became governor again. It was one of the most effective commercials I ever ran, because it was a strong response to a low blow, and because the facts spoke for themselves.

I was also glad that Roger and Mother hadn't let themselves get too hurt by White's bringing up Roger's drug problem. After he got out of prison, Roger served six months in a halfway house in Texas, and then moved to north Arkansas, where he worked for a friend of ours in a quick-stop service station. He was about to move to Nashville, Tennessee, and was healthy enough not to let the old story drag him down. Mother was happy with Dick Kelley, and by now knew that politics was a rough game in which the only answer to a low blow is winning.

In November, I won with 64 percent, including a staggering 75 percent in Little Rock. I was gratified that the victory gave me the opportunity to smash the suggestion that I had abused the governor's office and the implication that drugs had something to do with it. Despite the tough campaign, I wasn't very good at holding a grudge. Over the years, I came to like Frank White and his wife, Gay, and to enjoy being on programs with him. He had a great sense of humor, he loved Arkansas, and I was sad when he died in 2003. Thankfully, I also reconciled with Jack Stephens.

As far as I was concerned, the campaign against Faubus and White was a battle against Arkansas' past and against the emerging politics of personal destruction. I wanted to focus the people on the issues and on the future, by defending our education reforms and promoting our economic initiatives. The **Memphis Commercial Appeal** reported that "Clinton's stump speeches in the area sound as much like seminars on the economy as pleas for votes and most political analysts agree that the strategy is working."

I often told the story of my visit to the Arkansas Eastman chemical plant in rural Independence County. During the tour, my host kept saying that all the anti-pollution equipment was run by computers and he wanted me to meet the guy who was running them. He built him up so much that by the time I got to the computer control room, I expected to meet someone who was a cross between Albert

Einstein and the Wizard of Oz. Instead, the man running the computers was wearing cowboy boots, jeans with a belt adorned with a big silver rodeo buckle, and a baseball cap. He was listening to country music and chewing tobacco. The first thing he said to me was "My wife and I are going to vote for you, because we need more jobs like this." This guy raised cattle and horses—he was pure Arkansas—but he knew his prosperity depended more on what he knew than on how much he could do with his hands and back. He had seen the future and he wanted to go there.

In August, when the National Governors Association met in Hilton Head, South Carolina, I became the chairman and celebrated my fortieth birthday. I had already agreed to serve as chairman of the Education Commission of the States, a group dedicated to gathering the best education ideas and practices and spreading them across the nation. Lamar Alexander had also appointed me to be the Democratic co-chairman of the governors' task force on welfare reform, to work with the White House and Congress to develop a bipartisan proposal to improve the welfare system so that it would promote work, strengthen families, and meet children's basic needs. Though I had secured an increase in Arkansas' meager monthly welfare benefits in 1985, I wanted welfare to be a way station on the road to independence.

I was excited with these new responsibilities. I was both a political animal and a policy wonk, always eager to meet new people and explore new ideas. I thought the work would enable me to be a better governor, strengthen my network of national contacts, and gain a better understanding of the emerging global economy and how America should deal with its challenges.

As 1986 drew to a close, I took a quick trip to Taiwan to address the Tenth Annual Conference of Taiwanese and American Leaders about our future relations. The Taiwanese were good customers for Arkansas soybeans and a wide variety of our manufactured products, from electric motors to parking meters. But America's trade deficit was large and growing, and four in ten American workers had suffered declining incomes in the previous five years. Speaking for all the governors, I acknowledged America's responsibility to cut our deficit to bring down interest rates and increase domestic demand, to restructure and reduce the debt of our Latin American neighbors, to relax export controls on high-technology products, and to improve the education and productivity of our workforce. Then I challenged the Taiwanese to reduce trade barriers and invest more of their huge cash reserves in America. It was my first speech on global economics to a foreign audience. Making it forced me to sort out exactly what I thought should be done and who should do it.

By the end of 1986, I had formed some basic convictions about the nature of the modern world, which later developed into the so-called New Democrat philosophy that was the backbone of my 1992 campaign for President. I outlined them in a speech to the year-end management meeting of Gannett, the newspaper chain that had just bought the **Arkansas Gazette.**

> . . . these are the new rules that I believe should provide the framework within which we make policy today:
>
> (1) Change may be the only constant in today's American economy. I was at an old country church celebration in Arkansas about three months ago to

celebrate its 150th anniversary. There were about seventy-five people there, all packed in this small wooden church. After the service, we went out under the pine trees to have a potluck lunch, and I found myself talking to an old man who was obviously quite bright. Finally, I asked him, "Mister, how old are you?" He said, "I'm eighty-two." "When did you join this church?" "Nineteen sixteen," he said. "If you had to say in one sentence, what is the difference between our state now and in 1916?" He was quiet for a moment, then said, "Governor, that's pretty easy. In 1916 when I got up in the morning I knew what was going to happen, but when I get up in the morning now, I don't have any idea." That is about as good a one-sentence explanation about what has happened to America as Lester Thurow could give. . . .

(2) Human capital is probably more important than physical capital now. . . .

(3) A more constructive partnership between business and government is far more important than the dominance of either.

(4) As we try to solve problems which arise out of the internationalization of American life and the changes in our own population, cooperation in every area is far more important than conflict. . . . We have to share responsibilities and opportunities—we're going up or down together.

(5) Waste is going to be punished . . . it appears to me that we are spending billions of dollars of investment capital increasing the debt of corporations without increasing their productivity. More debt should mean increased productivity, growth,

and profitability. Now it means, too often, less employment, less investment for research and development, and forced restructuring to service nonproductive debt. . . .

(6) A strong America requires a resurgent sense of community, a strong sense of mutual obligations, and a conviction that we cannot pursue our individual interests independent of the needs of our fellow citizens. . . .

If we want to keep the American dream alive for our own people and preserve America's role in the world, we must accept the new rules of successful economic, political, and social life. And we must act on them.

Over the next five years, I would refine my analysis of globalization and interdependence and propose more initiatives to respond to them, juggling as best I could my desire to be a good governor and to have a positive impact on national policy.

In 1987, my agenda for the legislative session, "Good Beginnings, Good Schools, Good Jobs," was consistent with the work I was doing with the National Governors Association under the theme "Making America Work." In addition to recommendations that built on our previous efforts in education and economic development, I asked the legislature to help me get the growing number of poor children off to a good start in life by increasing health-care coverage for poor mothers and children, starting with prenatal care in order to lower the infant-mortality rate and reduce avoidable damage to newborns; to increase parenting education for mothers of at-risk children; to provide more special education in early childhood to kids with learning problems; to increase the availability of affordable child care; and to strengthen child-support enforcement.

From Hillary, I had learned most of what I knew about early-childhood development and its importance to later life. She had been interested in it as long as I'd known her, and had taken a fourth year at Yale Law School to work on children's issues at the Yale Child Study Center and Yale–New Haven Hospital. She had worked hard to import to Arkansas an innovative preschool program from Israel called HIPPY, which stands for Home Instruction Programs for Preschool Youngsters, a program that helps to develop both parenting skills and children's ability to learn. Hillary set up HIPPY programs all across the state. We both loved going to the graduation exercises, watching the children show their stuff and seeing the parents' pride in their kids and themselves. Thanks to Hillary, Arkansas had the largest program in the country, serving 2,400 mothers, and their children showed remarkable progress.

The main focus of my economic development efforts was to increase investment and opportunity for poor people and distressed areas, most of them in rural Arkansas. The most important proposal was to provide more capital to people who had the potential to operate profitable small businesses but couldn't borrow the money to get started. The South Shore Development Bank in Chicago had been instrumental in helping unemployed carpenters and electricians set themselves up in business on the city's South Side to renovate abandoned buildings that otherwise would have been condemned. As a result, the whole area recovered.

I knew about the bank because one of its employees, Jan Piercy, had been one of Hillary's best friends at Wellesley. Jan told us South Shore got the idea to fund artisans who were skilled but not creditworthy by conventional standards from the work of the Grameen Bank of Bangladesh, founded by Muhammad Yunus, who had studied economics at Vanderbilt University before going home to help his people. I arranged to meet him for breakfast in Washington one morning, and he explained how his "micro-credit" program worked. Village women who had skills and a reputation for honesty but no assets were organized in teams. When the first borrower repaid her small loan, the next one in line got hers, and so on. When I first met Yunus, the Grameen Bank already had made hundreds of thousands of loans, with a repayment rate higher than that for commercial lenders in Bangladesh. By 2002, Grameen had made them to more than 2.4 million people, 95 percent of them poor women.

If the idea worked in Chicago, I thought it would work in economically distressed areas in rural Arkansas. As Yunus said in an interview, "Anywhere anybody is rejected by the banking system, you have room for a Grameen-type program." We set up the Southern Development Bank Corporation in Arkadelphia. The Development Finance Authority put up some of the initial money, but most of it came from corporations that Hillary and I asked to invest in it.

When I became President, I secured congressional approval for a national loan program modeled on the Grameen Bank, and featured some of our success stories at a White House event. The U.S. Agency for International Development also funded two million micro-credit loans a year in poor villages in Africa, Latin America, and East Asia. In 1999, when I went to South Asia, I visited Muhammad Yunus and some of the people he'd set up in business, including women who'd used the loans to buy cell phones, which they charged villagers to use to call their relatives and friends in America and Europe. Muhammad Yunus should have been awarded the Nobel Prize in Economics years ago.

My other major interest was welfare reform. I asked the legislature to require recipients with children three years old or over to sign a contract committing themselves to a course of independence, through literacy, job training, and work. In February, I went to Washington with several other governors to testify before the House Ways and Means Committee on welfare prevention and reforms. We asked Congress to give us the tools to "promote work, not welfare; independence, not dependence." We argued that more should be done to keep people off welfare in the first place, by reducing adult illiteracy, teen pregnancy, the school dropout rate, and alcohol and drug abuse. On welfare reform, we advocated a binding contract between the recipient and the government, setting out the rights and responsibilities of both parties. Recipients would commit to strive for independence in return for the benefits, and the government would commit to help them, with education and training, medical care, child care, and job placement. We also asked that all welfare recipients with children age three or older be required to participate in a work program designed by the states, that each welfare recipient have a caseworker committed to a successful transition to self-sufficiency, that efforts to collect child-support payments be intensified, and that a new formula for cash assistance be established consistent with each state's cost of living. Federal law allowed states to set monthly benefits wherever they chose as long as they weren't lower than they had been in the early seventies, and they were all over the place.

I had spent enough time talking to welfare recipients and caseworkers in Arkansas to know that the vast majority of them wanted to work and support their families. But they faced formidable barriers, beyond the obvious ones of low skills, lack of work experience, and inability to pay for child care. Many of the people I met had no cars or access to public transportation. If they took a low-wage job, they would lose food stamps and medical coverage under Medicaid. Finally, many of them just didn't believe they could make it in the world of work and had no idea where to begin.

At one of our governors' meetings in Washington, along with my welfare reform co-chair, Governor Mike Castle of Delaware, I organized a meeting for other governors on welfare reform. I brought two women from Arkansas who had left welfare for work to testify. One young woman from Pine Bluff had never been on an airplane or an escalator before the trip. She was restrained but convincing about the potential of poor people to support themselves and their children. The other witness was in her mid to late thirties. Her name was Lillie Hardin, and she had recently found work as a cook. I asked her if she thought able-bodied people on welfare should be forced to take jobs if they were available. "I sure do," she answered. "Otherwise we'll just lay around watching the soaps all day." Then I asked Lillie what was the best thing about being off welfare. Without hesitation, she replied, "When my boy goes to school and they ask him, 'What does your mama do for a living?' he can give an answer." It was the best argument I've ever heard for welfare reform. After the hearing, the governors treated her like a rock star.

When I tackled welfare reform as President, I was

always somewhat amused to hear some members of the press characterize it as a Republican issue, as if valuing work was something only conservatives did. By 1996, when Congress passed a bill I could sign, I had been working on welfare reform for more than fifteen years. But I didn't consider it a Democratic issue. Or even a governors' issue. Welfare reform was about Lillie Hardin and her boy.

TWENTY-FOUR

Thanks to the four-year term, the dedication and ability of my staff and cabinet, a good working relationship with the legislature, and the strength of my political organization, I also had the space to move into the national political arena.

Because of the visibility I got from my work on education, economics, and welfare reform, and my chairmanships of the National Governors Association and the Education Commission of the States, I received a lot of invitations to speak out of state in 1987. I accepted more than two dozen of them, in fifteen states. While only four were Democratic Party events, they all served to broaden my contacts and to heighten speculation that I might enter the presidential race.

Although I was only forty in the spring of 1987, I was interested in making the race, for three reasons. First, by historical standards the Democrats had an excellent chance to recapture the White House. It seemed clear that Vice President Bush would be the nominee of the Republican Party, and up until then only vice president to win the presidency directly from that office had been Martin Van Buren, in 1836, who succeeded Andrew Jackson in the last election in which there was no effective opposition to the Democratic Party. Second, I felt very strongly that the country had to change direction. Our growth was fueled primarily by big increases in defense spending and large tax cuts that disproportionately benefited the wealthiest Americans and drove up the deficit. The big deficits led to high interest rates, as the government competed with private borrowers for money, and that in turn drove up the value of the dollar, making imports cheaper and American exports more expensive. At a time when Americans were beginning to improve their productivity and competitive position, we were still losing manufacturing jobs and farms. Moreover, because of the budget deficit, we weren't investing enough in the education, training, and research required to maintain high wages and low unemployment in the global economy. That's why 40 percent of the American people had suffered a decline in real income since the mid-1970s.

The third reason I was seriously considering entering the race is that I thought I understood what was happening and could explain it to the American people. Also, because I had a strong record on crime, welfare reform, accountability in education, and fiscal responsibility, I didn't think the Republicans could paint me as an ultra-liberal Democrat who didn't embrace mainstream values and who thought there was a government program for every problem. I was convinced that if we could escape the "alien" box the Republicans had put us in since 1968, except for President Carter's success in 1976, we could win the White House again.

It was a tall order, because it's not easy to get people to change their political frame of reference, but I thought I might be able to do it. So did several of my fellow governors. When I went to the Indianapolis 500 race in the spring, I ran into Governor Bob Kerrey of Nebraska. I liked Bob a lot and thought he, too, would be a good presidential candidate. He had won the Medal of Honor in

Vietnam and, like me, was a fiscal conservative and social progressive who had been elected in a state far more Republican than Arkansas. To my surprise, Bob encouraged me to run and said he'd be my chairman in the midwestern states if I did.

There was one obstacle at home to my running for President: Dale Bumpers was seriously considering it. I had been encouraging him to run since late 1974. He almost did in 1984, and he had an excellent chance to win this time. He had served in the marines in World War II, had been a great governor, and was the best speaker in the Senate. I knew that Dale would be a good President and that he would have a better chance to win than I would. I would have been happy to support him. I wanted our side to win and change the direction of the country.

On March 20, as I was jogging down Main Street in Little Rock, a local reporter chased me down to say that Senator Bumpers had just issued a statement saying he wouldn't run for President. He just didn't want to do it. A few weeks earlier, Governor Mario Cuomo of New York had made the same decision. I told Hillary and Betsey I wanted to take a serious look at the race.

We raised a little money for the exploratory effort, and Betsey sent people to do spadework in Iowa, New Hampshire, and some of the southern states that would vote in a bloc the next year on "Super Tuesday" shortly after the New Hampshire primary. On May 7, the primary looked even more winnable when Senator Gary Hart, who had almost upset Vice President Mondale in 1984, withdrew from the race after his relationship with Donna Rice was exposed. I thought Gary had made an error by challenging the press to tail him to see if they could find any dirt, but I felt bad for him, too. He was a brilliant, innovative politician who was always thinking about America's big challenges and what to do about them. After the Hart affair, those of us who had not led perfect lives had no way of knowing what the press's standards of disclosure were. Finally I concluded that anyone who believed he had something to offer should just run, deal with whatever charges arose, and trust the American people. Without a high pain threshold, you can't be a successful President anyway.

I set July 14 as a deadline for making a decision. Several of my old friends from past political battles came down to Little Rock, including Mickey Kantor, Carl Wagner, Steve Cohen, John Holum, and Sandy Berger. They all thought I should run; it seemed too good a chance to pass up. Still, I was holding back. I knew I was ready to be a good candidate, but I wasn't sure I had lived long enough to acquire the wisdom and judgment necessary to be a good President. If elected, I would be forty-two, about the same age Theodore Roosevelt was when he was sworn in after President McKinley's assassination, and a year younger than John Kennedy when he was elected. But they had both come from wealthy, politically prominent families, and had grown up in a way that made them comfortable in the circles of power. My two favorite Presidents, Lincoln and FDR, were fifty-one when they took office, fully mature and in command of themselves and their responsibilities. Ten years later, on my fifty-first birthday, Al Gore gave me an account of the Cherokee Indian Nation's view of the aging process. The Cherokees believe a man does not reach full maturity until he is fifty-one.

The second thing that bothered me was the difficulties a campaign would pose for my governorship. Nineteen eighty-seven was the deadline for implementing the school standards. I had already called one special session to raise money for schools and overcrowded prisons. It had been a knockdown fight that had strained my relations with several legislators, and it very nearly ended in failure before we scraped together enough votes at the last minute to do what had to be done. I knew that, in all probability, I'd have to call another special session in early 1988. I was determined to fully implement the school standards and build on them; it was the only chance most poor kids in my state had for a better future. Chelsea's elementary school was about 60 percent black, and more than half the kids were from low-income families. I remember how one little boy she invited to her birthday party at the mansion almost didn't come because he couldn't afford to buy her a present. I was determined to give that little boy a better chance than his parents had had.

The **Arkansas Gazette,** which had supported me in every campaign, ran an editorial arguing that I shouldn't run for both of the reasons that concerned me. While acknowledging my strong potential for national leadership, the **Gazette** said, "Bill Clinton is not ready to be President" and "Governor Clinton is needed in Arkansas."

Ambition is a powerful force, and the ambition to be President has led many a candidate to ignore both his own limitations and the responsibilities of the office he currently holds. I always thought I could rise to any occasion, stand the most withering fire, and do two or three jobs at once. In 1987, I might have made a decision rooted in self-confidence and driven by ambition, but I didn't. What finally decided the question for me was the one part of my life politics couldn't reach: Chelsea. Carl Wagner, who was also the father of an only daughter, told me I'd have to reconcile myself to being away from Chelsea for most of the next sixteen months. Mickey Kantor was talking me through it when Chelsea asked me where we were going for summer vacation. When I said I might not be able to take one if I ran for President, Chelsea replied, "Then Mom and I will go without you." That did it.

I went into the dining room of the Governor's Mansion, where my friends were eating lunch, told them I wasn't running, and apologized for bringing them all down. Then I went to the Excelsior to make my announcement to a few hundred supporters. I did my best to explain how I had come so close, yet backed away:

> I need some family time; I need some personal time. Politicians are people too. I think sometimes we forget it, but they really are. The only thing I or any other candidate has to offer in running for President is what's inside. That's what sets people on fire and gets their confidence and their votes, whether they live in Wisconsin or Montana or New York. That part of my life needs renewal. The other, even more important reason for my decision is the certain impact that this campaign would have had on our daughter. The only way I could have won, getting in this late, after others had been working up to two years, would be to go on the road full-time from now until the end, and to have Hillary do the same. . . . I've seen a lot of kids grow up under these pressures and a long, long time ago I made a promise to myself that if I was ever lucky enough to have a child, she would never grow up wondering who her father was.

Though she had said she would support me whichever way I went, Hillary was relieved. She thought I should finish the work I had started in Arkansas and keep building a national base of support. And she knew it was not a good time for me to be away from our families. Mother was having problems in her anesthesia work, Roger had been out of prison only a couple of years, and Hillary's parents were moving to Little Rock. In January 1983, during my swearing-in speech to the legislature, Hugh Rodham had slumped in his chair. He had suffered a massive heart attack and was rushed to the University Medical Center for quadruple-bypass surgery. I was with him when he woke up. After I realized he was lucid, I said, "Hugh, the speech wasn't good enough to give anyone a heart attack!" In 1987, he had a minor stroke. Hugh and Dorothy didn't need to stay up in Park Ridge alone. We wanted them nearby, and they were looking forward to the move, mostly to be near their only grandchild. Still, it would be a big adjustment for them.

Finally, Hillary was happy I didn't run because she disagreed with the conventional wisdom that the Democrats were likely to win in 1988. She didn't think the Reagan Revolution had run its course and believed that, despite the Iran-Contra affair, George Bush would win as a more moderate version of Reagan. Four years later, when prospects for victory looked much darker, with President Bush's approval ratings over 70 percent, Hillary encouraged me to run. As usual, she was right both times.

After the decision was announced, I felt as though the weight of the world had been lifted from my shoulders. I was free to be a father, husband, and governor, and to work and speak on national issues unencumbered by immediate ambitions.

In July, Hillary, Chelsea, and I went to the summer governors' conference in Traverse City, Michigan, to wrap up my year as chairman. I was succeeded by New Hampshire governor John Sununu, who promised to continue our work for welfare reform, and with whom I had a good relationship. After we adjourned, the Democratic governors went to Mackinaw Island, where Governor Jim Blanchard brought us together to meet with all our presidential candidates, including Senator Al Gore, Senator Paul Simon, Senator Joe Biden, Congressman Dick Gephardt, the Reverend Jesse Jackson, former governor Bruce Babbitt of Arizona, and Governor Mike Dukakis. I thought we had a good field, but I favored Dukakis. In Massachusetts he had presided over a successful high-tech economy, had balanced budgets, and had advanced both education and welfare reform. He was governing as a "New Democrat," and he knew what it was like to lose an election to negative attacks and make a successful comeback. Even though most Americans thought of Massachusetts as a liberal state, I believed we could sell him because he was a successful governor and would avoid the errors that had sunk us in previous elections. Besides, we were friends. Mike was relieved when I didn't enter the race and gave me an early birthday present, a T-shirt inscribed with the words "Happy 41st. Clinton in '96. You'll only be 49!"

At the end of the meeting, Jim Blanchard put on a terrific rock-and-roll concert featuring Motown artists from the sixties, including the Four Tops, Martha Reeves and the Vandellas, and Jr. Walker, a legendary tenor sax player who could make the horn play an octave higher than most of us mere mortals could. Near the end of the show, a young woman came up to me and invited me to play the sax with all the groups on the Motown standard "Dancin' in the Street." I hadn't played a note in three years. "Is there any sheet music?" I asked. "No," she said. "What key is it in?" She answered, "I don't have a clue." "Can I have a couple of minutes to warm up the horn?" Again, "No." I gave the only possible answer: "Okay, I'll do it." I went up to the stage. They gave me a horn, promptly attached a mike to the bell, and the music started. I played as softly as I could until I tuned the horn and figured out the key. Then I joined in and did pretty well. I still keep a picture of Jr. Walker and me doing a riff together.

September was a busy month. With the new school year starting, I appeared on NBC's **Meet the Press** along with Bill Bennett, who had succeeded Terrel Bell as President Reagan's secretary of education. I got along well with Bennett, who appreciated my support for accountability and teaching kids basic values in school, and he didn't disagree when I said the states needed more federal help to pay for early-childhood programs. When Bennett criticized the National Education Association as an obstacle to accountability, I said I thought the NEA was doing better on that score and reminded him that Al Shanker, leader of the other big teachers union, the American Federation of Teachers, supported both accountability and values education.

Unfortunately, my relationship with Bill Bennett didn't fare well after I became President and he began promoting virtue for a living. Although he had once inscribed a book to me with the words "To Bill Clinton, the Democrat who makes sense," he apparently came to believe that either he had been wrong or I had lost whatever sense I had when he wrote those words.

Around the time of the **Meet the Press** interview, Senator Joe Biden, the chairman of the judiciary committee, asked me to testify against Judge Robert Bork, who had been nominated to the U.S. Supreme Court by President

Reagan. I knew Joe wanted me because I was a white southern governor; the fact that I had been Bork's student in Constitutional Law was an added bonus. Before I agreed, I read most of Bork's articles, important judicial opinions, and published reports of his speeches. I concluded that Judge Bork should not go on the Supreme Court. In an eight-page statement, I said I liked and respected Bork as a teacher and thought President Reagan should have considerable latitude in his appointments, but I still believed the nomination should be rejected by the Senate. I argued that Bork's own words demonstrated that he was a reactionary, not a mainstream conservative. He had criticized almost every major Supreme Court decision expanding civil rights except **Brown** v. **Board of Education.** In fact, Bork had been one of two lawyers, along with William Rehnquist, to advise Barry Goldwater to vote against the Civil Rights Act of 1964. As a southerner, I knew how important it was not to reopen the wounds of race by disturbing those decisions. Bork had the most restrictive view on what the Supreme Court can do to protect individual rights of anyone who had been nominated to the Supreme Court in decades. He thought "dozens" of court decisions needed to be reversed. For example, he said a married couple's right to use contraceptives was no more deserving of privacy protection from government action than a utility's right to pollute the air. In fact, as his ruling against Arkansas in the Grand Gulf case showed, he thought utilities and other business interests were entitled to **more** protection than individual citizens from government actions he disagreed with. However, when it came to protecting business interests, he threw judicial restraint out the window in favor of activism. He even said federal courts shouldn't enforce antitrust laws because they were based on a flawed economic theory. I asked the Senate not to take the risk that Judge Bork would act on his long-held convictions rather than on the more moderate assurances he was then giving in the confirmation process.

I had to file the testimony rather than give it in person, because the hearings were delayed and I had to leave for a trade mission to Europe. In late October, the Senate rejected the Bork nomination, 58–42. I doubt that my testimony influenced a single vote. President Reagan then nominated Judge Antonin Scalia, who was as conservative as Bork but hadn't said and written as much to prove it. He sailed through. In December 2000, in the case of **Bush** v. **Gore,** he wrote the Saturday opinion of the Supreme Court granting an unprecedented injunction to stop counting votes in Florida. Three days later, by a 5–4 vote, the Supreme Court gave the election to George W. Bush, partly on the ground that the outstanding disputed ballots couldn't be counted by midnight of that day as Florida law required. Of course not: the Supreme Court had stopped the counting of legal votes three days before. It was an act of judicial activism that might have made even Bob Bork blush.

After the trade mission, Hillary and I joined John Sununu and Governor Ed DiPrete of Rhode Island for a meeting with our Italian counterparts in Florence. It was the first trip to Italy for Hillary and me, and we fell in love with Florence, Siena, Pisa, San Gimignano, and Venice. I was also fascinated by the economic success of northern Italy, which had a higher per capita income than Germany. One of the reasons for the region's prosperity seemed to be the extraordinary cooperation of small-business people in sharing facilities and administrative and marketing costs, as northern Italian artisans had been doing for centuries, since the development of medieval guilds. Once more I had found an idea I thought might work in Arkansas. When I got home, we helped a group of unemployed sheet-metal workers set up businesses and cooperate in cost-sharing and marketing as I had observed Italian leatherworkers and furniture makers doing.

In October, America's economy took a big jolt when the stock market fell more than 500 points in one day, the biggest one-day drop since 1929. By coincidence, the richest man in America, Sam Walton, was sitting in my office when the market closed. Sam was the leader of the Arkansas Business Council, a group of prominent businesspeople euphemistically known as "the Good Suit Club." They were committed to improving education and the economy in Arkansas. Sam excused himself to see what had happened to Wal-Mart stock. All his wealth was tied up in the company. He'd lived in the same house for decades and drove an old pickup truck. When Sam came back, I asked him how much he'd lost. "About a billion dollars," he said. In 1987, that was still a lot of money, even to Sam Walton. When I asked him if he was worried, he said, "Tomorrow I'm going to fly to Tennessee to see the newest Wal-Mart. If there are plenty of cars in the parking lot I won't be worried. I'm only in the stock market to raise money to open more stores and to give our employees a stake in the company." Almost all of the people who worked for Wal-Mart owned some of its stock. Walton was a stark contrast to the new breed of corporate executives who insisted on big pay increases even when their companies and workers weren't doing well, and on golden parachutes when their companies failed. When the collapse of many stocks in the first years of the new century exposed a new wave of corporate greed and corruption, I thought back to that day in 1987 when Sam Walton lost a billion dollars of his wealth. Sam was a Republican. I doubt he ever voted for me. I didn't agree with everything Wal-Mart did back then and I don't agree with some of the company's practices that have become more common since he died. As I said, Wal-Mart doesn't "buy American" as much as it used to. It's been accused of using large numbers of illegal immigrants. And, of course, the company is anti-union. But America would be better off if all our companies were run by people dedicated enough to see their own fortunes rise and fall with those of their employees and stockholders.

I ended 1987 with my third speech of the decade at the Florida Democratic convention, saying as I always did that we had to face the facts and get the American people to see them as we did. President Reagan had promised to cut taxes, raise defense spending, and balance the budget. He did the first two but couldn't do the third because supply-side economics defies arithmetic. As a result, we had exploded the national debt, failed to invest in our future, and allowed wages to decline for 40 percent of our people. I knew the Republicans were proud of their record, but I looked at it with the perspective of the two old dogs watching young kids break-dancing. One old dog says to the other, "You know, if we did that, they'd worm us."

I told the Florida Democrats, "We have to do nothing less than create a new world economic order and secure the place of the American people within it." The central arguments I made were "We've got to pay the price today to secure tomorrow" and "We're all in it together."

In retrospect, my speeches in the late eighties seem

interesting to me because of their similarity to what I would say in 1992 and what I tried to do as President.

In 1988, I traveled to thirteen states and the District of Columbia to speak on topics about evenly divided between politics and policy. The policy speeches mostly concerned education and the need for welfare-reform legislation, which we were hoping would pass the Congress by the end of the year. But the most important political speech for my future was one called "Democratic Capitalism," which I delivered to the Democratic Leadership Council in Williamsburg, Virginia, on February 29. From then on, I got more active in the DLC, because I thought it was the only group committed to developing the new ideas Democrats needed both to win elections and do right by the country. In Williamsburg, I spoke about the need to make access to the global economy "democratic"—that is, available to all citizens and communities. I had become a convert to William Julius Wilson's argument, articulated in his book **The Truly Disadvantaged,** that there were no race-specific solutions to hard-core unemployment and poverty. The only answers were schools, adult education and training, and jobs. Meanwhile, at home, I continued to wrestle with budget problems facing schools and prisons, to promote my agenda for "good beginnings, good schools, and good jobs," and to push for tax-reform and lobbying-reform legislation. Eventually, because the legislature wouldn't pass them, both these items were put on the ballot for the next election. The interest groups advertised heavily against them. Lobbying reform passed, and tax reform failed.

Governor Dukakis was moving to secure the Democratic nomination for President. A couple of weeks before our convention opened in Atlanta, Mike asked me to nominate him. He and his campaign leaders told me that, though he was leading in the polls against Vice President Bush, the American people didn't know him very well. They had concluded that the nominating speech was an opportunity to introduce him as a leader whose personal qualities, record in office, and new ideas made him the right person for the presidency. Because I was his colleague, his friend, and a southerner, they wanted me to do it and to take the entire allotted time, about twenty-five minutes. This was a departure from the usual practice, which was to have three people representing different groups within our party give five-minute nominating speeches. No one paid much attention to them, but they made the speakers and their constituents happy.

I was flattered by the invitation, but wary. As I've said, conventions are loud meet-and-greet affairs where the words coming from the platform are usually just background music, except for the keynote address and the presidential and vice-presidential acceptance speeches. I had been to enough conventions to know that another long speech would bomb unless the delegates and media were prepared for it and the conditions in the hall remained conducive to it. I explained to the Dukakis people that the speech would work only if I spoke with the lights down and the Dukakis floor operation worked to keep the delegates quiet. Also, they couldn't clap too much or it would substantially increase the length of the speech. I told them I knew that was going to be a lot of trouble, and if they didn't want to do it, I'd give him a rousing five-minute endorsement instead.

On the day of the speech, July 20, I brought a copy of my remarks to Mike's suite and showed it to him and his people. I told them that, as written, it would take about twenty-two minutes to deliver, and if there wasn't too much applause we could stay within the twenty-five-minute window. I described how I could cut 25 percent of the speech, or 50 percent, or 75 percent, if they thought that would be better. A couple of hours later I called back to see what they wanted me to do. I was told to give it all. Mike wanted America to know him as I did.

That night, I was introduced and walked out to strong music. As I began to speak, the lights were dimmed. It was all downhill after that. I wasn't through three sentences before the lights came up again. Then every time I mentioned Mike's name, the crowd roared. I knew right then I should scrap the speech in favor of the five-minute option, but I didn't. The real audience was watching on television. If I could ignore the distractions in the hall, I could still tell the folks at home what Mike wanted them to hear:

> I want to talk about Mike Dukakis. He's come so far, so fast that everybody wants to know what kind of person he is, what kind of governor he's been, and what kind of President he'll be.
>
> He's been my friend a long time. I want you to know my answer to those questions, and why I believe we should make Mike Dukakis the first American President born of immigrant parents since Andrew Jackson.

As I proceeded to answer the questions, the convention got back to talking, except to cheer when Mike's name was mentioned. I felt as if the speech was a two hundred–pound rock I was pushing up a hill. I later joked that I knew I was in trouble when, at the ten-minute mark, the American Samoan delegation started roasting a pig.

A few minutes later, the ABC and NBC networks started roasting me, showing the distracted convention hall and asking when I was going to finish. Only CBS and the radio networks ran the entire speech without critical commentary. The convention press people obviously hadn't been told how long I was expected to speak, or what I was trying to do. Also, the way I wrote the speech was all wrong. In an attempt to tell Mike's story without too much interruption by applause, I made it both too conversational and too "teachy." It was a big mistake to think I could speak only to people watching on TV without regard to how I would go over with the delegates.

I had some good lines, but, alas, the biggest applause I got was near the painful end, when I said, "In closing. . . ." It was thirty-two minutes of total disaster. I kidded Hillary afterward that I wasn't sure just how badly I'd bombed until we were walking out of the arena and she started going up to total strangers and introducing me as her first husband.

Fortunately, Mike Dukakis wasn't hurt by my misadventure. He got good reviews for naming Lloyd Bentsen as his running mate; they both gave good speeches; and the ticket left Atlanta with a hefty lead in the polls. On the other hand, I was a dead man walking.

On July 21, Tom Shales wrote a devastating piece in the **Washington Post** that summed up the press reaction to my speech: "As Jesse Jackson had electrified the hall on Tuesday, Governor Bill Clinton of Arkansas calcified it Wednesday night." He called it "Windy Clinty's classic clinker," and described in agonizing detail what the networks did to fill time until I finished.

When we woke up the next morning, Hillary and I knew I had jumped into another pit I'd have to dig myself out of. I had no idea how to begin, except to laugh at myself. My first public response was: "It wasn't my finest hour. It wasn't even my finest hour and a half." I kept my game face on, but I promised myself I would never again abandon my own instincts about a speech. And except for a brief moment in my speech to Congress on health care in 1994, I didn't.

I was never so glad to get back home in my life. Arkansans were mostly supportive. My paranoid supporters thought I'd been set up by somebody. Most people just thought I'd sacrificed my normal spark and spontaneity to the shackles of a written speech. Robert "Say" McIntosh, a volatile black restaurateur with whom I'd had an on-again, off-again relationship, rose to my defense, slamming the media coverage and hosting a free lunch at the state Capitol for anyone who turned in a postcard or letter hitting back at one of my national media critics. More than five hundred people showed up. I got about seven hundred letters on the speech, 90 percent of them positive. Apparently the people who wrote them had all heard the speech on radio or watched it on CBS, where Dan Rather at least waited until it was over to get his digs in.

A day or so after I returned, I got a call from my friend Harry Thomason, producer of the successful TV show **Designing Women,** which his wife, Linda Bloodworth, wrote. Harry was the brother of Danny Thomason, who sang next to me in the church choir. Hillary and I had gotten to know him and Linda in my first term when he came back to Arkansas to film a Civil War television movie, **The Blue and the Gray.** Harry told me I could make silk out of this sow's ear, but I had to move fast. He suggested I go on the Johnny Carson show and poke fun at myself. I was still shell-shocked and told him I needed a day to think about it. Carson had been having a field day with the speech in his monologues. One of his more memorable lines was "The speech went over about as well as a Velcro condom." But there really wasn't much to consider—I couldn't end up any worse off than I already was. The next day I called Harry and asked him to try to set up the Carson appearance. Carson normally didn't invite politicians on the show, but apparently he made an exception because I was too good a punching bag to pass up, and because I agreed to play the sax, which he could use as an excuse to keep his ban at least on nonmusical politicians. The sax argument was Harry's idea, not the last clever one he would think up for me.

A couple of days later, I was on a plane to California, with Bruce Lindsey and my press secretary, Mike Gauldin. Before the show, Johnny Carson came by the room where I was waiting and said hello, something he almost never did. I guess he knew I had to be hurting and wanted to put me at ease. I was slated to come onstage shortly after the show started, and Carson began by telling the audience not to worry about my appearance because "we've got plenty of coffee and extra cots in the lobby." Then he introduced me. And introduced me. And introduced me. He dragged it out forever by telling everything his researchers could find out about Arkansas. I thought he was going to take longer than I did in Atlanta. When I finally came out and sat down, Carson took out a huge hourglass and put it down next to me so that the whole world could see the sand running down. This performance would be time limited. It was hilarious. It was even funnier to me because I'd brought my own hourglass, which the studio people said I absolutely could not take out. Carson asked me what had happened in Atlanta. I told him I wanted to make Mike Dukakis, who wasn't known for his oratorical skills, look good, and "I succeeded beyond my wildest imagination." I told him Dukakis liked the speech so much, he wanted me to go to the Republican convention to nominate Vice President Bush, too. Then I claimed I'd blown the speech on purpose, because "I always wanted to be on this show in the worst way, and now I am." Johnny then asked if I thought I had a political future. I deadpanned an answer: "It depends on how I do on this show tonight." After we traded one-liners for a few minutes and got good laughs from the studio audience, Johnny invited me to play the sax with Doc Severinsen's band. We did an upbeat version of "Summertime," which went over at least as well as the jokes. Then I settled in to enjoy the next guest, the famous English rocker Joe Cocker, as he sang his latest hit, "Unchain My Heart."

After it was over, I was relieved and thought it had gone about as well as possible. Harry and Linda threw a party for me with some of their friends, including two other Arkansans, Oscar-winning actress Mary Steenburgen, and Gil Gerard, whose first claim to fame was his starring role in **Buck Rogers in the 25th Century.**

I took a red-eye flight home. The next day, I learned that the Carson show had earned good ratings nationwide and astronomical ones in Arkansas. Normally, not enough Arkansans stayed up late enough to earn those ratings, but the honor of the state was at stake. When I walked into the state Capitol, a hometown crowd was there to clap, cheer, and hug me for my performance. At least in Arkansas, the Carson show had put the Atlanta debacle behind me.

Things seemed to be looking up for me, and the rest of

America, too. CNN named me the political winner of the week, after dubbing me its big loser just the week before. Tom Shales said that I had "recovered miraculously" and that "people who watch television love this kind of comeback story." But it wasn't quite over. In August, Hillary, Chelsea, and I went to Long Island, New York, to spend a few days on the beach with our friend Liz Robbins. I was asked to umpire at the annual charity softball game between artists and writers who spend summers there. I still have a picture of myself calling balls and strikes on the pitching of Mort Zuckerman, now publisher of the New York **Daily News** and **U.S. News & World Report.** When I was introduced on the field, the announcer joked that he hoped I didn't take as long to make the calls as I did to finish the speech in Atlanta. I laughed, but I was groaning inside. I didn't know what the crowd thought until the inning was over. A tall man stood up in the stands, walked out on the field, and came up to me. He said, "Don't pay any attention to the criticism. I actually listened to the speech and I liked it a lot." It was Chevy Chase. I had always liked his movies. Now he had a fan for life.

Neither my bad speech nor the good Carson show had much to do with the real work I did as governor, but the ordeal had taught me all over again that how people perceive politicians has a big impact on what they can accomplish. It had also given me a healthy dose of humility. I knew that for the rest of my life I would be more sensitive to people who found themselves in embarrassing or humiliating situations. I had to admit to Pam Strickland, an **Arkansas Democrat** reporter I really respected, "I'm not so sure it's bad for politicians to get knocked on their rear every now and then."

Unfortunately, while things were looking up for me, they weren't going so well for Mike Dukakis. George Bush had given a marvelous acceptance speech at his convention, offering a "kinder, gentler" Reaganism and telling us to "read my lips: no new taxes." Moreover, the vice president's kinder, gentler approach didn't extend to Mike Dukakis. Lee Atwater and company went after him like a pack of rabid dogs, saying Mike didn't believe in pledging allegiance to the flag or being tough on criminals. An "independent" group with no overt ties to the Bush campaign ran an ad featuring a convicted killer named Willie Horton, who had been released on a Massachusetts prison-furlough program. Not coincidentally, Horton was black. His opponents were performing reverse plastic surgery on Dukakis, who didn't help himself by not responding quickly and vigorously to the attacks and by allowing himself to be photographed in a tank wearing a helmet that made him look more like **MAD Magazine**'s Alfred E. Neuman than a potential Commander in Chief of the armed forces.

In the fall, I flew up to Boston to see what I could do to help. By then Dukakis had fallen well behind in the polls. I pleaded with the people in the campaign to hit back; to at least tell the voters that the federal government, of which Bush was a part, furloughed prisoners too. But they never did it enough to suit me. I met Susan Estrich, the campaign manager, whom I liked and who I thought was shouldering too much of the blame for Mike's problems, and Madeleine Albright, a professor at Georgetown who had worked in the Carter White House. She was the foreign policy advisor. I was very impressed with her intellectual clarity and toughness, and resolved to keep in touch with her.

Dukakis found his voice in the last three weeks of the campaign, but he never recovered the New Democrat image that the negative ads and his insufficiently aggressive debate performances had destroyed. In November, Vice President Bush defeated him 54 to 46 percent. We didn't carry Arkansas either, though I tried. Dukakis was a good man and a fine governor. He and Lloyd Bentsen would have served our country well in the White House. But the Republicans had defined him right out of the race. I couldn't blame them for sticking with a strategy that worked, but I didn't think it was good for America.

In October, while the campaign for President was in the homestretch, I was involved in two exciting policy developments. I began a new initiative with the governors of our neighbor states, Ray Mabus of Mississippi and Buddy Roemer of Louisiana, to revive our economies. Both were young, articulate, Harvard-educated progressives. To highlight our commitment, we signed a compact on a barge in the middle of the Mississippi River at Rosedale. Not long afterward, we took a trade mission to Japan together. And we supported the successful effort of Senator Bumpers and Congressman Mike Espy of Mississippi to establish a Lower Mississippi Delta Development Commission to study and make recommendations to improve the economies of poor counties on both sides of the river, from southern Illinois to New Orleans, where the Mississippi flows into the Gulf of Mexico. The all-white counties in the northern part of the Delta region were in about as bad shape as the heavily black counties in the south. All three governors served on the Delta commission. For a year, we had hearings up and down the river in small towns time had passed by, and we came up with a report that led to the establishment of a full-time office and an ongoing effort to improve the economy and quality of life in the poorest part of America outside the Native American tribal lands.

On October 13, I was invited to the White House for President Reagan's signing of the long-awaited welfare-reform bill. It was a true bipartisan accomplishment, the work of Democratic and Republican governors; Democratic congressman Harold Ford of Tennessee and Republican congressman Carroll Campbell of South Carolina; House Ways and Means Committee chairman Dan Rostenkowski and Senate Finance Committee chairman Pat Moynihan, who knew more about the history of welfare than anyone else; and the White House staff. I was impressed by, and appreciative of, the way the Congress and the White House had worked with the governors. Harold Ford even invited Republican governor Mike Castle of Delaware and me to participate in his subcommittee's meeting to "mark up" the bill into the final version to be presented for a vote. I hoped and believed the legislation would help move more people from welfare to work, while providing more support to their children.

I was also glad to see President Reagan go out of office on a positive note. He had been badly battered by the illegal Iran-Contra affair, which the White House had approved, and which might have led to his impeachment had the Democrats been half as ruthless as Newt Gingrich. Despite my many disagreements with Reagan, I liked him personally, and I enjoyed listening to his stories when I sat at his table at the White House dinner for the governors and when a few of the governors had lunch with him after his last address to us in 1988. Reagan was something of a mystery to me, at once friendly and distant. I was never sure how much he knew about the human consequences of his harshest policies, or whether he was using the hard-core right or was being used by them; the books about him don't give a definitive answer, and because he developed Alzheimer's disease, we'll probably never know. Regardless, his own life is both more interesting and more mysterious than the movies he made.

I spent the last three months of 1988 getting ready for the next legislative session. In late October, I released a seventy-page booklet, **Moving Arkansas Forward into the 21st Century,** outlining the program I would present to the legislature in January. It reflected the work and recommendations of more than 350 citizens and public officials who had served on boards and commissions dealing with our most critical challenges. The booklet was filled with specific innovative ideas, including school health clinics to fight teen pregnancy; health coverage through schools for uninsured children; parents' and students' right to choose to attend a public school other than the one in their geographical area; expansion of the HIPPY preschool program to all seventy-five counties; a report card on every school, every year, comparing students' performance with the previous year and with other schools in the state; a provision for state takeover of failing school districts; and a big expansion of the adult literacy program, designed to make Arkansas the first state to "obliterate adult illiteracy among working-age citizens."

I was particularly excited about the literacy initiative, and the prospect of turning illiteracy from a stigma into a challenge. The previous fall, when Hillary and I went to a PTA meeting at Chelsea's school, a man had come up to me and said he'd seen me on television talking about literacy. He told me he had a good job but had never learned to read. Then he asked if I could get him into a literacy program without his employer knowing about it. I happened to know the employer and was sure he'd be proud of the man, but he was afraid, so my office got him into a reading program without his employer's knowledge. After that incident, I began to say illiteracy was nothing to be ashamed of, but doing nothing about it would be.

For all its sweep and new specifics, the program's central theme was the same one I had been hammering away on for the last six years: "Either we invest more in human capital and develop our people's capacity to cooperate or we are headed for long-term decline." Our old strategy of selling Arkansas as a beautiful state with hardworking people, low wages, and low taxes had lost its relevance a decade earlier, due to the new realities of the global economy. We had to keep working to change it.

After stumping the state for the rest of the year, I presented the program to the legislature on January 9, 1989. During the speech, I introduced Arkansans who supported it and the increased taxes necessary to pay for it: a school board president who had never voted for me but had been converted to the cause of education reform; a welfare mother who had enrolled in our work program and finished high school, started college, and gotten a job; a World War II veteran who had just learned to read; and the manager of the new $500 million Nekoosa Paper mill in Ashdown, who told the legislators he had to have a better-educated workforce because "our productivity plan requires our workers to know statistics, and a lot of them don't understand that."

I argued that we could afford to raise taxes. Our unemployment rate was still above the national average, down to 6.8 percent from 10.6 percent six years earlier. We ranked forty-sixth in per capita income, but were still forty-third in per capita state and local taxes.

At the end of my address, I noted that, a few days earlier, Representative John Paul Capps, a friend and strong supporter of my program, was quoted in the press as saying that the people "were getting sick and tired of Bill Clinton giving the same old speech." I told the legislature that I was sure many people were tired of hearing me say the same things, but that "the essence of political responsibility is being able to concentrate on what is really important for a long period of time until the problem is solved." I said I would talk about something else "when the unemployment rate is below the national average and income above the national average in our state . . . when no company passes us by because they think we can't carry the load in the new world economy . . . when no young person in this state ever has to leave home to find a good job." Until then, "we've got to do our duty."

I got some inspiration for giving the same old speech when Tina Turner came to Little Rock for a concert. After working through her new repertoire, Tina closed the show with her first top-ten hit, "Proud Mary." As soon as the band started playing it, the crowd went wild. Tina walked up to the mike, smiled, and said, "You know, I've been singing this song for twenty-five years. But it gets better every time I do it!"

I was hoping my old song was still effective, too, but there was evidence to support John Paul Capps's assertion that Arkansans, including the legislators, were growing tired of my constant urgings. The legislature passed most of my specific reform proposals, but wouldn't raise the taxes necessary to fund the more expensive initiatives in health care and education, including another large increase in teacher salaries and the expansion of early-childhood education to three- and four-year-olds. An early January poll showed that a majority of voters supported greater spending on education and that I was ahead of other prospective candidates for governor in 1990, but the poll also indicated that half the respondents wanted a new governor.

Meanwhile, some of my own first-rate people were getting tired too, and wanted to go on to other challenges, including the exuberant state chairman of the Democratic Party, Lib Carlisle, a businessman I'd talked into taking the position when it would only take, I told him, a half day a week. He later joked that I must have been referring to the time he'd have left for his own business.

Fortunately, talented new people were still willing to come serve. One of the best, and most controversial, appointments I made was Dr. Joycelyn Elders to be director of the Department of Health. I told Dr. Elders I wanted to do something about teen pregnancy, which was a huge problem in Arkansas. When she advocated the establishment of school-based health clinics that, if the local school boards approved, would provide sex education and promote both abstinence and safe sex, I supported her. There were already a couple of clinics in operation, and they seemed to be popular and successful in reducing out-of-wedlock births.

Our efforts generated a firestorm of opposition from fundamentalists, who favored a "just say no" policy. It was bad enough in their eyes that Dr. Elders was pro-choice. Now they claimed that our efforts to set up school-based clinics would lead to sexual encounters by hordes of

young people who would never even have considered
doing such a thing if Joycelyn hadn't promoted the clinics.
I doubted that Dr. Elders and her ideas even occurred to
overheated teenagers in the backseats of their cars. It was a
fight worth making.

When I became President, I appointed Joycelyn
Elders surgeon general, and she was very popular with
the public-health community for her continued willingness to stick her neck out for sound, if controversial,
health policies. In December 1994, after we had suffered
staggering losses in the midterm congressional elections
to the Republican right, Dr. Elders made headlines again
for suggesting that teaching children to masturbate
might be a good way to reduce the likelihood of teen
pregnancy. At the time, I had all I could handle to maintain the support of skittish congressional Democrats,
and I was determined to fight the Republicans on their
radical proposals to cut education, health care, and environmental protection. Now I faced the prospect that
Gingrich and company could divert the attention of the
press and the public away from their budget cuts by pil-
lorying us. At any other time, we probably could have
faced the heat, but I had already loaded the Democrats
down with my controversial budget, NAFTA, the failed
health-care effort, and the Brady bill and the assault
weapons ban, which the National Rifle Association had
used to beat about a dozen of our House members. I
decided I had to ask for her resignation. I hated to,
because she was honest, able, and brave, but we had
already shown enough political tone-deafness to last
through several presidential terms. I hope someday she'll
forgive me. She did a lot of good with the two appointments I gave her.

The biggest staff loss I sustained in 1989 was Betsey Wright. In early August she announced that she was taking a leave of absence for several weeks. I asked Jim Pledger to do double duty at Finance and Administration and as her temporary replacement. Betsey's announcement caused a lot of gossip and speculation, because everyone knew she ran a tight ship in the governor's office and kept a close eye on everything that was going on in state government. John Brummett, the acerbic columnist for the **Arkansas Gazette,** wrote a column wondering whether our trial separation might end in divorce. He thought not, because we were too important to each other. That we were, but Betsey needed to get away. She had been working herself to death since my defeat in 1980, and it was taking its toll. We were both workaholics who got more irritable when we were exhausted. In 1989, we were trying to do a lot in a difficult climate, and we too often took our frustrations out on each other. At the end of the year, Betsey formally resigned as chief of staff after a decade of selfless service. In early 1990, I named Henry Oliver, a retired FBI agent and former chief of police in Fort Smith, as Betsey's successor. Henry didn't really want to do it, but he was my friend and believed in what we were trying to do, so he gave me a good year.

Betsey came back in the '92 campaign to help defend me against attacks on my record and my personal life. Then, after a stint in Washington with Anne Wexler's lobbying firm early in my presidency, she went home to Arkansas to live in the Ozarks. Most Arkansans will never know the large role she played in giving them better schools, more jobs, and an honest, effective state government, but they should. I couldn't have accomplished much of what I did as governor without her. And without her, I never would have survived the Arkansas political wars to become President.

At the beginning of August, President Bush announced that he was inviting the nation's governors to an education summit the following month. We met September 27 and 28 at the University of Virginia in Charlottesville. Many of the Democrats were skeptical of the meeting, because the President and his secretary of education, Lauro Cavazos, made it clear the meeting was not a prelude to a large increase in federal support for education. I shared their concern, but was I excited by the prospect that the summit could produce a road map for the next steps in education reform, just as the **Nation at Risk** report had done in 1983. I believed the President's interest in education reform was genuine, and agreed with him that there were important things we could do without new federal money. For example, the administration supported giving parents and students the right to choose a public school other than the one to which they were assigned. Arkansas had just become the second state after Minnesota to adopt the proposal, and I wanted the other forty-eight states to follow suit. I also believed that, if the summit produced the right kind of report, governors could use it to build public support for more investment in education. If people knew what they would get for their money, their aversion to new taxes might lessen. As the co-chairman of the Governors' Task Force on Education, along with Governor Carroll Campbell of South Carolina, I wanted to build a consensus among the Democrats, then to work with the Republicans on a statement reflecting the outcome of the summit.

President Bush opened the meeting with a brief but

eloquent speech. Afterward, we all took a stroll around the central lawn to give the photographers something for the evening news and morning papers, then went to work. The President and Mrs. Bush hosted a dinner that night. Hillary sat at the President's table and got into a debate with him about how bad America's infant-mortality rate was. The President couldn't believe it when she said eighteen countries did a better job than we did in keeping babies alive until the age of two. When she offered to get him the evidence, he said he would find it himself. He did, and the next day he gave me a note for Hillary saying she was right. It was a gracious gesture that reminded me of the day in Kennebunkport six years earlier when he had personally escorted three-year-old Chelsea to the bathroom.

When Carroll Campbell was called home to deal with an emergency, I was left to work out the details of a summit statement with the NGA chairman, Republican governor Terry Branstad of Iowa; the association's education staffer, Mike Cohen; and my aide, Representative Gloria Cabe. Laboring until well after midnight, several of us hammered out a statement committing the governors and the White House to development of a set of specific education goals to be achieved by the year 2000. Unlike the standards movement of the last decade, these goals would be focused on outputs, not inputs, obligating all of us to achieve certain results. I argued that we would look foolish unless we came out of Charlottesville with a bold commitment that would put new energy into education reform.

From the start, most of the governors were behind the cause and supported the idea of making the summit the start of something big. Some of the President's people weren't so sure. They were afraid of committing him to a big idea that could get him into trouble by raising expectations of new federal funding. Because of the deficit and the President's "no new taxes" pledge, that wasn't in the cards. In the end, the White House came around, thanks to John Sununu, who was then the White House chief of staff. Sununu convinced his White House colleagues that the governors couldn't go home empty-handed, and I promised to minimize public pressure from the governors for more federal money. The final summit declaration said, "The time has come, for the first time in U.S. history, to establish clear national performance goals, goals that will make us internationally competitive."

At the end of the summit, President Bush hand-wrote me a very cordial note, thanking me for working with his staff on the summit and saying he wanted to keep education reform "out there above the fray" as we headed into the 1990 midterm election. I wanted that, too. The governors' education committee immediately began a process to develop the goals, working with the White House domestic-policy advisor, Roger Porter, who had gone to Oxford as a Rhodes scholar a year after I did. We worked furiously over the next four months to reach agreement with the White House in time for the President's State of the Union address.

By the end of January 1990, we had agreed on six goals for the year 2000:

- By the year 2000, all children in America will start school ready to learn.
- By the year 2000, the high school graduation rate will increase to at least 90 percent.
- By the year 2000, American students will leave grades four, eight, and twelve having demonstrated competency in challenging subject matter including English,

mathematics, science, history, and geography; and every school in America will ensure that all students learn to use their minds well, so they may be prepared for responsible citizenship, further learning, and productive employment in our modern economy.

- By the year 2000, U.S. students will be first in the world in science and mathematics achievement.
- By the year 2000, every adult in America will be literate and will possess the knowledge and skills necessary to compete in a global economy and exercise the rights and responsibilities of citizenship.
- By the year 2000, every school in America will be free of drugs and violence and will offer a disciplined environment conducive to learning.

On January 31, I sat in the gallery of the House of Representatives as President Bush announced these goals, said they were developed jointly by the White House and the Governors' Task Force on Education, and reported that they would be part of a more comprehensive goals-and-objectives statement that we would present to all the governors at their winter meeting the next month.

The document the governors adopted in late February was a worthy successor to the 1983 **Nation at Risk** report. I was proud to have been a part of it, impressed by the knowledge and commitment of my fellow governors, and grateful to the President, John Sununu, and Roger Porter. For the next eleven years, as governor and President, I worked hard to reach the national education goals. We had set the bar high. When you set a high bar and reach for it, even if you fall short, you wind up well ahead of where you started.

. . .

I spent the last months of 1989 trying to decide what to do with the rest of my life. There were good arguments against running for a fifth term. I was discouraged by my inability to raise the funds necessary to keep moving forward in education, early-childhood development, and health care. I could stop after ten years, look back on a decade of real accomplishments under difficult circumstances, and leave open the option of running for President in 1992. Finally, if I ran again, I might not win. I had already served longer than anyone but Orval Faubus. And the polls indicated that a lot of people wanted a new governor.

On the other hand, I loved both politics and policy. And I didn't want to leave office with the bad taste of 1989's money failures in my mouth. I still had an able, energetic, and extremely honest team. The whole time I was governor, only twice had I been offered money to make a decision a particular way. A company that wanted to win the bid to provide medical services in the prison system offered me a substantial amount through a third party. I had the company taken off the bid list. A county judge asked me to see an elderly man who wanted a pardon for his nephew. The old fellow had had no contact with state government in decades and obviously thought he was doing what he had to do when he offered me $10,000 for the pardon. I told the man it was lucky for him I was hard of hearing, because he might have just committed a crime. I suggested that he go home and give the money to his church or a charity, and said I'd look into his nephew's case.

On most days, I still looked forward to going to work, and I had no idea what I'd do if I gave it up. At the end of October, I went out to the state fair, as I did every year.

That year, I sat at a booth for several hours and talked to anyone who wanted to see me. Along toward the end of the day, a man in overalls who looked to be about sixty-five dropped by to visit. It was an enlightening experience. "Bill, are you gonna run again?" he asked. "I don't know," I replied. "If I do, will you vote for me?" "I guess so. I always have," he answered. "Aren't you sick of me after all these years?" I inquired. He smiled and said, "No, I'm not, but everybody else I know is." I chuckled and answered, "Don't they think I've done a good job?" He shot back, "Sure they do, but you got a paycheck every two weeks, didn't you?" It was a classic example of another of Clinton's laws of politics: All elections are about the future. I was supposed to do a good job, just like everyone else who worked for a living. A good record is helpful mostly as evidence that you'll do what you say if reelected.

In November, the Berlin Wall, symbol of the Cold War divide, fell. Like all Americans, I cheered at the sight of young Germans tearing it down and taking chunks of it for souvenirs. Our long standoff against Communist expansion in Europe was ending with the victory of freedom, thanks to the united front presented by NATO and the constancy of American leaders from Harry Truman to George Bush. I thought back to my own trip to Moscow almost twenty years earlier, the eagerness of young Russians for information and music from the West, and the hunger for freedom that it represented. Not long afterward, I received two pieces of the Berlin Wall from my longtime friend David Ifshin, who had been in Berlin on that fateful night of November 9 and joined in with the Germans in chipping away at the wall. David had been an intense and visible opponent of the Vietnam War. His joy at the fall of the wall symbolized the promise that all Americans saw in the post–Cold War era.

In December, my old pastor and mentor, W. O. Vaught, lost his battle with cancer. He had retired from Immanuel a few years earlier and was replaced by Dr. Brian Harbour, a fine young pastor who represented the dwindling ranks of progressive Southern Baptists with whom I identified. Dr. Vaught had remained active in retirement until his illness made him too weak to travel and speak. A couple of years earlier, he had come to visit me in the Governor's Mansion. He said he wanted to tell me three things. First, he said he knew I was concerned about the morality of capital punishment, though I had always supported it. He told me that the biblical commandment "Thou shall not kill" did not forbid lawful executions, because the root Greek word did not cover all killing. He said the literal meaning of the commandment was "Thou shall not commit murder." Second, he said he was concerned about fundamentalist attacks on me for my pro-choice position on abortion. He wanted me to know that, while he believed abortion was usually wrong, the Bible did not condemn it, nor did it say life begins at conception, but when life has been "breathed into" a baby, when it is slapped on the behind after being taken out of the mother's body. I asked him about the biblical statement that God knows us even when we are in our mother's womb. He replied that the verse simply refers to God being omniscient, and that it might as well have said God knew us even before we were in our mother's womb, even before anyone in our direct line was born.

The final thing Dr. Vaught said took me aback. He said, "Bill, I think you're going to be President someday. I think you'll do a good job, but there's one thing above all you must remember: God will never forgive you if you don't stand by Israel." He believed God intended the Jews to be at home in the Holy Land. While he didn't disagree that the Palestinians had been mistreated, he said the answer to their problem had to include peace and security for Israel.

In mid-December, I went to see Dr. Vaught. He was wasting away, too weak to leave his bedroom. He asked me to move his Christmas tree into his bedroom so that he could enjoy it in his last days. Fittingly, Dr. Vaught died on Christmas Day. Jesus never had a more faithful follower. And I never had a more faithful pastor and counselor. Now I would have to navigate the path he had predicted, and the perils of my own soul, without him.

TWENTY-FIVE

While I was trying to decide whether to run again, the governor's race was shaping up to be a real donnybrook, whether I ran or not. Years of pent-up ambitions were being unleashed. On the Democratic side, Jim Guy Tucker, Attorney General Steve Clark, and Rockefeller Foundation president Tom McRae, whose grandfather had been governor, all announced they would run. They were all friends of mine, and had good ideas and progressive records. On the Republican side, the contest was even more interesting. It involved two formidable former Democrats: Congressman Tommy Robinson, who didn't like Washington, and Sheffield Nelson, former president of Arkansas-Louisiana Gas Company, who said he had switched parties because the Democratic Party had moved too far to the left. It was the standard explanation white southerners gave, but more interesting coming from him because he had supported Senator Ted Kennedy against President Carter in 1980.

Robinson and Nelson, and their backers, all onetime friends, went after one another with a vengeance, in a race full of name-calling and mudslinging, which included Robinson's charge that Nelson and Jerry Jones, a long-time friend of both men who owned some of the gas fields that supplied Arkla, were rapacious businessmen who soaked Arkla's ratepayers for personal gain, and Nelson's charge that Robinson was unstable and unfit to be governor. About all they agreed on was that I had raised taxes too much and had too little to show for it in terms of educational improvement and economic development.

On the Democratic side, Steve Clark withdrew from the race, leaving Jim Guy Tucker and Tom McRae, who took a different approach, more clever than that of the Republicans, to discourage me from running. They said I'd done a lot of good, but I was out of new ideas and out of time. Ten years as governor was long enough. I couldn't get anything done in the legislature anymore, and four more years would give me too much control over all aspects of state government. McRae had met with "focus groups" of representative voters who said they wanted to continue the direction I'd set in economic development, but were open to new ideas from a new leader. I thought there was something to their argument, but I didn't believe they could get more out of our conservative anti-tax legislators than I could.

Finally, still uncertain of what to do, I set a March 1 deadline to announce my decision. Hillary and I hashed it over dozens of times. There was some press speculation that she would run if I didn't. When asked about it, I said she'd be a great governor but I didn't know if she would run. When I discussed it with her, Hillary said she'd cross that bridge if I decided not to run, but what she might do should be no part of my decision. She knew, before I did, that I wasn't ready to hang it up.

In the end I couldn't bear the thought of walking away from a decade of hard work, with my last year marked by repeated failures to fund further improvements in education. I never was one for quitting, and whenever I was tempted, something always happened to give me heart. In the mid-eighties, when our economy was in the tank, I was about to land a new industry for a county where one in four people was unemployed. At the last minute, Nebraska offered the company an extra million dollars and I lost the deal. I was crushed and felt I had failed the whole county. When Lynda Dixon, my secretary, saw me slumped in my chair with my head in my hands, she tore off the daily scripture reading from the devotional calendar she kept on her desk. The verse was Galatians 6:9: "Let us not grow weary while doing good, for in due season we shall reap if we do not lose heart." I went back to work.

On February 11, I witnessed the ultimate testimonial to the power of perseverance. Early that Sunday morning, Hillary and I got Chelsea up and took her down to the kitchen of the Governor's Mansion to see what we told her would be one of the most important events she'd ever witness. Then we turned on the television and watched Nelson Mandela take the last steps in his long walk to freedom. Through twenty-seven years of imprisonment and abuse, Mandela had endured, and triumphed, to end apartheid, liberate his own mind and heart from hatred, and inspire the world.

At the March 1 press conference, I said I would run for a fifth term, "although the fire of an election no longer burns in me," because I wanted another chance to finish the job of improving education and modernizing the economy, and because I thought I could do a better job of it than the other candidates. I also promised to keep bringing new people into state government and to bend over backward to avoid abuse of power.

Looking back on it, I can see how the statement looked ambivalent and a touch arrogant, but it was an honest expression of how I felt, as I began the first campaign since 1982 that I could have lost. I got a break soon afterward, when Jim Guy Tucker decided to withdraw from the race and run for lieutenant governor instead, saying a divisive primary would only increase the chances of a Republican victory in the fall, no matter who won. Jim Guy had made a judgment that he could win the lieutenant governor's race easily, then become governor in four years. He was almost certainly right, and I was relieved.

Still, I couldn't take the primary for granted. McRae was waging a vigorous campaign and had a lot of friends and admirers around the state from his years of good work at the Rockefeller Foundation. When he made his formal announcement, he had a broom in his hand and said he wanted to make a clean sweep of state government, clearing out old ideas and career politicians. The broom tactic had worked for my neighbor David Boren when he ran for governor of Oklahoma in 1974. I was determined that it wouldn't work this time. Gloria Cabe agreed to manage the campaign, and she put together an effective organization. Maurice Smith raised the money. And I followed a simple strategy: to outwork my opponents, do my job, and continue to preach new ideas, including college scholarships for all high school students with a B average or better; and a "plant the future" initiative to plant ten million more trees a year for a decade to do our part to reduce greenhouse gases and global warming.

McRae was forced to become more critical of me, which I think made him somewhat uncomfortable, but which had some impact. All the candidates hit me for my involvement in national politics. In late March, I went to New Orleans to accept the chairmanship of the Democratic Leadership Council. I was convinced the group's ideas on welfare reform, criminal justice, education, and economic growth were crucial to the future of the Democra-

tic Party and the nation. The DLC's positions were popular in Arkansas, but my high profile was a potential liability in the race, so I got back home as soon as I could.

In April, the AFL-CIO refused for the first time to
endorse me. Bill Becker, their president, had never really
liked me. He thought the sales-tax increase was unfair to
working people, opposed the tax incentives I'd supported
to lure new jobs to Arkansas, and blamed me for the failure of the tax-reform referendum in 1988. He was also
furious that I had supported a $300,000 loan guarantee to
a business involved in a labor dispute. I spoke to the labor
convention, defending the tax increase for education and
expressing amazement that Becker would blame me for
the failure of tax reform, which I had supported but the
people voted against. I also stood by the loan guarantee
because it saved 410 jobs: the company sold its products
to Ford Motor Company, and the loan enabled it to build
a two-month inventory, without which Ford would have
canceled the firm's contract and put it out of business.
Within two weeks, eighteen local unions defied Becker
and endorsed me anyway. They didn't fall into the classic
liberal trap of making the perfect the enemy of the good.
If the people who voted for Ralph Nader in 2000 hadn't
made the same mistake, Al Gore would have been elected
President.

The only dramatic moment of the primary came when
I was out of state again. While I was in Washington presenting the report of the Delta Development Commission
to Congress, McRae called a press conference at the state
Capitol to criticize my record. He thought he would have
the Arkansas press all to himself. Hillary thought otherwise. When I called her the night before, she said she
thought she might show up at the conference. McRae had

a cardboard likeness of me by his side. He attacked me for being absent from the state, implied that I had refused to debate him, and began to criticize my record by posing questions for me and supplying the answers himself.

In the middle of McRae's routine, Hillary stepped out of the crowd and interrupted him. She said Tom knew I was in Washington promoting the Delta commission's recommendations, which would help Arkansas. She then produced a prepared summary of several years of Rockefeller Foundation reports praising my work as governor. She said that he had been right in the reports, and that Arkansas should be proud: "We've made more progress than any other state except South Carolina, and we're right up there with them."

It was unheard of for a candidate's wife, much less the first lady, to confront an opponent like that. Some people criticized Hillary for it, but most people knew she had earned the right to defend the work we had done together for years, and it broke McRae's momentum. When I got home, I lit into him for his attacks and went after his economic development strategy, saying he wanted to build a wall around Arkansas. I won the election with 55 percent of the vote over McRae and several other challengers, but Tom had run a smart campaign on a shoestring budget, and had done well enough to encourage the Republicans about their prospects in the fall.

Sheffield Nelson beat Tommy Robinson in the Republican primary and promised to run against me on my "tax and spend" record. The strategy was flawed. Nelson should have run as a moderate Republican, praised my work in education and economic development, and said ten years was long enough—I should be given a gold watch and a respectable retirement. By switching from his original position in support of the school standards and the sales-tax increase to pay for them, Nelson allowed me to escape the straitjacket of tired incumbency and run as the only candidate of positive change.

The fact that Nelson was running against the education program and taxes had the added benefit that, if I won, I could argue to the legislators that the people had voted for more progress. As we moved toward election day, the AFL-CIO finally endorsed me. The Arkansas Education Association "recommended" me because of my commitment to raising teacher salaries, Nelson's promise not to raise taxes for four years, and AEA president Sid Johnson's desire to bury the hatchet and get on with business.

Nelson, meanwhile, moved farther to the right, advocating a reduction in welfare benefits for illegitimate children and hitting me for vetoing a bill the National Rifle Association had pushed through the legislature. The bill would have prohibited local governments from enacting any restrictions on firearms or ammunition. It was a smart move by the NRA, because state legislators were invariably more rural and pro-gun than city councils, but I thought the bill was bad policy. If the Little Rock City Council wanted to ban cop-killer bullets in the face of increasing gang activity, I thought they should have the right to do so.

The work of the governor's office didn't stop for the campaign. In June, I approved the first executions in Arkansas since 1964. John Swindler was convicted of murdering an Arkansas policeman and two South Carolina teenagers. Ronald Gene Simmons killed his wife, three sons, four daughters, a son-in-law, a daughter-in-law, four grandchildren, and two people he had grudges against. Simmons wanted to die. Swindler didn't. They were both executed in June. I didn't have qualms about either of them, but I knew there were tougher cases awaiting us.

I had also begun to commute the sentences of a few murderers with life sentences, so that they could be eligible for parole. As I explained to the voters, I had not commuted a sentence for years, after the bad experience during my first term, but both the Prison Board and the Paroles and Pardons Board pleaded with me to resume commuting some lifers. Most states made lifers eligible for parole after serving several years. In Arkansas the governor had to commute their sentences. The decisions weren't easy or popular, but were necessary to keep peace and order in a prison system where 10 percent of the inmates were serving life terms. It's fortunate that many lifers are unlikely to repeat their crimes and can return to society without risk to others. This time, we made extensive efforts to contact the victims' families for comments. Surprisingly, many did not object. Also, most of those whose sentences were commuted were old or had committed their crimes when they were very young.

In mid-September, a disgruntled former employee of the Development Finance Authority first raised the "sex question" against me. Larry Nichols had made more than 120 phone calls from his office to conservative supporters of the Nicaraguan Contras, a cause the national Republicans strongly supported. Nichols's defense was that he was calling the Contra supporters to get them to lobby congressional Republicans to support legislation beneficial to his agency. His excuse didn't fly, and he was fired when the calls were discovered. Nichols called a press conference on the steps of the Capitol and accused me of using the finance agency's funds to carry on affairs with five women.

I drove into my parking place in front of the Capitol not long after Nichols had made his charges and was hit cold with the story by Bill Simmons of the Associated Press, the senior member of the political press and a good reporter. When Simmons asked me about the charges, I just suggested he call the women. He did, they all denied it, and the story basically died. None of the television stations or newspapers ran it. Only one conservative radio announcer who supported Nelson talked about it, actually naming one of the women, Gennifer Flowers. She threatened to sue him if he didn't stop. The Nelson campaign tried to stoke the rumors, but without corroboration or evidence.

At the end of the campaign, Nelson put on a television ad that was misleading but effective. The announcer raised a series of issues and asked what I would do about them. To each question, my own voice answered, "Raise and spend." Nelson's campaign had lifted those three words from a section in my State of the State address, in which I compared Arkansas' budget with that of the federal government. While Washington could engage in deficit spending, if we didn't have money, we had to "raise and spend, or not spend at all." I put out a response ad comparing Nelson's claim to what I had really said and told the voters that if they couldn't trust Nelson not to mislead them in the campaign, they couldn't trust him to be governor. A couple of days later, I was reelected, 57 to 43 percent.

The victory was sweet in many ways. The people had decided to let me serve fourteen years, longer than any other Arkansas governor in history. And for the first time, I had carried Sebastian County, which was then still the most hard-core Republican big county in the state. In a campaign appearance in Fort Smith, I had promised that if I did win there, Hillary and I would dance down Garrison Avenue, the town's main street. A couple of nights after the election, along with a few hundred supporters, we kept our commitment. It was cold and raining, but we danced away and enjoyed every minute of it. We had waited sixteen years for a general-election win there.

The only really dark moment of the general election was purely personal. In August, Mother's doctor discovered a lump in her right breast. Forty-eight hours later, while Dick, Roger, and I waited in the hospital, Mother had the lump removed. After the procedure, she was her usual chipper self and was back at work on the campaign in no time, though she faced months of chemotherapy. The cancer had aleady spread to twenty-seven nodes in her arm, but she didn't tell anyone this—including me. In fact, she never told us how bad it was until 1993.

In December, I resumed my work for the Democratic Leadership Council, launching the Texas DLC chapter in Austin. In my speech, I argued that, contrary to our liberal critics, we were good Democrats. We believed in keeping the American dream alive for all people. We believed in government, though not in the status quo. And we believed government was spending too much on yesterday and today—interest on debt, defense, more money for the same health care—and too little on tomorrow: education, the environment, research and development, the infrastructure. I said the DLC stood for a modern, mainstream agenda: the expansion of opportunity, not bureaucracy; choice in public schools and child care; responsibility and empowerment for poor people; and reinventing government, away from the top-down bureaucracy of the industrial era, to a leaner, more flexible, more innovative model appropriate for the modern global economy.

I was trying to develop a national message for the Democrats, and the effort fueled speculation that I might enter the presidential race in 1992. During the recent campaign, I had said on more than one occasion that I would serve out my term if elected. That's what I thought I would do. I was excited about the coming legislative session. Though I strongly disagreed with many of his decisions, like killing the Brady bill and vetoing the Family and Medical Leave Act, I liked President Bush and had a good relationship with the White House. Also, a campaign to defeat him looked hopeless. Saddam Hussein had invaded Kuwait, and the United States was beginning its buildup for the Gulf War, which in two months would drive the President's approval ratings into the stratosphere.

On the morning of January 15, 1991, with ten-year-old Chelsea holding the Bible for me, I took the oath of office in Little Rock for the last time. Following the custom, I delivered my informal address in the crowded chamber of the House of Representatives, then, at noon, made a more formal address at the public ceremony, which was held in the Capitol rotunda because of inclement weather. The new legislature had more women and blacks than ever. The Speaker of the House, John Lipton, and the president pro tempore of the Senate, Jerry Bookout, were progressives and strong supporters of mine. Jim Guy Tucker was lieutenant governor, probably the ablest person ever to hold the job, and we were working together, rather than at cross-purposes, for the first time in years.

I dedicated my inaugural address to the men and women from Arkansas serving in the Persian Gulf, and noted that it was appropriate that we were making a new beginning on Martin Luther King Jr.'s birthday, because "we must go forward into the future together or we will all be limited in what we achieve." Then I outlined the most ambitious program I had ever proposed, in education, health care, highways, and the environment.

In education, I proposed a big increase in adult literacy and training programs; apprenticeships for non-college-bound youths; college scholarships for all middle-class and low-income kids who took the required courses, made a B average, and stayed off drugs; preschool programs for poor kids; a new residential high school for math and science students; conversion of fourteen vo-tech schools into two-year colleges; and a $4,000 raise for teachers over two years. I asked the legislature to raise the sales tax half a cent and the corporate income tax half a percent to pay for them.

There were also several reform measures in my package, including health insurance for pregnant women and for children; the removal of more than 250,000 taxpayers, more than 25 percent of the total, from the state income tax rolls; and an income tax credit to offset the sales-tax increase for up to 75 percent of the taxpayers.

And for the next sixty-eight days, I worked to pass the program, bringing legislators to my office; going to their committee hearings to argue personally for bills; cornering them in the halls, at nighttime events, or early in the morning at the Capitol cafeteria; hanging around with them outside the chambers or in the cloakrooms; calling them late at night; and bringing opposing legislators and their allied lobbyists together to hammer out compromises. By the end of the session, virtually my entire program had passed. The tax proposals received between 76 and 100 percent of the vote in both houses, including the votes of a majority of Republican lawmakers.

Ernest Dumas, one of the state's most distinguished and astute columnists, said, "For education, it was one of the best legislative sessions in the state's history, arguably the best." Dumas noted that we also passed the largest highway program ever; greatly expanded health care for poor families; improved the environment by passing proposals for solid-waste recycling and reduction and for "weakening the hand of polluting industries at the state's pollution control agency"; and "spurned a few religious zealots" by providing school health clinics in poor communities.

The legislature had its biggest fight over the school health clinics. I favored allowing the clinics to distribute condoms if the local school board approved. So did the Senate. The more conservative House was devoutly anti-condom. Finally the legislature adopted a compromise offered by Representative Mark Pryor, who in 2002 became Arkansas' junior U.S. senator: no state money could be used to buy condoms, but if bought with other funds, they could be distributed. Bob Lancaster, a witty columnist for the **Arkansas Gazette,** wrote a hilarious article chronicling the struggle of the "condom Congress." He called it, with apologies to Homer, the "Trojans War."

The legislature also passed the National Rifle Association's bill to prohibit cities and counties from adopting local gun-control ordinances, the same measure I had vetoed in 1989. No southern legislature could say no to the NRA. Even in the more liberal Senate, this bill passed 26–7. At least I got the Senate to pass it late, so I could veto it after they went home and they couldn't override it. After the bill was sent to me, I had an extraordinary encounter with the young NRA lobbyist who came down from Washington to push the bill. He was very tall and well dressed and spoke with a clipped New England accent. One day he stopped me as I was crossing the rotunda from the House to the Senate side of the Capitol. "Governuh, Governuh, why don't you just let this bill become law without your signature?" I explained for the umpteenth time why I didn't support the bill. Then he burst out, "Look, Governuh, you're going to run for President next year, and when you do, we're going to beat your brains out in Texas if you veto this bill." I knew I was getting older and more seasoned when I didn't slug him. Instead, I smiled and said, "You don't get it. I don't like this bill. You know gun control will never be a problem in Arkansas. You've just got a chart on the wall in your fancy office in Washington with this bill at the top and all the states listed below. You don't give a damn about the merits of this bill. You just want to put a check by Arkansas on that chart. So you get your gun and I'll get mine. We'll saddle up and meet in Texas." As soon as the legislature went home, I vetoed the bill. Soon afterward, the NRA began running television ads attacking me. It wasn't until I began writing this account that I realized that in my confrontation with the NRA lobbyist, I had acknowledged that I was considering running for President. At the time, I didn't think there was a chance I'd do it. I just didn't like to be threatened.

After the session, Henry Oliver told me he wanted to leave. I hated to lose him, but after decades of proud service in the marines, the FBI, and local and state government, he had earned the right to go home. For the time being, Gloria Cabe and Carol Rasco took over his responsibilities.

I spent the next few months making sure our massive legislative program was well implemented and traveling the country for the Democratic Leadership Council. Because I was out there making the case for how we could regain "mainstream, middle-class" voters who "have left the party in droves for twenty years," the press continued to speculate that I might run in 1992. In an interview in April, I joked about it, saying, "As long as nobody runs, everybody can be on the list, and it's kind of nice. It makes my mother happy to read my name in the paper."

While I still didn't believe I could or should run, and President Bush's approval ratings were still above 70 percent in the afterglow of the Gulf War, I was beginning to think a DLC Democrat who could relate both to the party's traditional base and to swing voters might have a chance, because the country had serious problems that weren't being addressed in Washington. The President and his team seemed determined to coast to victory on the wings of the Gulf War. I had seen enough in Arkansas and in my travels around the country to know America couldn't coast through four more years. As 1991 unfolded, more and more people came to share that view.

In April, I went to Los Angeles to speak to a luncheon for Education First, a citizens' group dedicated to improving public education. After Sidney Poitier introduced me, I recounted three recent experiences with education in California that reflected both promise and peril for America's future. The promise I had seen more than a year earlier when I spoke at California State University in Los Angeles to students with roots in 122 other nations. Their diversity was a good omen for our ability to compete with and relate to the rest of the global community. The perils were evident when Hillary and I visited with sixth-graders in East Los Angeles. They were great kids who had big dreams and a deep desire for normal lives. They told us their number one fear was of being shot going to and from school. They also said they did practice drills crouching under their desks in the event of a drive-by shooting. The children's number two fear was that, when they turned thirteen, they would have to join a gang and smoke crack cocaine or face severe beatings from their contemporaries. My experience with those kids had a profound impact on me. They deserved better.

On another California trip, this time to discuss education with the Business Roundtable, a telephone company executive told me that 70 percent of his job applicants flunked the company's entrance examination, even though virtually all of them were high school graduates. I asked the audience if the United States, fresh from victory in the Gulf War, could hope to lead the post–Cold War world if childhood was dangerous and our schools were inadequate.

Of course, it was one thing to say the country had problems and quite another to say what the federal government should do about them, and to say it in a way that could be heard by citizens conditioned by the Reagan-Bush years to believe the federal government was the source of our problems, not the solution. Making that case was the mission of the Democratic Leadership Council.

In early May, I went to Cleveland to preside over the DLC convention. A year earlier, in New Orleans, we had issued a statement of principles intended to move beyond the tired partisan debate in Washington by creating a dynamic but centrist progressive movement of new ideas rooted in traditional American values. While the DLC had been criticized for being too conservative by some of our party's leading liberals, like Governor Mario Cuomo and the Reverend Jesse Jackson (who said DLC stood for

"Democratic Leisure Class"), the convention attracted an impressive array of creative thinkers, innovative state and local officials, and businesspeople concerned about our economic and social problems. Many prominent national Democrats, including several prospective presidential candidates, were also there. Among the speakers were Senators Sam Nunn, John Glenn, Chuck Robb, Joe Lieberman, John Breaux, Jay Rockefeller, and Al Gore. Besides me, the governors there were Lawton Chiles of Florida and Jerry Baliles of Virginia. The House members there mostly represented conservative constituencies, like Dave McCurdy of Oklahoma, or had an interest in national security and foreign policy, like Steve Solarz of New York. Former senator Paul Tsongas and former governor Doug Wilder of Virginia, both of whom would soon be running for President, were there. A number of talented black leaders participated, including Governor Wilder; Mayor Mike White of Cleveland; Vince Lane, the creative chairman of the Chicago Housing Authority; Congressman Bill Gray of Pennsylvania; and Congressman Mike Espy of Mississippi.

I opened the convention with a keynote address designed to make the case that America needed to change course and that the DLC could and should lead the way. I began with a litany of America's problems and challenges and a rebuke of the years of Republican neglect, then noted that the Democrats had not been able to win elections, despite Republican failures, "because too many of the people that used to vote for us, the very burdened middle class we are talking about, have not trusted us in national elections to defend our national interests abroad, to put their values into our social policy at home, or to take their tax money and spend it with discipline."

I applauded the leadership of the Democratic Party under Ron Brown, our first black chairman, whom I had supported. Brown had made a real effort to broaden the party's base, but we needed a message with specific proposals to offer the American people:

> The Republican burden is their record of denial, evasion, and neglect. But our burden is to give the people a new choice, rooted in old values, a new choice that is simple, that offers opportunity, demands responsibility, gives citizens more say, provides them responsive government—all because we recognize that we are a community. We are all in this together, and we are going up or down together.

The opportunity agenda meant economic growth through free and fair trade, as well as more investment in new technologies and in world-class education and skills. The responsibility agenda required something of all citizens: national service for young people in return for college aid; welfare reforms that required able-bodied parents to work but provided more support for their children; tougher child-support enforcement; more efforts by parents to keep their kids in school; a "reinvented" government, with less bureaucracy and more choices in child care, public schools, job training, elderly care, neighborhood policing, and the management of public housing. The community agenda required us to invest more in our millions of poor children, and to reach across the racial divide, to build a politics based on lifting up all Americans, not dividing them against one another.

I tried hard to break through all the either/or debates that dominated national public discourse. In the conventional Washington wisdom, you had to be for excellence or equity in education; for quality or universal access in health care; for a cleaner environment or more economic growth; for work or child-rearing in welfare policy; for labor or business in the workplace; for crime prevention or punishing criminals; for family values or more spending for poor families. In his remarkable book **Why Americans Hate Politics,** the journalist E. J. Dionne labels these as "false choices," saying in each instance that Americans thought we should not choose "either/or" but "both." I agreed, and tried to illustrate my beliefs with lines like "Family values will not feed a hungry child, but you cannot raise that hungry child very well without them. We need both."

I wound up the speech by citing the lesson I had learned in Professor Carroll Quigley's Western Civilization class more than twenty-five years earlier, that the future can be better than the past, and that each of us has a personal, moral responsibility to make it so: "That is what the new choice is all about, that is what we are here in Cleveland to do. We are not here to save the Democratic Party. We are here to save the United States of America."

That speech was one of the most effective and important I ever made. It captured the essence of what I had learned in seventeen years in politics and what millions of Americans were thinking. It became the blueprint for my campaign message, helping to change the public focus from President Bush's victory in the Gulf War to what we had to do to build a better future. By embracing ideas and values that were both liberal and conservative, it made voters who had not supported Democratic presidential candidates in years listen to our message. And by the rousing reception it received, the speech established me as perhaps the leading spokesman for the course I passionately believed America should embrace. Several people at the convention urged me to run for President, and I left Cleveland convinced that I had a good chance to capture the Democratic nomination if I did run, and that I had to consider entering the race.

In June, my friend Vernon Jordan asked me to go with him to Baden-Baden, Germany, to the annual Bilderberg Conference, which brings together prominent business and political leaders from the United States and Europe to discuss current issues and the state of our transatlantic relationship. I always enjoyed being with Vernon and was stimulated by my conversations with the Europeans, including Gordon Brown, a brilliant Scottish Labour Party member who would become chancellor of the exchequer when Tony Blair was elected prime minister. I found the Europeans generally supportive of President Bush's foreign policies but very concerned by the continued drift and weakness of our economy, which hurt them as well as us.

At Bilderberg, I ran into Esther Coopersmith, a Democratic activist who had served as part of our UN delegation during the Carter years. Esther was on her way to Moscow with her daughter Connie, and she invited me to join them to observe firsthand the changes that were unfolding in the last days of the Soviet Union. Boris Yeltsin was about to be elected president of the Russian Republic with an even more explicit repudiation of Soviet economics and politics than Gorbachev had espoused. It was a brief but interesting trip.

When I got back to Arkansas, I was convinced that a lot of America's challenges in foreign relations would involve economic and political issues that I understood and could handle if I were to run and actually become the President. Still, as July dawned, I was genuinely torn about what to do. I had told Arkansans in the 1990 election that I would finish my term. The success of the 1991 legislative session had given me a new burst of enthusiasm for my job. Our family life was great. Chelsea was happy in a new school, with good teachers, good friends, and her passion for ballet. Hillary was doing well in her law practice and enjoyed great popularity and respect in her own right. After years of high-tension political struggles, we were settled and happy. Moreover, President Bush still looked unbeatable. An early June poll in Arkansas showed that only 39 percent of the people wanted me to run, and that I would lose my own state to the President 57 to 32 percent, with the rest undecided. Moreover, I wouldn't be stepping into an empty primary field. Several other good Democrats seemed likely to run, so the nomination fight was sure to be hard. And history was against me. Only one governor of a small state had ever been elected President, Franklin Pierce of New Hampshire in 1852.

Beyond the political considerations, I genuinely liked President Bush and appreciated the way he and his White House had worked with me on education. Though I strongly disagreed with his economic and social policies, I thought he was a good man and nowhere near as ruthless or right-wing as most of the Reaganites. I didn't know what to do. In June, on a trip to California, I was picked up at the airport and driven to my speech by a young man named Sean Landres. He encouraged me to run for President and said he had found the perfect theme for the campaign. He then put on a tape of Fleetwood Mac's hit "Don't Stop Thinkin' About Tomorrow." It struck him, and me, as exactly what I was trying to say.

When I was in Los Angeles, I discussed the pros and cons of running with Hillary's friend Mickey Kantor, who by then had become a close friend and trusted advisor of mine as well. When we started, Mickey said I should hire him for a dollar, so our conversations would be privileged. A few days later, I sent him a check for a dollar, with a note that said I had always wanted a high-priced lawyer and was sending the check "in firm belief that you get what you pay for." I got a lot of good advice for that dollar, but I still didn't know what to do. Then came the phone call that changed things.

One July day, Lynda Dixon told me that Roger Porter was on the phone from the White House. As I've said, I had worked with Roger on the education goals project and had a high regard for his ability to be loyal to the President and still work with the governors. Roger asked me if I was going to run for President in 1992. I told him that I hadn't decided, that I was happier being governor than I'd been in years, that my family life was good and I was reluctant to disrupt it, but that I thought the White House was being too passive in dealing with the country's economic and social problems. I said I thought the President should use the enormous political capital he had as a result of the Gulf War to tackle the country's big issues. After five or ten minutes of what I thought was a serious conversation, Roger cut it off and got to the point. I'll never forget the first words of the message he had been designated to deliver: "Cut the crap, Governor." He said "they" had reviewed all the potential candidates against the President. Governor Cuomo was the most powerful speaker, but they could paint him as too liberal. All the senators could be defeated by attacks on their voting records. But I was different. With a strong record in economic development, education, and crime, and a strong DLC message, I actually had a chance to win. So if I ran, they would have to destroy me personally. "Here's how Washington works," he said. "The press has to have some-body in every election, and we're going to give them you." He went on to say the press were elitists who would believe any tales they were told about backwater Arkansas. "We'll spend whatever we have to spend to get whoever we have to get to say whatever they have to say to take you out. And we'll do it early."

I tried to stay calm, but I was mad. I told Roger that what he had just said showed what was wrong with the administration. They had been in power so long they thought they were entitled to it. I said, "You think those parking spaces off the West Wing are yours, but they belong to the American people, and you have to earn the right to use them." I told Roger that what he had said made me more likely to run. Roger said that was a nice sentiment, but he was calling as my friend to give me fair warning. If I waited until 1996, I could win the presi-dency. If I ran in 1992, they would destroy me, and my political career would be over.

After the conversation ended, I called Hillary and told her about it. Then I told Mack McLarty. I never heard from or saw Roger Porter again until he attended a recep-tion for the White House Fellows when I was President. I wonder if he ever thinks about that phone call and whether it influenced my decision.

Ever since I was a little boy I have hated to be threat-ened. As a kid, I got shot by a BB gun and slugged by a much bigger boy because I wouldn't walk away from threats. In the campaign and for eight years afterward, the Republicans would make good on theirs, and as Roger

Porter had predicted, they got lots of help from some members of the press. Like the childhood BB shot in my leg and the roundhouse blow to my jaw, their attacks hurt. The lies hurt, and the occasional truth hurt more. I just tried to keep focused on the job at hand and the impact of my work on ordinary people. When I could do that, it was easier to stand up against those who craved power for its own sake.

The next three months rushed by in a blur. At July 4 picnics in northeast Arkansas, I saw the first "Clinton for President" signs, but was encouraged by some to wait until 1996 to run and by others, who were angry at me for raising taxes again, not to run at all. When I went to Memphis for the dedication of the National Civil Rights Museum on the site of the Lorraine Motel, where Martin Luther King Jr. was slain, several citizens urged me to run, but Jesse Jackson was still upset about the DLC, which he saw as conservative and divisive. I hated to be at cross-purposes with Jesse, whom I admired, especially for his efforts to persuade black youngsters to stay in school and off drugs. Back in 1977, we had marked the twentieth anniversary of the integration of Little Rock Central High with a joint appearance at the school, in which he told the students to "open your brains and not your veins."

Drugs and youth violence were still big issues in 1991. On July 12, I traveled to Chicago, to visit the public-housing projects and see what they were doing to protect kids. In late July, I went to a Little Rock hospital to visit the black comedian Dick Gregory, who had been arrested for staging a sit-in in a store that sold drug paraphernalia, along with four members of a local anti-drug group, DIGNITY (Doing In God's Name Incredible Things Yourself). The group was led by black ministers and the local leader of the Black Muslims. It represented the kind of adult responsibility for solving our social problems that Jackson also espoused, the DLC advocated, and I thought was essential if we were going to turn things around.

In August, the campaign began to take shape. I gave speeches in a number of places and formed an exploratory committee, with Bruce Lindsey as treasurer. The committee allowed me to raise money to pay travel and other expenses without becoming a candidate. Two weeks later, Bob Farmer of Boston, who had been Dukakis's chief fund-raiser, resigned as treasurer of the Democratic National Committee to help me raise money. I began to get help from Frank Greer, an Alabama native who in 1990 had produced television commercials for me that had both intellectual and emotional appeal, and Stan Greenberg, a pollster who had done focus groups for the 1990 campaign and had conducted extensive research on the so-called Reagan Democrats and what it would take to bring them home. I wanted Greenberg to be my pollster. I hated to give up Dick Morris, but by then he had become so involved with Republican candidates and officeholders that he was compromised in the eyes of virtually all Democrats.

After we set up the exploratory committee, Hillary, Chelsea, and I went to the summer meeting of the National Governors Association in Seattle. My colleagues had just voted me the most effective governor in the country in the annual survey conducted by **Newsweek** magazine, and several of them urged me to run. When the NGA meeting concluded, our family took a boat from Seattle to Canada for a short vacation in Victoria and Vancouver.

As soon as I got home, I started touring the state, including a lot of unannounced stops, to ask my constituents if I should run and whether they would release me from my pledge to serve my full term if I did. Most people said I should run if I thought it was the right thing to do, though few thought I had a chance to win. Senator Bumpers, Senator Pryor, and our two Democratic congressmen, Ray Thornton and Beryl Anthony, all made supportive statements. Lieutenant Governor Jim Guy Tucker, House Speaker John Lipton, and Senate President Jerry Bookout assured me they would take care of the state in my absence.

Hillary thought I should run, Mother was strongly in favor of it, and even Chelsea wasn't against it this time. I told her I'd be there for the important things, like her ballet performance in **The Nutcracker** at Christmastime, her school events, the trip to Renaissance Weekend, and her birthday party. But I knew, too, that I'd miss some things: playing another duet with her on my sax at her piano recital; making Halloween stops, with Chelsea in her always unique costume; reading to her at night; and helping with her homework. Being her father was the best job I ever had; I just hoped I could do it well enough in the long campaign ahead. When I wasn't around, I missed it as much as she did. But the telephone helped, and the fax machine did too—we sent a lot of math problems back and forth. Hillary would be gone less than I would, but when we were both away, Chelsea had a good support system in her grandparents, Carolyn Huber, the Governor's Mansion's staff, and her friends and their parents.

On August 21, I got a big break when Senator Al Gore announced that he wouldn't run. He had run in 1988, and if he had run again in 1992 we would have split the vote in the southern states on Super Tuesday, March 10, making it much harder for me to win. Al's only son, Albert, had been badly injured when he was hit by a car. Al decided he had to be there for his family during his son's long, hard recovery, a decision I understood and admired.

In September, I visited Illinois again and spoke to the leading Democrats of Iowa, South Dakota, and Nebraska in Sioux City, Iowa, and to the Democratic National Committee in Los Angeles. The Illinois stop was particularly important because of the primary calendar. The nomination fight began with the Iowa caucuses, which I could pass up because Senator Tom Harkin of Iowa was running and was sure to win his home state. Then came New Hampshire, then South Carolina, then Maryland, Georgia, and Colorado. Then the eleven Super Tuesday southern states. Then Illinois and Michigan on March 17, St. Patrick's Day.

Senator Gore's campaign had been derailed four years earlier when he didn't follow his impressive showing in the southern states with other victories. I thought I could win in Illinois, for three reasons: Hillary was from there, I had worked in southern Illinois with the Delta Commission, and a number of prominent black leaders in Chicago had Arkansas roots. In Chicago, I met with two young political activists, David Wilhelm and David Axelrod, who would become involved in the campaign. They were idealistic, tempered by the fire of Chicago election battles, and in tune with my politics. Meanwhile, Kevin O'Keefe was driving all over the state, building the organization necessary to win.

Michigan voted on the same day as Illinois, and I hoped to do well there, too, thanks to former governor

Jim Blanchard, Wayne County executive Ed McNamara, and a lot of people, black and white, who had come to Michigan from Arkansas to work in the automobile plants. After Michigan and Illinois, the next big state to vote was New York, where my friend Harold Ickes was busy lining up support, and Paul Carey, son of former governor Hugh Carey, was raising money.

On September 6, I finished organizing the governor's office for the campaign when Bill Bowen agreed to become my executive secretary. Bill was the president of Commercial National Bank, one of the state's most respected business leaders, and the prime organizer behind the so-called Good Suit Club, the business leaders who had supported the successful education program in the 1991 legislature. Bowen's appointment reassured people that the state's business would be well taken care of while I was away.

In the weeks leading up to my announcement, I began to get a taste of the difference between running for President and a campaign for state office. First, abortion was a big issue, because it was assumed that if President Bush were reelected, he would have enough Supreme Court vacancies to fill to secure a majority for reversing **Roe** v. **Wade.** I had always supported **Roe** but opposed public funding of abortions for poor women, so my position didn't really please either side. It wasn't fair to poor women, but I had a hard time justifying funding abortions with the money of taxpayers who believed it was the equivalent of murder. Also, the question was really moot, since even the Democratic Congress had repeatedly failed to provide abortion funding.

Besides abortion, there were the personal questions. When asked if I had ever smoked marijuana, I said I had never broken the drug laws in America. It was a tacit but awkward admission that I had tried it in England. There were also a lot of rumors about my personal life. On September 16, at Mickey Kantor's and Frank Greer's urging, Hillary and I appeared at the Sperling Breakfast, a regular meeting of Washington journalists, to answer press questions. I didn't know if it was the right thing to do, but Mickey was persuasive. He argued that I had said before that I hadn't been perfect, people knew it, and "You might as well tell them and try to take the sting out of what may or may not happen later in the campaign."

When a reporter asked the question, I said that, like a lot of couples, we'd had problems, but we were committed to each other and our marriage was strong. Hillary backed me up. As far as I know, I was the only candidate who had ever said as much. It satisfied some of the reporters and columnists; for others, my candor simply confirmed that I was a good target.

I'm still not sure I did the right thing in going to the breakfast, or in getting onto the slippery slope of answering personal questions. Character is important in a President, but as the contrasting examples of FDR and Richard Nixon show, marital perfection is not necessarily a good measure of presidential character. Moreover, that wasn't really the standard. In 1992, if you had violated your marriage vows, gotten divorced, and remarried, the infidelity wasn't considered disqualifying or even newsworthy, while couples who stayed married were fair game, as if divorce was always the more authentic choice. Given the complexity of people's lives and the importance of both parents in raising children, that's probably not the right standard.

Notwithstanding the personal questions, I got more than my fair share of favorable press coverage in the early days from thoughtful journalists who were interested in my ideas and policies and in what I had done as governor. I also knew I could start the campaign with a core of enthusiastic supporters across the country thanks to the friends Hillary and I had made over the years, and lots of Arkansans who were willing to travel to other states to campaign for me. They were undeterred by the fact that I was virtually unknown to the American people and far behind in the polls. So was I. Unlike 1987, this time I was ready.

TWENTY-SIX

O ctober 3 was a beautiful autumn morning in
Arkansas, crisp and clear. I started the day that
would change my life in the usual way, with an
early-morning jog. I went out the back gate of the Governor's Mansion, through the old Quapaw Quarter, then
downtown to the Old State House. The grand old place,
where I had held my first reception when I was sworn in as
attorney general in 1977, was already decked out in American flags. After I ran past it, turned, and headed for
home, I saw a newspaper vending machine. Through the
glass, I could read the headline: "Hour Arrives for Clinton." On the way home, several passersby wished me well.
Back at the mansion I took a last look at my announcement speech. I had worked on it until well past midnight;
it was full of what I felt was good rhetoric and specific policy proposals, but still too long, so I cut a few lines.

At noon, I was introduced on the stage by our state
treasurer, Jimmie Lou Fisher, who had been with me since
1978. I started out a little awkwardly, probably because of
the conflicting feelings flooding through me. I was at once
reluctant to abandon the life I knew and eager for the
challenge, a little afraid but sure I was doing the right
thing. I spoke for more than half an hour, thanking my
family, friends, and supporters for giving me the strength
"to step beyond a life and job I love, to make a commitment to a larger cause: preserving the American dream,

restoring the hopes of the forgotten middle class, reclaiming the future for our children." I closed with a pledge to "give new life to the American dream" by forming a "new covenant" with the people: "more opportunity for all, more responsibility from everyone, and a greater sense of common purpose."

When it was over, I felt elated and excited, but maybe relieved more than anything else, especially after Chelsea wisecracked, "Nice speech, Governor." Hillary and I spent the rest of the day receiving well-wishers, and Mother, Dick, and Roger all seemed happy about it, as did Hillary's family. Mother acted as if she knew I would win. As well as I knew her, I couldn't be sure if it was truly how she felt or just another example of her "game face." That night we gathered around the piano with old friends. Carolyn Staley played, just as she had done since we were fifteen. We sang "Amazing Grace" and other hymns, and lots of songs from the sixties, including "Abraham, Martin, and John," a tribute to the fallen heroes of our generation. I went to bed believing we could cut through the cynicism and despair and rekindle the fire those men had lit in my heart.

Governor Mario Cuomo once said we campaign in poetry but we govern in prose. The statement is basically accurate, but a lot of campaigning is prose, too: putting together the nuts and bolts, going through the required rituals, and responding to the press. Day two of the campaign was more prose than poetry: a series of interviews designed to get me on television nationally and in major local markets, and to answer the threshold question of why I had gone back on my commitment to finish my term and whether that meant I was untrustworthy. I answered the questions as best I could and moved on to the campaign message. It was all prosaic, but it got us to day three.

The rest of the year was full of the frantic activity of a late-starting campaign: getting organized, raising money, reaching out to specific constituencies, and working New Hampshire.

Our first headquarters was in an old paint store on Seventh Street near the Capitol. I had decided to base the campaign out of Little Rock instead of Washington. It made travel arrangements a little more complicated, but I wanted to stick close to my roots and to get home often enough to be with my family and handle official business that required my presence. But staying in Arkansas also had another big benefit: it helped our young staff keep focused on the work at hand. They weren't distracted by the pervasive Washington rumor mill and they didn't get too carried away by the surprisingly favorable press coverage I received early in the campaign, or too depressed by the torrent of negative press soon to come.

After a few weeks, we had outgrown the paint store and moved nearby to the old office of the Department of Higher Education, which we used until we outgrew it, too, just before the Democratic convention. Then we moved again, downtown to the **Arkansas Gazette** building, which had become vacant a few months earlier upon the purchase and subsequent dismantling of the **Gazette** by the owner of the **Arkansas Democrat,** Walter Hussman. The **Gazette** building would be our home for the rest of the campaign, which, from my point of view, was the only good result of the loss of the oldest independent newspaper in America west of the Mississippi.

The **Gazette** had stood for civil rights in the fifties and sixties, and had staunchly supported Dale Bumpers, David Pryor, and me in our efforts to modernize education, social services, and the economy. In its glory days, it was one of the best papers in the country, bringing well-written and wide-ranging national and international stories to readers in the far corners of our state. In the 1980s, the **Gazette** began to face competition from Hussman's **Arkansas Democrat,** which until then had been a much smaller afternoon paper. The newspaper war that followed had a foreordained outcome, because Hussman owned other profitable media properties, which allowed him to absorb tremendous operating losses at the **Democrat** in order to take advertising and subscribers away from the **Gazette.** Not long before I announced for President, Hussman acquired the **Gazette** and consolidated its operations into his paper, renaming it the **Arkansas Democrat-Gazette.** Over the years, the **Democrat-Gazette** would help to make Arkansas a more Republican state. The overall tone of its editorial page was conservative and highly critical of me, often in very personal terms. In this the paper faithfully reflected the views of its publisher. Though I was sad to see the **Gazette** fall, I was glad to have the building. Perhaps I was hoping that the ghosts of its progressive past would keep us fighting for tomorrow.

We started out with an all-Arkansas staff, with Bruce Lindsey as campaign director and Craig Smith, who had handled my appointments to boards and commissions, as finance director. Rodney Slater and Carol Willis were already hard at work contacting black political, religious, and business leaders across the country. My old friend Eli Segal agreed to help me build a national staff.

I had already met with one person I was sure I wanted on the team, a talented young staffer for Congressman Dick Gephardt, the Democratic majority leader. George Stephanopoulos, the son of a Greek Orthodox priest, was a Rhodes scholar who had previously worked for my friend

Father Tim Healy when he ran the New York Public Library. I liked George immediately, and knew he could serve as a bridge to the national press and the congressional Democrats, as well as make a contribution to thinking through the intellectual challenges of the campaign.

Eli met with him, confirmed my judgment, and George came to work as deputy campaign manager in charge of communications. Eli also saw David Wilhelm, the young Chicago political operative whom I wanted on the team. We offered him the job of campaign manager, and he quickly accepted. David was, in political language, a "two-fer": besides managing the overall campaign, he would be a special help in Illinois. I was convinced that, with David as campaign manager, along with Kevin O'Keefe as a state organizer, we could now win a clear victory in Illinois to follow up on the anticipated sweep of the southern states on Super Tuesday. Soon afterward, we also persuaded another young Chicagoan, Rahm Emanuel, to join our campaign. Rahm had worked with Wilhelm in the successful campaigns of Mayor Richard Daley and Senator Paul Simon. He was a slight, intense man who had studied ballet and, though an American citizen, had served in the Israeli Army. Rahm was so aggressive he made me look laid-back. We made him finance director, a job in which an underfunded campaign needs an aggressor. Craig Smith went to work on our state campaign organizations, a job better suited to his considerable political skills. Soon Bruce Reed left the Democratic Leadership Council to become our policy director. Eli also interviewed two women who would play important roles in the campaign. Dee Dee Myers from California became the press secretary, a job that would require her to handle more incoming fire than she possibly could have anticipated. Though she was very young, she rose to the challenge. Stephanie Solien, from Washington State, became our political director. She was married to Frank Greer, but that's not why I hired her. Stephanie was smart, politically astute, and less hard-edged than most of the boys. She provided both the good work and the good chemistry every high-tension effort needs. As the campaign progressed, young people from all over America just showed up to pick up the extra load.

On the financial front, we made do in the beginning with generous early help from Arkansans, Bob Farmer's efforts in Massachusetts and with regular Democratic donors who would give just because he asked them, and donations from friends around the country that helped me qualify for matching funds from the federal government. To do that, a candidate must raise $5,000 in each of twenty states, in amounts not exceeding $250 per contribution. In some states, my governor friends took care of it. In Texas, my longtime supporter Truman Arnold raised a much-needed $30,000. Unlike many wealthy people, Truman seemed to become an even more committed Democrat as he got richer.

Somewhat surprisingly, a lot of people in the Washington, D.C., area wanted to help, in particular Democratic lawyer and fund-raiser Vic Raiser and my friend from Renaissance Weekend Tom Schnieder. In New York, I got invaluable early help not only from our friends Harold Ickes and Susan Thomases but also from Ken Brody, a Goldman Sachs executive who decided he wanted to get heavily involved in Democratic politics for the first time. Ken told me he had been a Republican because he thought the Democrats had a heart but their head was in the wrong place. Then, he said, he had gotten close enough to the national Republicans to see that they had a head but no heart, and decided to join the Democrats because he thought it was easier to change minds than hearts, and luckily for me, he figured I was the best place to start. Ken took me to a dinner with high-powered New York businesspeople, including Bob Rubin, whose tightly reasoned arguments for a new economic policy made a lasting impression on me. In every successful political campaign, people like Ken Brody somehow appear, bringing energy, ideas, and converts.

In addition to money-raising and organizing, I had to reach out to constituencies that were predominantly Democratic. In October, I spoke to a Jewish group in Texas, saying that Israel should trade land for peace; to blacks and Hispanics in Chicago; and to Democratic Party groups in Tennessee, Maine, New Jersey, and California, all of which were considered swing states, meaning they could go either way in the general election. In November, I spoke in Memphis to the convention of the Church of God in Christ, America's fastest-growing black denomination. I worked the South: Florida, South Carolina, Louisiana, and Georgia. Florida was important, because its December 15 straw poll at the Democratic convention would be the first contested vote. President Bush was beginning to slip in the polls and didn't help himself by saying that the economy was in good shape. I spoke to the National Education Association and the annual meeting of the American Israel Public Affairs Committee in Washington. I went south again to North Carolina, Texas, and Georgia. In the West, I made stops in Colorado and South Dakota; in Wyoming, where Governor Mike Sullivan endorsed me; and in the Republican stronghold of Orange County, California, where I picked up the support of Republican telecommunications executive Roger Johnson and others who were disillusioned with President Bush's economic policy.

While all this was going on, however, the main focus of the campaign was New Hampshire. If I ran poorly there, I might not do well enough in the states that followed to last until Super Tuesday. Though I was running dead last in the polls in mid-November, I liked my chances. New Hampshire is a small state, less than half the size of Arkansas, with very well-informed primary voters who take seriously their responsibility to carefully evaluate the candidates and their positions. To compete effectively, a good organization and persuasive television ads are necessary, but nowhere near sufficient. You must also do well in an endless stream of small house parties, town meetings, rallies, and unscheduled handshaking. A lot of New Hampshire citizens won't vote for anyone who hasn't personally asked for their support. After all my years in Arkansas politics, that kind of campaigning was second nature to me.

Even more than the political culture, the economic distress and the inevitable emotional trauma it spawned made me feel at home in New Hampshire. It was like Arkansas ten years earlier. After prospering throughout the 1980s, New Hampshire had the nation's fastest-growing welfare and food-stamp rolls, and the highest rate of bankruptcies. Factories were closing and banks were in trouble. Lots of people were unemployed and genuinely afraid—afraid of losing their homes and their health insurance. They didn't know if they would be able to send their kids to college. They doubted Social Security would be solvent when they reached their retirement years. I knew how they felt. I had known many Arkansans in similar situations. And I thought I knew what needed to be done to turn things around.

The campaign organization began with two gifted young people, Mitchell Schwartz and Wendy Smith, who moved to Manchester and opened the state headquarters. They were soon joined by Michael Whouley, a Boston Irishman and world-class organizer, and my friend of forty years Patty Howe Criner, who moved up from Little Rock to explain and defend me and my record. Before long we had a big steering committee co-chaired by two lawyers I'd met through the DLC, John Broderick and Terry Schumaker, whose office, fortuitously, was in the same building that more than a century earlier had housed the law office of Governor Franklin Pierce.

The competition was stiff. All the announced candidates were running hard in New Hampshire. Senator Bob Kerrey, the Medal of Honor winner and former Nebraska governor, attracted a lot of interest because he was a political maverick: a fiscal conservative and a social liberal. The centerpiece of his campaign was a sweeping proposal to provide health coverage for all Americans, a big issue in a state where the number of people losing their health insurance was rising daily after a decade in which the cost of health insurance nationally had risen at three times the overall rate of inflation. Kerrey also had a powerful argument that his military record and his popularity in conservative Republican Nebraska made him the most electable Democrat against President Bush.

Senator Tom Harkin of Iowa was the Senate's leading advocate for the rights of the disabled; an authority on science and technology issues, which were important to the growing number of New Hampshire suburban voters; and a longtime ally of the labor movement. He argued that it would take an authentic populist campaign to win in November, not a DLC message, which he said had no appeal to "real" Democrats.

Former senator Paul Tsongas of Lowell, Massachusetts, had retired at a young age from a successful career in the Senate to battle cancer. He had become a fitness fanatic who swam vigorously, and publicly, to demonstrate that he was cured and able to be President. Tsongas argued that his premature brush with mortality had liberated him from conventional political constraints, making him more willing than the rest of us to tell voters hard truths they didn't necessarily want to hear. He had some interesting ideas, which he put forward in a widely distributed campaign booklet.

Governor Doug Wilder had made history by becoming Virginia's first African-American governor. He argued that his ability to win in a conservative southern state and his record on education, crime, and balanced budgets proved his electability.

Soon after I entered the race, former governor Jerry Brown of California also announced. Jerry said he wouldn't take contributions in amounts over $100 and tried to position himself as the only genuine reformer in the race. The focus of his campaign became a proposal to scrap the complex tax code in favor of a uniform "flat" tax of 13 percent on all Americans. In 1976, as a young governor, Jerry entered the late primaries and won several of them in a last-minute effort to stop Jimmy Carter. In 1979, I served with him in the National Governors Association, where I came to appreciate his quick mind and often unusual analysis of current events. The only quality his unique political persona lacked was a sense of humor. I liked Jerry, but he took every conversation awfully seriously.

For more than two months after I announced, the campaign was shadowed by the specter that there might be yet another candidate, Governor Mario Cuomo of New York. Cuomo was a huge figure in Democratic politics, our finest orator and a passionate defender of Democratic values during the Reagan-Bush years. Many people thought the nomination was his for the asking, and for a good while I thought he would ask. He took some hard shots at the DLC, at me, and at my ideas on welfare reform and national service. I was magnanimous in public, but I fumed in private and said some things about Mario I regret. I think I was so stung by his criticism because I had always admired him. In mid-December he finally announced that he wouldn't run. When some of my hard comments about him became public during the New Hampshire primary, all I could do was apologize. Thank goodness, he was big enough to accept it. In the years ahead, Mario Cuomo would become a valued advisor and one of my strongest defenders. I wanted to put him on the Supreme Court, but he didn't want that job, either. I think he loved his life in New York too much to give it up, a fact the voters didn't fully appreciate when they denied him a fourth term in 1994.

At the outset of the campaign, I thought my strongest competitor in New Hampshire would be Harkin or Kerrey. Before long, it was clear that I had been mistaken: Tsongas was the man to beat. His hometown was practically on the New Hampshire state line; he had a compelling life story; he demonstrated the toughness and determination to win; and, most important, he was the only other candidate who was competing with me on the essential battleground of ideas, message, and specific, comprehensive proposals.

Successful presidential campaigns require three basic things. First, people have to be able to look at you and imagine you as President. Then you have to have enough money and support to become known. After that, it's a battle of ideas, message, and issues. Tsongas met the first two criteria and was out to win the ideas battle. I was determined not to let him do it.

I scheduled three speeches at Georgetown to flesh out my New Covenant theme with specific proposals. They were delivered to students, faculty, supporters, and good press coverage in beautiful, old, wood-paneled Gaston Hall, in the Healy Building. On October 23, the topic was responsibility and community; on November 20, economic opportunity; on December 12, national security.

Together, these speeches allowed me to articulate the ideas and proposals I had developed over the previous decade as governor and with the Democratic Leadership Council. I had helped to write, and deeply believed in, the DLC's five core beliefs: Andrew Jackson's credo of opportunity for all and special privileges for none; the basic American values of work and family, freedom and responsibility, faith, tolerance, and inclusion; John Kennedy's ethic of mutual responsibility, asking citizens to give something back to their country; the advancement of democratic and humanitarian values around the world, and prosperity and upward mobility at home; and Franklin Roosevelt's commitment to innovation, to modernizing government for the information age and encouraging people by giving them the tools to make the most of their own lives.

I was amazed by some of the criticisms of the DLC from the Democratic left, who accused us of being closet Republicans, and from some members of the political press, who had comfortable little boxes marked "Democrat" and "Republican." When we didn't fit neatly in their ossified Democratic box, they said we didn't believe in anything. The proof was that we wanted to win national elections, something Democrats apparently weren't supposed to do.

I believed the DLC was furthering the best values and principles of the Democratic Party with new ideas. Of course, some liberals honestly disagreed with us on welfare reform, trade, fiscal responsibility, and national defense. But our differences with the Republicans were clear. We were against their unfair tax cuts and big deficits; their opposition to the Family and Medical Leave bill and the Brady bill; their failure to adequately fund education or push proven reforms, instead of vouchers; their divisive tactics on racial and gay issues; their unwillingness to protect the environment; their anti-choice stance; and much more. We also had good ideas, like putting 100,000 community police on the streets; doubling the Earned Income Tax Credit to make work more attractive and life better for families with modest incomes; and offering young people a chance to do community service in return for assistance to pay for college.

The principles and proposals I advocated could hardly be called Republican-lite or lacking in conviction. Instead, they helped to modernize the Democratic Party and later would be adopted by resurgent center-left parties all over the world, in what would be called the "Third Way." Most important, the new ideas, when implemented, would prove to be good for America. The 1991 Georgetown speeches gave me the invaluable opportunity to demonstrate that I had a comprehensive agenda for change and was serious about implementing it.

Meanwhile, back in New Hampshire, I put out a campaign booklet of my own, outlining all the specific proposals made in the Georgetown speeches. And I scheduled as many town meetings as possible. One of the early ones was held in Keene, a beautiful college town in the southern part of the state. Our campaign workers had put up flyers around town, but we didn't know how many people would show up. The room we rented held about two hundred. On the way to the meeting, I asked a veteran campaigner how many people we needed to avoid embarrassment. She said, "Fifty." And how many to be judged a success? "A hundred and fifty." When we arrived, there were four hundred people. The fire marshal made us put half of them in another room, and I had to do two meetings. It was the first time I knew we could do well in New Hampshire.

Usually I talked for fifteen minutes or so and spent an hour or more answering questions. At first I worried about being too detailed and "policy wonky" in the answers, but I soon realized that people were looking for substance over style. They were really hurting and wanted to understand what was happening to them and how they could get out of the fix they were in. I learned a lot just listening to the questions I got from people at those town meetings and other campaign stops.

An elderly couple, Edward and Annie Davis, told me they often had to choose between buying their prescription drugs and buying food. A high school student said her unemployed father was so ashamed he couldn't look at his family over dinner; he just hung his head. I met veterans in American Legion halls and found they were more concerned with the deterioration of health care at Veterans Administration hospitals than with my opposition to the Vietnam War. I was especially moved by the story of Ron Machos, whose son Ronnie was born with a heart problem. He had lost his job in the recession and couldn't find another one with health insurance to cover the large medical costs he knew were coming. When the New Hampshire Democrats held a convention to hear from all the candidates, a group of students carrying a CLINTON FOR PRESIDENT banner, who had been recruited by their teacher, my old friend from Arkansas Jan Paschal, led me to the podium. One of them made a particular impression on me. Michael Morrison was in a wheelchair, but it didn't slow him down. He was supporting me because he was being raised by a single mother on a modest income, and he thought I was committed to giving all kids a chance to go to college and get a good job.

By December, the campaign was on a roll. On December 2, James Carville and his partner, Paul Begala, joined us. They were colorful characters and a hot political property, having recently helped elect Governor Bob Casey and Senator Harris Wofford in Pennsylvania, and Governor Zell Miller in Georgia. Zell first got Carville on the phone for me so that I could set up a meeting with him and Begala. Like Frank Greer and me, they were part of an endangered but hardy political species, white southern Democrats. Carville was a Louisiana Cajun and ex-marine who had a great strategic sense and a deep commitment to progressive politics. He and I had a lot in common, including strong-willed, down-to-earth mothers whom we adored. Begala was a witty dynamo from Sugar Land, Texas, who blended aggressive populism with his Catholic social conscience. I wasn't the only candidate who wanted to hire them, and when they signed on, they brought energy, focus, and credibility to our efforts.

On December 10, I spoke to the Conference of Presidents of Major American Jewish Organizations, and two days later I delivered the third and final Georgetown speech, on national security. I got a lot of help with the speeches from my longtime friend Sandy Berger, who had been deputy director of policy planning in the State Department during the Carter years. Sandy recruited three other Carter-era foreign policy experts to help— Tony Lake, Dick Holbrooke, and Madeleine Albright— along with a bright, Australian-born expert on the Middle East, Martin Indyck. All would play important roles in the years ahead. In mid-December, it was enough that they helped me cross the threshold of understanding and competence in foreign affairs.

On December 15, I won the nonbinding Florida straw poll at the state Democratic convention with 54 percent of the delegates. I knew many of them from my three visits to the convention in the 1980s, and I had by far the strongest campaign organization, headed by Lieutenant Governor Buddy McKay. Hillary and I also worked the delegates hard, as did her brothers, Hugh and Tony, who lived in Miami, and Hugh's wife, Maria, a Cuban-American lawyer.

Two days after the Florida win, an Arkansas fund-raiser netted $800,000 for the campaign, far more than had ever before been raised at a single event there. On December 19, the **Nashville Banner** became the first newspaper to endorse me. On December 20, Governor Cuomo said he wouldn't run. Then Senator Sam Nunn and Governor Zell Miller of Georgia gave the campaign a huge boost when they endorsed me. Georgia's primary came just before Super Tuesday, along with Maryland's and Colorado's.

Meanwhile, President Bush's troubles mounted, as Pat Buchanan announced his intention to enter the GOP primaries with a George Wallace–like attack on the President from the right. Conservative Republicans were upset with the President for signing a $492 billion deficit-reduction package passed by the Democratic Congress because, in addition to spending cuts, it contained a five-cent gas-tax increase. Bush had brought the Republican convention to its feet in 1988 with his famous line "Read my lips—no new taxes." He did the responsible thing in signing the deficit-reduction package, but in doing so he broke his most visible campaign commitment and violated the anti-tax theology of his party's right-wing base.

The conservatives didn't direct all their fire at the President; I got my fair share, too, from a group called ARIAS, which stood for Alliance for the Rebirth of an Independent American Spirit. ARIAS was led in part by Cliff Jackson, an Arkansan whom I'd known and liked at Oxford, but who was now a conservative Republican with a deep personal animosity toward me. When ARIAS ran TV, radio, and newspaper ads attacking my record, we responded quickly and aggressively. The attacks might have done the campaign more good than harm, because answering them highlighted my accomplishments as governor, and because the source of the attacks made them suspect among New Hampshire Democrats. Two days before Christmas, a New Hampshire poll placed me second to Paul Tsongas and closing fast. The year ended on a good note.

On January 8, Governor Wilder withdrew from the race, reducing the competition for African-American voters, especially in the South. At about the same time, Frank Greer produced a great television ad, highlighting New

Hampshire's economic problems and my plan to remedy them, and we moved ahead of Tsongas in public polls. By the second week of January, our campaign had raised $3.3 million in less than three months, half of it from Arkansas. It seems a paltry sum today, but it was good enough to lead the field in early 1992.

The campaign seemed to be on track until January 23, when the Little Rock media received advance notice of a story in the February 4 issue of the tabloid newspaper **Star,** in which Gennifer Flowers said she had carried on a twelve-year affair with me. Her name had been on the list of five women Larry Nichols alleged I had affairs with during the 1990 governor's race. At the time, she had strongly denied it. At first we didn't know how seriously the press would take her about-face, so we stuck with the schedule. I took a long drive to Claremont, in southwestern New Hampshire, to tour a brush factory. The people who ran it wanted to sell their products to Wal-Mart, and I wanted to help them. At some point, Dee Dee Myers went into the plant's small office and called headquarters. Flowers was claiming that she had tapes of ten phone conversations with me that supposedly proved the truth of her allegations.

A year earlier, Flowers's lawyer had written a letter to a Little Rock radio station threatening a libel suit because one of its talk-show hosts had repeated some of the allegations in a Larry Nichols press release, saying the station had "wrongfully and untruthfully" accused her of having an affair. We didn't know what was on whatever tapes Flowers might have, but I remembered the conversations clearly, and I didn't think there could be anything damaging on them. Flowers, whom I'd known since 1977 and had recently helped get a state job, had called me to complain that the media were harassing her even at the place she was singing at night, and that she felt her job was threatened. I commiserated with her, but I hadn't thought it was a big deal. After Dee Dee went to work trying to discover more about what the **Star** was planning to publish, I called Hillary and told her what was going on. Fortunately, she was staying at the Georgia Governor's Mansion on a campaign trip, and Zell and Shirley Miller were wonderful to her.

The Flowers story hit with explosive force, and it proved irresistible to the media, though some of the stories cast doubt on her accusations. The press reported that Flowers had been paid for the story, and that she had vigorously denied an affair a year earlier. The media, to their credit, exposed Flowers's false claims about her education and work history. These reports, however, were dwarfed by the allegations. I was dropping in the New Hampshire polls, and Hillary and I decided we should accept an invitation from the CBS program **60 Minutes** to answer questions about the charges and the state of our marriage. It was not an easy call. We wanted to defend against the scandal coverage and to get back to the real issues without demeaning ourselves and adding fuel to the fire of personal-destruction politics, which I had deplored even before it burned me. I had already said I hadn't lived a perfect life. If that was the standard, someone else would have to be elected President.

We taped the program at the Ritz-Carlton in Boston on Sunday morning, January 26, for showing later that night, after the Super Bowl. We talked to the interviewer, Steve Kroft, for over an hour. He began by asking if Flowers's story was true. When I said it wasn't, he asked if I had

had any affairs. Perhaps I should have used Rosalynn Carter's brilliant response to a similar question in 1976: "If I had, I wouldn't tell you." Since I wasn't as blameless as Mrs. Carter, I decided not to be cute. Instead, I said that I had already acknowledged causing pain in my marriage, that I had already said more about the subject than any other politician ever had and would say no more, and that the American people understood what I meant.

Kroft, unbelievably, asked me again. His only goal in the interview was to get a specific admission. Finally, after a series of questions about Gennifer Flowers, he got around to Hillary and me, referring to our marriage as an "arrangement." I wanted to slug him. Instead, I said, "Wait a minute. You're looking at two people who love each other. This is not an arrangement or an understanding. This is a marriage." Hillary then said she was sitting in the interview with me "because I love him and I respect him and I honor what he's been through and what we've been through together. And you know, if that's not enough for people, then heck, don't vote for him." After the early mud wrestling, Kroft grew more civil, and there were some good exchanges about Hillary's and my life together. They were all cut out when the long interview was edited, down to about ten minutes, apparently because the Super Bowl shortened the program.

At some point during the session, the very bright, very hot overhead light above the couch Hillary and I were sitting on came loose from its tape on the ceiling and fell. It was directly above Hillary's head, and if it had hit her, she could have been burned badly. Somehow I saw it out of the corner of my eye and jerked her over onto my lap a split second before it crashed on the spot where she had been sitting. She was scared, and rightly so. I just stroked her hair and told her that it was all right and that I loved her. After the ordeal, we flew home to watch the show with Chelsea. When it was over, I asked Chelsea what she thought. She said, "I think I'm glad you're my parents."

The next morning I flew to Jackson, Mississippi, for a breakfast organized by former governor Bill Winter and Mike Espy, both of whom had endorsed me early. I was uncertain whether anyone would come and what the reception would be. To my immense relief, they had to get extra chairs for a larger-than-expected crowd that seemed genuinely glad to see me. So I went back to work.

It wasn't over, however. Gennifer Flowers gave a press conference to a packed house in New York's Waldorf-Astoria Hotel. She repeated her story and said she was sick of lying about it. She also acknowledged that she had been approached by a "local Republican candidate" who asked her to go public, but she declined to name him. Some of her tapes were played at the press conference, but except for proving that I had talked to her on the telephone, a fact I hadn't denied, the content of the tapes was anticlimactic, given all the hoopla about them.

Despite some later coverage, the Flowers media circus was ending. I think the chief reason was that we had managed to put it in the right perspective on **60 Minutes.** The public understood that I hadn't been perfect and wasn't pretending to be, but people also knew that there were many more important issues confronting the country. And a lot of people were repelled at the "cash for trash" aspects of the coverage. At about this time, Larry Nichols decided to drop his lawsuit, and he issued a public apology for, in his words, trying to "destroy" me: "The media has made a circus out of this thing and now it's gone way too far. When that **Star** article first came out, several women called asking if I was willing to pay them to say that they had had an affair with Bill Clinton. This is crazy." Questions were raised about the tapes that were played at Flowers's press conference. The **Star** declined to release the original tapes. A Los Angeles television station retained an expert who stated that while he didn't know that the tape was, in his words, "doctored," it definitely had been "selectively edited." CNN also ran some critical coverage, based on the analysis of its own expert.

As I've said, I first met Gennifer Flowers in 1977 when I was attorney general and she was a television reporter for a local station who often interviewed me. Soon afterward, she left Arkansas to pursue an entertainment career, I believe as a backup singer for country music star Roy Clark. At some point, she moved to Dallas. In the late eighties, she moved back to Little Rock to be near her mother and called to ask me to help her find a state job to supplement her income from singing. I referred her to Judy Gaddy on my staff, who was responsible for referring the many job seekers who asked for help with state employment to various agencies. After nine months, Flowers finally got a position paying less than $20,000 a year.

Gennifer Flowers struck me as a tough survivor who'd had a less-than-ideal childhood and disappointments in her career but kept going. She was later quoted in the press as saying that she might vote for me and, on another occasion, that she didn't believe Paula Jones's allegations of sexual harassment. Ironically, almost exactly six years after my January 1992 appearance on **60 Minutes,** I had to give a deposition in the Paula Jones case, and I was asked questions about Gennifer Flowers. I acknowledged that, back in the 1970s, I had had a relationship with her that I should not have had. Of course, the whole line of questioning had nothing to do with Jones's spurious sexual-harassment claim; it was just a part of the long, well-financed attempt to damage and embarrass me personally and politically. But I was under oath, and of course, if I hadn't done anything wrong, I couldn't have been embarrassed. My critics leapt on it. Ironically, even though they were sure the rest of the deposition was untruthful, this one answer they accepted as fact. The fact is, there was no twelve-year affair. Gennifer Flowers still has a suit against James Carville, Paul Begala, and Hillary for allegedly slandering her. I don't wish her ill, but now that I'm not President anymore, I do wish she'd let them be.

A few days after the firestorm broke, I called Eli Segal and pleaded with him to come down to Little Rock to be a mature, settling presence in the headquarters. When he asked how I could want the help of someone like him, who had worked only in losing presidential campaigns, I cracked, "I'm desperate." Eli laughed and came, becoming the campaign's chief of staff in charge of the central office, finances, and the campaign plane. Early in the month, Ned McWherter, Brereton Jones, and Booth Gardner, respectively the governors of Tennessee, Kentucky, and Washington, endorsed me. Those who had already done so, including Dick Riley of South Carolina, Mike Sullivan of Wyoming, Bruce King of New Mexico, George Sinner of North Dakota, and Zell Miller of Georgia, reaffirmed their support. So did Senator Sam Nunn, with the caveat that he wanted to "wait and see" what further stories came out.

A national poll said that 70 percent of the American people thought the press shouldn't report on the private lives of public figures. In another, 80 percent of the

Democrats said their votes wouldn't be affected even if the Flowers story was true. That sounds good, but 20 percent is a lot to give up right off the bat. Nevertheless, the campaign picked up steam again, and it seemed that at least we could finish a strong second to Tsongas, which I thought would be good enough to get me to the southern primaries.

Then, just as the campaign seemed to be recovering, there was another big shock when the draft story broke. On February 6, the **Wall Street Journal** ran a story on my draft experience and on my relationship with the ROTC program at the University of Arkansas in 1969. When the campaign began, I was unprepared for the draft questions, and I mistakenly said I had never had a draft deferment during my Oxford years; in fact, I did have one from August 7 through October 20, 1969. Even worse, Colonel Eugene Holmes, who had agreed to let me join the program, now claimed that I had misled him to get out of the draft. In 1978, when reporters asked him about the charge, he said he had dealt with hundreds of cases and didn't recall anything specific about mine. Coupled with my own misstatement that I had never had a deferment, the story made it seem that I was misleading people about why I wasn't drafted. That wasn't true, but at the time I couldn't prove it. I didn't remember and didn't find Jeff Dwire's tape relaying his friendly conversation with Holmes in March 1970, after I was out of the ROTC program and back in the draft. Jeff was dead, as was Bill Armstrong, the head of my local draft board. And all draft records from that period had been destroyed.

Holmes's attack surprised me, because it contradicted his earlier statements. It's been suggested that Holmes may have had some help with his memory from his daughter Linda Burnett, a Republican activist who was working for President Bush's reelection.

Closer to the election, on September 16, Holmes would issue a more detailed denunciation questioning my "patriotism and integrity" and saying again that I had deceived him. Apparently, the statement was drafted by his daughter, with "guidance" from the office of my old opponent, Congressman John Paul Hammerschmidt, and had been revised by several Bush campaign officials.

A few days after the story broke, and just a week from election day in New Hampshire, Ted Koppel, anchor of ABC's **Nightline,** called David Wilhelm and said that he had a copy of my now famous draft letter to Colonel Holmes, and that ABC would be doing a story about it. I had forgotten all about the letter, and ABC agreed to send us a copy, which they graciously did. When I read it, I could see why the Bush campaign was sure that the letter and Colonel Holmes's revised account of the ROTC episode would sink me in New Hampshire.

That night Mickey Kantor, Bruce Lindsey, James Carville, Paul Begala, George Stephanopoulos, Hillary, and I met in one of our rooms at the Days Inn Motel in Manchester. We were getting killed in the press. Now there was a double-barreled attack on my character. All the television pundits said I was dead as a doornail. George was curled up on the floor, practically in tears. He asked if it wasn't time to think about withdrawing. Carville paced the floor, waving the letter around and shouting, "Georgie! Georgie! That's crazy. This letter is our friend. Anyone who actually reads it will think he's got character!" Though I loved his "never say die" attitude, I was calmer than he was. I knew that George's only political experience had been in Washington, and that, unlike us, he might actually believe the press should decide who was worthy and who wasn't. I asked, "George, do you still think I'd be a good President?" "Yes," he said. "Then get up and go back to work. If the voters want to withdraw me, they'll do it on election day. I'm going to let them decide."

The words were brave, but I was dropping in the polls like a rock in a well. I was already in third place, and it looked as if I might fall into single digits. On Carville's and Mickey Kantor's advice, we took out an ad in the **Manchester Union Leader** containing the full text of the letter, and bought two thirty-minute segments on television to let voters call in and ask me about the charges and whatever else was on their minds. One hundred fifty Arkansans dropped what they were doing and came to New Hampshire to go door-to-door. One of them, Representative David Matthews, had been a law student of mine and one of the strongest supporters of my legislative programs and my campaigns at home. David was an eloquent and persuasive speaker who soon became my chief surrogate after Hillary. After he warmed up the crowd for me at several rallies, I think some people thought he should have been the candidate. Six hundred more Arkansans listed their names and home phone numbers in a full-page ad in the **Union Leader,** urging New Hampshire Democrats to call them if they wanted to know the truth about their governor. Hundreds of calls were made.

Of all the Arkansans who came to help, no one made a bigger difference than my closest childhood friend, David Leopoulos. After the Flowers story broke, David heard TV commentators say I was finished. He was so upset, he got in his car and drove three days to New Hampshire. He couldn't afford a plane ticket. When he reached our head-

quarters, Simon Rosenberg, my young press aide, scheduled him for an interview on a Boston radio station with a
large New Hampshire audience. He hit it out of the park,
just by talking about our forty-year friendship and making me seem more human. Then he spoke to a gathering
of our discouraged volunteers from across the state. When
he finished, he had them in tears and full of resolve for the
final push. David worked the state for a whole week,
doing radio interviews and passing out homemade flyers
with pictures of our childhood friends as proof that I was
a real person. At the end of his journey, I saw him at a rally
in Nashua, where he hooked up with fifty other
Arkansans, including Carolyn Staley, my old jazz partner
Randy Goodrum, and my grade-school friend Mauria
Aspell. The "Friends of Bill" probably saved the campaign
in New Hampshire.

A few days before the election, I went down to New
York for a long-planned fund-raiser. I wondered if anyone
would come, even if only to see a dead man walking. As I
made my way through the Sheraton Hotel kitchen to the
ballroom, I shook hands with the waiters and kitchen
workers, as I always did. One of the waiters, Dimitrios
Theofanis, engaged me in a brief conversation that made
him a friend for life. "My nine-year-old boy studies the
election in school and he says I should vote for you. If I
do, I want you to make my boy free. In Greece, we were
poor but we were free. Here, my boy can't play in the park
across the street alone or walk down the street to school by
himself because it is too dangerous. He's not free. So if I
vote for you, will you make my boy free?" I almost cried.
Here was a man who actually cared about what I could do
for his son's safety. I told him that community police officers, who would walk the blocks and know the residents,

could help a lot, and that I was committed to funding 100,000 of them.

I was already feeling better, but when I walked into the ballroom, my spirits soared: seven hundred people were there, including my Georgetown friend Denise Hyland Dangremond and her husband, Bob, who had come from Rhode Island to show moral support. I went back to New Hampshire thinking I might survive.

In the last few days of the campaign, Tsongas and I had a heated disagreement over economic policy. I had proposed a four-point plan to create jobs, help businesses get started, and reduce poverty and income inequality: cut the deficit in half in four years, with spending reductions and tax increases on the wealthiest Americans; increase investment in education, training, and new technologies; expand trade; and cut taxes modestly for the middle class and a lot more for the working poor. We had done our best to cost out each proposal, using figures from the Congressional Budget Office. In contrast to my plan, Tsongas said that we should just focus on cutting the deficit, and that the country couldn't afford the middle-class tax cut, though he was for a cut in the capital gains tax, which would benefit wealthy Americans most. He called me a "pander bear" for proposing the tax cuts. He said he'd be the best friend Wall Street ever had. I shot back that we needed a New Democrat economic plan that helped both Wall Street and Main Street, business and working families. A lot of people agreed with Tsongas's contention that the deficit was too big for my tax cuts, but I thought we had to do something about the two-decade growth in income inequality and the shift of the tax burden to the middle class in the 1980s.

While I was glad to debate the relative merits of our competing economic plans, I was under no illusion that the questions about my character had gone away. As the campaign drew to a close, I told an enthusiastic crowd in Dover what I really believed about the "character issue":

> It has been absolutely fascinating to me to go through the last few weeks and see these so-called character issues raised, conveniently, after I zoomed to the top by talking about your problems and your future and your lives.
>
> Well, character is an important issue in a presidential election, and the American people have been making character judgments about their politicians for more than two hundred years now. And most of the time they've been right, or none of us would be here today. I'll tell you what I think the character issue is: Who really cares about you? Who's really trying to say what he would do specifically if he were elected President? Who has a demonstrated record of doing what they're talking about? And who is determined to change your life rather than to just get or keep power? . . .
>
> I'll tell you what I think the character issue in this election is: How can you have the power of the presidency and never use it to help people improve their lives 'til your life needs saving in an election? That's a character issue. . . .
>
> I'll tell you something. I'm going to give you this election back, and if you'll give it to me, I won't be like George Bush. I'll never forget who gave me a second chance, and I'll be there for you 'til the last dog dies.

"'Til the last dog dies" became the rallying cry for our troops in the last days of the New Hampshire campaign.

Hundreds of volunteers worked furiously. Hillary and I shook every hand we could find. The polls were still discouraging, but the pulse felt better.

On election morning, February 18, it was cold and icy. Young Michael Morrison, Jan Paschal's wheelchair-bound student, woke in anticipation of working a polling place for me. Unfortunately, his mother's car wouldn't start. Michael was disappointed but not deterred. He rode his motorized wheelchair out into the cold morning and onto the shoulder of the slick road, then wheeled himself into the winter wind for two miles to reach his duty station. Some people thought the election was about the draft and Gennifer Flowers. I thought it was about Michael Morrison; and Ronnie Machos, the little boy with a hole in his heart and no health insurance; and the young girl whose unemployed father hung his head in shame over the dinner table; and Edward and Annie Davis, who didn't have enough money to buy food and the medicine they needed; and the son of an immigrant waiter in New York who couldn't play in the park across the street from where he lived. We were about to find out who was right.

That night, Paul Tsongas won with 35 percent, but I finished a strong second with 26 percent, well ahead of Kerrey with 12 percent, Harkin with 10 percent, and Brown with 9 percent. The rest of the votes went to write-ins. At the urging of Joe Grandmaison, a New Hampshire supporter I'd known since the Duffey campaign, I spoke to the media early, and at Paul Begala's suggestion said New Hampshire had made me "the Comeback Kid." Tsongas had annihilated me in the precincts closest to the Massachusetts state line. From ten miles north into New Hampshire, I had actually won. I was elated and profoundly grateful. The voters had decided that my campaign should go on.

I had come to love New Hampshire, to appreciate its idiosyncrasies, and to respect the seriousness of its voters, even those who chose someone else. The state had put me through the paces and made me a better candidate. So many people had befriended Hillary and me and lifted us up. A surprising number of them worked in my administration, and I kept in touch with several more over the next eight years, including hosting a New Hampshire Day at the White House.

New Hampshire demonstrated just how deeply the American people wanted their country to change. On the Republican side, Pat Buchanan's upstart campaign had won 37 percent of the vote, and the President's national approval ratings had dropped below 50 percent for the first time since the Gulf War. Although he still led both Paul Tsongas and me in the polls, the Democratic nomination was clearly worth having.

After New Hampshire, the rest of the primaries and caucuses came on at such a pace that the kind of "retail" politics New Hampshire demands became impossible to replicate. On February 23, Tsongas and Brown were the victors in the Maine caucuses, with Tsongas receiving 30 percent and Brown 29 percent. I was a distant third at 15 percent. With the exception of Iowa, the states with a caucus system drew far fewer people into the delegate-selection process than primaries did. Thus, the caucuses favored candidates with a hard core of intense supporters. They usually, but not always, were more left-leaning than the Democrats as a whole, and well to the left of the general election voters. On February 25, voters in the South Dakota primary gave more support to their neighbors Bob Kerrey and Tom Harkin than to me, though I made a respectable showing on just one trip to a rally at a horse ranch.

March was a big month. It opened with primaries in Colorado, Maryland, and Georgia. I had a lot of friends in Colorado, and former governor Dick Lamm was my Rocky Mountain coordinator, but the best I could do was a three-way split with Brown and Tsongas. Brown got 29 percent, I received 27 percent, with Tsongas right behind at 26 percent. In Maryland, I started out with a strong organization, but some supporters shifted to Tsongas when I dipped in the New Hampshire polls. He defeated me there.

Georgia was the big test. I hadn't won a primary yet, and I had to win there, and win convincingly. It was the largest state to vote on March 3 and the first in the South. Zell Miller had moved the primary date up a week, to separate Georgia from the southern Super Tuesday states. Georgia was an interesting state. Atlanta is a diverse, cosmopolitan city, with one of the highest concentrations of corporate headquarters of any other city in America. Outside Atlanta, the state is culturally conservative. For example, despite his great popularity, Zell had tried and failed to get the state legislature to take the Confederate cross off the state flag, and when his successor, Governor Roy Barnes, did it, he was defeated for reelection. The state also has a large military presence, long protected by its congressional leaders. It was no accident that Sam Nunn was chairman of the Senate Armed Services Committee. When the draft story broke, Bob Kerrey said that when I got to Georgia, the voters would split me open like a "soft peanut," a clever hit, because Georgia grows more peanuts than any other state. A couple of days after the New Hampshire vote, I flew to Atlanta. When my plane landed, I was met by Mayor Maynard Jackson, an old friend, and Jim Butler, a prosecuting attorney and Vietnam veteran who smiled and said he was one soldier who didn't want to split me open like a soft peanut.

The three of us rode downtown for a rally in a shopping mall. I got onto the stage with a large crowd of prominent Democrats who were supporting me. Before long, the stage built for the occasion couldn't support all of us; it just collapsed, throwing bodies everywhere. I wasn't hurt, but one of my co-chairs, Calvin Smyre, an African-American state representative, wasn't so lucky. He fell and broke his hip. Later, Craig Smith joked to Calvin that he was the only one of my supporters who literally "busted his ass" for me. He sure did. But so did Zell Miller, Congressman John Lewis, and a lot of other Georgians. And so did a number of Arkansans who had organized themselves into the "Arkansas Travelers." The Travelers campaigned in almost every state with a presidential primary. They always made a difference, but they were particularly effective in Georgia. The political press said that to go forward I had to win decisively there, with at least 40 percent of the vote. Thanks to my friends and my message, I won 57 percent.

The following Saturday, in South Carolina, I picked up my second win, with 63 percent of the vote. I had a lot of help from Democratic officials, plus former governor Dick Riley, and friends from Renaissance Weekend. Tom Harkin made a last-ditch effort to derail me, and Jesse Jackson, a South Carolina native, went around the state with him criticizing me. Despite the attacks, and the crass response to them I carelessly made at a radio station in a room with a live microphone, other black leaders stayed hitched. I received a large majority of the black vote, as I had in Georgia. I think it surprised my opponents, all of whom had strong convictions and good records on civil rights. But I was the only southerner, and both I and the Arkansas blacks supporting me brought years of personal connections to black political, educational, business, and religious leaders all across the South and beyond.

As in Georgia, I also got good support from white primary voters. By 1992, most of the whites who wouldn't support a candidate with close ties to the black community had already become Republicans. I got the votes of those who wanted a President to reach across racial lines to attack the problems that plagued all Americans. The Republicans tried to keep this group's numbers small by turning every election into a culture war, and turning every Democrat into an alien in the eyes of white voters. They knew just what psychological buttons to push to get white voters to stop thinking, and when they got away with it, they won. Besides trying to win the primary, I was trying to keep enough white voters thinking to be competitive in the South in the general election.

After Georgia, Bob Kerrey withdrew from the race. After South Carolina, Tom Harkin did, too. Only Tsongas, Brown, and I headed into Super Tuesday, with its eight primaries and three caucuses. Tsongas defeated me badly in the primaries in his home state of Massachusetts and neighboring Rhode Island, and won the caucuses in Delaware. But the southern and border states made the day a rout for our campaign. In all the southern primaries—in Texas, Florida, Louisiana, Mississippi, Oklahoma, and Tennessee—I won a majority of the vote. In Texas, with the help of friends I'd made in the 1972 McGovern campaign and a big majority among Mexican-Americans, I won with 66 percent. In all the other primary states I did better than that, except for Florida, which, after a hotly contested race, went 51 percent Clinton, 34 percent Tsongas, 12 percent Brown. I also won the caucuses in Hawaii, thanks to Governor John Waihee, and in Missouri, where Lieutenant Governor Mel Carnahan endorsed me, despite having his own primary campaign for governor. He won anyway.

After Super Tuesday, I had just a week to cement my strategy of building an insurmountable lead in Illinois and Michigan. Only a month earlier, I had been in free fall, with all the media "experts" predicting my demise. Now I was in the lead. However, Tsongas was still very much alive. On the day after Super Tuesday, he quipped that, because of my strong showing in the southern primaries, he would consider me as his vice-presidential running mate. The next day he, too, was in the Midwest, questioning my character, my record as governor, and my electability. For him the character issue was the middle-class tax cut. A new poll showed that around 40 percent of the American people also doubted my honesty, but I doubted that they were thinking about the tax issue.

There was nothing to do but stick to my strategy and press on. In Michigan, I visited the small town of Barton, near Flint, where a large majority of the residents had come from Arkansas, looking for jobs in the auto industry. On March 12, I spoke in Macomb County, near Detroit, the prototypical home of the Reagan Democrats, voters who had been lured away from our party by Reagan's anti-government, strong-defense, tough-on-crime message. In fact, these suburban voters had begun voting Republican in the 1960s, because they thought the Democrats no longer shared their values of work and family, and were too concerned with social programs, which they tended to see as taking their tax money and giving it to blacks and wasteful bureaucrats.

I told a full house at Macomb County Community College that I would give them a new Democratic Party, with economic and social policies based on opportunity for and responsibility from all citizens. That included corporate executives earning huge salaries without regard to their performance, working people who refused to upgrade their skills, and poor people on welfare who could work. Then I told them we couldn't succeed unless they were willing to reach across racial lines to work with all people who shared those values. They had to stop voting along the racial divide, because "the problems are not racial in nature. This is an issue of economics, of values."

The next day, I gave the same message to a few hundred black ministers and other activists at the Reverend Odell Jones's Pleasant Grove Baptist Church in inner-city Detroit. I told the black audience, many of whom had Arkansas roots, that I had challenged the white voters in Macomb County to reach across the racial divide, and now I was challenging them to do the same, by accepting the responsibility part of my agenda, including welfare reform, tough child-support enforcement, and anti-crime efforts that would promote the values of work, family, and safety in their neighborhoods. The twin speeches got quite a bit of attention, because it was unusual for a politician to challenge Macomb County whites on race or inner-city blacks on welfare and crime. When both groups responded strongly to the same message, I wasn't surprised. In their heart of hearts, most Americans know that the best social program is a job, that the strongest social institution is the family, and that the politics of racial division are self-defeating.

In Illinois, I visited a sausage factory with black, Hispanic, and Eastern European immigrant employees to highlight the company's commitment to giving all employees who hadn't finished high school access to a GED program. I met a new citizen from Romania who said he would cast his first vote for me. I worked in the black and Hispanic communities with two young activists, Bobby Rush and Luis Gutierrez, both of whom would later be elected to Congress. I toured an energy-efficient housing project with a young Hispanic community leader, Danny Solis, whose sister Patti went to work for Hillary in the campaign and has been with her ever since. And I marched in Chicago's St. Patrick's Day parade, to the cheers of supporters and jeers of opponents, both enhanced by the beer that was in ample supply at bars along the parade route.

Two days before the election, I debated Paul Tsongas and Jerry Brown on television in Chicago. They knew it was make-or-break time, and they went after me. Brown grabbed the spotlight with a harsh attack on Hillary, saying that I had steered state business to the Rose firm to increase her income and that a poultry company her firm represented got special treatment from the Department of Pollution Control and Ecology because of her. The charges were ridiculous and the vehemence with which Jerry made them angered me. I explained the facts, as I had done when Frank White attacked Hillary's law practice in the 1986 governor's race. The Rose firm had represented the State of Arkansas in the bond business since 1948. It represented the state against the utilities that wanted Arkansas to pay for the Grand Gulf nuclear plant. Hillary had all legal fees paid by the state deleted from the firm's income before her partnership share was calculated, so she didn't receive any benefit from them, as even rudimentary research would have shown. Moreover, there was no evidence that the Rose firm's clients secured special favors from any state agency. I shouldn't have lost my temper, but the charges were plainly baseless. Subconsciously, I suppose I also felt guilty that Hillary had been forced to defend me so much, and I was glad to be able to rise to her defense.

Everyone who knew her knew she was scrupulously honest, but not everyone knew her, and the attacks hurt. On the morning after the debate, we were shaking hands at the Busy Bee Coffee Shop in Chicago when a reporter asked her what she thought of Brown's charges. She gave a good answer about trying to have both a career and a family life. The reporter then asked if she could have avoided the appearance of a conflict. Of course, that's exactly what she did and what she should have said. But she was tired and stressed. Instead, she said, "I suppose I could have stayed home and baked cookies and had teas, but what I decided to do was fulfill my profession, which I entered before my husband was in public life. And I've worked very, very hard to be as careful as possible, and that's all I can tell you."

The press picked up the "tea and cookies" remark and played it as a slam on stay-at-home mothers. The Republican culture warriors had a field day, portraying Hillary as a "militant feminist lawyer" who would be the ideological leader of a "Clinton-Clinton administration" that would push a "radical feminist" agenda. I hurt for her. Over the years, I don't know how many times I'd heard her champion the importance of ensuring choices for women, including the choice to stay home with their children, a decision most mothers, single and married, simply couldn't afford anymore. Also, I knew she liked to bake cookies and have her women friends for tea. With one off-the-cuff remark, she had given our opponents another weapon to do what they did best—divide and distract the voters.

It was all forgotten the next day when we won in Illinois, Hillary's home state, with 52 percent to 25 percent for Tsongas and 15 percent for Brown, and in Michigan, with 49 percent to 27 percent for Brown and 18 percent for Tsongas. If Brown's attack on Hillary had any effect, it probably hurt him in Illinois. Meanwhile, President Bush handily defeated Pat Buchanan in both states, effectively ending his challenge. Although the division in the Republican ranks was good for me, I was glad to see Buchanan defeated. He had played to the dark side of middle-class insecurity. For example, in one southern state he visited a Confederate cemetery but wouldn't even walk across the street to visit the black cemetery.

After a great celebration in Chicago's Palmer House Hotel, complete with Irish green confetti in honor of the holiday, we got back to business. On the surface, the campaign was in great shape. Underneath, things weren't so clear. One new poll showed me running even with President Bush. Another, however, showed me well behind, even though the President's job approval had dropped to 39 percent. A survey of Illinois voters as they left their polling places said half the Democrats were unhappy with their choice of presidential candidates. Jerry Brown was unhappy, too. He said he might not support me if I won the nomination.

On March 19, Tsongas withdrew from the campaign, citing financial problems. That left Jerry Brown as my only opponent as we headed toward the Connecticut primary on March 24. It was assumed I would win in Connecticut, because most of the Democratic leaders had endorsed me, and I had friends there going back to my law school days. Though I campaigned hard, I was worried. It just didn't feel good. The Tsongas supporters were mad at me for driving him from the race; they were going to vote for him anyway or switch to Brown. By contrast, my supporters had a hard time getting stirred up, because they thought I had the nomination in the bag. I was worried that a low turnout could cost me the election. That's exactly what happened. The turnout was around 20 percent of the registered Democrats, and Brown beat me, 37 to 36 percent. Twenty percent of the voters were die-hard Tsongas supporters who stood by their man.

The next big test was in New York on April 7. Now that I had lost in Connecticut, if I didn't win in New York, the nomination would be in danger again. With its tough, insatiable twenty-four-hour news cycle and its rough-and-tumble interest group politics, New York seemed to be the ideal place to derail my campaign.

TWENTY-SEVEN

In politics, there's nothing quite like a New York election. First, there are three geographically and psychologically distinct regions of the state: New York City with its five very different boroughs; Long Island and the other suburban counties; and upstate. There are large black and Hispanic populations, the nation's largest population of Jewish Americans, plus well-organized groups of Indians, Pakistanis, Albanians, and just about any other ethnic group you can imagine. There is also a lot of diversity within New York's black and Hispanic populations— New York's Hispanics include people from Puerto Rico and all the Caribbean nations, including more than 500,000 from the Dominican Republic alone.

My outreach to the ethnic communities was organized by Chris Hyland, a Georgetown classmate who lived in lower Manhattan, one of the most ethnically diverse neighborhoods in America. When Hillary and I visited a group of elementary school students displaced by the attack on the World Trade Center in September 2001, we found children from eighty different national and ethnic groups. Chris started by buying about thirty ethnic newspapers and locating the leaders mentioned in them. After the primaries, he organized a fund-raiser in New York with 950 ethnic leaders, then moved to Little Rock to organize ethnic groups across the country, making an important contribution to victory in the general election, and laying the foundation for our continuing unprecedented contact with ethnic communities once we got to the White House.

The unions, especially the public employee groups, have a huge presence and are politically astute and effective. In New York City, the politics of the primary were further complicated by the fact that both party regulars and liberal reformers were active and often saw themselves at odds with each other. Gay-rights groups were organized and vocal about the need to do more about AIDS, which in 1992 still claimed more victims in America than any other country. The press was an ever-present cacophony of traditional newspapers, led by the **New York Times,** the tabloids, vigorous local TV stations, and talk radio—all in hot competition for the latest story.

While the New York campaign didn't really begin until after the Connecticut primary, I had been working the state for months with the invaluable help and expert advice of Harold Ickes, the namesake and son of FDR's famous secretary of the interior. By 1992, we had been friends for more than twenty years. Harold is a thin, intense, brilliant, passionate, and occasionally profane man, a unique blend of liberal idealism and practical political skills. As a young man, he'd worked as a cowboy out west and had been badly beaten working for civil rights in the South. In campaigns, he was a loyal friend and a ferocious opponent who believed in the power of politics to change lives. He knew the personalities, issues, and power struggles of New York like the back of his hand. If I was about to go through hell, I was at least making the trip with a man who stood a chance of getting me out alive.

In December 1991, Harold, who had already helped

line up important support in Manhattan, Brooklyn, and the Bronx, arranged for me to speak to the Queens Democratic Committee. He suggested we ride the subway from Manhattan to the meeting. My being a country boy on the subway got more press coverage than my speech, but the appearance was important. Shortly afterward, the Queens Democratic chairman, Congressman Tom Manton, endorsed me. So did Queens congressman Floyd Flake, who was also the minister of Allen African Methodist Episcopal Church.

In January, I visited a high school in Brooklyn to observe Martin Luther King Jr.'s birthday with African-American congressman Ed Towns and the Brooklyn Democratic chair, Clarence Norman. The kids talked a lot about the problem of guns and knives in their school. They wanted a President who would make their lives safer. I went to a debate in the Bronx, moderated by the borough president, Fernando Ferrer, who would become a supporter. I took the ferry to Staten Island and campaigned there. In Manhattan, the borough president, Ruth Messinger, worked hard for me, as did her young aide, Marty Rouse, who helped me make inroads into the gay community. Victor and Sara Kovner convinced a number of the liberal reformers to support me and became good friends. Guillermo Linares, who was one of the first Dominicans elected to the city council, became one of the first prominent Latinos to endorse me. I campaigned on Long Island and in Westchester County, where I now live.

The unions made a bigger difference in New York than in any previous primary. Among the largest and most active were the New York affiliates of AFSCME, the American Federation of State, County, and Municipal

Employees. After I appeared before its executive board, AFSCME was the first big union to endorse me. I had worked closely with AFSCME as governor, and had become a dues-paying member. But the real reason for the endorsement was that the union's president, Gerald McEntee, decided that he liked me and that I could win. McEntee was a good man to have on your side. He was effective, fiercely loyal, and didn't mind a tough fight. I also had the support of the United Transportation Union and, by the end of March, the Communications Workers of America and the International Ladies' Garment Workers Union. The teachers were helpful, even though I had not yet received a formal endorsement. In addition to the unions, I also had a strong group of business supporters, mobilized by Alan Patricot and Stan Schuman.

The most important and enduring encounter I had with an ethnic group was with the Irish. Late one night, I met with the Irish Issues Forum organized by Bronx assemblyman John Dearie. Harold Ickes and New York City tax commissioner Carol O'Cleireacain had helped me prepare. The legendary Paul O'Dwyer, who was about eighty-five, and his son Brian were there, as were Niall O'Dowd, editor of the **Irish Voice,** journalist Jimmy Breslin, Queens comptroller Peter King, a Republican, and about a hundred other Irish activists. They wanted me to promise to appoint a special representative to push for an end to the violence in Northern Ireland on terms that were fair to the Catholic minority. I had also been encouraged to do this by Boston mayor Ray Flynn, an ardent Irish Catholic and a strong supporter of mine. I had been interested in the Irish issue since "the Troubles" began in 1968, when I was at Oxford. After a lengthy discussion, I said I would do it and that I would push for an end to dis-

crimination against Northern Ireland's Catholics in economics and other areas. Though I knew it would infuriate
the British and strain our most important transatlantic
alliance, I had become convinced that the United States,
with its huge Irish diaspora, including people who fun-
neled money to the Irish Republican Army, might be able
to facilitate a breakthrough.

Soon I put out a strong statement reaffirming my commitment, drafted by my foreign policy aide Nancy Soderberg. My law school classmate former congressman Bruce
Morrison, of Connecticut, organized Irish-Americans for
Clinton. The group would play a major role in the campaign and in the work we would do afterward. As Chelsea
noted in her Stanford senior thesis on the Irish peace
process, I first got involved in the Irish issue because of the
politics of New York, but it became one of the great passions of my presidency.

In an ordinary Democratic primary, a campaign with
this kind of support would be assured an easy victory. But
this was not an ordinary primary. First, there was the
opposition. Jerry Brown was working like a demon, determined to rally the liberal voters in this last, best chance to
stop my campaign. Paul Tsongas, encouraged by his showing in Connecticut, let it be known that he wouldn't mind
his supporters voting for him one more time. The presidential candidate of the New Alliance Party, an articulate,
angry woman named Lenora Fulani, did what she could
to help them, bringing her supporters to a health-care
event I held in a Harlem hospital and shouting down my
speech.

Jesse Jackson practically moved to New York to help
Brown. His most important contribution was to persuade
Dennis Rivera, head of one of the city's largest and most

active unions, Service Employees International Union Local 1199, not to endorse me and to help Jerry instead. Brown returned the favor by saying that, if nominated, he would name Jesse as his running mate. I thought Brown's announcement would help him among New York's black voters, but it also galvanized a lot of new support for me in the Jewish community. Jackson was believed to be too close to Black Muslim leader Louis Farrakhan, who was known for anti-Semitic remarks. Still, Jesse's support was a net plus for Brown in New York.

Then there was the media. The big papers had been camping out in Arkansas for weeks, looking for whatever they could find on my record and my personal life. The **New York Times** had started the ball rolling in early March with the first of its Whitewater stories. In 1978, Hillary and I, along with Jim and Susan McDougal, took out bank loans of more than $200,000 to invest in land along the White River in northwest Arkansas. Jim was a land developer whom I had met when he ran Senator Fulbright's office in Little Rock. We hoped to subdivide the property and sell it at a profit to retirees who had begun moving to the Ozarks in large numbers in the sixties and seventies. McDougal had been successful in all his previous land ventures, including one in which I had invested a few thousand dollars and earned a modest profit. Unfortunately, in the late seventies, interest rates went through the roof, the economy slowed, land sales dropped, and we lost money on the venture.

By the time I became governor again in 1983, McDougal had bought a small savings-and-loan and named it Madison Guaranty Savings and Loan. A few years later, he retained the Rose Law Firm to represent it. When the savings-and-loan crisis hit America, Madison was facing insolvency and sought to inject new cash into the operation by selling preferred stock and forming a subsidiary to provide brokerage services. To do this, McDougal had to get permission from the state securities commissioner, Beverly Bassett Schaffer, whom I had appointed. Beverly was a first-class lawyer, the sister of my friend Woody Bassett, and the wife of Archie Schaffer, Senator Dale Bumpers' nephew.

The **Times** article was one of a series of articles on Whitewater. The reporter questioned whether there was a conflict in Hillary's representing an entity regulated by the state. She had personally signed one letter to Commissioner Schaffer explaining the preferred stock proposal. The reporter also implied that Madison had received special treatment in getting its "novel" financing proposals approved and that Schaffer had not exercised appropriate oversight over the institution when it was failing.

The facts did not support the accusations and innuendos. First, the financing proposals the commissioner approved were normal for the time, not novel. Second, as soon as an independent audit showed Madison to be insolvent, in 1987, Schaffer pushed federal regulators to shut it down, well before they were willing to do so. Third, Hillary had billed Madison for a grand total of twenty-one hours of legal work at the Rose Law Firm over a two-year period. Fourth, we never borrowed any money from Madison, but we did lose money on the Whitewater investment. That's the essential Whitewater picture. The **New York Times** reporter clearly was talking to Sheffield Nelson and other adversaries of mine in Arkansas who would have been happy to create "character problems" in other areas besides the draft and Flowers. In this case, doing so required ignoring inconvenient facts and misrepresenting the record of a dedicated public servant like Schaffer.

The **Washington Post** weighed in with an article designed to show I'd been too close to the poultry industry and had failed to stop it from spreading the waste from its chicken and hog operations onto farmland. A little animal waste made good fertilizer, but when the volume of waste was too great for the land to absorb, rain washed it into streams, polluting them so that they were unsafe for fishing and swimming. In 1990 the state Department of Pollution Control and Ecology found that more than 90 percent of the streams in northwest Arkansas, where the poultry industry was concentrated, were polluted. We spent several million dollars trying to correct the problem, and two years later, the Pollution Control people said over 50 percent of the streams met the standard for recreational use. I got the industry to agree to a set of "best management practices" to clean up the rest. I was criticized for not mandating an industry cleanup—something easier said than done. The Democratic Congress could not do it; the agricultural interests had enough influence to get themselves completely exempted from federal regulations when Congress passed the Clean Water Act. Poultry was Arkansas' biggest business and number one employer and very influential in the state legislature. Under the circumstances, I thought we had done a pretty good job, though it was the weakest spot in an otherwise solid environmental record. Both the **Washington Post** and the **New York Times** wound up doing articles on the subject, with the **Post** suggesting by late March that the Rose Law Firm had somehow gotten the state to go easy on the poultry industry.

I tried to keep things in perspective. The press had an obligation to examine the record of someone who might be President. Most reporters knew nothing about Arkansas or me when they started. Some of them had negative preconceptions about a poor, rural state and the people who lived there. I had also been identified as 1992's "character problem" candidate; that made the media vulnerable to whatever dirt they were handed to support the preconception.

Intellectually, I understood all this, and I remembered and appreciated the positive coverage I had received earlier in the campaign. Nevertheless, it felt more and more as if the investigative stories were being prepared on the basis of "shoot first, ask questions later." Reading them felt like an out-of-body experience. The press seemed determined to prove that everyone who thought I was fit to be President was a fool: the Arkansas voters who had elected me five times; my fellow governors, who had voted me the most effective governor in the country; the education experts who had praised our reforms and progress; lifelong friends who were campaigning for me all over the country. In Arkansas, even my honest adversaries knew I worked hard and wouldn't take a nickel to see the cow jump over the moon. Now it seemed I had snookered all these people from the age of six on. At one point, when things got really bad in New York, Craig Smith told me he didn't read the papers anymore, "because I don't recognize the person they're talking about."

Near the end of March, Betsey Wright, who was at Harvard doing a stint at the Kennedy School, came to my rescue. She had worked hard for years to build our progressive record and to run a tight ethical operation. She had a prodigious memory, knew the records, and was more than willing to fight with reporters to set the record straight. When she moved into the headquarters as director of damage control, I felt much better. Betsey stopped a lot of factually incorrect stories, but she couldn't stop them all.

On March 26, the smoke seemed to clear a little when Senator Tom Harkin, the Communications Workers of America, and the International Ladies' Garment Workers Union endorsed me. I was also helped when Governor Cuomo and New York senator Pat Moynihan criticized Jerry Brown's 13 percent flat-tax proposal and said it would hurt New York. It was a rare day in the campaign; the news was dominated by people concerned with issues and their impact on people's lives.

On March 29, I was back in the soup again, with a problem of my own making. Jerry Brown and I were in a televised candidates' forum on WCBS in New York when a reporter asked me if I had ever tried marijuana at Oxford. This was the first time I had ever been asked that specific question directly. In Arkansas, when asked generally if I had ever used marijuana, I had given an evasive answer, saying I had never broken the drug laws of the United States. This time, I gave a more direct and answer: "When I was in England, I experimented with marijuana a time or two and I didn't like it. I didn't inhale and I never tried it again."

Even Jerry Brown said the press should lay off because the issue wasn't relevant.

But the press had found another character issue. As for the "didn't inhale" remark, I was stating a fact, not trying to minimize what I had done, as I tried to explain until I was blue in the face. What I should have said was that I couldn't inhale. I had never smoked cigarettes, didn't inhale with the pipe I occasionally smoked at Oxford, and tried but failed to inhale the marijuana smoke. I don't know why I even mentioned it; maybe I thought I was being funny, or perhaps it was just a nervous reaction to a subject I didn't want to discuss. My account was corroborated by the respected English journalist Martin Walker, who later wrote an interesting and not altogether flattering book on my presidency, **Clinton: The President They Deserve.** Martin said publicly that he'd been at Oxford with me and had seen me try but fail to inhale at a party. By then it was too late. My unfortunate account of my marijuana misadventures was cited by pundits and Republicans throughout 1992 as evidence of my character problem. And I had given late-night TV hosts fodder for years of jokes.

As the old country song goes, I didn't know whether to "kill myself or go bowling." New York was suffering from severe economic and social problems. The Bush policies were making things worse. Yet every day seemed to be punctuated by television and print reporters shouting "character" questions at me. Radio talk-show host Don Imus called me a "redneck bozo." When I went on Phil Donahue's television show, all he did for twenty minutes was ask me questions about marital infidelity. After I gave my standard answer, he kept on asking. I rebuffed him and the audience cheered. He kept right on.

Whether I had a character problem or not, I sure had a reputation problem, one I had been promised by the White House more than six months earlier. Because the President is both the head of state and the Chief Executive of the government, he is in a sense the embodiment of people's idea of America, so reputation is important. Presidents going back to George Washington and Thomas Jefferson have guarded their reputations jealously: Washington, from criticism of his expense accounts during the Revolutionary War; Jefferson, from stories about his weakness for women. Before he became President, Abraham Lincoln suffered from debilitating episodes of depression. Once he was unable to leave his house for a whole month. If he had had to run under modern conditions, we might have been deprived of our greatest President.

Jefferson even wrote about the obligation of a President's associates to protect his reputation at all costs: "When the accident of situation is to give us a place in history, for which nature had not prepared us by corresponding endowments, it is the duty of those about us carefully to veil from the public eye the weaknesses, and still more, the vices of our character." The veil had been ripped from my weaknesses and vices, both real and imagined. The public knew more about them than about my record, message, or whatever virtues I might have. If my reputation was in tatters, I might not be able to be elected no matter how much people agreed with what I wanted to do, or how well they thought I might do it.

In the face of all the character attacks, I responded as I always did when my back was against the wall—I plowed on. In the last week of the campaign, the clouds began to lift. On April 1, during a meeting with President Bush at the White House, President Carter made a widely reported comment that he supported me. It couldn't have come at a better time. No one had ever questioned Carter's character, and his reputation had continued to grow after he left the presidency, because of his good works at home and around the world. In one comment, he more than made up for the problems he had caused me during the Cuban refugee crisis in 1980.

On April 2, Jerry Brown was booed in a speech to the

Jewish Community Relations Council in New York for suggesting Jesse Jackson as his running mate. Meanwhile, Hillary and I spoke to a large crowd at a midday rally on Wall Street. I got some boos, too, for referring to the eighties as a decade of greed and opposing a cut in the capital gains tax. After the speech, I worked the crowd, shaking hands with supporters and trying to convince the dissenters.

Meanwhile, we poured the whole campaign operation into the state. Besides Harold Ickes and Susan Thomases, Mickey Kantor was camped out in a hotel suite, joined by Carville, Stephanopoulos, Stan Greenberg, and Frank Greer and his partner, Mandy Grunwald. As always, Bruce Lindsey was with me. His wife, Bev, came up, too, to make sure all the public events were well planned and executed. Carol Willis organized a busload of black Arkansans to come to New York City to talk about what I had done as governor for and with blacks. Black ministers from home called counterparts in New York to ask for pulpit time for our people on the Sunday before the election. Lottie Shackleford, a Little Rock city director and Vice-Chair of the National Democratic Committee, spoke in five churches that Sunday. Those who knew me were putting a dent in the Reverend Jackson's efforts to bring a big majority of New York's black voters to Brown.

Some people in the press were coming around. Maybe the tide was turning; I even got a cordial reception on Don Imus's radio show. **Newsday** columnist Jimmy Breslin, who cared a lot about the Irish issue, wrote, "Say what you want, but do not say that he quits." Pete Hamill, the New York **Daily News** columnist whose books I'd read and enjoyed, said, "I've come to respect Bill Clinton. It's the late rounds and he's still there." The **New York Times** and the **Daily News** endorsed me. Amazingly, so did the **New York Post,** which had been more relentless in its attacks than any other paper. Its editorial said: "It speaks strongly to his strength of character that he has already survived a battering by the press on personal questions unprecedented in the history of American politics. . . . He has continued to campaign with remarkable tenacity. . . . In our view, he has manifested extraordinary grace under pressure."

On April 5, we got good news from Puerto Rico, where 96 percent of the voters supported me. Then, on April 7, with a low turnout of about a million voters, I carried New York with 41 percent. Tsongas finished second with 29 percent, just ahead of Brown at 26 percent. A majority of African-Americans cast their ballots for me. That night I was battered and bloodied but elated. My one-sentence take on the campaign was a line from a gospel song I'd heard in Anthony Mangun's church: "The darker the night, the sweeter the victory."

When I was doing research for this book, I read the account of the New York primary in **The Comeback Kid** by Charles Allen and Jonathan Portis. In it, the authors refer to something Levon Helm, the drummer for the Band and an Arkansas native, said in the great rock documentary **The Last Waltz** about what it's like for a southern boy to come to New York hoping to make it into the big time: "You just go in the first time and you get your ass kicked and you take off. Soon as it heals up, you come back and you try it again. Eventually, you fall right in love with it."

I didn't have the luxury of taking time off to heal, but I knew just how he felt. Like New Hampshire, New York had tested and taught me. And like Levon Helm, I had come to love it. After our rocky start, New York became one of my strongest states for the next eight years.

On April 7, we also won in Kansas, Minnesota, and Wisconsin. On April 9, Paul Tsongas announced that he would not reenter the race. The fight for the nomination was effectively over. I had more than half the 2,145 delegates I needed to be nominated, and had only Jerry Brown to compete with the rest of the way in. But I was under no illusions about how badly damaged I had been, or how little I could do about it before the Democratic convention in July. I was also exhausted. I had lost my voice and put on a lot of weight, about thirty pounds. I had gained the weight in New Hampshire, most of it in the last month of the campaign, when I suffered from a flu bug that filled my chest with fluid at night so I couldn't sleep for more than an hour without waking to cough. I kept alert on adrenaline and Dunkin' Donuts, and I had a bulging waistline to prove it. Harry Thomason bought me some new suits, so that I didn't look like a balloon about to burst.

After New York, I went home for a week to rest my voice, start getting back in shape, and think about how to get out of the hole I was in. While I was in Little Rock, I won the Virginia caucuses and received the endorsement of the leaders of the AFL-CIO. On April 24, the United Auto Workers endorsed me, and on April 28, I won a large majority in the Pennsylvania primary. Pennsylvania could have been tough. Governor Bob Casey, whom I admired for his tenacity in running three times before he won, had been very critical of me. He was strongly anti-abortion. As he struggled with his own life-threatening health problems, the issue became more and more important to him, and he had a hard time supporting pro-choice candidates.

So did a lot of other pro-life Democrats in the state. Still, I always felt good about Pennsylvania. The western part of the state reminded me of north Arkansas. I related well to the people in Pittsburgh and in the smaller cities in the middle of the state. And I loved Philadelphia. I carried the state with 57 percent. More important, exit polls showed that more than 60 percent of the Democrats who voted thought I had the integrity to serve as President, up from 49 percent in the New York exit polls. The integrity number improved because I had had three weeks to run a positive issue-oriented campaign in a state that badly wanted to hear it.

The Pennsylvania victory was welcome, but overshadowed by the prospect of a formidable new challenger, H. Ross Perot. Perot was a Texas billionaire who had made his fortune with EDS, Electronic Data Systems, a company that did a lot of government work, including some for Arkansas. He had become nationally known when he financed and engineered the rescue of EDS employees from Iran after the fall of the Shah. He had a blunt but effective speaking style, and he was convincing a lot of Americans that, with his business acumen, financial independence, and penchant for bold action, he could do a better job of running the country than either President Bush or I.

By the end of April, several published polls had him running ahead of the President, with me in third place. I found Perot to be an interesting man and was fascinated by his phenomenal early popularity. If he entered the race, I thought his boom would play itself out, but I couldn't be sure. So I stuck to my knitting, picking up the endorsement of "super delegates"—current and former elected officials who had a guaranteed vote at the convention.

One of the first super delegates to come out for me was Senator Jay Rockefeller of West Virginia. Jay had been my friend since we sat together at governors' meetings. And since New Hampshire, he had been giving me advice on health care, which he knew more about than I did.

On April 29, the day after the Pennsylvania vote, Los Angeles erupted in riots, after an all-white jury in neighboring Ventura County acquitted four white Los Angeles police officers of charges involving the beating of Rodney King, a black man, in March 1991. A bystander had videotaped the beating, and the tape had been released and shown on televisions across America. It looked as if King had offered no resistance when stopped, but was beaten brutally anyway.

The verdict inflamed the black community, which had long felt that the Los Angeles Police Department was riddled with racism. After a three-day rampage in South Central Los Angeles, more than 50 people were dead, more than 2,300 were injured, thousands of people had been arrested, and damages from looting and burning were estimated to be higher than $700 million.

On Sunday, May 3, I was in Los Angeles to speak to the Reverend Cecil "Chip" Murray's First AME Church about the need to heal our racial and economic rifts. And I toured the damaged areas with Maxine Waters, who represented South Central Los Angeles in Congress. Maxine was a smart, tough politician who had endorsed me early, despite her long friendship with Jesse Jackson. The streets looked like a war zone, full of burned and looted buildings. As we walked, I noticed a grocery store that appeared to be intact. When I asked Maxine about it, she said the store had been "protected" by people from the neighborhood, including gang members, because its owner, a white businessman named Ron Burkle, had been good to the community. He hired local people, all the employees were union members with health insurance, and the food was of the same quality as that in Beverly Hills groceries and sold at the same prices. At the time, that was unusual: because inner-city residents are less mobile, their stores often had inferior food at higher prices. I had met Burkle for the first time just a few hours earlier, and I resolved to get to know him better. He became one of my best friends and strongest supporters.

At a meeting in Maxine's house, I listened as South Central residents related stories about their problems with the police, the tension between Korean-American merchants and their black customers, and the need for more jobs. I pledged to support initiatives to empower inner-city residents, by initiating enterprise zones to encourage private investment and community development banks to make loans to low- and moderate-income people. I learned a lot on the trip, and it got good press coverage. It also made an impression in the city that I cared enough to come before President Bush did. The lesson was not lost on perhaps the best politician in the talented Bush family: in 2002, President George W. Bush came to Los Angeles for the tenth anniversary of the riots.

During the rest of May, a series of primary victories added to my delegate total, including a 68 percent win in Arkansas on the twenty-sixth, rivaling the best I'd ever done in a contested primary at home. Meanwhile, I campaigned in California, hoping to complete my fight for the nomination in Jerry Brown's home state. I called for federal aid to make our schools safer and for an all-out effort to turn back the tide of AIDS in America. And I began the search for a vice-presidential nominee. I entrusted the vetting process to Warren Christopher, a Los Angeles lawyer who had been President Carter's deputy secretary of state, and who had a well-deserved reputation for competence and discretion. In 1980, Chris had negotiated the release of our hostages in Iran. Sadly, their release was delayed until the day of President Reagan's inauguration, proof that all leaders play politics, even in a theocracy.

Meanwhile, Ross Perot's still-undeclared candidacy continued to gather steam. He resigned as chairman of his company and continued to rise in the polls. Just as I was about to wrap up the nomination, the papers were filled with headlines like "Clinton Set to Clinch Nomination, but All Eyes Are on Perot," "U.S. Primary Season Near End, Perot Man to Watch," and "New Poll Shows Perot Leading Bush and Clinton." Perot was unburdened by President Bush's record or my primary battle scars. For the Republicans, he must have seemed a Frankenstein's monster of their own making: a businessman who had slipped into the space created by their assault on me. For Democrats, he was also a bad dream, proof that the President could be defeated, but perhaps not by their wounded nominee.

On June 2, I won the primaries in Ohio, New Jersey, New Mexico, Alabama, Montana, and California, where I defeated Brown 48 to 40 percent. Finally, I had clinched the nomination. Of all the primary votes cast in 1992, I had received more than 10.3 million, or 52 percent. Brown got nearly 4 million votes, 20 percent; Tsongas received about 3.6 million, 18 percent; the rest were cast for the other candidates and those who voted for uncommitted delegates.

But the big story that night was the willingness of so

many voters in both parties, according to exit polls, to desert their parties' nominees to vote for Perot. It put a big damper on our celebration at the Los Angeles Biltmore. As Hillary and I watched the returns in my suite, even I was having trouble maintaining my congenital optimism. Not long before we were scheduled to go down to the ballroom to give a victory speech, Hillary and I had a visitor—Chevy Chase. Just as he had done on Long Island four years earlier, he showed up at a low moment to lift my spirits. This time, we were joined by his movie partner Goldie Hawn. By the time they finished making jokes about the absurd situation we were in, I was feeling better and ready to roll on.

Once again, press pundits said I was dead. Now Perot was the man to beat. A Reuters news service story captured the situation in one line: "Bill Clinton, who struggled for months to avoid publicity about his personal life, Friday faced an even worse political curse—being ignored." President Nixon predicted that Bush would beat Perot in a close race, with me a distant third.

Our campaign had to regain momentum. We decided to reach out to specific constituencies and the general public directly, and to keep pushing the issues. I went on Arsenio Hall's late-night TV show, which was especially popular with younger viewers. I wore sunglasses and played "Heartbreak Hotel" and "God Bless the Child" on my sax. I answered viewers' questions on **Larry King Live.** On June 11 and 12, the Democratic platform committee produced a draft that reflected my philosophy and campaign commitments, and avoided the polarizing language that had hurt us in the past.

On June 13, I appeared before the Reverend Jesse Jackson's Rainbow Coalition. At the outset, both Jesse and I saw it as an opportunity to bridge our differences and build a united front for the campaign. It didn't work out that way. The night before I spoke, the popular rap artist Sister Souljah addressed the coalition. She was a bright woman who could have an impact on young people. A month earlier, in an interview in the **Washington Post** after the Los Angeles riots, she had made some astounding comments: "If black people kill black people every day, why not have a week and kill white people? . . . So if you're a gang member and you would normally be killing somebody, why not kill a white person?"

I suppose Sister Souljah thought she was simply expressing the anger and alienation of young blacks and telling them to stop killing one another. But that's not what she said. My staff, especially Paul Begala, argued that I had to say something about her remarks. Two of my most important core concerns were combating youth violence and healing the racial divide. After challenging white voters all across America to abandon racism, if I kept silent on Sister Souljah I might look weak or phony. Near the end of my talk, I said of her remarks, "If you took the words 'white' and 'black' and reversed them, you might think David Duke was giving that speech. . . . We have an obligation, all of us, to call attention to prejudice whenever we see it."

The political press reported my comments as a calculated attempt to appeal to moderate and conservative swing voters by standing up to a Democratic core constituency. That's how Jesse Jackson saw it, too. He thought I had abused his hospitality to make a demagogic pitch to white voters. He said Sister Souljah was a fine person who had done community service work and I owed her an apology. And he threatened not to support me, even suggesting he might back Ross Perot. Actually, I had considered condemning Sister Souljah's remarks as soon as she made them, when I was in Los Angeles for a meeting of the Show Coalition, an entertainment group. In the end I didn't do it, because the Show Coalition event was for charity and I didn't want to politicize it. When the Rainbow Coalition brought us on virtually back to back, I decided I had to speak up.

At the time, I didn't really understand the rap culture. Over the years, Chelsea often told me it was full of highly intelligent but profoundly alienated young people and urged me to learn more about it. Finally, in 2001, she gave me six rap and hip-hop CDs and made me promise to listen to them. I did. While I still preferred jazz and rock, I enjoyed a lot of the music, and I saw that she was right about the intelligence, and the alienation. But I think I was right to speak out against Sister Souljah's apparent advocacy of race-based violence, and I believe most African-Americans agreed with what I said. Still, after Jesse criticized me, I resolved to try harder to reach out to inner-city young people who felt left out and left behind.

On June 18, I had my first meeting with Boris Yeltsin, who was in Washington to see President Bush. When foreign leaders visit another country, it is customary for them to meet with the leader of the political opposition. Yeltsin was polite and friendly, but slightly patronizing. I had been a big admirer of his since he stood up on a tank to oppose an attempted coup ten months earlier. On the other hand, he plainly preferred Bush and thought the President was going to be reelected. At the end of our talk, Yeltsin said I had a good future even if I didn't get elected this time. I thought he was the right man to lead post–Soviet Russia, and I left the meeting convinced I could work with him if I succeeded in disappointing him about the outcome of the election.

I added a needed bit of levity to the campaign that week. Vice President Dan Quayle said he intended to be the "pit bull terrier" of the election campaign. When asked about it, I said Quayle's claim would strike terror into the heart of every fire hydrant in America.

On June 23, I turned serious again, reissuing my economic plan with minor revisions based on the latest government report that the deficit would be larger than previously estimated. It was risky, because in order to keep my pledge to cut the deficit in half in four years, I had to trim the middle-class tax-cut proposal. The Republicans on Wall Street didn't like the plan either, because I proposed to raise income taxes on the wealthiest Americans and corporations; both were paying a much smaller percentage of the total tax load after twelve years of Reagan and Bush. We couldn't cut the deficit in half with spending cuts only, and I felt that those who had benefited most in the 1980s should pay half the cost. And I was determined not to fall into the "rosy scenarios" trap the Republicans had followed for twelve years, in which they constantly overestimated revenues and underestimated outlays in order to avoid hard choices. The revised economic plan was put together under the supervision of my new economic policy aide, Gene Sperling, who had left the staff of Governor Mario Cuomo in May to join the campaign. He was brilliant, rarely slept, and worked like a demon.

By the end of June, the vigorous public outreach and policy efforts were beginning to show results. A June 20 poll had the race a three-way dead heat. It wasn't all my doing. Perot and President Bush were engaged in a bitter, highly personal argument. There was plainly no love lost between the two Texans, and there were some bizarre elements to their spat, including Perot's strange claim that Bush had conspired to disrupt his daughter's wedding.

While Perot was fighting with Bush over his daughter, I took a day away from the campaign to pick Chelsea up at the end of her annual trip to northern Minnesota for a German-language summer camp. Chelsea started pushing to go to camp when she was only five, saying she wanted to "see the world and have adventures." The Concordia Language Camps in Minnesota's lake country featured several villages that were replicas of those in the countries whose languages were being taught. When the young people checked in, they got new names and some foreign currency, then spent the next two or four weeks speaking the language of the village. Concordia had villages speaking the Western European and Scandinavian languages, as well as Chinese and Japanese. Chelsea chose the German camp and went every summer for several years. It was a wonderful experience and an important part of her childhood.

I spent the first weeks of July picking a running mate. After exhaustive research, Warren Christopher recommended I consider Senator Bob Kerrey; Senator Harris Wofford of Pennsylvania, who had worked with Martin Luther King Jr. and in President Kennedy's White House; Congressman Lee Hamilton of Indiana, the highly respected chairman of the House Foreign Affairs Committee; Senator Bob Graham of Florida, with whom I'd become friends when we served as governors together; and Senator Al Gore of Tennessee. I liked them all. Kerrey and I had worked together as governors, and I didn't hold the tough things he had said in the campaign against him. He was a figure who could attract Republican and independent voters. Wofford was a deeply moral advocate of health-care reform and civil rights. He also had a good relationship with Governor Bob Casey, which could ensure my winning Pennsylvania. Hamilton was impressive for his knowledge of foreign affairs and his strength in a conservative district in southeastern Indiana. Graham was one of the three or four best governors of the 150 or so I served with over twelve years, and he would almost certainly bring Florida into the Democratic column for the first time since 1976.

In the end, I decided to ask Al Gore. At first, I didn't think I would. On our previous encounters, the chemistry between us had been correct but not warm. His selection defied the conventional wisdom that the vice-presidential candidate should provide political and geographic balance: We were from neighboring states. He was even younger than I was. And he, too, was identified with the New Democrat wing of the party. I believed his selection would work precisely because it didn't have the traditional kind of balance. It would present America with a new generation of leadership and prove I was serious about taking the party and the country in a different direction. I also thought his selection would be good politics in Tennessee, the South, and other swing states.

Moreover, Al would provide balance in a far more important way: He knew things I didn't. I knew a lot about economics, agriculture, crime, welfare, education, and health care, and had a good grasp of the major foreign policy issues. Al was an expert on national security, arms control, information technology, energy, and the environment. He was one of ten Senate Democrats to support President Bush in the first Gulf War. He had attended the global biodiversity conference in Rio de Janeiro, and strongly disagreed with President Bush's decision not to support the treaty that came out of it. He had recently written a best-selling book, **Earth in the Balance,** arguing that problems like global warming, the depletion of the ozone layer, and the destruction of rain forests required a radical reorientation of our relationship to the environment. He had given me an autographed copy of the book the previous April. I read it, learned a lot, and agreed with his argument. Besides knowing more about subjects that we'd have to deal with if elected, Al understood Congress and the Washington culture far better than I did. Most important, I thought he would be a good President if something happened to me, and I thought he'd have an excellent chance to be elected after I finished.

I set up shop in a Washington hotel to meet with a few people I was considering. Al came over late one night, at eleven, to minimize the chance of being seen by the press. The hour was more comfortable for me than for him, but he was alert and in good spirits. We talked for two hours about the country, the campaign, and our families. He was obviously devoted to and proud of Tipper and his four children. Tipper was an interesting person, an accomplished woman who had become famous for her campaign against violent and vulgar lyrics in contemporary music, and who had a passionate and well-informed interest in improving mental-health care. After our talk, I liked him and was convinced that he, and Tipper, would be a big addition to our campaign.

On July 8, I called Al and asked him to be my running mate. The next day, he and his family flew to Little Rock for the announcement. The picture of all of us standing together on the back porch of the Governor's Mansion was big news across the nation. Even more than the words we spoke, it conveyed the energy and enthusiasm of young leaders committed to positive change. The next day, after Al and I went for a jog in Little Rock, we flew to his hometown, Carthage, Tennessee, for a rally and a visit with his parents, both of whom had a large influence on him. Al Gore Sr. had been a three-term U.S. senator, a supporter of civil rights, and an opponent of the Vietnam War, positions that helped to defeat him in 1970 but that also ensured him an honored place in American history. Al's mother, Pauline, was equally impressive. When it was rare for women to do so, she had graduated from law school and then briefly practiced law in southwest Arkansas.

On July 11, Hillary, Chelsea, and I flew to New York for the Democratic convention. We had had a good five weeks, while Bush and Perot fought with each other. For the first time, some polls showed me in the lead. With four nights of television coverage, the convention would either strengthen our position or undermine it. In 1972 and 1980, Democrats had been crippled by showing the American people a divided, dispirited, undisciplined party. I was determined not to let that happen again. So was DNC chairman Ron Brown. Harold Ickes and Alexis Herman, Ron's deputy and the CEO of the convention, took charge of our operation to make sure we showcased unity, new ideas, and new leaders. It didn't hurt that rank-and-file Democrats were desperate to win after twelve years of Republican control of the White House. Still, we had plenty to do to pull the party together and project a more positive image. For example, our research showed that most Americans didn't know that Hillary and I had a child, and thought I had grown up in wealth and privilege.

Conventions are heady affairs for the nominee. This one was especially so. After months of being told I was lower than a snake's belly, I was now being held up as a paragon of all things good and true. In New Hampshire and afterward, with all the character attacks, I had to fight to keep my temper in check and minimize my tendency to whine when exhausted. Now I had to rein in my ego and remember not to get carried away by all the praise and positive press.

As the convention opened, we were making good progress on party unity. Tom Harkin had endorsed me earlier. Now Bob Kerrey, Paul Tsongas, and Doug Wilder made supportive comments. So did Jesse Jackson. Only Jerry Brown held out. Harkin, who had become one of my favorite politicians, said Jerry was on an ego trip. There was also a minor flap when Ron Brown refused to let Governor Bob Casey speak to the convention, not because he wanted to speak against abortion but because he wouldn't agree to endorse me. I was inclined to let Casey talk, because I liked him, respected the convictions of pro-life Democrats, and thought we could get a lot of them to vote for us on other issues and on my pledge to make abortion "safe, legal, and rare." But Ron was adamant. We could disagree on the issues, he said, but no one should get the microphone who wasn't committed to victory in November. I respected the discipline with which he had rebuilt our party, and I deferred to his judgment.

The opening night of the convention featured seven of our women candidates for the U.S. Senate. Hillary and Tipper also made brief appearances. Then came the keynote speeches by Senator Bill Bradley, Congresswoman Barbara Jordan, and Governor Zell Miller. Bradley and Jordan were more famous and gave good talks, but Miller brought the audience to tears with this story:

> My father, who was a teacher, died when I was two weeks old, leaving a young widow with two small children. But with my mother's faith in God—and Mr. Roosevelt's voice on the radio—we kept going. After my father's death, my mother with her own hands cleared a small piece of rugged land. Every day she waded into a neighbor's cold mountain creek, carrying out thousands of smooth stones to build a house. I grew up watching my mother complete that house from the rocks she'd lifted from the creek and cement she mixed in a wheelbarrow—cement that today still bears her handprints. Her son bears her handprints, too. She pressed her pride and her hopes and her dreams deep into my soul. So, you see, I know what Dan Quayle means when he says it's best for children to have two parents. You bet it is. And it would be good if they could all have trust funds, too. We can't all be born rich, handsome, and lucky. And that's why we have a Democratic Party.

He then extolled the contributions of every Democratic President from FDR through Carter, and said we believed government could improve education, human rights, civil rights, economic and social opportunity, and the environment. He attacked Republicans for policies favoring the wealthy and special-interest groups, and supported my plans on the economy, education, health care, crime, and welfare reform. It was a strong New Democrat message, exactly what I wanted the country to hear. When Zell Miller was elected to the Senate in 2000, Georgia had become more conservative and so had he. He became one of President Bush's strongest supporters, voting for huge tax cuts that exploded the deficits and disproportionately benefited the wealthiest Americans, and budgets that threw poor children out of after-school programs, unemployed workers out of job training, and uniformed police off the streets. I don't know what caused Zell to change his views on what was best for America, but I will always remember what he did for me, the Democrats, and America in 1992.

The second day featured a presentation of the platform, and strong speeches by President Carter, Tom Harkin, and Jesse Jackson. When Jesse decided to support me, he went all the way, with a barn burner that brought the house down. However, the most emotional part of the evening was devoted to health care. Senator Jay Rockefeller talked about the need for health insurance for all Americans. His point was illustrated by my New Hampshire friends Ron and Rhonda Machos, who were by then expecting their second child and were saddled with $100,000 in medical bills from little Ronnie's open-heart surgery. They said they felt like second-class citizens, but they knew me and I was their "best hope for the future."

Two of the featured health-care speakers were people with AIDS: Bob Hattoy and Elizabeth Glaser. I wanted them to bring the reality of a problem too long ignored by politicians into America's living rooms. Bob was a gay man who worked for me. He said, "I don't want to die. But I don't want to live in an America where the President sees me as the enemy. I can face dying because of a disease, but not because of politics." Elizabeth Glaser was a beautiful, intelligent woman, the wife of Paul Michael Glaser, who had starred in the successful TV series **Starsky and**

Hutch. She had been infected when she hemorrhaged during the birth of her first child and received a transfusion contaminated with the virus. She passed it on to her daughter through her breast milk and to her next child, a son, in utero. By the time she spoke to the convention, Elizabeth had founded the Pediatric AIDS Foundation, lobbied hard for more money for research and care, and lost her daughter, Ariel, to AIDS. She wanted a President who would do more about it. Not long after I was elected, Elizabeth, too, lost her fight with AIDS. It was heartbreaking to Hillary, me, and countless others who loved her and followed her lead. I am thankful that her son, Jake, survives, and that his father and Elizabeth's friends have carried on her work.

By the third day of the convention, a national poll showed me in first place, with a double-digit lead over President Bush. I started the morning with a jog in Central Park. Then Hillary, Chelsea, and I had a real treat when Nelson Mandela came to our suite for a visit. He was the convention guest of Mayor David Dinkins. Properly, he said he wasn't taking sides in the election, but he expressed appreciation for the Democrats' long opposition to apartheid. Mandela wanted the United Nations to send a special envoy to investigate an outbreak of violence in South Africa, and I said I would support his request. His visit was the beginning of a great friendship for all of us. Mandela plainly liked Hillary, and I was really struck by the attention he paid to Chelsea. In the eight years I was in the White House, he never talked to me without asking about her. Once, during a phone conversation, he asked to speak to her, too. I've seen him show the same sensitivity to children, black and white, who crossed his path in South Africa. It speaks to his fundamental greatness.

Wednesday was a big night at the convention, with rousing speeches by Bob Kerrey and Ted Kennedy. There was a moving film tribute to Robert Kennedy, introduced by his son, Congressman Joe Kennedy of Massachusetts. Then Jerry Brown and Paul Tsongas spoke. Jerry bashed President Bush. So did Paul Tsongas, but he spoke up for Al Gore and me, too. After all he'd been through, it was a brave and classy thing to do.

Then came the big moment: Mario Cuomo's nominating speech. He was still our party's best orator, and he didn't disappoint. With lofty rhetoric, stinging rebukes, and well-reasoned arguments, Cuomo made the case that it was time for "someone smart enough to know; strong enough to do; sure enough to lead: the Comeback Kid, a new voice for a new America." After Congresswoman Maxine Waters and Congressman Dave McCurdy of Oklahoma, my other nominators, spoke, the roll was called.

Alabama passed to Arkansas so that my home state could cast the first votes. Our Democratic chair, George Jernigan, who had run against me for attorney general sixteen years earlier, gave the honor to another Clinton delegate. Then my mother simply said, "Arkansas proudly casts our forty-eight votes for our favorite son and my son, Bill Clinton." I wondered what Mother was thinking and feeling, beyond her bursting pride; whether her mind wandered back forty-six years, to the twenty-three-year-old widow who gave me life, or back over all the troubles she had borne with a bright smile to give me and my brother as normal a life as possible. I loved watching her and was grateful that someone had thought to let her start the tide rolling.

As the roll call continued, Hillary, Chelsea, and I were

making our way to Madison Square Garden from our hotel and stopped inside Macy's department store, where we gathered to watch the voting on television. When Ohio cast 144 votes for me, I crossed the majority threshold of 2,145 and was finally the official Democratic nominee. During the demonstration that followed, the three of us walked onto the stage. I was the first candidate to come to the convention before the night of my acceptance speech since John Kennedy did it in 1960. In brief remarks, I said, "Thirty-two years ago another young candidate who wanted to get the country moving again came to the convention to say a simple thank you." I wanted to identify with the spirit of John Kennedy's campaign, to thank my nominators and the delegates, and "to tell you that tomorrow night I will be the Comeback Kid."

Thursday, July 16, was the final day of the convention. So far, we had had three great days, in the hall and on television. We had showcased not only our national leaders but also our rising stars, as well as ordinary citizens. We had hammered home our new ideas. But it would all count for nothing unless Al Gore and I were effective in our acceptance speeches. The day began with a surprise, as had so many days in this wild campaign season: Ross Perot withdrew from the race. I called him, congratulated him on his campaign, and said I agreed with him on the need for fundamental political reform. He declined to endorse either President Bush or me, and I went into the convention's last night unsure whether his withdrawal would help or hurt.

After Al Gore was nominated by acclamation, he gave a rip-roaring speech, which he began by saying he'd dreamed as a boy growing up in Tennessee that he would, one day, be the warm-up act for Elvis, the nickname the staff gave me during the campaign. Al then launched into a litany of the Bush administration's failings, saying after each one, "It's time for them to go." After he did it a couple of times, the delegates took over for him, sending sparks throughout the hall. Then he extolled my record, outlined the challenges we faced, and talked about his family and our obligation to leave a stronger, more united nation to the next generation. Al had given a really good speech. He had done his part. Now it was my turn.

Paul Begala wrote the first draft of the speech. We were trying to do a lot with it—biography, campaign rhetoric, and policy. And we were trying to appeal to three different groups—hard-core Democrats, independents and Republicans dissatisfied with the President but unsure of me, and people who didn't vote at all because they didn't think it made a difference. Paul, as always, had some great lines. And George Stephanopoulos had kept notes of the ones that had worked best on the stump during the primary campaign. Bruce Reed and Al From helped sharpen the policy section. To bring me on, my friends Harry and Linda Bloodworth Thomason produced a short film entitled "The Man from Hope." It pumped the crowd up, and I walked onto the platform to tremendous applause.

The speech started slowly, with a bow to Al Gore, thanks to Mario Cuomo, and a salute to my primary opponents. Then came the message: "In the name of all those who do the work and pay the taxes, raise the kids and play by the rules, in the name of the hardworking Americans who make up our forgotten middle class, I proudly accept your nomination for President of the United States. I am a product of that middle class, and when I am President, you will be forgotten no more."

Next, I told the story of the people who had had the

greatest impact on me, beginning with my mother, from her travails as a young widow with a baby to support to her current struggle with breast cancer, saying, "Always, always, always she taught me to fight." I talked about my grandfather and how he taught me "to look up to people other folks looked down on." And I paid tribute to Hillary for teaching me that "all children can learn and that each of us has a duty to help them do it." I wanted America to know that my fighting spirit started with my mother, my commitment to racial equality started with my grandfather, and my concern for the future of all our children started with my wife.

And I wanted people to know that everybody could be part of our American family: "I want to say something to every child in America tonight who is out there trying to grow up without a mother or father: I know how you feel. You are special too. You matter to America. And don't ever let anybody tell you you can't become whatever you want to be."

For the next several minutes, I laid out my critique of the Bush record and my plan to do better. "We have gone from first to thirteenth in the world in wages since Reagan and Bush took office." . . . "Four years ago he promised 15 million new jobs by this time, and he's over 14 million short." . . . "The incumbent President says unemployment always goes up a little before a recovery begins, but unemployment only has to go up one more person before a real recovery can begin. And Mr. President, you are that man." I said my New Covenant of opportunity, responsibility, and community would give us "an America in which the doors of college are thrown open again to the sons and daughters of stenographers and steelworkers," "an America in which middle-class incomes, not middle-class taxes, are going up," "an America in which the rich are not soaked, but the middle class is not drowned either," "an America where we end welfare as we know it."

Then I made an appeal for national unity. To me, it was the most important part of the speech, something I had believed in since I was a little boy:

Tonight every one of you knows deep in your heart that we are too divided. It is time to heal America.

And so we must say to every American: Look beyond the stereotypes that blind us. We need each other. All of us, we need each other. We don't have a person to waste. And yet for too long politicians have told most of us that are doing all right that what's really wrong with America is the rest of us. Them.

Them, the minorities. Them, the liberals. Them, the poor, them, the homeless, them, the people with disabilities. Them, the gays.

We've gotten to where we've nearly them'ed ourselves to death. Them and them and them.

But this is America. There is no them; there is only us. One nation, under God, indivisible, with liberty and justice for all.

That is our Pledge of Allegiance and that's what the New Covenant is all about. . . .

As a teenager I heard John Kennedy's summons to citizenship. And then, as a student at Georgetown, I heard that call clarified by a professor named Carroll Quigley, who said to us that America was the greatest nation in history because our people had always believed in two great ideas: that tomorrow can be better than today, and that every one of us has a personal, moral responsibility to make it so.

That kind of future entered my life the night our daughter, Chelsea, was born. As I stood in that delivery room, I was overcome with the thought that God had given me a blessing my own father never knew: the chance to hold my child in my arms.

Somewhere at this very moment, a child is being born in America. Let it be our cause to give that child a happy home, a healthy family, and a hopeful future. Let it be our cause to see that that child has a chance to live to the fullest of her God-given capacities. . . . Let it be our cause that we give this child a country that is coming together, not coming apart—a country of boundless hopes and endless dreams; a country that once again lifts its people and inspires the world.

Let that be our cause, our commitment, and our New Covenant.

My fellow Americans, I end tonight where it all began for me: I still believe in a place called Hope. God bless you and God bless America.

When my speech was over and the applause had died down, the convention ended with a song written for the occasion by Arthur Hamilton and my old friend and fellow high-school musician Randy Goodrum, "Circle of Friends." It was sung by the Broadway star Jennifer Holiday, backed by the Philander Smith College Choir from Little Rock; ten-year-old Reggie Jackson, who had wowed the convention Monday night singing "America the Beautiful"; and my brother, Roger. Before long they had us all singing "Let's join a circle of friends, one that begins and never ends."

It was a perfect end to the most important speech I'd

ever delivered. And it worked. We were widening the circle. Three different polls showed my message had strongly resonated with the voters, and we had a big lead, of twenty or more points. But I knew we couldn't hold that margin. For one thing, the Republican cultural base of white voters with a deep reluctance to vote for any Democratic presidential candidate was about 45 percent of the electorate. Also, the Republicans had not held their convention yet. It was sure to give President Bush a boost. Finally, I'd just had six weeks of good press coverage and a week of direct, completely positive access to America. It was more than enough to push all the doubts about me into the recesses of public consciousness, but, as I well knew, not enough to erase them.

TWENTY-EIGHT

The next morning, July 17, Al, Tipper, Hillary, and I drove over to New Jersey to begin the first of several bus tours across America. They were designed to bring us into small towns and rural areas never visited in modern presidential campaigns, which had become dominated by rallies in major media markets. We hoped the bus tour, the brainchild of Susan Thomases and David Wilhelm, would keep the excitement and momentum of the convention going.

The trip was a 1,000-mile jaunt through New Jersey, Pennsylvania, West Virginia, Ohio, Kentucky, Indiana, and Illinois. It was filled with stump speeches and hand-shaking at scheduled and unscheduled stops. On the first day, we worked our way through eastern and central Pennsylvania, reaching our last stop, York, at 2 a.m. Thousands of people had waited up for us. Al gave his best 2 a.m. version of the stump speech. I did the same, and then we shook supporters' hands for the better part of an hour before the four of us collapsed for a few hours' sleep. We spent the next day riding across Pennsylvania, bonding with each other as well as the crowds, growing more and more relaxed and excited, buoyed by the enthusiasm of people who came out to see us at the rallies or just along the highway. At a truck stop in Carlisle, Al and I climbed up into the big trucks to shake hands with drivers. At a Pennsylvania Turnpike rest stop, we tossed a football in the parking lot. Somewhere on the trip we even fit in a round of miniature golf. On the third day, we worked our way out of western Pennsylvania and into West Virginia, where we toured Weirton Steel, a large integrated producer that the employees had bought from its former owner and kept running. That night we went to Gene Branstool's farm near Utica, Ohio, for a cookout with a couple hundred farmers and their families, then stopped in a nearby field, where ten thousand people were waiting. I was stunned by two things: the size of the crowd and the size of the corn crop. It was the tallest and thickest I had ever seen, a good omen. The next day we visited Columbus, Ohio's capital city, then made our way into Kentucky. As we crossed the state line, I was convinced we could win Ohio, as Jimmy Carter had done in 1976. It was important. Since the Civil War, no Republican had won the presidency without capturing Ohio.

On the fifth and final day, after a big rally in Louisville, we drove through southern Indiana and into southern Illinois. All along the way, people were standing in fields and along the road waving our signs. We passed a big combine all decked out in an American flag and a Clinton-Gore poster. By the time we got to Illinois, we were late, as we were every day, because of all the unscheduled stops. We didn't need any more of them, but a small group was standing at a crossroads holding a big sign that said "Give us eight minutes and we'll give you eight years!" We stopped. The last rally of the evening was one of the most remarkable of the campaign. When we pulled into Vandalia, thousands of people holding candles had filled the square around the old state Capitol Building where Abraham Lincoln had served a term in the legislature before the seat of government was moved to Springfield. It was very late when we finally pulled into St. Louis for another short night.

The bus tour was a smashing success. It took us, and the national media, to places in the American heartland too often overlooked. America saw us reaching out to the people we had promised to represent in Washington, which made it harder for the Republicans to paint us as cultural and political radicals. And Al, Tipper, Hillary, and I had gotten to know one another in a way that would have been impossible without those long hours on the bus.

The next month we did four more bus tours, this time shorter ones of one or two days. The second tour took us up the Mississippi River, from St. Louis to Hannibal, Missouri, Mark Twain's hometown, to Davenport, Iowa, up through Wisconsin, and all the way to Minneapolis, where Walter Mondale held a crowd of ten thousand for two hours by giving them regular updates on our progress.

The most memorable moment of the second bus tour came in Cedar Rapids, Iowa, where, after a meeting on biotechnology and a tour of the Quaker Oats packaging plant, we held a rally in the parking lot. The crowd was large and enthusiastic, except for a loud group of opponents holding pro-life signs and jeering at me from the back. After the speeches, I got off the stage and began working the crowd. I was surprised to see a white woman wearing a pro-choice button and holding a black baby in her arms. When I asked her whose child it was, she beamed and said, "She's my baby. Her name is Jamiya." The woman told me that the child was born HIV-positive in Florida, and she had adopted her, even though she was a divorcée struggling to raise two children on her own. I'll never forget that woman holding Jamiya and proudly proclaiming, "She's my baby." She, too, was pro-life, just the kind of person I was trying to give a better shot at the American dream.

Later in the month, we did a one-day tour of California's San Joaquin Valley, and two-day trips through Texas and what we'd missed of Ohio and Pennsylvania, ending up in western New York. In September we bused through south Georgia. In October we did two days in Michigan and, in one hectic day, made ten towns in North Carolina.

I had never seen anything like the sustained enthusiasm the bus trips engendered. Of course, part of it was that people in small towns weren't accustomed to seeing presidential candidates up close—places like Coatesville, Pennsylvania; Centralia, Illinois; Prairie du Chien, Wisconsin; Walnut Grove, California; Tyler, Texas; Valdosta, Georgia; and Elon, North Carolina. But mostly it was the connection our bus made between the people and the campaign. It represented both the common touch and forward progress. In 1992, Americans were worried but still hopeful. We spoke to their fears and validated their enduring optimism. Al and I developed a good routine. At each stop, he would list all of America's problems and say, "Everything that should be down is up, and everything that should be up is down." Then he would introduce me and I'd tell people what we intended to do to fix it. I loved those bus tours. We motored through sixteen states and in November won thirteen of them.

After the first bus tour, one national poll showed me with a two-to-one lead over President Bush, but I didn't take it too seriously because he hadn't really started to campaign. He began in the last week of July, with a series of attacks. He said that my plan to trim defense increases would cost a million jobs; that my health-care plan would be a government-run program "with the compassion of the KGB"; that I wanted "the largest tax increase in history"; and that he would set a better "moral tone" as President than I would. His aide Mary Matalin edged out Dan Quayle in the race for the campaign's pit bull, calling me a "sniveling hypocrite." Later in the campaign, with Bush sinking, a lot of his careerist appointees started leaking to the press that it was anybody's fault but theirs. Some of them were even critical of the President. Not Mary. She stood by her man to the end. Ironically, Mary Matalin and James Carville were engaged and soon would be married. Although they were from opposite ends of the political spectrum, they were equally aggressive true believers whose love added spice to their lives, and whose politics enlivened both the Bush campaign and mine.

In the second week of August, President Bush persuaded James Baker to resign as secretary of state and return to the White House to oversee his campaign. I thought Baker had done a good job at State, except on Bosnia, where I felt the administration should have opposed the ethnic cleansing more vigorously. And I knew he was a good politician who would make the Bush campaign more effective.

Our campaign needed to be more effective, too. We had won the nomination by organizing around the primary schedule. Now that the convention was behind us, we needed much better coordination among all the forces, with a single strategic center. James Carville took it on. He needed an assistant. Because Paul Begala's wife, Diane, was expecting their first child, he couldn't come to Little Rock full-time, so reluctantly, I gave up George Stephanopoulos from the campaign plane. George had demonstrated a keen understanding of how the twenty-four-hour news cycle worked, and now knew we could fight bad press as well as enjoy the good stories. He was the best choice.

James put all the elements of the campaign—politics, press, and research—into a big open space in the old newsroom of the **Arkansas Gazette** building. It broke down barriers and built a sense of camaraderie. Hillary said it was like a "war room," and the name stuck. Carville put a sign on the wall as a constant reminder of what the campaign was about. It had just three lines:

Change vs. More of the Same
The Economy, stupid
Don't forget health care

Carville also captured his main battle tactic in a slogan he had printed on a T-shirt: "Speed Kills . . . Bush." The War Room held meetings every day at 7 a.m. and 7 p.m. to assess Stan Greenberg's overnight polls, Frank Greer's latest ads, the news, and the attacks from Bush, and to formulate responses to the attacks and unfolding events. Meanwhile, young volunteers worked around the clock, pulling in whatever information they could get from our satellite dish, tracking the news and the opposition on their computers. It's all routine stuff now, but then it was new, and our use of technology was essential to the campaign's ability to meet Carville's goal of being focused and fast.

Once we knew what we wanted to say, we got the message out, not only to the media but to our "rapid-response" teams in every state, whose job it was to transmit it to our supporters and local news outlets. We sent pins with "Rapid-Response Team" on them to those who agreed to do daily duty. By the end of the campaign, thousands of people were wearing them.

By the time I got my morning briefing from Carville, Stephanopoulos, and whoever else needed to be on call that day, they could lay out exactly where we were and what we needed to do. If I disagreed, we argued. If there was a close policy or strategic call, I made it. But mostly I just listened in amazement. Sometimes I complained about what wasn't going well, like speeches I thought were long on rhetoric and short on argument and substance, or the backbreaking schedule that was more my fault than theirs. Because of allergies and exhaustion, I griped too much in the mornings. Luckily, Carville and I were on the same wavelength, and he always knew when I was serious and when I was just blowing off steam. I think the others on call came to understand it too.

The Republicans held their convention in Houston in the third week of August. Normally, the opposition goes underground during the other party's convention. Though I would follow the usual practice and keep a low profile, our rapid-response operation would be out in force. It had to be. The Republicans had no choice but to throw the kitchen sink at me. They were way behind, and their slash-and-burn approach had worked in every election since 1968, except for President Carter's two-point victory in the aftermath of Watergate. We were determined to use the rapid-response team to turn the Republican attacks back on them.

On August 17, as their convention opened, I still had a twenty-point lead, and we rained on their parade a little when eighteen corporate chief executives endorsed me. It was a good story, but it didn't divert the Republicans from their game plan. They started off by calling me a "skirt chaser" and a "draft dodger," and accused Hillary of wanting to destroy the American family by allowing children to sue their parents whenever they disagreed with parental disciplinary decisions. Marilyn Quayle, the vice president's wife, was particularly critical of Hillary's alleged assault on "family values." The criticisms were based on a wildly distorted reading of an article Hillary had written when she was in law school, arguing that, in circumstances of abuse or severe neglect, minor children had legal rights independent of their parents. Almost all Americans would agree with a fair reading of her words, but, of course, since so few people had seen her article, hardly anyone who heard the charges knew whether they were true or not.

The main attraction on the Republicans' opening night was Pat Buchanan, who sent the delegates into a frenzy with his attacks on me. My favorite lines included his assertion that, while President Bush had presided over the liberation of Eastern Europe, my foreign policy experience was "pretty much confined to having had breakfast once at the International House of Pancakes" and his characterization of the Democratic convention as "radicals and liberals . . . dressed up as moderates and centrists in the greatest single exhibition of cross-dressing in American political history." The polls showed Buchanan hadn't helped Bush, but I disagreed. His job was to stop the hemorrhaging on the right by telling conservatives who wanted change that they couldn't vote for me, and he did it well.

The Clinton-bashing continued throughout the convention, with our rapid-response operation firing back. The Reverend Pat Robertson referred to me as "Slick Willie" and said I had a radical plan to destroy the American family. Since I had been for welfare reform before

Robertson figured out that God was a right-wing Republican, the charge was laughable. Our rapid-response team beat it back. They were also especially good at defending Hillary from the anti-family attacks, comparing the Republicans' treatment of her to their Willie Horton tactics against Dukakis four years earlier.

To reinforce our claim that the Republicans were attacking me because all they cared about was holding on to power, while we wanted power to attack America's problems, Al, Tipper, Hillary, and I had dinner with President and Mrs. Carter on August 18. Then we all spent the next day—both Tipper's and my birthday—building a house with members of Habitat for Humanity. Jimmy and Rosalynn Carter had supported Habitat for years. The brainchild of Millard Fuller, a friend of ours from Renaissance Weekend, Habitat uses volunteers to build houses for and with poor people, who then pay for the cost of the materials. The organization had already become one of America's largest home builders and was expanding into other countries. Our work presented a perfect contrast to the shrill attacks of the Republicans.

President Bush made a surprise visit to the convention on the night he was nominated, as I had, bringing his entire all-American-looking family. The next night, he gave an effective speech, wrapping himself in God, country, and family, and asserting that, unfortunately, I didn't embrace those values. He also said that he had made a mistake in signing the deficit-reduction bill with its gas-tax hike and that, if reelected, he'd cut taxes again. I thought his best line was saying I would use "Elvis economics" to take America to "Heartbreak Hotel." He contrasted his service in World War II with my opposition to Vietnam by saying, "While I bit the bullet, he bit his nails."

Now the Republicans had had their free shot at America, and though the conventional wisdom was that they had been too negative and extreme, the polls showed they had cut into my lead. One poll had the race down to ten points, another to five. I thought that was about right, and that if I didn't blow the debates or make some other error, the final margin would be somewhere between what the two surveys showed.

President Bush left Houston in a feisty mood, comparing his campaign to Harry Truman's miraculous comeback victory in 1948. He also went around the country doing what only incumbents can do: spending federal money to get votes. He pledged aid to wheat farmers and the victims of Hurricane Andrew, which had devastated much of south Florida, and he offered to sell 150 F-16 fighter planes to Taiwan and 72 F-15s to Saudi Arabia, securing jobs in defense plants located in critical states.

In late August, we both appeared before the American Legion Convention in Chicago. President Bush got a better reception than I did from his fellow veterans, but I did better than expected by confronting the draft issue and my opposition to the Vietnam War head-on. I said I still believed the Vietnam War was a mistake, but "if you choose to vote against me because of what happened twenty-three years ago, that's your right as an American citizen, and I respect that. But it is my hope that you will cast your vote while looking toward the future." I also got a good round of applause by promising new leadership at the Department of Veterans Affairs, whose director was unpopular with the veterans' groups.

After the American Legion meeting, I got back to my message of changing America's direction in economic and social policy, bolstered by a new study showing that the rich were getting richer while poor Americans were getting poorer. In early September, I was endorsed by two important environmental groups, the Sierra Club and the League of Conservation Voters. And I went to Florida a few days after President Bush did to observe the damage from Hurricane Andrew. I had dealt with a lot of natural disasters as governor, including floods, droughts, and tornadoes, but I had never seen anything like this. As I walked down streets littered with the wet ruins of houses, I was surprised to hear complaints from both local officials and residents about how the Federal Emergency Management Agency was handling the aftermath of the hurricane. Traditionally, the job of FEMA director was given to a political supporter of the President who wanted some plum position but who had had no experience with emergencies. I made a mental note to avoid that mistake if I won. Voters don't choose a President based on how he'll handle disasters, but if they're faced with one, it quickly becomes the most important issue in their lives.

On Labor Day, the traditional opening of the general election campaign, I went to Harry Truman's hometown of Independence, Missouri, to rally working people to our cause. Truman's outspoken daughter, Margaret, helped by saying at the rally that I, not George Bush, was the rightful heir to her father's legacy.

On September 11, I went to South Bend, Indiana, to deliver an address to the students and faculty at Notre Dame, America's most famous Catholic university. On the same day, President Bush was in Virginia to address the conservative Christian Coalition. I knew Catholics across the country would take notice of both events. The church hierarchy agreed with Bush's opposition to abortion, but I was far closer to the Catholic positions on economic and social justice. The Notre Dame appearance bore a striking resemblance, with roles reversed, to John Kennedy's 1960 speech to the Southern Baptist ministers. Paul Begala, a devout Catholic, helped prepare my remarks, and Boston mayor Ray Flynn and Senator Harris Wofford came along to lend moral support. I was nearly halfway through the speech before I could tell how it was going. When I said, "All of us must respect the reflection of God's image in every man and woman, and so we must value their freedom, not just their political freedom, but their freedom of conscience in matters of family and philosophy and faith," there was a standing ovation.

After Notre Dame, I went out west. In Salt Lake City, I made my case to the National Guard Convention, where I was well received, because my reputation for leading the Arkansas National Guard was good, and because I was introduced by Congressman Les Aspin, the respected chairman of the House Armed Services Committee. In Portland, Oregon, we had an amazing rally. Over ten thousand people filled the downtown streets, with many more leaning out of their office windows. During the speeches, supporters threw hundreds of roses onto the stage, a nice gesture in Oregon's City of Roses. For more than an hour after the event, I went up and down the streets, shaking hands with what seemed like thousands of people.

On September 15, the western swing got its biggest boost when thirty high-tech leaders in traditionally Republican Silicon Valley endorsed me. I had been working on Silicon Valley since the previous December, with the help of Dave Barram, vice president of Apple Computer. Dave had been recruited to the campaign by Ira Magaziner, my friend from Oxford, who had worked with

high-tech executives and knew that Barram was a Democrat. Many of Barram's Republican cohorts shared his dis-
illusionment with the economic policies of the Bush
administration and its failure to appreciate the explosive
potential of Silicon Valley's entrepreneurs. A few days
before my first trip, according to the **San Jose Mercury
News,** President Bush's trade representative, Carla Hills,
had endorsed the view that "it makes no difference
whether the United States exports potato chips or silicon
chips." The high-tech executives disagreed, and so did I.

Among those who came out for me were prominent
Republicans like John Young, president of Hewlett-
Packard; John Sculley, chairman of Apple Computer;
investment banker Sandy Robertson; and one of Silicon
Valley's few open Democrats at the time, Regis McKenna.
At our meeting in the Technology Center of Silicon Valley
at San Jose, I also issued a national technology policy,
which Dave Barram had worked for months to help me
prepare. In calling for greater investment in scientific and
technological research and development, including specific projects important to Silicon Valley, I staked out a
position at odds with the Bush administration's aversion
to government-industry partnerships. At the time, Japan
and Germany were outperforming America economically,
in part because government policy in those countries was
targeted to support potential areas of growth. By contrast,
American policy was to subsidize politically powerful,
established interests like oil and agriculture, which were
important but which had much less potential than technology to generate new jobs and new entrepreneurs. The
high-tech leaders' announcement provided an enormous
boost to the campaign, giving credibility to my claim to
be pro-business as well as pro-labor, and linking me to the

economic forces that most represented positive change and growth.

While I was garnering support for rebuilding the economy and reforming health care, the Republicans were working hard to tear me down. President Bush, in his convention speech, had accused me of raising taxes 128 times in Arkansas and enjoying it every time. In early September, the Bush campaign repeated the charge again and again, though the **New York Times** said it was "false," the **Washington Post** called it highly "exaggerated" and "silly," and even the **Wall Street Journal** said it was "misleading." The Bush list included a requirement that used-car dealers post a $25,000 bond, modest fees for beauty pageants, and a one-dollar court cost imposed on convicted criminals. Conservative columnist George Will said that, by the President's criteria, "Bush has raised taxes more often in four years than Clinton has in ten."

The Bush campaign devoted most of the rest of September to attacking me on the draft. President Bush said over and over that I should "just tell the truth" about it. Even Dan Quayle felt free to go after me on it, despite the fact that his family connections had gotten him into the National Guard and away from Vietnam. The vice president's main point seemed to be that the media weren't giving my case the same critical scrutiny he had received four years earlier. Apparently he hadn't followed the news out of New Hampshire and New York.

I got some good help in countering the draft attack. In early September, Senator Bob Kerrey, my Medal of Honor–winning primary opponent, said it shouldn't be an issue. Then on the eighteenth, on the back lawn of the Arkansas Governor's Mansion, I received the endorsement of Admiral Bill Crowe, who had been chairman of the Joint Chiefs of Staff under President Reagan and briefly under Bush. I was very impressed by Crowe's straightforward, down-home manner and deeply grateful that he would stick his neck out for someone he barely knew but had come to believe in.

The political impact of what Bush and I were doing was uncertain. Some of his convention edge had worn off, but throughout September the polls bounced back and forth between a lead of 9 and 20 percent for me. The basic dynamic of the campaign had been set: Bush claimed to represent family values and trustworthiness, while I was for economic and social change. He said I was untrustworthy and anti-family, while I said he was dividing America and holding us back. On any given day, a substantial number of voters were torn between which one of us was better.

Besides the issues dispute, we spent September arguing about the debates. The bipartisan national commission recommended three of them, with different formats. I accepted immediately, but President Bush didn't like the commission's debate formats. I claimed his objections were a fig leaf to cover his reluctance to defend his record. The disagreement continued for most of the month, which forced all three of the scheduled debates to be canceled. As they were, I went to each of the proposed debate sites to campaign, making sure the disappointed citizens knew who had cost their cities their moment in the national spotlight.

The worst thing to happen to us in September was far more personal than political. Paul Tully, the veteran Irish organizer Ron Brown had sent to Little Rock to coordinate the Democratic Party's efforts with ours, dropped dead in his hotel room. Tully was only forty-eight, an old-school political pro and a fine man we had all come to adore and depend on. Just as we were entering the home-stretch, another of our leaders was gone.

The month ended with some surprising developments. Earvin "Magic" Johnson, the HIV-positive former All-Star guard of the Los Angeles Lakers, abruptly resigned from the National Commission on HIV/AIDS and endorsed me, disgusted with the administration's lack of attention to, and action on, the AIDS problem. President Bush changed his mind about the debates and challenged me to four of them. And, most surprising, Ross Perot said he was thinking of reentering the presidential race, because he didn't think the President or I had a serious plan to reduce the deficit. He criticized Bush for his no-tax pledge and said I wanted to spend too much money. Perot invited both campaigns to send delegations to meet him and discuss the matter.

Because neither of us knew which of us would be hurt more if Perot got back in, and we both wanted his support if he didn't, each campaign sent a high-level team to meet with him. Our side was uneasy about it, because we thought he had already decided to run and this was just high theater to increase his prestige, but in the end I agreed that we ought to keep reaching out to him. Senator Lloyd Bentsen, Mickey Kantor, and Vernon Jordan went on my behalf. They got a cordial reception, as did the Bush people. Perot announced that he had learned a lot from both groups. Then a couple of days later, on October 1, Perot announced that he felt compelled to get back into the race as a "servant" of his volunteers. He had been helped by quitting the race back in July. In the ten weeks he was out of it, the memory of his nutty fight with Bush the previous spring had faded, while the President and I had kept each other's problems fresh in the public mind. Now the voters and the press took him even more seriously because the two of us had courted him so visibly.

As Perot was getting back in, we finally reached an agreement with the Bush people on debates. There would be three of them, plus a vice-presidential debate, all crammed into nine days, between October 11 and 19. In the first and third, we would be questioned by members of the press. The second would be a town hall meeting in which citizens would ask the questions. At first, the Bush people didn't want Perot in the debates, because they thought he would be attacking the President, and any extra votes he garnered would come from potential Bush supporters rather than those who might go for me. I said I had no objection to Perot's inclusion, not because I agreed that Perot would hurt Bush more—I wasn't convinced of that—but because I felt that, in the end, he would have to be included and I didn't want to look like a chicken. By October 4, both campaigns agreed to invite Perot to participate.

In the week leading up to the first debate, I finally endorsed the controversial North American Free Trade Agreement, which the Bush administration had negotiated with Canada and Mexico, with the caveat that I wanted to negotiate side agreements ensuring basic labor and environmental standards that would be binding on Mexico. My labor supporters were worried about the loss of low-wage manufacturing jobs to our southern neighbor and strongly disagreed with my position, but I felt compelled to take it, for both economic and political reasons. I was a free-trader at heart, and I thought America had to support Mexico's economic growth to ensure long-term stability in our hemisphere. A couple of days later, more than 550 economists, including nine Nobel Prize winners, endorsed my economic program, saying it was more likely than the President's proposals to restore economic growth.

Just as I was determined to focus on economics in the run-up to the debates, the Bush camp was equally determined to keep undermining my character and reputation for honesty. They were facilitating a search request with the National Records Center in Suitland, Maryland, for all the information in my passport files on my forty-day trip to northern Europe, the Soviet Union, and Czechoslovakia back in 1969–70. Apparently, they were chasing down bogus rumors that I had gone to Moscow to pursue anti-war activities or had tried to apply for citizenship in another country to avoid the draft. On October 5, there were news reports that the files had been tampered with. The passport story dragged out all month. Though the FBI said the files had not been tampered with, what had occurred put the Bush campaign in a bad light. A senior State Department political appointee pushed the National Records Center, which had more than 100 million files, to put the search of mine ahead of two thousand other requests that had been filed earlier, and that normally took months to process. A Bush appointee also ordered the U.S. embassies in London and Oslo to conduct an "extremely thorough" search of their files for information on my draft status and citizenship. At some point, it was revealed that even my mother's passport files were searched. It was hard to imagine that even the most paranoid right-wingers could think that a country girl from Arkansas who loved the races was subversive.

Later, it came out that the Bush people had also asked John Major's government to look into my activities in England. According to news reports, the Tories complied, although they claimed their "comprehensive" but fruitless search of their immigration and naturalization documents was in response to press inquiries. I know they did some further work on it, because a friend of David Edwards's told David that British officials had questioned him about what David and I did in those long-ago days. Two Tory campaign strategists came to Washington to advise the Bush campaign on how they might destroy me the way the Conservative Party had undone Labour Party leader Neil Kinnock six months earlier. After the election, the British press fretted that the special relationship between our two countries had been damaged by this unusual British involvement in American politics. I was determined that there would be no damage, but I wanted the Tories to worry about it for a while.

The press had a field day with the passport escapade, and Al Gore called it a "McCarthyite abuse of power." Undeterred, the President kept asking me to explain the trip to Moscow and continued to question my patriotism. In an interview on CNN with Larry King, I said I loved my country and had never considered giving up my American citizenship. I don't think the public paid much attention to the passport flap one way or the other, and I was kind of amused by the whole thing. Of course it was an abuse of power, but a pathetically small one compared with Iran-Contra. It just showed how desperate the Bush people were to hang on to power, and how little they had to offer for America's future. If they wanted to spend the last month of the campaign barking up the wrong tree, that was fine with me.

In the days leading up to the first debate, I worked hard to be well prepared. I studied the briefing book diligently and participated in several mock-debate sessions. President Bush was played by Washington lawyer Bob Barnett, who had performed the same role four years earlier for Dukakis. Perot's stand-in was Congressman Mike Synar of Oklahoma, who had Ross's sayings and accent down pat. Bob and Mike wore me out in tough encounters before each debate. After each of our sessions, I was just glad I didn't have to debate them; the election might have turned out differently.

The first debate was finally held on Sunday, October 11, Hillary's and my seventeenth wedding anniversary, at Washington University in St. Louis. I went into it encouraged by the endorsements in that morning's editions of the **Washington Post** and the **Louisville Courier-Journal.** The **Post** editorial said, "This country is drifting and worn down; it badly needs to be reenergized and given new direction. Bill Clinton is the only candidate with a chance of doing that." That was exactly the argument I wanted to make in the debate. Yet despite my lead in the polls and the **Post** endorsement, I was on edge, because I knew I had the most to lose. In a new Gallup poll, 44 percent of the respondents said they expected me to win the debate, and 30 percent said they could be swayed by it. President Bush and his advisors had decided the only way to sway that 30 percent was to beat people over the head with my alleged character problems until the message sunk in. Now, in addition to the draft, the Moscow trip, and the citizenship rumor, the President was attacking me for participating in anti-war demonstrations in London "against the United States of America, when our kids are dying halfway around the world."

Perot got the first question from one of three journalists, who rotated in a process moderated by Jim Lehrer of

The MacNeil/Lehrer NewsHour. He was given two minutes to say what separated him from the other two candidates. Ross said he was supported by the people, not parties or special interests. Bush and I got one minute to respond. I said I represented change. The President said he had experience. We then discussed experience. Then President Bush was given his moment: "Are there important issues of character separating you from these two men?" He hit me on the draft. Perot responded that Bush had made his mistakes as a mature man in the White House, not as a young student. I said that Bush's father, as a U.S. senator from Connecticut, was right to criticize Senator Joe McCarthy for attacking the patriotism of loyal Americans, and the President was wrong to attack my patriotism, and that what America needed was a President who would bring our country together, not divide it.

We went on like that for an hour and a half, discussing taxes, defense, the deficit, jobs and the changing economy, foreign policy, crime, Bosnia, the definition of family, the legalization of marijuana, racial divisions, AIDS, Medicare, and health-care reform.

All of us did reasonably well. After the debate the press was hustled by each candidate's "spinners" saying why their man had won. I had three good ones in Mario Cuomo, James Carville, and Senator Bill Bradley. One of President Bush's boosters, Charlie Black, invited the press to watch a new TV ad attacking me on the draft. The spinners could have some effect on the news stories about the debate, but those who had watched it had already formed their opinions.

I thought that, on balance, I gave the best answers in terms of specifics and arguments, but that Perot did better in presenting himself as folksy and relaxed. When Bush said Perot didn't have government experience, Perot said the President "had a point. I don't have any experience in running up a $4 trillion debt." Perot had big jug ears, which were accentuated by his short crew cut. On the deficit he said, "We've got to collect taxes" to eliminate it, but if anyone had a better idea, "I'm all ears." By contrast, I was a bit tight and at times seemed almost overprepared.

The good news was that the President gained no ground. The bad news was that Perot looked credible again. In the beginning, if he rose in the polls, his support would come from genuinely undecided voters or from those leaning toward both the President and me. But I well knew that if Ross rose much above 10 percent, most of his new voters would be those who wanted change but still weren't quite comfortable with me. The post-debate polls showed that among those who watched, a significant number now had more confidence in my ability to be President. They also showed that more than 60 percent of those who watched viewed Perot more favorably than they had before the debate. With three weeks to go, he was keeping the race unpredictable.

Two nights later, on October 13, in the vice-presidential debate in Atlanta, Al Gore clearly got the better of Dan Quayle. Perot's running mate, retired admiral James Stockdale, was likable but a non-factor, and his performance took a little steam out of the momentum Perot had gained after the St. Louis debate. Quayle was effective in staying on message: Clinton wanted to raise taxes and Bush wouldn't; Clinton had no character and Bush did. He repeated what, in retrospect, was one of my worst public statements. In early 1991, after the Congress authorized President Bush to attack Iraq, I was asked how I would have voted. I was for the resolution, but I answered, "I guess I would have voted with the majority if it was a close vote. But I agree with the arguments the minority made." At the time, I hadn't thought I would be running for President in 1992. Both Arkansas senators had voted against authorizing the war. They were my friends, and I just didn't want to embarrass them publicly. When I entered the race, the comment looked wishy-washy and slick. Al's strategy was to hit back briefly on Quayle's attacks and keep talking about our positive plans for America. His best line was in response to Quayle's support for congressional term limits, a pet cause for conservatives: "We're fixin' to limit one."

Two nights later, on October 15, we had the second debate, in Richmond, Virginia. This was the one I wanted, a town hall meeting where we would be questioned by a representative group of local undecided voters.

My big worry this time was my voice. It was so bad right before the first debate that I could hardly speak above a whisper. When I had lost it during the primary, I saw a specialist in New York and got a voice coach, who taught me a set of exercises to open my throat and push the sound up through my sinus cavities. They involved humming; singing pairs of vowels, back to back, always beginning with **e,** like **e-i, e-o, e-a**; and repeating certain phrases to get the feel of pushing the sound up through the damaged cords. My favorite phrase was "Abraham Lincoln was a great orator." Whenever I said it, I thought about Lincoln's high, almost squeaky voice, and the fact that at least he was smart enough not to lose it. When my voice was off, a lot of the young staffers good-naturedly poked fun at me by repeating the humming exercises. It was funny, but losing my voice wasn't. A politician without a voice isn't worth much. When you lose yours repeatedly, it's frightening, because there's always the lurking fear that it won't come back. When it first happened, I thought my allergies had caused it. Then I learned that the problem was acid reflux, a relatively common condition in which stomach acid comes back up the esophagus and scalds the vocal cords, usually during sleep. Later, when I began to take medication and sleep on a wedge to elevate my head and shoulders, it got better. On the eve of the second debate, I was still struggling.

Carole Simpson of ABC News moderated the debate with questions from the audience. The first question, about how to guarantee fairness in trade, went to Ross Perot. He gave an anti-trade answer. The President gave a pro-trade response. I said I was for free and fair trade and we needed to do three things: make sure our trading partners' markets were as open as ours; change the tax code to favor modernizing plants at home rather than moving them abroad; and stop giving low-interest loans and job-training funds to companies that move to other countries when we didn't provide the same assistance to needy companies at home.

After trade we went to the deficit, then to negative campaigning. Bush hit me again for demonstrating against the Vietnam War in England. I replied, "I'm not interested in his character. I want to change the character of the presidency. And I'm interested in what we can trust him to do and what you can trust me to do and what you can trust Mr. Perot to do for the next four years."

After that, we discussed a series of issues—the cities, highways, gun control, term limits, and health-care costs. Then came the question that turned the debate. A woman asked, "How has the national debt personally affected each of your lives? And if it hasn't, how can you honestly find a cure for the economic problems of the common people if you have no experience in what's ailing them?" Perot went first, saying the debt caused him to "disrupt my private life and my business to get involved in this activity." He said he wanted to lift the debt burden from his children and grandchildren. Bush had a hard time saying how he had been affected personally. The questioner kept pushing him, saying she'd had friends who had been laid off, who couldn't make their mortgage and car payments. Then, strangely, Bush said he'd been to a black church and read in the bulletin about teen pregnancies. Finally, he said it's not fair to say you can't know what a problem is like unless you have it. When my turn came, I said I'd been governor of a small state for twelve years. I knew people by name who had lost their jobs and businesses. I'd met a lot more in the last year all over the country. I had run a state government and seen the human consequences of cuts in federal services. Then I told the questioner that the debt was a big problem, but not the only reason we had no growth: "We're in the grip of a failed economic theory." At one point during these exchanges, President Bush made a bad moment worse for himself by nervously looking at his watch. It made him seem even more out of touch. Though we moved on to other matters, like Social Security, pensions, Medicare, America's responsibilities as a superpower, education, and the possibility of an African-American or a woman being elected President, the debate was essentially over after our answers to the woman's question about the personal impact of the debt on us.

President Bush was effective in his closing statement by asking the audience to think about who they wanted to be President if our country faced a major crisis. Perot spoke well about education, the deficit, and the fact that he'd paid more than a billion dollars in taxes, "and for a guy that started out with everything he owned in the trunk of his car, that ain't bad." I began by saying that I had tried to answer the questions "specifically and pointedly." I highlighted Arkansas' programs in education and jobs and the support I had from twenty-four retired generals and admirals and several Republican businesspeople. I then said, "You have to decide whether you want change or not." I urged them to help me replace "trickle-down" economics with "invest-and-grow" economics.

I loved the second debate. Whatever questions they had about me, real voters most wanted to know about things that affected their lives. A CBS News post-debate poll of 1,145 voters said 53 percent of them thought I had won, compared with 25 percent for Bush and 21 percent for Perot. Five debate coaches interviewed by the Associated Press said that I had won, based on style, specifics, and my obvious comfort level with a format I'd been working with throughout the campaign, and long before that in Arkansas. I liked direct contact with citizens, and I trusted their unfiltered judgment.

As we headed into the third debate, a CNN/**USA Today** poll had my lead back to fifteen points, 47 percent to 32 percent for Bush to 15 percent for Perot.

Hillary and I went into Ypsilanti with our crew a day early to prepare for the last debate on the campus of the Michigan State University in East Lansing. As they had for the two previous debates, Bob Barnett and Mike Synar put me through my paces. I knew this would be the roughest ride for me. President Bush was a tough, proud man who was finally fighting hard to hold on to his job. And I was sure that, sooner or later, Perot, too, would turn his fire on me.

More than 90 million people watched the last debate on October 19, the largest audience we had drawn. We were questioned half the time by Jim Lehrer, half the time by a panel of journalists. It was President Bush's best per-formance. He accused me of being a tax-and-spend lib-eral, a Jimmy Carter clone, and a waffler who couldn't make up his mind. On the waffling issue I had a pretty good retort: "I can't believe he's accused me of taking two sides of an issue. He said 'trickle-down economics is voodoo economics' and now he's its biggest practitioner." When he hit the Arkansas economy, I got to reply that Arkansas had always been a poor state, but in the last year we were first in job creation, fourth in the percentage increase in manufacturing jobs, fourth in the percentage increase in personal income, and fourth in the decline in poverty, with the second-lowest state and local tax burden in the country: "The difference between Arkansas and the United States is that we're going in the right direction and this country's going in the wrong direction." I said that, instead of apologizing for signing the deficit-reduction plan with its gas-tax increase, the President should have acknowledged that his error was in saying "Read my lips" in the first place. Perot took us both on, saying he had grown up five blocks from Arkansas and my experience as governor of such a small state was "irrelevant" to presiden-tial decision making, and accusing Bush of telling Saddam Hussein that the United States would not respond if he invaded northern Kuwait. We both whacked him back.

The second half of the debate featured questions by the panel of journalists. On the whole, it was more structured and less feisty, a bit like the first debate. However, there were some made-for-TV moments. Helen Thomas of United Press International, the senior White House correspondent, asked me: "If you had it to do over again, would you put on the nation's uniform?" I said I might answer the draft questions better, but I still thought Vietnam was a mistake. I then noted that we'd had some pretty good non-veteran Presidents, including FDR, Wilson, and Lincoln, who opposed the Mexican War. When I said Bush had made news in the first debate by saying he would put James Baker in charge of economic policy, but I would make news by putting myself in charge of economic policy, Bush got off a good line: "That's what worries me." The three of us brought the debates to an end with effective closing statements. I thanked the people for watching and caring about the country, and said again that I wasn't interested in attacking anyone personally. I complimented Ross Perot on his campaign and raising the profile of the deficit. And I said of President Bush, "I honor his service to our country, I appreciate his efforts, and I wish him well. I just believe it's time to change. . . . I know we can do better."

It's hard to say who won the third debate. I did a good job defending Arkansas and my record, and in discussing the issues, but I may have qualified too many of my answers. I had seen enough Presidents who had to change course to want my hands tied later by blanket statements in the debates. With his back against the wall, President Bush did well on everything except his attack on my record in Arkansas; that would work only in an unanswered paid ad, where the voters couldn't hear the facts. He was better at questioning what kind of President I would be, playing into the perception of Democrats as being weak on foreign policy and tax-happy, and reminding people that the last southern Democratic governor to be elected President presided over a period of high interest rates and inflation. Perot was witty and comfortable in his own skin, which I thought would reassure his supporters and perhaps sway some of the undecided voters. Three of the post-debate polls showed me winning the debate, but the CNN/**USA Today** poll, the only one to show Perot the victor, said 12 percent had changed their preference after the debate, more than half of them going to Perot.

Still, on balance, the debates were good for me. More Americans thought I had the ability to be a good President, and the give-and-take on the issues allowed me a chance to push my positive proposals. I wish we could have done them for two more weeks. Instead, we headed for the homestretch, a frenzied rush to as many states as possible, with the airwaves full of negative ads from my opponents, and a shot against Bush from me featuring his most famous statement: "Read my lips." Frank Greer and Mandy Grunwald did a good job with our ads, and our rapid-response team answered theirs effectively, but it wasn't the same as having all the candidates in one room. Now they were coming after me, and I had to hang on.

On October 21, the campaign got a little comic relief when Burke's Peerage, England's leading genealogical authority, said that President Bush and I were both descendants of thirteenth-century English royalty and were distant cousins, at least twenty times removed. Our common ancestor was King John. Bush was descended through John's son King Henry III, making him Queen Elizabeth's thirteenth cousin. Appropriately, my royal connections were both less impressive and offset by equally strong democratic ties. My Blythe kinfolk were descendants of both Henry III's sister Eleanor and her husband, Simon de Montfort, Earl of Leicester, who defeated the king in battle and forced him to accept the most representative parliament up to that time. Alas, in 1265 the king broke his oath to honor the Parliament, a breach that led to the battle of Evesham, in which poor Simon was killed. The spokesman for Burke's Peerage said that Simon's body "was hacked into a multitude of pieces, bits being sent out around the country—a finger, perhaps, to a village, a foot to a town—to show what happened to democrats." Now that I knew that the roots of my differences with the President went back seven hundred years, I suppose I couldn't blame his campaign for being faithful to the tactics of his ancestors. Burke's Peerage also traced the Blythes back to the village of Gotham, which, according to English legend, was a haunt of madmen. I knew I had to be a little crazy to run for President, but I hated to think it was genetic.

On October 23, our campaign got another boost from the high-tech sector when the leaders of more than thirty computer-software companies, including Microsoft executive vice president Steve Ballmer, endorsed me. But it wasn't over. A week after the last debate, a CNN/**USA Today** poll had my lead over President Bush down to seven points, 39 to 32 percent, with Perot at 20 percent. Just as I had feared, Perot's advertising, coupled with President Bush's attacks on me, were moving votes to Perot at my expense. On October 26, while campaigning in North Carolina, Al Gore and I tried to keep the lead by hitting the Bush administration over "Iraqgate," the channeling of U.S. government–backed credits to Iraq through the Atlanta branch of a bank owned by the Italian government. Ostensibly for agricultural purposes, the credits had been siphoned off by Saddam Hussein to rebuild his military and weapons program after the Iran-Iraq war. Two billion dollars of the credits were never repaid, leaving

U.S. taxpayers with the bill. The banker in Atlanta who was indicted for his role in the fraud negotiated a sweetheart plea bargain with the U.S. attorney's office, which, unbelievably, was headed by a Bush appointee who had represented Iraqi interests in the credit flap shortly before his appointment, although he said he had recused himself from this investigation. By the time Al and I mentioned it, the FBI, the CIA, and the Justice Department were all investigating each other for what they had or hadn't done in the affair. It was a real mess, but probably too complicated to affect any voters this late in the campaign.

Perot was still the wild card. On October 29, a Reuters news article began: "If President George Bush wins reelection, he will owe a major debt of gratitude to a tough-talking Texas billionaire who dislikes him." The article went on to say that the debates had altered Perot's image, allowing him to double his support, mostly at my expense, and taking away the monopoly I had had on the "change" issue. That day's CNN/**USA Today** poll had my lead down to two points, though five other polls and Stan Greenberg's poll for our campaign had the margin holding at seven to ten points. Whatever the number, the race was still volatile.

During the last week, I campaigned as hard as I could. So did President Bush. On Thursday, at a campaign rally in suburban Michigan, he referred to Al Gore and me as "bozos," a comparison to the clown Bozo, who probably found the reference more unflattering than we did. On the Friday before the election, Iran-Contra special prosecutor Lawrence Walsh, a Republican from Oklahoma, indicted President Reagan's defense secretary, Caspar Weinberger, and five others, with a note in the indictment suggesting that President Bush had played a greater role in and knew more about the illegal sales of arms to Iran authorized by the Reagan White House than he had previously admitted. Whether it would hurt him or not, I didn't know; I was too busy to think about it. The timing was ironic, though, considering the strenuous efforts the administration had made to dig into my passport files and the pressure they had been applying, which we didn't know about at the time, to get the U.S. attorney in Arkansas, a Bush appointee, to implicate me in the investigation of the failure of Madison Guaranty Savings and Loan.

Over the last weekend, Bush directed all his paid media fire at me. And Perot, believing 30 percent of my support was "soft" and could shift to him at the last minute, finally joined in, big-time. He spent a reported $3 million on thirty-minute television "infomercials," trashing Arkansas. He said if I was elected, "we'll all be plucking chickens for a living." The program listed twenty-three areas where Arkansas ranked near the bottom of all states. Apparently, he no longer thought Arkansas was irrelevant. Our team had a big argument about whether to respond. Hillary wanted to go after Perot. I thought we at least had to defend Arkansas. We had done well by never letting any charge go unanswered. Everyone else thought the attacks were too little, too late, and we should just stick with the game plan. Reluctantly, I agreed. My team had been right about the big questions so far, and I was too tired and keyed up to trust my judgment over theirs.

I began the weekend with a morning rally that filled a high school football stadium in Decatur, Georgia, outside Atlanta. Governor Zell Miller, Senator Sam Nunn, Congressman John Lewis, and other Democrats who had stuck with me all the way were there. But the big draw was

Hank Aaron, the baseball star who had broken Babe Ruth's home-run record in 1974. Aaron was a genuine local hero, not only for his baseball exploits but also for his work on behalf of poor children after he laid down his bat. There were 25,000 people at the Georgia rally. Three days later, I would carry Georgia by just 13,000 votes. From then on, Hank Aaron loved to kid me that he had personally delivered Georgia's electoral votes with his Saturday-morning plug. He may have been right.

After Georgia, I campaigned in Davenport, Iowa, then flew to Milwaukee, where I did my last televised town hall meeting and cut my last television spot, urging people to vote, and vote for change. On Sunday night, after campaign stops in Cincinnati and Scranton, the Rodhams' hometown, we flew to New Jersey for a big rally at the Meadowlands, a musical extravaganza featuring rock, jazz, and country musicians and movie stars who were supporting me. Then I played sax and danced with Hillary before 15,000 people at the Garden State Park racetrack in Cherry Hill, New Jersey, where a horse named Bubba Clinton, the name my brother had called me by since he was a toddler, had recently won a race at 17-to-1 odds. My odds were better now, but they had once been far longer. One man who bet 100 pounds on me in April with a London bookmaker when the odds were 33 to 1 made about $5,000. There's no telling what he could have made if he'd placed the bet in early February when I was being battered in New Hampshire.

Hillary and I woke up Monday morning in Philadelphia, the birthplace of our democracy, and the first leg of a four thousand–mile, eight-state, round-the-clock campaign swing. While Al and Tipper Gore campaigned in other battleground states, three Boeing 727s, decorated in red, white, and blue, took Hillary, me, our staff, and a horde of media on the twenty-nine-hour jaunt. At Philadelphia's Mayfair Diner, the first stop, when a man asked me what would be the first thing I would do if elected, I replied, "I'm going to thank God." On to Cleveland. With my voice failing again, I said, "Teddy Roosevelt once said we should speak softly and carry a big stick. Tomorrow, I want to talk softly and carry Ohio." At an airport rally outside Detroit, flanked by several of Michigan's elected officials and union leaders who had worked so hard for me, I croaked, "If you will be my voice tomorrow, I will be your voice for four years." After stops in St. Louis and Paducah, Kentucky, we flew to Texas for two visits. The first was in McAllen, deep in South Texas near the Mexican border where I had been stranded with Sargent Shriver twenty years earlier. It was after midnight when we got to Fort Worth, where the crowd was kept awake by the famous country-rocker Jerry Jeff Walker. When I got back to the plane, I learned that my staff had bought four hundred dollars' worth of mango ice cream from the Menger Hotel in San Antonio, just across the street from the Alamo. They had all heard me say how much I loved that ice cream, which I had discovered when working in the McGovern campaign in 1972. There was enough of it to feed the three planeloads of weary travelers all night.

Meanwhile, back at headquarters in Little Rock, James Carville had gathered our people, more than a hundred of them, for a last meeting. After George Stephanopoulos introduced him, James gave an emotional speech, saying that love and work were the two most precious gifts a person could give, and thanking all our people, most of them very young, for those gifts.

We flew from Texas to Albuquerque, New Mexico, for a very early-morning rally with my old friend Governor Bruce King. Afterward, at about 4 a.m., I devoured a breakfast of Mexican food, then headed for Denver, the last stop. We had a big, enthusiastic early-morning crowd. After Mayor Wellington Webb, Senator Tim Wirth, and my partner in education reform Governor Roy Roemer fired them up, Hillary gave the speech and I forced my last campaign words of gratitude and hope through swollen vocal cords. Then it was home to Little Rock.

Hillary and I were greeted at the airport by Chelsea, other family members, friends, and our headquarters staff. I thanked them for all they'd done, then left with my family for the drive to our polling place, the Dunbar Community Center, which is in a mostly African-American neighborhood less than a mile from the Governor's Mansion. We spoke to the folks gathered around the center and signed in with the election officials there. Then, just as she had done since she was six, Chelsea went into the voting booth with me. After I closed the curtain, Chelsea pulled down the lever by my name, then hugged me tight. After thirteen months of backbreaking effort, it was all that was left for us to do. When Hillary finished voting, the three of us embraced, went outside, answered a few press questions, shook a few hands, and went home.

For me, election days have always embodied the great mystery of democracy. No matter how hard pollsters and pundits try to demystify it, the mystery remains. It's the one day when the ordinary citizen has as much power as the millionaire and the President. Some people use it and some don't. Those who do choose candidates for all kinds of reasons, some rational, some intuitive, some with certainty, others skeptically. Somehow, they usually pick the right leader for the times; that's why America is still around and doing well after more than 228 years.

I had entered the race largely because I thought I was right for these times of dramatic change in how Americans live, work, raise children, and relate to the rest of the world. I had worked for years to understand how political leaders' decisions play out in people's lives. I believed I understood what needed to be done and how to do it. But I also knew I was asking the American people to take a big gamble. First, they weren't used to Democratic Presidents. Then there were the questions about me: I was very young; was the governor of a state most Americans knew little about; had opposed the Vietnam War and avoided military service; held liberal views on race and rights for women and gays; often seemed slick when I spoke of achieving ambitious goals that, at least on the surface, seemed mutually exclusive; and had lived a far from perfect life. I had worked my heart out to convince the American people that I was a risk worth taking, but the constantly shifting polls and the resurgence of Perot showed that many of them wanted to believe in me but still harbored doubts. On the stump, Al Gore asked voters to think about what headline they wanted to read the day after the election: "Four More Years," or "Change Is on the Way." I thought I knew what their answer would be, but on that long November day, like everyone else, I had to wait to find out.

When we got home, the three of us watched an old John Wayne movie until we dozed off for a couple of hours. In the afternoon, I went jogging with Chelsea downtown and stopped at McDonald's for a cup of water, as I had countless times before. After I got back to the

Governor's Mansion, I didn't have to wait much longer. The returns started to come in early, at about 6:30 p.m. I was still in my jogging clothes when I was projected the winner in several states in the East. A little over three hours later, the networks projected me the overall winner, when Ohio went our way by 90,000 votes out of almost 5 million cast, a victory margin of less than 2 percent. It seemed fitting, because Ohio had been one of the states to guarantee me the nomination in the June 2 primaries, and the state whose votes had officially put me over the top at our convention in New York. The turnout was huge, the highest since the early 1960s, with more than 100 million people voting.

When all 104,600,366 votes were counted, the final margin of victory was about 5.5 percent. I finished with 43 percent of the vote, to 37.4 percent for President Bush and 19 percent for Ross Perot, the best showing for a third-party candidate since Teddy Roosevelt garnered 27 percent with his Bull Moose Party in 1912. Our baby-boom ticket did best among voters over sixty-five and those under thirty. Our own generation apparently had more doubts about whether we were ready to lead the country. The late Bush-Perot tag-team attack on Arkansas had shaved two or three points off our high-water mark a few days before the election. It had hurt, but not badly enough.

The victory margin in the electoral college was larger. President Bush won eighteen states with 168 electoral votes. I received 370 electoral votes from thirty-two states and the District of Columbia, including every state that borders the Mississippi River from north to south except Mississippi, and all the New England and mid-Atlantic states. I also won in some unlikely places, like Georgia,

Montana, Nevada, and Colorado. Eleven states were decided by 3 percent or less: Arizona, Florida, Virginia, and North Carolina went for the President; besides Ohio, Georgia, Montana, Nevada, New Hampshire, Rhode Island, and New Jersey voted narrowly for me. I received 53 percent of the vote in Arkansas, my highest total, and won twelve other states by 10 percent or more, including some large ones: California, Illinois, Massachusetts, and New York. While Perot kept me from getting a majority of the popular vote, his presence on the ballot almost certainly added to my margin in the electoral college.

How did Americans come to choose their first baby-boom President, the third youngest in history, only the second governor of a small state, carrying more baggage than an ocean liner? Surveys of voters leaving the polls indicated that the economy was by far the biggest issue for them, followed by the deficit and health care, with the character issue trailing. In the end, I had won the debate over what the election was about. In a presidential campaign, that is more important than whether the voters agree with a candidate on specific issues. But the economy alone didn't do it. I was also helped by James Carville and a brilliant campaign team who kept me and everyone else focused and on message through all the ups and downs; by Stan Greenberg's insightful polling and Frank Greer's effective paid media; by able people who led the campaign at the grass roots; by a Democratic Party united by Ron Brown's skill and the desire to win after a dozen years in the wilderness; by extraordinarily high levels of support from minorities and women, who also elected a Congress with six female senators and forty-seven female members of the House, up from twenty-eight; by the initial disunity and overconfidence among the Republicans; by surprisingly positive press coverage in the general election, in stark contrast to the going-over I got in the primaries; by the extraordinary performance of Al and Tipper Gore in the campaign, and the generational change we all represented; and by the New Democrat philosophy and ideas I had developed in Arkansas and with the DLC. Finally, I was able to win because Hillary and my friends stayed with me through the fire, and because I didn't give up when I got beat up.

Early on election night, President Bush called to congratulate me. He was gracious and pledged a smooth transition, as did Dan Quayle. After a last look at my victory speech, Hillary and I said a prayer thanking God for our blessings and asking for divine guidance in the work ahead. Then we got Chelsea and drove down to the Old State House for the big event.

The Old State House was my favorite building in Arkansas, full of my state's history and my own. It was the place where I had received well-wishers when I was sworn in as attorney general sixteen years earlier, and where I had announced for President thirteen months ago. We walked onto the stage to greet Al and Tipper and the thousands of people who had filled the downtown streets. I was overwhelmed when I looked out into the faces of all those people, so full of happiness and hope. And I was filled with gratitude. I loved seeing my mother's tears of joy, and I hoped that my father was looking down on me with pride.

When I started this remarkable odyssey, I could never have anticipated how hard it would be, or how wonderful. The people in the crowd and millions like them had done their part. Now I had to prove them right. I began by saying, "On this day, with high hopes and brave hearts, in massive numbers, the American people have voted to make a new beginning." I asked those who had voted for President Bush and Ross Perot to join me in creating a "re-United States," then closed with these words:

> This victory was more than a victory of party; it was a victory for those who work hard and play by the rules, a victory for people who felt left out and left behind and want to do better. . . . I accept tonight the responsibility that you have given me to be the leader of this, the greatest country in human history. I accept it with a full heart and a joyous spirit. But I ask you to be Americans again, too, to be interested not just in getting but in giving, not just in placing blame but in assuming responsibility, not just in looking out for yourselves but in looking out for others, too. . . . Together, we can make the country that we love everything it was meant to be.

TWENTY-NINE

On the day after the election, awash in congratulatory calls and messages, I went to work on what is called the transition. Is it ever! There was no time to celebrate, and we didn't take much time to rest, which was probably a mistake. In just eleven weeks, my family and I had to make the transition from our life in Arkansas into the White House. There was so much to do: select the cabinet, important sub-cabinet officials, and the White House staff; work with the Bush people on the mechanics of the move; begin briefings on national security and talk to foreign leaders; reach out to congressional leaders; finalize the economic proposals I would present to Congress; develop a plan to implement my other campaign commitments; deal with a large number of requests for meetings and the desire of many of our campaign workers and major supporters to know as soon as possible whether they would be part of the new administration; and respond to unfolding events. There would be a lot of them in the next seventy days, especially overseas: in Iraq, where Saddam Hussein was seeking relief from UN sanctions; Somalia, where President Bush had dispatched U.S. troops on a humanitarian mission to avert mass starvation; and Russia, where the economy was in shambles, President Yeltsin faced growing opposition from ultra-nationalists and unconverted Communists, and the withdrawal of Russian troops from the Baltic nations had been delayed. The "to do" list was growing.

Several weeks earlier, we had quietly established a transition-planning operation in Little Rock, under a board that included Vernon Jordan, Warren Christopher, Mickey Kantor, former San Antonio mayor Henry Cisneros, Doris Matsui, and former Vermont governor Madeleine Kunin. The staff director was Gerald Stern, who was on leave from his job as executive vice president of Occidental Petroleum. Obviously, we didn't want to look as if we'd taken the outcome of the election for granted, so the operation was kept low-key, with an unlisted telephone number and no sign on the door of the offices on the thirteenth floor of the Worthen Bank building.

When George Stephanopoulos came over to the mansion on Wednesday, Hillary and I asked him to continue being our communications director in the White House. I would have been happy to have James Carville there too, to help develop strategy and keep us on message, but he didn't think he was suited to government and two days earlier he had cracked to reporters, "I wouldn't live in a country whose government would hire me."

On Wednesday afternoon, I met with the transition board and received my first briefing papers. At 2:30 p.m., I held a short press conference on the back lawn of the Governor's Mansion. Because President Bush was in another tense situation with Iraq, I emphasized that America "has only one President at a time," and that "America's foreign policy remains solely in his hands."

On my second day as President-elect, I spoke with a few foreign leaders, and went to the office to take care of some state business and thank the governor's staff for the fine job they had done while I was away. That night we had a party for the campaign staff. I was still so hoarse I could barely squeak out "Thank you." I spent most of the time shaking hands and walking around with signs on my shirt that said, "Sorry, I can't talk," and "You did a good job."

On Friday, I named Vernon Jordan as chairman and Warren Christopher as director of my transition board. The announcement of their appointments was well received in Washington and in Little Rock, where both were respected by the campaign staff, many of whom were beginning to show predictable and understandable signs of exhaustion, irritability, and anxiety about the future, as the euphoria of our victory wore off.

In the second week of the transition, the pace picked up. I spoke about Middle East peace with Israeli prime minister Yitzhak Rabin, Egyptian president Hosni Mubarak, and Saudi Arabia's King Fahd. Vernon and Chris filled out most of the senior transition staff with Alexis Herman, deputy chair of the Democratic Party, and Mark Gearan, who had managed Al Gore's campaign, as deputy directors; DLC president Al From in domestic policy; Sandy Berger, along with my campaign aide Nancy Soderberg in foreign policy; and Gene Sperling and my old Rhodes classmate Bob Reich, then a Harvard professor and author of several thought-provoking books on the global economy, in economic policy. The vetting of all candidates for important positions would be overseen by Tom Donilon, a sharp Washington lawyer and longtime Democratic activist. Donilon's job was important; defeating a President's appointments because of financial or personal problems in their backgrounds or previously unexamined opinions had become a regular part of Washington political life. Our vetters were supposed to make sure that anyone who was willing to serve could survive the scrutiny.

A few days later, former South Carolina governor Dick Riley joined the transition team to oversee the sub-cabinet appointments. Riley had a backbreaking job. At one point, he was getting more than three thousand résumés, as well as a couple of hundred phone calls, a day. Many of the calls were from members of Congress and governors who expected him to return the calls personally. So many people who had contributed to our victory wanted to serve that I was worried about able, deserving people falling through the cracks, and some of them did.

The third week of the transition was devoted to reaching out to Washington. I invited House Speaker Tom Foley, House majority leader Dick Gephardt, and Senate majority leader George Mitchell to Little Rock for dinner and a morning meeting. It was important for me to get off on the right foot with the Democratic leaders. I knew I had to have their support to succeed, and they knew the American people would hold us all accountable for breaking the partisan gridlock in Washington. It would require some compromise on my part and theirs, but after our meetings I was confident we could work together.

On Wednesday, I went to Washington for two days to meet with President Bush, other congressional Democrats, and the Republican leaders in Congress. My meeting with the President, scheduled to last an hour, went almost twice that long and was both cordial and helpful. We talked about a wide variety of issues, and I found the President's review of our foreign policy challenges particularly insightful.

From the White House, I drove two miles into north Washington, to a neighborhood beset by poverty, unemployment, drugs, and crime. On Georgia Avenue, I got out of the car and walked for a block, shaking hands and talking to merchants and other citizens about their problems and what I could do to help. Eight people had been killed the previous year within a mile of where I stopped. I got food from a Chinese takeout where the workers operated behind bulletproof glass for safety. Parents of school-aged children said they were frightened because so many of their kids' classmates brought guns to school. The people who lived in Washington's inner city were often forgotten by Congress and the White House, despite the fact that the federal government still retained substantial control over the city's affairs. I wanted the city's residents to know I cared about their problems and wanted to be a good neighbor.

On Thursday, I went for a morning jog, running out the door of the Hay-Adams Hotel, just across Lafayette Square from the White House, down a street filled with homeless people who had spent the night there, over to the Washington Monument and the Lincoln Memorial, then back to the McDonald's near the hotel. I got a cup of coffee and met a fifty-nine-year-old man who told me he'd lost his job and everything he had in the recession. I walked back to the hotel thinking about that man, and how I could manage to keep in touch with the problems of people like him from behind the wall that surrounds every President.

Later, after breakfast with fourteen Democratic congressional leaders, I had a private visit with the Senate minority leader, Bob Dole. I had always respected Dole, because of his courageous recovery from his World War II wounds and because he had worked with Democrats on issues like food stamps and disability rights. On the other hand, he was a partisan, and had wasted no time on election night in saying that because I didn't "even win by a majority . . . there's not a clear mandate there." Therefore, Dole said, his responsibility was "to bring our party together, to reach out to try to attract independent and Perot supporters to put up our own agenda." Dole and I had a good talk, but I left the meeting unsure of what our relationship, or his agenda, would be. After all, Dole wanted to be President too.

I also had a cordial meeting with the House minority leader, Bob Michel, an old-fashioned conservative from Illinois, but I regretted that the Republican whip, Newt Gingrich of Georgia, was away on vacation. Gingrich was the political and intellectual leader of the conservative Republicans in the House, and he believed a permanent Republican majority could be forged by uniting the cultural and religious conservatives with voters who were anti–big government and anti-tax. He had skewered President Bush for signing the Democrats' deficit-reduction package in 1990 because it contained a gas-tax increase. I could only imagine what he intended to do to me.

Back at the hotel, I met with General Colin Powell, chairman of the Joint Chiefs of Staff. Having risen to the highest ranks with the support of Presidents Reagan and Bush, Powell would serve his last nine months as chairman under a very different Commander in Chief. He was opposed to my proposal to allow gays to serve in the military, even though during the Gulf War, which made him a popular hero, the Pentagon had knowingly allowed more than one hundred gays to serve, dismissing them only after the conflict, when they were no longer needed. Despite our differences, General Powell made it clear that he would serve as best he could, including giving me his honest advice, which is exactly what I wanted.

Hillary and I ended our Washington stay with a dinner party given by Pamela Harriman. The previous night, Vernon and Ann Jordan had also invited some people to have dinner with us. These parties, along with a later one given by Katharine Graham, were designed to introduce Hillary and me to important people in Washington's political, press, and business circles. To most of them, we were still strangers.

After spending a last Thanksgiving in the Governor's Mansion with my family, including our annual visit to a shelter that a friend of ours ran for women and children who had fled from domestic abuse, Hillary and I flew with Chelsea and her friend Elizabeth Flammang to Southern California for a little rest with our friends the Thomasons and for a courtesy call on President Reagan. Reagan had set up shop in a very nice building located on property once used by Twentieth Century Fox to produce movies. I really enjoyed the visit. Reagan was a great storyteller, and after eight years in the White House he had some good ones I wanted to hear. At the close of the meeting, he gave me a jar of his trademark jelly beans, colored red, white, and blue. I would keep it in my office for eight years.

In December, I got down to the business that people hire Presidents to do: making decisions. Since I had promised to focus on the economy "like a laser beam," I began with that. On December 3, I had a one-on-one meeting at the Governor's Mansion with Alan Greenspan, chairman of the Federal Reserve Board. The Fed chairman has enormous influence over the economy, largely through the Fed's setting of short-term interest rates, which in turn affect long-term rates on business and consumer loans, including home mortgages. Because Greenspan was a brilliant student of all aspects of the economy and a seasoned Washington power player, his pronouncements in speeches and congressional testimony carried great weight. I knew Greenspan was a conservative Republican who was probably disappointed by my election, but I thought we could work together for three reasons: I believed in the independence of the Federal Reserve; like Greenspan, I thought it was essential to cut the deficit; and he, too, had once been a tenor saxophone player, who, like me, had decided he'd be better off doing something else for a living.

A week later, I began my cabinet announcements with my economic team, starting with Lloyd Bentsen, the chairman of the Senate Finance Committee, as secretary of the Treasury. Bentsen was a pro-business Democrat who still had concern for ordinary people. Tall and lean with a patrician bearing, he came from a wealthy South Texas family, and after service as a bomber pilot in Italy during World War II he was elected to the U.S. House of Representatives. After three terms there, he left the House to go into business, then, in 1970, was elected to the Senate, defeating Congressman George H. W. Bush. I liked Bentsen and thought he would be perfect for the Treasury job: he was respected on Wall Street, effective with Congress, and committed to my goals of restoring growth and reducing poverty. Bentsen's deputy secretary would be Roger Altman, vice chairman of the Blackstone Group investment firm and a lifelong Democrat and financial whiz who would strengthen our team and our ties to Wall Street. The other Treasury appointee, Larry Summers, who would become undersecretary for international affairs, was the youngest tenured professor at Harvard at the age of twenty-eight. He was even brighter than his reputation had led me to believe.

I chose Leon Panetta, the California congressman who chaired the House Budget Committee, to be the director of the Office of Management and Budget (OMB), always a critical position but especially important for me, because I was committed to crafting a budget that both reduced the deficit and increased spending in areas vital to our long-term prosperity, like education and technology. I didn't know Leon before I interviewed him, but I was very impressed with his knowledge, energy, and down-to-earth manner. I named the other finalist for the OMB job, Alice Rivlin, as Leon's deputy. Like him, she was a deficit "hawk," and sensitive to people who needed federal help.

I asked Bob Rubin to take on a new job: coordinating economic policy in the White House as chair of a National Economic Council, which would operate in much the same way the National Security Council did, bringing all the relevant agencies together to formulate and implement policy. I had become convinced that the federal government's economic policy making was neither as organized nor as effective as it could be. I wanted to bring together not only the tax and budget functions of Treasury and the OMB, but also the work of the Commerce Department, the Office of the U.S. Trade Representative, the Council of Economic Advisers, the Export-Import Bank, the Labor Department, and the Small Business Administration. We had to utilize every possible resource to implement the kind of comprehensive, sophisticated economic program necessary to benefit every income group and every region. Rubin was just the man to do it. Somehow he managed to be understated and intense at the same time. He had been co-chairman of Goldman Sachs, the big New York investment firm, and if he could balance all of its egos and interests, he had a good chance to succeed with the job I had given him. The National Economic Council represented the biggest change in White House operations in years, and thanks to Rubin, it would serve America well.

I announced that Laura Tyson, a respected economics professor at the University of California at Berkeley, would be chair of the Council of Economic Advisers. Laura impressed me with her knowledge of technology, manufacturing, and trade, the microeconomic issues I felt had been too long ignored in the making of national economic policy.

I also named Bob Reich labor secretary. The Labor post had languished under Reagan and Bush, but I saw it as a big part of our economic team. Bob had written some good books on the need for greater labor-management cooperation and the importance of both flexibility and security in the modern workplace. I believed he could both defend labor's interests in the health, safety, and welfare of working men and women and secure key labor support for our new economic policy.

I asked Ron Brown to be the commerce secretary, fulfilling a campaign commitment to elevate the importance of a department that had been considered a "second tier" agency for too long. With his unique mixture of brains and bravado, Ron had brought the DNC back from the dead, uniting its liberal and labor bases with those who embraced the new approach of the Democratic Leadership Council. If anyone could enliven the Commerce bureaucracy to advance America's commercial interests, he could. Ron would become the first African-American secretary of commerce and one of the most effective leaders the department ever had.

On the day I announced Ron Brown's appointment, I

also resigned as governor of Arkansas. I could no longer devote any time to the job, and Lieutenant Governor Jim Guy Tucker was more than ready and able to take over. One disappointing thing about leaving office in December was that I fell twenty-four days short of breaking Orval Faubus's record as my state's longest-serving governor.

On December 14 and 15, with the major economic positions filled, I hosted an economic summit in Little Rock. We had been working on it for six weeks, under the leadership of Mickey Kantor; John Emerson, a friend of Hillary's who had supported me in California; and Erskine Bowles, a successful North Carolina businessman who had supported me for President because of my New Democrat philosophy and my support for fetal-tissue research. Diabetes ran in Erskine's family, and he believed, as I did, that the research was essential to unlocking the mysteries of diabetes and other presently incurable medical conditions.

When the conference was announced, everybody in America seemed to want to attend, and we had a hard time keeping the crowd small enough to fit into the hall at the Little Rock Convention Center while leaving adequate space for the enormous number of press people from all over the world who wanted to cover it. Finally, they pared the list of delegates down to 329, ranging from heads of Fortune 500 companies to Silicon Valley executives to shop owners, and including labor leaders, academics, an Alaskan homesteader, and the chief of the Cherokee Indian Nation, whose imposing name was Wilma Mankiller.

When the conference opened, the atmosphere was electric, almost as if it were a rock concert for policy makers. The media called it a "wonkfest." The panels produced some keen insights and new ideas, and clarified the choices I faced. There was an overwhelming consensus that my number one priority should be to reduce the deficit, even if it meant less of a middle-class tax cut, or giving up on one altogether. "Mickey's Retreat," as we called the conference, was a smashing success, and not just in the eyes of the policy wonks. A poll released after the conference indicated that 77 percent of the American people approved of my preparations for taking over the presidency.

The economic conference sent a loud and clear message that, as I had promised, America was moving forward, away from trickle-down to invest-and-grow economics, away from neglect of those who were losing ground in the changing global economy to an America that once again offered opportunity to every responsible citizen. Eventually I would name Mickey Kantor to be U.S. trade representative, Erskine Bowles to head the Small Business Administration, and John Emerson to the White House staff. If anyone had earned a place on the team, they had.

Just before the economic conference, I announced that Mack McLarty would be White House chief of staff. It was an unusual choice because while Mack had served on two federal commissions under President Bush, he was hardly a Washington insider, a fact that concerned him. He told me he would prefer another job more suited to his business background. Nevertheless, I pressed Mack to accept the position, because I was convinced he could organize the White House staff to function smoothly and create the kind of team atmosphere in which I wanted to work. He was disciplined and intelligent; he had great negotiating skills and the ability to keep up with and follow through on many things at once. He was also a loyal friend of more than forty years, and I knew I could count on him not to shield me from diverse points of view and sources of information. In the first months of our tenure, both he and I would suffer from some of our tone deafness about Washington's political and press culture, but thanks to Mack, we also would accomplish a lot and create a spirit of cooperation that many previous White House staffs lacked.

Between December 11 and 18, I moved closer to my goal of naming the most diverse administration in history. On the eleventh, I named University of Wisconsin chancellor Donna Shalala as secretary of health and human services and Carole Browner, the state of Florida's environmental director, to head the Environmental Protection Agency. Hillary and I had known Shalala, a four-foot eleven-inch dynamo of Lebanese ancestry, for years. I didn't know Browner before I interviewed her, but was impressed with her; my friend Governor Lawton Chiles thought highly of her; and Al Gore wanted her to have the job. Both women would serve my entire eight years, building long lists of important achievements. On the fifteenth, the story broke that I would ask Dr. Joycelyn Elders, the Arkansas Health Department director, the second black woman to graduate from the University of Arkansas Medical School and a national authority on pediatric diabetes, to be U.S. surgeon general, America's top public-health official.

On the seventeenth, I announced the selection of Henry Cisneros to be secretary of housing and urban development. With his unusual combination of great political gifts and a caring heart, Henry had become the most popular Hispanic politician in America. He was well qualified for the job, with a brilliant record as mayor in revitalizing San Antonio. I also named Jesse Brown, an African-American ex-marine and Vietnam veteran, who was the executive director of the Disabled American Veterans, to be secretary of the Department of Veterans Affairs.

On December 21, I named Hazel O'Leary, an African-American utility executive from Northern States Power Company in Minnesota, to be secretary of energy, and Dick Riley, to be secretary of education. Hazel was an expert on natural gas, and I wanted to support its development because it was cleaner than oil and coal, and in ample supply. Dick and I had been friends for years. His modest manner was deceptive. He had long endured an agonizing spinal condition, despite which he had built a successful legal and political career and a fine family. And he had been a great education governor. In the campaign, I had often cited an article saying Arkansas had made more progress in education in the last ten years than any other state except South Carolina.

On Tuesday, December 22, I announced my entire national security team: Warren Christopher as secretary of state, Les Aspin as secretary of defense, Madeleine Albright as ambassador to the United Nations, Tony Lake as national security advisor, Jim Woolsey as director of the Central Intelligence Agency, and Admiral Bill Crowe as head of the President's Foreign Intelligence Advisory Board.

Christopher had been President Carter's deputy secretary of state and had played a major role in negotiating the release of American hostages from Iran. He had served me well in the vice-presidential and cabinet selection processes and shared my basic foreign policy objectives.

Some people thought his personality was too restrained for him to be effective, but I knew he could get things done.

I asked Les Aspin to be secretary of defense after it became clear that Sam Nunn wouldn't accept the appointment. As chairman of the House Armed Services Committee, Aspin probably knew more about defense than anyone else in the House of Representatives, understood the security challenges of the post–Cold War world, and was committed to modernizing our military to meet them.

I had been impressed with Madeleine Albright, a popular professor at Georgetown University, since I first met her during the Dukakis campaign. A native of Czechoslovakia and friend of Václav Havel, she was a passionate and articulate advocate of democracy and freedom. I thought she would be an ideal spokesperson for us at the United Nations in the post–Cold War era. Because I also wanted her counsel on national security matters, I elevated the UN ambassador's job to cabinet rank.

The national security advisor decision was difficult for me, because both Tony Lake and Sandy Berger had done a great job educating and advising me on foreign policy throughout the campaign. Tony was a little older and Sandy had worked for him in the Carter State Department, but I had known Sandy longer and better. In the end, the matter was resolved when Sandy came to me and suggested that I appoint Tony national security advisor and make him the deputy.

The CIA job was filled last. I wanted to appoint Congressman Dave McCurdy of Oklahoma chairman of the House Intelligence Committee, but much to my disappointment, he declined. I had met Jim Woolsey, a longtime figure in the Washington foreign policy establishment, in late 1991 at a national security discussion Sandy Berger organized with a diverse group of Democrats and independents with more robust views on national security and defense than our party typically projected. Woolsey was clearly intelligent and interested in the job. After one interview, I offered it to him.

After the national security announcements, I was close to meeting my self-imposed deadline of appointing the cabinet by Christmas. On Christmas Eve day we made it: in addition to officially announcing Mickey Kantor's appointment, I nominated Congressman Mike Espy of Mississippi to be secretary of agriculture; Federico Peña, the former mayor of Denver, as secretary of transportation; former Arizona governor Bruce Babbitt as secretary of the interior; and Zoë Baird, the general counsel for Aetna Life and Casualty, to be the first female attorney general.

Espy was active in the DLC, understood agricultural issues, and, along with Congressmen Bill Jefferson of New Orleans and John Lewis of Atlanta, was one of the first prominent black leaders outside Arkansas to endorse me. I didn't know Peña well, but he had been a fine mayor and had spearheaded the building of Denver's massive new airport. The airline industry was in trouble and needed a transportation secretary who understood its problems. Bruce Babbitt had been one of my favorite fellow governors. Brilliant, iconoclastic, and witty, he had won election in traditionally Republican Arizona and had succeeded as an activist, progressive governor. I hoped he could pursue our environmental agenda with less fallout in the western states than President Carter had suffered.

Originally, I had hoped to make Vernon Jordan attorney general. He had been a distinguished civil rights lawyer and was well thought of in corporate America. But Vernon, like James Carville, was determined not to come into government. When he bowed out in early December, during a talk on the back porch of the Governor's Mansion, I considered several people before ultimately choosing Zoë Baird.

I didn't know Zoë until I interviewed her. In addition to her work as Aetna's counsel, she had served in the Carter White House, had been an advocate for the poor, and, though she was only forty, seemed to have an unusually mature understanding of the attorney general's role and the challenges she would face.

Though I would later elevate some other positions to cabinet level, including those of drug czar, director of the Small Business Administration, and director of the Federal Emergency Management Agency, I had made the Christmas deadline with a cabinet of unquestionable competence and unprecedented diversity.

It was a good story, but not the main one of the day. President Bush gave a big Christmas present to some former associates, and potentially to himself, when he pardoned Caspar Weinberger and five others who had been indicted in the Iran-Contra scandal by Independent Counsel Lawrence Walsh. Weinberger's trial was about to get under way, and President Bush was likely to be called as a witness. Walsh angrily denounced the pardons as completing a six-year cover-up, saying it "undermines the principle that no man is above the law. It demonstrates that powerful people with powerful allies can commit serious crimes in high office—deliberately abusing the public trust—without consequence." Since now none of the defendants could be called to testify in court under oath, if there were any more facts to come out, they probably never would. Just two weeks earlier, Walsh had learned that the President and his lawyer, Boyden Gray, had failed for more than a year to hand over Bush's own contemporaneous notes relating to Iran-Contra, despite repeated requests to do so.

I disagreed with the pardons and could have made more of them but didn't, for three reasons. First, the President's pardon power is absolute under our Constitution. Second, I wanted the country to be more united, not more divided, even if the split would be to my political advantage. Finally, President Bush had given decades of service to our country, and I thought we should allow him to retire in peace, leaving the matter between him and his conscience.

On the day after Christmas, I got a pleasant surprise when it was announced that **Time** magazine would name me "Man of the Year," saying that I had been given the opportunity "to preside over one of the periodic reinventions of the country—those moments when Americans dig out of their deepest problems by reimagining themselves." When asked about the honor, I said I was flattered by it but worried about the troubled world, about getting bogged down because there was so much to do, and about whether the move to Washington would be good for Chelsea. Chelsea would do just fine, but my other concerns proved to be well founded.

Hillary, Chelsea, and I spent New Year's in Hilton Head at Renaissance Weekend, as we had been doing every year for nearly a decade. I loved being with old friends, playing touch football on the beach with kids and a few rounds of golf with a new set of clubs Hillary had given me. I enjoyed attending the discussion panels, where I always learned things from people who talked about everything from science to politics to love. That year, I especially liked one entitled "What I'd Tell the President over a Brown Bag Lunch."

Meanwhile, President Bush was going out in full stride. He visited our troops in Somalia, then called me to say he was headed to Russia to sign a strategic arms limitation treaty, START II, with Boris Yeltsin. I supported the treaty and said I was prepared to push its ratification in the Senate. Bush was also being helpful to me, telling other world leaders he wanted me to "succeed as President" and that they would find me "a good man to work with" on important problems.

On January 5, Hillary and I announced that we would enroll Chelsea in a private school, Sidwell Friends. Until that time, she had always been in public schools, and there were some good ones in the District of Columbia. After discussing it with Chelsea, we decided on Sidwell primarily because it guaranteed her privacy. She was about to turn thirteen, and Hillary and I wanted to give her the chance to live out her teenage years as normally as possible. She wanted that, too.

On January 6, with only two weeks to go before the inauguration, and the day before my first meeting with my economic team, the Bush administration's OMB director, Richard Darman, announced that the coming year's budget deficit would be even higher than previously estimated. (My staff was convinced Darman had known about the larger deficit earlier and had delayed his bad-news announcement until after the election.) Regardless, now it was going to be much more difficult to juggle the competing priorities: to cut the deficit in half without weakening the fragile economic recovery in the short run; to find the right combination of spending cuts and tax increases necessary to reduce the deficit and increase spending in areas vital to our long-term economic prosperity; and to ensure more tax fairness for middle- and lower-income working people.

The next day, the economic team gathered around the dining-room table in the Governor's Mansion to discuss our dilemma and explore which policy choices would produce the most growth. According to traditional Keynesian economic theory, governments should run deficits in bad economic times and balanced budgets or surpluses in good times. Therefore, the combination of tough spending cuts and tax increases necessary to halve the deficit seemed to be the wrong medicine for the present moment. That's why FDR, after being elected on a promise to balance the budget, abandoned deficit reduction in favor of big spending to put people back to work and stimulate the private economy.

The problem with applying the traditional analysis to current conditions was that under Reagan and Bush, we had built in a large structural deficit that persisted in good times and bad. When President Reagan took office, the national debt was $1 trillion. It tripled during his eight years, thanks to the big tax cuts in 1981 and increases in spending. Under President Bush, the debt continued to increase again, by one-third, in just four years. Now it totaled $4 trillion. Annual interest payments on the debt were the third-largest item in the federal budget after defense and Social Security.

The deficit was the inevitable result of so-called supply-side economics, the theory that the more you cut taxes, the more the economy will grow, with the growth producing more tax revenue at lower rates than previously had been collected at higher ones. Of course it didn't work, and the deficits exploded throughout the recovery of the 1980s. Though supply-side theory was bad arithmetic and lousy economics, the Republicans stayed with it because of their ideological aversion to taxes, and because, in the short run, supply-side was good politics. "Spend more, tax less" sounded good and felt good, but it had put our country in a deep hole and left a cloud over our children's future.

Coupled with our large trade deficit, the budget deficit required us to import tremendous amounts of capital every year to finance our overspending. To attract that kind of money and avoid a precipitous drop in the value of the dollar, we had to keep interest rates far higher than they should have been during the economic downturn that preceded my election. Those high interest rates inhibited economic growth and amounted to a huge indirect tax on middle-class Americans who paid more for home mortgages, car payments, and all other purchases financed through borrowing.

After we sat down to work, Bob Rubin, who was running the meeting, called on Leon Panetta first. Leon said the deficit had gotten worse because tax revenues were down in the sluggish economy, while spending was up, as more people qualified for government assistance and health-care costs soared. Laura Tyson said that if current conditions continued, the economy would probably grow at a rate of 2.5 to 3 percent over the next years, not enough to lower unemployment much or to ensure a sustained recovery. Then we got down to the meat of the coconut, as Alan Blinder, another of my economic advisors, was asked to analyze whether a strong deficit-reduction package would spur growth and new jobs by bringing down interest rates, since the government wouldn't provide as much competition with the private sector in borrowing money. Blinder said that would happen, but that the positive effects would be offset for a couple of years by the negative economic impact of less government spending or higher taxes, unless the Federal Reserve and the bond market responded to our plan by lowering interest rates substantially. Blinder thought that after so many false promises on deficit reduction over the last few years, a strong positive response by the bond market was unlikely. Larry Summers disagreed, saying that a good plan would convince the market to lower rates because there was no threat of inflation as the economy recovered. He cited the experience of some Asian countries to support his view.

This was the first of many exchanges we would have about the power over the lives of ordinary Americans exercised by thirty-year-old bond traders. Often my loud complaints about this, and Bob Rubin's retorts to them, were funny, but the issue was dead serious. With national unemployment stuck at above 7 percent, we had to do something. Tyson and Blinder seemed to be saying that, for the long-term health of the economy, we had to cut the deficit, but that doing so would slow down growth in the short term. Bentsen, Altman, Summers, and Panetta bought the bond-market argument and believed deficit reduction would accelerate economic growth. Rubin was just running the meeting, but I knew he agreed with them. So did Al Gore.

Bob Reich missed the meeting but sent me a memo the next day, arguing that while the debt was a higher percentage of the gross domestic product than it should be, investment in education, training, and non-defense research and development were all at a much lower percentage of GDP than in the pre-Reagan years, and underinvestment was hurting the economy as much as the big deficits. He said the goal should not be to cut the deficit in half but to return it, and investments, to the percentage of GDP they had been before the Reagan-Bush years. He argued that the investments would increase productivity, growth, and employment, enabling us to reduce the deficit, but if we went for deficit reduction only, a stagnant economy with anemic revenues couldn't cut it in half anyway. I think Gene Sperling pretty much agreed with Reich.

While I was mulling it all over, we moved on to a discussion about how to achieve the deficit reduction we needed. In my campaign plan, **Putting People First,** I had proposed more than $140 billion in budget cuts. With the deficit numbers higher, we would have to cut more to reach my goal of halving the deficit in four years. That led to the first of many discussions of what should be cut. For example, you could save a lot by reducing the cost-of-living allowances, called COLAs, on Social Security, but as Hillary pointed out, almost half of all Americans over sixty-five relied on Social Security to live above the poverty line; the COLA cut would hurt them. We didn't have to make final decisions, and couldn't without discussing it with congressional leaders, but it was obvious that, whatever we ultimately decided, it wouldn't be easy.

In the campaign, in addition to the budget cuts, I had also proposed raising a comparable amount in new revenues, all from wealthy individuals and corporations. Now, to cut the deficit in half we would have to raise more revenues, too. And we would almost certainly have to scrap the broad-based middle-class tax cut, though I was still determined to cut taxes for working families earning about $30,000 a year or less by doubling the Earned Income Tax Credit. Those people's incomes had been losing ground for twenty years, and they needed the help; moreover, we had to make lower-income jobs more attractive than public assistance if we were to be successful in moving people from welfare to work. Lloyd Bentsen went over the list of possible tax increases, saying that any tax would be hard to pass and the most important thing was to prevail. If our plan failed in Congress, it could endanger my presidency. Bentsen said we should present a number of options to Congress, so that if I failed to pass one or two, I could still claim success and avoid being crippled politically.

After the tax presentation, Roger Altman and Larry Summers argued for a short-term stimulus package to go with the deficit-reduction plan. They recommended about $20 billion of spending and business-tax reductions that at best would give the economy a boost, and at the least would prevent it from sliding back into a recession, which they thought was about a 20 percent possibility. Then Gene Sperling made a presentation of options for new investments, arguing for the most expensive one, about $90 billion, which would meet all my campaign commitments immediately.

After the presentations, I decided the deficit hawks were right. If we didn't get the deficit down substantially, interest rates would remain high, preventing a sustained, strong economic recovery. Al Gore strongly agreed. But, as we discussed how much deficit reduction we needed, I was concerned about the short-term drag that Laura Tyson and Alan Blinder predicted—and Roger Altman and Gene Sperling feared—might occur. After nearly six hours, we were headed in the deficit-reduction direction. Clearly, economic policy making, at least in this environment, was not science, and if it was art, it had to be beautiful in the eyes of the beholders in the bond market.

A week later, we held a second meeting in which I abandoned the middle-class tax cuts; agreed to look at savings in Social Security, Medicare, and Medicaid; and supported Al Gore's suggestion of a broad-based energy tax, called a BTU tax, on the heat content of energy at the wholesale level. Al said that while the BTU tax would be controversial in states that produced coal, oil, and natural gas, it would fall on all sectors of the economy, lessening the burden on ordinary consumers, and would promote energy conservation, something we badly needed more of.

For several hours more, we again debated how much deficit reduction we had to try for, beginning five years out and working back to the present. Gore took a hard line, saying if we went for the biggest possible reduction, we'd get credit for courage and create a new reality, making it possible to do previously unthinkable things, like requiring Social Security beneficiaries above a certain income level to pay income tax on their benefits. Rivlin agreed with him. Blinder said it might work if the Fed and the bond market believed us. Tyson and Altman were skeptical about avoiding short-term economic contractions. Sperling and Reich, who was present at this meeting, held out for more investments.

So did Stan Greenberg, Mandy Grunwald, and Paul Begala, who weren't part of the meetings and were afraid I was sacrificing everything I believed in under the influence of people who weren't part of our campaign and didn't care about the ordinary Americans who had elected me. In late November, Stan had sent me a memo saying my honeymoon with voters would be short-lived unless I moved quickly to address the problem of jobs and declining incomes. Sixty percent of those who said their finances had worsened in 1992, about a third of the electorate, had voted for me. He thought I could lose them with this plan. George Stephanopoulos, who sat in on the meetings, had to try to explain to Stan and his allies that the deficit was killing the economy, and that if we didn't fix it, there would be no economic recovery and no tax revenues to spend on education, middle-class tax cuts, or anything else. Bentsen and Panetta wanted as much deficit reduction as we could pass in Congress, an amount less than Gore and Rivlin advocated, but still a lot. Rubin, as moderator, was again keeping his own counsel, but I sensed he was with Bentsen and Panetta. After hearing everyone out, so was I.

At some point, I asked Bentsen how much we'd have to reduce the deficit to rally the bond market. He said about $140 billion in the fifth year, with a five-year total of $500 billion. I decided to go with the $500 billion figure, but even with new spending cuts and revenue increases, we still might not be able to meet the target of cutting the deficit in half by the end of my first term. It all depended on the rate of growth.

Because of the possibility that our strategy would produce a short-term slowdown, we searched for ways to promote more growth. I met with executives of the Big Three automakers and Owen Bieber, president of the United Auto Workers, who said that while Japanese cars had almost 30 percent of the American market, Japan was still largely closed to American cars and auto-parts suppliers. I asked Mickey Kantor to find a way to open the Japanese market more. Representatives of the fast-growing biotechnology industry told me that our research-and-development tax credit should be extended and made refundable for young firms, which often didn't make enough money to claim the full credit under current law. They also wanted stronger protection for their patents against unfair competition, and modifications in and acceleration of the product-approval process of the Food and Drug Administration. I told the team to analyze their proposals and make a recommendation. Finally, I authorized the development of the $20 billion one-shot stimulus proposal to increase economic activity in the short run.

I hated to give up the middle-class tax cut, but with the deficit numbers worse, there was no choice. If our strategy worked, the middle class would see direct benefits worth far more than a tax cut—in the form of lower home mortgages and lower interest rates on things like car payments, credit card purchases, and student loans. We also wouldn't be able to increase spending as much as I had proposed in the campaign, at least at first. But if deficit reduction brought interest rates down and growth up, tax revenues would increase, and I could still meet my investment objectives over four years. That was a big "if."

There was also another big "if." The strategy would work only if Congress adopted it. After Bush's defeat, the Republicans were more anti-tax than ever, so few, if any, of them would vote for any plan I put up with new taxes in it. A lot of Democrats who came from conservative districts would also be wary of tax votes, and liberal Democrats from safe seats might not support the budget if the cuts were too steep in programs they believed in.

After a campaign during which the economic problems of America were center stage, in a time when growth was lagging all over the world, I would begin my presidency with an economic strategy for which there was no precedent. It could bring enormous benefits if I could convince Congress to pass the budget, and if it got the hoped-for response from the Federal Reserve and the bond market. There were compelling arguments for it, but the most important domestic decision of my presidency was still one big gamble.

While most of the transition was occupied by the cabinet and other appointments and the development of our economic program, a number of other things were going on. On January 5, I held a meeting leading to the announcement that I would temporarily continue President Bush's policy of intercepting and returning Haitians who were trying to reach the United States by boat, a policy I had strongly criticized during the election. After Haiti's elected president, Jean-Bertrand Aristide, was overthrown by Lieutenant General Raoul Cedras and his allies in 1991, Haitian sympathizers of Aristide had begun to flee the island. When the Bush administration, which appeared to be more sympathetic to Cedras than I was, began to return the refugees, there were loud protests from the human rights community. I wanted to make it easier for Haitians to seek and obtain political asylum in the United States, but was concerned that large numbers of them would perish in trying to get here in rickety boats on the high seas, as about four hundred had done just a week earlier. So, on the advice of our security team, I said that, instead of taking in all the Haitians who could survive the voyage to America, we would beef up our official presence in Haiti and speed up asylum claims there. In the meantime, for safety reasons, we would continue to stop the boats and return the passengers. Ironically, while human rights groups criticized the announcement, and the press characterized it as going back on my campaign pledge, President Aristide supported my position. He knew we would bring more Haitians to the United States than the Bush administration had, and he didn't want his people to drown.

On January 8, I flew to Austin, Texas, where I had lived and worked for McGovern more than twenty years earlier. After a reunion lunch with old friends from those days at Scholtz's Beer Garden, I held my first meeting since the election with a foreign leader, Mexico's president, Carlos Salinas de Gortari. Salinas was deeply committed to the North American Free Trade Agreement (NAFTA), which he had negotiated with President Bush. We were hosted by my longtime friend Governor Ann Richards, who was also a big supporter of NAFTA. I wanted to meet with Salinas early to make it clear that I cared about Mexico's prosperity and stability, and to make my case to him for the importance of labor and environmental side agreements to strengthen the treaty, and for greater cooperation against narco-trafficking.

On the thirteenth, my nominee for attorney general, Zoë Baird, got into hot water when it came out that she had employed two illegal immigrants as household help and had paid the employer's portion of Social Security taxes on them only recently, when she came into consideration for the Justice post. The employment of illegal immigrants was not that uncommon then, but it was a particular problem for Zoë, because the attorney general oversees the Immigration and Naturalization Service. With Zoë's early confirmation unlikely, the incumbent assistant attorney general for the civil division, Stuart Gerson, would serve as acting attorney general. We also sent

Webb Hubbell, the associate attorney general–designate, over to the Justice Department to look after things.

Over the next two days, we announced several more White House staff appointments. Besides George Stephanopoulos as communications director, I named Dee Dee Myers the first female White House press secretary; put Eli Segal in charge of creating the new national service program; and made Rahm Emanuel the director of political affairs, and Alexis Herman director of public liaison. I was bringing several people up from Arkansas: Bruce Lindsey would handle personnel, including appointments to boards and commissions; Carol Rasco would be my assistant for domestic policy; Nancy Hernreich, my scheduler in the governor's office, would oversee Oval Office operations, with an office just outside mine; David Watkins would oversee the administrative functions of the White House; Ann McCoy, the Governor's Mansion administrator, came to work in the White House; and my lifelong friend Vince Foster agreed to come to the counsel's office.

Among those who didn't come out of the campaign were my choice for White House counsel, Bernie Nussbaum, Hillary's colleague on the 1974 Nixon impeachment inquiry staff; Ira Magaziner, my Oxford classmate, who would work with us on health-care reform; Howard Paster, an experienced Washington lobbyist, who would manage our congressional relations; John Podesta, an old friend from the Duffey campaign, as staff secretary; Katie McGinty, Al Gore's choice for our environmental policy person; and Betty Currie, Warren Christopher's secretary in the transition, who would do the same job for me. Andrew Friendly, a young Washington, D.C., native would be the President's aide, going with me to every appointment and on every trip, making sure I read my briefing paper, and keeping in touch with the White House when we were away. Al had his own staff, with fellow Tennessean Roy Neel as chief of staff. So did Hillary, whose chief of staff, Maggie Williams, was an old friend of hers.

I also stated my support for David Wilhelm, my campaign manager, to succeed Ron Brown as chairman of the Democratic Committee. David was young and didn't have Ron Brown's public presence, but almost no one did. His strength was grassroots organizing, and our party badly needed revitalization at the state and local levels. Now that we had the White House, I figured Al Gore and I would have to shoulder the lion's share of the fund-raising and public pronouncements anyway.

Besides the appointments, I issued a statement strongly supporting the military action President Bush had taken in Iraq and, for the first time, said I would press for the trial of Serbian president Slobodan Milosevic for war crimes. It would take too long for that to happen.

During this period, I also hosted a lunch for evangelical ministers at the Governor's Mansion. My pastor, Rex Horne, suggested that I do it, and put together the invitation list. Rex thought it would be helpful to have an informal discussion with them so that at least I'd have some lines of communication into the evangelical community. About ten ministers came, including nationally known figures like Charles Swindoll, Adrian Rogers, and Max Lucado. We also invited Hillary's minister at Little Rock's First United Methodist Church, Ed Matthews, a wonderful man who we knew would stick with us if the lunch deteriorated into a war of words. I was especially impressed by the young, articulate pastor of Willow Creek Community Church near Chicago, Bill Hybels. He had built his church from scratch into one of the largest single congregations in America. Like the others, he disagreed with me on abortion and gay rights, but he was interested in other issues, too, and in what kind of leadership it would take to end the gridlock and reduce the partisan bitterness in Washington. For eight years, Bill Hybels came to see me on a regular basis, to pray with me, counsel me, and check on what he called my "spiritual health." We argued from time to time. Sometimes we even agreed. But always he would be a blessing to me.

At the beginning of my last week in Arkansas, with moving vans in the driveway, I gave a farewell interview to Arkansas reporters, confessing to mixed emotions of pride and regret at leaving home: "I've been happy and proud and sad almost on the point of tears a couple of times. . . . I love my life here." One of my final tasks before leaving for Washington was personal. Chelsea had a pet frog she had initially gotten for a school science project. While we were taking our cat, Socks, with us, Chelsea decided she wanted to free the frog so that it could lead a "normal life." She asked me to do it, so on my last day in Arkansas, I jogged down to the Arkansas River, took the shoebox the frog was in, climbed down a steep bank to the water, and let the frog go. At least one of us was returning to normal life.

The rest of us were excited about our new adventure, but apprehensive, too. Chelsea hated to leave her friends and the world she knew, but we told her she could have her pals come to stay with us often. Hillary was wondering how she'd feel without the independence of a paying job, but she was eager to be a full-time First Lady, both to pursue the policy work she loved and to perform the traditional duties of the office. She had surprised me with the amount of time she had already spent studying the history of the White House, the various functions she would be responsible for there, and the important contributions of her predecessors. Whenever Hillary undertook a new challenge, she was always on edge at first, but once she got the hang of it, she relaxed and enjoyed herself. I couldn't blame her for being a little nervous. I was too.

The transition period had been hectic and hard. In retrospect, we did a good job picking a cabinet and sub-cabinet officials who were able and who reflected the diversity of America, but I made a mistake in not appointing a prominent Republican to a cabinet post as a demonstration of my desire to build bipartisan cooperation. I also kept my commitment to put the economy first, with a first-rate team, the economic summit, and a decision-making process that was well informed and subject to thorough debate. And as I had pledged, Al Gore was a full partner in the incoming administration, involved in all the strategy meetings and the cabinet and White House staff selections, while maintaining a high public profile.

During and after the transition, I was criticized for not following through on my campaign commitments to cut middle-class taxes, halve the deficit in four years, and take in the Haitian boat people. With respect to the first two issues, when I replied that I was simply responding to the worse-than-expected deficit projections, some critics said I had to know the Bush administration was lowballing the deficit until after the election, and therefore I shouldn't have used official government figures in putting together my economic plan. I didn't take those criticisms too seriously. By contrast, I thought some of the criticism on the Haitian issue was justified, given the unqualified statements I had made during the campaign. Still, I was determined to bring more asylum seekers to the United States safely, and eventually to restore President Aristide. If I succeeded, my commitment would be fulfilled.

I was also being criticized for appointing Zoë Baird, for my tendency to want to know everything that was going on, and for taking too much time in making decisions. There was some merit to the hits. Zoë hadn't concealed the nanny issue; we had simply underestimated its significance. As for my management style, I knew I had a lot to learn, and I had used the transition to absorb as much about as many aspects of the President's job as I could. For example, I don't regret a minute of the time I spent coming to grips with the economy during the transition. It stood me in good stead for the next eight years. On the other hand, I had always had a tendency to try to do too much, which also contributed to physical exhaustion, irritability, and my well-deserved reputation for tardiness.

I knew that the transition was only a foretaste of what the presidency would be like: everything happening at once. I would have to delegate more and have a better-organized decision-making process than I had as governor. However, the fact that so many sub-cabinet positions had not been finalized had more to do with the fact that the Democrats had been out of power for twelve years. We had to replace a lot of people, we were committed to casting a wide net for diversity, and there were a great number of people with a claim to be considered. Moreover, the required vetting process had gotten so complicated that it took too much time, as federal investigators pored over every piece of paper and ran down every petty rumor to find people who were bulletproof in the face of political and press assaults.

Looking back, I think the major shortcomings of the transition were two: I spent so much time on the cabinet that I hardly spent any time on the White House staff, and I gave almost no thought to how to keep the public's focus on my most important priorities, rather than on competing stories that, at the least, would divert public attention from the big issues and, at worst, could make it appear that I was neglecting those priorities.

The real problem with the staff was that most of them came out of the campaign or Arkansas, and had no experience in working in the White House or dealing with Washington's political culture. My young staffers were talented, honest, and dedicated, and I felt I owed many of them the chance to serve the country by working in the White House. In time, they would get their sea legs and do very well. But in the critical early months, both the staff and I would do a lot of on-the-job learning, and some of the lessons would prove to be quite costly.

We also didn't give messaging anything close to the amount of attention that we had in the election, though it's harder in government, even for the President, to get out the message you want every day. As I said, everything happens at once, and any controversy is more likely to dominate the news than a policy decision, no matter how important the decision might be. That's what happened with the Zoë Baird and gays-in-the-military controversies. Though they took up only a small part of my time, people watching the evening news could be forgiven for thinking I spent my time on nothing else. If we had thought more about this challenge and worked harder on it during the transition, I'm sure we would have handled it better.

Despite the problems, I believed our transition had gone reasonably well. So, apparently, did the American people. Before I left for Washington, an NBC News/**Wall Street Journal** poll gave me a 60 percent favorability rating, up from just 32 percent in May. Hillary was doing even better; 66 percent saw her as "a positive role model for American women," up from 39 percent in the earlier survey. Another poll taken by a bipartisan organization said that 84 percent of the people approved of my performance since the election. President Bush's job approval was up, too, nearly twenty points, to 59 percent. Our fellow citizens had regained their optimism about America, and they were giving me a chance to succeed.

On January 16, when Hillary, Chelsea, and I said good-bye to the friends who came to the Little Rock airport to see us off, I thought of Abraham Lincoln's moving farewell remarks to the people of Springfield, Illinois, as he left the train station on his journey to the White House: "My friends—No one, not in my situation, can appreciate my feeling of sadness at this parting. To this place, and the kindness of these people, I owe everything. . . . Trusting in [God], who can go with me, and remain with you and be everywhere for good, let us confidently hope that all will yet be well." I didn't say it as well as Lincoln, but I did my best to convey that message to my fellow Arkansans. Without them, I wouldn't have been getting on that airplane.

We were flying to Virginia, where we would begin the inaugural events at Monticello, Thomas Jefferson's home. On the flight, I thought about the historical significance of my election and the momentous challenges ahead. The election represented a generational shift in America, from the World War II veterans to the baby boomers, who were alternately derided as spoiled and self-absorbed, and lauded as idealistic and committed to the common good. Whether liberal or conservative, our politics were forged by Vietnam, civil rights, and the tumult of 1968, with its protests, riots, and assassinations. We were also the first generation to feel the full force of the women's movement, the impact of which people were about to observe in the White House. Hillary would be the most professionally accomplished First Lady in history. Now that she had resigned from her law practice and her boards, my income would be the sole support of our family for the first time since we married, and she would be free to use her enormous talent as a full-time partner in our work. I thought she could have a more positive impact than any First Lady since Eleanor Roosevelt. Of course, such activism would make her more controversial with those who thought First Ladies should stay above the fray, or who disagreed with us politically, but that, too, was part of what our generational change meant.

Clearly, we represented a changing of the guard, but could we meet the tests of these tumultuous times? Could we restore the economy, social progress, and the legitimacy of government? Could we blunt the rise of religious, racial, and ethnic strife across the globe? In the words of the **Time** magazine citation in its "Man of the Year" edition, could we lead Americans to "dig out of their deepest problems by reimagining themselves"? Despite our victory in the Cold War and the rise of democracy around the world, powerful forces were dividing people and tearing at the fragile fabric of communities, both at home and abroad. In the face of these challenges, the American people had taken a chance on me.

About three weeks after the election, I had received a remarkable letter from Robert McNamara, who, as secretary of defense under Presidents Kennedy and Johnson, had prosecuted the Vietnam War. He had been moved to write me by a news story he read about my friendship with my Oxford roommate Frank Aller, who had resisted the draft and had killed himself in 1971. This is what he said:

> For me—and I believe for the nation as well—the Vietnam war finally ended the day you were elected president. By their votes, the American people, at long last, recognized that the Allers and the Clintons, when they questioned the wisdom and morality of their government's decisions relating to Vietnam, were no less patriotic than those who served in uniform. The anguish with which you and your friends debated our actions in 1969 was painful for you then and, I am sure, the resurrection of the issues during the campaign reopened old wounds. But the dignity with which you met the attacks, and your refusal to draw back from the belief that it is the responsibility of all citizens to question the basis for any decision to send our youth to war, has strengthened the nation for all time.

I was moved by McNamara's letter, and by similar ones I received from Vietnam veterans. Just before the election, Bob Higgins, an ex-marine from Hillsboro, Ohio, sent me his Vietnam service medal because of my stand against the war and "the way you have conducted yourself in the bitter campaign." A few months earlier, Ronald Murphy of Las Vegas had given me his Purple Heart, and Charles Hampton from Marmaduke, Arkansas, had sent me the Bronze Star he earned for valor in Vietnam. All told, in 1992, Vietnam veterans sent me five Purple Hearts, three Vietnam service medals, a combat infantry badge, and my fellow Arkansan's Bronze Star. I framed most of them and hung them in my private hall off the Oval Office.

As my plane headed down into the beautiful Virginia landscape, which gave birth to four of our first five Presidents, I was thinking of those veterans and their medals, hoping that at last we could heal the wounds of the 1960s, and praying that I would prove worthy of their sacrifices, their support, and their dreams.

THIRTY

On Sunday, January 17, Al and Tipper Gore, Hillary, and I began inaugural week with a tour of Monticello, followed by a discussion of Thomas Jefferson's importance to America with young people.

After the event, we boarded our bus for the 120-mile trip to Washington. The bus symbolized our commitment to giving the federal government back to the people. Besides, we cherished the fond memories it held, and we wanted one last ride. We stopped for a brief church service in the pretty Shenandoah Valley town of Culpeper, then made our way to Washington. Just as in the campaign, there were well-wishers, and a few critics, along the way.

By the time we got to the capital, the public events of our inaugural, entitled "An American Reunion: New Beginnings, Renewed Hope," were already under way. Harry Thomason, Rahm Emanuel, and Mel French, a friend from Arkansas who would become chief of protocol in my second term, had organized an extraordinary series of events, with as many as possible free of charge or within the price range of the working people who had elected me. On Sunday and Monday, the Mall between the Capitol Building and the Washington Monument was filled by an outdoor festival featuring food, music, and crafts. That night we had a "Call for Reunion" concert on the steps of the Lincoln Memorial, with a star-studded lineup including Diana Ross and Bob Dylan, who thrilled the crowd of 200,000 that filled the space from the stage all the way back to the Washington Monument. Standing beneath Lincoln's statue, I gave a short speech appealing for national unity, saying that Lincoln "gave new life to Jefferson's dream that we are all created free and equal."

After the concert, the Gores and my family led a procession of thousands of people carrying flashlights across the Potomac River on Memorial Bridge to the Lady Bird Johnson Circle just outside Arlington National Cemetery. At 6 p.m., we rang a replica of the Liberty Bell, to start "Bells of Hope" ringing all across America and even aboard the space shuttle **Endeavour.** Then there was a fireworks display followed by several receptions. By the time we got back to Blair House, the official guest residence just across the street from the White House, we were tired but exhilarated, and before falling asleep I took some time to review the latest draft of my inaugural address.

I still wasn't satisfied with it. Compared with my campaign speeches, it seemed stilted. I knew it had to be more dignified, but I didn't want it to drag. I did like one passage, built around the idea that our new beginning had "forced the spring" to come to America on this cold winter day. It was the brainchild of my friend Father Tim Healy, former president of Georgetown University. Tim had died suddenly of a heart attack while walking through Newark airport a few weeks after the election. When friends went to his apartment, they found in his typewriter the beginning of a letter to me that included suggested language for the inaugural speech. His phrase "force the spring" struck all of us, and I wanted to use it in his memory.

Monday, January 18, was the holiday celebrating Martin Luther King Jr.'s birthday. In the morning I held a reception for the diplomatic representatives of other nations in the inner quadrangle at Georgetown, addressing them from the steps of Old North Building. It was the same spot on which George Washington stood in 1797 and the great French general and Revolutionary War hero Lafayette spoke in 1824. I told the ambassadors that my foreign policy would be built on three pillars—economic security at home, restructuring the armed forces to meet the new challenges of the post–Cold War world, and support for democratic values across the globe. The day before, President Bush had ordered an air strike on a suspected weapons-production site in Iraq, and on this day, U.S. planes hit Saddam Hussein's air-defense positions. I supported the effort to bring Saddam into full compliance with UN resolutions and asked the diplomats to emphasize that to their governments. After the diplomatic event, I spoke to Georgetown students and alumni, including many of my old classmates, urging them to support my national service initiative.

From Georgetown, we drove to Howard University for a ceremony honoring Dr. King, then to a luncheon at the beautiful Folger Library for more than fifty people Al, Tipper, Hillary, and I met during the campaign who had made a strong impression on us. We called them "Faces of Hope," because of their courage in the face of adversity or their innovative ways of dealing with contemporary challenges. We wanted to thank these people for inspiring us, and to remind everyone, amidst the glamour of the inaugural week, that a lot of Americans were still having a hard time.

The Faces of Hope included two former members of rival gangs in Los Angeles who joined forces after the riots to give kids a better future; two of the Vietnam veterans who had sent me their medals; a school principal who had created a violence-free magnet school in Chicago's highest-crime neighborhood, with students who regularly scored above state and national learning levels; a Texas judge who had created an innovative program for troubled kids; a young Arizona boy who had made me more aware of the family pressures caused by the extra hours his father had to work; a Native American doctor from Montana who worked to improve mental-health services to her people; men who had lost their jobs to low-wage foreign competition; people struggling with costly health problems the government didn't help with; a young entrepreneur scrapping for venture capital; people who ran community centers for broken families; a policeman's widow whose husband was killed by a mental patient who bought a handgun without a background check; an eighteen-year-old financial wizard who was already working on Wall Street; a woman who had started a large recycling program at her plant; and many others. Michael Morrison, the young man who drove his wheelchair down an icy New Hampshire highway to work for me, was there. So was Dimitrios Theofanis, the Greek immigrant from New York who had asked me to make his boy free.

All of the Faces of Hope had taught me something about the pain and promise of America in 1992, but none more than Louise and Clifford Ray, whose three sons were hemophiliacs who had contracted the HIV virus through transfusions of tainted blood. They also had a daughter who was not infected. Frightened people in their small Florida community pushed to have the Ray boys removed from school, fearing that their children could be infected if one of them started bleeding and the blood got on them. The Rays filed a lawsuit to keep the kids in class and settled it out of court, then decided to move to Sarasota, a larger city where the school officials welcomed them. The oldest son, Ricky, was obviously very ill and fighting to hang on to his life. After the election, I called Ricky in the hospital to encourage him and invite him to the inauguration. He was looking forward to coming, but he didn't make it; at fifteen, he lost his fight, just five weeks before I became President. I was so glad that the Rays came to the luncheon anyway. When I took office, they championed the cause of hemophiliacs with AIDS, and successfully lobbied Congress for the passage of the Ricky Ray Hemophilia Relief Fund. But it took eight long years, and their grief still wasn't over. In October 2000, three months before the end of my presidency, the Rays' second son, Robert, died of AIDS at twenty-two. If only anti-retroviral therapy had been available a few years earlier. Now that it is, I spend a lot of time trying to get the medicine to many of the Ricky Rays across the world. I want them to be Faces of Hope, too.

On Tuesday morning, Hillary and I started the day with a visit to the graves of John and Robert Kennedy at Arlington National Cemetery. Accompanied by John Kennedy Jr., Ethel Kennedy, several of her children, and Senator Ted Kennedy, I knelt at the eternal flame and said a short prayer, thanking God for their lives and service and asking for wisdom and strength in the great adventures just ahead. At noon, I hosted a lunch for my fellow governors at the Library of Congress, thanking them for all I had learned from them in the past twelve years. After an afternoon event at the Kennedy Center highlighting America's children, we drove out to the Capitol Centre in Landover, Maryland, for the Gala Concert, where Barbra Streisand,

Wynton Marsalis, k.d. lang, rock legends Chuck Berry and Little Richard, Michael Jackson, Aretha Franklin, Jack Nicholson, Bill Cosby, the Alvin Ailey Dance Theater, and other artists kept us entertained for hours. Fleetwood Mac brought the crowd to its feet with our campaign theme song, "Don't Stop Thinkin' About Tomorrow."

After the concert, there was a late-night prayer service at the First Baptist Church, and it was after midnight when I got back to Blair House. Though it was getting better, I still wasn't satisfied with the inaugural address. My speechwriters, Michael Waldman and David Kusnet, must have been tearing their hair out, because as we practiced between one and four in the morning on inauguration day, I was still changing it. Bruce Lindsey, Paul Begala, Bruce Reed, George Stephanopoulos, Michael Sheehan, and my wordsmith friends Tommy Caplan and Taylor Branch stayed up with me. So did Al Gore. The terrific staff at Blair House was used to taking care of foreign heads of state who kept all kinds of hours, so they were ready with gallons of coffee to keep us awake and snacks to keep us in a reasonably good humor. By the time I went to bed for a couple of hours' sleep, I was feeling better about the speech.

Wednesday morning dawned cold and clear. I began the day with an early-morning security briefing, then I received instructions on how my military aide would handle the launching of our nuclear weapons. The President has five military aides, one outstanding young officer from each service branch; one of them is near him at all times.

Though a nuclear exchange seemed unthinkable with the Cold War over, assuming the control of our arsenal was a sober reminder of the responsibilities just a few hours away. There's a difference between knowing about the presidency and actually being President. It's hard to describe in words, but I left Blair House with my eagerness tempered by humility.

The last activity before the inauguration was a prayer service at the Metropolitan African Methodist Episcopal Church. It was important to me. With input from Hillary and Al Gore, I had picked the participating clergy, the singers, and the music. Hillary's family and mine were there. Mother was beaming. Roger was grinning, and enjoying the music. Both our pastors from home participated in the service, as did Al and Tipper's ministers, and George Stephanopoulos's father, the Greek Orthodox dean of the Holy Trinity Cathedral in New York. Father Otto Hentz, who, almost thirty years earlier, had asked me to consider becoming a Jesuit, said a prayer. Rabbi Gene Levy from Little Rock and Imam Wallace D. Mohammad spoke. Several black clergymen who were friends of mine participated, with Dr. Gardner Taylor, one of America's greatest preachers of any race or denomination, giving the principal address. My Pentecostal friends from Arkansas and Louisiana sang, along with Phil Driscoll, a fabulous singer and trumpeter Al knew from Tennessee, and Carolyn Staley sang "Be Not Afraid," one of my favorite hymns and a good lesson for the day. Tears welled up in my eyes several times during the service, and I left it uplifted and ready for the hours ahead.

We went back to Blair House to look at the speech for the last time. It had gotten a lot better since 4 a.m. At ten, Hillary, Chelsea, and I walked across the street to the White House, where we were met on the front steps by President and Mrs. Bush, who took us inside for coffee with the Gores and the Quayles. Ron and Alma Brown were also there. I wanted Ron to share a moment he had done so much to make possible. I was struck by how well President and Mrs. Bush dealt with a painful situation and a sad parting—it was obvious that they had become close to several members of the staff and would miss and be missed by them. At about 10:45, we all got into limousines. Following tradition, President Bush and I rode together, with Speaker Foley and Wendell Ford, the gravelly-voiced senator from Kentucky who was co-chairman of the Joint Congressional Committee on Inaugural Ceremonies and who had worked hard for the narrow victory that Al and I had won in his state.

Fortunately, the ongoing Capitol restoration project had required the last three inaugurations to be held on the building's west front. Before that, they had taken place on the other side, facing the Supreme Court and the Library of Congress. Most of the people who came could not have seen the ceremonies from that viewpoint. The crowd, which filled the large grounds of the Capitol and spilled back over onto the Mall and up Constitution and Pennsylvania avenues, was estimated by the National Park Service to be between 280,000 and 300,000 people. Whatever the number, the throng was big, and full of all kinds of people, old and young, of all races and faiths, from all walks of life. I was happy that so many people who had made this day possible were there to share in it.

Many of the FOBs who came illustrated the extent to which I was indebted to my personal friends: Marsha Scott and Martha Whetstone, who organized my campaigns in northern California, were old friends from Arkansas; Sheila Bronfman, leader of the Arkansas Travelers, had lived around the corner from Hillary and me when I was attorney general; Dave Matter, my leader in western Pennsylvania, had succeeded me as class president at George-town; Bob Raymar and Tom Schneider, two of my most important fund-raisers, were friends from law school and Renaissance Weekend. There were so many people like them who had made this day possible.

The ceremony started at 11:30. All the principals walked out onto the platform according to protocol order with their congressional escorts. President Bush went just before me, with the Marine Band, under Colonel John Bourgeois, playing "Hail to the Chief" for both of us. I gazed out onto the vast crowd.

Then Al Gore took the oath of office, administered by Supreme Court Justice Byron White. The oath was originally going to be administered by retired Supreme Court Justice Thurgood Marshall, a great civil rights lawyer whom President Johnson had made the first black on the high court, but he had fallen ill. It would have been unusual for a retired justice to do the honors, but Marshall's son, Thurgood Jr., was on Gore's staff. Another son, John, was a Virginia state trooper who had led our inaugural motorcade from Monticello to Washington. Marshall died four days after the inauguration. He was mourned, missed, and deeply appreciated by the legions of Americans who remembered what America was like before he set out to change it.

After the oath, the great mezzo-soprano Marilyn Horne, whom I had first met when she performed in Little Rock a few years earlier, sang a medley of classic American songs. Then it was my turn. Hillary stood to my left, holding our family Bible. With Chelsea on my right, I put my left hand on the Bible, raised my right hand, and repeated the oath of office after Chief Justice Rehnquist, solemnly swearing to "faithfully execute" the office of the

President, and "to the best of my ability, preserve, protect, and defend the Constitution of the United States, so help me God."

I shook hands with the chief justice and President Bush, then hugged Hillary and Chelsea and told them I loved them. Then Senator Wendell Ford called me to the podium as "the President of the United States." I began by placing the present moment in the stream of American history:

> Today we celebrate the mystery of American renewal. This ceremony is held in the depth of winter. But, by the words we speak and the faces we show the world, we force the spring. A spring reborn in the world's oldest democracy, that brings forth the vision and courage to reinvent America. When our founders boldly declared America's independence to the world and our purposes to the Almighty, they knew that America, to endure, would have to change. . . . Each generation of Americans must define what it means to be an American.

After a salute to President Bush, I described the current situation:

> Today, a generation raised in the shadows of the Cold War assumes new responsibilities in a world warmed by the sunshine of freedom but threatened still by ancient hatreds and new plagues. Raised in unrivaled prosperity, we inherit an economy that is still the world's strongest, but is weakened. . . . Profound and powerful forces are shaking and remaking our world, and the urgent question of our time is whether we can make change our friend and not our

enemy. . . . There is nothing wrong with America that cannot be cured by what is right with America.

Still, I warned, "It will not be easy; it will require sacrifice. . . . We must provide for our nation the way a family provides for its children." I asked my fellow citizens to think of posterity, "the world to come—the world for whom we hold our ideals, from whom we have borrowed our planet, and to whom we bear sacred responsibility. We must do what America does best: offer more opportunity to all and demand responsibility from all."

I said that, in our time,

there is no longer a clear division between what is foreign and what is domestic. The world economy, the world environment, the world AIDS crisis, the world arms race—they affect us all. . . . America must continue to lead the world we did so much to make.

I closed the speech with a challenge to the American people, telling them that, by their votes, they had "forced the spring," but that government alone could not create the nation they wanted: "You, too, must play your part in our renewal. I challenge a new generation of young Americans to a season of service. . . . There is so much to be done. . . . From this joyful mountaintop of celebration, we hear a call to service in the valley. We have heard the trumpets. We have changed the guard. And now, each in our way, and with God's help, we must answer the call."

Although several commentators panned the speech, saying it was devoid of both ringing phrases and compelling specifics, I felt good about it. It had flashes of eloquence, it was clear, it said we were going to reduce the deficit while increasing critical investments in our future, and it challenged the American people to do more to help those in need and to heal our divisions. And it was short, the third-shortest inaugural address in history, after Lincoln's second inaugural, the greatest of them all, and Washington's second speech, which lasted less than two minutes. Essentially, Washington just said, Thanks, I'm going back to work, and if I don't do a good job, reprimand me. By contrast, William Henry Harrison gave the longest address in history, in 1841, speaking without a coat on a cold day for well over an hour and catching a bad case of pneumonia, which cost him his life thirty-three days later. At least I was mercifully and uncharacteristically brief, and the people knew how I saw the world and what I intended to do.

By far the most beautiful words of the day were spoken by Maya Angelou, a tall woman with a deep strong voice whom I had asked to write a poem for the occasion, the first poet to do so since Robert Frost spoke at President Kennedy's inauguration in 1961. I had followed Maya's career since I'd read her memoir, **I Know Why the Caged Bird Sings,** which recounts her early years as a traumatized mute girl in a poor black community in Stamps, Arkansas.

Maya's poem, "On the Pulse of Morning," riveted the crowd. Built on powerful images of a rock to stand on, a river to rest by, and a tree with roots in all the cultures and kinds that make up the American mosaic, the poem issued a passionate plea in the form of a neighborly invitation:

> Lift up your faces, you have a piercing need
> For this bright morning dawning for you.
> History, despite its wrenching pain,
> Cannot be unlived, and if faced

With courage, need not be lived again.
Lift up your eyes upon
The day breaking for you.
Give birth again
To the dream.

. . . .

Here on the pulse of this new day
You may have the grace to look up and out
And into your sister's eyes, and into
Your brother's face, your country
And say simply
Very simply
With hope
Good morning.

Billy Graham ended our good morning with a brief benediction, and Hillary and I left the stage to accompany the Bushes down the back steps of the Capitol, where the presidential helicopter, Marine One, was waiting to take them on the first leg of their journey home. We went back inside for lunch with the Congressional Committee, then drove up Pennsylvania Avenue toward the viewing stand in front of the White House for the inaugural parade. With Chelsea, we got out of the car and walked the last few blocks of the route so that we could wave to the crowds packed several deep along the way.

After the parade, we went into our new home for the first time, with only about two hours to greet the staff, rest, and get ready for the evening. Miraculously, the movers had gotten all our belongings in during the inaugural ceremonies and the parade.

At seven, we started our evening marathon with a dinner, followed by visits to all eleven inaugural balls. My brother sang for me at the MTV Youth Ball, and at another I played a tenor saxophone duet on "Night Train" with Clarence Clemons. However, at most of the balls Hillary and I would first say a few words of thanks, then dance to a few bars of one of our favorite songs, "It Had to Be You," showing off her beautiful purple gown. Meanwhile, Chelsea was off with friends from Arkansas at the Youth Ball, and Al and Tipper kept their own schedule. At the Tennessee ball, Paul Simon regaled them with his hit "You Can Call Me Al." At the Arkansas Ball, I introduced Mother to Barbra Streisand and told them both I thought they'd get along. They did more than that. They became fast friends, and Barbra called my mother every week until she died. I still have a picture of them walking hand in hand on that inaugural evening.

When we got back to the White House, it was after 2 a.m. We had to be up the next morning for a public reception, but I was too excited to go right to bed. We had a full house: Hillary's parents, Mother and Dick, our siblings, Chelsea's friends from home, and our friends Jim and Diane Blair and Harry and Linda Thomason. Only our parents had retired.

I wanted to look around. We had been in the second-floor living quarters before, but this was different. It was beginning to sink in that we actually lived there and would have to make it a home. Most of the rooms had high ceilings and beautiful but comfortable furniture. The presidential bedroom and living room face the south, with a small room off the bedroom that would become Hillary's sitting room. Chelsea had a bedroom and study across the hall, just beyond the formal dining room and the small kitchen. At the other end of the hall were the main guest bedrooms, one of which had been Lincoln's

office and has one of his handwritten copies of the Gettysburg Address.

Next to the Lincoln Bedroom is the Treaty Room, so
named because the treaty ending the Spanish-American
War was signed there in 1898. For several years it had
been the private office of the President, usually configured
with multiple televisions so the Chief Executive could
watch all the news programs at once. I believe President
Bush had four TVs there. I decided I wanted it to be a
quiet place where I could read, reflect, listen to music, and
hold small meetings. The White House carpenters made
me floor-to-ceiling bookshelves, and the staff brought up
the table on which the Spanish-American War treaty had
been signed. In 1869, it had been Ulysses Grant's cabinet
table, with space for the President and his seven department heads to sit around it. Since 1898 it had been used
for the signing of all treaties, including the temporary
nuclear test ban under President Kennedy and the Camp
David Accords under President Carter. Before the year
was out, I would be using it too.

I filled out the room with a late-eighteenth-century
Chippendale sofa, the oldest piece of furniture in the
White House collection, and an antique table bought by
Mary Todd Lincoln, on which we put the silver commemorative cup from the 1898 treaty. When I got my books
and CDs in, and hung some of my old pictures, including
an 1860 photo of Abraham Lincoln and Yousuf Karsh's
famous photograph of Churchill, the place had a comfortable, peaceful atmosphere in which I would spend countless hours in the years ahead.

On my first day as President, I started out by taking
Mother down to the Rose Garden, to show her exactly
where I had stood when I shook hands with President

Kennedy almost thirty years ago. Then, in a departure from traditional practice, we opened the White House to the public, providing tickets to two thousand people who had been selected in a postcard lottery. Al, Tipper, Hillary, and I stood in line shaking hands with the ticket holders, then with others who waited in the cold rain for their time to walk through the lower south entrance into the Diplomatic Reception Room to say hello. One determined young man without a ticket had hitchhiked overnight to the White House with his sleeping bag. After six hours, we had to stop, so I went outside to speak to the rest of the crowd gathered on the South Lawn. That night, Hillary and I stood in line for another few hours, to greet our friends from Arkansas and classmates from Georgetown, Wellesley, and Yale.

A few months after the inauguration, a book was published filled with beautiful photographs that capture the excitement and meaning of the inaugural week, with an explanatory text written by Rebecca Buffum Taylor. In her epilogue to the book, Taylor writes:

> A shift in political values takes time. Even if successful, its clarity must wait until months or years have passed, until the lens has been extended and recedes again, until far and middle distance merge with what can be seen today.

The words were penetrating, and probably correct. But I couldn't wait years, months, or even days to see if the campaign and the inauguration had effected a shift in values, deepening the roots and broadening the reach of the American community. I had too much to do, and once again the work quickly turned from poetry to prose, not all of it pretty.

THIRTY-ONE

The next year involved an amazing combination of major legislative achievements, frustrations and successes in foreign policy, unforeseen events, personal tragedy, honest errors, and clumsy violations of the Washington culture, which, when combined with compulsive leaking by a few staffers, ensured press coverage that often resembled what I'd experienced during the New York primary.

On January 22, we announced that Zoë Baird had withdrawn her name from consideration for attorney general. Since we had learned about her employment of illegal immigrant workers and her failure to pay Social Security taxes for them during the vetting process, I had to say that we had failed to evaluate the matter properly, and that I, not she, was responsible for the situation. Zoë had not misled us in any way. When the household workers were hired, she had just gotten a new job, and her husband had the summer off from teaching. Apparently, each assumed the other had handled the tax matter. I believed her and kept working for her nomination for three weeks after she first offered to withdraw it. Later, I appointed Zoë to the Foreign Intelligence Advisory Board, where she made a real contribution to the work Admiral Crowe's group did.

On the same day, the press became infuriated with the new White House when we denied them the privilege, which they'd had for years, of walking from the press room, located between the West Wing and the residence, up to the press secretary's office on the first floor near the Cabinet Room. This strolling allowed them to hang out in the halls and pepper whoever came by with questions. Apparently, a couple of people high up in the Bush administration had mentioned to their new counterparts that this arrangement impeded efficiency and increased leaks, and the decision was made to change it. I don't recall being consulted about it, but perhaps I was. The press raised the roof, but we stuck with the decision, figuring they'd get over it. There's no question that the new policy contributed to freer movement and conversation among the staff, but it's hard to say it was worth the animosity it engendered. And since, in the first few months, the White House leaked worse than a tar-paper shack with holes in the roof and gaps in the walls, it's impossible to say that confining the press to quarters did much good.

That afternoon, the anniversary of **Roe** v. **Wade,** I issued executive orders ending the Reagan-Bush ban on fetal-tissue research; abolishing the so-called Mexico City rule, which prohibited federal aid to international planning agencies that were in any way involved in abortions; and reversing the Bush "gag rule" barring abortion counseling at family planning clinics that receive federal funds. I had pledged to take these actions in the campaign, and I believed in them. Fetal-tissue research was essential to finding better treatments for Parkinson's disease, diabetes, and other conditions. The Mexico City rule arguably led to more abortions, by reducing the availability of information on alternative family planning measures. And the gag rule used federal funds to prevent family planning clinics from telling pregnant women—often frightened, young, and alone—about an option the Supreme Court had declared a constitutional right. Federal funds still could not be used to fund abortions, at home or abroad.

On January 25, Chelsea's first day at her new school, I announced that Hillary would head a task force to come up with a comprehensive health-care plan, working with Ira Magaziner as the lead staff person, domestic policy advisor Carol Rasco, and Judy Feder, who had led our health-care transition team. I was pleased that Ira had agreed to work on health care. We had been friends since 1969, when he had come to Oxford as a Rhodes scholar a year after I did. Now a successful businessman, he had worked on the campaign economic team. Ira believed delivering universal health coverage was both morally and economically imperative. I knew he would give Hillary the kind of support she needed for the grueling task ahead of us.

Heading up the effort to reform health care was an unprecedented thing for a First Lady to do, as was my decision to give Hillary and her staff offices in the West Wing, where the policy action is, as opposed to the traditional office space in the East Wing, where the social affairs of the White House are run. Both decisions were controversial; when it came to the First Lady's role, it seemed Washington was more conservative than Arkansas. I decided Hillary should lead the health-care effort because she cared and knew a lot about the issue, she had time to do the job right, and I thought she would be able to be an honest broker among all the competing interests in the health-care industry, government agencies, and consumer groups. I knew the whole enterprise was risky; Harry Truman's attempt to provide universal health coverage had nearly destroyed his presidency, and Nixon and Carter never even got their bills out of committee.

With the most Democratic Congress in decades, Lyndon Johnson got Medicare for the elderly and Medicaid for the poor, but didn't even try to insure the rest of those without coverage. Nevertheless, I thought we should try for universal coverage, which every other wealthy nation had long enjoyed, for both health and economic reasons. Almost 40 million people had no health insurance, yet we were spending 14 percent of our gross national product on health care, 4 percent more than Canada, the country with the next-highest rate.

On the night of the twenty-fifth, at their urgent request, I met with the Joint Chiefs of Staff to discuss the gays-in-the-military issue. Earlier in the day, the **New York Times** had reported that, because of strong military opposition to the change, I would delay issuing formal regulations lifting the ban for six months, while the views of senior officers, as well as practical problems, were considered. It was a reasonable thing to do. When Harry Truman ordered the racial integration of the military, he had given the Pentagon even more time to figure out how to carry it out in a way that was consistent with its primary mission of maintaining a well-prepared, cohesive fighting force with high morale. In the meantime, Secretary Aspin would tell the military to stop asking recruits about their sexual orientation and to stop discharging homosexual men and women who had not been discovered to have committed a homosexual act, which was a violation of the Uniform Code of Military Justice.

The Joint Chiefs' early request for a meeting created a problem. I was more than willing to hear them out, but I didn't want the issue to get any more publicity than it already was receiving, not because I was trying to hide my position, but because I didn't want the public to think I was paying more attention to it than to the economy. That's exactly what the congressional Republicans wanted the American people to think. Senator Dole was already talking about passing a resolution removing my authority to lift the ban; he clearly wanted this to be the defining issue of my first weeks in office.

In the meeting, the chiefs acknowledged that there were thousands of gay men and women serving with distinction in the 1.8 million–member military, but they maintained that letting them serve openly would be, in General Powell's words, "prejudicial to good order and discipline." The rest of the Joint Chiefs were with the chairman. When I raised the fact that it apparently had cost the military $500 million to kick 17,000 homosexuals out of the service in the previous decade, despite a government report saying there was no reason to believe they could not serve effectively, the chiefs replied that it was worth it to preserve unit cohesion and morale.

The chief of naval operations, Admiral Frank Kelso, said the navy had the greatest practical problems, given the close and isolated living arrangements on ships. The army chief, General Gordon Sullivan, and U.S. Air Force General Merrill McPeak were opposed, too. But the most adamant opponent was the commandant of the Marine Corps, General Carl Mundy. He was concerned about more than appearances and practicalities. He believed that homosexuality was immoral, and that if gays were permitted to serve openly, the military would be condoning immoral behavior and could no longer attract the finest young Americans. I disagreed with Mundy, but I liked him. In fact, I liked and respected them all. They had given me their honest opinions, yet had made it clear that if I ordered them to take action they'd do the best job they could, although if called to testify before Congress they would have to state their views frankly.

A couple of days later, I had another night meeting on the issue, with members of the Senate Armed Services Committee, including Senators Sam Nunn, James Exon, Carl Levin, Robert Byrd, Edward Kennedy, Bob Graham, Jeff Bingaman, John Glenn, Richard Shelby, Joe Lieberman, and Chuck Robb. Nunn, while opposed to my position, had agreed to the six-month delay. Some of my staffers were upset with him for his early and forceful opposition, but I wasn't; after all, he was personally conservative, and as chairman of the committee, he honored the military culture and saw it as his duty to protect it. He was not alone. Charlie Moskos, the Northwestern University sociologist who had worked with Nunn and me on the DLC national-service proposal and who said he had known a gay officer during the Korean War, was also against lifting the ban, saying that it preserved the "expectation of privacy" to which soldiers living in close quarters were entitled. Moskos said we should stick with what the great majority of military people wanted, because the main thing we needed in the military was the ability and willingness to fight. The problem I saw with his argument, and Sam Nunn's, is that they could have been used with equal force against Truman's order on integration or against current efforts to open more positions to women in the military.

Senator Byrd took a harder line than Nunn, echoing what I had heard from General Mundy. He believed homosexuality was a sin; said he would never let his grandson, whom he adored, join a military that admitted gays; and asserted that one reason the Roman Empire fell was the acceptance of pervasive homosexual conduct in the Roman legions from Julius Caesar on down. In contrast to Byrd and Nunn, Chuck Robb, who was conservative on many issues and had survived heated combat in Vietnam, supported my position, based on his wartime contact with men who were both gay and brave. He wasn't the only Vietnam combat veteran in Congress who felt that way.

The cultural divide was partly, but not completely, partisan and generational. Some younger Democrats opposed lifting the ban, while some older Republicans were for lifting it, including Lawrence Korb and Barry Goldwater. Korb, who had enforced the ban as an assistant secretary of defense under Reagan, said it was not necessary for maintaining the quality and strength of our forces. Goldwater, a former chairman of the Senate Armed Services Committee, a veteran, and the founder of the Arizona National Guard, was an old-fashioned conservative with libertarian instincts. In a statement published in the **Washington Post,** he said that allowing gays to serve was not a call for cultural license but a reaffirmation of the American value of extending opportunity to responsible citizens and limiting the reach of government into people's private lives. In his typically blunt way, he said he didn't care whether a soldier **was** straight, but whether he could **shoot** straight.

As things turned out, Goldwater's support and all my arguments were academic. The House passed a resolution opposing my position by more than three to one. The Senate opposition was not as great but was still substantial. That meant that if I persisted, the Congress would overturn my position with an amendment to the defense appropriations bill that I couldn't easily veto, and even if I did, the veto would be overridden in both houses.

While all this was going on, I saw a poll showing that by 48 to 45 percent the public disagreed with my position. The numbers didn't look too bad for such a controversial issue, but they were, and they showed why Congress thought it was a dcad-bang loser for them. Only 16 percent of the electorate strongly approved of lifting the ban, while 33 percent very strongly disapproved. Those were the people whose votes could be influenced by a congressman's position. It's hard to get politicians in swing districts to take a 17 percent deficit on any issue into an election. Interestingly, the biggest divisions were these: self-identified born-again Christians opposed my position 70 to 22 percent, while people who said they knew homosexuals personally approved of it 66 to 33 percent.

With congressional defeat inevitable, Les Aspin worked with Colin Powell and the Joint Chiefs on a compromise. Almost exactly six months later, on July 19, I went to the National Defense University at Fort McNair to announce it to the officers in attendance. "Don't ask, don't tell" basically said that if you say you're gay, it's presumed that you intend to violate the Uniform Code of Military Justice and you can be removed, unless you can convince your commander you're celibate and therefore not in violation of the code. But if you don't say you're gay, the following things will not lead to your removal: marching in a gay-rights parade in civilian clothes; hanging out in gay bars or with known homosexuals; being on homosexual mailing lists; and living with a person of the same sex who is the beneficiary of your life insurance policy. On paper, the military had moved a long way, to "live and let live," while holding on to the idea that it couldn't acknowledge gays without approving of homosexuality and compromising morale and cohesion. In practice it often didn't work out that way. Many anti-gay officers simply ignored the new policy and worked even harder to root out homosexuals, costing the military millions of dollars that would have been far better spent making America more secure.

In the short run, I got the worst of both worlds—I lost the fight, and the gay community was highly critical of me for the compromise, simply refusing to acknowledge the consequences of having so little support in Congress, and giving me little credit for lifting another ban on gays, the ban against serving in critical national security positions, or for the substantial number of gays and lesbians who were working throughout the administration. By contrast, Senator Dole won big. By raising the issue early, and repeatedly, he guaranteed it so much publicity that it appeared I was working on little else, which caused a lot of Americans who had elected me to fix the economy to wonder what on earth I was doing and whether they'd made a mistake.

I was finding it a challenge to keep another campaign commitment: cutting the White House staff by 25 percent. It was a nightmare for Mack McLarty, especially since we had a more ambitious agenda than the previous administration's and were getting more than twice as much mail. On February 9, just a week before I was slated to announce my economic program, I proposed the 25 percent reduction, cutting the staff by 350 people, down to 1,044 employees. Everybody took a hit; even Hillary's office would be smaller than Barbara Bush's, though she would take on greater responsibilities. The reduction I regretted most was the elimination of twenty career positions in the correspondence section. I would have preferred to reduce their numbers by attrition, but Mack said there was no other way to meet the goal. Besides, we had to have some money to modernize the White House. The staff couldn't even send and receive e-mail, and the phone system hadn't been changed since the Carter years. We couldn't do conference calls, but anyone could press one of the big lighted extension buttons and listen in on someone else's conversation, including mine. Soon we had a better system installed.

We also beefed up one part of the White House staff: the casework operation that was designed to help individual citizens who had personal problems with the federal government, often involving an effort to obtain disability, veterans, or other benefits. Usually citizens call on their U.S. senators or representatives for help in such matters, but because I had run a highly personalized campaign, many Americans felt they could call on me. I got an especially memorable request on February 20, when Peter Jennings, the ABC news anchor, moderated a televised "Children's Town Meeting" in the White House, in which young people between the ages of eight and fifteen asked me questions. The kids asked if I helped Chelsea with her homework, why no women had been elected President, what I would do to help Los Angeles after the riots, how health care would be paid for, and whether I could do anything to stop violence in schools. A lot of them were interested in the environment.

But one of the children wanted help. Anastasia Somoza was a beautiful girl from New York City who was confined to a wheelchair because of cerebral palsy. She explained that she had a twin sister, Alba, who also had cerebral palsy but who, unlike her, couldn't speak. "So because she can't speak, they put her in a special education class. But she uses computers to speak. And I would like her to be in a regular education class just like me." Anastasia said she and her parents were convinced that Alba could do regular schoolwork if given a chance. Federal law required children with disabilities to be educated in the "least restrictive" environment, but the critical decision about what is least restrictive is made at the child's school. It took about a year, but eventually Alba got into a regular class.

Hillary and I kept in touch with the Somoza family, and in 2002, I spoke at the girls' high school graduation. They both went on to college, because Anastasia and her parents were determined to give Alba all the opportunities she deserved, and weren't shy about asking others, including me, to help. Every month, the agency liaison who headed the casework operation sent me a report on the people we'd helped, along with a few of the moving thank-you letters they sent.

In addition to the staff cuts, I announced an executive order to cut administrative expenses 3 percent throughout the government, and a reduction in the salaries of top appointees and in their perks, like limousine service and private dining rooms. In a move that would prove to be a tremendous morale booster, I changed the rules of the White House Mess to allow more junior staff to use what had been the private preserve of high-level White House officials.

Our young staffers were working long hours and weekends, and it seemed foolish to me to require them all to leave for lunch, order in, or bring a paper bag with food from home. Besides, access to the White House Mess implied that they, too, were important. The mess was a wood-paneled room with good food prepared by navy personnel. I ordered lunch from it almost every day and enjoyed going down to visit with the young people who worked in the kitchen. Once a week they served Mexican dishes I especially liked. After I left office, the mess was again closed to all but senior staff. I believe our policy was good for morale and productivity.

With all the extra work and fewer people to do it, we would have to rely more than ever not only on those junior staffers, but also on the thousand-plus volunteers who put in long hours, some of them virtually full-time. The volunteers opened the mail, sent form replies when appropriate, filled requests for information, and did countless other tasks, without which the White House would have been far less responsive to the American people. All the volunteers got in return for their efforts, apart from the satisfaction of serving, was an annual thank-you reception Hillary and I hosted for them on the South Lawn. The White House couldn't function without them.

Besides the specific cuts I had already decided on, I was convinced that with a longer-term systematic approach, we could save a lot more money and improve government services. In Arkansas, I had initiated a Total Quality Management program that had achieved positive results. On March 3, I announced that Al Gore would lead a six-month review of all federal operations. Al took to the job like a duck to water, bringing in outside experts and consulting widely with government employees. He kept at it for eight years, helping us to eliminate hundreds of programs and 16,000 pages of regulations, to reduce the federal workforce by 300,000, making this the smallest federal government since 1960, and to save $136 million in tax money.

While we were getting organized and dealing with the controversies in the press, most of my time in January and

February was devoted to filling in the details of the economic plan. On Sunday, January 24, Lloyd Bentsen appeared on **Meet the Press.** He was supposed to give nonspecific answers to all questions regarding the details of the plan, but he went a little further than that, announcing that we would propose a consumption tax of some kind and that a broad-based energy tax was under consideration. The next day, interest rates on the government's thirty-year bond fell from 7.29 to 7.19 percent, the lowest rate in six years.

Meanwhile, we were struggling with the budget details. All the spending cuts and taxes that raised real money were controversial. For example, when I met with Senate and House leaders on the budget, Leon Panetta suggested that we have a one-time three-month delay in increasing the Social Security cost-of-living allowance. Most experts agreed that the COLA was too high, given the low rate of inflation, and the delay would save $15 billion over five years. Senator Mitchell said that the suggested delay was regressive and unfair, and that he couldn't support it. Neither would the other senators. We'd have to find that $15 billion elsewhere.

Over the weekend of January 30–31, I brought the cabinet and senior White House staff to Camp David, the presidential retreat in Maryland's Catoctin Mountains. Camp David is a beautiful wooded site, with comfortable cabins and recreational facilities, staffed by men and women from the navy and the Marine Corps. It was the perfect setting for us to get to know one another better and talk about the year ahead. I also invited Stan Greenberg, Paul Begala, and Mandy Grunwald. They felt that they had been shut out of the transition, and that an obsession with the deficit had overtaken every other objective I had advanced in the campaign. They thought Al and I were courting disaster by disregarding the deeper concerns and interests of the people who had elected us. I sympathized with them. For one thing, they hadn't been in on the hours of discussions that led most of us to the conclusion that if we didn't deal with the deficit, we couldn't achieve sustained strong growth and that my other campaign commitments, at least those that cost money, would die in the stagnant backwater of a sluggish economy.

I let Mandy and Stan start the discussion. Mandy outlined the anxiety of the middle class about jobs, retirement, health care, and education. Stan said that voters' most important concerns were, in order, jobs, health-care reform, welfare reform, and then deficit reduction, and that if deficit reduction was going to require the middle class to pay more taxes, I had darn sure better do something else for them. Hillary then described how we'd failed in Arkansas in my first term by doing too many things at once, without a clear story line and an effort to prepare people for a long, sustained struggle. Then she told them about the success we'd had the second time around, by focusing on one or two issues every two years, and laying out long-term goals, along with short-term benchmarks of progress against which we could be judged. That kind of approach, she said, enabled me to develop a story line people could understand and support. In response, someone pointed out that we couldn't develop a story line as long as we were awash in leaks, all of which concerned the most controversial proposals. After the weekend, the consultants tried to come up with a communications strategy that would take us beyond the daily leaks and controversies.

The rest of the retreat was devoted to more informal, personal conversations. On Saturday night there was a session, run by a facilitator who was a friend of Al Gore's, in which we were supposed to bond by sitting in a group, taking turns telling something about ourselves the others didn't know. Though the exercise got mixed reviews, I actually enjoyed it, and managed to confess that, as a child, I was overweight and often ridiculed. Lloyd Bentsen thought the whole exercise was silly and went back to his cabin; if there was something about him the rest of us didn't know, it was intentional. Bob Rubin stayed, but said he didn't have anything to say—apparently such group unburdening wasn't the key to his success at Goldman Sachs. Warren Christopher did participate, probably because he was the most disciplined man on the planet and thought this baby-boomer version of Chinese water torture would somehow strengthen his already considerable character. All in all, the weekend was helpful, but the real bonding would come in the fires of the struggles, victories, and defeats that lay ahead.

On Sunday night, we were back in the White House to host the annual National Governors Association dinner. It was Hillary's first formal event as First Lady, and she was nervous, but it went well. The governors were concerned about the economy, which diminished state revenues, forcing them to cut services, raise taxes, or both. They understood the necessity of reducing the deficit, but didn't want it to come at their expense, in the form of responsibilities shifting from the federal government to the states without funds being provided to pay for them.

On February 5, I signed my first bill into law, keeping another campaign commitment. With the Family and

Medical Leave Act, the United States at last joined more than 150 other countries in guaranteeing workers some time off when a baby is born or a family member is sick. The bill's principal sponsor, my longtime friend Senator Chris Dodd of Connecticut, had worked for years to enact it. President Bush had vetoed it twice, saying it would prove too burdensome for business. While the legislation had some strong Republican supporters, most Republicans had voted against it for the same reason. I believed that family leave would be good for the economy. With most parents in the workforce, by choice or necessity, it is imperative that Americans be able to do well both on the job and at home. People who are worried about their infants or their sick parents are less productive than those who go to work knowing they've done right by their families. During my time as President, more than thirty-five million people would take advantage of the Family and Medical Leave law.

In the next eight years, and even after I left office, more people would mention it to me than any other bill I signed. Many of their stories were powerful. Early one Sunday morning, when I came in from my jog, I ran into a family touring the White House. One of the children, a teenage girl, was in a wheelchair and obviously very ill. I greeted them and said that if they'd wait for me to shower and get dressed for church, I'd take them into the Oval Office for a picture. They waited and we had a good visit. I especially enjoyed my talk with the brave young girl. As I walked away, her father grabbed my arm and turned me around, saying, "My little girl is probably not going to make it. The last three weeks I've spent with her have been the most important of my life. I couldn't have done it without the family leave law."

In early 2001, when I took my first shuttle flight from New York to Washington as a private citizen, one of the flight attendants told me that both her parents had been desperately ill at the same time, one with cancer, the other with Alzheimer's. She said there was no one to care for them in their last days except her and her sister, and they wouldn't have been able to do it without the family leave law. "You know, the Republicans are always talking about family values," she said, "but I think how your parents die is an important part of family values."

On February 11, as we worked to finish the economic plan, I finally got an attorney general, having decided, after a false start or two, on Janet Reno, the prosecuting attorney of Dade County, Florida. I had known about and admired Janet's work for years, especially her innovative "drug courts," which gave first-time offenders the chance to avoid going to jail if they agreed to undergo drug treatment and check in regularly with the court. My brother-in-law Hugh Rodham had worked in the Miami drug court as an attorney with the public defender's office. At his invitation, I had attended two sessions of the court myself in the 1980s, and was struck by the unusual but effective way the prosecutor, defense lawyer, and judge worked together to convince the defendants that this was their last opportunity to stay out of prison. The program was very successful, with a much lower recidivism rate than the prison system, at far less cost to the taxpayers. In the campaign, I had pledged to support federal funding to establish drug courts based on the Miami model all across the country.

Senator Bob Graham gave Reno a glowing endorsement when I called him. So did my friend Diane Blair, who had gone to Cornell with her thirty years earlier. So did Vince Foster, who was a very good judge of people. After he interviewed Janet, he called me and said in his droll way, "I think we've got a live one." Reno also was immensely popular with her constituents, based on her reputation as a no-nonsense, tough but fair prosecutor. She was a native Floridian, about six feet tall, and had never married. Public service was her life, and she had performed it well. I thought she could strengthen the often-frayed relationships between federal law enforcement and its state and local counterparts. It concerned me a little that, like me, she was a stranger to Washington's ways, but in Miami she had had extensive experience working with federal authorities on immigration and narcotics cases, and I thought she would learn enough to get along.

Over the weekend, we worked hard to finish the economic plan. Paul Begala had come to work in the White House a couple of weeks earlier, in large measure to help me explain what I was about to do in a way that was consistent with my campaign message of restoring opportunity for the middle class, something he believed most members of the economic team didn't care enough about. Begala felt that the entire team should stress three points: that deficit reduction is not an end in itself, but the means to achieve the real objectives—economic growth, more jobs, and higher incomes; that our plan represented a fundamental change in the way government had been working, ending the irresponsibility and unfairness of the past by asking the wealthy big corporations, and other special interests that had benefited disproportionately from the tax cuts and deficits of the 1980s to pay their fair share of cleaning up the mess; and that we should not say we were asking people to "sacrifice" but to "contribute" to America's renewal, a more patriotic and positive formulation.

Begala wrote a memo containing his arguments and suggesting a new theme: "It's NOT the deficit, stupid." Gene Sperling, Bob Reich, and George Stephanopoulos agreed with Paul, and were glad to have some inside help in arguing the message.

While all this was going on in public, we were struggling hard with some big questions. By far the largest was whether to include health-care reform along with the economic plan in the omnibus Budget Reconciliation Act. There was a compelling argument for doing so: first, the budget, unlike all other legislation, isn't subject to the filibuster rule, the Senate practice that allows just forty-one senators to kill any bill by debating it to death, blocking a vote until the Senate has to move on to other business. Since the Senate had forty-four Republicans, the probability that they would at least try to filibuster health care was high.

Hillary and Ira Magaziner badly wanted health care in the budget, the congressional leaders were open to it, and Dick Gephardt had urged Hillary to do it, because he was sure the Republican senators would try to filibuster health care if it were proposed by itself. George Mitchell was sympathetic for another reason: If health-care reform were introduced as a separate bill, it would be referred to the Senate Finance Committee, whose chairman, Senator Pat Moynihan of New York, was, to put it mildly, skeptical that we could come up with a workable health-care plan so quickly. Moynihan recommended that we first do welfare reform, and spend the next two years developing a health-care proposal.

The economic team was adamantly opposed to including health care in the budget, and they had good reasons, too. Ira Magaziner and many health-care economists believed, correctly as it turned out, that greater competition in the health-care marketplace, which our plan would promote, would produce significant savings without price controls. But the Congressional Budget Office would not give credit for these savings in any budget we presented. Thus, to provide universal coverage, we had either to include a provision for backup price controls in the plan, raise taxes and cut other spending even further, or reduce the deficit target, which might adversely affect our strategy to lower interest rates.

I decided to delay the decision until after I put the details of the economic plan before the people and the Congress. Not long afterward, the decision was made for me. On March 11, Senator Robert Byrd, the senior Senate Democrat and ultimate authority on the body's rules, told us he would not make an exception for health care to the "Byrd rule," which prohibited the inclusion of nongeneric items in the budget-reconciliation bill. We had enlisted everyone we could think of to make the case to Byrd, but he was adamant that health-care reform could not be construed as part of the basic budget process. Now, if the Republicans could sustain a filibuster, our health-care plan would be dead on arrival.

In the second week of February, we decided to kick the health-care can down the road and complete the rest of the economic plan. I had become deeply immersed in the details of budgeting, determined to understand the human impact of our decisions. Most of the team wanted to cut farm supports and other rural programs, which they thought were unjustifiable. Alice Rivlin pushed hard for the cuts, suggesting I could then say I had ended welfare for farmers "as we know it." It was a takeoff on one of my best campaign lines, a pledge to "end welfare as we know it." I reminded my mostly urban budgeteers that farmers were good people who had chosen hard work in an uncertain environment, and though we had to make some cuts in their programs, "we don't have to enjoy it." Since we couldn't restructure the whole farm program, reduce the subsidies in other nations' budgets, or eliminate all the foreign barriers to our food exports, we ended up reducing the existing farm benefits modestly. But I didn't enjoy it.

Another thing we had to consider in proposing cuts, of course, was whether they had a chance to pass. For example, someone said we could save a lot of money by eliminating all the so-called highway-demonstration projects, which were specific spending items members of Congress obtained for their districts or states. When the suggestion came up, my new congressional liaison, Howard Paster, shook his head in disbelief. Paster had worked in both the House and Senate and for both Democratic and Republican lobbying firms. A New Yorker with a brusque, candid manner, Howard snapped, "How many votes does the bond market have?" Of course, he knew we had to convince the bond market that our deficit-reduction plan was credible, but he wanted us to remember that it first had to pass, and inflicting personal pain on members of Congress was unlikely to prove a successful strategy.

Some of the proposals we considered were so absurd they were comical. When someone suggested we impose fees for Coast Guard services, I asked how they would work. It was explained that the Coast Guard was quite often called upon to bring in boats that were in distress, often due to the negligence of the operators. I laughed and said, "So when we pull up alongside, or throw down a rope from a helicopter, before we do the rescue, we're going to ask, 'Visa? MasterCard?' " We let that one go, but eventually we did come up with more than 150 budget cuts.

Deciding on the tax increases was no easier than choosing the budget cuts. The toughest issue for me was the BTU tax. It was bad enough that I was going back on my commitment to cut middle-class taxes; now I was told we had to raise them, both to reach the $140 billion deficit reduction target in the fifth year and to turn the psychology of the bond market. The middle class had been shafted in the eighties, and Bush had been crippled by signing a gas-tax increase. In one fell swoop, if I proposed the BTU tax I would make the Republicans the anti-tax party again, largely to satisfy the hunger of the prosperous interest-rate setters for a little middle-class pain, in this case about $9 a month in direct costs, rising to $17 when indirect costs, in the form of higher prices for consumer products, were included. Lloyd Bentsen said that he had never had any fallout from voting for energy taxes, and that Bush was hurt by signing the 1990 gas-tax increase because of his "read my lips" pledge and the fact that the most militant anti-taxers were hard-core Republicans. Gore again pushed for the BTU tax, saying it would promote energy conservation and independence.

Finally, I gave in, but made some other changes in Treasury's tax proposals that I hoped would reduce the tax burden on average Americans. I insisted that we include in the budget the full $26.8 billion cost of my campaign proposal to more than double the tax cut for millions of working families with incomes of $30,000 or less, called the Earned Income Tax Credit (EITC), and for the first time offer a more modest EITC to more than 4 million working poor Americans without dependents. This proposal would ensure that, even with the energy tax, working families with incomes of $30,000 or less would still receive a meaningful tax cut. On the campaign trail, I had said at virtually every stop, "No one with children who works full-time should live in poverty." In 1993, there were a lot of people in that situation. After we doubled the EITC, more than four million of them moved out of poverty into the middle class during my presidency.

As we were trying to close the deal, Laura Tyson said she felt she had to point out that there was no significant economic difference between a fifth-year reduction of $140 billion and one of $120 or $125 billion. Congress would probably pare back whatever I proposed anyway. She argued that, if it eased our political problems or was simply better policy, we would save ourselves some headaches by reducing the figure to $135 billion or even a little less. Reich, Sperling, Blinder, Begala, and Stephanopoulos all agreed with her. The others held out for the high number. Bentsen said we could save $3 billion by dropping the estimated cost of welfare reform from the budget. I agreed. After all, we hadn't developed our proposal yet, and the number was just a guess. We knew we'd have to spend more on training, child care, and transportation to help poor people move from welfare to work, but if we moved enough people off the rolls, the net cost might go down, not up. Moreover, I believed we could pass welfare reform separately with bipartisan support.

Later, Lloyd Bentsen added a final piece to the plan, removing the $135,000 earnings cap on the 1.45 percent payroll tax that funded Medicare. This was necessary to make sure that our numbers on extending Medicare's solvency added up, but it did ask for more from the wealthiest Americans, whose top rate we were already proposing to raise to 39.6 percent, and who would almost certainly never cost the Medicare program as much as they would now pay into it. When I asked Bentsen about it, he just smiled and said he knew what he was doing. He was confident that he and other high-income Americans who would pay the extra tax would more than make it back in the stock market boom that our economic program would spark.

On Monday, February 15, I gave my first televised address from the Oval Office, a ten-minute outline of the economic program I would unveil two days later to a joint session of Congress. Even though the economy was in a statistical recovery, it was a jobless one, burdened by the quadrupling of the debt in the last twelve years. Since all the deficits were the result of the tax cuts for the wealthy, soaring health costs, and increases in defense spending, we were investing less in "the things that make us stronger and smarter, richer and safer," like education, children, transportation, and local law enforcement. At the rate we were going, our living standards, which usually doubled every twenty-five years, wouldn't do so again for another one hundred years. Reversing the trend would require a dramatic change in our national priorities, with a combination of tax increases and spending cuts to reduce the deficit and invest more in our future. I said that I had hoped to pursue this course without asking more of middle-class Americans, because they had borne hardships and had been treated unfairly in the previous twelve years, but the deficit had grown far beyond the earlier estimates on which I had built my budget proposals in the campaign. Now "more Americans must contribute today so that all Americans can do better tomorrow." However, unlike what had happened in the 1980s, most of the new taxes would be paid by wealthier Americans; "for the first time in more than a decade, we're all in this together." In addition to deficit reduction, my economic plan would provide incentives to businesses to create new jobs; a short-term stimulus to add 500,000 jobs right away; investments in education and training, with special programs to help displaced defense workers; welfare reform and the big increase in the EITC; Head Start opportunities and vaccinations for all children who need them; and the national service initiative to allow young people to earn money for college in return for serving in their communities. I acknowledged that these proposals would not be easily or quickly implemented, but when they were, we could "restore the vitality of the American dream."

On Wednesday night, in the address to Congress, I explained the strategy behind the plan and outlined the specifics. Its guiding principles were four: to shift more public and private spending from consumption to investment in order to create more jobs; to honor work and family; to produce a budget with conservative estimates, not the unrealistic "rosy scenario" figures that had been used in the past; and to pay for the changes with real cuts in spending and fair taxes.

To create more jobs, I proposed a permanent investment tax credit for small businesses, which employed 40 percent of the workforce but were creating most of our new jobs, and the establishment of community development banks and empowerment zones, two of my campaign commitments, which were designed to bring new loans and investments into poor areas. I also asked for more money for roads, bridges, mass transit, high-tech information systems, and environmental cleanups to increase productivity and employment.

On education, I recommended increased investments in and higher standards for public schools, and incentives to encourage more students to go to college, including my national service initiative. I complimented Congress on passing the family leave law, and asked them to follow up with tougher child-support enforcement. On crime, I asked for passage of the Brady bill, military-style boot camps for first-time nonviolent offenders, and my proposal to put 100,000 new police on the streets.

I then asked Congress to help me change the way government worked, by enacting campaign finance reform and registration requirements for lobbyists, and eliminating the tax deduction for lobbyists' expenses. I committed to reduce the size of the federal workforce by 100,000, and to cut administrative expenses, saving $9 billion. I asked Congress to help me slow spiraling health-care costs, and said that we could continue modest defense downsizing but that our responsibilities as the world's only superpower required us to spend enough to keep our military the best trained and equipped in the world.

I saved taxes for last, recommending that we increase the top income tax rate from 31 to 36 percent on incomes over $180,000, with a 10 percent surcharge on incomes over $250,000; raise the corporate income tax rate from 34 to 36 percent on incomes over $10 million; end the tax subsidy that made it more profitable for a company to shut down its American operations and move overseas than to reinvest at home; subject more of the income of the best-off Social Security recipients to taxation; and enact the BTU tax. The income tax rates would increase on only the top 1.2 percent of earners; the Social Security increase would apply to 13 percent of recipients; and the energy tax would cost about $17 per month for people with incomes of $40,000 or more a year. For families with incomes of $30,000 or less, the EITC would more than offset the cost of the BTU tax. The taxes and budget would enable us to reduce the deficit by about $500 billion over five years at present economic estimates.

At the end of the speech, I did my best to bring home the magnitude of the deficit problem, pointing out that if present trends continued, within a decade the annual deficit would increase to at least $635 billion a year from this year's $290 billion, and that interest payments on our accumulated debt would become America's largest budget item, taking more than twenty cents of every tax dollar. To show I was serious about deficit reduction, I invited Alan Greenspan to sit with Hillary in the First Lady's box in the House gallery. To show he was serious about it, Greenspan came, overcoming his understandable reluctance to make what could be seen as a political appearance.

After the speech, which was generally well received, all the commentators noted that I had abandoned the middle-class tax cut. So I had, but a lot of my other promises were fulfilled in the economic plan. Over the next few days, Al Gore, the cabinet members, and I fanned out across the country to sell it. Alan Greenspan praised it. So did Paul Tsongas, who said the Clinton who spoke to Congress was not the Clinton he ran against, which, of course, is what my political advisors and some congressional Democrats were worried about.

There were enough important and controversial proposals in the speech to keep Congress busy for the rest of the year, not to mention the other legislation that already was, or soon would be, on their calendar. I knew that there would be a lot of ups and downs before the economic program passed, and that I wouldn't be able to spend all of my time pushing it. Foreign problems and domestic developments wouldn't permit it.

On the home front, February ended in violence. On the twenty-sixth, a bomb exploded at Manhattan's World Trade Center, killing six people and injuring more than one thousand. The investigation quickly revealed it to be the work of terrorists from the Middle East, who hadn't covered their tracks very well. The first arrests were made March 4; eventually, six of the conspirators were convicted in federal court in New York and each sentenced to 240 years in prison. I was pleased with the effectiveness of our law-enforcement work, but troubled by the evident vulnerability of our open society to terror. My national security team began to devote more attention to terror networks and what we could do to protect ourselves and free societies around the world against them.

On February 28, four agents from the Bureau of Alcohol, Tobacco, and Firearms were killed and sixteen others wounded at the onset of a confrontation with a religious cult, the Branch Davidians, at their compound outside Waco, Texas. The Davidians were suspected of illegal firearms violations. The sect's messianic leader, David Koresh, believed he was Christ reincarnate, the only person who knew the secret of the seven seals referred to in the book of Revelation. Koresh had almost hypnotic mind control over the men, women, and children who followed him; a large arsenal of weapons, which he was obviously prepared to use; and enough food to hold out for a long time. The standoff between the Davidians and the FBI dragged out for almost two months. During that time, several adults and children left, but most of them stayed, with Koresh promising to surrender but always finding an excuse to delay doing so.

On Sunday night, April 18, Janet Reno came to the White House to tell me that the FBI wanted to storm the compound, apprehend Koresh and any of his followers who had taken part in killing the agents or some other crime, and free the rest of them. Janet said she was concerned by FBI reports that Koresh was sexually abusing children, most of them pre-teens, and that he might be planning a mass suicide. The FBI had also told her that it couldn't keep so many of its resources tied down in one place forever. They wanted to raid the compound the next day, using armored vehicles to break holes in the buildings, then blast tear gas into them, a maneuver they estimated would force all the members to surrender within two hours. Reno had to approve the assault and wanted my okay first.

Several years earlier, I had faced a similar situation as governor. A right-wing extremist group had established a compound in the mountains of north Arkansas. Among the men, women, and children who lived there were two suspects wanted for murder. The people lived in several cabins, each of which had a trapdoor that led to a dugout from which they could fire on approaching authorities. And they had a lot of weapons to fire. The FBI wanted to storm them, too. At a meeting I convened with the FBI, our state police, and cooperating law-enforcement people from Missouri and Oklahoma, I listened to the FBI's case, then said that before I could approve the action, I wanted someone who'd fought in the jungles of Vietnam to fly over the place in a helicopter and make an assessment. The battlewise veteran who made the inspection for me returned to say, "If those people can shoot at all, you'll lose

fifty men in the assault." I called off the raid, put a blockade around the camp, cut off food-stamp aid to the several
families who had been receiving it, and prevented anyone
who left the premises to get supplies from going back.
Eventually the holdouts gave in, and the suspects were
apprehended with no loss of life.

When Janet made her case to me, I thought we should
try what had worked in Arkansas before we approved the
FBI raid. She countered that the FBI was tired of waiting;
that the standoff was costing the government a million
dollars a week and tying up law-enforcement resources
needed elsewhere; that the Branch Davidians could hold
out longer than the Arkansas people had; and that the
possibilities of child sexual abuse and mass suicide were
real, because Koresh was crazy and so were many of his
followers. Finally, I told her that if she thought it was the
right thing to do, she could go ahead.

The next day, as I watched CNN on a television just
outside the Oval Office, I saw Koresh's compound in
flames. The raid had gone terribly wrong. After the FBI
fired the tear gas into the buildings where the people were
holed up, the Davidians started a fire. It got worse when
they opened the windows to let the tear gas out and also
let in a hard wind off the Texas plains, which stoked the
flames. When it ended, more than eighty people had died,
including twenty-five children; only nine survived. I knew
I needed to speak to the press and take responsibility for
the fiasco. So did Dee Dee Myers and Bruce Lindsey. But
several times during the day, when I wanted to go ahead,
George Stephanopoulos urged me to wait, saying we
didn't know whether anyone was still alive or whether, if
Koresh heard my words, he might snap and kill them, too.
Janet Reno did appear before the cameras, explained what

happened, and took full responsibility for the raid. As the first woman to hold the attorney general's post, she thought it was important not to pass the buck. By the time I finally talked to the press about Waco, Reno was being praised and I was being criticized for letting her take the fall.

For the second time in less than twenty-four hours, I had accepted advice that ran counter to my instincts. I didn't blame George. He was young and cautious and had given me his honest, albeit mistaken, opinion. But I was furious at myself, first for agreeing to the raid against my better judgment, then for delaying a public acknowledgment of responsibility for it. One of the most important decisions a President has to make is when to take the advice of the people who work for him and when to reject it. Nobody can be right all the time, but it's a lot easier to live with bad decisions that you believed in when you made them than with those your advisors say are right but your gut says are wrong. After Waco, I resolved to go with my gut.

Perhaps one reason I didn't trust my instincts enough is that the administration was being hammered hard in Washington and I was being second-guessed at every turn. After a great initial appearance on Capitol Hill, Hillary was being criticized for the closed meetings of her health-care task force. Since they were consulting with hundreds of people, nothing they did was secret; they were simply trying to move with dispatch over many immensely complicated matters to reach my overly ambitious goal of presenting a health-care plan to Congress within one hundred days. The task force heard testimony from over 1,100 groups, had more than 200 meetings with members of Congress, and held public meetings all around the country. Its reputation for being secretive was exaggerated. In the end, the task force operation proved too unwieldy and was allowed to expire, and we couldn't make the hundred-day deadline anyway.

As if all this weren't enough, I also suffered the defeat of my short-term stimulus package, which was designed to create 500,000 jobs by getting money out quickly to cities and states for infrastructure projects. The economy was still growing slowly, it needed the boost, and the modest nonrecurring expenditures wouldn't have made our deficit problem worse. The House passed the bill handily and the Senate was for it, too, but Bob Dole had more than forty Republican senators who were willing to filibuster it. After the first filibuster vote, we should have tried to negotiate a smaller package with Dole, or accepted a less ambitious compromise proposal offered by Senators John Breaux and David Boren, two conservative Democrats. Senator Robert Byrd, who was handling the proposal, was adamant that if we didn't bend, we could break the filibuster. But we couldn't, and finally admitted defeat on April 21, two days after Waco.

In my first term, the Republicans resorted to the filibuster to an unprecedented extent, thwarting the will of the congressional majority, out of either conviction or a desire to prove that I couldn't lead. Senator George Mitchell had to have twelve votes to break filibusters just in my first hundred days.

On March 19, we suffered a personal blow that put politics in perspective when Hillary's dad had a massive stroke. Hillary rushed to his bedside at St. Vincent's Hospital in Little Rock, with Chelsea and my brother-in-law Tony. Dr. Drew Kumpuris, Hugh's doctor and our friend, told Hillary that her father had suffered severe brain damage and was in a deep coma from which, in all probability, he would never emerge. I got there two days later. Hillary, Chelsea, Dorothy, and his sons, Hugh and Tony, had been taking turns talking, even singing, to Hugh, who looked as if he was just sleeping peacefully. We didn't know how long he would last, and I could stay only a day. I left Hillary in the good company of her family, the Thomasons, Carolyn Huber, who had known Hugh ever since her days as the administrator of the Governor's Mansion, and Lisa Caputo, Hillary's press secretary and a favorite of Hugh's because like him she came from eastern Pennsylvania, near his hometown of Scranton.

The next Sunday, I flew home again for a couple of days. I wanted to be with my family, even though there was nothing to do but wait. The doctor told us that Hugh was essentially brain dead. Over the weekend, the family decided to take him off the machine that was breathing for him, and we all said prayers and good-byes, but Hugh didn't go for it. His strong old heart just kept beating. Though I had been able to attend to most of my duties in Arkansas, I had to return to Washington on Tuesday. I hated to leave, knowing it was the last time I'd ever see my father-in-law. I loved Hugh Rodham, with his no-nonsense gruffness and fierce family loyalty. I was grateful that he had accepted me into the fold twenty years earlier, when I was scruffy, penniless, and, worst of all, a Democrat. I would miss our pinochle games and political arguments, and just knowing he was around.

On April 4, with Hugh still hanging on, Hillary had to return to Washington, too, to get Chelsea back to school after spring break, and to get back to work. She had promised to give a speech on April 6 at the University of

Texas at Austin for Liz Carpenter, who had been Lady Bird Johnson's press secretary. Liz pressed her not to cancel, and she decided to go. At a time when she was grief-stricken, she reached deep inside herself to say that, as we moved into the new millennium, "we need a new politics of meaning. We need a new ethos of individual responsibility and caring. We need a new definition of civil society which answers the unanswerable questions posed by both the market forces and the governmental ones, as to how we can have a society that fills us up again and makes us feel that we are part of something bigger than ourselves." Hillary had been moved to make this argument by reading an article written by Lee Atwater shortly before he died at forty of cancer. Atwater had become famous and feared for his ruthless attacks on Democrats while working for Presidents Reagan and Bush. As he faced death, he found that a life devoted only to getting power, wealth, and prestige left a lot to be desired, and he hoped that in a parting shot, he could push us to a higher purpose. In Austin, on April 6, bearing her own sorrow, Hillary tried to define that purpose. I loved what she said and was proud of her for saying it.

The next day, Hugh Rodham died. We had a memorial service for him in Little Rock, then took him home to Scranton for the funeral at the Court Street Methodist Church. I eulogized the man who had put aside his Republican convictions to work for me in 1974, and who, through a lifetime of learning from personal experience, had let go of all the bigotries he had grown up with. He lost his racism when he worked with a black man in Chicago. He lost his homophobia when he was befriended and looked after by his gay neighbors, a doctor and a nurse, in Little Rock. He had grown up in football-fanatical eastern Pennsylvania, where the Catholic stars went to Notre Dame and the Protestant ones like him played for Penn State. The divide revealed a prejudice against Catholics that was also part of Hugh's upbringing. He gave that up, too. We all thought it fitting that his last days were spent in St. Vincent's Hospital, where the Catholic nuns took loving care of him.

THIRTY-TWO

Though most of the headlines of my early months in office concerned the effort to define, defend, and pass my economic plan; gays in the military; and Hillary's health-care work, foreign policy was always there, an ever-present part of my daily routine and concern. The general impression among Washington observers was that I wasn't too interested in foreign affairs and wanted to spend as little time as possible on them. It's true that the overwhelming focus of the campaign had been on domestic issues; our economic troubles demanded that. But, as I had said over and over, increasing global interdependence was erasing the divide between foreign and domestic policy. And the "new world order" President Bush had proclaimed after the fall of the Berlin Wall was rife with chaos and big, unresolved questions.

Early on, my national security advisor, Tony Lake, had declared that success in foreign affairs is often defined by preventing or defusing problems before they develop into headaches and headline grabbers. "If we do a really good job," he said, "the public may never know it, because the dogs won't bark." When I took office, we had a whole kennel full of barking hounds, with Bosnia and Russia howling the loudest, and several others, including Somalia, Haiti, North Korea, and Japan's trade policy, growling in the background.

The breakup of the Soviet Union and the collapse of

communism in the Warsaw Pact nations raised the prospect that Europe might become democratic, peaceful, and united for the first time in history. Whether it would happen turned on four great questions: Would East and West Germany be reunited; would Russia become a truly democratic, stable, nonimperial nation; what would happen to Yugoslavia, a cauldron of diverse ethnic provinces, which had been held together by the iron will of Marshal Tito; and would Russia and the former Communist countries be integrated into the European Union and the transatlantic NATO alliance with the United States and Canada?

By the time I became President, Germany had been reunited under the visionary leadership of Chancellor Helmut Kohl, with the strong support of President Bush and despite reservations in Europe about the political and economic power of a resurgent Germany. The other three questions were still open, and I knew that one of my most important responsibilities as President was to see that they were answered correctly.

During the election campaign, both President Bush and I had supported aid to Russia. At first I was more assertive than he was, but after prodding by former president Nixon, Bush announced that the G-7, the seven largest industrial nations—the United States, Germany, France, Italy, the United Kingdom, Canada, and Japan— would provide $24 billion to support democracy and economic reform in Russia. By the time Yeltsin came to Washington in June 1992 as Russia's president, he was grateful and openly supporting Bush's reelection. As I mentioned earlier, Yeltsin did agree to a courtesy meeting with me at Blair House on June 18, thanks to the friendship between Foreign Minister Andrei Kozyrev and Toby

Gati, one of my foreign policy advisors. It didn't bother me that Yeltsin was supporting Bush; I just wanted him to know that if I won, I would support him.

In November, a couple of days after the election, Yeltsin called to congratulate me and to urge me to come to Moscow as soon as possible to reaffirm America's support for his reforms in the face of mounting opposition at home. Yeltsin had a hard row to hoe. He had been elected president of Russia in June 1991, when Russia was still part of the crumbling Soviet Union. In August, Soviet president Mikhail Gorbachev was put under house arrest at his summer retreat on the Black Sea by conspirators intent on staging a coup d'état. Russian citizens took to the Moscow streets in protest. The defining moment of the drama came when Yeltsin, in office for just two months, climbed on a tank in front of the Russian White House, the parliamentary building under siege by the coup plotters. He urged the Russian people to defend their hard-won democracy. In effect, he was telling the reactionaries, "You may steal our freedom, but you'll have to do it over my dead body." Yeltsin's heroic clarion call galvanized domestic and international support, and the coup failed. By December, the Soviet Union had dissolved into a collection of independent states, and Russia had taken the Soviet seat on the United Nations Security Council.

But Yeltsin's problems were not over. Reactionary elements, smarting from their loss of power, opposed his determination to withdraw Soviet troops from the Baltic nations of Estonia, Lithuania, and Latvia. Economic disaster loomed, as the rotting remains of the Soviet economy were exposed to free-market reforms, which brought inflation and the sale of state-owned assets at low prices to a new class of ultra-rich businessmen called "oligarchs," who made America's robber barons of the late nineteenth century look like Puritan preachers. Organized-crime networks also moved into the vacuum created by the collapse of the Soviet state and spread their tentacles across the globe. Yeltsin had destroyed the old system, but had not yet been able to build a new one. He also had not developed a good working relationship with the Duma, Russia's parliament, partly because he was by nature averse to compromise, partly because the Duma was full of people who longed for the old order or an equally oppressive new one rooted in ultra-nationalism.

Yeltsin was up to his ears in alligators, and I wanted to help him. I was encouraged to do so by Bob Strauss, whom President Bush had sent to Moscow as our ambassador even though he was an ardent Democrat and a former chairman of the Democratic National Committee. Strauss said I could work with Yeltsin and give him good political advice, and he urged me to do both.

I was inclined to accept Yeltsin's invitation to go to Russia, but Tony Lake said Moscow shouldn't be my first foreign stop, and the rest of my team said it would divert attention from our domestic agenda. They made strong arguments, but the United States had a big stake in Russia's success, and we sure didn't want hard-liners, either Communists or ultra-nationalists, in control there. Boris made it easier when he suggested a meeting in a mutually acceptable third country.

About this time, I persuaded my old friend and Oxford housemate Strobe Talbott to leave **Time** magazine and come to work in the State Department to help us with policy on the former Soviet Union. By then, Strobe and I had been discussing Russian history and politics for almost twenty-five years. Ever since he translated and edited Khrushchev's memoirs, Strobe had known and cared more about Russia and the Russian people than anyone else I knew. He had a fine analytical mind and a fertile imagination behind his proper professorial façade, and I trusted both his judgment and his willingness to tell me the unvarnished truth. There was no position in the State Department hierarchy that described what I wanted Strobe to do, so he set out to create one, with the blessing of Warren Christopher and the help of Dick Holbrooke, an investment banker and veteran foreign policy hand who had provided advice during the campaign and who would become one of the most important figures in my administration.

Eventually, Strobe's new job had a title: ambassador-at-large and special advisor to the secretary of state on the new independent states of the former Soviet Union. He later became deputy secretary of state. I don't think five people could repeat Strobe's title, but everybody knew what he did: he was our "go to" man on Russia. For eight years, he was by my side in all my meetings with Presidents Yeltsin and Vladimir Putin, eighteen with Yeltsin alone. Since Strobe spoke fluent Russian and took copious notes, his participation with me and his own interactions with the Russians guaranteed a precision and accuracy in our work that would prove invaluable. Strobe chronicles our eight-year odyssey in his book **The Russia Hand,** which is remarkable not only for its insights but for the verbatim accounts of the colorful conversations I had with Yeltsin. Unlike what happens in most books of the genre, the quotes are not reconstructions; they are, for good or ill, what we actually said. Strobe's main point is that I became my own "Russia hand" because, while not an expert on Russia, I knew "one big thing: on the twin issues that had constituted the casus belli of the cold war—democracy versus dictatorship at home and cooperation versus competition abroad"—Yeltsin and I were, "in principle, on the same side."

During the transition period, I had talked to Strobe a lot about the deteriorating situation in Russia and the imperative of averting disaster. At Renaissance Weekend, Strobe and his wife, Brooke, who had campaigned full-time with Hillary and was about to become head of the White House Fellows program, were jogging with me on Hilton Head beach. We wanted to talk about Russia, but the leader of our group, the great Olympic hurdler Edwin Moses, set such a brisk pace that I couldn't keep up and talk at the same time. We came upon Hillary taking her morning walk, so the three of us had an excuse to slow down and visit. President Bush was in Moscow signing the START II treaty with Yeltsin. It was good news, though like everything progressive Yeltsin did, it was facing strong opposition in the Duma. I told Strobe that things were changing so much in Russia that we couldn't have a completely defensive strategy; we had to help solidify and accelerate positive developments, especially those that would improve the Russian economy.

In February, I went over to Strobe's house one night to see his family and talk about Russia. Strobe told me about a recent meeting he'd had with Richard Nixon, in which the former President had urged us to support Yeltsin heavily. The $24 billion assistance package President Bush had announced the previous spring hadn't done that, because the international financial institutions wouldn't release the money until Russia had restructured its economy. We needed to do something now.

In early March, Yeltsin and I agreed to meet on April 3 and 4 in Vancouver, Canada. On March 8, Richard Nixon called on me at the White House to urge me personally to support Yeltsin. After a brief visit with Hillary and Chelsea, in which he reminded them that he was raised a Quaker and that his daughters, like Chelsea, had gone to Sidwell Friends School, he got down to business, saying I would be remembered as President more for what I did with Russia than for my economic policy. Later that night, I called Strobe to report on the Nixon conversation and to stress again how important it was that we do something at Vancouver to help Russia, with a high-impact follow-up at the annual G-7 summit in Tokyo in July. All through March, as I got updates from our foreign policy team and Larry Summers and his assistant David Lipton at Treasury, I pushed them to think bigger and do more.

Meanwhile, in Moscow, the Duma was reducing Yeltsin's power and endorsing the fruitless inflationary policies of the Russian Central Bank. On March 20, Yeltsin struck back with a speech announcing a public referendum for April 25 to determine whether he or the Duma ran the country; until then, he said, his presidential decrees would remain in effect, no matter what the Duma did. I watched the speech on one of two television sets in my private dining room off the Oval Office. The other TV was showing the NCAA tournament basketball game between the Arkansas Razorbacks and St. John's University. I had a dog in both hunts.

My entire foreign policy team and I had a vigorous debate about how I should respond to Yeltsin's speech. They all cautioned restraint, because Yeltsin was stretching the limits of his constitutional authority, and because he might lose. I disagreed. Yeltsin was in the fight of his life against the old Communists and other reactionaries. He was going to the people with a referendum. And I didn't care about the risk of losing—I reminded our team that I had lost plenty of times myself. I had no interest in hedging my bets, and instructed Tony Lake to draft a statement of strong support. When he presented it to me, I made it even stronger and gave it to the press. In this case, I went with my gut instincts and placed a bet that Russia would stick with Yeltsin, and stay on the right side of history. My optimism was bolstered by Arkansas' come-from-behind victory in the ball game.

Finally, in March, I got an assistance program I could support: $1.6 billion in direct aid to help Russia stabilize its economy, including money to provide housing for decommissioned military officers, positive work programs for now underemployed and frequently unpaid nuclear scientists, and more assistance in dismantling nuclear weapons under the recently enacted Nunn-Lugar program; food and medicine for those suffering from shortages; aid to support small business, independent media outlets, nongovernmental organizations, political parties, and labor unions; and an exchange program to bring tens of thousands of students and young professionals to the United States. The aid package was four times what the previous administration had allocated and three times what I had originally recommended.

Although a public poll said that 75 percent of the American people were opposed to giving Russia more money, and we were already in a hard fight for the economic plan, I felt we had no choice but to press ahead. America had spent trillions of dollars in defense to win the Cold War; we couldn't risk reversal over less than $2 billion and a bad poll. To the surprise of my staff, the congressional leaders, including the Republicans, agreed with me. At a meeting I convened to push the plan, Senator Joe Biden, the chairman of the Foreign Relations Committee, strongly endorsed the aid package. Bob Dole came around on the argument that we didn't want to foul up the post–Cold War era the way the victors in World War I had done. Their shortsightedness contributed mightily to World War II, in which Dole had served so heroically. Newt Gingrich was passionately in favor of helping Russia, saying it was a "great defining moment" for America and we had to do the right thing. As I told Strobe, Newt was trying to "out-Russia" me, which I was only too happy to have him do.

When Yeltsin and I got together on April 3, the meeting began a little awkwardly, with Yeltsin explaining that he had to walk a fine line between receiving U.S. assistance to help Russia's transition to democracy and looking as if he was under America's thumb. When we got to the details of our aid package, he said he liked it but needed more for housing for the military people he was bringing home from the Baltic states, many of whom were actually living in tents. After we resolved that issue, Yeltsin abruptly went on the offensive, demanding that I repeal the Jackson-Vanik amendment, a 1974 law tying U.S. trade to free immigration from Russia, and end the observance of Captive Nations Week, which highlighted Soviet domination of countries like Poland and Hungary that were now free. Both these laws were largely symbolic, without real impact on our relations, and I couldn't expend the political capital to change them and at the same time succeed in getting real help to Russia.

After the first session, my people worried that I'd let Yeltsin harangue me the way Khrushchev had hectored

Kennedy in their famous meeting in Vienna in 1961. They didn't want me to look weak. I wasn't worried about that, because the historical analogy was flawed. Yeltsin wasn't trying to make me look bad as Khrushchev had done to Kennedy; he was trying to make himself look good against enemies at home who were trying to do him in. In the week before our summit, they had tried to impeach him in the Duma. They had failed, but the motion got a lot of votes. I could take a little bombastic posturing if it helped to keep Russia on the right road.

In the afternoon, we agreed on a way to institutionalize our cooperation, with a commission headed by Vice President Gore and Russian prime minister Viktor Chernomyrdin. The idea was developed by Strobe and Georgi Mamedov, the Russian deputy foreign minister, and it worked better than any of us could have imagined, thanks largely to the consistent and concentrated efforts made over the years by Al Gore and his Russian counterparts in working through a host of difficult, contentious problems.

On Sunday, April 4, we met in a more formal setting to discuss security issues, with Yeltsin and his advisors sitting across the table from me and mine. As before, Yeltsin began aggressively, demanding that we change our arms control positions and open American markets to Russian products like satellite rocket launchers without requiring export controls that would prohibit Russian sales of military technology to America's adversaries like Iran and Iraq. With the help of our hard-nosed expert, Lynn Davis, I hung tough on export controls and rebuffed the arms control demands by referring them to our staffs for further study.

The atmosphere brightened when we moved on to economics. I described the economics package as "cooperation," not "assistance," then asked Lloyd Bentsen to outline the proposals we would make to the G-7 in Tokyo. Yeltsin became alarmed when he realized that we couldn't get him any money before the April 25 referendum. Though I couldn't give Boris the $500 million check he wanted, at the press conference following our final session I made it plain that a lot of money was coming, because the United States supported Russia's democracy, its reforms, and its leader.

I left Vancouver with more confidence in Yeltsin and a better understanding of the magnitude of his challenges and his visceral determination to overcome them. And I liked him. He was a big bear of a man, full of apparent contradictions. He had grown up in primitive conditions that made my childhood look like a Rockefeller's, and he could be crude, but he had a fine mind capable of grasping the subtleties of a situation. He would attack one minute and embrace the next. He seemed by turns coldly calculating and genuinely emotional, petty and generous, mad at the world and full of fun. Once when we were walking through my hotel together, a Russian journalist asked him if he was happy with our meeting. He responded quickly, "Happy? One cannot be happy outside the presence of a beautiful woman. But I am satisfied." As everyone knows, Yeltsin had a fondness for vodka, but, by and large, in all our dealings he was alert, well prepared, and effective in representing his country. Compared with the realistic alternatives, Russia was lucky to have him at the helm. He loved his country, loathed communism, and wanted Russia to be both great and good. Whenever anyone made a snide remark about Yeltsin's drinking, I was reminded of what Lincoln allegedly said when Washington snobs made the same criticism of General Grant, by far his most aggressive and successful commander in the Civil War: "Find out what he drinks, and give it to the other generals."

When I got back to Washington, I increased the aid package again, proposing $2.5 billion for all the former Soviet states, with two-thirds going to Russia. On April 25, a large majority of Russian voters supported Yeltsin, his policies, and his desire for a new Duma. After a little more than one hundred days in office, we had made great strides in bolstering Yeltsin and Russian democracy. Unfortunately, the same could not be said about our efforts to end the slaughter and ethnic cleansing in Bosnia.

In 1989, as the Soviet Union crumbled and communism's demise in Europe accelerated, the question of what political philosophy would replace it was being answered in different ways in different countries. The westernmost part of the former Soviet empire plainly preferred democracy, a cause championed for decades by immigrants to the United States from Poland, Hungary, Czechoslovakia, and the Baltic states. In Russia, Yeltsin and other democrats were fighting a rear-guard action against Communists and ultra-nationalists. In Yugoslavia, as the nation struggled to reconcile the competing claims of its ethnic and religious constituencies, Serbian nationalism prevailed over democracy under the leadership of the country's dominant political figure, Slobodan Milosevic.

By 1991, Yugoslavia's westernmost provinces, Slovenia and Croatia, both predominantly Catholic, had declared independence from Yugoslavia. Fighting then broke out between Serbia and Croatia, and spilled over into Bosnia, the most ethnically diverse province of Yugoslavia, where Muslims constituted about 45 percent of the population, Serbs were just over 30 percent, and Croatians about 17 percent. The so-called ethnic differences in Bosnia were really political and religious. Bosnia had been the meeting place of three imperial expansions: the Catholic Holy Roman Empire from the west, the Orthodox Christian movement from the east, and the Muslim Ottoman Empire from the south. In 1991, the Bosnians were governed by a coalition of national unity headed by the leading Muslim politician, Alija Izetbegovic, and including the militant Serbian nationalist leader Radovan Karadzic, a Sarajevo psychiatrist.

At first Izetbegovic wanted Bosnia to be an autonomous multi-ethnic, multi-religious province of Yugoslavia. When Slovenia and Croatia were recognized by the international community as independent nations, Izetbegovic decided that the only way Bosnia could escape Serbian dominance was to seek independence, too. Karadzic and his allies, who were tied closely to Milosevic, had a very different agenda. They were supportive of Milosevic's desire to turn as much of Yugoslavia as he could hold on to, including Bosnia, into a Greater Serbia. On March 1, 1992, a referendum was held on whether Bosnia should become an independent nation in which all citizens and groups would be treated equally. The result was an almost unanimous approval of independence, but only two-thirds of the electorate voted. Karadzic had ordered the Serbs to stay away from the polls and most of them did. By then, Serb paramilitary forces had begun killing unarmed Muslims, driving them from their homes in Serb-dominated areas in the hope of carving up Bosnia into ethnic enclaves, or "cantons," by force. This cruel policy came to be known by a curiously antiseptic name: ethnic cleansing.

The European Community envoy, Lord Carrington, tried to get the parties to agree to peacefully divide the country into ethnic regions but failed, because there was no way to do it without leaving large numbers of one group on land controlled by another, and because many Bosnians wanted to keep their country together, with the different groups living together in peace, as they had done successfully for most of the previous five hundred years.

In April 1992, the European Community recognized Bosnia as an independent state for the first time since the fifteenth century. Meanwhile, Serbian paramilitary forces continued to terrorize Muslim communities and kill civilians, all the while using the media to convince local Serbs that it was they who were under attack from the Muslims and who had to defend themselves. On April 27, Milosevic announced a new state of Yugoslavia comprising Serbia and Montenegro. He then made a show of withdrawing his army from Bosnia, while leaving armaments, supplies, and Bosnian Serb soldiers under the leadership of his handpicked commander, Ratko Mladic. The fighting and killing raged throughout 1992, with European Community leaders struggling to contain it and the Bush administration, uncertain of what to do and unwilling to take on another problem in an election year, content to leave the matter in Europe's hands.

To its credit, the Bush administration did urge the United Nations to impose economic sanctions on Serbia, a measure initially opposed by Secretary-General Boutros Boutros-Ghali, the French, and the British, who said they wanted to give Milosevic a chance to stop the very violence he had incited. Finally, sanctions were imposed in late May, but with little effect, as supplies continued to reach the Serbs from friendly neighbors. The United Nations also continued to maintain the arms embargo against the Bosnian government that originally had been imposed against all Yugoslavia in late 1991. The problem with the embargo was that the Serbs had enough weapons and ammunition on hand to fight for years; therefore, the only consequence of maintaining the embargo was to make it virtually impossible for the Bosnians to defend themselves. Somehow they managed to hold out throughout 1992, acquiring some arms by capturing them from Serb forces, or in small shipments from Croatia that managed to evade the NATO blockade of the Croatian coast.

In the summer of 1992, as television and print media finally brought the horror of a Serb-run detention camp in northern Bosnia home to Europeans and Americans, I spoke out in favor of NATO air strikes with U.S. involvement. Later, when it became clear that the Serbs were engaging in the systematic slaughter of Bosnian Muslims, especially targeting local leaders for extermination, I suggested lifting the arms embargo. Instead, the Europeans focused on ending the violence. British prime minister John Major attempted to get the Serbs to lift the siege of Bosnian towns and put their heavy weapons under UN supervision. At the same time, many private and government humanitarian missions were launched to provide food and medicine, and the United Nations sent in eight thousand troops to protect the aid convoys.

In late October, just before our election, Lord David Owen, the new European negotiator, and the UN negotiator, former U.S. secretary of state Cyrus Vance, put forward a proposal to turn Bosnia into a number of autonomous provinces that would be responsible for all government functions except defense and foreign affairs, which would be handled by a weak central government. The cantons were sufficiently numerous, with the dominant ethnic groups geographically divided in a way that Vance and Owen thought would make it impossible for the Serb-controlled areas to merge with Milosevic's Yugoslavia to form a Greater Serbia. There were several problems with their plan, the two largest of which were that the sweeping powers of the canton governments made it clear that Muslims couldn't safely return to their homes in Serb-controlled areas, and that the vagueness of the canton boundaries invited continued Serb aggression intended to expand their areas, as well as the ongoing, though less severe, conflict between Croats and Muslims.

By the time I became President, the arms embargo and European support for the Vance-Owen plan had weakened Muslim resistance to the Serbs, even as evidence of their slaughter of Muslim civilians and violations of human rights in detention camps continued to surface. In early February, I decided not to endorse the Vance-Owen plan. On the fifth, I met with Prime Minister Brian Mulroney of Canada and was pleased to hear him say he didn't like it either. A few days later, we completed a Bosnian policy review, with Warren Christopher announcing that the United States would like to negotiate a new agreement and would be willing to help enforce it.

On February 23, UN Secretary-General Boutros-Ghali agreed with me on an emergency plan to airdrop humanitarian supplies to the Bosnians. The next day, in my first meeting with John Major, he too supported the airdrops. The airdrops would help a lot of people stay alive, but would do nothing to address the causes of the crisis.

By March, we seemed to be making some progress.

Economic sanctions had been strengthened and seemed to be hurting the Serbs, who were also concerned about the possibility of military action by NATO. But we were a long way from a unified policy. On the ninth, in my first meeting with French president François Mitterrand, he made clear to me that, although he had sent five thousand French troops to Bosnia as part of a UN humanitarian force to deliver aid and contain the violence, he was more sympathetic to the Serbs than I was, and less willing to see a Muslim-led unified Bosnia.

On the twenty-sixth, I met with Helmut Kohl, who deplored what was happening and who, like me, had favored lifting the arms embargo. But we couldn't budge the British and French, who felt lifting the embargo would only prolong the war and endanger the UN forces on the ground that included their troops but not ours. Izetbegovic was also in the White House on the twenty-sixth to meet with Al Gore, whose national security aide, Leon Fuerth, was responsible for our success in making the embargo more effective. Both Kohl and I told Izetbegovic we were doing our best to get the Europeans to take a stronger stand to support him. Five days later, we succeeded in getting the United Nations to extend a "no fly" zone over all of Bosnia, to at least deprive the Serbs of the benefit of their monopoly on airpower. It was a good thing to do, but it didn't slow the killing much.

In April, a team of U.S. military, diplomatic, and humanitarian aid personnel returned from Bosnia urging that we intervene militarily to stop the suffering. On the sixteenth, the United Nations accepted our recommendation for declaring a "safe area" around Srebrenica, a town in eastern Bosnia where Serb killing and ethnic cleansing had been especially outrageous. On the twenty-second, at the dedication of the U.S. Holocaust Memorial Museum, Holocaust survivor Elie Wiesel publicly pleaded with me to do more to stop the violence. By the end of the month, my foreign policy team recommended that if we could not secure a Serbian cease-fire, we should lift the arms embargo against the Muslims and launch air strikes against Serb military targets. As Warren Christopher left for Europe to seek support for this policy, the Bosnian Serb leader, Radovan Karadzic, hoping to avoid the air strikes, finally signed the UN peace plan, even though his assembly had rejected it just six days earlier. I didn't believe for a minute that his signature signaled a change in his long-term objectives.

At the end of our first one hundred days, we were nowhere near a satisfactory solution to the Bosnian crisis. The British and French rebuffed Warren Christopher's overtures and reaffirmed their right to take the lead in dealing with the situation. The problem with their position, of course, was that if the Serbs could take the economic hit of the tough sanctions, they could continue their aggressive ethnic cleansing without fear of further punishment. The Bosnian tragedy would drag on for more than two years, leaving more than 250,000 dead and 2.5 million driven from their homes, until NATO air attacks, aided by Serb military losses on the ground, led to an American diplomatic initiative that would bring the war to an end.

I had stepped into what Dick Holbrooke called "the greatest collective security failure of the West since the 1930s." In his book **To End a War,** Holbrooke ascribes the failure to five factors: (1) a misreading of Balkan history, holding that the ethnic strife was too ancient and ingrained to be prevented by outsiders; (2) the apparent loss of Yugoslavia's strategic importance after the end of the Cold War; (3) the triumph of nationalism over democracy as the dominant ideology of post-Communist Yugoslavia; (4) the reluctance of the Bush administration to undertake another military commitment so soon after the 1991 Iraq war; and (5) the decision of the United States to turn the issue over to Europe instead of NATO, and the confused and passive European response. To Holbrooke's list I would add a sixth factor: some European leaders were not eager to have a Muslim state in the heart of the Balkans, fearing it might become a base for exporting extremism, a result that their neglect made more, not less, likely.

My own options were constrained by the dug-in positions I found when I took office. For example, I was reluctant to go along with Senator Dole in unilaterally lifting the arms embargo, for fear of weakening the United Nations (though we later did so in effect, by declining to enforce it). I also didn't want to divide the NATO alliance by unilaterally bombing Serb military positions, especially since there were European, but no American, soldiers on the ground with the UN mission. And I didn't want to send American troops there, putting them in harm's way under a UN mandate I thought was bound to fail. In May 1993, we were still a long way from a solution.

At the end of the first one hundred days of a new presidency, the press always does an assessment of how well the new administration is doing in keeping its campaign promises and dealing with the other challenges that have arisen. The consensus of the reviews was that my initial performance was mixed. On the positive side of the ledger, I had created a National Economic Council in the

White House and put together an ambitious economic program to reverse twelve years of trickle-down economics, and it was making progress in the Congress. I had signed the family leave law, and the "motor voter" law to make voter registration easier, and had reversed the Reagan-Bush abortion policies, including the ban on fetal-tissue research and the gag rule. I had reduced the size of the White House staff, despite its increasing workload; for example, we received more mail in the first three and a half months than had come to the White House in all of 1992. I had also ordered a reduction of 100,000 in total federal employment, and put Vice President Gore in charge of finding new savings and better ways to serve the public with a "reinventing government" initiative whose considerable results would eventually prove the skeptics wrong. I had sent legislation to Congress to create my national service program, to double the Earned Income Tax Credit and create empowerment zones in poor communities, and to dramatically cut the cost of college loans, saving billions of dollars for both students and taxpayers. I had put health-care reform on a fast track and had taken strong action to strengthen democracy and reform in Russia. And I was blessed with a hardworking and able staff and cabinet who, apart from the leaks, worked well together, without the backbiting and infighting that had characterized many previous administrations. After a slow start, I had filled more required presidential appointments in the first hundred days than President Reagan or President Bush had in the same period of time, not bad considering how cumbersome and overly intrusive the whole appointments process had become. At one point, Senator Alan Simpson, the witty Republican whip from Wyoming, joked to me that the process was so overdone that he "wouldn't even want to have dinner with someone who could be confirmed by the U.S. Senate."

On the negative side, I had temporarily dropped the middle-class tax cut in the face of the growing deficit; lost the stimulus program to a Republican filibuster; maintained the Bush policy of forcibly returning Haitian refugees, though we were taking in more Haitians by other means; lost the gays-in-the-military fight; delayed presenting the health-care plan beyond my hundred-day goal; mishandled at least the public part of the Waco raid; and failed to convince Europe to join with the United States in taking a stronger stand in Bosnia, although we had increased humanitarian aid, strengthened sanctions against Serbia, and created an enforceable no-fly zone.

One reason my scorecard was mixed was that I was trying to do so much in the face of determined Republican opposition and mixed feelings among the American people about how much government could or should do. After all, the people had been told for twelve years that government was the source of all our problems, and was so incompetent it couldn't organize a two-car parade. Clearly, I had overestimated how much I could do in a hurry. The country had been going in one direction for more than a decade, living with wedge politics, reassuring bromides about how great we were, and the illusory, though fleeting, comforts of spending more and taxing less today and ignoring the consequences for tomorrow. It was going to take more than a hundred days to turn things around.

In addition to the pace of change, I may have overestimated the amount of change I could achieve, as well as how much of it the American people could digest. In one post–hundred-days analysis, a Vanderbilt University political scientist, Erwin Hargrove, observed, "I wonder whether the president isn't spreading himself too thin." He was probably right, but there was so much to do, and I didn't stop trying to do it all at once until the voters hit me between the eyes with a two-by-four in the 1994 midterm elections. I had let my sense of urgency blot out the memory of another of my laws of politics: Everyone is for change in general, but against it in particular, when they themselves have to change.

The public struggles of the first hundred days didn't occur in a vacuum; at the same time, my family was adjusting to a dramatic change in our way of life and dealing with the loss of Hillary's dad. I loved being President and Hillary was deeply committed to her health-care work. Chelsea liked her school and was making new friends. We enjoyed living in the White House, hosting the social events, and having our friends stay with us.

The White House staff was getting used to a first family that kept longer, and later, hours. Though I came to rely on them and greatly value their service, it took me a while to get used to all the help I had in the White House. As governor, I'd lived in a mansion with a fine staff, and had been driven everywhere by the state police security detail. But on weekends, Hillary and I usually cooked for ourselves, and I drove the car to church on Sundays. Now I had valets who laid my clothes out every morning, packed for my trips, and went along to unpack and steam the wrinkles out; butlers who stayed late, came early, and worked weekends, serving me food and bringing me diet drinks and coffee; navy stewards who performed those same functions when I was in the Oval Office and traveling; a kitchen staff who prepared food for us even on weekends; ushers to take me up and down in the elevator and bring me papers to sign and memos to read at all hours; round-the-clock medical care; and the Secret Service, who wouldn't even let me ride in the front seat, much less drive.

One of the things I liked best about living in the White House was the fresh flowers that filled the residence and office spaces. The White House always had beautifully arranged flowers. It's one of the things I would miss most after I left.

When we moved in, Hillary redid the little kitchen so that we could eat dinner there at night when it was just the three of us. The upstairs dining room was beautiful, but too big and formal for our taste unless we had guests. Hillary also fixed up the solarium on the third floor, a bright room that leads out to a balcony and the White House roof. We turned it into a family room. Whenever we had relatives or friends staying with us, we always gravitated to the solarium, to talk, watch TV, and play cards or board games. I became addicted to Master Boggle and a game called UpWords; it's basically a three-dimensional Scrabble game in which you get more points not by using odd letters or landing on certain spaces, but by building words upon words. I tried to get my family and friends into UpWords, succeeding with some more than others. My brother-in-law Hugh played countless games of UpWords with me, and Roger liked it. But Hillary, Tony, and Chelsea preferred our old standby, pinochle. I continued to play hearts with my staff and we all got hooked on a new card game that Steven Spielberg and Kate Capshaw taught us when they were visiting. It had a perfect name for Washington political life: Oh Hell!

The Secret Service had been with me since the New Hampshire primary, but once I got into the White House,

I presented a challenge to them with my morning jogs. I had several jogging routes. Sometimes I drove out to Haines Point, which had a three-mile route around a public golf course. It was flat, but could be tough in the winter when the winds off the Potomac were strong. From time to time I also ran at Fort McNair, which has an oval route on the grounds of the National Defense University. My favorite jog by far was just to run out the Southwest Gate of the White House to the Mall, then up to the Lincoln Memorial, back down to the Capitol, and home. I met a lot of interesting people on those runs, and never tired of running through American history. When the Secret Service finally asked me to stop because of security concerns, I did, but I missed it. To me, these public runs were a way to keep in touch with the world beyond the White House. To them, with the memory of John Hinckley's assassination attempt on President Reagan never far from their minds and with more knowledge than I had of the hate mail I was getting, my contacts with the public were a worrisome risk to be managed.

Al Gore helped me a lot in the early days, encouraging me to keep making hard decisions and put them behind me, and giving me a continuing crash course in how Washington works. Part of our regular routine was having lunch alone in my private dining room once a week. We took turns saying grace, then proceeded to talk about everything from our families to sports, books, and movies to the latest items on his agenda or mine. We kept our lunch schedule up for eight years, except when one of us was gone for several days at a stretch. Though we had a lot in common, we were very different, and the lunches kept us closer than we otherwise would have been in the Washington pressure cooker, and eased my adjustment to my new life.

All things considered, I felt pretty good, personally and politically, about the first one hundred days. Still, I was under a lot of stress. So was Hillary. For all our excitement and commitment, we were tired going in, not having taken any real time off after the election. Then we were denied the honeymoon traditionally given new Presidents, partly because of the way the gays-in-the military issue surfaced early, perhaps because we made the press angry by restricting access to the West Wing. Hillary's father's death was a painful loss to her. I missed Hugh, too, and for a while, it was harder for both of us to operate at the top of our games. Though we very much enjoyed the work, the physical and emotional toll of the first hundred days was considerable.

THIRTY-THREE

W hile deficit reduction was essential to my economic strategy, it was not sufficient to build a sustained, widely shared recovery. In the early months, we filled out the agenda with initiatives to expand trade, increase investment in education and training, and promote a host of micro-economic issues aimed at particular trouble spots or targets of opportunity. For example, I offered proposals to help military and civilian personnel who had lost their jobs as a result of the post–Cold War decline in defense spending; urged our major federal research labs—Los Alamos and Sandia in New Mexico, and Livermore in California—to use the massive scientific and technological resources that had helped win the Cold War to develop new technologies with commercial applications; announced a micro-loan program to support budding entrepreneurs, including welfare recipients eager to get off the rolls, who often had good ideas but couldn't meet the credit standards of traditional lenders; increased the volume of Small Business Administration loans, especially to women and minorities; and named a National Commission to Ensure a Strong and Competitive Airline Industry, chaired by former Virginia governor Jerry Baliles. The airline manufacturers and carriers were in trouble because of the economic downturn, fewer orders for military planes, and stiff competition from the European manufacturer Airbus.

I also offered plans to help communities develop commercial uses for the military facilities that would be closed as defense was downsized. As governor, I had dealt with the closing of an air force base, and I was determined to give more aid to those facing the same challenge now. Since California was, by itself, the world's sixth-largest economy, and it had been hit especially hard by defense downsizing and other problems, we developed a special plan to promote recovery there. John Emerson had the responsibility of riding herd on the project and other matters of concern to his native state. He was so unrelenting in doing so that he became known around the White House as the "Secretary of California."

One of the most effective things we did was to reform the regulations governing financial institutions under the 1977 Community Reinvestment Act. The law required federally insured lenders to make an extra effort to give loans to low- and modest-income borrowers, but before 1993 it had never had much impact. After the changes we made, between 1993 and 2000, banks would offer more than $800 billion in home mortgage, small-business, and community development loans to borrowers covered by the law, a staggering figure that amounted to well over 90 percent of all the loans made in the twenty-three years of the Community Reinvestment Act.

May was an interesting month, and valuable for my continuing political education. On the fifth, I awarded my first Presidential Medal of Freedom to my old mentor Senator Fulbright on his eighty-eighth birthday. Al Gore's father was at the ceremony, and when he reminded Fulbright that he himself was only eighty-five, Fulbright replied, "Albert, if you behave yourself, you'll make it, too." I admired both men for what they'd done for America; I wondered if I would live as long as they had; if so, I hoped I could wear the years as well.

In the third week of the month, I went to California to emphasize the investments in the economic plan for education and inner-city development at a town hall meeting in San Diego, a community college in Van Nuys with a large Hispanic enrollment, and a sporting-goods store in South Central Los Angeles where the riots had occurred a year earlier. I especially enjoyed the last event. The athletic store, called the Playground, had a basketball court out back, which had become a gathering place for young people. Ron Brown was with me, and we took some of the kids and played each other in an impromptu basketball game, after which I talked about the potential of empowerment zones to create more successful businesses like the Playground in poor communities all across America. I'm pretty sure this was the first time a President ever played basketball with inner-city kids in their backyard, and I hoped that pictures of the game would send a message to America about the new administration's priorities, and to young people in particular that I cared about them and their futures.

Unfortunately, most Americans never heard about the basketball game because I got a haircut. I hadn't found a barber in Washington yet; I couldn't go back to Arkansas every three weeks to see Jim Miles, and my hair was too long. Hillary had had her hair done by a man in Los Angeles, Cristophe Schatteman, who was a friend of the Thomasons and whom I liked very much. I asked Cristophe if he would be willing to give me a quick trim. He agreed to do it and met me in my private quarters on Air Force One. Before we started, I asked the Secret Service not once, but twice, to make sure I wouldn't cause any delay in takeoffs or landings if I put off our departure for a few minutes. They checked with the airport personnel, who said it would be no problem. Then I asked Cristophe just to make me presentable as quickly as possible. He did, in ten minutes or so, and we took off.

The next thing I knew, there was a story out that I had kept two runways tied up for an hour, inconveniencing thousands of people, while I got a $200 haircut from a fancy hairdresser who was known only by his first name. Forget the basketball game with inner-city kids; the irresistible news was that I had shed my Arkansas roots and populist politics for an expensive indulgence. It was a great story, but it wasn't true. First of all, I didn't pay $200 for the ten-minute trim. Second, I didn't keep anybody waiting to take off or land, as the Federal Aviation Administration records showed when they were finally released a few weeks later. I was appalled that anyone would think I'd do such a thing. I might have been President, but Mother would still have given me a whipping if I'd kept a lot of people waiting an hour while I got a haircut, much less a $200 one.

The haircut story was crazy. I didn't handle it well, because I got angry, which is always a mistake. A big part of its attraction was that Cristophe was a Hollywood hairdresser. Many people in Washington's political and press establishment have a love-hate relationship with Hollywood. They like to mix with movie and television stars but tend to view the entertainment community's political interests and commitments as somehow less authentic than their own. In fact, most people in both groups are good citizens with a lot in common. Someone once said that politics is show business for ugly people.

A few weeks later, **Newsday,** a Long Island newspaper,

obtained the Federal Aviation Administration records of flight activities at the Los Angeles airport that day, proving that the reported delays had never occurred. **USA Today** and a few other papers also printed a correction.

One thing that probably kept the haircut story alive and mostly uncorrected was something that had nothing to do with it. On May 19, on the advice of David Watkins, who was in charge of administrative operations at the White House, and with the concurrence of the White House counsel's office, Mack McLarty fired the seven employees of the White House Travel Office. The office makes all arrangements for the press when they travel with the President, and bills their employers for the costs. Hillary and I had both asked Mack to look into the Travel Office operations because she was told that the office allowed no competitive bidding on its charter flights, and I got a complaint from a White House reporter about bad meals and high costs. After an audit by the accounting firm KPMG Peat Marwick turned up an off-the-books ledger with $18,000 not properly accounted for and other irregularities, the employees were dismissed.

Once I mentioned the reporter's complaint to Mack, I forgot all about the Travel Office until the firings were announced. The reaction of the press corps was extremely negative. They liked the way they had been cared for, especially on foreign trips. And they had known the people in the Travel Office for years and couldn't imagine that they would do anything wrong. Many in the press felt the Travel Office staff virtually worked for them, not the White House, and felt they should have at least been notified, if not fully consulted, as the investigation proceeded. Despite the criticism, the reconstituted Travel Office provided the same services with fewer federal employees at lower costs to the press.

The Travel Office affair proved to be a particularly powerful example of the culture clash between the new White House and the established political press. The director of the Travel Office was later indicted for embezzlement based on Travel Office funds found in his personal account, and, according to press reports, he offered to plead guilty to a lesser charge and spend a few months in jail. Instead, the prosecutor insisted on going to trial on the felony charge. After several famous journalists testified for him as character witnesses, he was acquitted. Despite investigations of the Travel Office by the White House, the General Accounting Office, the FBI, and the independent counsel's office, no evidence of wrongdoing, conflicts of interest, or criminality by anyone at the White House was ever found, nor did anyone dispute the Travel Office's financial problems and mismanagement found in the Peat Marwick audit.

I couldn't believe the American people were seeing me primarily through the prism of the haircut, the Travel Office, and gays in the military. Instead of a President fighting to change America for the better, I was being portrayed as a man who had abandoned down-home for uptown, a knee-jerk liberal whose mask of moderation had been removed. I had recently done a television interview in Cleveland in which a man said he no longer supported me because I was spending all my time on gays in the military and Bosnia. I replied that I'd just done an analysis of how I'd spent my time in the first hundred days: 55 percent on the economy and health care, 25 percent on foreign policy, 20 percent on other domestic issues. When he asked how much time I'd spent on gays in the military, and I told him just a few hours, he simply replied, "I don't believe you." All he knew was what he read and saw.

The Cleveland encounter and the haircut and Travel Office fiascoes were object lessons about how little all of us outsiders knew about what mattered in Washington, and how the failure of understanding could blot out our efforts to communicate what we were doing to improve what really mattered to the rest of America. A few years later, Doug Sosnik, one of my wittiest staffers, coined a phrase that captured the buzz saw we had walked into. When we were about to leave for Oslo on a trip to promote the Middle East peace process, Sharon Farmer, my lively African-American photographer, said she wasn't looking forward to the trip to cold Norway. "That's okay, Sharon," Doug replied. "It's not a 'home game' for you. Nobody likes the 'away games.' " Midway through 1993, I was just hoping my entire term wouldn't be one long "away game."

I did some serious thinking about the trouble I was in. It seemed to me that the roots of the problem were these: the White House staff had too little experience in, and too few connections with, Washington's established power centers; we were trying to do too many things at once, creating an impression of disarray and preventing the people from hearing what we had actually accomplished; our lack of a clear message made otherwise minor issues look as if I was governing on the cultural and political left, not from the dynamic center, as I had promised; the impression was being reinforced by the one-note Republican attack that my budget plan was nothing but a big tax increase; and I had been blind to the considerable political obstacles I faced. I was elected with 43 percent of the vote; I had underestimated how hard it would be to turn Washington around after twelve years on a very different course, and how politically—even psychologically—jarring the changes would be to Washington's main players; many Republicans never considered my presidency legitimate in the first place and were acting accordingly; and the Congress, with a Democratic majority with its own way of doing things and a Republican minority determined to prove I was too liberal and couldn't govern, was not about to pass all the legislation I wanted as quickly as I wanted to pass it.

I knew I had to change, but just like everyone else, I found that was harder to do myself than to recommend to others. Still, I managed to make two changes that were particularly helpful. I persuaded David Gergen, a friend from Renaissance Weekend and veteran of three Republican administrations, to come into the White House as counselor to the President, to help us with organization and communication. In his **U.S. News & World Report** column David had given some thoughtful advice, some of it quite critical, with which I agreed; he liked and respected Mack McLarty; he was a bona fide member of the Washington establishment who thought and kept score the way they did; and for the sake of the country, he wanted us to succeed. For the next several months, David had a calming impact on the White House, immediately moving to improve relations with the press by restoring their direct access to the communications office, something we should have done long before.

Along with Gergen's appointment, we made some other staff changes: Mark Gearan, Mack McLarty's able and popular deputy chief of staff, would replace George

Stephanopoulos as communications director, with Dee Dee Myers staying as press secretary and taking over the daily briefings; and George would move to a new senior advisor position, to help me coordinate policy, strategy, and day-to-day decisions. At first he was disappointed not to be doing the daily press briefings any longer, but he soon mastered a job much like the one he had done in the campaign, and he did it so well that his influence and impact within the White House increased.

The other positive change we made was to unclutter my day, providing two hours in the middle of most days for me to read, think, rest, and make phone calls. It would make a big difference.

Things were looking up by the end of the month, when the House passed my budget, 219–213. The Senate then took it up, and immediately scrapped the BTU tax in favor of a 4.3-cents-a-gallon increase in the gasoline tax and more spending cuts. The bad news was that the gas tax would promote less energy conservation than the BTU tax; the good news was that it would cost middle-class Americans less, only about $33 a year.

On May 31, my first Memorial Day as President, after the traditional ceremony in Arlington National Cemetery, I went to another ceremony at the newly opened section of the Vietnam Veterans Memorial, a long black marble wall with the names of all the members of the U.S. armed forces who had been killed or were missing in the war etched on it. Early that morning I had jogged over to the wall from the White House to look at the names of my friends from Hot Springs. I knelt at the spot where my friend Bert Jeffries's name was, touched it, and said a prayer.

I knew it would be a tough event, full of people for whom the Vietnam War continued to be the defining moment in their lives and to whom the thought of someone like me as Commander in Chief was abhorrent. But I was determined to go, to face those who still held my views on Vietnam against me, and to tell all Vietnam veterans that I honored their service and that of their fallen comrades and would work to resolve the still-open cases of prisoners of war and soldiers still listed as missing in action.

Colin Powell introduced me with conviction and class, strongly signaling the respect he thought I should receive as Commander in Chief. Nevertheless, when I got up to speak, loud protesters attempted to drown me out. I spoke to them directly:

> To all of you who are shouting, I have heard you. I ask you now to hear me. . . . Some have suggested that it is wrong for me to be here with you today because I did not agree a quarter of a century ago with the decision made to send the young men and women to battle in Vietnam. Well, so much the better. . . . Just as war is freedom's cost, disagreement is freedom's privilege, and we honor it here today. . . . The message of this memorial is quite simple: these men and women fought for freedom, brought honor to their communities, loved their country, and died for it. . . . There's not a person in this crowd today who did not know someone on this wall. Four of my high school classmates are there. . . . Let us continue to disagree, if we must, about the war. But let us not let it divide us as a people any longer.

The event started roughly, but ended well. Robert McNamara's prediction that my election had ended the

Vietnam War wasn't quite accurate, but maybe we were getting there.

June began with a disappointment that was both personal and political, as I withdrew my nomination of Lani Guinier, a University of Pennsylvania professor, a longtime lawyer for the NAACP Legal Defense Fund, and my law school classmate, to be the first career civil rights lawyer to head the Civil Rights Division. After I named her in April, the conservatives went after Guinier with a vengeance, attacking her as a "quota queen" and accusing her of advocating the abandonment of the constitutional principle of "one man, one vote" because she had supported a system of cumulative voting, under which each voter would get as many votes as there are contested seats on a legislative body, and could cast all the votes for a single candidate. In theory, cumulative voting would dramatically increase the odds of minority candidates being elected.

At first, I didn't pay too much attention to the rantings of the right, thinking that what they really disliked about Guinier was her long record of successful civil rights fights, and that, as she made the rounds of the Senate, she would win enough votes to be confirmed easily.

I was wrong. My friend Senator David Pryor came to see me and urged me to withdraw Lani's nomination, saying that her interviews with the senators were going poorly, and reminding me that we also had an economic program to pass and not a vote to spare. Majority Leader George Mitchell, who had been a federal judge before he came to the Senate, strongly agreed with David; he said Lani couldn't be confirmed and we needed to end it as soon as possible. I was informed that Senators Ted Kennedy and Carol Moseley Braun, the Senate's only African-American member, felt the same way.

I decided I had better read Lani's articles. They made a persuasive case for her position, but were in conflict with my support for affirmative action and opposition to quotas, and seemed to abandon one man, one vote in favor of one man, many votes: spread them out however you like.

I asked her to come see me so that we could talk it through. As we discussed the problem in the Oval Office, Lani was understandably offended by the battering she had taken, amazed that anyone would see the academic musings in her articles as a serious obstacle to her confirmation, and dismissive of the difficulties her nomination presented to the senators whose votes she needed, perhaps through several filibusters. My staff had told her we didn't have the votes to confirm her, but she declined to withdraw, feeling she had a right to be voted on. Finally, I told her that I felt I had to withdraw her nomination, that I hated to do it, but we were going to lose, and though it was cold comfort, her withdrawal would make her a heroine in the civil rights community.

In the aftermath, I was heavily criticized for abandoning a friend in the face of political pressure, mostly by people who didn't know what was going on in the background. Eventually, I nominated Deval Patrick, another brilliant African-American lawyer with a strong civil rights background, to lead the Civil Rights Division, and he did a fine job. I still admire Lani Guinier, and regret that I lost her friendship.

I spent much of the first two weeks of June picking a Supreme Court justice. A few weeks earlier, Byron "Whizzer" White had announced his retirement after thirty-one years on the High Court. As I said earlier, I first wanted to appoint Governor Mario Cuomo, but he wasn't interested. After reviewing more than forty candidates, I settled on three: my Interior Secretary Bruce Babbitt, who had been attorney general of Arizona before becoming governor; Judge Stephen Breyer, chief judge of the First Circuit Court of Appeals in Boston, who had compiled an impressive record on the bench; and Judge Ruth Bader Ginsburg of the United States Court of Appeals for the District of Columbia circuit, a brilliant woman with a compelling life story whose record was interesting, independent, and progressive. I met with Babbitt and Breyer and was convinced they both would be good justices, but I hated to lose Babbitt at Interior, as did large numbers of environmentalists who called the White House to urge that I keep him there, and Breyer had a minor "nanny" problem, though Senator Kennedy, who was pushing him hard, assured me that he would be confirmed.

Like everything else that happened in the White House in the early months, my interviews with both men leaked, so I decided to see Ginsburg in my private office in the residence of the White House on a Sunday night. I was tremendously impressed with her. I thought that she had the potential to become a great justice, and that, at the least, she could do the three things I felt a new justice needed to do on the Rehnquist Court, which was closely divided between moderates and conservatives: decide cases on the merits, not on ideology or the identities of the parties; work with the conservative Republican justices to reach consensus when possible; and stand up to them when necessary. In one of her articles, Ginsburg had written: "The greatest figures of the American judiciary have been independent thinking individuals with open but not empty minds; individuals willing to listen and to learn. They have exhibited a readiness to reexamine their own premises, liberal or conservative, as thoroughly as those of others."

When we announced her appointment, it hadn't leaked. The press had written that I intended to appoint Breyer, based on a tip from a leaker who didn't know what he was talking about. After Judge Ginsburg made her brief but moving statement, one of the reporters said her appointment gave the impression that my decision to appoint her, rather than Breyer, reflected a certain "zig-zag quality" to the process of decision making in the White House. He then asked whether I could refute that impression. I didn't know whether to laugh or cry. I replied, "I have long since given up the thought that I could disabuse some of you of turning any substantive decision into anything but political process." Apparently, when it came to appointments, the name of the game wasn't supposed to be "follow the leader" but "follow the leaker." I have to confess that I was almost as happy about surprising the press as I was with the choice I had made.

In the last week of June, the Senate finally passed my budget by only 50–49, with one Democrat and one Republican not voting, and Al Gore breaking the tie. No Republican voted for it, and we lost six conservative Democrats. Senator David Boren of Oklahoma, whom I had known since 1974, when he first ran for governor and I ran for Congress, gave us a vote to stave off defeat, but indicated that he would oppose the final bill unless it contained more spending cuts and fewer taxes.

Now that the Senate and House had approved the budget plans, they would have to reconcile their differences and then we'd have to fight for passage in both houses all over again. Since we had won by such small margins in both places, any concession made by one chamber to the other could lose a vote or two, all it would take to defeat the whole package. Roger Altman came over from Treasury with his chief of staff, Josh Steiner, to set up a "war room" to organize the campaign for final passage. We needed to know where every vote was, and what we could argue or offer to wavering members to get a majority. After all the blood we'd spilled over minor issues, this was a fight worth making. For the next six and a half weeks, the economic future of the country, not to mention the future of my presidency, hung in the balance.

On the day after the Senate passed the budget, I ordered the military into action for the first time, firing twenty-three Tomahawk missiles into Iraq's intelligence headquarters, in retaliation for a plot to assassinate President George H. W. Bush during a trip he had made to Kuwait. More than a dozen people involved in the plot had been arrested in Kuwait on April 13, one day before the former President had been scheduled to arrive. The materials in their possession were conclusively traced to Iraqi intelligence, and on May 19 one of the arrested Iraqis confirmed to the FBI that the Iraqi intelligence service was behind the plot. I asked the Pentagon to recommend a course of action, and General Powell came to me with the missile attack on the intelligence headquarters as both a proportionate response and an effective deterrent. I felt we would have been justified in hitting Iraq harder, but Powell made a persuasive case that the attack would deter further Iraqi terrorism, and that dropping bombs on more targets, including presidential palaces, would have been unlikely to kill Saddam Hussein and almost certain to kill more innocent people. Most of the Tomahawks hit the target, but four of them overshot, three landing in an upscale Baghdad neighborhood and killing eight civilians. It was a stark reminder that no matter how careful the planning and how accurate the weapons, when that kind of fire-power is unleashed, there are usually unintended consequences.

On July 6, I was in Tokyo for my first international meeting, the sixteenth annual G-7 summit. Historically, these meetings had been talkfests, with few meaningful policy commitments and little follow-up coming out of them. We didn't have the luxury of another meeting where nothing happened. The world economy was dragging, with growth in Europe the slowest in more than a decade, and in Japan the slowest in nearly two decades. We were making some headway on the economic front; in the last five months, over 950,000 more Americans had found work, about as many new jobs as the economy had produced in the previous three years.

I went to Japan with an agenda: to get the agreement of European and Japanese leaders to coordinate their internal economic policies with ours, in order to raise the level of global growth; convince Europe and Japan to drop tariffs on manufacturing goods, which would create jobs in all our countries and increase the chances of finishing the seven-year-old Uruguay Round of world trade talks by the December 15 deadline; and send a clear, unified signal of financial and political support for Yeltsin and Russian democracy.

The odds of success on any of these items, much less all three, were not great, in part because none of the leaders were particularly strong coming into the meeting. Between the tough medicine in my economic plan and the bad press over problems, both real and imagined, my public approval had dropped steeply since the inauguration. John Major was hanging on in England, but was hurt by constant unfavorable comparison to his predecessor, Margaret Thatcher, something the Iron Lady did nothing to discourage. François Mitterrand was a fascinating, brilliant man, a Socialist in his second seven-year term, who was limited in what he could deliver by the fact that the French prime minister and his governing coalition, who controlled economic policy, were from opposing political parties. Carlo Ciampi, the Italian prime minister, was a former governor of the Italian Central Bank and a modest man who was known for riding his bicycle to work. Despite his intelligence and appeal, he was hampered by the fractured and inherently unstable Italian political environment. Kim Campbell, Canada's first female prime minister, was an impressive, clearly dedicated person who had just taken office after the resignation of Brian Mulroney. She was essentially finishing Mulroney's long run at the helm, with the polls showing a rising tide of support for the opposition leader, Jean Chrétien. Our host, Kiichi Miyazawa, was widely regarded as a lame duck in a Japanese political system in which the long monopoly of the Liberal Democratic Party was coming to an end. Miyazawa may have been a lame duck, but he was an impressive one, with sophisticated understanding of the world. He spoke colloquial English about as well as I did. And he was also a patriot who wanted the G-7 meeting to reflect well on his country.

The conventional wisdom held that Helmut Kohl, the long-serving German chancellor, was also in trouble, because his poll numbers were down and his Christian Democratic Party had suffered some recent losses in local elections, but I thought Kohl still had plenty of life in his leadership. He was a huge man, about my height and weighing well over three hundred pounds. He spoke with great conviction in a direct, often brusque manner, and he was a world-class storyteller with a good sense of humor. And in more than size he was the largest figure on the European continent in decades. He had reunified Germany, funneling massive sums of money from West to East Germany to lift the incomes of those who had made far less under communism. Kohl's Germany had become the largest financial supporter of Russian democracy. He was also the leading force behind the emerging European Union, and he was in favor of admitting Poland, Hungary, and the Czech Republic into both the EU and the NATO alliance. Finally, Kohl was deeply troubled by Europe's passivity in Bosnia and thought, as I did, that the United Nations should lift the arms embargo because it was unfair to the Bosnian Muslims. On all the great questions facing Europe, he was on the right side, and pushing hard for his point of view. He felt if he got the big things right, the polls would follow. I liked Helmut Kohl a lot. Over the next several years, through many meals, visits, and phone calls, we would forge a political and personal bond that would bear great fruit for Europeans and Americans alike.

I was optimistic about the prospects for the G-7 because I was bringing a strong agenda to the meeting and because I believed all the other leaders were smart enough to know that the best way to get out of trouble at home was to do something meaningful in Tokyo. Just as the conference opened, we crossed one threshold, when our trade ministers agreed that all of us would lower tariffs to zero on ten different manufacturing sectors, opening markets for hundreds of billions of dollars' worth of trade. It was Mickey Kantor's first victory as our trade ambassador.

He had proved to be a tough, effective negotiator, with skills that eventually would produce more than two hundred agreements, sparking an expansion of trade that would account for almost 30 percent of our economic growth over the next eight years.

After we agreed on a generous aid package, the G-7 meeting also left no doubt that the rich nations were all committed to helping Russia. On the matter of coordinating our economic policies, the results were more ambiguous. I was working to bring the deficit down, and Germany's central bank had just lowered interest rates, but Japan's willingness to stimulate its economy and open its borders to more foreign trade and competition remained unclear. That was progress I'd have to achieve in our bilateral talks with the Japanese, which began right after the G-7 meeting.

In 1993, because Japan was dealing with economic stagnation and political uncertainty, I knew it would be hard to get changes in trade policy, but I had to try. Clearly our large trade deficit with Japan was due in part to protectionism. For example, they wouldn't buy our skis, saying they weren't the right width. I had to find a way to push open Japanese markets without damaging our important security partnership, which was essential to building a stable future for Asia. While I was making these points in a speech to Japanese students at Waseda University, Hillary went on her own charm offensive in Japan, finding an especially warm reception among the increasingly large number of young, well-educated working women.

Prime Minister Miyazawa agreed in principle to my suggestion that we achieve a framework agreement committing ourselves to specific measurable steps to improve our trade relationship. So did the Japanese Foreign Ministry, whose senior civil servant, the father of Japan's new crown princess, was determined to reach an agreement. The big obstacle was the Ministry of International Trade and Industry (MITI), whose leaders felt that their policies had made Japan a great power and saw no reason to change. Late one night, after we finished our talks, representatives of the two ministries were literally screaming their arguments at each other in the lobby of the Hotel Okura. Our staffs got as close as they could to an agreement, with Mickey Kantor's deputy, Charlene Barshefsky, driving such a hard bargain the Japanese called her "Stonewall." Then Miyazawa and I got together over a traditional Japanese meal at the Hotel Okura to see if we could resolve the remaining differences. We did, in what was later called the "Sushi Summit," though Miyazawa always joked that the sake we drank contributed more than the sushi to the final outcome.

The framework agreement committed America to reduce its budget deficit and Japan to take steps over the next year to open its markets in automobile and auto parts, computers, telecommunications, satellites, medical equipment, financial services, and insurance, with objective standards for measuring success on specific timetables. I was convinced that the agreement would be economically beneficial to both the United States and Japan and that it would help Japanese reformers succeed in leading their remarkable nation to its next era of greatness. Like most such agreements, it didn't produce all one could hope for in either country, but it was still a very good thing.

As I left Japan for Korea, the press reports back home said that my first G-7 meeting was a triumph for my personal diplomacy with the other leaders and my outreach to the Japanese people. It was nice to get some positive press coverage, and even better to have met the objectives we set for the G-7 and the Japanese negotiations. I had enjoyed getting to know and work with the other leaders. And after the G-7, I felt more confident in my ability to advance America's interests in the world and understood why so many Presidents preferred foreign policy to the frustrations they faced on the home front.

In South Korea, I visited our troops along the DMZ, which had divided North and South Korea since the armistice ending the Korean War was signed. I walked out onto the Bridge of No Return, stopping about ten feet from the stripe of white paint dividing the two countries and staring at the young North Korean soldier guarding his side in the last lonely outpost of the Cold War. In Seoul, Hillary and I were the guests of President Kim Yong-Sam in the official guest residence, which had an indoor swimming pool. When I went for a dip, music suddenly filled the air. I found myself swimming to many of my favorite tunes, from Elvis to jazz, a nice example of Korea's famous hospitality. After a meeting with the president and a speech to the parliament, I left South Korea grateful for our long alliance and determined to maintain it.

THIRTY-FOUR

I returned to the rigors of Washington. In the third
week of July, on the recommendation of Janet Reno, I
dismissed the director of the FBI, William Sessions,
after he refused to resign despite numerous problems
within the agency. We had to find a replacement. Bernie
Nussbaum urged me to choose Louis Freeh, a former FBI
agent whom President Bush had appointed to the federal
bench in New York after a stellar career as a federal prosecutor. When I met with Freeh, I asked him what he
thought about the FBI's assertion at Waco that they had
proceeded with the raid because it was wrong to keep so
many of their resources tied down in one place for so long.
Without knowing what I thought, he said forthrightly
that he disagreed: "They get paid to wait." That impressed
me. I knew Freeh was a Republican, but Nussbaum
assured me that he was a professional and a stand-up guy
who would not use the FBI for political purposes. We
scheduled the announcement for the twentieth. The day
before, when word got out about the appointment, a
retired FBI agent who was a friend of mine called Nancy
Heinrich, who ran the Oval Office operations, to tell me
not to do it. He said Freeh was too political and self-
serving for the current climate. It gave me pause, but I
sent word back that it was too late; the offer had been
extended and accepted. I would just have to trust Bernie
Nussbaum's judgment.

When we announced Freeh's appointment in a morning ceremony in the Rose Garden, I noticed Vince Foster
standing at the back, near one of the grand old magnolia
trees planted by Andrew Jackson. Vince had a smile on his
face, and I remember thinking he must be relieved that he
and the counsel's office were working on things like
Supreme Court and FBI appointments, instead of answering endless questions about the Travel Office. The whole
ceremony seemed perfect, almost too good to be true. It
was, in more ways than one.

That night I appeared on Larry King's show from the
library on the ground floor of the White House to talk
about my battle for the budget and whatever else was on
his and his callers' minds. Like everyone else, I liked Larry
King. He has a good sense of humor and a human touch,
even when he's asking tough questions. About forty-five
minutes into the program, things were going so well that
Larry asked me if I'd do an extra thirty minutes, so that we
could take more questions from viewers. I agreed immediately and was looking forward to it, but at the next break
Mack McLarty showed up and said we had to end the
interview after an hour. At first I was irritated, thinking
my staff was worried that I might make a mistake if I kept
going, but the look in Mack's eyes told me something else
was going on.

After Larry and I wrapped up the interview and I shook
hands with his crew, Mack walked me upstairs to the residence. Holding back tears, he told me Vince Foster was
dead. Vince had left the Rose Garden after the ceremony
for Louis Freeh, driven out to Fort Marcy Park, and shot
himself with an old revolver that was a family heirloom.
We had been friends virtually all our lives. Our backyards
had touched when I lived with my grandparents in Hope.

We had played together even before Mack and I started kindergarten. I knew Vince had been upset by the Travel Office controversy and held himself responsible for the criticism directed at the counsel's office. He had also been wounded by questions raised about his competence and integrity in several **Wall Street Journal** editorials.

Just the night before, I had called Vince to invite him to watch a movie with me. I was hoping to give him some encouragement, but he had already gone home for the night and said he needed to spend some time with his wife, Lisa. I did my best in our phone conversation to persuade him to shrug off the **Journal** editorials. The **Journal** was a fine paper, but not that many people read its editorials; most of those who did were, like the editorial writers, conservatives who were lost to us anyway. Vince listened, but I could tell I hadn't convinced him. He had never been subject to public criticism before and, like so many people when they're pounded in the press for the first time, he seemed to think that everyone had read the negative things said about him and believed them.

After Mack told me what had happened, Hillary called me from Little Rock. She already knew and was crying. Vince had been her closest friend at the Rose firm. She was frantically searching for an answer we would never completely find—why this had happened. I did my best to convince her there was nothing she could have done, all the while wondering what **I** could have done. Then Mack and I went over to Vince's house to be with the family. Webb and Suzy Hubbell were there, as were several of Vince's friends from Arkansas and the White House. I tried to console everyone, but I was hurting too, and feeling, as I had when Frank Aller killed himself, angry at Vince for doing it and angry at myself for not seeing it coming and doing something, anything, to try to stop it. I was also sad for all my friends from Arkansas who had come to Washington wanting nothing more than to serve and do good, only to find their every move second-guessed. Now Vince, the tall, handsome, strong, and self-assured person they felt was the most stable of them all, was gone.

For whatever reason, Vince came to the end of his rope. In his briefcase, Bernie Nussbaum found a note that had been torn into little pieces. When put back together, it said, "I was not meant for the job in the spotlight of public life in Washington. Here ruining people is considered sport. . . . The public will never believe the innocence of the Clintons and their loyal staff." Vince was overwhelmed, exhausted, and vulnerable to attacks by people who didn't play by the same rules he did. He was rooted in the values of honor and respect, and uprooted by those who valued power and personal assault more. And his untreated depression stripped him of the defenses that allowed the rest of us to survive.

The next day I spoke to the staff, telling them that there are things in life we can't control and mysteries we can't understand; that I wanted them to take more care with themselves, their friends, and their families; and that we couldn't "deaden our sensitivities by working too hard." That last bit of advice had always been easier for me to give than to take.

We all went to Little Rock for Vince's funeral at St. Andrew's Catholic Cathedral, then drove home to Hope, to lay Vince to rest in the cemetery where my grandparents and father were buried. Many people with whom we'd gone to kindergarten and grade school were there. By then, I had given up trying to understand Vince's depression and suicide in favor of accepting them and being grateful for his life. In my eulogy at the funeral, I tried to capture all of Vince's wonderful qualities, what he meant to all of us, how much good he'd done at the White House, and how profoundly honorable he was. I quoted from Leon Russell's moving "A Song for You": "I love you in a place where there's no space or time. I love you for in my life you are a friend of mine."

It was summertime, and the watermelon crop had begun to come in. Before I left town, I stopped at Carter Russell's place and sampled both the red- and yellow-meated ones. Then I discussed the finer points of Hope's main product with the traveling press, who knew I needed a respite from the pain and were uncommonly kind to me that day. I flew back to Washington thinking Vince was home, where he belonged, and thanking God that so many people cared about him.

The next day, July 24, I welcomed the current class of American Legion Boys Nation senators to the White House, on the thirtieth anniversary of my coming to the Rose Garden to meet President Kennedy. A number of my fellow delegates were also there for the reunion. Al Gore was lobbying hard for our economic plan, but he broke away for a couple of minutes to tell the boys, "I have only one word of advice. If you can manage somehow to get a picture of you shaking hands with President Clinton, it might come in handy later on." I shook hands and posed for pictures with all of them, as I would do in six of my eight years in the White House, for both Boys and Girls Nation. I hope some of those photos turn up in campaign ads one day.

I spent the rest of the month and the early days of

August lobbying individual representatives and senators on the economic plan. Roger Altman's war room was working the public side, having me do telephone press conferences in states whose members of Congress could go either way. Al Gore and the cabinet were making literally hundreds of calls and visits. The outcome was uncertain, and tilting away from us, for two reasons. The first was Senator David Boren's proposal to scrap any energy tax; keep most, but not all, of the taxes on the high-income Americans, and make up the difference by eliminating much of the Earned Income Tax Credit; reduce the cost-of-living adjustments for Social Security and military and civilian pensions; and cap expenditures for Medicare and Medicaid below the projected requirements for new recipients and cost increases. Boren couldn't pass his proposal out of committee, but he gave Democrats from conservative states a place to go. It was also endorsed by Democratic senator Bennett Johnston of Louisiana and Republican senators John Danforth of Missouri and Bill Cohen of Maine.

When the budget had first passed, 50–49, with Al Gore breaking the tie, Bennett Johnston had voted against it, along with Sam Nunn, Dennis DeConcini of Arizona, Richard Shelby of Alabama, Richard Bryan of Nevada, and Frank Lautenberg of New Jersey. Shelby was already drifting toward the Republican Party in an increasingly Republican state; Sam Nunn was a hard no; DeConcini, Bryan, and Lautenberg were worried about the anti-tax mood in their states. As I've said, I had made it the first time without them because two senators, one Republican and one Democrat, didn't vote. The next time, they would all show up. With all the Republicans against us, if Boren voted no and none of the others changed, I would lose

51–49. Besides those six, Senator Bob Kerrey was also saying he might vote against the program. Our relationship had been strained by the presidential campaign, and Nebraska was a heavily Republican state. Still, I was optimistic about Kerrey because he was genuinely committed to reducing the deficit, and he was very close to the Senate Finance Committee chairman, Pat Moynihan, who was strongly supporting my plan.

In the House of Representatives, I had a different problem. Every Democrat knew he or she had maximum leverage, and many were bargaining with me over details of the plan or for help on specific issues. Many of the Democrats who came from anti-tax districts were especially afraid of voting for another increase in the gas tax only three years after Congress had last raised it. Besides the Speaker and his leadership team, my strongest supporter was the powerful chairman of the House Ways and Means Committee, Illinois congressman Dan Rostenkowski. Rostenkowski was a superb legislator who combined a fine mind with Chicago street skills, but he was being investigated for converting public funds to political uses, and the assumption was that the investigation would reduce his influence over other members. Every time I met with members of Congress, the press would ask me about Rostenkowski. To his everlasting credit, Rosty bulled right ahead, rounding up votes and telling his colleagues they had to do the right thing. He was still effective, and he had to be. The slightest misstep could lose a vote or two, plunging us off the razor's edge into defeat.

In early August, as the budget drama moved to its climax, Warren Christopher finally secured the agreement of the British and the French to conduct NATO air strikes in Bosnia, but the strikes could occur only if both NATO and the UN approved them, the so-called dual key approach. I was afraid we could never turn both keys, because Russia had a veto on the Security Council and was closely tied to the Serbs. The dual key would prove to be a frustrating impediment to protecting the Bosnians, but it marked another step in the long, tortuous process of moving Europe and the UN to a more aggressive posture.

By August 3, we had settled on a final budget plan, with $255 billion in budget cuts and $241 billion in tax increases. Some Democrats were still worried that any gas-tax increase would kill us with those middle-class voters who were angry anyway about not getting a tax cut. Conservative Democrats said it didn't do enough to reduce the deficit through cutting spending on the entitlements of Medicare, Medicaid, and Social Security. More than 20 percent of our savings already came from reducing future payments to doctors and hospitals under Medicare, plus another big chunk from subjecting more of the Social Security income of better-off retirees to taxation. That's all I could do without losing more votes in the House than we could gain.

That night, in a televised address from the Oval Office, I made one last pitch for public support for the plan, saying it would create eight million jobs in the next four years, and announcing that I would sign an executive order the following day to establish a deficit-reduction trust fund, assuring that all the new taxes and spending cuts would be used for that purpose only. The trust fund was especially important to Senator Dennis DeConcini of Arizona, and I credited him for the idea in the TV address. Of the six senators who had voted against the plan the first time, DeConcini was my only hope. I had had the others to dinner, met with and called them, and had their closest friends in the administration lobby them, to no avail. If DeConcini didn't change, we were beat.

The next day, he did, saying he would vote yes because of the trust fund. Now, if Bob Kerrey stayed with us we would get fifty votes in the Senate, and Al Gore could break the tie again. But before we got there, the budget first had to pass the House. We had one more day to find a majority of 218 votes, and we still weren't there. More than thirty Democrats were wavering. They were afraid of the taxes, though we had done printouts for each of the members showing how many people in their districts would get a tax cut under the EITC, as compared with those who would get an income tax increase. In many cases, the ratio was ten to one or better, and in barely more than a dozen were their constituents so well off that the district would see more tax increases than decreases. Still, they were all worried about the gas tax. I could have passed the plan easily had I dropped the gas tax and offset the loss by abandoning the EITC tax cut. It would have been far less politically damaging. Poor working people had no lobbyists in Washington; they would never have known. But I would have. Besides, if we were going to soak the rich, the bond market wanted us to spray the middle class with a little bit of pain.

That afternoon, Leon Panetta and House majority leader, Dick Gephardt, who was working tirelessly for the budget, had struck a deal with Congressman Tim Penny of Minnesota, the leader of a group of conservative Democrats who wanted more spending cuts, promising the budget cutters another vote during the fall appropriations process to cut spending even more. Penny was satisfied, and his approval brought us seven or eight more votes.

```
patron's name:WILLIAMS, WILBUR EUGE

    title:My life
   author:Clinton, Bill, 1946
  item id:300001250993329 .
     due:12/3/2004,23:59
```

We lost two of our earlier yes votes when Billy Tauzin of Louisiana, who later became a Republican, and Charlie Stenholm of Texas, who represented a district where most of the voters were Republican, said they would vote no. They hated the gas tax and said the unified Republican opposition to the plan had convinced their constituents that it was nothing but a tax increase.

Less than an hour before the vote, I spoke with Congressman Bill Sarpalius from Amarillo, Texas, who had voted against the plan in May. In our fourth phone conversation of the day, Bill said he had decided to vote for the plan, because so many more of his constituents would get tax cuts than tax increases, and because Energy Secretary Hazel O'Leary had pledged to shift more government work to the Pantex plant in his district. We made many commitments like that. Someone once said that the two things people should never watch being made are sausages and laws. It was ugly, and uncertain.

When the voting began, I still didn't know whether we were going to win or lose. After David Minge, who represented a rural district in Minnesota, said he would vote no, it all came down to three people: Pat Williams of Montana, Ray Thornton of Arkansas, and Marjorie Margolies-Mezvinsky of Pennsylvania. I really didn't want Margolies-Mezvinsky to have to vote with us. She was one of the very few Democrats who represented a district with more constituents who'd get tax hikes than tax cuts, and in her campaign she had promised not to vote for any tax increases. It was a tough vote for Pat Williams, too. Far more of his constituents would get tax cuts than tax increases, but Montana was a huge, sparsely populated state where people had to drive long distances, so the gas tax would hit them harder than most Americans. But Pat Williams was a good politician and a tough populist who deplored what trickle-down economics had done to his people. There was at least a chance that he could survive the vote.

Compared with Williams and Margolies-Mezvinsky, Thornton had an easy vote. He represented central Arkansas, where there were far more people who would get a tax cut than a tax increase. He was popular and could not have been blown out of his seat with a stick of dynamite. He was my congressman, and my presidency was on the line. And he had lots of cover: both Arkansas senators, David Pryor and Dale Bumpers, were strong supporters of the plan. But in the end Thornton said no. He had never voted for a gas tax before and he wouldn't start now, not to get the deficit down, not to revive the economy, not to save my presidency or the career of Marjorie Margolies-Mezvinsky.

Finally, Pat Williams and Margolies-Mezvinsky came down the aisle and voted yes, giving us a one-vote victory. The Democrats cheered their courage and the Republicans jeered. They were especially cruel to Margolies-Mezvinsky, waving and singing, "Good-bye, Margie." She had earned an honored place in history, with a vote she shouldn't have had to cast. Dan Rostenkowski was so happy he had tears in his eyes. Back in the White House, I let out a whoop of joy, and relief.

The next day, the drama moved to the Senate. Thanks to George Mitchell and his leadership team, and our lobbying, we had held all the senators from the first vote except David Boren. Dennis DeConcini had bravely stepped into his place, but the outcome was still in doubt, because Bob Kerrey remained uncommitted. On Friday he met with me for ninety minutes, then, about an hour and a half before the vote, he spoke on the Senate floor, saying directly to me, "I could not and should not cast a vote that brings down your presidency." While he would vote yes, he said I would have to do more to control entitlement spending. I agreed to work with him on this. He was pleased with that, as well as with my acceptance of Tim Penny's proposal for an October vote on more cuts.

Kerrey's vote made it a 50–50 tie. Then, just as he had in the first vote on June 25, Al Gore, as president of the Senate, cast the tie-breaking vote. In a statement after the vote, I thanked George Mitchell and all the senators who "voted for change," and Al Gore for "his unwavering contribution in the landslide." Al loved to joke that whenever he voted, we always won.

I signed the legislation on August 10. It reversed twelve years in which the national debt had quadrupled with deficits built on overly optimistic revenue numbers and an almost theological belief that low taxes and high levels of spending would somehow bring enough growth to balance the budget. At the ceremony I specifically acknowledged those senators and representatives whose support never wavered from beginning to end, and who therefore were never mentioned in the news stories. Every yes voter in both houses of the Congress could rightfully say that, but for him or her, we would not be here today.

We had come a long way since those heated debates around the dining-room table in Little Rock the previous December. All by themselves, the Democrats had replaced a wrongheaded but deeply embedded economic theory with a sensible one. Our new economic idea had become reality.

Unfortunately, the Republicans, whose policies had created the problem in the first place, had done a good job portraying the plan as nothing but a tax increase. It was true that most of the spending cuts kicked in later than the tax increases, but that was also true of the alternative budget offered by Senator Dole. In fact, Dole's plan had an even higher percentage of its cuts in the last two years of the five-year budget than mine did. It simply takes time to reduce defense and health spending; you can't slash it all at once. Moreover, our "future" investments in education, training, research, technology, and the environment were already at unacceptably low levels, having been held down in the eighties as tax cuts, defense appropriations, and health costs soared. My budget began to reverse that trend.

Predictably, the Republicans said my economic plan would cause the sky to fall in, calling it a "job killer" and a "one-way ticket to recession." They were wrong. Our bond market gambit would work beyond our wildest dreams, bringing lower interest rates, a soaring stock market, and a booming economy. Just as Lloyd Bentsen had predicted, the wealthiest Americans would get their tax money back, and more, in investment income. The middle class would get their gas-tax money back many times over, in lower home mortgage rates and lower interest costs for car payments, student loans, and credit card purchases. Working families with modest incomes benefited from the Earned Income Tax Credit right away.

In later years I was often asked what great new idea my economic team and I brought to economic policy making. Rather than give a complicated explanation of the bond market/deficit-reduction strategy, I always gave a one-word answer: "arithmetic." The American people had been told for more than a decade that their government was a gluttonous leviathan swallowing their hard-earned tax dollars to no good end. Then the same politicians who told them that, and served up tax cuts to starve the evil beast, would turn right around and spend themselves to reelection, leaving the false impression that the voters could have programs they didn't pay for, and that the only reason we had big deficits was wasteful spending on foreign aid, welfare, and other programs for poor people, a tiny fraction of the budget. Spending on "them" was bad; spending and tax cuts for "us" were good. As my fiscally conservative friend Senator Dale Bumpers used to say: "You let me write $200 billion a year in hot checks and I'll show you a good time, too."

We had brought arithmetic back to the budget, and broken America of a bad habit. Unfortunately, though the benefits began to accrue right away, the people wouldn't feel them for some time. In the meantime, my fellow Democrats and I bore the brunt of the public's withdrawal pains. I couldn't expect gratitude. Even with an abscessed tooth, nobody likes to go to the dentist.

THIRTY-FIVE

After the budget passed, Congress went on its August recess and I was eager to take my family on vacation for two much-needed weeks on Martha's Vineyard. Vernon and Ann Jordan had arranged for us to stay on the edge of Oyster Pond in a cottage that belonged to Robert McNamara.

But before I could leave, there was a busy week of work. On the eleventh I nominated Army General John Shalikashvili to succeed Colin Powell as chairman of the Joint Chiefs of Staff when Colin's term ended in late September. Shali, as everyone called him, had entered the army as a draftee and risen through the ranks to his current position as the commander of NATO and U.S. forces in Europe. He was born in Poland, to a family from Georgia in the former Soviet Union. Before the Russian Revolution, his grandfather had been a general in the czar's army and his father had been an officer, too. When Shali was sixteen, his family moved to Peoria, Illinois, where he taught himself English by watching John Wayne movies. I thought he was the right man to lead our forces in the post–Cold War world, especially given all the problems in Bosnia.

In mid-month, Hillary and I flew to St. Louis, where I signed the Mississippi River flood relief legislation, after an enormous flood had caused the upper Mississippi River to overrun its banks all the way from Minnesota and the Dakotas down to Missouri. The bill-signing ceremony marked my third visit to the flooded areas. Farms and businesses had been destroyed, and some small towns within the hundred-year flood plain had been completely wiped out. On every trip, I marveled at the number of citizens from all over America who just showed up to help.

Then we flew on to Denver, where we welcomed Pope John Paul II to the United States. I had a productive meeting with His Holiness, who supported our mission in Somalia and my desire to do more in Bosnia. After we finished, he graciously received all the Catholics on the White House staff and on my Secret Service detail who had been able to come to Denver with me. The next day I signed the Colorado Wilderness Act, my first major environmental legislation, protecting more than 600,000 acres of national forests and public lands in the National Wilderness Preservation System.

Then I went on to Tulsa, Oklahoma, to speak to my old colleagues at the National Governors Association about health care. Though the ink was barely dry on the budget plan, I wanted to get started on health care and thought the governors might help, because the rising costs of Medicaid, state employees' health insurance, and health care for the uninsured were a big burden on state budgets.

On the nineteenth, my forty-seventh birthday, I announced that Bill Daley of Chicago would become the chair of our task force on the North American Free Trade Agreement. Six days earlier, with Canada and Mexico, we had completed the side deals to NAFTA on labor and environmental rights, which I had promised in the campaign, as well as one protecting our markets from import "surges." Now that they were in place, I was ready to go all out to pass NAFTA in the Congress. I thought Bill Daley was the ideal person to head the campaign for it. He was a

Democratic lawyer from Chicago's most famous political family; his brother was the city's mayor, as his father had been before him, and he had good relationships with several labor leaders. NAFTA would be a very different fight from the budget. A lot of Republicans would support it, and we had to find enough Democrats to go along over the objections of the AFL-CIO.

After the Daley announcement we finally flew off to Martha's Vineyard. That night the Jordans hosted a birthday party for me, with old friends and some new ones. Jackie Kennedy Onassis and her companion, Maurice Tempelsman, came, along with Bill and Rose Styron, and Katharine Graham, the publisher of the **Washington Post** and one of the people I most admired in Washington. The next day we went sailing and swimming with Jackie and Maurice, Ann and Vernon, Ted and Vicki Kennedy, and Ed and Caroline Kennedy Schlossberg. Caroline and Chelsea climbed up on a high platform of Maurice's yacht and jumped into the water. They dared Hillary to follow suit, and Ted and I urged her on. Only Jackie encouraged her to take a safer route to the water. With her usual good judgment, Hillary listened to Jackie.

I spent the next ten days hanging around Oyster Pond, catching crabs with Hillary and Chelsea, walking on the beach that bordered the pond and the Atlantic Ocean, getting to know some of the people who lived in the area year-round, and reading.

The vacation ended all too quickly, and we returned to Washington to the start of Chelsea's first year in high school, Hillary's campaign for health-care reform, Al Gore's first recommendations for savings through his National Performance Review, and a newly redecorated Oval Office. I loved working there. It was always light and open, even on cloudy days, because of the tall windows and glass door toward the south and east. At night the indirect lighting reflected off the curved ceiling, which added light and made it comfortable to work at home. The room was elegant yet inviting, and I always felt comfortable there, alone or in large groups. Kaki Hockersmith, a decorator friend from Arkansas, helped us with a new, brighter look: gold curtains in blue trim, gold high-back chairs, couches upholstered in gold-and-red stripes, and a beautiful deep blue rug with the presidential seal in the center, mirroring the one on the ceiling overhead. Now I liked it even better.

September was also the biggest foreign policy month of my presidency. On September 8, President Izetbegovic of Bosnia came to the White House. The threat of NATO air strikes had succeeded in restraining the Serbs and getting peace talks going again. Izetbegovic assured me that he was committed to a peaceful settlement as long as it was fair to the Bosnian Muslims. If one was reached, he wanted my commitment to send NATO forces, including U.S. troops, to Bosnia to enforce it. I reaffirmed my intention to do so.

On September 9, Yitzhak Rabin called to tell me that Israel and the PLO had reached a peace agreement. It was achieved in secret talks the parties held in Oslo, which we were informed of shortly before I took office. On a couple of occasions, when the talks were in danger of being derailed, Warren Christopher had done a good job of keeping them on track. The talks were kept confidential, which enabled the negotiators to deal candidly with the most sensitive issues and agree on a set of principles that both sides could accept. Most of our work lay in the future, in helping with the immensely difficult task of resolving the tough issues, hammering out the terms of implementation, and raising the money to finance the costs of the agreement, from increased security for Israel to economic development and refugee relocation and compensation for the Palestinians. I had already gotten encouraging signs of financial support from other countries, including Saudi Arabia, where King Fahd, though still angry about Yasser Arafat's support for Iraq in the Gulf War, was supportive of the peace process.

We were still a long way from a comprehensive solution, but the Declaration of Principles was a huge step forward. On September 10, I announced that the Israeli and Palestinian leaders would sign the agreement on the South Lawn of the White House on Monday, the thirteenth, and that because the PLO had renounced violence and recognized Israel's right to exist, the United States would resume its dialogue with them. A couple of days before the signing, the press asked me if Arafat would be welcome at the White House. I said that it was up to the parties directly involved to decide who would represent them in the ceremony. In fact, I badly wanted Rabin and Arafat to attend and urged them to do so; if they didn't, no one in the region would believe they were fully committed to implementing the principles, and, if they did, a billion people across the globe would see them on television and they would leave the White House even more committed to peace than when they arrived. When Arafat said he would be there, I again asked Rabin to come. He accepted, though he was still a bit on edge about it.

In retrospect, the leaders' decision to come may look easy. At the time, it was a gamble for both Rabin and Arafat, who couldn't be sure how their people would react.

Even if a majority of their constituents supported them, extremists on both sides were bound to be inflamed by the compromises on fundamental issues inherent in the Declaration of Principles. Rabin and Arafat showed both vision and guts in consenting to come and speak. The agreement would be signed by Foreign Minister Shimon Peres and Mahmoud Abbas, better known as Abu Mazen, both of whom had been intimately involved in the Oslo negotiations. Secretary Christopher and Russian foreign minister Andrei Kozyrev would witness the accord.

On the morning of the thirteenth, the atmosphere around the White House was alive with excitement as well as tension. We had invited more than 2,500 people to the event, which George Stephanopoulos and Rahm Emanuel had labored over. I was especially happy Rahm was working on this because he had served in the Israeli army. President Carter, who had negotiated the Camp David Accords between Egypt and Israel, would be there. So would President Bush, who, with Gorbachev, had co-sponsored talks in Madrid in 1991 involving Israel, the Palestinians, and the Arab states. President Ford was invited but couldn't get to Washington before the celebration dinner in the evening. All former secretaries of state and national security advisors who had worked for peace over the past twenty years were also invited. Chelsea was taking the morning off from school, as were the Gore children. This was something they didn't want to miss.

The night before, I had gone to bed at ten, early for me, and awakened at three in the morning. Unable to go back to sleep, I got my Bible and read the entire book of Joshua. It inspired me to rewrite some of my remarks, and to wear a blue tie with golden horns, which reminded me of those Joshua had used to blow down the walls of Jericho. Now the horns would herald the coming of a peace that would return Jericho to the Palestinians.

We had two minor flaps early in the morning. When I was told that Arafat intended to appear in his trademark garb, a kaffiyeh and an olive green uniform, and that he might want to dress it up with the revolver he often wore on his hip, I balked and sent word that he couldn't bring the gun. He was here to make peace; the pistol would send the wrong message, and he certainly would be safe without it. He agreed to come unarmed. When the Palestinians saw that they were identified in the agreement as the "Palestinian delegation," not the PLO, they balked. Israel agreed to the preferred designation.

Then there was the question of whether Rabin and Arafat would shake hands. I knew Arafat wanted to do it. Before arriving in Washington, Rabin had said he would do the handshake "if it will be needed," but I could tell he didn't want to. When he arrived at the White House, I raised the subject. He avoided making a commitment, telling me how many young Israelis he had buried because of Arafat. I told Yitzhak that if he was really committed to peace, he'd have to shake Arafat's hand to prove it. "The whole world will be watching, and the handshake is what they will be looking for." Rabin sighed, and in his deep, world-weary voice, said, "I suppose one does not make peace with one's friends." "Then you'll do it?" I asked. He almost snapped at me, "All right. All right. But no kissing." The traditional Arab greeting was a kiss on the cheek, and he wanted no part of that.

I knew Arafat was a great showman and might try to kiss Rabin after the handshake. We had decided that I would shake hands with each of them first, then sort of motion them together. I was sure that if Arafat didn't kiss me, he wouldn't try kissing Rabin. As I stood in the Oval Office discussing it with Hillary, George Stephanopoulos, Tony Lake, and Martin Indyk, Tony said he knew a way I could shake hands with Arafat while avoiding a kiss. He described the procedure and we practiced it. I played Arafat and he played me, showing me what to do. When I shook his hand and moved in for the kiss, he put his left hand on my right arm where it was bent at the elbow, and squeezed; it stopped me cold. Then we reversed roles and I did it to him. We practiced it a couple of more times until I felt sure Rabin's cheek would remain untouched. We all laughed about it, but I knew avoiding the kiss was deadly serious for Rabin.

Just before the ceremony, all three delegations gathered in the large oval Blue Room on the main floor of the White House. The Israelis and the Palestinians still weren't talking to each other in public, so the Americans went back and forth between the two groups as they moved around the rim of the room. We looked like a bunch of awkward kids riding a slow-moving carousel.

Mercifully, it was over before long, and we walked downstairs to start the ceremony. Everyone else walked out on cue, leaving Arafat, Rabin, and me alone for a moment. Arafat said hello to Rabin and held out his hand. Yitzhak's hands were firmly grasped behind his back. He said tersely, "Outside." Arafat just smiled and nodded his understanding. Then Rabin said, "You know, we are going to have to work very hard to make this work." Arafat replied, "I know, and I am prepared to do my part."

We walked out into the bright sunshine of a late-summer day. I opened the ceremony with a brief welcome and words of thanks, support, and encouragement for the leaders and their determination to achieve a "peace of the brave." Peres and Abbas followed me with brief speeches, then sat down to sign the agreement. Warren Christopher and Andrei Kozyrev witnessed it while Rabin, Arafat, and I stood behind and to the right. When the signing was completed, all eyes shifted to the leaders; Arafat stood on my left and Rabin to my right. I shook hands with Arafat, with the blocking maneuver I had practiced. I then turned and shook hands with Rabin, after which I stepped back out of the space between them and spread my arms to bring them together. Arafat lifted his hand toward a still reluctant Rabin. When Rabin extended his hand, the crowd let out an audible gasp, followed by thunderous applause, as they completed the kissless handshake. All the world was cheering, except for diehard protesters in the Middle East who were inciting violence, and demonstrators in front of the White House claiming we were endangering Israel's security.

After the handshake, Christopher and Kozyrev made brief remarks, then Rabin moved to the microphone. Sounding like an Old Testament prophet, he spoke in English, and directly to the Palestinians: "We are destined to live together, on the same soil in the same land. We, the soldiers who have returned from battles stained with blood . . . , say to you today, in a loud and clear voice: Enough of blood and tears. Enough! . . . We, like you, are people—people who want to build a home, to plant a tree, to love, to live side by side with you in dignity, in affinity as human beings, as free men." Then, quoting the book of Koheleth, which Christians call Ecclesiastes, Rabin said, "To everything there is a season and a time to every purpose under heaven. A time to be born and a time to die, a time to kill and a time to heal, . . . a time of war and a time of peace. The time for peace has come." It was a magnificent speech. He had used it to reach out to his adversaries.

When Arafat's time came, he took a different tack. He had already reached out to the Israelis with smiles, friendly gestures, and his eager handshake. Now, in a rhythmic, singsong voice, he spoke to his people in Arabic, recounting their hopes for the peace process and reaffirming the legitimacy of their aspirations. Like Rabin, he promoted peace, but with an edge: "Our people do not consider that exercising the right to self-determination could violate the rights of their neighbors or infringe on their security. Rather, putting an end to their feelings of being wronged and of having suffered an historic injustice is the strongest guarantee to achieve coexistence and openness between our two peoples and future generations."

Arafat had chosen generous gestures to speak to the Israelis and tough words to reassure the doubters back home. Rabin had done the reverse. He had been heartfelt and genuine toward the Palestinians in his speech; now he used body language to reassure his doubters back in Israel. All the while Arafat was speaking, he looked uncomfortable and skeptical, so ill at ease that he gave the impression of someone who was dying to excuse himself. Their different tactics, side by side, made for a fascinating and revealing juxtaposition. I made a mental note to take it into account in future negotiations with them. But I shouldn't have worried. Before long, Rabin and Arafat would develop a remarkable working relationship, a tribute to Arafat's regard for Rabin and the Israeli leader's uncanny ability to understand how Arafat's mind worked.

I closed the ceremony by bidding the descendants of Isaac and Ishmael, both children of Abraham, "Shalom, salaam, peace," and urging them to "go as peacemakers."

After the event I had a brief meeting with Arafat and a private lunch with Rabin. Yitzhak was drained from the long flight and the emotion of the occasion. It was an amazing turn in his eventful life, much of which had been spent in uniform, fighting the enemies of Israel, including Arafat. I asked him why he had decided to support the Oslo talks and the agreement they produced. He explained to me that he had come to realize that the territory Israel had occupied since the 1967 war was no longer necessary to its security and, in fact, was a source of insecurity. He said that the intifada that had broken out some years before had shown that occupying territory full of angry people did not make Israel more secure, but made it more vulnerable to attacks from within. Then, in the Gulf War, when Iraq fired Scud missiles into Israel, he realized that the land did not provide a security buffer against attacks with modern weapons from the outside. Finally, he said, if Israel were to hold on to the West Bank permanently, it would have to decide whether to let the Arabs there vote in Israeli elections, as those who lived within the pre-1967 borders did. If the Palestinians got the right to vote, given their higher birthrate, within a few decades Israel would no longer be a Jewish state. If they were denied the right to vote, Israel would no longer be a democracy but an apartheid state. Therefore, he concluded, Israel should give up the territory, but only if doing so brought real peace and normal relations with its neighbors, including Syria. Rabin thought he could make a deal with Syrian president Hafez al-Assad before or soon after the Palestinian process was completed. Based on my conversations with Assad, so did I.

Over time, Rabin's analysis of the meaning of the West Bank to Israel would become widely accepted among pro-peace Israelis, but in 1993 it was novel, insightful, and courageous. I had admired Rabin even before meeting him in 1992, but that day, watching him speak at the ceremony and listening to his argument for peace, I had seen the greatness of his leadership and his spirit. I had never met anyone quite like him, and I was determined to help him achieve his dream of peace.

After the lunch, Rabin and the Israelis flew home for the High Holy Days and the task of selling the agreement to the Knesset, the Israeli parliament, stopping on the way in Morocco to brief King Hassan, who had long taken a moderate position toward Israel, on the agreement.

That night Hillary and I hosted a celebratory dinner for about twenty-five couples, including President and Mrs. Carter, President and Mrs. Ford, and President Bush, six of the nine living secretaries of state, and Democratic and Republican congressional leaders. The Presidents had agreed to come, not only to celebrate the peace breakthrough, but also to participate in the public kickoff of the campaign for NAFTA the next day. During the evening I took all of them up to my office on the residence floor, where we took a picture to commemorate a rare occasion in American history when four Presidents dined together at the White House. After the dinner the Carters and Bush accepted our invitation to spend the night. The Fords declined, for a very good reason: they had booked the Washington hotel suite in which they had spent their first night as a married couple.

The next day we kept the momentum for peace going, as Israeli and Jordanian diplomats signed an agreement that moved them closer to a final peace, and several hundred Jewish and Arab-American businesspeople gathered at the State Department to commit themselves to a joint effort to invest in the Palestinian areas when conditions were peaceful enough to permit a stable economy to develop.

Meanwhile, the other Presidents joined me at a signing ceremony for the NAFTA side agreements in the East Room of the White House. I made the case that NAFTA would be good for the economies of the United States, Canada, and Mexico, creating a giant market of nearly 400 million people; that it would strengthen U.S. leadership in our hemisphere and in the world; and that the failure to pass it would make the loss of jobs to low-wage competition in Mexico more, not less, likely. Mexico's tariffs were two and a half times as high as ours, and even so, next to Canada, it was the largest purchaser of U.S. products. The mutual phaseout of tariffs had to be a net plus to us.

Then Presidents Ford, Carter, and Bush spoke up for NAFTA. They were all good, but Bush was especially effective, and wittily generous to me. He complimented my speech by saying, "Now I understand why he's inside looking out and I'm outside looking in." The Presidents gave bipartisan gravitas to the campaign, and we needed all the help we could get. NAFTA faced intense opposition from an unusual coalition of liberal Democrats and conservative Republicans, who shared a fear that a more open relationship with Mexico would cost America good jobs without helping ordinary Mexicans, who they believed would continue to be underpaid and overworked no matter how much money their employers made out of trading with the United States. I knew they might be right about the second part, but I believed NAFTA was essential, not just to our relationships with Mexico and Latin

America but also to our commitment to building a more integrated, cooperative world.

Though it was becoming clear that a vote on health-care reform would not come until the following year, we still had to get our bill up to Capitol Hill so that the legislative process could begin. At first, we considered just sending an outline of the proposal to the committees of jurisdiction and letting them write the bill, but Dick Gephardt and others insisted that our chances of success would be better if we started off with specific legislation. After a meeting with congressional leaders in the Cabinet Room, I suggested to Bob Dole that we work together on legislation. I did it because Dole and his chief of staff, an impressive former nurse named Sheila Burke, genuinely cared about health care, and, in any case, if I produced a bill he didn't like, he could filibuster it to death. Dole declined to work on drafting a joint proposal, saying I should just present my own bill and we'd work out a compromise later. When he said that, he may have meant it, but it didn't turn out that way.

I was scheduled to present the health-care plan to a joint session of Congress on September 22. I was feeling upbeat. That morning I had signed the bill creating AmeriCorps, the national service program; it was one of my most important personal priorities. I also nominated Eli Segal, who had shepherded the bill through Congress, to be the first chief executive of the Corporation for National Service. Attendees at the signing ceremony on the back lawn of the White House included young people who had answered my call to do community service that summer; two old veterans of FDR's Civilian Conservation Corps, whose projects still marked the American landscape; and Sargent Shriver, the first director of the Peace Corps. Thoughtfully, Sarge had lent me one of the pens President Kennedy had used thirty-two years earlier to sign the Peace Corps legislation, and I used it to bring AmeriCorps into being. Over the next five years, nearly 200,000 young Americans would join the ranks of Ameri-Corps, a larger number than had served in the entire forty-year history of the Peace Corps.

On the evening of the twenty-second, I felt confident as I walked down the aisle of the House Chamber and looked up at Hillary sitting in the balcony with two of America's most famous doctors, the pediatrician Dr. T. Berry Brazelton, a longtime friend of hers, and Dr. C. Everett Koop, who had served as President Reagan's surgeon general, a position he used to educate the nation about AIDS and the importance of preventing its spread. Both Brazelton and Koop were advocates of health-care reform who would lend credibility to our efforts.

My confidence slipped when I glanced at the Tele-PrompTer to begin my speech. It wasn't there. Instead, I was looking at the beginning of the speech to Congress on the economic plan that I'd delivered in February. The budget had been enacted more than a month earlier; Congress didn't need to hear that speech again. I turned to Al Gore, who was sitting in his customary seat behind me, explained the problem, and asked him to get George Stephanopoulos to fix it. Meanwhile I started the speech. I had a written copy with me and I knew what I wanted to say anyway, so I wasn't too worried, though it was a bit distracting to see all those irrelevant words scrolling by on the TelePrompTer. At the seven-minute mark, the right text finally came up. I don't think anyone knew the difference at the time, but it was reassuring to get my crutch back.

As simply and directly as I could, I explained the problem—that our system cost too much and covered too few—and outlined the basic principles of our plan: security, simplicity, savings, choice, quality, and responsibility. Everyone would have coverage, through private insurers, that would not be lost when there was an illness or a job change; there would be far less paperwork because of a uniform minimum-benefit package; we would reap large savings through lower administrative costs, which were then significantly higher than those of other wealthy nations, and a crackdown on fraud and abuse. According to Dr. Koop, that could save tens of billions of dollars.

Under our plan, Americans would be able to choose their own health plan and keep their own doctors, choices that were vanishing for more and more Americans whose insurance was carried by health maintenance organizations (HMOs), which tried to hold down costs by restricting patient choices and conducting extensive reviews before approving expensive treatments. Quality would be assured by the issuance of report cards on health-care plans to consumers, and the provision of more information to doctors. Responsibility would be enforced across the board against health insurance companies that wrongfully denied care, providers who padded their bills, drug companies that overcharged, lawyers who brought bogus suits, and citizens whose irresponsible choices weakened their health and exploded costs to everyone else.

I proposed that all employers provide health insurance, as 75 percent of them were already doing, with a discount for small-business owners who otherwise couldn't afford the insurance. The subsidy would be paid for by an increase in cigarette taxes. Self-employed people would be able to deduct all the costs of their health-care premiums from their taxable incomes.

If the system I proposed had been adopted, it would have reduced inflation in health-care costs, spread the burden of paying for health care more fairly, and provided health security to millions of Americans who didn't have it. And it would have put an end to the kinds of horrible injustices I had personally encountered, like the case of a woman who had to give up a $50,000-a-year job that supported her six children because her youngest child was so ill she couldn't keep her health insurance, and the only way for the mother to get health care for the child was to go on welfare and sign up for Medicaid; or the case of a young couple with a sick child whose only health insurance came through one parent's employer, a small non-profit corporation with twenty employees. The child's care was so costly that the employer was given the choice by its insurer of firing the employee with the sick child or raising the premiums of all the other employees by $200. I thought America could do better than that.

Hillary, Ira Magaziner, Judy Feder, and all those who helped them had crafted a plan that we could implement while reducing the deficit. And contrary to how it was later portrayed, health experts generally praised it at the time as moderate and workable. It certainly wasn't a government takeover of the health-care system, as its critics charged, but that story came later. On the night of the twenty-second, I was just glad that the TelePrompTer was working.

Toward the end of September, Russia dashed back into the headlines, as hard-line parliamentarians tried to depose Yeltsin. In response, he dissolved parliament and called new elections for December 12. We used the crisis to increase support for our Russian aid package, which passed the House, 321–108, on September 29 and the Senate, 87–11, on September 30.

By Sunday, October 3, the conflict between Yeltsin and his reactionary opponents in the Duma erupted into a battle on the streets of Moscow. Armed groups carrying hammer-and-sickle flags and portraits of Stalin fired rocket-propelled grenades into the building that housed a number of Russian television stations. Other reform leaders in former Communist countries, including Václav Havel, issued statements in support of Yeltsin, and I did, too, telling reporters that it was clear that Yeltsin's opponents had started the violence, that Yeltsin had "bent over backwards" to avoid using excessive force, and that the United States would support him and his effort to hold free and fair elections for parliament. The next day Russian military forces shelled the parliament building and threatened to storm it, forcing the surrender of the rebellion's leaders. Aboard Air Force One, on my way to California, I called Yeltsin with a message of support.

The battle in Moscow's streets was the top news story across the world that night, but the news in America led with a different story, which marked one of the darkest days of my presidency and made famous the phrase "Black Hawk Down."

In December 1992, President Bush, with my support, had sent U.S. troops to Somalia to help the UN after more than 350,000 Somalis had died in a bloody civil war, which brought famine and disease in its wake. At the time, Bush's national security advisor, General Brent Scowcroft, had told Sandy Berger they would be home before my inauguration. That didn't happen because Somalia had no functioning government, and without our troop presence, armed thugs would have stolen the supplies the UN had been providing and starvation would have set in again. Over the next several months, the United Nations sent in about 20,000 troops and we reduced the American force to just over 4,000, down from 25,000. After seven months, crops were growing, starvation had ended, refugees were returning, schools and hospitals were reopening, a police force had been created, and many Somalis were engaged in a process of reconciliation moving toward democracy.

Then, in June, the clan of Somali warlord Mohammed Aidid killed twenty-four Pakistani peacekeepers. Aidid, whose armed thugs controlled a good part of the capital city of Mogadishu and didn't like the reconciliation process, wanted to control Somalia. He thought he had to run the UN out to do so. After the Pakistanis were killed, Secretary-General Boutros-Ghali and his representative for Somalia, retired American Admiral Jonathan Howe, became determined to get Aidid, believing the UN mission could not succeed unless he was brought to justice. Because Aidid was well protected by heavily armed forces, the United Nations was unable to apprehend him and asked the United States to help. Admiral Howe, who had been a deputy to Brent Scowcroft in the Bush White House, was convinced, especially after the Pakistani peacekeepers were killed, that arresting Aidid and putting him on trial was the only way to end the clan-based conflicts that kept Somalia mired in violence, failure, and chaos.

Just a few days before he retired as chairman of the Joint Chiefs of Staff, Colin Powell came to me with a recommendation that I approve a parallel American effort to capture Aidid, though he thought we had only a 50 percent chance of getting him, with a 25 percent chance of getting him alive. Still, he argued, we couldn't behave as if we didn't care that Aidid had murdered UN forces who were serving with us. Repeated UN failures to capture Aidid had only raised his status and tarnished the humanitarian nature of the UN mission, I agreed.

The American commander of the Rangers was Major General William Garrison. The army's Tenth Mountain Division, headquartered in Fort Drum, New York, also had troops in Somalia under the overall commander of U.S. forces there, General Thomas Montgomery. They both reported to Marine General Joseph Hoar, the commander of the U.S. Central Command at MacDill Air Force Base in Tampa, Florida. I knew Hoar and had great confidence in his judgment and ability.

On October 3, acting on a tip that two of Aidid's top aides were in Mogadishu's "Black Sea" neighborhood, which he controlled, Major General Garrison ordered the Army Rangers to mount an assault on the building where the men were thought to be. They flew into Mogadishu in Black Hawk helicopters in broad daylight. It was a much riskier operation during the day than it would have been on a dark night, when helicopters and troops are less visible and their night-vision devices give them the ability to operate as well as they can in daylight. Garrison decided to take the risk because his troops had carried out three previous daylight operations successfully.

The Rangers stormed the building and captured Aidid's lieutenants and some lesser figures. Then the raid went terribly wrong. Aidid's forces fought back, downing two of the Black Hawks. The pilot of the first copter was pinned in the wreckage. The Rangers would not abandon him: they never leave their men on the field of battle, dead or alive. When they went back in, the real fireworks began. Before long, ninety U.S. soldiers were surrounding the copter, engaged in a massive shootout with hundreds of Somalis. Eventually, General Montgomery's Rapid Deployment Force entered the action, but the Somali resistance was strong enough to prevent the rescue operation from succeeding throughout the night. When the battle was over, nineteen Americans were dead, dozens were wounded, and Black Hawk pilot Mike Durant had been captured. More than five hundred Somalis were dead and over a thousand wounded. Enraged Somalis dragged the body of the slain Black Hawk crew chief through the streets of Mogadishu.

Americans were outraged and astounded. How had our humanitarian mission turned into an obsession with getting Aidid? Why were American forces doing Boutros-Ghali's and Admiral Howe's bidding? Senator Robert Byrd called for an end to "these cops-and-robbers operations." Senator John McCain said, "Clinton's got to bring them home." Admiral Howe and General Garrison wanted to pursue Aidid; according to their sources in Mogadishu, many of his clan allies had fled the city and it wouldn't take much to finish the job.

On the sixth, our national security team convened in the White House. Tony Lake had also brought in Robert Oakley, who had been America's top civilian in Mogadishu from December through March. Oakley believed that the United Nations, including his old friend Admiral Howe, had made a mistake by isolating Aidid from the political process and by becoming so obsessed with tracking him down. By extension, he disagreed with our decision to try to apprehend Aidid for the UN.

I had a lot of sympathy for General Garrison and the men who wanted to go back and finish the job. I was sick about the loss of our troops and I wanted Aidid to pay. If getting him was worth eighteen dead and eighty-four wounded Americans, wasn't it worth finishing the job? The problem with that line of reasoning was that if we went back in and nabbed Aidid, dead or alive, then we, not the UN, would own Somalia, and there was no guarantee that we could put it together politically any better than the UN had. Subsequent events proved the validity of that view: after Aidid died of natural causes in 1996, Somalia remained divided. Moreover, there was no support in Congress for a larger military role in Somalia, as I learned in a White House meeting with several members; most of them demanded an immediate withdrawal of our forces. I strongly disagreed, and in the end we compromised on a six-month transition period. I didn't mind taking Congress on, but I had to consider the consequences of any action that could make it even harder to get congressional support for sending American troops to Bosnia and Haiti, where we had far greater interests at stake.

In the end, I agreed to dispatch Oakley on a mission to get Aidid to release Mike Durant, the captured pilot. His instructions were clear: The United States would not retaliate if Durant was released immediately and unconditionally. We would not trade the people who had just been captured. Oakley delivered the message and Durant was freed. I beefed up our forces and set a fixed date for their withdrawal, giving the UN six more months to establish control or set up an effective Somali political organization. After Durant's release, Oakley opened negotiations with Aidid and eventually secured a truce of sorts.

The battle of Mogadishu haunted me. I thought I knew how President Kennedy felt after the Bay of Pigs. I was responsible for an operation that I had approved in general but not in its particulars. Unlike the Bay of Pigs, it was not a failure in strictly military terms—Task Force Ranger had arrested Aidid's lieutenants by dropping into the middle of Mogadishu in broad daylight, executing its complex and difficult mission, and enduring unexpected losses with courage and skill. But the losses shocked America, and the battle that produced them was inconsistent with our larger humanitarian mission and the UN's.

What plagued me most was that when I approved the use of U.S. forces to apprehend Aidid, I did not envision anything like a daytime assault in a crowded, hostile neighborhood. I assumed we would try to get him when he was on the move, away from large numbers of civilians and the cover they gave his armed supporters. I thought I was approving a police action by U.S. troops who had far better capacity, equipment, and training than their UN counterparts. Apparently, that's also what Colin Powell thought he was asking me to approve; when I discussed it with him after I left the White House and he was secretary of state, Powell said he would not have approved an operation like that one unless it was conducted at night. But we hadn't discussed that, nor apparently had anyone else imposed any parameters on General Garrison's range of options. Colin Powell had retired three days before the raid and John Shalikashvili had not yet been confirmed as his replacement. The operation was not approved by General Hoar at CentCom or by the Pentagon. As a result, instead of authorizing an aggressive police operation, I had authorized a military assault in hostile territory.

In a handwritten letter to me the day after the fight, General Garrison took full responsibility for his decision to go forward with the raid, outlining his reasons for the decision: the intelligence was excellent; the force was experienced; the capacity of the enemy was known; the tactics were appropriate; planning for contingencies had been done; an armored reaction force would have helped, but might not have reduced U.S. casualties, because the task-force troops would not leave behind their fallen comrades, one of whom was pinned in the wreckage of his helicopter. Garrison closed his letter by saying, "The Mission was a success. Targeted individuals were captured and extracted from the target. . . . President Clinton and Secretary Aspin need to be taken off the blame line."

I respected Garrison and agreed with his letter, except for the last point. There was no way I could, or should, be taken off the "blame line." I believe the raid was a mistake, because carrying it out in the daytime underestimated the strength and determination of Aidid's forces and the attendant possibility of losing one or more of the helicopters. In wartime, the risks would have been acceptable. On a peacekeeping mission, they were not, because the value of the prize was not worth the risk of significant casualties and the certain consequences of changing the nature of our mission in the eyes of both Somalis and Americans. Arresting Aidid and his top men because the UN forces couldn't do it was supposed to be incidental to our operations there, not its main purpose. It was worth doing under the right circumstances, but when I gave my consent to General Powell's recommendation, I should also have required prior approval of the Pentagon and the White House for any operations of this magnitude. I certainly don't blame General Garrison, a fine soldier whose career was unfairly damaged. The decision he made, given his instructions, was defensible. The larger implications of it should have been determined higher up.

In the weeks ahead, I visited several of the wounded soldiers at Walter Reed Army Hospital and had two moving meetings with the families of the soldiers who had lost their lives. In one, I was asked tough questions by two grieving fathers, Larry Joyce and Jim Smith, a former Ranger who had lost a leg in Vietnam. They wanted to know what their sons had died for and why we had changed course. When I gave the Medal of Honor, posthumously, to Delta snipers Gary Gordon and Randy Shugart for their heroism in trying to save Mike Durant and his helicopter crew, their families were still in great pain. Shugart's father was furious at me, and angrily told me that I wasn't fit to be Commander in Chief. After the price he'd paid, he could say anything he wanted as far as I was concerned. I couldn't tell if he felt the way he did because I had not served in Vietnam, because I had approved the policy that led to the raid, or because I had declined to go back after Aidid after October 3. Regardless, I didn't believe the emotional, political, or strategic benefits of catching or killing Aidid justified further loss of life on either side, or a greater shifting of responsibility for Somalia's future from the UN to the United States.

After Black Hawk Down, whenever I approved the deployment of forces, I knew much more about what the risks were, and made much clearer what operations had to be approved in Washington. The lessons of Somalia were not lost on the military planners who plotted our course in Bosnia, Kosovo, Afghanistan, and other trouble spots of the post–Cold War world, where America was often asked to step in to stop hideous violence, and too often expected to do it without the loss of lives to ourselves, our adversaries, or innocent bystanders. The challenge of dealing with complicated problems like Somalia, Haiti, and Bosnia inspired one of Tony Lake's best lines: "Sometimes I really miss the Cold War."

THIRTY-SIX

I spent much of the rest of October dealing with the aftermath of Somalia and fending off efforts in Congress to limit my ability to commit American troops to Haiti and Bosnia.

On the twenty-sixth we finally celebrated a light moment, Hillary's first birthday in the White House. It was a surprise costume party. Her staff had arranged for us to dress up like James and Dolley Madison. When she got back from a long day of health-care work, she was led upstairs in a totally dark White House to find her costume. She came downstairs, looking wonderful in her hoop skirt and wig, to find me in white wig and colonial tights, and several of her staff dressed up like her in all her manifestations, with different hairdos and in different roles, from pushing health care to making tea and cookies. With my hair going white anyway, my wig looked good, but I looked ridiculous in the tights.

The next day, dressed in normal clothes, Hillary and I personally delivered our health-care legislation to Congress. Hillary had been briefing members of Congress from both parties for weeks and getting rave reviews. Many House Republicans had praised our efforts, and Senator John Chafee of Rhode Island, who represented the Senate Republicans, said that while he disagreed with parts of our plan, he thought we could work together to produce a good compromise. I was beginning to believe we might actually have an honest debate that would produce something close to universal coverage.

Our critics had a field day with the bill's length, 1,342 pages. Every year Congress passes bills more than a thousand pages long dealing with less profound and complex subjects. Moreover, our bill would have eliminated far more pages of laws and regulations than it proposed to add. Everyone in Washington knew that, but the American people didn't. The bill's length gave credibility to the effective ads the health insurance companies were already running against the plan. They featured two actors as a normal-looking couple named Harry and Louise, who talked wearily about their fears that the government was going to "force us to pick from a few health plans designed by government bureaucrats." The ads were completely misleading but clever and widely seen. In fact, the bureaucratic costs imposed by the insurance companies were a big reason Americans paid more for health care but still didn't have the universal coverage that citizens in every other prosperous nation took for granted. The insurance companies wanted to keep the profits of an inefficient and unfair system; tapping into the well-known skepticism of Americans about any major government action was the best way to do it.

In early November, **Congressional Quarterly** reported that I had enjoyed a higher success rate with Congress than any President in his first year since President Eisenhower in 1953. We had passed the economic plan, reduced the deficit, and implemented many of my campaign promises, including the EITC expansion, the empowerment zones, a capital gains tax cut for small business, the childhood immigration initiative, and student-loan reform. Congress had also approved national service, the Russian aid package, the motor voter bill, and the family leave law. Both houses of Congress had passed versions of my crime bill, which would begin funding the 100,000 community police officers I had promised during the campaign. The economy had already produced more private-sector jobs than had been produced in the previous four years. Interest rates were still low, and investment was up.

Al Gore's campaign mantra was coming true. Now everything that should be up was up and everything that should be down was down, with one big exception. Despite the successes, my approval ratings were still low. On November 7, in a special **Meet the Press** interview I did with Tim Russert and Tom Brokaw on the show's forty-sixth anniversary, Russert asked me why my ratings were down. I told him I didn't know, though I had a few ideas.

A few days earlier I had read a list of our accomplishments to a group from Arkansas who were visiting the White House. When I finished, one of my home staters said, "Then there must be a conspiracy to keep this a secret; we don't hear about any of this." Part of the fault was mine. As soon as I finished a task, I moved on to the next one, without doing a lot of follow-up communications. In politics, if you don't toot your own horn, it usually stays untooted. Part of the problem was the constant intrusion of crises like Haiti and Somalia. Part of it was the nature of the press coverage. The haircut, the Travel Office, and stories about the White House staff and our decision-making process were, I believed, either wrongly or overly reported.

A few months earlier, a national survey had shown

that I had received an unusually high amount of negative press coverage. I had brought some of it on myself in mishandling press relations early. And maybe the press, which was so often called liberal, was in fact more conservative than I was, at least when it came to changing how things were supposed to work in Washington. Certainly they had different notions of what was important. Also, most of the people covering me were young, trying to build their careers in a system of twenty-four-hour news coverage where every story was expected to have a political edge and there were no kudos from colleagues for positive stories. This was almost inevitable in an environment where the print and network news media faced more competition from cable channels and where the lines between traditional press, tabloids, partisan publications, and political talk shows on TV and radio were being blurred.

The Republicans also deserved a lot of credit for the fact that my poll ratings were worse than my performance: they had been effective in their constant attacks and negative characterizations of the health-care and economic plans, and they had made the most of my mistakes. Since I had been elected, Republicans had won special U.S. Senate elections in Texas and Georgia, governors' races in Virginia and New Jersey, and the mayoral races in New York and Los Angeles. In each case, the outcome was determined by decisive local factors, but I sure didn't have much positive influence. People didn't yet feel the economy getting better, and the old anti-tax, anti-government rhetoric still had a lot of juice. Finally, some of the things we were doing that would help millions of Americans were either too complex for easy consumption, like the Earned Income Tax Credit, or too controversial to avoid being politically damaging, even when they were good policy.

November offered two examples of sound policy and questionable politics. After Al Gore plainly bested Ross Perot in a heavily watched TV debate on NAFTA, it passed the House, 234–200. Three days later the Senate followed suit, 61–38. Mark Gearan reported to the press that Al and I had called or seen two hundred members of Congress, and the cabinet had made nine hundred calls. President Carter also helped, calling members of Congress all day long for a week. We also had to make deals on a wide range of issues; the lobbying effort for NAFTA looked even more like sausage making than the budget fight had. Bill Daley and our whole team had won a great economic and political victory for America, but like the budget, it came at a high price, dividing our party in Congress and infuriating many of our strongest supporters in the labor movement.

The Brady bill also passed in November, after the Senate Republicans backed off a filibuster inspired by the National Rifle Association. I signed the bill, with Jim and Sarah Brady in attendance. Ever since John Hinckley Jr. shot Jim in Hinckley's attempt to assassinate President Reagan, Jim and Sarah had crusaded for sensible gun-safety laws. They had worked for seven years to pass a bill requiring a waiting period for all handgun purchases so that the buyers' backgrounds could be checked for criminal or mental-health problems. President Bush had vetoed an earlier version of the Brady bill because of the intense opposition of the NRA, which said it infringed on the constitutional right to keep and bear arms. The NRA believed the brief waiting period was an unacceptable burden on lawful gun buyers and declared that we could achieve the same result by increasing the penalties for illegally buying guns. Most Americans were for the Brady bill, but once it passed, it was no longer a voting issue with them. By contrast, the NRA was determined to defeat as many members of Congress who voted against them as possible. By the time I left office, the Brady background checks had kept more than 600,000 felons, fugitives, and stalkers from buying handguns. It had saved countless lives. But, like the budget, it exposed many of those brave enough to vote for it to harsh attacks, which were effective enough to drive several of them from office.

Not everything positive I did was controversial. On the sixteenth, I signed the Religious Freedom Restoration Act, which was intended to protect a reasonable range of religious expression in public areas like schools and workplaces. The bill was designed to reverse a 1990 Supreme Court decision giving states more authority to regulate religious expression in such areas. America is full of people deeply committed to their very diverse faiths. I thought the bill struck the right balance between protecting their rights and the need for public order. It was sponsored in the Senate by Ted Kennedy and Republican Orrin Hatch of Utah, and passed 97–3. The House adopted it by a voice vote. Though the Supreme Court later struck it down, I remain convinced it was a good and needed piece of legislation.

I always felt that protecting religious liberty and making the White House accessible to all religious faiths was an important part of my job. I assigned a member of the White House public liaison staff to be our bridge to the religious communities. I attended every one of the National Prayer

Breakfasts that are held each year as Congress begins its work, speaking and staying for the entire event so that I could visit with the people of different faiths and political parties who came to pray for God's guidance in our work. And every year when Congress resumed after the August recess, I hosted an interfaith breakfast in the State Dining Room that allowed me to hear the concerns of religious leaders and share mine with them. I wanted to keep open the lines of communication to them, even those who disagreed with me, and work with them whenever I could on social problems at home and humanitarian problems around the world.

I believe strongly in separation of church and state, but I also believe that both make indisputable contributions to the strength of our nation, and that on occasion they can work together for the common good without violating the Constitution. Government is, by definition, imperfect and experimental, always a work in progress. Faith speaks to the inner life, to the search for truth and the spirit's capacity for profound change and growth. Government programs don't work as well in a culture that devalues family, work, and mutual respect. And it's hard to live by faith without acting on the scriptural admonitions to care for the poor and downtrodden, and to "love thy neighbor as thyself."

I was thinking about the role of faith in our national life in mid-November when I traveled to Memphis to address the convocation of the Church of God in Christ at Mason Temple Church. There had been a number of news reports about the rising tide of violence against children in African-American neighborhoods, and I wanted to discuss with the ministers and laypeople what we could do about it. There were obvious economic and social forces behind the disappearance of work in our inner cities, the break-down of the family, the problems in schools, and the rise of welfare dependency, out-of-wedlock births, and violence. But the crushing combination of difficulties had created a culture that accepted as normal the presence of violence and the absence of work and two-parent families, and I was convinced that government alone could not change that culture. Many black churches were beginning to address these issues, and I wanted to encourage them to do more.

When I got to Memphis, I was among friends. The Church of God in Christ was the fastest-growing African-American denomination. Its founder, Charles Harrison Mason, received the inspiration for his church's name in Little Rock, on a spot where I had helped lay a plaque two years earlier. His widow was in the church that day. The presiding bishop, Louis Ford of Chicago, had played a leading role in the presidential campaign.

Mason Temple is hallowed ground in the history of civil rights. Martin Luther King Jr. had preached his last sermon there, on the night before he was killed. I evoked the spirit of King and his uncanny prediction that his life might not last much longer to ask my friends to examine honestly "the great crisis of the spirit that is gripping America today."

Then I put away my notes and gave what many commentators later said was the best speech of my eight years as President, speaking to friends from my heart in the language of our shared heritage:

> If Martin Luther King were to reappear by my side today and give us a report card on the last twenty-five years, what would he say? You did a good job, he

would say, voting and electing people who formerly were not electable because of the color of their skin. . . . You did a good job, he would say, letting people who have the ability to do so live wherever they want to live, go wherever they want to go in this great country. . . . He would say you did a good job creating a black middle class . . . in opening opportunity.

But, he would say, I did not live and die to see the American family destroyed. I did not live and die to see thirteen-year-old boys get automatic weapons and gun down nine-year-olds just for the kick of it. I did not live and die to see young people destroy their own lives with drugs and then build fortunes destroying the lives of others. That is not what I came here to do. I fought for freedom, he would say, but not for the freedom of people to kill each other with reckless abandon, not for the freedom of children to have children and the fathers of the children walk away from them and abandon them as if they don't amount to anything. I fought for people to have the right to work but not to have whole communities and people abandoned. This is not what I lived and died for.

I did not fight for the right of black people to murder other black people with reckless abandon. . . .

There are changes we can make from the outside in; that's the job of the President and the Congress and the governors and the mayors and the social service agencies. And then there's some changes we're going to have to make from the inside out, or the others won't matter. . . . Sometimes there are no answers from the outside in; sometimes all the answers have to come from the values and the stirrings and the voices that speak to us from within. . . .

Where there are no families, where there is no order, where there is no hope . . . who will be there to give structure, discipline, and love to these children? You must do that. And we must help you.

So in this pulpit, on this day, let me ask all of you in your heart to say: We will honor the life and the work of Martin Luther King. . . . Somehow, by God's grace, we will turn this around. We will give these children a future. We will take away their guns and give them books. We will take away their despair and give them hope. We will rebuild the families and the neighborhoods and the communities. We won't make all the work that has gone on here benefit just a few. We will do it together, by the grace of God.

The Memphis speech was a hymn of praise to a public philosophy rooted in my personal religious values. Too many things were falling apart; I was trying to put them together.

On November 19 and 20, I went back to putting things together, flying to Seattle for the first-ever leaders' meeting of the Asia-Pacific Economic Cooperation organization. Before 1993, APEC had been a forum for finance ministers to discuss economic issues. I had suggested that the leaders themselves should meet every year to discuss our common interests, and I wanted to use our first meeting, on Blake Island, just off the coast of Seattle, to pursue three objectives: a free-trade area covering the Americas and the Asian Pacific nations; an informal discussion of political and security issues; and the creation of habits of cooperation, which clearly were going to be more important than ever in the twenty-first century. The Asia-Pacific nations accounted for half the world's output and presented some of its most challenging political and security problems. In the past, the United States had never dealt with the region with the kind of comprehensive approach we followed toward Europe. I thought it was the moment to do so.

I enjoyed my time with the new Japanese prime minister, Morihiro Hosokawa, a reformer who had broken the Liberal Democratic Party's monopoly on power and who had continued to open Japan economically. I was also glad for the chance to talk at length with China's president, Jiang Zemin, in a more informal setting. We still had differences over human rights, Tibet, and economics, but we had a shared interest in building a relationship that would not isolate but integrate China into the global community. Both Jiang and Hosokawa shared my concern about the looming crisis with North Korea, which seemed determined to become a nuclear power, something I was determined to avoid and would need their help to accomplish.

Back in Washington, Hillary and I hosted our first state dinner, for South Korean president Kim Yong-Sam. I always enjoyed the official state visits. They were the most ritualized events to occur at the White House, beginning with the official welcoming ceremony. Hillary and I would stand at the South Portico of the White House to greet our guests as they drove up. After greeting them, we would walk out onto the South Lawn for a brief receiving line, and the visiting dignitary and I would stand onstage, facing an impressive array of uniformed men and women from our armed services. The military band would play both nations' national anthems, after which I would escort my visitor on a review of the troops. We would then walk back to the stage to give brief remarks, often pausing on the way to wave to a crowd of schoolchildren, citizens from the visiting nation who were living in the United States, and Americans who had roots in the other country.

Before the state dinner, Hillary and I would host a small reception for the visiting delegation in the Yellow Oval Room on the residence floor. Al and Tipper, the secretary of state, the secretary of defense, and a few others would join us to visit with foreign guests. After the reception, a military honor guard of one man or woman from each service would escort us down the stairs past the portraits of my predecessors to a receiving line for the guests. During dinner, which was usually in the State Dining Room (with larger groups, dinner would be in the East Room or outside under a tent), we would be entertained by the U.S. Marine Corps Strolling Strings or their counterparts from the air force; I was always thrilled when they entered the room. After dinner, we had musical entertainment, often selected to suit the tastes of our guest. For example, Václav Havel wanted to hear Lou Reed, whose hard-driving music had inspired Havel's partisans in Czechoslovakia's Velvet Revolution. I took every opportunity I could to bring all kinds of musicians to the White House. Over the years we had Earth, Wind and Fire, Yo-Yo Ma, Placido Domingo, Jessye Norman, and many other classical, jazz, blues, Broadway, and gospel musicians as well as dancers from several disciplines. For the entertainment, we usually had room to invite more guests than could be accommodated at the dinner. Afterward, anyone who wanted to stay returned to the foyer of the White House for dancing. Usually, the honored guests were tired and soon left for Blair House, the official guest residence. Hillary and I would stay for a dance or two, then go upstairs while the revelers stayed at it for another hour or so.

In late November, I participated in the annual tradition going back to President Coolidge, of pardoning a Thanksgiving turkey, after which Hillary, Chelsea, and I left for a long Thanksgiving weekend at Camp David. I had a lot to be thankful for. My approval ratings were rising again, and American Airlines announced the settlement of its five-day-old strike. The strike could have been quite damaging to the economy; it was settled with the intense and skillful involvement of Bruce Lindsey. I was happy that my fellow citizens could fly home for the holiday.

Thanksgiving at Camp David became an annual tradition with our families and a few friends. We always had our Thanksgiving meal in Laurel, the largest cabin on the grounds, with its big dining and conference room, a large open space with a fireplace and television, and a private office for me. And we went by the dining hall to greet the navy and marine personnel and their families who kept the camp going. At night we watched movies and bowled. And at least once over the weekend, no matter how cold and rainy it was, Hillary's brothers, Roger, and I would play golf with whoever else was brave enough to go with us. Amazingly, Dick Kelley always played, though he was already almost eighty in 1993.

I loved every one of our Thanksgivings at Camp David, but the first one was special, because it was Mother's last. By late November, her cancer had spread and contaminated her bloodstream. She had to have blood transfusions every day just to stay alive. I didn't know how much longer she could last, but the transfusions made her look deceptively healthy and she was determined to live each day to the fullest. She enjoyed the football games on television, the meals, and visiting with the young servicemen and -women at the Camp David bar. The last thing she wanted to talk about was death. She was too alive to dwell on it.

On December 4, I went to California again, to hold an economic summit on the state's continuing difficulties, and spoke to a large group of people in the entertainment community, at the headquarters of Creative Artists Agency, asking them to join me in a partnership to reduce the massive amount of violence the media directed at young people, as well as the culture's assault on family and work. Over the next two weeks, I kept two of my commitments from the budget battle: I went to Marjorie Margolies-Mezvinsky's district for the conference on entitlements, and I appointed Bob Kerrey as co-chair, along with Senator John Danforth of Missouri, of a commission to study Social Security and other entitlements.

On December 15, I hailed the joint declaration of British prime minister John Major and Irish prime minister Albert Reynolds, which proposed a framework for the peaceful resolution of the Troubles in Northern Ireland. It was a wonderful Christmas present, one that I hoped would give me an opportunity to play a role in resolving a problem I had first become interested in as a student at Oxford. On the same day, I named an old friend from the McGovern days, John Holum, to head the Arms Control and Disarmament Agency and used the occasion to emphasize my nonproliferation agenda: ratification of the convention controlling chemical weapons, achieving a comprehensive nuclear test ban treaty, achieving permanent extension of the Nuclear Non-Proliferation Treaty (NPT), which expired in 1995, and fully funding the Nunn-Lugar program to secure and destroy Russian nuclear weapons and material.

On December 20, I signed a bill that was especially important to Hillary and me. The National Child Protection Act provided for a national database that any child-care provider could use to check the background of any job applicant. It was the brainchild of the writer Andrew Vachss, in response to stories of children subject to awful abuse in child-care centers. Most parents had to work, and therefore had to leave their preschool children in day care. They had a right to know their children would be safe and well cared for.

The Christmas season gave Hillary and me the chance to see Chelsea perform twice: in **The Nutcracker** with the Washington Ballet Company, where she went for class every day after school, and in a Christmas skit at the church we had chosen, Foundry United Methodist, on Sixteenth Street, not far from the White House. We liked Foundry's pastor, Phil Wogaman, and the fact that the church included people of various races, cultures, incomes, and political affiliations, and openly welcomed gays.

The White House is special at Christmastime. Every year a large Christmas tree is brought in for the oval Blue Room on the main floor. It is decorated, as are all the public rooms, according to the year's theme. Hillary made American crafts the theme of our first Christmas. Artisans from around the country gave us Christmas ornaments and other works in glass, wood, and metal. Every Christmas, the State Dining Room has a huge gingerbread

White House, which kids especially enjoy seeing. In 1993, about 150,000 people came through the White House during the holidays to see the decorations.

We also got another big tree for the Yellow Oval Room on the residence floor, and filled it with ornaments Hillary and I had been collecting since our first Christmas together. Traditionally, Chelsea and I put on most of the ornaments, following a practice we began as soon as she was old enough. Between Thanksgiving and Christmas we hosted a large number of receptions and parties for Congress, the press, the Secret Service, the residence staff, the White House staff and cabinet, other administration officials and supporters from around the country, family, and friends. Hillary and I would stand in line for hours, greeting people and taking pictures, as choirs and other musical groups from around the country performed throughout the house. It was an exhausting but happy way to thank the people who made our work possible and our lives richer.

Our first Christmas was especially important to me because I knew that, like our first Camp David Thanksgiving, it would almost certainly be our last one with Mother. We persuaded her and Dick to come spend a week with us, which she agreed to do when I promised I'd take her home in time for her to get ready to go to Las Vegas for Barbra Streisand's much-heralded New Year's Eve concert. Barbra really wanted her to come, and Mother was determined to go. She loved Barbra, and in her mind, Las Vegas was the closest thing she'd seen to heaven on earth. I didn't know what she'd do if it turned out there was no gambling or fancy entertainment in the afterlife.

While we were enjoying Christmas, Whitewater became an issue once more. For the previous several weeks, the

Washington Post and the **New York Times** had been chasing rumors that Jim McDougal might be indicted again. In 1990, he had been tried and acquitted on charges arising out of the failure of Madison Guaranty. Apparently, the Resolution Trust Corporation was looking into whether McDougal had made illegal campaign contributions to politicians, including me. During the campaign, we had commissioned a report that proved we had lost money on the Whitewater investment. My campaign contributions were a matter of public record, and neither Hillary nor I had ever borrowed any money from Madison. I knew the whole Whitewater business was simply an attempt by my enemies to discredit me and impair my ability to serve.

Nonetheless, Hillary and I decided we should hire a lawyer. David Kendall had been at Yale Law School with us. He had represented clients in savings-and-loan cases and understood how to organize and synthesize complex and apparently unconnected material. There was a brilliant mind behind David's modest Quaker demeanor, and a willingness to fight against injustice. He had been jailed for his civil rights activity in Mississippi during Freedom Summer in 1964, and had argued death penalty cases for the NAACP Legal Defense Fund. Best of all, David Kendall was a terrific human being who would see us through the darkest moments of the years ahead with strength, judgment, and a great sense of humor.

On December 18, Kendall told us that the **American Spectator,** a right-wing monthly magazine, was about to publish an article by David Brock in which four Arkansas state troopers claimed they had procured women for me when I was governor. Only two of the troopers agreed to be interviewed on CNN. There were some allegations in the story that could be easily disproved, and the two troopers had credibility problems of their own, unrelated to their allegations against me: they had been investigated for insurance fraud involving a state vehicle they wrecked in 1990. David Brock later apologized to Hillary and me for the story. If you want to know more, read his brave memoir, **Blinded by the Right,** in which he reveals the extraordinary efforts made to discredit me by wealthy right-wingers with ties to Newt Gingrich and some adversaries of mine in Arkansas. Brock acknowledges that he allowed himself to be used in the smear by people who didn't care whether the damaging information they paid for was true or not.

The trooper story was ridiculous, but it hurt. It hit Hillary hard because she thought we'd left all that behind in the campaign. Now she knew it might never end. For the moment, there was nothing to do but carry on and hope the story would blow over. While it was raging, we went to the Kennedy Center one night for a performance of Handel's **Messiah.** When Hillary and I appeared in the President's box on the balcony, the large audience stood and cheered. We were moved by the kind and spontaneous gesture. I didn't realize how upset I had been until I felt tears of gratitude fill my eyes.

After a memorable Christmas week, Hillary, Chelsea, and I flew Mother and Dick home to Arkansas. Hillary and Chelsea stayed with Dorothy in Little Rock, and I drove with Mother and Dick to Hot Springs. We all went to dinner with some of my friends from high school at Rocky's Pizza, one of Mother's favorite haunts, just across the street from the racetrack. After dinner Mother and Dick wanted to go to bed, so I took them home, then went bowling with my friends, after which we came back to the little house on Lake Hamilton to play cards and talk until the early hours of the morning.

The next day Mother and I sat alone together over a cup of coffee for what turned out to be our last visit. She was upbeat as always, saying the only reason the trooper story came out when it did was that my poll ratings had rebounded in the last month to their highest level since my inauguration. Then she chuckled and said she knew the two troopers weren't the "brightest lights on the horizon," but she sure wished "the boys would find some other way to make a living."

For a brief moment I got her to think about the sand running out of the hourglass. She was working on her memoirs with a fine collaborator from Arkansas, James Morgan, and she had put her entire story on tape, but there were still several chapters in the drafting stage. I asked her what she wanted to happen if she didn't finish them. She smiled and said, "You're going to finish them, of course." I said, "What are my instructions?" She said I should check the facts, change anything that was wrong, and clarify anything that was confusing. "But I want this to be my story in my words. So don't change it unless you think I've been too hard on someone who's still alive." With that, she went back to discussing politics and her trip to Las Vegas.

Later that day I kissed Mother good-bye, drove to Little Rock to pick up Hillary and Chelsea, and flew to Fayetteville to see the number one–ranked Arkansas Razorbacks play basketball, then on to the Renaissance Weekend with our friends Jim and Diane Blair. After a jam-packed year, so full of highs and lows, it was good to have a few days with old friends. I walked on the beach, played touch football with the kids and golf with my friends, went to the panels, and enjoyed the company.

But my thoughts were never far from Mother. She was a marvel, still beautiful at seventy, even after a mastectomy, chemotherapy treatments that took all her hair and forced her to wear a wig, and daily blood transfusions that would have put most people in bed. She was ending her life as she had lived it, going all out, grateful for her blessings, without a shred of self-pity for her pain and illness, and eager for the adventures of every new day she could get. She was relieved that Roger's life was on track, and convinced that I was mastering my job. She would have loved to live to be one hundred, but if her time was up, so be it. She had found her peace with God. He could call her home, but He would have to catch her on the run.

THIRTY-SEVEN

The year 1994 was one of the hardest of my life, one in which important successes in foreign and domestic policy were overshadowed by the demise of health-care reform and an obsession with bogus scandal. It began with personal heartbreak and ended in political disaster.

On the night of January 5, Mother called me at the White House. She had just returned home from her trip to Las Vegas. I told her I had been calling her hotel room for several days and never found her in. She laughed and said she had been out day and night, having the time of her life in her favorite city, and she didn't have time to sit around waiting for the phone to ring. She had loved Barbra Streisand's concert, and was especially pleased that Barbra had introduced her and dedicated a song to her. Mother was in high spirits and seemed strong; she just wanted to check in and tell me she loved me. It wasn't much different from the countless calls we'd shared over the years, usually on Sunday nights.

About 2 a.m. the phone rang again, waking Hillary and me. Dick Kelley was on the line, crying. He said, "She's gone, Bill." After a perfect but exhausting week, Mother had just gone to sleep and died. I knew it was coming, but I wasn't ready to let her go. Now our last phone conversation seemed too routine, too full of idle chitchat; we had talked like people who think they have forever to talk to each other. I was aching to redo it, but all I could do was tell Dick that I loved him, that I was so grateful to him for making her last years happy, and that I'd get home as quickly as I could. Hillary knew what had happened from my end of the conversation. I hugged her and wept. She said something about Mother and her love of life, and I realized that the phone conversation was just the kind Mother would have chosen to be our last one. My mother was always about life, not death.

I called my brother, who I knew would be devastated. He worshipped Mother, all the more because she never gave up on him. I told him he had to hold up for her and keep building his life. Then I called my friend Patty Howe Criner, who had been part of our lives for more than forty years, and asked her to help Dick and me with the funeral arrangements. Hillary woke Chelsea and we told her. She had already lost a grandfather, and she and Mother, whom she called Ginger, had a close, tender relationship. On the wall of her study room, she had a terrific pen-and-ink portrait of Mother by Hot Springs artist Gary Simmons, entitled **Chelsea's Ginger.** It was moving to watch my daughter coming to terms with the loss of someone else she loved, trying to express her grief and keep her composure, letting go and holding on. **Chelsea's Ginger** is hanging in her room in Chappaqua today.

Later that morning we put out a release announcing Mother's death, which was all over the news immediately. By coincidence, Bob Dole and Newt Gingrich were on the morning news programs. Undeterred by the moment, interviewers asked about Whitewater; to one, Dole replied that it "cries out" for the appointment of an independent counsel. I was stunned. I would have thought that even the press and my adversaries would take a time-out on the day of my mother's death. To his credit, a few years later Dole apologized to me. By then, I better understood what had happened. Washington's narcotic of choice is power. It dulls the senses and clouds the judgment. Dole was not even close to being its worst abuser. I was touched by his apology.

That same day Al Gore went to Milwaukee to deliver a foreign-policy speech I had agreed to make, and I flew home. Dick and Mother's house was full of their friends, family, and the food Arkansas folks bring to ease common grieving. We all laughed and told stories about her. The next day Hillary and Chelsea arrived, as did some of Mother's other friends from out of state, including Barbra Streisand and Ralph Wilson, the owner of the Buffalo Bills, who had invited Mother to the Super Bowl the previous year when he learned she was a huge Bills fan.

No church was big enough to hold all Mother's friends and it was too cold to hold the funeral service at her preferred venue, the racetrack, so we scheduled it for the Convention Center. About three thousand people came, including Senator Pryor, Governor Tucker, and all my college roommates. But most of the attendees were simple working people whom Mother had met and befriended over the years. All the women from her "birthday club" were there, too. There were twelve members, each with a birthday in a different month. They celebrated them together over monthly lunches. After Mother died, as she requested, the other women picked a replacement; and they renamed their group the Virginia Clinton Kelley Birthday Club.

The Reverend John Miles presided over the service, referring to Mother as an "American original." "Virginia," he said, "was like a rubber ball; the harder life put her down, the higher she bounced." Brother John reminded the crowd of Mother's automatic response to every problem: "That's no hill for a stepper."

The service featured the hymns she loved. We all sang "Amazing Grace" and "Precious Lord, Take My Hand." Her friend Malvie Lee Giles, who once lost her voice completely, then got it back "from God" with an extra octave to spare, sang "His Eye Is on the Sparrow," and Mother's favorite, "A Closer Walk with Thee." Our Pentecostal friend Janice Sjostrand sang a powerful hymn Mother had heard at my inaugural church service, "Holy Ground." When Barbra Streisand, who was sitting behind me, heard Janice, she touched my shoulder and shook her head in amazement. When the service was over, she asked, "Who is that woman and what is that music? It's magnificent!" Barbra was so inspired by Mother's funeral music that she made her own album of hymns and inspirational songs, including one written in Mother's memory, "Leading with Your Heart."

After the funeral we drove Mother home to Hope. All along the way, people were standing by the road to show their respect. She was buried in the cemetery across the street from where her father's store had been, in the plot that had long awaited her, beside her parents and my father. It was January 8, the birthday of her favorite man outside the family, Elvis Presley.

After a reception at the Sizzlin' Steakhouse, we drove to the airport to fly back to Washington. There was no time to grieve; I had to go back to putting things together. As soon as I dropped Hillary and Chelsea off, I left for a long-planned trip to Europe to establish a process for opening NATO's door to the Central European nations in a way that wouldn't cause Yeltsin too many problems in Russia. I was determined to do everything I could to create a Europe that was united, free, democratic, and secure for the first time in history. I had to make sure NATO expansion didn't simply lead to a new division of Europe farther to the east.

In Brussels, after a speech in the city hall to a group of young Europeans, I received a special gift. Belgium was celebrating the hundredth anniversary of the death of my favorite Belgian, Adolphe Sax, inventor of the saxophone, and the mayor of Dinant, Sax's hometown, presented me with a beautiful new Selmer tenor sax made in Paris.

The next day the NATO leaders approved my Partnership for Peace proposal to increase our security cooperation with Europe's new democracies until we could achieve the expansion of NATO itself.

On January 11, I was in Prague with Václav Havel, twenty-four years to the week after my first trip there as a student. Havel, a small, soft-spoken man with dancing eyes and a biting wit, was a hero to the forces of freedom everywhere. He had been in prison for years and used the time to write eloquent and provocative books. When he was released, he led Czechoslovakia through a peaceful Velvet Revolution, then oversaw the orderly division of the country into two states. Now he was the president of the Czech Republic, eager to build a successful market economy and to claim the security of NATO membership. Havel was a good friend of our UN ambassador, Madeleine Albright, who was born in Czechoslovakia and delighted in every opportunity she had to speak with him in their native tongue.

Havel took me to one of the jazz clubs that had been hotbeds of support for his Velvet Revolution. After the group played a couple of tunes, he brought me up to meet the band and presented me with another new saxophone, this one made in Prague by a company that, in Communist times, had produced saxophones for the military bands throughout the Warsaw Pact nations. He invited me to play it with the band. We did "Summertime" and "My Funny Valentine," with Havel enthusiastically joining in on the tambourine.

On the way to Moscow, I stopped briefly in Kiev to meet with Ukraine's president, Leonid Kravchuk, to thank him for the agreement that he, Yeltsin, and I would sign the following Friday, committing Ukraine to eliminate 176 intercontinental ballistic missiles and 1,500 nuclear warheads targeted at the United States. Ukraine was a large country of sixty million people with great potential. Like Russia, it was wrestling with the question of exactly what kind of future it wanted. Kravchuk faced considerable opposition in parliament to getting rid of his nuclear weapons, and I wanted to support him.

Hillary met me in Moscow. She brought Chelsea, too, because we didn't want her to be alone right after Mother's death. Staying together in the guest quarters of the Kremlin and seeing Moscow in the dead of winter would be a good distraction for all of us. Yeltsin knew I was hurting because he also had recently lost his mother, whom he adored.

Whenever we had a chance we took to the streets, shopping for Russian artifacts and buying bread at a small bakery. I lit a candle for Mother at Kazan Cathedral, now fully restored from the ravages of Stalinism, and visited the patriarch of the Russian Orthodox Church in the hospital. On January 14, after an impressive welcoming ceremony in the Kremlin's St. George's Hall, a massive white room with high arches and columns with the names of more than two hundred years of Russia's war heroes emblazoned in gold, Yeltsin and I signed the nuclear agreement with Ukranian president Kravchuk, and held talks about economic and security initiatives.

In the press conference afterward, Yeltsin expressed his appreciation for the American aid package and the one approved at the Tokyo G-7 meeting, for the commitment of $1 billion more in each of the next two years, and for our decision to reduce tariffs on five thousand Russian products. He gave a qualified endorsement of the Partnership for Peace, on the strength of my commitment to work out a special cooperative agreement between NATO and Russia. I was also pleased that we had agreed, as of May 30, not to target our nuclear missiles against each other or any other country, and that the United States would buy $12 billion worth of highly enriched uranium from Russia over the next twenty years, gradually removing it from any possibility of being used to make weapons.

I thought all these actions were good for both the United States and Russia, but not everyone agreed. Yeltsin was having some problems with his new parliament, especially with Vladimir Zhirinovsky, the leader of a sizable bloc of militant nationalists who wanted to return Russia to imperial glory and were convinced I was trying to reduce its power and reach. To push back a bit, I repeated my mantra that the Russian people should define their greatness in terms relevant to the future, not the past.

After the press conference, I did a town hall meeting with young people at the Ostankino television station. They asked questions about all the current issues, but they also wanted to know whether American students could learn anything from Russia, how old I was when I first thought of becoming President, what advice I could give a young Russian who wanted to go into politics, and how I wanted to be remembered. The students made me hopeful about the future of Russia. They were intelligent, idealistic, and fiercely committed to democracy.

The trip was going well, advancing important American interests in building a safer, freer world, but you would never have known it back home, where the only thing the politicians and press wanted to talk about was Whitewater. I even got questions about it on my trip from the American press accompanying me. Even before I left, the **Washington Post** and the **New York Times** had joined the Republicans in demanding that Janet Reno appoint an independent counsel. The only new development in recent months was that David Hale, a Republican who had been indicted in 1993 for defrauding the Small Business Administration, had said I had asked him to make a loan to Susan McDougal for which she was ineligible. I had not done so.

The standard for appointing an independent counsel under both the old law, which had expired, and the new one being considered by Congress was "credible evidence" of wrongdoing. In its January 5 editorial calling for an independent counsel in Whitewater, the **Washington Post** explicitly acknowledged that "there has been no credible charge in this case that either the President or Mrs. Clinton did anything wrong." Nevertheless, the **Post** said the public interest demanded an independent counsel, because Hillary and I had been partners in the Whitewater real estate deal (on which we lost money), before McDougal bought Madison Guaranty (from which we had never borrowed money). Even worse, we had apparently failed to take the full tax deduction for our losses. It was probably the first time in history when the flames of outrage against a politician were fanned because of money he lost, loans he didn't receive, and a tax deduction he didn't take. The **Post** said the Justice Department was headed by presidential appointees who couldn't be trusted to investigate me or to decide whether someone else should investigate me.

The independent counsel law was enacted in reaction to President Nixon's firing of Watergate special prosecutor Archibald Cox, who had been appointed by Nixon's attorney general and therefore was an executive branch employee subject to termination. Congress recognized both the need for independent investigations of alleged wrongdoing by the President and his major appointees and the danger of giving unlimited power to an unaccountable prosecutor with limitless resources. That's why the law required credible evidence of wrongdoing. Now the press was saying the President should agree to an independent counsel **without** such evidence, whenever anyone with whom he had ever been associated was being investigated.

In the Reagan-Bush years, more than twenty people were convicted of felonies by independent counsels. After six years of investigations and a finding by Senator John Tower's commission that President Reagan had authorized the illegal sales of arms to the Nicaraguan rebels, Iran-Contra prosecutor Lawrence Walsh indicted Caspar Weinberger and five others, but President Bush pardoned them. The only independent counsel investigation into a President's activities before he took office involved President Carter, who was investigated for a disputed loan to a peanut warehouse he and his brother, Billy, owned. The special prosecutor the President requested finished his investigation in six months, exonerating the Carters.

By the time I got to Moscow, several Democratic senators and President Carter had joined the Republicans and
the press in calling for an independent counsel, though
they couldn't give a reason that approached credible evidence of wrongdoing. Most of the Democrats didn't
know a thing about Whitewater; they were just anxious
to show they didn't object to Democratic Presidents
being investigated, and they didn't want to be on the
other side of the **Washington Post** and the **New York
Times.** They also probably thought that Janet Reno
could be trusted to appoint a professional prosecutor who
would deal with the problem promptly. Regardless, it was
clear that we had to do something, in Lloyd Bentsen's
words, "to lance the boil."

When I arrived in Moscow, I got on a conference call
with my staff, David Kendall, and Hillary, who was still
in Washington, to discuss what we should do. David Gergen, Bernie Nussbaum, and Kendall were against asking
for an independent counsel, because there were no
grounds for one, and if we got unlucky, an unscrupulous
prosecutor could pursue an endless disruptive investigation. Moreover, it wouldn't have to last long to bankrupt
us; I had the lowest net worth of any President in modern
history. Nussbaum, a world-class lawyer who had worked
with Hillary on the congressional Watergate inquiry, was
adamantly against a special prosecutor. He called it "an
evil institution," because it gave unaccountable prosecutors the ability to do anything they wanted; Bernie said I
owed it to the presidency, and to myself, to resist a special
prosecutor with everything I had. Nussbaum also pointed
out that the **Washington Post**'s disdain for the Justice
Department's inquiry was unfounded, since my records
were being reviewed by a career prosecutor who had been

nominated for a Justice Department position by President Bush.

Gergen agreed, but argued forcefully that I should turn over all our records to the **Washington Post.** So did Mark Gearan and George Stephanopoulos. David said Len Downie, the **Post**'s executive editor, had achieved his spurs with Watergate and had convinced himself we were covering something up. The **New York Times** seemed to think so, too. Gergen thought the only way to defuse the pressure for an independent counsel was to produce the documents.

All the lawyers—Nussbaum, Kendall, and Bruce Lindsey—were against releasing the records because, while we had agreed to give the Justice Department everything we'd found, the records were incomplete and scattered, and we were still in the process of rounding them up. They said as soon as we couldn't answer a question or produce a document, the press would return to the drumbeat for an independent counsel. In the meantime, we'd get lots of bad stories full of innuendo and speculation.

The rest of my staff, including George Stephanopoulos and Harold Ickes, who had come to work as deputy chief of staff in January, thought that because the Democrats were taking the path of least resistance, the special prosecutor was inevitable, and we should just go on and ask for it, so we could get back to the people's business. I asked Hillary what she thought. She said that asking for the prosecutor would set a terrible precedent, basically changing the standard from requiring credible evidence of wrongdoing to giving in whenever a media frenzy could be stirred up, but that it had to be my decision. I could tell she was tired of fighting my staff.

I told everyone on the call that I wasn't worried about

an investigation, because I hadn't done anything wrong and neither had Hillary, nor did I have any objections to releasing the records. After all, we had endured a lot of irresponsible Whitewater stories since the campaign. My instincts were to release the records and fight the prosecutor, but if the consensus was to do the reverse, I could live with it. Nussbaum was distraught, predicting that whoever was appointed would be frustrated when nothing was there, and would keep widening the investigation until he found something someone I knew had done wrong. He said if I felt I had to do more, we should just dump the records on the press and even offer to testify before the Senate Judiciary Committee. Stephanopoulos thought that was a terrible idea because of all the publicity it would generate. He said Reno would appoint an independent counsel who would satisfy the press and the whole thing would be over in a few months. Bernie disagreed, saying that if Congress passed a new independent counsel law and I signed it, which I had promised to do, the judges on the Washington, D.C., Court of Appeals would appoint a new prosecutor and start all over again. George got angry, saying Bernie was paranoid and it would never happen. Bernie knew that Chief Justice Rehnquist would name the panel and it would be dominated by conservative Republicans. He laughed nervously at George's outburst and said maybe the chances of a second prosecutor were only fifty-fifty.

After further discussion I asked to speak with just Hillary and David Kendall. I told them I thought we had to go along with the consensus of the nonlegal staff for a special prosecutor. After all, I had nothing to hide, and all the clamor was diverting the attention of Congress and the country from our larger agenda. The next day the

White House asked Janet Reno to appoint a special prosecutor. Though I had said I could live with it, I almost didn't live through it.

It was the worst presidential decision I ever made, wrong on the facts, wrong on the law, wrong on the politics, wrong for the presidency and the Constitution. Perhaps I did it because I was completely exhausted and grieving over Mother; it took all the concentration I could muster just to do the job I had left her funeral to do. What I should have done is release the records, resist the prosecutor, give an extensive briefing to all the Democrats who wanted it, and ask for their support. Of course, it might not have made any difference. At the time I wasn't that worried about it, because I knew I hadn't broken any laws, and I still believed that the press wanted the truth.

Within a week Janet Reno appointed Robert Fiske, a Republican former prosecutor from New York, who would have completed his investigation in a timely way had he been left to do his job. Of course, Fiske was not allowed to finish, but I'm getting ahead of myself. For now, agreeing to the special prosecutor was like taking aspirin for a cold; it brought temporary relief. Very temporary.

On the way home from Russia, after a brief stop in Belarus, I flew to Geneva, for my first meeting with President Assad of Syria. He was a ruthless but brilliant man who had once wiped out a whole village as a lesson to his opponents, and whose support of terrorist groups in the Middle East had isolated Syria from the United States. Assad rarely left Syria, and when he did it was almost always to come to Geneva to meet with foreign leaders. On our visit, I was impressed by his intelligence and his almost total recall of detailed events going back more than twenty years. Assad was famous for long meetings—he could go on for six or seven hours without taking a break. I, on the other hand, was tired and needed to drink coffee, tea, or water to stay awake. Fortunately, the meeting ran only a few hours. Our discussion produced the two things I wanted: Assad's first explicit statement that he was willing to make peace and establish normal relations with Israel, and his commitment to withdraw all Syrian forces from Lebanon and respect its independence once a comprehensive Middle East peace was reached. I knew the success of the meeting resulted from more than personal chemistry. Assad had received a lot of economic support from the former Soviet Union; that was gone now, so he needed to reach out to the West. To do that, he had to stop supporting terrorism in the region, which would be easy to do if he made an agreement with Israel that succeeded in giving back to Syria the Golan Heights, lost in the 1967 war.

I returned to Washington to a whole series of those all-too-typical days when everything happens at once. On the seventeenth, Los Angeles was struck with the most costly earthquake in U.S. history, which caused billions of dollars of damage to homes, hospitals, schools, and businesses. I flew out on the nineteenth with James Lee Witt, director of the Federal Emergency Management Agency (FEMA), to view the damage, including a large stretch of interstate highway that had completely split open. On the twentieth, virtually the entire cabinet and I met with Mayor Dick Riordan and other state and local leaders in an airplane hangar in Burbank to plan emergency efforts. Thanks to a remarkable partnership, the recovery occurred quickly: the main freeway was rebuilt in three months; FEMA gave financial help to more than 600,000 families and businesses; and thousands of homes and businesses were rebuilt with Small Business Administration loans. The entire effort involved more than $16 billion in direct aid. I was distressed for Californians; they'd borne the brunt of the recession and the defense downsizing, suffered severe fires, and now the earthquake. One of the local officials joked to me that he was just waiting for a plague of locusts. His sense of humor reminded me of Mother Teresa's famous observation that she knew God would never give her a heavier burden than she could carry, but sometimes she wished He didn't have so much confidence in her. I returned to Washington to do an interview with Larry King on the first anniversary of the start of my presidency, telling him that I liked my job, even on the bad days. After all, I hadn't signed up to have a good time, but to change the country.

A few days later, President Assad's eldest son, whom he had groomed to succeed him, was killed in a car accident. When I called to express my condolences, Assad was obviously heartbroken, a reminder that the worst thing that can happen in life is losing a child.

That week I named the deputy secretary of defense, Bill Perry, to succeed Les Aspin, who had resigned as secretary not long after the day of Black Hawk Down. We had conducted an exhaustive search, and all the while the best candidate had been right under our noses. Perry had led several defense-related organizations, been a professor of mathematics and engineering, and done a superb job at the Pentagon, promoting Stealth technology, procurement reform, and realistic budgeting. He was a soft-spoken, modest man whose demeanor disguised a surprising toughness. He would turn out to be one of my best appointments, probably the finest secretary of defense since General George Marshall.

On the twenty-fifth, I gave my State of the Union address. It's the only time in a year when a President gets the chance to speak to the American people, unfiltered, for a whole hour, and I wanted to make the most of it. After a tribute to the late House Speaker Tip O'Neill, who had died the day before Mother, I summarized the long list of congressional achievements in 1993, saying that the economy was producing jobs; that millions of Americans had saved money by refinancing their homes at lower rates; that only 1.2 percent of the American people had had their income taxes increased; that the deficit would be 40 percent lower than previously predicted; and that we would reduce the federal payrolls by more than 250,000 instead of the 100,000 I had previously promised.

The rest of the speech was an outline of my 1994 agenda, beginning with education. I asked Congress to pass my Goals 2000 initiative to help public schools reach the national education goals the governors and the Bush administration had given the country, through reforms like school choice, charter schools, and connecting all our schools to the Internet by 2000; and to measure schools' progress toward reaching the goals the old-fashioned way, by whether our students were learning what they needed to know.

I also asked for more investments in new job-creating technologies and defense conversion projects; urged passage of the crime bill and a ban on assault weapons; and promoted three environmental laws: a Safe Drinking Water Act, a revitalized Clean Water Act, and a reformed Superfund program. The Superfund was a public/private partnership to clean up polluted sites that had been

abandoned and had become ugly, unusable health hazards. It was important to me and to Al Gore, and by the
time we left office we had cleaned up three times as
many Superfund sites as the Reagan and Bush administrations combined.

I then asked Congress to pass both welfare reform and
health-care reform in 1994. One million people were on
the welfare rolls because it was the only way they could get
health care for their children. When people left welfare for
low-wage jobs without benefits, they were in the incredible position of paying taxes to support the Medicaid program, which provided health care for families that had
stayed on welfare. At some time during each year, nearly
sixty million Americans found themselves without health
insurance. More than eighty million Americans had "preexisting conditions," health problems that meant they
were paying more for insurance, if they could get it, and
often couldn't change jobs without losing it. Three out of
four Americans had policies with "lifetime limits" on how
much of their health-care costs would be covered, meaning they could lose their insurance just when they needed
it most. The system hurt small businesses, too; their premiums were 35 percent higher than those paid by large
businesses and government. To control costs, more and
more Americans were being forced into health maintenance organizations, which restricted patients in their
choice of a doctor, and doctors in their choice of care, and
forced health-care professionals to spend more and more
time on paperwork and less on their patients. All these
problems were rooted in one fundamental fact: we had a
crazy-quilt pattern of coverage in which insurance companies called the shots.

I told the Congress I knew it was hard to change the

system. Roosevelt, Truman, Nixon, and Carter had all tried and failed. The effort virtually destroyed Truman's presidency, driving his approval ratings below 30 percent and helping the Republicans gain control of the Congress. This happened because, for all our problems, most Americans had some kind of coverage, liked their doctors and hospitals, and knew we had a good system of health-care delivery. All those things were still true. Those who profited from the way health care was financed were spending huge sums to convince the Congress and the people that fixing what was wrong with the health-care system would destroy what it did right.

I thought my argument was effective except for one thing: at the end of the health-care portion of the speech, I held up a pen and said I would use it to veto any bill that didn't guarantee health insurance to all Americans. I did it because a couple of my advisors had said that people wouldn't think I had the strength of my convictions unless I demonstrated that I wouldn't compromise. It was an unnecessary red flag to my opponents in Congress. Politics is about compromise, and people expect Presidents to win, not posture for them. Health-care reform was the hardest of all hills to climb. I couldn't do it alone, without compromise. As it turned out, my error didn't matter, because Bob Dole would decide to kill any health-care reform.

In the short run, the State of the Union speech dramatically increased public support for my agenda. Newt Gingrich later said to me that after hearing the speech, he told the House Republicans that if I could persuade the congressional Democrats to deliver on my proposals, our party would be in the majority for a long time. Newt sure didn't want that, so, like Bob Dole, he would try to keep as much from happening before the midterm elections as possible.

In the last week of January, we had a heated debate with our foreign policy team over whether to grant a visa to Gerry Adams, leader of Sinn Fein, the political arm of the Irish Republican Army. America had great significance to both sides in the Irish conflict. For years, ardent American supporters of the IRA had provided funds for its violent activities. Sinn Fein had a larger number of partisans here among Irish Catholics who disowned terrorism but wanted to see an end to discrimination against their co-religionists and more political autonomy, with Catholic participation, in Northern Ireland. The British and the Irish Protestants had their supporters, too, who deplored any dealings with Sinn Fein because of its ties to the IRA, and who believed that we had no business meddling in the affairs of the United Kingdom, our strongest ally. That argument had carried the day with all my predecessors, including those sympathetic to the legitimate grievances of Northern Ireland's Catholics. Now, with the Declaration of Principles, we had to revisit it.

In the declaration, for the first time ever, the UK pledged that the status of Northern Ireland would be determined by the wishes of its citizens, and Ireland renounced its historic claim to the six counties in the north until a majority of its people voted to change its status. The more moderate Unionist and Irish Nationalist parties were cautiously supportive of the agreement. The Reverend Ian Paisley, leader of the extreme Democratic Unionist Party, was outraged by it. Gerry Adams and Sinn Fein said they were disappointed because the principles lacked specificity as to how the peace process would operate and how Sinn Fein would be able to participate in it. Notwithstanding the ambiguous responses, the British and Irish governments clearly had created pressure on all the parties to work with them for peace.

From the time the declaration was issued, Adams's allies in America had been asking me to grant him a visa to visit the United States. They said it would increase his standing and his ability to get involved in the process and to press the IRA toward giving up violence. John Hume, leader of the moderate Social Democratic and Labour Party, who had built a career on nonviolent action, said he had changed his position on giving Adams a visa; he now thought it would advance the peace process. A number of Irish-American activists agreed, including my friend Bruce Morrison, who had organized our outreach to the Irish-American community in 1992, and our ambassador to Ireland, Jean Kennedy Smith. There was support in Congress from her brother, Senator Ted Kennedy; Senators Chris Dodd, Pat Moynihan, and John Kerry; and New York congressmen Peter King and Tom Manton. House Speaker Tom Foley, who had long been active in Irish issues, remained strongly opposed to the visa.

In early January, Irish prime minister Albert Reynolds informed us that, like John Hume, he now favored granting the visa because Adams was working for peace, and he felt the visa would give him leverage to move the IRA away from violence and into the peace process. The British government remained vehemently opposed to the visa, because of the long history of IRA terror and because Adams had neither renounced violence nor embraced the Declaration of Principles as the basis for settling the problem.

I told Albert Reynolds I would consider a visa if Adams had a formal invitation to speak in the United States.

Shortly afterward, Adams, along with the leaders of Northern Ireland's other parties, was invited to participate in a peace conference in New York hosted by an American foreign policy group. This put the visa question front and center, where it became the first important issue on which my foreign policy advisors couldn't reach a consensus.

Warren Christopher and the State Department, including our ambassador to Great Britain, Ray Seitz, were strongly opposed to issuing the visa, arguing that since Adams wouldn't renounce violence, it would make us look soft on terrorism and that it could do irreparable damage to our vaunted "special relationship" with Great Britain, including our ability to secure British cooperation on Bosnia and other important matters. The Justice Department, the FBI, and the CIA agreed with State. Their unanimous opinion was entitled to great weight.

Three people were working the Irish issue at the National Security Council: Tony Lake, NSC staff director Nancy Soderberg, and our European affairs person, Army Major Jane Holl. With my support, they were taking an independent look at the visa question, while trying to reach a consensus position with the State Department, working through Undersecretary Peter Tarnoff. The NSC team became convinced that Adams favored an end to IRA violence, full participation by Sinn Fein in the peace process, and a democratic future for Northern Ireland. Their analysis made sense. The Irish were beginning to prosper economically, Europe as a whole was moving toward greater economic and political integration, and tolerance for terrorism among the Irish had dropped. On the other hand, the IRA was a tough nut to crack, full of hard men who had built a life on hatred of the British and the Ulster Unionists, and for whom the idea of peaceful coexistence and continuing to be a part of the UK was anathema. Since the population of the northern counties was about 10 percent more Protestant than Catholic, and the Declaration of Principles committed both Ireland and the UK to a democratic future based on majority rule, Northern Ireland was likely to remain a part of the UK for some time to come. Adams understood that, but he also knew that terror wouldn't bring victory and he seemed genuine when he said he wanted the IRA to give it up in return for an end to discrimination against and isolation of Catholics.

Based on this analysis, the NSC determined that we should grant the visa, because it would boost Adams's leverage within Sinn Fein and the IRA, while increasing American influence with him. That was important, because unless the IRA renounced violence and Sinn Fein became a part of the peace process, the Irish problem could not be resolved.

The debate raged on until a few days before the conference was scheduled to open, with both the British government and Adams's allies in the Congress and the Irish-American community turning up the heat. I listened carefully to both sides, including an impassioned last-minute plea not to do it from Warren Christopher and a message from Adams saying the Irish people were taking risks for peace and I should take a risk, too. Nancy Soderberg said she had come around on the visa because she was convinced that Adams was serious about making peace and that at present he couldn't say more about his desire to move away from violence than he already had without damaging his position within Sinn Fein and the IRA. Nancy had advised me on foreign policy since the campaign, and I had developed great respect for her judgment. I was also impressed that Tony Lake agreed with her. As my national security advisor, he had to deal with the British on many other issues that could be adversely affected by the visa. He also understood the implications of the decision in terms of our overall efforts to combat terrorism. Vice President Gore also clearly grasped the larger context in which the decision had to be made, and he favored the visa, too. I decided to issue it, but to restrict it so that Adams couldn't do any fund-raising or travel outside New York during his three-day stay.

The British were furious. They thought Adams was just a fast-talking deceiver who had no intention of giving up the violence that had included an attempt to assassinate Margaret Thatcher and had already claimed the lives of thousands of British citizens, including innocent children, government officials, and a member of the royal family, Lord Mountbatten, who had overseen the end of British rule in India. The Unionist parties boycotted the conference because Adams was coming. For days John Major refused to take my phone calls. The British press was filled with articles and columns saying I had damaged the special relationship between our countries. One memorable headline read: "Slimy Snake Adams Spits Venom at Yanks."

Some of the press implied that I had issued the visa to appeal to the Irish vote in America and because I was still angry at Major for his attempts to help President Bush during the campaign. It wasn't true. I had never been as upset with Major as the British believed, and I admired him for sticking his neck out with the Declaration of Principles; he had a slim majority in Parliament and needed the votes of the Irish Unionists to keep it. Moreover, I despised terrorism, as did the American people; politically, there was a lot more downside than upside to the decision. I was granting the visa because I thought it was the best shot we had to bring the violence to an end. I remembered Yitzhak Rabin's adage: You do not make peace with your friends.

Gerry Adams came to the United States on January 31 and received a warm reception from Irish-Americans sympathetic to the cause. During the visit he promised to push Sinn Fein to make concrete positive decisions. Afterward the British accelerated their efforts to get political talks going with the Northern Irish parties, and the Irish government increased its pressure on Sinn Fein to cooperate. Seven months later the IRA declared a cease-fire. The visa decision had worked. It was the beginning of my deep engagement in the long, emotional, complicated search for peace in Northern Ireland.

On February 3, I began the day at my second National Prayer Breakfast. Mother Teresa was the guest speaker, and I argued that we should emulate her in bringing more humility and a spirit of reconciliation to politics. That afternoon I did a little reconciliation work myself, lifting our long trade embargo on Vietnam, based on remarkable cooperation from the Vietnamese government in resolving POW and MIA cases and in returning the remains of slain servicemen to the United States. My decision was strongly supported by Vietnam veterans in Congress, especially Senators John Kerry, Bob Kerrey, and John McCain, and Congressman Pete Peterson of Florida, who had been a prisoner of war in Vietnam for more than six years.

In the second week of February, after the brutal shelling of the Sarajevo marketplace by Bosnian Serbs had killed dozens of innocent people, NATO finally voted, with the approval of the UN secretary-general, to bomb the Serbs if they didn't move their heavy guns more than a dozen miles away from the city. It was long overdue, but still not a vote without risk for the Canadians, whose forces in Srebrenica were surrounded by the Serbs, or for the French, British, Spanish, and Dutch, who also had relatively small, and vulnerable, numbers of troops on the ground.

Soon afterward, the heavy weapons were removed or put under UN control. Senator Dole was still pushing for a unilateral lifting of the arms embargo, but for the moment I was willing to stick with it, because we had finally gotten a green light for the NATO air strikes, and because I didn't want others to use our unilateral abandonment of the Bosnian embargo as an excuse to disregard the embargoes we supported in Haiti, Libya, and Iraq.

In the middle of the month, Hillary and Chelsea left for Lillehammer, Norway, to represent America at the Winter Olympics, and I flew down to Hot Springs for a day to see Dick Kelley. It had been five weeks since Mother's funeral, and I wanted to check on him. Dick was lonely in their little house, where Mother's presence was still strong in every room, but the old navy veteran was getting his sea legs back and thinking about how to get on with his life.

I spent the next two weeks plugging health-care reform and the crime bill in different venues across the country, and dealing with foreign policy. We got a piece of good news when Saudi Arabia agreed to buy $6 billion worth of American planes, after intense efforts by Ron Brown, Mickey Kantor, and Transportation Secretary Federico Peña.

We also got a shock when the FBI arrested thirty-one-year veteran CIA agent Aldrich Ames and his wife, breaking one of the biggest espionage cases in American history. For nine years, Ames had made a fortune giving up information that led to the deaths of more than ten of our sources inside Russia, and had done severe damage to our intelligence capability. After years of trying to catch a spy they knew was there, the FBI, with CIA cooperation, finally nailed him. The Ames case called into question both the vulnerability of our intelligence apparatus and our policy toward Russia: if they were spying on us, shouldn't we cancel or suspend aid to them? In a bipartisan congressional meeting and in responses to press questions, I argued against suspending aid. Russia was engaged in an internal struggle between yesterday and tomorrow; yesterday's Russia was spying on us, but our aid was being used to support tomorrow's Russia, by strengthening democracy and economic reform, and securing and destroying its nuclear weapons. Besides, the Russians weren't the only ones with spies.

Toward the end of the month, a militant Israeli settler, outraged at the prospect of turning the West Bank back to the Palestinians, gunned down several worshippers at the Mosque of Abraham in Hebron. The murderer had struck during the Muslim holy month of Ramadan, at a site sacred to both Muslims and Jews because it is thought to be the burial site of Abraham and his wife, Sarah. It seemed clear that his intention was to spark a violent reaction that would derail the peace process. To head that off, I asked Warren Christopher to contact Rabin and Arafat and invite them to send negotiators to Washington as soon as possible and have them stay until they had settled on concrete actions to implement their agreement.

On February 28, NATO fighters shot down four Serb planes for violating the no-fly zone, the first military action in the forty-four-year history of the alliance. I hoped that the air strikes, along with our success in relieving the siege of Sarajevo, would convince the allies to take a stronger posture toward Serb aggression in and around the embattled towns of Tuzla and Srebrenica as well.

One of those allies, John Major, was in America that day to talk about Bosnia and Northern Ireland. I took him first to Pittsburgh, where his grandfather had worked in the steel mills in the nineteenth century. Major seemed to enjoy retracing his roots to the industrial heartland of America. That night he stayed at the White House, the first foreign leader to do so during my tenure. The next day we held a press conference, which was unmemorable except for the larger message it sent: that our disagreement over the Adams visa would not undermine the Anglo-American relationship or keep us from working together closely on Bosnia and other issues. I found Major to be serious, intelligent, and, as I said earlier, genuinely committed to resolving the Irish problem, despite the fact that the very effort to do so posed a threat to his already precarious situation in Parliament. I thought he was a better leader than his press coverage often suggested, and after our two days together we maintained a friendly and productive working relationship.

THIRTY-EIGHT

While I was hard at work on foreign affairs, the new world of Whitewater was beginning to take shape at home. In March, Robert Fiske began his job in earnest by sending out subpoenas to several members of the White House staff, including Maggie Williams and Lisa Caputo, who worked for Hillary and were friends of Vince Foster's. Mack McLarty set up a Whitewater Response Team, led by Harold Ickes, to coordinate responses to questions from Fiske and from the press; to free the rest of the staff, and me, to do the public work we came to Washington to do; and to minimize conversations our staff might have about Whitewater among themselves or with Hillary or me. Any such conversations could only expose our young staffers to depositions, political attacks, and big legal bills. A lot of people had already acquired a vested interest in finding something wrong; if there was nothing illegal in our long-ago land deal, perhaps they could catch someone doing something wrong in the handling of it.

The system worked well enough for me. After all, I had learned how to lead parallel lives as a child: most of the time, I could shut out all the accusations and innuendo and go on with my work. I knew it would be harder to cope with for those who had never lived with the constant threat of arbitrary and destructive attacks, especially in an atmosphere in which there was a presumption of guilt attached to any charge. To be sure, there were some legal experts, like Sam Dash, who talked about how cooperative we were compared with the Reagan and Nixon administrations, because we didn't resist subpoenas and we turned all our records over to the Justice Department and then to Fiske. But the goalposts had been moved: unless Hillary and I could prove ourselves innocent of whatever charges any adversary could come up with, most of the questions would be asked, and the stories written, in a tone of intense suspicion; the underlying current was that we must have done something wrong.

For example, as our financial records found their way into the press, the **New York Times** reported that, starting with a $1,000 investment, Hillary had made $100,000 in the commodities market in 1979, with the help of Jim Blair. Blair was one of my closest friends; he did help Hillary and a number of his other friends in trading commodities, but she took her own risks, paid more than $18,000 in brokerage fees, and, following her own instincts, got out of the market before it dropped. Leo Melamed, the Republican former chairman of the Chicago Mercantile Exchange, on which agricultural commodities are traded, reviewed all of Hillary's trades and said there was nothing wrong with them. It didn't matter. For years, the critics would refer to Hillary's commodity profit as prima facie evidence of corruption.

The presumption of wrongdoing was reflected in a **Newsweek** story saying Hillary did not put up her own money for her "sweet deal," with an analysis that it said was based on the expert opinion of Professor Marvin Chirelstein of Columbia Law School, one of the nation's leading authorities on corporate law and contracts, who had taught me at Yale and who had been asked by our lawyer to review our tax returns for 1978–79, the period of the Whitewater investment. Chirelstein disputed the **Newsweek** story, saying, "I never said anything like that," and that he was "outraged" and "humiliated."

About the same time, **Time** magazine ran a cover photograph purporting to show George Stephanopoulos peering over my shoulder as I sat at my desk fretting over Whitewater. In fact, the photo captured an earlier routine scheduling meeting at which several people were present. At least two others were in the original picture. **Time** simply cropped them out.

In April, Hillary held a press conference to answer questions about her commodity trades and Whitewater. She did a fine job and I was proud of her. She even got a laugh from the press corps when she acknowledged that her belief in a "zone of privacy" might have made her less responsive to press questions about her past personal dealings than she should have been, but that "after resisting for a long time, I've been rezoned."

The presumption of guilt imposed on us was extended to others. For example, Roger Altman and Bernie Nussbaum were both heavily criticized for discussing criminal referrals issued against Madison Guaranty by the Resolution Trust Corporation, because the RTC was a part of the Treasury Department and Altman was overseeing it temporarily. Presumably, the critics thought Nussbaum could have been trying to influence the RTC proceedings. In fact, the discussions were a result of the need to answer press questions arising out of leaks about the Madison investigation, and they had been approved by the Treasury Department's ethics counsel.

Edwin Yoder, an old-fashioned progressive columnist,

said Washington was being overtaken by "ethical cleansers." In a column on the Nussbaum-Altman meeting, he said:

I wish someone would begin by explaining to me why it is so very wicked for White House staff to want information from elsewhere within the executive branch about charges and rumors concerning the president. . . .

Robert Fiske found the contacts between the White House and the Treasury Department to be legal, but that didn't stop the smearing of Nussbaum and Altman. Back then, all our political appointees needed to be read their Miranda warnings three times a day. Bernie Nussbaum resigned in early March; he never got over my foolish decision to ask for an independent counsel, and he didn't want to be a source of further problems. Altman would leave government service a few months later. They were both able, honest public servants.

In March, Roger Ailes, a longtime Republican operative who had become president of CNBC, accused the administration of "a cover-up with regard to Whitewater that includes . . . land fraud, illegal contributions, abuse of power . . . suicide cover-up—possible murder." So much for the "credible evidence of wrongdoing" standard.

William Safire, the **New York Times** columnist who had been a speechwriter for Nixon and Agnew, and who seemed determined to prove that all their successors were just as bad as they were, was especially avid in his unsupported assertions that Vince's death was linked to illegal conduct by Hillary and me. Of course, Vince's suicide note had said exactly the reverse, that we had done nothing wrong, but that didn't prevent Safire from speculating that Vince had improperly kept records damaging to us in his office.

We now know that a lot of the so-called information that fueled the damaging but erroneous stories was fed to the press by David Hale and the right-wingers who adopted him for their own purposes. In 1993, Hale, the Republican municipal judge in Little Rock, was charged with defrauding the Small Business Administration of $900,000 in federal funds that were supposed to have been used to make loans to minority businesses through his company, Capital Management Services (a later GAO audit indicated he had defrauded the SBA of $3.4 million). Instead, he gave the money to himself through a series of dummy corporations. Hale discussed his plight with Justice Jim Johnson, the old Arkansas racist who had run against Win Rockefeller for governor in 1966 and against Senator Fulbright in 1968. Johnson took Hale under his wing, and in August put him in contact with a conservative group called Citizens United, whose principals were Floyd Brown and David Bossie. Brown had produced the infamous Willie Horton ads against Mike Dukakis in 1988. Bossie had helped him write a book for the 1992 campaign entitled **Slick Willie: Why America Cannot Trust Bill Clinton,** in which the authors gave "special thanks" to Justice Jim Johnson.

Hale claimed that I had pressed him to lend $300,000 from Capital Management to a company owned by Susan McDougal, for the purpose of giving it out to leading Arkansas Democrats. In return, McDougal would lend Hale more than $800,000 from Madison Guaranty, enabling him to get another million dollars from the Small Business Administration. It was an absurd and untrue story, but Brown and Bossie peddled it hard. Apparently, Sheffield Nelson also helped, by pushing it to his contact at the **New York Times,** Jeff Gerth.

By March 1994, the media was wringing its hands about some documents shredded by the Rose firm; one of the boxes that held the papers had Vince Foster's initials on it. The firm explained that the shredding involved material unrelated to Whitewater and was a normal procedure involving papers that were no longer needed. No one in our White House knew about the routine destruction of unneeded records unrelated to Whitewater at the Rose firm. Moreover, we had nothing to cover up, and there still wasn't a bit of evidence to indicate that we did.

It got so bad that even the highly respected journalist David Broder referred to Bernie Nussbaum as "unfortunate" for allegedly tolerating arrogance and abuse of power that led to "the all-too-familiar words—investigation, subpoena, grand jury, resignation" that had "echoed through Washington again this past week." Broder even compared the "war rooms" that managed our campaigns for the economic plan and NAFTA to Nixon's enemies list.

Nussbaum was unfortunate, all right; there would have been no investigation, subpoenas, or grand jury if I had listened to him and refused to give in to the demands for an independent counsel to "clear the air." Bernie's real offense was that he thought I should abide by the rule of law and accepted standards of propriety, rather than the constantly shifting standards of the Whitewater media, which were designed to produce the very results they professed to deplore. Nussbaum's successor, longtime Washington attorney Lloyd Cutler, had a justifiably good reputation in the Washington establishment. In the coming months, his presence and advice would help a great deal, but he couldn't turn the Whitewater tide.

Rush Limbaugh was having a field day on his show, wallowing in the Whitewater mud. He claimed that Vince had been murdered in an apartment Hillary owned, and that his body had been moved to Fort Marcy Park. I could not imagine how that made Vince's wife and kids feel. Later, Limbaugh falsely charged that "journalists and others working on or involved in Whitewatergate have been beaten and harassed in Little Rock. Some have died."

Not to be outdone by Limbaugh, former Republican congressman Bill Dannemeyer called for congressional hearings on the "frightening" number of people connected to me who had died "under other than natural circumstances." Dannemeyer's grisly list included my campaign finance co-chairman, Vic Raiser, and his son, who had died tragically in a plane crash on a trip to Alaska in 1992, and Paul Tully, the political director of the Democratic Party who had died of a heart attack while working on the campaign in Little Rock. I had delivered eulogies at both funerals, and later appointed Vic's widow, Molly, as chief of protocol.

Jerry Falwell outdid Dannemeyer by releasing **Circle of Power,** a video about "countless people who mysteriously died" in Arkansas; the film implied that I was somehow responsible. Then came Falwell's sequel, **The Clinton Chronicles,** which he promoted on his television show, **The Old Time Gospel Hour.** The video featured Dannemeyer and Justice Jim Johnson, and accused me of being involved with cocaine smuggling, having witnesses killed, and arranging the murders of a private investigator and the wife of a state trooper. A lot of the "witnesses" were paid for their testimonials, and Falwell sold a great many videos.

As Whitewater unfolded, I tried to keep some perspective, and to remember that not everyone was caught up in the hysteria. For example, **USA Today** ran a fair story on

Whitewater that included interviews with Jim McDougal, who said Hillary and I didn't do anything wrong, and Chris Wade, the real estate agent in north Arkansas who supervised the Whitewater land, who also said we were telling the truth about our limited involvement with the property.

I could understand why right-wingers like Rush Limbaugh, Bill Dannemeyer, Jerry Falwell, and a paper like the **Washington Times** would say such things. The **Washington Times** was avowedly right-wing, financed by the Reverend Sun Myung Moon, and edited by Wes Pruden Jr., whose father, the Reverend Wesley Pruden, had been chaplain of the White Citizens' Council in Arkansas and an ally of Justice Jim Johnson's in their lost crusade against civil rights for blacks. What I couldn't believe was that the **New York Times,** the **Washington Post,** and others in the media I had always respected and trusted had been sucker punched by the likes of Floyd Brown, David Bossie, David Hale, and Jim Johnson.

Around this time I hosted a dinner at the White House to observe Black History Month. Among the attendees were my old law school professor Burke Marshall and his friend Nicholas Katzenbach, who had done so much to advance civil rights in the Kennedy Justice Department. Nick came up to me and told me that he was on the board of the **Washington Post** and that he was ashamed of the paper's coverage of Whitewater and the "terrible damage" that had been done to me and the presidency over charges that didn't amount to a hill of beans: "What is this about?" he asked. "It sure isn't about the public interest."

Whatever it was about, it was working. A poll in March said that half the people thought Hillary and I were lying about Whitewater, and a third of them thought we had done something illegal. I have to confess that Whitewater, especially the attacks on Hillary, took a bigger toll on me than I thought it would. The charges were baseless and unsupported by any reliable evidence. I had other problems, but except for occasionally being hardheaded, Hillary was above reproach. It killed me to see her hurt by one false charge after another, all the more so because I had made things worse by giving in to the naïve notion that an independent counsel would clear the air. I had to work hard to keep my anger in check, and I didn't always succeed. The cabinet and staff seemed to understand and tolerate my occasional flare-ups, and Al Gore helped me get through them. Though I kept working hard and continued to love my job, my normally sunny disposition and innate optimism would be put to one severe test after another.

It helped to laugh about it. Every spring there are three press dinners, hosted by the Gridiron Club, the White House correspondents, and the radio and television correspondents. They give the press an opportunity to poke fun at the President and other politicians, and the President gets a chance to reply. I looked forward to these occasions because they allowed all of us to let our guards down a little, and because they reminded me that the press was not a monolith and was made up mostly of good people trying to be fair. Also, as Proverbs says, "A happy heart doeth good like medicine, but a broken spirit drieth the bones."

I was in pretty good spirits on April 12 at the Radio and Television Correspondents' dinner, and I got off some good lines, like "I really am delighted to be here. If you believe that I've got some land in northwest Arkansas I'd like to show you"; "Some say my relations with the press have been marked by self-pity. I like to think of it as the outer limits of my empathy. I feel my pain"; "It's three days before April fifteenth, and most of you have to spend more time on my taxes than your own"; and "I still believe in a place called Help!"

The work of what Hillary would later call the "vast right-wing conspiracy" has been chronicled in great detail by Sidney Blumenthal in **The Clinton Wars** and by Joe Conason and Gene Lyons in **The Hunting of the President.** As far as I know, none of their factual assertions have been refuted. When those books were published, the people in the mainstream media who had been part of the Whitewater mania ignored their charges, dismissed the authors as being too sympathetic to Hillary and me, or blamed us for the way we handled the Whitewater problem and for complaining. I'm sure we could have handled it better, but so could they.

In the early days of Whitewater, one of my friends was forced to resign his government post because of something he had done wrong before he came to Washington. The Rose Law Firm filed a complaint against Webb Hubbell with the Arkansas Bar Association for allegedly overcharging his clients and padding his expenses. Webb resigned from the Justice Department, but assured Hillary there was nothing to the charges, saying that the whole problem arose because his wealthy but irascible father-in-law, Seth Ward, had refused to pay the Rose firm for the costs of a patent infringement case they had lost. It seemed plausible, but it wasn't true.

It turned out that Webb **had** overcharged his clients, and in so doing, had injured the Rose firm and reduced the income of all his partners, including Hillary. If his case had played out normally, he probably would have reached an agreement with the law firm to repay it for the cost of reimbursing its clients and would have lost his license for a year or two. The bar association might or might not have referred him to the state prosecuting attorney; if it had, Hubbell probably would have been able to avoid going to prison by reimbursing the firm. Instead, Webb was caught up in the independent counsel's net.

When the facts first came out, I was stunned. Webb and I had been friends and golfing partners for years, and I thought I knew him well. I still think he's a good man who made a bad mistake, one he had to pay too high a price for, because he refused to become a pawn in Starr's game.

While all this was going on, I stayed on the other track of my parallel lives, the one I came to Washington to pursue. In March, I devoted considerable time to pushing two bills that I thought would help workers without college degrees. Most people could no longer keep one job or even stay with one employer for their entire working lives, and the churning job market treated them in markedly different ways. Our 6.5 percent unemployment rate was misleading; it was 3.5 percent for college graduates, more than 5 percent for those with two years of college, over 7 percent for high school graduates, and more than 11 percent for high school dropouts. At events in Nashua and Keene, New Hampshire, I said I wanted to convert the program of unemployment benefits into a reemployment system with a broader range of better-designed training programs. And I wanted Congress to approve a school-to-work program, to provide one or two years of high-quality training for young people who didn't want to get a four-year college degree. By the end of the month, I was able to sign the Goals 2000 bill. Finally, we had a congressional commitment to meet the national education goals I had worked on back in 1989, to measure students' progress toward them, and to encourage local school districts to adopt the most promising reforms. It was a good day for Secretary Dick Riley.

On March 18, Presidents Alija Izetbegovic of Bosnia and Franjo Tudjman of Croatia were at the White House to sign an agreement negotiated with the help of my special envoy, Charles Redman, that established a federation in the areas of Bosnia in which their populations were in a majority, and set up a process to move toward a confederation with Croatia. The fighting between Muslims and Croatians had not been as severe as that in which both sides had engaged with the Bosnian Serbs, but the agreement was still an important step toward peace.

The last days of March marked the beginning of a serious crisis with North Korea. After agreeing in February to let inspectors from the International Atomic Energy Agency (IAEA) check their declared nuclear sites on March 15, North Korea blocked them from completing their work. The reactor they were studying operated on fuel rods. Once the rods had been exhausted for their original purpose, the spent fuel could be reprocessed into plutonium in sufficient quantities to make nuclear weapons. North Korea also was planning to build two larger reactors, which would have produced many more spent fuel rods. The rods were a dangerous asset in the hands of the most isolated country in the world, a poor one that could not even feed its own people and might feel the temptation to sell the plutonium to the wrong buyer. Within a week I had decided to send Patriot missiles to South Korea and to ask the UN to impose economic sanctions against

North Korea. As Bill Perry told a group of editors and reporters on March 30, I was determined to stop North Korea from developing a nuclear arsenal, even at the risk of war. In order to make absolutely certain that the North Koreans knew we were serious, Perry continued the tough talk over the next three days, even saying that we would not rule out a preemptive military strike.

Meanwhile, Warren Christopher made sure our message had the right balance. The State Department said we preferred a peaceful solution, and our ambassador to South Korea, Jim Laney, described our position as one of "watchfulness, firmness, and patience." I believed that if North Korea really understood our position, as well as the economic and political benefits it could realize by abandoning its nuclear program in favor of cooperation with its neighbors and the United States, we could work it out. If we didn't, Whitewater would soon look like the sideshow it was.

On March 26, I was in Dallas for a happy weekend off, to serve as best man in my brother's wedding to Molly Martin, a beautiful woman he'd met when, after spending a few years in Nashville, he'd moved to Los Angeles in the hope of reviving his singing career. I was really happy for Roger.

On the day after the wedding, we all went to see the Arkansas Razorbacks defeat the University of Michigan in the NCAA Basketball Tournament quarterfinals. That week **Sports Illustrated** had me on the cover in a Razorback jogging suit; the article inside included a picture of me palming a basketball. After the kind of coverage I'd been getting, the piece was manna from heaven. A week later I was in the arena in Charlotte, North Carolina, when Arkansas won the national championship, defeating Duke 76–72.

On April 6, Justice Harry Blackmun announced his retirement from the Supreme Court. Hillary and I had become friends of Justice Blackmun and his wife, Dotty, through Renaissance Weekend. He was a fine man, an excellent justice, and a sorely needed moderate voice on the Rehnquist Court. I knew I owed the country a worthy replacement. My first choice was Senator George Mitchell, who had announced his retirement from the Senate a month earlier. He was a good majority leader, he had been loyal and extremely helpful to me, and it was far from certain that we could hold on to his seat in the November election. I didn't want him to leave the Senate but was excited by the prospect of appointing George to the Supreme Court. He had been a federal judge before coming to the Senate, and would be a big personality on the Court, someone who could move votes and whose voice would be heard, even in dissent. For the second time in five weeks, Mitchell turned me down. He said that if he were to leave the Senate at this time, whatever chance we had to pass health care would evaporate, hurting the American people, the Democrats up for reelection, and my presidency.

I quickly settled on two other prospects: Judge Stephen Breyer, who had already been vetted; and Judge Richard Arnold, chief judge of the Eighth Circuit Court of Appeals, which sits in St. Louis and includes Arkansas within its jurisdiction. Arnold was a former aide to Dale Bumpers who came from a long line of distinguished Arkansas lawyers. He was probably the most brilliant man on the federal bench. He graduated at the top of his class at Yale and at Harvard Law School, and had learned Latin and Greek, in part so that he could read early biblical texts. I probably would have appointed him, except for the fact that he had been treated for cancer and his prognosis was not clear. My Republican predecessors had filled the federal courts with young conservatives who would be around a long time, and I didn't want to risk giving them another position. In May, I made the decision to nominate Judge Breyer. He was equally qualified, and I had been impressed with him in our earlier interview after Justice White resigned. Breyer would be confirmed easily. Richard Arnold, I'm happy to say, is still serving on the Eighth Circuit and still plays an occasional round of golf with me.

Early in April, NATO bombed in Bosnia again, this time to stop the Serbs' siege of Gorazde. On the same day, mass violence raged in Rwanda. A plane crash killing the Rwandan president and the president of Burundi sparked the beginning of a horrendous slaughter inflicted by leaders of the majority Hutu on the Tutsis and their Hutu sympathizers. The Tutsis constituted only 15 percent of the population but were thought to have disproportionate economic and political power. I ordered the evacuation of all Americans and sent troops to guarantee their safety. Within one hundred days, more than 800,000 people in a country of only 8 million would be murdered, most of them with machetes. We were so preoccupied with Bosnia, with the memory of Somalia just six months old, and with opposition in Congress to military deployments in faraway places not vital to our national interests that neither I nor anyone on my foreign policy team adequately focused on sending troops to stop the slaughter. With a few thousand troops and help from our allies, even making allowances for the time it would have taken to deploy them, we could have saved lives. The failure to try to stop Rwanda's tragedies became one of the greatest regrets of my presidency.

In my second term, and after I left office, I did what I could to help the Rwandans put their country and their lives back together. Today, at the invitation of President Paul Kagame, Rwanda is one of the countries in which my foundation is working to stem the tide of AIDS.

On April 22, Richard Nixon died, one month and a day after writing a remarkable seven-page letter to me about his recent trip to Russia, Ukraine, Germany, and England. Nixon said I had earned the respect of the leaders he visited and could not let Whitewater or any other domestic issue "divert attention from our major foreign policy priority—the survival of political and economic freedom in Russia." He was worried about Yeltsin's political position and the rise of anti-Americanism in the Duma, and he urged me to keep my close relationship with Yeltsin, but also to reach out to other democrats into Russia; to improve the design and administration of our foreign aid program; and to put a leading businessman in charge of getting more private investment into Russia. Nixon said the ultra-nationalist Zhirinovsky should be exposed "for the fraud he is," rather than suppressed, and that we should seek "to keep the bad guys—Zhirinovsky, Rutskoi, and the Communists—divided, and to try to get the good guys—Chernomyrdin, Yavlinski, Shahrai, Travkin—to coalesce if possible in a united front for responsible reform." Finally, Nixon said I should not spread directed aid dollars all over the former Soviet Union, but concentrate our resources beyond Russia on Ukraine: "It is indispensable." The letter was a tour de force, Nixon at his best in the eighth decade of his life.

All the living former Presidents came to President Nixon's funeral on the grounds of his presidential library and birthplace. I was somewhat surprised when his family asked me to speak, along with Bob Dole, Henry Kissinger, and California governor Pete Wilson, who as a young man had worked for Nixon. In my remarks, I expressed appreciation for his "wise counsel, especially with regard to Russia," and I remarked on his continuing vigorous and clearheaded interest in America and the world, mentioning his call and letter to me a month before his death. I referred to Watergate only by indirection, with a plea for reconciliation: "Today is a day for his family, his friends, and his nation to remember President Nixon's life in totality . . . may the day of judging President Nixon on anything less than his entire life and career come to an end." Some of my party's Nixon-haters didn't like what I said. Nixon had done a lot more than Watergate with which I disagreed—the enemies list, the prolongation of the Vietnam War and the expanded bombing, the Red-baiting of his opponents for the House and Senate in California. But he had also opened the door to China, signed bills establishing the Environmental Protection Agency, the Legal Services Corporation, and the Occupational Safety and Health Administration, and had supported affirmative action. Compared with the Republicans who took over the party in the 1980s and 1990s, President Nixon was a wild-eyed liberal.

On the day after the funeral, I called in to the Larry King show because he was interviewing Dick Kelley and James Morgan about Mother's book, **Leading with My Heart,** which was just coming out. I told Larry that when I got back from the foreign trip I had taken after her funeral, I found myself halfway to the phone in our kitchen before I realized I couldn't call her on Sunday night anymore. It would be months before the urge to make that call stopped coming over me.

On April 29, with virtually the entire cabinet in attendance, I hosted Native American and Native Alaskan tribal leaders on the South Lawn, apparently bringing them to the White House for the first time since the 1820s. Some of them were so wealthy from Indian gaming that they flew to Washington in their own planes. Others, who lived on isolated reservations, were so poor they had to "pass the hat" among their tribes to collect enough money for a plane ticket. I pledged to respect their rights of self-determination, tribal sovereignty, and religious freedom, and to work hard to improve the federal government's relations with them. And I signed executive orders to guarantee that our commitments would be kept. Finally, I pledged to do more to support education, health care, and economic development for the poorest tribes.

By the end of April, it was clear that we had lost the health-care communications battle. A **Wall Street Journal** article on April 29 described the $300 million misinformation campaign that had been run against us:

> The baby's scream is anguished, the mother's voice desperate. "Please," she pleads into the phone as she seeks help for her sick child.
>
> "We're sorry; the government health center is closed now," says the recording on the other end of the line. "However, if this is an emergency, you may call 1-800-GOVERNMENT." She tries it, only to be greeted by another recording: "We're sorry, all health-care representatives are busy now. Please stay on the line and our first available . . ."

"Why did they let the government take over?" she asks plaintively. "I need my family doctor back."

The story goes on to say that the only problem with the radio spot, produced by a Washington-based group called Americans for Tax Reform, is that it isn't true.

Another massive campaign of direct mail, by a group called the American Council for Health Reform, maintained that under the Clinton plan people would face five years in jail if they bought extra health care. In fact, our plan explicitly stated that people were free to purchase any health-care services they wanted.

The ad campaign was false, but it was working. In fact, a **Wall Street Journal**/NBC News poll, published March 10 in an article titled "Many Don't Realize It's the Clinton Plan They Like," showed that when people were asked about our health plan, a majority opposed it. But when asked about what they wanted in a health plan, the major provisions that were actually in our plan were all supported by more than 60 percent of the people. The article said, "When the group is read a description of the Clinton bill without identifying it as the President's plan and of the four other leading proposals in Congress, the Clinton plan is the first choice of everyone in the room."

The poll authors, one Republican and one Democrat, are quoted as saying, "The White House should find this both satisfying and sobering. Satisfying because the basic ideas which they have drawn up are the right ideas in the view of many people. But sobering because they clearly have communicated very little to the public and in that respect have ceded too much to the interest groups."

Despite this, Congress was moving forward. The bill had been referred to five committees in Congress, three in

The inauguration and an inaugural ball, January 20, 1993

Al Gore and I with the cabinet: (standing, from left) Madeleine Albright, Mack McLarty, Mickey Kantor, Laura Tyson, Leon Panetta, Carol Browner, Lee Brown; (seated, from bottom left) Lloyd Bentsen, Janet Reno, Mike Espy, Robert Reich, Henry Cisneros, Hazel O'Leary, Richard Riley, Jesse Brown, Federico Peña, Donna Shalala, Ron Brown, Bruce Babbitt, Les Aspin, and Warren Christopher

Al and I praying at our weekly lunch

With Mother, Dick Kelley, a
Champ, in Hot Springs

Mack McLarty and I
attending the Summit of the
Americas, in Santiago, Chile

In the residence private study, with
Presidents George Bush, Jimmy Carter,
and Gerald Ford on the eve of the
announcement of the campaign for
NAFTA

With the White
House residence
butlers and staff

With Hillary in Wyoming

Mother, Roger, and I celebrate our last Christmas together.

Chelsea in *The Nutcracker*

Ron Brown and I playing an impromptu basketball game in South Central Los Angeles

Al and I, on the South Lawn, announcing the elimination of forklifts of government regulations, part of our Reinventing Government initiative

Straightening Prime Minister Yitzhak Rabin's tie. It would be our last time together.

Right: Tony Lake informs me of Rabin's death.

Arriving on Marine One, with Bruce Lindsey and Erskine Bowles

Below: Bosnia briefing in the White House Situation Room

Above, left: With AmeriCorps volunteers at a tornado site in Arkansas

Above, right: Chelsea's graduation from Sidwell Friends

Rahm Emanuel and Leon Panetta brief me in the Oval Office dining room.

Below, left: Riding with Harold Ickes in Montana

With Hillary

Al and I on the edge of the Grand Canyon establishing the Grand Staircase–Escalante National Monument

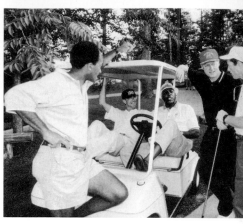

On the golf course with Frank Raines, Erskine Bowles, Vernon Jordan, and Max Chapman

A strategy meeting in the Yellow Oval Room

With Republican leaders Representative Newt Gingrich and Senator Bob Dole in the Cabinet Room

With Democratic leaders Representative Richard Gephardt and Senator Tom Daschle in the Oval Office

Russian president Boris Yeltsin and I in Hyde Park, New York

With German chancellor Helmut Kohl at Warburg Castle

Reading "'Twas the Night Before Christmas" to children in the East Room with Hillary and Chelsea

Chelsea and I at Ron Brown's funeral

Our friends Queen Noor and King Hussein join Hillary and me on the Truman Balcony.

Above: Speaking about America's bridge to the twenty-first century at Arizona State University

Right: Promoting education at an event in California

Celebrating our 1996 victory aboard Air Force One

Signing an executive order with representatives of Native American Tribal Governments

Visiting with the troops in Kuwait

Briefing in Shepherdstown, West Virginia, with my Middle East team: Madeleine Albright, Dennis Ross, Martin Indyk, Rob Malley, Bruce Reidel, and Sandy Berger. Deputy Chief of Staff Maria Echaveste is at far right.

Below: With the economic team in the Oval Office

Playing cards with Bruce Lindsey, Doug Sosnik, and Joe Lockhart on Marine One

With White House valets Fred Sanchez and Lito Bautista, my doctor Connie Mariano, valet Joe Fama, and Oval Office steward Bayani Nelvis

My legal team: Cheryl Mills, Bruce Lindsey, David Kendall, Chuck Ruff, and Nicole Seligman

Oval Office steward Glen Maes shows Al and me the cake he made for my birthday.

Left: Playing with Buddy and my nephews Zachary and Tyler on the South Lawn

Below: Socks briefing the press

South African president Nelson Mandela and I in the cell on Robben Island, where he had spent the first eighteen of his twenty-seven years in captivity

With Japanese prime minister Keizo Obuchi in Tokyo

With Chinese president Jiang Zemin in the Oval Office

The Vallenato Children performing in Cartagena, with Chelsea and the president of Colombia, Andrés Pastrana

The G-8 meeting in Denver: (left to right) Jacques Delors, Tony Blair, Ryutaro Hashimoto, Helmut Kohl, Boris Yeltsin, me, Jacques Chirac, Jean Chrétien, Romano Prodi, and Wim Kok

With the cabinet: (first row) Bruce Babbitt, William Cohen, Madeleine Albright, me, Larry Summers, Janet Reno; (second row) George Tenet, Togo West, Bill Richardson, Andrew Cuomo, Alexis Herman, Dan Glickman, John Podesta, William Daley, Donna Shalala, Rodney Slater, Richard Riley, Carol Browner; (back row) Thurgood Marshall, Jr., Bruce Reed, James Lee Witt, Charlene Barshefsky, Martin Baily, Jack Lew, Barry McCaffrey, Aida Alvarez, Gene Sperling, and Sandy Berger

Above, left: With Tony Blair at Chequers

Above, right: Hillary and I touring a Kosovar refugee camp in Macedonia

Left: Hillary and I with a newborn child named Bill Clinton in Wanyange, Uganda

Below: Addressing a crowd of more than 500,000 in Independence Square, Ghana

Commemorating the thirty-fifth anniversary of the voting rights march in Selma, Alabama, by crossing the Edmund Pettus Bridge with Jesse Jackson, Coretta Scott King, John Lewis, and other veterans of the civil rights movement who had marched arm in arm with Martin Luther King, Jr.

Camp David Middle East peace summit, with Prime Minister Ehud Barak, Chairman Yasser Arafat, and my Arabic translator and Middle East advisor, Gemal Helal

Hillary, Chelsea, and I at an MIA excavation site in Vietnam, with the Evert family

Being showered with rose petals in a traditional ceremony in Naila, India

With Gerry Adams, John Hume, and David Trimble on St. Patrick's Day 2000

Addressing a crowd in Market Square, Dundalk, Northern Ireland

Bringing the Internet into America's classrooms, with Dick Riley

The special agents in charge, presidential protective division, United States Secret Service, with Nancy Hernreich, director of Oval Office Operations, and my secretary Betty Currie

Above: With my presidential aides Doug Band, Kris Engskov, Stephen Goodin, and Andrew Friendly

Below: Celebrating with my staff after my final address to the nation

February 7, 2000: Hillary announces her campaign for the Senate

Chelsea and I wait for Hillary as she cast her first vote as a candidate, Chappaqua New York.

My last moments in the Oval Office after placing the traditional letter to its next occupant on the *Resolute* desk

the House and two in the Senate. The House Labor committee voted out a health-care bill in April that was actually more comprehensive than our bill. The other four committees were hard at work trying to forge consensus.

The first week of May was another example of everything happening at once. I answered the questions of international journalists in a global forum sponsored by President Carter's center at CNN's headquarters in Atlanta; signed the School-to-Work bill; congratulated Rabin and Arafat for their agreement on handling the handover of Gaza and Jericho; lobbied the House of Representatives to pass a ban on deadly assault weapons; cheered its passage by two votes, in the face of fierce opposition from the NRA; announced that the United States would increase its assistance to South Africa in the aftermath of its first full and fair election, and that Al and Tipper Gore, Hillary, Ron Brown, and Mike Espy would head our delegation to President Mandela's inauguration; held a White House event to highlight the special problems of women without health insurance; tightened sanctions on Haiti because of the continued killing and mutilation of Aristide supporters by Lieutenant General Raoul Cedras; appointed Bill Gray, head of the United Negro College Fund and former chairman of the House Budget Committee, to be special advisor to me and Warren Christopher on Haiti; and got sued by Paula Jones. It was just another week at the office.

Paula Jones had first appeared in public the previous February at the Conservative Political Action Committee convention in Washington, D.C., where Cliff Jackson introduced her, allegedly for the purpose of "clearing her name." In David Brock's **American Spectator** article based on the allegations of the Arkansas state troopers, one of their charges was that I had met with a woman in a Little Rock hotel suite who later told the trooper who had taken her there that she wanted to be my "regular girl-friend." Though she was identified in the article only as Paula, Jones claimed her family and friends recognized her when they read the article. She said she wanted to clear her name, but instead of suing the **Spectator** for libel, she accused me of sexually harassing her and said that, after she rebuffed my unwanted advances, she was denied the annual pay raises normally given to state employees. At the time she was a clerical employee of the Arkansas Industrial Development Commission. Initially, Jones's debut with Cliff Jackson didn't get much publicity, but on May 6, two days before the statute of limitations expired, she filed suit against me, seeking $700,000 for my alleged harassment.

Before she filed the suit, Jones's first lawyer had made contact with a man in Little Rock who got in touch with my office, telling us that the lawyer had said that her case was weak and that if I would pay her $50,000 and help her and her husband, Steve, who turned out to be a conservative Clinton hater, get jobs in Hollywood, she wouldn't sue me. I didn't pay because I hadn't sexually harassed her, and contrary to her other allegation, she had received her annual pay increases. Now I had to hire another lawyer to defend myself, Washington attorney Bob Bennett.

I spent most of the rest of May campaigning for the health-care and crime bills across the country, but there were always other things going on as well. By far the best of them was the birth of our first nephew, Tyler Cassidy

Clinton, whom Roger and Molly brought into the world on May 12.

On the eighteenth, I signed an important Head Start reform bill, on which Secretaries Shalala and Riley had worked hard; it increased the number of poor children served by the preschool program, improved its quality, and provided services for children under three for the first time with our new Early Head Start initiative.

The next day I welcomed Prime Minister P. V. Narasimha Rao of India to the White House. The Cold War and clumsy diplomacy had kept India and the United States apart for too long. With a population of nearly one billion, India was the world's largest democracy. Over the previous three decades, tensions with China had driven it closer to the Soviet Union, and the Cold War had pushed the United States closer to India's neighbor Pakistan. Since becoming independent, the two nations had been involved in a bitter, seemingly endless dispute over Kashmir, the predominantly Muslim region in northern India. With the Cold War over, I thought I had an opportunity, as well as an obligation, to improve U.S.-India relations.

The main sticking point was the conflict between our efforts to limit the spread of nuclear weapons and India's drive to develop them, which the Indians saw as a necessary deterrent to China's nuclear arsenal and a prerequisite to its becoming a world power. Pakistan had developed a nuclear program, too, creating a dangerous situation on the Indian subcontinent. I believed that their nuclear arsenals made both India and Pakistan less secure, but the Indians didn't see it that way and were determined not to let the United States interfere with what they saw as their legitimate prerogative to proceed with their nuclear program. Even so, the Indians wanted to improve our relations as much as I did. While we didn't resolve our differences, Prime Minister Rao and I broke the ice and began a new chapter in Indo-U.S. relations, which continued to warm throughout my two terms and afterward.

On the day I met with Prime Minister Rao, Jackie Kennedy Onassis died after a battle with cancer. She was only sixty-four. Jackie was the most private of our great public icons, to most people an indelible image of elegance, grace, and grieving. To those lucky enough to know her, she was what she seemed to be, but much more—a bright woman full of life, a fine mother and good friend. I knew how much her children, John and Caroline, and her companion, Maurice Tempelsman, would miss her. Hillary would miss her, too; she had been a source of constant encouragement, sound advice, and genuine friendship.

At the end of May, I had to decide whether to extend most-favored-nation status to China. MFN was actually a slightly misleading term for normal trade relations without any extra tariffs or other barriers. America already had a sizable trade deficit with China, one that would grow over the years as the United States purchased between 35 and 40 percent of Chinese exports annually. After the violence in Tiananmen Square and the crackdown on dissidents that followed, Americans from across the political spectrum felt the Bush administration had been too quick to reestablish normal relations with Beijing. During the election campaign I had been critical of President Bush's policy, and in 1993 I had issued an executive order requiring progress on a range of issues from emigration to human rights to forced prison labor before I would extend MFN to China. In May, Warren Christopher sent me a report saying that all the emigration cases had been resolved; that we had signed a memorandum of understanding on how to deal with the prison labor issue; and that for the first time China had said that it would adhere to the Universal Declaration of Human Rights. On the other hand, Christopher said, there were still human rights abuses in the arrest and detention of peaceful political dissidents and the repression of Tibet's religious and cultural traditions.

China was extremely sensitive to other nations "interfering" in its political affairs. The Chinese leaders also felt that they were managing all the change they could handle with their economic modernization program and attendant huge population shifts from inland provinces to booming coastal cities. Because our engagement had produced some positive results, I decided, with the unanimous support of my foreign policy and economic advisors, to extend MFN and, for the future, to delink our human rights efforts from trade. The United States had a big stake in bringing China into the global community. Greater trade and involvement would bring more prosperity to Chinese citizens; more contacts with the outside world; more cooperation on problems like North Korea, where we needed it; greater adherence to the rules of international law; and, we hoped, the advance of personal freedom and human rights.

In the first week of June, Hillary and I went to Europe to honor the fiftieth anniversary of D-day, June 6, 1944, when the United States and its allies crossed the English Channel and stormed the beaches of Normandy. It was the largest naval invasion in history and marked the beginning of the end of World War II in Europe.

The trip began in Rome, with a visit to the Vatican to

see the pope and Italy's new prime minister, Silvio Berlusconi, the country's biggest media owner and a political novice, who had put together an interesting coalition that included an extreme right-wing party that evoked comparisons with fascism. Despite his incomplete recovery from a broken leg, His Holiness Pope John Paul II was vigorous in discussing world issues, ranging from whether religious liberty could be secured in China to the possibilities of cooperation with moderate Muslim countries to our differences over how best to limit population explosion and promote sustainable development in poor nations.

Berlusconi was, in some ways, Italy's first television-age politician: charismatic, strong-willed, and determined to bring his own brand of discipline and direction to Italy's notoriously unstable political life. His critics accused him of trying to impose a neo-fascist order on Italy, a charge he strongly denied. I was pleased with Berlusconi's assurances that he was committed to preserving democracy and human rights, maintaining Italy's historic partnership with the United States, and fulfilling Italy's NATO responsibilities in Bosnia.

On June 3, I spoke at the American cemetery at Nettuno, once scarred by battle, now lush with pine and cypress trees. Row after row of marble headstones display the names of the 7,862 soldiers buried there. The names of another 3,000 Americans whose bodies were never found are inscribed in the chapel nearby. All of them died too young, in the liberation of Italy. This was the battle theater in which my father had served.

The next day we were in England, at Mildenhall Air Force Base near Cambridge, where we went to another American cemetery, this one with the names of 3,812 airmen, soldiers, and sailors who had been based there, and another Wall of the Missing with more than 5,000 names on it, including two who never returned from their flights over the English Channel: Joe Kennedy Jr., the oldest of the Kennedy children, who everyone thought would become the politician in the family; and Glenn Miller, the American bandleader whose music was all the rage in the 1940s. At the event the Air Force Band played Miller's theme song, "Moonlight Serenade."

After a meeting with John Major at Chequers, the fifteenth-century country residence of the British prime minister, Hillary and I attended a mammoth dinner in Portsmouth, where I was seated next to the queen. I was taken with her grace and intelligence and the clever manner in which she discussed public issues, probing me for information and insights without venturing too far into expressing her own political views, which was taboo for the British head of state. Her Majesty impressed me as someone who, but for the circumstance of her birth, might have become a successful politician or diplomat. As it was, she had to be both, without quite seeming to be either.

After the dinner we were guests of the royal family on their yacht, the HMS **Britannia,** where we had the pleasure of spending time with the Queen Mother, who at ninety-three was still lively and lovely, with luminous, piercing eyes. The following morning, the day before D-day, we all attended the Drumhead Service, the religious ceremony for "the Forces Committed" to battle. Princess Diana, who was separated but not divorced from Prince Charles, also came. After saying hello to Hillary and me, she went out into the crowd to shake hands with her fellow countrymen, who were obviously happy to see her. During the little time I had spent with Charles and Diana, I liked them both and wished that life had dealt them a different hand.

When the service was over, we boarded the **Britannia** for lunch and sailed out into the English Channel, to begin the crossing among a huge fleet of ships. After a short sail, we said good-bye to the royal family and boarded a small boat crewed by U.S. Navy SEALs, which took us to the aircraft carrier **George Washington** for the rest of the voyage. Hillary and I enjoyed dinner with some of the six thousand sailors and marines who manned the ship, and I worked on my speeches.

On D-day, I spoke at Pointe du Hoc, Utah Beach, and the U.S. cemetery in Colleville-sur-Mer. Each site was filled with veterans from World War II.

I also took a walk on Utah Beach with three veterans, one of whom had won the Medal of Honor for heroism on that fateful day fifty years earlier. This was his first trip back. He told me we were standing almost exactly where he had landed in 1944. Then he pointed up the beach and told me his brother had landed a few hundred yards in that direction. He said, "It's funny how life works out. I won the Medal of Honor and my brother was killed." "You still miss him, don't you?" I asked. I'll never forget his reply: "Every day, for fifty years."

At the ceremony, I was introduced by Joe Dawson of Corpus Christi, Texas, who, as a young captain, was credited as being the first officer to successfully reach the top of the forbidding bluffs of Normandy under withering German fire. Almost 9,400 Americans died on D-day, including thirty-three pairs of brothers, a father and his son, and eleven men from tiny Bedford, Virginia. I acknowledged that those who survived and had returned to the scene of their triumph "may walk with a little less spring in their step and their ranks are growing thinner. But let us never forget, when they were young, these men saved the world."

The next day I was in Paris to meet with Mayor Jacques Chirac, speak to the French National Assembly in the Palais Bourbon, and attend a dinner hosted by President François Mitterrand at the Elysée Palace. Mitterrand's dinner ended about midnight, and I was surprised when he asked me if Hillary and I would like to see the "New Louvre," the magnificent creation of Chinese-American architect I. M. Pei. Mitterrand was seventy-seven and in ill health, but he was eager to show off France's latest masterpiece. When François, U.S. ambassador Pamela Harriman, Hillary, and I arrived, we found that our tour guide was none other than Pei himself. We looked at the magnificent glass pyramid, the restored and adapted old buildings, and the excavated Roman ruins for more than an hour and a half. Mitterrand's energy never flagged as he supplemented Pei's narrative to make sure we didn't miss anything.

The final day of the trip was a personal one, a return to Oxford to receive an honorary degree. It was one of those perfect English spring days. The sun was shining, a breeze was blowing, and the trees, wisteria, and flowers were all in bloom. In brief remarks, I referred to the D-day commemoration, then said, "History does not always give us grand crusades, but it always gives us opportunities." We had plenty of them, at home and abroad: restoring economic growth, extending the reach of democracy, ending environmental destruction, building a new security in Europe, and halting "the spread of nuclear weapons and terrorism." Hillary and I had had an unforgettable week, but it was time to get back to those "opportunities."

The day after I returned, Senator Kennedy's Labor and Human Resources Committee reported out a health-care reform bill. It was the first time legislation providing universal coverage had ever even made it out of a full congressional committee. One Republican, Jim Jeffords of Vermont, had voted for it. Jeffords encouraged me to keep reaching out to Republicans. He said that with a couple of amendments that wouldn't gut the bill we could pick up a few more votes.

Our euphoria was short-lived. Two days later, Bob Dole, after having told me earlier that we would work out a compromise on the issue, announced that he would block any health-care legislation and make my program a major issue in the November congressional elections. A few days later, Newt Gingrich was quoted as saying the Republican strategy was to make health-care reform unpassable by voting against improving amendments. He was as good as his word. On June 30, the House Ways and Means Committee voted out a universal coverage bill without a single Republican vote.

The Republican leaders had received a memorandum from William Kristol, former chief of staff to Vice President Dan Quayle, urging them to kill health-care reform. Kristol said the Republicans couldn't afford to allow anything to pass; a success on health care would present a "serious political threat to the Republican Party," while its demise would be a "monumental setback for the President." At the end of May, at a Memorial Day retreat, the Republican congressional leaders decided to adopt Kristol's position. I wasn't surprised that Gingrich would follow Kristol's hard line; his goal was to win the House and push the country to the right. Dole, on the other hand, was genuinely interested in health care and knew we needed to reform the system. But he was running for President. All he had to do was to hold forty-one of his fellow Republicans for a fili-buster and we were sunk.

On June 21, I transmitted to Congress a welfare reform bill designed by Donna Shalala, Bruce Reed, and their topflight policy people to make welfare "a second chance, not a way of life." The bill was the product of months of consultations with every affected interest group, from governors to people on welfare. The legislation required able-bodied people to go to work after two years on wel-fare, during which time the government would provide education and training for them. If there was no private-sector job available, the welfare recipient would be required to take a government-subsidized one.

Other provisions were designed to make sure recipients wouldn't be worse off economically in the workforce than they had been on welfare, including more money for child-support enforcement, and continuing health and nutritional coverage for a transition period under Medi-caid and the food stamp program. These changes, plus the large EITC tax cut for low-wage workers enacted in 1993, would be more than enough to make even low-wage jobs more attractive than welfare. Of course, if we passed health-care reform, lower-income workers would have permanent, not just temporary, health coverage, and wel-fare reform would be even more successful.

I also proposed to end the perverse incentive in the pre-sent system under which young teen mothers received more aid if they moved out of their homes than if they continued to live with their parents and stayed in school. And I urged Congress to toughen the child-support enforcement law, to force absent parents to come up with more of the startling $34 billion worth of court-ordered, but still unpaid, child support. Secretary Shalala had already granted several states "waivers" from existing federal rules to pursue many of these reforms, and they were producing results: the welfare rolls were already dropping sharply.

June was a big month for international affairs: I tightened sanctions on Haiti; Hillary and I hosted a state dinner for the emperor and empress of Japan, both highly intelligent, gentle people who spread goodwill for their country wherever they went; and I met with King Hussein of Jordan, and the presidents of Hungary, Slovakia, and Chile. By far the biggest foreign policy issue, however, was North Korea.

As I mentioned earlier, North Korea had prevented inspections by the IAEA to make sure their spent fuel rods were not being reprocessed into plutonium for nuclear weapons. In March, when the inspections were stopped, I had pledged to seek UN sanctions against North Korea and refused to rule out military action. It got worse after that. In May, North Korea began to discharge fuel from a reactor in a way that prevented the inspectors from adequately monitoring its operation and determining what use was being made of the spent fuel.

President Carter called me on June 1 and said he would like to go to North Korea to try to resolve the problem. I sent Ambassador Bob Gallucci, who was handling the matter for us, down to Plains, Georgia, to brief Carter on the seriousness of the North Korean violations. He still wanted to go, and after consulting with Al Gore and my national security team, I decided it was worth trying. About three weeks earlier, I had received a sobering estimate of the staggering losses both sides would suffer if war broke out. I was in Europe for D-day, so Al Gore called Carter and told him that I had no objection to his going

to North Korea as long as President Kim Il Sung understood that I would not agree to a suspension of the sanctions unless North Korea let the inspectors do their jobs,
agreed to freeze its nuclear program, and committed to a
new round of talks with the United States on building a
non-nuclear future.

On June 16, President Carter called from Pyongyang
and then did a live interview on CNN saying that Kim
would not expel the inspectors from its nuclear complex
as long as good-faith efforts were made to resolve the differences over international inspections. Carter then said
that because of this "very positive step," our administration should ease its sanction efforts and start high-level
negotiations with North Korea. I replied that if North
Korea was prepared to freeze its nuclear program, we
would return to talks, but it wasn't clear to me that North
Korea had agreed to that.

Based on previous experience, I was unwilling to trust
North Korea and would leave the sanctions hanging until
we received official confirmation of North Korea's change
in policy. Within a week we got it, when President Kim
sent me a letter confirming what he had told Carter and
accepting our other preconditions for talks. I thanked
President Carter for his efforts and announced that North
Korea had agreed to all our conditions, and that North
and South Korea had agreed to discuss a possible meeting
between their presidents. In return, I said that the United
States was willing to start talks with North Korea in
Geneva the following month, and that while they were
taking place we would suspend our sanctions efforts.

At the end of June, I announced several staff changes that
I hoped would better equip us to deal with our large leg-

islative agenda and the elections just four months away. A few weeks earlier Mack McLarty had told me he thought it was time for him to change jobs. He had taken a lot of hits for the Travel Office and had endured countless press stories criticizing our decision-making process. Mack suggested that I appoint Leon Panetta chief of staff, because he had a good understanding of Congress and the press and would run a tight ship. When word got out about Mack, others also favored Leon for the job. Mack said he would like to try to build bridges to moderate Republicans and conservative Democrats in Congress, and to oversee our preparations for the Summit of the Americas, to be held in Miami in December.

I thought Mack had done a better job than he had gotten credit for, managing a much smaller White House with a much heavier workload, and playing a pivotal role in our victories on the economic plan and NAFTA. As Bob Rubin often said, Mack had established a collegial atmosphere within the White House and with the cabinet that many previous administrations never achieved. This environment had helped us to get a lot done, both in Congress and with the government agencies. It had also encouraged the kind of free and open debate that led to criticism of our decision-making process, but that, given the complexity and novelty of many of our challenges, led to better decisions.

Moreover, I doubted there was much we could do, apart from reducing the leaks, to avoid the negative press coverage. Professor Thomas Patterson, an authority on the media's role in elections, had recently published an important book, **Out of Order,** which helped me to better understand what was going on, and to take it less personally. Patterson's thesis was that press coverage of presidential campaigns had become steadily more negative over the past twenty years or so, as the press had come to see itself as the "mediator" between candidates and the public, with the responsibility to tell the voters how they should view the candidates and what was wrong with them. In 1992, Bush, Perot, and I had all received more negative than positive coverage.

In his postscript to the 1994 edition of **Out of Order,** Patterson said that, after the '92 election, the media for the first time had taken its negative bias from the campaign straight into its coverage of the administration. Now, he said, a President's news coverage "depends less on his actual performance in office than on the media's cynical bias. The press nearly always magnifies the bad and underplays the good." For example, the nonpartisan Center for Media and Public Affairs said that, on my handling of domestic policy issues, the coverage was 60 percent negative, mostly focusing on broken campaign commitments, even though, as Patterson said, I had kept "dozens" of my campaign commitments and that I was a President who "should have acquired a reputation for fulfilling his promises," in part by prevailing in Congress on 88 percent of contested votes, a mark bettered only by Eisenhower in 1953 and Johnson in 1965. Patterson concluded that the negative coverage drove down not only my approval rating but also public support for my programs, including health care, and thus "imposed extraordinary costs on the Clinton presidency and the national interest."

In the summer of 1994, Thomas Patterson's book helped me to see that there might be nothing I could do to change the press coverage. If that was true, I had to learn to handle it better. Mack McLarty had never sought the chief of staff's job, and Leon Panetta was willing to take on the challenge. He had already built a record at OMB that would be hard to improve on—our first two budgets were the first in seventeen years to be adopted by Congress on time; the budgets guaranteed three years of deficit reduction in a row for the first time since Truman was President; and perhaps most impressive, they brought the first reduction in discretionary domestic spending in twenty-five years, while still providing increases for education, Head Start, job training, and new technologies. Perhaps as chief of staff, Leon could more clearly communicate what we had done and were trying to accomplish for America. I named him, and appointed Mack counselor to the President, with the job description he had recommended.

THIRTY-NINE

June brought the first real action from Robert Fiske. He had decided to conduct an independent inquiry into Vince Foster's death since so many questions had been raised about it in the media and by Republicans in Congress. I was glad Fiske was looking at it. The scandal machine was trying to get blood out of a turnip, and maybe this would shut them up and give Vince's family some relief.

Some of the charges and antics would have been funny except for the tragedy involved. One of the loudest and most sanctimonious of the "Foster was murdered" crowd was Republican congressman Dan Burton of Indiana. In an attempt to prove that Vince couldn't have killed himself, Burton went out in his backyard and shot a revolver into a watermelon. It was nutty. I never could figure out what Burton was trying to prove.

Fiske interviewed Hillary and me. It was a straightforward, professional session, and afterward I knew he would be thorough and believed he would finish his inquiry in a timely fashion. On June 30, he issued preliminary findings on Vince's death, as well as on the much-ballyhooed conversations between Bernie Nussbaum and Roger Altman. Fiske said that Vince's death was a suicide and found no evidence that it had anything to do with Whitewater. He also found that Nussbaum and Altman had not acted improperly.

From then on, Fiske was scorned by the conservative Republicans and their allies in the media. The **Wall Street Journal** had already pushed the press to be even more aggressive in writing stories critical of Hillary and me, however much they might later be "overtaken by other facts." Some conservative commentators and members of Congress began calling for Fiske's resignation. Senator Lauch Faircloth of North Carolina was especially vocal, spurred on by a new staff member, David Bossie, who had been Floyd Brown's partner in Citizens United, a right-wing group that had already spread a lot of false stories about me.

On the same day that Fiske issued his report, I drove another nail in my own coffin by signing the new independent counsel law. The law permitted Fiske to be reappointed, but the "Special Division" of the D.C. Circuit Court of Appeals could also remove him and appoint another prosecutor, starting the process all over again. Under the statute, the judges on the Special Division would be selected by Chief Justice Rehnquist, who had been an extremely conservative Republican activist before he came to the Supreme Court.

I wanted Fiske to be grandfathered in, but my new head of legislative affairs, Pat Griffin, said some Democrats were afraid it wouldn't look good. Lloyd Cutler said there was nothing to worry about because Fiske was clearly independent and there was no way he would be replaced. He told Hillary he would "eat his hat" if it happened.

In early July, I returned to Europe for the G-7 summit in Naples. On the way, I stopped in Riga, Latvia, to meet with the leaders of the Baltic states and celebrate the withdrawal of Russian troops from Lithuania and Latvia, a move we had helped to speed up by providing a large number of housing vouchers for Russian officers who wanted to go home. There were still Russian troops in Estonia, and President Lennart Meri, a filmmaker who had always opposed Russian domination of his country, was determined to get them out as soon as possible. After the meeting there was a moving celebration in Riga's Freedom Square, where I was welcomed by about forty thousand people waving flags in gratitude for America's steadfast support of their newfound freedom.

The next stop was Warsaw, to meet with President Lech Walesa and emphasize my commitment to bringing Poland into NATO. Walesa had become a hero, and free Poland's natural choice for president, by leading the Gdansk shipyard workers' revolt against communism more than a decade earlier. He was deeply suspicious of Russia and wanted Poland in NATO as soon as possible. He also wanted more American investment in Poland, saying the country's future required more American generals, "starting with General Motors and General Electric."

That night Walesa hosted a dinner to which he invited leaders of all political views. I listened with fascination to a heated argument between Mrs. Walesa, a feisty mother of eight children, and a legislative leader who was also a potato farmer. She was railing against communism, while he argued that farmers had been better off under communism than they were today. I thought they were going to come to blows. I tried to help by reminding the legislator that even under communism the Polish farms were in private hands; all the Polish Communists had done was to purchase the food and sell it in Ukraine and Russia. He conceded the point, but said he had always had a market and a good price for his crops. I told him he had never been under a completely Communist system like Russia's, where the farms themselves were collectivized. Then I explained how the American system worked, and how all successful free-market systems also had some form of cooperative marketing and price supports. The farmer remained skeptical, and Mrs. Walesa remained adamant. If democracy is about free and unfettered debate, it had certainly taken hold in Poland.

My first day at the Naples summit was devoted to Asia. Kim Il Sung had died the previous day, just as talks with North Korea resumed in Geneva, throwing the future of our agreement with North Korea into doubt. The other G-7 member with a big interest in the issue was Japan. There had been tensions between the Japanese and the Koreans for decades, going back before World War II. If North Korea had nuclear weapons, there would be great pressure on Japan to develop a nuclear deterrent, an action that, given their own painful experience, the Japanese did not want to take. The new Japanese prime minister, Tomi-ichi Murayama, who had become Japan's first socialist prime minister by joining in a coalition with the Liberal Democratic Party, assured me that our solidarity on North Korea would remain intact. Out of respect for Kim Il Sung's death, the Geneva talks were suspended for a month.

The most important decisions we made in Naples were to provide an aid package to Ukraine and to include Russia in the political part of all future summits. Bringing Russia into the prestigious circle gave Yeltsin and other reformers pushing for closer ties to the West a big boost, and guaranteed that our future gatherings would be more interesting. Yeltsin was always entertaining.

Chelsea, Hillary, and I loved Naples, and after the meetings, we took a day to see Pompeii, which the Italians had done a marvelous job of recovering from the ashes of the volcano that engulfed the town in A.D. 79. We saw wall paintings with colors that had retained their rich texture, including some that were first-century versions of political posters; open-air food stands that were early precursors of today's fast-food restaurants; and the remains of several bodies remarkably preserved by the ashes, among them a man lying with his hand over the face of his obviously pregnant wife, with two other children beside them. It was a powerful reminder of the fragile and fleeting nature of life.

The European trip ended in Germany. Helmut Kohl took us to visit his hometown, Ludwigshafen, before I flew to Ramstein Air Base to see our troops, many of whom would soon be leaving the military in the post–Cold War downsizing. The servicemen and -women at Ramstein, just like their counterparts in the U.S. Navy I had met in Naples, mentioned only one domestic issue to me: health care. Most of them had children, and in the military they had taken health coverage for granted. Now they worried that because of defense downsizing they were going home to a country that would no longer provide health care for their kids.

Berlin was booming, full of construction cranes, as the city prepared to resume its role as the capital of a united Germany. Hillary and I walked with the Kohls out of the Reichstag along the line where the Berlin Wall had stood and through the magnificent Brandenburg Gate. President Kennedy and President Reagan had given memorable speeches just outside the gate on the western side of the wall. Now I was standing on a podium on the eastern side of unified Berlin, facing an enthusiastic crowd of fifty thousand Germans, many of them young people wondering about their future in a very different world from the one their parents had known.

I urged the Germans to lead Europe toward greater unity. If they did so, I pledged in German, "Amerika steht an Ihrer Seite jetzt und für immer." (America is on your side, now and forever.) The Brandenburg Gate had long been a symbol of its time, sometimes a monument to tyranny and a tower of conquest, but now it was what its builders had meant it to be, a gateway to the future.

When I returned home, the foreign policy work continued. Increased repression in Haiti had led to a new flood of boat people and the suspension of all commercial air traffic. By the end of the month, the UN Security Council had approved an invasion to dislodge the dictatorship, an action that seemed more and more inevitable.

On July 22, I announced a large increase in emergency aid to Rwandan refugees, with U.S. military forces establishing a base in Uganda to support round-the-clock shipments of relief supplies to the tremendous number of refugees in camps near the Rwandan border. I also ordered the military to establish a safe water supply and distribute as much clean water as possible to those at risk of cholera and other diseases, and announced that the United States would be delivering twenty million oral rehydration therapy packages over the next two days to help stem the cholera outbreak. Within a week we had delivered more than 1,300 tons of food, medicine, and other supplies, and were producing and distributing more than 100,000 gallons of safe water a day. The entire effort would require about 4,000 troops and cost nearly $500 million, but even after all the slaughter, it would still save many lives.

On July 25, King Hussein and Prime Minister Rabin came to town to sign the Washington declaration, formally ending the state of belligerency between Jordan and

Israel and committing themselves to negotiating a full peace agreement. They had been talking secretly for some time, and Warren Christopher had worked hard to facilitate their agreement. The next day, the two leaders spoke to a joint session of Congress, and the three of us held a press conference to reaffirm our commitment to a comprehensive peace involving all the parties to the Middle East conflict.

The Israeli-Jordanian agreement stood in stark contrast to recent terrorist attacks against a Jewish center in Buenos Aires, and others in Panama and London, all of which Hezbollah was believed to be responsible for. Hezbollah was armed by Iran and aided by Syria in conducting operations against Israel from southern Lebanon. Since the peace process could not be completed without an agreement between Israel and Syria, Hezbollah's activities presented a serious potential obstacle. I had called President Assad to tell him about the Israeli-Jordanian announcement, to ask him to support it, and to assure him that Israel and the United States were still committed to successful negotiations with his country. Rabin left the door open to talks with Syria by saying that the Syrians could limit but not end Hezbollah's activities. Hussein responded that not just Syria but the entire Arab world should follow Jordan's lead and reconcile with Israel.

I closed the press conference by saying that Hussein and Rabin must have "put peace in the air all over the world." Boris Yeltsin had just informed me that he and President Meri had agreed that all Russian troops would be withdrawn from Estonia by August 31.

In August it gets hot in Washington, and Congress usually leaves town. In 1994, Congress stayed in session almost the entire month to deal with crime and health care. Both the Senate and House had passed versions of the crime bill, which provided 100,000 more community police, tougher penalties for repeat offenders, and more funds for both prison construction and prevention programs to keep young people out of trouble.

When the conference committee met to resolve the differences between the Senate and House crime bills, the Democrats folded the assault weapons ban into the compromise bill. As I've said, the ban had passed the House as a separate matter by only two votes, in the face of furious opposition by the National Rifle Association. The NRA had already lost the fight to defeat the Brady bill and was determined to prevail on this one, so that Americans would retain their right to "keep and bear" rapid-fire large-magazine weapons designed for one purpose only: to kill a great many people in a hurry. These weapons worked; crime victims shot with them were three times more likely to die than those whose assailants fired regular handguns.

The conference decided to combine the ban with the crime bill because, while we had a clear majority for the ban in the Senate, we didn't have the sixty votes necessary to break a certain filibuster by NRA supporters. The Democrats in the conference knew it would be much harder to filibuster the overall crime bill than the assault weapons ban standing alone. The problem with the strategy was that it forced the House Democrats from rural pro-gun districts to vote on the assault weapons ban all over again, risking the failure of the whole bill, and putting them at risk of losing their seats if they voted for it.

On August 11, the House defeated the new crime bill,

225–210, on a procedural vote, with 58 Democrats voting against it and only 11 Republicans voting for it. A few of the Democratic "no" votes were liberals who opposed the bill's expansion of the death penalty, but most of our defectors were voting with the NRA. A sizable group of Republicans said they wanted to support the bill, including the assault weapons ban, but thought it spent too much money overall, especially on prevention programs. We were in trouble on one of my most important campaign commitments, and I had to do something to turn it around.

The next day, before the National Association of Police Officers in Minneapolis, with Mayor Rudy Giuliani of New York and Mayor Ed Rendell of Philadelphia, I tried to frame the choice as one between the police and the people on one side and the NRA on the other. Surely we had not reached the point where the only way to keep congressional seats safe was to leave the American people and police officers in greater danger.

Three days later, at a ceremony in the Rose Garden, the issue was put in even sharper focus by Steve Sposato, a Republican businessman whose wife had been killed when a deranged man with an assault weapon went on a shooting spree in the San Francisco office building where she worked. Sposato, who had brought his young daughter, Megan, with him, made a compelling appeal for the assault weapons ban.

Late in the month, the crime bill came to a vote again. Unlike health care, we were working on crime through good-faith bipartisan negotiation. This time we won, 235–195, having picked up almost 20 Republican votes by negotiating a substantial cut in the costs of the bill. Some liberal Democrats were persuaded to change their votes on the strength of the bill's prevention programs, and a few more Democrats from pro-gun districts stuck their necks out. Four days later, Senator Joe Biden shepherded the crime bill through the Senate, 61–38, when 6 Republicans provided the votes necessary to break a filibuster. The crime legislation would have a profoundly positive impact, helping to usher in the largest sustained drop in crime on record.

Just before the House vote, Speaker Tom Foley and majority leader Dick Gephardt had made a last-ditch appeal to me to remove the assault weapons ban from the bill. They argued that many Democrats who represented closely divided districts had already cast a very difficult vote for the economic program, and had already defied the NRA once on the Brady bill vote. They said that if we made them walk the plank again on the assault weapons ban, the overall bill might not pass, and that if it did, many Democrats who voted for it would not survive the election in November. Jack Brooks, the House Judiciary Committee chairman from Texas, told me the same thing. Brooks had been in the House for more than forty years and was one of my favorite congressmen. He represented a district full of NRA members and had led the effort to defeat the assault weapons ban when it first came to a vote. Jack was convinced that if we didn't drop the ban, the NRA would beat a lot of Democrats by terrifying gun owners.

I was troubled by what Foley, Gephardt, and Brooks had said, but I was convinced that our members could win a debate with the NRA over the issue in their backyards. Dale Bumpers and David Pryor knew how to explain their votes to Arkansans. Senator Howell Heflin of Alabama, whom I had known almost twenty years, had an ingenious explanation for his support of the crime bill. He said he had never voted for gun control, but the crime bill banned only nineteen assault weapons, and he didn't know anyone who owned those weapons. On the other hand, the bill expressly prohibited restrictions on owning hundreds of other weapons, including "every weapon I am familiar with."

It was a persuasive point, but not everyone could make it the way Howell Heflin did. Foley, Gephardt, and Brooks were right and I was wrong. The price of a safer America would be heavy casualties among its defenders.

Maybe I was pushing the Congress, the country, and the administration too hard. At my press conference on August 19, a reporter asked me a very perceptive question: "I was wondering if you've thought about this, that as a President elected with 43 percent, you may be trying to do too much, too fast . . . exceeding your mandate," by pushing through so much legislation with so little Republican support. Even though we had accomplished a lot, I was wondering about that, too. I wouldn't have to wonder much longer.

While we were winning on the crime bill, we kept on losing with health care. In early August, George Mitchell introduced a compromise bill to increase the percentage of the insured population to 95 percent without an employer mandate, leaving open the possibility of imposing one in later years to get to 100 percent, if the bill's voluntary procedures didn't succeed in doing so. I announced my support for Mitchell's bill the next day, and we began to shop it to moderate Republicans, but it was no use. Dole was determined to defeat any meaningful reform; it was good politics. On the day the crime bill passed, the Senate recessed for two weeks with no further action on health care. Dole had failed in his efforts to kill the crime bill, but he had prevailed in derailing health care.

The other big news in August was in the parallel world of Whitewater. After I signed the independent counsel statute, Chief Justice Rehnquist appointed Judge David Sentelle to head the Special Division that had responsibility for naming independent counsels under the new law. Sentelle was an ultra-conservative protégé of Senator Jesse Helms, who had decried the influence of "leftist heretics" who wanted America to become a "collectivist, egalitarian, materialistic, race-conscious, hyper-secular, and socially permissive state." The three-member panel also contained another conservative judge, so Sentelle could do whatever he wanted.

On August 5, Sentelle's panel fired Robert Fiske and replaced him with Kenneth Starr, who had been a court of appeals judge and solicitor general in the Bush administration. Unlike Fiske, Starr had no prosecutorial experience, but he had something far more important: he was much more conservative and partisan than Fiske. In a terse statement Judge Sentelle said he was replacing Fiske with Starr to guarantee the "appearance of independence," a test Fiske could not meet because he was "affiliated with the incumbent administration." It was an absurd argument. Fiske was a Republican whose only affiliation with the administration was that Janet Reno had appointed him to a job he did not seek. Had the Special Division re-appointed him, there would have been no more affiliation.

In his place, Judge Sentelle's panel appointed someone with not an apparent but a real and blatant conflict of interest. Starr had been an outspoken proponent of the Paula Jones lawsuit, appearing on TV and even offering to write a friend-of-the-court brief on her behalf. Five former presidents of the American Bar Association criticized the Starr appointment because of its apparent political bias. So did the **New York Times,** after it emerged that Judge Sentelle had had lunch with Fiske's biggest critic, Senator Lauch Faircloth, and Jesse Helms just a couple of weeks before the Fiske-Starr switch. The three said they were just discussing prostate problems.

Of course, Starr had no intention of stepping aside. His bias against me was the very reason he was chosen and why he took the job. We now had a bizarre definition of an "independent" counsel: he had to be independent of me, but it was fine to be closely tied to my political enemies and legal adversaries.

The Starr appointment was unprecedented. In the past, there had been an effort to ensure that special prosecutors would be not only independent but also fair and respectful of the institution of the presidency. Leon Jaworski, the Watergate special prosecutor, was a conservative Democrat who had supported President Nixon for reelection in 1972. Lawrence Walsh, the Iran-Contra prosecutor, was an Oklahoma Republican who had supported President Reagan. I had never wanted the Whitewater inquiry to be a "home game," in Doug Sosnik's words, but I thought I was at least entitled to a neutral field. It was not to be. Since there was nothing to Whitewater, the only way to use the investigation against me was to turn it into one long "away game." Robert Fiske was too fair and too fast for that job. He had to go.

Lloyd Cutler didn't eat his hat, but less than a week after the Starr appointment he left, too, having fulfilled his commitment to serve a brief stint in the counsel's office. I replaced him with Abner Mikva, a former Illinois

congressman and court of appeals judge with an impeccable reputation and a clearheaded view of the forces we
were up against. I was sorry that, after such a long and distinguished career, Lloyd had to learn that people he
thought he knew and could trust were playing by different
rules than he was.

When Congress left town, we took off for Martha's Vineyard again. Hillary and I needed some time off. So did Al
Gore. A few days earlier he had ruptured his Achilles ten-
don in a basketball game. It was a painful injury, requiring
a prolonged recovery. Al would come back stronger than
before, using his forced immobility to work out with
weights. In the meantime, on crutches, he traveled to
forty states and four foreign countries, including Egypt,
where he brokered a compromise on the sensitive issue of
population control at the Cairo Conference on Sustainable Development. He also continued overseeing the
Reinventing Government Initiative. By mid-September,
we had already achieved savings of $47 billion, enough to
pay for the entire crime bill; begun a competitive venture
with the automakers to develop a "clean car"; cut the
application form for an SBA loan from a hundred pages to
one; reformed FEMA so that it was no longer the least
popular federal agency but the most admired one, thanks
to James Lee Witt; and saved more than $1 billion
through cancellations of unneeded construction projects
under Roger Johnson's leadership at the General Services
Administration. Al Gore was doing a lot on one good leg.
    Our week on the Vineyard was interesting for several
reasons. Vernon Jordan set up a golf game with Warren
Buffett and Bill Gates, America's wealthiest men. I liked
them both, and was particularly impressed that Buffett

was a die-hard Democrat who believed in civil rights, fair taxation, and a woman's right to choose.

The most memorable evening for me was a dinner at Bill and Rose Styron's, where the guests of honor were the superb Mexican writer Carlos Fuentes and my literary hero, Gabriel García Márquez. García Márquez was friends with Fidel Castro, who, in an effort to export some of his problems to us, was in the process of unleashing a mass exodus of Cubans to the United States, reminiscent of the Mariel boat lift, which had caused me so many problems in 1980. Thousands of Cubans, at great risk to themselves, had set out in small boats and rafts for the ninety-mile voyage to Florida.

García Márquez was opposed to the U.S. embargo on Cuba and tried to talk me out of it. I told him that I would not lift the embargo, but that I supported the Cuban Democracy Act, which gave the President authority to improve relations with Cuba in return for greater movement toward freedom and democracy there. I also asked him to tell Castro that if the influx of Cubans continued, he would get a very different response from the United States than he had received in 1980 from President Carter. "Castro has already cost me one election," I said. "He can't have two." I relayed the same message through President Salinas of Mexico, who had a good working relationship with Castro. Not long afterward, the United States and Cuba reached an agreement by which Castro pledged to stem the exodus, and we promised to take twenty thousand more Cubans each year through the normal process. Castro faithfully observed the accord for the remainder of my term. Later, García Márquez would joke that he was the only man who was friends with both Fidel Castro and Bill Clinton.

After we discussed Cuba, García Márquez lavished most of his attention on Chelsea, who said she had read two of his books. He later told me that he didn't believe a fourteen-year-old girl could understand his work, so he launched into an extended discussion with her about **One Hundred Years of Solitude.** He was so impressed that he later sent her an entire set of his novels.

The only business I did on vacation involved Ireland. I granted a visa to Joe Cahill, a seventy-six-year-old hero to Irish Republicans. In 1973, Cahill had been convicted of gunrunning in Ireland, and he continued to promote violence for years afterward. I gave him a visa because he now wanted to promote peace among the IRA's American supporters, as part of an understanding under which the IRA would, at long last, announce a cease-fire. Cahill came to America on August 30, and the next day the IRA announced a total cessation of violence, opening the way for Sinn Fein's participation in the peace talks. It was a victory for Gerry Adams and for the Irish government.

When we returned from our vacation, we moved into Blair House for three weeks while the White House air-conditioning system was being repaired. A massive stone-by-stone restoration of the nearly two-hundred-year-old exterior, begun during the Reagan administration, was also still going on. A portion of the White House would be covered by scaffolding all through my first term.

Our family always enjoyed the time we spent in Blair House, and this extended visit was no exception, though it caused us to miss a dramatic moment back across the street. On September 12 an inebriated man who was disappointed with his life broke into a small airplane and took off for downtown Washington and the White

House. He was trying either to kill himself by crashing into the building or to stage a landing on the South Lawn, like the one executed by a young German pilot in Moscow's Red Square a few years earlier. Unfortunately, his little Cessna hit the ground too late for the landing, bounced over the hedge and under the giant magnolia tree on the west side of the entrance, then slammed into the large stone base of the White House, killing him instantly. A few years later, another troubled man with a pistol vaulted the White House fence before he was wounded and apprehended by officers of the Uniformed Division of the Secret Service. The White House was a magnet for more than ambitious politicians.

The crisis in Haiti came to a head in September. General Cedras and his thugs had intensified their reign of terror, executing orphaned children, raping young girls, killing priests, mutilating people and leaving body parts in the open to terrify others, and slashing the faces of mothers with machetes while their children watched. By this time, I had been working for a peaceful solution for two years, and I was fed up. More than a year earlier, Cedras had signed an agreement to give up power, but when the time came to leave, he simply refused to go.

It was time to throw him out, but public opinion and congressional sentiment were strongly against it. Though the Congressional Black Caucus, Senator Tom Harkin, and Senator Chris Dodd supported me, the Republicans were solidly opposed, and most Democrats, including George Mitchell, thought I was just taking them out onto another precipice without public support or congressional authorization. There was even division within the administration. Al Gore, Warren Christopher, Bill Gray, Tony

Lake, and Sandy Berger were for it. Bill Perry and the Pentagon were not, but they had been working on an invasion plan in case I ordered them to proceed.

I thought we had to go forward. Innocent people were being slaughtered in our own backyard, and we were already spending a small fortune taking care of Haitian refugees. The United Nations was unanimous in supporting the ouster of Cedras.

On September 16, in a last-minute attempt to avoid an invasion, I sent President Carter, Colin Powell, and Sam Nunn to Haiti to try to persuade General Cedras and his supporters in the military and parliament to peacefully accept Aristide's return and Cedras's departure from the country. For different reasons, they all disagreed with my determination to use force to restore Aristide. Though the Carter Center had monitored Aristide's overwhelming election victory, President Carter had developed a relationship with Cedras and was skeptical of Aristide's commitment to democracy. Nunn was opposed to Aristide's return until parliamentary elections were held, because he didn't trust Aristide to protect minority rights without an established countervailing force in parliament. Powell thought only the military and the police could govern Haiti, and that they would never work with Aristide.

As subsequent events would prove, there was some merit to their arguments. Haiti was deeply divided economically and politically and had no previous experience with democracy, no significant middle class, and little of the institutional capacity required to operate a modern state. Even if Aristide was returned without a hitch, he might not succeed. Still, he had been elected overwhelmingly, and Cedras and his crew were killing innocent people. We could at least stop that.

Despite their reservations, the distinguished trio pledged to faithfully communicate my policy. They wanted to avoid a violent American entry, which could make matters even worse. Nunn spoke to members of Haiti's parliament; Powell told the Haitian military leaders in graphic terms what would happen if the United States invaded; and Carter worked on Cedras.

The next day I went to the Pentagon to review the invasion plan with General Shalikashvili and the Joint Chiefs, and, by teleconference, with Admiral Paul David Miller, the commander of the overall operation, and Lieutenant General Hugh Shelton, commander of the Eighteenth Airborne Corps, who would lead our troops onto the island. The invasion plan called for a unified operation involving all branches of the military. Two aircraft carriers were in the waters off Haiti, one transporting Special Operations forces and the other carrying soldiers from the Tenth Mountain Division. Air force planes were set to provide necessary air support. The marines were assigned to occupy Cap Haitien, Haiti's second-largest city. Planes carrying Eighty-second Airborne Division paratroopers would fly out of North Carolina and drop them over the island at the outset of the assault. Navy SEALs would go in early and scan designated areas. They had already done a test run that morning, coming out of the water and onto land without incident. Most troops and equipment were to enter Haiti in an operation called "RoRo," for "roll on, roll off"; troops and vehicles would roll onto landing vessels for the trip to Haiti, then roll off on the Haitian shoreline. When the mission was accomplished, the process would be reversed. Besides the U.S. forces, we had support from twenty-five other countries that had joined the UN coalition.

As the deadline for our attack approached, President Carter called me pleading for more time to persuade Cedras to leave. Carter desperately wanted to avoid a forced invasion. So did I. Haiti had no military capability; it would be like shooting fish in a barrel. I agreed to give him three more hours, but made it clear that any agreement he made with the general could not include another delay in the handover to Aristide. Cedras couldn't have more time to murder children, rape young girls, and slash women's faces. We had already spent $200 million taking care of the Haitians who had left their country. I wanted them to be able to go home.

In Port-au-Prince, as the three-hour deadline ran out, an angry mob gathered outside the building where the Americans were still talking. Every time I talked with Carter, Cedras had proposed a different deal, but they all gave him some wiggle room to hang around and delay Aristide's return. I rejected them all. With the danger outside and the deadline for invasion at hand, Carter, Powell, and Nunn kept trying to persuade Cedras, to no avail. Carter pleaded for more time. I agreed to another delay, until 5 p.m. The planes with the paratroopers were scheduled to arrive just after dark, at about six. If the three of them were still there negotiating then, they would be in much greater danger from the mob.

At 5:30 p.m. they were still in place and already in greater peril, because Cedras knew the operation had begun. He had had someone watching the airstrip in North Carolina, when our sixty-one planes carrying the paratroopers took off. I called President Carter and told him that he, Colin, and Sam had to leave immediately. The three of them made one last appeal to the titular head of Haiti, eighty-one-year-old President Emile Jonassaint, who at last told them he would choose peace instead of war. When all the cabinet members but one agreed with him, Cedras finally relented, less than an hour before the skies over Port-au-Prince would have been filled with parachutes. Instead, I ordered the planes to turn around and come home.

The next day General Shelton led the first of the fifteen-thousand-member multinational force into Haiti without a shot being fired. Shelton cut a striking figure. He was about six feet five inches tall, with chiseled features and a slow southern drawl. Though he was a couple of years older than I, he still did regular parachute jumps with his troops. He looked as if he could have deposed Cedras all by himself. I had visited General Shelton not long before at Fort Bragg, after a plane crash at nearby Pope Air Force Base had killed several servicemen. On Shelton's office wall were pictures of two great Confederate Civil War generals, Robert E. Lee and Stonewall Jackson. When I saw Shelton on television as he stepped ashore, I remarked to one of my staff that America had come a long way if a man who revered Stonewall Jackson could be the liberator of Haiti.

Cedras promised to cooperate with General Shelton and to leave power by October 15, as soon as the general amnesty law required by the UN agreement was passed. Although I almost had to forcibly remove them from Haiti, Carter, Powell, and Nunn had done a courageous job under difficult and potentially dangerous circumstances. A combination of dogged diplomacy and imminent force had avoided bloodshed. Now it was up to Aristide to honor his commitment of "no to violence, no to vengeance, yes to reconciliation." As with so many such statements, this would prove to be easier said than done.

Because the restoration of democracy in Haiti occurred without incident, it didn't turn out to have the negative impact the Democrats had feared. We should have been in good shape going into the elections: the economy was producing 250,000 jobs a month, with unemployment dropping from over 7 percent to under 6 percent; the deficit was coming down; we had passed important legislation on crime, education, national service, trade, and family leave; and I was making headway on our foreign policy agenda with Russia, Europe, China, Japan, the Middle East, Northern Ireland, Bosnia, and Haiti. But despite the record and the results, we were in trouble heading into the last six weeks of the election, for a variety of reasons: many people hadn't felt the economic improvements yet; no one believed the deficit was coming down; most people were unaware of the legislative victories and didn't know or didn't care about the foreign policy progress; the Republicans and their media and interest group allies had constantly and effectively attacked me as a wild-eyed liberal who wanted to tax them into the poorhouse and take their doctors and guns away; and the general press coverage was overwhelmingly negative.

The Center for Media and Public Affairs issued a report saying that in my first sixteen months, there was an average of nearly five negative comments a night on the evening network news programs, far more than the first President Bush had received in his first two years. The center's director, Robert Lichter, said I had the "misfortune of being president at the dawning of an age that combines attack-dog journalism with tabloid news." There were some exceptions, of course. Jacob Weisberg wrote that "Bill Clinton has been more faithful to his word than any other chief executive in recent memory," but that "voters mistrust Clinton in part because the media keeps telling them not to trust him." Jonathan Alter wrote in

Newsweek, "In less than two years, Bill Clinton had already achieved more domestically than John F. Kennedy, Gerald Ford, Jimmy Carter and George Bush combined. Although Richard Nixon and Ronald Reagan often had their way with Congress, **Congressional Quarterly** says it's Clinton who has had the most legislative success of any President since Lyndon Johnson. The standard for measuring results domestically should not be the coherence of the process but how actual lives are touched and changed. By that standard, he's doing well."

Alter may have been right, but if so, it was a well-kept secret.

FORTY

Things grew worse as September drew to a close. Acting baseball commissioner Bud Selig announced that the players' strike couldn't be resolved and he was canceling the rest of the season, and the World Series, for the first time since 1904. Bruce Lindsey, who had helped to settle the airline strike, tried to resolve the standoff. I even invited the representatives of the players and owners to the White House, but we couldn't settle it. If our national pastime was being canceled, things could not be going in the right direction.

On September 26, George Mitchell formally threw in the towel on health-care reform. Senator Chafee had continued to work with him, but he couldn't bring enough Republicans along to break Senator Dole's filibuster. The $300 million that the health insurance and other lobbies had spent to stop health-care reform was well invested. I put out a brief statement saying I would try again next year.

Though I had felt for months that we were beaten, I was still disappointed, and I felt bad that Hillary and Ira Magaziner were taking the rap for the failure. It was unfair for three reasons. First, our proposals were not the big government–run nightmare that the health-insurance companies' ad campaigns had made them out to be; second, the plan was the best Hillary and Ira could do, given the charge from me: universal coverage without a tax increase; and finally, it wasn't they who had derailed health-care reform—Senator Dole's decision to kill any meaningful compromise had done that. I tried to cheer up Hillary by telling her that there were bigger mistakes in life than "getting caught red-handed" trying to provide health insurance to forty million Americans who were without it.

In spite of our defeat, all the work Hillary, Ira Magaziner, and the rest of our people had done would not be in vain. In the years ahead, many of our proposals would find their way into law and practice. Senator Kennedy and Republican senator Nancy Kassebaum of Kansas would pass a bill guaranteeing that workers wouldn't lose their insurance when they changed jobs. And in 1997, we would pass the Children's Health Insurance Program (CHIP), providing health care to millions of children in the largest expansion of health insurance since Medicaid was enacted in 1965. CHIP would help bring about the first decline in twelve years in the number of Americans without health insurance.

There would be many other health-care victories as well: a bill allowing women to stay in the hospital for more than twenty-four hours after childbirth, ending HMO-ordered "drive-by" deliveries; increased coverage for mammograms and prostate screenings; a diabetes self-management program called the most important advance since insulin by the American Diabetes Association; large increases in biomedical research and in the care and treatment of HIV/AIDS at home and abroad; childhood immunization rates above 90 percent for the first time; and the application by executive order of a patient's "bill of rights" guaranteeing the choice of a doctor and the right to prompt, adequate treatment for the eighty-five million Americans covered by federally funded plans.

But that was all in the future. For now, we had taken a good shellacking. That's the image people would take into the elections.

Near the end of the month, Newt Gingrich gathered more than three hundred Republican incumbents and candidates for a rally on the Capitol steps to sign a "Contract with America." The details of the contract had been percolating for some time. Newt had put them together to show that the Republicans were more than naysayers; they had a positive agenda. The contract was something new to American politics. Traditionally, midterm elections had been fought seat by seat. National conditions and a President's level of popularity could be a boost or a drag, but the conventional wisdom held that local factors were more important. Gingrich was convinced that the conventional wisdom was wrong. He boldly asked the American people to give the Republicans a majority, saying, "If we break this contract, throw us out. We mean it."

The contract called for a constitutional balanced budget amendment and the line-item veto, which enables the President to delete specific items in appropriations bills without having to veto the entire piece of legislation; stiffer penalties for criminals and repeal of the prevention programs in my crime bill; welfare reform, with a two-year limit on able-bodied recipients; a $500 child tax credit, another $500 credit for the care of a parent or grandparent, and tougher child-support enforcement; repeal of the taxes on upper-income Social Security recipients that were part of the 1993 budget; a 50 percent cut in the capital gains tax, and other tax cuts; an end to unfunded federal mandates on state and local government; a large increase in defense spending; tort reform to limit punitive damages; term limits for senators and representatives; a requirement that Congress, as an employer, follow all laws it has imposed on other employers; a reduction in congressional committee staffs by a third; and a requirement that 60 percent of each house of Congress approve any future tax increase.

I agreed with many of the particulars of the contract. I was already pushing welfare reform and tougher child-support enforcement, and had long supported the line-item veto and ending unfunded mandates. I liked the family tax credits. Though several of the specifics were appealing, the contract was, at its core, a simplistic and hypocritical document. In the twelve years before I became President, the Republicans, with the support of a few Democrats in Congress, had quadrupled the national debt by cutting taxes and increasing spending; now that Democrats were reducing the deficit, they wanted the Constitution to require a balanced budget, even as they recommended large tax cuts and big increases in defense spending without saying what other spending they would cut to pay for them. Just as they had done in the 1980s and would do again in the 2000s, the Republicans were trying to abolish arithmetic. As Yogi Berra said, it was déjà vu all over again, but in a nice new package.

Besides giving the Republicans a national platform for the 1994 campaign, Gingrich provided them with a list of words to use in defining their Democratic opponents. His political action committee, GOPAC, published a pamphlet entitled **Language: A Key Mechanism of Control.** Among the "contrasting words" Newt suggested for labeling Democrats were: betray, cheat, collapse, corruption, crisis, decay, destruction, failure, hypocrisy, incompetent, insecure, liberal, lie, pathetic, permissive, shallow, sick, traitors. Gingrich was convinced that if he could institutionalize that kind of name-calling, he could define the Democrats into a minority party for a long time.

The Democrats thought the Republicans had made a critical error in announcing the contract, and proceeded to attack it by showing the large cuts in education, health care, and environmental protection that would be necessary to fund the tax cuts, increase defense, and balance the budget. They even renamed Newt's plan the "Contract **on** America." They were absolutely right, but it didn't work. Post-election polls would show that the public knew only two things about the contract: that the Republicans had a plan, and that balancing the budget was part of it.

Beyond attacking the Republicans, the Democrats were determined to fight the election the old-fashioned way, state by state, district by district. I had already done a lot of fund-raisers for them, but not a single one for a national campaign to advertise what we had accomplished, or what our future agenda would be in contrast to the Republican contract.

We capped off another productive legislative year on September 30, the last day of the fiscal year, by passing all thirteen appropriation bills on time, something that hadn't happened since 1948. The appropriations represented the first back-to-back years of deficit reduction in two decades, reducing the federal payroll by 272,000, and still increasing investments in education and other important areas. It was an impressive achievement, but nowhere near as attention-grabbing as the balanced budget amendment.

I limped into October with approval ratings of around 40 percent, but good things would happen that month to improve my standing and apparently to increase the Democrats' election prospects. The only sad development was the resignation of Agriculture Secretary Mike Espy. Janet Reno had asked for a court-appointed independent counsel to look into allegations of wrongdoing by Espy involving acceptance of gifts, such as sports tickets and trips. Judge Sentelle's panel appointed Donald Smaltz, another Republican activist, to investigate Espy. I was heartsick about it. Mike Espy had supported me through thick and thin in 1992. He had left a safe seat in Congress, where even the white voters of Mississippi supported him, to become the first black agriculture secretary, and he had done an excellent job, including raising the standards for food safety.

The October news was mostly positive. On October 4, Nelson Mandela came to the White House for a state visit. His smile always brightened even the darkest days, and I was glad to see him. We announced a joint commission to promote mutual cooperation, to be headed by Vice President Gore and Deputy President Thabo Mbeki, Mandela's likely successor. The joint commission idea was working so well with Russia that we wanted to try it in another country that was important to us, and South Africa certainly was. If Mandela's reconciliation government succeeded, it could lift all of Africa and inspire similar efforts in trouble spots around the world. I also announced assistance for housing, electricity, and health care for South Africa's poor, densely populated townships; rural economic initiatives; and an investment fund to be headed by Ron Brown.

While I was meeting with Mandela, the Senate followed the House in passing, with broad bipartisan support, the last important piece of my education agenda from the campaign, the Elementary and Secondary Education Act. The bill ended the practice of uncritically giving poor children a watered-down curriculum; too often, children from disadvantaged backgrounds were put in special education classes, not because they lacked normal learning capacity, but because they had fallen behind in poor schools and had too little support at home. Dick Riley and I were convinced that, with smaller classes and extra attention from teachers, they could catch up. The bill also contained incentives to increase parental involvement; gave federal support to allow students and parents to choose a public school other than the one to which they were assigned; and funded public charter schools designed to promote innovation and allowed to operate free of school district requirements that can stifle creativity. In just two years, in addition to the ESEA, bipartisan supporters in Congress had enacted Head Start reform; put the National Education Association goals into law; reformed the student loan program; created the national service program; passed the school-to-work program to create apprenticeships for high school graduates who don't go on to college; and dramatically increased our commitment to adult education and lifelong learning.

The education package was one of the most important achievements of my first two years in office. Although it would increase the quality of learning and economic opportunities for millions of Americans, almost no one knew about it. Because education reforms had broad support in both parties, the efforts to pass them generated relatively little controversy, and therefore weren't considered particularly newsworthy.

We ended the first week of the month on a high note, when the unemployment rate fell to 5.9 percent, the lowest since 1990 (down from over 7 percent when I took office), with 4.6 million new jobs. Later in the month, economic growth in the third quarter of the year was pegged at 3.4 percent, with inflation at 1.6 percent. NAFTA was making a contribution to the growth. Overall exports to Mexico were up 19 percent in just a year, with car and truck exports up 600 percent.

On October 7, Iraq massed a large number of troops just two and a half miles from the Kuwait border, raising the specter of another Gulf War. With strong international support, I rapidly deployed 36,000 troops to Kuwait, backed up by an aircraft carrier battle group and fighter planes. I also ordered an updated list of targets for our Tomahawk missiles. The British announced they would beef up their forces as well. On the ninth, the Kuwaitis moved most of their 18,000-man army to the border. The next day, the Iraqis, surprised by the strength and speed of our response, announced that they would pull back their forces, and within a month the Iraqi parliament recognized Kuwait's sovereignty, borders, and territorial integrity. A couple of days after the immediate Iraq crisis passed, the Protestant paramilitary groups in Northern Ireland announced that they would join the IRA in observing a complete cease-fire.

The good news spilled over into the third week of October. On the fifteenth, President Aristide returned to Haiti. Three days later I announced that after sixteen months of intense negotiations, we had reached an agreement with North Korea to end the threat of nuclear proliferation on the Korean peninsula. The agreed framework, signed in Geneva on October 21 by our negotiator, Bob Gallucci, and the North Koreans, committed North Korea to freeze all activity at existing nuclear reactors and allow them to be monitored; ship 8,000 unloaded fuel rods out of the country; dismantle its exist-ing nuclear facilities; and ultimately account for the spent fuel it had produced in the past. In return, the United States would organize an international consortium to build light water reactors that didn't produce usable amounts of weapons-grade material; we would guarantee 500,000 tons of heavy oil per year; trade, investment, and diplomatic barriers would be reduced; and the United States would give formal assurances against the use or the threat to use nuclear weapons against North Korea.

Three successive administrations had tried to bring North Korea's nuclear program under control. The pact was a tribute to the hard work of Warren Christopher and Ambassador Bob Gallucci, and to our clear determination not to allow North Korea to become a nuclear power, or a seller of nuclear weapons and materials.

After I left office, the United States learned that in 1998 North Korea had begun to violate the spirit if not the letter of the agreement by producing highly enriched uranium in a laboratory—enough, perhaps, to make one or two bombs. Some people said this development called the validity of our 1994 agreement into question. But the plutonium program we ended was much larger than the later laboratory effort. North Korea's nuclear reactor pro-gram, had it proceeded, would have produced enough weapons-grade plutonium to make several nuclear weapons a year.

On October 17, Israel and Jordan announced that they had reached a peace agreement. Yitzhak Rabin and King Hussein invited me to witness the signing ceremony on October 26, in the Wadi Araba border crossing in the great Rift Valley. I accepted, in the hope that I could use the trip to push for progress on the other Middle East tracks. I stopped first in Cairo, where President Mubarak and I met with Yasser Arafat. We encouraged him to do more to combat terrorism, especially by Hamas, and pledged to help resolve his differences with the Israelis concerning the delayed turnover of designated areas to Palestinian control.

The next day I witnessed the ceremony and thanked the Israelis and Jordanians for their courage in leading the way to peace. It was a hot and clear day, and the breathtaking backdrop of the Rift Valley was perfect for the grandeur of the occasion, but the sun was so bright bouncing off the desert sand that it almost blinded me. I nearly passed out, and if my alert presidential aide, Andrew Friendly, hadn't come to my rescue with sunglasses, I might have fainted and spoiled the whole occasion.

After the ceremony Hillary and I drove the short distance with King Hussein and Queen Noor to their vacation home in Aqaba. It was Hillary's birthday, and they gave her a cake with trick candles Hillary couldn't blow out, prompting me to kid her that her advancing years had diminished her lung capacity. Both Hussein and Noor were intelligent, gracious, and visionary. Noor, a Princeton graduate, was the daughter of a distinguished Arab-American father and Swedish mother. Hussein was a short but powerfully built man with a winning smile, a dignified manner, and wise eyes. He had survived several assassination attempts in his long reign, and he knew well that "taking risks for peace" was far more than a fine-sounding phrase. Hussein and Noor became real friends of ours. We laughed a lot together, forgetting our duties whenever we could in favor of stories about our lives, our kids, and our shared interests, including horses and motorcycles. In the years ahead, Noor would join us in vacation sing-alongs in Wyoming; I would go to their home in Maryland for one of Hussein's birthday parties; and Hillary and Noor would talk often. They were a blessing in our lives.

Later that day I became the first American President to speak to the Jordanian parliament in Amman. The best-received lines in the speech were directed to the Arab world at large: "America refuses to accept that our civilizations must collide. We respect Islam . . . the traditional values of Islam, devotion to faith and good work, to family and society, are in harmony with the best of American ideals. Therefore, we know our people, our faiths, our cultures can live in harmony with each other."

The next morning I flew to Damascus, the oldest continuously inhabited city in the world, to see President Assad. No American President had been there in twenty years because of Syria's support for terrorism and its domination of Lebanon. I wanted Assad to know that I was committed to a Syrian-Israeli peace based on UN Resolutions 242 and 338, and that, if an agreement were reached, I would work hard to improve relations with his country. I took some heat for going to Syria because of its support for Hezbollah and other violent anti-Israeli groups, but I knew there would never be security and stability in the region unless Syria and Israel were reconciled. My meeting with Assad produced no big breakthrough, but he did give me some encouraging hints about how we might move forward. It was clear that he wanted to make peace, but when I suggested that he ought to go to Israel, reach out to the Israeli citizens, and make his case in the Knesset as Anwar Sadat had done, I could tell that I was beating a dead horse. Assad was brilliant but literal-minded and extremely cautious. He enjoyed the security of his beautiful marble palace and his daily routine in Damascus, and he couldn't imagine taking the political risk of flying to Tel Aviv. As soon as our meeting and the obligatory press conference were over, I flew to Israel to tell Rabin what I'd learned.

In a speech to the Knesset, Israel's parliament, I thanked and praised Rabin and assured the Knesset members that as Israel took steps toward peace, the United States would move to enhance its security and economic progress. It was a timely message because Israel had recently suffered yet another deadly terrorist attack. Unlike the Palestinian agreement, which many Israelis opposed, the Jordan peace pact had the support of nearly everyone in the Knesset, including the leader of the Likud opposition, Benjamin "Bibi" Netanyahu. The Israelis admired and trusted King Hussein; they remained uncertain about Arafat.

On the twenty-eighth, after an emotional visit to Yad Vashem, Israel's magnificent Holocaust memorial, Hillary and I said good-bye to Yitzhak and Leah Rabin, and I flew to Kuwait to see the emir and to thank our troops for forcing the withdrawal of Iraqi forces from the Kuwait border through their rapid deployment to the area. After Kuwait, I flew to Saudi Arabia for a few hours to see King Fahd. I had been impressed by Fahd's call, in early 1993, asking me to stop the ethnic cleansing of the Bosnian Muslims. On this occasion, Fahd received me warmly and thanked me for America's rapid move to defuse the crisis with Iraq. It had been a successful and encouraging visit, but I had to go home to face the election music.

FORTY-ONE

By October, the polls we were getting didn't look too bad, but the atmosphere on the campaign trail still didn't feel good. Before we left for the Middle East, Hillary had called our old pollster Dick Morris for his assessment. Dick took a survey for us and the results were discouraging. He said that most people didn't believe that the economy was getting better or that the deficit was declining; that they didn't know about any of the good things the Democrats and I had done; and that the attacks on Gingrich's contract weren't working.

My approval rating had risen above 50 percent for the first time in a while, and voters responded positively when told about the family leave law, the 100,000 new police in the crime bill, the education standards and school reform, and our other achievements. Dick said we could cut our losses if the Democrats would stop talking about the economy, the deficit, and the contract, and concentrate instead on their popular legislative accomplishments. And he recommended that when I returned to Washington, I should stay off the campaign trail and remain "presidential," saying and doing things that would reinforce my higher ratings. Morris believed that would do more to help the Democrats than my plunging back into the political fray. Neither recommendation was followed.

The Democrats had no mechanism to move a new message quickly into every contested state and congressional district where it would make a difference; though I had done a lot of fund-raising for individual candidates and the House and Senate campaign committees, they had wanted to spend the money in the traditional way.

I called back to the White House from the Middle East trip and said I thought that, on my return, I should stay at work and make news rather than go back to the campaign trail. When I got home I was surprised to find my schedule packed with trips to Pennsylvania, Michigan, Ohio, Rhode Island, New York, Iowa, Minnesota, California, Washington, and Delaware. Apparently, when my own poll numbers started rising, Democrats around the country asked that I campaign for them. They had been there for me; now I had to be there for them.

While campaigning, I tried to keep emphasizing our shared accomplishments: signing the California Desert Protection Act, which protected 7.5 million acres of magnificent lands in the wilderness and national park systems; highlighting the large financial benefits of the new direct student-loan program at the University of Michigan; and doing as many radio interviews about our record as I could. But I also did big rallies with boisterous crowds, where I had to speak loudly to be heard. My campaign riffs were effective for the party faithful, but not for the larger audience who saw them on television; on TV, the hot campaign rhetoric turned a statesman-like President back into the politician the voters weren't sure about. Going back on the campaign trail, while understandable and perhaps unavoidable, was a mistake.

On November 8, we got the living daylights beat out of us, losing eight Senate seats and fifty-four House seats, the largest defeat for our party since 1946, when the Democrats were routed after President Truman tried to get health insurance for all Americans. The Republicans were rewarded for two years of constant attacks on me and for their solidarity on the contract. The Democrats were punished for too much good government and too little good politics. I had contributed to the demise by allowing my first weeks to be defined by gays in the military; by failing to concentrate on the campaign until it was too late; and by trying to do too much too fast in a news climate in which my victories were minimized, my losses were magnified, and the overall impression was created that I was just another pro-tax, big-government liberal, not the New Democrat who had won the presidency. Moreover, the public mood was still anxious; people didn't feel their lives were improving and they were sick of all the fighting in Washington. Apparently they thought divided government would force us to work together.

Ironically, I had hurt the Democrats by both my victories and my defeats. The loss of health care and the passage of NAFTA demoralized many of our base voters and depressed our turnout. The victories on the economic plan with its tax increases on high-income Americans, the Brady bill, and the assault weapons ban inflamed the Republican base voters and increased their turnout. The turnout differential alone probably accounted for half of our losses, and contributed to a Republican gain of eleven governorships. Mario Cuomo lost in New York with a miserable Democratic turnout. In the South, thanks largely to an extraordinary effort by the Christian Coalition, Republicans routinely ran five or six points ahead of their positions in the pre-election polls. In Texas, George W. Bush defeated Governor Ann Richards, despite the fact that she had a 60 percent job approval rating.

The NRA had a great night. They beat both Speaker

Tom Foley and Jack Brooks, two of the ablest members of Congress, who had warned me this would happen. Foley was the first Speaker to be defeated in more than a century. Jack Brooks had supported the NRA for years and had led the fight against the assault weapons ban in the House, but as chairman of the Judiciary Committee he had voted for the overall crime bill even after the ban was put into it. The NRA was an unforgiving master: one strike and you're out. The gun lobby claimed to have defeated nineteen of the twenty-four members on its hit list. They did at least that much damage and could rightly claim to have made Gingrich the House Speaker. In Oklahoma, Congressman Dave McCurdy, a DLC leader, lost his Senate race because of, in his words, "God, gays, and guns."

On October 29, a man named Francisco Duran, who had driven all the way from Colorado, protested the crime bill by opening fire on the White House with an assault weapon. He got off twenty to thirty rounds before he was subdued. Luckily, no one was hurt. Duran may have been an aberration, but he reflected the almost pathological hatred I had engendered among paranoid gun owners with the Brady bill and the assault weapons ban. After the election I had to face the fact that the law-enforcement groups and other supporters of responsible gun legislation, though they represented the majority of Americans, simply could not protect their friends in Congress from the NRA. The gun lobby outspent, outorganized, outfought, and outdemagogued them.

The election had a few bright spots. Ted Kennedy and Senator Dianne Feinstein prevailed in tough campaigns. So did my friend Senator Chuck Robb of Virginia, who defeated conservative talk-show host Oliver North of Iran-Contra fame, with the help of an endorsement from his

Republican colleague Senator John Warner, who liked Robb and couldn't stand the thought of North in the Senate.

In the Upper Peninsula of Michigan, Congressman Bart Stupak, a former police officer, survived a tough challenge in his conservative district by going on the offensive to defend himself against the charge that his vote for the economic plan hurt his constituents. Stupak ran ads comparing the exact number of those who got tax cuts with those who had gotten tax increases. The ratio was about ten to one.

Senator Kent Conrad and Congressman Earl Pomeroy were reelected in North Dakota, a conservative Republican state, because they, like Stupak, aggressively defended their votes and made sure the voters knew the good things that had been accomplished. Perhaps it was easier to counter the blizzard of negative TV ads in a small state or a rural district. Regardless, if more of our members had done what Stupak, Conrad, and Pomeroy did, we would have won more seats.

The two heroes of the budget battle in the House met different fates. Marjorie Margolies-Mezvinsky lost her wealthy suburban Pennsylvania district, but Pat Williams survived in rural Montana.

I was profoundly distressed by the election, far more than I ever let on in public. We probably would not have lost either the House or the Senate if I had not included the gas tax and the tax on upper-income Social Security recipients in the economic plan, and if I had listened to Tom Foley, Jack Brooks, and Dick Gephardt about the assault weapons ban. Of course, if I had made those decisions, I would have had to drop the EITC tax cut for lower-income working families, or accept less deficit reduction, with the attendant risk of an unfavorable response from the bond market; and I would have left more police officers and children at the mercy of assault weapons. I remained convinced that those hard decisions were good for America. Still, too many Democrats had paid a big price at the hands of voters who nevertheless would later reap the benefits of their courage in greater prosperity and safer streets.

We might not have lost either house if, as soon as it became clear that Senator Dole would filibuster any meaningful health reform, I had announced a delay in health care until we reached a bipartisan consensus, and had taken up and passed welfare reform instead. That would have been popular with alienated middle-class Americans who voted in droves for Republicans, and, unlike different decisions on the economic plan and the assault weapons ban, this course of action would have helped the Democrats without hurting the American people.

Gingrich had proved to be a better politician than I was. He understood that he could nationalize a midterm election with the contract, with incessant attacks on the Democrats, and with the argument that all the conflicts and bitter partisanship in Washington the Republicans had generated must be the Democrats' fault since we controlled both Congress and the White House. Because I had been preoccupied with the work of the presidency, I hadn't organized, financed, and forced the Democrats to adopt an effective national counter-message. The nationalization of midterm elections was Newt Gingrich's major contribution to modern electioneering. From 1994 on, if one party did it and the other didn't, the side without a national message would sustain unnecessary losses. It happened again in 1998 and 2002.

Though far more Americans had received tax cuts than

income tax increases, and we had reduced the government to a much smaller size than it had been under Reagan and Bush, the Republicans also won on their same old promises of lower taxes and smaller government. They were even rewarded for problems they had created; they had killed health care, campaign finance reform, and lobbying reform with Senate filibusters. In that sense, Dole deserves a lot of credit for the Republican landslide, too; most people couldn't believe that a minority of forty-one senators could defeat any measure except the budget. All the voters knew was that they didn't yet feel more prosperous or more secure; there was too much fighting in Washington and we were in charge; and the Democrats were for big government.

I felt much as I did when I was defeated for reelection as governor in 1980: I had done a lot of good, but no one knew it. The electorate may be operationally progressive, but philosophically it is moderately conservative and deeply skeptical of government. Even if I had enjoyed more balanced press coverage, the voters probably would have had a hard time sorting out what I had accomplished in all the flurry of activity. Somehow I had forgotten the searing lesson of my 1980 loss: You can have good policy without good politics, but you can't give the people good government without both. I would not forget it again, but I never got over all those good people who lost their seats because they helped me dig America out of the deficit hole of Reaganomics, made our streets safer, and tried to provide health insurance to all Americans.

On the day after the election, I tried to make the best of a bad situation, promising to work with the Republicans and asking them "to join me in the center of the public debate where the best ideas for the next generation of

American progress must come." I suggested we work together on welfare reform and the line-item veto, which I supported. For the time being, there was nothing more I could do.

Many of the pundits already were predicting my demise in 1996, but I was more hopeful. The Republicans had convinced many Americans that the Democrats and I were too liberal and too tied to big government, but time was on my side for three reasons: because of our economic plan, the deficit would keep coming down and the economy would continue to improve; the new Congress, especially the House, was well to the right of the American people; and, despite their campaign promises, the Republicans would soon be proposing cuts in education, health care, and aid to the environment to pay for their tax cuts and defense increases. It would happen because that's what ultra-conservatives wanted to do, and because I was determined to hold them to the laws of arithmetic.

FORTY-TWO

Within a week of the election, I was hard at work again, as were the Republicans. On November 10, I named Patsy Fleming as national AIDS policy director, in recognition of her outstanding work in developing our AIDS policy, which included a 30 percent increase in overall AIDS funding, and I outlined a series of new initiatives to combat AIDS. The announcement was dedicated to the guiding light of the AIDS fight, Elizabeth Glaser, who was desperately ill with AIDS and would die in three weeks.

The same day, I announced that the United States would no longer enforce the arms embargo in Bosnia. The move had strong support in Congress and was necessary because the Serbs had resumed their aggression, with an assault on the town of Bihac; by late November, NATO was bombing Serb missile sites in the area. On the twelfth, I was en route to Indonesia for the annual APEC leaders' meeting, where the eighteen Asian-Pacific nations committed themselves to creating an Asian free market by 2020, with the wealthier nations doing so by 2010.

On the home front, Newt Gingrich, basking in the afterglow of his big victory, kept up the withering personal attacks that had proved so successful in the campaign. Just before the election, he had taken a page from his pamphlet of smear words, calling me "the enemy of normal Americans." On the day after the election, he called

Hillary and me "counterculture McGovernicks," his ultimate condemnation.

The epithet Gingrich hurled at us was correct in some respects. We had supported McGovern, and we weren't part of the culture that Gingrich wanted to dominate America: the self-righteous, condemning, Absolute Truth–claiming dark side of white southern conservatism. I was a white Southern Baptist who was proud of my roots and confirmed in my faith. But I knew the dark side all too well. Since I was a boy, I had watched people assert their piety and moral superiority as justifications for claiming an entitlement to political power, and for demonizing those who begged to differ with them, usually over civil rights. I thought America was about building a more perfect union, widening the circle of freedom and opportunity, and strengthening the bonds of community across the lines that divide us.

Even though I was intrigued by Gingrich and impressed by his political skills, I didn't think much of his claim that his politics represented America's best values. I had been raised not to look down on anyone and not to blame others for my own problems or shortcomings. That's exactly what the "New Right" message did. But it had enormous political appeal because it offered both psychological certainty and escape from responsibility: "they" were always right, "we" were always wrong; "we" were responsible for all the problems, even though "they" had controlled the presidency for all but six of the last twenty-six years. All of us are vulnerable to arguments that let us off the hook, and in the 1994 election, in an America where hardworking middle-class families felt economic anxiety and were upset by the pervasiveness of crime, drugs, and family dysfunction, there was an audience for the Gingrich message, especially when we didn't offer a competing one.

Gingrich and the Republican right had brought us back to the 1960s again; Newt said that America had been a great country until the sixties, when the Democrats took over and replaced absolute notions of right and wrong with more relativistic values. He pledged to take us back to the morality of the 1950s, in order to "renew American civilization."

Of course there were political and personal excesses in the 1960s, but the decade and the movements it spawned also produced advances in civil rights, women's rights, a clean environment, workplace safety, and opportunities for the poor. The Democrats believed in and worked for those things. So did a lot of traditional Republicans, including many of the governors I'd served with in the late 1970s and 1980s. In focusing only on the excesses of the 1960s, the New Right reminded me a lot of the carping that white southerners did against Reconstruction for a century after the Civil War. When I was growing up, we were still being taught how mean the Northern forces were to us during Reconstruction, and how noble the South was, even in defeat. There was something to it, but the loudest complaints always overlooked the good done by Lincoln and the national Republicans in ending slavery and preserving the Union. On the big issues, slavery and the Union, the South was wrong.

Now it was happening again, as the right wing used the excesses of the sixties to obscure the good done in civil rights and other areas. Their blanket condemnation reminded me of a story Senator David Pryor used to tell about a conversation he'd had with an eighty-five-year-old man who told him he had lived through two world wars, the Depression, Vietnam, the civil rights movement, and all the other upheavals of the twentieth century. Pryor said, "You sure have seen a lot of changes." "Yeah," the old man replied, "and I was against every one of them!"

Still, I didn't want to demonize Gingrich and his crowd as they had done to us. He had some interesting ideas, especially in the areas of science, technology, and entrepreneurialism, and he was a committed internationalist in foreign policy. Also, I had thought for years that the Democratic Party needed to modernize its approach, to focus less on preserving the party's industrial-age achievements and more on meeting the challenges of the information age, and to clarify our commitment to middle-class values and concerns. I welcomed the chance to compare our New Democrat ideas on economic and social problems with those embodied in the "Contract with America." Politics at its best is about the competition of ideas and policy.

But Gingrich didn't stop there. The core of his argument was not just that his ideas were better than ours; he said his **values** were better than ours, because Democrats were weak on family, work, welfare, crime, and defense, and because, being crippled by the self-indulgent sixties, we couldn't draw distinctions between right and wrong.

The political power of his theory was that it forcefully and clearly confirmed the negative stereotypes of Democrats that Republicans had been working to embed in the nation's consciousness since 1968. Nixon had done it; Reagan had done it; and George Bush had done it, too, when he turned the 1988 election into a referendum on Willie Horton and the Pledge of Allegiance. Now Newt had taken the art of "reverse plastic surgery" to a whole new level of sophistication and harshness.

The problem with his theory was that it didn't fit the facts. Most Democrats were tough on crime, supported welfare reform and a strong national defense, and had been much more fiscally responsible than the New Right Republicans. Most were also hardworking, law-abiding Americans who loved their country, worked in their communities, and tried to raise their children well. Never mind the facts; Gingrich had his story line down pat, and he applied it every chance he got.

Soon he would charge, without a shred of evidence, that 25 percent of my White House aides were recent drug users. Then he said that Democratic values were responsible for the large number of out-of-wedlock births to teen mothers, whose babies should be taken away from them and put into orphanages. When Hillary questioned whether infants separated from their mothers would really be better off, he said she should watch the 1938 movie **Boys Town,** in which poor boys are raised in a Catholic orphanage, well before the dreaded 1960s ruined us all.

Gingrich even blamed the Democrats and their "permissive" values for creating a moral climate that encouraged a troubled South Carolina woman, Susan Smith, to drown her two young sons in October 1994. When it came out that Smith might have been unbalanced because she had been sexually abused as a child by her ultra-conservative stepfather, who was on the board of his local chapter of the Christian Coalition, Gingrich was unfazed. All sins, even those committed by conservatives, were caused by the moral relativism the Democrats had imposed on America since the 1960s.

I kept waiting for Gingrich to explain how the Democrats' moral bankruptcy had corrupted the Nixon and Reagan administrations and led to the crimes of Watergate and Iran-Contra. I'm sure he could have found a way. When he was on a roll, Newt was hard to stop.

As we headed into December, a little sanity crept back into political life when the House and the Senate passed the Global Agreement on Tariffs and Trade, GATT, with large bipartisan majorities. The agreement reduced tariffs worldwide by a whopping $740 billion, opening previously closed markets to American products and services, giving poor countries a chance to sell products to consumers beyond their borders, and providing for the establishment of the World Trade Organization to create uniform trade rules and adjudicate disputes. Ralph Nader and Ross Perot campaigned hard against the pact, claiming it would have horrible consequences, from a loss of American sovereignty to an increase in abusive child labor. Their vocal opposition had little effect; the labor movement was less intensely opposed to GATT than it had been to NAFTA, and Mickey Kantor had done a good job in making the case for GATT to Congress.

Almost unnoticed in the comprehensive legislation that included GATT was the Retirement Protection Act of 1994. The problem of underfunded pensions was first brought to my attention by a citizen at the Richmond debate during the campaign. The bill required corporations with large underfunded plans to increase their contributions, and it stabilized the national pension insurance system and provided better protection to forty million Americans. The Retirement Protection Act and GATT were the last in a long line of major legislative achievements in my first two years, and, given the election results, bittersweet ones.

In early December, Lloyd Bentsen resigned as secretary

of Treasury, and I appointed Bob Rubin to succeed him. Bentsen had done a remarkable job, and I didn't want him to leave, but he and his wife, B.A., wanted to return to private life. The choice of a successor was easy: Bob Rubin had built the National Economic Council into the most important innovation in White House decision making in decades, was respected on Wall Street, and wanted the economy to work for all Americans. Soon afterward, I named Laura Tyson to succeed Bob at the National Economic Council.

After hosting a state dinner for the new president of Ukraine, Leonid Kuchma, I flew to Budapest, Hungary, for only eight hours, to attend the meeting of the Conference on Security and Cooperation in Europe and sign a series of denuclearization agreements with President Yeltsin, Prime Minister Major, and the presidents of Ukraine, Kazakhstan, and Belarus. It should have produced good news coverage about our shared determination to reduce our arsenals by several thousand warheads and to prevent the spread of nuclear weapons to other nations. Instead, the story coming out of Budapest was Yeltsin's speech criticizing me for trading in the Cold War for a "cold peace" by rushing NATO enlargement to include the Central European nations. In fact, I had done the reverse, by establishing the Partnership for Peace as an interim step to include a much larger number of countries; by setting up a deliberate process for adding new NATO members; and by working hard to establish a NATO-Russian partnership.

Since I had no advance warning about Yeltsin's speech, and he spoke after I did, I was stunned and angry, because I didn't know what had set him off and because I had no opportunity to respond. Apparently, Yeltsin's advisors had convinced him that NATO would admit Poland, Hungary, and the Czech Republic in 1996, just when he would be running for reelection against the ultra-nationalists, who hated NATO expansion, and I would be running against the Republicans, who supported it.

Budapest was embarrassing, a rare moment when people on both sides dropped the ball, but I knew it would pass. A few days later, Al Gore went to see Yeltsin when he was in Moscow for the fourth meeting of the Gore-Chernomyrdin Commission for Economic, Scientific and Technical Cooperation. Boris told him that he and I were still partners, and Al assured Yeltsin that our NATO policy hadn't changed. I wasn't about to jam him for domestic political reasons, any more than I would let him keep NATO's doors closed indefinitely.

On December 9, I was in Miami to open the Summit of the Americas, the first meeting of all the hemisphere's leaders since 1967. The thirty-three democratically elected leaders of Canada, Central and South America, and the Caribbean were there, including forty-one-year-old President Aristide of Haiti and his neighbor, President Joaquín Balaguer of the Dominican Republic, who was eighty-eight years old, blind, and infirm, but mentally still sharp as a tack.

I had initiated the summit to promote a free trade area in all the Americas, from the Arctic Circle to Tierra del Fuego; to strengthen democracy and effective government throughout the region; and to show that America was determined to be a good neighbor. The gathering was a big success. We committed ourselves to establishing a free trade area of the Americas by 2005, and left feeling that we were going into the future together, a future where, in the words of the great Chilean poet Pablo

Neruda, "There is no such thing as a lone struggle, no such thing as a lone hope."

On December 15, I gave a televised address to outline my proposals for middle-class tax cuts in the coming budgets. The move was opposed by some people in the administration and criticized by some in the media as an attempt to copy the Republicans, or as a belated attempt to return to a 1993 campaign promise the voters had punished me for not keeping. For both policy and political reasons, I was trying to get back in the tax-cut hunt with the Republicans before the new Congress convened. The GOP contract contained tax proposals that I thought were unaffordable and too heavily tilted to upper-income Americans. On the other hand, the United States was still suffering from two decades of middle-class income stagnation, the main reason people hadn't felt the economy improving. We had made a dent in the problem by doubling the Earned Income Tax Credit. Now the right kind of tax cuts could raise middle-class incomes without derailing deficit reduction or our ability to invest in the future, and would fulfill my 1992 campaign commitment.

In the speech, I proposed a Middle-Class Bill of Rights, including a $500 child tax credit for families with incomes of $75,000 or less; tax deductibility for college tuition; expanded Individual Retirement Accounts (IRAs); and the conversion of the funds the government was spending on dozens of job-training programs into cash vouchers that would go directly to workers so they could choose their own training program. I told the American people that we could finance the tax package through further cost savings from Al Gore's Reinventing Government initiative and still keep reducing the deficit.

Just before Christmas, Al Gore and I announced the

designation of the first cities and rural communities as "empowerment zones," making them eligible, under the 1993 economic plan, for tax incentives and federal funds to spur job development in places that had been left behind in previous recoveries.

December 22 was Dee Dee Myers's last day as press secretary. She had done a good job under difficult circumstances. Dee Dee had been with me in the snows of New Hampshire. Since then we had weathered a lot of storms and played countless games of hearts together. I knew she would do well when she left, and she did.

After our annual New Year's trip to Renaissance Weekend, Hillary and I took a couple of extra days off to go home, so that we could see her mother and Dick Kelley, and I could go duck hunting with friends in eastern Arkansas. Every year, when the ducks fly south from Canada for the winter, one of the two main flyways is down the Mississippi River. Many of them land in the rice paddies and ponds of the Arkansas Delta, and over the last few years several farmers had established duck hunting camps on their land, both for their own enjoyment and to supplement their incomes.

It's wonderful seeing the ducks fly at morning light. We also saw large geese high overhead, flying in perfect V formation. Only two ducks came down within shooting range that cloudy morning, and the guys who were with me let me shoot them both. They had more days to hunt than I did. I pointed out to the reporters who were along that all our guns were protected by the crime bill and that we didn't need assault weapons to bag the ducks, including one I got with a lucky shot from about seventy yards.

The next day Hillary and I attended the dedication of William Jefferson Clinton Elementary Magnet School in

Sherwood, just outside North Little Rock. It was a beautiful facility, with a multi-purpose room named for my mother and a library named for Hillary. I confess that I liked having my name on a new school; no one owed more to his teachers than I did.

I needed that trip home. I had worked like a dog for two years. I had gotten so much done, but often "couldn't see the forest for the trees." The coming year was going to present a new set of challenges. To meet them, I needed more chances to recharge my batteries and water my roots.

As I returned to Washington, I was looking forward to watching the Republicans try to keep their campaign promises, and to the battle to preserve and fully implement all the legislation enacted the previous two years. When Congress passes a new law, the work of the executive branch has just begun. For example, the crime bill provided funding for 100,000 new police in our communities. We had to set up an office in the Justice Department to distribute the funds, establish criteria for eligibility for them, create and administer an application process, and monitor how the money was spent, so that we could make progress reports to Congress and the American people.

On January 5, I had my first meeting with the new congressional leaders. Besides Bob Dole and Newt Gingrich, the Republican team included Senator Trent Lott of Mississippi, and two Texans, Congressman Dick Armey, the House majority leader, and Congressman Tom DeLay, the House majority whip. The new Democratic leaders were Senator Tom Daschle of South Dakota and Congressman Dick Gephardt, as well as the Senate Democratic whip, Wendell Ford of Kentucky, and his counterpart in the House, David Bonior of Michigan.

Though the meeting with the congressional leaders was cordial, and there were some areas of the GOP contract on which we could work together, I knew there was no way we could avoid several heated struggles over important matters about which we had honest differences. Clearly, I and my entire team would have to be very focused and disciplined, in both our actions and our communications strategy. When a reporter asked me whether our relations would be marked by "compromise or combat," I responded, "My answer to that is, Mr. Gingrich will whisper in your right ear and I will whisper in your left ear."

When the congressmen left, I went into the press room to announce that Mike McCurry would be the new press secretary. Until then, Mike had been Warren Christopher's spokesman at State. During the presidential campaign, as press secretary for Senator Bob Kerrey, he had taken some pretty hard shots at me. I didn't care about that; he was supposed to be against me in the primary season, and he had done a good job at State explaining and defending our foreign policy.

We had some more new blood on our team. Erskine Bowles had come to the White House from the Small Business Administration as deputy chief of staff, switching jobs with Phil Lader. Erskine was especially well suited to the mixture of careful compromise and guerrilla war that would characterize our relations with the new Congress, because he was a gifted entrepreneur and world-class deal maker who knew when to hold and when to fold. He would support Panetta well and provide skills that complemented those of Leon's other deputy, the hard-charging Harold Ickes.

Like so many months, January was filled with both good and bad news: Unemployment was down to 5.4 percent, with 5.6 million new jobs; Kenneth Starr showed his "independence" when, unbelievably, he said he was going to reinvestigate Vince Foster's death; Yitzhak Rabin's government was threatened when nineteen Israelis were killed by two terrorist bombs, an act that weakened support for his peace efforts; and I signed the first bill of the new Congress, one I strongly supported, requiring the nation's lawmakers to comply with all the requirements they imposed on other employers.

On January 24, I gave the State of the Union address to the first Republican Congress in forty years. It was a delicate moment; I had to be conciliatory without seeming weak, strong without looking hostile. I began by asking Congress to put aside "partisanship and pettiness and pride" and suggesting that we work together on welfare reform, not to punish the poor but to empower them. I then introduced perhaps the best example of the potential of America's welfare recipients, Lynn Woolsey, a woman who had worked her way off welfare all the way to becoming a member of the House of Representatives from California.

Then I challenged the Republicans on several fronts. If they were going to vote for a balanced budget amendment, they should say **how** they proposed to balance the budget and whether they would cut Social Security. I asked them not to abolish AmeriCorps, as they had threatened to do. If they wanted to strengthen the crime bill, I would work with them, but I would oppose repealing proven prevention programs, the plan to put 100,000 more police on the streets, or the assault weapons ban. I said I would never do anything to infringe on legitimate firearms ownership and use, "but a lot of people laid down their seats in Congress so that police officers and kids wouldn't have to lay down their lives under a hail of assault weapon attacks, and I will not let that be repealed."

I finished the speech with an outreach to the Republicans, pushing my middle-class tax cuts but saying I would work with them on the issue, admitting that on health care, "We bit off more than we could chew," but asking them to work with me step by step, and to start by making sure people didn't lose their health insurance when they changed jobs or a family member was sick; and seeking their support for a bipartisan foreign policy agenda.

The State of the Union is not only the President's chance to speak for an unfiltered hour to the American people each year; it is also one of the most important rituals in American politics. How many times the President is interrupted by applause, especially standing ovations; what provokes the Democrats or Republicans to clap, and what they seem to agree on; the reactions of important senators and representatives; and the symbolic significance of the people chosen to sit in the First Lady's box are all noted by the press and witnessed by the American people on television. For this State of the Union, I had a speech designed to last fifty minutes, allowing ten minutes for applause. Because there was so much conciliation, as well as some meaty confrontation, the applause interruptions, more than ninety of them, took the speech to eighty-one minutes.

By the time of the State of the Union, we were two weeks into one of the biggest crises of my first term. On the evening of January 10, after Bob Rubin was sworn in as secretary of Treasury in the Oval Office, he and Larry Summers stayed to meet with me and a few of my advisors about the financial crisis in Mexico. The value of the peso had been declining precipitously, undermining Mexico's ability to borrow money or to repay existing debts. The problem was exacerbated because, as Mexico's condition deteriorated, in order to raise money it had issued short-term debt instruments called **tesobonos,** which had to be repaid in dollars. As the value of the peso continued to decline, it took more and more of them to finance the dollar value of Mexico's short-term debt. Now, with only $6 billion in reserves, Mexico had $30 billion of payments due in 1995, $10 billion in the first three months of the year.

If Mexico defaulted on its obligations, the economic "meltdown," as Bob Rubin tried to avoid calling it, could accelerate, with massive unemployment, inflation, and, very likely, a steep and prolonged recession because the international financial institutions, other governments, and private investors would all be unwilling to put more money at risk there.

As Rubin and Summers explained, the economic collapse of Mexico could have severe consequences for the United States. First, Mexico was our third-largest trading partner. If it couldn't buy our products, American companies and employees would be hurt. Second, economic dislocation in Mexico could lead to a 30 percent increase in illegal immigration, or half a million more people each year. Third, an impoverished Mexico would almost certainly become more vulnerable to increased activity by illegal drug cartels, which were already sending large quantities of narcotics across the border into the United States. Finally, a default by Mexico could have a damaging impact on other countries, by shaking investors' confidence in emerging markets in the rest of Latin America, Central Europe, Russia, South Africa, and other countries we were trying to help modernize and prosper. Since about 40 percent of American exports went to developing countries, our economy could be hurt badly.

Rubin and Summers recommended that we ask the Congress to approve $25 billion in loans to allow Mexico to pay its debt on schedule and retain the confidence of creditors and investors, in return for Mexico's commitment to financial reforms and more timely reporting on its financial condition, in order to prevent this from happening again. They warned, however, that risks were attached to their recommendation. Mexico might fail anyway and we could lose whatever money we had extended. If the policy succeeded, it could create the problem economists call "moral hazard." Mexico was on the brink of collapse not only because of flawed government policies and weak institutions, but also because investors had continued to finance its operations long past the point of prudence. By giving the money to Mexico to repay wealthy investors for unwise decisions, we might create an expectation that such decisions were risk free.

The risks were compounded by the fact that most Americans didn't understand the consequences to the American economy of a Mexican default. Most congressional Democrats would think the bailout proved that NAFTA was ill advised in the first place. And many of the newly elected Republicans, especially in the House, didn't share the Speaker's enthusiasm for international affairs. A surprising number of them didn't even have passports. They wanted to restrict immigration from Mexico, not send billions of dollars there.

After I listened to the presentation, I asked a couple of questions, then said we had to go forward with the loan. I thought the decision was clear-cut, but not all my advisors agreed. Those who wanted to speed my political recovery after the crushing midterm defeat thought I was nuts, or, as we say in Arkansas, "three bricks shy of a full load." When George Stephanopoulos heard Treasury's $25 billion figure for the loan, he thought Rubin and Summers must have meant $25 **million**; he thought I was about to shoot myself in the foot. Panetta favored the loan, but warned that if Mexico didn't repay us, it could cost me the election in 1996.

The risks were considerable, but I had confidence in Mexico's new president, Ernesto Zedillo, an economist with a doctorate from Yale who had stepped into the breach when his party's original candidate for president, Luis Colosio, was assassinated. If anybody could bring Mexico back, Zedillo could.

Besides, we simply couldn't stand aside and let Mexico fail without trying to help. In addition to the economic problems it would cause both for us and for the Mexicans, we would be sending a terrible signal of selfishness and shortsightedness throughout Latin America. There was a long history of Latin American resentment of America as arrogant and insensitive to their interests and problems. Whenever America reached out in genuine friendship— with FDR's Good Neighbor Policy, JFK's Alliance for Progress, and President Carter's return of the Panama Canal—we did better. During the Cold War, when we supported the overthrow of democratically elected leaders, backed dictators, and tolerated their human rights abuses, we got the reaction we deserved.

I called the congressional leaders to the White House, explained the situation, and asked for their support. All of them pledged it, including Bob Dole and Newt Gingrich, who aptly described the Mexico problem as "the first crisis of the twenty-first century." As Rubin and Summers made the rounds on Capitol Hill, we picked up support from Senator Paul Sarbanes of Maryland, Senator Chris Dodd, and Republican senator Bob Bennett of Utah, a highly intelligent, old-fashioned conservative who quickly grasped the consequences of inaction and would stick with us throughout the crisis. Several governors were also supportive, including Bill Weld of Massachusetts, who had a great interest in Mexico, and George W. Bush of Texas, whose state, along with California, would be hardest hit if the Mexican economy collapsed.

Despite the merits of the case and the support of Alan Greenspan, it became obvious by the end of the month that we weren't doing well in Congress. Anti-NAFTA Democrats were sure the aid package was a step too far, and the new Republican members were in open revolt.

By the end of the month, Rubin and Summers had begun to consider acting unilaterally, by providing the money to Mexico out of the Exchange Stabilization Fund. The fund was created in 1934, when America took the dollar off the gold standard, and was used to minimize currency fluctuations; it had about $35 billion and could be used by the Treasury secretary with the President's approval. On the twenty-eighth, the need for American action took on even greater urgency when the Mexican finance minister called Rubin and told him default was imminent, with more than a billion dollars' worth of **tesobonos** coming due the following week.

The matter came to a head on Monday night, January 30. Mexico's reserves were down to $2 billion, and the value of the peso had dropped another 10 percent during the day. That evening, Rubin and Summers came to the White House to see Leon Panetta and Sandy Berger, who was handling the issue for the National Security Council. In blunt terms, Rubin told them, "Mexico has about forty-eight hours to live." Gingrich called to say he couldn't pass the aid package for another two weeks, if at all. Dole had already said the same thing. They had tried, as had Tom Daschle and Dick Gephardt, but the opposition was too strong.

I returned to the White House from a fund-raiser at about 11 p.m. and went to Leon's office to hear the grim message. Rubin and Summers briefly restated the consequences of a Mexican default, then said we needed "only" $20 billion in loan guarantees, not $25 billion, because International Monetary Fund director Michel Camdessus had put together almost $18 billion in aid that the IMF would extend if the United States acted; combined with smaller contributions from other countries and the World Bank, that brought the total aid package to just under $40 billion.

Though they favored going forward, Sandy Berger and Bob Rubin again pointed out the risks. A newly published poll in the **Los Angeles Times** said the American people opposed helping Mexico by 79 percent to 18 percent. I replied, "So a year from now, when we have another million illegal immigrants, we're awash in drugs from Mexico, and lots of people on both sides of the Rio Grande are out of work, when they ask me, 'Why didn't you do something?' what will I say? That there was a poll that said 80 percent of Americans were against it? This is something we have to do." The meeting lasted about ten minutes.

The next day, January 31, we announced the aid package with money from the Exchange Stabilization Fund. The loan agreement was signed a couple of weeks later at the Treasury Building, to howls of protest in Congress and grumbles among our G-7 allies, who were upset that the IMF director had made the $18 billion commitment to Mexico, and to us, without their prior approval. The first money was released in March, after which we continued to make regular disbursements, even though things didn't really get better in Mexico for several months. By the end of the year, however, investors had entered the Mexican markets again and foreign exchange reserves had begun to build up. Ernesto Zedillo had also instituted the reforms he had promised.

Though it was tough at first, the aid package worked. In 1982, when the Mexican economy collapsed, it had taken almost a decade for growth to return. This time, after a year of severe recession, the Mexican economy started to grow again. After 1982, it had taken seven years for Mexico to regain access to the capital markets. In 1995, it took only seven months. In January 1997, Mexico repaid its loan in full, with interest, more than three years ahead of schedule. Mexico had borrowed $10.5 billion of the $20 billion we made available, and it paid a total of $1.4 billion in interest, almost $600 million more than the money would have earned had it been invested in U.S. Treasury notes, as other Exchange Stabilization Fund monies were. The loan turned out to be not only good policy but also a good investment.

New York Times columnist Tom Friedman called the Mexican loan guarantee "the least popular, least understood, but most important foreign policy decision of the Clinton Presidency." He may have been right. As for popular opposition, 75 percent of the people had also opposed the Russian aid package; my decision to restore Aristide in Haiti was unpopular; and my subsequent actions in Bosnia and Kosovo met with initial popular resistance. Polls can be helpful in telling a President what the American people think, and which arguments may be most persuasive at a particular time, but they cannot dictate a decision that requires looking down the road and around the corner. The American people hire a President to do the right thing for our country over the long run. Helping Mexico was the right thing for America. It was the only sensible economic course, and by taking it, we proved ourselves to be, once again, a good neighbor.

On February 9, Helmut Kohl came to see me. He had just been reelected, and he confidently predicted that I would be as well. He told me we were living in turbulent times, but the end would bring me out all right. At the press conference after our meeting, Kohl paid a moving tribute to Senator Fulbright, who had died shortly after midnight at the age of eighty-nine. Kohl said he came from a generation who, when they were students, "wanted nothing more than to obtain a Fulbright scholarship," and that, across the world, Fulbright's name was associated "with openness, with friendship, and with people striving together." At the time of his passing, more than 90,000 Americans and 120,000 students from other countries had been Fulbright scholars.

　　I had gone to Senator Fulbright's home to visit him not long before he died. He had had a stroke and his speech was somewhat impaired, but his eyes were bright, his mind was working, and we had a good last visit. Fulbright would loom large in American history—as I said at his memorial service, "Always the teacher and always the student."

On February 13, Laura Tyson and the other members of the Council of Economic Advisers, Joe Stiglitz and Martin

Baily, gave me a copy of the latest **Economic Report of the President.** It highlighted our progress since 1993, as well as the persistent problems of income stagnation and inequality. I used the occasion to push the Middle-Class Bill of Rights and my proposal to increase the minimum wage by 90 cents over two years, from $4.25 to $5.15 an hour. The raise would benefit 10 million workers, adding $1,800 a year to their incomes. Half the increase was necessary just to get the minimum wage (after inflation) back to what it had been in 1991, the last time it was raised.

The minimum wage was a favorite cause of most Democrats, but most Republicans opposed minimum wage increases, claiming that they cost jobs by increasing the cost of doing business. There was little evidentiary support for their position. Indeed, some young labor economists had recently found that a moderate minimum wage increase might lead to a modest increase—not decrease—in employment. I had recently seen a television interview with a minimum wage worker in a factory in southwest Virginia. When asked about rumors that the increase might cause her employer to lay off her and other co-workers and do more work with machines, the woman smiled and told the interviewer, "Honey, I'll take my chances."

In the fourth week of February, Hillary and I paid a two-day state visit to Canada, where we stayed at the American ambassador's residence with Ambassador Jim and Janet Blanchard. Jim and I had become friends in the 1980s, when he was governor of Michigan. Canada is our largest trading partner and closest ally. We share the longest unguarded border in the world. In 1995, we were working together on Haiti, on helping Mexico, and on NATO, NAFTA, the Summit of the Americas, and

APEC. While we had occasional disputes over trade in wheat and timber and over salmon-fishing rights, our friendship was broad and deep.

We spent a lot of time with Prime Minister Jean Chrétien and his wife, Aline. Chrétien would become one of my best friends among world leaders, a strong ally, confidant, and frequent golfing partner.

I also spoke to the Canadian parliament, thanking them for our economic and security partnerships and the rich cultural contributions of Canadians to American life, including Oscar Peterson, my favorite jazz pianist; singer-songwriter Joni Mitchell, who wrote "Chelsea Morning"; and Yousuf Karsh, the great photographer who had become famous for his portrait of Churchill scowling after Karsh jerked the omnipresent cigar out of his hand, and who had photographed Hillary and me in less forbidding poses.

March got off to a good start, at least from my point of view, when the Senate failed, by only one vote, to get the two-thirds majority necessary to pass the balanced budget amendment. Though the amendment was popular, virtually every economist thought it was a bad idea because it restricted the ability of the government to run deficits under appropriate circumstances during a recession or a national emergency. Before 1981, America had not had much of a deficit problem; only after twelve years of trickle-down economics had quadrupled the national debt did politicians begin to argue that they would never make responsible economic decisions unless forced to do so by a constitutional amendment.

While the debate was going on, I urged the new Republican majority, who were pushing the amendment, to say exactly how they were going to balance the budget.

I had produced a budget less than a month into my term; they had been in control of Congress for nearly two months and had still not presented one. They were finding it difficult to transform their campaign rhetoric into specific recommendations.

Soon, the Republicans offered a taste of the budget to come by proposing a package of cuts, called rescissions, in the current year's budget. The cuts they chose proved that the Democrats had been right on target in their criticism of the contract during the campaign. The GOP rescissions included the elimination of 15,000 AmeriCorps positions, 1.2 million summer jobs for young people, and $1.7 billion in education funds, including nearly half of our drug-prevention funds, at a time when drug use among young people was still rising. Worst of all, they wanted to cut the school lunch program and WIC, the nutrition program for women, infants, and children under five, which, until then, had always had strong support from both Republicans and Democrats. The White House and the Democrats had a field day fighting those cuts.

Another GOP proposal that met stiff resistance was its move to eliminate the Department of Education, which, like the school lunch program, had always enjoyed strong bipartisan support. When Senator Dole said the department had done more harm than good, I joked that he might be right, because for most of the time since its inception, the department had been under the control of Republican secretaries of education. By contrast, Dick Riley was doing far more good than harm.

While pushing back on the Republican proposals, I was also promoting our agenda in ways that didn't require congressional approval and demonstrated that I had gotten the message from the last election. In the middle of

March, I announced a regulatory reform effort developed by Al Gore's Reinventing Government project that focused on improving our environmental protection efforts through providing market incentives to the private sector, rather than imposing detailed regulations; the 25 percent reduction in paperwork requirements would save them 20 million work hours per year.

The "Rego" effort was working. We had already reduced the federal workforce by more than 100,000 and eliminated 10,000 pages of federal personnel manuals; soon we would earn almost $8 billion by auctioning slices of the broadcast spectrum for the first time; and eventually we would scrap 16,000 pages of federal regulations with no harm to the public interest. All the Rego changes were developed according to a simple credo: protect people, not bureaucracy; promote results, not rules; get action, not rhetoric. Al Gore's highly successful initiative confounded our adversaries, elated our allies, and escaped the notice of most of the public because it was neither sensational nor controversial.

By my third St. Patrick's Day as President, the occasion had grown from a celebration into an annual opportunity for the United States to advance the peace process in Northern Ireland. That year, I was giving the traditional Irish greeting, **céad míle fáilte,** "a hundred thousand welcomes," to a new Irish prime minister, John Bruton, who was continuing the peace policy of his predecessor. At noon, I met Gerry Adams for the first time at the Capitol, as Newt Gingrich hosted his first St. Patrick's Day Speaker's luncheon. I had given Adams a second visa after Sinn Fein had agreed to discuss with the British government the IRA's laying down of arms, and had invited him, along with John Hume and representatives of Northern Ireland's other main political parties, both Unionist and Republican, to the St. Patrick's Day reception at the White House that night.

When Adams showed up at the lunch, John Hume encouraged me to go over and shake hands with him, so I did. At the White House reception that night, the assembled crowd listened to a superb Irish tenor, Frank Patterson. Adams was having such a good time that he wound up singing a duet with Hume.

All this may sound routine now, but at the time it represented a sea change in American policy, one the British government and many in our own State Department still opposed. Now I was consorting not only with John Hume, the champion of peaceful change, but with Gerry Adams, whom the British still considered a terrorist. Physically, Adams was a striking contrast to the gentle, slightly rumpled, professorial Hume. He was bearded, taller, younger, and leaner, hardened by his years on the edge of destruction. But Adams and Hume shared some important traits. Behind their glasses were eyes that revealed intelligence, conviction, and that uniquely Irish mixture of sadness and humor born of hopes often dashed but never abandoned. Against all odds, they both were trying to free their people from the shackles of the past. Before long, David Trimble, who led the largest Unionist party, would join them at the White House on St. Patrick's Day and in the quest for peace.

On March 25, Hillary began her first extended overseas trip without me, a twelve-day visit to Pakistan, India, Nepal, Bangladesh, and Sri Lanka. She took Chelsea along on what would be an important effort for the

United States and a grand personal odyssey for them both. While the rest of my family was far away, I traveled closer to home, going to Haiti to visit the troops, meet with President Aristide, exhort the people of Haiti to embrace a peaceful democratic future, and participate in the handover of authority from our multinational force to the United Nations. In six months, forces from thirty nations had worked together under American leadership to remove more than 30,000 weapons and explosive devices from the streets and train a permanent police force. They had ended repressive violence; reversed the outmigration of Haitians, who were now coming home; and protected democracy in our hemisphere. Now the United Nations mission of more than 6,000 military personnel, 900 police officers, and dozens of economic, political, and legal advisors would take over for eleven months, until the election and inauguration of a new president. The United States would play a part, but our force levels and expenses would drop, as thirty-two other nations stepped forward to participate.

In 2004, after President Aristide resigned and flew into exile amidst renewed violence and strife, I thought back to what Hugh Shelton, the commander of the American forces, had told me: "The Haitians are good people and they deserve a chance." Aristide certainly made mistakes and was often his own worst enemy, but the political opposition never really cooperated with him. Also, after the Republicans took over Congress in 1995, they were unwilling to give the financial assistance that might have made a difference.

Haiti will never develop into a stable democracy without more help from the United States. Still, our intervention saved lives and gave Haitians their first taste of the democracy they had voted for. Even with Aristide's serious problems, the Haitians would have been far worse off under Cedras and his murderous coup. I remain glad that we gave Haiti a chance.

The Haitian intervention also provided strong evidence of the wisdom of multilateral responses in the world's trouble spots. Nations working together, and through the UN, spread the responsibilities and costs of such operations, reduce resentment against the United States, and build invaluable habits of cooperation. In an increasingly interdependent world, we should work this way whenever we can.

FORTY-THREE

———————————

I spent the first two and a half weeks of April meeting with world leaders. Prime Minister John Major, President Hosni Mubarak, and Prime Minister Benazir Bhutto of Pakistan and Prime Minister Tansu Ciller of Turkey, two intelligent, very modern women leaders of Muslim countries, came to see me.

Meanwhile, Newt Gingrich gave a speech on his first hundred days as Speaker. To hear him tell it, you would think the Republicans had revolutionized America overnight, and in the process changed our form of government to a parliamentary system under which he, as prime minister, set the course for domestic policy, while I, as President, was restricted to handling foreign affairs.

For the moment, the Republicans were dominating the news, based on the novelty of their control of Congress and their assertions that they were making big changes. Actually, they had enacted only three relatively minor parts of their contract, all of which I supported. The hard decisions were still ahead of them.

In a speech to the American Society of Newspaper Editors, I spelled out the parts of the contract I agreed with, on which I would seek compromise, and those I opposed and would veto. On April 14, four days after Senator Dole announced his candidacy for President, I quietly filed for reelection. On the eighteenth, I held a press conference and was asked more than twenty questions about a wide variety of topics, foreign and domestic. The next day they would all be forgotten and there would be only two words on the lips of every American: Oklahoma City.

In late morning I learned that a truck bomb had exploded outside the Alfred P. Murrah Federal Building in Oklahoma City, leaving the building a rubble and killing an unknown number of people. I immediately declared a state of emergency and sent an investigative team to the site. When the magnitude of the recovery effort became apparent, firefighters and other emergency workers came from all over the country to help Oklahoma City dig through the rubble in a desperate attempt to find any survivors.

America was riveted and heartbroken by the tragedy; it claimed the lives of 168 people, including nineteen children who were in the building's day-care center when the bomb exploded. Most of the dead were federal employees who worked for the several agencies that had offices in the Murrah Building. Many people assumed that Islamic militants were responsible, but I cautioned against jumping to conclusions about the perpetrators' identity.

Soon after the bombing, Oklahoma lawmen arrested Timothy McVeigh, an alienated military veteran who had come to hate the federal government. By the twenty-first, McVeigh was in FBI custody and had been arraigned. He had chosen April 19 to bomb the federal building because it was the anniversary of the FBI raid on the Branch Davidians at Waco, an event that, to right-wing extremists, represented the ultimate exercise of arbitrary, abusive government power. Anti-government paranoia had been building in America for years, as more and more people took the historical skepticism of Americans toward government to a level of outright hatred. This animus led to the rise of armed militia groups that rejected the legitimacy of federal authority and asserted the right to be a law unto themselves.

The atmosphere of hostility was intensified by right-wing radio talk-show hosts, whose venomous rhetoric pervaded the airwaves daily, and by Web sites encouraging people to rise up against the government and offering practical assistance, including easy-to-follow instructions on how to make bombs.

In the wake of Oklahoma City, I tried to comfort and encourage those who had lost their loved ones, and the country at large, and to step up our efforts to protect Americans from terrorism. In the more than two years since the World Trade Center bombing, I had increased counterterrorism resources for the FBI and CIA and instructed them to work together more closely. Our law-enforcement efforts had succeeded in returning several terrorists to the United States for trial after they fled to foreign countries and in preventing terrorist attacks on the United Nations, on the Holland and Lincoln tunnels in New York City, and on planes flying out of the Philippines to America's West Coast.

Two months before Oklahoma City, I had sent anti-terrorism legislation to Congress asking, among other things, for one thousand more law-enforcement officials to fight terrorism; a new counterterrorism center under the direction of the FBI to coordinate our efforts; and approval to use military experts, normally prohibited from involvement in domestic law enforcement, to help with terrorist threats and incidents within the country involving chemical, biological, and nuclear weapons.

After Oklahoma City, I asked the congressional leaders for expedited consideration of the legislation and, on

May 3, proposed amendments to strengthen it: greater law-enforcement access to financial records; authority to conduct electronic surveillance on suspected terrorists when they move from place to place, without having to go back to court for a new order to tap each specific site; increased penalties for knowingly providing firearms or explosives for terrorist acts against current or former federal employees and their families; and a requirement that markers, called taggants, be put into all explosive materials so that they could be traced. Some of these measures were bound to be controversial, but, as I said to a reporter on May 4, terrorism "is the major threat to the security of Americans." I wish I had been wrong.

On Sunday, Hillary and I flew to Oklahoma City for a memorial service at the Oklahoma State Fairgrounds. The service had been organized by Cathy Keating, the wife of Governor Frank Keating, whom I had first met more than thirty years earlier when we were students at Georgetown. Frank and Cathy were obviously still in a lot of pain, but they and the mayor of Oklahoma City, Ron Norick, had risen to the challenge of the search-and-recovery operation and of meeting Oklahomans' need for grieving. At the service, the Reverend Billy Graham got a standing ovation when he said, "The spirit of this city and of this nation will not be defeated." In moving remarks, the governor said that if anyone thought Americans had lost the capacity for love and caring and courage, they should come to Oklahoma.

I tried to speak for the nation in saying, "You have lost too much, but you have not lost everything. And you have certainly not lost America, for we will stand with you for as many tomorrows as it takes." I shared a letter I had received from a young widow and mother of three whose husband had been killed by the terrorist downing of Pan Am 103 over Lockerbie, Scotland, in 1988. She asked those who had lost loved ones not to turn their hurt into hate, but instead to do the things their loved ones had "left undone, thus ensuring they did not die in vain." After Hillary and I met with some of the victims' families, I needed to remember those wise words too. One of the Secret Service agents killed was Al Whicher, who had served on my detail before going to Oklahoma; his wife and three children were among the families there.

So often referred to by the demeaning term "federal bureaucrats," the slain employees had been killed because they served us, helping the elderly and disabled, supporting farmers and veterans, enforcing our laws. They were family members, friends, neighbors, PTA members, and workers in their communities. Somehow they had been morphed into heartless parasites of tax dollars and abusers of power, not only in the twisted minds of Timothy McVeigh and his sympathizers but also by too many others who bashed them for power and profit. I promised myself that I would never use the thoughtless term "federal bureaucrat" again, and that I would do all I could to change the atmosphere of bitterness and bigotry out of which this madness had come.

Whitewater World didn't stop for Oklahoma City. The day before Hillary and I left for the memorial service, Ken Starr and three aides came to the White House to question us. I was accompanied to the session in the Treaty Room by Ab Mikva and Jane Sherburne of the White House counsel's office, and my private attorneys, David Kendall and his partner Nicole Seligman. The interview was uneventful, and when it concluded, I asked Jane Sherburne to show Starr and his deputies the Lincoln Bedroom, with its furniture brought to the White House by Mary Todd Lincoln and a copy of the Gettysburg Address, which Lincoln had written in his own hand after the fact so that it could be auctioned to raise money for war veterans. Hillary thought I was being too nice to them, but I was just behaving as I'd been raised to do, and I hadn't yet given up all my illusions that the inquiry would, in the end, follow a legitimate course.

During the same week my longtime friend Senator David Pryor announced that he would not seek reelection in 1996. We had known each other for nearly thirty years. David Pryor and Dale Bumpers were far more than just my home-state senators; we had served consecutively as governor, and together we had helped to keep Arkansas a progressive Democratic state as most of the South moved into the Republican fold. Pryor and Bumpers had been invaluable to my work and my peace of mind, not only because they had supported me on tough issues but because they were my friends, men who had known me a long time. They could make me listen and laugh, and reminded their colleagues that I wasn't the person they kept reading about. After David retired, I would have to get him on the golf course to obtain the advice and perspective that were near at hand as long as he was in the Senate.

At the White House correspondents' dinner on April 29, my remarks were brief, and except for a line or two, I didn't try to be funny. Instead, I thanked the assembled press for their powerful and poignant coverage of the Oklahoma City tragedy and the herculean recovery effort, assured them that "we are going to get through this, and when we do, we'll be even stronger," and closed with W. H. Auden's words:

> In the deserts of the heart
> Let the healing fountain start.

On May 5, at the Michigan State University commencement, I spoke not only to the graduates but also to the armed militia groups, many of which were active in remote areas of rural Michigan. I said that I knew that most militia members, while they dressed up on weekends in fatigues and conducted military exercises, had not broken any laws, and I expressed appreciation for those who had condemned the bombing. Then I attacked those who had gone beyond harsh words to advocating violence against law-enforcement officers and other government employees, while comparing themselves to the colonial militias, "who fought for the democracy you now rail against."

For the next few weeks, in addition to hammering away at those who condoned violence, I asked all Americans, including radio talk-show hosts, to weigh their words more carefully, to make sure that they did not encourage violence in the minds of people less stable than themselves.

Oklahoma City prompted millions of Americans to reassess their own words and attitudes toward government and toward people whose views differed from their own. In so doing, it began a slow but inexorable moving away from the kind of uncritical condemnation that had become all too prevalent in our political life. The haters and extremists didn't go away, but they were on the defensive and, for the rest of my term, would never quite regain the position they had enjoyed before Timothy McVeigh took the demonization of government beyond the limits of humanity.

In the second week of May, I boarded Air Force One to fly to Moscow to celebrate the fiftieth anniversary of the end of World War II in Europe. Even though Helmut Kohl, François Mitterrand, John Major, Jiang Zemin, and other leaders were scheduled to be there, my decision was controversial because Russia was involved in a bloody battle against separatists in the predominantly Muslim republic of Chechnya, civilian casualties were mounting, and most outside observers thought that Russia had used excessive force and insufficient diplomacy.

I made the trip because our nations were allies in World War II, which had claimed the lives of one in eight Soviet citizens: twenty-seven million of them died in battle or from disease, starvation, and freezing. Also, we were allies once again, and our partnership was essential to Russia's economic and political progress, to our cooperation in securing and destroying nuclear weapons, to the orderly expansion of NATO and the Partnership for Peace, and to our fight against terrorism and organized crime. Finally, Yeltsin and I had two thorny issues to resolve: the problem of Russia's cooperation with Iran's nuclear program and the question of how to handle NATO expansion in a way that would bring Russia into the Partnership for Peace and wouldn't cost Yeltsin the election in 1996.

On May 9, I stood with Jiang Zemin and several other leaders in Red Square as we watched a military parade featuring old veterans marching shoulder to shoulder, often holding hands and leaning against one another to steady themselves as they paraded one last time for Mother Russia. The next day, after the commemorative ceremonies, Yeltsin and I met in St. Catherine's Hall in the Kremlin. I started the meeting with Iran, telling Yeltsin that we had worked together to get all the nuclear weapons out of Ukraine, Belarus, and Kazakhstan; now we had to make sure that we didn't allow states that could harm us both, like Iran, to become nuclear powers. Yeltsin was prepared for this; he immediately said no centrifuges would be sold and suggested we refer the question of the reactors, which Iran claimed it wanted for peaceful purposes only, to the Gore-Chernomyrdin commission. I agreed, provided Yeltsin would publicly commit to Russia's not giving Iran nuclear technology that could be used for military purposes. Boris said okay and we shook hands on it. We also agreed to begin visits to Russia's biological weapons plants in August, as part of a broader effort to reduce the threat of biological and chemical weapons proliferation.

On the question of NATO enlargement, after I told Yeltsin indirectly that we wouldn't push it before his election in 1996, he finally agreed to join the Partnership for Peace. Although he didn't agree to announce his decision publicly, for fear of being seen as conceding too much, he promised that Russia would sign the documents by May 25, and that was good enough for me. The trip had been a success.

On the way home, I stopped in Ukraine for another World War II ceremony, a speech to university students, and a moving visit to Babi Yar, the hauntingly beautiful wooded ravine where, almost fifty-four years earlier, the Nazis had slaughtered more than 100,000 Jews and several thousand Ukrainian nationalists, Soviet prisoners of war, and Gypsies. Just the day before, the United Nations had voted to permanently extend the Nuclear Nonproliferation Treaty, which had been the bedrock of our efforts to contain the proliferation of nuclear weapons for more than twenty-five years. Since several nations were still trying to obtain them, the extension of NPT was one of my most important nonproliferation objectives. Babi Yar and Oklahoma City were sober reminders of the human capacity for evil and destruction; they reinforced the importance of the NPT and the agreement I had made restricting Russian nuclear sales to Iran.

By the time I got back to Washington, the Republicans had begun to move on their proposals, and I spent most of the rest of the month trying to beat them back, threatening to veto their rescission package, their attempts to weaken our clean water program, and the large cuts they had proposed in education, health care, and foreign aid.

In the third week of May, I announced that, for the first time since the beginning of the Republic, the two blocks of Pennsylvania Avenue that front the White House would be closed to vehicular traffic. I agreed to this decision reluctantly, after a panel of experts from the Secret Service, Treasury, and past Republican and Democratic administrations told me that it was necessary to secure the White House from a bomb. In the aftermath of Oklahoma City and the Japanese subway attack, I felt I had to go along with the recommendation, but I didn't like it.

By the end of the month, Bosnia was back in the news. The Serbs tightened their blockade around Sarajevo, and their snipers began firing on innocent children again. On May 25, NATO conducted air strikes on the Serb stronghold of Pale, and the Serbs, in retaliation, seized UN peacekeepers and chained them to ammunition dumps in Pale as hostages against further strikes; they also killed two UN soldiers from France in the seizure of a UN outpost.

Our airpower had been used extensively in Bosnia to conduct the longest-lasting humanitarian mission in history; to enforce the no-fly zone, which kept the Serbs from bombing Bosnian Muslims; and to maintain a fire-free zone around Sarajevo and other populated areas. Along with the UN peacekeepers and the embargo, our pilots had made a real difference: casualties had dropped from 130,000 in 1992 to under 3,000 in 1994. Nonetheless, the war was still raging, and more would have to be done to bring it to an end.

The other main foreign policy developments in June occurred around the G-7 summit hosted by Jean Chrétien in Halifax, Nova Scotia. Jacques Chirac, who had just been elected president of France, stopped by to see me on his way to Canada. Chirac had warm feelings for America. As a young man, he had spent time in our country, including a brief period working in a Howard Johnson's restaurant in Boston. He had an insatiable curiosity about a wide variety of issues. I liked him a lot, and liked the fact that his wife was also in politics, with a career of her own.

Despite the good chemistry between us, our relationship had been somewhat strained by his decision to resume testing France's nuclear weapons while I was trying to get worldwide support for a comprehensive nuclear test-ban treaty, a goal of every American President since Eisenhower. After Chirac assured me that when the tests were completed he would support the treaty, we moved on to Bosnia, where he was inclined to be tougher on the Serbs than Mitterrand had been. He and John Major were supporting the creation of a rapid reaction force to respond to attacks on UN peacekeepers, and I pledged U.S. military support to help them and the other UN forces get into and out of Bosnia if they and the regular peacekeepers had to be withdrawn. But I also told Chirac that if the force didn't work and the UN troops were forced out of Bosnia, we would have to lift the arms embargo.

At the G-7, I had three objectives: to secure greater cooperation among the allies on terrorism, organized crime, and narco-trafficking; to identify major financial crises quickly and handle them better, with more timely and accurate information and with investments in developing nations to reduce poverty and promote environmentally responsible growth; and to resolve a serious trade dispute with Japan.

The first two were easily achieved; the third was a real problem. In two and a half years, we had made progress with Japan, completing fifteen separate trade agreements. However, in the two years since Japan had pledged to open its markets to U.S. automobiles and auto parts, the sector that accounted for more than half our total bilateral trade deficit, we had made almost no headway at all. Eighty percent of American dealerships sold Japanese cars; only 7 percent of Japanese dealerships sold cars from any other country, and rigid government regulation kept our parts out of Japan's repair market. Mickey Kantor had reached the limits of his patience and had recommended putting a 100 percent tariff on Japanese luxury cars. In a meeting with Prime Minister Murayama, I told him that because of our security relationship and the sluggish Japanese economy, the United States would continue to negotiate with Japan, but we had to have action soon. By the end of the month we had it. Japan agreed that two hundred dealerships would offer U.S. cars immediately, and a thousand would do so within five years; that the regulations keeping our parts out would be changed; and that Japanese automakers would increase their production in the United States and use more American-made parts.

During the entire month of June, I was also embroiled in the unfolding battle with the Republicans over the budget. On the first day of the month, I went to a farm in Billings, Montana, to highlight the differences between my approach to agriculture and that of the Republicans in Congress. The agricultural aid program had to be reauthorized in 1995, and therefore was part of the budget debate. I told the farm families that while I favored a modest reduction in overall agricultural spending, the Republican plan cut assistance too sharply and did too little for family farmers. For several years, Republicans had done better than Democrats in rural America because they were more culturally conservative, but when push came to shove, the Republicans cared more about large agribusiness than family farmers.

I also went horseback riding, mostly because I liked to ride and loved the broad sweep of the Montana landscape, but also because I wanted to show that I wasn't a cultural alien rural Americans couldn't support. After the farm event, my advance man, Mort Engleberg, had asked one of our hosts what he thought of me. The farmer replied, "He's all right. And he ain't anything like they make him out to be." I heard that a lot in 1995, and just hoped I wouldn't have to bring perception into line with reality one voter at a time.

Our ride got interesting when one of my Secret Service

agents fell off his horse; the agent was unhurt, but the horse took off like a rocket across the open range. To the amazement of the press and the Montanans watching, my deputy chief of staff, Harold Ickes, rode off after the runaway steed at a blistering pace, chased him down, and returned him to his owner. Harold's exploit seemed totally at odds with his image as a high-strung, urban, liberal activist. As a young man, he had worked on ranches out west, and he hadn't forgotten how to ride.

On June 5, Henry Cisneros and I unveiled a "National Homeownership Strategy" of one hundred things we were going to do to increase home ownership to two-thirds of the population. The big decline in the deficit had kept mortgage rates low even as the economy picked up, and in a couple of years, we would reach Henry's goal for the first time in American history.

At the end of the first week of June, I vetoed my first bill, the $16 billion GOP rescission package, because it cut too much out of education, national service, and the environment, while leaving untouched unnecessary highway demonstration projects, courthouses, and other federal buildings that were pet projects of Republican members. They may have hated government in general, but, like most incumbents, they still wanted to spend themselves to reelection. I offered to work with the Republicans to cut even more spending, but said it would have to come out of pork-barrel projects and other nonessential spending, not investments in our children and our future. A couple of days later, I had another reason to fight for those investments, as Hillary's brother Tony and his wife, Nicole, gave us a new nephew—Zachary Boxer Rodham.

I was still trying to find the right balance between confrontation and accommodation when I went to Claremont, New Hampshire, for a town meeting with Speaker Gingrich. I had said I thought it would be good for Newt to talk to people in New Hampshire as I had in 1992, and he took me up on it. We both made positive opening comments about the need for honest debate and cooperation rather than the kind of name-calling sound bites that make the evening news. Gingrich even joked that he had followed my campaign example by stopping at a Dunkin' Donuts shop on the way to the meeting.

In the course of answering questions from citizens, we agreed to work together for campaign finance reform, even shaking hands on it; talked about other areas where we saw eye to eye; had an interesting, civilized disagreement about health care; and disagreed about the utility of the United Nations and whether Congress should fund AmeriCorps.

The discussion with Gingrich was well received in a country weary of partisan warfare. Two of my Secret Service agents, who almost never said anything to me about politics, told me how glad they were to see the two of us in a positive discussion. The next day, at the White House Conference on Small Business, several Republicans said the same thing. If we could have continued in the same vein, I believe the Speaker and I could have resolved most of our differences in a way that would have been good for America. At his best, Newt Gingrich was creative, flexible, and brimming over with new ideas. But that wasn't what had made him Speaker; his searing attacks on the Democrats had done that. It's hard to restrain the source of your power, as Newt was reminded the next day when he was criticized by Rush Limbaugh and the conservative **Manchester Union Leader** for being too pleasant to me. It was a mistake he wouldn't often repeat in the future, at least not in public.

After the meeting I went to Boston for a fund-raiser for Senator John Kerry, who was up for reelection and would likely face a tough opponent in Governor Bill Weld. I had a good relationship with Weld, perhaps the most progressive of all the Republican governors, but I didn't want to lose Kerry in the Senate. He was one of the Senate's leading authorities on the environment and high technology. He had also devoted an extraordinary amount of time to the problem of youth violence, an issue he had cared about since his days as a prosecutor. Caring about an issue in which there are no votes today but which will have a big impact on the future is a very good quality in a politician.

On June 13, in a nationally televised address from the Oval Office, I offered a plan to balance the budget in ten years. The Republicans had proposed to do it in seven, with big spending cuts in education, health care, and the environment, and large tax cuts. By contrast, my plan had no cuts in education, health services for the elderly, the family supports necessary to make welfare reform work, or essential environmental protections. It restricted tax cuts to middle-income people, with an emphasis on helping Americans pay for the rapidly rising costs of a college education. Also, by taking ten years instead of seven to get to balance, my plan's annual contractionary impact would be less, reducing the risk of slowing economic growth.

The timing and substance of the speech were opposed by many congressional Democrats and some members of my cabinet and staff, who thought it was too early to get into the budget debate with the Republicans; their public support was dropping now that they were making decisions instead of just saying no to me, and a lot of Democrats thought it was foolish to get in their way with a plan of my own before it was absolutely necessary to put one out. After the beating we'd taken during my first two years, they thought the Republicans should have to endure at least a year of their own medicine.

It was a persuasive argument. On the other hand, I was the President; I was supposed to lead, and we had already cut the deficit by a third with no Republican support. If I later had to veto Republican budget bills, I wanted to do so after demonstrating a good-faith effort to make honorable compromises. Besides, in New Hampshire, the Speaker and I had pledged to try to work together. I wanted to hold up my end of the bargain.

My budget decision was supported by Leon Panetta, Erskine Bowles, most of the economic team, the Democratic deficit hawks in Congress, and Dick Morris, who had been advising me since the '94 elections. Most of the staff didn't like Dick because he was difficult to deal with, liked to go around established White House procedures, and had worked for Republicans. He also had some off-the-wall ideas from time to time and wanted to politicize foreign policy too much, but I had worked with him long enough to know when to accept, and when to reject, his advice.

Dick's main advice was that I had to practice the politics of "triangulation," bridging the divide between Republicans and Democrats and taking the best ideas of both. To many liberals and some in the press corps, triangulation was compromise without conviction, a cynical ploy to win reelection. Actually, it was just another way of articulating what I had advocated as governor, with the DLC, and in 1992 during the campaign. I had always tried to synthesize new ideas and traditional values, and to change government policies as conditions changed. I wasn't splitting the difference between liberals and conservatives; instead, I was trying to build a new consensus. And, as the coming showdown with the Republicans over the budget would show, my approach was far from lacking in conviction. Eventually, Dick's role would become known to the public and he would become a regular part of our weekly strategy sessions, which were normally held every Wednesday night. He also brought in Mark Penn and his partner, Doug Schoen, to do polling for us. Penn and Schoen were a good team who shared my New Democrat philosophy and would remain with me for the rest of my presidency. Soon we would also be joined by veteran media consultant Bob Squier and his partner, Bill Knapp, who understood and cared about policy as well as promotion.

On June 29, I finally reached an agreement with the Republicans on the rescission bill, once they restored more than $700 million for education, AmeriCorps, and our safe drinking water program. Senator Mark Hatfield, the chairman of the Senate Appropriations Committee and an old-fashioned progressive Republican, had worked closely with the White House to make the compromise possible.

The next day in Chicago, with police officers and citizens who had been wounded by assault weapons, I defended the assault weapons ban and asked Congress to support Senator Paul Simon's legislation to close a big loophole in the law banning cop-killer bullets. The policeman who introduced me said he had survived severe combat in Vietnam without a mark, but had nearly been killed by a criminal who used an assault weapon to riddle his body with bullets. Current law already banned the bullets that pierced protective vests worn by police officers, but the banned ammunition was defined not by its armor-piercing capability, but by what the ammunition was made of; ingenious entrepreneurs had discovered other elements, not mentioned in the law, that could also be made into bullets that pierced vests and killed cops.

The National Rifle Association was sure to fight the bill, but they were down a little from their high-water mark in 1994. After their executive director had referred to federal law-enforcement officers as "jackbooted thugs," former President Bush had resigned from the organization in protest. A few months earlier, at an event in California, the comedian Robin Williams had lampooned the NRA's opposition to banning cop-killer bullets with a good line: "Of course we can't ban them. Hunters need them. Somewhere out there in the woods, there's a deer wearing a Kevlar vest!" As we headed into the second half of 1995, I hoped Robin's joke and President Bush's protest were harbingers of a larger trend toward common sense on the gun issue.

In July, the partisan fights abated a little. On the twelfth, at James Madison High School in Vienna, Virginia, I continued efforts to bring the American people together, this time on the subject of religious liberty.

There was a lot of controversy about how much religious expression could be allowed in public schools. Some school officials and teachers believed that the Constitution prohibited any of it. That was incorrect. Students were free to pray individually or together; religious clubs were entitled to be treated like any other extracurricular organizations; in their free time, students were free to read religious texts; they could include their religious views in their homework as long as they were relevant to the assignment; and they could wear T-shirts promoting their religion if they were allowed to wear those that promoted other causes.

I asked Secretary Riley and Attorney General Reno to prepare a detailed explanation of the range of religious expression permitted in schools and to provide copies to every school district in America before the start of the next school year. When the booklet was issued, it substantially reduced conflict and lawsuits, and in so doing won support across the religious and political spectrum.

I had long been working on the issue, having established a White House liaison to faith communities, and signed the Religious Freedom Restoration Act. Near the end of my second term, Professor Rodney Smith, an expert on the First Amendment, said my administration had done more to protect and advance religious liberty than any since James Madison's. I don't know if that's accurate, but I tried.

A week after the religious liberty event, I was faced with the biggest current challenge to building a more united American community: affirmative action. The term refers to preferences given to racial minorities or women by governmental entities in employment, contracts for products and services, access to small-business loans, and admissions to universities. The purpose of affirmative action programs is to reduce the impact of long-term systemic exclusion of people based on race or gender from opportunities open to others in our society. The policy began under Kennedy and Johnson and was expanded under the Nixon administration, with strong bipartisan support, out of recognition that the impact of past discrimination could not be overcome by simply outlawing discrimination from now on, coupled with a desire to avoid requiring strict quotas, which could lead to benefits going to unqualified people and reverse discrimination against white males.

By the early 1990s, opposition to affirmative action had built up: from conservatives who said that any race-based preferences amounted to reverse discrimination and therefore were unconstitutional; from whites who had lost out on contracts or university admissions to blacks or other minorities; and from those who believed that affirmative action programs, while well intentioned, were too often abused or had achieved their purpose and outlived their usefulness. There were also some progressives who were uncomfortable with race-based preferences and who urged that the criteria for preferential treatment be redefined in terms of economic and social disadvantage.

The debate intensified when the Republicans won control of Congress in 1994; many of them had promised to end affirmative action, and after twenty years of stagnant middle-class incomes, their position appealed to working-class whites and small-business people, as well as to white students and their parents who were disappointed when they were rejected by the college or university of their choice.

Matters came to a head in June 1995, when the Supreme Court decided the case of **Adarand Constructors, Inc.** v. **Peña,** in which a white contractor sued the secretary of transportation to invalidate a contract awarded to a minority bidder under an affirmative action program. The Court ruled that the government could continue to act against "the lingering effects of racial discrimination," but that, from now on, race-based programs would be subject to the high standard of review called "strict scrutiny," which required the government to show that it had a compelling interest in solving a problem and that the problem could not be addressed effectively by a narrower non-race-based remedy. The Supreme Court decision required us to revisit federal affirmative action programs. Civil rights leaders wanted to keep them strong and comprehensive, while many Republicans were urging that they be abandoned altogether.

On July 19, after intense consultations with both proponents and critics of the policy, I offered my response to the **Adarand** decision, and to those who wanted to abolish affirmative action altogether, in a speech at the National Archives. In preparation, I had ordered a comprehensive review of our affirmative action programs, which concluded that affirmative action for women and minorities had given us the finest, most integrated military in the world, with 260,000 new positions made available to women in the last two and a half years alone; the Small Business Administration had dramatically increased loans to women and minorities without reducing loans to white males or giving loans to unqualified applicants; large private corporations with affirmative action programs reported that increasing the diversity of their workforces had increased their productivity and competitiveness in the global marketplace; government procurement policies had helped to build women- and minority-owned firms, but had on occasion been misused and abused; and there was still a need for affirmative action because of continuing racial and gender disparities in employment, income, and business ownership.

Based on these findings, I proposed to crack down on fraud and abuse in the procurement programs and do a better job of moving firms out of them once they could compete; to comply with the **Adarand** decision by focusing set-aside programs on areas where both the problem and the need for affirmative action were provable; and to do more to help distressed communities and disadvantaged people, no matter what their race or gender. We would retain the principle of affirmative action but reform its practices to ensure that there were no quotas, no preferences for unqualified persons or companies, no reverse discrimination against whites, and no continuation of programs after their equal opportunity purpose had been achieved. In a phrase, my policy was "Mend it, but don't end it."

The speech was well received by the civil rights, corporate, and military communities, but it didn't persuade everyone. Eight days later Senator Dole and Congressman Charles Canady of Florida introduced bills to repeal all federal affirmative action laws. Newt Gingrich had a more positive response, saying he didn't want to get rid of affirmative action until he came up with something to replace it that still gave a "helping hand."

While I was searching for common ground, the Republicans spent much of July moving their budget proposals through the Congress. They proposed big cuts in education and training. The Medicare and Medicaid cuts were so large that they increased substantially the out-of-pocket costs for seniors, who, because of medical inflation, were already paying a higher percentage of their income for health care than they had before the programs were created in the 1960s. The Environmental Protection Agency cuts were so severe that they would effectively end enforcement of the Clean Air and Clean Water acts. They voted to abolish AmeriCorps and cut assistance for the nation's homeless population in half. They effectively ended the family planning program that previously had been supported by Democrats and Republicans alike as a way to help prevent unwanted pregnancies and abortions. They wanted to slash the foreign aid budget, already only 1.3 percent of total federal spending, weakening our ability to fight terrorism and the spread of nuclear weapons, open new markets for American exports, and support the forces of peace, democracy, and human rights around the world.

Unbelievably, just five years after President Bush had signed the Americans with Disabilities Act, which had passed with large bipartisan majorities, the Republicans even proposed to cut the services and supports necessary for disabled people to exercise their rights under the law. After the disability cuts were made public, I got a call one night from Tom Campbell, my roommate for four years at Georgetown. Tom was an airline pilot who made a comfortable living but was by no means wealthy. In an agitated voice, he said he was concerned about the proposed budget cuts for the disabled. His daughter Ciara had cerebral palsy. So did her best friend, who was being raised by a single mother working at a minimum-wage job to which she traveled one hour each way every day by bus. Tom asked some questions about the budget cuts and I answered them. Then he said, "So let me get this straight. They're going to give me a tax cut and cut the aid Ciara's friend and her mother get to cover the costs of the child's wheelchair and the four or five pairs of expensive special shoes she has to have every year and the transportation assistance the mother gets to travel to and from her minimum-wage job?" "That's right," I said. He replied, "Bill, that's immoral. You've got to stop it."

Tom Campbell was a devout Catholic and an ex-marine who had been raised in a conservative Republican home. If the New Right Republicans had gone too far for Americans like him, I knew I could beat them back. On the last day of the month, Alice Rivlin announced that the improving economy had led to a lower deficit than we had expected, and that we could now balance the budget in nine years without the harsh GOP cuts. I was closing in on them.

FORTY-FOUR

There were three positive developments in foreign affairs in July: I normalized relations with Vietnam, with the strong support of most Vietnam veterans in Congress, including John McCain, Bob Kerrey, John Kerry, Chuck Robb, and Pete Peterson; Saddam Hussein released two Americans who had been held prisoner since March, after a strong plea from Congressman Bill Richardson; and South Korean President Kim Young-Sam, in Washington for the dedication of the Korean War Memorial, strongly endorsed the agreement we had made with North Korea to end its nuclear program. Because Jesse Helms and others had criticized the deal, Kim's support was helpful, especially since he had been a political prisoner and advocate for democracy when South Korea was still an authoritarian state.

Unfortunately, the good news was dwarfed by what was happening in Bosnia. After being reasonably quiet for most of 1994, things had begun to go wrong at the end of November, when Serb warplanes attacked Croatian Muslims in western Bosnia. The attack was a violation of the no-fly zone, and in retaliation NATO bombed the Serb airfield, but didn't destroy it or all the planes that had flown.

In March, when the cease-fire President Carter had announced began to unravel, Dick Holbrooke, who had left his post as ambassador to Germany to become assistant secretary of state for European and Canadian affairs, sent our special envoy to the former Yugoslavia, Bob Frasure, to see Milosevic in the futile hope of ending the Bosnian Serb aggression and securing at least limited recognition for Bosnia in return for lifting the UN sanctions on Serbia.

By July, the fighting was in full swing again, with the Bosnian government forces making some gains in the middle of the country. Instead of trying to regain the lost territory, General Mladic decided to attack three isolated Muslim towns in eastern Bosnia, Srebrenica, Zepa, and Gorazde. The towns were filled with Muslim refugees from nearby areas, and though they had been declared UN safe areas, they were protected by only a small number of UN troops. Mladic wanted to take the three towns so that all of eastern Bosnia would be controlled by the Serbs, and he was convinced that, as long as he held UN peacekeepers hostage, the UN would not allow NATO to bomb in retaliation. He was right, and the consequences were devastating.

On July 10, the Serbs took Srebrenica. By the end of the month they had also taken Zepa, and refugees who escaped from Srebrenica had begun to tell the world of the horrifying slaughter of Muslims there by Mladic's troops. Thousands of men and boys were gathered in a soccer field and murdered en masse. Thousands more were trying to escape through the heavily wooded hills.

After Srebrenica was overrun, I pressured the UN to authorize the rapid reaction force we had discussed at the G-7 meeting in Canada a few weeks earlier. Meanwhile, Bob Dole was pushing to lift the arms embargo. I asked him to postpone the vote and he agreed. I was still trying to find a way to save Bosnia that restored the effectiveness of the UN and NATO, but by the third week of July, Bosnian Serbs had made a mockery of the UN and, by extension, of the commitments of NATO and the United States. The safe areas were far from safe, and NATO action was severely limited because of the vulnerability of European troops who couldn't defend themselves, much less the Muslims. The Bosnian Serb practice of UN hostage-taking had exposed the fundamental flaw of the UN's strategy. Its arms embargo had kept the Bosnian government from achieving military parity with the Serbs. The peacekeepers could protect the Bosnian Muslims and Croatians only as long as the Serbs believed NATO would punish their aggression. Now the hostage-taking had erased that fear and given the Serbs a free hand in eastern Bosnia. The situation was slightly better in central and western Bosnia, because the Croatians and Muslims had been able to obtain some arms despite the UN embargo.

In an almost desperate attempt to regain the initiative, the foreign and defense ministers of NATO met in London. Warren Christopher, Bill Perry, and General Shalikashvili went to the conference determined to reverse the building momentum for a withdrawal of UN forces from Bosnia and, instead, to increase NATO's commitment and authority to act against the Serbs. Both the loss of Srebrenica and Zepa and the move in Congress to lift the arms embargo had strengthened our ability to push for more aggressive action. At the meeting, the ministers eventually accepted a proposal developed by Warren Christopher and his team to "draw a line in the sand" around Gorazde and to remove the "dual key" decision making that had given the UN veto authority over NATO action. The London conference was a turning point; from then on, NATO would be much more assertive. Not long

afterward, the NATO commander, General George Joulwan, and our NATO ambassador, Robert Hunter, succeeded in extending the Gorazde rules to the Sarajevo safe
area.

In August, the situation took a dramatic turn. The
Croatians launched an offensive to retake the Krajina, a
part of Croatia that the local Serbs had proclaimed their
territory. European and some American military and
intelligence officials had recommended against the action
in the belief that Milosevic would intervene to save the
Krajina Serbs, but I was rooting for the Croatians. So was
Helmut Kohl, who knew, as I did, that diplomacy could
not succeed until the Serbs had sustained some serious
losses on the ground.

Because we knew Bosnia's survival was at stake, we had
not tightly enforced the arms embargo. As a result, both
the Croatians and the Bosnians were able to get some
arms, which helped them survive. We had also authorized
a private company to use retired U.S. military personnel
to improve and train the Croatian army.

As it turned out, Milosevic didn't come to the aid of the
Krajina Serbs, and Croatian forces took Krajina with little
resistance. It was the first defeat for the Serbs in four years,
and it changed both the balance of power on the ground
and the psychology of all the parties. One Western diplomat in Croatia was quoted as saying, "There was almost a
signal of support from Washington. The Americans have
been spoiling for a chance to hit the Serbs, and they are
using Croatia as their proxy to do the deed for them." On
August 4, in a visit with veteran ABC News correspondent
Sam Donaldson at the National Institutes of Health,
where he was recovering from cancer surgery, I acknowledged that the Croatian offensive could prove helpful in

resolving the conflict. Ever the good journalist, Donaldson filed a report on my comments from his hospital bed.

In an effort to capitalize on the shift in momentum, I sent Tony Lake and Undersecretary of State Peter Tarnoff to Europe (including Russia) to present a framework for peace that Lake had developed and to have Dick Holbrooke lead a team to begin a last-ditch effort to negotiate an end to the conflict with the Bosnians and Milosevic, who claimed not to control the Bosnian Serbs, though everyone knew they could not prevail without his support. Just before we launched the diplomatic mission, the Senate followed the House in voting to lift the arms embargo and I vetoed the bill to give our effort a chance. Lake and Tarnoff immediately took off to make the case for our plan, then met with Holbrooke on August 14 to report that the allies and Russians were supportive, and that Holbrooke could begin his mission at once.

On August 15, after a briefing from Tony Lake on Bosnia, Hillary, Chelsea, and I left for a vacation in Jackson Hole, Wyoming, where we had been invited to spend a few days at the home of Senator Jay and Sharon Rockefeller. We all needed the time off, and I was really looking forward to the prospect of hiking and horseback riding in the Grand Tetons; rafting the Snake River; visiting Yellowstone National Park to see Old Faithful, the buffalo and moose, and the wolves we had brought back to the wild; and playing golf at the high altitude, where the ball goes a lot farther. Hillary was working on a book about families and children, and she was looking forward to making headway on it at the Rockefellers' spacious, light-filled ranch house. We did all those things and more, but the enduring memory of our vacation was about Bosnia, and heartbreak.

On the day my family went to Wyoming, Dick Holbrooke left for Bosnia with an impressive team, including Bob Frasure; Joe Kruzel; Air Force Colonel Nelson Drew; and Lieutenant General Wesley Clark, director of strategic policy for the Joint Chiefs and a fellow Arkansan I had first met at Georgetown in 1965.

Holbrooke and his team landed in the Croatian coastal city of Split, where they briefed the Bosnian foreign minister, Muhamed Sacirbey, on our plans. Sacirbey was the eloquent public face of Bosnia on American television, a handsome, fit man who, as a student in the United States, had been a starting football player at Tulane University. He had long sought greater American involvement in his beleaguered nation and was glad the hour had finally come.

After Split, the U.S. team went to Zagreb, Croatia's capital, to see President Tudjman, then flew to Belgrade to meet with Slobodan Milosevic. This inconclusive meeting was remarkable only for the fact that Milosevic refused to guarantee the safety of our team's plane from Bosnian Serb artillery if they flew from Belgrade into the airport at Sarajevo, their next stop. That meant they had to fly back to Split, from which they would helicopter to a landing spot, then take off for a two-hour drive to Sarajevo over the Mount Igman road, a narrow, unpaved route with no guardrails at the edges of its steep slopes and great vulnerability to nearby Serb machine gunners who regularly shot at UN vehicles. The EU negotiator, Carl Bildt, had been shot at when he traveled the road a few weeks earlier, and there were many wrecked vehicles in the ravines between Spilt and Sarajevo, some of which had simply slid off the road.

On August 19, my forty-ninth birthday, I started the

day by playing golf with Vernon Jordan, Erskine Bowles, and Jim Wolfensohn, the president of the World Bank. It was a perfect morning until I heard about what had happened on the Mount Igman road. First from a news report, and later in an emotional phone call with Dick Holbrooke and Wes Clark, I learned that our team had set out for Sarajevo with Holbrooke and Clark riding in a U.S. Army Humvee, and Frasure, Kruzel, and Drew following behind in a French armored personnel carrier (APC) painted UN white. About an hour into the trip, at the top of a steep incline, the road gave way on the APC, and it somersaulted down the mountain and exploded into flames. Besides the three members of our team, there were two other Americans and four French soldiers in the vehicle. The APC had caught fire when the live ammunition it was carrying exploded. In a brave attempt to help, Wes Clark rappelled down the mountain with a rope tied to a tree trunk and tried to get into the burning vehicle to rescue the men still trapped inside, but it was too damaged and scalding hot.

It was also too late. Bob Frasure and Nelson Drew had been killed in the tumbling fall down the mountain. The others all got out, but Joe Kruzel soon died of his injuries, and one French soldier also perished. Frasure was fifty-three, Kruzel fifty, Drew forty-seven; all were patriotic public servants and good family men who died too young trying to save the lives of innocent people a long way from home.

The next week, after the Bosnian Serbs lobbed a mortar shell into the heart of Sarajevo, killing thirty-eight people, NATO began three days of air strikes on Serb positions. On September 1, Holbrooke announced that all the parties would meet in Geneva for talks. When the Bosnian

Serbs did not comply with all of NATO's conditions, the air strikes resumed and continued until the fourteenth, when Holbrooke succeeded in getting an agreement signed by Kradzic and Mladic to end the siege of Sarajevo. Soon the final peace talks would begin in Dayton, Ohio. Ultimately they would bring an end to the bloody Bosnian war. When they did, their success would be in no small measure a tribute to three quiet American heroes who did not live to see the fruits of their labors.

While the August news was dominated by Bosnia, I continued to argue with the Republicans on the budget; noted that a million Americans had lost their health insurance in the year since the failure of health-care reform; and took executive action to limit the advertising, promotion, distribution, and marketing of cigarettes to teenagers. The Food and Drug Administration had just completed a fourteen-month study confirming that cigarettes were addictive, harmful, and aggressively marketed to teenagers, whose smoking rates were on the rise.

The teen smoking problem was a tough nut to crack. Tobacco is America's legal addictive drug; it kills people and adds untold billions to the cost of health care. But the tobacco companies are politically influential, and the farmers who raise the tobacco crop are an important part of the economic, political, and cultural life of Kentucky and North Carolina. The farmers were the sympathetic face of the tobacco companies' effort to increase their profits by hooking younger and younger people on cigarettes. I thought we had to do something to push them back. So did Al Gore, who had lost his beloved sister, Nancy, to lung cancer.

On August 8, we got a break in our efforts to eliminate

the vestiges of Iraq's weapons of mass destruction program when two of Saddam Hussein's daughters and their husbands defected to Jordan and were given asylum by King Hussein. One of the men, Hussein Kamel Hassan al-Majid, had headed Saddam's secret effort to develop weapons of mass destruction and would supply valuable information on Iraq's remaining WMD stocks, the size and significance of which contradicted what the UN inspectors had been told by Iraqi officials. When confronted with the evidence, the Iraqis simply acknowledged that Saddam's son-in-law was telling the truth and took the inspectors to the sites he had identified. After six months in exile, Saddam's relatives were induced to return to Iraq. Within a couple of days, both sons-in-law were killed. Their brief journey to freedom had provided the UN inspectors with so much information that more chemical and biological stocks and laboratory equipment were destroyed during the inspections process than during the Gulf War.

August was also a big month in Whitewater World. Kenneth Starr indicted Jim and Susan McDougal and Governor Jim Guy Tucker on charges unrelated to Whitewater, and the Senate and House Republicans held hearings all month. In the Senate, Al D'Amato was still trying to prove there was something more to Vince Foster's death than a depression-induced suicide. He hauled Hillary's staff and friends before the committee for bullying questioning and ad hominem attacks. D'Amato was especially unpleasant to Maggie Williams and his fellow New Yorker Susan Thomases. Senator Lauch Faircloth was even worse, scoffing at the notion that Williams and Thomases could have had so many phone conversations about Vince Foster just to share their grief. At the time, I thought that if

Faircloth really didn't understand their feelings, his own life must have been lived in an emotional wilderness. The fact that Maggie had passed two lie detector tests about her actions in the aftermath of Vince's death didn't temper D'Amato's and Faircloth's accusatory questioning.

In the House Banking Committee, Chairman Jim Leach was behaving much like D'Amato. From the beginning, he trumpeted every bogus charge against Hillary and me, alleging that we had made, not lost, money on Whitewater, had used Madison Guaranty funds for personal and political expenses, and had engineered David Hale's SBA fraud. He kept promising "blockbuster" revelations, but they never materialized.

In August, Leach held a hearing starring L. Jean Lewis, the Resolution Trust Corporation investigator who had named Hillary and me as witnesses in a criminal referral shortly before the 1992 election. At the time, the Bush Justice Department inquired about Lewis's referral and the Republican U.S. attorney in Arkansas, Charles Banks, told them that there was no case against us, that it was an attempt to influence the election, and that to launch an investigation at that time would amount to "prosecutorial misconduct."

Nevertheless, Leach referred to Lewis as a "heroic" public servant whose investigation had been thwarted after my election. Before the hearings began, documents were released that supported our position, including Banks's letter refusing to pursue Lewis's allegations because of lack of evidence, and internal FBI cables and Justice Department evaluations saying that "no facts can be identified to support the designation" of Hillary and me as material witnesses. Although there was almost no press coverage of the documents refuting Lewis, the hearings fizzled.

By the time of the August hearings and Starr's latest round of indictments, I had settled into a routine of handling press questions about Whitewater with as little public comment as possible. I had learned from the press coverage over the gays-in-the-military issue that if I gave a meaty answer to a question on whatever the press was obsessing about, it would be on the evening news, blocking out whatever else I was doing in the public interest that day, and the American people would think I was spending all my time defending myself instead of working for them, when in fact Whitewater took up very little of my own time. On a scale of 1 to 10, a 7 answer on the economy was better than a 10 answer on Whitewater. So, with the help of constant reminders from my staff, I held my tongue on most days, but it was hard. I had always hated abuse of power, and as false charges flew, evidence of our innocence was ignored, and more blameless people were hounded by Starr, I was seething inside. No one can be as angry as I was without doing himself harm. It took me too long to figure that out.

September began with a memorable trip to Hawaii to commemorate the fiftieth anniversary of the end of World War II, followed by Hillary's trip to Beijing to address the United Nations Fourth World Conference on Women. Hillary gave one of the most important speeches delivered by anyone in our administration during our entire eight years, asserting that "human rights are women's rights" and condemning their all-too-frequent violation by those who sold women into prostitution, burned them when their marriage dowries were deemed too small, raped them in wartime, beat them in their homes, or subjected them to genital mutilation, forced abortions, or sterilization on them. Her speech got a standing ovation and struck a responsive chord with women all over the world, who knew now, beyond a doubt, that America was pulling for them. Once again, despite the abuse she had been taking on Whitewater, Hillary had come through for a cause she deeply believed in, and for our country. I was so proud of her; the unfair hard knocks she had endured had done nothing to dull the idealism that I had fallen in love with so long ago.

By the middle of the month, Dick Holbrooke had persuaded the foreign ministers of Bosnia, Croatia, and Yugoslavia to agree on a set of basic principles as a framework to settle the Bosnian conflict. Meanwhile, NATO air strikes and cruise missile attacks continued to pound Bosnian Serb positions, and Bosnian and Croatian military gains reduced the percentage of Bosnia controlled by the Serbs from 70 to 50 percent, close to what a negotiated settlement would likely require.

September 28 capped off a good month in foreign policy, as Yitzhak Rabin and Yasser Arafat came to the White House for the next big step in the peace process, the signing of the West Bank accord, which turned over a substantial portion of land to Palestinian control.

The most significant event occurred away from the cameras. The signing ceremony was scheduled to occur at noon, but first Rabin and Arafat met in the Cabinet Room to initial the annex to the agreement, three copies that included twenty-six different maps, each reflecting literally thousands of decisions the parties had reached on roads, crossings, settlements, and holy sites. I was also asked to initial the pages as the official witness. About midway through the process, when I had stepped outside to take a call, Rabin came out and said, "We have a problem." On one of the maps, Arafat had spotted a stretch of road that was marked as under Israeli control but that he was convinced the parties had agreed to turn over to the Palestinians. Rabin and Arafat wanted me to help resolve the dispute. I took them into my private dining room and they began to talk, with Rabin saying he wanted to be a good neighbor and Arafat replying that, as descendants of Abraham, they were really more like cousins. The interplay between the old adversaries was fascinating. Without saying a word, I turned and walked out of the room, leaving them alone together for the first time. Sooner or later, they had to develop a direct relationship, and today seemed the right moment to begin.

Within twenty minutes they had reached an agreement that the disputed crossing should go to the Palestinians. Because the world was waiting for the ceremony and we were already late, there was no time to change the map. Instead, Rabin and Arafat agreed to its modification with a handshake, then signed the maps before them, legally binding themselves to the incorrect designation of the disputed road.

It was an act of personal trust that would have been unthinkable not long before. And it was risky for Rabin. Several days later, with Israelis evenly divided on the West Bank accord, Rabin survived a no-confidence vote in the Knesset by only one vote. We were still walking a tightrope, but I was optimistic. I knew the handover would proceed according to the handshake, and it did. It was the handshake even more than the official signing that convinced me that Rabin and Arafat would find a way to finish the job of making peace.

The fiscal year ended on September 30, and we still didn't have a budget. When I wasn't working on Bosnia and the

Middle East, I had spent the entire month traveling the country campaigning against the Republicans' proposed cuts in Medicare and Medicaid, food stamps, the direct student-loan program, AmeriCorps, environmental enforcement, and the initiative to put 100,000 new police officers on the street. They were even proposing to cut back the Earned Income Tax Credit, thus raising taxes on lower-income working families at the same time they were trying to cut taxes for the wealthiest Americans. At virtually every stop, I pointed out that our fight was not about whether to balance the budget and reduce the burden of unnecessary government, but how to do it. The big dispute involved what responsibilities the federal government should assume for the common good.

In response to my attacks, Newt Gingrich threatened to refuse to raise the debt limit and thus put America in default if I vetoed their budget bills. Raising the debt limit was merely a technical act that recognized the inevitable: as long as America continued to run deficits, the annual debt would increase, and the government would be required to sell more bonds to finance it. Increasing the debt limit simply gave the Treasury Department authority to do that. As long as Democrats were in the majority, Republicans could cast symbolic votes against raising the debt limit and pretend that they hadn't contributed to the necessity to do it. Many Republicans in the House had never voted to raise the debt limit and didn't relish doing so now, so I had to take Gingrich's threat seriously.

If America defaulted on its debt, the consequences could be severe. In more than two hundred years, the United States had never failed to pay its debts. Default would shake investor confidence in our reliability. As we headed into the final showdown, I couldn't deny that

Newt had a bargaining chip, but I was determined not to be blackmailed. If he followed through on his threat, he would be hurt, too. Default ran the risk of increasing interest rates, and even a small increase would add hundreds of billions of dollars to home mortgage payments. Ten million Americans had variable-rate mortgages tied to federal interest rates. If Congress didn't raise the debt limit, people could pay what Al Gore called a "Gingrich surcharge" on their monthly mortgage payments. The Republicans would have to think twice before letting America go into default.

In the first week of October, the pope came to America again, and Hillary and I went to meet him at Newark's magnificent Gothic cathedral. As we had in Denver and at the Vatican, His Holiness and I met alone and mostly talked about Bosnia. The pope encouraged our efforts for peace, with an observation that stuck with me: he said the twentieth century had begun with a war in Sarajevo, and I must not allow the century to end with a war in Sarajevo.

When our meeting concluded, the pope gave me a lesson in politics. First, he left the cathedral for a spot a couple of miles away so that he could drive back in his "popemobile," with its roof of clear, bulletproof glass, waving to the people who had crowded the streets. By the time he reached the church, the congregation was seated. Hillary and I were in the front pew with local and state officials and prominent New Jersey Catholics. The massive oak doors opened, revealing the pontiff in his resplendent white cassock and cape, and the crowd stood and began to clap. As the pope began to walk down the aisle with his arms spread out to touch hands with people on either side of the aisle, the applause turned into cheers and roars. I noticed a group of nuns standing on their pews and screaming like teenagers at a rock concert. When I asked a man near me about it, he explained that they were Carmelites, members of an order that lived a cloistered existence completely apart from society. The pope had given them a dispensation to come to the cathedral. He sure knew how to build a crowd. I just shook my head and said, "I'd hate to have to run against that man."

On the day after I met with the pope, we made progress on Bosnia, as I announced that all the parties had agreed to a cease-fire. A week later Bill Perry stated that a peace agreement would require NATO to send troops to Bosnia to enforce it. Moreover, since our responsibility to participate in NATO missions was clear, he did not believe we were required to seek advance approval from Congress. I thought Dole and Gingrich might be relieved not to have a vote on the Bosnia mission; they were both internationalists who knew what we had to do, but there were many Republicans in both chambers who strongly disagreed.

On October 15, I reinforced my determination to end the Bosnian war and hold those who had perpetrated war crimes accountable when I went to the University of Connecticut with my friend Senator Chris Dodd to inaugurate the research center named for his father. Before going to the Senate, Tom Dodd had been the executive trial counsel at the Nuremberg War Crimes Tribunal. In my remarks, I strongly endorsed the existing war crimes tribunals for the former Yugoslavia and Rwanda, to which we were contributing money and personnel, and supported the establishment of a permanent tribunal to deal with war crimes and other atrocities that violated human rights. Eventually, the idea would take root in the International Criminal Court.

While I was dealing with Bosnia at home, Hillary was off on another trip, this time to Latin America. In the post–Cold War world, with America the world's only military, economic, and political superpower, every nation wanted our attention, and it was usually in our interest to give it. But I couldn't go everywhere, especially during the budget struggles with Congress. As a result, both Al Gore and Hillary made an unusually large number of important foreign trips. Wherever they went, people knew they spoke for the United States, and for me, and on every trip, without fail, they strengthened America's standing in the world.

On October 22, I flew to New York to celebrate the fiftieth anniversary of the United Nations, using the occasion to call for greater international cooperation in the fight against terrorism, the spread of weapons of mass destruction, organized crime, and narco-trafficking. Earlier in the month, Sheikh Omar Abdel Rahman and nine others had been found guilty in the first World Trade Center bombing case, and not long before, Colombia had arrested several leaders of the infamous Cali drug cartel. In my address I outlined an agenda to build on those successes, including universal adherence to anti–money laundering practices; freezing the assets of terrorists and narco-traffickers, as I had just done with respect to Colombian cartels; a no-sanctuary pledge for members of terrorist or organized crime groups; shutting down the gray markets that provided arms and false identification papers to terrorists and narco-traffickers; intensified efforts to destroy drug crops and decrease demand for drugs; an international network to train police officers and provide them with the latest technology; ratification of the Chemical Weapons Convention; and strengthening of the Biological Weapons Convention.

The next day I returned to Hyde Park for my ninth meeting with Boris Yeltsin. Yeltsin had been ill and was under a lot of pressure at home from the ultra-nationalists over NATO expansion and the aggressive role the United States was playing in Bosnia at the expense of the Bosnian Serbs. He had given a tough speech the day before at the UN, which was mostly for domestic consumption, and I could tell he was stressed out.

To put him more at ease, I flew him to Hyde Park in my helicopter so that he could see the beautiful foliage along the Hudson River on an unseasonably warm fall day. When we arrived, I took him out to the front yard of the old house with its sweeping view of the river, and we talked awhile, sitting in the same chairs Roosevelt and Churchill had used when the prime minister visited there during World War II. Then I brought him into the house to show him a bust of Roosevelt sculpted by a Russian artist, a painting of the President's indomitable mother done by the sculptor's brother, and the handwritten note FDR had sent to Stalin informing him that the date for D-day had been set.

Boris and I spent the morning talking about his precarious political situation. I reminded him that I had done everything I could to support him, and though we disagreed on NATO expansion, I would try to help him work through it.

After lunch we retuned to the house to talk about Bosnia. The parties were about to come to the United States to negotiate what we all hoped would be a final pact, the success of which depended on both a multinational NATO-led force and the participation of Russian troops, to reassure the Bosnian Serbs that they too would be treated fairly. Finally, Boris agreed to send troops, but said they could not serve under NATO commanders, though he would be glad to have them serve "under an American general." I assented, as long as it was understood that his troops would not in any way interfere with NATO's command and control.

I regretted that Yeltsin was in so much trouble back home. Yes, he had made his share of mistakes, but against enormous odds he had also kept Russia going in the right direction. I still thought he would come out ahead in the election.

At the press conference after our meeting, I said that we had made progress on Bosnia and that we would both push for the ratification of START II and work together to conclude a comprehensive nuclear test-ban treaty in 1996. It was a good announcement, but Yeltsin stole the show. He told the press that he was leaving our meeting with more optimism than he had brought to it, because of all the press reports saying that our summit "was going to be a disaster. Well, now, for the first time, I can tell you that you're a disaster." I almost fell over laughing, and the press laughed too. All I could say to them in response was "Be sure you get the right attribution there." Yeltsin could get away with saying the darnedest things. There's no telling how he would have answered all the Whitewater questions.

October was relatively quiet on the home front, as the budget pot slowly simmered toward a boil. Early in the month, Newt Gingrich decided not to bring the lobbying-reform legislation to a vote and I vetoed the legislative appropriations bill. The lobbying bill required lobbyists to disclose their activities and prohibited them from giving lawmakers gifts, travel, and meals beyond a modest limit. The Republicans were raising a lot of money from lobbyists by writing legislation that gave tax breaks, subsidies, and relief from environmental regulations to a wide array of interest groups. Gingrich saw no reason to disturb a beneficial situation. I vetoed the legislative appropriations bill because, apart from the appropriations act for military construction, it was the only budget bill Congress had passed as the new fiscal year started, and I didn't think Congress should be taking care of itself first. I didn't want to veto the bill and had asked the Republican leaders just to hold it until we had finished a few other budget bills, but they sent it to me anyway.

While the budget battle continued, Energy Secretary Hazel O'Leary and I received a report from my Advisory Committee on Human Radiation Experiments detailing thousands of experiments done on humans at universities, hospitals, and military bases during the Cold War. Most of them were ethical, but a few were not: in one experiment scientists injected plutonium into eighteen patients without their knowledge; in another, doctors exposed indigent cancer patients to excessive radiation, knowing they would not benefit from it. I ordered a review of all current experimentation procedures and pledged to seek compensation in all appropriate cases. The release of this formerly classified information was part of a wider disclosure policy I followed throughout my tenure. We had already declassified thousands of documents from World War II, the Cold War, and President Kennedy's assassination.

At the end of the first week of October, Hillary and I took a weekend off to fly to Martha's Vineyard for the wedding of our good friend Mary Steenburgen to Ted Danson. We had been friends since 1980; our children had played together since they were young, and Mary had worked her heart out for me all over the country in 1992. I was thrilled when she and Ted met and fell in love, and their wedding was a welcome relief from the strains of Bosnia, Whitewater, and the budget battle.

At the end of the month, Hillary and I celebrated our twentieth wedding anniversary. I got her a pretty diamond ring to mark a milestone in our lives and to make up for the fact that when she agreed to marry me, I didn't have enough money to buy her an engagement ring. Hillary loved the little diamonds across the thin band, and wore the ring as a reminder that, through all our ups and downs, we were still very much engaged.

FORTY-FIVE

Saturday, November 4, started out to be a hopeful day. The Bosnian peace talks had begun three days earlier at Wright-Patterson Air Force Base in Dayton, Ohio, and we had just won a vote in Congress to beat back seventeen anti-environment riders to the EPA budget. I had prerecorded my usual Saturday-morning radio address, assailing the cuts that were still in the EPA budget, and was enjoying a rare, relaxing day, until 3:25 p.m., when Tony Lake called me in the residence to tell me that Yitzhak Rabin had been shot while leaving a huge peace rally in Tel Aviv. His assailant was not a Palestinian terrorist but a young Israeli law student, Yigal Amir, who was bitterly opposed to turning over the West Bank, including land occupied by Israeli settlements, to the Palestinians.

Yitzhak had been rushed to the hospital, and for a good while we didn't know how badly he'd been wounded. I called Hillary, who was upstairs working on her book, and told her what had happened. She came down and held me for a while as we talked about how Yitzhak and I had been together just ten days before when he had come to the United States to present me with the United Jewish Appeal's Isaiah Award. It was a happy night. Yitzhak, who hated to dress up, showed up for the black-tie event in a dark suit with a regular tie. He borrowed a bow tie from my presidential aide, Steve Goodin, and I straightened it for him just before we walked out. When Yitzhak presented the award to me, he insisted that, as the honoree, I stand on his right, even though protocol dictated that foreign leaders stand on the President's right. "Tonight we reverse the order," he said. I replied that he was probably right to do so before the United Jewish Appeal because, "after all, they may be more your crowd than mine." Now I hoped against hope that we would laugh together like that again.

About twenty-five minutes after his first call, Tony called again to say that Rabin's condition was grave, but he knew nothing else. I hung up the phone and told Hillary I wanted to go down to the Oval Office. After talking to my staff and pacing the floor for five minutes, I wanted to be alone, so I grabbed a putter and a couple of golf balls and headed for the putting green on the South Lawn, where I prayed to God to spare Yitzhak's life, hit the ball aimlessly, and waited.

After ten or fifteen minutes I saw the door to the Oval Office open and looked up to watch Tony Lake walking down the stone pathway toward me. I could tell by the look on his face that Yitzhak was dead. When Tony told me, I asked him to go back and prepare a statement for me to read.

In the two and a half years we had worked together, Rabin and I had developed an unusually close relationship, marked by candor, trust, and an extraordinary understanding of each other's political positions and thought processes. We had become friends in that unique way people do when they are in a struggle that they believe is great and good. With every encounter, I came to respect and care for him more. By the time he was killed, I had come to love him as I had rarely loved another man. In the back of my mind, I suppose I always knew he had put his life at risk, but I couldn't imagine him gone, and I didn't know what I would or could do in the Middle East without him. Overcome with grief, I went back upstairs to be with Hillary for a couple of hours.

The next day Hillary, Chelsea, and I went to Foundry Methodist Church with our guests from Little Rock, Vic and Susan Fleming and their daughter Elizabeth, one of Chelsea's closest friends from back home. It was All Saints' Day, and the service was full of evocations of Rabin. Chelsea and another young girl read a lesson from Exodus about Moses confronting God in the burning bush. Our pastor, Phil Wogaman, said that the site in Tel Aviv where Rabin "laid down his life has become a holy place."

After Hillary and I took communion, we left the church and drove to the Israeli embassy to see Ambassador and Mrs. Rabinovich and sign the condolence book, which lay on a table in the embassy's Jerusalem Hall alongside a large photograph of Rabin. By the time we arrived, Tony Lake and Dennis Ross, our special envoy to the Middle East, were already there, sitting in silent respect. Hillary and I signed the book and then went home to get ready to fly to Jerusalem for the funeral.

We were accompanied by former Presidents Carter and Bush, the congressional leadership and three dozen other senators and representatives, General Shalikashvili, former secretary of state George Shultz, and several prominent business leaders. As soon as we landed, Hillary and I went to the Rabin home to see Leah. She was heartbroken, but trying to put on a brave front for her family and her country.

The funeral was attended by King Hussein and Queen Noor, President Mubarak, and other world leaders. Arafat wanted to come, but was persuaded not to because of the risk and the potentially divisive impact of his presence in Israel. It was also a risk for Mubarak, who had recently survived an assassination attempt himself, but he took it. Hussein and Noor were devastated by Rabin's death; they genuinely cared about him and thought he was essential to the peace process. For each of his Arab partners, Yitzhak's assassination was a painful reminder of the risks they, too, were running for peace.

Hussein gave a magnificent eulogy, and Rabin's granddaughter Noa Ben Artzi–Pelossof, then doing her service in the Israeli army, moved the audience by speaking to her grandfather: "Grandpa, you were the pillar of fire before the camp, and now we are just a camp left alone in the dark, and we're so cold." In my remarks, I tried to rally the people of Israel to keep following their fallen leader. That very week, Jews around the world were studying that portion of the Torah in which God commanded Abraham to sacrifice his beloved son Isaac, or Yitzhak; once Abraham demonstrated his willingness to obey, God spared the boy. "Now God tests our faith even more terribly, for he has taken our Yitzhak. But Israel's covenant with God, for freedom, for tolerance, for security, for peace—that covenant must hold. That covenant was Prime Minister Rabin's life's work. Now we must make it his lasting legacy." I closed with **"Shalom, chaver."**

Somehow those two words, **Shalom, chaver**—Goodbye, friend—had captured the feelings of Israelis about Rabin. I had a number of Jewish staff members who spoke Hebrew and knew how I felt about Rabin; I am still grateful that they gave me the phrase. Shimon Peres later told me that **chaver** means more than mere friendship; it evokes the comradeship of soul mates in common cause.

Soon **Shalom, chaver** began to appear on billboards and bumper stickers all across Israel.

After the funeral I held a few meetings with other leaders at the King David Hotel, with its magnificent view of the Old City, then headed back to Washington. It was almost 4:30 a.m. when we touched down at Andrews Air Force Base, and all the weary travelers staggered off the plane to get whatever rest they could before the budget battle moved into its final phase.

Ever since the new fiscal year had begun on October 1, the government had been running on a continuing resolution (CR), which authorized funding for departments until their new budgets were enacted. It wasn't all that unusual for a new fiscal year to begin without Congress passing a couple of appropriations bills, but now we had the whole government on a CR, with no end in sight. By contrast, in my first two years, the Democratic Congress had approved the budgets on time.

I had offered a plan to balance the budget in ten years, and then one to balance it in nine, by 2004, but the Republicans and I were still far apart on our budgets. All my experts believed the GOP cuts in Medicare and Medicaid, education, the environment, and the EITC were larger than they needed to be to finance their tax cuts and reach balance, even in seven years. We had differences over the estimates of economic growth, medical inflation, and anticipated revenues. When they controlled the White House, the Republicans had consistently overestimated revenues and underestimated spending. I was determined not to make that mistake, and had always used conservative estimates that had enabled us to beat our deficit reduction targets.

Now that they controlled the Congress, the Republicans had gone too far in the other direction, underestimating economic growth and revenues and overestimating the rate of medical inflation, even as they promoted HMOs as a surefire way to slow it down. Their strategy appeared to be the logical extension of William Kristol's advice in his memo to Bob Dole, urging that he block all action on health care. If they could cut funding for Medicare, Medicaid, education, and the environment, middle-class Americans would see fewer benefits from their tax dollars, feel more resentful paying taxes, and become even more receptive to their appeals for tax cuts and their strategy of waging campaigns on divisive social and cultural issues like abortion, gay rights, and guns.

President Reagan's budget director, David Stockman, had acknowledged that his administration had intentionally run huge deficits to create a crisis that would "starve" the domestic budget. They succeeded partially, underfunding but not eliminating investments in our common future. Now the Gingrich Republicans were trying to use a balanced budget with unreasonable revenue and spending assumptions to finish the job. I was determined to stop them; the future direction of our nation hung in the balance.

On November 10, three days before the expiration of the continuing resolution, Congress sent me a new one that threw down the gauntlet: the price for keeping the government open was signing a new CR that increased Medicare premiums 25 percent, cut funding for education and the environment, and weakened environmental laws.

The following day, just a week after Rabin's assassination, I gave my radio address on the Republican attempts to pass their budget through the back door of the CR. It was Veterans Day, so I pointed out that eight million of the seniors whose Medicare premiums would be raised were veterans. There was no need for the GOP's draconian cuts: the combined rates of unemployment and inflation were at a twenty-five-year low; federal employment as a percentage of the overall workforce was the smallest since 1933; and the deficit was down. I still wanted to balance the budget, but in a way that was "consistent with our fundamental values" and "without threats and without partisan rancor."

On Monday night the Congress finally sent me an extension of the debt limit. It was worse than the CR, another backdoor effort to pass the budget cuts and weaken environmental laws. The legislation also stripped from the secretary of the Treasury the fund management flexibility he had had since the Reagan years to avoid defaults under extraordinary circumstances. Even worse, it lowered the debt limit again after thirty days, virtually ensuring a default.

Gingrich had been threatening since April to shut the government down and put America in default if I didn't accept his budget. I couldn't tell whether he really wanted to do it or whether he simply believed all the press coverage during my first two years that, in the face of ample evidence to the contrary, had portrayed me as too weak, too willing to abandon commitments, too eager to compromise. If so, he should have paid more attention to the evidence.

On November 13, with the existing CR scheduled to expire at midnight, the negotiators met one more time to try to resolve our differences before the government shutdown. Dole, Gingrich, Armey, Daschle, and Gephardt were there, as were Al Gore, Leon Panetta, Bob Rubin,

Laura Tyson, and other members of our team. The atmosphere was already tense when Gingrich started the meeting by complaining about our TV ads. We had started
running ads in targeted states in June to highlight administration achievements, beginning with the crime bill.
When the budget debate heated up after Labor Day, we
put up new ads targeting the proposed Republican cuts,
especially in Medicare and Medicaid. After Newt carried
on for a while, Leon Panetta tersely reminded him of all
the terrible things he'd said about me before the 1994
election: "Mr. Speaker, you don't have clean hands."

Dole tried to calm things, saying that he didn't want
the government to shut down. At that point, Dick Armey
broke in to say Dole didn't speak for the House Republicans. Armey was a big man who always wore cowboy
boots and seemed to be in a constant state of agitation. He
launched into a tirade about how the House Republicans
were determined to be true to their principles, and how
angry he was that my TV ads on the Medicare cuts had
frightened his elderly mother-in-law. I replied that I didn't
know about his mother-in-law, but if the Republican budget cuts were to become law, large numbers of elderly people would be forced out of nursing homes or lose their
home health care.

Armey replied gruffly that if I didn't give in to them,
they would shut the government down and my presidency
would be over. I shot back, saying I would never allow
their budget to become law, "even if I drop to 5 percent in
the polls. If you want your budget, you'll have to get
someone else to sit in this chair!" Not surprisingly, we
didn't make a deal.

After the meeting, Daschle, Gephardt, and my team
were elated by my confrontation with Armey. Al Gore said

he just wished everyone in America had heard my declaration, except I should have said I didn't care if I fell to zero in the polls. I looked back at him and said, "No, Al. If we drop to 4 percent, I'm caving." We all laughed, but our insides were still in knots.

I vetoed both the CR and the debt ceiling bill, and the next day at noon large portions of the federal government shut down. Almost 800,000 workers were sent home, disrupting the lives of millions of Americans who needed their applications for Social Security, veterans benefits, and business loans processed, their workplaces inspected for safety, their national parks open for visits, and much more. After the vetoes, Bob Rubin took the unusual step of borrowing $61 billion from retirement funds to pay our debt and avert default for a while longer.

Not surprisingly, the Republicans tried to blame me for the shutdown. I was afraid they'd get away with it, given their success at blaming me for the partisan divide in the '94 election. Then I got a break when, at a breakfast with reporters on the fifteenth, Gingrich implied that he had made the CR even harsher because I'd snubbed him during the flight back from Rabin's funeral by not talking to him about the budget and asking him to leave the plane by the back ramp instead of the front one with me. Gingrich said, "It's petty but I think it's human . . . nobody has talked to you and they ask you to get off the plane by the back ramp. . . . You just wonder, where is their sense of manners?" Perhaps I should have discussed the budget on the way home, but I couldn't bring myself to think about anything but the purpose of the sad trip and the future of the peace process. I did visit with the Speaker and the congressional delegation, as a photograph of Newt, Bob Dole, and me talking on the plane showed. As for getting off the back of the plane, my staff thought they were being courteous, because that was the exit closest to the cars that were picking up Gingrich and the others. And it was four-thirty in the morning; there were no cameras around. The White House released the photo of our conversation, and the press lampooned Gingrich's complaints.

On the sixteenth, at a news conference, I continued to ask the Republicans to send me a clean CR and to begin good-faith budget negotiations, even as they threatened to send me another one with all the same problems. The night before, I signed the Department of Transportation appropriations bill, only the fourth of the needed thirteen, and canceled my scheduled trip to the Asia Pacific leaders' meeting in Osaka, Japan.

On November 19, I made a move toward the Republicans, saying that, in principle, I would work for a seven-year balanced budget agreement but would not commit to the GOP tax and spending cuts. The economy had continued to grow, with the deficit dropping more than expected; Panetta, Alice Rivlin, and our economics team believed we could now get to balance in seven years without the harsh cuts the Republicans were pushing. I signed two more appropriations bills, for the legislative branch and for the Treasury Department, the Postal Service, and general government operations. With six of the thirteen bills signed, about 200,000 of the 800,000 federal employees were back at work.

On the morning of November 21, Warren Christopher called me from Dayton to say that the presidents of Bosnia, Croatia, and Serbia had reached a peace agreement to end the war in Bosnia. The agreement preserved

Bosnia as a single state to be made up of two parts, the Bosnian Croat Federation and the Bosnian Serb Republic, with a resolution of the territorial disputes over which the war was begun. Sarajevo would remain the undivided capital city. The national government would have responsibility for foreign affairs, trade, immigration, citizenship, and monetary policy. Each of the federations would have its own police force. Refugees would be able to return home, and free movement throughout the country would be guaranteed. There would be international supervision of human rights and police training, and those charged with war crimes would be excluded from political life. A strong international force, commanded by NATO, would supervise the separation of forces and keep the peace as the agreement was being implemented.

The Bosnian peace plan was hard-won and its particulars contained bitter pills for both sides, but it would bring an end to four bloody years that claimed more than 250,000 lives and caused more than two million people to flee their homes. American leadership was decisive in pushing NATO to be more aggressive and in taking the final diplomatic initiative. Our efforts were immeasurably helped by the Croatian and Bosnian military gains on the ground, and the brave and stubborn refusal of Izetbegovic and his comrades to give up in the face of Bosnian Serb aggression.

The final agreement was a tribute to the skills of Dick Holbrooke and his negotiating team; to Warren Christopher, who at critical points was decisive in keeping the Bosnians on board and in closing the deal; to Tony Lake, who initially conceived and sold our peace initiative to our allies and who, with Holbrooke, pushed for the final talks to be held in the United States; to Sandy Berger, who chaired the deputies' committee meetings, which kept people throughout the national security operation informed of what was going on without allowing too much interference; and to Madeleine Albright, who strongly supported our aggressive posture in the United Nations. The choice of Dayton and Wright-Patterson Air Force Base was inspired, and carefully chosen by the negotiating team; it was in the United States, but far enough away from Washington to discourage leaks, and the facilities permitted the kind of "proximity talks" that allowed Holbrooke and his team to hammer out the tough details.

On November 22, after twenty-one days of isolation in Dayton, Holbrooke and his team came to the White House to receive my congratulations and discuss our next steps. We still had a big selling job on the Hill and with the American people, who, according to the latest polls, were proud of the peace agreement but were still overwhelmingly opposed to sending U.S. troops to Bosnia. After Al Gore kicked off the meeting by saying that the military testimony to date had not been helpful, I told General Shalikashvili that I knew he supported our involvement in Bosnia but that many of his subordinates remained ambivalent. Al and I had orchestrated our comments to emphasize that it was time for everybody in the government, not just the military, to get with the program. They had the desired effect.

We already had strong support from some important members of Congress, especially Senators Lugar, Biden, and Lieberman. Others offered a more qualified endorsement, saying that they wanted a clear "exit strategy." To add to their numbers, I began to invite members of Congress to the White House, while sending Christopher,

Perry, Shalikashvili, and Holbrooke to the Hill. Our challenge was complicated by the ongoing debate over the budget; the government was open for the time being, but the Republicans were threatening to shut it down again on December 15.

On November 27, I took my case for U.S. involvement in Bosnia to the American people. Speaking from the Oval Office, I said that our diplomacy had produced the Dayton accords and that our troops had been requested not to fight, but to help the parties implement the peace plan, which served our strategic interests and advanced our fundamental values.

Because twenty-five other nations had already agreed to participate in a force of sixty thousand, only a third of the troops would be Americans. I pledged that they would go in with a clear, limited, achievable mission and would be well trained and heavily armed to minimize the risk of casualties. After the address I felt that I had made the strongest case I could for our responsibility to lead the forces of peace and freedom, and hoped that I had moved public opinion enough so that Congress would at least not try to stop me from sending in the troops.

In addition to the arguments made in my speech, standing up for the Bosnians had another important benefit to the United States: it would demonstrate to Muslims the world over that the United States cared about them, respected Islam, and would support them if they rejected terror and embraced the possibilities of peace and reconciliation.

On November 28, after signing a bill to provide more than $5 billion for transportation projects that included my "zero tolerance" drinking standard for drivers under twenty-one, I left for a trip to the UK and Ireland to pursue another important peace initiative. Through all the activity in the Middle East and Bosnia and discussions over the budget, we had continued to work hard on Northern Ireland. On the eve of my trip, and with our urging, Prime Ministers Major and Bruton announced a breakthrough in the Irish peace process: a "twin tracks" initiative that provided for separate talks on arms decommissioning and the resolution of political issues; all parties, including Sinn Fein, would be invited to participate in talks overseen by an international panel, which George Mitchell had agreed to chair. It was nice to fly into good news.

On the twenty-ninth, I met with John Major and spoke to Parliament, where I thanked the British for their support of the Bosnian peace process and their willingness to play a major role in the NATO force. I commended Major for his pursuit of peace in Northern Ireland, quoting John Milton's lovely line, "Peace hath her victories, no less renowned than war." I also had my first meeting with the impressive young opposition leader, Tony Blair, who was in the process of reviving the Labour Party with an approach remarkably similar to what we had tried to do with the DLC. Meanwhile, back home, the Republicans had reversed their position on lobbying reform, and the House passed it without a dissenting vote, 421–0.

The next day I flew to Belfast as the first American President ever to visit Northern Ireland. It was the beginning of two of the best days of my presidency. On the road in from the airport, there were people waving American flags and thanking me for working for peace. When I got to Belfast, I made a stop on the Shankill Road, the center of Protestant Unionism, where ten people had been killed by an IRA bomb in 1993. The only thing most of the Protestants knew about me was the Adams visa. I wanted them to know I was working for a peace that was fair to them, too. As I bought some flowers, apples, and oranges from a local shop, I talked to people and shook a few hands.

In the morning I spoke to the employees and other attendees at Mackie International, a textile machine manufacturer that employed both Catholics and Protestants. After being introduced by two children who wanted peace, one Protestant, the other Catholic, I asked the audience to listen to the kids: "Only you can decide between division and unity, between hard lives and high hopes." The IRA's slogan was "Our day will come." I urged the Irish to say to those who still clung to violence, "You are the past, your day is over."

Afterward, I stopped on the Falls Road, the heart of Belfast's Catholic community. I visited a bakery and began to shake hands with a quickly growing crowd of citizens. One of them was Gerry Adams. I told him that I was reading **The Street,** his book of short stories about the Falls, and that it gave me a better feel for what the Catholics had been through. It was our first public appearance together, and it signaled the importance of his commitment to the peace process. The enthusiastic crowd that quickly gathered was obviously pleased at the way things were going.

In the afternoon Hillary and I helicoptered to Derry, the most Catholic city in Northern Ireland and John Hume's hometown. Twenty-five thousand cheering people filled the Guildhall Square and the streets leading to it. After Hume introduced me, I asked the crowd a simple question: "Are you going to be someone who defines yourself in terms of what you are against or what you are for?

Will you be someone who defines yourself in terms of who you aren't or who you are? The time has come for the peacemakers to triumph in Northern Ireland, and the United States will support them as they do."

Hillary and I ended our day by returning to Belfast for the official lighting of the city's Christmas tree just outside city hall, before a crowd of about fifty thousand people, which was fired up by the singing of Northern Ireland's own Van Morrison: "Oh, my mama told me there'll be days like this." We both spoke; she talked about the thousands of letters we had received from schoolchildren expressing their hopes for peace, and I quoted from one written by a fourteen-year-old girl from County Armagh: "Both sides have been hurt. Both sides must forgive." Then I ended my remarks by saying that for Jesus, whose birth we celebrated, "no words more important than these: 'Blessed are the peacemakers, for they shall inherit the earth.' "

After the tree lighting, we attended a reception, to which all the party leaders were invited. Even the Reverend Ian Paisley, the fiery leader of the Democratic Unionist Party, came. Though he wouldn't shake hands with the Catholic leaders, he was only too happy to lecture me on the error of my ways. After a few minutes of his hectoring, I decided the Catholic leaders had gotten the better end of the deal.

Hillary and I left the reception for our night at the Europa Hotel. On that first trip to Ireland, even our choice of lodging carried great symbolism. The Europa had been bombed on more than one occasion during the Troubles; now it was safe for the President of the United States to stay there.

It was the end of a perfect day, which even included some progress back home, as I signed the Department of

Defense Appropriations Act, in which the congressional leaders had provided funding for our troop deployments in Bosnia. Dole and Gingrich had come through, in exchange for a few billion dollars of extra spending that even the Pentagon said was unnecessary.

The next morning we flew into Dublin, where the streets were lined with even bigger and more enthusiastic crowds than we had seen in the north. Hillary and I met with President Mary Robinson and Prime Minister Bruton, then went to a site outside the Bank of Ireland on the Trinity College Green, where I spoke to 100,000 people waving Irish and American flags and cheering. By that time I had been joined by a large number of Irish-American congressmen; Secretary Dick Riley and Peace Corps director Mark Gearan; the Irish-American mayors of Chicago, Pittsburgh, and Los Angeles; my very Irish stepfather, Dick Kelley; and Secretary of Commerce Ron Brown, who had worked on our economic initiatives for Northern Ireland and kidded the rest of us about his being "black Irish." Once more, I urged the sea of people to set an example that would inspire the world.

When the event was over, Hillary and I walked back into the majestic Bank of Ireland to greet Bono, his wife, Ali, and other members of the Irish rock band U2. Bono was a big supporter of the peace process, and for my efforts he gave me a gift he knew I'd appreciate: a book of William Butler Yeats's plays inscribed by the author and by Bono, who wrote, irreverently, "Bill, Hillary, Chelsea—This guy wrote a few good lyrics—Bono and Ali." The Irish aren't known for understatement, but Bono pulled it off.

I left the College Green to address the Irish parliament, reminding them that all of us had to do more to bring the tangible benefits of peace to ordinary Irish citizens; as Yeats said: "Too long a sacrifice can make a stone of the heart."

Then I went to Cassidy's Pub, to which we had invited some of my distant relatives through my maternal grandfather, whose family had come from Fermanagh.

Feeling full of my Irishness, I went from the pub to the American ambassador's residence, where Jean Kennedy Smith had arranged a brief meeting with the opposition leader, Bertie Ahern, who would soon become prime minister and my newest partner for peace. I also met Seamus Heaney, the Nobel Prize–winning poet whom I'd quoted in Derry the day before.

The next morning, as I flew to see our troops in Germany, I had the feeling that my trip had shifted the psychological balance in Ireland. Until then, the advocates of peace had to argue their case to the skeptics, while their adversaries could just say no. After those two days, the burden had shifted to the opponents of peace to explain themselves.

In Baumholder, General George Joulwan, the NATO commander, briefed me on the military plan and assured me that the morale of the troops about to go to Bosnia was high. I met briefly with Helmut Kohl to thank him for his commitment to send four thousand German soldiers, then flew to Spain to thank Prime Minister Felipe González, the current EU president, for Europe's support. I also acknowledged the leadership of NATO's new secretary-general, the former Spanish foreign minister Javier Solana, an exceptionally able and delightful man who inspired the confidence of all his NATO leaders, no matter how large their egos.

Three days after I got home, I vetoed the Private Securities Litigation Reform Act, because it went too far in limiting access to our courts to innocent investors victimized by securities fraud. Congress overrode my veto, but in 2001, when all the problems with Enron and WorldCom arose, I knew I had done the right thing. I also vetoed another Republican budget. They had made a few changes and tried to make it harder to veto by including their welfare reform bill, but it still cut health and education, raised taxes on the working poor, and relaxed rules that kept pension funds from being depleted for non-pension purposes, less than a year after the Democratic Congress had stabilized America's pension system.

The next day I submitted my own seven-year balanced budget plan. The Republicans panned it because it didn't accept all their estimates for revenues and expenses. We were $300 billion apart over seven years, not an insurmountable difference in an annual budget of $1.6 trillion. I was confident we would eventually reach an agreement, though it might take another government shutdown to get us there.

In mid-month, Shimon Peres came to see me for the first time as prime minister, to reaffirm Israel's intention to turn over Gaza, Jericho, other major cities, and 450 villages in the West Bank to the Palestinians by Christmas, and to release at least another 1,000 Palestinian prisoners before the coming Israeli elections. We also discussed Syria, and I was encouraged enough by what Shimon said to call President Assad and ask him to see Warren Christopher about it.

On the fourteenth, I flew to Paris for a day, for the official signing of the agreement ending the Bosnian war. I met with the presidents of Bosnia, Croatia, and Serbia, and went to a lunch with them hosted by Jacques Chirac at the Elysée Palace. Slobodan Milosevic was sitting across from me, and we talked for a good while. He was intelligent, articulate, and cordial, but he had the coldest look in his eyes I had ever seen. He was also paranoid, telling me he was sure Rabin's assassination was the result of betrayal by someone in his security service. Then he said that everyone knew that's what had happened to President Kennedy, too, but that we Americans "have been successful in covering it up." After spending time with him, I was no longer surprised by his support of the murderous outrages of Bosnia, and I had the feeling that I would be at odds with him again before long.

When I came home to the budget war, the Republicans shut down the government again and it sure didn't feel as if Christmas was on the way, though seeing Chelsea dance in **The Nutcracker** brightened my mood considerably. This time the shutdown was somewhat less severe because about 500,000 federal employees deemed "essential" were allowed to work without pay until the government reopened. But benefits to veterans and poor kids still weren't being paid. It wasn't much of a Christmas present to the American people.

On the eighteenth, I vetoed two more appropriations bills, one for the Department of the Interior, the other for the Departments of Veterans Affairs and Housing and Urban Development. The next day I signed the Lobbying Disclosure Act, after the House Republicans reversed their opposition, and vetoed a third appropriations bill, for the Departments of Commerce, State, and Justice. This one was really something: it eliminated the COPS program in the face of clear evidence that more police on the beat reduced crime; it eliminated all the drug courts, like those that had been promoted by Janet Reno when she was a prosecuting attorney, which reduced crime and drug abuse; it eliminated the Commerce Department's Advanced Technology Program, which many Republican businesspeople supported because it helped them become more competitive; and it severely cut funding for legal services for the poor and for foreign operations.

By Christmas, I had felt for some time that if left to our own devices, Senator Dole and I could have resolved the budget impasse fairly easily, but Dole had to be careful. He was running for President, and Senator Phil Gramm was running against him with Gingrich-like rhetoric, in Republican primaries in which the electorate was well to the right of the country as a whole.

After breaking for Christmas, I vetoed one more budget bill, the National Defense Authorization Act. This one was tough because the legislation included a military pay increase and a larger military housing allowance, both of which I strongly supported. Nevertheless, I felt I had to do it because the bill also mandated the complete deployment of a national missile defense system by 2003, well before a workable system could be developed or would be needed; moreover, such action would violate our commitments under the ABM Treaty and jeopardize Russia's implementation of START I and its ratification of START II. The bill also restricted the President's ability to commit troops in emergencies and interfered too much with important management prerogatives of the Defense Department, including its actions to redress the threat of weapons of mass destruction under the Nunn-Lugar program. No responsible President, Republican or Democrat, could have allowed that defense bill to become law.

During the last three days of the year our forces deployed to Bosnia, and I worked with the congressional leaders on the budget, including one seven-hour session. We made some progress, but broke for New Year's without agreement on the budget or on ending the shutdown. In the first session of the 104th Congress, the new Republican majority had enacted only 67 bills, as compared with 210 in the first year of the previous Congress. And only 6 of the 13 appropriations bills were law, three full months after the beginning of the fiscal year. As our family headed down to Hilton Head for Renaissance Weekend, I wondered whether the American people's votes in the '94 elections had produced the results they wanted.

And I thought about the last two emotionally draining, exhausting, jam-packed months, and the fact that the enormity of the events—Rabin's death, the Bosnian peace and the deployment of our troops, the progress in Northern Ireland, the herculean budget fight—had done nothing to slow down the worker bees in Whitewater World.

On November 29, as I was making my way to Ireland, Senator D'Amato's committee called L. Jean Lewis to testify again about how her investigation of Madison Guaranty had been thwarted after I became President. During her appearance before Congressman Leach's committee the previous August, she had been so badly discredited by government documents and her own tape-recorded conversations with Resolution Trust Corporation attorney April Breslaw that I was amazed D'Amato would call her back. On the other hand, hardly anybody knew of the problems with Lewis's testimony, and D'Amato received a lot of publicity, as Leach had, by simply leveling charges that were unsupported and were actually disproved by subsequent testimony.

Lewis once again repeated her claim that her investigation was thwarted after I was elected. Richard Ben-Veniste, the committee's minority counsel, confronted her with evidence that, contrary to her sworn deposition, she had tried repeatedly to push federal authorities to act on her referral of Hillary and me as material witnesses in Whitewater before the election, not after I became President, and had told an FBI agent that she was "altering history" by her actions. When Senator Paul Sarbanes read to Lewis from the 1992 letter of U.S. Attorney Chuck Banks saying that acting on her referral would constitute "prosecutorial misconduct," then referred to a 1993 Justice Department appraisal of Lewis's inadequate knowledge of federal banking law, Lewis cried, slumped in her chair, and was led away, never to return.

Less than a month later, in mid-December, the complete Whitewater story finally came out, when the RTC inquiry from Pillsbury, Madison & Sutro was released. The report was written by Jay Stephens, who, like Chuck Banks, was a Republican former U.S. attorney whom I had replaced. It said, as had the preliminary report in June, that there were no grounds for a civil suit against us in Whitewater, much less any criminal action, and it recommended that the investigation be closed.

This was what the **New York Times** and the **Washington Post** had wanted to know when they called for an independent counsel. I eagerly awaited their coverage. Immediately after the RTC report was released, the **Post** mentioned it in passing, in the eleventh paragraph of a front-page story about an unrelated subpoena battle with Starr, and the **New York Times** didn't run a word. The **Los Angeles Times, Chicago Tribune,** and **Washington Times** ran an Associated Press story of about four hundred words on the inside pages of their papers. The TV networks didn't cover the RTC report, though. ABC's Ted Koppel mentioned it on **Nightline,** then dismissed its importance, because there were so many "new" questions. Whitewater wasn't about Whitewater anymore. It was about whatever Ken Starr could dig up on anybody in Arkansas or my administration. In the meantime, some Whitewater reporters were actually covering up evidence of our innocence. To be fair, a few journalists took note. **Washington Post** writer Howard Kurtz wrote an article pointing out the way the RTC report had been buried, and Lars-Erik Nelson, a columnist for the New York **Daily News,** who had been a correspondent in the Soviet Union, wrote, "The secret verdict is in: There was nothing for the Clintons to hide . . . in a bizarre reversal of those Stalin-era trials in which innocent people were convicted in secret, the President and the First Lady have been publicly charged and secretly found innocent."

I was genuinely confused by the mainstream press coverage of Whitewater; it seemed inconsistent with the more careful and balanced approach the press had taken on other issues, at least since the Republicans won the Congress in 1994. One day, after one of our budget meetings in October, I asked Senator Alan Simpson of Wyoming to stay a moment to talk. Simpson was a conservative Republican, but we had a pretty good relationship because of the friendship we had in common with his governor, Mike Sullivan. I asked Alan if he thought Hillary and I had done anything wrong in Whitewater. "Of course not," he said. "That's not what this is about. This is about making the public think you did something wrong. Anybody who looked at the evidence would see that you didn't." Simpson laughed at how willing the "elitist" press was to swallow anything negative about small, rural places like Wyoming or Arkansas and made an interesting observation: "You know, before you were elected, we Republicans believed the press was liberal. Now we have a more sophisticated view. They are liberal in a way. Most of them voted for you, but they think more like your right-wing critics do, and that's much more important." When I asked him to explain, he said, "Democrats like you and Sullivan get into government to help people. The right-wing extremists don't think government can do much to improve on human nature, but they do like power. So does the press. And since you're President, they both get power the same way, by hurting you." I appreciated Simpson's candor and I thought about what he said for months. For a long time, whenever I was angry about the Whitewater press coverage I would tell people about Simpson's analysis. When I finally just accepted his insight as accurate, it was liberating, and it cleared my head for the fight.

Despite my anger over Whitewater and my puzzlement about what was behind the press coverage of it, I headed into 1996 feeling fairly optimistic. In 1995, we had helped save Mexico, gotten through Oklahoma City and increased the focus on terrorism, preserved and reformed affirmative action, ended the war in Bosnia, continued the Middle East peace process, and helped make progress in Northern Ireland. The economy had continued to improve, and so far I was winning the budget fight with the Republicans, a battle that in the beginning seemed likely to doom my presidency. It could still lead to that, but as we headed into 1996 I was ready to see it through to the end. As I had told Dick Armey, I didn't want to be President if the price of doing so was meaner streets, weaker health care, fewer educational opportunities, dirtier air, and more poverty. I was betting that the American people didn't want those things either.

FORTY-SIX

By January 2, we were back to the budget negotiations. Bob Dole wanted to make a deal to reopen the government, and after a couple of days so did Newt Gingrich. In one of our budget meetings, the Speaker admitted that in the beginning he had thought he could keep me from vetoing the GOP budget by threatening to shut the government down. In front of Dole, Armey, Daschle, Gephardt, Panetta, and Al Gore, he said frankly, "We made a mistake. We thought you would cave." Finally, on the sixth, with a severe blizzard covering Washington, the impasse was broken, as Congress sent me two more continuing resolutions that put all the federal employees back to work, though they still didn't restore all government services. I signed the CRs and sent the Congress my plan for a balanced budget in seven years.

The next week, I vetoed the Republican welfare reform bill, because it did too little to move people from welfare to work and too much to hurt poor people and their children. The first time I vetoed the Republican welfare reform proposal, it had been a part of their budget. Now a number of their budget cuts were simply put in a bill with the label "welfare reform" on it. Meanwhile, Donna Shalala and I had already gone far in reforming the welfare system on our own. We had given fifty separate waivers to thirty-seven states to pursue initiatives that were pro-work and pro-family. Seventy-three percent of America's welfare recipients were covered by these reforms, and the welfare rolls were dropping.

As we headed into the State of the Union speech on the twenty-third, we seemed to be making some progress on a budget agreement, so I used the address to reach out to the Republicans, rally the Democrats, and explain to the American people my position on both the budget debate, and on the larger question that the budget battle presented: What was the proper role of government in the global information age? The basic theme of the speech was "the era of big government is over. But we cannot go back to the time when our citizens were left to fend for themselves." This formulation reflected my philosophy of getting rid of yesterday's bureaucratic government while advocating a creative, future-oriented, "empowering government"; it also fairly described our economic and social policies and Al Gore's "Rego" initiative. By then my case was bolstered by the success of our economic policy: nearly eight million new jobs had been created since the inauguration and a record number of new businesses had been started for three years in a row. U.S. automakers were even outselling their Japanese competitors in America for the first time since the 1970s.

After offering again to work with the Congress to balance the budget in seven years and pass welfare reform, I outlined a legislative agenda concerning families and children, education and health care, and crime and drugs. It emphasized programs that reflected basic American values and the idea of citizen empowerment: the V-chip, charter schools, public school choice, and school uniforms. I also named General Barry McCaffrey to be America's new drug czar. At the time, McCaffrey was commander in chief of the Southern Command, where he had worked to stop cocaine from being sent to America from Colombia and elsewhere.

The most memorable moment of the evening came near the end of the speech, when, as usual, I introduced the people sitting in the First Lady's box with Hillary. The first person I mentioned was Richard Dean, a forty-nine-year-old Vietnam veteran who had worked for the Social Security Administration for twenty-two years. When I told Congress that he had been in the Murrah Building in Oklahoma City when it was bombed, risked his life to reenter the ruins four times, and saved the lives of three women, Dean got a huge standing ovation from the entire Congress, with the Republicans leading the cheers. Then came the zinger. As the applause died down, I said, "But Richard Dean's story doesn't end there. This last November, he was forced out of his office when the government shut down. And the second time the government shut down, he continued helping Social Security recipients, but he was working without pay. On behalf of Richard Dean . . . I challenge all of you in this chamber: let's never, ever shut the federal government down again."

This time the gleeful Democrats led the applause. The Republicans, knowing that they had been trapped, looked glum. I didn't think I had to worry about a third government shutdown; its consequences now had a human, heroic face.

Defining moments like that don't happen by accident. Every year we used the State of the Union as an organizing tool for the cabinet and staff to come up with new policy ideas, and then we worked hard on how best to present them. On the day of the speech, we held several rehearsals in the movie theater located between the residence and the East Wing. The White House Communications Agency, which also recorded all my public statements, set up a TelePrompTer and a podium, and various staff members moved in and out through the day in an informal process managed by my communications director, Don Baer. We all worked together, listening to each sentence, imagining how it would be received in the Congress and in the country, and improving the language.

We had defeated the philosophy behind the "Contract with America" by winning the government shutdown debate. Now the speech offered an alternative philosophy of government and, through Richard Dean, showed that federal employees were good people performing valuable services. It wasn't much different from what I had been saying all along, but in the aftermath of the shutdown, millions of Americans heard and understood it for the first time.

We began the year in foreign policy with Warren Christopher hosting talks between the Israelis and Syrians at Wye River Plantation in Maryland. Then, on January 12, I flew overnight to the U.S. Air Force base in Aviano, Italy, that had been the center of our NATO air operations over Bosnia, where I boarded one of our new C-17 transport planes for the flight to Taszar Air Base in Hungary, from which our troops were deploying into Bosnia. I had fought in 1993 to keep the C-17 from being eliminated in the defense downsizing. It was an amazing plane with remarkable cargo capacity and the ability to operate in difficult conditions. The Bosnian mission was using twelve C-17s, and I had to fly one into Tuzla; the regular Air Force One, a Boeing 747, was too big.

After meeting with Hungarian President Arpad Goncz and seeing our troops in Taszar, I flew on to Tuzla in northeastern Bosnia, the area for which the United States was responsible. In less than a month and despite terrible weather, seven thousand of our troops and more than two thousand armored vehicles had crossed the flooded Sava River to reach their duty stations. They had turned an airfield with no lights or navigational equipment into one that was open for business around the clock. I thanked the troops and personally delivered a birthday present to a colonel whose wife had charged me with the duty when I stopped in Aviano. I met with President Izetbegovic, then flew on to Zagreb, Croatia, to see President Tudjman. Both of them were satisfied with the implementation of the peace agreement so far and very glad U.S. troops were part of it.

By the time I got back to Washington, it had been a long day, but an important one. Our troops were involved in NATO's first deployment beyond its members' borders. They were working with the soldiers of their Cold War adversaries Russia, Poland, the Czech Republic, Hungary, and the Baltic states. Their mission was pivotal to creating a united Europe, yet it was being criticized in Congress and in coffee shops across America. The troops were at least entitled to know why they were in Bosnia and how strongly I supported them.

Two weeks later the Cold War continued to fade into history as the Senate ratified the START II treaty, which President Bush had negotiated and submitted to the Senate three years earlier, just before he left office. Together with the START I treaty, which we had put into force in December 1994, START II would eliminate two-thirds of the nuclear arsenals the United States and the former Soviet Union had maintained at the height of the Cold War, including the most destabilizing nuclear weapons, the multiple-warhead intercontinental ballistic missiles.

Along with START I and II, we had signed an agreement to freeze North Korea's nuclear program, had led the effort to make the Nuclear Nonproliferation Treaty permanent, and were working to safeguard and ultimately dismantle nuclear weapons and materials under the Nunn-Lugar program. In congratulating the Senate on START II, I asked them to continue making America more secure by passing the Chemical Weapons Convention and my anti-terrorism legislation.

On January 30, Prime Minister Victor Chernomyrdin of Russia came to the White House for his sixth meeting with Al Gore. After they finished their commission business, Chernomyrdin came to see me to brief me on events in Russia and Yeltsin's prospects for reelection. Just before our meeting, I spoke to President Suleyman Demirel and Prime Minister Tansu Ciller of Turkey. They told me that Turkey and Greece were on the brink of military confrontation and implored me to intervene to stop it. They were about to go to war over two tiny Aegean islets called Imia by the Greeks and Kardak by the Turks. Both countries claimed the islets, but Greece apparently had acquired them in a treaty with Italy in 1947. Turkey denied the validity of the Greek claim. There were no people living there, though Turks often sailed to the larger islet for picnics. The crisis was triggered when some Turkish journalists had torn down a Greek flag and put up a Turkish one.

It was unthinkable that two great countries with a real dispute over Cyprus would actually go to war over ten acres of rock islets inhabited by only a couple of dozen sheep, but I could tell that Ciller was genuinely afraid it could happen. I interrupted the Chernomyrdin meeting to get briefed, then placed a series of calls, first to Greek prime minister Konstandinos Simitis, then to Demirel and Ciller again. After all the talk back and forth, the two sides agreed to hold their fire, and Dick Holbrooke, who was already working on Cyprus, stayed up all night to get the parties to agree to resolve the problem through diplomacy. I couldn't help laughing to myself at the thought that whether or not I succeeded in making peace in the Middle East, Bosnia, or Northern Ireland, at least I had saved some Aegean sheep.

Just when I thought things couldn't get any weirder in Whitewater World, they did. On January 4, Carolyn Huber found copies of Hillary's records for work the Rose firm had done for Madison Guaranty in 1985 and 1986. Carolyn had been our assistant at the Governor's Mansion and had come to Washington to help us with our personal papers and correspondence. She had already assisted David Kendall in turning over fifty thousand pages of documents to the independent counsel's office, but for some reason this copy of the billing records wasn't among them. Carolyn found it in a box she had moved to her office from the third-floor residence storage area the previous August. Apparently, the copy had been made in the 1992 campaign; it had Vince Foster's notes on it, because he was handling press questions for the Rose firm at the time.

On the surface, it must have looked suspicious. Why were the records turning up after all this time? If you had seen the disordered array of papers we brought up from Arkansas, you wouldn't have been surprised. I'm amazed that we found as much material as we did in a timely fashion. At any rate, Hillary was glad the records had been found; they proved her contention that she had done only a modest amount of work for Madison Guaranty. In a few weeks, the RTC would issue a report saying just that.

But that's not how the independent counsel, congressional Republicans, and the Whitewater reporters played it. In his **New York Times** column, William Safire called Hillary a "congenital liar." Carolyn Huber was called up to Congress to testify before Al D'Amato's committee on January 18. And on the twenty-sixth, Kenneth Starr hauled Hillary before the grand jury for four hours of questioning.

Starr's summons was a cheap, sleazy publicity stunt. We had turned the records over voluntarily as soon as we found them, and they proved the truth of Hillary's account. If Starr had more questions, he could have come to the White House to ask them, as he had done three times before, rather than make her the first First Lady to appear before a grand jury. In 1992, President Bush's White House counsel, Boyden Gray, had withheld his boss's diary for more than a year, until after the election, in direct violation of a subpoena from the Iran-Contra prosecutor. No one put Gray or Bush before a grand jury, and the press uproar was nowhere near as great.

I was more troubled by the attacks on Hillary than on those directed at me. Because I was helpless to stop them, all I could do was stand by her, telling the press that America would be a better place "if everybody in this country had the character my wife has." Hillary and I explained to Chelsea what was going on; she didn't like it but seemed to take it in stride. She knew her mother a lot better than her assailants did.

Still, it was wearing on all of us. I had been struggling

for months to keep my anger from interfering with my work, as I dealt with the budget fight, Bosnia, Northern Ireland, and Rabin's death. But it had been very hard; now I was anxious for Hillary and Chelsea as well. I was also concerned about all the other people being pulled into the congressional hearings and into Starr's net who were being hurt emotionally and financially.

Five days after the billing records were turned over, Hillary was scheduled to do an interview with Barbara Walters so that she could discuss her new book, **It Takes a Village.** Instead, the interview turned into a session on the billing records. **It Takes a Village** became a bestseller anyway, as Hillary bravely set out from Washington on a book tour across the country and found legions of friendly and supportive Americans who cared more about what she had to say about improving children's lives than about what Ken Starr, Al D'Amato, William Safire, and their friends had to say about her.

Those boys certainly seemed to get a big kick out of beating up on Hillary. My only consolation was the sure knowledge, rooted in twenty-five years of close observation, that she was a lot tougher than they would ever be. Some guys don't like that in a woman, but it was one of the reasons I loved her.

In early February, as the presidential campaign kicked into high gear, I returned to New Hampshire to highlight both the positive impact of my policies there and my commitment not to forget about the state after I took office. Although I had no primary opponent, I wanted to carry New Hampshire in November, and I needed to deal with the one issue I thought could keep me from doing it: guns.

One Saturday morning, I went to a diner in Manchester full of men who were deer hunters and NRA members. In impromptu remarks, I told them that I knew they had defeated their Democratic congressman, Dick Swett, in 1994 because he voted for the Brady bill and the assault weapons ban. Several of them nodded in agreement. Those hunters were good men who had been frightened by the NRA; I thought they could be stampeded again in 1996 only if no one presented them with the other side of the argument in language they could understand. So I gave it my best shot: "I know the NRA told you to defeat Congressman Swett. Now, if you missed a day, or even an hour, in the deer woods because of the Brady bill or the assault weapons ban, I want you to vote against me, too, because I asked him to support those bills. On the other hand, if you didn't, then they didn't tell you the truth, and you need to get even."

A few days later, at the Library of Congress, I signed the Telecommunications Act, a sweeping overhaul of the laws affecting an industry that was already one-sixth of our economy. The act increased competition, innovation, and access to what Al Gore had dubbed the "information superhighway." There had been months of sparring over complex economic issues, with the Republicans favoring greater concentration of ownership in media and telecommunications markets, and the White House and the Democrats supporting greater competition, especially in local and long-distance telephone service. With Al Gore taking the lead for the White House and Speaker Gingrich in his positive entrepreneurial mode, we reached what I thought was a fair compromise, and in the end the bill passed almost unanimously. It also contained a requirement that new television sets include the V-chip, which I had first endorsed at the Gores' annual family conference, to allow parents to control their children's access to programs; by the end of the month, executives from most of the television networks would agree to have a rating system for their programs in place by 1997. Even more important, the act mandated discounted Internet access rates for schools, libraries, and hospitals; the so-called E-rate would eventually save public entities about $2 billion a year.

The next day, the bloom came off the Irish rose, as Gerry Adams called to tell me the IRA had ended its cease-fire, allegedly because of foot-dragging by John Major and the Unionists, including their insistence on IRA arms decommissioning in return for Sinn Fein's participation in the political life of Northern Ireland. Later that day a bomb exploded at Canary Wharf in London.

The IRA would keep it up for more than a year, at great cost to themselves. While they killed two soldiers and two civilians and injured many others, they suffered the deaths of two IRA operatives, the breakup of their bombing team in Britain, and the arrest of numerous IRA operatives in Northern Ireland. By the end of the month, peace vigils were being held all over Northern Ireland to demonstrate the continuing support of ordinary citizens for peace. John Major and John Bruton said they would resume talks with Sinn Fein if the IRA reinstated its cease-fire. With John Hume's support, the White House decided to maintain contact with Adams, waiting for the moment when the march toward peace could resume.

The peace process in the Middle East was also threatened in late February, as two Hamas bombs killed twenty-six people. With elections coming up in Israel, I assumed

Hamas was trying to defeat Prime Minister Peres and provoke the Israelis to elect a hard-line government that would not make peace with the PLO. We pushed Arafat to do more to prevent terrorist acts. As I had told him when we signed the original agreement back in 1993, he could never be the most militant Palestinian again, and if he tried to keep one foot in the peace camp and the other on the terrorist side he would eventually be undone.

We also had trouble closer to home when Cuba shot down two civilian planes flown by the anti-Castro group Brothers to the Rescue, killing four men. Castro hated the group and the leaflets critical of him that it had dropped over Havana in the past. Cuba claimed the planes were shot in its airspace. They weren't, but even if they had been, the downings still would have violated international law.

I suspended charter flights to Cuba, restricted travel by Cuban officials in the United States, expanded the reach of Radio Martí, which beamed pro-democracy messages into Cuba, and asked Congress to authorize compensation out of Cuba's blocked assets in the United States to the families of the men who were killed. Madeleine Albright asked the United Nations to impose sanctions and went to Miami to deliver a fiery speech to the Cuban-American community, telling them that the shootdown reflected cowardice, "not **cojones**." Her macho remarks made her a heroine among South Florida's Cubans.

I also committed to signing a version of the Helms-Burton bill, which stiffened the embargo against Cuba and restricted the President's authority to lift it without congressional approval. Supporting the bill was good election-year politics in Florida, but it undermined whatever chance I might have if I won a second term to lift the embargo in return for positive changes within Cuba. It almost appeared that Castro was trying to force us to maintain the embargo as an excuse for the economic failures of his regime. If that wasn't the objective, then Cuba had made a colossal error. I later received word from Castro, indirectly of course, that the shootdown was a mistake. Apparently he had issued earlier orders to fire on any aircraft that violated Cuban airspace and had failed to withdraw them when the Cubans knew the Brothers to the Rescue planes were coming.

In the last week of the month, after visiting areas devastated by recent flooding in Washington, Oregon, Idaho, and Pennsylvania, I met with the new Japanese prime minister in Santa Monica, California. Ryutaro Hashimoto had been Mickey Kantor's counterpart before becoming the head of the Japanese government. An avid practitioner of kendo, a Japanese martial art, Hashimoto was a tough, intelligent man who enjoyed combat of all kinds. But he was also a leader with whom we could work; he and Kantor had concluded twenty trade agreements, our exports to Japan were up 80 percent, and our bilateral trade deficit had declined for three years in a row.

The month ended on a high note as Hillary and I celebrated Chelsea's sixteenth birthday by taking her to see **Les Misérables** at the National Theatre, then hosting a busload of her friends for a weekend at Camp David. We liked all Chelsea's friends, and we loved seeing them shooting at one another with paintball guns in the woods, bowling and playing other games, and generally being kids as their high school years were drawing to a close. The best part of the weekend for me was giving Chelsea a driving lesson around the Camp David compound. I missed driving and wanted Chelsea to enjoy it, and to do it safely and well.

The Middle East peace process was shaken again in the first weeks of March when, on successive days, a new round of Hamas bombs in Jerusalem and Tel Aviv killed more than thirty people and wounded many more. Among the dead were children, a Palestinian nurse who lived and worked among her Jewish friends, and two young American women. I met with their families in New Jersey and was deeply moved by their steadfast commitment to peace as the only way to prevent more children from being killed in the future. In a televised address to the people of Israel, I stated the obvious, that the terrorist acts were "aimed not just at killing innocent people but at killing the growing hope for peace in the Middle East."

On March 12, Jordan's King Hussein flew on Air Force One with me to a Summit of Peacemakers hosted by President Mubarak in Sharm el-Sheikh, a beautiful resort on the Red Sea favored by European scuba-diving enthusiasts. Hussein had come to see me at the White House a few days earlier to condemn the Hamas bombings and was determined to rally the Arab world to the cause of peace. I really enjoyed the long flight with him. We had always gotten along well, but we had become closer friends and allies in the aftermath of Rabin's assassination.

Leaders of twenty-nine nations from the Arab world, Europe, Asia, and North America, including Boris Yeltsin and UN Secretary-General Boutros Boutros-Ghali, joined Peres and Arafat at Sharm el-Sheikh. President Mubarak and I co-chaired the meeting. We and our staffs had worked day and night to ensure that we would come out of the conference with a clear and concrete commitment to fighting terror and preserving the peace process.

For the first time, the Arab world stood with Israel in condemning terror and promising to work against it. The united front was essential to give Peres the support necessary to keep the peace process going and to reopen Gaza, so that the thousands of Palestinians who lived there but had jobs in Israel could go back to work; it was also necessary to give Arafat the backing to make an all-out effort against the terrorists, without which Israeli support for peace would collapse.

On the thirteenth, I flew to Tel Aviv to discuss specific steps the United States could take to help the Israeli military and police. In a meeting with Prime Minister Peres and his cabinet, I pledged $100 million in support and asked Warren Christopher and CIA director John Deutch to stay in Israel to accelerate the implementation of our joint efforts. In the press conference with Peres after our meeting, I acknowledged the difficulty of providing complete protection from "young men who have bought some apocalyptic version of Islam and politics that causes them to strap their bodies with bombs" in order to commit suicide and kill innocent children. But I said we could improve our capacity to prevent such events and to break up the networks of money and national support that made them possible. I also used the occasion to urge congressional action on the anti-terrorism legislation that had been held up for more than a year.

After the press conference and a question-and-answer session with young Israeli students in Tel Aviv, I met with the Likud Party leader, Benjamin Netanyahu. The Hamas bombings had made a Likud victory in the election more likely. I wanted Netanyahu to know that if he won, I would be his partner in the fight against terror, but I also wanted him to stick with the peace process.

I couldn't go home without making the trip up Mount Herzl to visit Rabin's grave. I knelt, said a prayer, and, following Jewish custom, placed a small stone on Yitzhak's marble marker. I also took another small rock from the ground around the grave home with me as a reminder of my friend and the job he had left for me to do.

While I was preoccupied with trouble in the Middle East, China roiled the waters of the Taiwan Strait by "test"-firing three missiles close to Taiwan in an apparent attempt to discourage the Taiwanese politicians from pushing for independence in the election campaign then under way. Ever since President Carter normalized relations with mainland China, the United States had followed a consistent policy of recognizing "one China" while continuing to have good relations with Taiwan, and saying that the two sides should resolve their differences peacefully. We had never said whether we would or wouldn't come to the defense of Taiwan if it were attacked.

It seemed to me that the Middle East and Taiwan were polar opposite foreign policy problems. If nothing was done by political leaders in the Middle East, things would get worse. By contrast, I thought that if the politicians in China and Taiwan didn't do anything foolish, the problem would resolve itself over time. Taiwan was an economic powerhouse that had moved from dictatorship to democracy. It wanted no part of the mainland's bureaucratic communism. On the other hand, Taiwanese businesspeople were investing heavily in China, and there was travel back and forth. China liked the Taiwanese investment, but could not agree to give up its claim to sovereignty over the island; finding the right balance between economic pragmatism and aggressive nationalism was a constant challenge for China's leaders, especially during election season in Taiwan. I thought China had gone too far with the missile tests, and quickly, but without fanfare, I ordered a carrier group from the U.S. Navy's Pacific fleet to sail to the Taiwan Strait. The crisis passed.

After a rocky start in February, Bob Dole won all the Republican primaries in March, wrapping up his party's nomination with a late-month victory in California. Even though Senator Phil Gramm, who ran to the right of Dole, would have been easier to beat, I was pulling for Dole. No election is a sure thing, and if I lost, I believed the country would be in more solid and more moderate hands with him.

While Dole was moving toward the nomination, I campaigned in several states, including an event in Maryland with General McCaffrey and Jesse Jackson to highlight our efforts to stem teen drug use, and a stop at Harman International, a manufacturer of premier speakers in Northridge, California, to announce that the economy had produced 8.4 million jobs in just over three years since I took office; I had promised 8 million in four years. Middle-class incomes were also beginning to rise. In the last two years, two-thirds of the new jobs created were in industries that paid above the minimum wage.

During the course of the month, we didn't reach agreement on the appropriations bills still outstanding, so I signed three more CRs and sent my budget for the next fiscal year up to Capitol Hill. Meanwhile, the House continued to follow the NRA, voting to repeal the assault weapons ban and to delete from the anti-terrorism legislation sections the gun lobby opposed.

At the end of the month, I initiated an effort to accelerate the approval of anti-cancer drugs by the Food and Drug Administration. Al Gore, Donna Shalala, and FDA administrator David Kessler had worked to cut the average approval process for new drugs from thirty-three months in 1987 to just under a year in 1994. The latest approval for an AIDS drug was issued in just forty-two days. It was important for the FDA to determine how drugs would affect the body before they were approved, but the process should be as speedy as safety permitted; lives were riding on it.

Finally, on March 29, eight months after Bob Rubin and I had first requested it, I signed a bill to increase the debt limit. The Damocles sword of default was no longer hanging over our budget negotiations.

On April 3, with springtime in full bloom in Washington, I was working in the Oval Office when I received word that the air force jet carrying Ron Brown and a U.S. trade and investment delegation he had organized to increase the economic benefits of peace to the Balkans had flown off course in bad weather and crashed into St. John's Mountain near Dubrovnik, Croatia. Everyone on board was killed. Barely a week earlier, on their trip to Europe, Hillary and Chelsea had been on the same plane with some of the same crew members.

I was devastated. Ron was my friend and my best political advisor in the cabinet. As chairman of the DNC, he had brought the Democratic Party back from our loss in 1988 and played a pivotal role in uniting the Democrats for the 1992 election. In the aftermath of the 1994 congressional election losses, Ron had remained upbeat, lifting everyone's spirits with his confident prediction that we were doing the right things on the economy and would win in 1996. He had revitalized the Commerce Department, modernizing the bureaucracy and using it to further not only our economic objectives but our larger interests in the Balkans and Northern Ireland. He had also worked hard to increase U.S. exports to ten "emerging markets" that were sure to loom large in the twenty-first century, including Poland, Turkey, Brazil, Argentina, South Africa, and Indonesia. After he died I received a letter from a business executive who had worked with him, saying he was "the finest Secretary of Commerce the United States ever had."

Hillary and I drove to Ron's house to see his wife, Alma, and his children, Tracey and Michael, and Michael's wife, Tammy. They were part of our extended family, and I was relieved to see them already surrounded by loving friends and dealing with their loss by telling Ron Brown stories; there were many worth repeating from the long journey he had traveled from his boyhood home at the old Hotel Teresa in Harlem to the pinnacle of American politics and public service.

When we left Alma, we went downtown to the Commerce Department to talk to the employees, who had lost both their leader and their friends. One of those who died was a young man Hillary and I knew well. Adam Darling was the idealistic and spunky son of a Methodist minister who had entered our lives in 1992 when he made news by riding his bicycle across America to support the Clinton-Gore ticket.

A few days later, just two weeks before the first anniversary of the Oklahoma City bombing, Hillary and I planted a dogwood on the back lawn of the White House in memory of Ron and the other Americans who had died in Croatia. Then we flew to Oklahoma City to dedicate a new day-care center to replace the one lost in the bombing and to visit with the victims' families who were there. At the University of Central Oklahoma, in nearby Edmond, I told the students that while we had apprehended more terrorists in the last three years than in any other previous time in our history, terror required us to do more: it was the threat of their generation just as nuclear war had been the threat for those of us who had grown up during the Cold War.

The next afternoon we made the sad trip to Dover Air Force Base in Delaware, where America brings home those who have died in service to the nation. After the caskets had been solemnly carried off the plane, I read the names of all who had perished on Ron Brown's plane and reminded those in attendance that tomorrow was Easter, which for Christians marks the passage from loss and despair to hope and redemption. The Bible says, "Though we weep through the night, joy will come in the morning." I took that verse as my theme for Ron's eulogy on April 10 at the National Cathedral, because for all of us who knew him, Ron was always our joy in the morning. I looked at his casket and said, "I want to say to my friend just one last time: Thank you; if it weren't for you, I wouldn't be here." We laid Ron to rest in Arlington National Cemetery; by then I was so exhausted and grief-stricken after the terrible ordeal that I could hardly stand. Chelsea, hiding her tears behind sunglasses, put her arm around me and I laid my head on her shoulder.

In the awful week between the crash and the funeral, I carried on with my duties as best I could. First, I signed the new farm bill. Just two weeks earlier, I had signed legislation that improved the farm credit system, to make more loans available to farmers at lower interest rates. Although I thought the new farm bill failed to provide an adequate safety net for family farms, I signed it anyway because if the current law expired without a replacement, farmers would have to plant their next crop under the completely inadequate support program put in place back in 1948. Also, the bill had many provisions I did support: greater flexibility for farmers in choosing what crops to plant without losing aid; money for economic development in rural communities; funds to help farmers prevent soil erosion, air and water pollution, and the loss of wetlands; and $200 million to begin work on one of my top environmental priorities, the restoration of Florida's Everglades, which had been damaged by extensive development and sugarcane growing.

On the ninth I signed legislation granting the President a line-item veto. Most governors had the authority and every President since Ulysses Grant in 1869 had sought it. The provision was also part of the Republican "Contract with America," and I had endorsed it in my 1992 campaign. I was pleased that it had finally passed, and I thought its main utility would be in the leverage it gave future Presidents to keep wasteful items out of budgets in the first place. Signing the bill had one significant downside: Senator Robert Byrd, the most respected authority in Congress on the Constitution, considered it an unconstitutional infringement on the legislative branch by the executive. Byrd hated the line-item veto with a passion most people reserve for more personal injuries, and I don't think he ever forgave me for signing the bill.

On the day of Ron Brown's memorial service, I vetoed a

bill that banned a procedure its proponents called "partial-birth" abortion. The legislation as described by its anti-abortion advocates was highly popular; it prohibited a type of late-term abortion that seemed so heartless and cruel that many pro-choice citizens thought it should be banned. It was a bit more complicated than that. As far as I could determine, the procedure was rare, and it was pre-dominantly performed on women whose doctors had told them it was necessary to preserve their own lives or health, often because they were carrying hydrocephalic babies who were certain to die before, during, or shortly after child-birth. The question was how badly damaged the mothers' bodies would be if they carried their doomed babies to term, and whether doing so could render them unable to bear other children. In such cases, it was far from clear that banning the operation was "pro-life."

I thought it should be a decision for the mother and her doctor. When I vetoed the bill, I stood with five women who had undergone partial-birth abortions. Three of them, a Catholic, an evangelical Christian, and an Orthodox Jew, were devoutly pro-life. One of them said she had prayed to God to take her life and spare her child, and all of them said they had consented to the late-term procedure only because their doctors had told them their babies could not have lived, and they wanted to be able to have other children.

If you consider how long it took me to explain why I vetoed the bill, you understand why it was terrible poli-tics to do so. I vetoed it because no one had shown me evidence that the women's advocates had been untruthful in saying the procedure was necessary or that there was another alternative procedure that would have protected the mothers and their reproductive capacity. I had offered to sign a bill banning all late-term abortions except in cases where the life or health of the mother was at risk. Several states still permitted them, and such action could have prevented far more abortions than the partial-birth bill, but the anti-abortion forces in Congress killed it. They were looking for a way to erode **Roe** v. **Wade;** besides, there was no political advantage to a bill that even most pro-choice senators and representatives would support.

On April 12, I named Mickey Kantor secretary of commerce and his able deputy, Charlene Barshefsky, the new U.S. trade representative. I also named Frank Raines, vice chairman of Fannie Mae, the Federal National Mortgage Association, to be head of the Office of Management and Budget. Raines had the right combination of intellect, knowledge of the budget, and political skills to succeed at OMB, and was the first African-American ever to hold the job.

On April 14, Hillary and I boarded Air Force One for a busy one-week trip to Korea, Japan, and Russia. On South Korea's beautiful Cheju Island, President Kim Young-Sam and I proposed that we convene four-party talks with North Korea and China, the other signers of the forty-six-year-old armistice concluding the Korean War, in order to provide a framework within which North and South Korea could talk and, we hoped, make a final peace agreement. North Korea had been saying it wanted peace, and I believed we had to discover whether they were serious about it.

I flew from South Korea to Tokyo, where Prime Minister Hashimoto and I issued a declaration designed to reaffirm and modernize our security relationship, including greater cooperation in counterterrorism, which the Japanese were eager for after the sarin gas subway attack. The United States also pledged to maintain its troop presence of about 100,000 in Japan, Korea, and the rest of East Asia, while reducing our profile on the Japanese island of Okinawa, where criminal incidents involving U.S. military personnel had increased opposition to our presence there. America had a big economic stake in maintaining peace and stability in Asia. The Asians bought half our exports, and those purchases supported three million jobs.

Before leaving Japan, I visited U.S. forces from the Seventh Fleet aboard the USS **Independence,** attended an elegant state dinner hosted by the emperor and empress at the Imperial Palace, made a speech to the Japanese Diet, and enjoyed a lunch hosted by the prime minister that featured American-born sumo wrestlers and an outstanding Japanese jazz saxophonist.

To reinforce the importance of American-Japanese ties, I had named former vice president Walter Mondale as our ambassador. His prestige and skill at handling difficult problems sent an unmistakable message to the Japanese that they were important to the United States.

We flew on to St. Petersburg, Russia. On April 19, the first anniversary of the Oklahoma City bombing, Al Gore went to Oklahoma to speak for the administration, while I marked the occasion during a visit to the Russian military cemetery and prepared for a summit on nuclear safety with Boris Yeltsin and the G-7 leaders. Yeltsin had suggested the summit to highlight our commitment to the Comprehensive Test Ban Treaty, START I and START II, and our joint efforts to secure and destroy nuclear weapons and materials. We also agreed to improve safety at nuclear power plants, end the dumping of nuclear materials in the oceans, and help Ukrainian president Leonid Kuchma close the Chernobyl power plant within four years. Ten years after the tragic accident there, it was still running.

On the twenty-fourth, I was back home, but not out of foreign affairs. President Elias Hrawi of Lebanon was at the White House at a tense moment in the Middle East. In response to a barrage of Katyusha rockets fired into Israel from southern Lebanon by Hezbollah, Shimon Peres had ordered retaliatory attacks that killed many civilians. I had much sympathy for Lebanon; it was caught up in the conflict between Israel and Syria, and was full of terrorist operatives. I reaffirmed America's steadfast support for UN Security Council Resolution 425, which calls for a truly independent Lebanon.

The news from the Middle East was not all bad. While I was meeting with the Lebanese president, Yasser Arafat persuaded the PLO executive council to amend its charter to recognize Israel's right to exist, a policy shift very important to the Israelis. Two days later Warren Christopher and our Middle East envoy, Dennis Ross, secured an agreement among Israel, Lebanon, and Syria to end the Lebanese crisis and enable us to get back to the business of peace.

Shimon Peres came to see me at the end of the month to sign an anti-terrorism cooperative agreement that included $50 million for our joint efforts to reduce Israel's vulnerability to the kind of suicide bombings that had recently caused such havoc and heartbreak.

Just a week earlier, I had signed the anti-terrorism legislation that the Congress had finally passed, a full year after Oklahoma City. In the end, the bill had won strong bipartisan support after the deletion of the provisions requiring traceable markers in black and smokeless powder and giving federal authorities the ability to conduct the kind of roving wiretaps on suspected terrorists that already could be used against organized crime figures. The bill would give us more tools and resources to prevent terrorist attacks, disrupt terrorist organizations, and increase controls over chemical and biological weapons. The Congress also agreed to let us put chemical taggants in plastic explosives and left open the option requiring them in other types of explosives not clearly prohibited by the law.

April was another interesting month in Whitewater World. On the second, Kenneth Starr appeared in the Fifth Circuit Court of Appeals in New Orleans on behalf of four big tobacco companies that, at the same time, were engaged in a heated dispute with my administration over their marketing of cigarettes to teenagers and how much authority the FDA had to stop them. Starr didn't see any conflict of interest in keeping up a lucrative law practice in which he was paid large sums by my adversaries. **USA Today** had already revealed that in a court appearance defending the Wisconsin school voucher program, which I opposed, Starr had been paid not by the state but by the ultra-conservative Bradley Foundation. Starr was investigating the Resolution Trust Corporation for its inquiry into the conduct of our accuser, L. Jean Lewis, while the RTC was negotiating with his law firm to settle a suit the agency had filed against the firm for its negligence in its representation of a failed Denver savings-and-loan institution. And, of course, Starr had offered to go on television to defend Paula Jones's lawsuit. Robert Fiske had been removed as the Whitewater independent counsel on the tenuous claim that his appointment by Janet Reno created the appearance of a conflict of interest. Now we had a prosecutor with real conflicts.

As I said, Starr and his allies in Congress and on the federal courts had created a new definition of "conflict of interest": anyone who might remotely be favorable or, as in Fiske's case, even fair to Hillary and me was by definition conflicted; Ken Starr's blatant political and economic conflicts of interest and the extreme bias against me they reflected presented no problem at all to his assumption of unlimited and unaccountable authority to go after us and many other innocent people.

Starr and his allies' curious view of what constituted a conflict of interest was never more apparent than in their treatment of Judge Henry Woods, a highly respected veteran jurist and former FBI agent who was assigned to preside over the trial of Governor Jim Guy Tucker and others whom Starr had indicted on federal charges completely unrelated to Whitewater. They involved the purchase of cable television stations. At first, neither Starr nor Tucker objected to Woods hearing the case; he was a Democrat but had never been close to the governor. Judge Woods dismissed the indictments after he determined that Starr had exceeded his authority under the independent counsel law because the charges had nothing to do with Whitewater.

Starr appealed Woods's decision to the Eighth Circuit Court and requested that the judge be thrown off the case for bias. The members of the appeals panel that heard the case were conservative Republicans appointed by Reagan and Bush. The lead judge, Pasco Bowman, rivaled David Sentelle in his right-wing politics. Without even giving Judge Woods an opportunity to defend himself, the court not only reversed his decision and reinstated the indictment but also kicked him off the case, citing not court records, but newspaper and magazine articles critical of him. One of the articles filled with false charges was written by Justice Jim Johnson in the right-wing **Washington Times.** After the ruling Woods pointed out that he was the only judge in American history to be removed from a case on the basis of press articles. When another enterprising defense lawyer appealed to the Eighth Circuit to get a trial judge removed and cited the Woods case as precedent, a different, less ideological panel refused the request and criticized the Woods decision, saying it was both unprecedented and unjustified. Of course it was, but there were different rules for Whitewater.

On April 17, even the **New York Times** couldn't take it any longer. Calling Starr "defiantly blind to his appearance problems and indifferent to the special obligation he owes to the American people" for his refusal "to divest himself of his own political and financial baggage," the **Times** said Starr should step down. I couldn't deny that the grand old paper still had a conscience; they didn't want Hillary and me handed over to a lynch mob. The rest of the Whitewater media was silent on the subject.

On April 28, I gave four and a half hours of videotaped testimony in another Whitewater trial. In this one, Starr had indicted Jim and Susan McDougal and Jim Guy Tucker for misappropriating funds from Madison Guaranty and from the Small Business Administration. The loans were not repaid, but the prosecutors didn't dispute that the defendants intended to repay them; instead, they were charged with crimes arising from the fact that the borrowed money was used for purposes other than those described on the loan application papers.

The trial had nothing to do with Whitewater, Hillary,

or me. I mention it here because David Hale dragged me into it. He had swindled the SBA out of millions of dollars and was cooperating with Starr in hopes of getting a reduced prison sentence. In his testimony at the trial, Hale repeated his charge that I had pressured him to make a $300,000 loan to the McDougals.

I testified that Hale's account of his conversations with me was false and that I knew nothing of the dealings between the parties that had given rise to the charges. The defense attorneys believed that once the jury knew that Hale had lied about my role in his dealings with the McDougals and Tucker, his entire testimony would be compromised and the prosecutor's case would collapse, and therefore the defendants themselves did not need to testify. There were two difficulties with the strategy. First, against all advice, Jim McDougal insisted on testifying in his own defense. He had done so in a previous trial arising out of the collapse of Madison Guaranty in 1990, and he had been acquitted. But the manic depression from which he suffered had progressed since then, and according to many observers, his rambling, erratic testimony damaged not just himself but also Susan and Jim Guy Tucker, who did not testify in their own defense, even after McDougal had unwittingly imperiled them.

The other problem was that the jury didn't have all the facts about David Hale's connections to my political adversaries; some of them weren't yet known, and others were ruled inadmissible by the judge. The jury didn't know about the money and support Hale had been receiving from a clandestine effort known as the Arkansas Project.

The Arkansas Project was funded by the ultra-conservative billionaire Richard Mellon Scaife from Pittsburgh, who had also pumped money into the **American Spectator** to fund its negative stories on Hillary and me. For example, the project had paid one former state trooper $10,000 for the ridiculous yarn accusing me of drug smuggling. Scaife's people also worked closely with allies of Newt Gingrich. When David Brock was working on the **Spectator** article featuring the two Arkansas state troopers who claimed they had procured women for me, Brock had received not only his salary from the magazine but also secret payments from Chicago businessman Peter Smith, the finance chairman of Newt's political action committee.

Most of the Arkansas Project's efforts centered on David Hale. Working through Parker Dozhier, a former aide to Justice Jim Johnson, the project set up a haven for Hale at Dozhier's bait shop outside Hot Springs, where Dozhier gave Hale cash and the use of his car and fishing cabin while Hale was cooperating with Starr. During this time Hale also received free legal advice from Ted Olson, a friend of Starr's and a lawyer for the Arkansas Project and the **American Spectator.** Olson later became the solicitor general in President George W. Bush's Justice Department after a Senate hearing in which he was less than candid about his work for the Arkansas Project.

For whatever reasons, the jury convicted all three defendants on several of the charges against them. In his closing, the lead OIC prosecutor went out of his way to state that I was not "on trial" and that there had "been no allegations of wrongdoing" directed at me. But Starr now had what he really wanted: three people he could pressure to give him something damaging on us in order to avoid a jail sentence. Since there was nothing to tell, I didn't worry about it, though I regretted the cost to the taxpayers of Starr's far-flung efforts, and the mounting casualties among people in Arkansas whose principal sin was that they had known Hillary and me before I became President.

I also had serious doubts about the jury verdict. Jim McDougal's mental illness had progressed to the point where he was probably not competent to stand trial, much less testify. And I felt that Susan McDougal and Jim Guy Tucker might have been convicted only because they were caught up in Jim McDougal's downward mental spiral and David Hale's desperate effort to save himself.

May was a relatively quiet month on the legislative front, which enabled me to do some campaigning in several states and to enjoy some of the ceremonial duties of the presidency, including the presentation of a Congressional Gold Medal to Billy Graham, the annual WETA-TV "In Performance" concert on the South Lawn, featuring Aaron Neville and Linda Ronstadt, and a state visit from the Greek president, Constantinos Stephanopoulos. When we were involved in high-stakes foreign and domestic problems, I often had a hard time relaxing enough to fully enjoy such things.

On May 15, I announced the latest round of community policing grants, which brought us to 43,000 of the 100,000 new police officers I'd promised. That same day Bob Dole announced that he was resigning from the Senate to pursue his presidential campaign full-time. He called to tell me of his decision and I wished him well. It was the only sensible course for him; he didn't have time to campaign against me and be majority leader, and the positions the Senate and House Republicans were taking on the budget and other matters were hurting him in his presidential race.

The next day I called for a global ban on anti-personnel land mines. There were about 100 million land mines, mostly relics of past wars, just beneath the surface of the earth in Europe, Asia, Africa, and Latin America. Many of them had been there for decades but were still lethal; twenty-five thousand people were killed or maimed by them every year. The damage they were doing, especially to children in places like Angola and Cambodia, was awful. There were a lot of them in Bosnia, too; the only casualty our troops had suffered came when an army sergeant was killed trying to pick up a land mine. I committed the United States to destroy four million of our own so-called dumb, or non–self-destructing, mines by 1999 and to help other nations with their demining efforts. Soon we would be financing more than half the cost of demining worldwide.

Unfortunately, what should have been a life-affirming event was marked by yet another tragedy, as I announced that our chief of naval operations, Admiral Mike Boorda, had died that afternoon of a self-inflicted gunshot wound. Boorda was the first enlisted man ever to rise through the ranks to the navy's highest position. His suicide was triggered by news stories alleging that he had worn two Vietnam battle ribbons on his uniform that he hadn't earned. The facts were in dispute and, in any case, should not have diminished his standing after a long career marked by devotion, stellar service, and evident courage. Like Vince Foster, he had never had his honor and integrity questioned before. There's a big difference between being told that you are no good at your job and being told that you're just no good.

In mid-May, I signed the reauthorization of the Ryan White CARE Act, which funded medical and support services for people with HIV and AIDS, the leading cause of death for Americans between the ages of twenty-five and forty-four. Now we had doubled the money available for AIDS care since 1993, and one-third of the 900,000 people with HIV were receiving services under the act.

That same week I also signed a bill known as Megan's Law. Named after a little girl who had been killed by a sex offender, the legislation gave states the power to notify communities of the presence of violent sex offenders; several studies had shown they are rarely rehabilitated.

After the ceremony I flew to Missouri to campaign with Dick Gephardt. I really admired Gephardt, a hard-working, smart, kind man who looked twenty years younger than he was. Even though he was the Democratic leader in the House, he regularly came home on weekends to go into neighborhoods and knock on his constituents' doors to talk with them. Often, Dick would give me a list of things he wanted me to do for his district. While lots of congressmen asked for things from time to time, the only other member who regularly provided me a typed "to do" list was Senator Ted Kennedy.

At the end of the month, I announced that the Veterans Administration would provide compensation to Vietnam veterans for a series of severe illnesses, including cancers, liver disorders, and Hodgkin's disease, that were associated with exposure to Agent Orange, a cause long championed by Vietnam veterans, Senators John Kerry and John McCain, and by the late Admiral Bud Zumwalt.

On May 29, I stayed up until well past midnight watching the election returns in Israel. It was a real cliffhanger, as Bibi Netanyahu defeated Shimon Peres by less than 1 percent of the vote. Peres won the Arab vote by a large majority, but Netanyahu beat him badly enough among Jewish voters, who made up more than 90 percent of the electorate, to win. He did it by promising to be tougher on terrorism and slower with the peace process, and by using American-style television ads, including some attacking Peres that were made with the help of a Republican media advisor from New York. Peres resisted the pleas of his supporters to answer the ads until the very end of the campaign, and by then it was too late. I thought Shimon had done a good job as prime minister, and he had given his entire life to the state of Israel, but in 1996, by a narrow margin, Netanyahu proved to be a better politician. I was eager to determine whether and how he and I could work together to keep the peace process going.

In June, against the backdrop of the presidential campaign, I focused on two issues, education and the disturbing rash of black church burnings then sweeping the country. At the Princeton University commencement, I outlined a plan to open the doors of college to all Americans and to make at least two years of college as universally available as high school: a tax credit modeled on Georgia's Hope Scholarships of $1,500 (the average cost of community college tuition) for two years of higher education; a tax deduction of $10,000 a year for all higher education beyond the first two years; a $1,000 scholarship to students in the top 5 percent of every high school graduating class; funds to increase college work-study positions from 700,000 to 1 million; and annual increases in Pell Grants for lower-income students.

In mid-month I went to Grover Cleveland Middle School in Albuquerque, New Mexico, to support the community's curfew program, one of several such efforts across the country requiring young people to be in their homes after a certain hour on school nights; they had led to a decline in crime and an improvement in student learning. I also endorsed the policy of requiring school uniforms for elementary and middle school students. Almost without exception, school districts that required uniforms experienced higher student attendance, less violence, and increased student learning. The distinctions between poor and wealthier students diminished as well.

Some of my critics ridiculed my emphasis on what they called "small bore" issues like curfews, uniforms, character education programs, and the V-chip, saying it was all politics, as well as a reflection of my inability to pass big programs in the Republican Congress. That was inaccurate. At the time, we were also implementing the large education and crime programs passed in my first two years, and I had another major education initiative before Congress. But I knew that federal money and laws could only give Americans the tools to make their lives better; the real changes still had to be effected by citizens at the grassroots level. Partly as a result of our promotion of school uniforms, more and more school districts embraced them, with positive results.

On June 12, I was in Greeleyville, South Carolina, to dedicate the new Mount Zion African Methodist Episcopal Church, after the congregation's old church had been burned. Less than a week earlier, a church in Charlotte, North Carolina, had become the thirtieth black church to be burned in the previous eighteen months. The whole black community in America was in an uproar and expected me to do something about it. I endorsed bipartisan legislation to make it easier for federal prosecutors to punish those who burn houses of worship, and pledged federal loan guarantees to support low-interest loans for the rebuilding efforts. The church burnings seemed to feed off one another, much as a rash of synagogue defacements had in 1992. They weren't connected by a conspiracy, but by a contagion of the heart, a hatred of those who are different.

During this time, I also had to acknowledge a problem in my White House operation so severe that I felt it was the first issue of my administration that merited an independent investigation.

In early June, news reports revealed that three years earlier, in 1993, my White House Office of Personnel Security had obtained from the FBI hundreds of FBI file summaries on people who had been cleared for entry into the Bush and Reagan White Houses. The files had been obtained when the office was attempting to replace security files on current White House employees, since those files had been taken away by the departing Bush administration for deposit in the Bush Library. The White House had no business possessing confidential FBI reports on Republicans. I was outraged when I heard about it.

On June 9, Leon Panetta and I apologized for the incident. Within a week, Louis Freeh announced that the FBI had wrongly turned over 408 files to the White House. A few days later, Janet Reno asked Ken Starr to investigate the files case. In 2000, the OIC found that the incident had been simply a mistake. The White House had not engaged in any kind of political espionage—the Secret Service had given the Personnel Security Office an outdated list of White House employees, which included Republicans' names, and this was the list that had been sent to the White House.

Late in June, at the annual Gore family conference in

Nashville, I called for an expansion of the family leave law to allow people to take up to twenty-four hours a year, or three more workdays, to attend parent-teacher conferences at their children's school or to take their children, or a spouse, or their parents for routine medical care.

The problem of balancing work and family was weighing heavily on me because of the toll it was taking on the White House. Bill Galston, a brilliant member of the Domestic Policy Council staff whom I had first met through the DLC and who was a continuous source of good ideas, had recently resigned to spend more time with his ten-year-old son: "My boy keeps asking where I am. You can get somebody else to do this job; no one else can do that job. I have to go home."

My deputy chief of staff, Erskine Bowles, who had become a close friend and golfing partner and who was a superb manager and our best liaison to the business community, was going home, too. His wife, Crandall, a Wellesley classmate of Hillary's, ran a big textile company and had to travel a lot. Two of their kids were in college; their youngest was about to start his senior year in high school. Erskine told me he loved his job, "but my boy should not be at home alone in his last year in high school. I don't want him ever to wonder whether he was the most important thing in the world to his parents. I'm going home."

I respected and agreed with the decisions Bill and Erskine had made, and I was thankful that Hillary and I lived and worked in the White House so we had no long commutes to and from work, and at least one of us was almost always with Chelsea for dinner at night and when she got up in the morning. But the experience of my staff members brought home the fact that all too many Americans, in all kinds of jobs earning widely different incomes, went to work every day worried sick that they were neglecting their kids for their jobs. The United States provided less support for balancing work and family than any other wealthy nation, and I wanted to change that.

Unfortunately, the Republican majority in Congress were opposed to imposing any new requirements on employers. A young boy had recently approached me and offered to tell me a joke; as he said, "Once you become President, it's hard to find a joke you can tell in public." Here it is: "Being President with this Congress is like standing in the middle of a cemetery. There are a lot of people under you, but nobody is listening." He was one smart kid.

At the end of the month, as I was preparing to leave for Lyon, France, for the annual G-7 conference, which would primarily be devoted to terrorism, nineteen air force personnel were killed and almost three hundred Americans and others were injured when terrorists drove a truck containing a powerful bomb to a security barrier just outside Khobar Towers, a military housing complex in Dhahran, Saudi Arabia. When an American patrol approached the truck, two of its occupants fled and the bomb exploded. I sent an FBI team of more than forty investigators and forensic experts to work with Saudi authorities. King Fahd called me to express his condolences and solidarity, and to pledge the commitment of his government to apprehend and punish the men who had killed our airmen. Eventually, Saudi Arabia would execute the people it determined to be responsible for the attack.

The Saudis had allowed us to establish the base after the Gulf War in the hope that having U.S. forces "prepositioned" in the Gulf would deter further aggression by Saddam Hussein and allow us to respond quickly if deterrence was unsuccessful. It achieved that objective, but the base also made our forces more vulnerable to terrorists in the region. The security provisions at Khobar were plainly inadequate; the truck had been able to get too close to the building because our people and the Saudis had underestimated the ability of terrorists to build a bomb that powerful. I appointed General Wayne Downing, former commander in chief of the U.S. Special Operations Command, head of a commission to recommend what steps we should take to make our troops stationed overseas more secure.

As we prepared for the G-7 summit, I asked my staff to draw up recommended steps that the international community could take to work together more effectively against global terrorism. At Lyon, the leaders agreed to more than forty of them, including speeding up the extradition and prosecution of terrorists, doing more to seize the resources that funded their violence, improving our internal defenses, and limiting terrorists' access to high-tech communications equipment as much as possible.

By 1996, my administration had settled on a strategy for fighting terror that focused on preventing serious incidents, capturing and punishing terrorists through international cooperation, interrupting the flow of money and communications to terrorist organizations, cutting off access to weapons of mass destruction, and isolating and imposing sanctions on nations that support terrorism. As President Reagan's bombing raid on Libya in 1986 and the attack I ordered on Iraq's intelligence headquarters in 1993 demonstrated, American power could deter states that were directly involved in terrorist acts against us; neither nation attempted another one. However, it was more difficult to get at non-state terrorist organizations; the military and economic pressures that were effective against nations were not as easily applied to them.

The strategy had brought many successes—we had prevented several planned terrorist attacks, including attempts to bomb the Holland and Lincoln tunnels in New York and to blow up several planes flying from the Philippines to the United States, and had brought terrorists back to the United States from all over the world to stand trial. On the other hand, terror is more than a form of international organized crime; because of their stated political objectives, terrorist groups often enjoy both state sponsorship and popular support. Moreover, getting to the bottom of the networks could raise difficult and dangerous questions, as the Khobar Towers investigation did when the possibility of Iran's support for the terrorists was raised. Even if we had a good defense against attacks, would law enforcement be a sufficient offensive strategy against terrorists? If not, would greater reliance on military options work? In the middle of 1996, it was clear that we didn't have all the answers on how to deal with attacks on Americans in this country and overseas, and that the problem would be with us for years to come.

The summer began with good news at home and abroad. Boris Yeltsin had been forced into a runoff on July 3 against the ultra-nationalist Gennady Zyuganov. The first election was close, but Boris won the runoff handily, after a vigorous campaign across all his country's eleven time zones that included American-style campaign events and TV ads. The election was a ratification of Yeltsin's leadership to secure democracy, modernize the economy, and reach out to the West. Russia still had a number of problems, but I believed it was moving in the right direction.

Things were moving in the right direction in America, too, as the unemployment rate dropped to 5.3 percent, with 10 million new jobs, economic growth at 4.2 percent for the quarter, and a deficit that had dropped to less than half what it was when I took office. Wages were also rising. The next day the stock market fell 115 points, prompting me to tease Bob Rubin again about how much Wall Street hated it when average Americans did well. Actually, it was more complicated than that. The market is about the future; when things are really good, investors tend to think they'll get worse. Soon they changed their minds, and the market resumed its upward movement.

On July 17, TWA Flight 800 exploded off Long Island, killing some 230 people. At the time everyone assumed—wrongly, as it turned out—that this was a terrorist act; there was even speculation that the plane had been downed by a rocket fired from a boat in Long Island Sound. While I cautioned against jumping to conclusions, it was clear that we had to do more to strengthen aviation safety.

Hillary and I went to Jamaica, New York, to meet with the victims' families, and I announced new measures to increase air travel security. We had been working on the problem since 1993, with a proposal to modernize the air traffic control system; add more than 450 safety inspectors and the issuance of uniform safety standards; and test new high-tech explosive detection machines. Now I said we would hand-search more luggage and screen more bags on domestic and international flights, and would require preflight inspections of every plane cargo hold and cabin before every flight. I also asked Al Gore to head a commission to review aviation safety and security and the air traffic control system, and report back in forty-five days.

Just ten days after the crash, we had an undisputed terrorist incident when a pipe bomb exploded at the Olympics in Atlanta, killing two people. Hillary and I had gone to the opening ceremonies, which featured Muhammad Ali lighting the Olympic flame. Hillary and Chelsea loved the Olympics and spent more time attending the events than I did, but I was able to visit with the American team, as well as with athletes from several other nations. Irish, Croatian, and Palestinian athletes thanked me for America's efforts to bring peace to their homelands. North and South Korean Olympians sat at adjoining tables in the dining room and talked to each other. The Olympics symbolized the world at its best, bringing people together across old divisions. The pipe bomb planted by a homegrown terrorist who had still not been apprehended was a reminder of how vulnerable the forces of openness and cooperation were to those who rejected the values and rules required to build an integrated global community.

On August 5, at George Washington University, I gave an extended analysis of how terrorism would affect our future, saying that it had become "an equal-opportunity destroyer, with no respect for borders." I outlined the steps we were taking to combat "the enemy of our generation" and said we would prevail if we maintained our confidence and our leadership as the world's "indispensable force for peace and freedom."

The rest of August was taken up with bill signings, the party conventions, and a positive development in Whitewater World. With the election approaching and the budget fight at least temporarily resolved, members of Congress in both parties were eager to give the American people evidence of bipartisan progress. As a result, they produced a raft of progressive legislation the White House had been fighting for. I signed the Food Quality Protection Act, to increase the safeguarding of vegetables, fruits, and grains from harmful pesticides; the Safe Drinking Water Act, to reduce pollution and provide $10 billion in loans to upgrade municipal water systems in the wake of deaths and illnesses caused by the contamination of drinking water by cryptosporidium; and the bill to increase the minimum wage by 90 cents an hour, give small businesses tax relief for new investments in equipment and for hiring new employees, make it easier for small businesses to offer their employees pension plans with a new 401(k) plan, and provide a new incentive that was very important to Hillary, a $5,000 tax credit for adopting a child, with $6,000 for a child with special needs.

In the last week of the month, I signed the Kennedy-Kassebaum bill, which helped millions of people by allowing them to take their health insurance from job to job while prohibiting insurance companies from denying anyone coverage because of a preexisting health problem. I also announced the Food and Drug Administration's final rule to protect young people from the dangers of tobacco. It required young people to prove their age with an ID card before buying cigarettes and significantly restricted advertising and vending machine placement by tobacco companies. We had made some enemies in the tobacco industry, but I thought the effort would save some lives.

On August 22, I signed a landmark welfare reform bill, which had passed with bipartisan majorities of more than 70 percent in both houses. Unlike the two bills I had vetoed, the new legislation retained the federal guarantee of medical care and food aid, increased federal child-care assistance by 40 percent to $14 billion, contained the measures I wanted for tougher child-support enforcement, and gave states the ability to convert monthly welfare payments into wage subsidies as an incentive for employers to hire welfare recipients.

Most advocates for the poor and for legal immigration, and several people in my cabinet, still opposed the bill and wanted me to veto it because it ended the federal guarantee of a fixed monthly benefit to welfare recipients, had a five-year lifetime limit on welfare benefits, cut overall spending on the food stamp program, and denied food stamps and medical care to low-income legal immigrants. I agreed with the last two objections; the hit on legal immigrants was particularly harsh and, I thought, unjustifiable. Shortly after I signed the bill, two high officials in the Department of Health and Human Services, Mary Jo Bane and Peter Edelman, resigned in protest. When they left, I praised them for their service and for following their convictions.

I decided to sign the legislation because I thought it was the best chance America would have for a long time to change the incentives in the welfare system from dependence to empowerment through work. In order to maximize the chances of success, I asked Eli Segal, who had done such a good job in setting up AmeriCorps, to organize a Welfare to Work Partnership to enlist employers who would commit to hiring welfare recipients. Eventually, twenty thousand companies in the partnership would hire more than one million people off welfare.

At the signing ceremony, several former welfare recipients spoke up for the bill. One of them was Lillie Hardin, the Arkansas woman who had so impressed my fellow governors ten years earlier when she said the best thing about leaving welfare for work was that "when my boy goes to school and they ask him, 'What does your mama do for a living?' he can give an answer." Over the next four years, the results of welfare reform would prove Lillie Hardin right. By the time I left office, the welfare rolls had been reduced from 14.1 million to 5.8 million, a 60 percent decrease; and child poverty was down 25 percent to its lowest point since 1979.

Signing the welfare reform bill was one of the most important decisions of my presidency. I had spent most of my career trying to move people from welfare to work, and ending welfare "as we know it" had been a central promise of my 1992 campaign. Though we had pursued welfare reforms through granting waivers from the existing system to most states, America needed legislation that changed the emphasis of assistance to the poor from dependence on welfare checks to independence through work.

The Republicans held their convention in San Diego in mid-month, nominating Bob Dole and his choice for vice president, former New York congressman, secretary of housing and urban development, and Buffalo Bills star quarterback Jack Kemp. Kemp was an interesting man, a free-market conservative with a genuine commitment to bringing economic opportunity to poor people and an openness to new ideas from all quarters, and I thought he would be an asset to Dole's campaign.

The Republicans didn't make the mistake of opening with harsh right-wing rhetoric as they had done at their convention in 1992. Featuring Colin Powell, Senator Kay

Bailey Hutchison, Representative Susan Molinari, and Senator John McCain, they presented a more moderate, positive, and forward-looking image to the American people. Elizabeth Dole gave an impressive and effective nominating speech for her husband, leaving the podium to speak in a conversational way as she walked among the delegates. Dole gave a good speech, too, focusing on his lifetime of duty, his tax cuts, and his advocacy of traditional American values. He derided me for being part of a baby boomer "elite who never grew up, never did anything real, never sacrificed, never suffered, and never learned." He promised to build a bridge back to a better past of "tranquillity, faith, and confidence in action." Dole also took a swipe at Hillary for the theme of her book, that "it takes a village" to raise a child, saying that Republicans thought parents raised children while Democrats thought government should do the job. Dole's attack wasn't too harsh, and in a couple of weeks Hillary and I would have our chances to answer him.

While the Republicans were in San Diego, our family went to Jackson Hole, Wyoming, for the second time. This time I was finishing up a short book, **Between Hope and History,** which highlighted the policies of my first term through stories of individual Americans who had been positively affected by them, and articulated where I wanted to take our country in the next four years.

On August 12, we went back to Yellowstone National Park for the only public business of our vacation, as I signed an agreement that stopped a planned gold mine on property adjacent to the park. The agreement was the welcome result of cooperative efforts by the mining company, citizens' groups, and members of Congress and the White House environmental team, headed by Katie McGinty.

On the eighteenth, Hillary, Chelsea, and I were in New York City for a big party celebrating my fiftieth birthday at Radio City Music Hall. Afterward, I was saddened to learn that the plane carrying the equipment back to Washington from our Wyoming stay had crashed, killing all nine people on board.

The next day we joined Al and Tipper Gore in Tennessee, where we celebrated the birthday Tipper and I shared by helping to rebuild two rural churches, one white and one black, that had been burned in the recent rash of church burnings.

In the last week of the month, the nation's attention turned to the Democratic National Convention in Chicago. By then our campaign, chaired by Peter Knight, was well organized, and it was working closely with the White House through Doug Sosnick and Harold Ickes, who had overseen our convention organization. I was excited about going to Chicago because it was Hillary's hometown, had played a pivotal role in my 1992 victory, and had made good use of many of my most important initiatives in education, economic development, and crime control.

On August 25, in Huntington, West Virginia, Chelsea and I began a four-day train trip to Chicago. Hillary had gone ahead of us to be there when the convention opened. We had leased a wonderful old train we dubbed the "21st Century Express" for the trip through Kentucky, Ohio, Michigan, and Indiana to Chicago. We made fifteen stops along the way and slowed down as we passed through small towns so that I could wave to the people who had gathered by the tracks. I could feel from the excitement of the crowds that the train was connecting with the American people just as the bus tours had in 1992, and I could see from the expressions on people's faces that they felt much better about the condition of the country and about their own lives. When we stopped in Wyandotte, Michigan, for an education event, two children introduced me by reading **The Little Engine That Could.** The book and their enthusiastic reading captured the return of America's innate optimism and self-confidence.

On many stops we picked up friends, supporters, and local officials who wanted to be aboard for the next leg of the trip. I especially enjoyed sharing the leisurely travel with Chelsea, as we stood on the caboose, waved to the crowds, and talked about everything under the sun. Our relationship was as close as ever, but she was changing, growing into a mature young woman with her own opinions and interests. More and more, I found myself amazed at how she saw the world.

Our convention opened on the twenty-sixth, with appearances by Jim and Sarah Brady, who appreciated the support the Democrats had given to the Brady bill, and Christopher Reeve, the actor who, after being paralyzed in a fall from a horse, had inspired the nation with his courageous fight to recover and his advocacy for more research into spinal cord injuries.

On the day of my speech, our campaign was rocked by press reports that Dick Morris had frequently been with a prostitute in his hotel room when he was in Washington working for me. Dick resigned from the campaign, and I put out a statement saying that he was my friend and a superb political strategist who had done "invaluable work" over the past two years. I regretted his departure, but he was obviously under enormous stress and he needed time to work through his problems. I knew Dick was resilient and felt sure he would be back in the political arena before long.

My acceptance speech was easy to give because of the record: the lowest combined rate of unemployment and inflation in twenty-eight years; 10 million new jobs; 10 million people getting the minimum wage increase; 25 million Americans benefiting from the Kennedy-Kassebaum bill; 15 million working Americans with a tax cut; 12 million taking advantage of the family leave law; 10 million students saving money through the Direct Student Loan Program; 40 million workers with more pension security.

I stated that we were going in the right direction and, referring to Bob Dole's speech in San Diego, said, "with all respect, we do not need to build a bridge to the past; we need to build a bridge to the future . . . let us resolve to build that bridge to the twenty-first century." The "Bridge to the 21st Century" became the theme of the campaign and the next four years.

As good as the record was, I knew that all elections are about the future, so I outlined my agenda: higher school standards and universal access to college; a balanced budget that protected health care, education, and the environment; targeted tax cuts to support home ownership, long-term care, college education, and child-rearing; more jobs for people on welfare and more investment in poor urban and rural areas; and some new initiatives to fight crime and drugs and clean the environment.

I knew that if the American people saw the election as a choice between building a bridge to the past and building a bridge to the future, we would win. Bob Dole had unintentionally given me the central message of the 1996 campaign. On the day after the convention closed, Al, Tipper, Hillary, and I kicked off my last campaign with a bus tour, beginning in Cape Girardeau, Missouri, with Governor

Mel Carnahan, who had been with me since early 1992, going through southern Illinois and western Kentucky, and winding up in Memphis, after several stops in Tennessee, with former governor Ned Ray McWherter, a huge bear of a man who was the only person I ever heard call the vice president "Albert." Ned Ray was worth so many votes that I didn't care what he called Al, or me for that matter.

In August, Kenneth Starr lost his first big case, one that reflected just how desperate he and his staff were to pin something on me. Starr had indicted the two owners of the Perry County Bank, lawyer Herby Branscum Jr. and accountant Rob Hill, on charges arising out of my 1990 gubernatorial campaign.

The indictment stated that Branscum and Hill had taken about $13,000 from their own bank for legal and accounting services they did not perform in order to reimburse themselves for political contributions they had made, and that they had instructed the man who ran the bank for them not to report two cash withdrawals of more than $10,000 each from my campaign account to the Internal Revenue Service as required by federal law.

The indictment also named Bruce Lindsey, who had served as my campaign treasurer, as an "unindicted co-conspirator," alleging that when Bruce withdrew the money to pay for our election day "get out the vote" activities, he had urged the bankers not to file the required report. Starr's people had threatened Bruce with an indictment, but he called their bluff; there was nothing wrong with our contributions or the way they had been spent, and Bruce had no motive for asking the bank not to make the required filing on it: we would be making all the information public in three weeks as required by Arkansas state election law. Since the contributions and their expenditure were legal and our public report was accurate, Starr's people knew Bruce hadn't committed a crime, so they settled for smearing him as an unindicted co-conspirator.

The charges against Branscum and Hill were absurd. First, they wholly owned the bank; if they did not impair the bank's liquidity, they could take money out of it as long as they paid income taxes on it, and there was no suggestion that they had not done so in this case. As to the second charge, the law that requires a bank to report cash deposits or withdrawals of $10,000 or more is a good one; it permits the government to follow large amounts of "dirty money" from criminal enterprises like money laundering or drug dealing. The reports filed with the government are checked every three to six months but are not open to the public. As of 1996, there had been two hundred prosecutions for failure to file the reports required by the act, but only twenty of them were for failures to report withdrawals. All of those involved money that was tainted by an illegal enterprise. Until Starr came along, no one had ever been indicted for a negligent failure to report deposits or withdrawals of legitimate funds.

Our campaign money was undisputably clean money that had been withdrawn at the end of the campaign to pay for our efforts to call voters and offer rides to the polls on election day. We had filed the required public report within three weeks after the election, detailing how much money we had spent and how we had spent it. Branscum, Hill, and Lindsey simply had no motive to hide from the government a legal cash withdrawal that would be a matter of public record in less than a month.

That didn't stop Hickman Ewing, Starr's deputy in Arkansas, who was just as obsessed as Starr with going after us and not nearly as good at disguising it. He threatened to send Neal Ainley, who ran the bank for Branscum and Hill and who had been responsible for filing the reports, to prison unless he testified that Branscum, Hill, and Lindsey had ordered him not to file it, even though Ainley had earlier denied any wrongdoing by them. The poor man was a little fish caught in a powerful net; he changed his story. Initially charged with five felonies, Ainley was now allowed to plead to two misdemeanors.

As in the earlier trial of the McDougals and Tucker, I testified on videotape at the request of the defendants. Though I had not been involved in the withdrawals, I was able to say I had not appointed Branscum and Hill to the two state boards on which they served in return for their contributions to my campaign.

After a vigorous defense, Branscum and Hill were acquitted on the reporting charges, and the jury deadlocked on the question of whether they had falsely reported the purposes for which they had withdrawn funds from their own bank. I was relieved that Herby, Rob, and Bruce Lindsey were cleared, but sickened by the abuse of prosecutorial power, the enormous legal costs my friends had been forced to bear, and the staggering costs to the taxpayers of a prosecution over the $13,000 of reimbursements the defendants got from their own bank and the failure to file federal reports on two legal and publicly reported withdrawals of campaign funds.

There were noneconomic costs as well: FBI agents working for Starr went to Rob Hill's teenage son's school and dragged him out of class for questioning. They could have talked to him after school or during lunch or on the weekend. Instead, they humiliated the young man in hopes of pressuring his father into telling them something that would damage me, whether it was true or not.

After the trial, several jurors burned the independent counsel's office with comments like "It's a waste of money. . . . I would hate to see the government waste more money on Whitewater"; "If they're going to spend my tax dollars, they need stronger evidence"; "If anyone is untouchable it is OIC [Office of Independent Counsel]." One juror who identified himself as an "anti-Clinton" person said, "I would have loved for them to have a little more evidence, but they didn't." Even conservative Republicans who lived in the real world, as opposed to Whitewater World, knew the independent counsel had gone too far.

As bad as Starr's treatment of Branscum and Hill was, it was a tea party compared with what he was about to do to Susan McDougal. On August 20, Susan was sentenced to two years in prison. Starr's people had offered to keep her out of jail if she gave them information implicating Hillary or me in some illegal activity. On the day she was sentenced, when Susan repeated what she had said from the beginning—that she knew of nothing either of us had done wrong—she was served with a subpoena to appear before the grand jury. She appeared, but refused to answer the prosecutors' questions, fearing that they would charge her with perjury because she wouldn't lie and tell them what they wanted to hear. Judge Susan Webber Wright found her in contempt of court and sent her to jail for an indefinite period until she agreed to cooperate with the special prosecutor. She would remain confined for eighteen months, often under miserable conditions.

September opened with the campaign on a roll. Our convention had been a success, and Dole was tarred by his association with Gingrich and the government shutdown. Even more important, the country was in good shape, and the voters no longer saw issues like crime, welfare, fiscal responsibility, foreign policy, and defense as the exclusive province of the Republican Party. Polls showed that my job and personal approval ratings were around 60 percent, with the same percentage of people saying they felt comfortable with me in the White House.

On the other hand, I expected to be weaker in some parts of America because of my positions on the cultural issues—guns, gays, and abortion—and, at least in North Carolina and Kentucky, on tobacco. Also, it seemed certain that Ross Perot would receive far fewer votes than he had in 1992, making it harder for me to carry a couple of states where he had taken more votes from President Bush than from me. Still, on balance, I was in much better shape this time around. All through September the campaign drew large, enthusiastic crowds, or "October crowds," as I called them, beginning with nearly thirty thousand people at a Labor Day picnic in De Pere, Wisconsin, near Green Bay.

Since presidential elections are decided by electoral votes, I wanted to use our momentum to bring a couple of new states into our column and to force Senator Dole to spend time and money in states a Republican could normally take for granted. Dole wanted to do the same thing to me by contesting California, where I was opposing a popular ballot initiative to end affirmative action in college admissions and where he had helped himself by holding the GOP convention in San Diego.

My main target was Florida. If I could win there and hold most of the states I had won in '92, the election was over. I had worked hard in Florida for four years: helping the state recover from Hurricane Andrew; holding the Summit of the Americas there; announcing the relocation of the U.S. military's Southern Command from Panama to Miami; working to restore the Everglades; and even making inroads into the Cuban-American community, which normally had given Republicans more than 80 percent of its votes in presidential elections ever since the Bay of Pigs. I was also blessed with a good organization in Florida and the strong support of Governor Lawton Chiles, who had great rapport with voters in the more conservative areas of central and northern Florida. Those people liked Lawton in part because he hit back when attacked. As he said, "No redneck wants a dog that won't bite." In early September, Lawton went with me to north Florida to campaign and to honor retiring Congressman Pete Peterson, who had spent six and a half years as a prisoner of war in Vietnam and whom I had recently nominated to be our first ambassador there since the end of the war.

I spent most of the rest of the month in states I'd won in '92. On a western swing, I also campaigned in Arizona, a state that hadn't voted for a Democrat for President since 1948, but that I thought I could carry because of its growing Hispanic population and the discomfort of many of the state's moderate and traditional conservative voters with the more extreme politics of the Republican Congress.

On the sixteenth, I received the endorsement of the

Fraternal Order of Police. The FOP usually endorsed Republicans for President, but our White House had worked with them for four years to put more police on the streets, take guns out of the hands of criminals, and ban cop-killer bullets; they wanted four more years of that kind of cooperation.

Two days later, I announced one of the most important environmental accomplishments of my entire eight years in office, the establishment of the 1.7 million–acre Grand Staircase–Escalante National Monument in the remote and beautiful red rock area of southern Utah, which contains fossils of dinosaurs and the remains of the ancient Anasazi Indian civilization. I had the authority to do so under the Antiquities Act of 1906, which allows the President to protect federal lands of extraordinary cultural, historic, and scientific value. I made the announcement with Al Gore on the edge of the Grand Canyon, which Theodore Roosevelt had first protected under the Antiquities Act. My action was necessary to stop a large coal mine that would have fundamentally changed the character of the area. Most of the Utah officials and many who wanted the mining operation's economic boost were against it, but the land was priceless, and I thought the monument designation would bring in tourism income that over time would more than offset the loss of the mine.

Apart from the size and exuberance of the crowds, the September events offered anecdotal evidence that things were going our way. After a rally in Longview, Texas, as I was shaking hands in the crowd, I met a single mother of two who had left welfare to serve in AmeriCorps and was using its scholarship money to go to Kilgore Junior College; another woman who had used the family leave law when her husband became ill with cancer; and a Vietnam veteran who was grateful for the health and disability benefits for children born with spina bifida as a result of their fathers' exposure to Agent Orange during the war. He had his twelve-year-old daughter with him. The child had spina bifida and had already endured a dozen operations in her short life.

The rest of the world didn't stop for our campaign. In the first week of September, Saddam Hussein was making trouble again, assaulting and occupying the town of Irbil in the Kurdish area of northern Iraq, in violation of restrictions imposed on him at the end of the Gulf War. Two Kurdish factions had been vying for control of the area; after one of them decided to support Saddam, he had attacked the other. I ordered bomb and missile attacks on the Iraqi forces and they withdrew.

On the twenty-fourth, I went to New York for the opening session of the United Nations, where I was the first of many world leaders to sign the Comprehensive Test Ban Treaty, using the pen with which President Kennedy had signed the Limited Test Ban Treaty thirty-three years earlier. In my remarks, I outlined a broader agenda to reduce the threat of weapons of mass destruction, urging the UN members to bring the Chemical Weapons Convention into force, strengthen the compliance provisions of the Biological Weapons Convention, freeze the production of fissile materials for use in nuclear weapons, and ban the use, production, stockpiling, and transfer of anti-personnel land mines.

While the UN was discussing nonproliferation, the Middle East exploded again. The Israelis had opened a tunnel that ran under the Temple Mount in Jerusalem's

Old City. The ruins of the Temples of Solomon and Herod were under the mount, atop which stood the Dome of the Rock and the Al-Aqsa Mosque, two of the holiest sites to Muslims. Since the Israelis took East Jerusalem in the 1967 war, the Temple Mount, called Haram al-Sharif by the Arabs, had been under the control of Muslim officials; when the tunnel was opened, the Palestinians saw it as a threat to their religious and political interests, and riots and shooting broke out. After three days, more than sixty people had died, with many more wounded. I called on both sides to end the violence and get back to implementing the peace agreement, while Warren Christopher burned up the phone lines with Prime Minister Netanyahu and Chairman Arafat to stop the bloodshed. On Christopher's advice, I invited Netanyahu and Arafat to the White House to talk things over.

I ended the month by signing a health-care appropriations bill that ended so-called drive-by deliveries, by guaranteeing a minimum of forty-eight hours of coverage to mothers and newborns; provided medical assistance to children of Vietnam veterans who were born with spina bifida, as I mentioned earlier; and required the same annual and lifetime coverage limits in health insurance policies for mental and physical illness. The breakthrough in mental-health care was a tribute not only to the work of mental-health advocacy groups but also to the personal efforts of Senator Pete Domenici of New Mexico, Senator Paul Wellstone of Minnesota, and Tipper Gore, whom I had named my official advisor on mental-health policy.

I spent the first two days of October with Netanyahu, Arafat, and King Hussein, who had agreed to join us to try to get the peace process back on track. At the end of our talks, Arafat and Netanyahu asked me to field all the press questions. I said that while we had not yet resolved the tunnel issue, both sides had agreed to begin immediate talks in the region with a view toward ending the violence and returning to the peace process. In our meeting, Netanyahu had reaffirmed his commitment to implement the agreements made before he took office, including the withdrawal of Israeli troops from Hebron. Not long afterward, the tunnel was sealed again, consistent with the commitment both parties had made to do nothing to change the status quo in Jerusalem until it was negotiated.

On the third, I was back on the campaign trail again, stopping for a rally in Buffalo, New York, a city that had always been good to me, on the way to Chautauqua, to prepare for my first presidential debate with Bob Dole in Hartford, Connecticut, on October 6. Our whole team was there, including my media advisor, Michael Sheehan. George Mitchell came in to play Bob Dole in the mock debates. He cleaned my clock at first, but I got better with practice. In between sessions, Erskine Bowles and I got in a round of golf. My golf game was getting better. In June, I had finally scored below 80 for the first time, but I still couldn't beat Erskine when his game was on.

The debate itself turned out to be civilized, and educational for people who were interested in our different philosophies of government and positions on the issues. There were a few fireworks when Dole hit me for scaring seniors with my ads criticizing the Medicare cuts in the Republican budget I had vetoed, and he repeated his claim from his convention speech that I had filled the administration with young elitists who "never grew up, never did anything real, never sacrificed, never suffered, and never learned" and who wanted "to fund with your earnings their dubious and self-serving schemes." I shot back that one of the young "elitists" who worked for me in the White House had grown up in a house trailer, and as for the charge that I was too liberal, "that's what their party always drags out when they get in a tight race. It's sort of their golden oldie . . . I just don't think that dog will hunt anymore."

The second debate was scheduled ten days later in San Diego. In the interim, Hillary, Al, Tipper, and I visited the massive AIDS quilt that covered the Mall in Washington, with separate squares in honor of people who had died; two of those commemorated were friends of Hillary's and mine. I was gratified that the death rate from AIDS was coming down, and I was determined to keep pushing for more research to develop lifesaving medicines.

Mickey Kantor had negotiated a town hall format for the San Diego debate. On the sixteenth, citizens at the University of San Diego asked good questions, and Dole and I answered them without hitting each other until the end. In his closing statement, Dole appealed to his base, reminding people that I opposed term limits as well as constitutional amendments to balance the budget and to protect the American flag, and forbid restrictions on voluntary school prayer. I closed with a summary of my proposals for the next four years. At least people knew what the choice was.

With two weeks to go until the election, the polls showed me with a twenty-point lead, and 55 percent of the vote. I wish the survey hadn't been released; it took some of the life out of our campaign when our supporters thought the election was over. I kept working hard, concentrating on our pickup targets, Arizona and Florida, and the states we'd won before, including three of those I was most worried about, Nevada, Colorado, and Georgia. On October 25, we had a great rally in Atlanta, where my longtime friend Max Cleland was in a tight race for the U.S. Senate. Sam Nunn gave a particularly effective argument for my reelection, and I left the state thinking we might have a chance.

On November 1, I headed into the homestretch of the campaign with a morning rally at Santa Barbara City College. On a warm, sunny day, a large crowd gathered on the campus hillside overlooking the Pacific Ocean. Santa Barbara was a good place to end the California campaign, a once solidly Republican area that had been trending our way.

From Santa Barbara, I flew on to Las Cruces, New Mexico, then to El Paso and the biggest crowd of the campaign, as more than forty thousand people came out to the airport to show their support, and finally to San Antonio and the traditional rally at the Alamo. I knew we couldn't win Texas, but I wanted to honor the loyalty of the state's Democrats, especially the Hispanics who had stuck with me.

As we headed into the last three days of the campaign, I had a choice to make. Senate candidates from several relatively small states were asking me to campaign for them. Mark Penn said that if I spent the last days of the campaign doing that, instead of going to the larger states, I might not get a majority of the vote, for several reasons. First, our campaign's momentum had been slowed in the last two weeks by allegations that the DNC had received several hundred thousand dollars in illegal campaign contributions from Asians, including people I had known when I was governor. When I heard about it, I was angry; my finance chair, Terry McAuliffe, had made sure the

contributions to our campaign were reviewed scrupulously, and the DNC was also supposed to have a vetting
operation to reject questionable contributions. There
were clearly problems with the DNC clearance procedures. All I could say was that any unlawful contributions
should be returned immediately. Regardless, the controversy seemed certain to hurt us on election day. Second,
Ralph Nader was running on the Green Party ticket and
would take some votes away from me on the left. Third,
Ross Perot, who had entered the campaign in October,
too late to get into the debates, wasn't doing nearly as well
as he had in 1992, but he was ending this campaign as he
had the previous one, with vicious attacks on me. He said
that I would be "totally occupied for the next two years in
staying out of jail," and called me a "draft dodger" who
was tainted by "ethical lapses, corrupt campaign financing, and a lax attitude toward drug use." Finally, voter
turnout was likely to be well below that of 1992, because
the voters had been told for several weeks that the campaign was over.

Mark Penn advised me that if I wanted to win a majority of the votes, I needed to fly into the large media markets in the big states and ask people to go to the polls.
Otherwise, he said, with the outcome not in doubt, lower-
income Democrats were far less likely than more affluent
or ideologically driven Republicans to vote. I was already
scheduled to be in Florida and New Jersey, and on Mark's
advice we added a stop in Cleveland. Beyond that, I
scheduled appearances in the Senate race states:
Louisiana, Massachusetts, Maine, New Hampshire, Kentucky, Iowa, and South Dakota. In the presidential race,
only Kentucky was in doubt; I was well ahead in all the
others except South Dakota, where I expected the Repub-

licans to come home to Dole at the end. I decided to go to these states because I thought it was worth two or three points off my vote total to elect more Democrats to the Senate, and the candidates in six of the seven states had helped me in '92 or in the Congress.

On Sunday, November 3, after attending services at St. Paul's AME Church in Tampa, I flew to New Hampshire to support our Senate candidate, Dick Swett; to Cleveland, where Mayor Mike White and Senator John Glenn gave me a last-minute boost; and to Lexington, Kentucky, for a rally at the state university with Senator Wendell Ford, Governor Paul Patton, and our Senate candidate, Steve Beshear. I knew it was going to be tough to hold Kentucky because of the tobacco issue, and I was heartened by the presence on the stage of the University of Kentucky basketball coach, Rick Pitino. In a state where everyone loved the basketball team and nearly half of them disliked me, Pitino's presence was helpful and a gutsy move on his part.

By the time I got to Cedar Rapids, Iowa, it was 8 p.m. I really wanted to be there for Tom Harkin, who was in a tight race for reelection. Tom had strongly supported me in the Senate, and after the '92 primary he and his wife, Ruth, a lawyer who was serving with the administration, had become close friends of mine.

The last stop of the night was Sioux Falls, South Dakota, where Democratic congressman Tim Johnson had a real chance to unseat incumbent Republican Larry Pressler. Both Johnson and his chief supporter, Senator Tom Daschle, had been very good to me. As Senate minority leader, Daschle had been invaluable to the White House during the budget fights and the shutdown; when he asked me to come to South Dakota, I couldn't say no.

It was nearly midnight when I got up in the Sioux Falls Arena and Convention Center to speak "at the last rally of the last campaign I will ever run." Because it was my final speech, I gave them the whole load on the record, the budget fight, and what I wanted to do for the next four years. Since I was in a rural state like Arkansas, I told them a joke. I said the Republicans' budget reminded me of the story of a politician who wanted to ask a farmer to vote for him but was reluctant to come into his yard because a barking dog was there. The politician asked the farmer, "Does your dog bite?" "No," the farmer replied. When the politician walked through the yard toward the farmer, the dog bit him. "I thought you said your dog didn't bite!" he shouted. The farmer replied, "Son, that ain't my dog." The budget was their dog.

The election went as Mark Penn predicted: there was a record low turnout, and I won 49 to 41 percent. The electoral vote was 379 to 159, as I lost three states I had carried in 1992, Montana, Colorado, and Georgia, and won two new ones, Arizona and Florida, for a net gain of nine electoral votes.

Underneath the aggregate numbers, subtle differences in the state totals between 1992 and 1996 revealed the extent to which cultural factors influenced the election in some states, while more traditional economic and social matters dominated in others. All competitive elections are determined by such shifts, and in 1996 they told me a lot about what mattered to different groups of Americans. For example, in Pennsylvania, a state with many NRA members and pro-life voters, my winning percentage was the same as it had been in 1992, thanks to a bigger margin in Philadelphia and a strong vote in Pittsburgh, while my vote went down in the rest of the state because of guns and my veto of the partial-birth abortion bill. In Missouri, the same factors cut my victory margin almost in half, from 10 to 6 percent. I still got a majority in Arkansas, but my victory margin was slightly smaller than in 1992; in Tennessee, the margin was cut from 4.5 to 2.5 percent.

In Kentucky, tobacco and guns cut our margin from 3 to 1 percent. For the same reasons, though I was ahead in North Carolina all the way to the end, I lost by 3 percent. In Colorado, I went from a 4 percent victory in 1992 to a 1.5 percent loss because the '92 Perot voters in the West were more likely to vote Republican in '96 and because the Republicans had gained 100,000 registered voters on the Democrats since 1992, partly as a result of the large number of Christian Right organizations that had located their headquarters in the state. In Montana, I lost this time around largely because, as in Colorado, the lower vote for Perot meant more votes for Senator Dole than for me.

In Georgia, the last poll had me ahead by 4 percent; I lost by 1 percent. The Christian Coalition deserved a lot of credit for that; in 1992, they had cut my margin from 6 percent to under 1 percent with heavy distribution of their "voting guides" in conservative churches the Sunday before the election. Democrats had worked black churches like that for years, but the Christian Coalition, at least in Georgia, was particularly effective at it, changing the outcome by 5 percent in both 1992 and 1996. I was disappointed to lose Georgia, but glad that Max Cleland survived by getting a few more white votes than I did. The South was tough because of the cultural issues; the only southern state to give me a substantially larger victory margin in 1996 was Louisiana, which went from 4.5 to 12 percent.

By contrast, my winning percentage increased a good deal in less culturally conservative or more economically sensitive states. My margin over the Republicans was up 10 percent or more in 1996 over 1992 in Connecticut, Hawaii, Maine, Massachusetts, New Jersey, New York, and Rhode Island. We held on to our big '92 margins in Illinois, Minnesota, Maryland, and California, and substantially increased the edge in Michigan and Ohio. Despite the gun issue, I also gained 10 percent over my '92 margin in New Hampshire. And I held on for a 1 percent victory in Nevada, largely because of my opposition to dumping America's nuclear waste there without scientific evidence that it was safe to do so, and the constant publicity my position received thanks to my friend and Georgetown classmate Brian Greenspun, the president and editor of the **Las Vegas Sun,** who felt passionately about the issue.

On balance, I was happy with the results. I had won more electoral votes than in 1992, and four of the seven Senate candidates I had campaigned for won: Tom Harkin, Tim Johnson, John Kerry, and, in Louisiana, Mary Landrieu. But the fact that my share of the vote was considerably lower than my job rating, my personal approval rating, the percentage of people who said they felt comfortable with my presidency, was a sober reminder of the power of cultural issues like guns, gays, and abortion, especially among white married couples in the South, the intermountain West, and the rural Midwest, and among white men all across the country. All I could do was to keep searching for common ground, keep trying to temper the bitter partisanship in Washington, and keep doing my best as President.

The atmosphere at the victory rally at the Old State

House in Little Rock was quite different this time around. The crowd was still large, but the celebration was marked not so much by shouting exuberance as by a genuine happiness that our nation was in better shape and that the American people had approved of the job I was doing.

Because the election had not been in doubt for several weeks, it was easy to miss its significance. After the 1994 elections, I had been ridiculed as an irrelevant figure, destined for defeat in 1996. In the early stages of the budget fight, with the government shutdown looming, it had been far from clear that I would prevail or that the American people would support my stance against the Republicans. Now I was the first Democratic President to be elected to a second term since FDR in 1936.

FORTY-SEVEN

O n the day after the election, I was back at the White House for a celebration on the South Lawn with my staff, cabinet, other appointees, campaign workers, and Democratic Party officials. In my remarks, I mentioned that the night before, as I waited for the election results, I had held a reunion with people who had worked for me in Arkansas when I was attorney general and governor, and that "I told them something I want to tell you—that is, I have always been a very hardworking, kind of hard-driving person. I'm always focused on the matter before me. Sometimes I don't say 'Thank you' enough. And I've always been kind of hard on myself, and sometimes I think, just by omission, I'm too hard on the people who work here."

Our team had accomplished a lot in the last four years under extreme duress. This was the result of my own early mistakes, the first two years of intensely negative press coverage, the loss of Congress in '94, the financial and emotional toll of Whitewater, too much personal tragedy, and the constant demands inherent in trying to turn the country around. I had done my best to keep my own and everybody else's spirits up, and to keep us all from being too distracted by the tragedies, the trash, and the mishaps. Now that the American people had given us another term, I was hoping that in the next four years we would be freer to do the public's business without the turmoil and strife of the first term.

I had been inspired by a statement made in late October by the archbishop of Chicago, Joseph Cardinal Bernardin, a tireless advocate for social justice whom Hillary and I knew and admired very much. Bernardin was desperately ill and didn't have long to live when he said, "A dying person does not have time for the peripheral or the accidental . . . it is wrong to waste the precious gift of time given to us on acrimony and division."

In the week after the election, several people central to the administration announced their intention to leave by the end of the year, including Leon Panetta and Warren Christopher. Chris had lived on an airplane for four years, and Leon had seen us through the budget battles, not to mention staying up on election night playing hearts with me. Both of them wanted to go home to California and to a more normal life. They had served me and the nation well, and I would miss them. On November 8, I announced that Erskine Bowles would become the new chief of staff. His youngest child was off to college now, and Erskine was free to serve again, though it would cost him an arm and a leg to do so, as he once again gave up his lucrative business ventures.

Thank goodness, Nancy Hernreich and Betty Currie were staying. By this time, Betty knew most of my friends around the country, could handle a lot of the phone traffic, and was a wonderful help to me in the office. Nancy understood the dynamics of our office and my need for both involvement in and distance from the details of the day-to-day work. She did everything she could to make it easier for me to do my job, and kept the Oval Office operations in great shape. My then presidential aide, Stephen Goodin, was leaving, but we had lined up a good replacement: Kris Engskov, who had been at the White House from the start and whom I first met in north Arkansas way back in 1974 during my first campaign. Since the President's aide sat just outside the Oval Office door, was with me all of the time, and was always by my side, it was good to have someone I'd known so long and who liked so much doing the job. I was also glad to have Janis Kearny, the White House diarist. Janis had been the editor of the **Arkansas State Press**, Little Rock's black newspaper, and she was keeping meticulous records of all our meetings. I don't know what I would have done without my Oval Office team.

A week later, after I announced an eighteen-month extension of our mission in Bosnia, Hillary and I were on our way to Australia, the Philippines, and Thailand for a combination of work and a vacation that we needed. We began with three days of pure fun in Hawaii, then flew on to Sydney, Australia. After a meeting with Prime Minister John Howard, a speech to the Australian parliament in Canberra, and a day in Sydney, including an unforgettable game with one of the greatest golfers of our time, Greg Norman, we flew north to Port Douglas, a coastal resort on the Coral Sea near the Great Barrier Reef. While there, we walked through the Daintree Rainforest with an aboriginal guide, toured a wildlife preserve where I cuddled a koala named Chelsea, and snorkeled around the magnificent reef. Like coral reefs the world over, it was threatened by ocean pollution, global warming, and physical abuse. Just before we went out to see it, I announced America's support for the International Coral Reef Initiative, which was designed to prevent further destruction of reefs everywhere.

We flew from Australia to the Philippines for the fourth Asian Pacific leaders' meeting, hosted by President Fidel Ramos. The principal result of the conference was an agreement I had worked for that eliminated all tariffs on an array of computers, semiconductors, and telecommunications technology by 2000, a move that would result in more exports and more high-wage jobs for America.

We visited Thailand to honor the king's fiftieth year on the throne of one of America's oldest allies in Southeast Asia: the United States had signed a treaty of amity and commerce with the king of Siam in 1833. King Bhumibol Adulyadej was an accomplished pianist and a big jazz fan. I presented him with a golden anniversary gift any jazz aficionado would appreciate, a large portfolio of photographs of jazz musicians, autographed by the superb jazz photographer Herman Leonard.

We got home in time for our traditional Thanksgiving at Camp David. This year our group included our two delightful young nephews, Roger's son, Tyler, and Tony's son, Zach. Watching them play together made the spirit of the season come alive.

In December, I had to reconstitute a large part of my administration. Bill Perry, John Deutch, Mickey Kantor, Bob Reich, Hazel O'Leary, Laura Tyson, and Henry Cisneros were all leaving. We were losing valuable people in the White House, too. Harold Ickes was returning to his law practice and consulting business, and Deputy Chief of Staff Evelyn Lieberman was going to the State Department to head the Voice of America.

Early in the month I announced my new national security team: Madeleine Albright as secretary of state; Bill Cohen, former Republican senator from Maine, as secretary of defense; Tony Lake as CIA director; Bill Richardson as UN ambassador; and Sandy Berger as national security advisor. Albright had done an outstanding job at the United Nations and understood the challenges we faced, especially in the Balkans and the Middle East. I thought she had earned the chance to be the first female secretary of state. Bill Richardson had proved himself to be a skilled diplomat by his efforts in North Korea and Iraq, and I was pleased when he agreed to become America's first Hispanic ambassador to the United Nations.

Bill Cohen was an articulate, youthful-looking politician who had been an innovative thinker on defense issues for years. He had helped to craft the START I treaty and had played a key role in the legislation that reorganized and strengthened the military command structure in the 1980s. I wanted a Republican in the cabinet, liked and respected Cohen, and thought he could fill Bill Perry's very big shoes. When I pledged to him that I would never politicize defense decisions, he accepted the job. I hated to lose John Deutch at the CIA. He had done a fine job as deputy secretary of defense, then had stepped into the tough CIA job after Jim Woolsey's brief tenure. Tony Lake's work at the National Security Council had given him a unique understanding of the strengths and weaknesses of our intelligence operations, which were especially critical now with the threat of terrorism on the rise.

I didn't consider anyone other than Sandy Berger for the job of national security advisor. We had been friends for more than twenty years. He felt comfortable bringing me bad news and disagreeing with me at meetings, and he had done a superb job on a whole range of issues in the first term. Sandy's analytical powers were considerable. He thought through problems to the end, seeing potential pitfalls that others missed, without being paralyzed by them. He understood my strengths and weaknesses and how to make the most of the former and minimize the latter. He also never allowed his ego to get in the way of good decision making.

George Stephanopoulos was leaving, too. He had told me not long before the election that he was burned out and had to go. Until I read his memoir, I had no idea how difficult the pressure-packed years had been for him, or how hard he had been on himself, and me. George was going on to a career in teaching and television, where I hoped he would be happier.

Within two weeks I had filled the remaining vacancies in the cabinet. I named Bill Daley of Chicago to be secretary of commerce after Mickey Kantor, to my regret, told me he wanted to return to private life. Daley was a talented man who had led our campaign for NAFTA. Charlene Barshefsky had been acting trade representative in the eight months since Mickey Kantor had gone to Commerce. She was doing a terrific job, and it was time to take the word "acting" out of her title.

I also appointed Alexis Herman to succeed Bob Reich at the Labor Department; Assistant HUD Secretary Andrew Cuomo to follow Henry Cisneros at HUD; Federico Peña to replace Hazel O'Leary at Energy; Rodney Slater, the federal highway administrator, to succeed Peña as secretary of transportation; Aida Alvarez to become head of the Small Business Administration; Gene Sperling to head the National Economic Council on the departure of Laura Tyson; Dr. Janet Yellen, who had taught Larry Summers at Harvard, to be chair of the Council of Economic Advisers; Bruce Reed to be my domestic policy advisor, replacing Carol Rasco, who was going to the Department of Education to run our America Reads program; and Sylvia Matthews, a brilliant young woman who worked for Bob Rubin, to replace Harold Ickes as deputy chief of staff.

Bob Reich had done a good job at the Department of Labor and as a member of the economic team, but it was becoming difficult for him; he disagreed with my economic and budget policies, believing I had put too much emphasis on deficit reduction and invested too little in education, training, and new technologies. Bob also wanted to go home to Massachusetts to his wife, Clare, and their sons.

I was heartsick about losing Henry Cisneros. We had been friends since before I ran for President, and he had done a brilliant job at HUD. For more than a year, Henry had been subject to an investigation by an independent counsel for making incorrect statements about his personal expenses in his FBI vetting interview for the HUD job. The law made it a crime for a nominee to make a "material" misstatement, one that would affect the confirmation process. Senator Al D'Amato, whose committee had recommended Cisneros's confirmation, wrote a letter saying that Henry's misstatement of the details of his expenses would not have affected his vote or that of any other senator on the committee. Prosecutors from the Justice Department's public integrity office argued against a special prosecutor.

Unfortunately, Janet Reno referred the Cisneros case to Judge Sentelle's panel anyway. True to form, they saddled him with a Republican special prosecutor: David Barrett, an active partisan who, though accused of no wrongdoing, reportedly had close ties with officials who were convicted in the HUD scandals of the Reagan administration. No one had accused Henry of any impropriety in his job, but he had been plunged into Whitewater World anyway. Henry's legal bills had left him deeply in debt and he had two kids in college. He had to earn more money to support his family and pay his lawyers. I was just thankful he had stayed for the full four years.

Though I had made a lot of changes, I thought we could maintain the spirit of camaraderie and teamwork that had marked the first term. Most of the new appointees were transferring from other positions in the administration, and many of my cabinet members were staying put.

There were several interesting developments in foreign policy in December. On the thirteenth, the UN Security Council, with the strong support of the United States, selected a new secretary-general, Kofi Annan of Ghana. Annan was the first person from sub-Saharan Africa to hold the post. As the UN undersecretary for peacekeeping during the previous four years, he had supported our efforts in Bosnia and Haiti. Madeleine Albright thought he was an exceptional leader and had urged me to support him, as had Warren Christopher, Tony Lake, and Dick Holbrooke. Kofi was an intelligent, impressive man with a quiet but commanding presence. He had given most of his professional life in service to the United Nations, but he was not blind to its shortcomings, nor wedded to its bad habits. Instead, he was committed to making the UN's operations more efficient and more accountable. That was important on the merits and vital to my ability to persuade the congressional Republicans to pay our UN dues. We were $1.5 billion in arrears, and since 1995, when the Republicans took over, the Congress had refused to pay until the UN reformed itself. I thought the refusal to pay our back dues was irresponsible and damaging to both the UN and the United States, but I agreed that reform was imperative.

In the Middle East, Prime Minister Netanyahu and Chairman Arafat were trying to resolve their differences, with Netanyahu going to Gaza for three hours of talks on Christmas Eve day. As the year ended, my envoy, Dennis Ross, was shuttling back and forth between them, trying to close a deal on the turnover of Hebron to the Palestinians. It wasn't done yet, but I began 1997 with more hope for the peace process than I'd had in months.

After spending the first days of the New Year on St. Thomas in the U.S. Virgin Islands, a part of our nation Presidents rarely visit, my family went home to get ready for the inauguration and my fifth year as President. In many ways, it would be the most normal year of my presidency so far. For most of the year, Whitewater World was just a low-grade fever that spiked up from time to time with the campaign finance investigations, and I was free to do my job.

In the run-up to the inauguration, we held a series of events to emphasize that things were going in the right direction, highlighting 11.2 million new jobs in the previous four years, the largest decline in the crime rate in twenty-five years, and a 40 percent drop in the student-loan default rate.

I corrected an old injustice by giving the Congressional Medal of Honor to seven African-American veterans of World War II. Amazingly, no Medals of Honor had ever been awarded to blacks who served in that war. The selections were made after an exhaustive study of battle records. Six of the medals were awarded posthumously, but one of the recipients, seventy-seven-year-old Vernon Baker, was at the White House for the ceremony. He was an impressive man of quiet dignity and clear intelligence: as a young lieutenant in Italy more than fifty years earlier, he had single-handedly wiped out three enemy machine-gun units, an observer post, and a dugout. When asked how he had dealt with discrimination and prejudice after having given so much to his country, Baker said he had lived his life by a simple creed: "Give respect before you expect it, treat people the way you want to be treated, remember the mission, set the example, keep going." It sounded good to me.

A day after the Medal of Honor ceremony, Prime Minister Netanyahu and Chairman Arafat called me to say they had finally reached an agreement on the Israeli deployment in Hebron, bringing to a successful conclusion the talks we had launched in September. The Hebron deal was a relatively small part of the peace process, but it was the first time Netanyahu and Arafat had accomplished something together. If it had not been achieved, the entire peace process would have been in grave peril. Dennis Ross had been working with them virtually around the clock for a couple of weeks, and both King Hussein and Warren Christopher had pressed the parties to agree in the closing days of the negotiations. President Mubarak weighed in, too, when I called him for help at one o'clock in the morning in Cairo at the end of Ramadan. The Middle East was like that; it often took all hands on board to get things done.

Three days before the inauguration I awarded the Presidential Medal of Freedom to Bob Dole, noting that from his service in World War II, in which he was badly wounded coming to the aid of a fallen comrade, through all the ups and downs of his political career, Dole had "turned adversity to advantage and pain to public service, embodying the motto of the state he loved and went on to serve so well: **Ad astra per aspera,** to the stars through difficulties." Though we had been opponents and dis-agreed on many issues, I liked Dole. He could be mean and tough in a fight, but he lacked the fanaticism and hunger for personal destruction that characterized so many of the hard-right Republicans who now dominated his party in Washington.

I had had a fascinating visit with Dole a month earlier. He came to see me with a little toy for our cat, Socks, which he said was from his dog. We discussed the election, foreign policy, and the budget negotiations. The press was still buzzing about campaign finance abuses. Besides the DNC, the Republican National Committee and the Dole campaign had committed some violations. I had been criticized for inviting supporters to spend the night at the White House and for hosting morning coffees with administration members, supporters, contributors, and others who had no political ties to us.

I asked Dole, based on his years of experience, whether politics and politicians in Washington were more or less honest than they had been thirty years earlier. "Oh, it's not close," he said. "Much more honest today." Then I asked, "Would you agree that people think things are less hon-est?" "Sure," he said, "but they're wrong about it."

I was strongly supporting the new campaign finance reform bill sponsored by Senator John McCain and Sena-tor Russ Feingold, but I doubted that its passage would increase public confidence in the integrity of politicians. Fundamentally, the press objected to the influence of money on campaigns, though most of the money was spent on media advertising. Unless we were to legislate free or reduced-cost airtime, which the media generally opposed, or to adopt public financing of campaigns, an option with little public or congressional support, the media would continue to be the largest consumer of campaign dollars, even as they pilloried politicians for raising the funds to pay them.

In my inaugural address, I painted the most vivid picture I could of what America might be in the twenty-first century, and said that the American people had not "returned to office a President of one party and a Congress of another . . . to advance the politics of petty bickering and extreme partisanship they plainly deplored," but to work together on "America's mission."

The inaugural ceremonies, like our November victory celebration, were more serene, even relaxed, this time around, though the morning church service was enlivened by the fiery sermons of the Reverends Jesse Jackson and Tony Campolo, an Italian evangelical from Philadelphia who was perhaps the only white preacher in America who could keep up with Jesse. The atmosphere at the congressional luncheon was friendly, as I noted that the new Senate majority leader, Trent Lott of Mississippi, and I shared a profound debt to Thomas Jefferson: if he hadn't decided to buy the vast Louisiana Territory from France, neither of us would have been there. Ninety-four-year-old Senator Strom Thurmond was seated next to Chelsea and told her, "If I were seventy years younger, I'd court you!" No wonder he had lived so long. Hillary and I attended all fourteen inaugural balls; at one of them I got to dance with my beautiful daughter, now a senior in high school. She wouldn't be home much longer, and I savored the moment.

On the day after the inauguration, as a result of an investigation going back several years, the House of Representatives voted to reprimand Speaker Gingrich and fine him $300,000 for several violations of House ethics rules arising out of the use of tax-exempt funds for political purposes that had been given by his supporters to allegedly charitable organizations, and for several untruthful responses to congressional investigators about his activities. The counsel for the House Ethics Committee said that Gingrich and his political supporters had violated the tax laws and that there was evidence the Speaker had intentionally misled the committee about it.

In the late 1980s, Gingrich had led the charge to remove Jim Wright as Speaker of the House because his supporters had bought, in bulk, copies of a privately published book of Wright's speeches, in an alleged attempt to get around House rules prohibiting members from accepting speaking fees. Though the charges against Gingrich were much more serious, the Republican whip, Tom DeLay, complained that the fine and reprimand were out of proportion to the offense and an abuse of the ethics process. When I was asked about the affair, I could have urged the Justice Department or the U.S. attorney to investigate the charges of tax evasion and false statements to Congress; instead, I said the House should handle it "and then we should get back to the people's business." Two years later, when the shoe was on the other foot, Gingrich and DeLay would not be so charitable.

Shortly before the inauguration, in preparation for the second term and the State of the Union, I had gathered about eighty members of the White House staff and the departments for an all-day meeting at Blair House to focus on two things: the meaning of what we had done in the first four years and what we were going to do for the next four.

I believed the first term produced six important accomplishments: (1) restoring economic growth by replacing supply-side economics with our more disciplined "invest and grow" policy; (2) resolving the debate over the role of government in our lives by demonstrating that it is neither the enemy nor the solution, but the instrument to give our people the tools and conditions to make the most of their own lives; (3) reaffirming the primacy of community as the operative political model for America, and rejecting divisions by race, religion, gender, sexual orientation, or political philosophy; (4) replacing rhetoric with reality in our social policy, actually proving government action could make a difference in areas like welfare and crime if it reflected common sense and creative thinking, rather than just tough talk and hot rhetoric; (5) reestablishing the family as the primary unit of society, one that government could strengthen with policies like the family leave law, the Earned Income Tax Credit, the minimum wage increase, the V-chip, the anti–teen smoking initiative, efforts to increase adoption, and new reforms in health and education; (6) and reasserting America's leadership in the post–Cold War world as a force for democracy, shared prosperity, and peace, and against the new security threats of terror, weapons of mass destruction, organized crime, narco-trafficking, and racial and religious conflicts.

These accomplishments gave us a foundation from which we could launch America into the new century. Because the Republicans were in control of Congress and because it is more difficult to enact large reforms when times are good, I wasn't sure how much we could achieve in my second term, but I was determined to keep trying.

During the State of the Union on February 4, I first asked the Congress to conclude the unfinished business of our country: balancing the budget, passing the campaign finance reform bill, and completing the process of welfare reform by providing more incentives to employers and states to hire recipients and more training, transportation, and child-care support to help people go to work. I also asked for the restoration of health and disability benefits for legal immigrants, which the Republicans had cut off in 1996 to make room in the budget for their tax cuts.

Looking to the future, I asked Congress to join me in making education our number one priority because "every eight-year-old must be able to read; every twelve-year-old must be able to log on to the Internet; every eighteen-year-old must be able to go to college; and every adult American must be able to keep on learning for a lifetime." I offered a ten-point plan to achieve these goals, including the development of national standards and tests to measure progress in meeting them; certification of 100,000 "master teachers" by the National Board for Professional Teaching Standards, up from only 500 in 1995; the America Reads tutoring initiative for eight-year-olds, which sixty college presidents had already agreed to support; more children in preschool; public school choice in every state; character education in every school; a multi-billion-dollar school construction and repair program, the first since just after World War II, to repair run-down facilities and help build new ones in school districts so over-crowded that classes were being held in trailers; the $1,500 HOPE Scholarship tax credit for the first two years of college and a $10,000 tuition tax deduction for all higher education after high school; a "GI Bill" for America's workers to give a skill grant to adults who needed further training; and a plan to connect every classroom and library to the Internet by 2000.

I told the Congress and the American people that one of America's greatest strengths in the Cold War had been a bipartisan foreign policy. Now, with education critical to our security in the twenty-first century, I asked that we approach it in the same way: "Politics must stop at the schoolhouse door."

I also asked the Congress to support the other commitments I had made to the American people in my campaign: the expansion of the family leave law; a large increase in AIDS research to develop a vaccine; an extension of health insurance to the children of low-income working people who couldn't afford it on their own; a comprehensive assault on juvenile crime, violence, drugs, and gangs; a doubling of the number of empowerment zones and the number of toxic waste sites cleaned up; and the continued expansion of community service programs.

In foreign policy, I asked for support for the expansion of NATO; the North Korean nuclear agreement; the extension of our Bosnian mission; our increasing engagement with China; "fast track" authority in trade negotiations, which requires Congress to vote on trade agreements up or down without amendments; a weapons modernization program at the Pentagon to meet new security challenges; and ratification of the Chemical Weapons Convention, which I thought would go a long way toward protecting America from terrorist attacks with poison gas.

In the speech, I tried to reach out to Republicans as well as Democrats, telling them that I would defend any member's vote on the right kind of balanced budget and quoting a scripture verse, Isaiah 58:12: "thou shalt be called, The repairer of the breach, The restorer of paths to dwell in." In one way or another, that's what I had been trying to do for most of my life.

The media's limited appetite for policy, compared with

breaking scandal, became humorously apparent near the end of my speech. I had what I thought was a fine closing: I pointed out that "a child born tonight will have almost no memory of the twentieth century. Everything that child will know about America will be because of what we do now to build a new century." I reminded all who were listening that there were just over a thousand days until that new century, "a thousand days to build a bridge to a land of new promise." While I was making my pitch, the networks split the television screen so that viewers could also watch the jury render its verdict in the civil suit against O. J. Simpson over the murder of his wife, a suit brought after the jury in the criminal case failed to convict him. The television audience heard the civil jury rule against Simpson and my exhortations about the future simultaneously. I felt fortunate that I wasn't cut off completely, and that the public response to the speech was still positive.

Two days later I presented my budget plan to Congress. The budget brought America into balance in five years; increased investment in education by 20 percent, including the largest increase in college aid in fifty years since the GI Bill; cut spending in hundreds of other programs; provided targeted middle-class tax relief, including a $500-per-child tax credit; secured the Medicare Trust Fund, which was about to go broke, for ten years; provided health insurance to five million uninsured children, respite care for families caring for a loved one with Alzheimer's, and, for the first time, mammograms for older women under Medicare; and reversed the downward spiral in international affairs spending so that we could do more to promote peace and freedom and to fight terrorism, weapons proliferation, and narco-trafficking.

Unlike two years earlier, when I had forced the Republicans to make their harsh budget proposals public before coming forward with my own, I went first. I thought it was the right thing to do, and also good politics. Now when the Republicans presented their budget, with its bigger tax cuts for upper-income people, they would have to cut back on my education and health-care proposals to pay for them. This wasn't 1994; the public had figured things out, and the Republicans wanted to get reelected. I felt sure that, within a few months, Congress would pass a balanced budget that would be pretty close to my plan.

A couple of weeks later, another attempt to pass the balanced budget amendment to the Constitution failed in the Senate as Senator Bob Torricelli of New Jersey decided to vote against it. It was a courageous vote. New Jersey was an anti-tax state, and Bob had voted for the amendment as a congressman. I hoped that his bravery would get us past the posturing and on to the business of actually balancing the budget.

In mid-month we got another economic boost when American-led negotiations in Geneva produced an agreement to liberalize world trade in telecommunications services, opening 90 percent of the markets to U.S. firms. The negotiations were launched by Al Gore and conducted by Charlene Barshefsky. Their work was certain to bring new jobs and services at lower prices to Americans, and to spread the benefits of new technologies across the world.

Around this time I was in Boston with Mayor Tom Menino. Crime, violence, and drug use were going down in America, but they were still on the rise among people under eighteen, though not in Boston, where no child had died from gun violence in eighteen months, a remarkable achievement for a large city. I proposed child trigger locks on guns to prevent accidental shootings, a massive anti-drug advertising campaign, required drug tests for young people seeking driver's licenses, and reforms in the juvenile justice system, including the kind of probation and after-school services that Boston had implemented so successfully.

There were some interesting developments in Whitewater World in February. On the seventeenth, Kenneth Starr announced he would leave his post on August 1 to become dean of the Pepperdine University Law School in southern California. He had obviously decided that Whitewater was a dry hole and this was a graceful way out, but he received heavy criticism for his decision. The press said it looked bad because his Pepperdine position had been funded by Richard Mellon Scaife, whose funding of the Arkansas Project was not yet public knowledge, but who was widely recognized as an extreme right-winger with an animus toward me. I thought their objection was flimsy; Starr was already earning lots of money representing political opponents of my administration while serving as independent counsel, and he would in fact reduce his conflicts of interest by going to Pepperdine.

What really rocked Starr was all the heat he got from the Republican right and the three or four reporters who were deeply vested in finding something we'd done wrong, or at least in continuing the torment. By then, Starr had already done a lot for them: he had saddled a lot of people with big legal bills and damaged reputations, and, at enormous cost to taxpayers, had managed to drag the investigation out for three years, even after the RTC report said there was no basis for any civil or criminal action against Hillary and me. But the right wing and the Whitewater press knew that if Starr quit, it was a tacit admission that there was "no there there." After they beat him up for four days he announced he would stay on. I didn't know whether to laugh or cry.

The press was also still writing about fund-raising in the 1996 campaign. Among other things, they were agitated that I had invited people who had contributed to my campaign in 1992 to spend the night at the White Hosue, even though, as with all guests, I paid for the costs of meals and other refreshments. The implication was that I had been selling overnights in the White House to raise money for the DNC. It was ridiculous. I was an incumbent President who led in the polls from start to finish; raising money was no problem, and even if it had been, I would never have used the White House in that way. At the end of the month, I released a list of all overnight guests in the first term. There were hundreds of them, about 85 percent of whom were relatives, friends of Chelsea's, foreign visitors and other dignitaries, or people whom Hillary and I had known before I started running for President. As for my supporters from '92 who were also my friends, I wanted as many of them as possible to have the honor of spending the night in the White House. Often, given the long hours I worked, the only time I had to visit with people in an informal way was late at night. There was never a single case when I raised money because of this practice. My critics seemed to be saying that the only people who shouldn't be overnight guests were friends and supporters. When I released the list, many people on it were questioned by the press. One reporter called Tony Campolo and asked if he'd given me a contribution. When he said he had, he was asked how much. "I think $25," he said, "but it might have been $50." "Oh," the reporter replied, "we don't want to talk to you," and hung up.

The month ended on a happy note, as Hillary and I took Chelsea and eleven of her girlfriends to dinner at the Bombay Club restaurant in Washington for her seventeenth birthday, and later to New York to see some plays, and Hillary won a Grammy Award for the audio version of **It Takes a Village.** She has a great voice, and the book was full of stories she loved to tell. The Grammy was another reminder that at least beyond the Washington Beltway, a lot of Americans were interested in the same things we were.

In mid-February, Prime Minister Netanyahu came to see me to discuss the current state of the peace process, and Yasser Arafat did the same in early March. Netanyahu was constrained politically in what he could do beyond the Hebron deal. The Israelis had just begun to elect their prime minister directly, so Netanyahu had a four-year term, but he still had to put together a majority coalition in the Knesset. If he lost his coalition on the right, he could form a national unity government with Peres and the Labor Party, but he didn't want to do that. The hardliners in his coalition knew this and were making it difficult for him to keep moving toward peace by opening the Gaza airport or even letting all the Palestinians from Gaza come back to work in Israel. Psychologically, Netanyahu faced the same challenge Rabin had: Israel had to give up something concrete—land, access, jobs, an airport—in return for something far less tangible: the best efforts of the PLO to prevent terrorist attacks.

I was convinced Netanyahu wanted to do more, and afraid that if he couldn't, Arafat would find it more difficult to keep the lid on violence. To further complicate matters, whenever the peace process slowed, or the Israelis retaliated for a terrorist attack or began another building program in a West Bank settlement, there was likely to be a UN Security Council resolution condemning Israel for its continued violation of UN resolutions, and doing so in a way that suggested what the negotiated settlement should be. The Israelis depended on the United States to veto such measures, which we normally did. That enabled us to maintain our influence with them, but weakened our claim to be an honest broker with the Palestinians. I had to keep reminding Arafat that I was committed to the peace process and that only the United States could help bring it about, because the Israelis trusted America, not the European Union or Russia, to protect its security.

When Arafat came to see me I tried to work through the next steps with him. Not surprisingly, he saw things differently from Netanyahu; he thought he was supposed to prevent all violence and wait around for Netanyahu's politics to permit Israel to honor its commitments under the peace agreement. I had developed a comfortable working relationship with both leaders by then and had decided the only realistic option was to keep the process from falling apart by staying in constant touch, putting things back on track when they **did** fall apart, and maintaining momentum, even if it came in baby steps.

On the night of March 13, after appearances in North Carolina and south Florida, I went to Greg Norman's house in Hobe Sound to visit with him and his wife, Laura. It was a very pleasant evening, and the time got away from us. Before I knew it, it was after one o'clock in the morning, and since we were supposed to play in a golf tournament a few hours later, I got up to leave. As we were walking down the steps, I didn't see the last one. My right foot came down on the step's edge and I began to fall. Had I fallen forward, the worst that could have happened was scratched palms. Instead, I jerked backward, heard a loud pop, and fell. The sound was so loud that Norman, who was a few feet in front of me, heard it, turned around, and caught me, or I would have been hurt far worse than I was.

An ambulance took me on the forty-minute drive to St. Mary's Hospital, a Catholic institution the White House medical team had chosen because it had an excellent emergency room. I was there for the rest of the night in agonizing pain. When an MRI revealed that I'd torn 90 percent of my right quadriceps, I was flown back to Washington. Hillary met Air Force One at Andrews Air Force Base and watched as they lowered me out of the belly of the plane in a wheelchair. She had been scheduled to leave for Africa, but delayed her trip to get me through the necessary surgery at Bethesda Naval Hospital.

About thirteen hours after my injury, a fine surgical team led by Dr. David Adkison gave me an epidural, put on some music by Jimmy Buffett and Lyle Lovett, and talked me through the surgery. I could see what they were doing in a glass panel above the operating table: the doctor drilled holes in my kneecap, pulled the torn muscle through them, sutured the ends to the solid part of the muscle, and put me back together. After it was over, Hillary and Chelsea helped me get through one horrible day of pain; then things began to get better.

The thing I dreaded most was the six months of rehabilitation, and not being able to jog and play golf. I would be on crutches for a couple of months and in a soft leg brace after that. And for a while I was still vulnerable to falling and reinjuring myself. The White House staff rigged my shower up with safety rails so that I could keep my balance. Soon I learned how to dress myself with the help of a little stick. I could do everything but put on my socks. The medical staff at the White House, headed by Dr. Connie Mariano, was available around the clock. The navy gave me two great physical therapists, Dr. Bob Kellogg and Nannette Paco, who worked with me every day. Even though I had been told I'd gain weight during my period of immobility, by the time the physical therapists were through with me, I had lost fifteen pounds.

When I got home from the hospital, I had less than a week to get ready to meet Boris Yeltsin in Helsinki, and a big issue to deal with before then. On the seventeenth, Tony Lake came to see me and asked me to withdraw his nomination for director of central intelligence. Senator Richard Shelby, the chairman of the Intelligence Committee, had delayed Lake's confirmation hearings largely on the grounds that the White House had not informed the committee of our decision to stop enforcing the arms embargo against Bosnia in 1994. I was not required by law to tell the committee and had decided that it was better not to do so in order to keep it from leaking. I knew a strong bipartisan majority of the Senate favored lifting the embargo; in fact, not long afterward, they voted for a resolution asking me to stop enforcing it.

Though I got along with Shelby well enough, I thought he was far off base in holding up Lake's confirmation and unnecessarily hampering the operations of the CIA. Tony had some strong Republican supporters, including Senator Lugar, and would have been voted out of committee and confirmed had it not been for Shelby, but he was worn down after working seventy- and eighty-hour weeks for four years. And he didn't want to risk hurting the CIA with further delays. If it had been up to me, I would have carried on the fight for a year if that's what it took to get a vote. But I could see Tony had had enough. Two days later I nominated George Tenet, the acting CIA director who had been John Deutch's deputy and before that had served as my senior aide for intelligence on the NSC, and staff director of the Senate Intelligence Committee. He was confirmed easily, but I still regret the raw deal handed to Lake, who had given thirty years to advancing America's security interests and had played a major role in so many of our foreign policy successes in my first term.

My doctors didn't want me to go to Helsinki, but staying home wasn't an option. Yeltsin had been reelected and NATO was about to vote to admit Poland, Hungary, and the Czech Republic; we had to have an agreement on how to proceed.

The flight was long and uncomfortable, but the time passed quickly as I discussed with Strobe Talbott and the rest of the team what we could do to help Yeltsin live with NATO expansion, including getting Russia into the G-7 and the World Trade Organization. At a dinner that night hosted by President Martti Ahtisaari of Finland, I was glad to see Yeltsin in good spirits and apparently recovering from open-heart surgery. He had lost a lot of weight and was still pale, but he was back to his old buoyant and aggressive self.

The next morning we got down to business. When I told Boris I wanted NATO both to expand and to sign an agreement with Russia, he asked me to commit secretly— in his words, "in a closet"—to limiting future NATO expansion to the Warsaw Pact nations, thus excluding the states of the former Soviet Union, like the Baltics and

Ukraine. I said I couldn't do that because, first of all, it wouldn't remain secret, and doing so would undermine the credibility of the Partnership for Peace. Nor would it be in America's or Russia's interest. NATO's governing mission was no longer directed against Russia but against the new threats to peace and stability in Europe. I pointed out that a declaration that NATO would stop its expansion with the Warsaw Pact nations would be tantamount to announcing a new dividing line in Europe, with a smaller Russian empire. That would make Russia look weaker, not stronger, whereas a NATO-Russia agreement would boost Russia's standing. I also urged Yeltsin not to foreclose the possibility of future Russian membership.

Yeltsin was still afraid of the domestic reaction to expansion. At one point when we were alone, I asked, "Boris, do you really think I would allow NATO to attack Russia from bases in Poland?" "No," he replied, "I don't, but a lot of older people who live in the western part of Russia and listen to Zyuganov do." He reminded me that, unlike the United States, Russia had been invaded twice—by Napoleon and by Hitler—and the trauma of those events still colored the country's collective psychology and shaped its politics. I told Yeltsin that if he would agree to NATO expansion and the NATO-Russia partnership, I would make a commitment not to station troops or missiles in the new member countries prematurely, and to support Russian membership in the new G-8, the World Trade Organization, and other international organizations. We had a deal.

Yeltsin and I also faced two arms control problems at Helsinki: the reluctance of the Russian Duma to ratify START II, which would reduce both our nuclear arsenals by two-thirds from their Cold War peak; and the growing opposition in Russia to America's development of missile defense systems. When the Russian economy collapsed and the military budget was slashed, the START II treaty had turned into a bad deal for them. It required both countries to dismantle their multiple-warhead missiles, called MIRVs, and provided for parity in both sides' single-warhead arsenals. Since Russia relied more heavily than the United States on MIRVs, the Russians would have to build a considerable number of single-warhead missiles to regain parity, and they couldn't afford to do it. I told Yeltsin I didn't want START II to give us strategic superiority and suggested that our teams come up with a solution that included adopting targets for a START III treaty that would take both countries down to between 2,000 and 2,500 warheads, an 80 percent reduction from the Cold War high, and a number sufficiently small so that Russia wouldn't have to build new missiles to be at parity with us. There was some reluctance in the Pentagon to go that low, but General Shalikashvili believed it was safe to do so, and Bill Cohen backed him. Within a short time, we agreed to extend the deadline for START II from 2002 to 2007 and to have START III come into effect the same year, so that Russia would never be at a strategic disadvantage.

On the second issue, since the 1980s the United States had been exploring missile defense, beginning with President Reagan's idea of a sky-based system that would shoot down all hostile missiles and thus free the world from the specter of nuclear war. There were two problems with the idea: it wasn't yet technically feasible, and a national missile defense system (NMD) would violate the Anti-Ballistic Missile Treaty, which forbade such systems because if one country had an NMD and the other didn't, the latter's nuclear arsenal might no longer be a deterrent to an attack by the nation with the NMD.

Les Aspin, my first secretary of defense, had shifted the emphasis of our efforts away from developing defenses that could shoot down long-range Russian missiles to funding a theater missile defense (TMD) that could protect our soldiers and other people from shorter-range missiles like those being developed by Iran, Iraq, Libya, and North Korea. They were a real danger; in the Gulf War twenty-eight of our soldiers had been killed by an Iraqi Scud missile.

I strongly supported the TMD program, which was permitted by the ABM Treaty and which, as I told Yeltsin, might someday be used to defend both our nations on a common battlefield, in the Balkans or elsewhere. The problem Russia had with our position was that it was unclear what the dividing line was between theater missile defense and the larger ones prohibited by the treaty. The new technologies developed for TMD might later be adaptable for use against ABMs, in violation of the treaty. Eventually, both sides agreed to a technical definition of the dividing line between permissible programs and prohibited ones that allowed us to proceed with the TMD.

The Helsinki summit was an unexpected success, thanks in no small measure to Yeltsin's capacity to imagine a different future for Russia, in which it would affirm its greatness in terms other than territorial domination, and his willingness to stand against prevailing opinion in the Duma and sometimes even within his own government. Though our work never realized its full potential because the Duma still refused to ratify START II, the stage was set for a successful NATO summit in July in Madrid to move us further along the road to a united Europe.

When I got home, the reaction was generally favorable, though Henry Kissinger and some other Republicans criticized me for agreeing not to deploy nuclear weapons and foreign troops closer to Russia in the new member states. Yeltsin got hit hard by the old Communists, who said he had caved in to me on the important issues. Zyuganov said Yeltsin had let "his friend Bill kick him in the rear." Yeltsin had just kicked Zyuganov in the rear in the election by fighting for tomorrow's Russia instead of yesterday's. I thought he would weather this storm, too.

When Hillary and Chelsea got home from Africa, they regaled me with their adventures. Africa was important to America, and Hillary's trip, much like her earlier one to South Asia, emphasized our commitment to supporting leaders and ordinary citizens in their efforts to find peace, prosperity, and freedom and to roll back the tide of AIDS.

On the last day of the month, I announced the appointment of Wes Clark to succeed General George Joulwan as the commander in chief, U.S. European Command, and Supreme Allied Commander of the NATO forces in Europe. I admired both men. Joulwan had vigorously supported an aggressive NATO stance in Bosnia, and Clark had been an integral part of Dick Holbrooke's negotiating team. I felt he was the best person to continue our firm commitment to peace in the Balkans.

In April, I saw King Hussein and Prime Minister Netanyahu in an attempt to keep the peace process from falling apart. Violence had broken out again, in the wake of an Israeli decision to build new housing in Har Homa, an Israeli settlement on the outskirts of East Jerusalem. Every time Netanyahu took a step forward, as with the Hebron agreement, his governing coalition made him do something that drove a wedge between Israel and the Palestinians. During the same period, a Jordanian soldier had gone berserk and killed seven Israeli schoolchildren. King Hussein immediately went to Israel and apologized. That diffused the tensions between Israel and Jordan, but Arafat was left with the continuing demand of the United States and Israel that he suppress terror while living with the Har Homa project, which he felt contradicted Israel's commitment not to change areas on the ground that were supposed to be resolved in the negotiations.

When King Hussein came to see me, he was worried that the step-by-step peace process that had been working under Rabin couldn't succeed now because of the political constraints on Netanyahu. Netanyahu was concerned about that, too; he had expressed some interest in trying to accelerate the process by moving to the difficult final status issues quickly. Hussein thought that if this could be done, we should try. When Netanyahu came to the White House a few days later, I told him I would support this approach, but in order to get Arafat to agree, he would have to find a way to follow through on the interim steps the Palestinians had already been promised, including the opening of the Gaza airport, safe passage between Gaza and the Palestinian areas in the West Bank, and economic assistance.

I spent most of the month in an intense effort to convince the Senate to ratify the Chemical Weapons Convention: calling and meeting with members of Congress; agreeing with Jesse Helms to move the Arms Control and Disarmament Agency and the U.S. Information Agency into the State Department in return for his allowing a vote on the CWC, which he opposed; and holding an event on the South Lawn with distinguished Republicans and military supporters of the treaty, including Colin Powell and James Baker, to counter conservative Republican opposition from people like Helms, Caspar Weinberger, and Donald Rumsfeld.

I was surprised at the conservative opposition, since all our military leaders strongly supported the CWC, but it reflected the right's deep skepticism about international cooperation in general and its desire to maintain maximum freedom of action now that the United States was the world's only superpower. Near the end of the month, I reached an agreement with Senator Lott to add some language that he felt strengthened the treaty. Finally, with Lott's support, the CWC was ratified, 74–26. Interestingly, I watched the Senate vote on television with Japanese prime minister Ryutaro Hashimoto, who was in town to meet with me the next day, and I thought he would like to see the ratification after what Japan had suffered in the sarin gas attack.

On the home front, I named Sandy Thurman of Atlanta, one of America's foremost AIDS advocates, to head the Office of National AIDS Policy. Since 1993 our overall investment in combating HIV and AIDS had increased 60 percent, we had approved eight new AIDS drugs and nineteen others for AIDS-related conditions, and the death rate was going down in America. Still, we were a long way from a vaccine or a cure, and the problem had exploded in Africa, where we weren't doing enough. Thurman was bright, energetic, and forceful; I knew she would keep us all on our toes.

On the last day of April, Hillary and I made public Chelsea's decision to attend Stanford in the fall. In her typically methodical way, Chelsea had also visited Harvard, Yale, Princeton, Brown, and Wellesley, and had been to several of them twice to get a feel for the academic and social life of each institution. Given her excellent grades and test scores, she had been accepted by all of them, and Hillary had hoped she would stay closer to home. I always suspected Chelsea would like to get far away from Washington. I just wanted her to go to a school where she would learn a lot, make good friends, and enjoy herself. But her mother and I were going to miss her badly. Having Chelsea at home in our first four years in the White House, going to her school and ballet events, and getting to know her friends and their parents had been a joy, repeatedly reminding us, no matter what else was going on, of what a blessing our daughter was.

Economic growth in the first quarter of 1997 was reported to be 5.6 percent, which pushed the estimated deficit down to $75 billion, about a quarter of what it was when I took office. On May 2, I announced that, at long last, I had reached a balanced budget agreement with Speaker Gingrich and Senator Lott and the congressional negotiators for both parties. Senator Tom Daschle also announced his support for the agreement; Dick Gephardt did not, but I was hoping he would come around once he had a chance to review it. The deal was much easier to make this time because economic growth had brought unemployment below 5 percent for the first time since 1973, boosting payrolls, profits, and tax revenues.

In broad terms, the agreement extended the life of Medicare for a decade, while providing the annual mammogram and diabetes screening initiatives I wanted; extended health coverage to five million children, the largest expansion since the passage of Medicaid in the 1960s; contained the largest increase in education spending in thirty years; gave more incentives to businesses to hire welfare recipients; restored health benefits to disabled legal immigrants; funded the cleanup of five hundred more toxic waste sites; and provided tax relief close to the amount I had recommended.

I met the Republicans halfway on the amount of Medicare savings, which I now believed we could achieve with good policy changes that didn't hurt senior citizens, and the Republicans accepted a smaller tax cut, the child health insurance program, and the big education increase. We got about 95 percent of the new investments I had recommended in the State of the Union, and the Republicans took about two-thirds of the tax cut figure they had originally proposed. The tax cuts would now be far smaller than the Reagan tax reduction of 1981. I was elated that the countless hours of meetings, begun in late 1995 under the threat of a government shutdown, had produced the first balanced budget since 1969, and a good one to boot. Senator Lott and Speaker Gingrich had worked with us in good faith, and Erskine Bowles, with his negotiating skills and common sense, had kept things going with them and the principal congressional negotiators at critical moments.

Later in the month, when the budget agreement was brought to a vote in a resolution, 64 percent of the House Democrats joined 88 percent of the House Republicans in voting for it. In the Senate, where Tom Daschle was supporting the agreement, Democrats were in favor of the agreement even more strongly than Republicans, 82 to 74 percent.

I took some criticism from Democrats who objected to the tax cut or to the fact that we were making the agreement at all. They argued that if we did nothing, the budget would be balanced the next year or the year afterward anyway because of the 1993 plan only Democrats had voted for; now we were going to let Republicans share the credit. That was true, but we were also going to get the biggest increase in higher education aid in fifty years, health care for five million kids, and middle-class tax cuts I supported.

On the fifth, Mexican Independence Day, I left for a trip to Mexico, Central America, and the Caribbean. Little over a decade earlier, our neighbors had been plagued with civil wars, coups, dictators, closed economies, and desperate poverty. Now every nation in the hemisphere except one was a democracy, and the region as a whole was our largest trading partner; we exported twice as much to the Americas as to Europe and almost 50 percent more than to Asia. Still, there was too much poverty in the region, and we had serious problems with drugs and illegal immigration.

I took a number of cabinet members and a bipartisan congressional delegation to Mexico with me as we announced new agreements designed to reduce illegal immigration and the influx of drugs across the Rio Grande. President Zedillo was an able, honest man with a strong supporting team, and I was sure he would try his best to deal with these problems. While I knew we could do better, I doubted there was a completely satisfactory solution to either of the two problems. There were a number of contributing factors to take into account. Mexico was poorer than the United States; the border was long; millions of Mexicans had relatives in our country; and many illegal immigrants came to the United States looking for work, often at low-paying, demanding jobs most Americans didn't want to do. As for drugs, our demand was a magnet for them, and the drug cartels had a lot of money with which to bribe Mexican officials and plenty of hired guns to intimidate or kill those who didn't want to cooperate. Some Mexican border police were offered five times their annual salary to look the other way on just one drug shipment. One honest prosecutor in northern Mexico had been shot more than one hundred times right in front of his house. These were tough problems, but I thought the implementation of our agreements would help.

In Costa Rica, a beautiful country with no permanent military organization and perhaps the most advanced environmental policy in the world, President José María Figueres hosted the Central American leaders for a meeting that focused on trade and the environment. NAFTA had inadvertently hurt Central America and the Caribbean nations by putting them at a competitive disadvantage with Mexico in trading with the United States. I wanted to do what I could to rectify the inequity. The next day I made the same point in Bridgetown, Barbados, where Prime Minister Owen Arthur hosted the first meeting ever held between a U.S. President and all the leaders of the Caribbean nations in their own territory.

Immigration was also a big issue at both meetings. Many Central Americans and people from the Caribbean nations were working in the United States and sending money back home to their families, providing a major source of income in the smaller nations. The leaders were worried about the anti-immigration stance Republicans had taken and wanted my assurances that there would be no mass deportations. I gave it to them, but also said we had to enforce our immigration laws.

At the end of the month I flew to Paris for the signing of the NATO-Russia Founding Act. Yeltsin had kept his Helsinki commitment: NATO's Cold War adversary was now its partner.

After a stop in the Netherlands to celebrate the fiftieth anniversary of the Marshall Plan, I flew to London for my first official meeting with the new British prime minister, Tony Blair. His Labour Party had won a big victory over the Tories in the recent election as a result of Blair's leadership, Labour's more modern and more moderate message, and the natural ebbing of support for the Conservatives after their many years in power. Blair was young, articulate, and forceful, and we shared many of the same political views. I thought he had the potential to be an important leader for the UK and all of Europe, and was excited about the prospect of working with him.

Hillary and I went to dinner with Tony and Cherie Blair at a restaurant in a restored warehouse district on the Thames. We felt like old friends from the start. The British press was fascinated by the similarity in our philosophies and politics, and the questions they asked seemed to have an impact on the American press traveling with me. For the first time, I had the feeling that they were beginning to believe there was something more than rhetoric to my New Democrat approach.

On June 6, my mother's birthday, I gave the commencement address at Chelsea's graduation ceremony at Sidwell Friends School. Teddy Roosevelt had spoken to the Sidwell students almost a century earlier, but I was there in a different role, not as a President but as a father. When I asked Chelsea what she wanted me to say, she replied, "Dad, I want you to be wise, briefly," then added, "The girls want you to be wise; the boys just want you to be funny." I wanted the speech to be my gift to her, and I was up until three in the morning the night before the commencement writing it out, over and over again.

I told Chelsea and her classmates that on this day their parents' "pride and joy are tempered by our coming separation from you . . . we are remembering your first day in school and all the triumphs and travails between then and now. Though we have raised you for this moment of departure and we are very proud of you, a part of us longs to hold you once more as we did when you could barely walk, to read to you just one more time **Goodnight Moon** or **Curious George** or **The Little Engine That Could.**" I said that an exciting world beckoned and they had almost limitless choices, and I reminded them of Eleanor Roosevelt's adage that no one can make you feel inferior without your permission: "Do not give them permission."

When Chelsea walked up to get her diploma, I hugged her and told her I loved her. After the ceremony several parents thanked me for saying what they were thinking and feeling, then we went back to the White House for a graduation party. Chelsea was touched to see the entire residence staff gathered to congratulate her. She had come a long way from the young girl with braces we had brought to the White House four and a half years earlier, and she had only just begun.

Soon after Chelsea's graduation, I accepted the recommendation of the National Bioethics Advisory Commission that human cloning was "morally unacceptable" and proposed that Congress ban it. It had become an issue since the cloning of Dolly the sheep in Scotland. Cloning technology had been used for some time to increase agricultural production and to achieve biomedical advances in the treatment of cancer, diabetes, and other disorders. It held great promise for producing replacement skin, cartilage, and bone tissue for burn and accident victims, and nerve tissue to treat spinal cord injuries. I didn't want to interfere with all that, but thought we should draw the line at human cloning. Just a month earlier I had apologized for the unconscionable and racist syphilis experiments performed on hundreds of black men decades earlier by the federal government in Tuskegee, Alabama.

In mid-June, I went to the University of California at San Diego to speak about America's continuing struggle to rid itself of racial discrimination and make the most of our growing diversity. The United States still suffered from discrimination, bigotry, hate crimes, and great disparities in income, education, and health care. I appointed a seven-member commission chaired by the distinguished scholar John Hope Franklin to educate America about the state of race relations and to make recommendations to help build "One America" in the twenty-first century. I would coordinate the efforts through a new White House office headed by Ben Johnson.

In late June, Denver served as the host city for the annual G-7 meeting. I had pledged to Yeltsin that Russia would be fully included, but the finance ministers opposed the move because of Russia's economic weaknesses. Since Russia depended on the financial support of the international community, they felt it shouldn't be in on the G-7's financial decision making. I could understand why the finance ministers needed to meet and make decisions without Russia, but the G-7 was also a political organization; being in it would symbolize Russia's importance to the future and strengthen Yeltsin at home. We had already called this meeting the Summit of Eight. In the end, we voted to take Russia in as a full member of the new G-8, but to allow the finance ministers of the other seven nations to continue to meet on appropriate matters. Now Yeltsin and I had both kept our Helsinki commitments.

At about this time, Mir Aimal Kansi, who was believed to be responsible for murdering two CIA employees and wounding three others at CIA headquarters in 1993, was brought back to the United States from Pakistan to stand trial after intense efforts to secure his extradition by the FBI, the CIA, and the Departments of State, Justice, and Defense. It was strong evidence of our determination to track down terrorists and bring them to justice.

A week later, after a heated debate, the House of Representatives voted to continue normal trade relations with China. Although the motion carried by eighty-six votes, it sparked strong opposition from conservatives and liberals who disapproved of China's human rights and trade policies. I also supported more political freedom in China, and had recently invited the Dalai Lama and Hong Kong human rights activist Martin Lee to the White House to highlight my support for the cultural and religious integrity of Tibet and for maintaining Hong Kong's democracy now that the UK had restored it to China. I thought the trade relationship could be improved only through negotiations leading to China's entry into the World Trade Organization. Meanwhile, we needed to stay involved with, not isolate, China. Interestingly, Martin Lee agreed, and supported the continuation of our trade relationship.

Soon afterward, I flew home to Hope for the funeral of Oren Grisham, my ninety-two-year-old uncle Buddy, who had played such a large role in my life. When I got to the funeral home, his family and I immediately started swapping funny stories about him. As one of my relatives said, he was the salt of the earth and the spice of life. According to Wordsworth, the best portion of a good man's life is his little, unremembered acts of kindness and love. Buddy had showered them on me when I was young and fatherless. In December, Hillary gave me a beautiful chocolate Labrador retriever to keep me company with Chelsea gone. He was a good-natured, high-spirited, intelligent dog. I named him Buddy.

In early July, Hillary, Chelsea, and I, after a couple of relaxing days with King Juan Carlos and Queen Sofia on the island of Majorca, were in Madrid for the NATO meeting. I had a fruitful discussion with the Spanish president, José María Aznar, who had just decided to fully integrate Spain into NATO's command structure. Then NATO voted to admit Poland, Hungary, and the Czech Republic, and made clear to the two dozen other nations that had joined the Partnership for Peace that NATO's door remained open to new members. From the beginning of my presidency, I had pushed for the expansion of NATO and believed this historic step would help both to unify Europe and to maintain the trans-Atlantic alliance.

The next day we signed a partnership agreement with Ukraine, and I left for stops in Poland, Romania, and Denmark to reinforce the meaning of NATO expansion. There were large, enthusiastic crowds in Warsaw, Bucharest, and Copenhagen. In Poland, they were celebrating their new NATO membership. In Bucharest, about 100,000 people chanted "U.S.A, U.S.A.!" to demonstrate their support for democracy and their desire to enter NATO as soon as possible. In Copenhagen, on a bright sunny day, the size and enthusiasm of the crowd reflected an affirmation of our alliance and an appreciation of the fact that I was the first sitting President ever to visit Denmark.

By mid-month, I was back at work in the White House, proposing legislation to ban discrimination based on genetic screening. Scientists were rapidly unlocking the mysteries of the human genome, and their discoveries were likely to save millions of lives and revolutionize health care. But genetic testing would also reveal an individual's propensity to develop various illnesses, like breast cancer or Parkinson's. We couldn't allow the results of genetic tests to be the basis for denying health insurance or access to a job, and we didn't want to discourage people from undergoing them out of fear that the results would be used against them rather than to lengthen their lives.

At about the same time, the IRA restored the cease-fire it had broken in February 1996. I had pushed hard for the cease-fire, and it would hold this time, making it possible at last for the Irish to find their way through the thicket of accumulated hurt and suspicion to a shared future.

As July was drawing to a close, we still hadn't been able to agree on a detailed budget consistent with the earlier, more general agreement with the Republicans. We remained at odds over the size and shape of the tax cuts and over the allocation of new funds. While our team continued to negotiate with Congress, I went on with the rest of my job, asserting that, contrary to the dominant opinion in Congress, global warming was a reality and that we had to cut our greenhouse gas emissions, and holding a forum with Al Gore and other federal and state officials at Incline Village, Nevada, on the condition of Lake Tahoe.

Tahoe was one of the deepest, purest, cleanest lakes in the world, but its quality was degrading as a result of development, air pollution from traffic, and direct pollution from fuel that was discharged into the water from inefficient motorboats and Jet Ski engines. There was broad bipartisan support in California and Nevada for restoring the lake, and Al and I were determined to do everything possible to help.

At the end of the month, after I spoke to the National Governors Association in Las Vegas, Governor Bob Miller took me and several of my former colleagues to play golf with Michael Jordan. I had started playing again only two weeks earlier and was still wearing a soft leg brace for protection. I didn't really think I needed it anymore, so I took it off for the golf match.

Jordan was a great golfer, a long if sometimes erratic driver who also had a great short game. I got some insight into why he had won so many NBA championships when our group played a short par-five hole. All five of us had a good chance to make a birdie four. Jordan looked at his forty-five-foot downhill breaking putt and said, "Well, I guess I have to make this to win the hole." I could tell by the look in his eyes that he actually expected to make the difficult putt. He did, and won the hole.

Jordan told me I'd play better if I put my leg brace back on: "Your body doesn't need it anymore, but your mind doesn't know it yet." One reason I wasn't playing better is that I was constantly on the phone to the White House for an update on the budget negotiations, as we made last-minute offers and compromises in an effort to conclude them.

A little more than halfway through the match, Rahm Emanuel called to say we had a deal. Then Erskine called to confirm it and tell me how good it was. We got all our education and health money, the tax cut was modest, about 10 percent of the Reagan cut in '81, the Medicare savings were manageable, the middle-class tax cuts were in, the capital gains tax rate would be reduced from 28 to 20 percent, and everyone agreed that the budget would be balanced by 2002, and probably before then if the economy kept growing. Erskine and our whole team, especially my legislative aide, John Hilley, had done a great job. I was so happy I parred the next three holes, with my leg brace back on.

The next day we had a big celebration on the South Lawn with all the members of Congress and the administration who had worked on the budget. The atmosphere was euphoric and the speeches were warm, generous, and bipartisan, although I did go out of my way to thank the Democrats, especially Ted Kennedy, Jay Rockefeller, and Hillary, for the children's health plan. Because the deficit had already been reduced by more than 80 percent from its $290 billion high in 1993, the agreement was basically a progressive budget, with middle-class tax cuts I supported and the Republican capital gains cut. In addition to the health, education, and tax cut provisions, it raised the cigarette tax fifteen cents a pack to help pay for the children's health insurance, restored $12 billion in disability and health benefits to legal immigrants, doubled the number of empowerment zones, and gave us the money to continue cleaning up the environment.

With all the sweetness and light at the White House that day, it was hard to remember that we'd been at each other's throats for more than two years. I didn't know how long the good feelings would last, but I'd worked hard to keep things more civil during the stressful negotiations. A few weeks earlier Trent Lott, who was miffed about having lost a minor legislative battle to the White House, had called me a "spoiled brat" on one of the Sunday-morning talk shows. A few days after Lott's remarks I called and told him I knew what had happened and not to give it a second thought. After a hard week he had awakened on Sunday morning feeling bad and wishing he had never agreed to do the TV interview. He was tired and irritable, and when the interviewer goaded him about me he took the bait. He laughed and said, "That's exactly what happened," and the matter was behind us.

Most people who work hard under a lot of pressure occasionally say things they wish they hadn't; I certainly had. Usually, I didn't even read what the Republicans were saying about me, and if a harsh comment came to my attention I tried to ignore it. People hire Presidents to act for them; getting agitated about personal slights interferes with that. I'm glad I called Trent Lott and wish I'd made more calls like it in similar situations.

I didn't feel the same sense of detachment toward Ken Starr's continuing efforts to coerce people into making false charges against Hillary and me, and to prosecute those who refused to lie for him. In April, Jim McDougal, having changed his story to suit Starr and his deputy in Arkansas, Hick Ewing, finally went to jail with a recommendation from Starr that his sentence be shortened. Starr had done the same thing for David Hale.

Starr's coddling of McDougal and Hale was in sharp contrast to his treatment of Susan McDougal, who was still being held in prison for contempt because of her refusal to answer Starr's questions before the grand jury. After a brief period in an Arkansas county jail, to which she was led in handcuffs, leg manacles, and a waist chain,

Susan was transferred to a federal facility, where she was kept apart from the other prisoners in a medical unit for a few months. She was then taken to a Los Angeles jail to answer charges there that she had embezzled funds from a former employer. When newly discovered documentary evidence shredded the prosecution's case, she was acquitted. Meanwhile, she was forced to spend twenty-three hours a day in a windowless cell block usually inhabited by convicted murderers. She was also forced to wear a red dress, normally worn only by murderers and child molesters. After a few months of that, she was put in a Plexiglas cell in the middle of a jail pod; she couldn't talk to other inmates, watch television, or even hear outside sounds. On the prison bus to her court appearances, she was put in a separate cage otherwise reserved for dangerous criminals. Her Hannibal Lecter–like confinement finally came to an end on July 30, after the American Civil Liberties Union filed a suit alleging that McDougal was being held in "barbaric" conditions at Starr's request, in an attempt to coerce her to testify.

Years later, when I read McDougal's book, **The Woman Who Wouldn't Talk,** it sent chills up my spine. She could have ended her suffering at any time, and made a lot of money to boot, just by telling the lies Starr and Hick Ewing wanted her to tell. How she stood up to them I'll never know, but the sight of her in chains finally began to penetrate the shield the Whitewater reporters had erected around Starr and his staff.

Late in the spring, the Supreme Court ruled unanimously that the Paula Jones suit could go forward while I was still in the White House, dismissing my attorneys' arguments that the work of the presidency should not be interrupted by the suit, since it could be litigated at the end of my term. The Court's previous decisions had indicated that a sitting President could not be the subject of a civil suit arising out of his official actions while President because the defense would be too distracting and time-consuming. The Court said that adopting a principle of delay in involving a President's unofficial acts could cause harm to the other party in the suit, so Jones's suit should not be delayed. Besides, the Court said, defending the suit wouldn't be unduly burdensome or time-consuming for me. It was one of the most politically naïve decisions the Supreme Court had made in a long time.

On June 25 the **Washington Post** reported that Kenneth Starr was investigating rumors that twelve to fifteen women, including Jones, had been involved with me. He said he had no interest in my sex life; he just wanted to question anyone with whom I might have had a conversation about Whitewater. Eventually Starr would deploy scores of FBI agents, as well as taxpayer-funded private investigators, to look into the subject in which he professed no interest.

By the end of July, I was getting concerned about the FBI, for reasons far more important than the bureau's sex inquiries for Ken Starr. There had been a whole series of missteps on Louis Freeh's watch: botched reports from the FBI forensic laboratory that threatened several pending criminal cases; large cost overruns on two computer systems designed to upgrade the National Crime Information Center and to provide quick fingerprint checks to police officers all across the country; the release of FBI files on Republican officials to the White House; and the naming and apparent attempted entrapment of Richard Jewell, a suspect in the Olympic bombing case who was subsequently cleared. There was also a criminal inquiry under way into the conduct of Freeh's deputy, Larry Potts, in the deadly standoff at Ruby Ridge in 1992, for which the FBI had been heavily criticized and Potts had been censured before Freeh appointed him.

Freeh had been criticized in the press and by Republicans in Congress, who cited the FBI missteps as the reason for their refusal to pass the provision in my anti-terrorism legislation that would have given the agency wiretap authority to track suspected terrorists as they moved from place to place.

There was one sure way for Freeh to please the Republicans in Congress and get the press off his back: he could assume an adversarial position toward the White House. Whether out of conviction or necessity, Freeh had begun to do just that. When the files case became public, his initial reaction was to blame the White House and decline to accept any responsibility for the FBI. When the campaign finance story broke, he wrote Janet Reno a memo that was leaked to the press, urging her to appoint an independent counsel. When reports surfaced of possible attempts by the Chinese government to funnel illegal contributions to members of Congress in 1996, lower-level agents briefed people well down the chain of command in the National Security Council about it and urged them not to tell their superiors. When Madeleine Albright was preparing to go to China, the White House counsel, Chuck Ruff, a respected former U.S. attorney and Justice Department official, asked the FBI for information about Beijing's plans to influence the government. This was clearly something the secretary of state needed to know about before meeting with the Chinese, but Freeh personally ordered the FBI not to send its prepared reply, despite the fact that it had been approved by the Justice Department and two of Freeh's top assistants.

I didn't believe Freeh was foolish enough to think the Democratic Party would knowingly accept illegal contributions from the Chinese government; he was just trying to avoid criticism from the press and the Republicans, even if it damaged our foreign policy operations. I thought back to the call I had received the day before I appointed Freeh from the retired FBI agent in Arkansas pleading with me not to name him and warning that he would sell me down the river the minute it would benefit him to do so.

Whatever Freeh's motives, the behavior of the FBI toward the White House was just one more example of how crazy Washington had become. The country was in good shape and getting better, and we were advancing peace and prosperity throughout the world, yet the mindless search for scandal continued. A few months earlier Tom Oliphant, the thoughtful and independent-minded **Boston Globe** columnist, summed up the situation well:

> The grand and vainglorious forces running The Great American Scandal Machine are very big on how things seem. The machine's lifeblood is appearances, which generate questions, creating more appearances, all in turn generating a righteous frenzy that demands intense inquiry by super-scrupulous inquisitors who must at all costs be independent. The frenzy, of course, can be resisted only by the complicit and the guilty.

August began with good and bad news. Unemployment was down to 4.8 percent, the lowest since 1973, and confidence in the future remained high in the aftermath of the bipartisan balanced budget agreement. On the other hand, the cooperation didn't extend to the appointments process: Jesse Helms was holding up my nomination of the Republican governor of Massachusetts, Bill Weld, to be ambassador to Mexico because he felt Weld had insulted him, and Janet Reno told the American Bar Association that there were 101 vacant federal judgeships because the Senate had confirmed only nine of my nominees in 1997, none for the court of appeals.

After a two-year hiatus, our family went back to Martha's Vineyard for our August vacation. We stayed at the home of our friend Dick Friedman near Oyster Pond. I celebrated my birthday by going for a jog with Chelsea, and I persuaded Hillary to play her annual round of golf with me at the Mink Meadows public course. She had never liked golf, but once a year she humored me by strolling around a few holes. I also played a lot of golf with Vernon Jordan at the wonderful old Farm Neck course. He liked the game a lot more than Hillary did.

The month ended as it began, with both good and bad news. On the twenty-ninth, Tony Blair invited Sinn Fein to join the Irish peace talks, giving the party formal standing for the first time. On the thirty-first, Princess Diana was killed in an auto crash in Paris. Less than a week later, Mother Teresa died. Hillary was very saddened by their deaths. She had known and liked both of them very much, and she represented the United States at both funerals, flying first to London, then to Calcutta a few days later.

During August, I also had to announce a major disappointment: the United States would not be able to sign the international treaty banning land mines. The circumstances leading to our exclusion were almost bizarre. The United States had spent $153 million on demining all over the world since 1993; we had recently lost a plane with nine people on board after depositing a demining team in southwest Africa; we had trained more than 25 percent of the world's demining experts; and we had destroyed 1.5 million of our own mines, with another 1.5 million scheduled to be destroyed by 1999. No other nation had done as much as America to rid the world of dangerous land mines.

Near the end of negotiations on the treaty, I had asked for two amendments: an exception for the heavily marked UN-sanctioned minefield along the Korean border, which protected the people of South Korea and our troops there; and a rewording of the provision approving anti-tank missiles that covered those manufactured in Europe but not ours. Ours were just as safe and worked better to protect our troops. Both amendments were rejected, partly because the Landmine Conference was determined to pass the strongest possible treaty in the wake of the death of its most famous champion, Princess Diana, and partly because some people at the conference just wanted to embarrass the United States or bully us into signing the treaty as it was. I hated not to be part of the international agreement because it undermined our leverage in trying to stop the manufacture and use of more land mines, some of which could be bought for as little as three dollars each, but I couldn't put the safety of our troops or the people of South Korea at risk.

On September 18, Hillary and I took Chelsea to Stanford. We wanted her new life to be as normal as possible and had worked with the Secret Service to make sure she would be assigned young agents who would dress informally and be as unobtrusive as they could be. Stanford had agreed to bar media access to her on campus. We enjoyed the welcoming ceremonies and visits with the other parents, after which we took Chelsea to her dorm room and helped her move in. Chelsea was happy and excited; Hillary and I were a little sad and anxious. Hillary tried to deal with it by scurrying around and helping Chelsea organize things, even lining her drawers with Contac paper. I had carried her luggage up the stairs to her room, then fixed her bunk bed. After that, I just stared out the window, as her mother got on Chelsea's nerves with all the fixing up. When the student speaker at the convocation, Blake Harris, had said to all the parents that our children would miss us "in about a month and for about fifteen minutes," we all laughed. I hoped it was true, but we sure would miss her. When it was time to go, Hillary had pulled herself together and was ready. Not me; I wanted to stay for dinner.

On the last day of September, I attended the retirement ceremony of General John Shalikashvili and gave him the Presidential Medal of Freedom. He had been a superb chairman of the Joint Chiefs, supporting the expansion of NATO, the creation of the Partnership for Peace, and the deployment of our troops in more than forty operations, including Bosnia, Haiti, Iraq, Rwanda, and the Taiwan Strait. I had really enjoyed working with him. He was intelligent, straight-talking, and completely committed to the welfare of our men and women in uniform. As his replacement I named General Hugh Shelton, who had so impressed me with his handling of the Haiti operation.

The early fall was largely devoted to foreign affairs, as I took my first trip to South America. I traveled to Venezuela, Brazil, and Argentina to express the importance of Latin America to America's future and to keep pushing the idea of a free trade area covering all the Americas. Venezuela was our number one oil supplier and had always made more petroleum available to the United States when we needed it, from World War II to the Gulf War. My visit was brief and uncomplicated; its highlight was a speech to the people of Caracas at the tomb of Simón Bolívar.

Brazil was a different story. There had long been tensions between our two countries; many Brazilians had long resented the United States. Brazil was the leader of the Mercosur trading bloc, which also included Argentina, Paraguay, and Uruguay, and which had a larger volume of trade with Europe than with the United States. On the other hand, the Brazilian president, Henrique Cardoso, was a modern, effective leader who wanted a good relationship with the United States and who understood that a stronger partnership with us would help him to modernize his country's economy, reduce its chronic poverty, and increase its influence in the world.

I had been fascinated by Brazil since the great jazz saxophonist Stan Getz popularized its music in America in the 1960s, and ever since then I had wanted to see its cities and beautiful landscapes. I also respected and liked Cardoso. He had already been to Washington on a state visit, and I thought he was one of the most impressive leaders I had met. I wanted to affirm our mutual dedication to a closer economic partnership and to support his policies, especially those to sustain Brazil's vast rain forest, which had been severely reduced by overclearing, and to improve education. Cardoso had initiated an intriguing program called **bolsa escola,** which made monthly cash payments to poor Brazilians if their children attended school at least 85 percent of the time.

There was an interesting moment in our press conference, which, besides several questions on American-Brazilian relations and climate change, included four from the American press on the ongoing controversy back home over the financing of the '96 campaign. A reporter asked if it embarrassed me or the country to have such questions asked on a foreign trip. I replied, "That's a decision for you. You have to decide what questions you're going to ask. I can't be embarrassed about how you decide to do your job."

After a visit to a school in a poor neighborhood in Rio de Janeiro with Brazil's soccer legend Pelé, Hillary and I went to Brasília for a state dinner at the presidential residence, where Henrique and Ruth Cardoso gave us a taste of the Brazilian music I had loved for more than thirty years, a women's percussion ensemble playing pulsating rhythms on different-sized metal plates tied to their bodies, and a fabulous singer from Bahia, Virginia Rodrigues.

Argentina's President Carlos Menem had been a strong ally of the United States, supporting America in the Gulf War and in Haiti and adopting a strong free-market economic policy. He hosted a barbeque at the Rural Center in Buenos Aires that included tango lessons for Hillary and me and a demonstration of Argentine horsemanship: a man riding around the rodeo arena standing atop two broad-shouldered stallions.

President Menem also took us to Bariloche, a beautiful resort town in Patagonia, to discuss global warming and what I hoped would be our common response to the problem. The international conference on climate change was coming up in December in Kyoto, Japan. I strongly favored setting aggressive targets for the reduction of greenhouse gas emissions for both developed and developing nations, but I wanted to achieve the targets not through regulations and taxes but through market incentives to promote energy conservation and the use of clean energy technology. Bariloche was a perfect site to highlight the importance of the environment. Just across the cold, clear lake from the Llao Llao Hotel where we stayed, Hillary and I walked through the magical Arrayanes forest, with its barkless myrtle trees. The trees were stained orange by tannic acid and were cool to the touch. Their survival resulted from perfect soil, clean water, clean air, and a moderate climate. The right action against climate change would preserve the fragile, unique trees and the stability of much of the rest of our planet.

On October 26, back in Washington, Capricia Marshall, Kelly Craighead, and the rest of Hillary's staff put together a big fiftieth birthday celebration for her under a tent on the South Lawn. Chelsea came home to surprise her. There were tables with food and music from every decade of her life, with people standing by them who had known her in each period: from Illinois in the fifties, Wellesley in the sixties, Yale in the seventies, and Arkansas in the eighties.

The next day, Jiang Zemin came to Washington. I invited him to the residence for an informal meeting that night. After almost five years of working with him, I was impressed with Jiang's political skills, his desire to integrate China into the world community, and the economic growth that had accelerated under his leadership and that of his prime minister, Zhu Rongji, but I was still concerned about China's continued suppression of basic freedoms and its imprisonment of political dissidents. I asked Jiang to release some dissidents and told him that in order

for the United States and China to have a long-term partnership, our relationship had to have room for fair, honest
disagreement.

When Jiang said he agreed, we proceeded to debate
how much change and freedom China could accommodate without risking internal chaos. We didn't resolve our
differences, but our mutual understanding increased, and
after Jiang went back to Blair House, I went to bed thinking that China would be forced by the imperatives of
modern society to become more open, and that in the new
century it was more likely that our nations would be partners than adversaries.

The next day at our press conference, Jiang and I
announced that we would increase our cooperation to
stop the spread of weapons of mass destruction; work
together on the peaceful use of nuclear energy, and on
fighting organized crime, drug trafficking, and alien
smuggling; expand America's efforts to promote the rule
of law in China by helping to train judges and lawyers;
and cooperate to protect the environment. I also pledged
to do all I could to bring China into the World Trade
Organization. Jiang echoed my remarks and told the press
we had also agreed to regular summit meetings and the
opening of a direct telephone "hot-line" to assure that we
could maintain direct communication.

When we opened the floor to questions, the press asked
the inevitable ones about human rights, Tiananmen
Square, and Tibet. Jiang seemed a little taken aback but
maintained his good humor, essentially repeating what he
had said to me on the subjects the night before, and
adding that he knew he was visiting a democracy where
the people were free to voice their different opinions. I
replied that while China was on the right side of history

on so many issues, on the human rights issue "we believe the policy of the government is on the wrong side of history." A couple of days later, in a speech at Harvard, President Jiang acknowledged that mistakes had been made in dealing with the demonstrators at Tiananmen Square. China often moved at a pace that seemed maddeningly slow to Westerners, but it was not impervious to change.

October brought two developments on the legal front. After Judge Susan Webber Wright dismissed with prejudice (meaning they could not be refiled) two of the four counts in Paula Jones's lawsuit, I offered to settle it. I didn't want to, because it would take about half of everything Hillary and I had saved over twenty years, and because I knew, on the basis of the investigative work my legal team had done, that we would win the case if it ever went to trial. But I didn't want to waste any days in the three years I had left on it.

Jones refused to accept the settlement unless I also apologized for sexually harassing her. I couldn't do that because it wasn't true. Not long afterward, her lawyers petitioned the court to be released of their duties. Soon they were replaced by a Dallas firm closely associated with and funded by the Rutherford Institute, another right-wing legal foundation financed by my opponents. Now there was no longer even a pretense that Paula Jones was the real plaintiff in the case that bore her name.

Early in the month, the White House turned over videotapes of forty-four of the much-discussed White House coffees to the Justice Department and the Congress. They proved what I'd said all along, that the coffees were not fund-raisers, but wide-ranging and often interesting discussions with some people who were supporters and some who weren't. The only thing most of the critics could do was to complain that they weren't released sooner.

Soon after that, Newt Gingrich announced that he didn't have the votes to pass the fast-track trade legislation in the House. I had worked very hard for months to pass it. In an attempt to get more votes from my party, I had pledged to Democrats that I would negotiate trade agreements with labor and environmental provisions, and told them that I had secured Chile's agreement to put such requirements into the bilateral agreement we were working on. Unfortunately, I couldn't persuade very many of them, because the AFL-CIO, which was still angry about losing the NAFTA vote, had made the fast-track vote a test of whether Democrats were for or against labor. Even Democrats who agreed with me on the merits were reluctant to face a reelection campaign without the AFL-CIO's financial and organizational support. Several conservative Republicans conditioned their vote on whether or not I would impose further restrictions on U.S. policy for international family planning. When I wouldn't do it, I lost their votes. The Speaker had also worked to pass the bill, but at the end we were still six votes short at best. Now I would just have to continue making individual trade agreements and hope that Congress wouldn't kill them with amendments.

In mid-month we had a new crisis in Iraq, when Saddam expelled six American members of the UN weapons inspection teams. I ordered the USS **George Washington** carrier group to the region, and a few days later the inspectors returned.

The Kyoto global warming talks opened on December 1. Before they were over, Al Gore flew to Japan to help our chief negotiator, Undersecretary of State Stu

Eizenstat, get an agreement we could sign, with firm targets but without undue restrictions on how to achieve them and with a call for developing countries like China and India to participate; within thirty years they would surpass the United States as emitters of greenhouse gases (the United States is now the world's leading emitter). Unless the changes were made, I couldn't submit the treaty to Congress; it would be difficult to pass in the best of circumstances. With the support of Prime Minister Hashimoto, who wanted Kyoto to be a success for Japan, and other friendly nations including Argentina, the negotiations produced an agreement I was happy to support, with targets I thought we could meet, if Congress would enact the tax incentives necessary to promote the production and purchase of more conservation technologies and clean energy products.

In the days before Christmas, Hillary, Chelsea, and I went to Bosnia to encourage the people in Sarajevo to stay on the path of peace and to meet with the troops in Tuzla. Bob and Elizabeth Dole joined our delegation, along with several military leaders and a dozen members of Congress of both parties. Elizabeth was the president of the American Red Cross, and Bob had just agreed to my request to head the International Commission on Missing Persons in the former Yugoslavia.

On the day before Christmas the United States agreed to put up $1.7 billion to provide financial support to the faltering South Korean economy. It marked the beginning of our commitment to solving the Asian financial crisis, which would grow much worse in the coming year. South Korea had just elected a new president, Kim Dae Jung, a longtime democracy activist who had been sentenced to execution in the 1970s until President Carter intervened on his behalf. I had first met Kim on the steps of Los Angeles City Hall in May 1992, when he proudly told me he represented the same new approach to politics that I did. He was both brave and visionary, and I wanted to support him.

As we headed to Renaissance Weekend and a new year, I looked back on 1997 with satisfaction, hoping the worst of the partisan wars had passed in the wake of all that had been accomplished: the balanced budget; the largest increase in college aid in fifty years; the biggest increase in children's health coverage since 1965; the expansion of NATO; the Chemical Weapons Convention; the Kyoto accord; sweeping reforms of our adoption laws and of our Food and Drug Administration to speed the introduction of lifesaving medicines and medical devices; and the One America initiative, which had already involved millions of people in conversations about the current state of race relations. It was an impressive list, but it would not be enough to bridge the ideological divide.

FORTY-EIGHT

When 1998 began, I had no idea it would be the strangest year of my presidency, full of personal humiliation and disgrace, policy struggles at home and triumphs abroad, and, against all odds, a stunning demonstration of the common sense and fundamental decency of the American people. Because everything happened at once, I was compelled as never before to live parallel lives, except that this time the darkest part of my inner life was in full view.

January began on a positive note, with three major initiatives: (1) a 50 percent increase in the number of Peace Corps volunteers, primarily to support the new democracies that had emerged since the fall of communism; (2) a $22 billion child-care program to double the number of children in working families receiving child-care subsidies, provide tax credits to encourage employees to make child care available to their employees, and expand before- and after-school programs to serve 500,000 children; and (3) a proposal to allow people to "buy into" Medicare, which covered Americans sixty-five and older, at age sixty-two, or at age fifty-five if they had lost their jobs. The program was designed to be self-financing through modest premiums and other payments. It was needed because so many Americans were leaving the workforce early, through downsizing, layoffs, or choice, and couldn't find affordable insurance elsewhere after they lost their employer-based coverage.

In the second week of the month, I went to South Texas, one of my favorite places in America, to urge the largely Hispanic student body at Mission High School to help close the gap between the college-going rates of Hispanic young people and the rest of the student population by taking full advantage of the tremendous increase in college aid the Congress had authorized in 1997. While there, I was informed of the collapse of Indonesia's economy, and my economic team went to work on the next casualty of the Asian financial crisis; Deputy Treasury Secretary Larry Summers went to Indonesia to secure the government's agreement to implement the reforms necessary to receive assistance from the International Monetary Fund.

On the thirteenth, trouble broke out in Iraq again as Saddam's government blocked an American-led UN inspection team from doing its job, the beginning of a protracted effort by Saddam to coerce the United Nations into lifting sanctions in return for continuing the weapons inspections. The same day, the Middle East moved toward crisis as Prime Minister Netanyahu's government, which still had not completed the overdue opening of the Gaza airport or provided safe passage between Gaza and the West Bank, put the entire peace process in danger by voting to keep control of the West Bank indefinitely. The only bright spot on the world horizon in January was the White House signing of a NATO partnership with the Baltic nations, which was designed to formalize our security relationship and reassure them that the ultimate goal of all the NATO nations, including the United States, was the full integration of Estonia, Lithuania, and Latvia into NATO and other multilateral institutions.

On the fourteenth, I was in the East Room of the White House with Al Gore to announce our push for a

Patients' Bill of Rights, to provide Americans in managed care plans with some basic treatment guarantees that were being denied all too frequently, and Hillary was being questioned by Ken Starr for the fifth time. The topic on this occasion was how the FBI files on Republicans got to the White House, something she knew nothing about.

My deposition in the Jones case came three days later. I had gone over a series of possible questions with my lawyers and thought I was reasonably well prepared, though I didn't feel well that day and certainly wasn't looking forward to my encounter with the Rutherford Institute lawyers. The presiding judge, Susan Webber Wright, had given Jones's lawyers broad permission to delve into my private life, allegedly to see if there was a pattern of sexual harassment involving any women who had held or sought state employment when I was governor or federal employment when I was President, during a time period from five years before Jones's alleged harassment to the present day. The judge had also given the Jones lawyers strict instructions not to leak the contents of any deposition or other aspects of their investigation.

The stated objective could have been achieved less intrusively by simply directing me to answer yes or no to questions about whether I had ever been alone with women working for the government; then the lawyers could have asked the women whether I had ever harassed them. However, that would have rendered the deposition useless. By this time, everyone involved in the case knew there was no evidence of sexual harassment. I was certain that the lawyers wanted to force me to acknowledge any kind of involvement with one or more women that they could then leak to the press, in violation of the judge's confidentiality order. As it turned out, I didn't know the half of it.

After I was sworn in, the deposition began with a request from the Rutherford Institute lawyers that the judge accept a definition of "sexual relations" that they had purportedly found in a legal document. Basically, the definition covered most intimate contact beyond kissing by the person being asked the question, if it was done for gratification or arousal. It seemed to require both a specific act and a certain state of mind on my part, and did not include any act by another person. The lawyers said they were trying to spare me embarrassing questions.

I was there for several hours, only ten or fifteen minutes of which were devoted to Paula Jones. The rest of the time was spent on a variety of topics with no connection to Jones, including a great many questions about Monica Lewinsky, who had worked in the White House in the summer of 1995 as an intern and then in a staff job from December through early April, when she was transferred to the Pentagon. The lawyers asked, among other things, how well I knew her, whether we had ever exchanged gifts, whether we had ever talked on the phone, and if I had had "sexual relations" with her. I discussed our conversations, acknowledged that I had given her gifts, and answered no to the "sexual relations" question.

The Rutherford Institute lawyers kept asking the same questions with slight variations over and over again. When we took a break, my legal team was perplexed, because Lewinsky's name had shown up on the plaintiff's list of potential witnesses only in early December, and she had been given a subpoena to appear as a witness two weeks later. I didn't tell them about my relationship with her, but I did say I was unsure of exactly what the curious definition of sexual relations meant. So were they. At the beginning of the deposition, my attorney, Bob Bennett, had invited the Rutherford Institute lawyers to ask specific and unambiguous questions about my contact with women. At the end of the discussion of Lewinsky, I asked the lawyer who was questioning me if there wasn't something more specific he wanted to ask me. Once again he declined to do so. Instead he said, "Sir, I think this will come to light shortly, and you'll understand."

I was relieved but somewhat concerned that the lawyer seemed not to want to ask specific questions, nor to want to get my answers to them. If he had asked such questions, I would have answered them truthfully, but I would have hated it. During the government shutdown in late 1995, when very few people were allowed to come to work in the White House and those who were there were working late, I'd had an inappropriate encounter with Monica Lewinsky and would do so again on other occasions between November and April, when she left the White House for the Pentagon. For the next ten months, I didn't see her, although we talked on the phone from time to time.

In February 1997, Monica was among the guests at an evening taping of my weekly radio address, after which I met with her alone again for about fifteen minutes. I was disgusted with myself for doing it, and in the spring, when I saw her again, I told her that it was wrong for me, wrong for my family, and wrong for her, and I couldn't do it anymore. I also told her that she was an intelligent, interesting person who could have a good life, and that if she wanted me to, I would try to be her friend and help her.

Monica continued to visit the White House, and I saw her on some of those occasions, but nothing improper occurred. In October, she asked me to help her get a job in New York, and I did. She had received two offers and accepted one, and late in December, she came to the White House to say good-bye. By then, she had received her subpoena in the Jones case. She said she didn't want to be deposed, and I told her some women had avoided questioning by filing affidavits saying that I had not sexually harassed them.

What I had done with Monica Lewinsky was immoral and foolish. I was deeply ashamed of it and I didn't want it to come out. In the deposition, I was trying to protect my family and myself from my selfish stupidity. I believed that the contorted definition of "sexual relations" enabled me to do so, though I was worried enough about it to invite the lawyer interrogating me to ask specific questions. I didn't have to wait long to find out why he declined to do so.

On January 21, the **Washington Post** led with a story that I had had an affair with Monica Lewinsky, and that Kenneth Starr was investigating charges that I had encouraged her to lie about it under oath. The story first emerged publicly early on the eighteenth, on an Internet site. The deposition had been a setup; nearly four years after he first offered to help Paula Jones, Starr had finally gotten into her case.

In the summer of 1996, Monica Lewinsky had begun talking to a co-worker, Linda Tripp, about her relationship with me. A year later, Tripp had started taping their telephone conversations. In October 1997, Tripp offered to play the tapes for a **Newsweek** reporter and did play them for Lucianne Goldberg, a conservative Republican publicist. Tripp was subpoenaed in the Jones case, though she was never on any witness list provided to my attorneys.

Late on Monday, January 12, 1998, Tripp phoned

Starr's office, described her secret taping of Lewinsky, and made arrangements to turn over those tapes. She was concerned about her own criminal liability, because the kind of taping she had done was a felony under Maryland law, but Starr's people promised to protect her. The next day Starr had FBI agents wire Tripp so that she could secretly record a conversation with Lewinsky over lunch at the Pentagon City Ritz-Carlton. A couple of days later, Starr asked the Justice Department for permission to expand his authority to encompass the investigation of Lewinsky, apparently being less than truthful about the basis for his request.

On the sixteenth, the day before my deposition, Tripp arranged to meet Lewinsky again at the hotel. This time Monica was greeted by FBI agents and attorneys who took her to a hotel room, questioned her for several hours, and discouraged her from calling a lawyer. One of Starr's lawyers told her she should cooperate if she wanted to avoid going to jail and offered her an immunity deal that expired at midnight. Lewinsky was also pressured to wear a wire to secretly tape conversations with people involved in the alleged cover-up. Finally, Monica was able to call her mother, who contacted her father, from whom she had long been divorced. He got in touch with a lawyer, William Ginsburg, who advised her not to accept the immunity deal until he learned more about the case, and who blasted Starr for holding his client "for eight or nine hours without an attorney" and for pressuring her to wear a wire to entrap others.

After the story broke, I called David Kendall and assured him that I had not suborned perjury or obstructed justice. It was clear to both of us that Starr was trying to create a firestorm to force me from office. He was off to a flying start, but I thought that if I could survive the public pounding for two weeks, the smoke would begin to clear, the press and the public would focus on Starr's tactics, and a more balanced view of the matter would emerge. I knew I had made a terrible mistake, and I was determined not to compound it by allowing Starr to drive me from office. For now, the hysteria was overwhelming.

I went on doing my job, and I stonewalled, denying what had happened to everyone: Hillary, Chelsea, my staff and cabinet, my friends in Congress, members of the press, and the American people. What I regret the most, other than my conduct, is having misled all of them. Since 1991 I had been called a liar about everything under the sun, when in fact I had been honest in my public life and financial affairs, as all the investigations would show. Now I was misleading everyone about my personal failings. I was embarrassed and wanted to keep it from my wife and daughter. I didn't want to help Ken Starr criminalize my personal life, and I didn't want the American people to know I'd let them down. It was like living in a nightmare. I was back to my parallel lives with a vengeance.

On the day the story broke, I did a previously scheduled interview with Jim Lehrer for the PBS **NewsHour.** I responded to his questions by saying that I had not asked anyone to lie, which was true, and that "there is no improper relationship." Although the impropriety was over well before Lehrer asked the question, my answer was misleading, and I was ashamed of telling Lehrer that; from then on, whenever I could, I just said I never asked anybody not to tell the truth.

While all this was going on, I had to keep doing my job. On the twentieth, I met with Prime Minister Netanyahu at the White House to discuss his plans for a phased withdrawal from the West Bank. Netanyahu had made a decision to move the peace process forward as long as he had "peace with security." It was a bold move because his governing coalition was shaky, but he could see that if he didn't act, the situation would quickly get out of hand.

The next day Arafat came to the White House. I gave him an encouraging report of my meeting with Netanyahu, assured him that I was pushing the prime minister to fulfill Israel's obligation under the peace process, reminded him of the Israeli leader's political problems, and stated, as I always did, that he had to keep fighting terror if he wanted Israel to move forward. The next day Mir Aimal Kansi was sentenced to death for the murder of the two CIA agents in January 1993, the first terrorist act to occur during my presidency.

By January 27, the day of the State of the Union address, the American people had been deluged with a week of coverage of Starr's inquiry, and I had spent a week dealing with it. Starr had already issued subpoenas to a number of White House staff people and for our records. I had asked Harold Ickes and Mickey Kantor to help deal with the controversy. The day before the speech, at the urging of Harold and Harry Thomason, who felt I had been too tentative in my public comments, I reluctantly appeared once more before the press to say "I did not have sexual relations" with Lewinsky.

On the morning of the speech, on NBC's **Today** show, Hillary said that she didn't believe the charges against me and that a "vast right-wing conspiracy" had been trying to destroy us since the 1992 campaign. Starr issued an indignant statement complaining that Hillary had questioned his motives. Though she was right about the nature of our opposition, seeing Hillary defend me made me even more ashamed about what I had done.

Hillary's difficult interview and my mixed reaction to it clearly exemplified the bind I had put myself in: As a husband, I had done something wrong that I needed to apologize and atone for; as President, I was in a legal and political struggle with forces who had abused the criminal and civil laws and severely damaged innocent people in their attempt to destroy my presidency and cripple my ability to serve.

Finally, after years of dry holes, I had given them something to work with. I had hurt the presidency and the people by my misconduct. That was no one's fault but my own. I didn't want to compound the error by letting the reactionaries prevail.

By 9 p.m., when I walked into the packed House chamber, the tension was palpable both there and in living rooms across America, where more people were watching my State of the Union address than since I delivered my first one. The big question was whether I would mention the controversy. I began with what was not in dispute. The country was in good shape, with fourteen million new jobs, rising incomes, the highest rate of home ownership ever, the fewest people on the welfare rolls in twenty-seven years, and the smallest federal government in thirty-five years. The 1993 economic plan had cut the deficit, projected to be $357 billion in 1998, by 90 percent, and the previous year's balanced budget plan would get rid of it entirely.

Then I outlined my plan for the future. First, I proposed that before spending the coming surpluses on new programs or tax cuts, we should save Social Security for the baby boomers' retirement. In education, I recommended funding to hire 100,000 new teachers and to cut class size to eighteen in the first three grades; a plan to help communities modernize or build five thousand schools; and assistance to help schools end the practice of "social promotion," by providing funds for extra learning in after-school or summer-school programs. I reiterated my support for a Patients' Bill of Rights, opening Medicare to Americans between the ages of fifty-five and sixty-five, expanding the Family and Medical Leave Act, and called for a large enough expansion in federal child-care assistance to provide support for one million more children.

On the security front, I asked for congressional support in combating "an unholy axis of new threats from terrorists, international criminals, and drug traffickers"; Senate approval of the expansion of NATO; and continued funding for our mission in Bosnia and our efforts to confront the hazards of chemical and biological weapons and the outlaw states, terrorists, and organized criminals seeking to acquire them.

The last section of my speech dealt with appeals to bring America together and look to the future: tripling the number of empowerment zones in poor communities; launching a new clean water initiative for our rivers, lakes, and coastal waters; providing $6 billion in tax cuts and research funds for the development of fuel-efficient cars, clean-energy homes, and renewable energy; financing the "next generation" Internet to transmit information up to a thousand times faster; and funding the Equal Employment Opportunity Commission, which, because of congressional hostility, didn't have the resources to handle sixty thousand backlogged cases alleging discrimination in the workplace. I also proposed the largest increase in history for the National Institutes of Health, the National

Cancer Institute, and the National Science Foundation so that "ours will be the generation that finally wins the war against cancer and begins a revolution in our fight against all deadly diseases."

I closed the speech thanking Hillary for leading our millennium campaign to preserve America's treasures, including the tattered old Star Spangled Banner, which inspired Francis Scott Key to write our national anthem during the War of 1812.

There wasn't a word in the address about the scandal, and the biggest new idea had been to "save Social Security first." I was afraid Congress would get into a bidding war for the coming surpluses and squander them on tax cuts and spending before we had dealt with the baby boomers' retirement. Most Democrats agreed with me, and most Republicans didn't, though over the coming years we would hold a series of bipartisan forums around the country in which, despite everything else that was going on, we searched for common ground, arguing about how to provide for retirement security rather than whether to do so.

Two days after the speech, Judge Wright ordered that all evidence related to Monica Lewinsky be excluded from the Jones case because it was "not essential to the core issues," making Starr's inquiry into my deposition even more questionable, since perjury requires a false statement about a "material" matter. On the last day of the month, ten days after the firestorm began, the **Chicago Tribune** published a poll showing that my job approval rating had risen to 72 percent. I was determined to show the American people that I was on the job and getting results for them.

On February 5 and 6, Tony and Cherie Blair came to the United States for a two-day state visit. They were a sight for sore eyes for both Hillary and me. They made us laugh, and Tony gave me strong support in public, emphasizing our common approach to economic and social problems and to foreign policy. We took them to Camp David for a dinner with Al and Tipper Gore, and held a state dinner at the White House with entertainment by Elton John and Stevie Wonder. After the event Hillary told me that Newt Gingrich, who had been seated at her table with Tony Blair, had said the charges against me were "ludicrous," and "meaningless" even if true, and weren't "going anywhere."

At our press conference, after Tony said that I was not just his colleague but his friend, Mike Frisby, a reporter for the **Wall Street Journal,** finally asked the question I had been waiting for. He wanted to know whether, given the pain and all the issues about my personal life, "at what point do you consider that it's just not worth it, and do you consider resigning the office?" "Never," I answered. I said I had tried to take the personal venom out of politics, but the harder I tried, "the harder others have pulled in the other direction." Still, "I would never walk away from the people of this country and the trust they've placed in me," so "I'm just going to keep showing up for work."

In mid-month, as Tony Blair and I continued to build support around the world for launching air strikes on Iraq in response to the expulsion of the UN inspectors, Kofi Annan secured a last-minute agreement from Saddam Hussein to resume the inspections. It seemed that Saddam never moved except when forced to do so.

Besides plugging my new initiatives, I spent time working for the McCain-Feingold campaign finance reform bill, which the Senate Republicans killed at the end of the month; swearing in a new surgeon general, Dr. David Satcher, the director of the Centers for Disease Control;

touring tornado damage in central Florida; announcing the first grants to help communities strengthen their efforts to prevent violence against women; and raising funds to help Democrats in the coming election.

In late January and in February, several White House staffers were called before the grand jury. I felt terrible that they had been caught up in all this, especially Betty Currie, who had tried to befriend Monica Lewinsky and was now being punished for it. I also felt bad that Vernon Jordan had been caught up in the maelstrom. We had been close friends for so long, and time and again I had seen him help people who needed it. Now he was being targeted because of me. I knew he hadn't done anything wrong and hoped someday he would be able to forgive me for the mess I had gotten him into.

Starr also subpoenaed Sidney Blumenthal, a journalist and old friend of Hillary's and mine who had come to work in the White House in July 1997. According to the **Washington Post,** Starr was exploring whether Sid's criticism of him amounted to an obstruction of justice. It was a chilling indication of how thin-skinned Starr was, and how willing to use the power of his office against anyone who criticized him. Starr also subpoenaed two private investigators who had been hired by the **National Enquirer** to run down a rumor that he had been having an affair with a woman in Little Rock. The rumor was false, apparently a case of mistaken identity, but again, it reflected a double standard. He was using FBI agents and private investigators to look into my life. When a tabloid looked at his, he went after them.

Starr's tactics were beginning to draw the attention of the press. **Newsweek** published a two-page chart, "Conspiracy or Coincidence," which traced the connections of more than twenty conservative activists and organizations that had promoted and financed the "scandals" Starr was investigating. The **Washington Post** ran a story in which a number of former federal prosecutors expressed discomfort not just with Starr's new focus on my private conduct, "but with the arsenal of weapons he has deployed to try to make his case against the president."

Starr was particularly criticized for forcing Monica Lewinsky's mother to testify against her will. Federal guidelines, which Starr was supposed to follow, said that family members should ordinarily not be forced to testify unless they were part of the criminal activity being investigated, or there were "overriding prosecutorial concerns." By early February, according to an NBC News poll, only 26 percent of the American people thought Starr was conducting an impartial inquiry.

The saga continued into March. My deposition in the Jones case was leaked, obviously by someone on the Jones side. Although the judge had repeatedly warned the Rutherford Institute lawyers not to leak it, no one was ever sanctioned. On the eighth, Jim McDougal died in a federal prison in Texas, a sad and ironic end to his long downward slide. According to Susan McDougal, Jim had changed his story to suit Starr and Hick Ewing because he desperately wanted to avoid dying in jail.

In mid-month, **60 Minutes** ran an interview with a woman named Kathleen Willey, who claimed I had made an unwanted advance toward her while she was working in the White House. It wasn't true. We had evidence that cast doubt on her story, including the affidavit of her friend Julie Hiatt Steele, who said Willey had asked her to lie by saying she had told Steele about the alleged episode shortly after it happened, when in fact she hadn't.

Willey's husband had killed himself, leaving her responsible for more than $200,000 of outstanding debt. Within a week, news stories reported that after I called her to offer my condolences on her husband's death, she had told people I was coming to his funeral; this was after the alleged incident. Eventually we released about a dozen letters Willey had written to me, again after the alleged encounter, saying things like she was my "number one fan" and that she wanted to help me "in any way that I can." After a report that she had sought $300,000 to tell her story to a tabloid or in a book, the story faded away.

I mention Willey's sad tale here because of what Starr did with it. First, in a highly unusual move, he gave her "transactional immunity"—complete protection against any kind of criminal prosecution—provided she told him the "truth." When she was caught being untruthful about some embarrassing details involving another man, Starr just gave her immunity again. By contrast, when Julie Hiatt Steele, a registered Republican, refused to change her story and lie for Starr, he indicted her. Even though she wasn't convicted, it ruined her financially. Starr's office even sought to challenge the legality of her adoption of a baby from Romania.

On St. Patrick's Day, I met with the leaders of all of the political parties in Northern Ireland that were participating in the political process, and had extended visits with Gerry Adams and David Trimble. Tony Blair and Bertie Ahern wanted to reach an agreement. My role was basically to keep reassuring and pushing all the parties into the framework George Mitchell was constructing. There were hard compromises still ahead, but I thought we were getting there.

A few days later, Hillary and I flew to Africa, far away from the clamor at home. Africa was a continent that America had too often ignored, and one that I believed would play a large role for good or ill in the twenty-first century. I was really glad Hillary was going with me; she had loved the trip she and Chelsea had made to Africa the previous year, and we needed the time away together.

The visit began in Ghana, where President Jerry Rawlings and his wife, Nana Konadu Agyemang, got us off to a rousing start with a ceremony in Independence Square; it was filled with more than half a million people. We were flanked on the stage by tribal kings draped in bright-colored native kente cloth and entertained by African rhythms played by several Ghanaians on by far the largest drum I had ever seen.

I liked Rawlings and respected the fact that after seizing power in a military coup, he was elected and reelected president, and was committed to relinquishing his office in 2000. Besides, we had an indirect family connection: when Chelsea was born, the doctor was assisted by a wonderful Ghanaian midwife who had come to Arkansas to continue her education. Hillary and I came to like Hagar Sam very much and were pleased to learn she had also helped to deliver the four Rawlings children.

On the twenty-fourth, we were in Uganda to meet with President Yoweri Museveni and his wife, Janet. Uganda had come a long way since the stifling dictatorship of Idi Amin. Just a few years earlier, it had had the highest AIDS rate in Africa. With a campaign called "the big noise," the death rate had been cut in half through a focus on abstinence, education, marriage, and condoms.

The four of us went to two small villages, Mukono and Wanyange, to highlight the importance of education and of American-financed micro-credit loans. Uganda had tripled education funding in the previous five years and had made a real effort to educate girls as well as boys. The schoolchildren we visited in Mukono wore nice pink uniforms. They were obviously bright and interested, but their learning materials were inadequate; the map on the classroom wall was so old it still included the Soviet Union. In Wanyange, the village cook had expanded her operation and another woman had diversified her chicken-raising business to include rabbits with micro-credit loans funded by U.S. aid. We met a woman with a two-day-old baby. She let me hold the infant boy as the White House photographer took a picture of two guys named Bill Clinton.

The Secret Service didn't want me to go to Rwanda because of ongoing security problems, but I felt that I had to. As a concession to the security issue, I met at the Kigali airport with the leaders of the country and with survivors of the genocide. President Pasteur Bizimungu, a Hutu, and Vice President Paul Kagame, a Tutsi, were trying to put the country back together. Kagame was the nation's most powerful political leader; he had decided that it would advance the reconciliation process to begin with a president from the majority Hutu tribe. I acknowledged that the United States and the international community had not acted quickly enough to stop the genocide or to prevent the refugee camps from becoming havens for the killers, and I offered to help the nation rebuild and to support the war crimes tribunal that would hold accountable the perpetrators of the genocide.

The survivors told me their stories. The last speaker was a dignified woman who said her family had been identified to the rampaging killers as Tutsis by Hutu neighbors whose children had played with hers for years. She was badly wounded by a machete and left for dead. She awoke in a pool of her own blood to find her husband and six children lying dead beside her. She told Hillary and me that she had cried out to God in despair that she had survived, then came to understand "that my life must have been spared for a reason, and it could not be something as mean as vengeance. So I do what I can to help us start again." I was overwhelmed; that magnificent woman had made my problems seem pathetically small. She had deepened my resolve to do whatever I could to help Rwanda.

I began the first visit by any American President to South Africa in Cape Town, with a speech to the parliament in which I said I had come "in part to help the American people see the new Africa with new eyes." It was fascinating to me to witness the supporters and victims of apartheid working together. They didn't deny the past or hide their current disagreements, but they seemed confident that they could build a common future. It was a tribute to the spirit of reconciliation that emanated from Mandela.

The next day Mandela took us to visit Robben Island, where he had spent the first eighteen years of his captivity. I saw the rock quarry where he had worked and the cramped cell where he was kept when he wasn't breaking rocks. In Johannesburg, I called on Deputy President Thabo Mbeki, who had been meeting with Al Gore twice a year on our common agenda and was almost certain to be Mandela's successor; dedicated a commercial center named after Ron Brown, who had loved South Africa; and visited a primary school. Hillary and I went to church with Jesse Jackson in Soweto, the teeming township that had produced so many of the anti-apartheid activists.

By this time I had developed a real friendship with Mandela. He was remarkable not only because of his astonishing journey from hatred to reconciliation during twenty-seven years in prison, but also because he was both a tough-minded politician and a caring person who, despite his long confinement, never lost his interest in the personal side of life or his ability to show love, friendship, and kindness.

We had one especially meaningful conversation. I said, "Madiba [Mandela's colloquial tribal name, which he asked me to use], I know you did a great thing in inviting your jailers to your inauguration, but didn't you really hate those who imprisoned you?" He replied, "Of course I did, for many years. They took the best years of my life. They abused me physically and mentally. I didn't get to see my children grow up. I hated them. Then one day when I was working in the quarry, hammering the rocks, I realized that they had already taken everything from me except my mind and my heart. Those they could not take without my permission. I decided not to give them away." Then he looked at me, smiled, and said, "And neither should you."

After I caught my breath, I asked him another question. "When you were walking out of prison for the last time, didn't you feel the hatred rise up in you again?" "Yes," he said, "for a moment I did. Then I thought to myself, 'They have had me for twenty-seven years. If I keep hating them, they will still have me.' I wanted to be free, and so I let it go." He smiled again. This time he didn't have to say, "And so should you."

The only vacation day on the trip came in Botswana, which had the highest per capita income in sub-Saharan Africa and the highest AIDS rate in the world. We went

on a safari in Chobe National Park and saw lions, ele-
phants, impalas, hippos, crocodiles, and more than
twenty different species of birds. We got very close to a
mother elephant and her child—apparently too close. She
raised her trunk and sprayed us with water. It made me
laugh to think how happy the Republicans would have
been if they could have seen their party's mascot watering
me. Late in the afternoon we took a leisurely boat ride
down the Chobe River; Hillary and I held hands and
counted our blessings as we watched the sun go down.

Our last stop was Senegal, where we visited the Door of
No Return on Gorée Island, the point from which so
many Africans were taken to slavery in North America. As
I had in Uganda, I expressed my regret over America's
responsibility for slavery and the long, hard struggle of
African-Americans for freedom. I introduced the large
delegation with me "representing over thirty million
Americans that are Africa's great gift to America," and
pledged to work with the Senegalese and all Africans for a
better future. I also visited a mosque with President
Abdou Diouf, out of respect for Senegal's overwhelmingly
Muslim population; a village that had recovered a section
of desert with the help of American aid; and Senegalese
troops being trained by American military personnel as
part of the African Crisis Response Initiative, which my
administration had initiated, our effort to better prepare
Africans to stop wars and prevent other Rwandas.

The trip was the longest and most comprehensive ever
taken to Africa by an American President. The bipartisan
congressional delegation and the prominent citizens who
accompanied me, as well as the specific programs I was
supporting, including the Africa Growth and Opportunity Act, demonstrated to Africans that we were turning a

new page in our shared history. For all its problems, Africa was a hopeful place. I had seen it in the faces of the massive crowds in the cities, in those of the schoolchildren and villagers in the bush and on the edge of the desert. And Africa had given me a great gift: in the wisdom of a Rwandan widow and of Nelson Mandela, I had found more peace of mind to face what lay ahead.

On April 1, while we were still in Senegal, Judge Wright granted my lawyers' motion for a summary judgment in the Jones case, dismissing it without a trial, because she found that Jones had produced no credible evidence to support her claim. The dismissal exposed the raw political nature of Starr's investigation. Now he was pursuing me on the theory that I had given a false statement in a deposition the judge had said was not relevant, and that I had obstructed justice in a case that had no merit in the first place. No one was even talking about Whitewater anymore. On April 2, to no one's surprise, Starr said he would press on.

A few days later Bob Rubin and I announced that the United States would block the importation of 1.6 million assault weapons. Although we had banned the manufacture of nineteen different assault weapons in the 1994 crime bill, ingenious foreign gun makers were trying to evade the law by making modifications on guns whose only purpose was to kill people.

Good Friday, April 10, was one of the happiest days of my presidency. Seventeen hours past the deadline for a decision, all the parties in Northern Ireland agreed to a plan to end thirty years of sectarian violence. I had been up most of the night before, trying to help George Mitchell close the deal. Besides George, I talked to Bertie

Ahern, and to Tony Blair, David Trimble, and Gerry Adams twice, before going to bed at 2:30 a.m. At five, George woke me with a request to call Adams again to seal the deal.

The agreement was a fine piece of work, calling for majority rule and minority rights; shared political decision making and shared economic benefits; continued ties to the United Kingdom and new ties to Ireland. The process that produced the pact began with the determination of John Major and Albert Reynolds to seek peace, continued when John Bruton succeeded Reynolds, and was completed by Bertie Ahern, Tony Blair, David Trimble, John Hume, and Gerry Adams. My first visa to Adams and the subsequent intense engagement of the White House made a difference, and George Mitchell handled the negotiations brilliantly.

Of course, the main credit went to those who had to make the hard decisions, the Northern Irish leaders, Blair, and Ahern, and to the people of Northern Ireland who had chosen the promise of peace over a poisoned past. The agreement would have to be ratified in a referendum by the voters of Northern Ireland and the Irish Republic on May 22. With a touch of Irish eloquence, it became known as the Good Friday accord.

At around that time, I also flew to the Johnson Space Center in Houston to discuss our newest shuttle mission to conduct twenty-six experiments on the impact of space on the human body, including how the brain adapts and what happens to the inner ear and the human balance system. One of the crew was in the audience, seventy-seven-year-old senator John Glenn. After flying 149 combat missions in World War II and Korea, John had been one of America's first astronauts more than thirty-five years earlier. He was retiring from the Senate and was itching to go into space once more. NASA's director, Dan Goldin, and I were strongly in favor of Glenn's participation because our space agency wanted to study the effects of space on aging. I had always been a strong supporter of the space program, including the International Space Station and the upcoming mission to Mars; John Glenn's last hurrah gave us a chance to show the practical benefits of space exploration.

I then flew to Chile for a state visit and the second Summit of the Americas. After the long, harsh dictatorship of General Augusto Pinochet, Chile seemed firmly committed to democracy under the leadership of President Eduardo Frei, whose father had also been president of Chile in the 1960s. Shortly after the summit, Mack McLarty resigned as my special envoy to the Americas. By then my old friend had made more than forty trips to the region in the four years since he had taken the job and, in so doing, had sent an unmistakable message that the United States was committed to being a good neighbor.

The month ended on two high notes. I held a reception for members of Congress who had voted for the 1993 budget, including those who had lost their seats for doing so, to announce that the deficit had been completely eliminated for the first time since 1969. It was a development that would have been unthinkable when I took office, and impossible without the hard vote for the economic plan in 1993. On the last day of the month, the Senate voted, 80–19, to approve another of my major priorities—bringing Poland, Hungary, and the Czech Republic into NATO.

In mid-May our efforts to ban nuclear testing were shaken when India conducted five underground tests. Two weeks later, Pakistan responded with six tests of its own. India claimed its nuclear weapons were needed as a deterrent to China; Pakistan said it was responding to India. Public opinion in both nations strongly supported the possession of nuclear weapons, but it was a dangerous proposition. For one thing, our national security people were convinced that, unlike the United States and the Soviet Union in the Cold War, India and Pakistan knew little about each other's nuclear capabilities and policies for using them. After the Indian tests, I urged Pakistan's prime minister Nawaz Sharif not to follow suit, but he couldn't resist the political pressure.

I was deeply concerned about India's decision, not only because I considered it so dangerous, but also because it set back my policy of improving Indo-U.S. relations and made it harder for me to secure Senate ratification of the Comprehensive Test Ban Treaty. France and the UK had already done so, but there was a growing sense of isolation and unilateralism in Congress, as evidenced by the failure of the fast-track legislation and the refusal to pay our UN dues or our contribution to the International Monetary Fund. The IMF funding was especially important. With an Asian financial crisis threatening to spread to fragile economies in other parts of the world, the IMF needed to be able to organize an aggressive and well-funded response. The Congress was compromising the stability of the global economy.

While the nuclear testing controversy was unfolding, I had to leave on another trip, to the annual G-8 summit being held in Birmingham, England. On the way, I stopped in Germany for a meeting with Helmut Kohl at Sans Souci, the palace of Frederick the Great; for a celebration marking the fiftieth anniversary of the Berlin airlift; and for a public appearance with Kohl at a General Motors Opel plant in Eisenach, in the former East Germany.

Kohl was in a tough fight for reelection, and my appearances with him beyond the airlift ceremonies raised a few questions, especially since his Social Democratic Party opponent, Gerhard Schroeder, was running on a platform that was a lot like what Tony Blair and I were advocating. Helmut had already served longer than any German chancellor except Bismarck, and he was behind in the polls. But he had been America's friend, and mine, and no matter how the election came out, his legacy was secure: a reunited Germany, a strong European Union, a partnership with democratic Russia, and German support for ending the Bosnian war. Before I left Germany, I also had a good talk with Schroeder, who had risen from modest beginnings to the summit of German politics. He struck me as tough, smart, and clearheaded about what he wanted to do. I wished him well, and told him that if he won I would do whatever I could to help him succeed.

When I arrived in Birmingham, I saw that the city had undergone a remarkable revival and was much more beautiful than it had been when I first visited there almost thirty years earlier. The conference had a useful agenda, calling for international economic reforms; greater cooperation against drug trafficking, money laundering, and trafficking in women and children; and a specific alliance between the United States and the European Union against terrorism. However important, it was overshadowed by unfolding world events: the Indian nuclear tests; the political and economic collapse of Indonesia; the stalled peace process in the Middle East; the looming prospect of war in Kosovo; and the coming referendum on the Good Friday accord. We condemned the Indian nuclear tests, reaffirmed our support for the Nuclear Non-proliferation and Comprehensive Test Ban treaties, and said we wanted a global treaty to stop the production of fissile materials for nuclear weapons. On Indonesia, we urged both economic and political reforms, which seemed unlikely to occur because the country's finances were in such a terrible mess that the necessary reforms would make life even harder for ordinary Indonesians in the short run. Within a couple of days, President Suharto resigned, but Indonesia's problems did not leave with him. They would soon claim more of my time. Nothing could be done on the Middle East for the moment, until the Israeli political situation was sorted out.

In Kosovo, the southernmost province of Serbia, the majority of the people were Albanian Muslims who were chafing under Milosevic's rule. After Serbian attacks on the Kosovars earlier in the year, the United Nations had placed an arms embargo on the former Yugoslavia (Serbia and Montenegro) and several nations had imposed economic sanctions on Serbia. A Contact Group consisting of the United States, Russia, and several European nations was working to defuse the crisis. The G-8 supported the Contact Group's efforts, but soon we would have to do more.

Again, the only good news was in Northern Ireland. More than 90 percent of Sinn Fein party members had endorsed the Good Friday accord. With both John Hume and Gerry Adams working for it, a huge Catholic vote in favor of the agreement was certain. Protestant opinion was more closely divided. After consulting with the parties, I decided not to go from Birmingham to Belfast to speak in person for the agreement. I didn't want to give Ian Paisley any ammunition to attack me as an outsider telling the

Northern Irish what to do. Instead, Tony Blair and I met with reporters and did two lengthy television interviews with the BBC and CNN supporting the referendum.

On May 20, two days before the vote, I also delivered a brief radio address to the people of Northern Ireland, pledging America's support if they voted for "a lasting peace for yourselves and your children." That's exactly what they did. The Good Friday accord was approved by 71 percent of the people in Northern Ireland, including a solid majority of Protestants. In the Irish Republic, more than 90 percent of the people voted for it. I was never more proud of my Irish heritage.

After a stop in Geneva to urge the World Trade Organization to adopt a more open decision-making process, take more account of labor and environmental conditions in trade negotiations, and listen to the representatives of ordinary citizens who felt left out of the global economy, I flew home to America, but not away from the world's problems.

That week, at the commencement ceremony of the U.S. Naval Academy, I outlined an aggressive approach to deal with sophisticated global terrorist networks, including a plan to detect, deter, and defend against attacks on our power systems, water supplies, police, fire and medical services, air traffic control, financial services, telephone systems, and computer networks, and a concerted effort to prevent the spread and use of biological weapons and protect our people from them. I proposed to strengthen the inspection system of the Biological Weapons Convention; vaccinate our armed forces against biological threats, especially anthrax; train more state and local officials and National Guard personnel to respond to biological attacks; upgrade our system of detection and warning;

stockpile medicines and vaccines against the most likely biological attacks; and increase research and development to create the next generation of vaccines, medicines, and diagnostic tools.

Over the previous several months I had become particularly worried about the prospect of a biological attack, perhaps with a weapon that had been genetically engineered to resist existing vaccines and medicines. The previous December, at Renaissance Weekend, Hillary and I had arranged to have dinner with Craig Venter, a molecular biologist whose company was attempting to finish sequencing the human genome. I asked Craig about the possibility that genetic mapping would permit terrorists to develop synthetic genes, reengineer existing viruses, or combine smallpox with another deadly virus to make it even more harmful.

Craig said those things were possible and urged me to read Richard Preston's new novel, **The Cobra Event,** a thriller about a mad scientist's efforts to reduce the world's population by infecting New York City with a "brainpox," a combination of smallpox and an insect virus that destroys nerves. When I read the book I was surprised that Preston's acknowledgments included more than one hundred scientists, military and intelligence experts, and officials in my own administration. I urged several cabinet members and Speaker Gingrich to read it.

We had begun working on the biological warfare issue in 1993, after the World Trade Center bombing made it clear that terrorism could strike at home, and a defector from Russia had told us that his country had huge stocks of anthrax, smallpox, Ebola, and other pathogens, and had continued to produce them even after the demise of the Soviet Union. In response, the mandate of the Nunn-

Lugar program was broadened to include cooperation with Russia on biological as well as nuclear weapons.

After the sarin gas release in the Tokyo subway in 1995, the Counterterrorism Security Group (CSG), headed by National Security Council staffer Richard Clarke, began to focus more on planning defenses against chemical and biological attacks. In June 1995, I signed Presidential Decision Directive (PDD) 39 to allocate responsibilities among various government agencies for preventing and dealing with such attacks, and for reducing terrorists' capabilities through covert action and aggressive efforts to capture terrorists abroad. In the Pentagon, a few military and civilian leaders were interested in the issue, including the commandant of the Marine Corps, Charles Krulak, and Richard Danzig, the undersecretary of the navy. In late 1996, the Joint Chiefs endorsed Danzig's recommendation to vaccinate the entire military force against anthrax, and Congress moved to tighten control over biological agents in American labs, after a fanatic, using false identification, was caught buying three vials of plague virus from a lab for about $300.

By late 1997, when it became clear that Russia had even larger stocks of germ warfare agents than we had believed, I authorized American cooperation with scientists who had worked at the institutes where a lot of the bioweapons had been built in the Soviet era, in the hope of finding out exactly what was going on and preventing them from providing their expertise or biological agents to Iran or other high bidders.

In March 1998, Dick Clarke gathered about forty members of the administration at Blair House for a "table top exercise" on handling terrorist attacks of smallpox, a chemical agent, and a nuclear weapon. The results were troubling. With smallpox, it took them too much time and the loss of too many lives to bring the epidemic under control. The stocks of antibiotics and vaccines were inadequate, the quarantine laws were antiquated, the public-health systems were in bad shape, and the state emergency plans were not well developed.

A few weeks later, at my request, Clarke assembled seven scientists and emergency response experts, including Craig Venter; Joshua Lederberg, a Nobel Prize–winning biologist who had spent decades crusading against biological weapons; and Jerry Hauer, director of Emergency Management in New York City. Along with Bill Cohen, Janet Reno, Donna Shalala, George Tenet, and Sandy Berger, I met with the group for several hours to discuss the threat and what to do about it. Although I had been up most of the previous night helping to close the Irish peace agreement, I listened carefully to their presentation and asked a lot of questions. Everything I heard confirmed that we were not prepared for bio-attacks, and that the coming ability to sequence and reconfigure genes had profound implications for our national security. As the meeting was breaking up, Dr. Lederberg gave me a copy of a recent issue of the **Journal of the American Medical Association** devoted to the threat of bioterrorism. After reading it, I was even more concerned.

Less than a month later, the group sent me a report containing its recommendations for spending almost $2 billion over the next four years to improve public-health capabilities, build a national stockpile of antibiotics and vaccines, especially against smallpox, and increase research into the development of better medicines and vaccines through genetic engineering.

On the day of the Annapolis speech, I signed two more

presidential directives on terrorism. PDD-62 created a ten-point counterterrorism initiative, assigning responsibility to various government agencies for specific functions, including the apprehension, return, and prosecution of terrorists and the disruption of their networks; preventing terrorists from acquiring weapons of mass destruction; managing the aftermath of attacks; protecting critical infrastructure and cybersystems; and protecting Americans at home and overseas.

PDD-62 also established the position of National Coordinator for Counterterrorism and Infrastructure Protection; I appointed Dick Clarke, who had been our point person on anti-terrorism from the start. He was a career professional who had served under Presidents Reagan and Bush, and was appropriately aggressive in his efforts to organize the government to fight terror. PDD-63 established a National Infrastructure Protection Center to prepare for the first time a comprehensive plan to protect our critical infrastructure, such as transportation, telecommunications, and water systems.

At the end of the month, Starr tried and failed again to force Susan McDougal to testify before the grand jury; questioned Hillary for nearly five hours and for the sixth time; and indicted Webb Hubbell again on tax charges. Several former prosecutors questioned the propriety of Starr's highly unusual move; essentially Hubbell was being charged again for overcharging his clients because he hadn't paid taxes on the money. To make matters worse, Starr also indicted Hubbell's wife, Suzy, because she had signed their joint income tax returns, and Webb's friends, accountant Mike Schaufele and lawyer Charles Owen, because they had given Hubbell advice on his financial affairs, free of charge, when he was in trouble. Hubbell was blunt in his response: "They think by indicting my wife and my friends that I will lie about the President and the First Lady. I will not do so . . . I'm not gonna lie about the President. I'm not gonna lie about the First Lady, or anyone else."

In early May, Starr continued his strategy of intimidation by indicting Susan McDougal on charges of criminal contempt and obstruction of justice for her continuing refusal to talk to the grand jury, the same offense for which she had already served eighteen months for civil contempt. This one took the cake. Starr and Hick Ewing couldn't bully Susan McDougal into lying for them and it was driving them nuts. Although it would take Susan nearly another year to prove it, she was tougher than they were, and in the end she would be vindicated.

In June, Starr finally got into a little hot water. After Steven Brill published an article in **Brill's Content** on Starr's operation that highlighted the OIC's strategy of unlawful news leaks, and reported that Starr had admitted the leaks in a ninety-minute interview, Judge Norma Holloway Johnson ruled that there was "probable cause" to believe that Starr's office had engaged in "serious and repetitive" leaks to the news media and that David Kendall could subpoena Starr and his deputies to find the source of the leaks. Because the judge's decision involved grand jury proceedings, it was rendered in secret. Strangely, it was one aspect of Starr's operation that was not leaked to the press.

On May 29, Barry Goldwater died at the age of eighty-nine. I was saddened by his passing. Although we were of different parties and philosophies, Goldwater had been uncommonly kind to Hillary and me. I also respected him for being a genuine patriot and an old-fashioned libertarian who thought the government should stay out of citizens' private lives and who believed political combat should focus on ideas, not personal attacks.

I spent the rest of the spring lobbying for my legislative program and doing the business at hand: issuing an executive order to prohibit discrimination against gays in federal civilian employment; supporting Boris Yeltsin's new economic reform program; receiving the emir of Bahrain at the White House; addressing the UN General Assembly session on global drug trafficking; hosting a state visit for South Korean president Kim Dae Jung; holding a National Ocean Conference in Monterey, California, where I extended the ban on oil drilling off the California coast for fourteen years; signing a bill that provided funds to buy bulletproof vests for the 25 percent of our law-enforcement officers who didn't have them; speaking at three university commencements; and campaigning for Democrats in six states.

It was a busy but fairly normal month, except for an unhappy trip I took to Springfield, Oregon, where a troubled fifteen-year-old boy armed with a semiautomatic weapon had killed and wounded several of his classmates. It was the latest in a series of school shootings that included lethal incidents in Jonesboro, Arkansas; Pearl, Mississippi; Paducah, Kentucky; and Edinboro, Pennsylvania.

The killings were both heartbreaking and perplexing, because the overall juvenile crime rate was finally declining. It seemed to me that the violent outbursts were due, at least in part, to the excessive glorification of violence in our culture and the easy availability of deadly weapons to children. In all the school shooting cases, including several others in which no deaths had occurred, the young perpetrators seemed to be enraged, alienated, or in the grip of some dark philosophy of life. I asked Janet Reno and Dick Riley to put together a guide for teachers, parents, and students on the early warning signals troubled young people frequently exhibited, with suggested strategies on how to deal with them.

I went to the high school in Springfield to meet with the victims' families, listen to accounts of what had happened, and speak to the students, teachers, and citizens. They were traumatized, wondering how such a thing could have occurred in their community. Often at times like this, I felt all I could do was share people's grief, reassure them that they were good men and women, and encourage them to pick up the pieces and go on.

As spring turned to summer, it was time for my long-planned visit to China. Although the United States and China still had significant differences over human rights, religious and political freedom, and other matters, I was looking forward to the trip. I thought Jiang Zemin had done well on his trip to the United States in 1997 and he was eager to have me reciprocate.

The trip was not free of controversy in either country. I would be the first President to go to China since the suppression of pro-democracy forces in Tiananmen Square in 1989. The charges of Chinese attempts to influence the '96 election had not been resolved. Also, some Republicans were attacking me for allowing American companies to launch commercial satellites into space on Chinese missiles, though the satellite technology was not accessible to the Chinese, and the process had begun under the Reagan administration and continued during the Bush years in order to save money for U.S. companies. Finally, many Americans feared that China's trade policies and its tolerance of the illegal reproduction and sale of American books, movies, and music were causing job losses in the United States.

On the Chinese side, many officials resented our criticism of Chinese human rights policies as interference in their internal affairs, while others believed that, for all my positive talk, American policy was to contain, not cooperate, with China in the twenty-first century.

With a quarter of the world's population and a rapidly growing economy, China was bound to have a profound economic and political impact on America and the world. If at all possible, we had to build a positive relationship. It would have been foolish not to go.

In the week before I left, I nominated UN Ambassador Bill Richardson to succeed Federico Peña as secretary of energy, and Dick Holbrooke to become the new UN ambassador. Richardson, a former congressman from New Mexico, where two of the Energy Department's important research labs were located, was a natural for the job. Holbrooke had the skills to solve our UN dues problem and the experience and intellect to make a major contribution to our foreign policy team. With trouble brewing in the Balkans again, we needed him.

Hillary, Chelsea, and I arrived in China on the night of June 25, along with Hillary's mother, Dorothy, and a delegation that included Secretary Albright, Secretary Rubin, Secretary Daley, and six members of Congress, including John Dingell of Michigan, the longest-serving member of the House. John's presence was important because Michigan's dependence on the automobile industry made it a center of protectionist sentiment. I was gratified that he wanted to see China firsthand, to make his own judgment about whether China should join the WTO.

We began the trip at the ancient capital of Xi'an, where the Chinese put on an elaborate and beautiful welcoming ceremony. The next day we had the opportunity to walk among the rows of the famous terra-cotta warriors, and to have a roundtable discussion with Chinese citizens in the small village of Xiahe.

We got down to business two days later, when President Jiang Zemin and I met and held a press conference that was televised live all over China. We frankly discussed our differences as well as our commitment to building a strategic partnership. It was the first time the Chinese people had ever seen their leader actually debate issues like human rights and religious liberty with a foreign head of state. Jiang had grown more confident in his ability to deal with such issues in public and he trusted me to disagree in a respectful way, as well as to stress our common interests in ending the Asian financial crisis, advancing nonproliferation, and promoting reconciliation on the Korean peninsula.

When I advocated more freedom and human rights in China, Jiang responded that America was highly developed, while China still had a per capita income of $700 a year. He emphasized our different histories, cultures, ideologies, and social systems. When I urged Jiang to meet with the Dalai Lama, he said the door was open if the Dalai Lama would first state that Tibet and Taiwan were part of China, and added that there were already "several channels of communication" with the leader of Tibetan Buddhism. I got a laugh from the Chinese audience when I said I thought that if Jiang and the Dalai Lama did meet, they would like each other very much. I also tried to make some practical suggestions to move forward on human rights. For example, there were still Chinese citizens in prison for offenses no longer on the books. I suggested they be released.

The main point of the press conference was the debate itself. I wanted Chinese citizens to see America supporting human rights that we believe are universal, and I wanted Chinese officials to see that greater openness wouldn't cause the social disintegration that, given China's history, they understandably feared.

After the state dinner hosted by Jiang Zemin and his wife, Wang Yeping, he and I took turns conducting the People's Liberation Army Band. The next day my family attended Sunday church services at Chongwenmen Church, Beijing's earliest Protestant church, one of the few houses of worship the government had sanctioned. Many Christians were meeting secretly in homes. Religious liberty was important to me, and I was pleased when Jiang agreed to let me send a delegation of American religious leaders, including a rabbi, a Catholic archbishop, and an evangelical minister, to pursue the matter further.

After we toured the Forbidden City and the Great Wall, I held a question-and-answer session with students at Beijing University. We discussed human rights in China, but they also asked me about human rights problems in the United States and about what I could do to increase the American people's understanding of China. These were fair questions from young people who wanted their country to change but were still proud of it.

Premier Zhu Rongji hosted a lunch for the delegation in which we discussed the economic and social challenges facing China, as well as the remaining issues we still had to resolve in order to bring China into the World Trade Organization. I was strongly in favor of doing so, in order to continue China's integration into the global economy, and to increase both its acceptance of international rules of law and its willingness to cooperate with the United States and other nations on a whole range of other issues. That night President Jiang and Madame Wang invited us to dine alone with them at their official residence, which lay beside a placid lake inside the compound that housed China's most important leaders. The more time I spent with Jiang, the more I liked him. He was intriguing, funny, and fiercely proud, but always willing to listen to different points of view. Even though I didn't always agree with him, I became convinced that he believed he was changing China as fast as he could, and in the right direction.

From Beijing we went to Shanghai, which seemed to have more construction cranes than any other city in the world. Hillary and I had a fascinating discussion about China's problems and potential with a group of younger Chinese, including professors, businesspeople, a consumer advocate, and a novelist. One of the most enlightening experiences of the entire trip was a radio call-in show I did with the mayor. There were some good but predictable questions for me on economic and security matters, but the mayor got more questions than I did; his callers were interested in better education and more computers, and worried about the traffic congestion as a result of the city's growing prosperity and expansion. It struck me that if citizens were complaining to the mayor about traffic jams, Chinese politics was evolving in the right direction.

Before going home, we flew to Guilin for a meeting with environmentalists concerned about the destruction of forests and the loss of unique wildlife, and a leisurely boat trip down the Li River, which flows through a stunning landscape marked by large limestone formations that looked as if they had burst up through the landscape of the gentle countryside. After Guilin, we made a stop in Hong Kong to see Tung Chee-hwa, the chief executive chosen by the Chinese after the British left. An intelligent, sophisticated man who had lived in America for several years, Tung had his hands full balancing the boisterous Hong Kong political culture with the much more conformist Chinese central government. I also met again with democracy advocate Martin Lee. The Chinese had promised to let Hong Kong keep its much more democratic political system, but I had the clear impression that the details of their reunion were still being worked out, and that neither side was fully satisfied with the present state of affairs.

In mid-July, Al Gore and I held an event at the National Academy of Sciences to highlight our administration's efforts to avoid computer meltdowns at the dawn of the new millennium. There was widespread concern that many computer systems would not make the change to the year 2000, which would cause havoc in the economy and disrupt the affairs of millions of Americans. We organized an exhaustive effort led by John Koskinen to make sure all government systems were ready for the new millennium and to help the private sector make the adjustment. We wouldn't know for sure whether we had been successful until the date arrived.

On the sixteenth, I signed another of my priorities into law, the Child Support Performance and Incentive Act. We had already increased collections 68 percent since

1992; 1.4 million more families were now receiving child support. This bill penalized states that did not automate their child-support files and gave financial rewards to those that were successful in meeting performance goals.

Around this time I announced the purchase of eighty billion bushels of wheat for distribution to poor nations with food shortages. Grain prices were down, and the purchase would both meet a humanitarian need and raise the price of wheat as much as thirteen cents a bushel for hard-pressed farmers. Because a severe heat wave was destroying crops in parts of the country, I also asked Congress to pass an emergency farm aid package.

Toward the end of the month, Mike McCurry announced that he would resign as White House press secretary in the fall, and I named his deputy, Joe Lockhart, who had served as press secretary for my reelection campaign, to succeed him. McCurry had done a fine job in a demanding position, answering tough questions, explaining the administration's policies with clarity and a quick wit, and working long hours with around-the-clock availability. He wanted to see his kids grow up. I liked Joe Lockhart a lot, and the press seemed to like him, too. Besides, he liked to play cards with me; we would have a smooth transition.

In July, as I continued to push my agenda at home, Dick Holbrooke flew to Belgrade to see Milosevic in an attempt to resolve the Kosovo crisis; Prime Minister Hashimoto resigned after election losses in Japan; Nelson Mandela got married to Graça Machel, the lovely widow of a former president of Mozambique and a leading figure in the struggle to stop the use of children in Africa's wars; and Ken Starr continued to build his case against me.

He insisted on taking the testimony of several of my

Secret Service agents, including Larry Cockell, the head of my detail. The Secret Service had resisted this, and former President Bush had written two letters opposing it. Except when the President is on the residence floor of the White House, the Secret Service is always with him or just outside the door of whatever room he is in. Presidents depend on the Secret Service to protect them, and to protect their confidences. The agents overhear all kinds of conversations involving national security, domestic policy, political conflicts, and personal struggles. Their dedication, professionalism, and discretion had served Presidents of both parties and the nation well. Now Starr was willing to put all that at risk—to investigate not espionage, or Watergate-like abuses of the FBI, or Iran-Contra–like willful defiance of the law, but whether I had given false answers and encouraged Monica Lewinsky to do the same in response to questions asked in bad faith, in a case that had been thrown out of court because it had no merit in the first place.

By the end of the month, Starr had granted Monica Lewinsky immunity from prosecution in return for her testimony before the grand jury, and had subpoenaed me to testify as well. On the twenty-ninth, I agreed to testify voluntarily and the subpoena was withdrawn. I can't say I was looking forward to it.

Early in August, I met with ten Indian tribal leaders in Washington to announce a comprehensive effort to increase educational, health care, and economic opportunities for Native Americans. My assistant for intergovernmental affairs, Mickey Ibarra, and Lynn Cutler, my liaison to the tribes, had worked hard on the initiative and it was sorely needed. Although the United States was enjoying its lowest unemployment rate in twenty-eight years, the lowest crime rate in twenty-five years, and the smallest percentage of our citizens on welfare in twenty-nine years, Native American communities that had not grown wealthy from gambling operations were still in bad shape. Fewer than 10 percent of Native Americans went to college, they were three times more likely to suffer from diabetes as white Americans, and they still had the lowest per capita income of any American ethnic group. Some of the tribal communities had unemployment rates in excess of 50 percent. The leaders were encouraged by the new steps we were taking, and after the meeting I had some hope that we could help them.

The next day the American embassies in Tanzania and Kenya were hit by bombs that exploded within five minutes of each other, killing 257 people, including 12 Americans, and injuring 5,000 others. The initial evidence indicated that Osama bin Laden's network, which became known as al Qaeda, had launched the attacks. In late February, bin Laden had issued a fatwa calling for attacks on American military and civilian targets anywhere in the world. In May, he had said his supporters would hit U.S. targets in the Gulf and talked about "bringing the war home to America." In June, in an interview with an American journalist, he had threatened to bring down U.S. military aircraft with anti-aircraft missiles.

By this time, we had been following bin Laden for years. Early in my first term, Tony Lake and Dick Clarke had pressed the CIA for more information about the wealthy Saudi, who had been expelled from his own country in 1991, had lost his citizenship in 1994, and had taken up residence in Sudan.

At first, bin Laden seemed to be a financier of terrorist operations, but over time we would learn that he was the head of a highly sophisticated terrorist organization, with access to large amounts of money beyond his own fortune, and with operatives in several countries, including Chechnya, Bosnia, and the Philippines. In 1995, after the war in Bosnia, we had thwarted mujahedin attempts to take over there and, in cooperation with local officials, had also stopped a plot to blow up a dozen planes flying out of the Philippines to the West Coast, but bin Laden's transnational network continued to grow.

In January 1996, the CIA had established a station focused exclusively on bin Laden and his network within its Counterterrorism Center, and shortly thereafter we began to urge Sudan to expel bin Laden. Sudan was then a virtual safe haven for terrorists, including the Egyptians who had tried to kill President Mubarak the previous June and who had succeeded in assassinating his predecessor, Anwar Sadat. The nation's leader, Hasan al-Turabi, shared bin Laden's radical views, and the two of them were involved in a whole host of business ventures, running the gamut from legitimate operations to weapons manufacturing and support for terrorists.

As we pressed Turabi to expel bin Laden, we asked Saudi Arabia to take him. The Saudis didn't want him back, but bin Laden finally left Sudan in mid-1996, apparently still on good terms with Turabi. He moved to Afghanistan, where he found a warm welcome from Mullah Omar, leader of the Taliban, a militant Sunni sect that was bent on establishing a radical Muslim theocracy in Afghanistan.

In September 1996, the Taliban captured Kabul and started seizing other areas of the country. By the end of the year, the CIA's bin Laden unit had developed significant information on him and his infrastructure. Almost a year later, Kenyan authorities arrested a man they believed was involved in a terrorist plot against the U.S. Embassy there.

In the week after the bombings, I kept up my regular schedule, traveling to Kentucky, Illinois, and California to promote the Patients' Bill of Rights and our clean water initiative, and to help Democrats up for election in those states. Beyond the public events, I spent most of my time with our national security team discussing how we were going to respond to the African attacks.

On August 13, there was a memorial service at Andrews Air Force Base for ten of the twelve American victims. The people bin Laden believed deserved to die just because they were Americans included a career diplomat I had met twice and his son; a woman who had just spent her vacation caring for her aged parents; an Indian-born foreign service officer who had traveled the world working for her adopted country; an epidemiologist working to save African children from disease and death; a mother of three small children; a proud new grandmother; an accomplished jazz musician with a day job in the foreign service; an embassy administrator who had married a Kenyan; and three sergeants, one each in the army, the air force, and the Marine Corps.

By all accounts, bin Laden was poisoned by the conviction that he was in possession of the absolute truth and therefore free to play God by killing innocent people. Since we had been going after his organization for several years, I had known for some time that he was a formidable adversary. After the African slaughter I became intently focused on capturing or killing him and with destroying al Qaeda.

One week after the embassy bombings, and after videotaping an address to the people of Kenya and Tanzania, whose losses were far greater than ours, I met with the national security principals. The CIA and FBI both confirmed that al Qaeda was responsible and reported that some of the perpetrators had already been arrested.

I had also received an intelligence report that al Qaeda had plans to attack yet another embassy, in Tirana, Albania, and that our enemies thought America was vulnerable because we would be distracted by the controversy over my personal behavior. We closed the Albanian embassy, sent in heavily armed marines to guard it, and began working with local authorities to break up the al Qaeda cell there. But we still had other embassies in countries with al Qaeda operations.

The CIA also had intelligence that bin Laden and his top staff were planning a meeting at one of his camps in Afghanistan on August 20 to assess the impact of their attacks and plan their next operations. The meeting would provide an opportunity to retaliate and perhaps wipe out much of the al Qaeda leadership. I asked Sandy Berger to manage the process leading up to a military response. We had to pick targets, move the necessary military assets into place, and figure out how to handle Pakistan. If we launched air strikes, our planes would pass over Pakistan's airspace.

Although we were trying to work with Pakistan to defuse tensions on the Indian subcontinent, and our two nations had been allies during the Cold War, Pakistan supported the Taliban and, by extension, al Qaeda. The Pakistani intelligence service used some of the same camps that bin Laden and al Qaeda did to train the Taliban and insurgents who fought in Kashmir. If Pakistan found out about our planned attacks in advance, it was likely that Pakistani intelligence would warn the Taliban or even al

Qaeda. On the other hand, Deputy Secretary of State Strobe Talbott, who was working to minimize the chances of military conflict on the Indian subcontinent, was afraid that if we didn't tell the Pakistanis, they might assume the flying missiles had been launched at them by India and retaliate, conceivably even with nuclear weapons.

We decided to send the vice chairman of the Joint Chiefs of Staff, General Joe Ralston, to have dinner with the top Pakistani military commander at the time the attacks were scheduled. Ralston would tell him what was happening a few minutes before our missiles invaded Pakistani airspace, too late to alert the Taliban or al Qaeda, but in time to avoid having them shot down or sparking a counterattack on India.

My team was worried about one other thing: my testimony before the grand jury in three days, on August 17. They were afraid that it would make me reluctant to strike, or that if I did order the attack, I would be accused of doing it to divert public attention from my problems, especially if the attack didn't get bin Laden. I told them in no uncertain terms that their job was to give me advice on national security. If the recommendation was to strike on the twentieth, then that's what we would do. I said I would handle my personal problems. Time was running out on that, too.

FORTY-NINE

On Saturday morning, August 15, with the grand jury testimony looming and after a miserable, sleepless night, I woke up Hillary and told her the truth about what had happened between me and Monica Lewinsky. She looked at me as if I had punched her in the gut, almost as angry at me for lying to her in January as for what I had done. All I could do was tell her that I was sorry, and that I had felt I couldn't tell anyone, even her, what had happened. I told her that I loved her and I didn't want to hurt her or Chelsea, that I was ashamed of what I had done, and that I had kept everything to myself in an effort to avoid hurting my family and undermining the presidency. And after all the lies and abuse we had endured from the start of my presidency, I didn't want to be run out of office in the flood tide that followed my deposition in January. I still didn't fully understand why I had done something so wrong and stupid; that understanding would come slowly, in the months of working on our relationship that lay ahead.

I had to talk to Chelsea, too. In some ways, that was even harder. Sooner or later, every child learns that her parents aren't perfect, but this went far beyond the normal. I had always believed that I had been a good father. Chelsea's high school years and her freshman year in college had already been clouded by four years of intensely personal attacks on her parents. Now Chelsea had to learn that her father not only had done something terribly wrong, but had not told her or her mother the truth about it. I was afraid that I would lose not only my marriage, but my daughter's love and respect as well.

The rest of that awful day was dominated by another terrorist act. In Omagh, Northern Ireland, a breakaway faction of the IRA that did not support the Good Friday accord murdered twenty-eight people in a crowded shopping section of the city with a car bomb. All the parties to the peace process, including Sinn Fein, denounced the bombing. I issued a statement condemning the butchery, extending my sympathy to the victims' families, and urging the parties of peace to redouble their efforts. The outlaw group, which called itself the Real IRA, had about two hundred members and supporters, enough to cause real trouble, but not enough to disrupt the peace process: the Omagh bombing showed the utter insanity of going back to the old ways.

On Monday, after spending what time I could preparing, I went downstairs to the Map Room for four hours of testimony. Starr had agreed not to bring me down to the courthouse, probably because of the adverse reaction he got when he made Hillary do it. However, he insisted on videotaping my testimony, allegedly because one of the twenty-four grand jurors couldn't attend the session. David Kendall said the grand jury was welcome to come to the White House if Starr would not videotape my "secret" testimony. He refused; I suspected that he wanted to send the videotape to Congress, where it could be released without getting him into more hot water.

The grand jury was watching the proceedings on closed-circuit television back at the courthouse while Starr and his interrogators did their best to turn the videotape into a pornographic home movie, asking me questions designed to humiliate me and to so disgust the Congress and the American people that they would demand my resignation, after which he might be able to indict me. Samuel Johnson once said that nothing concentrates the mind as much as the prospect of one's own destruction. Moreover, I believed that a lot more was at stake than what might happen to me.

After the preliminaries, I asked to make a brief statement. I admitted that "on certain occasions in 1996 and once in 1997" I engaged in wrongful conduct that included inappropriate intimate contact with Monica Lewinsky; that the conduct, while morally wrong, did not constitute "sexual relations" as I understood the definition of the term that Judge Wright accepted at the request of the Jones lawyers; that I took full responsibility for my actions; and that I would answer to the best of my ability all the OIC's questions relating to the legality of my actions, but would not say more about the specifics of what had happened.

The principal OIC interrogator then took me through a long list of questions dealing with the definition of "sexual relations" that Judge Wright had imposed. I acknowledged that I had not been trying to be helpful to the Jones lawyers because they, like the OIC, had engaged in repeated unlawful leaks, and since they knew by then that their case had no merit, I believed that their objective in the deposition was to elicit damaging new information from me for the purpose of leaking it. I said that of course I didn't know that by the time I testified Starr's office had already become heavily involved.

Now Starr's lawyers were trying to capitalize on the setup by getting me on videotape discussing things in graphic detail that no one should ever have to talk about publicly.

When the OIC lawyer continued to complain about my deposition answers on the sex questions, I reminded him that both my lawyer and I had invited Jones's attorneys to ask specific follow-up questions, and that they declined to do so. I said it was now clear to me that they didn't do so because they were no longer trying to get a damaging admission that they could leak to the press. Instead, they were working for Starr. They wanted the deposition to lay the basis for forcing my resignation, or impeachment, or perhaps even an indictment. So they didn't ask follow-up questions "because they were afraid I would give them a truthful answer. . . . They were trying to set me up and trick me. And now you seem to be complaining that they didn't do a good enough job." I confessed that I "deplored" what the Rutherford Institute lawyers had done in Jones's name—the tormenting of innocent people, the illegal leaking, the pursuit of a bogus, politically motivated suit—"but I was determined to walk through the minefield of this deposition without violating the law, and I believe I did."

I did acknowledge that I had misled everyone who asked about the story after it broke. And I said over and over again that I never asked anyone to lie. When the agreed-upon four hours had expired, I had been asked many questions six or seven times, as the lawyers tried hard to turn my interrogation into admissions that were humiliating and incriminating. That's what the, to date, whole four-year $40 million investigation had come down to: parsing the definition of sex.

I finished the testimony at about six-thirty, three and a half hours before I was scheduled to address the nation. I was visibly upset when I went up to the solarium to see friends and staff who had gathered to discuss what had just happened, including White House counsel Chuck Ruff, David Kendall, Mickey Kantor, Rahm Emanuel, James Carville, Paul Begala, and Harry and Linda Thomason. Chelsea was there, too, and to my relief, at about eight, Hillary joined in.

We had a discussion about what I should say. Everyone knew I had to admit that I had made an awful mistake and had tried to hide it. The question was whether I should also take a shot at Starr's investigation and say it was time to end it. The virtually unanimous opinion was that I should not. Most people already knew that Starr was out of control; they needed to hear my admission of wrongdoing and witness my remorse. Some of my friends had given what they thought was strategic advice; others were genuinely appalled by what I had done. Only Hillary refused to express an opinion, instead encouraging everyone to leave me alone to write my statement.

At ten o'clock I told the American people about my testimony, said I was solely and completely responsible for my personal failure, and admitted misleading everyone, "even my wife." I said I was trying to protect myself and my family from intrusive questions in a politically inspired lawsuit that had been dismissed. I also said that Starr's investigation had gone on too long, cost too much, and hurt too many people, and that two years earlier, another investigation, a truly independent one, had found no wrongdoing by Hillary or me in Whitewater. Finally, I committed to doing my best to repair my family life, and I hoped we could repair the fabric of our nation's life by stopping the pursuit of personal destruction and prying into private lives, and moving on. I believed every word I said, but my anger hadn't worn off enough for me to be as contrite as I should have been.

The next day we left for Martha's Vineyard on our annual vacation. Usually I counted the days until we could get away for some family time; this year, though I knew we needed it, I wished that I was working around the clock instead. As we walked out to the South Lawn to get on the helicopter, with Chelsea between Hillary and me and Buddy walking beside me, photographers took pictures that revealed the pain I had caused. When there were no cameras around, my wife and daughter were barely speaking to me.

I spent the first couple of days alternating between begging for forgiveness and planning the strikes on al Qaeda. At night Hillary would go up to bed and I slept on the couch.

On my birthday General Don Kerrick, Sandy Berger's staffer, flew to Martha's Vineyard to go over the targets recommended by the CIA and the Joint Chiefs—the al Qaeda camps in Afghanistan and two targets in Sudan, a tannery in which bin Laden had a financial interest and a chemical plant the CIA believed was being used to produce or store a chemical used in the production of VX nerve gas. I took the tannery off the list because it had no military value to al Qaeda and I wanted to minimize civilian casualties. The hit on the camps would be timed to coincide with the meeting the intelligence indicated bin Laden and his top people would be having.

At 3 a.m. I gave Sandy Berger the final order to proceed, and U.S. Navy destroyers in the northern Arabian Sea launched cruise missiles at the targets in Afghanistan, while missiles were fired at the Sudanese chemical plant from ships in the Red Sea. Most of the missiles hit the targets, but bin Laden was not in the camp where the CIA thought he would be when the missiles hit it. Some reports said he had left the camp only a couple of hours earlier, but we never knew for sure. Several people associated with al Qaeda were killed, as were some Pakistani officers who were reported to be there to train Kashmiri terrorists. The Sudanese chemical plant was destroyed.

After announcing the attacks in Martha's Vineyard, I flew back to Washington to speak to the American people for the second time in four days, telling them I had ordered the strikes because al Qaeda was responsible for the embassy bombings, and bin Laden was "perhaps the preeminent organizer and financier of international terrorism in the world today," a man who had vowed to wage a terrorist war on America with no distinction between military personnel and civilians. I said that our attacks were not aimed against Islam "but against fanatics and killers," and that we had been fighting against them on several fronts for years and would continue to do so, because "this will be a long, ongoing struggle."

Around the time I spoke of the long struggle, I signed the first of a series of orders to prepare for it by using all the tools available. Executive Order 13099 imposed economic sanctions on bin Laden and al Qaeda. Later the sanctions were extended to the Taliban as well. To date, we had not been effective in disrupting terrorists' financial networks. The executive order invoked the International Emergency Economic Powers Act, which we had earlier used successfully against the Cali drug cartel in Colombia.

I had also asked General Shelton and Dick Clarke to develop some options for dropping commando forces into Afghanistan. I thought that if we took out a couple of al Qaeda's training operations it would show them how serious we were, even if we didn't get bin Laden or his top lieutenants. It was clear to me that the senior military didn't want to do this, perhaps because of Somalia, perhaps because they would have to send in the Special Forces without knowing for certain where bin Laden was, or whether we could get our troops back out to safety. At any rate, I continued to keep the option alive.

I also signed several Memoranda of Notification (MONs) authorizing the CIA to use lethal force to apprehend bin Laden. The CIA had been authorized to conduct its own "snatch operation" against bin Laden the previous spring, months before the embassy bombings, but it lacked the paramilitary capability to do the job. Instead, it contracted with members of local Afghan tribes to get bin Laden. When field agents or the Afghan tribals were apparently uncertain of whether they had to try to capture bin Laden before they used deadly force, I made it clear that they did not. Within a few months I had extended the lethal force authorization by expanding the list of targeted bin Laden associates and the circumstances under which they could be attacked.

By and large, the response of the congressional leaders of both parties to the missile strikes was positive, in large part because they had been well briefed and Secretary Cohen had assured his fellow Republicans that the attack and its timing were justified. Speaker Gingrich said, "The United States did exactly the right thing today." Senator Lott said the attacks were "appropriate and just." Tom Daschle, Dick Gephardt, and all the Democrats were supportive. Soon I was heartened by the arrest of Mohamed Rashed, an al Qaeda operative who was a suspect in the Kenyan embassy bombing.

Some people criticized me for hitting the chemical

plant, which the Sudanese government insisted had nothing to do with the production or storage of dangerous chemicals. I still believe we did the right thing there. The CIA had soil samples taken at the plant site that contained the chemical used to produce VX. In a subsequent terrorist trial in New York City, one of the witnesses testified that bin Laden had a chemical weapons operation in Khartoum. Despite the plain evidence, some people in the media tried to push the possibility that the action was a real-life version of **Wag the Dog,** a movie in which a fictional President starts a made-for-TV war to distract public attention from his personal problems.

The American people had to absorb the news of the strike and my grand jury testimony at the same time. **Newsweek** ran an article reporting that the public's reaction to my testimony and television address about it was "calm and measured." My job rating was 62 percent, with 73 percent supporting the missile strikes. Most people thought I had been dishonest in my personal life but remained credible on public issues. By contrast, **Newsweek** said, "the first reaction of the pundit class was near hysteria." They were hitting me hard. I deserved a whipping, all right, but I was getting it at home, where it should have been administered.

For now, I just hoped that the Democrats wouldn't be pushed by the media pounding into calling for my resignation, and that I would be able to repair the breach I had caused with my family and with my staff, cabinet, and the people who had believed in me through all the years of constant attacks.

After the speech I went back to the Vineyard for ten days. There was not much thaw on the family front. I made my first public appearance since my grand jury testimony, traveling to Worcester, Massachusetts, at the invitation of Congressman Jim McGovern, to promote the Police Corps, an innovative program that provided college scholarships to people who committed to becoming law-enforcement officers. Worcester is an old-fashioned blue-collar city; I was somewhat apprehensive about the kind of reception I would get there, and was encouraged to find a large enthusiastic crowd at an event attended by the mayor, both senators, and four Massachusetts congressmen. Many people in the crowd urged me to keep doing my job; several said they had made mistakes in their lives, too, and were sorry that mine had been aired in public.

On August 28, the thirty-fifth anniversary of Martin Luther King Jr.'s famous "I have a dream" speech, I went to a commemorative service at Union Chapel in Oak Bluffs, which had been a vacation mecca for African-Americans for more than a century. I shared the platform with Congressman John Lewis, who had worked with Dr. King and was one of the most powerful moral forces in American politics. He and I had been friends for a long time, going back well before 1992. He was one of my earliest supporters and had every right to condemn me. Instead, when he rose to speak, John said that I was his friend and brother, that he had stood with me when I was up and would not leave me when I was down, that I had been a good President, and that if it were up to him, I would continue to be. John Lewis will never know how much he lifted my spirits that day.

We returned to Washington at the end of the month to face another tremendous problem. The Asian financial crisis had spread and was now threatening to destabilize the entire global economy. The crisis had begun in Thailand in 1997, then infected Indonesia and South Korea, and now it had spread to Russia. In mid-August, Russia had defaulted on its foreign debt, and by the end of the month the Russian collapse had caused large drops in stock markets across the world. On August 31, the Dow Jones industrial average dropped 512 points, following a drop of 357 just four days earlier; all the gains of 1998 were wiped out.

Bob Rubin and his international economics team had been working on the financial crisis since Thailand's trouble began. Although the details of each nation's problem were somewhat different, there were some common elements: flawed banking systems, bad loans, crony capitalism, and a general loss of confidence. The situation was aggravated by the lack of economic growth in Japan over the past five years. With no inflation and a 20 percent savings rate, the Japanese could stand it, but the absence of growth in Asia's largest economy increased the adverse consequences of bad policies elsewhere. Even the Japanese were getting restless; the stagnant economy had contributed to the election losses that had led to the recent resignation of my friend Ryutaro Hashimoto as prime minister. China, with the region's fastest-growing economy, had kept the crisis from growing even worse by refusing to devalue its currency.

The general formula for recovery in the 1990s was the extension of sizable loans from the International Monetary Fund and wealthy countries in return for necessary reforms in the affected nations. The reforms were invariably politically difficult. They always forced change on entrenched interests and often required fiscal austerity that made things harder on ordinary citizens in the short

run, though it brought a quicker recovery and more stability in the long run.

The United States had supported the IMF efforts in
Thailand, Indonesia, and South Korea, and had made
contributions in the last two cases. The Treasury Department decided not to put money into Thailand because the
$17 billion already available was sufficient and because
the Exchange Stabilization Fund, which we had used to
help Mexico, had some new, albeit temporary, restrictions
imposed on it by Congress. The restrictions had expired
by the time the other nations needed help, but I regretted
not making at least a modest contribution to the Thai
package. State, Defense, and the NSC all wanted to do it
because Thailand was our oldest ally in Southeast Asia. So
did I, but we let Treasury make the call. On the economics and in terms of domestic politics it was the correct
decision, but it sent the wrong message to Thais and
across Asia. Bob Rubin and I didn't make too many policy
errors; I believe this was one of them.

We certainly didn't have the Thai problem with Russia.
The United States had been supporting the Russian economy since my first year in office, and we had contributed
almost a third of the $23 billion IMF package in July.
Unfortunately, the first disbursement of about $5 billion
from the package had virtually disappeared overnight, as
the ruble was devalued and Russians began to move large
sums of their own money out of the country. Russia's
problems were aggravated by the irresponsible inflationary
policies of its central bank and by the Duma's refusal to
establish an effective system to collect taxes. The tax rates
were high enough, maybe too high, but most taxpayers
didn't pay them.

Right after we got back from Martha's Vineyard,

Hillary and I took a quick trip to Russia and Northern Ireland with Madeleine Albright, Bill Daley, Bill Richardson, and a bipartisan congressional delegation. Ambassador Jim Collins invited a group of leaders of the Duma to his residence, Spaso House. I tried hard to convince them that no nation could escape the discipline of the global economy, and that if they wanted foreign loans and investment, Russia would have to collect taxes, stop printing money to pay bills and bail out troubled banks, avoid crony capitalism, and pay debts. I don't think I made many converts.

My fifteenth meeting with Boris Yeltsin went as well as it could, given his problems. The Communists and ultranationalists were blocking his reform proposals in the Duma. He had tried to create a more effective tax collection system by executive action, but he still couldn't stop the central bank from printing too much money, which only encouraged greater capital flight from the ruble to more stable currencies and discouraged foreign credit and investment. For now, all I could do was encourage him and say the rest of the IMF money would be available as soon as it could make a difference. If we released it now, the funds would disappear as quickly as the first installment had.

We did make one positive announcement, saying that we would remove from each of our nuclear programs about fifty tons of plutonium—enough to make thousands of bombs—and render the material incapable of being used to make weapons in the future. With terrorist groups as well as hostile nations trying to get their hands on fissile material, it was an important step that could save countless lives.

After a speech to the new Northern Ireland Assembly

in Belfast in which I encouraged the members to continue to implement the Good Friday accord, Hillary and I went with Tony and Cherie Blair, George Mitchell, and Mo Mowlan, the UK secretary of state for Northern Ireland, to Omagh to meet with victims of the bombing. Tony and I spoke as best we could, then we all moved among the families, listening to their stories, seeing the children who had been scarred, and being struck by the victims' steady determination to stay on the path of peace. During the Troubles someone had painted a provocative question on a Belfast wall: "Is there life before death?" Amidst the cruel carnage of Omagh, the Irish were still saying yes.

Before leaving for Dublin, we and the Blairs attended a Gathering for Peace in Armagh, the base from which St. Patrick brought Christianity to Ireland and now the spiritual center in Northern Ireland for both Catholics and Protestants. I was introduced by a lovely seventeen-year-old girl, Sharon Haughey, who had written to me when she was just fourteen, asking me to help end the fighting with a simple solution: "Both sides have been hurt. Both sides will have to forgive."

In Dublin, Bertie Ahern and I spoke with the press after our meeting. An Irish reporter said, "It usually seems to take a visit from you to give the peace process a boost. Will we need to see you again?" I replied that for their sake I hoped not, but for my own sake I hoped so. Then Bertie said my quick response to the Omagh tragedy had galvanized the parties to make decisions quickly that "might have taken weeks and months." Just two days earlier, Martin McGuinness, the chief Sinn Fein negotiator, had announced that he would oversee the arms decommissioning process for Sinn Fein. Martin was Gerry Adams's top aide and a powerful force in his own right. The announcement sent a signal to David Trimble and the Unionists that for Sinn Fein and the IRA, violence, as Adams had said, "is a thing of the past, over, done with, and gone." In our private meeting, Bertie Ahern told me that after Omagh, the IRA had warned the Real IRA that if they ever did anything like that again, the British police would be the least of their worries.

The first question I got from an American reporter was a request to reply to the stinging rebuke I had received the day before on the floor of the Senate from my longtime friend Joe Lieberman. I replied, "I agree with what he said . . . I made a bad mistake, it was indefensible, and I'm sorry about it." Some of our staff were upset that Joe attacked me while I was overseas, but I wasn't. I knew he was a devoutly religious man who was angry about what I had done, and he had carefully avoided saying that I should be impeached.

Our last stop in Ireland was in Limerick, where fifty thousand supporters of peace filled the streets, including the relatives of one member of our delegation, Congressman Peter King of New York, who had brought his mother home for the event. I told the crowd that my friend Frank McCourt had memorialized the old Limerick in **Angela's Ashes,** but I liked the new one better.

On September 9, Ken Starr sent his 445-page report to Congress, alleging eleven impeachable offenses. Even with all the crimes of Watergate, Leon Jaworski hadn't done that. The independent counsel was supposed to report his findings to Congress if he found "substantial and credible" evidence to support an impeachment; Congress was supposed to decide whether there were grounds for impeachment. The report was made public on the eleventh; Jaworski's never was. In Starr's report, the word "sex" appeared more than five hundred times; Whitewater was mentioned twice. He and his allies thought they could wash away all their sins over the last four years in my dirty laundry.

On September 10, I called the cabinet to the White House and apologized to them. Many of them didn't know what to say. They believed in what we were doing and appreciated the opportunity I had given them to serve, but most of them felt I had been selfish and stupid and had left them hanging for eight months. Madeleine Albright led off, saying that I had done wrong and she was disappointed, but our only option was to go back to work. Donna Shalala was tougher, saying it was important for leaders to be good people as well as to have good policies. My longtime friends James Lee Witt and Rodney Slater talked about the power of redemption, and quoted scripture. Bruce Babbitt, a Catholic, talked about the power of confession. Carol Browner said she had been forced to talk with her son about subjects she never thought she'd have to discuss with him.

Listening to my cabinet, I really understood for the first time the extent to which the exposure of my misconduct and my dishonesty about it had opened a Pandora's box of emotions in the American people. It was easy enough to say that I had been through a lot in the past six years, and that Starr's inquisition had been awful and the Jones lawsuit was bogus and politically motivated; easy enough to say that even a President's personal life should remain private. But once what I had done was out there in all its stark ugliness, people's evaluations of it were inevitably a reflection of their own personal experiences, marked not only by their convictions but also by their own fears, disappointments, and heartbreak.

My cabinet's honest and very different reactions gave me a direct sense of what was going on in conversations all across America. As the impeachment hearings grew closer, I received many letters from friends and strangers alike. Some of the letter writers offered touching words of support and encouragement; some told their own stories of failure and recovery; some expressed outrage over the actions of Starr; some were full of condemnation and disappointment over what I had done; and still others reflected a combination of all these views. Reading the letters helped me to deal with my own emotions, and to remember that if I wanted to be forgiven, I had to forgive.

The atmosphere in the Yellow Oval Room remained awkward and tense until Bob Rubin spoke. Rubin was the one person in the room who best understood what my life had been like for the last four years. He had been through an exhaustive investigation of Goldman Sachs that featured one of his partners being hauled away in handcuffs before he was cleared. After several others had spoken, Rubin said, with characteristic bluntness, "There's no question you screwed up. But we all make mistakes, even big ones. In my opinion, the bigger issue is the disproportion of the media coverage and the hypocrisy of some of your critics." The atmosphere got better after that. I'm grateful that no one quit. We all went back to work.

On September 15, I hired Greg Craig, a fine lawyer and old friend of Hillary's and mine from law school, to work with Chuck Ruff, David Kendall, Bruce Lindsay, Cheryl Mills, Lanny Breuer, and Nicole Seligman on my defense team. On the eighteenth, just as I knew they would, the House Judiciary Committee voted on a straight party-line vote to release the video of my grand jury testimony to the public.

A few days later, Hillary and I hosted our annual break-fast for religious leaders at the White House. We usually discussed shared public concerns. This time I asked for their prayers during my personal travail:

> I have been on quite a journey these last few weeks to get to the end of this, to the rock-bottom truth of where I am and where we all are. I agree with those who have said that in my first statement after I testified, I was not contrite enough. I don't think there is a fancy way to say that I have sinned.

I said that I was sorry for all who had been hurt—my family, friends, staff, cabinet, and Monica Lewinsky and her family; that I had asked for their forgiveness; and that I would pursue counseling from pastors and others to find, with God's help, "a willingness to give the very forgiveness I seek, a renunciation of the pride and the anger which cloud judgment, lead people to excuse and compare and to blame and complain." I also said I would mount a vigorous defense in response to the charges against me and would intensify my efforts to do my job "in the hope that with a broken spirit and a still strong heart I can be used for greater good."

I had asked three pastors to counsel me at least once a month for an indefinite period: Phil Wogaman, our minister at Foundry Methodist Church; my friend Tony Campolo; and Gordon MacDonald, a minister and author of several books I had read on living one's faith. They would more than fulfill their commitment, usually coming to the White House together, sometimes separately. We would pray, read scripture, and discuss some things I had never really talked about before. The Reverend Bill Hybels from Chicago also continued to come to the White House regularly, to ask searching questions designed to check my "spiritual health." Even though they were often tough on me, the pastors took me past the politics into soul-searching and the power of God's love.

Hillary and I also began a serious counseling program, one day a week for about a year. For the first time in my life, I actually talked openly about feelings, experiences, and opinions about life, love, and the nature of relationships. I didn't like everything I learned about myself or my past, and it pained me to face the fact that my childhood and the life I'd led since growing up had made some things difficult for me that seemed to come more naturally to other people.

I also came to understand that when I was exhausted, angry, or feeling isolated and alone, I was more vulnerable to making selfish and self-destructive personal mistakes about which I would later be ashamed. The current controversy was the latest casualty of my lifelong effort to lead parallel lives, to wall off my anger and grief and get on with my outer life, which I loved and lived well. During the government shutdowns I was engaged in two titanic struggles: a public one with Congress over the future of our country, and a private one to hold the old demons at bay. I had won the public fight and lost the private one.

In so doing, I had hurt more than my family and my administration. It was also damaging to the presidency and the American people. No matter how much pressure I was under, I should have been stronger and behaved better.

There was no excuse for what I did, but trying to come to grips with why I did it gave me at least a chance to finally unify my parallel lives.

In the long counseling sessions and our conversations about them afterward, Hillary and I also got to know each other again, beyond the work and ideas we shared and the child we adored. I had always loved her very much, but not always very well. I was grateful that she was brave enough to participate in the counseling. We were still each other's best friend, and I hoped we could save our marriage.

Meanwhile, I was still sleeping on a couch, this one in the small living room that adjoined our bedroom. I slept on that old couch for two months or more. I got a lot of reading, thinking, and work done, and the couch was pretty comfortable, but I hoped I wouldn't be on it forever.

As the Republicans intensified their criticism of me, my supporters started to stand up. On September 11, eight hundred Irish-Americans gathered on the South Lawn as Brian O'Dwyer presented me with an award named after his late father, Paul, for my role in the Irish peace process. Brian's remarks and the crowd's response to them left no doubt about why they were really there.

A few days later, Václav Havel came to Washington for a state visit, telling the press I was his "great friend." As the press continued to ask questions about impeachment, resignation, and whether I had lost my moral authority to lead, Havel said America had many different faces: "I love most of these faces. There are some I don't understand. I don't like to speak about things which I don't understand."

Five days after that I went to New York for the opening session of the UN General Assembly, to deliver a speech on the world's shared obligations to fight terrorists: to give them no support, sanctuary, or financial assistance; to bring pressure on states that do; to step up extradition and prosecutions; to sign the global anti-terror conventions and strengthen and enforce the ones designed to protect us against biological and chemical weapons; to control the manufacture and export of explosives; to raise international standards for airport security; and to combat the conditions that breed terror. It was an important speech, especially at that time, but the delegates in the cavernous hall of the General Assembly were also thinking about events in Washington. When I stood up to speak, they responded with an enthusiastic and prolonged standing ovation. It was unheard of for the normally reserved UN, and I was profoundly moved. I wasn't sure whether the unprecedented act was more a gesture of support for me or opposition to what was going on in Congress. While I was speaking to the UN about terrorism, all the television networks were showing the videotape of my grand jury testimony.

The next day, at the White House, I held a reception for Nelson Mandela with African-American religious leaders. It was his idea. The Congress had voted to give him the Congressional Gold Medal and he was to receive it the following day. Mandela called to say he suspected the timing of the award was no accident: "As the President of South Africa I cannot decline this award. But I would like to come a day early and tell the American people what I think about what the Congress is doing to you." And that's exactly what he did, saying that he had never seen a reception at the UN like the one I had received, that the world needed me, and that my adversaries should leave me alone. The pastors applauded their approval.

As good as Mandela was, the Reverend Bernice King, Martin Luther King Jr.'s daughter, stole the show. She said that even great leaders sometimes commit grievous sins; that King David had done something far worse than

I had in arranging the death in battle of Bathsheba's husband, who was David's loyal soldier, so that David could marry her; and that David had to atone for his sin and was punished for it. No one could tell where Bernice was going until she got to the closing: "Yes, David committed a terrible sin and God punished him. But David remained king."

Meanwhile, I kept working, pushing my proposal for school modernization and construction funds in Maryland, Florida, and Illinois; talking to the National Farmers Union about agriculture; giving an important address on modernizing the global financial system at the Council on Foreign Relations; meeting with the Joint Chiefs on the readiness of our armed forces; drumming up support for another minimum wage increase at the International Brotherhood of Electrical Workers union; receiving the final report of the President's Advisory Commission on Race from John Hope Franklin; holding a dialogue with Tony Blair, Italian prime minister Romano Prodi, and President Peter Stoyanov of Bulgaria on the applicability to other nations of the "Third Way" philosophy Tony and I had embraced; having my first meeting with the new Japanese prime minister, Keizo Obuchi; bringing Netanyahu and Arafat to the White House in an attempt to get the peace process going; and appearing at more than a dozen campaign events for Democrats in six states and Washington, D.C.

On September 30, the last day of the fiscal year, I announced that we had run a budget surplus of about $70 billion, the first one in twenty-nine years. Although the press was focused on little besides the Starr report, there were, as always, a lot of other things going on, and they had to be dealt with. I was determined not to let the public's business grind to a halt and was gratified that the White House staff and cabinet felt the same way. No matter what was in the daily news, they kept doing their job.

In October the House Republicans, led by Henry Hyde and his colleagues on the Judiciary Committee, continued to push for my impeachment. The committee Democrats, led by John Conyers of Michigan, fought them tooth and nail, arguing that even if the worst charges against me were true, they didn't amount to the "high crimes and misdemeanors" the Constitution required for impeachment. The Democrats were right on the law, but the Republicans had the votes; on October 8 the House voted to open an inquiry into whether I should be impeached. I wasn't surprised; we were just a month away from the midterm elections and the Republicans were running a single-issue campaign: get Clinton. After the election I believed the moderate Republicans would look at the facts and the law and decide against impeachment in favor of a resolution of censure or reprimand—which is what Newt Gingrich had received for false statements and apparent violations of the tax laws.

Many of the pundits were predicting disaster for the Democrats. The conventional wisdom was that we would lose twenty-five to thirty-five seats in the House and four to six seats in the Senate because of the controversy. It seemed a safe bet to most people in Washington. The Republicans had $100 million more than the Democrats to spend, and more Democrats than Republicans were up for reelection in the Senate. Among the contested Senate seats, the Democrats seemed sure to pick up the one in Indiana, where the candidate was Governor Evan Bayh, while Ohio governor George Voinovich seemed certain to win the seat being vacated by John Glenn for the Republicans. That left seven seats up in the air, five currently held by Democrats and only two by Republicans.

I disagreed with the conventional wisdom for several reasons. First, a majority of Americans disapproved of the way Starr was conducting himself, and resented the fact that the Republican Congress was more interested in hurting me than in helping them. Almost 80 percent disapproved of the release of my grand jury videotape, and overall approval of the Congress had dropped to 43 percent. Second, as Gingrich had shown with the "Contract with America" in 1994, if the public believed one party had a positive agenda and the other didn't, the party with the plan would win. The Democrats were united with a midterm program for the first time ever: save Social Security first before spending the surplus on new programs or tax cuts; put 100,000 teachers in our schools; modernize old schools and build new ones; raise the minimum wage; and pass the Patients' Bill of Rights. Finally, a sizable majority of Americans were opposed to impeachment; if Democrats ran on their plan and against impeachment, I thought they might actually be able to win the House.

I did some political events at the beginning and end of October, most of them near Washington, in settings designed to emphasize the issues our candidates were stressing. Otherwise, I spent most of the month on the job. There was plenty of work to do, by far the most important of which involved the Middle East. Madeleine Albright and Dennis Ross had been laboring for months to get the peace process back on track, and Madeleine had finally gotten Arafat and Netanyahu together when they were in New York for the UN General Assembly session. Neither of them was ready to take the next steps or to be seen by his own constituents as compromising too much, but both were concerned that the deteriorating situation could easily get out of hand, especially if Hamas launched a new round of attacks.

The next day, the leaders came down to Washington to see me, and I announced plans to bring them back to the United States within a month to hammer out an agreement. In the interim, Madeleine went to the region to see them. They met on the border between Israel and Gaza, then Arafat took them to his guest house for lunch, making the hard-liner Netanyahu the first Israeli prime minister to go into Palestinian Gaza.

Months of work had gone into preparation of the summit. Both parties wanted the United States to work with them on the hard decisions and believed that the high drama of the event would help them sell those decisions back home. Of course, in any summit there's always a risk that the two sides won't be able to reach an agreement, and that the high-profile effort will damage all involved. My national security team was worried about the possibility of failure and its consequences. Both Arafat and Netanyahu had staked out tough positions in public, and Bibi had bolstered his rhetoric by naming Ariel Sharon, the most hard-line of the prominent Likud leaders, foreign minister. Sharon had referred to the 1993 peace agreement as "national suicide" for Israel. It was impossible to know whether Netanyahu had given Sharon the portfolio to have someone to blame if the summit failed or to provide himself cover on the right if it succeeded.

I thought the summit was a good idea and was eager to hold it. It seemed to me that we didn't have much to lose, and I always preferred failure in a worthy effort to inaction for fear of failure.

On the fifteenth, we kicked things off at the White House, then the delegations moved to the Wye River Conference Center in Maryland. It was well suited to the task at hand; the public meeting and dining spaces were comfortable, and the living quarters were laid out in such a way that the delegations could each have all their people staying together and at a fair distance from the other side.

Originally, we had planned for the summit to last four days; it would end two days before Netanyahu had to be back in Israel to open the new session of the Knesset. We agreed on the usual rules: neither side was bound by interim agreements on specific issues until a complete accord was reached, and the United States would draft the final agreement. I told them I would be there as much as I could, but would helicopter back to the White House at night, no matter how late, so that I could work in the office the next morning to sign legislation and continue negotiating with Congress on the budget bills. We were in the new fiscal year, but less than a third of the thirteen appropriations bills had been passed and signed into law. The marines who ran HMX1, the presidential helicopter, did a great job for me over eight years, but during Wye River they were even more invaluable, staying on duty to fly me back to the White House at two and three o'clock in the morning after the late sessions.

At the first dinner I urged Arafat and Netanyahu to think about how they could help each other cope with their domestic opposition. They thought and talked for four days, but were exhausted from trying and were nowhere near an agreement. Netanyahu told me we couldn't reach agreement on all the issues and suggested a partial one: Israel would withdraw from 13 percent of the West Bank and the Palestinians would dramatically improve cooperation on security, following a plan developed with the help of CIA director George Tenet, who enjoyed the confidence of both sides.

Late that night I met alone with Ariel Sharon for the first time. The seventy-year-old former general had been part of Israel's creation and all its subsequent wars. He was unpopular among Arabs not only for his hostility to trading land for peace but also for his role in the Israeli invasion of Lebanon in 1982, in which a large number of unarmed Palestinian refugees were killed by the Lebanese militia that was allied with Israel. During our meeting, which ran more than two hours, I mostly asked questions and listened. Sharon was not without sympathy for the plight of the Palestinians. He wanted to help them economically, but did not believe giving up the West Bank was in Israel's security interest, nor did he trust Arafat to fight terror. He was the only member of the Israeli delegation who would not shake hands with Arafat. I enjoyed hearing Sharon talk about his life and his views, and when we finished, at nearly three in the morning, I had a better understanding of how he thought.

One thing that surprised me was how hard he pushed me to pardon Jonathan Pollard, a former U.S. Navy intelligence analyst who had been convicted in 1986 of spying for Israel. Rabin and Netanyahu had previously asked for Pollard's release, too. It was obvious that this was an issue in Israeli domestic politics and that the Israeli public didn't think the United States should have punished Pollard so severely since it was to an ally that he had sold highly sensitive information. The case would come up again before we finished. Meanwhile, I continued to work with the leaders and to talk with their team members, including the Israeli defense minister, Yitzhak Mordechai;

Arafat's senior advisors Abu Ala and Abu Mazen, both of whom would later become Palestinian prime ministers; Saeb Erekat, Arafat's chief negotiator; and Mohammed Dahlan, the thirty-seven-year-old security chief in Gaza. Both the Israelis and the Palestinians were diverse, impressive groups. I tried to spend time with all of them; there was no telling who might make a decisive case for peace when they were alone in their separate delegations.

When we hadn't reached consensus by Sunday night, the parties agreed to extend the talks, and Al Gore joined me to add his powers of persuasion to our team, which included Sandy Berger, Rob Malley, and Bruce Reidel from the White House, and Secretary Albright, Dennis Ross, Martin Indyk, Aaron Miller, Wendy Sherman, and Toni Verstandig from the State Department. Every day they would take turns working on their Israeli and Palestinian counterparts on various issues, always looking for that streak of light that might break through the clouds.

The State Department translator, Gemal Helal, also played a unique role in these and other negotiations. The members of both delegations spoke English, but Arafat always conducted business in Arabic. Gemal was usually the only other person in the room during my one-on-one meetings with Arafat. He understood the Middle East and the role each member of the Palestinian delegation played in their deliberations, and Arafat liked him. He would become an advisor on my team. On more than one occasion, his insight and his personal connection with Arafat would prove invaluable.

On Monday I felt we were making headway again. I kept pushing Netanyahu to give Arafat the benefits of peace—the land, the airport, the safe passage between Gaza and the West Bank, a port in Gaza—so that he would be strong enough to fight terror, and I pressed Arafat not only to increase his efforts on security but to call the Palestinian National Council together to formally revise the Palestinian Covenant, excising the language calling for the destruction of Israel. The PLO Executive Council had already renounced the provisions, but Netanyahu thought Israeli citizens would never believe they had a partner for peace until the elected Palestinian Assembly voted to delete the offensive language from the charter. Arafat didn't want to call the council into session because he thought he might not be able to control the outcome. Palestinians the world over were eligible to vote for council members, and many of the expatriates were not as supportive of the compromises inherent in the peace process and of his leadership as were the Palestinians living in Gaza and the West Bank.

On the twentieth, King Hussein and Queen Noor joined us. Hussein was in the United States for cancer treatments at the Mayo Clinic. I had kept him briefed on our progress and problems. Although he was weakened by his illness and the chemotherapy treatments, he said he would come to Wye if I thought it would help. After talking to Noor, who assured me that he wanted to come, and that they would be fine in whatever guest quarters were available, I told Hussein we could use all the help we could get. It is difficult to describe or overstate the impact Hussein's presence had on the talks. He had lost a lot of weight, and the chemotherapy had taken all of his hair, even his eyebrows, but his mind and heart were still strong. He was very helpful, talking common sense to both sides, and the very sight of him diminished the posturing and pettiness that are a usual part of all such negotiations.

On the twenty-first, we had reached agreement only on the security issue, and it looked as if Netanyahu might celebrate his forty-ninth birthday by leaving the failed talks. The next day I came back to stay for the duration. After the two sides met alone for two hours, they came up with an ingenious way to get the Palestinian Council to vote on changing the charter: I would go to Gaza to address the group with Arafat, who would then ask for a show of support by raised hands or clapping or stamping of feet. Sandy Berger, although he was supportive of the plan, warned that it was a risky move for me. That was true, but we were asking the Israelis and Palestinians to take bigger risks; I agreed to do it.

That night we were still hung up on Arafat's demand for the release of one thousand Palestinian prisoners from Israeli jails. Netanyahu said he couldn't release Hamas members or others "with blood on their hands," and he thought no more than five hundred could be let go. I knew we were at a breaking point and had asked Hussein to come to the large cabin where we were dining to talk to both delegations together. When he entered the room, his regal aura, luminous eyes, and simple eloquence seemed magnified by his physical decline. In his deep, sonorous voice, he said that history would judge us all, that the differences remaining between the parties were trivial compared with the benefits of peace, and that they had to achieve it for the sake of their children. His unspoken message was equally clear: I may not have long to live; it's up to you not to let the peace die.

After Hussein left, we kept going, with everyone staying in the dining room and collecting around different tables to keep working on various issues. I told my team we were out of time, and I wasn't going to bed. My strategy for success had now boiled down to endurance; I was determined to be the last man standing. Netanyahu and Arafat also knew it was now or never. They and their teams stayed with us through the long night.

Finally, at about 3 a.m., I worked out a deal on the prisoners with Netanyahu and Arafat, and we just kept plowing ahead until we finished. It was almost seven in the morning. There was one more obstacle: Netanyahu was threatening to scuttle the whole deal unless I released Pollard. He said I had promised him I would do so at an earlier meeting the night before, and that's why he had agreed on the other issues. In fact, I had told the prime minister that if that's what it took to make peace, I was inclined to do it, but I would have to check with our people.

For all the sympathy Pollard generated in Israel, he was a hard case to push in America; he had sold our country's secrets for money, not conviction, and for years had not shown any remorse. When I talked to Sandy Berger and George Tenet, they were adamantly opposed to letting Pollard go, as was Madeleine Albright. George said that after the severe damage the Aldrich Ames case had done to the CIA, he would have to resign if I commuted Pollard's sentence. I didn't want to do it, and Tenet's comments closed the door. Security and the commitments by the Israelis and Palestinians to work together against terror were at the heart of the agreement we had reached. Tenet had helped the sides to work out details and had agreed that the CIA would support their implementation. If he left, there was a real chance Arafat would not go forward. I also needed George in the fight against al Qaeda and terrorism. I told Netanyahu that I would review the case seriously and try to work through it with Tenet and the national security team, but that Netanyahu was better off with a security agreement that he could count on than he would have been with the release of Pollard.

Finally, after we talked again at length, Bibi agreed to stay with the agreement, but only on the condition that he could change the mix of prisoners to be released, so that he would free more ordinary criminals and fewer who had committed security offenses. That was a problem for Arafat, who wanted the release of people he considered freedom fighters. Dennis Ross and Madeleine Albright went to his cabin and convinced him that this was the best I could do. Then I went to see him to thank him; his last-minute concession had saved the day.

The agreement provided the Palestinians more land on the West Bank, the airport, a seaport, a prisoner release, safe passage between Gaza and the West Bank, and economic aid. In return, Israel would get unprecedented cooperation in the fight against violence and terror, the jailing of specific Palestinians whom Israelis had identified as the source of continuing violence and killing, the change in the Palestinian Covenant, and a quick start on the final status talks. The United States would provide aid to help Israel meet the security costs of redeployment and support for Palestinian economic development, and would play a central role in cementing the unprecedented security cooperation the two sides had agreed to embrace.

As soon as we finally shook hands on the deal, we had to rush back to the White House to announce it. Most of us had been up for almost forty hours straight and could have used a nap and shower, but it was Friday afternoon, and we had to finish the ceremony before sundown, the beginning of the Jewish Sabbath. The ceremony began at 4 p.m. in the East Room. After Madeleine Albright and Al Gore spoke, I outlined the particulars of the agreement and thanked the parties. Then Netanyahu and Arafat made gracious and upbeat remarks. Bibi was very statesman-like and Arafat renounced violence in unusually strong words. Hussein warned that the enemies of peace would try to undo the agreement with violence and urged the people on both sides to stand behind their leaders, and to replace destruction and death with a shared future for the children of Abraham "that is worthy of them under the sun."

In a gesture of friendship and an appreciation of what the Republicans in Congress were up to, Hussein said that he had been friends with nine Presidents, "But on the subject of peace . . . never—with all the affection I held for your predecessors—have I known someone with your dedication, clearheadedness, focus, and determination . . . and we hope you will be with us as we see greater success and as we help our brethren move ahead towards a better tomorrow."

Then Netanyahu and Arafat signed the agreement, just before the sun went down and Shabbat began. The Middle East peace was still alive.

While the talks were going on at Wye River, Erskine Bowles was managing intense negotiations with Congress over the budget. He had told me he was going to leave after the election, and he wanted to make the best agreement he could. We had a lot of leverage because the Republicans wouldn't dare shut the government down again, and they had wasted a lot of time in the previous months squabbling among themselves and attacking me instead of finishing their business.

Erskine and his team adroitly maneuvered through the details of the budget bills, giving a concession here and there in order to secure funding for our big priorities. We announced agreement on the afternoon of the fifteenth, and the next morning there was a celebration of it in the Rose Garden with Tom Daschle, Dick Gephardt, and our entire economic team. The final deal saved the surplus for Social Security reform and provided funding for the first installment of the 100,000 new teachers, a large increase in after-school and summer school programs, and our other education priorities. We secured a solid relief package for farmers and ranchers and scored impressive environmental gains: funding for the clean water initiative to restore 40 percent of our lakes and rivers that were still too polluted for fishing and swimming, as well as money to combat global warming and continue our efforts to protect precious lands from development and pollution. And after eight months of deadlock, we also won approval for America's contribution to the International Monetary Fund, enabling the United States to continue our efforts to end the financial crisis and stabilize the world economy.

Not all of our agenda passed, so we had plenty of ammunition for the last two and a half weeks of the campaign. The Republicans had blocked the Patients' Bill of Rights for the HMOs; killed the tobacco legislation, with its cigarette tax increase and anti–teen smoking measures for the big tobacco companies; filibustered campaign finance reform in the Senate, despite unanimous Senate Democratic support for it after it had passed the House; defeated the minimum wage increase; and, most surprising to me, refused to pass my proposal to build or repair five thousand schools. They also refused to pass the tax credit on the production and purchase of clean energy and energy conservation devices. I kidded Newt Gingrich that I had finally found a tax cut that he was against.

Still, it was a superb budget, given the political compo-
sition of Congress, and a real tribute to the negotiating
skills of Erskine Bowles. After negotiating the balanced
budget in 1997, he had come through again. As I said, he
had "a great closing act."

Four days later, just before I left again for Wye River, I
named John Podesta to succeed Erskine, who had strongly
recommended him for the job. I had known John for
nearly thirty years, since Joe Duffey's campaign for the
Senate in 1970. He had already served as White House
staff secretary and deputy chief of staff; he understood
Congress and had helped guide our economic, foreign,
and defense policies; he was an ardent environmentalist;
and except for Al Gore, he knew more about information
technology than anyone else in the White House. He had
the right personal qualities, too: a fine mind, a tough hide,
a dry wit, and he was a better hearts player than Erskine
Bowles. John gave the White House an exceptionally able
leadership team, with Deputy Chiefs of Staff Steve Ricchetti and Maria Echaveste and his aide, Karen Tramon-
tano.

Through our trials and triumphs, our golf matches and
card games, Erskine and I had become close friends. I
would miss him, especially on the golf course. On many
tough days Erskine and I would go out to Army-Navy golf
course for a quick round. Until my friend Kevin O'Keefe
left the counsel's office, he often joined us. We were always
accompanied around the course by Mel Cook, a retired
military man who worked there and knew the place like
the back of his hand. Sometimes I would play four or five
holes before hitting a decent shot, but eventually the
beauty of the layout and my love for the game would drive
away the pressures of the day. I kept up my trips to Army-

Navy, but I always missed Erskine. At least he was leaving me in good hands with Podesta.

Rahm Emanuel had left, too. Since he had started with me as campaign finance director in 1991, he had married and started a family, and he wanted to provide for them. Rahm's great gift was putting ideas into action. He saw the potential in issues everyone else missed, and he stayed on top of the details that often determine success or failure. After our defeat in 1994, he had played a major role in bringing my image back into line with reality. Within a few years Rahm would be back in Washington, as a congressman from Chicago, the city he thought should be capital of the world. I replaced him with Doug Sosnik, the White House political director, who was almost as aggressive as Rahm, understood politics and the Congress, always told me the downside of every situation without wanting me to give in to it, and was a shrewd hearts player. Craig Smith took over the political director's job, the same position he had had in the 1992 campaign.

On the morning of the twenty-second, not long before I left for the last, never-ending day at Wye River, Congress adjourned after having sent me the administration's bill to establish three thousand charter schools in America by 2000. In the last week of the month, Prime Minister Netanyahu survived a no-confidence vote in the Knesset on the Wye River accord, and the presidents of Ecuador and Peru, with help from the United States, settled a contentious border dispute that had threatened to erupt into armed conflict. At the White House, I welcomed the new president of Colombia, Andrés Pastrana, and supported his courageous efforts to end the decades-old conflict with guerrilla groups. I also signed the International Religious Freedom Act of 1998 and appointed Robert Seiple, formerly head of World Vision U.S., a Christian charity, to be the secretary of state's special representative for international religious freedom.

As the campaign drew to a close, I made several stops in California, New York, Florida, and Maryland and went with Hillary to Cape Canaveral, Florida, to see John Glenn blast into space; the Republican National Committee began a series of television ads attacking me; Judge Norma Holloway Johnson ruled that there was probable cause to believe that Starr's office had violated the law against grand jury leaks twenty-four times; and news reports indicated that, according to DNA tests, Thomas Jefferson had fathered several children with his slave Sally Hemings.

On November 3, despite the huge Republican financial advantage, the attacks on me, and the pundits' predictions of the Democrats' demise, the elections went our way. Instead of the predicted loss of four to six Senate seats, there was no change. My friend John Breaux, who had helped me restore the New Democrat image of the administration after the '94 election and was a staunch foe of impeachment, was overwhelmingly reelected in Louisiana. In the House of Representatives, the Democrats actually won back five seats, the first time the President's party had done so in the sixth year of a presidency since 1822.

The election had presented a simple choice: the Democrats wanted to save Social Security first, hire 100,000 teachers, modernize schools, raise the minimum wage, and pass the Patients' Bill of Rights. The Republicans were against all that. By and large they ran a single-issue campaign, on impeachment, although in some states they also ran anti-gay ads, essentially saying that if the

Democrats won Congress, we would force every state to recognize gay marriages. In states like Washington and Arkansas, the message was reinforced by pictures of a gay couple kissing or at a church altar. Not long before the election, Matthew Shepard, a young gay man, was beaten to death in Wyoming because of his sexual orientation. The whole country was moved, especially after his parents bravely talked about it in public. I couldn't believe the Far Right would run the gay-bashing ads in the wake of Shepard's death, but they always needed an enemy. The Republicans were also weakened because they were deeply divided over the late October budget agreement; the most conservative members thought they had given away the store and gotten nothing in return.

In the months before the elections, I had decided that the "sixth-year jinx" was way overrated, that citizens historically had voted against the President's party in the sixth year because they thought that the presidency was winding down, that the energy and new ideas were running out, and that they might as well give the other side a chance. In 1998, they saw me working on the Middle East and other foreign and domestic issues right up to the election, and they knew we had an agenda for the coming two years. The impeachment campaign galvanized the Democrats to vote in larger numbers than they had in 1994, and blocked any other message swing voters might have heard from the Republicans. By contrast, the incumbent Republican governors who essentially ran on my platform of fiscal responsibility, welfare reform, commonsense crime-control measures, and strong support for education did very well. In Texas, Governor George W. Bush, after handily defeating my old friend Garry Mauro, gave his victory speech in front of a banner that said "Opportunity, Responsibility," two-thirds of my 1992 campaign slogan.

Large turnouts of African-American voters helped a young lawyer named John Edwards defeat North Carolina senator Lauch Faircloth, Judge Sentelle's friend and one of my harshest critics, and in South Carolina, black voters propelled Senator Fritz Hollings to a come-from-behind victory. In New York, Congressman Chuck Schumer, an outspoken opponent of impeachment with a strong record on crime, easily defeated Senator Al D'Amato, who had spent much of the last several years attacking Hillary and her staff in his committee hearings. In California, Senator Barbara Boxer won reelection and Gray Davis was elected governor with far higher margins than their pre-election polls indicated, and the Democrats picked up two House seats on the anti-impeachment momentum and a large turnout of Hispanic and African-American voters.

In the House elections, we won back the seat that Marjorie Margolies-Mezvinsky had lost in 1994 when our candidate, Joe Hoeffel, who had lost in 1996, ran again and opposed impeachment. In Washington State, Jay Inslee, who had been defeated in 1994, won his seat back. In New Jersey, a physics professor named Rush Holt was behind by 20 percent ten days before the election. He pushed one TV ad highlighting his opposition to impeachment, and won a seat no Democrat had held in a century.

We all did our best to close the vast fund-raising gap and I taped telephone messages that were directed to the homes of Hispanics, blacks, and other likely Democratic voters. Al Gore campaigned vigorously all over the country, and Hillary probably made more appearances than anybody else. When her foot became badly swollen during a campaign stop in New York, a blood clot was discovered behind her right knee and she was put on blood thinners. Dr. Mariano wanted her to stay in bed for a week, but she kept going, giving confidence as well as support to our candidates. I was really concerned about her, but she was determined to push on. As angry as she was with me, she was even more upset about what Starr and the Republicans were trying to do.

Surveys by James Carville and Stan Greenberg and by Democratic pollster Mark Mellman had indicated that, nationwide, voters were 20 percent more likely to vote for a Democrat who said that I should be censured by the Congress and that we should get on with the public's business than for a Republican who favored impeachment. After the results came in, Carville and others implored all the challengers with a chance to win to adopt this strategy. Its power was evident even in races we lost narrowly that the Republicans should have won easily. For example, in New Mexico, Democrat Phil Maloof, who had just lost a special election in June by six points and was down by ten a week before the November election, began anti-impeachment ads the weekend before the election. He won on election day, but lost the election by one percent because a third of the voters had cast early ballots before they heard his message. I believe the Democrats would have won the House if more of our challengers had run on our positive program and against impeachment. Many of them didn't do so because they were afraid; they simply couldn't believe the plain evidence in the face of the massively negative coverage I had received, and the near-universal view of the pundits that what Starr and Henry Hyde were doing would be bad for Democrats rather than Republicans.

On the day after the election I called Newt Gingrich to talk about some business; when the conversation got around to the election, he was very generous, saying that as a historian and "the quarterback for the other team," he wanted to congratulate me. He hadn't believed we could do it, he said, and it was a truly historic achievement. Later in November, Erskine Bowles called to tell me about a very different conversation he had had with Gingrich. Newt told Erskine that they were going to go forward with the impeachment despite the election results and the fact that many moderate Republicans didn't want to vote for it. When Erskine asked Newt why they would proceed with impeachment instead of other possible remedies such as censure or reprimand, the Speaker replied, "Because we can."

The right-wing Republicans who controlled the House believed that they had now paid for impeachment so they should just go on and do it before the new Congress came in. They thought that by the next election there would be no more impeachment losses because the voters would have other things on their minds. Newt and Tom DeLay believed that they could bring most of the moderates into line through pressure—from right-wing talk shows and activists in their districts; with threats to cut off campaign funds, or to come up with opponents in the Republican primary, or to take leadership positions away; or with offers of new leadership positions or other benefits.

The right-wingers in the House caucus were seething over their defeat. Many actually believed they had lost because they had given in to too many White House demands in the last two budget negotiations. In fact, if they had run on the balanced budgets of 1997 and 1998, the Children's Health Insurance Program, and the

100,000 teachers, they would have done well, just as the Republican governors had. But they were too ideological and angry to do that. Now they were going to seize back control of the Republican agenda through impeachment.

I had already had four showdowns with the radical right: the '94 election, which they won, and the budget shutdown, the '96 election, and the '98 election, which went our way. In the interim I had tried to work in good faith with Congress to keep the country moving forward. Now, in the face of overwhelming public opinion against impeachment, and the clear evidence that nothing I was alleged to have done rose to the level of an impeachable offense, they were coming back for another bitter ideological fight. There was nothing to do but suit up and take the field.

FIFTY

Within a week of the election, two high-profile Washington politicians announced they wouldn't run again, and we were in the teeth of a new crisis with Saddam Hussein. Newt Gingrich stunned us all by announcing that he was resigning as Speaker and from the House. Apparently, he had a deeply divided caucus, was facing an assault on his leadership because of the election losses, and didn't want to fight anymore. After several moderate Republicans made clear that, based on the election results, impeachment was a dead issue, I had mixed feelings about the Speaker's decision. He had supported me on most foreign policy decisions, had been frank about what his caucus was really up to when the two of us talked alone, and, after the government shutdown battle, had shown flexibility in working out honorable compromises with the White House. Now he had the worst of both worlds: the moderate-to-conservative Republicans were upset because the party had offered no positive program in the '98 elections, and for a solid year had done nothing but attack me; his right-wing ideologues were upset because they thought he had worked with me too much and demonized me too little. The ingratitude of the right-wing cabal that now controlled the Republican caucus must have galled Gingrich; they were in power only because of his brilliant strategy in the 1994 election and his years of organizing and proselytizing before then.

Newt's announcement got more headlines, but the retirement of New York senator Pat Moynihan would have a bigger impact on my family. On the night Moynihan said he wouldn't seek reelection, Hillary got a call from our friend Charlie Rangel, the congressman from Harlem and ranking member of the House Ways and Means Committee, urging her to run for Moynihan's seat. Hillary told Charlie she was flattered but couldn't imagine doing such a thing.

She didn't completely close the door, and I was glad. It sounded like a pretty good idea to me. We had intended to move to New York after my term ended, with me spending a fair amount of time in Arkansas at my library. New Yorkers seemed to like having high-profile senators: Moynihan, Robert Kennedy, Jacob Javits, Robert Wagner, and many others had been seen as representatives of both the citizens of New York and the nation at large. I thought Hillary would do a great job in the Senate and that she would enjoy it. But that decision was months away.

On November eighth, I brought my national security team to Camp David to discuss Iraq. A week earlier Saddam Hussein had kicked the UN inspectors out again, and it seemed almost certain that we'd have to take military action. The UN Security Council had voted unanimously to condemn Iraq's "flagrant violations" of UN resolutions, Bill Cohen had gone to the Middle East to line up support for air strikes, and Tony Blair was ready to participate.

A few days later the international community took the next big step in our bid to stabilize the global financial situation with a $42 billion aid package to Brazil, $5 billion of it in U.S. taxpayers' money. Unlike the aid packages to Thailand, South Korea, Indonesia, and Russia, this one

was coming before the country was on the brink of
default, consistent with our new policy of trying to prevent failure and its spread to other nations. We were doing
our best to convince international investors that Brazil
was committed to reform and had the cash to fight off
speculators. And this time, the IMF loan conditions
would be less stringent, preserving programs to help the
poor and encouraging Brazilian banks to keep making
loans. I didn't know whether it would work, but I had a
lot of confidence in President Henrique Cardoso, and as
Brazil's major trading partner, the United States had a big
stake in his success. It was another of those risks worth
taking.

On the fourteenth, I asked Al Gore to represent the
United States at the annual APEC meeting in Malaysia,
the first leg of a long-scheduled trip to Asia. I couldn't go,
because Saddam was still trying to impose unacceptable
conditions on the return of the UN inspectors; in
response, we were preparing to launch air strikes at sites
our intelligence indicated were connected to his weapons
program, as well as other military targets. Just before the
attacks were launched, with the planes already on their
way, we received the first of three letters from Iraq addressing our objections. Within hours, Saddam had backed
down completely, and had committed to resolving all outstanding issues raised by the inspectors, to giving them
unfettered access to all sites without any interference, to
turning over all relevant documents, and to accepting all
UN resolutions on weapons of mass destruction. I was
skeptical, but I decided to give him one more chance.

On the eighteenth, I left for Tokyo and Seoul. I wanted
to go to Japan to establish a working relationship with
Keizo Obuchi, the new prime minister, and to try to influ-

ence Japanese public opinion to support the tough reforms necessary to end more than five years of economic stagnation. I liked Obuchi and thought he had a chance to tame the turbulent Japanese political scene and serve for several years. He was interested in American-style hands-on politics. As a young man in the 1960s, he had come to the United States and talked his way into meeting with then attorney general Robert Kennedy, who became his political hero. After our meeting Obuchi took me to the streets of Tokyo, where we shook hands with school-children who were holding Japanese and American flags. I also did a televised town hall meeting in which the famously reticent Japanese surprised me with their open, blunt questions, not only about Japan's current challenges but also about whether I had ever visited victims of Hiroshima and Nagasaki; how Japan could get fathers to spend more time with their children, as I had with Chelsea; how many times a month I ate dinner with my family; how I was coping with all the pressures of the presidency; and how I had apologized to Hillary and Chelsea.

In Seoul, I supported both Kim Dae Jung's continuing efforts to move beyond the economic crisis and his outreach to North Korea, so long as it was clear that neither of us would allow the proliferation of missiles, nuclear weapons, or other weapons of mass destruction. We were both concerned about the recent North Korean test launch of a long-range missile. I had asked Bill Perry to head a small group to review our Korea policy, and to recommend a road map to the future that would maximize the chances of North Korea abandoning its weapons and missile programs and reconciling with South Korea, while minimizing the risks of its failure to do so.

At the end of the month Madeleine Albright and I

hosted a conference at the State Department to support economic development for the Palestinians, with Yasser Arafat, Jim Wolfensohn of the World Bank, and representatives of the European Union, the Middle East, and Asia. The Israeli cabinet and the Knesset had supported the Wye River accord, and it was time to get some investment into Gaza and the West Bank to give the beleaguered Palestinians a taste of the benefits of peace.

While all this was going on, Henry Hyde and his colleagues kept pushing their agenda, sending me eighty-one questions that they demanded be answered with "admit or deny," and releasing twenty-two hours of the Tripp-Lewinsky tapes. Tripp's taping of those conversations without Lewinsky's permission, after her lawyer explicitly told her the taping was criminal and she should not do it again, was a felony under Maryland's criminal law. She was indicted for it, but the trial judge refused to allow the prosecutor to call Lewinsky as a witness to prove the conversations occurred, ruling that the immunity Starr had given Tripp to testify about her unlawful violation of Lewinsky's privacy prevented Lewinsky from testifying against her. Once more, Starr had succeeded in protecting lawbreakers who played ball with him even as he indicted innocent people who would not lie for him.

During this period Starr also indicted Webb Hubbell for a third time, claiming that he had misled federal regulators about work he and the Rose Law Firm had done for another failed financial institution. It was Starr's last, almost desperate attempt to break Hubbell and force him to say something damaging about Hillary or me.

On the nineteenth of November, Kenneth Starr appeared before the House Judiciary Committee, making comments that, like his report, went far beyond the scope of his responsibility to report the facts he had found to Congress. The Starr report had already been criticized for omitting one big piece of evidence helpful to me: Monica Lewinsky's adamant assertion that I never asked her to lie.

Three surprising things came out of Starr's testimony. The first was his announcement that he had found no wrongdoing on my part or Hillary's in the Travel Office and FBI file investigations. Congressman Barney Frank of Massachusetts asked him when he had reached those conclusions. "Some months ago," replied Starr. Frank then asked him why he waited until after the election to exonerate me on these charges, when he had submitted his report "with a lot of negative stuff about the President" before the election. Starr's brief response was confused and evasive.

Second, Starr admitted he had talked to the press, on background, a violation of the grand jury secrecy rules. Finally, he denied under oath that his office had tried to get Monica Lewinsky to wear a wire to record conversations with Vernon Jordan, me, or other people. When confronted with the FBI form proving that he had, he was evasive. The **Washington Post** reported that "Starr's denials . . . were shattered by his own FBI reports."

The fact that Starr had admitted violating the law on grand jury secrecy and had given false testimony under oath didn't slow him or the committee Republicans down a bit. They thought different rules applied to the home team.

The next day Sam Dash resigned as Starr's ethics advisor, saying that Starr had "unlawfully" injected himself into the impeachment process with his remarks at the congressional hearing. As my mother used to say, Dash was "a day late and a dollar short": Starr hadn't cared about the lawfulness of his behavior for a long time.

Shortly before Thanksgiving, the House Republicans returned to Washington to elect Bob Livingston of Louisiana, the chairman of the Appropriations Committee, as the new Speaker of the House. He would take office in January when the new session of Congress began. At the time, most people thought the movement to impeach me was stalled. Several moderate Republicans had said that they were opposed to it, and that the election had been a clear message that the American people wanted the Congress to reprimand or censure me and get on with the public's business.

In the middle of the month, I settled the Paula Jones case for a large amount of money and no apology. I hated to do it because I had won a clear victory on the law and the facts in a politically motivated case. Jones's lawyers had appealed her case to the Eighth Circuit Court of Appeals, but the governing case law was clear: if the Court of Appeals followed its own decisions, I would win the appeal. Unfortunately, the three-judge panel assigned to hear the case was headed by Pasco Bowman, the same ultra-conservative judge who had removed Judge Henry Woods from one of the Whitewater cases on the basis of spurious newspaper articles after Woods had rendered a decision Starr didn't like. Pasco Bowman, like Judge David Sentelle in Washington, had shown that he was willing to make exceptions to the normal rules of law in Whitewater-related cases.

Part of me almost wanted to lose the appeal so that I could go to court, get all the documents and depositions released, and show the public what my adversaries had been up to. But I had promised the American people I would spend the next two years working for them; I had no business spending five more minutes on the Jones case. The settlement took about half our life savings and we were already deeply in debt with legal bills, but I knew that if I stayed healthy, I could make enough money to take care of my family and pay those bills after I left office. So I settled a case I had already won and went back to work.

My promise to leave the Jones case behind would be tested once more, and severely. In April 1999, Judge Wright sanctioned me for violating her discovery orders and required me to pay her travel costs and the Jones lawyers' deposition expenses. I strongly disagreed with Wright's opinion but could not dispute it without getting into the very factual issues I was determined to avoid and taking more time away from my work. It really burned me up to pay the Jones lawyers' expenses; they had abused the deposition with questions asked in bad faith and in collusion with Starr, and they had repeatedly defied the judge's order not to leak. The judge never did anything to them.

On December 2, Mike Espy was acquitted on all charges brought against him by independent counsel Donald Smaltz. Smaltz had followed Starr's playbook in the Espy investigation, spending more than $17 million and indicting everybody he could in an effort to force them to say something damaging against Mike. The jury's stinging rebuke made Smaltz and Starr the only two independent counsels ever to lose jury trials.

A few days later, Hillary and I flew to Nashville for a memorial service for Al Gore's father, Senator Albert Gore Sr., who had died at ninety at his home in Carthage, Tennessee. The War Memorial Auditorium was full, with people from all walks of life who had come to pay their respects to a man whose Senate service included his role in building the interstate highway system, his refusal to sign the segregationist Southern Manifesto in 1956, and his courageous opposition to the Vietnam War. I had admired Senator Gore since I was a young man, and always enjoyed the chances my association with Al gave me to be with him. Senator and Mrs. Gore had campaigned hard for Al and me in 1992, and I got a big kick out of hearing the Senator give his old-fashioned stump speeches full of fire and brimstone.

The music at the memorial service was moving, especially when we heard an old tape of Senator Gore as a rising young politician playing the fiddle in Constitution Hall in 1938. Al delivered the eulogy, a loving and eloquent tribute to the father, the man, and the public servant. After the service I told Hillary I wished everyone in America could have heard it.

In mid-month, just as I was about to leave for Israel and Gaza to keep my commitments under the Wye River accord, the House Judiciary Committee voted, again along straight party lines, in favor of impeaching me for perjury in the deposition and the grand jury testimony, and for obstruction of justice. They also passed a fourth count accusing me of giving false answers to their questions. It was a truly bizarre proceeding. Chairman Hyde refused to set a standard for what constituted an impeachable offense, or to call any witnesses with direct knowledge of the matters in dispute. He took the position that a vote for impeachment was simply a vote to send the Starr report on to the Senate, which could determine whether the report was factually accurate and whether my removal from office was warranted.

A bipartisan group of prosecutors told the committee that no normal prosecutor would charge me with perjury on the evidence in this case, and a panel of distinguished historians, including Arthur Schlesinger of City University of New York, C. Vann Woodward of Yale, and Sean Wilentz of Princeton, said that what I was alleged to have done did not meet the framers' standard of impeachment—that is, a "high crime or misdemeanor" committed in the exercise of executive power. This had long been the accepted understanding, and their interpretation was backed up by an open letter to Congress signed by four hundred historians. For example, in the Watergate case, the House Judiciary Committee voted against impeaching President Nixon for alleged income tax evasion because it had nothing to do with his performance in office. But all this was entirely irrelevant to Hyde, to his equally hostile counsel, David Schippers, and to the right-wingers who controlled the House.

Ever since the election, Tom DeLay and his staff had been firing up the right-wing networks to demand my impeachment. The radio talk shows were pushing it hard, and moderates were beginning to hear from anti-Clinton activists in their home districts. They were convinced they could get enough moderate members of Congress to forget about the popular opposition to impeachment by making them fear the retaliation of disappointed Clinton haters.

In the context of this strategy, the Hyde committee's vote against a censure resolution was as important as its votes for the impeachment articles. Censure was the preferred option of 75 percent of the American people; if a censure motion were to be presented to the House, the moderate Republicans would vote for it and impeachment would be dead. Hyde claimed that Congress didn't have the authority to censure the President; it was impeachment or nothing. In fact, Presidents Andrew Jackson and James Polk had both been censured by Congress. The censure resolution was voted down by the committee, again on a partisan vote. The full House would not be able to vote on what most Americans wanted. Now it was just a question of how many moderate Republicans could be "persuaded."

After the committee vote, Hillary and I flew to the Middle East. We had a meeting and dinner with Prime Minister Netanyahu, lit candles on a menorah for Hanukkah, and visited Rabin's grave with his family. The next day Madeleine Albright, Sandy Berger, Dennis Ross, Hillary, and I helicoptered into densely populated Gaza to cut the ribbon on the new airport and have lunch with Arafat in a hotel overlooking Gaza's long, beautiful Mediterranean beach. And I gave the speech to the Palestinian National Council that I had pledged to deliver at Wye River. Just before I got up to speak, almost all the delegates raised their hands in support of removing the provision calling for the destruction of Israel from their charter. It was the moment that made the whole trip worthwhile. You could almost hear the sighs of relief in Israel; perhaps Israelis and Palestinians actually could share the land and the future after all. I thanked the delegates, told them I wanted their people to have concrete benefits from peace, and asked them to stay with the peace process.

It wasn't an idle plea. Less than two months after the triumph at Wye River, the negotiations were in trouble again. Even though Netanyahu's cabinet had narrowly approved the agreement, his coalition didn't really favor it, making it virtually impossible for him to proceed with troop redeployment and prisoner releases, or to move on to the even more difficult final status issues, including the question of Palestinian statehood and whether the eastern section of Jerusalem would become the capital of Palestine. The previous day's amendment of the Palestinian charter helped Netanyahu with the Israeli public, but his own coalition was a much harder crew to convince. It looked as if he would either have to form a more broad-based government of national unity or call elections.

On the morning after my speech to the Palestinians, Netanyahu, Arafat, and I met at the Erez border crossing to try to energize the implementation of Wye River and decide how to move to the final status issues. Afterward, Arafat took Hillary and me to Bethlehem. He was proud to have custody of a site so holy to Christians, and he knew it would mean a lot to us to visit it close to Christmas.

After we left Arafat, we joined Prime Minister Netanyahu for a visit to Masada. I was impressed that so much work had been done since Hillary and I had first been there in 1981 to recover the remains of the fortress where Jewish martyrs had fought to the death for their convictions. Bibi seemed somewhat pensive and subdued. He had gone beyond his political safety zone at Wye River, and his future was uncertain. There was no way to know whether the chances he had taken would bring Israel closer to lasting peace or bring an end to his government.

We bid the prime minister farewell and flew home to another conflict. Six days earlier, on just the second day of renewed UN inspections in Iraq, some inspectors had been denied access to Saddam's Ba'ath Party headquarters. On the day we returned to Washington, the chief UN weapons inspector, Richard Butler, reported to Kofi Annan that Iraq had not kept its commitments to cooperate with him and had even imposed new restrictions on the inspectors' work.

The next day the United States and the United Kingdom launched a series of attacks from airplanes and with cruise missiles on Iraq's suspected chemical, biological, and nuclear lab sites and its military capacity to threaten its neighbors. In my address to the American people that evening, I noted that Saddam had previously used chemical weapons on Iranians and Kurds in northern Iraq and had fired Scud missiles at other countries. I said I had called off an attack four weeks earlier because Saddam had promised full compliance. Instead, the inspectors had repeatedly been threatened, "so Iraq has abused its final chance."

At the time the strikes were launched, our intelligence indicated that substantial amounts of biological and chemical materials that had been in Iraq at the end of the Gulf War as well as some missile warheads were still unaccounted for, and that some elementary laboratory work toward acquiring a nuclear weapon was being done. Our military experts felt that unconventional weapons might have become even more important to Saddam because his conventional military forces were much weaker than they had been before the Gulf War.

My national security team was unanimous in the belief that we should hit Saddam as soon as the Butler report was issued, to minimize the chances that Iraq could disperse its forces and protect its biological and chemical stocks. Tony Blair and his advisors agreed. The Anglo-American assault lasted four days, with 650 air sorties and 400 cruise missiles, all carefully targeted to hit military and national security targets and to minimize civilian casualties. After the attack we had no way to know how much of the proscribed material had been destroyed, but Iraq's ability to produce and deploy dangerous weapons had plainly been reduced.

Although they talked about Saddam as if he were the devil himself, some of the Republicans were in a snit over the attacks. Several of them, including Senator Lott and Representative Dick Armey, criticized the timing of the attacks, saying I had ordered them in order to delay the House vote on impeachment. The next day, after several Republican senators had expressed support for the raid, Lott backed off his comments. Armey never did; he, DeLay, and their minions had worked hard to get their more moderate colleagues in line, and they were in a hurry to vote on impeachment before some of them started thinking again.

On December 19, not long before the House began to vote on impeachment, Speaker-designate Bob Livingston announced his retirement from the House in the wake of public disclosure of his own personal problems. I learned later that seventeen conservative Republicans had come to him and said he had to quit, not because of what he had done, but because he had become an obstacle to my impeachment.

Barely six weeks after the American people had plainly sent them a message against impeachment, the House passed two of the four articles of impeachment approved by the Hyde committee. The first, accusing me of lying to the grand jury, passed 228–206, with five Republicans voting against it. The second, alleging that I had obstructed justice by suborning perjury and hiding gifts, passed 221–212, with twelve Republicans voting no. The two charges were inconsistent. The first was based on the perceived differences between Monica Lewinsky's description of the details of our encounters in the Starr report and my grand jury testimony; the second ignored the fact that she also had testified that I never asked her to lie, a fact supported by all the other witnesses. The Republicans apparently believed her only when she disagreed with me.

Shortly after the election, Tom DeLay and company began roping in the moderate Republicans. They got some votes by depriving moderates of the chance to vote for censure, then telling them that since they wanted to reprimand me in some way, they should feel free to vote for impeachment, because I'd never be convicted and removed from office since the Republicans couldn't get the required two-thirds vote for removal in the Senate. A few days after the House vote, four moderate Republican House members—Mike Castle of Delaware, James Greenwood of Pennsylvania, and Ben Gilman and Sherwood Boehlert of New York—wrote to the **New York Times** saying that their votes for impeachment didn't mean they thought I should be removed.

I don't know all the individual carrots and sticks that were used on the moderates, but I did find out about some of them. One Republican committee chairman was plainly distraught when he told a White House aide that he didn't want to vote for impeachment but he would lose his chairmanship if he voted against it. Jay Dickey, an Arkansas Republican, told Mack McLarty he might lose his seat on the Appropriations Committee if he didn't vote to impeach me. I was disappointed when Jack Quinn, a Buffalo, New York, Republican who had been a frequent guest at the White House and who had told several people, including me, that he was opposed to impeachment, did an about-face and announced that he would vote for three articles. I had carried his district by a large majority in 1996, but a vocal minority of his constituents had apparently put a lot of heat on him. Mike Forbes, a Long Island Republican who had supported me in the impeachment battle, changed when he was offered a new leadership position on Livingston's team. When Livingston resigned, the offer evaporated.

Five Democrats also voted for impeachment. Four of them came from conservative districts. The fifth said he had wanted to vote for censure, then bought the argument that he was doing the next best thing. The Republicans who voted against impeachment included Amo Houghton of New York and Chris Shays of Connecticut, two of the most progressive and independent House Republicans; Connie Morella of Maryland, also a progressive whose district had voted overwhelmingly for me in 1996; and two conservatives, Mark Souder of Indiana and Peter King of New York, who simply refused to go along with their party's leadership in converting a constitutional question into a test of party loyalty.

Peter King, with whom I had worked on Northern Ireland, withstood weeks of enormous pressure, including threats to destroy him politically if he did not vote for impeachment. In several television interviews, King made a simple argument to his fellow Republicans: I'm against impeachment because if President Clinton were a Republican, you'd be against it, too. The pro-impeachment Republicans who appeared on the programs with him never had a good response to that. The right-wingers thought every person had a price or a breaking point, and more often than not they were right, but Peter King had an Irish soul: he loved the poetry of Yeats; he was not afraid to fight for a lost cause; and he was not for sale.

Although the pro-impeachment forces were said to have had prayer meetings in DeLay's office to seek God's support for their divine mission, the impeachment drive was fundamentally neither about morality nor the rule of law, but about power. Newt Gingrich had said it all in one phrase; they were doing it "because we can." My impeachment wasn't about my indefensible personal conduct; there was plenty of that on their side, too, and it was beginning to come out, even without a bogus lawsuit and a special prosecutor to do the digging. It wasn't about whether I had lied in a legal proceeding; when Newt Gingrich was found to have given false testimony several times during the House Ethics Committee investigation into the apparently unlawful practices of his political action committee, he got a reprimand and a fine from the same crowd that had just voted to impeach me. When Kathleen Willey, who had immunity from Starr as long as she told him what he wanted to hear, lied, Starr just gave her immunity again. When Susan McDougal wouldn't lie for him, he indicted her. When Herby Branscum and Rob Hill wouldn't lie for him, he indicted them. When Webb Hubbell wouldn't lie for him, he indicted him a second and a third time, and indicted his wife, his lawyer, and his accountant, only to drop the charges against the three of them later. When David Hale's first story about me was disproved, Starr let him change it until Hale finally came up with a version that was not disprovable. Jim McDougal's former partner and my old friend, Steve Smith, offered to take a lie-detector test regarding his assertion that Starr's people had prepared a typewritten statement for him to read to the grand jury and kept pressuring him to do so, even after he had told them repeatedly that it was a lie. Starr himself didn't tell the truth under oath about trying to get Monica Lewinsky to wear a wire.

And the House vote certainly wasn't about whether the House managers' accusations constituted impeachable offenses as historically understood. If the Watergate standard had been applied to my case, there would have been no impeachment.

This was about power, about something the House Republican leaders did because they could, and because they wanted to pursue an agenda I opposed and had blocked. I have no doubt that many of their supporters out in the country believed that the drive to remove me from office was rooted in morality or law, and that I was such a bad person it didn't matter whether or not my conduct fit the constitutional definition of impeachability. But their position didn't meet the first test of all morality and just law: The same rules apply to everyone. As Teddy Roosevelt once said, no man is above the law, but "no man is below the law either."

In the partisan wars that had raged since the mid-1960s, neither side had been completely blameless. I had thought the Democrats wrong to examine the movie tastes of Judge Bork and the drinking habits of Senator John Tower. But when it came to the politics of personal destruction, the New Right Republicans were in a class by themselves. My party sometimes didn't seem to understand power, but I was proud of the fact that there were some things Democrats wouldn't do just because they could.

Shortly before the House vote, Robert Healy wrote an article in the **Boston Globe** about a meeting that had occurred between Speaker Tip O'Neill and President Reagan in the White House in late 1986. The Iran-Contra story was out; White House aides John Poindexter and Oliver North had broken the law and lied about it to Congress. O'Neill did not ask the President if he had known about or authorized the lawbreaking. (Republican senator John Tower's bipartisan commission later found that Reagan did know about it.) According to Healy, O'Neill simply told the President that he would not permit an impeachment proceeding to go forward; he said he had lived through Watergate and wouldn't put the country through such an ordeal again.

Tip O'Neill may have been a better patriot than Gingrich and DeLay, but they and their allies were more effective in concentrating power and using it to whatever extent they could against their adversaries. They believed that, in the short run, might makes right, and they didn't care what they put the country through. It certainly didn't matter to them that the Senate wouldn't remove me. They thought if they trashed me long enough, the press and the public would eventually blame me for their bad behavior, as well as for my own. They badly wanted to brand me with a big "I," and believed that for the rest of my life and for some time thereafter, the fact of my impeachment would loom far larger than the circumstances of it, and that before long no one would even talk about what a hypocritical farce the whole process had been, and how it was the culmination of years of unconscionable conduct by Kenneth Starr and his cohorts.

Just after the vote, Dick Gephardt brought a large group of the House Democrats who had defended me to the White House so that I could thank them and we could show unity for the battle ahead. Al Gore gave a stirring defense of my record as President, and Dick made an impassioned plea to the Republicans to stop the politics of personal destruction and get on with the nation's business. Hillary commented to me afterward that the event almost had the feel of a victory rally. In a way it was. The Democrats had stood up not just for me but, far more importantly, for the Constitution.

I certainly hadn't wanted to be impeached, but I was consoled by the fact that the only other time it had happened, to Andrew Johnson in the late 1860s, there were also no "high crimes and misdemeanors"; just like this case, that was a politically motivated action by a majority party in Congress that couldn't restrain itself.

Hillary was more upset about the partisan political nature of the House proceedings than I was. As a young lawyer, she had served on John Doar's staff for the House Judiciary Committee during Watergate, when there was a serious, balanced, bipartisan effort to fulfill the constitutional mandate of defining and finding high crimes and misdemeanors in the official actions of the President.

From the beginning, I had believed that the best way to win the final showdown with the Far Right was for me to keep doing my job and let others handle the defense. During the proceedings in the House and Senate, that's what I tried to do, and many people told me they appreciated it.

The strategy worked better than it might have. The release of the Starr report and the determination of the Republicans to proceed with impeachment brought with them a marked shift in the media coverage. As I've said, the media was never a monolith; now even those who had previously been willing to give Starr a free ride began to point out the involvement of right-wing groups in the cabal, the abusive tactics of the OIC, and the unprecedented nature of what the Republicans were doing. And the TV talk shows began to show more balance, as commentators like Greta Van Sustren and Susan Estrich, and guests like lawyers Lanny Davis, Alan Dershowitz, Julian Epstein, and Vincent Bugliosi made sure that both sides of the case were heard. Members of Congress also made the case, including Senator Tom Harkin, House Judiciary Committee members Sheila Jackson Lee, and Bill Delahunt, himself a former prosecutor. Professors Cass Sunstein of the University of Chicago and Susan Bloch of Georgetown released a letter on the unconstitutionality of the impeachment process signed by four hundred legal scholars.

As we headed into 1999, the unemployment rate was down to 4.3 percent and the stock market had rebounded to an all-time high. Hillary had hurt her back while making a Christmas visit to employees in the Old Executive Office Building, but it was getting better, after her doctor told her to stop wearing high heels on the hard marble floors. Chelsea and I decorated the tree and went on our annual Christmas shopping spree.

My best Christmas presents that year were the expressions of kindness and support from ordinary citizens. A thirteen-year-old girl from Kentucky wrote me to say that I'd made a mistake, but I couldn't quit, because my opponents were "mean." And an eighty-six-year-old white man from New Brunswick, New Jersey, after telling his family he was going to Atlantic City for the day, instead rode the train to Washington, where he took a cab to the Reverend Jesse Jackson's house. When he was greeted by Jesse's mother-in-law, he told her he was there because the Reverend Jackson was the only person he knew of who talked to the President, and he wanted to send me a message: "Tell the President not to quit. I was around when the

Republicans tried to destroy Al Smith [our presidential nominee in 1928] for being a Catholic. He can't give in to them." The man got back in his cab, returned to Union Station, and took the next train home. I called that man to say thank you. Then my family and I went to Renaissance Weekend and into the new year.

FIFTY-ONE

O n January 7, Chief Justice William Rehnquist officially opened the impeachment trial in the Senate,
and Ken Starr indicted Julie Hiatt Steele, the
Republican woman who wouldn't lie to back up Kathleen
Willey's story.

A week later, the House impeachment managers made
a three-day presentation of their case. They now wanted
to call witnesses, something they hadn't done in their own
hearings, with the exception of Kenneth Starr. One of the
managers, Asa Hutchinson from Arkansas, who had prosecuted my brother's drug case as U.S. attorney in the
1980s, said the Senate had to let them call witnesses,
because if he were a prosecutor, he couldn't indict me for
obstruction of justice, the issue he was charged with handling, based on the meager record the House had sent to
the Senate! On the other hand, another of the House
managers argued that the Senate had no right to judge
whether my alleged offenses met the constitutional standard of impeachment; he said the House had done that
for them and the Senate should be bound by their opinion, despite the fact that the Hyde committee had refused
to articulate a standard for judging what conduct was
impeachable.

In his closing argument to the Senate, Henry Hyde
finally gave his interpretation of the constitutional meaning of impeachment when he said in essence that trying to

spare oneself embarrassment over private misconduct was more of a justification for removal from office than misleading the nation about an important matter of state. My mother had raised me to look for the good in everybody. When I watched the vituperative Mr. Hyde, I was sure there must be a Dr. Jekyll in there somewhere, but I was having a hard time finding him.

On the nineteenth, my legal team began its three days of response. Chuck Ruff, the White House counsel and a former U.S. attorney, led off, arguing for two and a half hours that the charges were untrue and that even if the senators thought they **were** true, the offenses did not come close to meeting the constitutional standard for impeachment, much less removal. Ruff was a mild-mannered man who had been wheelchair-bound for most of his life. He was also a powerful advocate, who was offended by what the House managers had done. He shredded their evidentiary arguments and reminded the Senate that a bipartisan panel of prosecutors had already said that no responsible prosecutor would bring a perjury charge on the facts before them.

I thought Ruff's best moment was when he caught Asa Hutchinson red-handed in a telling misrepresentation of fact. Hutchinson had told the Senate that Vernon Jordan began helping Monica Lewinsky to get a job only after he learned she would be a witness in the Jones case. The evidence proved that Vernon had done so several weeks before he knew or could have known that, and that at the time Judge Wright made the decision to allow Lewinsky to be called as a witness (a decision that she later reversed), Vernon was on a plane to Europe. I didn't know whether Asa had misled the Senate because he thought that the senators wouldn't figure it out or because he thought that they, like the House managers, wouldn't care whether the presentation was accurate or not.

The next day Greg Craig and Cheryl Mills addressed the specific charges. Greg noted that the article charging me with perjury failed to cite a single specific example of it and instead tried to bring my deposition in the Jones case into play, even though the House had voted against the article of impeachment dealing with that. Craig also pointed out that some of the allegations of perjury now being made to the Senate were never made by Starr or any House member during the debates in the Judiciary Committee or on the floor of the House. They were making up their case as they moved along.

Cheryl Mills, a young African-American graduate of Stanford Law School, spoke on the sixth anniversary of the day she began her work in the White House. She dealt brilliantly with two of the obstruction of justice charges, presenting facts that the House managers couldn't dispute but had not told the Senate about and that proved their claims of obstruction of justice to be nonsense. Cheryl's finest moment was her closing. Responding to suggestions by Republican Lindsey Graham of South Carolina and others that my acquittal would send a message that our civil rights and sexual harassment laws are unimportant, she said, "I can't let their comments go unchallenged." Black people all over America knew that the drive to impeach me was being led by right-wing white southerners who had never lifted a finger for civil rights.

Cheryl pointed out that Paula Jones had had her day in court and a female judge had found that she didn't have a case. She said that we revered men like Jefferson, Kennedy, and King, all of whom were imperfect but "struggled to do humanity good," and that my record on civil rights and women's rights was "unimpeachable": "I stand here before you today because President Bill Clinton believed I could stand here for him. . . . It would be wrong to convict him on this record."

On the third and final day of our presentation, David Kendall led off with a cool, logical, and systematic dismantling of the charge that I had obstructed justice, citing Monica Lewinsky's repeated assertions that I never asked her to lie and once again detailing the House managers' misstatements or omissions of critical facts.

My defense was closed by Dale Bumpers. I had asked Dale to do it because he was a fine trial lawyer, a careful student of the Constitution, and one of the best orators in America. He had also known me a long time and had just left the Senate after serving twenty-four years. After loosening his former colleagues up with a few jokes, Dale said that he had been reluctant to appear because he and I had been close friends for twenty-five years and had worked together for the same causes. He said that while he knew the Senate might discount his defense as the words of a friend, he had come not to defend me but to defend the Constitution, "the most sacred document to me next to the Holy Bible."

Bumpers opened his argument by bashing Starr's investigation: "Javert's pursuit of Jean Valjean in **Les Misérables** pales by comparison." He said, "After all those years . . . the President was found guilty of nothing, official or personal . . . we are here today because the President suffered a terrible moral lapse."

He chided the House managers for having no compassion. Then came the most dramatic moment of Dale's speech: "Put yourself in his position . . . we are, none of us, perfect . . . he should have thought of all that beforehand. And indeed he should have, just as Adam and Eve should have"—now he pointed at the senators—"just as **you** and **you** and **you** and **you** and millions of other people who have been caught in similar circumstances should have thought of it before. As I say, none of us is perfect."

Dale then said that I had already been punished severely for my mistake, that the people didn't want me removed, and that the Senate should listen to the world leaders who had stood up for me, including Havel, Mandela, and King Hussein.

He closed with an erudite and detailed history of the Constitutional Convention's deliberations on the impeachment provision, saying that our framers took it from English law, which plainly covered offenses "distinctly 'political' against the state." He pleaded with the Senate not to defile the Constitution, but instead to hear the American people "calling on you to rise above politics . . . and do your solemn duty."

Bumpers' speech was magnificent, by turns erudite and emotional, earthy and profound. If the Senate roll had been called at that moment, there wouldn't have been many votes for removal. Instead, the process would drag out for three more weeks, as the House managers and their allies tried to find a way to persuade more Republican senators to vote with them. After the two sides had made their presentations, it was clear that all the Democratic senators and several Republicans were going to vote no.

While the Senate was sitting in trial, I was doing what I always did at this time of the year—getting ready for the State of the Union speech and promoting around the country the new initiatives that would be in it. The speech was scheduled for the nineteenth, the same day my defense opened in the Senate. Some Republican senators had urged me to delay the speech, but I wasn't about to do that. The impeachment had already cost the American people lots of their hard-earned tax dollars, diverted the Congress from pressing business, and weakened the fabric of the Constitution. If I had delayed my speech, it would have sent a message to the American people that their business had been put on the back burner.

If possible, the atmosphere at this State of the Union was even more surreal than it had been the previous year. As always, I entered the Capitol and was taken to the Speaker's quarters, which were now occupied by Dennis Hastert of Illinois, a stocky former wrestling coach who was quite conservative but less abrasive and confrontational than Gingrich, Armey, and DeLay. Before long, a bipartisan delegation of senators and representatives came to take me to the House chamber. We shook hands and talked as if nothing else in the world was going on. When I was introduced and began to walk down the aisle, the Democrats cheered loudly as most Republicans clapped politely. Since the aisle splits the Republicans and Democrats, I expected to spend the trip down to the podium shaking hands on the Democratic side and was surprised that, for whatever reason, several Republican House members held out their hands, too.

I began with a salute to the new Speaker, who had said he wanted to work with the Democrats in a spirit of civility and bipartisanship. It sounded good and he might have meant it, since the impeachment vote in the House had occurred before he became Speaker. So I accepted his offer.

By 1999, our economic expansion was the longest in history, with eighteen million new jobs since I took office, real wages going up, income inequality finally going down a little, and the lowest peacetime unemployment rate since 1957. The state of our union was stronger than ever, and I outlined a program to make the most of it, beginning with a series of initiatives to create a secure retirement for the baby boom generation. I proposed to commit 60 percent of the surplus over the next fifteen years to extend the solvency of the Social Security Trust Fund until 2055, an increase of more than twenty years, a small portion of it to be invested in mutual funds; an end to the limit on what Social Security recipients could earn without penalty; and more generous payments to elderly women, who were twice as likely as men their age to live in poverty. I also proposed to use 16 percent of the surplus to add ten years to the life of the Medicare Trust Fund; a $1,000 long-term–care tax credit for the elderly and disabled; the option to let people between the ages of fifty-five and sixty-five buy into Medicare; and a new pension initiative, USA Accounts, which would take 11 percent of the surplus to provide tax credits to citizens who opened their own retirement accounts, and to match a portion of the savings of workers with more modest incomes. This was perhaps the largest proposal ever made to help modest-income families save and create wealth.

I also proposed a large package of education reforms, arguing that we should change the way we spent the more than $15 billion a year of education aid to "support what works and stop supporting what doesn't work," by requiring states to end social promotion, turn around failing schools or shut them down, improve the quality of the teaching force, issue report cards on every school, and adopt sensible discipline policies. I again asked Congress to provide funds to build or modernize five thousand schools and to approve a sixfold increase in the number of college scholarships for students who would commit to teaching in underserved areas.

To give more support to families, I recommended a minimum wage increase, expanded family leave, a child-care tax credit, and trigger locks on guns so that children could not fire them accidentally. I also asked Congress to pass the Equal Pay and Employment Non-Discrimination acts; to establish a new American Private Investment Corporation to help raise $15 billion to create new businesses and jobs in poor communities; to enact the Africa Trade and Development Act to open more of our markets to African products; and to fund a $1 billion Lands Legacy initiative to preserve natural treasures, and a package of tax cuts and research money to fight global warming.

On national security, I asked for funds to guard computer networks against terrorists, and to protect communities from chemical and biological attacks; to increase research into vaccines and treatments; to increase the Nunn-Lugar nuclear safety program by two-thirds; to support the Wye River accord; and to reverse the decline in military spending that had begun at the end of the Cold War.

Before closing, I honored Hillary for her leadership in the Millennium Project and in representing America so well all over the world. She was sitting in her box with the home-run–hitting Chicago Cubs star Sammy Sosa, who had joined her on a recent trip to his native Dominican Republic. After all she had been through, Hillary got an even bigger round of applause than Sammy. I ended "the last State of the Union address of the twentieth century" by reminding the Congress that "perhaps, in the daily press of events, in the clash of controversy, we don't see our own time for what it truly is, a new dawn for America."

On the day after the speech, with the highest job approval ratings I had ever had, I flew to Buffalo, with Hillary and Al and Tipper Gore, to speak to an overflow crowd of more than twenty thousand at the Marine Midland Arena. Once again, in spite of all that was going on, the State of the Union address, with its full agenda for the year ahead, had struck a responsive chord with the American people.

I ended the month with a major speech at the National Academy of Sciences, outlining my proposals to protect America from terrorist attacks with biological and chemical weapons and from cyberterrorism; a trip home to Little Rock to view tornado damage in my old neighborhood, including the loss of several old trees on the grounds of the Governor's Mansion; a visit to St. Louis to welcome Pope John Paul II back to the United States; a meeting with a large bipartisan congressional delegation in the East Room to discuss the future of Social Security and Medicare; and a memorial service for my friend Governor Lawton Chiles of Florida, who had died suddenly not long before. Lawton had given me courage for the current fight with one of his favorite sayings: If you can't run with the big dogs, you ought to stay on the porch.

On February 7, King Hussein lost his fight against cancer. Hillary and I immediately left for Jordan with a delegation that included Presidents Ford, Carter, and Bush. I was very grateful for their willingness, on short notice, to honor a man we had all worked with and admired. The next day we walked in his funeral procession for almost a mile, attended the memorial service, and paid our respects to Queen Noor, who was heartbroken. So were Hillary and I. We had enjoyed some wonderful times with Hussein and Noor in Jordan and in the United States. I remembered with particular pleasure a meal the four of us had shared on the Truman Balcony of the White House not long before the king died. Now he was gone, and the world was a poorer place.

After meetings with the new monarch, Hussein's son Abdullah, as well as Prime Minister Netanyahu, President Assad, President Mubarak, Tony Blair, Jacques Chirac, Boris Yeltsin, and President Suleyman Demirel of Turkey, I flew home to await the Senate vote on my future. Though the outcome wasn't in doubt, the behind-the-scenes maneuvering had been interesting. Several Republican senators were upset with the House Republicans for putting them through the trial, but whenever the right wing turned the pressure up, most of them backed down and went along with dragging the whole thing out. When Senator Robert Byrd moved to have the charges dismissed as having no merit, David Kendall's partner, Nicole Seligman, made an argument on the law and the facts that most senators knew was undebatable. Nevertheless, Byrd's motion was defeated. When Senator Strom Thurmond told his Republican colleagues early on that the votes weren't there to remove me and the process should be stopped, he was overruled in the Republican caucus.

One Republican senator who was opposed to impeachment kept us informed of what was going on among his colleagues. Several days before the vote, he said there were only thirty Republican votes for the perjury count and forty to forty-five for the obstruction of justice count. They were nowhere near the two-thirds majority the Constitution requires for removal. A few days before the vote, the senator told us that the House Republicans had said they would be humiliated if neither count got at least a token majority of the votes, and their Senate colleagues had better not humiliate them if they wanted the House to stay in Republican hands after the next election. The senator reported that they would have to whittle the number of Republican "no" votes down.

On February 12 the impeachment motions failed. The vote on the perjury count failed by 22 votes, 45–55, and the vote on the obstruction of justice count failed by 17 votes, 50–50, with all the Democrats and Republican senators Olympia Snowe and Susan Collins of Maine, Jim Jeffords of Vermont, Arlen Specter of Pennsylvania, and John Chafee of Rhode Island voting no on both counts. Senators Richard Shelby of Alabama, Slade Gorton of Washington, Ted Stevens of Alaska, Fred Thompson of Tennessee, and John Warner of Virginia voted no on the perjury count.

The vote itself was anticlimactic, coming three weeks after the close of my defense. Only the margin of defeat was in doubt. I was just glad the ordeal was over for my family and my country. After the vote I said that I was profoundly sorry for what I had done to trigger the events and the great burden they imposed on the American people, and that I was rededicating myself to "a time of reconciliation and renewal for America." I took one question: "In your heart, sir, can you forgive and forget?" I replied, "I believe any person who asks for forgiveness has to be prepared to give it."

After the impeachment ordeal, people often asked me how I got through it without losing my mind, or at least the ability to keep doing the job. I couldn't have done it if the White House staff and cabinet, including those who were angry and disappointed over my conduct, hadn't stayed with me. It would have been much harder if the American people hadn't made an early judgment that I should remain President and stuck with it. If more congressional Democrats had bailed out when it looked like the safe thing to do in January, after the story broke, or in August, after I testified to the grand jury, it would have been tough; instead, they rose to the challenge. Having the support of world leaders like Mandela, Blair, Hussein, Havel, Crown Prince Abdullah, King Kim Dae Jung, Chirac, Cardoso, Zedillo, and others whom I admired helped to keep my spirits up. When I compared them with my enemies, as disgusted as I still was with myself, I figured I couldn't be all bad.

The love and support of friends and strangers made a big difference; those who wrote to me or said a kind word in a crowd meant more than they will ever know. The religious leaders who counseled me, visited me at the White House, or called to pray with me reminded me that, notwithstanding the condemnations I had received from some quarters, God is love.

But the biggest factors in my ability to survive and function were personal. Hillary's brothers and my brother were wonderfully supportive. Roger joked to me that it was nice to finally be the brother who wasn't in trouble. Hugh came up from Miami every week to play UpWords, talk sports, and make me laugh. Tony came over for our family pinochle matches. My mother-in-law and Dick Kelley were great to me.

Despite everything, our daughter still loved me and wanted me to stand my ground. And, most important, Hillary stood with me and loved me through it all. From the time we first met, I had loved her laugh. In the midst of all the absurdity, we were laughing again, brought back together by our weekly counseling and our shared determination to fight off the right-wing coup. I almost wound up being grateful to my tormentors: they were probably the only people who could have made me look good to Hillary again. I even got off the couch.

During the long year between the deposition in the Jones case and my acquittal in the Senate, on most of the nights when I was home in the White House I spent two to three hours alone in my office, reading the Bible and books on faith and forgiveness, and rereading **The Imitation of Christ** by Thomas à Kempis, the **Meditations** of Marcus Aurelius, and several of the most thoughtful letters I had received, including a series of mini-sermons from Rabbi Menachem Genack of Englewood, New Jersey. I was particularly affected by **Seventy Times Seven,** a book about forgiveness by Johann Christoph Arnold, the elder of Bruderhof, a Christian community with members in the northeastern United States and in England.

I still have poems, prayers, and quotations that people sent me or put into my hand at public events. And I have two stones with the New Testament verse John 8:7 inscribed on them. In what many people believe was Jesus' last encounter with his critics, the Pharisees, they brought to him a woman caught in the act of adultery and said the law of Moses commanded them to stone her to death. They taunted Jesus: "What sayest thou?" Instead of answering, Jesus leaned over and wrote on the ground with his finger, as if he had not heard them. When they continued to ask, he stood and said: "He that is without sin among you, let him first cast a stone at her." Those who heard him, "being convicted by their own conscience, went out one by one, beginning at the eldest, even unto the last." When Jesus was alone with the woman, he asked her, "Where are those thine accusers? hath no man condemned thee?" She answered, "No man, Lord," and Jesus replied, "Neither do I condemn thee."

I had had a lot of stones cast at me, and through my own self-inflicted wounds I had been exposed to the whole world. In some ways it was liberating; I had nothing more to hide. And as I tried to understand why I had made my own mistakes, I also attempted to figure out why my adversaries were so consumed with hatred, and so willing to say and do things inconsistent with their professed moral convictions. I had always looked with a jaundiced eye at other people's attempts to psychoanalyze me, but it did seem to me that many of my bitterest critics among the Far Right political and religious groups and the most judgmental members of the press had sought safety and security in positions where they could judge and not be judged, hurt and not be hurt.

My sense of my own mortality and human frailty and the unconditional love I'd had as a child had spared me the compulsion to judge and condemn others. And I believed my personal flaws, no matter how deep, were far less threatening to our democratic government than the power lust of my accusers. In late January, I had received a moving letter from Bill Ziff of New York, a businessman I'd never met but whose son was a friend of mine. He said that he was sorry for the pain Hillary and I had endured but that much good had come of it, because the Americans people had shown maturity and judgment in seeing through "the demonizing mullahs in our midst. Though it was never your intention, you have done more to expose their underlying agenda than any President in history, including Roosevelt."

Whatever the motives of my adversaries, it became clear, on those solitary nights in my upstairs office, that if I wanted compassion from others, I needed to show it, even to those who didn't respond in kind. Besides, what did I have to complain about? I would never be a perfect person, but Hillary was laughing again, Chelsea was still doing well at Stanford, I was still doing a job I loved, and spring was on the way.

FIFTY-TWO

On February 19, a week after the Senate vote, I gave the first posthumous pardon ever granted by a President, to Henry Flipper, the first black graduate of West Point, who, because of his race, had been wrongfully convicted of conduct unbecoming an officer 117 years earlier. Such actions by a President may seem unimportant compared with the power of current events, but correcting historical mistakes matters, not only to the descendants of those who were wronged but to us all.

In the last week of the month, Paul Begala announced his departure from the White House. I had relished having Paul there, because he had been with me since New Hampshire and he was smart, funny, combative, and effective. He also had small children who deserved more time with their father. Paul had stuck with me through the impeachment battle; now he needed to leave.

The only news out of Whitewater World was the lopsided vote of the American Bar Association, 384–49, on a resolution calling for the repeal of the independent counsel law, and a news report saying the Justice Department was investigating whether Kenneth Starr had deceived Janet Reno about his office's involvement with the Jones case and about the reasons he gave her for adding the Lewinsky matter to his jurisdiction.

March began with the announcement that after months of complex negotiations, the administration had succeeded in preserving the largest unprotected stand of old-growth redwoods in the world, the Headwaters Forest in northern California. The next week I took a four-day trip to Nicaragua, El Salvador, Honduras, and Guatemala to highlight a new era of democratic cooperation in a region in which, not long before, America had supported repressive regimes with horrible human rights records as long as they were anti-Communist. Viewing the aftermath of natural disasters that American troops were helping with, speaking to the parliament in El Salvador, where recent adversaries in a bloody civil war now sat together in peace, apologizing for America's past actions in Guatemala—all these seemed to me to be signs of a new era of democratic progress I was committed to support.

By the time I returned, we were moving toward another Balkan war, this time in Kosovo. The Serbs had launched an offensive against rebellious Kosovar Albanians a year earlier, killing many innocent people; some women and children were burned in their own homes. The last round of Serb aggression had sparked another exodus of refugees and had increased the desire of Kosovar Albanians for independence. The killings were all too reminiscent of the early days of Bosnia, which, like Kosovo, bridged the divide between European Muslims and Serb Orthodox Christians, a dividing line along which there had been conflict from time to time for six hundred years.

In 1974, Tito had given Kosovo autonomy, allowing it self-government and control over its schools. In 1989, Milosevic had taken autonomy away. The tensions had been rising ever since, and had exploded after the independence of Bosnia was secured in 1995. I was determined not to allow Kosovo to become another Bosnia. So was Madeleine Albright.

By April 1998, the United Nations had imposed an arms embargo, and the United States and its allies had imposed economic sanctions on Serbia for its failure to end the hostilities and begin a dialogue with the Kosovar Albanians. By the middle of June, NATO had begun to plan for a range of military options to end the violence. As summer came, Dick Holbrooke was back in the region to try to find a diplomatic solution for the standoff.

In mid-July, Serb forces again attacked armed and unarmed Kosovars, beginning a summer of aggression that would force 300,000 more Kosovar Albanians to leave their homes. In late September, the UN Security Council had passed another resolution demanding an end to hostilities, and at month's end we sent Holbrooke on yet another mission to Belgrade to try to reason with Milosevic.

On October 13, NATO had threatened to attack Serbia within four days unless the UN resolutions were observed. The air strikes were delayed when four thousand Yugoslav special police officers were withdrawn from Kosovo. Things got better for a while, but in January 1999 the Serbs were killing innocents in Kosovo again, and NATO air strikes seemed inevitable. We decided to try diplomacy one more time, but I wasn't optimistic. The parties' objectives were far apart. The United States and NATO wanted Kosovo to have the political autonomy it had enjoyed under the Yugoslav constitution between 1974 and 1989, until Milosevic took it away, and we wanted a NATO-led peacekeeping force to guarantee the peace and the safety of Kosovo's civilians, including the Serb minority. Milosevic wanted to keep control of

Kosovo, and was opposed to any foreign troop deployments there. The Kosovar Albanians wanted independence. They were also divided among themselves. Ibrahim Rugova, the head of the shadow government, was a softspoken man with a penchant for wearing a scarf around his neck. I was convinced we could make a peace agreement with him, but not so sure about the other main Kosovar faction, the Kosovo Liberation Army (KLA), led by a young man named Hacim Thaci. The KLA wanted independence and believed it could actually go toe-to-toe with the Serbian army.

The parties met at Rambouillet, France, on February 6, to work out the details of an agreement that would restore autonomy, protect the Kosovars from oppression with a NATO-led operation, disarm the KLA, and allow the Serb army to continue to patrol the border. Madeleine Albright and her British counterpart, Robin Cook, pursued this policy aggressively. After a week of negotiations coordinated by U.S. Ambassador Chris Hill and his counterparts from the European Union and Russia, Madeleine found that our position was opposed by both sides: the Serbs didn't want to agree to a NATO peacekeeping force, and the Kosovars didn't want to agree to accept autonomy unless they were also guaranteed a referendum on independence. And the KLA weren't happy about having to disarm, partly because they weren't sure they could rely on the NATO forces to protect them. Our team decided to write the agreement in a way that would delay the referendum but not deny it forever.

On February 23, the Kosovar Albanians, including Thaci, accepted the agreement in principle, returned home to sell it to their people, and in mid-March traveled to Paris to sign the finished document. The Serbs boycotted the ceremony, as forty thousand Serbian troops massed in and around Kosovo and Milosevic said again that he would never agree to foreign troops on Yugoslavian soil. I sent Dick Holbrooke back to see him one last time, but even Dick couldn't budge him.

On March 23, after Holbrooke left Belgrade, NATO Secretary-General Javier Solana, with my full support, directed General Wes Clark to begin air strikes. On the same day, by a bipartisan majority of 58–41, the Senate voted to support the action. Earlier in the month, the House had voted 219–191 to support sending U.S. troops to Kosovo if there was a peace agreement. Among the prominent Republicans voting for the proposal were the new Speaker, Dennis Hastert, and Henry Hyde. When Congressman Hyde said America should stand up against Milosevic and ethnic cleansing, I smiled and thought to myself that maybe Dr. Jekyll was in there somewhere after all.

While a majority of Congress and all our NATO allies favored the air strikes, Russia did not. Prime Minister Yevgeny Primakov was on his way to the United States to meet with Al Gore. When Al notified him that a NATO attack on Yugoslavia was imminent, Primakov ordered his plane to turn around and take him back to Moscow.

On the twenty-fourth, I spoke to the American people about what I was doing and why. I explained that Milosevic had stripped the Kosovars of their autonomy, denying them their constitutionally guaranteed rights to speak their own language, run their own schools, and govern themselves. I described the Serb atrocities: killing civilians, burning villages, and driving people from their homes, sixty thousand in the last five weeks, a quarter million in all. Finally, I put the current events in the context of the wars Milosevic had already waged against Bosnia and Croatia, and the destructive impact of his killing on the future of Europe.

The bombing campaign had three objectives: to show Milosevic we were serious about stopping another round of ethnic cleansing, to deter an even bloodier offensive against innocent civilians in Kosovo, and, if Milosevic didn't throw in the towel soon, to seriously damage the Serbs' military capacity.

That night the NATO air strikes began. They would last for eleven weeks, as Milosevic continued to kill Kosovar Albanians and drive almost one million people from their homes. The bombs would inflict great damage on the military and economic infrastructure of Serbia. Alas, on a few occasions they would miss their intended targets and take the lives of people we were trying to protect.

Some people argued that our position would have been more defensible if we had sent in ground troops. There were two problems with that argument. First, by the time the soldiers were in position, in adequate numbers and with proper support, the Serbs would have done an enormous amount of damage. Second, the civilian casualties of a ground campaign would probably have been greater than the toll from errant bombs. I didn't find the argument that I should pursue a course that would cost more American lives without enhancing the prospects of victory very persuasive. Our strategy would often be second-guessed, but never abandoned.

At the end of the month, as the stock market closed above 10,000 for the first time ever, up from 3,200 when I took office, I sat down for an interview with CBS-TV's Dan Rather. After an extended discussion of

Kosovo, Dan asked me whether I expected to be the husband of a United States senator. By then, many New York officials had joined Charlie Rangel in asking Hillary to consider the race. I told Rather that I had no idea what she would do, but that if she ran and won, "she would be magnificent."

In April, the Kosovo conflict intensified as we extended the bombing to downtown Belgrade, hitting the Interior Ministry, Serbia's state television headquarters, and Milosevic's party headquarters and his home. We also dramatically increased our financial support and troop presence in neighboring Albania and Macedonia to help them deal with the large number of refugees flooding in. By the end of the month, when Milosevic still hadn't folded, opposition to our policy was coming from both directions. Tony Blair and some members of Congress thought it was time to send in ground troops, while the House of Representatives voted to deny the use of troops without prior approval of Congress.

I still believed the air campaign would work, and hoped we could avoid sending ground troops until their mission was to keep the peace. On April 14, I called Boris Yeltsin to request Russian troop participation in a post-conflict peacekeeping force, as in Bosnia. I thought a Russian presence would help protect the Serb minority and might give Milosevic a face-saving way out of his opposition to foreign troops.

A lot of other things happened in April. On the fifth, Libya finally handed over two suspects in the bombing of Pan Am 103 over Lockerbie, Scotland, in 1988. They would be tried before Scottish judges in The Hague. The White House had been deeply involved in the issue for years. I had pressed the Libyans to do it, and the White

House had reached out to the families of victims, keeping them informed and approving the construction of a memorial to their loved ones in Arlington National Cemetery. It was the beginning of a thaw in U.S.–Libyan relations.

In the second week of the month, Chinese premier Zhu Rongji made his first trip to the White House in the hope of resolving the remaining obstacles to China's entry into the World Trade Organization. We had made substantial progress in closing the gaps between us, but problems remained, including our desire for greater access to China's auto market, and China's insistence on a five-year limit for our "surge" agreement, under which the United States could limit a sudden large increase in Chinese imports when it occurred for other than normal economic reasons. It was an important issue in America because of the surge we had experienced in imported steel from Russia, Japan, and elsewhere.

Charlene Barshefsky told me that the Chinese had moved a long way and we should close the deal while Zhu was in the United States to avoid weakening him at home. Madeleine Albright and Sandy Berger agreed with her. The rest of the economic team—Rubin, Summers, Sperling, and Daley—along with John Podesta and my legislative aide Larry Stein, disagreed. They thought that without more progress, Congress would reject the deal and kill China's entry into the WTO.

I met with Zhu in the Yellow Oval Room the night before the start of his official visit. I told him frankly that my advisors were split but that we would work all night if it was important to have the deal done while he was in the United States. Zhu said if the timing was bad we could wait.

Unfortunately the false story that we had a deal leaked, so that when it didn't happen, Zhu was hurt for the concessions he had made and I was criticized as having turned away a good agreement under pressure from the opponents of China's entry into the WTO. The story was reinforced by a spate of anti-China stories circulating in the media. The allegations that the Chinese government had steered funds into the 1996 campaign had not been resolved, and Wen Ho Lee, a Chinese-American employee of our national energy lab in Los Alamos, New Mexico, had been accused of stealing sensitive technology for China. All of my team wanted China in the WTO this year; now it was going to be harder to achieve.

On April 12, a jury rendered its verdict in Kenneth Starr's case against Susan McDougal, who had been charged with obstruction of justice and criminal contempt for her continued refusal to testify before the grand jury. She was acquitted on the obstruction of justice charge and, according to press reports, the jury deadlocked 7–5 for acquittal on the contempt charges. It was an amazing verdict. McDougal admitted that she had refused a court order to testify because she didn't trust Starr and his chief deputy, Hick Ewing. She testified that, now, in open court, she would be glad to answer any questions that the OIC had wanted to ask in the secret grand jury proceedings. She said that even though she had been offered immunity, she had refused to cooperate with the OIC because Starr and his staff had repeatedly tried to get her to lie to incriminate Hillary or me, and she believed that if she testified truthfully before the grand jury he would indict her for her refusal to lie. To close her defense, she called Julie Hiatt Steele, who testified that Starr had done exactly that to her, indicting her after she twice refused to lie for him in a grand jury proceeding.

The victory couldn't give Susan McDougal her lost years back, but her vindication was a stunning setback for Starr, and a sweet triumph for all the other people whose lives and savings he had destroyed.

On the twentieth, America suffered another horrible school shooting. At Columbine High School in Littleton, Colorado, two heavily armed students opened fire on their classmates, killing twelve students and injuring more than twenty others before turning their guns on themselves. It could have been even worse. One teacher, who later died from his wounds, led many students to safety. Medics and police officers saved more lives. A week later, with a bipartisan group of members of Congress and mayors, I announced some measures to make it harder for guns to fall into the wrong hands: applying the Brady law's prohibition on gun ownership to violent juveniles; closing the "gun show loophole" to require background checks on people who bought guns at such events rather than at gun stores; cracking down on illegal gun trafficking; and prohibiting juveniles from owning assault rifles. I also proposed funds to help schools develop successful violence prevention and conflict-resolution programs like the one I had just observed at T. C. Williams High School in Alexandria, Virginia.

Senate majority leader Trent Lott called my initiative a "typical knee-jerk reaction," and Tom DeLay accused me of exploiting Columbine for political gain. But the legislation's principal sponsor, Congresswoman Carolyn McCarthy of New York, wasn't interested in politics; her husband had been killed and her son badly wounded on a commuter train by a deranged man with a handgun he should never have been able to possess. The NRA and its supporters blamed our violent culture. I agreed that children were exposed to too much violence; that's why I was supporting Al and Tipper Gore's drive to get V-chips into new TVs so that parents could limit children's exposure to excessive violence. But the violence in our culture only strengthened the argument for doing more to keep guns away from children, criminals, and mentally unstable people.

At the end of the month, Hillary and I hosted the largest gathering of heads of state ever to meet in Washington, as the leaders of NATO and the states in its Partnership for Peace gathered to celebrate the fiftieth anniversary of NATO, and to reaffirm our determination to prevail in Kosovo. Afterward, Al From of the DLC and Sidney Blumenthal put together another of our "Third Way" conferences to highlight the values, ideas, and strategies Tony Blair and I shared with Gerhard Schroeder of Germany, Wim Kok of the Netherlands, and the new Italian prime minister, Massimo D'Alema. By this time, I was focused on building a global consensus on economic, social, and security policies that I thought would serve America and the world well when my term was over by strengthening the forces of positive interdependence and weakening those of disintegration and destruction. The Third Way movement and the broadening of NATO's alliance and its mission had moved us a fair distance in the right direction, but as with so many of the best-laid plans, they would later be overtaken and redirected by events, principally the growing hostility to globalization and the rising tide of terror.

In early May, shortly after Jesse Jackson persuaded Milosevic to release three U.S. servicemen the Serbs had captured along their border with Macedonia, we lost two American soldiers when their Apache helicopter crashed in a training exercise; they would be the only U.S. casualties in the conflict. Boris Yeltsin sent Victor Chernomyrdin to see me to discuss Russia's interest in ending the war and its apparent willingness to participate in the peacekeeping force afterward. Meanwhile, we kept the pressure up, as I authorized 176 more aircraft for Wes Clark.

On May 7, we suffered the worst political setback of the conflict when NATO bombed the Chinese embassy in Belgrade, killing three Chinese citizens. I soon learned that the bombs had hit their intended target, which had been erroneously identified on the basis of old CIA maps as a Serbian government building used for military purposes. It was the kind of mistake we had worked hard to avoid. The military was mostly using aerial photography for targeting. I had begun meeting with Bill Cohen, Hugh Shelton, and Sandy Berger several times a week to go over the high-profile targets in an attempt to maximize damage to Milosevic's aggression while minimizing civilian casualties. I was dumbfounded and deeply upset by the mistake and immediately called Jiang Zemin to apologize. He wouldn't take the call, so I publicly and repeatedly apologized.

Over the next three days, protests escalated all over China. They were especially intense around the American embassy in Beijing, where Ambassador Sasser found himself besieged. The Chinese said they believed the attack was deliberate and declined to accept my apologies. When I finally talked with President Jiang on the fourteenth, I apologized again and told him I was sure he didn't believe I would knowingly attack his embassy. Jiang replied that he knew I wouldn't do that, but said he did believe that there were people in the Pentagon or the CIA who didn't favor my outreach to China and could have rigged the maps intentionally to cause a rift between us. Jiang had a hard time believing that a nation as technologically advanced as we were could make such a mistake.

I had a hard time believing it, too, but that's what happened. Eventually we got beyond it, but it was tough going for a while. I had just named Admiral Joe Prueher, who was retiring as commander in chief of our forces in the Pacific, to be the new U.S. ambassador to China. He was very respected by the Chinese military, and I believed he would be able to help repair the relationship.

By late May, NATO had approved a 48,000-troop peacekeeping force to go into Kosovo after the conflict was concluded, and we had begun quiet discussions about the possibility of sending in ground troops earlier if it became clear that the air campaign wasn't going to prevail before people were trapped in the mountains by winter. Sandy Berger was preparing a memo for me on options, and I was ready to send troops in if necessary, but I still believed the air war would succeed. On the twenty-seventh, Milosevic was indicted by the war crimes prosecutor in The Hague.

There was a great deal of activity in the rest of the world in May. In mid-month, Boris Yeltsin survived his own impeachment vote in the Duma. On the seventeenth, Prime Minister Netanyahu was defeated for reelection by the Labor Party leader, retired general Ehud Barak, the most decorated soldier in Israeli history. Barak was a brilliant Renaissance man: he had done graduate work in economic engineering systems at Stanford, was a concert-level classical pianist, and repaired clocks as a hobby. He had been in politics only a few years, and his close-cropped hair, intense stare, and blunt, staccato speaking style were more reflective of his military past than of the more murky political waters he now had to navigate. His victory was a clear signal that Israelis saw in him what they had seen in his role model, Yitzhak Rabin: the possibility of peace with security. Equally important, Barak's large victory margin had given him the chance to have a governing coalition in the Knesset that would support the hard steps to peace, something Prime Minister Netanyahu had never had.

The next day Jordan's King Abdullah came to see me, full of hope for peace and determination to be a worthy successor to his father. He clearly understood the challenges facing his nation and the peace process. I was also struck by his understanding of economics and the contribution that more growth could make to peace and reconciliation. After the meeting I was convinced that the king and his equally impressive wife, Queen Rania, would be positive forces in the region for a long time to come.

On May 26, Bill Perry delivered a letter from me to Kim Jong Il, North Korea's leader, proposing a road map to the future in which America would provide a broad range of assistance to him if, but only if, he gave up his attempts to develop nuclear weapons and long-range missiles. In 1998, North Korea had taken the constructive step of ending its tests of such missiles, and I thought Perry's mission had a fair chance to succeed.

Two days later, Hillary and I were at a DLC retreat at White Oak Plantation in northern Florida, which has the largest wild game preserve in the United States. I got up at four in the morning to watch the inaugural ceremonies for Nigeria's new president, former general Olusegun Obasanjo, on TV. Ever since gaining independence, Nigeria had been riddled by corruption, regional and religious strife, and deteriorating social conditions. Despite its large oil production, the country suffered periodic power outages and fuel shortages. Obasanjo had taken power briefly in a military coup in the 1970s, then had kept his promise to step aside as soon as new elections could be held. Later, he had been imprisoned for his political views and, while incarcerated, had become a devout Christian and had written books about his faith. It was hard to imagine a bright future for sub-Saharan Africa without a more successful Nigeria, by far its most populous nation. After listening to his compelling inaugural address, I hoped Obasanjo would be able to succeed where others had failed.

On the home front, I started the month with an important clean-air announcement. We had already reduced toxic air pollution from chemical plants by 90 percent, and had set tough standards to reduce smog and soot that would prevent millions of cases of childhood asthma. On May 1, I said that after extensive consultation with industry, environmental, and consumer groups, EPA administrator Carol Browner would promulgate a rule to require all passenger vehicles, including gas-guzzling SUVs, to meet the same pollution standards, and that we would cut the sulfur content of gasoline by 90 percent over five years.

I announced a new crime initiative, releasing the funds to complete our efforts to put 100,000 police on the streets (more than half of them were already in service);

expanding the COPS program to hire 50,000 more police officers in the highest-crime areas; and making it a federal crime to possess biological agents that could be turned into terrorist weapons without a legitimate, peaceful purpose for having them.

The twelfth was a day I had hoped would never come; Bob Rubin was returning to private life. I believed he had been the best and most important Treasury secretary since Alexander Hamilton in the early days of our Republic. Bob had also been the first head of the National Economic Council. In both positions he had played a decisive role in our efforts to restore economic growth and spread its benefits to more Americans, to prevent and contain financial crisis abroad, and to modernize the international financial system to deal with a global economy in which more than one trillion dollars crossed national borders every day. He had also been a rock of stability during the impeachment ordeal, not only speaking up at the meeting when I apologized to my cabinet, but also constantly reminding our people that they should be proud of what they were doing, and cautioning them not to be too judgmental. One of our younger people said that Bob had told him that if he lived long enough, he would do something he'd be ashamed of, too.

When Bob came into the administration he was probably the wealthiest person on our team. After he supported the 1993 economic plan, with its tax increase for the highest-income Americans, I used to joke that "Bob Rubin came to Washington to help me save the middle class, and when he leaves, he'll be one of them." Now that Bob was moving back into private life, I didn't think I'd have to worry about that anymore.

I named Bob's able deputy secretary, Larry Summers, to

succeed him. Larry had been in the thick of all the major economic questions of the last six years, and he was ready. I also named Stu Eizenstat, the undersecretary of state for economic affairs, to be deputy Treasury secretary. Stu had handled a lot of important assignments well, none more important than the so-called Nazi Gold matter. Edgar Bronfman Sr. had sparked our interest in it by contacting Hillary, who got things moving with an initial meeting. Eizenstat then spearheaded our attempt to secure justice and compensation for Holocaust survivors and their families whose assets had been looted as they were being packed off to concentration camps.

Soon afterward, Hillary and I flew to Colorado to meet with students and families from Columbine High School. A few days earlier the Senate had adopted my proposals to ban the import of large ammunition clips that were being used to evade the assault weapons ban, and to ban the possession of assault weapons by juveniles. And in the face of intense lobbying by the NRA, Al Gore had broken a 50–50 tie to pass the proposal to close the gun show loophole in the Brady law's requirement of background checks.

Although the community was still grieving, the students at Columbine were coming back, and they and their parents seemed determined to do something to reduce the chances of further Columbines. They knew that though there had been several school shootings before theirs, it was Columbine that had finally pierced the soul of America. I told them that they could help America build a safer future because of what they had endured. Although Congress would not close the gun show loophole, in the 2000 election, because of Columbine, the voters in conservative Colorado would pass a measure to do so in their state by an overwhelming margin.

Whitewater World was still alive and well in May, as Kenneth Starr, despite his defeat in the Susan McDougal trial, pursued his case against Julie Hiatt Steele. The case ended in a hung jury; in conservative northern Virginia, it was another setback for the independent counsel and his tactics. After all Starr's efforts to get into the Jones case, the only person who was indicted as a result was Steele, another innocent bystander who refused to lie. Starr's office had now conducted four trials and lost three.

In June, the punishing bombing raids on the Serbs finally broke Milosevic's will to resist. On the second, Victor Chernomyrdin and Finnish president Martti Ahtisaari personally handled NATO's demands to Milosevic. The next day Milosevic and the Serbian parliament agreed to them. Predictably, the next few days were full of tension and disputes over the details, but on the ninth NATO and Serbian military officials agreed to a prompt withdrawal of Serb forces from Kosovo and the deployment of an international security force with a unified NATO chain of command. The next day Javier Solana instructed General Clark to suspend NATO's air operations, the UN Security Council passed a resolution welcoming the end of the war, and I announced to the American people that, after seventy-nine days, the bombing campaign was over, the Serb forces were withdrawing, and the one million men, women, and children driven from their land would be able to go home. In an Oval Office address to the nation, I thanked our armed forces for their superb performance and the American people for their stand against ethnic cleansing and their generous support of the refugees, many of whom had come to America.

Allied Commander Wes Clark had managed the campaign with skill and determination, and he and Javier

Solana had done yeoman's work in holding the alliance together and in never wavering in our steadfast commitment to victory on the bad days as well as the good ones. So had my entire national security team. Even though when the bombing wasn't over in a week we were constantly second-guessed, Bill Cohen and Hugh Shelton had remained convinced that the air campaign would work if we could hold the coalition together for two months. Al Gore, Madeleine Albright, and Sandy Berger had all remained cool under fire in the nail-biting, roller-coaster weeks we had just been through together. Al had played a critical role in keeping our relationship with Russia intact by staying in contact with Victor Chernomyrdin and making sure that we and the Russians had a common position when Chernomyrdin and Ahtisaari went to Serbia to try to persuade Milosevic to give up his futile resistance.

On the eleventh, I took a congressional delegation to Whiteman Air Force Base in Missouri to say a special word of thanks to the crews and support personnel on B-2 stealth bombers, which flew all the way from Missouri to Serbia and back, nonstop, to perform the night-time bombing operations for which the B-2 was especially well suited. In all, 30,000 sorties were flown in the Kosovo campaign. Only two planes were lost, and their crews were recovered safely.

After the raids succeeded, John Keegan, perhaps the foremost living historian of warfare, wrote a fascinating article in the British press about the Kosovo campaign. He admitted frankly that he had not believed the bombing would work and that he had been wrong. He said the reason such campaigns had failed in the past is that most bombs had missed their targets. The weaponry used in

Kosovo was more precise than that used in the first Gulf War; and though some bombs went astray in Kosovo and Serbia, far fewer civilians were killed than in Iraq. I'm also still convinced that fewer civilians died than would have perished if we had put in ground troops, a bridge I would nevertheless have crossed rather than let Milosevic prevail. The success of the air campaign in Kosovo marked a new chapter in military history.

There was one more tense moment before things settled down. Two days after hostilities officially ended, fifty vehicles carrying about two hundred Russian troops rushed into Kosovo from Bosnia and occupied the Pristina airport without advance agreement from NATO, four hours before the NATO troops authorized by the UN arrived. The Russians asserted their intention to keep control of the airport.

Wes Clark was livid. I didn't blame him, but I knew we weren't on the verge of World War III. Yeltsin was getting a lot of criticism at home for cooperating with us from ultra-nationalists whose sympathies lay with the Serbs. I thought he was just throwing them a temporary bone. Soon the British commander, Lieutenant General Michael Jackson, resolved the situation without incident, and on June 18, Secretary Cohen and the Russian defense minister reached an agreement under which Russian troops would join the UN-sanctioned NATO forces in Kosovo. On June 20, the Yugoslav military completed its withdrawal, and just two weeks later the UN High Commissioner for Refugees estimated that more than 765,000 refugees had already returned to Kosovo.

As we had learned from our experience in Bosnia, even after the conflict there would still be a great deal of work ahead in Kosovo: getting the refugees home safely; clearing the minefields; rebuilding homes; providing food, medicine, and shelter to the homeless; demilitarizing the Kosovo Liberation Army; creating a secure environment for both Kosovar Albanians and the minority Serb population; organizing a civilian administration; and restoring a functioning economy. It was a big job, most of which would be performed by our European allies, even as America had borne the lion's share of responsibility for the air war.

Despite the challenges ahead, I felt an enormous sense of relief and satisfaction. Slobodan Milosevic's bloody ten-year campaign to exploit ethnic and religious differences in order to impose his will on the former Yugoslavia was on its last legs. The burning of villages and killing of innocents was history. I knew it was just a matter of time before Milosevic was history, too.

On the day we reached the agreement with Russia, Hillary and I were in Cologne, Germany, for the annual G-8 summit. It turned out to be one of the most important such meetings of my entire eight years. In addition to celebrating the successful end to the Kosovo conflict, we endorsed our finance ministers' recommendations to modernize the international financial institutions and our national policies to meet the challenges of the global economy, and we announced a proposal, which I strongly supported, for a massive millennium debt-relief initiative for poor countries if they agreed to put all the savings into education, health care, or economic development. The initiative was consistent with a chorus of calls for debt relief from all over the world, led by Pope John Paul II and my friend Bono.

After the summit we flew on to Slovenia to thank the

Slovenians for supporting NATO in Kosovo and helping the refugees, then to Macedonia, where President Kiro Gligorov, despite his country's own economic hardships and ethnic tensions, had taken in 300,000 refugees. At the camp in Skopje, Hillary, Chelsea, and I got to visit with some of them and hear the horrible stories of what they had endured. We also met members of the international security force who were stationed there. It was my first chance to thank Wes Clark in person.

Politics began to heat up in June. Al Gore announced for President on the sixteenth. His likely opponent was Governor George W. Bush, the preferred candidate of both the Republican Party's right wing and its establishment. Bush had already raised more money than Al and his primary opponent, former New Jersey senator Bill Bradley, combined. Hillary was moving closer to getting into the Senate race in New York. By the time we left the White House she would have helped me in my political career for more than twenty-six years. I was more than happy to support her for the next twenty-six.

As we entered the political season, I was far more concerned about maintaining the momentum for action in Congress and in my own government. Traditionally, when presidential politics begin to heat up and the President isn't part of it, inertia sets in. Some of the Democrats thought they would be better off if little new legislation was passed; then they could run against a Republican "do nothing" Congress. Many Republicans just didn't want to give me any more victories. I was surprised at how bitter some of them still seemed to be four months after the impeachment battle, especially since I hadn't been hammering them in public or in private.

I tried to wake up every morning without bitterness

and to keep working in a spirit of reconciliation. The Republicans seemed to have reverted to the theme they had trumpeted since 1992: I was a person without character who could not be trusted. During the Kosovo conflict some Republicans almost seemed to be rooting for us to fail. One Republican senator justified his colleagues' tepid support for what our troops were doing by saying I had lost their trust; they were blaming me for their own failure to oppose ethnic cleansing.

It seemed to me that the Republicans were trying to put me in a lose-lose situation. If I went around wearing a hair shirt, they would say I was too damaged to lead. If I was happy, they would say I was gloating and acting as if I'd gotten away with something. Six days after my acquittal in the Senate, I had gone to New Hampshire to celebrate the seventh anniversary of my New Hampshire primary. Some of my congressional critics said I shouldn't have been happy, but I was happy—and for good reasons: all my old friends came out to see me; I met a young man who said he'd cast his first vote for me, and I had done exactly what I said I would do; and I met a woman who said I had inspired her to get off welfare and go back to school to become a nurse. By 1999, she was a member of the New Hampshire Board of Nursing. Those were the people I got into politics for.

At first I couldn't for the life of me figure out how the Republicans and some commentators could say I'd gotten away with anything. The public humiliation, the pain to my family, the huge debts from legal bills and settling the Jones suit after I'd won it, the years of press and legal abuse Hillary had endured, and the helplessness I felt as countless innocent people in Washington and Arkansas were persecuted and ruined financially—these things took a terrible toll on me. I had apologized and tried to demonstrate my sincerity in the way I'd treated and worked with the Republicans. But none of it was enough. It would never be enough, for one simple reason: I had survived and continued to serve and fight for what I believed. First, last, and always, my struggle with the New Right Republicans was about power. I thought power came from the people and they should give it and take it away. They thought the people had made a mistake in electing me twice, and they were determined to use my personal mistakes to justify their continuing assault.

I was sure that my more positive strategy was the right thing for me as a person and for my ability to do my job. I wasn't as sure it was good politics. The more the Republicans pounded away at me, the more the memories of what Ken Starr had done or how they had behaved during impeachment faded. The press is naturally focused on today's story, not yesterday's, and conflict makes news. That tends to reward the aggressor, whether the underlying attack is fair or not. Soon, instead of asking me whether I could forgive and forget, the press was asking those earnest-sounding questions again about whether I had the moral authority to lead. The Republicans were barking away at Hillary, too, now that, instead of being a sympathetic figure standing by her flawed man, she was a strong woman finding her own way in politics. Yet, on balance, I still felt good about where things stood: the country was moving in the right direction, my job rating was high, and we still had plenty to do.

Although I would always regret what I had done wrong, I will go to my grave being proud of what I had fought for in the impeachment battle, my last great showdown with the forces I had opposed all of my life—those who had defended the old order of racial discrimination and segregation in the South and played on the insecurities and fears of the white working class in which I grew up; who had opposed the women's movement, the environmental movement, the gay-rights movement, and other efforts to expand our national community as assaults on the natural order; who believed government should be run for the benefit of powerful entrenched interests and favored tax cuts for the wealthy over health care and better education for children.

Ever since I was a boy I had been on the other side. At first, the forces of reaction, division, and the status quo were represented by anti–civil rights Democrats. When the national party under Truman, Kennedy, and Johnson began to embrace the cause of civil rights, the southern conservatives migrated to the Republican Party, which, beginning in the 1970s, formed an alliance with the rising religious right-wing movement.

When the New Right Republicans had taken power in Congress in 1995, I had blocked their most extreme designs and had made further progress in economic, social, and environmental justice the price of our cooperation. I understood why the people who equated political, economic, and social conservatism with God's will hated me. I wanted an America of shared benefits, shared responsibilities, and equal participation in a democratic community. The New Right Republicans wanted an America in which wealth and power were concentrated in the hands of the "right" people, who maintained majority support by demonizing a rolling succession of minorities whose demands for inclusion threatened their hold on power. They also hated me because I was an apostate, a white southern Protestant who could appeal to the very people they had always taken for granted.

Now that my private sins had been publicly aired, they would be able to throw stones until the day I died. I was letting go of my anger about it, but I was glad that, by accident of history, I had had the good fortune to stand against this latest incarnation of the forces of reaction and division, and in favor of a more perfect union.

FIFTY-THREE

In early June, I gave a radio address to increase awareness of mental-health issues with Tipper Gore, whom I had named my official advisor for mental health and who recently had courageously revealed her own treatment for depression. Two days later, Hillary and I joined Al and Tipper for a White House Conference on Mental Health, in which we dealt with the staggering personal, economic, and social costs of untreated mental illness.

For the rest of the month, I highlighted our gun safety proposals; our efforts to develop an AIDS vaccine; my efforts to include environmental and labor rights issues in trade talks; the report of the President's Foreign Intelligence Advisory Board on security at the Energy Department's weapons labs; a plan to restore health and disability benefits to legal immigrants; a proposal to allow Medicaid to cover disabled Americans who couldn't meet the costs of treatments if they lost their health-care coverage because they entered the workforce; legislation to help older children who leave foster care to make the adjustment to independent living; and a plan to modernize Medicare and extend the life of its trust fund.

I had been looking forward to July. I thought it would be a predictable, positive month. I would announce that we were taking the bald eagle off the endangered species list, and Al Gore would outline our plan to complete the restoration of the Florida Everglades. Hillary would begin her "listening tour" at Senator Moynihan's farm at Pindars Corners in upstate New York, and I would take a tour of poor communities across the country to promote my "New Markets" initiative to attract more investment to areas that were still not part of our recovery. All those things happened, but so did events that were unplanned, troublesome, or tragic.

Prime Minister Nawaz Sharif of Pakistan called and asked if he could come to Washington on July 4 to discuss the dangerous standoff with India that had begun several weeks earlier when Pakistani forces under the command of General Pervez Musharraf crossed the Line of Control, which had been the recognized and generally observed boundary between India and Pakistan in Kashmir since 1972. Sharif was concerned that the situation Pakistan had created was getting out of control, and he hoped to use my good offices not only to resolve the crisis but also to help mediate with the Indians on the question of Kashmir itself. Even before the crisis, Sharif had asked me to help in Kashmir, saying it was as worthy of my attention as the Middle East and Northern Ireland. I had explained to him then that the United States was involved in those peace processes because both sides wanted us. In this case, India had strongly refused the involvement of any outside party.

Sharif's moves were perplexing because that February, Indian prime minister Atal Behari Vajpayee had traveled to Lahore, Pakistan, to promote bilateral talks aimed at resolving the Kashmir problem and other differences. By crossing the Line of Control, Pakistan had wrecked the talks. I didn't know whether Sharif had authorized the invasion to create a crisis he hoped would get America involved or had simply allowed it in order to avoid a confrontation with Pakistan's powerful military. Regardless, he had gotten himself into a bind with no easy way out.

I told Sharif that he was always welcome in Washington, even on July 4, but if he wanted me to spend America's Independence Day with him, he had to come to the United States knowing two things: first, he had to agree to withdraw his troops back across the Line of Control; and second, I would not agree to intervene in the Kashmir dispute, especially under circumstances that appeared to reward Pakistan's wrongful incursion.

Sharif said he wanted to come anyway. On July 4, we met at Blair House. It was a hot day, but the Pakistani delegation was used to the heat and, in their traditional white pants and long tunics, seemed more comfortable than my team. Once more, Sharif urged me to intervene in Kashmir, and again I explained that without India's consent it would be counterproductive, but that I would urge Vajpayee to resume the bilateral dialogue if the Pakistani troops withdrew. He agreed, and we released a joint statement saying that steps would be taken to restore the Line of Control and that I would support and encourage the resumption and intensification of bilateral talks once the violence had stopped.

After the meeting, I thought perhaps Sharif had come in order to use pressure from the United States to provide himself cover for ordering his military to defuse the conflict. I knew he was on shaky ground at home, and I hoped he would survive, because I needed his cooperation in the fight against terrorism.

Pakistan was one of the few countries with close ties to the Taliban in Afghanistan. Before our July 4 meeting, I had asked Sharif on three occasions for help in apprehending Osama bin Laden: in our meeting the previous

December, at King Hussein's funeral, and in a June phone conversation and follow-up letter. We had intelligence reports that al Qaeda was planning attacks on U.S. officials and facilities in various places around the world and perhaps in the United States as well. We had been successful in breaking up cells and arresting a number of al Qaeda members, but unless bin Laden and his top lieutenants were apprehended or killed, the threat would remain. On July 4, I told Sharif that unless he did more to help, I would have to announce that Pakistan was in effect supporting terrorism in Afghanistan.

On the day I met with Sharif, I also signed an executive order placing economic sanctions on the Taliban, freezing its assets and prohibiting commercial exchanges. Around this time, with Sharif's support, U.S. officials also began to train sixty Pakistani troops as commandos to go into Afghanistan to get bin Laden. I was skeptical about the project; even if Sharif wanted to help, the Pakistani military was full of Taliban and al Qaeda sympathizers. But I thought we had nothing to lose by exploring every option.

The day after the Sharif meeting, I started the New Markets tour, beginning in Hazard, Kentucky, with a large delegation including several business executives, congressmen, cabinet members, the Reverend Jesse Jackson, and Al From.

I was glad that Jackson was making the tour and that we were starting in Appalachia, America's poorest all-white area. Jesse had long worked to bring more private-sector investment to poor areas, and we had grown even closer during the impeachment year, when he had strongly supported my whole family and made a special effort to reach out to Chelsea. From Kentucky we traveled to Clarksdale, Mississippi; East St. Louis, Illinois; the Pine Ridge Reservation in South Dakota; a Hispanic neighborhood in Phoenix, Arizona; and the Watts neighborhood in Los Angeles.

Even though America had had two years of unemployment rates just above 4 percent, all the communities I visited and many like them suffered from unemployment that was far higher than that and per capita incomes well below the national average. The unemployment rate at Pine Ridge was over 70 percent. Yet everywhere we went, I met intelligent, hardworking people who were capable of contributing much more to the economy.

I thought doing more to get investment into these areas was both the right thing to do and economically smart. We were already enjoying the largest economic expansion in history, with a rapidly growing rate of productivity. It seemed to me there were three ways to continue to increase growth without inflation: sell more products and services overseas; increase the workforce participation of particular populations, like welfare recipients; and bring growth to new markets in America where investment was too low and unemployment too high.

We were doing well in the first two areas, with more than 250 trade agreements and welfare reform. And we had made a good start on the third, with more than 130 empowerment zones and enterprise communities, community development banks, and aggressive enforcement of the Community Reinvestment Act. But too many communities had been left behind. I was putting together a legislative proposal to increase available capital to inner cities, rural towns, and Indian reservations by $15 billion. Since it would promote free enterprise, I hoped to get strong bipartisan support and was encouraged by the fact that Speaker Hastert seemed especially interested in the effort.

On July 15, Ehud and Nava Barak accepted an invitation to spend the night at Camp David with Hillary and me. We had an enjoyable dinner, and Ehud and I stayed up talking until nearly three in the morning. It was clear that he wanted to complete the peace process and believed that his big election victory gave him a mandate to do so. He was interested in doing something substantive at Camp David, especially after I showed him the building where most of the negotiations President Carter mediated between Anwar Sadat and Menachem Begin had taken place in 1978.

At the same time I was also occupied with trying to get the Northern Ireland peace process back on track. There was a deadlock caused by a disagreement between Sinn Fein and the Unionists over whether the IRA's decommissioning could occur after the new government was formed or had to come before it. I explained the situation to Barak, who was intrigued by the differences and similarities between the Irish problems and his own.

The next day John Kennedy Jr., his wife, Carolyn, and her sister Lauren were killed when the small plane John was flying crashed off the coast of Massachusetts. I had liked John ever since I had met him in the 1980s when he was a law student working as an intern in Mickey Kantor's firm in Los Angeles. He had come to one of my first New York campaign events in 1991, and not long before they perished I had enjoyed showing Carolyn and John the residence floors of the White House. Ted Kennedy gave another magnificent eulogy for a fallen family member: "Like his father, he had every gift."

On July 23, King Hassan II of Morocco died at the age

of seventy. He had been an ally of the United States, and a supporter of the Middle East peace process, and I had enjoyed a good personal relationship with him. Again on short notice, President Bush agreed to fly to Morocco for the funeral with Hillary, Chelsea, and me. I walked behind the king's horse-drawn casket with President Mubarak, Yasser Arafat, Jacques Chirac, and other leaders on a three-mile route through downtown Rabat. Well over one million people lined the streets, ululating and shouting in grief and respect to their fallen monarch. The deafening din of the huge, emotional throng made the march one of the most incredible events I had ever participated in. I think Hassan would have approved.

After a brief meeting with Hassan's son and heir, King Mohammed VI, I flew home for a couple of days of work, then left again for Sarajevo, where I joined several European leaders as we committed to a stability pact for the Balkans, an agreement to support the region's short-term needs and long-term growth by providing greater access to our markets for Balkan products; working for the inclusion of southeastern European countries into the WTO; and providing investment funds and credit guarantees to encourage private investment.

The rest of the summer flew by as I continued to disagree with the Republicans over the budget and the size and distribution of their proposed tax cut; Dick Holbrooke was finally confirmed as UN ambassador after an unconscionable delay of fourteen months; and Hillary moved closer to declaring her Senate candidacy.

In August, we took two trips to New York to look for a home. On the twenty-eighth, we visited a late-nineteenth-century farmhouse with a large addition from 1989 in

Chappaqua, about forty miles from Manhattan. The old part of the house was charming, the new part spacious and full of light. The instant I walked upstairs into the master bedroom I told Hillary we had to buy the house. It was part of the 1989 addition; it had extra-high ceilings with a row of glass doors facing the backyard, and had two huge windows on the other walls. When Hillary asked me why I was so sure, I replied, "Because you're about to start a hard campaign. There'll be some bad days. This beautiful room is bathed in light. You'll wake up every morning in a good humor."

Later in August, I traveled to Atlanta to give the Medal of Freedom to President and Mrs. Carter for the extraordinary work they had done as private citizens since leaving the White House. A couple of days later, in a White House ceremony, I gave the award to several other distinguished Americans, including President Ford and Lloyd Bentsen. The other recipients were civil rights, labor, democracy, and environmental activists. All were less famous than Ford and Bentsen, but each had made unique and enduring contributions to America.

I did a little campaigning, going to Arkansas with Al Gore for meetings with local farmers and black leaders from across the South and a large fund-raiser full of people from my old campaigns. I also spoke and played saxophone at an event for Hillary on Martha's Vineyard, and appeared with her at events in New York, including a stop at the state fair in Syracuse, where I was right at home with the farmers. I enjoyed campaigning for both Hillary and Al, and I was beginning to look forward to a time when, after a lifetime of being helped by others, I could end my life in politics the way I'd started it, campaigning for other people I believed in.

In early September, Henry Cisneros finally resolved his case with independent counsel David Barrett, who had indicted him, unbelieveably, on eighteen felony counts for understating personal expenses to the FBI during his 1993 interview. On the day before his trial began, Barrett, who knew he had an unwinnable case, offered Cisneros a deal: a guilty plea to one misdemeanor, a $10,000 fine, and no jail time. Henry took it to avoid the crushing legal expense of a long trial. Barrett had spent more than $9 million of the taxpayers' money to torment a good man for four years. Just a few weeks earlier, the independent counsel law had expired.

Most of September was devoted to foreign policy. Early in the month Madeleine Albright and Dennis Ross were in Gaza to support Ehud Barak and Yasser Arafat as they agreed on the next steps to implement the Wye River accord, approving a port for the Palestinians, a road connecting the West Bank and Gaza, the handover of 11 percent of the West Bank, and the release of 350 prisoners. Albright and Ross then went to Damascus to urge President Assad to respond to Barak's desire for peace talks with him soon.

On the ninth, I made my first trip to New Zealand for the APEC summit. Chelsea went with me, while Hillary stayed home to campaign. The big news at the summit involved Indonesia and the support its military had given to the violent suppression of the pro-independence movement in East Timor, a long-troubled Roman Catholic enclave in the world's most populous Muslim country. Most of the APEC leaders favored an international peace-keeping mission for East Timor, and Australian prime minister John Howard was willing to take the lead. At first the Indonesians were opposed to it, but soon they would be forced to relent. An international coalition was formed to send troops to East Timor under the leadership of Australia, and I pledged to Prime Minister Howard that I would send a couple of hundred American troops to provide the logistical support our allies needed.

I also met with President Jiang to discuss WTO issues, held joint discussions with Kim Dae Jung and Keizo Obuchi to reaffirm our common position on North Korea, and had my first meeting with Boris Yeltsin's new prime minister and chosen successor, Vladimir Putin. Putin presented a stark contrast to Yeltsin. Yeltsin was large and stocky; Putin was compact and extremely fit from years of martial arts practice. Yeltsin was voluble; the former KGB agent was measured and precise. I came away from the meeting believing Yeltsin had picked a successor who had the skills and capacity for hard work necessary to manage Russia's turbulent political and economic life better than Yeltsin now could, given his health problems; Putin also had the toughness to defend Russia's interests and protect Yeltsin's legacy.

Before we left New Zealand, Chelsea and I and my staff took some time to enjoy the beautiful country. Prime Minister Jenny Shipley and her husband, Burton, hosted us in Queenstown, where I played golf with Burton, Chelsea explored caves with the Shipley kids, and several of my staff went bungee jumping off a high bridge. Gene Sperling tried to goad me into trying it, but I told him I'd had about all the free falls I could stand.

Our last stop was the International Antarctic Center in Christchurch, America's launching station for our operations in Antarctica. The center contained a large training module in which the frigid conditions of Antarctica were replicated. I went there to highlight the problem of global warming. Antarctica is a great cooling tower for our planet, with ice more than two miles thick. A huge chunk of Antarctic ice, about the size of Rhode Island, had recently broken free as a result of thawing. I released previously classified satellite photos of the continent to aid in studying the changes that were occurring. The biggest thrill of the event for Chelsea and me was the presence of Sir Edmund Hillary, who had explored the South Pole in the 1950s, was the first man to reach the top of Mount Everest, and, most important, was the man Chelsea's mother had been named for.

Soon after I returned to America, I went to New York to open the last UN General Assembly of the twentieth century, urging the delegates to adopt three resolutions: to do more to fight poverty and put a human face on the global economy; to increase our efforts to prevent or quickly stop the killing of innocents in ethnic, religious, racial, or tribal conflicts; and to intensify our efforts to prevent the use of nuclear, chemical, or biological weapons by irresponsible nations or terrorist groups.

At the end of the month I got back to domestic affairs, vetoing the latest Republican tax cut because it was "too big, too bloated," and put too great a burden on America's economy. Under the budget rules, the bill would have forced large cuts in education, health care, and environmental protection. It would have prevented us from extending the life of the Social Security and Medicare trust funds, and from adding a much-needed prescription drug benefit to Medicare.

We were going to have a surplus this year of about $100 billion, but the proposed GOP tax cut would cost nearly $1 trillion over a decade. Republicans' justification for it was based on projected surpluses. On this issue I was far more conservative than they were. If the projections were wrong, the deficits would return, and, with them, higher interest rates and slower growth. Over the previous five years, Congressional Budget Office estimates had been off by an average of 13 percent a year, though our administration's had been closer to the mark. It was an irresponsible risk. I asked the Republicans to work with the White House and the Democrats in the same spirit that had produced the bipartisan welfare reform bill in 1996 and the Balanced Budget Act in 1997.

On September 24, Hillary and I hosted an event in the Old Executive Office Building to celebrate the success of bipartisan efforts to increase the adoption of children out of the foster-care system. They had increased almost 30 percent in the two years since our legislation had passed. I paid tribute to Hillary, who had been working on the issue for more than twenty years, and to perhaps the most ardent supporter of the reforms in the House, Tom DeLay, himself an adoptive parent.

I would have liked a few more moments like that, but with this one exception, DeLay didn't believe in consorting with the enemy.

Partisanship returned in early October, when the Senate rejected, on a party-line vote, my nomination of Judge Ronnie White to a federal district judgeship. White was the first African-American man to serve on the Missouri Supreme Court and was a highly regarded judge. He was defeated after Missouri's conservative senator John Ashcroft, who was in a tough fight for reelection against Governor Mel Carnahan, grossly distorted White's record on the death penalty. White had voted to uphold 70 percent of the death penalty cases that had come before him.

On more than half of those he had voted to reverse, he was part of a unanimous state supreme court ruling. Ashcroft got his Republican colleagues to go along with the smear because he thought it would help him and hurt White's supporter Governor Carnahan with pro–death penalty voters in Missouri.

Ashcroft wasn't alone in completely politicizing the confirmation process. By this time, Senator Jesse Helms had refused for years to allow the Senate to vote on a black judge for the Fourth Circuit Court of Appeals, even though there had never been an African-American on the court. And the Republicans wondered why African-Americans wouldn't vote for them.

Our partisan differences extended even to the nuclear test ban treaty, which had been supported by every Republican and Democrat President since Eisenhower. The Joint Chiefs were for it, and our nuclear experts said tests weren't necessary to check the reliability of our weapons. But we didn't have the votes of two-thirds of the senators necessary to ratify the treaty, and Trent Lott tried to get me to promise not to raise it for the rest of my term. I couldn't figure out whether the Senate Republicans had really moved that far to the right of their own party's traditional position or just didn't want to give me another victory. Regardless, their refusal to ratify the test ban treaty weakened America's ability to argue that other nations shouldn't develop or test nuclear weapons.

I continued doing political events for Al Gore and the Democrats, including two with gay activists who were strongly supportive of both Al and me because of the substantial number of openly gay and lesbian citizens serving in the administration, and because of our strong support of the Employment Nondiscrimination Act and the hate crimes bill, which made crimes committed against people because of their race, disability, or sexual orientation a federal offense. I also went to New York whenever I could to support Hillary. Her likely opponent was New York mayor Rudy Giuliani, who was a combative, controversial figure but was much less conservative than the national Republicans. I had had a cordial relationship with him, largely because of our shared support for the COPS program and gun safety measures.

George W. Bush seemed well on his way to winning the Republican nomination, as several of his challengers dropped out, leaving only Senator John McCain with any chance of stopping him. I had been impressed with Bush's campaign since I first saw him articulate his "compassionate conservative" theme in a farm setting in Iowa. I thought it was a brilliant formulation, virtually the only argument he could make to swing voters against an administration with approval ratings in the 65 percent range. He couldn't dispute the fact that we had 19 million new jobs, the economy was still growing, and crime was down for the seventh year in a row. Instead, his compassionate conservative message to the swing voters was this: "I'll give you the same good conditions you have now, with a smaller government and a bigger tax cut. Wouldn't you like that?" On most issues, Bush was in line with the conservative congressional Republicans, though he had criticized their budget for being harsh to the poor because it raised taxes for low-income Americans by cutting back on the Earned Income Tax Credit, while reducing taxes on the wealthiest Americans.

Although Bush was a formidable politician, I still thought Al Gore would win, despite the fact that only two previous vice presidents, Martin Van Buren and George

H. W. Bush, had been elected directly from the vice presidency, because the country was in good shape and our administration had strong support. All vice presidents who run for President have two problems: most people don't know what they've done and don't give them credit for the accomplishments of the administration, and they tend to get typecast as number two men. I had done everything I could to help Al avoid those problems by giving him many high-profile assignments and making sure he received public recognition for his invaluable contribution to our successes. Yet even though he was indisputably the most active and influential vice president in history, there was still a gap between perception and reality.

The biggest challenge Al faced was how to show independence while still getting the benefit of our record. He had already said he disagreed with my personal misconduct but was proud of what we had accomplished for the American people. Now I thought he should say that no matter who became the next President, change was inevitable; the question for the voters was whether we would keep changing in the right way or make a U-turn to the failed policies of the past. Governor Bush was clearly advocating a return to trickle-down economics. We had tried it that way for twelve years and our way for seven. Our way worked better, and we had the evidence to prove it.

The campaign gave Al the chance to remind voters that I was leaving, but that the Republicans who had pursued impeachment and supported Starr were staying. America needed a President to stand up to them so that they couldn't abuse their power like that again, or succeed in implementing the harsh policies I had stopped in the budget battles, beginning with the government shutdown.

There was ample evidence, less than a year old, that if the voters saw the election as a choice for the future and were reminded of what the Republicans had done, the advantage would shift markedly to the Democrats.

When a few people in the press began pushing the theory that I could cost Al the election, I had a funny telephone conversation with him about it. I said I was interested only in his winning, and if I thought it would help I would stand on the doorstep of the **Washington Post**'s headquarters and let him lash me with a bullwhip. He deadpanned, "Maybe we ought to poll that." I laughed and said, "Let's see whether it works better with my shirt on or off."

On October 12, Pakistan's prime minister Nawaz Sharif was overthrown in a military coup headed by General Musharraf, who had led the Pakistani armed forces over the Line of Control in Kashmir. I was concerned about the loss of democracy, and urged the restoration of civilian rule as soon as possible. Musharraf's ascendancy had one immediate consequence: the program to send Pakistani commandos into Afghanistan to catch or kill Osama bin Laden was canceled.

In mid-month, Ken Starr announced he was stepping down. Judge Sentelle's panel replaced him with Robert Ray, who was on Starr's staff and before that had been on the staff of Donald Smaltz during the failed attempt to convict Mike Espy. Near the end of my term, Ray wanted his pound of flesh, too: a written statement admitting that I had given false testimony in my deposition, and an agreement to accept a temporary suspension of my law license in return for Ray's shutting down the independent counsel's investigation. I doubted that he would actually indict me, given the fact that a bipartisan panel of prosecutors had testified at the impeachment proceedings that no responsible prosecutor would do so. But I was ready to get on with my life and didn't want to complicate Hillary's new life in politics. However, I couldn't agree to intentionally giving false testimony because I didn't believe I had. After carefully rereading my deposition and finding a couple of instances in which I gave answers that were not accurate, I gave Ray a statement that said that though I had tried to testify lawfully, some of my responses were false. He accepted the statement. After almost six years and $70 million in tax money, Whitewater was over.

Not everyone wanted a pound of flesh. In the middle of the month, I invited my high school classmates to the White House for our thirty-fifth high school reunion—as I had done five years earlier, for our thirtieth. I had loved my high school years and always enjoyed seeing my classmates. On this occasion several of them told me that their lives had gotten better over the last seven years. The son of one of them said that he thought I had been a good president, but "the most proud I ever was of you was when you stood up to that impeachment thing." I heard that often from people who'd felt helpless in the face of their own mistakes and misfortunes; somehow the fact that I had just kept going struck a chord with them, because that's what they had had to do.

At the end of the month, a Senate filibuster killed campaign finance reform again; we marked the fifth anniversary of AmeriCorps, in which 150,000 Americans had now served; Hillary and I held a White House Conference on Philanthropy in the hope of increasing the amount and impact of charitable giving; and we celebrated her birthday with a "Broadway for Hillary" event reminiscent of what Broadway stars had done for me back in 1992.

I began November by going to Oslo, where the negotiations between the Israelis and Palestinians had begun, to observe the fourth anniversary of Yitzhak Rabin's assassination, honor his memory, and join with the parties in rededicating ourselves to the peace process. Norwegian prime minister Kjell Bondevik had decided that an Oslo event might move the process forward. Our ambassador, David Hermelin, an irrepressible man of Norwegian-Jewish descent, tried to do his part by serving kosher hot dogs to both Barak and Arafat. Shimon Peres and Leah Rabin were there, too. The event had the desired effect, though I was convinced that both Barak and Arafat already wanted to complete the peace process and would do so in 2000.

Around this time several members of the press began to ask me about my legacy. Would I be known for bringing prosperity? For being a peacemaker? I tried to formulate an answer that captured not only concrete achievements but also the sense of possibility and community I wanted America to embody. The truth is, though, I didn't have time to think about such things. I wanted to press ahead until the last day. The legacy would take care of itself, probably long after I was dead.

On November 4, I began another New Markets tour, this time to Newark, Hartford, and Hermitage, Arkansas, the little town I had helped get living facilities for its migrant tomato workers in the late seventies. The tour ended in Chicago with Jesse Jackson and Speaker Hastert, who had decided to support the initiative. Jesse was looking resplendent in a fine pin-striped suit, and I kidded him about dressing up "like a Republican today" for the

Speaker. I was encouraged by Hastert's support and confident we would pass legislation in the coming year.

In the second week of the month, I joined Al From for the first online presidential town hall meeting. Since I had been President, the number of Web sites had grown from 50 sites to 9 million, and new pages were being added at a rate of 100,000 per hour. The voice recognition software that converted my responses to type is routine today but was novel then. Two people asked me what I was going to do after I left the White House. I hadn't figured it all out yet, but I had begun to make plans for my presidential library.

I had thought a lot about the library and its exhibits on my years as President. Each President has to raise all the funds to build his library, plus an endowment to maintain the facility. The National Archives then provides the staff to organize and care for its contents. I had pored over the work of several architects and had visited many of the presidential libraries. The overwhelming majority of people who visit them come to see the exhibits, but the building has to be built in a way that preserves the records. I wanted the exhibit space to be open, beautiful, and full of light, and I wanted the material presented in a way that demonstrated America's movement into the twenty-first century.

I chose Jim Polshek and his firm as my architects, largely because of his design for the Rose Center for Earth and Space in New York, a huge glass-and-steel structure with a massive globe inside. I asked Ralph Applebaum to do the exhibits, because I thought his work on the Holocaust Museum in Washington was the best I had ever seen. I had already begun working with both of them. Before it was over, Polshek would say I was the worst client he had ever had: if he came to see me after a six-month hiatus with only a minor change in the drawings, I would notice and ask him about it.

I wanted to situate the library in Little Rock because I felt I owed it to my native state and because I thought the library should be in the heartland of America where people who didn't travel to Washington or New York would have direct access to it. The city of Little Rock, on the initiative of Mayor Jim Dailey and city board member Dr. Dean Kumpuris, had offered twenty-seven acres of land along the Arkansas River in the old section of town, which was being revitalized and was not far from the Old State Capitol, the scene of so many important events in my life.

Beyond the library, I knew that I wanted to write a book about my life and the presidency and that I would have to work hard for three or four years to pay my legal bills, buy our home—two homes, if Hillary won the Senate race—and put aside some money for her and Chelsea. Then I wanted to devote the rest of my life to public service. Jimmy Carter had made a real difference in his post-presidential years, and I thought I could, too.

In mid-month, on the day I left for a ten-day trip to Turkey, Greece, Italy, Bulgaria, and Kosovo, I hailed Kofi Annan's announcement that President Glafcos Clerides of Cyprus and Turkish Cypriot leader Rauf Denktash would begin "proximity talks" in New York in early December. Cyprus had received its independence from the UK in 1960. In 1974, the president of Cyprus, Archbishop Makarios, was deposed in a coup orchestrated by the Greek military regime. In response, the Turkish military sent troops to the island to protect the Turkish Cypriots, dividing the country and creating a de facto Turkish enclave of independence in the north. Many Greeks in the north of Cyprus left their homes and moved south. The island had been divided ever since, and tensions had remained high between Turkey and Greece. Greece wanted to end the Turkish military presence in Cyprus and find a resolution that would at least allow the Greeks the possibility of returning to the north. I had tried for years to solve the problem and hoped the secretary-general's effort would succeed. It did not, and I would leave office disappointed that Cyprus remained an obstacle to Greek-Turkish reconciliation and to Turkey's being fully embraced by Europe.

We also finally reached agreement with the Republican leadership on three of my important budget priorities: funding the 100,000 new teachers, doubling the number of children in after-school programs, and, at long last, paying our back dues to the United Nations. Somehow, Madeleine Albright and Dick Holbrooke had worked it out with Jesse Helms and the other UN skeptics. It took Dick longer than making peace in Bosnia, but I'm not sure anyone else could have done it.

Hillary, Chelsea, and I arrived in Turkey for a five-day visit, an unusually long stay. I wanted to support the Turks in the aftermath of two devastating earthquakes, and to encourage them to continue to work with the United States and Europe. Turkey was a NATO ally and was hoping to be admitted to the European Union, a development I had been strongly supporting for years. It was one of a handful of countries whose future course would have a large impact on the twenty-first–century world. If it could resolve the Cyprus problem with Greece, reach an accommodation with its restive and sometimes repressed Kurdish minority, and maintain its identity as a secular Muslim democracy, Turkey could be the West's gateway to a new Middle East. If peace in the Middle East fell victim to a rising tide of Islamic extremism, a stable, democratic Turkey could be a bulwark against its spread into Europe.

I was glad to see President Demirel again. He was a large-minded man who wanted Turkey to be a bridge between East and West. I made my pitch for that vision to Prime Minister Bülent Ecevit and to the Turkish Grand National Assembly, urging them to reject isolationism and nationalism by resolving their problems with the Kurds and Greece and moving toward EU membership.

The next day I made the same arguments to American and Turkish business leaders in Istanbul, after a stop at a tent city near Izmit to meet with earthquake victims. We visited with some of the families who had lost everything, and I thanked all the nations that had helped the victims, including Greece. Not long after the Turkish quakes, Greece had an earthquake of its own, and the Turks had returned the favor. If earthquakes could bring them together, they should be able to work together when the ground stopped moving.

My whole trip became defined for the Turks by the visit to the quake victims. When I held a young child in my arms, he reached up and grabbed my nose, just as Chelsea used to do when she was a toddler. A photographer got a shot of it, and the picture was in all the Turkish papers the next day. One of them carried it with the headline, "He's a Turk!"

After my family visited the ruins of Ephesus, including one of the largest libraries in the Roman world and an open amphitheater where St. Paul had preached, I participated in a meeting of the fifty-four–nation Organization for Security and Cooperation in Europe, which had been organized in 1973 to advance democracy, human rights, and the rule of law. We were there to support the Stability Pact for the Balkans and a resolution of the continuing crisis in Chechnya that would end the terrorism against Russia and the excessive use of force against noncombatant Chechens. I also signed an agreement with the leaders of Kazakhstan, Turkmenistan, Azerbaijan, and Georgia committing the United States to support the development of two pipelines that would carry oil from the Caspian Sea to the West without going through Iran. Depending on what kind of future Iran chose to pursue, the pipeline agreement could prove to be of enormous consequence to the future stability of both the producing and consuming countries.

I was fascinated by Istanbul and its rich history as the capital of both the Ottoman Empire and the Roman Empire in the East. In another attempt to promote reconciliation, I visited the ecumenical patriarch of all the Orthodox churches, Bartholomew of Constantinople, and asked the Turks to reopen the Orthodox monastery in Istanbul. The patriarch gave me a beautiful scroll inscribed with what he knew was one of my favorite scriptural passages, from the eleventh chapter of Hebrews. It begins, "Faith is the assurance of things hoped for, the conviction of things not seen."

While I was in Turkey, the White House and Congress reached a budget agreement that, in addition to my education initiatives, provided funding for more police, the Lands Legacy initiative, our commitments under the Wye River accord, and the new debt-relief initiative for the poorest countries. The Republicans also agreed to give up their most damaging anti-environmental riders to the appropriation bills.

There was also good news in Northern Ireland, where

George Mitchell had reached an agreement with the parties to proceed simultaneously with a new government and decommissioning with the support of Tony Blair and Bertie Ahern. Bertie was with me in Turkey when we heard the news.

In Athens, after a thrilling early-morning tour of the Acropolis with Chelsea, and a public expression of regret over America's support of the repressive anti-democratic regime that took control of Greece in 1967, I reaffirmed my commitment to a fair resolution to the Cyprus problem as a condition of Turkey's EU membership and thanked Prime Minister Costas Simitis for staying with the allies in Kosovo. Because the Greeks and Serbs shared the Orthodox faith, it had been difficult for him. I left the meeting encouraged by the prime minister's openness to reconciliation with Turkey and its entry into the EU if the Cyprus problem could be resolved, in part because the two countries' foreign ministers, George Papandreou and Ismael Cem, were young, forward-looking leaders who were working together for a common future—the only course that made sense.

From Greece, I flew to Florence, where Prime Minister D'Alema hosted another of our Third Way conferences. This one had a distinctly Italian flavor, as Andrea Bocelli sang at the dinner and Academy Award–winning actor Roberto Benigni kept us in stitches. He and D'Alema were a well-matched pair—two lean, intense, passionate men who were always finding something to laugh about. When I met Benigni, he said, "I love you!" and jumped into my arms. I was thinking that maybe I should run for office in Italy; I had always loved it there.

This was by far our most substantive Third Way meeting. Tony Blair, EU president Romano Prodi, Gerhard

Schroeder, Henrique Cardoso, and French prime minister Lionel Jospin were all there as we worked to articulate a progressive consensus for domestic and foreign policies in the twenty-first century, and for reforms in the international financial system to minimize financial crises and intensify our efforts to spread the benefits and reduce the burdens of globalization.

On the twenty-second, Chelsea and I flew to Bulgaria, which I was the first American President to visit. In a speech to more than thirty thousand people in the shadow of the brightly lit Alexander Nevsky Cathedral, I pledged America's support for their hard-won freedom, their economic aspirations, and their partnership with NATO.

My last stop before going home for Thanksgiving was in Kosovo, where Madeleine Albright, Wes Clark, and I got a roaring welcome. I spoke to a group of citizens who kept interrupting my speech by shouting my name. I hated to break the mood, but I tried to get them to listen to my plea not to take out resentment over past wrongs by retaliating against the Serb minority, a point I made privately to the leaders of various factions in Kosovar politics. Later that day I went to Camp Bondsteel to thank the troops and share an early Thanksgiving dinner with them. They were clearly proud of what they had done, but Chelsea was a bigger hit with the young soldiers than I was.

While we were on the trip, I sent Charlene Barshefsky and Gene Sperling to China to try to close the deal for China's entry into the WTO. The agreement had to be good enough to enable us to pass legislation establishing permanent normal trade relations with China. Gene's presence would ensure that the Chinese knew that I was supporting the negotiations. The negotiations were difficult until the very end, when we got the protections against dumping and import surges and access to the automobile market that earned the support of Michigan Democratic congressman Sandy Levin. His support ensured congressional approval of permanent normal trade relations and thus China's entry into the WTO. Gene and Charlene had done a great job.

Shortly after Thanksgiving, David Trimble's Ulster Unionist Party approved the new peace agreement, and the new Northern Ireland government was formed with David Trimble as first minister and Seamus Mallon from John Hume's SDLP as deputy first minister. Sinn Fein's Martin McGuinness was named education minister. It would have been unthinkable not long before.

In December, when the members of the World Trade Organization met in Seattle, violent protests from anti-globalization forces rocked the downtown area. Most of the demonstrators were peaceful, however, and had legitimate grievances, as I told the convention delegates. The process of interdependence probably could not be reversed, but the WTO would have to be more open, and more sensitive to trade and environmental issues, and the wealthy countries that benefited from globalization would have to do more to bring its benefits to the other half of the world that was still living on less than two dollars a day. After Seattle, there would be more demonstrations at international financial meetings. I was convinced they would continue until we addressed the concerns of those who felt left out and left behind.

Early in December, I was able to announce that after seven years our economy had now created more than twenty million new jobs, 80 percent of them in job categories paying above our median wage, with the lowest

African-American and Hispanic unemployment rates ever recorded and the lowest female unemployment rate since 1953, when a far smaller percentage of women were in the workforce.

On December 6, I had a special visitor: eleven-year-old Fred Sanger, from St. Louis. Fred and his parents came to see me with representatives of the Make-a-Wish foundation, which helps seriously ill children fulfill their wishes. Fred had heart problems that required him to stay indoors a lot. He watched the news and knew a surprising amount about my work. We had a good conversation and stayed in touch for some time afterward. During my eight years in office, the Make-a-Wish people brought forty-seven children to see me. They always brightened my day and reminded me why I had wanted to be President.

In the second week of the month, after a telephone conversation with President Assad, I announced that, within a week, Israel and Syria would resume their negotiations in Washington at a site to be determined, with the goal of reaching an agreement as soon as possible.

On the ninth, I went back to Worcester, Massachusetts, the city that had welcomed me in the dark days of August 1998, for the funeral of six firefighters who had been killed in action. The heartbreaking tragedy had galvanized the community and all of America's firefighters; hundreds of them from across the country and several from overseas filled the city's convention center, a poignant reminder that the mortality rate of firemen is even higher than that of police officers.

A week later at the FDR Memorial, I signed the legislation that extended Medicare and Medicaid benefits to disabled people in the workforce. It was the most important piece of legislation for the disabled community since the passage of the Americans with Disabilities Act, allowing otherwise uninsurable people with AIDS, muscular dystrophy, Parkinson's, diabetes, or crippling injuries to "buy into" the Medicare program. The law would change the quality of life for countless people who would now be able to earn an income and enhance the quality of their lives. It was a tribute to the hard work of disability activists, especially my friend Justin Dart, a wheelchair-bound Wyoming Republican who was never without his cowboy hat and boots.

All during the Christmas season we were looking forward to New Year's Eve and the new millennium. For the first time in many years, our family would miss Renaissance Weekend to stay in Washington for the millennium celebration. It was all privately funded; my friend Terry McAuliffe raised several million dollars so that we could offer citizens a chance to enjoy the festivities, which included two days of public family activities at the Smithsonian Institution, and on the thirty-first a children's celebration in the afternoon and a concert on the Mall produced by Quincy Jones and George Stevens, with a big fireworks display. We also had a large dinner at the White House, filled with fascinating people from literary, artistic, musical, academic, military, and civic circles, and a long dance after the fireworks on the Mall.

It was a wonderful evening, but I was nervous the entire time. Our security team had been on high alert for weeks due to numerous intelligence reports that the United States would be hit with several terrorist attacks. Particularly since the embassy bombings in 1998, I had been focused intently on bin Laden and his al Qaeda supporters. We had rolled up a score of al Qaeda cells, captured terrorist operatives, broken up plots against us, and continued to urge Pakistan and Saudi Arabia to press Afghanistan to give bin Laden up. Now, with this new warning, Sandy Berger convened all of my top national security staff in the White House virtually every day for a month.

One man with bomb-making materials was arrested crossing the Canadian border in Washington State; he had planned to bomb the Los Angeles airport. Two terrorist cells in the Northeast and one in Canada were discovered and broken up. Planned attacks in Jordan were thwarted. The millennium came to America with lots of celebration and no terror, a tribute to the hard work of thousands of people, and perhaps to a bit of luck as well. Regardless, as the new year, the new century, and the new millennium began, I was filled with joy and gratitude. Our country was in excellent shape, and we were moving into the new era in good condition.

FIFTY-FOUR

Hillary and I began the first day of the new century and the last year of my presidency with a joint radio address to the American people, which was also televised live. We had stayed up with the revelers at the White House until about two-thirty in the morning, and we were tired but eager to mark this day. A remarkable worldwide celebration had taken place the night before: billions of people had watched on television as midnight broke first in Asia, then in Europe, then in Africa, South America, and finally North America. The United States was entering the new century of global interdependence with a unique combination of economic success, social solidarity, and national self-confidence, and with our openness, dynamism, and democratic values being celebrated the world over. Hillary and I said that we Americans had to make the most of this opportunity to keep making our own country better and to spread the benefits and share the burdens of the twenty-first–century world. That's what I intended to spend my last year doing.

Defying historical trends, the seventh year of my presidency had been full of achievement because we had continued to work on the public's business through the impeachment process and afterward, following the agenda laid out in the State of the Union address and dealing with problems and opportunities as they arose. The traditional winding down in the last half of a President's second term had not occurred. I was determined not to let it happen this year, either.

The new year brought the loss of one of my old partners, as Boris Yeltsin resigned and was succeeded by Vladimir Putin. Yeltsin had never fully recovered his strength and stamina after his heart surgery, and he believed Putin was ready to succeed him and able to put in the long hours the job required. Boris also knew that giving the Russian people the chance to see Putin perform would increase the chances that he would win the next election. It was both a wise and a shrewd move, but I was going to miss Yeltsin. For all his physical problems and occasional unpredictability, he had been a courageous and visionary leader. We trusted each other and had accomplished a lot together. On the day he resigned we talked on the phone for about twenty minutes, and I could tell he was comfortable with his decision. He left office as he had lived and governed, in his own unique way.

On January 3, I went to Shepherdstown, West Virginia, to open peace talks between Syria and Israel. Ehud Barak had pressed me hard to hold the talks early in the year. He was growing impatient over the peace process with Arafat, and was unsure whether their differences over Jerusalem could be resolved. By contrast, he had told me months before that he was prepared to give the Golan Heights back to Syria as long as Israel's concerns could be satisfied about its early-warning station on the Golan and its dependence on Lake Tiberias, otherwise known as the Sea of Galilee, for one-third of its water supply.

The Sea of Galilee is a unique body of water: the bottom part is salt water fed by underground springs, while the top layer is fresh water. Because fresh water is lighter, care had to be taken not to draw down the lake too much in any given year lest the covering layer of fresh water becomes too light to hold the salt water down. If the fresh water were to fall below a certain point, the salt water could rush upward and mix with it, taking out a water supply that is essential for Israel.

Before he was killed, Yitzhak Rabin had given me a commitment to withdraw from the Golan to the June 4, 1967, borders as long as Israel's concerns were satisfied. The commitment was given on the condition that I keep it "in my pocket" until it could be formally presented to Syria in the context of a complete solution. After Yitzhak's death, Shimon Peres reaffirmed the pocket commitment, and on this basis we had sponsored talks between the Syrians and the Israelis in 1996 at Wye River. Peres wanted me to sign a security treaty with Israel if it gave up the Golan, an idea that was suggested to me later by Netanyahu and would be advanced again by Barak. I had told them I was willing to do it.

Dennis Ross and our team had been making progress until Bibi Netanyahu defeated Peres in the election amid a rash of terrorist activity. Then the Syrian negotiations faltered. Now Barak wanted to start them up again, though as yet he was unwilling to reaffirm the precise words of the Rabin pocket commitment.

Barak had to contend with a very different Israeli electorate from the one Rabin had led. There were many more immigrants, and the Russians in particular were opposed to giving up the Golan. Natan Sharansky, who had become a hero in the West during his long imprisonment in the Soviet Union and had accompanied Netanyahu to Wye in 1998, explained the Russian Jews' attitude to me. He said they had come from the world's largest country to one of its smallest ones, and didn't believe in making Israel even smaller by giving up the Golan or the West Bank. They also considered Syria to be no threat to Israel. They weren't at peace but were not at war either. If Syria attacked Israel, the Israelis could win easily. Why give up the Golan?

While Barak didn't agree with this view, he had to contend with it. Nevertheless, he wanted to make peace with Syria, was confident the issues could be resolved, and wanted me to convene negotiations as soon as possible. By January, I had been working for more than three months with the Syrian foreign minister, Farouk al-Shara, and by telephone with President Assad to set the stage for the talks. Assad was not in good health and wanted to regain the Golan before he died, but he had to be careful. He wanted his son Bashar to succeed him, and apart from his own conviction that Syria should get back all the land it had occupied before June 4, 1967, he had to make an agreement that would not be subject to attack from forces within Syria whose support his son would need.

Assad's frailty and a stroke suffered by Foreign Minister Shara in the fall of 1999 heightened Barak's sense of urgency. At his request, I sent Assad a letter saying I thought Barak was willing to make a deal if we could resolve the definition of the border, the control of water, and the early-warning post, and that if they did reach agreement, the United States would be prepared to establish bilateral relations with Syria, a move Barak had urged. That was a big step for us, given Syria's past support of terrorism. Of course, Assad would have to stop supporting terrorism in order to achieve normal relations with the U.S., but if he had the Golan back, the incentive to support the Hezbollah terrorists who attacked Israel from Lebanon would evaporate.

Barak wanted peace with Lebanon, too, because he had committed to withdrawing Israeli forces from the country by the end of the year, and a peace agreement would make Israel safer from Hezbollah attacks along the border, and would not make it appear that Israel had withdrawn because of the attacks. As he well knew, no agreement with Lebanon would come without Syria's consent and involvement.

Assad replied a month later in a letter that appeared to back away from his previous position, perhaps because of the uncertainties in Syria that his and Shara's health problems had caused. However, a few weeks after that, when Madeleine Albright and Dennis Ross went to see Assad and Shara, who seemed completely recovered, Assad told them that he wanted to resume negotiations and was ready to make peace because he believed Barak was serious. He even agreed to have Shara negotiate, something he had not done before, as long as Barak would personally handle the Israeli side.

Barak accepted eagerly and wanted to begin immediately. I explained that we could not do it during the Christmas holidays, and he agreed to our timetable: preliminary talks in Washington in mid-December, to be resumed early in the New Year with my participation and to continue uninterrupted until agreement was reached. The Washington talks got off to a bit of a rocky start with an aggressive public statement by Shara. Nevertheless, in the private talks, when Shara suggested that we should start where the talks had left off in 1996, with Rabin's pocket commitment of the June 4 line provided Israel's needs were met, Barak responded that while he had made no commitment on territory, "we do not erase history." The two men then agreed that I could decide the order in which the issues—including borders, security, water, and peace—would be discussed. Barak wanted the negotiations to continue uninterrupted; that would require the Syrians to work through the end of Ramadan on January 7 and not go home to celebrate the traditional feast of Eid Al Fitr at the end of the fasting period. Shara agreed, and the two sides went home to prepare.

Although Barak had pushed hard for the early negotiations, he soon began to worry about the political consequences of giving up the Golan without having prepared the Israeli public for it. He wanted some cover: the resumption of the Lebanon track to be conducted by the Syrians in consultation with the Lebanese; the announcement by at least one Arab state of an upgrade of relations with Israel; clear security benefits from the United States; and a free-trade zone on the Golan. I agreed to support all these requests and took things a step further, calling Assad on December 19 and asking him to resume the Lebanese track at the same time as the Syrian talks and to help retrieve the remains of three Israelis still listed as missing in action from the Lebanon war almost twenty years earlier. Assad agreed to the second request and we sent a forensics team to Syria, but unfortunately the remains weren't where the Israelis thought they would be. On the first issue, Assad hedged, saying the Lebanese talks should resume once some headway had been made on the Syrian track.

Shepherdstown is a rural community a little more than an hour's drive from Washington; Barak had insisted on an isolated setting to minimize leaks, and the Syrians didn't want to go to Camp David or Wye River because other high-profile Middle East negotiations had occurred there. That was fine with me; the conference facilities in

Shepherdstown were comfortable, and I could get there from the White House in about twenty minutes by helicopter.

It quickly became apparent that the two sides were not that far apart on the issues. Syria wanted all of the Golan back but was willing to leave the Israelis a small strip of land, 10 meters (33 feet) wide, along the border of the lake; Israel wanted a wider strip of land. Syria wanted Israel to withdraw within eighteen months; Barak wanted three years. Israel wanted to stay in the early-warning station; Syria wanted it manned by personnel from the UN or perhaps from the U.S. Israel wanted guarantees on the quality and quantity of water flowing from the Golan into the lake; Syria agreed as long as it got the same guarantees on its water flow from Turkey. Israel wanted full diplomatic relations as soon as withdrawal began; Syria wanted something less until the withdrawal was complete.

The Syrians came to Shepherdstown in a positive and flexible frame of mind, eager to make an agreement. By contrast, Barak, who had pushed hard for the talks, decided, apparently on the basis of polling data, that he needed to slow-walk the process for a few days in order to convince the Israeli public that he was being a tough negotiator. He wanted me to use my good relationship with Shara and Assad to keep the Syrians happy while he said as little as possible during his self-imposed waiting period.

I was, to put it mildly, disappointed. If Barak had dealt with the Syrians before or if he had given us some advance notice, it might have been manageable. Perhaps, as a democratically elected leader, he had to pay more attention to public opinion than Assad did, but Assad had his own political problems, and had overcome his notorious aversion to high-level involvement with the Israelis because he trusted me and had believed Barak's assurances.

Barak had not been in politics long, and I thought he had gotten some very bad advice. In foreign affairs, polls are often useless; people hire leaders to win for them, and it's the results that matter. Many of my most important foreign policy decisions had not been popular at first. If Barak made real peace with Syria, it would lift his standing in Israel and across the world, and increase the chances of success with the Palestinians. If he failed, a few days of good poll numbers would vanish in the wind. As hard as I tried, I couldn't change Barak's mind. He wanted me to help keep Shara on board while he waited, and to do it in the isolated setting of Shepherdstown, where there were few distractions from the business at hand.

Madeleine Albright and Dennis Ross tried to think of creative ways to at least clarify Barak's commitment to the Rabin pocket commitment, including opening a back channel between Madeleine and Butheina Shaban, the only woman in the Syrian delegation. Butheina was an articulate, impressive woman who had always served as Assad's interpreter when we met. She had been with Assad for years, and I was sure she was in Shepherdstown to guarantee the president an unvarnished version of what was happening.

On Friday, the fifth day, we presented a draft peace agreement with the two sides' differences in brackets. The Syrians responded positively on Saturday night, and we began meetings on border and security issues. Again, the Syrians showed flexibility on both matters, saying they would accept an adjustment of the strip of land bordering Galilee to as much as 50 meters (164 feet), provided that

Israel accepted the June 4 line as the basis of discussion. There was some practical validity to this; apparently the lake had shrunk in size in the last thirty years. I was encouraged, but it quickly became apparent that Barak still had not authorized anyone on his team to accept June 4, no matter what the Syrians offered.

On Sunday, at a lunch for Ehud and Nava Barak at Madeleine Albright's farm, Madeleine and Dennis made a last pitch to Barak. Syria had shown flexibility on what Israel wanted, providing its needs were met; Israel had not responded in kind. What would it take? Barak said he wanted to resume the Lebanese negotiations. And if not, he wanted to break for several days and come back.

Shara was in no mood to hear this. He said that Shepherdstown was a failure, that Barak was not sincere, and that he would have to say as much to President Assad. At the last dinner, I tried again to get Barak to say something positive that Shara could take back to Syria. He declined, instead telling me privately that I could call Assad after we left Shepherdstown and say he would accept the June 4 line once the Lebanese negotiations resumed or were about to start. That meant Shara would go home empty-handed from negotiations he had been led to believe would be decisive, so much so that the Syrians had been willing to stay through the end of Ramadan and the Eid.

To make matters worse, the latest bracketed text of our treaty leaked in the Israeli press, showing the concessions that Syria had offered without getting anything in return. Shara was subjected to intense criticism at home. It was understandably embarrassing to him, and to Assad. Even authoritarian governments are not immune to popular opinion and powerful interest groups.

When I called Assad with Barak's offer to affirm the Rabin commitment and demarcate the border on the basis of it as long as the Lebanese negotiations also started, he listened without comment. A few days later, Shara called Madeleine Albright and rejected Barak's offer, saying the Syrians would open negotiations on Lebanon only after the border demarcation was agreed upon. They had been burned once by being flexible and forthcoming, and they weren't about to make the same mistake again.

For the time being we were stumped, but I thought we should keep trying. Barak still seemed to want the Syrian peace, and it was true that the Israeli public had not been prepared for the compromises that peace required. It was also still in Syria's interest to make peace, and soon. Assad was in ill health and had to pave the way for his son's succession. Meanwhile, there was more than enough still to do on the Palestinian track. I asked Sandy, Madeleine, and Dennis to figure out what we should do next, and turned my attention to other things.

On January 10, after a White House celebration with Muslims marking the end of Ramadan, Hillary and I went to the U.S. Naval Academy Chapel in Annapolis, Maryland, for the funeral of former chief of naval operations Bud Zumwalt, who had become our friend through Renaissance Weekend. After I took office, Bud had worked with us to provide aid to the families of servicemen who, like his late son, had become ill as a result of their exposure to Agent Orange during the Vietnam War. He had also lobbied the Senate to ratify the Chemical Weapons Convention. His personal support to our family during and after the House impeachment proceedings was a gift of kindness we would never forget. As I was dressing for the funeral, one of my valets, Lito Bautista, a Filipino-

American who had been in the navy for thirty years, said he was glad I was going to the service because Bud Zumwalt "was the best we ever had. He was for us."

That night I flew to the Grand Canyon, staying at the El Tovar Hotel in a room with a balcony right on the canyon's edge. Nearly thirty years earlier, I had seen the sun set over the Grand Canyon; now I wanted to watch it rise, lighting the layers of differently colored rocks from the top down. The next morning, after a sunrise just as beautiful as I had hoped it would be, Secretary of the Interior Bruce Babbitt and I designated three new national monuments and expanded a fourth in Arizona and California, including one million acres around the Grand Canyon and a stretch of thousands of small islands and exposed reefs along the California coast.

It was ninety-two years to the day since President Theodore Roosevelt had set aside the Grand Canyon itself as a national monument. Bruce Babbitt, Al Gore, and I had done our best to be faithful to Roosevelt's conservation ethic and to his admonition that we should always be taking what he called "the long look ahead."

On the fifteenth I commemorated Martin Luther King Jr.'s birthday in my Saturday morning radio address by marking the economic and social progress of African-Americans and Hispanics in the last seven years and pointing out how far we had to go: Though minority unemployment and poverty rates were at historically low levels, they were still far above the national average. We had also suffered a recent spate of hate crimes against victims because of their race or ethnicity—James Byrd, a black man dragged from the back of a pickup truck and killed by white racists in Texas; bullets fired at a Jewish school in Los Angeles; a Korean-American student, an

African-American basketball coach, and a Filipino postal worker all killed because of their race.

A few months earlier, at one of Hillary's millennium evenings at the White House, Dr. Eric Lander, director of the Whitehead Institute Center for Genome Research at MIT, and high-tech executive Vinton Cerf, who is known as the "Father of the Internet," discussed how digital chip technology had enabled the human genome project to succeed. The thing I remembered most clearly about the evening was Lander's statement that all human beings are more than 99.9 percent alike genetically. Ever since he said that, I had thought of all the blood that had been shed, all the energy wasted, by people obsessed with keeping us divided over that one-tenth of a percent.

In the radio address, I again asked the Congress to pass the hate-crimes bill, and asked the Senate to confirm a distinguished Chinese-American lawyer, Bill Lann Lee, as the new assistant attorney general for civil rights. The Republican majority had been holding him up; they seemed to have an aversion to many of my non-Caucasian nominees. My main guest that morning was Charlotte Fillmore, a one hundred–year-old former White House employee who decades earlier had had to enter the White House through a special door because of her race. This time we brought Charlotte through the front door to the Oval Office.

In the week leading up to the State of the Union address, I followed my usual custom of highlighting important initiatives that would be in the speech. This time I was incorporating two proposals Hillary and Al Gore were advocating on the campaign trail. I recommended allowing parents of children eligible for health insurance under the CHIP program to purchase insurance for themselves, a plan Al was promoting, and I supported making the first $10,000 of college tuition tax-deductible, an idea that Senator Chuck Schumer was pushing in Congress and Hillary was advocating in her campaign.

If all the parents and children who were income-eligible—about fourteen million—bought into the CHIP program, it would take care of about a third of our uninsured population. If people fifty-five and over were allowed to buy into Medicare as I had recommended, the two programs together would cut the number of uninsured Americans in half. If the tuition tax credit was adopted, along with the college aid expansions I had already signed into law, we could rightly claim to have opened the doors of college to all Americans. The college-enrollment rate had already risen to 67 percent, almost 10 percent higher than when I took office.

In a speech to scientists at California Institute of Technology, I unveiled a proposed increase of nearly $3 billion in research, which included $1 billion for AIDS and other biomedical purposes and $500 million for nanotechnology, and major increases for basic science, space, and clean energy. On the twenty-fourth, Alexis Herman, Donna Shalala, and I asked Congress to help close the 25 percent pay gap between men and women by passing the Paycheck Fairness Act, giving us the funds to clear up the large backlog of employment discrimination cases at the Equal Employment Opportunity Commission, and supporting the Labor Department's efforts to increase female employment in high-wage jobs in which women were underrepresented. For example, in most high-tech occupations, men outnumbered women by more than two to one.

On the day before the speech, I sat down with Jim

Lehrer of PBS's **NewsHour** for the first time since our interview two years earlier, right after the storm over my deposition broke. After we went through the achievements of the administration over the previous seven years, Lehrer asked me if I was worried about what historians were going to write about me. The **New York Times** had just published an editorial saying historians were beginning to say I was a politician with great natural talent and some significant accomplishments who had "missed the greatness that once seemed within his grasp."

He asked me about my reaction to the "what might have been" assessment. I said that it seemed to me that the time most like our own was at the turn of the last century, when we were also moving into a new era of economic and social change, and were being drawn into the world beyond our shores more than ever before. Based on what had happened then, I thought the tests of my service would be: Did we manage the transition of America into the new economy and an era of globalization well or not? Did we make social progress and change the way we approached our problems to fit the times? Were we good stewards of the environment? And what were the forces we stood against? I told him I felt comfortable with the answers to those questions.

Moreover, I had read enough history to know that it is constantly being rewritten. While I was in office, two major biographies of Grant had been published that dramatically revised the conventional assessment of his presidency upward. That sort of thing was going on all the time. Besides, as I told Lehrer, I was more focused on what I could accomplish in my last year than on what the future might think of me.

Beyond the domestic agenda, I told Lehrer that I

wanted to prepare our nation to deal with the biggest security challenges of the twenty-first century. The congressional Republicans' first priority was building a national missile defense system, but I said the main threat was "the likelihood that you'll have terrorists and narco-traffickers and organized criminals cooperating with each other, with smaller and smaller and more difficult to detect weapons of mass destruction and powerful traditional weapons. So we've tried to lay in a framework for dealing with cyberterrorism, bioterrorism, chemical terrorism. . . . Now, this is not in the headlines, but . . . I think the enemies of the nation-state in this interconnected world are likely to be the biggest security threat."

I was thinking about terrorism a great deal then because of the nail-biting two months we'd had leading up to the millennium celebration. The CIA, National Security Agency, FBI, and our entire counterterrorism group had worked hard to thwart several planned attacks in the United States and the Middle East. Now two submarines were in the northern Arabian Sea, ready to fire missiles at any point the CIA determined to be bin Laden's whereabouts. Dick Clarke's counterterrorism group and George Tenet were working hard to find him. I felt we were on top of the situation but still did not have either the offensive or defensive capabilities we needed to combat an enemy adept at finding the opportunities to attack innocent people that an increasingly open world offered.

Before the interview was over, Lehrer asked the question I knew was coming: if, two years ago, I had answered his question and other questions about my conduct differently right at the beginning, did I think that there might have been a different result and that I might not have been impeached? I told him that I didn't know, but that I deeply regretted having misled him and the American people. I still don't have the answer to his question, given the hysterical atmosphere that had engulfed Washington at the time. As I told Lehrer, I had apologized and tried to make amends for my mistakes. That was all I could do.

Then Lehrer asked if I took satisfaction in knowing that if there was a conspiracy to run me out of office, it hadn't worked. I believe that was as close as any journalist ever came in my presence to admitting the existence of the conspiracy they all knew existed but could not bring themselves to acknowledge. I told Jim I had learned the hard way that life always humbles you if you give in to anger or take too much satisfaction in having defeated someone, or think that no matter how bad your own sins are, those of your adversaries are worse. I had a year to go; there was no time to be angry or satisfied.

My last State of the Union address was a joy to deliver. We had more than twenty million new jobs, the lowest unemployment rate and smallest welfare rolls in thirty years, the lowest crime rate in twenty-five years, the lowest poverty rate in twenty years, the smallest federal workforce in forty years, the first back-to-back surpluses in forty-two years, seven years of declining teen pregnancies and a 30 percent increase in adoptions, and 150,000 young people who had served in AmeriCorps. Within a month we would have the longest economic expansion in American history, and by the end of the year we would have three consecutive surpluses for the first time in more than fifty years.

I was concerned that America would become complacent in our prosperity, so I asked our people not to take it for granted, but to take that "long look ahead" to the nation we could build in the twenty-first century. I offered more than sixty initiatives to meet an ambitious set of goals: every child would start school ready to learn and graduate ready to succeed; every family would be able to succeed at home and at work, and no child would be raised in poverty; the challenge of the baby boomers' retirement would be met; all Americans would have access to quality, affordable health care; America would be the safest big country on earth and debt-free for the first time since 1835; prosperity would come to every community; climate change would be reversed; America would lead the world toward shared prosperity and security and to the far frontiers of science and technology; and we would at last become one nation, united in all our diversity.

I did my best to reach out to Republicans and Democrats, recommending a mix of both tax cuts and spending programs to move toward the goals; greater support for faith-based efforts to fight poverty and drug abuse and help teen mothers; a tax break for charitable contributions by low- and moderate-income citizens who couldn't claim one now because they didn't itemize their deductions; tax relief from the so-called marriage penalty and another expansion of the EITC; greater incentives to teach English and civics to new immigrants; and passage of the hate crimes bill and the Employment Non-Discrimination Act. I also thanked the Speaker for his support of the New Markets initiative.

For the last time, I introduced the people sitting with Hillary who represented what we were trying to accomplish: the father of one of the students killed at Columbine, who wanted Congress to close the gun show loophole; a Hispanic father who proudly paid child support and who would benefit from the tax-relief package for working families I had proposed; an air force captain who had rescued a downed pilot in Kosovo, to illustrate the importance of finishing our work in the Balkans; and my friend Hank Aaron, who had spent his years after baseball working to help poor children and bridge the racial divide.

I closed with an appeal for unity, getting a laugh when I reminded Congress that even Republicans and Democrats were genetically 99.9 percent the same. I said, "Modern science has confirmed what ancient faiths have always taught: the most important fact of life is our common humanity."

The speech was criticized by one congressman who said I sounded like Calvin Coolidge in wanting to make America debt-free, and by some conservatives who said I was spending too much money on education, health care, and the environment. Most citizens seemed to be reassured that I was going to work hard in my last year, interested in the new ideas I was advancing, and supportive of my efforts to keep them focused on the future.

The last time America seemed to be sailing on such smooth seas was in the early sixties, with the economy booming, civil rights laws promising a more just future, and Vietnam a distant blip on the screen. Within six years the economy was sagging, there were race riots in the streets, John and Robert Kennedy and Martin Luther King Jr. had been killed, and Vietnam had consumed America, driven President Johnson from office, and ushered in a new era of division in our politics. Good times are to be seized and built upon, not coasted through.

After a stop in Quincy, Illinois, to hit the high points of my agenda, I flew to Davos, Switzerland, to address the World Economic Forum, an increasingly important annual gathering of international political and business leaders. I brought five cabinet members with me to discuss the popular uprising against globalization that we had witnessed in the streets of Seattle during the recent WTO meeting. The multinational corporations and their political supporters had largely been content to create a global economy that served their needs, believing that the growth resulting from trade would create wealth and jobs everywhere.

Trade in well-governed countries had helped lift many people out of poverty, but too many people in poor countries were left out: half the world still lived on less than $2 a day, a billion people lived on less than a dollar a day, and more than a billion people went to bed hungry every night. One in four people had no access to clean water. Some 130 million children never went to school at all, and 10 million children died every year of preventable diseases.

Even in wealthy countries, the constant churning of the economy was always dislocating some people, and the United States wasn't doing enough to get them back in the workforce at the same or higher pay. Finally, the global financial institutions had not been able to head off or mitigate crises in developing countries in a way that minimized damage to working people, and the WTO was perceived as being too captive to wealthy countries and multinational corporations.

In my first two years, when the Democrats were in the majority, I had gotten more money for training displaced workers and signed the NAFTA side agreements on the environment and labor standards. Afterward, the Republican Congress was less sympathetic to such efforts, especially those designed to reduce poverty and create new jobs in poor nations. Now it seemed to me that we had a chance to build a bipartisan consensus on at least three initiatives: the New Markets program, the trade bill for Africa and the Caribbean, and the Millennium Debt Relief effort.

The larger question was whether we could have a global economy without global social and environmental policies and more open governance by the economic decision makers, especially the WTO. I thought the anti-trade, anti-globalization forces were wrong in believing that trade had increased poverty. In fact, trade had lifted more people out of poverty and pulled more nations out of isolation. On the other hand, those who thought all we needed were unregulated flows of more than $1 trillion a day of capital and ever increasing trade were wrong, too.

I said globalization imposed on its beneficiaries the responsibility of sharing its gains and its burdens and empowering more people to participate in it. Essentially, I advocated a Third Way approach to globalization: trade plus a concerted effort to give people and nations the tools and conditions to make the most of it. Finally, I argued that giving people hope through economic growth and social justice was essential to our ability to persuade the twenty-first–century world to walk away from the modern horrors of terrorism and weapons of mass destruction and the old conflicts rooted in racial, religious, and tribal hatreds.

When the speech was over, I couldn't know if I'd succeeded in getting the thousand business leaders there to agree with me, but I felt that they had listened and at least were wrestling with the problems of our global interdependence and their own obligations to create a more unified world. What the movers and shakers of the world needed was a shared vision. When good people with energy act on a shared vision, most of the problems get worked out.

Back home, it was time for my last National Prayer Breakfast. Joe Lieberman, the event's first Jewish speaker, gave a fine talk on the values common to all faiths. I discussed the practical implications of his remarks: if we are admonished not to turn away strangers, to treat others as we would like to be treated, and to love our neighbors as ourselves, "who are our neighbors, and what does it mean to love them?" If we were virtually the same genetically, and our world was so interdependent that I had a cousin in Arkansas who played chess twice a week on the Internet with a man from Australia, we obviously had to broaden our horizons in the years ahead.

The direction of those years, of course, would be shaped by the outcome of this year's election. Al Gore and George W. Bush had both won handily in Iowa, as expected. Then the campaign moved on to New Hampshire, where voters in both parties' primaries delight in upsetting expectations. Al's campaign had gotten off to a rocky start, but when he moved his campaign headquarters to Nashville and began doing informal town hall meetings in New Hampshire, he really started connecting with voters, got better press coverage, and pulled ahead of Senator Bradley. After the State of the Union, in which I featured some of his important accomplishments, he picked up a few more points in the "bounce" we always received from the speech. Then Bradley began to attack him harshly. When Al didn't respond, Bradley cut into his lead, but Al held on to win 52–47 percent. After that, I knew he was home free for the nomination. He was going to carry the South and California big, and I thought he would do well in the large industrial states, too, especially after the AFL-CIO endorsed him.

John McCain defeated George W. Bush in New Hampshire 49–31 percent. It was a state tailor-made for McCain. They liked his independent streak and his support for campaign finance reform. The next big contest was in South Carolina, where McCain would be helped by his military background and the endorsements of two congressmen, but Bush had the backing of both the party establishment and the religious right.

On Sunday afternoon, February 6, Hillary, Chelsea, Dorothy, and I drove from Chappaqua to the State University of New York's campus in nearby Purchase for Hillary's formal announcement of her Senate candidacy. Senator Moynihan introduced her. He said that he had known Eleanor Roosevelt and that she "would love you." It was a sincere compliment and a funny one, since Hillary had taken a lot of good-natured ribbing for saying she had had imaginary conversations with Mrs. Roosevelt.

Hillary gave a terrific speech, one she had written carefully and practiced hard; it displayed how much she had learned about the concerns of the different regions of the state and how clearly she understood the choices voters were facing. She also had to explain why she was running; show that she understood why New Yorkers might be wary of voting for a candidate, even one they liked, who had never lived in the state until a few months before; and say what she would do as a senator. There was some discussion about whether I should speak. New York was one of my best states; at the time my job approval was over

70 percent there and my personal approval was at 60 percent. But we decided I shouldn't talk. It was Hillary's day, and the voters wanted to hear from her.

For the rest of the month, while politics dominated the news, I was dealing with a wide variety of domestic and foreign policy issues. On the home front, I endorsed a bipartisan bill to provide Medicaid coverage to lower-income women for breast and cervical cancer treatment; made a deal with Senator Lott to bring five of my judicial nominees to the Senate floor for a vote in return for appointing the person he wanted, a rabid foe of campaign finance reform, to the Federal Election Commission; argued with the Republicans over the Patients' Bill of Rights—they said they'd pass it as long as no one could bring a lawsuit to enforce it, and I argued that that would make it a bill of "suggestions"; dedicated the White House press room to James Brady, President Reagan's courageous press secretary; announced a record increase in funds for Native American education and health care; supported a change in food stamp regulations to allow welfare recipients who went to work to own a used car without losing their food aid; received an award from the League of United Latin American Citizens (LULAC) for my economic and social policies and for my major Hispanic appointments; and hosted the National Governors Association for the last time.

In foreign affairs, we dealt with a lot of headaches. On the seventh, Yasser Arafat suspended his peace talks with Israel. He was convinced that Israel was putting Palestinian issues on the back burner in favor of pursuing peace with Syria. There was some truth in it, and at the time, the Israeli public was more willing to make peace with the Palestinians, with all the difficulties that entailed, than to give up the Golan Heights and put the Palestinian talks at risk. We spent the rest of the month trying to get things going again.

On the eleventh, the UK suspended home rule in Northern Ireland, despite the IRA's last-minute assurance of an act of arms decommissioning to General John de Chastelain, the Canadian who was overseeing the process. I had gotten George Mitchell involved again, and we had done our best to help Bertie Ahern and Tony Blair avoid this day. The fundamental problem, according to Gerry Adams, was that the IRA wanted to disarm because their people had voted for it, not because David Trimble and the Unionists had made decommissioning the price of their continued participation in the government. Of course, without decommissioning, the Protestants would lose faith in the process, and eventually Trimble would be replaced, a result Adams and Sinn Fein did not want. Trimble could be dour and pessimistic, but beneath his stern Scots-Irish front was a brave idealist who was also taking risks for peace. At any rate, the sequencing issue had delayed establishment of the government for more than a year; now we were back to no government. It was frustrating, but I thought the impasse would be resolved because no one wanted to return to the bad old days.

On March 5, I commemorated the thirty-fifth anniversary of the voting rights march in Selma, Alabama, by walking across the Edmund Pettus Bridge as the civil rights demonstrators had on that "Bloody Sunday," risking their lives to gain the right to vote for all Americans. Many of the veterans of the civil rights movement who had marched with or supported Martin Luther King Jr. marched arm in arm again that day, including Coretta

Scott King, Jesse Jackson, John Lewis, Andrew Young, Joe Lowery, Julian Bond, Ethel Kennedy, and Harris Wofford.

In 1965, the Selma march galvanized the conscience of the nation. Five months later, President Johnson signed the Voting Rights Act into law. Before the Voting Rights Act, there were only 300 black elected officials at any level, and just three African-American congressmen. In 2000, there were nearly 9,000 black elected officials and 39 members of the Congressional Black Caucus.

In my remarks, I noted that Martin Luther King Jr. was right when he said that when black Americans "win their struggle to become free, those who have held them down will themselves be free for the first time." After Selma, white and black southerners crossed the bridge to the New South, leaving hatred and isolation behind for new opportunities and prosperity and political influence: Without Selma, Jimmy Carter and Bill Clinton would never have become President of the United States.

Now, as we crossed the bridge into the twenty-first century with the lowest unemployment and poverty rates and the highest home and business ownership rates among African-Americans ever recorded, I asked the audience to remember what was yet to be accomplished. As long as there were wide racial disparities in income, education, health, vulnerability to violence, and perceptions of fairness in the criminal justice system, as long as discrimination and hate crimes persisted, "we have another bridge to cross."

I loved that day in Selma. Once again, I was swept back across the years to my boyhood longing for and belief in an America without a racial divide. Once again, I returned to the emotional core of my political life in saying farewell to the people who had done so much to nourish it: "As long as Americans are willing to hold hands, we can walk with any wind, we can cross any bridge. Deep in my heart, I do believe, we shall overcome."

I spent most of the first half of the month campaigning for my gun safety measures: closing the gun show loophole, putting child trigger locks on guns, and requiring gun owners to have a photo-ID license showing that they had passed the Brady background check and had taken a gun safety course. America had been rocked by a series of tragic shooting deaths, one of them caused by a very young child firing a gun he had found in his apartment. The accidental gun death rate for children under fifteen in America was nine times higher than that of the twenty-five next largest economies combined.

Despite the crying need and rising public support for gun control, the NRA so far had kept anything from happening in Congress, though most gun manufacturers, to their credit, were now providing child trigger locks. On the gun show loophole, the NRA said, as it had in opposing the Brady bill, that it didn't object to instant background checks, but it didn't want anyone inconvenienced for the public's safety by having to endure a three-day waiting period. Already, 70 percent of the checks were completed in an hour, 90 percent in a day. A few took longer. If we didn't have a waiting period, people with bad records could buy their guns at closing time on Friday afternoon. The NRA was also adamantly against licensing gun owners, seeing it as the first step toward depriving them of the right to own weapons. It was a spurious argument; we had required driver's licenses for a long time, and no one had ever suggested banning automobile possession.

Still, I knew the NRA could scare a lot of people. I had grown up in the hunting culture in which its influence was greatest and had seen the devastating impact the NRA had had on the '94 congressional elections. But I had always felt most hunters and sports shooters were good citizens and would listen to a reasonable argument plainly stated. I knew I had to try, because I believed in what I was doing and because Al Gore had put himself squarely within the NRA's gunsights by endorsing the licensing idea even before I did.

On the twelfth, Wayne LaPierre, the executive vice president of the NRA, said that I needed a "certain level of violence" and was "willing to accept a certain level of killing" to further my political objectives, "and his vice president's, too." LaPierre's position was that we should prosecute gun crimes more severely and punish adults who recklessly allow children access to guns. The next day, in Cleveland, I answered him, saying that I agreed with his proposals for punishment but that I thought his position that no preventive measures were needed was nonsense. The NRA was even against banning cop-killer bullets. It was they who were willing to accept a certain level of violence and killing to keep their membership up and their ideology pure. I said I'd like to see LaPierre look into the eyes of the parents who had lost their children at Columbine, or in Springfield, Oregon, or Jonesboro, Arkansas, and say those things.

I didn't think I could beat the NRA in the House, but I was having a good time trying. I asked people how they would feel if the NRA's "no prevention, all punishment" strategy were applied to every aspect of our lives: getting rid of seat belts, air bags, and speed limits and adding five years to the sentences of reckless drivers who kill people;

and getting rid of airport metal detectors and adding ten years to the sentence of anyone who blows up a plane.

On my previous trip to Cleveland, I had visited an elementary school where AmeriCorps volunteers were tutoring young children in reading. A six-year-old boy looked up at me and asked, "Are you really the President?" When I said that I was, he replied, "But you're not dead yet!" He knew only about George Washington and Abraham Lincoln. I was running out of time, but with a high-class fight like this one on my hands, I knew the boy was right. I wasn't dead yet.

On March 17, I announced a breakthrough agreement between Smith & Wesson, one of the largest gun manufacturers, and federal, state, and local governments. The company agreed to include locking devices with its guns, to develop a "smart gun" that could be fired only by the adult who owned it, to cut off gun dealers who sold a disproportionate number of guns used in crimes, to require its dealers not to sell at gun shows unless background checks were conducted, and to design new guns that did not accept large-capacity magazines. It was a brave thing for the company to do. I knew Smith & Wesson would be subject to withering attacks from the NRA and from its competitors.

The presidential nominating process was over by the second week of March, as John McCain and Bill Bradley withdrew after Al Gore and George W. Bush won big victories in the sixteen Super Tuesday primaries and caucuses. Bill Bradley had run a serious campaign, and in pressing Al early he had made him a better candidate, as Al scrapped his endorsement-laden approach for a grassroots effort in which he looked more like a relaxed but aggressive challenger. Bush had righted his campaign after losing in New Hampshire by winning in South Carolina, aided by a telephone campaign into conservative white households reminding them that Senator McCain had a "black baby." McCain had adopted a child from Bangladesh, one of the many reasons I admired him.

Before the primaries were over, an ad hoc veterans' group supporting Bush accused McCain of betraying his country in the five and a half years he was a POW in North Vietnam. In New York, the Bush people attacked McCain for opposing breast cancer research. Actually, he had voted against a defense bill with some breast cancer money in it to protest all the pork-barrel spending included in the bill; the senator had a sister with breast cancer and had always voted for the appropriations that contained well over 90 percent of the cancer research funds. Senator McCain didn't hit back hard at the Bush campaign or the right-wing extremists for smearing him until it was too late.

The developments on the international front in March were largely positive. Barak and Arafat agreed to restart their talks. On my last St. Patrick's Day as President, Seamus Heaney read his poetry, we all sang "Danny Boy," and it was clear that, although the government was still down in Northern Ireland, no one was prepared to let the peace process die. I spoke with King Fahd of Saudi Arabia about the possibility of OPEC increasing its production. A year earlier, the price of oil had dropped to $12 a barrel, too low to meet the basic needs of producing countries. Now it was jumping to between $31 and $34, too high to avoid adverse effects in the consuming nations. I wanted to see the price stabilize at between $20 and $22 a barrel and hoped OPEC could increase production enough to do that; otherwise, the United States could have significant economic problems.

On the eighteenth, I left for a week-long trip to India, Pakistan, and Bangladesh. I was going to India to lay the foundation for what I had hoped would be a positive long-term relationship. We had wasted too much time since the end of the Cold War, when India had aligned itself with the Soviet Union principally as a counterweight to China. Bangladesh was the poorest country in South Asia, but a large one with some innovative economic programs and a friendly attitude toward the United States. Unlike Pakistan and India, Bangladesh was a non-nuclear nation that had ratified the Comprehensive Test Ban Treaty, which was more than could be said for the United States. My stop in Pakistan was the most controversial because of the recent military coup there, but I decided I had to go for several reasons: to encourage an early return to civilian rule and a lessening of tensions over Kashmir; to urge General Musharraf not to execute the deposed prime minister, Nawaz Sharif, who was on trial for his life; and to press Musharraf to cooperate with us on bin Laden and al Qaeda.

The Secret Service was strongly opposed to my going to Pakistan or Bangladesh because the CIA had intelligence that indicated al Qaeda wanted to attack me on one of those stops, either on the ground or during takeoffs or landings. I felt I had to go because of the adverse consequences to American interests of going only to India and because I didn't want to give in to a terrorist threat. So we took sensible precautions and proceeded. I believe it was the only request the Secret Service ever made that I refused.

Hillary's mother, Dorothy, and Chelsea were going

with me to India. We flew there first, where I left them in the good hands of our ambassador, my old friend Dick Celeste, the former Ohio governor, and his wife, Jacqueline. Then I took a reduced group on two small planes into Bangladesh, where I met with the prime minister, Sheikh Hasina. Later, I was forced to make another concession to security. I had been scheduled to visit the village of Joypura with my friend Muhammad Yunus to observe some of Grameen Bank's micro-credit projects. The Secret Service had determined that our party would be defenseless on the narrow roads or flying in a helicopter to the village, so we brought the villagers, including some schoolchildren, to the American embassy in Dacca, where they set up a classroom and some displays in the inner courtyard.

While I was in Bangladesh, thirty-five Sikhs were murdered in Kashmir by unknown killers intent on getting publicity tied to my visit. When I got back to Delhi, in my meeting with Prime Minister Vajpayee I expressed outrage and deep regret that terrorists had used my trip as an excuse to kill. I got on well with Vajpayee and hoped he would have an opportunity to reengage Pakistan before he left office. We didn't agree on the test ban treaty, but I already knew that, because Strobe Talbott had been working with Foreign Minister Jaswant Singh and others for months on nonproliferation issues. However, Vajpayee did join me in pledging to forgo future tests, and we agreed upon a set of positive principles that would govern our bilateral relationship, which had been cool for so long.

I also had a good visit with the leader of the opposition Congress Party, Sonia Gandhi. Her husband and mother-in-law, the grandson and daughter of Nehru, were both victims of political assassination. Sonia, an Italian by birth, had bravely remained in public life.

On the fourth day of my trip, I had the opportunity to address the Indian parliament. The Parliament Building is a large circular structure in which the several hundred parliamentarians sit tightly bunched at row after row of narrow tables. I spoke of my respect for India's democracy, diversity, and impressive strides in building a modern economy, frankly discussed our differences over nuclear issues, and urged them to reach a peaceful solution to the Kashmir problem. Somewhat to my surprise, I got a grand reception. They applauded by slapping the table, demonstrating that the Indians were as eager as I was for our long estrangement to end.

Chelsea, Dorothy, and I visited the Gandhi Memorial, where we were given copies of his autobiography and other writings, and we traveled to Agra, where the Taj Mahal, perhaps the world's most beautiful structure, was threatened by severe air pollution. India was working hard to establish a pollution-free zone around the Taj, and Foreign Minister Singh and Madeleine Albright signed an agreement for Indo-U.S. cooperation on energy and the environment, with the United States providing $45 million in USAID funds and $200 million from the Export-Import Bank to develop clean energy in India. The Taj was breathtaking, and I hated to leave.

On the twenty-third, I visited Naila, a small village near Jaipur. After the village women in their brightly colored saris greeted me by surrounding me and showering me with thousands of flower petals, I met with the elected officials who were working together across caste and gender lines that had traditionally divided Indians, and discussed the importance of micro-credit loans with the women of the local dairy cooperative.

The next day I went to the thriving high-tech city of Hyderabad as the guest of the state's chief minister, Chandrababu Naidu, an articulate and very modern political leader. We visited the HITECH Center, where I was amazed to see the variety of companies that were growing like wildfire, and a hospital where, along with USAID administrator Brady Anderson, I announced a grant of $5 million to help it deal with AIDS and tuberculosis. At the time, AIDS was just beginning to be recognized in India, and there was still a lot of denial. I hoped our modest grant would help increase public awareness and willingness to act before the AIDS problem in India reached Africa's epidemic proportions. My last stop was in Mumbai (Bombay), where I met with business leaders, then had an interesting conversation with young leaders at a local restaurant. I left India feeling that our nations had begun a solid relationship, but wishing I had another week to absorb the country's beauty and mystery.

On the twenty-fifth, I flew to Islamabad, the leg of the trip the Secret Service thought was most dangerous. I took as few people as possible, leaving most of our party behind, to fly on the larger plane to our refueling stop in Oman. Sandy Berger joked that he was a little older than I, and since we had been through so much in almost thirty years of friendship he might as well go along to Pakistan for the ride. Again we went in on two small planes, one with U.S. Air Force markings, the other, in which I was riding, painted plain white. The Pakistanis had cleared an area a mile wide around the runway to make certain that we couldn't be hit by a shoulder-fired missile. Nevertheless, landing was a bracing experience.

Our motorcade traveled an empty highway to the Presidential Palace for a meeting with General Musharraf and his cabinet and a televised address to the people of Pakistan. In the speech, I noted our long friendship through the Cold War and asked the Pakistani people to turn away from terror and nuclear weapons toward a dialogue with India on Kashmir, to embrace the test ban treaty, and to invest in education, health, and development rather than arms. I said I had come as a friend of Pakistan and the Muslim world who had stood against the slaughter of Muslims in Bosnia and Kosovo, spoken to the Palestinian National Council in Gaza, marched with the mourners at the funerals of King Hussein and King Hassan, and celebrated the end of Ramadan at the White House with American Muslims. The point I tried to make is that our world was not divided by religious differences, but between those who chose to live with the pain of the past and those who chose the promise of the future.

In my meetings with Musharraf, I saw why he had emerged from the complex, often violent culture of Pakistani politics. He was clearly intelligent, strong, and sophisticated. If he chose to pursue a peaceful, progressive path, I thought he had a fair chance to succeed, but I told him I thought terrorism would eventually destroy Pakistan from within if he didn't move against it.

Musharraf said he didn't believe Sharif would be executed, but he was noncommittal on the other issues. I knew he was still trying to solidify his position and was in a tough spot. Sharif subsequently was released into exile in Jedda, Saudi Arabia. When Musharraf began serious cooperation with the United States in the war against terror after September 11, 2001, it remained a risky course for him. In 2003, he survived two assassination attempts within days of each other.

On the way home, after the stop in Oman to see Sultan Qaboos and get our delegation back on Air Force One, I flew to Geneva to meet with President Assad. Our team had been working to get Barak to make a specific proposal on Syria for me to present. I knew it wouldn't be a final offer, and the Syrians would know it, too, but I thought that if Israel finally responded with the same flexibility the Syrians had shown at Shepherdstown, we might still be able to make a deal. It was not to be.

When I met Assad, he was friendly as I gave him a blue tie with a red-line profile of a lion, the English meaning of his name. It was a small meeting: Assad was joined by Foreign Minister Shara and Butheina Shaban; Madeleine Albright and Dennis Ross accompanied me, with the National Security Council's Rob Malley serving as notetaker. After some pleasant small talk, I asked Dennis to spread out the maps I had studied carefully in preparing for our talks. Compared with his stated position at Shepherdstown, Barak was now willing to accept less land around the lake, though he still wanted a lot, 400 meters (1,312 feet); fewer people at the listening station; and a quicker withdrawal period. Assad didn't want me even to finish the presentation. He became agitated and, contradicting the Syrian position at Shepherdstown, said that he would never cede any of the land, that he wanted to be able to sit on the shore of the lake and put his feet in the water. We tried for two hours to get some traction with the Syrians, all to no avail. The Israeli rebuff in Shepherdstown and the leak of the working document in the Israeli press had embarrassed Assad and destroyed his fragile trust. And his health had deteriorated even more than I knew. Barak had made a respectable offer. If it had come at Shepherdstown, an agreement might have emerged. Now, Assad's first priority was his son's succession, and he had obviously decided that a new round of negotiations, no matter how it came out, could put that at risk. In less than four years, I had seen the prospects of peace between Israel and Syria dashed three times: by terror in Israel and Peres's defeat in 1996, by the Israeli rebuff of Syrian overtures at Shepherdstown, and by Assad's preoccupation with his own mortality. After we parted in Geneva, I never saw Assad again.

That same day Vladimir Putin was elected president of Russia in the first round, with 52.5 percent of the vote. I called to congratulate him and hung up the phone thinking he was tough enough to hold Russia together and hoping he was wise enough to find an honorable way out of the Chechnya problem and committed enough to democracy to preserve it. He was soon off to a strong start, as the Duma ratified both START II and the Comprehensive Nuclear Test Ban Treaty. Now even the Russian Duma was more progressive on arms control than the U.S. Senate.

In April, I continued to travel the country pushing my education, gun safety, and technology access issues from the State of the Union address; established another national monument, Grand Sequoia, in California; vetoed the bill to put all America's low-level nuclear waste in Nevada because I didn't think all the legitimate questions had been answered; signed the bill ending the earnings limitations for retirees who were collecting Social Security; visited the people of the Navajo Nation in Shiprock in northern New Mexico to highlight our efforts to use the Internet to bring educational, health, and economic opportunities to remote communities; and dedicated the simple but powerful memorial to the victims of the Oklahoma City bombing, 168 empty chairs in rows on a small knoll flanked by two large entryways and overlooking a large reflecting pool.

April also brought the final act in the long saga of little Elián González. Several months earlier his mother had fled Cuba with him for the United States in a rickety boat. The boat capsized and she drowned after putting Elián in an inner tube to save his life. The boy was taken to Miami and put in the temporary custody of a great-uncle, who was willing to keep him. His father in Cuba wanted him back. The Cuban-American community made Elián's case a crusade, saying that his mother had died trying to bring her son to freedom and it would be wrong to send him back to Castro's dictatorship.

The governing law seemed clear. The Immigration and Naturalization Service was supposed to determine whether the boy's father was a fit parent; if he was, Elián had to be returned to him. An INS team went to Cuba and discovered that though Elián's parents were divorced, they had maintained a good relationship and had shared child-rearing duties. In fact, Elián had spent about half his time with his father, who lived closer to the boy's school. The INS found that Juan Miguel González was a fit parent.

Advocates for the American relatives took the case to court in an attempt to question the validity of the process in Cuba, thinking it might have been compromised by the presence of Castro's people at the hearing. Some sought to apply the normal state-law standard in child custody cases: what is in the best interest of the child? The Congress got in on the act, with various bills being proposed to keep Elián in the United States. Meanwhile, the Cuban-American community was whipped into a frenzy by permanent demonstrations outside the house of Elián's relatives and regular TV interviews with one of them, a highly emotional young woman.

Janet Reno, who had served as prosecuting attorney in Miami and had been a popular figure among Cuban-Americans, enraged them by stating that federal law should control the situation and Elián should be returned to his father. It wasn't easy for Janet. She told me that one of her former secretaries would hardly speak to her; the woman's husband had been jailed for fifteen years by Castro, and she had waited all that time for him to be released and reunited with her. Many Cuban-Americans and other immigrants believed the boy would be better off staying here.

I backed Reno, believing that the fact that Elián's father loved him and had been a good parent should count for more than the poverty or the closed and repressive politics of Cuba. Moreover, the United States had frequently tried to get children returned to our country who had been taken away, usually by parents who had lost child custody cases here. If we kept Elián, our arguments for the return of those children to their American parents would be weakened.

Eventually, the case became an election issue. Al Gore publicly disagreed with us, saying that he had problems with the INS process and that even if Elián's father was a fit parent, the boy might still be better off in America. It was a defensible position on the merits, and understandable, given the importance of Florida in the election. I had worked for eight years to strengthen our position in the state and among Cuban-Americans; at least in that community, the Elián case had wiped out most of our gains. Hillary saw the case as a child advocate and a parent: she backed our decision to reunite the boy and his father.

Early in the month Juan Miguel González came to America hoping to take custody of his son, in accordance with a federal court order. A couple of weeks later, after Janet Reno had tried for several days to secure the voluntary surrender of the boy, a group of four leading citizens—the president of the University of Miami, a highly regarded lawyer, and two respected Cuban-Americans—suggested that the Miami family hand over custody to the father in a secluded place where they could all be together for a few days to ease the transition. On Good Friday evening, I talked to Reno at midnight and they were still negotiating, but she was running out of patience. At two o'clock Saturday morning, John Podesta called to say the talks were still going on. At quarter to five, Podesta called again and said the Miami family was now refusing even to recognize the father's custody rights. Thirty minutes later, at five-fifteen, I got another call from John saying it was over. Reno had authorized a pre-dawn raid on the great-uncle's house by federal officials. It lasted three minutes, no one was hurt, and Elián was returned to his father. A small boy had become a pawn in the never-ending struggle against Castro.

Photographs of an obviously happy Elián with his father were published, and sentiment shifted markedly in favor of the reunification. I was confident we had followed the only course open to us, but I was still concerned that it could cost Al Gore Florida in November. Juan Miguel and Elián González remained in the United States a few more weeks, until the Supreme Court finally upheld the lower court's custody order. Mr. González could have stayed in the United States, but he wanted to take his son home to Cuba.

In May, I toured schools in Kentucky, Iowa, Minnesota, and Ohio to push our education package; hosted a state visit for Thabo Mbeki, who had just been elected president of South Africa; and promoted the China trade bill, which was necessary for China's admission into the WTO. Presidents Ford and Carter, along with James Baker and Henry Kissinger, came to the White House to promote it. This turned out to be a very difficult legislative fight—an especially tough vote for Democrats who depended on labor support—and I brought groups of a dozen or so members down to the residence for several weeks in an intensive effort to explain the importance of integrating China into the global economy.

On May 17, I gave my last service academy speech to the U.S. Coast Guard Academy in New London, Connecticut. In eight years I had now spoken to each of the service academies twice. Every class filled me with pride in the quality of young men and women who wanted to serve our country in uniform. I was also proud of the young people who came to our service academies from all over the world. This class included graduates from our Cold War adversaries Russia and Bulgaria.

I spoke to the new officers about the fateful struggle in which they would be engaged between the forces of integration and harmony and those of disintegration and chaos, a struggle in which globalization and information technology had magnified both the creative and destructive potential of humankind. I discussed the attacks that Osama bin Laden and al Qaeda had planned for the millennium, which were thwarted through hard work and domestic and international cooperation. To build on that work, I said that I was allocating another $300 million to our anti-terrorism budget; on top of the $9 billion request I had already sent to Congress, it amounted to an increase of more than 40 percent in three years.

After discussing other security challenges, I made the best case I could for an activist foreign policy, cooperating with others in a world in which no nation was protected any longer by geography or conventional military strength.

In late May, just before I left on a trip to Portugal, Germany, Russia, and Ukraine, I went to Assateague Island, Maryland, to announce a new initiative to protect our coral reefs and other marine treasures. We had already quadrupled funding for national marine sanctuaries. I signed an executive order to create a national protective network for our coasts, reefs, underwater forests, and other important structures, and I said we were going to permanently protect the coral reefs of the northwest Hawaiian Islands, more than 60 percent of America's total, stretching over 1,200 miles. It was the biggest conservation step I had taken since preserving 43 million roadless acres in our national forests, and a needed one, since ocean pollution was threatening reefs the world over, including the Great Barrier Reef in Australia.

I went to Portugal for the annual meeting between the United States and the European Union. Portuguese prime minister Antonio Guterres was serving as president of the European Council. He was a bright young physicist who was a member of our Third Way group, as was EU president Romano Prodi. We saw eye to eye on most things, and I enjoyed the meeting, as well as my first visit to Portugal. It was beautiful and warm, with friendly people and a fascinating history.

On June 2, I went with Gerhard Schroeder to the ancient city of Aachen to receive the Charlemagne Prize. In a sunny outdoor ceremony in a public space near the medieval city hall and the old cathedral holding Charlemagne's remains, I thanked Chancellor Schroeder and the German people for giving me an honor shared by Václav Havel and King Juan Carlos and rarely awarded to an American. I had done everything I could to help Europe become united, democratic, and secure, to expand and strengthen the transatlantic alliance, to reach out to Russia, and to end ethnic cleansing in the Balkans. It was gratifying to be recognized for it.

The next day Gerhard Schroeder hosted another of our Third Way conferences in Berlin. This time Gerhard, Jean Chrétien, and I were joined by three Latin Americans— Henrique Cardoso of Brazil, President Ricardo Lagos of Chile, and President Fernando de la Rúa of Argentina—as we outlined the kinds of progressive partnerships leaders of developed and developing countries should form. Tony Blair wasn't there because he and Cherie, already the parents of three children, had recently brought a fourth into the world, a boy they named Leo.

I flew into Moscow for my first meeting with Vladimir Putin since his election. We agreed to destroy another thirty-four metric tons each of weapons-grade plutonium, but could not reach accord on amending the ABM Treaty to enable the United States to deploy a national missile defense system. I wasn't too concerned about that; Putin probably wanted to wait to see how the U.S. election turned out. The Republicans had been enamored of missile defense since the Reagan era, and many of them wouldn't hesitate to abrogate the ABM Treaty in order to deploy it. Al Gore basically agreed with me. Putin didn't want to have to deal with this twice.

At the time, we didn't have a missile defense system reliable enough to deploy. As Hugh Shelton had said, shooting down an incoming missile was like "a bullet hitting a bullet." If we ever did develop a workable system, I thought that we should offer the technology to other nations and that, in so doing, we could probably persuade the Russians to amend the ABM Treaty. I wasn't at all sure that, even if it worked, erecting a missile defense system was the best way to spend the staggering sums it would cost. We were far more likely to face attacks from terrorists having smaller nuclear, chemical, or biological weapons.

Moreover, putting up a missile defense could actually expose the world to greater danger. For the foreseeable future, the system would knock out only a few missiles even if it worked. If the United States and Russia were to erect such a system, China would probably build more missiles to overcome it in order to maintain its deterrent capability. Then India would follow suit, as would Pakistan. The Europeans were convinced it was a terrible idea. But we didn't have to deal with all those issues until we had a system that worked, and so far, we didn't.

Before I left Moscow, Putin hosted a small dinner in the Kremlin with a jazz concert afterward, featuring Russian musicians from teenagers to an octogenarian. The finale began on a dark stage, a haunting series of tunes by my favorite living tenor saxophonist, Igor Butman. John Podesta, who loved jazz as much as I did, agreed with me that we had never heard a finer live performance.

I went to Ukraine to announce America's financial support for President Leonid Kuchma's decision to close the final reactor at the Chernobyl nuclear power plant by December 15. It had taken a long time, and I was glad to know that at least the problem would be resolved before I left. My last stop was an outdoor speech to a huge crowd of Ukrainians whom I urged to stay on the course of freedom and economic reform. Kiev was beautiful in the late spring sunshine, and I hoped its people could keep up the high spirits I had observed in the crowd. They still had many hurdles to clear.

On June 8, I flew to Tokyo for the day to pay my respects at the memorial service of my friend Prime Minister Keizo Obuchi, who had died of a stroke a few days before. The service was held in the indoor section of a soccer stadium, with a few thousand seats on the floor divided by an aisle in the middle, and several hundred more people sitting in balconies above. A stage had been constructed with a large ramp up the front and smaller ones on the side. Behind the stage was a wall covered in flowers twenty-five or thirty feet high. The flowers were beautifully arranged to show the Japanese rising sun against a pale blue sky. At the very top there was an indented space where at the beginning of the ceremony a military aide solemnly placed a box containing Obuchi's ashes. After his colleagues and friends had paid tribute to him, several young Japanese women appeared holding trays full of white flowers. Beginning with Obuchi's wife and children, members of the imperial family, and leaders of the government, the mourners all walked up the center ramp, bowed in respect before his ashes, and placed our flowers on a waist-high strip of wood that ran the entire length of the flowered wall.

After I bowed to my friend and placed my flower, I returned to the U.S. embassy to see our ambassador, former House Speaker Tom Foley. I turned on the television to see the ceremony still in progress. Thousands of Obuchi's fellow citizens were creating a cloud of sacred flowers against the rising sun. It was one of the most moving tributes I had ever witnessed. I stopped briefly at the reception to pay my respects to Mrs. Obuchi and Keizo's children, one of whom was in politics herself. Mrs. Obuchi thanked me for coming and gave me a beautiful enamel letter box that had belonged to her husband. Obuchi had been a friend to me, and to America. Our alliance was important, and he had valued it even as a young man. I wished he had had longer to serve.

Several days later, while I was participating in the Carleton College commencement exercises in Minnesota, an aide passed me a note informing me that President Hafez al-Assad had just died in Damascus, only ten weeks after our last meeting in Geneva. Although we had our disagreements, he had always been straightforward with me, and I had believed him when he said he had made a strategic choice for peace. Circumstances, miscommunication, and psychological barriers had kept it from happening, but at least we now knew what it would take for Israel and Syria to get there once both sides were ready.

As spring turned to summer, I hosted our largest state dinner ever, as more than four hundred people gathered under a tent on the South Lawn to honor King Mohammed VI of Morocco, one of whose ancestors was the first sovereign to recognize the United States shortly after our original thirteen states joined together.

The next day I corrected an old injustice, awarding the Congressional Medal of Honor to twenty-two Japanese-Americans who had volunteered to serve in Europe during

World War II after their families were interned in camps. One of them was my friend and ally Senator Daniel Inouye of Hawaii, who had lost an arm and very nearly his life in the war. A week later I nominated the first Asian-American to the cabinet: former congressman Norm Mineta of California agreed to serve for the remainder of my term as commerce secretary, replacing Bill Daley, who was leaving to become the chairman of Al Gore's campaign.

In the last week of the month, I held a gathering in the East Room of the White House, where almost two hundred years earlier Thomas Jefferson had spread out the path-breaking map of the western United States that his aide Meriwether Lewis had made on his courageous expedition from the Mississippi River to the Pacific Ocean in 1803. The crowd of scientists and diplomats had gathered to celebrate a twenty-first–century map: more than a thousand researchers in the United States, the UK, Germany, France, Japan, and China had decoded the human genome, identifying nearly all of the three billion sequences of our genetic code. After battling each other for years, Francis Collins, head of the government-funded international human genome project, and Celera president Craig Venter had agreed to publish their genetic data together later in the year. Craig was an old friend, and I had done my best to bring them together. Tony Blair joined us on a satellite hookup, giving me a chance to joke that his infant son's life expectancy had just gone up by about twenty-five years.

As the month drew to a close, I announced that our budget surplus would exceed $200 billion, with a ten-year projected surplus of over $4 trillion. Once again, I recommended that we lock away the Social Security surplus, about $2.3 trillion, and that we save about $550 billion for Medicare. It was beginning to look as if we could handle the baby boomers' retirement after all.

I also did a number of political events to support Democrats in Arizona and California and to help Terry McAuliffe raise the rest of the money we needed to put on our convention in Los Angeles in August. We were working closely with him and the Gore campaign through my political director Minyon Moore.

Most polls had Gore trailing Bush, and at my press conference on June 28, I was asked by an NBC News reporter whether Al was being held accountable for the "scandals" of the administration. I said there was no evidence that he was being punished for my mistakes; that the only wrongdoing he had been accused of involved campaign fund-raising, and he wasn't guilty; and that the other so-called scandals were bogus: "The word 'scandal' has been thrown around here like a clanging teapot for seven years." I also said I knew three things about Al Gore: he had had a more positive impact on our country as vice president than any of his predecessors; he had the right positions on the issues and would keep the prosperity going; and he understood the future, both its possibilities and its dangers. I believed if all the voters understood that, Al would win.

In the first week of July, I announced that our economy had now produced twenty-two million jobs since I took office, and went out to the Old Soldiers' Home a few miles north of the White House to protect the old cottage Abraham Lincoln and his family had used for a summer home when the Potomac generated hordes of mosquitoes and there was no air conditioning. Several other Presidents had used it, too. It was one of Hillary's Save America's Treasures projects, and we wanted to know the old place would be cared for when we left the White House.

On July 11, I opened a summit with Ehud Barak and Yasser Arafat at Camp David in an attempt to resolve the remaining obstacles to peace, or at least to narrow their differences so that we could finish before I left office, a result both leaders said they wanted.

They came to the summit with very different attitudes. Barak had pushed hard for the summit because the piecemeal approach of the 1993 agreement and the Wye River accord didn't work for him. The 180,000 Israeli settlers in the West Bank and Gaza were a formidable force. Every Israeli concession that failed to bring an end to terror and a formal Palestinian recognition that the conflict was over was a death by a thousand cuts. Barak had just survived a no-confidence vote in the Knesset by only two votes. He was also eager for a deal before September, when Arafat had threatened to unilaterally declare a state. Barak believed that if he could present a comprehensive peace plan to Israeli citizens, they would vote for it as long as Israel's fundamental interests were achieved: security, the protection of its religious and cultural sites on the Temple Mount, an end to the Palestinian claim to an unlimited right of return to Israel, and a declaration that the conflict was over.

Arafat, on the other hand, didn't want to come to Camp David, at least not yet. He had felt abandoned by the Israelis when they turned to the Syrian track, and was angry that Barak had not kept previous commitments to turn over more of the West Bank, including villages near Jerusalem. In Arafat's eyes, Barak's unilateral withdrawal from Lebanon and his offer to withdraw from the Golan had weakened him. While Arafat had patiently continued the peace process, Lebanon and Syria had benefited by taking a hard line. Arafat also said he needed two more weeks to develop his proposals. He wanted as close to a hundred percent of the West Bank and Gaza as he could get; complete sovereignty over the Temple Mount and East Jerusalem, except for the Jewish neighborhoods there; and a solution to the refugee problem that did not require him to give up the principle of the right of return.

As usual, each leader saw his own position more clearly than he saw the other side. There was not a high probability of success for the summit. I called it because I believed that the collapse of the peace process would be a near certainty if I didn't.

On the first day, I tried to get Arafat past his grievances to focus on the work ahead and to get Barak to agree on how to move through the issues, especially the most contentious ones: territory, settlements, refugees, security, and Jerusalem. As he had at Shepherdstown, Barak wanted to slow-walk things for a couple of days. It didn't matter that much this time—Arafat hadn't come with a set of negotiating points; this was all strange territory to him. In previous negotiations he would just hold out for the best offer he could get from Israel on issues such as land, an airport, connecting roads, and prisoner releases, then pledge his best efforts on the security front. Now if we were going to get this done, Arafat had some compromising of his own to do on concrete matters: He couldn't get a hundred percent of the West Bank or an unlimited right of return to a much smaller Israel. He also would have to meet some of Israel's security concerns about potential enemies east of the Jordan River.

I spent the first couple of days trying to get Arafat and Barak in the right frame of mind, while Madeleine, Sandy,

Dennis, Gemal Helal, John Podesta, and the rest of our team began working with their Israeli and Palestinian counterparts. I was immensely impressed with the quality of both delegations. They were all patriotic, intelligent, and hardworking, and they genuinely seemed to want an agreement. Most of them had known each other and their counterparts on the other side for years, and the chemistry between the two groups was quite good.

We tried to create a comfortable, informal atmosphere for the Israelis and Palestinians. In addition to our regular Middle East team, I asked Hillary's aide, Huma Abedin, to join us. An Arabic-speaking Muslim American raised in Saudi Arabia, Huma was an impressive young woman who understood the Middle East and was especially effective at making the Israeli and Palestinian delegates feel at home and at ease. Capricia Marshall, the White House social secretary, arranged for the White House butlers, chefs, and valets to come help the Camp David staff in making sure the meals were enjoyable. And Chelsea stayed with me the whole time, entertaining our guests and helping me deal with the endless hours of tension.

Most nights we all had dinner together at Laurel, the large gathering cabin at Camp David, which had dining facilities, a large den, a meeting room, and my private office. Breakfast and lunch were more informal, and the Israelis and Palestinians could often be seen talking among themselves in small groups. Sometimes it was business; often they were telling stories and jokes or relating family histories. Abu Ala and Abu Mazen were Arafat's oldest and longest-serving advisors. Abu Ala took a lot of kidding from the Israelis and the Americans for his family. His father was so prolific that the sixty-three-year-old Palestinian had an eight-year-old brother; the boy was younger than some of Abu's own grandchildren. Eli Rubinstein, the Israeli attorney general, knew more jokes than I did and told them better.

While the chemistry between the teams was good, the same could not be said of Arafat and Barak. I had put them in cabins close to mine and visited at length with both of them every day, but they didn't visit each other. Arafat continued to feel aggrieved. Barak didn't want to meet alone with Arafat; he was afraid that they would fall into the old patterns where Barak did all the giving and Arafat made no response in kind. Ehud spent most of the day in his cabin, much of it on the phone to Israel trying to hold his coalition together.

By this time, I had gotten to understand Barak better. He was brilliant and brave, and he was willing to go a long way on Jerusalem and on territory. But he had a hard time listening to people who didn't see things the way he did, and his way of doing things was diametrically opposed to honored customs among the Arabs with whom I'd dealt. Barak wanted others to wait until he decided the time was right, then, when he made his best offer, he expected it to be accepted as self-evidently a good deal. His negotiating partners wanted trust-building courtesies and conversations and lots of bargaining.

The culture clash made my team's job harder. They came up with a variety of strategies to break the impasse, and some progress was made after the delegations broke up into different groups to work on specific issues, but neither side had permission to go beyond a certain point.

On the sixth day, Shlomo Ben-Ami and Gilead Sher, with Barak's blessing, went well beyond previously stated Israeli positions in the hope of getting some movement from Saeb Erekat and Mohammed Dahlan, younger members of Arafat's team who we all believed wanted a deal. When the Palestinians didn't offer Barak anything in return for his moves on Jerusalem and territory, I went to see Arafat, taking Helal with me to interpret and Malley to take notes. It was a tough meeting, and it ended with my telling Arafat that I would end the talks and say he had refused to negotiate unless he gave me something to take back to Barak, who was off the wall because Ben-Ami and Sher had gone as far as they had and gotten nothing in return. After a while Arafat gave me a letter that seemed to say that if he was satisfied with the Jerusalem question, I could make the final call on how much land the Israelis kept for settlements and what constituted a fair land swap. I took the letter to Barak and spent a lot of time talking to him, often alone or with the NSC notetaker for Israel, Bruce Reidel. Eventually Barak agreed that Arafat's letter might mean something.

On the seventh day, July 17, we almost lost Barak. He was eating and working when he choked on a peanut and stopped breathing for about forty seconds, until Gid Gernstein, the youngest member of his delegation, administered the Heimlich maneuver. Barak was a tough customer; when he got his breath back, he went back to work as if nothing had happened. For the rest of us, nothing **was** happening. Barak had kept his entire delegation working with him all day long and into the night.

In any process like this, there are always periods of downtime, when some people are working and others aren't. You have to do something to break the tension. I spent several hours of my downtime playing cards with Joe Lockhart, John Podesta, and Doug Band. Doug had worked at the White House for five years while putting himself through graduate and law school at night, and in the spring had become my last presidential aide. He had an interest in the Middle East and was very helpful to me. Chelsea played cards, too. She made the highest Oh Hell! score in the entire two weeks at Camp David.

It was after midnight when Barak finally came to me with proposals. They were less than what Ben-Ami and Sher had already presented to the Palestinians. Ehud wanted me to present them to Arafat as U.S. proposals. I understood his frustration with Arafat, but I couldn't do that; it would have been a disaster, and I told him so. We talked until two-thirty. At three-fifteen he came back, and we talked another hour alone on the back porch of my cabin. Essentially he gave me the go-ahead to see if I could work out a deal on Jerusalem and the West Bank that he could live with and that was consistent with what Ben-Ami and Sher had discussed with their counterparts. That was worth staying up for.

On the morning of the eighth day, I was feeling both anxious and hopeful, anxious because I had been sched-uled to leave for the G-8 summit in Okinawa, which I had to attend for a variety of reasons, and hopeful because Barak's sense of timing and his enormous courage had kicked in. I delayed my departure for Okinawa by a day and met with Arafat. I told him that I thought he could get 91 percent of the West Bank, plus at least a symbolic swap of land near Gaza and the West Bank; a capital in East Jerusalem; sovereignty over the Muslim and Chris-tian quarters of the Old City and the outer neighborhoods of East Jerusalem; planning, zoning, and law-enforcement authority over the rest of the eastern part of the city; and custodianship but not sovereignty over the Temple Mount, which was known as Haram al-Sharif to the Arabs. Arafat balked at not having sovereignty over all of

East Jerusalem, including the Temple Mount. He turned the offer down. I asked him to think about it. While he fretted and Barak fumed, I called Arab leaders for support. Most wouldn't say much, for fear of undercutting Arafat.

On the ninth day, I gave Arafat my best shot again. Again he said no. Israel had gone much further than he had, and he wouldn't even embrace their moves as the basis for future negotiations. Again I called several Arab leaders for help. King Abdullah and President Ben Ali of Tunisia tried to encourage Arafat. They told me he was afraid to make compromises. It looked as if the talks were dead, and on disastrous terms. Both sides clearly wanted a deal, so I asked them to stay and work while I was in Okinawa. They agreed, though after I left, the Palestinians still refused to negotiate on the basis of the ideas I had advanced, saying they had already rejected them. Then the Israelis balked. That was in part my fault. Apparently I had not been as clear with Arafat as I thought I had been about what the terms of staying on should be.

I had left Madeleine and the rest of our team with a real mess. She took Arafat to her farm and Barak to the famous Civil War battlefield at nearby Gettysburg. It lightened them up, but nothing happened between them. Shlomo Ben-Ami and Amnon Shahak, himself a former general, had good talks with Mohammed Dahlan and Mohamed Rashid, but they were the most forward leaning of their respective groups; even if they agreed on everything, they probably couldn't get their leaders on board.

I returned on the thirteenth day of discussions, and we worked all night again, mostly on security issues. Then we did it again on the fourteenth day, going well past 3 a.m. before giving up when effective control over the Temple Mount and all East Jerusalem was not enough for Arafat without the word "sovereignty." In a last-ditch effort I offered to try to sell Barak on full sovereignty for East Jerusalem's outer neighborhoods, limited sovereignty over the inner ones, and "custodial" sovereignty over the Haram. Again Arafat said no. I shut down the talks. It was frustrating and profoundly sad. There was little difference between the two sides on how the affairs of Jerusalem would actually be handled; it was all about who got to claim sovereignty.

I issued a statement saying I had concluded that the parties could not reach agreement at this time given the historical, religious, political, and emotional dimensions of the conflict. To give Barak some cover back home and indicate what had occurred, I said that while Arafat had made clear that he wanted to stay on the path of peace, Barak had shown "particular courage, vision, and an understanding of the historical importance of this moment."

I said that the two delegations had shown each other a genuine respect and understanding unique in my eight years of peacemaking around the world, and for the first time had openly discussed the most sensitive matters in dispute. We now had a better idea of each side's bottom line and I still believed we had a chance to reach an agreement before the year was out.

Arafat had wanted to continue the negotiations, and on more than one occasion had acknowledged that he was unlikely to get a future Israeli government or American team so committed to peace. It was hard to know why he had moved so little. Perhaps his team really hadn't worked through the hard compromises; perhaps they wanted one session to see how much they could squeeze out of Israel before showing their hand. For whatever reasons, they had left Barak exposed in a precarious political situation. It was not for nothing that he was the most decorated soldier in the history of Israel. For all his brusque bullheadedness, he had taken great risks to win a more secure future for Israel. In my remarks to the press, I assured the people of Israel that he had done nothing to compromise their security and said they should be very proud of him.

Arafat was famous for waiting until the very last minute to make a decision, or "five minutes to midnight" as we used to say. I had only six months to go as President. I certainly hoped Arafat's watch kept good time.

FIFTY-FIVE

While the Camp David talks were going on, positive things happened elsewhere. Charlene Barshefsky completed a sweeping trade agreement with Vietnam, and the House adopted an amendment by my longtime supporter Maxine Waters that funded a down payment on our share of the Millennium Debt Relief effort. By this time debt relief had an amazing array of supporters, led by Bono.

By then Bono had become a fixture in Washington political life. He turned out to be a first-class politician, partly through the element of surprise. Larry Summers, who knew everything about economics but little about popular culture, came into the Oval Office one day and remarked that he'd just had a meeting on debt relief with "some guy named Bono—just one name—dressed in jeans, a T-shirt, and big sunglasses. He came to see me about debt relief, and he knows what he's talking about."

The trip to Okinawa was a big success, as the G-8 put some teeth into our commitment to have all the world's children in primary school by 2015. I led off with a $300 million program to provide one good meal a day to nine million children, provided they came to school to get the meal. The initiative had been brought to me by our ambassador to the UN food programs in Rome, George McGovern; McGovern's old partner in pioneering food stamps, Bob Dole; and Congressman Jim McGovern of Massachusetts. I also visited the U.S. forces in Okinawa, thanked Prime Minister Yoshiro Mori for letting them be stationed there, and pledged to reduce the tensions our presence had caused. It was my last G-8 summit, and I was sorry to rush through it to get back to Camp David. The other leaders had been very supportive of my initiatives over eight years, and we had accomplished a lot together.

Chelsea traveled to Okinawa with me. One of the best things about the year for both Hillary and me was that Chelsea was home for the last half of it. She had amassed far more credits in her first three years at Stanford than she needed to graduate so that she could spend the last six months in the White House with us. Now she would be dividing her time between campaigning for her mother and helping me with events in the White House and going with me on foreign trips. She did a great job on both counts, and her presence made life much better for her parents.

At the end of the month I resumed my battle with the Republicans over tax cuts. They still wanted to spend a decade's worth of projected surpluses on them, claiming that the money belonged to the taxpayers and we should give it back to them. It was a persuasive argument except for one thing: the surpluses were projected and the tax cuts would take effect whether the surpluses materialized or not. I attempted to illustrate the point by asking people to imagine that they had gotten one of those heavily advertised letters from well-known TV personality Ed McMahon that started with, "You may have already won $10 million." I said that the people who would spend $10 million upon receiving that letter should support the Republican plan; everyone else should "stick with us and keep the prosperity going."

August was a busy month. It began with the nomination of George W. Bush and Dick Cheney in Philadelphia. Hillary and I went to Martha's Vineyard for a couple of fund-raisers for her, then I flew to Idaho to visit firefighters who were fighting a large and dangerous forest fire. On the ninth, I awarded the Medal of Freedom to fifteen Americans, including the late senator John Chafee, Senator Pat Moynihan, Children's Defense Fund founder Marian Edelman, AIDS activist Dr. Mathilde Krim, Jesse Jackson, civil rights lawyer Judge Cruz Reynoso, and General Wes Clark, who had ended his brilliant military career by commanding our arduous campaign against Milosevic and his ethnic cleansing in Kosovo.

Amid a blizzard of political events, I did one completely nonpolitical one: I went to my friend Bill Hybels's Willow Creek Community Church in South Barrington, Illinois, near Chicago, for a conversation before several hundred people at Bill's ministers' leadership conference. We talked about when I decided to go into politics, where my family went to church and what it meant to me, why so many people still believed I had never apologized for my misconduct, how I used polls, what the most important elements of leadership were, and how I wanted to be remembered. Hybels had an uncanny way of stripping things down to basics and getting me to discuss things I normally would not talk about. I enjoyed taking a few hours away from politics and work to think about the inner life that politics often crowds out.

On August 14, opening night of the Democratic convention, Hillary gave a moving expression of thanks to the Democrats for their support and a mighty declaration of what was at stake in this year's election. Then, after my third convention film produced by Harry and Linda

Thomason, which outlined the accomplishments of our eight years, I was brought onstage to thunderous applause and inspirational music. When the noise died down, I said that the election was about one simple question: "Are we going to keep this progress and prosperity going?"

I asked the Democrats to make sure we applied President Reagan's 1980 standard for whether a party should continue in office: "Are we better off today than we were eight years ago?" The answer proved that Harry Truman was right when he said, "If you want to live like a Republican, you better vote for the Democrats." The crowd roared. We were better off, and not just economically. Jobs were up, but so were adoptions. The debt was down, but so was teen pregnancy. We were becoming both more diverse and more united. We had built and crossed our bridge to the twenty-first century, "and we're not going back."

I made the case for a Democratic Congress, saying that what we did with our prosperity was just as sure a test of America's character, values, and judgment as how we had dealt with adversity in the past. If we had a Democratic Congress, America would already have the Patients' Bill of Rights, a minimum wage increase, stronger equal-pay laws for women, and middle-class tax cuts for college tuition and long-term care.

I praised Hillary for thirty years of public service and especially her work in the White House for children and families, and said that just as she had always been there for our family, she would always be there for the families of New York and America.

Then I argued for Al Gore, emphasizing his strong convictions, good ideas, understanding of the future, and fundamental decency. I thanked Tipper for her mental-health advocacy and applauded Al's selection of Joe Lieberman, and spoke of our thirty-year friendship and Joe's work for civil rights in the South in the sixties. As the first Jewish-American ever to be on a major party's national ticket, Joe provided clear evidence of Al Gore's commitment to building One America.

I ended the speech with personal thanks and a personal plea:

> My friends, fifty-four years ago this week I was born in a summer storm to a young widow in a small southern town. America gave me the chance to live my dreams. And I have tried as hard as I knew how to give you a better chance to live yours. Now, my hair is a little grayer, my wrinkles are a little deeper, but with the same optimism and hope I brought to the work I loved so eight years ago, I want you to know my heart is filled with gratitude.
>
> My fellow Americans, the future of our country is now in your hands. You must think hard, feel deeply, and choose wisely. And remember . . . keep putting people first. Keep building those bridges. And don't stop thinking about tomorrow.

The next day Hillary, Chelsea, and I flew to Monroe, Michigan, for a "passing the torch" rally with Al and Tipper Gore. A good crowd in a battleground state sent Al off to Los Angeles to claim the nomination and become the leader of our party, and me to the local McDonald's, a stop I hadn't made in years.

The Bush-Cheney ticket had settled on a two-pronged campaign message. The positive argument was "compassionate conservatism," giving America the same good conditions we had provided, but with a smaller government and a bigger tax cut. The negative one was that they would elevate the moral tone and end bitter partisanship in Washington. That was, to say the least, disingenuous. I had done everything I knew to reach out to the Republicans in Washington; they had tried to demonize me from day one. Now they were saying, "We'll stop misbehaving if you give us the White House back."

The morality argument should have had no resonance, unless people believed Gore had done something wrong, especially with the super-straight Lieberman on the ticket. I wasn't on the ballot; it was both unfair and self-defeating for voters to blame them for my personal mistakes. I knew their strategy wouldn't work unless the Democrats accepted the legitimacy of the Republican argument and failed to remind voters of the impeachment fiasco and how much more damage the right wing could inflict if they controlled both the White House and the Congress. An NRA vice president had already boasted that if Bush were elected, the NRA would have an office in the White House.

After our convention, the polls showed Al Gore had come from behind to hold a narrow lead, and I accompanied Hillary to the Finger Lakes area of upstate New York for a couple of days of vacation and campaigning. She was running a different race from the one she had begun. Mayor Giuliani had withdrawn, and her new opponent, Long Island congressman Rick Lazio, presented a new challenge: he was attractive and smart, a less polarizing figure who was nevertheless more conservative than Giuliani.

I ended the month with two short trips. After meeting in Washington with Vicente Fox, the president-elect of Mexico, I flew to Nigeria to see President Olusegun

Obasanjo. I wanted to support his efforts to curb AIDS before Nigeria's infection rates reached the levels of southern African nations, and to highlight the recent passage of the African trade bill, which I hoped would help Nigeria's struggling economy. Obasanjo and I attended a gathering on AIDS at which a young girl spoke of her efforts to educate her schoolmates about the disease, and a man named John Ibekwe told the gripping story of his marriage to a woman who was HIV-positive, his becoming infected, and his frantic search to get the medicine for his wife that would enable their child to be born without the virus. Eventually John succeeded, and little Maria was born HIV-free. President Obasanjo asked Mrs. Ibekwe to come up onstage, where he embraced her. It was a touching gesture and sent a clear signal that Nigeria would not fall into the trap of denial that had contributed so much to the spread of AIDS in other countries.

From Nigeria, I flew to Arusha, Tanzania, to the Burundi peace talks, which Nelson Mandela had been chairing. Mandela wanted me to join him and several other African leaders for the closing session to exhort the leaders of Burundi's numerous factions to sign the agreement and avoid another Rwanda. Mandela gave me clear instructions: We were doing a good cop/bad cop routine. I would give a positive speech urging them to do the right thing, then Mandela would demand that the parties sign on to his proposal. It worked: President Pierre Buyoya and thirteen of the nineteen warring parties signed the agreement. Soon all but two of them would sign. Although it was a burdensome trip, going to the Burundi peace conference was an important way to demonstrate to Africa and the world that the United States was a peacemaker. As I said to myself before we began our

Camp David talks, "we're either going to succeed or get caught trying."

On August 30, I flew to Cartagena, Colombia, with Speaker Dennis Hastert and six other House members, Senator Joe Biden and three other senators, and several cabinet members. We all wanted to reinforce America's commitment to President Andrés Pastrana's Plan Colombia, which was intended to free his country of the narco-traffickers and terrorists who controlled about one-third of its territory. Pastrana had risked his life in an attempt to make peace, going alone to meet with the guerrillas in their lair. When he failed, he had asked the United States to help him defeat them with Plan Colombia. With Hastert's strong support, I had gotten more than $1 billion from Congress to do our part.

Cartagena is a beautiful old walled city. Pastrana took us out into the streets to meet officials who were fighting the narco-traffickers and some of the people who had been affected by the violence, including the widow of a police officer slain in the line of duty, one of hundreds killed for their honesty and bravery. Andrés also introduced Chelsea and me to an adorable group of young musicians who called themselves the Children of Vallenato, their home village in an area often ruled by violence. They sang and danced for peace in traditional native dress, and that evening in the streets of Cartagena, Pastrana, Chelsea, and I danced with them.

At the end of the first week of September, after vetoing a bill repealing the estate tax, announcing that I would defer a decision on deploying a missile defense system to my successor, and campaigning with Hillary at the New York State Fair, I went to the United Nations for its Millennium Summit. It was the largest assembly of world leaders ever gathered. My last UN speech was a brief but impassioned appeal for international cooperation on the issues of security, peace, and shared prosperity, in order to build a world that operated according to simple rules: "Everyone counts; everyone has a role to play; and we all do better when we help each other."

After the speech I walked out into the hall to sit with Madeleine Albright and Dick Holbrooke to listen to the next speaker: President Mohammed Khatami of Iran. Iran had held several elections in recent years, for the presidency, for parliament, and for municipal offices. In every case the reformers had won between two-thirds and 70 percent of the vote. The problem was that under the Iranian constitution, a council of Islamic fundamentalists led by Ayatollah Sayyed Ali Khamenei held enormous power; they could nullify certain legislation and prohibit candidates from running for office. And they controlled Iran's foreign intelligence operations and funded its support for terrorism. We had tried to reach out to Khatami and to promote more people-to-people contacts. I had also said that the United States was wrong to support the overthrow of an elected government in Iran in the 1950s. I hoped my gesture of respect would make more progress possible under the next President.

Kofi Annan and I hosted the traditional luncheon, and when it was over I followed my usual custom of standing by my table to shake hands with the leaders who stopped by on the way out. I thought I was at the end when I shook hands with a giant Namibian official, who towered over me. He then moved on, revealing a last greeter who had been invisible behind him: Fidel Castro. Castro stuck out his hand and I shook it, the first President to do so in more than forty years. He said he didn't wish to cause me any trouble but wanted to pay his respects before I left office. I replied that I hoped that someday our nations would be reconciled.

After the UN meetings, OPEC announced an increase in oil production of 800,000 barrels a day, Prime Minister Vajpayee of India came to Washington for a state visit, and on September 19, the Senate followed the House in approving the bill granting normal trade relations with China, thus clearing the way for its entry into the WTO. I was convinced that in time it would prove to be one of the most important foreign policy developments of my eight years.

Hillary had a good September. She won the primary on the twelfth and handily defeated Lazio in their debate moderated by Tim Russert in Buffalo. Lazio had three problems: he claimed that the still distressed economy of upstate New York had turned the corner; ran a misleading ad (for which he was called to account) that implied that Senator Moynihan was supporting him, not Hillary; and got in Hillary's face and tried to bully her into signing a pledge on campaign finance that was not credible. All Hillary had to do was keep her composure and answer the questions, which she did very well. A week later, a new poll showed her leading Lazio 48–39 percent, with new strength among suburban women.

On September 16, I bid an emotional farewell to a large, predominantly African-American crowd at the Congressional Black Caucus dinner, reviewing the record, making my case for Gore and Lieberman, and asking their support for well-qualified but still unconfirmed black judges. Then I threw away the script and closed with these words:

I thank you from the bottom of my heart. Toni
Morrison once said I was the first black President
this country ever had. And I would rather have that
than a Nobel Prize, and I'll tell you why. Because
somewhere, in the deep and lost threads of my own
memory, are the roots of understanding of what you
have known. Somewhere, there was a deep longing
to share the fate of the people who had been left out
and left behind, sometimes brutalized, and too often
ignored or forgotten.

I don't exactly know who all I have to thank for
that. But I'm quite sure I don't deserve any credit for
it, because whatever I did, I really felt I had no other
choice.

I made the same points a few days later, on September
20, to the Congressional Hispanic Caucus dinner, and to
the Bishops Conference of the Church of God in Christ,
where I noted that there were only 120 days left in my
presidency and that I would give them "120 hard days"
working with Congress and trying to make peace in the
Middle East. I knew I'd have an opportunity to win some
more victories as Congress wound down, but I wasn't so
sure about the Middle East.

Several days later my economic team was with me as I
announced that median income had risen by more than
$1,000 in the last year, taking it above $40,000 for the
first time in our history, and that the number of Americans without health insurance had dropped by 1.7 million
the previous year, the first major decline in twelve years.

On September 25, after weeks of efforts by our team to
get peace talks back on track, Barak invited Arafat to his

home for dinner. Near the end of the meal, I called and had a good talk with both of them. The next day both sides sent negotiators to Washington to take up where they had left off at Camp David. On the twenty-eighth, everything changed, as Ariel Sharon became the first leading Israeli politician to walk on the Temple Mount since Israel captured it in the 1967 war. At the time, Moshe Dayan had said that Muslim religious sites would be respected, and thereafter the mount was overseen by Muslims.

Arafat said he had asked Barak to prevent Sharon's stroll, which was clearly intended to affirm Israel's sovereignty over the site and to strengthen his hand against a challenge to his leadership of the Likud Party from former prime minister Netanyahu, who was now sounding more hawkish than Sharon. I had also hoped Barak would prevent Sharon's inflammatory escapade, but Barak told me he couldn't. Instead, Sharon was forbidden to enter the Dome of the Rock, or the Al-Aqsa Mosque, and was escorted to the Mount by a large number of heavily armed police officers.

I and others on our team had urged Arafat to prevent violence. It was a great opportunity for the Palestinians, for once, to refuse to be provoked. I thought Sharon should have been greeted with flowers by Palestinian children and told that when the Temple Mount was under Palestinian control, he would be welcome anytime. But as Abba Eban had said long ago, the Palestinians never miss an opportunity to miss an opportunity. The next day there were large Palestinian demonstrations near the Western Wall, during which Israeli police opened fire with rubber bullets on stone throwers and others. At least five people were killed and hundreds were wounded. As the violence persisted, two vivid images of its pain and futility emerged: a twelve-year-old Palestinian boy shot in the crossfire and dying in his father's arms, and two Israeli soldiers pulled from a building and beaten to death, with their lifeless bodies dragged through the streets and one of their assailants proudly showing his bloodstained hands to the world on television.

While the Middle East was exploding, the Balkans was getting better. In the last week of September, Slobodan Milosevic was defeated for the presidency of Serbia by Vojislav Kostunica in a campaign in which we had helped ensure that the election could not be stolen and Kostunica could get his message out. Milosevic tried to steal the election anyway, but massive demonstrations convinced him he couldn't get away with it, and on October 6, the prime mover behind the Balkan slaughters admitted defeat.

In early October, I hosted a meeting in the Cabinet Room for supporters of the debt-relief initiative. Reverened Pat Robertson was there. His strong support and that of the evangelical Christian community showed how broad and deep support for debt relief had become. In the House, the effort was being pushed by Maxine Waters, one of our most liberal members, and conservative Budget Committee chairman John Kasich. Even Jesse Helms was supporting it, thanks in no small measure to Bono's personal outreach to him. The early results were encouraging: Bolivia had spent $77 million on health and education; Uganda had doubled primary school enrollment; and Honduras was to go from six to nine years of mandatory schooling. I was aiming to get the rest of our contribution in the final budget agreement.

In the second week of the month, Hillary did well in her second, more civilized debate with Rick Lazio. I signed the China trade bill and thanked Charlene Barshefsky and Gene Sperling for their arduous trek to China to hammer out our agreement at the eleventh hour; signed into law my Lands Legacy Initiative and the new investments for Native American communities; and on October 11, in Chappaqua, met Hillary to celebrate our twenty-fifth wedding anniversary. It seemed like only yesterday when we were young and just beginning. Now our daughter was almost out of college and the White House years were almost over. I was confident Hillary would win the Senate race, and optimistic about what the future held for all of us.

My brief reverie was shattered the next day, when a small boat laden with explosives blew up beside the USS **Cole,** in port in Aden, Yemen. Seventeen sailors were killed in what was obviously a terrorist attack. We all thought it was the work of bin Laden and al Qaeda, but we couldn't be sure. The CIA went to work on it, and I sent officials from Defense, State, and the FBI to Yemen, where President Ali Saleh had promised to cooperate fully in the investigation and in bringing the murderers to justice.

Meanwhile, I continued to push the Pentagon and the national security team for more options to get bin Laden. We came close to launching another missile strike at him in October, but the CIA recommended that we call it off at the last minute, believing that the evidence of his presence was insufficiently reliable. The Pentagon recommended against putting Special Forces into Afghanistan, with all the attendant logistical difficulties, unless we had more reliable intelligence on bin Laden's whereabouts. That left bigger military options: a large-scale bombing campaign of all suspected campsites or a sizable invasion.

I thought neither was feasible without a finding of al Qaeda responsibility for the **Cole**. I was very frustrated, and I hoped that before I left office we would locate bin Laden for a missile strike.

After campaign stops in Colorado and Washington, I flew to Sharm el-Sheikh, Egypt, for a summit on the Middle East violence with President Mubarak, King Abdullah, Kofi Annan, and Javier Solana, now secretary-general of the European Union. All of them wanted to end the violence, as did Crown Prince Abdullah of Saudi Arabia, who was not there but had already weighed in on the subject. Barak and Arafat were present, but might as well have been on opposite sides of the world from each other. Barak wanted the violence stopped; Arafat wanted an inquiry into the alleged excessive use of force by the Israeli military and police. George Tenet worked out a security plan with both sides, and I had to sell it to Barak and Arafat, as well as a statement to be read at the end of the summit.

I told Arafat that I had intended to present a proposal to resolve the outstanding issues in the peace talks but couldn't do so until he agreed to the security plan. There could be no peace without shutting down the violence. Arafat agreed to the plan. We then worked until early in the morning on a statement for me to issue on behalf of all the parties. It contained three parts: a commitment to end the violence; the establishment of a fact-finding committee to look into what had caused the uprising and the conduct of both sides, appointed by the United States with the Israelis and Palestinians and in consultation with Kofi Annan; and a commitment to move forward with the peace talks. It sounds simple, but it wasn't. Arafat wanted a UN committee and immediate resumption of the talks.

Barak wanted a U.S. committee and enough delay to see whether the violence would subside. Mubarak and I finally met alone with Arafat and persuaded him to accept the statement. I couldn't have done it without Hosni. I had thought he was often too resistant to getting deeply involved in the peace process, but that night he was strong, clear, and effective.

When I returned to the United States, Hillary, Chelsea, and I went to Norfolk, Virginia, for a memorial service for victims of the USS **Cole** bombing and private meetings with their grieving families. Like the airmen at Khobar Towers, our sailors had been killed in a very different conflict from the kind they had been trained to fight. In this one, the enemy was elusive, everyone was a potential target, our enormous arsenal was not a deterrent, and the openness and information technology of the modern world were being used against us. I knew that eventually we would prevail in the struggle against bin Laden, but I didn't know how many innocent people would lose their lives before we figured out how to do it.

Two days later Hillary, Al and Tipper Gore, and I went to Jefferson City, Missouri, for a memorial service for Governor Mel Carnahan, his son, and a young aide who had been killed when their small plane crashed. Carnahan and I had been close since he endorsed me early in the 1992 campaign. He had been a fine governor and a leader in welfare reform, and at the time of his death he was in a tight race with the incumbent, John Ashcroft, in the U.S. Senate race. It was too late to put someone else on the ballot. A few days later, Jean Carnahan said that if the people of Missouri voted for her husband, she would serve. They did, and Jean served with distinction.

In the last days of October, as the presidential election

came down to the wire, I signed a trade agreement with Jordan's King Abdullah, continued to sign and veto bills, and campaigned in Indiana, Kentucky, Massachusetts, and New York, where I did several events for Hillary. The most fun was a birthday celebration in which Robert De Niro gave me instructions on how to talk like a real New Yorker.

Ever since the convention Al Gore had framed the election as a contest of "the people versus the powerful." That it was; every conceivable conservative interest group—the health insurance industry, the tobacco companies, the heavily polluting industries, the NRA, and many more—was for Governor Bush. The problem with the slogan was that it didn't give Al the full benefit of our record of economic and social progress or put into sharp relief Bush's explicit commitment to undo that progress. Also, the populist edge sounded to some swing voters as if Al, too, might change the economic direction of the country. Along toward the end of the month, Al started saying, "Don't put the prosperity at risk." By the first of November, he was moving up in the polls, though still down by about four points.

In the last week of the campaign, at Governor Gray Davis's request, I flew to California for two days of campaigning for the ticket and our congressional candidates, did a big event in Harlem for Hillary, then on Sunday went home to Arkansas to campaign for Mike Ross, who had served as my driver in the 1982 governor's campaign and was running against Republican congressman Jay Dickey.

I spent the day before the election and election day doing more than sixty radio interviews across the country urging people to vote for Al and Joe and our local Democrats. I had already recorded more than 170 radio ads and telephone messages to be dialed into homes of hard-core Democrats and minorities, asking them to vote for our candidates.

On election day, Hillary, Chelsea, and I voted at Douglas Grafflin Elementary School, our local polling station in Chappaqua. It was a strange and wonderful experience: strange because the school was the only place I'd ever voted outside Arkansas, and after twenty-six years in political life, my name wasn't on the ballot; wonderful because I got to vote for Hillary. Chelsea and I voted first, then hugged each other as we watched Hillary close the curtain and cast a ballot for herself.

Election night was a roller coaster. Hillary won her election, 55–43 percent, a much larger margin than she had in all the pre-election polls but one. I was so proud of her. New York had put her through the wringer, just as it had done to me in 1992. She had been up, down, and up again, but she kept her bearings and pressed ahead.

As we celebrated her victory at the Grand Hyatt Hotel in New York City, Bush and Gore were neck and neck. For weeks everyone had known the election would be close, with many commentators saying that Gore might lose the popular vote but still win the electoral college. Two days before the election, as I looked at the map and the latest polls, I told Steve Ricchetti that I was afraid the reverse could occur. Our base voters had been activated and would turn out as eagerly as the Republicans who wanted the White House back. Al was going to win big states by large margins, but Bush was going to win more small rural states, and they had an advantage in the electoral college because every state got one electoral vote for each House member plus two extra ones for its senators. Going into election day, I still thought Al would win because he had the momentum and he was right on the issues.

Gore did win, by more than 500,000 votes, but the electoral college was in doubt. The race came down to Florida, after Gore won a narrow victory of 366 votes in New Mexico, one of several states that were closer than they would have been had Ralph Nader not been on the ballot. I had asked Bill Richardson to spend the last week in his home state, and he may well have made the difference.

Of the states I had won in 1996, Bush picked up Nevada, Arizona, Missouri, Arkansas, Tennessee, Kentucky, Ohio, West Virginia, and New Hampshire. Tennessee had been growing increasingly Republican. In 1992, 1996, and 2000, the Democratic vote had held steady at between 47 and 48 percent. The NRA also hurt Al badly there and in several other states, including Arkansas. For example, Yell County, where the Clintons had settled a century earlier, is a populist, culturally conservative county a Democrat has to win to carry the state in a tight race. Gore lost it to Bush 50–47 percent. The NRA did that. I might have been able to turn it around, but it would have taken two or three days of rural work to do it, and I didn't know how big the problem was until I went home right before the election.

The gun lobby tried to beat Al in Michigan and Pennsylvania, and might have done so had it not been for a heroic effort by the local labor unions, which had a lot of NRA members themselves. They fought back by saying, "Gore won't take your gun away, but Bush will take your union away!" Unfortunately, in the rural areas of

Arkansas, Tennessee, Kentucky, West Virginia, Missouri, and Ohio, there weren't enough union members to win the war on the ground.

In Kentucky, our stand against the big tobacco companies marketing cigarettes to kids hurt Al in the tobacco-growing areas. In West Virginia, he was damaged by the failure of Weirton Steel, an employee-owned company; the employees and their families were convinced the collapse was caused by my failure to limit cheap imported steel from Russia and Asia during the Asian financial crisis. The evidence indicated that the company had failed for other reasons, but the Weirton workers thought otherwise and Al paid the price.

New Hampshire went for Bush by a margin of just over 7,000 because Nader got 22,198 votes. Even worse, Nader received more than 90,000 votes in Florida, where Bush was hanging on by a thread in an election contest that would drag on for more than a month.

As the Florida vote battle began, it was clear that we had picked up four seats in the Senate and one in the House. Three incumbent House Republicans were defeated, including Jay Dickey, who lost to Mike Ross in Arkansas, and the Democrats picked up four seats in California, prevailing in all but one of the contested races. Al was at a disadvantage going into the election recount in Florida because the chief election official, Secretary of State Katherine Harris, was a conservative Republican who was close to Governor Jeb Bush, and the state legislature that would certify the electors was dominated by conservative Republicans. On the other hand, the state supreme court, which presumably would have the final say on the counting of ballots, had more judges appointed by Democratic governors and was thought to be less partisan.

Two days later, still not knowing who my successor would be, I saw Arafat in the Oval Office. The violence was subsiding and I thought he might be serious about peace. I told him that I had only ten weeks left to make an agreement. In a private moment I held his arm, stared straight at him, and told him I also had a chance to make an agreement with North Korea to end its long-range missile production, but I would have to go there to do it. The whole trip would take a week or longer by the time I made the obligatory stops in South Korea, Japan, and China.

If we were going to make peace in the Middle East, I knew I would have to close the deal. I told Arafat I had done everything I could to get the Palestinians a state on the West Bank and Gaza while protecting the security of Israel. After all my efforts, if Arafat wasn't going to make peace, he owed it to me to tell me, so that I could go to North Korea to end another serious security threat. He pleaded with me to stay, saying that we had to finish the peace and that if we didn't do it before I left office, it would be at least five years before we'd be this close to peace again.

That night, we had a dinner to celebrate the two hundredth anniversary of the White House. Lady Bird Johnson, President and Mrs. Ford, President and Mrs. Carter, and President and Mrs. Bush were all there to mark the birthday of the people's house, which every President since John Adams had inhabited. It was a wonderful moment in American history, but a tense one for President and Mrs. Bush, who had to be on edge with their son's election hanging fire. I was glad they had come.

A few days later Chelsea and I went to Brunei for the annual APEC summit. Sultan Hassanal Bolkiah hosted our meeting in a beautiful new hotel and convention center. We made some headway on the reforms necessary to avoid another Asian financial crisis, and Singapore prime minister Goh Chok Tong and I agreed to start negotiations on a bilateral free-trade agreement. I also enjoyed a round of golf with Prime Minister Goh on a night golf course designed to help golfers manage the intense heat. I had instituted the APEC leaders' meeting back in 1993, and I was pleased with the expansion of the group and the work done since then. At my last APEC meeting I thought the effort had borne fruit, not simply in specific agreements, but also in building an institution that tied the United States to Asia in the new century.

After Brunei, Chelsea and I went to Vietnam for a historic visit to Hanoi, Ho Chi Minh City (the old Saigon), and a site where Vietnamese were working with Americans to unearth the remains of our men still listed as missing in action. Hillary flew in to join us from Israel, where she had gone to attend the funeral of Leah Rabin.

I met with the Communist Party leader, the president, the prime minister, and the mayor of Ho Chi Minh City. The higher the position, the more likely the leader was to sound like an old-style Communist. The party leader, Le Kha Phieu, tried to use my opposition to the Vietnam War to condemn what the United States had done as an imperialist act. I was angry about it, especially since he said it in the presence of our ambassador, Pete Peterson, who had been a prisoner of war. I told the leader in no uncertain terms that while I had disagreed with our Vietnam policy, those who had pursued it were not imperialists or colonialists, but good people who believed they were fighting communism. I pointed at Pete and said he hadn't spent six and a half years in the prison known as the Hanoi Hilton because he wanted to colonize Vietnam.

We had turned a new page with normalized relations, the trade agreement, and two-way cooperation on MIA issues; now was not the time to reopen old wounds. The president, Tran Duc Luong, was only a little less dogmatic.

Prime Minister Phan Van Khai and I had established a good relationship at the APEC meetings; a year earlier he had told me he appreciated my opposition to the war. When I said that the Americans who disagreed with me and supported the war were good people who wanted freedom for the Vietnamese, he replied, "I know." Khai was interested in the future and hoped the United States would give Vietnam assistance in caring for the victims of Agent Orange and developing its economy. The mayor of Ho Chi Minh City, Vo Viet Thanh, sounded like every good aggressive American mayor I knew. He bragged about balancing his budget, reducing his payroll, and working for more foreign investment. Besides the officials, I shook hands with a large crowd of friendly people who gathered spontaneously to greet us after an informal lunch at a local restaurant. They wanted to build a common future.

The trip to the MIA site was an experience none of us would ever forget. I thought back over the years to my high school classmates who had died in Vietnam and to the man I'd helped when I was in Moscow in 1970, who was searching for information about his missing son. The Americans working with the Vietnamese crew believed, based on information from local residents, that a missing pilot, Lieutenant Colonel Lawrence Evert, had crashed there more than thirty years earlier. His now grown children accompanied us to the site. Working knee-deep in mud with the Vietnamese, our soldiers cut the mud into large chunks, took it to a nearby shed, and sifted through it. They had already recovered parts of the plane and a uniform, and were close to having enough for an identification. The work was supervised by an American archaeologist who was himself a Vietnam veteran. He said this was the most rewarding dig in the world. The care and detail of their work was amazing, as were the efforts of the Vietnamese to help. Soon, the Everts found their father.

On the way home from Vietnam, I found out that Chuck Ruff, my White House counsel during the impeachment proceeding, had died suddenly. When I landed, I went to see his wife, Sue; Chuck was an extraordinary man who had led our defense team in the Senate with skill and courage.

The rest of November was consumed by the Middle East and the Florida recount, which was cut off with thousands of votes still uncounted in three big counties, a result unfair to Gore since it was obvious from the votes that had been thrown out for errors resulting from confusing ballots and flawed punch-card devices that thousands more Floridians had intended to vote for Gore than for Bush. Gore contested the election in court. At the same time, Barak and Arafat were meeting again in the Middle East. It wasn't clear to me whether we were going to win or lose either the battle for Florida or the struggle for peace.

On December 5, Hillary went to Capitol Hill for her initiation as a freshman senator. The night before, I kidded her about going to her first day of "Senator School," telling her she had to get a good night's sleep and wear a nice outfit. She was excited about it, and I was really happy for her.

Three days later, I traveled to Nebraska, the only state I

had not yet visited as President, for a speech at the University of Nebraska at Kearney. It was in effect a valedictory address in the heartland urging continued American leadership in the world beyond our borders. Meanwhile, the Florida Supreme Court ordered the inclusion of more recounted votes in Palm Beach and Dade counties, and the recount of 45,000 more votes according to the standard of Florida law: a ballot was to be counted only if the intent of the voter was clear. Bush's margin was now down to 154 votes.

Governor Bush immediately appealed to the U.S. Supreme Court to stop the recount. Several lawyers told me the Supreme Court wouldn't take the case; the mechanics of elections were a question of state law unless they were used to discriminate against a group of citizens, like racial minorities. Also, it is difficult to get a court-ordered injunction against an otherwise legal action, like an election recount or razing a building when the owner agrees. To do so, a party must show that irreparable harm would result unless the activity is stopped. In a 5–4 decision, Justice Scalia wrote an astonishingly honest opinion granting the injunction. What was the irreparable harm? Scalia said. That counting the ballots might "cast a cloud upon what [Bush] claims to be the legitimacy of his election." Well, he was right about that. If Gore got more votes than Bush in Florida, it would be harder for the Supreme Court to give Bush the presidency anyway.

We were having a Christmas reception at the White House that night, and I asked every lawyer who came through the receiving line if he or she had ever heard of such a ruling. No one had. The Court was to hand down another opinion shortly, on the underlying issue of whether the recount itself was constitutional. Now we knew they would kill it 5–4. I told Hillary that Scalia would never be allowed to write the second opinion; he had been too candid in this one.

On December 11, Hillary, Chelsea, and I flew to Ireland, to the land of my ancestors and the scene of so much of the peacemaking I had done. We stopped in Dublin to see Bertie Ahern, then went to Dundalk near the border for a massive rally in a city that was once a hotbed of IRA activity and was now a force for peace. The streets were bright with Christmas lights as the large crowd cheered wildly and sang "Danny Boy" to me. Seamus Heaney once said of Yeats: "His interest was to clear a space in the mind and in the world for the miraculous." I thanked the Irish for filling that space with the miracle of peace.

We went to Belfast, where I met with the Northern Irish leaders, including David Trimble, Seamus Mallon, John Hume, and Gerry Adams. Then we went with Tony and Cherie Blair, Bertie Ahern, and George Mitchell to a large meeting of both Catholics and Protestants in the Odyssey Arena. It was still somewhat unusual for them to gather together in Belfast. Some sharp disputes remained involving the new police force and the schedule and method of putting arms beyond use. I asked them to keep working on the problems and remember that the enemies of peace didn't need their approval: "All they need is your apathy." I reminded the audience that the Good Friday accord had given heart to peacemakers the world over, and cited the just announced agreement ending the bloody conflict between Eritrea and Ethiopia that the United States had helped broker. I closed by saying how much I had loved working with them for peace, "but the issue is not how I feel; it's how your kids are going to live."

After the event, my family flew to England to stay with

the Blairs at Chequers and listen to Al Gore give his concession speech. The night before, at 10 p.m., the Supreme Court had ruled, 7–2, that the Florida recount was unconstitutional because there were no uniform standards for defining the clear intent of the voter for purposes of a recount, and therefore different vote counters might count or interpret the same ballots differently. Therefore, the Court said, allowing any of the disputed votes to be counted, no matter how clear the voters' intent, would deny equal protection of the law to those whose ballots weren't counted. I disagreed strongly with the decision, but I was heartened that Justices Souter and Breyer wanted to send the case back to the Florida Supreme Court to set a standard and proceed with the recount in a hurry. The electoral college was meeting soon. The other five justices in the majority disagreed. By 5–4, the same five justices who had stopped the vote count three days earlier now said it had to give the election to Bush because under Florida law the recount had to be finished by midnight on that day anyway.

It was an appalling decision. A narrow conservative majority that had made a virtual fetish of states' rights had now stripped Florida of a clear state function: the right to recount votes the way it always had. The five justices who didn't want the votes counted by any standard claimed to advance equal protection by depriving thousands of people of their constitutional right to have their votes counted even if their intent was crystal clear. They said Bush should be awarded the election because the votes couldn't be counted in the next two hours, when, after already killing three days of recounting, they had delayed issuing the opinion until 10 p.m., to make absolutely sure the recount could not be completed on time. The five-vote majority didn't make any bones about what it was up to: the opinion clearly stated that the ruling could not be used as precedent in future election law cases; its reasoning was "limited to the present circumstances, for the problem of equal protection in election processes generally presents many complexities." If Gore had been ahead in the vote count and Bush behind, there's not a doubt in my mind that the same Supreme Court would have voted 9–0 to count the votes. And I would have supported the decision.

Bush v. **Gore** will go down in history as one of the worst decisions the Supreme Court ever made, along with the **Dred Scott** case, which said that a slave who escaped to freedom was still a piece of property to be returned to its owner; **Plessy** v. **Ferguson,** upholding the legality of racial segregation; the cases in the twenties and thirties invalidating legislative protections for workers, like minimum wage and maximum workweek laws, as violations of the property rights of employers; and the **Korematsu** case, in which the Supreme Court approved the blanket internment of Japanese-Americans in camps after Pearl Harbor. We had lived through and rejected the premises of all those previous reactionary decisions. I knew America would also get beyond this dark day when five Republican justices stripped thousands of their fellow Americans of their votes, just because they could.

Al Gore gave a marvelous concession speech. It was genuine, gracious, and patriotic. When I called to congratulate him, he told me that a friend who was a professional comedian had joked to him that he had gotten the best of both worlds: he had won the popular vote and didn't have to do the job.

The next morning, after Tony Blair and I talked a bit, I

walked outside, complimented Al, and pledged to work with President-elect Bush. Then Tony and Cherie accompanied Hillary, Chelsea, and me to the University of Warwick, where I gave another of my farewell speeches, this one on the approach to globalization our Third Way group had embraced: trade plus a global contract for economic empowerment, education, health care, and democratic governance. The speech also gave me a chance to publicly thank Tony Blair for his friendship and our partnership. I had treasured our times together and would miss them.

Before we left England, we went to Buckingham Palace, accepting Queen Elizabeth's kind invitation to tea. We had a pleasant visit, discussing the election and world affairs. Then Her Majesty took the unusual step of accompanying us down to the ground floor of the palace and walking us out to our car to say good-bye. She, too, had been gracious and kind to me over the past eight years.

On December 15, I reached an omnibus budget agreement with Congress, the last major legislative victory of my eight years. The education budget was especially good. Finally, I secured more than $1 billion to repair schools; the largest increase ever in Head Start; enough money to put 1.3 million students in after-school programs; a 25 percent increase in the fund to hire 100,000 teachers; and more funding for Pell Grants, for our Gear Up mentoring program, and for our efforts to turn around failing schools. The bill also included the New Markets initiative, a large increase in biomedical research, health-care coverage for welfare recipients and disabled people moving into the workforce, and the Millennium Debt Relief initiative.

John Podesta, Steve Ricchetti, my legislative aide Larry Stein, and our whole team had done a great job. My last

year, when I was supposed to be a lame duck, had
resulted in the passage of a surprising number of the State
of the Union recommendations. Besides those mentioned above, Congress had passed the Africa-Caribbean
trade bill, the China trade bill, the Lands Legacy initiative, and a large increase in child-care assistance to working families.

I was still deeply disappointed in the election outcome
and concerned about the Middle East, but after the visit
to Ireland and England and the budget victories, I was
finally getting into the Christmas spirit.

On the eighteenth, Jacques Chirac and Romano Prodi
came to the White House for my last meeting with European Union leaders. By then we were old friends, and I
was glad to receive them one last time. Jacques thanked
me for supporting the growth of the EU and transatlantic
relations. I responded that we had managed three great
questions well: the growth and expansion of the EU; the
expansion of NATO and the new relationship with Russia; and the problems of the Balkans.

While I was meeting with Chirac and Prodi, the Middle East teams began talks at Bolling Air Force Base in
Washington, Hillary received Laura Bush at the White
House, and our family went house shopping in Washington. The people of New York had decided she wasn't leaving town after all. Eventually we found a lovely house that
bordered Rock Creek Park in the embassy area off Massachusetts Avenue.

The next day President-elect Bush came to the White
House for the same meeting I had had with his father
eight years earlier. We talked about the campaign, White
House operations, and national security. He was putting
together an experienced team from past Republican

administrations who believed that the biggest security issues were the need for national missile defense and Iraq. I told him that based on the last eight years, I thought his biggest security problems, in order, would be Osama bin Laden and al Qaeda; the absence of peace in the Middle East; the standoff between nuclear powers India and Pakistan, and the ties of the Pakistanis to the Taliban and al Qaeda; North Korea; and then Iraq. I said that my biggest disappointment was not getting bin Laden, that we still might achieve an agreement in the Middle East, and that we had almost tied up a deal with North Korea to end its missile program, but that he probably would have to go there to close the deal.

He listened to what I had to say without much comment, then changed the subject to how I did the job. My only advice was that he should put together a good team and try to do what he thought was right for the country. Then we talked a little more politics.

Bush had been a very adept politician in 2000, building a coalition with moderate rhetoric and quite conservative-specific proposals. The first time I had seen him give his "compassionate conservative" speech in Iowa, I knew he had a chance to win. After the primaries he was badly positioned way out on the right and behind in the polls, but he had walked back to the center by moderating his rhetoric, urging the Republican Congress not to balance the budget on the backs of the poor, and even supporting my position on a couple of foreign policy issues. When he was governor, his conservatism had been leavened by the need to work with a Democratic state legislature and by the support he had received from Democratic lieutenant governor Bob Bullock, who wielded a lot of the day-to-day power under the Texas system. Now he would govern with a conservative Republican Congress. He had to choose his own way. After our meeting I knew he was fully capable of getting his way, but I couldn't tell whether it would be the path he had followed as governor or the one he had taken to defeat John McCain in the South Carolina primary.

December 23 was a fateful day for the Middle East peace process. After the two sides had been negotiating again for several days at Bolling Air Force Base, my team and I became convinced that unless we narrowed the range of debate, in effect forcing the big compromises up front, there would never be an agreement. Arafat was afraid of being criticized by other Arab leaders; Barak was losing ground to Sharon at home. So I brought the Palestinian and Israeli teams into the Cabinet Room and read them my "parameters" for proceeding. These were developed after extensive private talks with the parties separately since Camp David. If they accepted the parameters within four days, we would go forward. If not, we were through.

I read them slowly so that both sides could take careful notes. On territory, I recommended 94 to 96 percent of the West Bank for the Palestinians with a land swap from Israel of 1 to 3 percent, and an understanding that the land kept by Israel would include 80 percent of the settlers in blocs. On security, I said Israeli forces should withdraw over a three-year period while an international force would be gradually introduced, with the understanding that a small Israeli presence in the Jordan Valley could remain for another three years under the authority of the international forces. The Israelis would also be able to maintain their early-warning station in the West Bank with a Palestinian liaison presence. In the event of an "imminent and demonstrable threat to Israel's security," there would be provision for emergency deployments in the West Bank.

The new state of Palestine would be "nonmilitarized," but would have a strong security force; sovereignty over its airspace, with special arrangements to meet Israeli training and operational needs; and an international force for border security and deterrence.

On Jerusalem, I recommended that the Arab neighborhoods be in Palestine and the Jewish neighborhoods in Israel, and that the Palestinians should have sovereignty over the Temple Mount/Haram and the Israelis sovereignty over the Western Wall and the "holy space" of which it is a part, with no excavation around the wall or under the Mount, at least without mutual consent.

On refugees, I said that the new state of Palestine should be the homeland for refugees displaced in the 1948 war and afterward, without ruling out the possibility that Israel would accept some of the refugees according to its own laws and sovereign decisions, giving priority to the refugee populations in Lebanon. I recommended an international effort to compensate refugees and assist them in finding houses in the new state of Palestine, in the land-swap areas to be transferred to Palestine, in their current host countries, in other willing nations, or in Israel. Both parties should agree that this solution would satisfy UN Security Council Resolution 194.

Finally, the agreement had to clearly mark the end of the conflict and put an end to all violence. I suggested a new UN Security Council resolution saying that this agreement, along with the final release of Palestinian prisoners, would fulfill the requirements of resolutions, 242 and 338.

I said these parameters were nonnegotiable and were the best I could do, and I wanted the parties to negotiate a final status agreement within them. After I left, Dennis Ross and other members of our team stayed behind to clarify any misunderstanding, but they refused to hear complaints. I knew the plan was tough for both parties, but it was time—past time—to put up or shut up. The Palestinians would give up the absolute right of return; they had always known they would have to, but they never wanted to admit it. The Israelis would give up East Jerusalem and parts of the Old City, but their religious and cultural sites would be preserved; it had been evident for some time that for peace to come, they would have to do that. The Israelis would also give up a little more of the West Bank and probably a larger land swap than Barak's last best offer, but they would keep enough to hold at least 80 percent of the settlers. And they would get a formal end to the conflict. It was a hard deal, but if they wanted peace, I thought it was fair to both sides.

Arafat immediately began to equivocate, asking for "clarifications." But the parameters were clear; either he would negotiate within them or not. As always, he was playing for more time. I called Mubarak and read him the points. He said they were historic and he could encourage Arafat to accept them.

On the twenty-seventh, Barak's cabinet endorsed the parameters with reservations, but all their reservations were within the parameters, and therefore subject to negotiations anyway. It was historic: an Israeli government had said that to get peace, there would be a Palestinian state in roughly 97 percent of the West Bank, counting the swap, and all of Gaza, where Israel also had settlements. The ball was in Arafat's court.

I was calling other Arab leaders daily to urge them to pressure Arafat to say yes. They were all impressed with Israel's acceptance and told me they believed Arafat should take the deal. I have no way of knowing what they told him, though the Saudi ambassador, Prince Bandar, later told me he and Crown Prince Abdullah had the distinct impression Arafat was going to accept the parameters.

On the twenty-ninth, Dennis Ross met with Abu Ala, whom we all respected, to make sure Arafat understood the consequences of rejection. I would be gone. Ross would be gone. Barak would lose the upcoming election to Sharon. Bush wouldn't want to jump in after I had invested so much and failed.

I still didn't believe Arafat would make such a colossal mistake. The previous day I had announced that I would not travel to North Korea to close the agreement banning its production of long-range missiles, saying I was confident the next administration would consummate the deal based on the good work that had been done. I hated to give up on ending the North Korean missile program. We had stopped their plutonium and missile testing programs, and had refused to deal with them on other issues without involving South Korea, setting the stage for Kim Dae Jung's "sunshine policy." Kim's brave outreach offered more hope for reconciliation than at any time since the end of the Korean War, and he had just been awarded the Nobel Peace Prize for it. Madeleine Albright had made a trip to North Korea and was convinced that if I went, we could make the missile agreement. Although I wanted to take the next step, I simply couldn't risk being halfway around the world when we were so close to peace in the Middle East, especially after Arafat had assured me that he was eager for an agreement and had implored me not to go.

Besides the Middle East and the budget, a surprising number of other things had happened in the last thirty days. I marked the seventh anniversary of the Brady bill with the announcement that it had now prevented 611,000 felons, fugitives, and stalkers from buying handguns; observed World AIDS Day at Howard University with representatives from twenty-four African countries, saying that we had cut the death rate by more than 70 percent in the United States and now had to do much more in Africa and other places where the disease was raging; unveiled the design of my presidential library, a long, narrow glass-and-steel "bridge to the twenty-first century" jutting out above the Arkansas River; announced an effort to increase immunizations among inner-city children, whose vaccination rates remained far below the national average; signed my last veto, of a bankruptcy reform bill that was much harsher to lower-income debtors than to wealthy ones; issued strong regulations to protect the privacy of medical records; hailed India's decision to maintain its cease-fire in Kashmir and Pakistan's upcoming withdrawal of troops along the Line of Control; and announced new regulations to reduce unhealthy diesel fuel emissions from trucks and buses. Together with the year-old emissions standards on cars and SUVs, the new rules ensured that by the end of the decade, new vehicles would be up to 95 percent cleaner than those now on the road, preventing many thousands of cases of respiratory illness and premature death.

Three days before Christmas, I granted executive clemency or commutations of sentences to sixty-two people. I hadn't given many pardons in my first term and was anxious to deal with the backlog. President Carter had granted 566 clemencies in four years. President Ford had granted 409 in two and a half years. President Reagan's total was 406 in his eight years. President Bush had granted only 77, and they included the controversial pardons of the Iran-Contra figures, and the release of Orlando Bosch, an anti-Castro Cuban the FBI believed to be guilty of multiple murders.

My philosophy on pardons and commutations of sentences, developed while I was attorney general and governor of Arkansas, was conservative when it came to shortening sentences and liberal in granting pardons for nonviolent offenses once people had served their sentences and spent a reasonable amount of time afterward as law-abiding citizens, if for no other reason than to give them their voting rights back. There was a pardon office in the Justice Department that reviewed applications and made recommendations. I had been receiving them for eight years and had learned two things: the people over at Justice took too long to review the applications, and they recommended denial in almost all the cases.

I understood how it had happened. In Washington everything was political and almost every pardon was potentially controversial. If you were a civil servant, the only surefire way to stay out of trouble was to say no. The Justice Department's pardon office knew that they couldn't get heat for delaying cases or for recommending denials; a constitutional function vested in the President was slowly being transferred into the bowels of the Justice Department.

For the last several months, we had been pushing Justice hard to send us more files, and they were doing better.

Of the fifty-nine people I pardoned and the three whose sentences I commuted, most were people who'd made a mistake, served their time, and become good citizens. I also issued pardons in the so-called girlfriend cases. They involved women who had been arrested because their husbands or boyfriends had committed an offense, usually drug-related. The women were threatened with long sentences, even if they hadn't themselves been directly involved in the crime, unless they provided testimony against their men. Those who refused or didn't know enough to be helpful got long jail terms. In several cases, the men in question later cooperated with prosecutors and received shorter sentences than the women had. We had been working on these cases for months. I had already pardoned four of them the previous summer.

I also pardoned former House Ways and Means Committee chairman Dan Rostenkowski. Rostenkowski had done a lot for his country and had more than paid for his mistakes. And I pardoned Archie Schaffer, an executive of Tyson Foods who was caught in the Espy investigation and was facing a mandatory jail sentence for violating an old law Schaffer knew nothing about, because he had made travel arrangements, as instructed, so that Espy could come to a Tyson retreat.

After the Christmas clemencies, we were flooded with requests, many from people upset at the delay in the regular process. Over the next five weeks we worked through hundreds of requests, rejecting hundreds more and granting 140, bringing my eight-year total to 456, out of more than 7,000 petitions for clemency. My White House counsel Beth Nolan, Bruce Lindsey, and my pardon attorney, Meredith Cabe, worked through as many as they could, getting information and clearance from the Justice

Department. Some of the decisions were easy, like the cases of Susan McDougal and Henry Cisneros, who had been horribly mistreated by independent counsels; more girlfriend cases; and a large number of routine requests that probably should have been granted years earlier. One of them was a mistake based on inadequate information because the Justice Department didn't know that the man in question was under investigation in a different state. Most of the pardons were for people of modest means who had no way to break through the system.

The most controversial pardons went to Marc Rich and his partner, Pincus Green. Rich, a wealthy businessman, had left the United States for Switzerland shortly before he was indicted on tax and other charges for allegedly falsely reporting the price of certain oil transactions to minimize his tax liability. There were several such cases in the 1980s, when some oil was under price controls and some was not, inviting the dishonest to underestimate their income or to overcharge their customers. During that time, several people and companies were charged with violating the law, but the individuals were usually charged with a civil offense. It was extremely rare for tax charges to be prosecuted under the racketeering statutes, as Rich and Green were, and after they were charged, the Justice Department ordered U.S. attorneys to stop doing it. After he was indicted, Rich stayed overseas, mostly in Israel and Switzerland.

The government had allowed Rich's business to continue to operate after he agreed to pay $200 million in fines, more than four times the $48 million in taxes the government claimed he had evaded. Professor Marty Ginsburg, a tax expert and husband of Justice Ruth Bader Ginsburg, and Harvard Law professor Bernard Wolfman had reviewed the transactions in question and concluded that Rich's companies were right in their tax computations, which meant that Rich himself had not owed any taxes on these transactions. Rich agreed to waive the statute of limitations so that he could still be sued by the government in a civil action as all other offenders had been. Ehud Barak asked me three times to pardon Rich because of Rich's services to Israel and his help with the Palestinians, and several other Israeli figures in both major parties urged his release. Finally, the Justice Department said it had no objections and would lean toward granting the pardon if it advanced our foreign policy interests.

Most everyone thought I was wrong to pardon a wealthy fugitive whose ex-wife was a supporter of mine and who had retained one of my former White House counsels on his legal team, along with two prominent Republican lawyers. Rich had also been recently represented by Lewis "Scooter" Libby, Vice President–elect Dick Cheney's chief of staff. I may have made a mistake, at least in the way I allowed the case to come to my attention, but I made the decision based on the merits. As of May 2004, Rich still had not been sued by the Justice Department, a surprising development, since the burden of proof is much easier for the government to make in a civil case than in a criminal one.

Although I would later be criticized for some of the pardons I granted, I was more concerned by a few I didn't grant. For example, I thought Michael Milken had a persuasive case, because of the good work he had done on prostate cancer after his release from prison, but Treasury and the Securities and Exchange Commission were adamantly against my pardoning him, saying it would send the wrong signal at a time when they were trying to enforce high standards in the financial industry. The two cases I most regretted turning down were Webb Hubbell and Jim Guy Tucker. Tucker's case was on appeal and Hubbell had actually broken the law and had not been out of jail for the usual period before being considered for a pardon. But they both had been abused by Ken Starr's office for their refusal to lie. Neither of them would have endured a fraction of what they did had I not been elected President and fallen into Starr's clutches. David Kendall and Hillary strongly urged me to pardon them. Everyone else was adamantly against it. Finally, I gave in to my staff's hard-nosed judgment. I've regretted it ever since. I later apologized to Jim Guy Tucker when I saw him and will do the same to Webb one day.

Our Christmas was like all the others, but more savored because we knew it was our last at the White House. I would enjoy these last receptions more and the chance to see so many people who shared our time in Washington. I was looking more carefully now at all the ornaments Chelsea, Hillary, and I put on our tree, and at the bells, books, Christmas plates, stockings, pictures, and standing Santa Clauses with which we filled the Yellow Oval Room. I found myself taking time to walk into all the rooms on the second and third floors to look more closely at all the paintings and old furniture. And I finally got around to getting the White House ushers to provide me with a history of all the White House grandfather clocks, which I used as I studied them. The portraits of my predecessors and their wives took on a new meaning as Hillary and I realized we'd be among them before long. Both of us had chosen Simmie Knox to paint our portraits: we liked Knox's lifelike style, and he would be the first African-

American portraitist to have his work hang in the White House.

In the week after Christmas I signed a few more bills and appointed Roger Gregory to be the first African-American judge on the Fourth Circuit Court of Appeals. Gregory was well qualified, and Jesse Helms had blocked a black judge there long enough. It was a "recess" appointment, one a President can make for a year, when Congress is not in session. I was betting the new President wouldn't want an all-white court of appeals in the Southeast.

I also announced that with the budget just enacted, there would be enough money to pay $600 billion of the debt down over four years, and if we stayed on the present course, we would be debt-free by 2010, freeing up twelve cents of every tax dollar for tax cuts or new investments. Because of our fiscal responsibility, long-term interest rates were now, after all the growth, 2 percent lower than when I took office, reducing the costs of mortgages, car payments, business loans, and student loans. The low interest rates had put more money in people's pockets than tax cuts would have.

Finally, on the last day of the year, I signed the treaty by which America joined the International Criminal Court. Senator Lott and most Republican senators were strongly opposed to it, fearing that U.S. soldiers sent to foreign lands would be hauled before the court for political purposes. I had been concerned about that, too, but the treaty was now drafted in a manner that I was convinced would prevent that from happening. I had been among the first world leaders to call for an International War Crimes Tribunal, and I thought the United States should support it.

We passed up Renaissance Weekend again that year so that our family could spend the last New Year's at Camp

David. I still hadn't heard from Arafat. On New Year's Day, I invited him to the White House the next day. Before he came, he received Prince Bandar and the Egyptian ambassador at his hotel. One of Arafat's younger aides told us that they had pushed him hard to say yes. When Arafat came to see me, he asked a lot of questions about my proposal. He wanted Israel to have the Wailing Wall, because of its religious significance, but asserted that the remaining fifty feet of the Western Wall should go to the Palestinians. I told him he was wrong, that Israel should have the entire wall to protect itself from someone using one entrance of the tunnel that ran beneath the wall from damaging the remains of the temples beneath the Haram. The Old City has four quarters: Jewish, Muslim, Christian, and Armenian. It was assumed that Palestine would get the Muslim and Christian quarters, with Israel getting the other two. Arafat argued that he should have a few blocks of the Armenian quarter because of the Christian churches there. I couldn't believe he was talking to me about this.

Arafat was also trying to wiggle out of giving up the right of return. He knew he had to but was afraid of the criticism he would get. I reminded him that Israel had promised to take some of the refugees from Lebanon whose families had lived in what was now northern Israel for hundreds of years, but that no Israeli leader would ever let in so many Palestinians that the Jewish character of the state could be threatened in a few decades by the higher Palestinian birthrate. There were not going to be two majority-Arab states in the Holy Land; Arafat had acknowledged that by signing the 1993 peace agreement with its implicit two-state solution. Besides, the agreement had to be approved by Israeli citizens in a referendum. The right of return was a deal breaker. I wouldn't think of asking the Israelis to vote for it. On the other hand, I thought the Israelis would vote for a final settlement within the parameters I had laid out. If there was an agreement, I even thought Barak might be able to come back and win the election, though he was running well behind Sharon in the polls, in an electorate frightened by the intifada and angered by Arafat's refusal to make peace.

At times Arafat seemed confused, not wholly in command of the facts. I had felt for some time that he might not be at the top of his game any longer, after all the years of spending the night in different places to dodge assassins' bullets, all the countless hours on airplanes, all the endless hours of tension-filled talks. Perhaps he simply couldn't make the final jump from revolutionary to statesman. He had grown used to flying from place to place, giving mother-of-pearl gifts made by Palestinian craftsmen to world leaders and appearing on television with them. It would be different if the end of violence took Palestine out of the headlines and instead he had to worry about providing jobs, schools, and basic services. Most of the young people on Arafat's team wanted him to take the deal. I believe Abu Ala and Abu Mazen also would have agreed but didn't want to be at odds with Arafat.

When he left, I still had no idea what Arafat was going to do. His body language said no, but the deal was so good I couldn't believe anyone would be foolish enough to let it go. Barak wanted me to come to the region, but I wanted Arafat to say yes to the Israelis on the big issues embodied in my parameters first. In December the parties had met at Bolling Air Force Base for talks that didn't succeed because Arafat wouldn't accept the parameters that were hard for him.

Finally, Arafat agreed to see Shimon Peres on the thirteenth after Peres had first met with Saeb Erekat. Nothing came of it. As a backstop, the Israelis tried to produce a letter with as much agreement on the parameters as possible, on the assumption that Barak would lose the election and at least both sides would be bound to a course that could lead to an agreement. Arafat wouldn't even do that, because he didn't want to be seen conceding anything. The parties continued their talks in Taba, Egypt. They got close, but did not succeed. Arafat never said no; he just couldn't bring himself to say yes. Pride goeth before the fall.

Right before I left office, Arafat, in one of our last conversations, thanked me for all my efforts and told me what a great man I was. "Mr. Chairman," I replied, "I am not a great man. I am a failure, and you have made me one." I warned Arafat that he was single-handedly electing Sharon and that he would reap the whirlwind.

In February 2001, Ariel Sharon would be elected prime minister in a landslide. The Israelis had decided that if Arafat wouldn't take my offer he wouldn't take anything, and that if they had no partner for peace, it was better to be led by the most aggressive, intransigent leader available. Sharon would take a hard line toward Arafat and would be supported in doing so by Ehud Barak and the United States. Nearly a year after I left office, Arafat said he was ready to negotiate on the basis of the parameters I had presented. Apparently, Arafat had thought the time to decide, five minutes to midnight, had finally come. His watch had been broken a long time.

Arafat's rejection of my proposal after Barak accepted it was an error of historic proportions. However, many Palestinians and Israelis are still committed to peace.

Someday peace will come, and when it does, the final agreement will look a lot like the proposals that came out of Camp David and the six long months that followed.

On January 3, I sat in the Senate with Chelsea and the rest of Hillary's family as Al Gore administered the oath of office to New York's new senator. I was so excited I almost jumped over the railing. For seventeen more days we would both be in office, the first couple to serve in the White House and the Senate in American history. But Hillary was on her own now. About all I could do was ask Trent Lott not to be too hard on her and offer to be Hillary's caseworker for Westchester County.

The next day we held a White House event that for me was about Mother: a celebration of the Breast and Cervical Cancer Protection and Treatment Act of 2000, which allowed women without health insurance who were diagnosed with these cancers to have full Medicaid benefits.

On the fifth, I announced that we would protect sixty million acres of pristine national forest in thirty-nine states from road-building and logging, including the Tongass National Forest in Alaska, the last great temperate rain forest in America. The timber interests were against the move and I thought the Bush administration might try to undo it on economic grounds, but only 5 percent of the nation's timber came from national forests, and only 5 percent of that amount came from roadless areas. We could do without that tiny amount of logging to preserve another priceless national treasure.

After the announcement I drove out to Fort Myer to receive the traditional farewell tribute from the armed forces, a fine military ceremony that included the presentation of an American flag, a flag with the presidential seal, and medals from each of the service branches. They gave Hillary a medal, too. Bill Cohen noted that in appointing him I became the only President ever to ask an elected official of the opposite party to become secretary of defense.

Being President carries no greater honor than being Commander in Chief of men and women of every race and religion who trace their ancestry to every region on earth. They are the living embodiment of our national creed, **E pluribus unum.** I had seen them cheered in refugee camps in the Balkans, helping the victims of disasters in Central America, working against narco-traffickers in Colombia and the Caribbean, welcomed with open arms in the former Communist nations of Central Europe, manning distant outposts in Alaska, standing guard in the deserts of the Middle East, and patrolling the Pacific.

Americans know about our forces when they go into battle. There will never be a full account of the wars never fought, the losses never suffered, the tears never shed because American men and women stood guard for peace. I may have gotten off to a rocky start with the military, but I worked hard at being Commander in Chief, and I was confident that I was leaving our military in even better shape than I found it.

On Saturday, January 6, after a visit to the National Zoo to see the pandas, Hillary and I held a farewell party on the South Lawn with Al and Tipper for all the people who had worked or volunteered in the White House over the past eight years. Hundreds of people came, many from long distances. We talked and reminisced for several hours. Al got a rousing welcome when I introduced him as the people's choice in the recent election. When he asked for a show of hands of all the people who had married or had children during our time in the White House, I was amazed at the number of hands that shot up. No matter what the Republicans said, we were a pro-family party.

The White House social secretary, Capricia Marshall, who had supported me since 1991 and had been with Hillary since early in our first campaign, had arranged a special surprise for me. The curtain behind us rose to reveal Fleetwood Mac singing "Don't Stop Thinkin' About Tomorrow" one more time.

On Sunday, Hillary, Chelsea, and I went to Foundry United Methodist Church, where the Reverend Phil Wogaman invited Hillary and me to make farewell remarks to the congregation that had embraced us for eight years. Chelsea had made good friends there and had learned a lot working in a distant hollow of rural Kentucky on the church's Appalachian Service Project. The church members came from many races and nations, and were rich and poor, straight and gay, old and young. Foundry had supported Washington's homeless population and refugees in parts of the world where I tried to make peace.

I didn't know what I was going to say, but Wogaman had told the congregation that I would tell them what I anticipated my new life would be like. So I said that my faith would be tested by a return to commercial air travel and that I would be disoriented by walking into large rooms because no band would be playing "Hail to the Chief." And I said I would do whatever I could to be a good citizen, to lift the hopes and fortunes of those who deserve a better hand than they have been dealt, and to keep working for peace and reconciliation. Despite my best efforts for the last eight years, that kind of work still seemed to be in strong demand.

Later that night in New York City, I spoke to the pro-peace Israel Policy Forum. At the time we still had some hope of making peace. Arafat had said he accepted the parameters with reservations. The problem was that his reservations, unlike Israel's, were outside the parameters, at least on refugees and the Western Wall, but I treated the acceptance as if it were real, based on his pledge to make peace before I left office. The American-Jewish community had been very good to me. Some, like my friend Haim Saban and Danny Abraham were deeply involved with Israel and had given me helpful advice over the years. Many others simply supported my work for peace. Regardless of what happened, I thought I owed it to them to explain my proposal.

The next day, after presenting the Citizens Medal to twenty-eight deserving Americans, including Muhammad Ali, I went over to the Democratic Party headquarters to thank the chairmen, Mayor Ed Rendell of Philadelphia and Joe Andrew, and to give a plug to Terry McAuliffe, who had done so much for Al Gore and for me, and who now was campaigning to be the new party chair. After all the work he'd done, I couldn't believe Terry wanted the job, but if he did, I was for him. I told the people who'd slaved away at the party work without glory or recognition how much I appreciated them.

On the ninth, I began a farewell tour to places that had been especially good to me, Michigan and Illinois, where victories in the primaries on St. Patrick's Day 1992 had virtually assured me of the nomination. Two days later, I went to Massachusetts, which gave me the highest percentage of any state in '96, and to New Hampshire, where they had made me the Comeback Kid in early 1992. In between, I dedicated a statue of Franklin Roosevelt in his wheelchair at the FDR Memorial on the Mall. The disability community had lobbied hard for it, and most of the Roosevelt family had supported it. Of the more than 10,000 photos of FDR in his archives, only four depict him in his wheelchair. Disabled Americans had come a long way since then.

I said farewell to New Hampshire in Dover, where almost nine years earlier I had promised to be with them "'til the last dog dies." Many of my old supporters were in the audience. I called several by name, thanked them all, then gave them a full account of the record their hard work in that long-ago winter had made possible. And I asked them never to forget that, "even though I won't be President, I'll always be with you until the last dog dies."

On the eleventh through the fourteenth, I had parties for the cabinet, the White House staff, and friends at Camp David. On the night of the fourteenth, Don Henley gave us a wonderful solo concert after dinner in the Camp David Chapel. The next morning was our family's last Sunday in the beautiful chapel, where we had shared many services with the fine young sailors and marines who staffed the camp and their families. They had even let me sing with the choir, always leaving the sheet music in Aspen, our family cabin, on Friday or Saturday so that I could review it in advance.

On Monday, I spoke at the Martin Luther King Jr. holiday celebration at the University of the District of Columbia. Usually I marked the day by doing some community service work, but I wanted to take this opportunity to thank the District of Columbia for being my home for eight years. The D.C. representative in Congress, Eleanor Holmes Norton, and Mayor Tony Williams were good friends of mine, as were several city council members. I had worked to help them get needed legislation through Congress and to prevent unduly meddlesome laws from being enacted. The District still had a lot of problems, but it was in much better condition than it had been eight years earlier when I took my pre-inaugural walk down Georgia Avenue.

I also sent my last message to Congress: "The Unfinished Work of Building One America." It was based in large part on the final report of the Commission on Race and included a wide array of recommendations: further steps to close the racial divide in education, health care, employment, and the criminal justice system; special efforts to help low-income absent fathers succeed at parenting; new investments for Native American communities; improved immigration policies; passage of the hate crimes bill; reform of the voting laws; and the continuation of AmeriCorps and the White House Office on One America. We had made a lot of headway in eight years, but America was growing more diverse, and there was still much to be done.

On the seventeenth, I held my last ceremony in the East Room, as Bruce Babbitt and I announced eight more national monuments, two of them along the trail Lewis and Clark blazed in 1803 with their Indian guide Sacagawea and a slave named York. We had now protected more land in the lower forty-eight states than any administration since that of Theodore Roosevelt.

After the announcement, I left the White House on the last trip of my presidency, going home to Little Rock to address the Arkansas legislature. Some of my old pals were still in the state House or Senate, as were people who had gotten their start in politics working with me and a few who began by working against me. More than twenty

Arkansans who were then serving or had served with me in Washington joined me that day, as did three of my high school classmates who lived in the Washington area, and several Arkansans who had served as my liaisons to the legislature when I was governor. Chelsea came with me, too. We passed two of her schools on the way in from the airport, and I thought of how much she had grown up since Hillary and I had attended her school programs at Booker Arts Magnet School.

I tried to thank all the Arkansans who had helped me reach this day, beginning with two men who were no longer living, Judge Frank Holt and Senator Fulbright. I urged the legislators to keep pushing the federal government to support the states on education, economic development, health care, and welfare reform. Finally, I told my old friends that I would leave office in three days grateful that "somehow the mystery of this great democracy gave me the chance to go from a little boy on South Hervey Street in Hope, Arkansas, to the White House. . . . I may be the only person ever elected President who owed his election purely to his personal friends, without whom I could never have won." I left my friends and flew home to finish the job.

The next night, after a day working on last-minute business, I gave a brief farewell address to the nation from the Oval Office. After thanking the American people for giving me the chance to serve and briefly summarizing my philosophy and record, I offered three observations about the future, saying that we should stay on the path to fiscal responsibility; that our security and prosperity required us to lead in the fight for prosperity and freedom and against terrorism, organized crime, narco-trafficking, the spread of deadly weapons, environmental degradation, disease, and global poverty; and finally, that we must continue to "weave the threads of our coat of many colors into the fabric of one America."

I wished President-elect Bush and his family well and said I would "leave the presidency more idealistic, more full of hope than the day I arrived, and more confident than ever that America's best days lie ahead."

On the nineteenth, my last full day as President, I issued a statement on land mines, saying that since 1993 the United States had destroyed more than 3.3 million of our own land mines, spent $500 million to remove land mines in thirty-five countries, and was making a vigorous effort to find a sensible alternative to mines that would protect our troops as well. I asked the new administration to continue our global demining effort for ten more years.

When I got back to the residence it was late and we still weren't completely packed. There were boxes everywhere, and I still had to decide which clothes were going where—to New York, Washington, or Arkansas. Hillary and I didn't want to sleep; we just wanted to keep strolling from room to room. We felt as honored to be living in the White House on our last night as we had when we came home after our first inaugural balls. I never ceased to be thrilled by it all. It seemed almost unbelievable that it had been our home for eight years; now it was almost over.

I went back into the Lincoln Bedroom, read Lincoln's handwritten copy of the Gettysburg Address one last time, and stared at the lithograph of him signing the Emancipation Proclamation, on the very spot where I was standing. I went into the Queen's Room and thought of Winston Churchill spending three weeks there in the dif-

ficult days of World War II. I sat behind the Treaty Table
in my office looking at the empty bookshelves and bare
walls, thinking of all the meetings and calls I'd had in that
room on Northern Ireland, the Middle East, Russia,
Korea, and domestic struggles. And it was in this room
where I read my Bible and books and letters, and prayed
for strength and guidance all through 1998.

Earlier in the day I had pre-recorded my final radio
address, to be aired not long before I was to leave the White
House for the inaugural ceremony. In it I thanked the
White House staff, the residence staff, the Secret Service,
the cabinet, and Al Gore for all they had done to make my
service possible. And I kept my promise to work until the
last hour of the last day, releasing another $100 million to
fund more police officers; those new police had helped give
America the lowest crime rate in a quarter century.

Well past midnight, I went back to the Oval Office again
to clean up, pack, and answer a few letters. As I sat alone at
the desk, I thought about all that had happened during the
last eight years, and how quickly it would be over. Soon I
would observe the transfer of power and take my leave.
Hillary, Chelsea, and I would board Air Force One for a last
flight with the fine crew that had taken us to the far corners
of the world; our closest staff members; my new Secret Service detail; some of the career military staff such as Glen
Maes, the navy steward who baked all my specially decorated birthday cakes, and Glenn Powell, the air force
sergeant who made sure our luggage never got lost; and a
few of the folks who "brought me to the dance"—the Jordans, the McAuliffes, the McLartys, and Harry Thomason.

Several members of the press corps were also scheduled
to make the last trip. One of them, Mark Knoller of CBS
Radio, had covered me all eight years and had conducted

one of the many wrap-up interviews I had done in the past several weeks. Mark had asked me if I was afraid that "the best part of your life is over." I said I had enjoyed every part of my life and that in each stage I had been "absorbed, interested, and found something useful to do."

I was looking forward to my new life, to building my library, doing public service work through my foundation, supporting Hillary, and having more time for reading, golf, music, and unhurried travel. I knew I would enjoy myself and believed that if I stayed healthy I could still do a lot of good. But Mark Knoller had hit a soft spot with his question. I was going to miss my old job. I had loved being President, even on the bad days.

I thought about the note to President Bush I would write and leave behind in the Oval Office, just as his father had done for me eight years earlier. I wanted to be gracious and encouraging, as George Bush had been to me. Soon George W. Bush would be President of all the people, and I wished him well. I had paid close attention to what Bush and Cheney had said in the campaign. I knew they saw the world very differently from the way I did and would want to undo much of what I had done, especially on economic policy and the environment. I thought that they would pass their big tax cut and that before long we would be back to the big deficits of the 1980s, and in spite of Bush's encouraging comments on education and AmeriCorps, he would feel pressure to cut back on all domestic spending, including education, child care, after-school programs, police on the streets, innovative research, and the environment. But those were not my calls to make anymore.

I thought that the international partnerships that we had developed in the aftermath of the Cold War could be strained by the more unilateral approach of the Republicans—they were opposed to the test ban treaty, the climate change treaty, the ABM Treaty, and the International Criminal Court.

I had watched the Washington Republicans for eight years and imagined that President Bush would, from the outset of his term, be under pressure to abandon compassionate conservatism by the more right-wing leaders and interest groups now in control of his party. They believed in their way as deeply as I believed in mine, but I thought the evidence, and the weight of history, favored our side.

I couldn't control what happened to my policies and programs; few things are permanent in politics. Nor could I affect the early judgments on my so-called legacy. The history of America's move from the end of the Cold War to the millennium would be written and rewritten over and over. The only thing that mattered to me about my presidency was whether I had done a good job for the American people in a new and very different era of global interdependence.

Had I helped to form a "more perfect union" by widening the circle of opportunity, deepening the meaning of freedom, and strengthening the bonds of community? I had certainly tried to make America the twenty-first century's leading force for peace and prosperity, freedom and security. I had tried to put a more human face on globalization by urging other nations to join us in building a more integrated world of shared responsibilities, shared benefits, and shared values; and I had tried to lead America through its transition into this new era with a sense of hope and optimism about what we could do, and a sober sense of what the new forces of destruction could do to us. Finally, I had tried to build a new progressive politics rooted in new ideas and old values, and to support like-minded movements around the world. No matter how many of my specific initiatives the new administration and its congressional majority might undo, I believed that if we were on the right side of history, the direction I had taken into the new millennium would eventually prevail.

On my last night in the now-barren Oval Office, I thought of the glass case I had kept on the coffee table between the two couches, just a few feet away. It contained a rock Neil Armstrong had taken off the moon in 1969. Whenever arguments in the Oval Office heated up beyond reason, I would interrupt and say, "You see that rock? It's 3.6 billion years old. We're all just passing through. Let's calm down and go back to work."

That moon rock gave me a whole different perspective on history and the proverbial "long run." Our job is to live as well and as long as we can, and to help others to do the same. What happens after that and how we are viewed by others is beyond our control. The river of time carries us all away. All we have is the moment. Whether I had made the most of mine was for others to judge. It was almost dawn when I returned to the residence to do some more packing and share some private moments with Hillary and Chelsea.

The next morning, I returned to the Oval Office to write my note to President Bush. Hillary came down, too. We gazed out the windows to take a long, admiring look at the beautiful grounds where we had shared so many memorable times and I had thrown countless tennis balls to Buddy. Then she left me to write my letter. As I placed the letter on the desk, I called my staff in to say good-bye. We hugged, smiled, shed a few tears, and took a few pictures. Then I walked out of the Oval Office for the last time.

As I stepped out the door with my arms opened wide, I was greeted by members of the press there to capture the moment. John Podesta walked with me down the colonnade to join Hillary, Chelsea, and the Gores on the state floor, where we would soon greet our successors. The entire residence staff had gathered to say good-bye—the housekeeping staff, the kitchen staff, the florist, the grounds crew, the ushers, the butlers, my valets. Many of them had become like family. I looked into their faces and stored the memories, not knowing when I would see them again, and knowing that when I did, it would never be quite the same. They would soon have a new family who would need them as much as we had.

A small combo from the marine band was playing in the grand foyer. I sat down at the piano with Master Sergeant Charlie Corrado, who had played for Presidents for forty years. Charlie was always there for us, and his music had brightened a lot of days. Hillary and I had a last dance, and at about ten-thirty the Bushes and the Cheneys arrived. We drank coffee and chatted for a few minutes, then the eight of us got in the limousines, and I rode with George W. Bush for the drive down Pennsylvania Avenue to the Capitol.

Within an hour, the peaceful transfer of power that has kept our country free for more than two hundred years had taken place again. My family said good-bye to the new First Family and drove to Andrews Air Force Base for our last flight on the presidential plane that was no longer Air Force One for me. After eight years as President, and half a lifetime in politics, I was a private citizen again, but a very grateful one, still pulling for my country, still thinking about tomorrow.

EPILOGUE

I wrote this book to tell my story, and to tell the story of America in the last half of the twentieth century; to describe as fairly as I could the forces competing for the country's heart and mind; to explain the challenges of the new world in which we live and how I believe our government and our citizens should respond to them; and to give people who have never been involved in public life a sense of what it is like to hold office, and especially what it is like to be President.

While writing, I found myself falling back in time, reliving events as I recounted them, feeling as I did then and writing as I felt. During my second term, as the partisan battles I tried to defuse continued unabated, I also tried to understand how my time in office fit into the stream of American history.

That history is largely the story of our efforts to honor our founders' charge to form a "more perfect union." In calmer times, our country has been well served by our two-party system, with progressives and conservatives debating what to change and what to preserve. But when change is forced upon us by events, we are all tested, and thrown back to our fundamental mission to widen the circle of opportunity, deepen the meaning of freedom, and strengthen the bonds of our community. To me, that is what it means to make our union more perfect.

At every turning point, we have chosen union over

division: in the early days of the Republic, by building a national economic and legal system; during the Civil War, by preserving the Union and ending slavery; in the early twentieth century, as we moved from an agricultural to an industrial society, by making our government stronger to preserve competition, promote basic safeguards for labor, provide for the poor, the elderly, and the infirm, and protect our natural resources from plunder; and in the sixties and seventies, by advancing civil rights and women's rights. In each instance, while we were engaged in the struggle to define, defend, and expand our union, powerful conservative forces resisted, and as long as the outcome was in doubt, the political and personal conflicts were intense.

In 1993, when I took office, we were facing another historic challenge to the Union, as we moved from the industrial age into the global information age. The American people were faced with big changes in the way they lived and worked, and with big questions to be answered: Would we choose global economic engagement or economic nationalism? Would we use our unrivaled military, political, and economic power to spread the benefits and confront the emerging threats of the interdependent world or become Fortress America? Would we abandon our industrial-age government, with its commitments to equal opportunity and social justice, or reform it so as to retain its achievements while giving people the tools to succeed in the new era? Would our increasing racial and religious diversity fracture or strengthen our national community?

As President, I tried to answer these questions in a way that kept moving us toward a more perfect union, lifting people's vision, and bringing them together to build a new vital center for American politics in the twenty-first century. Two-thirds of our citizens supported my general approach, but on the controversial cultural questions and on the always appealing tax cuts, the electorate was more closely divided. With the outcome in doubt, bitter partisan and personal attacks raged, bearing a striking resemblance to those of the early Republic.

Whether my historical analysis is right or not, I judge my presidency primarily in terms of its impact on people's lives. That is how I kept score: all the millions of people with new jobs, new homes, and college aid; the kids with health insurance and after-school programs; the people who left welfare for work; the families helped by the family leave law; the people living in safer neighborhoods—all those people have stories, and they're better ones now. Life got better for all Americans because the air and water were cleaner and more of our natural heritage was preserved. And we brought more hope for peace, freedom, security, and prosperity to people all over the world. They have their stories, too.

When I became President, America was sailing into uncharted waters, into a world full of apparently disconnected positive and negative forces. Because I had spent a lifetime trying to bring together my own parallel lives and had been raised to value all people, and, as governor, had seen both the bright and dark sides of globalization, I felt I understood where my country was and how we needed to move into the new century. I knew how to put things together, and how hard it would be to do.

On September 11, things seemed to fall apart again as al Qaeda used the forces of interdependence—open borders, easy immigration and travel, easy access to information and technology—to murder close to 3,000 people, from more than seventy nations, in New York, Washington, D.C., and Pennsylvania. The world rallied around our loss and the American people in our determination to fight terrorism. In the years since, the battle has intensified, with understandable and honestly held differences at home and around the world about how best to pursue the war on terror.

The interdependent world we live in is inherently unstable, full of both opportunity and forces of destruction. It will remain so until we find our way from interdependence to a more integrated global community of shared responsibilities, shared benefits, and shared values. Building that kind of world, and defeating terror, cannot be done quickly; it will be the great challenge of the first half of the twenty-first century. I believe there are five things the United States should be doing to lead the way: fight terror and the spread of weapons of mass destruction and improve our defenses against them; make more friends and fewer terrorists by helping the 50 percent of the world not reaping the benefits of globalization to overcome poverty, ignorance, disease, and bad government; strengthen the institutions of global cooperation and work through them to promote security and prosperity and combat our shared problems, from terror to AIDS to global warming; continue to make America a better model of how we want the world to work; and work to end the age-old compulsion to believe that our differences are more important than our common humanity.

I believe the world will continue its forward march from isolation to interdependence to cooperation because there is no other choice. We have come a long way since our ancestors first stood up on the African savannah more than a hundred thousand years ago. In just the fifteen years since the end of the Cold War, the West has been largely reconciled to its old adversaries, Russia and China; more than half of the world's people are living under governments of their own choosing for the first time in history; there has been an unprecedented degree of global cooperation against terror and a recognition that we must do more to fight poverty, disease, and global warming and to get all the world's children in school; and America and many other free societies have shown that people of all races and religions can live together in mutual respect and harmony.

Our nation will not be undone by terror. We will defeat it, but we must take care that in so doing we do not compromise the character of our country or the future of our children. Our mission to form a more perfect union is now a global one.

As for myself, I'm still working on that list of life goals I made as a young man. Becoming a good person is a lifelong effort that requires letting go of anger at others and holding on to responsibility for the mistakes I've made. And it requires forgiveness. After all the forgiveness I've been given from Hillary, Chelsea, my friends, and millions of people in America and across the world, it's the least I can do. As a young politician, when I started going to black churches, for the first time I heard people refer to funerals as "homegoings." We're all going home, and I want to be ready.

In the meantime, I take great joy in the life Chelsea is building, the superb job Hillary is doing in the Senate, and my foundation's efforts to bring economic, educational, and service opportunities to poor communities in

America and across the world; to fight AIDS and bring low-cost medicine to those who need it; and to continue my lifelong commitment to racial and religious reconciliation.

Do I have regrets? Sure, both private and public ones, as I've discussed in this book. I leave it to others to judge how to balance the scales.

I've simply tried to tell the story of my joys and sorrows, dreams and fears, triumphs and failures. And I've tried to explain the difference between my view of the world and that held by those on the Far Right with whom I did battle. In essence they honestly believe they know the whole truth. I see things differently. I think Saint Paul had it right when he said that in this life we "see through a glass darkly" and "know in part." That's why he extolled the virtues of "faith, hope, and love."

I've had an improbable life, and a wonderful one full of faith, hope, and love, as well as more than my share of grace and good fortune. As improbable as my life has been, it would have been impossible anywhere but America. Unlike so many people, I have been privileged to spend every day working for things I've believed in since I was a little boy hanging around my grandfather's store. I grew up with a fascinating mother who adored me, have learned at the feet of great teachers, have made a legion of loyal friends, have built a loving life with the finest woman I've ever known, and have a child who continues to be the light of my life.

As I said, I think it's a good story, and I've had a good time telling it.

ACKNOWLEDGMENTS

I am particularly indebted to the many people without whom this book could not have been written. Justin Cooper gave up more than two years of his young life to work with me every day and, on many occasions in the last six months, all night. He organized and retrieved mountains of materials, did further research, corrected many errors, and typed the manuscript over and over from my illegible scrawling in more than twenty large notebooks. Many of the sections were rewritten a half dozen times or more. He never lost his patience, his energy never flagged, and by the time we got to the last lap, he sometimes seemed to know me and what I wanted to say better than I did. Though he is not responsible for its errors, this book is a testament to his gifts and efforts.

Before we began to work together, I was told that my editor, Robert Gottlieb, was the best there was at his craft. He turned out to be that and more. I only wish I'd met him thirty years earlier. Bob taught me about magic moments and hard cuts. Without his judgment and feel, this book might have been twice as long and half as good. He read my story as a person who was interested in but not obsessed with politics. He kept pulling me back to the human side of my life. And he convinced me to take out countless names of people who helped me along the way, because the general reader couldn't keep up with them all. If you're one of them, I hope you'll forgive him, and me.

A book this long and full requires a mammoth amount of fact checking. This lion's share of work was done by Meg Thompson, a brilliant young woman who carefully waded through the minutiae of my life for a year or so; then for the last few months she was assisted by Caitlin Klevorick and other young volunteers. They now have many examples of the fact that my memory is far from perfect. If any factual errors remain, it is not for lack of effort to correct them on their part.

I can't thank the people at Knopf enough, beginning with Sonny Mehta, the president and editor-in-chief. He believed in the project from the beginning and did his part to keep it going, including giving me an amazed look wherever and whenever I ran in to him over the last two years; a look that said something like, "Are you really going to finish on time?", and "Why are you here instead of at home writing?" Sonny's look always had the desired effect.

I also owe thanks to the many people at Knopf who helped. I am grateful that the editorial/production team at Knopf is as obsessed with accuracy and detail as I am (even with a book on a slightly accelerated pace as mine was) and especially appreciate the tireless efforts and meticulous work of managing editor Katherine Hourigan; the noble director of manufacturing Andy Hughes; indefatigable production editor Maria Massey; copy chief Lydia Buechler, copy editor Charlotte Gross, and proofreaders Steve Messina, Jenna Dolan, Ellen Feldman, Rita Madrigal, and Liz

Polizzi; design director Peter Andersen; jacket art director Carol Carson; the ever-helpful Diana Tejerina and Eric Bliss; and Lee Pentea.

In addition, I want to thank the many other people at Knopf who have helped me: Tony Chirico, for his valued guidance; Jim Johnston, Justine LeCates, and Anne Diaz; Carol Janeway and Suzanne Smith; Jon Fine; and the promotion/marketing talents of Pat Johnson, Paul Bogaards, Nina Bourne, Nicholas Latimer, Joy Dallanegra-Sanger, Amanda Kauff, Anne-Lise Spitzer, and Sarah Robinson. And thanks to the staff at North Market Street Graphics, Coral Graphics, and R. R. Donnelley & Sons.

Robert Barnett, a fine lawyer and longtime friend, negotiated the contract with Knopf; he and his partner Michael O'Connor worked with me throughout the project as foreign publishers joined in. I am very grateful to them. I appreciate the careful technical and legal review that David Kendall and Beth Nolan gave the manuscript.

When I was in the White House, beginning in late 1993, I met with my old friend Taylor Branch about once a month to do an oral history. Those contemporaneous conversations helped in recalling particular moments of the presidency. After I left the White House, Ted Widmer, a fine historian who worked in the White House as a speechwriter, did an oral history of my life before the presidency that helped me bring back and organize old memories. Janis Kearney, the White House diarist, left me with voluminous notes that enabled me to reconstruct day-to-day events.

The photographs were selected with the help of

Vincent Virga, who found many that captured special moments discussed in the book, and Carolyn Huber, who was with our family throughout our years in the Governor's Mansion and the White House. While I was President, Carolyn also organized all my private papers and letters from the time I was a little boy to 1974, an arduous task without which much of the first part of the book could not have been written.

I am deeply indebted to those who read all or part of the book and made helpful suggestions for additions, subtractions, reorganization, context, and interpretation, including Hillary, Chelsea, Dorothy Rodham, Doug Band, Sandy Berger, Tommy Caplan, Mary DeRosa, Nancy Hernreich, Dick Holbrooke, David Kendall, Jim Kennedy, Ian Klauss, Bruce Lindsey, Ira Magaziner, Cheryl Mills, Beth Nolan, John Podesta, Bruce Reed, Steve Ricchetti, Bob Rubin, Ruby Shamir, Brooke Shearer, Gene Sperling, Strobe Talbott, Mark Weiner, Maggie Williams, and my friends Brian and Myra Greenspun, who were with me when the first page was written.

Many of my friends and colleagues took time to do impromptu oral histories with me including Huma Abedin, Madeleine Albright, Dave Barram, Woody Bassett, Paul Begala, Paul Berry, Jim Blair, Sidney Blumenthal, Erskine Bowles, Ron Burkle, Tom Campbell, James Carville, Roger Clinton, Patty Criner, Denise Dangremond, Lynda Dixon, Rahm Emanuel, Al From, Mark Gearen, Ann Henry, Denise Hyland, Harold Ickes, Roger Johnson, Vernon Jordan, Mickey Kantor, Dick Kelley, Tony Lake, David Leopoulos, Capricia Marshall, Mack McLarty, Rudy Moore, Bob

Nash, Kevin O'Keefe, Leon Panetta, Betsey Reader, Dick Riley, Bobby Roberts, Hugh Rodham, Tony Rodham, Dennis Ross, Martha Saxton, Eli Segal, Terry Schumaker, Marsha Scott, Michael Sheehan, Nancy Soderberg, Doug Sosnik, Rodney Slater, Craig Smith, Gayle Smith, Steve Smith, Carolyn Staley, Stephanie Street, Larry Summers, Martha Whetstone, Delta Willis, Carol Willis, and several of my readers. I'm sure there are others I've forgotten; if so, I'm sorry and I appreciate their help as well.

My research was also helped greatly by many books written by members of the administration and others, and of course by the memoirs of Hillary and my mother.

David Alsobrook and the staff of the Clinton Presidential Materials Project were patient and persistent in recovering materials. I want to thank them all: Deborah Bush, Susan Collins, Gary Foulk, John Keller, Jimmie Purvis, Emily Robison, Rob Seibert, Dana Simmons, Richard Stalcup, Rhonda Wilson. And Arkansas historian David Ware. The archivists and historians at Georgetown and Oxford were also helpful.

While I was absorbed in writing for much of the last two and a half years, especially the last six months, the work of my foundation continued as we built the library and pursued our missions: fighting AIDS in Africa and the Caribbean and providing low cost drugs and testing around the world; increasing economic opportunity in poor communities in the United States, India, and Africa; promoting education and citizen service among young people at home and abroad; and advocating religious, racial, and ethnic reconciliation across the world. I want to thank those whose donations have made possible my foundation work, and the construction of the Presidential Library and the Clinton School of Public Service at the University of Arkansas. I am deeply indebted to Maggie Williams, my chief of staff, for all she did to keep things moving and for her help on the book. I want to thank members of my foundation and office staff for all they did to continue the work of the foundation and its programs while I was writing the book. A special word of thanks goes to Doug Band, my counselor, who helped me from the day I left the White House to build my new life and who struggled to protect my book-writing time on our travels across America and the world.

I also owe a debt to Oscar Flores, who keeps things going at my home in Chappaqua. On the many nights when Justin Cooper and I worked into the wee hours, Oscar went out of his way to make sure we remembered to have dinner and that we were well supplied with coffee.

Finally, I cannot list all the people who made the life chronicled in these pages possible—all the teachers and mentors of my youth; the people who worked on and contributed to all my campaigns; those who worked with me in the Democratic Leadership Council, National Governors Association, and all the other organizations that contributed to my education in public policy; those who worked with me for peace, security, and reconciliation around the world; those who made the White House run and my trips work; the thousands of gifted people who worked in my adminstrations as attorney general, governor, and President without whose dedicated service I would have little to say about my years in public life; those who provided security to me and my family; and my friends of a lifetime. None of them are responsible for the failures of my life, but for whatever good has come out of it they deserve much of the credit.

INDEX

The names of people who appear in the photograph inserts are followed by I (first insert) or II (second insert).

PHOTOGRAPHIC CREDITS

Photo inserts researched, edited, and designed by
Vincent Virga, with the assistance of
Carolyn Huber
Every effort has been made to identify copyright
holders; in case of oversight, and upon notification
to the publisher, corrections will be made in
the next edition.

PHOTO INSERT I

Unless otherwise noted, all photos are from the author's collection.

AP/Wide World Photos: page 15, lower right.

Arkansas Democrat-Gazette: page 5, top right; page 6, top left; page 10, top right; page 15, top.

Arsenio Hall Show, courtesy Paramount Pictures: page 15, lower left.

pfbentley/pfpix.com: page 13, center left and right, and bottom; page 14, center right and bottom.

Donald R. Broyles/Office of Governor Clinton: page 9, center left.

Clinton Presidential Materials Project: page 5, top left; page 14, top left, top right, and upper left.

Tipper Gore: page 13, top.

Harry Hamburg/New York *Daily News:* page 16, bottom.

Morning News of Northwest Arkansas: page 7, top.

Brooke Shearer: page 6, lower left.

Joseph Sohm/visionsofamerica.com: page 15, top right.